Writing is not something I can stop. I'm constantly writing in my head, with a pen on paper, on a computer, or scribbling in the dirt with my fingers.

— **Kristina Martinez**

(To read Kristina Martinez's paper, see page 85. To read her notes on the writing process, see Chapter 3.)

I enjoy writing, but I find it a challenge. Writing is demanding because it requires having ideas to throw down on the page. That is why I read. **Every time I read, I encounter ideas. They might be new, or they might be old, but each one enlivens my mind.** It's like taking a walk in the woods and seeing a deer; the encounter enriches a person with an experience that makes nature all the more precious.

— **Sunkyo Hong**

(To read Sunkyo Hong's paper, see page 714. To read his notes on the writing process, see Chapter 18.)

There are those experiences when I write something late at night and wake up the next morning and go back to what I have written and see it all differently (usually all wrong), but that experience is always so odd and strangely energizing. **I really enjoy going back to my drafts (most of them)—to play, distort, delete, add—and that silent energy tells me this writing world is a place I belong in.**

— **Alicia Abood**

(To read Alicia Abood's paper, see page 272. To read her notes on the writing process, see Chapter 9.)

Third Edition

Approaching Literature

Reading + Thinking + Writing

Peter Schakel

Hope College

Jack Ridl

Hope College

Bedford/St. Martin's

Boston ◆ New York

For Bedford/St. Martin's

Executive Editor: Stephen A. Scipione
Developmental Editor: Deja Earley
Production Editor: Annette Pagliaro Sweeney
Assistant Manager/Production: Joe Ford
Senior Marketing Manager: Adrienne Petsick
Editorial Assistant: Regina Tavani
Copy Editor: Mary Lou Wilshaw-Watts
Permissions Manager: Kalina K. Ingham
Senior Art Director: Anna Palchik
Text Design: Glenna Collett
Cover Design: Donna Lee Dennison
Cover Photo: Summer Fun by mitarart. Photo courtesy of Veer.
Composition: Cenveo Publisher Services
Printing and Binding: Quad/Graphics Taunton

President: Joan E. Feinberg
Editorial Director: Denise B. Wydra
Editor in Chief: Karen S. Henry
Director of Marketing: Karen R. Soeltz
Director of Production: Susan W. Brown
Associate Director, Editorial Production: Elise S. Kaiser
Managing Editor: Elizabeth M. Schaaf

Library of Congress Control Number: 2011926680

Manufactured in the United States of America.
6   5   4   3   2   1
f   e   d   c   b   a

For information, write: Bedford/St. Martin's, 75 Arlington Street, Boston, MA 02116
  (617-399-4000)

ISBN-13: 978-0-312-64099-6

Acknowledgments

  Ai, "Why Can't I Leave You?" from *Vice: New and Selected Poems* by Ai. Copyright © 1973 by Ai. Used by permission of W. W. Norton & Company, Inc.
  Agha Shahid Ali, "I Dream It Is Afternoon When I Return to Delhi" by Agha Shahid Ali, from *The Half-Inch Himalayas.* Copyright © 1987 by Agha Shahid Ali. Reprinted by permission of Wesleyan University Press.

Acknowledgments and copyrights are continued at the back of the book on pages 1489-98, which constitute an extension of the copyright page. It is a violation of the law to reproduce these selections by any means whatsoever without the written permission of the copyright holder.

Preface for Instructors

In the third edition of *Approaching Literature: Reading + Thinking + Writing*, as with previous editions, we have tried to make the book as fresh in its selections and as accessible and inclusive in its pedagogy as possible. When students are required to take literature courses, it is not uncommon that their experience with literature is minimal. As teachers, we do not see ourselves as guardians of literature's stronghold, but as its ambassadors and guides, reaching out to invite students to enjoy literature's beauty and be moved by its power and wisdom. This has been our guiding principle in preparing *Approaching Literature*.

We're sure our students are not the only ones who have asked for a choice of literature that speaks to them, to their wide interests, varied cultures, and unique circumstances. Therefore, we have tried to have the contents of this book reflect the extraordinary diversity of contemporary literature. However, we also want students to be introduced to important writers and works of the past, so they may come to see how timeless great literature can be and affirm its continued resonance. For example, the emotions of the narrator in James Joyce's "Araby" still speak to students, even if their own experiences of young love are more like what the spunky narrator of Katherine Min's "Courting a Monk" relates. Throughout, therefore, *Approaching Literature* mingles, juxtaposes, and connects recent and diverse writing with works from the traditional canon, often using the one as a gateway to the other.

We want students to understand that any literary work concerns itself with a multiplicity of things, not a single topic, theme, or view that readers must identify through some seemingly mysterious and esoteric method. Our approach, which teaches reading and writing as processes, affirms students' own experiences and cultural backgrounds as it enlarges their ways of perceiving and understanding. By savoring the lines of Julia Alvarez's poem "How I Learned to Sweep," by identifying what she learned in the learning, by comparing her "lesson" with similar lessons from their own lives, students are empowered to see that reading literature involves an exploration of *all* that can be discovered in a work, and that such exploration can start from wherever they are, whatever their background.

We introduce writing sequentially, starting with observations that students write in the margins of books as they read, and progressing by sensible, gradual steps to notes, journal writing, short critical papers, and longer research papers. We show how active reading can lead directly to student writing. The comments that students scribble in the margins of Don Nigro's *Letters from Quebec to Providence in the Rain* may culminate in a paper that compares the effects of jealousy in that short contemporary play with the tragic results of jealousy in Shakespeare's *Othello*. We also emphasize that each strategy and form of writing, while valuable in itself, is part of an overall repertoire of skills that apply in many other reading-writing situations beyond a literature course.

In brief, our intention in *Approaching Literature* was to invite students in, to create an accessible introduction to fiction, poetry, and drama for all students, whatever their previous exposure to literature. The general principles outlined here guided us in all of our work developing this book. This will become clearer in a more detailed look at how these principles have influenced and shaped specific elements in our text.

Features of *Approaching Literature*

A Common Ground for Exploring Contemporary and Classic Literature

Lucille Clifton has said, "In this polyglot we call America, literature *has* to include all voices. Nothing else makes sense." This anthology, of course, does not include all voices (what anthology could?) but it does include, juxtapose, and connect an uncommon number of fresh, contemporary works with some of the most frequently taught texts from the traditional canon. It uses current voices to help students recognize the relevance of older works, and older works to see the depth and significance of newer works.

Chapter 5, for example, includes three stories dealing with cars, one from the 1990s, one from the 1980s, and one from the 1950s, giving the students a way to see how some human experiences tend to remain consistent even though the particulars change with the passing of time. Observing in Dagoberto Gilb's short, humorous story "Love in L.A." (1993) how structure carries along the narrative, recognizing ways the author brings distinctive characters to life, and noticing both what an author emphasizes and leaves out prepare students for reading two stories with confrontational characters and situations that are a bit more demanding: Louise Erdrich's "The Red Convertible" (1984) and Flannery O'Connor's "A Good Man Is Hard to Find" (1955). Similarly, pairing two poems about monuments — Percy Bysshe Shelley's "Ozymandias" and Peter Blue Cloud's "Crazy Horse Monument" — provides an opportunity for students to compare differences in form, imagery, and attitude in a poem from nineteenth-century England and one from twentieth-century South Dakota.

A Student-Friendly Approach to Literature

We need hardly tell you that students enter introductory literature courses with varied levels of education and experience. *Approaching Literature* attempts to bridge those levels by addressing students in a way that does not presuppose prior knowledge of or experience with literature. We present information concisely, in step-by-step fashion, avoiding overly technical vocabulary. We pause frequently to summarize and remind (for example, every chapter ends with boxed checklists that serve as memory refreshers and quick references). Also, each chapter treating the literary elements begins accessibly with a very short story, poem, or play that sets an engaging tone for the chapter and provides illustrations for discussing the topic at hand. Further, we include pictures of the students whose papers we reprint, along with their comments about writing those papers at each stage of the process, in the expectation that your students will discover that their concerns are shared and their experiences reflected in the book.

A Focus on Active Reading

Right from the start, *Approaching Literature* invites students to become active readers. Our discussion of the reading process in Chapter 1 is built around a personal essay by Sherman Alexie and a story by Julia Alvarez, both of whom testify to how reading saved the lives of these writers. Seeing how these writers participate fully with a work, connecting with it intellectually, emotionally, and imaginatively, reveals reading as a vital part of one's life and serves as an inspiration and a model for students' own active reading. Throughout the book, "Approaching the Reading" prompts that follow stories, poems, and plays give students ways to reflect on and apply the techniques of reading they learn. By placing emphasis on what literary techniques and elements *do* and what readers do *with* them, we try to help students engage more deeply with literature and realize how enjoyable and meaningful stories, poems, and plays can be.

An Emphasis on Critical Thinking

Another central aim of this book is to foster habits and skills of critical thinking. By critical thinking, we mean two things: a set of skills for examining information and a developed ability to use those skills to guide one's responses. Critical thinking contrasts with passively taking in information and confining the reasons for remembering it only to comprehension. It is not just possessing a set of skills; it always involves using those skills in active, practical ways.

Accordingly, Chapter 1 stresses how students can develop habits of mind to engage fully with the texts they read—not simply to track what is going on in texts, but to enter them imaginatively, to ask questions of them, and to resist settling for trite or simple answers. Chapter 2 helps students see themselves as makers of knowledge, as they read with pens or pencils in hand, participate in discussions, analyze questions and topics, and construct argumentative theses and papers. Subsequent chapters on the elements of fiction, poetry, and drama discuss how to connect in personally important ways with literary texts, how to understand them on a level that goes beyond merely comprehending what is going on, how to interrogate, analyze, and value them — critical skills reinforced throughout the book by the reading prompts and writing assignments.

Practical Explanation of the Writing Process

Chapters 2, 3, 9, 18, and 24 lead students in a unified, cumulative, step-by-step way through the writing process. We begin with how to find possible topics to write about and how to shape these into successful topics by using critical thinking skills. We go on to show how to turn the organization and development of ideas into convincing, well-supported arguments. Each stage of the writing process is accompanied by student comments speaking to individual writing experiences, and the book provides five complete student papers, two of which are accompanied by rough drafts so students can see revision in action. Our aim is to offer the students who use the book models to follow that will give them confidence that they can do the work described in the chapters. The book provides, in addition, sample marginal annotations, journal entries, and exam answers to clarify the different forms of writing.

Clear, Sensible Guidance on Using Sources and Research

The new edition is particularly attentive to twenty-first-century research challenges and includes specific coverage of the benefits and pitfalls involved in using electronic resources. Chapter 3 guides students step by step through the literary research process, from finding material, to reading it, evaluating it, incorporating it effectively, citing it accurately, and avoiding plagiarism. Each step of writing instruction is accompanied by a first-person account of how a student writer moved from conception to completion. It offers thorough, detailed, easy-to-use information about parenthetical citations and bibliography form and an annotated sample paper that provides a clear, helpful model for handling various situations students may encounter.

A unique feature of this book is its appendix on reading critical essays, which provides practical instruction on how to approach and read the academic essay, a genre that in itself is unfamiliar to many students, and which students may be asked to use as sources in their own writing. This appendix includes a provocative critical essay on a story that students like: Susan Farrell's article "Fight vs. Flight: A Re-evaluation of Dee in Alice Walker's 'Everyday Use'" uses sources to build an argument for a more sympathetic view of Dee (Wangero) than many readers are inclined to give her. As a reading, the essay challenges students to think critically, as they reconsider the story from a different perspective, and to decide which approach to it seems more appropriate and helpful. As a model of writing, it features marginal annotations that show students what to look for in a critical essay, in particular rhetorical strategies that they can use in their own writing.

New to the Third Edition

Our goal in the third edition has been to make the book even more inclusive and accessible than the first and second editions. The choice of new literary works and the additions to our pedagogy reflect these dual concerns.

A Continuing Emphasis on Inclusiveness in Almost 100 New Selections

We've continued to look for the most engaging, contemporary and diverse literature, while also bringing in canonical selections that have stood the test of time. Specifically, we have selected 13 new stories, 75 new poems, and 10 new plays for this edition, many of them by authors who did not appear in the first edition (9 fiction writers, 34 poets, and 7 playwrights), including:

- new examples of contemporary fiction by Ann Beattie, Ray González, Dave Eggers, Ha Jin, Bharati Mukherjee, and ZZ Packer; contemporary poetry by Natasha Trethewey, Gerald Stern, Jo Carson, Chitra Banerjee Divakaruni, Luis J. Rodriguez, Tony Hoagland, and Jane Hirshfield; and contemporary drama by Suzan-Lori Parks, Mark Lambeck, and Marco Ramirez

- a dozen new selections from canonical writers such as William Wordsworth, John Donne, Robert Frost, Thomas Hardy, Joyce Carol Oates, William Shakespeare, Tennessee Williams, and Lorraine Hansberry

- double the amount of graphic literature, including new work by Marjane Satrapi, Richard McGuire, and Art Spiegelman

- a new author-in-depth casebook focusing on Judith Ortiz Cofer

Teachable Pairings and Clusters of Literary Works in the Anthology

- **Thematic pairings of classic and current literature.** In this edition we've embedded provocative pairings of literary works in the anthologies, and accompanied them with entry points that make the teachable, thematic connections clear. The pairings provide fresh access into enduring older works while suggesting intriguing ways to approach current writing that may be less familiar — for example, pairing Nathaniel Hawthorne's "Young Goodman Brown" with Ha Jin's "Saboteur"; William Wordsworth's "The world is too much with us" with Cheryl Savageau's "Bones — A City Poem"; and Tennessee Williams's *This Property Is Condemned* with Marco Ramirez's *I Am Not Batman*.

- **Clusters of Short-Short Works.** Our students delight in discovering that even the briefest literary works, when read closely, reveal startling and satisfying complexities. Accordingly, we offer a collection of very short literary works at the beginning of each genre's anthology, works such as Lydia Davis's "What She Knew," Randall Jarrell's "The Death of the Ball Turret Gunner," and Suzan-Lori Parks's *Father Comes Home from the Wars* that can be read quickly but examined deeply. Moreover, brief introductions to these sections explain how these forms — flash fiction, very short poems, and ten-minute plays — relate to the larger framework of the main genres.

Lively Biographical Asides Draw Students into the Literature

Students often assume that authors are remote, elevated beings who exist mainly in anthologies, an impression that traditional biographical notes do little to dispel. Such biographies are of course useful — in fact, *Approaching Literature* includes such notes in an appendix. But to augment these traditional notes, in this edition many selections are accompanied by brief call-outs that offer surprising and humanizing insights into the writers' lives. For example, did you know that Gwendolyn Brooks published 75 poems by the age of 16, that Wendell Berry doesn't use a computer, and that it's rumored Sophocles died by attempting to recite a lengthy passage of *Antigone* without taking a breath? Our hope is that these asides — some of which include photographs of the authors — will allow students to engage further with authors as well as with their work and therefore enliven their reading experience.

More Accessible Treatment of the Reading-to-Writing Process

The coverage of reading and writing in this edition has been revised throughout, making the stages of planning and writing clearer and easier to follow. For example, in addition to sentence-level streamlining in Chapters 1 and 2, the discussion of research papers has been updated and moved from near the end of the book to Chapter 3. This placement is immediately after the discussion of writing short papers about literature, so that students realize that research-based writing is on a continuum with less daunting writing tasks such as annotating and summarizing. Further, several student papers now include drafts, so students have useful examples of the revision process in action.

Additional Electronic and Print Resources for Teaching and Learning

Re:Writing for Literature. Marginal icons throughout the book send students to our best free and open resources (no codes required) at **bedfordstmartins.com/rewritinglit.** Students will find easy-to-access visual tutorials, reference materials, and support for working with sources.

- *VirtuaLit* Tutorials for Close Reading (Fiction, Poetry, Drama)
- *AuthorLinks* and Biographies
- Quizzes on Literary Works
- A Glossary of Literary Terms
- MLA-Style sample student papers
- Help for finding and citing sources, including Diana Hacker's *Research and Documentation Online*

Upgrade to Re:Writing Plus. Our library full of premium resources for today's classroom includes access to VideoCentral: Literature plus hundreds of additional readings — public domain short stories, poems, and plays — as well as tutorials, innovative writing help, and hundreds of models of writing. Preview Re:Writing Plus at **rewritingplus/catalog.**

Upgrade to VideoCentral: Literature. Our growing collection of more than fifty video interviews features authors such as Ha Jin and Chitra Banerjee Divakaruni. Preview VideoCentral: Literature at **bedfordstmartins/ videolit/catalog.** To package VideoCentral with student copies, use package ISBN-10: 1-457-60715-8 or ISBN-13: 978-1-457-60715-8.

Download Your Instructor's Manual. Available in print or online, the manual supports every selection in *Approaching Literature* with entry points, suggestions for opening discussions, provocative pairings for each selection, and useful teaching tips. Download the Instructor's Manual at **bedfordstmartins.com/approachinglit/catalog** or order the print manual using ISBN 978-0-312-61917-6.

Literary Reprints. Additional works of literature from any of Bedford/ St. Martin's literary reprint series are available at a special price with *Approaching Literature,* including volumes from the Bedford Cultural Editions, the Bedford Shakespeare Series, Case Studies in Contemporary Criticism, and Case Studies in Critical Controversy. To view a complete list of titles, visit the Bedford/ St. Martin's web site (**bedfordstmartins.com**) and click through "English" and "Literature and Linguistics" to reach "Literary Reprints."

Video and DVD Library. Selected videos and DVDs of plays and stories included in the text are available from Bedford/St. Martin's video library to qualified adopters. Please contact your Bedford/St. Martin's sales representative for more information.

Acknowledgments

We want to express again our appreciation to many colleagues at Hope College for their generous assistance and encouragement as we worked on the earlier editions of *Approaching Literature*: Ion Agheana, John Cox, Jane Currie, Miguel De La Torre, Natalie Dykstra, Curtis Gruenler, Stephen Hemenway, Charles Huttar, Rhoda Janzen, David Klooster, Marla Lunderberg, William Pannapacker, William Reynolds, Heather Sellers, Carla Vissers, and Jennifer Young — and especially to Jesus Montaño for his generous help in each edition. We want to thank Julie Ridl and Elizabeth Trembley for their help in selecting and discussing graphic literature for this edition. Sarah Baar, office manager for the English department at Hope College, assisted us with research, use of computers, and preparation of manuscript copy.

We are grateful also to our students at Hope College, from whom we learn as they learn, and especially to Alicia Abood, Kortney DeVito, Julian Hinson, Sunkyo Hong, Kristina Martinez, and Annie Otto for allowing us to include their writing in this edition.

We appreciate also the help given by colleagues elsewhere on the first edition, especially Sue Beebe, Southwest Texas State University; Daniel Cano, Santa Monica College; Emily Dial-Driver, Rogers State University; Tamara Kuzmenkov, Tacoma Community College; Laurie F. Leach, Hawaii Pacific University; Refugio Romo, Northwest Vista College; Tracy L. Schaelen, Southwestern College; William E. Sheidley, Colorado State University-Pueblo; James G. Van Belle, Edmonds Community College; and Sallie Wolf, Arapahoe Community College. We express thanks for those who provided help in shaping the second edition, especially Marilyn Boutwell, Long Island University, Brooklyn Campus; Janice Carello, SUNY Brockport; Dr. Keith Coplin, Colby Community College; Terence A. Dalrymple, Angelo State University; Robert T. Davis, University of West Florida; James Flavin, Shawnee State University; Sharon G. Levy, Northampton Community College; Mary E. Galvin, Palm Beach Community College; Donald Gilzinger Jr., Suffolk Community College; Peter Goldstein, Juniata College; Eunice Hargett, Broward Community College; Robin Havenick, Linn Benton Community College; Steve Kaufman, Minneapolis Community and Technical College; Erica Lara, Southwest Texas Junior College; Jeremy Saint Larance, West Liberty State College; Cara McClintock-Walsh, Northampton Community College; Janice McKay, SUNY College at Brockport; Jennifer Nader, Bergen Community College; Bill Nedrow, Triton College; Gregory M. Neubauer, West Liberty State College; Darlene Pagán, Pacific University; Melanie Fahlman Reid, Capilano College; Michelle Salman, Pima Community College; Nicole Staub, West Liberty State College; David Thomson, Henderson State University; Catherine Vedder, Kentucky State University; Sheri Weinstein, Kingsborough Community College, City University of New York; and Shari Weiss, San Francisco State University. And we're particularly grateful to those who helped us refine this new edition, especially Dianne O. Armstrong, Ventura College; Jeannie Boniecki, Naugatuck Valley Community College; Marilyn Boutwell, Long Island University; Andrea J. Cleary, Virginia Commonwealth University; Emily Dial-Driver, Rogers State University; Amanda Jane Eller, Westwood College; Priscilla Eng, Middlesex Community College; Martin J. Fertig, Montgomery County Community College; Tasha Haas, Kansas City Kansas Community College; Robin Havenick, Linn Benton Community College; Trevor Kearns, Greenfield Community College; Jeremy Larance, West Liberty University; Sonja Lynch, Wartburg College; Caroline Mains, Palo Alto College; Timothy F. McGinn, Northwest Arkansas Community College; Anna Lee McKennon, Mt. San Antonio College; Denise Nemec, Northwest Arkansas Community College; Traci Thomas-Card, University of Wisconsin, Eau Claire; and Sallie Wolf, Arapahoe Community College.

Finally, we want to thank those at Bedford/St. Martin's who made this book possible and worked hard on it. We are grateful to Charles Christensen and Joan Feinberg for their support of the project and their vision for what the book should be, and to Steve Scipione for his help in developing the book and his excellent advice on contents, style, and other aspects of each edition. And we are grateful to those who helped develop the current edition: to Denise Wydra and Karen Henry for their editorial insights; to Annette Pagliaro Sweeney for guiding the book expertly through the production process and for her patience and understanding as she dealt with our questions and requests; to Mary Lou Wilshaw-Watts for her attentive and knowledgeable copyediting; to Margaret Gorenstein for her careful and alert work on permissions; and Regina Tavani and Shannon Walsh for their tireless assistance with research and other details of revision. Finally, we want to express our gratitude to our editor, Deja Earley, who enriched the third edition in more ways than can be listed or measured, bringing her fresh vision, tireless energy, gentle candor, penetrating intelligence, warm support, and joyful spirit to every e-mail, idea, re-write, conversation, and comma. We are deeply indebted to her.

And we are profoundly grateful for the support of our wives, Julie Ridl and the late Karen Schakel.

Brief Contents

Preface for Instructors   v

Using This Book   xli

PART **1** **Approaching LITERATURE**   **1**

1 Reading Literature   3
2 Writing in Response to Literature   19
3 Writing a Literary Research Paper   55

PART **2** **Approaching FICTION**   **105**

4 Reading Fiction   107
5 Plot and Character   112
6 Point of View and Theme   159
7 Setting and Symbol   195
8 Tone, Style, and Irony   232
9 Writing about Fiction   265
10 Sherman Alexie — An Author in Depth   278
11 A Collection of Stories   313

PART **3** **Approaching POETRY**   **563**

12 Reading Poetry   565
13 Words and Images   570
14 Voice, Tone, and Sound   595
15 Figurative Language   627
16 Rhythm and Meter   652
17 Form and Type   674

18 Writing about Poetry   706
19 A Poet in Personal Context — Judith Ortiz Cofer   720
20 A Collection of Poems   757

PART 4 Approaching DRAMA 889

21 Reading Drama   891
22 Character, Conflict, and Dramatic Action   897
23 Setting and Structure   920
24 Writing about Drama   948
25 August Wilson's *Fences* — A Casebook   959
26 A Collection of Plays   1045

Biographical Sketches   **1371**

Appendix on Scansion   **1422**

Appendix on Reading Critical Essays   **1432**

Approaching Critical Theory   **1445**

Glossary of Literary Terms   **1469**

Index of Authors and Titles   **1499**

Contents

Preface for Instructors   v

Using This Book   xli

PART 1   Approaching LITERATURE   1

1   Reading Literature
Taking Part in a Process   3

SHERMAN ALEXIE, *Superman and Me*   4
"I was smart. I was arrogant. I was lucky. I read books late into the
night, until I could barely keep my eyes open."

The Nature of Reading   7

Active Reading   8

■ CHECKLIST on Active Reading   9

JULIA ALVAREZ, *Daughter of Invention*   10
"Back in the Dominican Republic, I was a terrible student. No one
could ever get me to sit down to a book. But in New York, I needed to
settle somewhere, and the natives were unfriendly, the country
inhospitable, so I took root in the language."

2   Writing in Response to Literature
Entering the Conversation   19

ALICE WALKER, *The Flowers*   20
"It seemed gloomy in the little cove in which she found herself. The air
was damp, the silence close and deep."

Writing in the Margins   21

Sample Student Annotations   23

Journal Writing   24

Sample Student Journal Entry   25

➤ **TIPS for Effective Journal Writing**   25

Writing Essay Examination Answers   26

    Sample Exam Answers: Less Effective and More Effective   28

Writing Short Papers   30

    Step 1. Prewriting: Finding a Topic   31   Step 2. Prewriting: Narrowing the Topic   32   Step 3. Prewriting: Deciding on an Approach   33

➤ **TIPS for Writing Literary Analysis Papers**   34

➤ **TIPS for Writing Comparison-Contrast Papers**   35

➤ **TIPS for Writing Social and Cultural Criticism Papers**   36

    Step 4. Prewriting: Framing a Thesis and Preparing an Outline   36
    Step 5. Writing: Developing and Supporting the Thesis   39
    Step 6. Revising, Proofreading, and Formatting   43

■ **CHECKLIST for Revising**   43

Sample Short Paper   46

    Kortney DeVito's Rough Draft   46   Kortney Devito's Final Draft with Her Notes: "The Death of Myop's Childhood"   47

➤ **TIPS for Writing a Successful Short Paper**   51

A Closer Look at HANDLING TITLES   52

A Closer Look at PUNCTUATING AND FORMATTING QUOTATIONS   53

3   Writing a Literary Research Paper
    Entering the Larger Conversation   **55**

The Research Process   56

    The Nature of Literary Research   56   Factual Research   56
    Primary Research   57   Secondary Research   57

Finding Materials   59

    Doing Library Searches—for Books   59   Doing Library Searches—for Articles   61   Doing Searches for Internet Sources   65

Evaluating Sources   68

Keeping Track of What You've Read   69

Writing a Research Paper   71

    Finding a Topic   71   Developing Ideas   73   Incorporating Sources   74   Documenting Sources   76   Step 1. In-Text Citations   77   Step 2. Works Cited Page   79

Revising, Proofreading, and Double-Checking   84

Sample Research Paper—Kristina Martinez's Final Draft: "The Structure of Story in Toni Morrison's 'Recitatif'"   85

A Closer Look at AVOIDING PLAGIARISM   91

A Closer Look at PREPARING A WORKS CITED PAGE   94

➤ **TIPS for Handling Online Sources**   104

PART **2** **Approaching FICTION** **105**

4 **Reading Fiction**
Responding to the Real World of Stories **107**

What Is Fiction? 107
Why Read Fiction? 108
Active Reading: Fiction 109
Rereading: Fiction 110

5 **Plot and Character**
Watching What Happens, to Whom **112**

DAGOBERTO GILB, *Love in L.A.* 113
"'We'll see you, Mariana,' he said holding out his hand. Her hand felt
so warm and soft he felt like he'd been kissed."

Reading for Plot 116
Starting the Action 116 Organizing the Action 116
Concluding the Action 120
Reading for Character 121
Techniques of Characterization 121 Categories of
Characterization 123 Qualities of Characterization 124
■ CHECKLIST on Reading for Plot and Character 125
Further Reading 125

LOUISE ERDRICH, *The Red Convertible* 126
"I was the first one to drive a convertible on my reservation. And of
course it was red, a red Olds. I owned that car along with my brother
Henry Junior."

FLANNERY O'CONNOR, *A Good Man Is Hard to Find* 134
"'You wouldn't shoot a lady, would you?' the grandmother said and
removed a clean handkerchief from her cuff and began to slap at her
eyes with it."

Approaching Graphic Fiction 146
LYNDA BARRY, *Today's Demon: Magic* 150
Responding through Writing 156
Writing about Plot and Character 156
➤ TIPS for Writing about Plot and Character 157
Writing about Connections 157
Writing Research Papers 158

6   Point of View and Theme
Being Alert to Angles, Open to Insights   159

SANDRA CISNEROS, *The House on Mango Street*   160
"*You live there? The way she said it made me feel like nothing. There. I lived there. I nodded.*"

Reading for Point of View   161

First-Person Narration   162   Third-Person Narration   164
Center of Consciousness   165   Interior Monologue   166
Stream of Consciousness   166

Reading for Theme   167

■ CHECKLIST for Reading about Point of View and Theme   168

Further Reading   169

ALICE WALKER, *Everyday Use*   169
"*Maggie will be nervous until after her sister goes: she will stand hopelessly in corners, homely and ashamed of the burn scars down her arms and legs. . . .*"

WILLIAM FAULKNER, *A Rose for Emily*   176
"*When Miss Emily Grierson died, our whole town went to her funeral: the men through a sort of respectful affection for a fallen monument, the women mostly out of curiosity to see the inside of her house. . . .*"

MARJANE SATRAPI, *The Cigarette* from *Persepolis*   185

Responding through Writing   192

Writing about Point of View and Theme   192

➤ TIPS for Writing about Point of View and Theme   193

Writing about Connections   194
Writing Research Papers   194

7   Setting and Symbol
Meeting Meaning in Places and Objects   195

Reading for Setting   195

ERNEST HEMINGWAY, *Hills Like White Elephants*   196
"'*Would you please please please please please please please stop talking?*'"

Setting as Place   200   Setting as Time   201   Setting as Cultural Context   202   The Effects of Setting   203   Setting and Atmosphere   203

Reading for Symbols   203

Recognizing Symbols   204   Literary Symbols   205   Symbols in "Hills Like White Elephants"   205

Reading for Allegory   207

■ **CHECKLIST on Reading for Setting and Symbol   207**

Further Reading   208

TONI CADE BAMBARA, *The Lesson*   208

"Back in the days when everyone was old and stupid or young and
foolish and me and Sugar were the only ones just right, this lady moved
on our block with nappy hair and proper speech and no makeup."

DAVID MEANS, *The Secret Goldfish*   215

"Everyone knows the story. The kids beg and plead: Please, please get
us a fish (or a dog), we'll feed it, we will, honest. . . ."

RICHARD MCGUIRE, *Here*   223

Responding through Writing   229

Writing about Setting and Symbol   229

➤ **TIPS for Writing about Setting and Symbol   230**

Writing about Connections   231

Writing Research Papers   231

8   Tone, Style, and Irony
Attending to Expression and Attitude   **232**

KATE CHOPIN, *The Story of an Hour*   233

"Knowing that Mrs. Mallard was afflicted with a heart trouble, great
care was taken to break to her as gently as possible the news of her
husband's death."

Reading for Tone   235

Reading for Style   237

Word Choice   237   Sentence Structure   238

Reading for Irony   239

Verbal Irony   239   Sarcasm   240   Dramatic Irony   240

Situational Irony   240

■ **CHECKLIST on Reading for Tone, Style, and Irony   241**

Further Reading   241

JAMES JOYCE, *Araby*   242

"I had never spoken to her, except for a few casual words, and yet her
name was like a summons to all my foolish blood."

KATHERINE MIN, *Courting a Monk*   247

"When I first saw my husband he was sitting cross-legged under a tree on
the quad, his hair as short as peach fuzz, large blue eyes staring upward,
the smile on his face so wide and undirected as to seem moronic."

ART SPIEGELMAN, from *Maus*   260

Responding through Writing   262

    Writing about Tone, Style, and Irony   262

    Writing about Connections   263

➤ **TIPS for Writing about Tone, Style, and Irony**   **264**

    Writing Research Papers   264

9   Writing about Fiction
Applying What You've Learned   265

Step 1. Prewriting: Finding a Topic   266   Step 2. Prewriting: Narrowing the Topic   267   Step 3. Prewriting: Deciding on an Approach   268 Step 4. Prewriting: Framing a Thesis   269 Step 5. Writing: Developing and Supporting the Thesis   269 Step 6. Revising, Proofreading, and Formatting   270

Sample Short Paper   272

    Alicia Abood's Rough Draft   272   Alicia Abood's Final Draft with Notes about Revisions: "A Lost Identity: Taking a Look at Jake in 'Love in L.A.'"   273

10   Sherman Alexie – An Author in Depth
"I've always had crazy dreams"   278

SHERMAN ALEXIE, *This Is What It Means to Say Phoenix, Arizona*   282
    "Thomas was a storyteller that nobody wanted to listen to. That's like being a dentist in a town where everybody has false teeth."

SHERMAN ALEXIE, *The Lone Ranger and Tonto Fistfight in Heaven*   291
    "Forget about the cowboys versus Indians business. The most intense competition on any reservation is Indians versus Indians."

TOMSON HIGHWAY, *Interview with Sherman Alexie*   295

ÅSE NYGREN, *A World of Story-Smoke: A Conversation with Sherman Alexie* (criticism)   297

JOSEPH L. COULOMBE, *The Approximate Size of His Favorite Humor: Sherman Alexie's Comic Connections and Disconnections in* The Lone Ranger and Tonto Fistfight in Heaven (criticism)   300

JEROME DENUCCIO, *Slow Dancing with Skeletons: Sherman Alexie's* The Lone Ranger and Tonto Fistfight in Heaven (criticism)   301

JAMES COX, *Muting White Noise: The Subversion of Popular Culture Narratives of Conquest in Sherman Alexie's Fiction* (criticism)   305

Responding through Writing   310

    Papers Using No Outside Sources   310

    Papers Using Limited Outside Sources   311

    Papers Involving Further Research   312

11 A Collection of Stories
Investigating Various Vistas   **313**

Flash Fiction   313

ANN BEATTIE, *Snow*   314
"This is a story, told the way you say stories should be told:
Somebody grew up, fell in love, and spent a winter with her lover
in the country."

LYDIA DAVIS, *What She Knew*   315
"The fact that she was an old man made it hard for her to be a young
woman."

DAVE EGGERS, *Accident*   315
"Walking over to their car, which you have ruined, it occurs to you
that if the three teenagers are angry teenagers, this encounter could be
very unpleasant."

RAY GONZALES, *The Jalapeño Contest*   316
"Freddy and his brother Tesoro have not seen each other in five years,
and they sit at the kitchen table in Freddy's house and have a jalapeño
contest."

JAMAICA KINCAID, *Girl*   317
". . . you mustn't speak to wharf-rat boys, not even to give directions . . ."

MICHAEL OPPENHEIMER, *The Paring Knife*   319
"I found a knife under the refrigerator while the woman I love and I
were cleaning our house."

Two Short Story Pairings   319

JOHN STEINBECK, *The Chrysanthemums*   320
"Underneath the wagon, between the hind wheels, a lean and rangy
mongrel dog walked sedately. Words were painted on the canvas,
in clumsy, crooked letters. 'Pots, pans, knives, sisors, lawn mores,
Fixed.'"

CHITRA BANERJEE DIVAKARUNI, *Clothes*   328
"It was the most expensive sari I had ever seen, and surely the most
beautiful. Its body was a pale pink, like the dawn sky over the
women's lake."

NATHANIEL HAWTHORNE, *Young Goodman Brown*   337
"What, my sweet, pretty wife, dost thou doubt me already, and we
but three months married!"

HA JIN, *Saboteur*   347
"They grabbed Mr. Chiu and clamped handcuffs around his
wrists. He cried, 'You can't do this to me. This is utterly
unreasonable.'"

Stories for Further Reading

ISABEL ALLENDE, *And of Clay Are We Created*   355
"They discovered the girl's head protruding from the mudpit, eyes wide open, calling soundlessly."

JAMES BALDWIN, *Sonny's Blues*   362
"I was scared, scared for Sonny. . . . A great block of ice got settled in my belly and kept melting there slowly all day long, while I taught my classes algebra."

RAYMOND CARVER, *What We Talk about When We Talk about Love*   386
"There was an ice bucket on the table. The gin and the tonic water kept going around, and we somehow got on the subject of love."

JUDITH ORTIZ COFER, *Nada*   395
"Almost as soon as Doña Ernestina got the telegram about her son's having been killed in Vietnam, she started giving her possessions away."

RALPH ELLISON, *Battle Royal*   402
"Each of us was issued a pair of boxing gloves and ushered out into the big mirrored hall, which we entered looking cautiously about us and whispering. . . ."

GABRIEL GARCÍA MÁRQUEZ, *A Very Old Man with Enormous Wings*   413
"He had to go very close to see that it was an old man, a very old man, lying face down in the mud, who, in spite of his tremendous efforts, couldn't get up, impeded by his enormous wings."

LANGSTON HUGHES, *Thank You, M'am*   418
"The woman said, 'You ought to be my son. I would teach you right from wrong. Least I can do right now is wash your face.'"

ZORA NEALE HURSTON, *Sweat*   421
"She squatted on the kitchen floor beside the great pile of clothes, sorting them into small heaps according to color, and humming a song in a mournful key, but wondering through it all where Sykes, her husband, had gone. . . ."

BEL KAUFMAN, *Sunday in the Park*   429
"The other boy suddenly stood up and with a quick, deliberate swing of his chubby arm threw a spadeful of sand at Larry. It just missed his head."

YIYUN LI, *The Princess of Nebraska*   432
"But that must be what was Yang's value—he made people fall in love with him, and the love led them astray, willingly, from their otherwise tedious paths."

TONI MORRISON, *Recitatif*   445
"It was one thing to be taken out of your own bed early in the morning—it was something else to be stuck in a strange place with a girl from a whole other race."

BHARATI MUKHERJEE, *The Management of Grief*   459
"A woman I don't know is boiling tea the Indian way in my kitchen. There are a lot of women I don't know in my kitchen, whispering, and moving tactfully."

HARUKI MURAKAMI, *Birthday Girl*   471
"[B]eing screamed at by an angry chef while lugging pumpkin gnocchi and seafood fritto misto to customers' tables was no way to spend one's twentieth birthday."

JOYCE CAROL OATES, *Where Are You Going, Where Have You Been?*   481
"Her name was Connie. She was fifteen and she had a quick, nervous giggling habit of craning her neck to glance into mirrors or checking other people's faces to make sure her own was all right."

TIM O'BRIEN, *The Things They Carried*   493
"As a first lieutenant and platoon leader, Jimmy Cross carried a compass, maps, code books, binoculars, and a .45-caliber pistol that weighed 2.9 pounds fully loaded. He carried a strobe light and the responsibility for the lives of his men."

TILLIE OLSEN, *I Stand Here Ironing*   506
"I stand here ironing, and what you asked me moves tormented back and forth with the iron."

ZZ PACKER, *Brownies*   512
"By our second day at Camp Crescendo, the girls in my Brownie troop had decided to kick the asses of each and every girl in Brownie Troop 909."

EDGAR ALLAN POE, *The Cask of Amontillado*   528
"The thousand injuries of Fortunato I had borne as I best could; but when he ventured upon insult, I vowed revenge."

KATHERINE ANNE PORTER, *The Jilting of Granny Weatherall*   533
"She flicked her wrist neatly out of Doctor Harry's pudgy careful fingers and pulled the sheet up to her chin. The brat ought to be in knee breeches."

LESLIE MARMON SILKO, *The Man to Send Rain Clouds*   540
"He had been dead for a day or more, and the sheep had wandered and scattered up and down the arroyo."

AMY TAN, *Two Kinds*   543
"My mother believed you could be anything you wanted to be in America."

JOHN UPDIKE, *A & P*   552
"In walks these three girls in nothing but bathing suits."

HELENA MARÍA VIRAMONTES, *The Moths*   557
"I was fourteen years old when Abuelita requested my help. And it seemed only fair."

PART **3**   **Approaching POETRY**   **563**

12 Reading Poetry
Realizing the Richness in Poems   **565**

What Is Poetry?   565
  What Does Poetry Do?   566
Why Read Poetry?   567
Active Reading: Poetry   567
Rereading: Poetry   568

13 Words and Images
Seizing on Sense and Sight   **570**

Reading for Denotation   571
  ROBERT HAYDEN, *Those Winter Sundays*   572
Reading for Connotation   573
  GWENDOLYN BROOKS, *The Bean Eaters*   574
Reading for Images   575
  MAXINE KUMIN, *The Sound of Night*   576
  WILLIAM CARLOS WILLIAMS, *The Red Wheelbarrow*   578
■ CHECKLIST on Reading for Words and Images   579
Further Reading   579
  RICHARD JONES, *OED*   580
  RON KOERTGE, *Q and A*   581
  ALLISON JOSEPH, *On Being Told I Don't Speak Like a Black Person*   582
  NATASHA TRETHEWEY, *History Lesson*   585
  ANITA ENDREZZE, *The Girl Who Loved the Sky*   586
  WENDELL BERRY, *The Peace of Wild Things*   588
  CATHY SONG, *Heaven*   589
Responding through Writing   591
  Writing about Words and Images   591
➤ TIPS for Writing about Words and Images   592
  Writing about Connections   593
  Writing Research Papers   594

14 Voice, Tone, and Sound
Hearing How Sense Is Said   **595**

Reading for Voice   595

    LI-YOUNG LEE, *Eating Alone*   596

    CHARLES BUKOWSKI, *my old man*   598

Reading a Dramatic Monologue   601

Reading for Tone   601

    THEODORE ROETHKE, *My Papa's Waltz*   602

Reading for Irony   603

    MARGE PIERCY, *Barbie Doll*   604

Reading for Sound   606

➤ **TIPS for Reading Poems Aloud**   606

    SEKOU SUNDIATA, *Blink Your Eyes*   607

    Alliteration 609   Assonance 610   Repetition 610   Rhyme 611

▪ **CHECKLIST on Reading for Voice, Tone, and Sound**   613

Further Reading   613

    GERALD STERN, *The Dog*   614

    JANE KENYON, *A Boy Goes into the World*   616

    PAT MORA, *La Migra*   617

    WILFRED OWEN, *Dulce et Decorum Est*   619

    YUSEF KOMUNYAKAA, *Facing It*   620

    ROBERT BROWNING, *My Last Duchess*   622

Responding through Writing   624

    Writing about Voice, Tone, and Sound   624

➤ **TIPS for Writing about Voice, Tone, and Sound**   625

    Writing about Connections   625

    Writing Research Papers   626

15 Figurative Language
Wondering What This Has to Do with That   **627**

Reading for Simile   628

    MARTÍN ESPADA, *Latin Night at the Pawnshop*   628

    LANGSTON HUGHES, *Harlem*   631

Reading for Metaphor   632

    DENNIS BRUTUS, *Nightsong: City*   633

Reading for Personification   634

    ANGELINA WELD GRIMKÉ, *A Winter Twilight*   635

Reading for Metonymy and Synecdoche   636

    EDWIN ARLINGTON ROBINSON, *Richard Cory*   637

Two Other Observations about Figures   639

    WILLIAM STAFFORD, *Traveling through the Dark*   639

■ CHECKLIST on Reading for Figurative Language   641

Further Reading   641

    ALFRED, LORD TENNYSON, *The Eagle*   642

    TED KOOSER, *Student*   642

    EMILY DICKINSON, *It sifts from Leaden Sieves*   643

    MARY OLIVER, *First Snow*   644

    JUDITH ORTIZ COFER, *Cold as Heaven*   646

    JULIA ALVAREZ, *How I Learned to Sweep*   647

Responding through Writing   649

    Writing about Figurative Language   649

    Writing about Connections   650

➤ TIPS for Writing about Figurative Language   650

    Writing Research Papers   651

16 Rhythm and Meter
Feeling the Beat, the Flux, and the Flow   652

Reading for Rhythm   652

    Line Length 653   Phrasings 653   Line Endings 653   Pauses 653
    Spaces 654   Word Choice and Combinations of Sounds 654

    E. E. CUMMINGS, *Buffalo Bill 's*   655

Reading for Meter   656

    PAUL LAURENCE DUNBAR, *We Wear the Mask*   659

■ CHECKLIST on Reading for Rhythm and Meter   661

Further Reading   661

    LUCILLE CLIFTON, *at the cemetery, walnut grove plantation, south carolina, 1989*   662

    LORNA DEE CERVANTES, *Freeway 280*   663

    SEAMUS HEANEY, *Mid-Term Break*   665

    ROBERT FROST, *The Road Not Taken*   666

GARY MIRANDA, *Love Poem* 668

A. K. RAMANUJAN, *Self-Portrait* 669

EMILY DICKINSON, *I'm Nobody! Who are you?* 669

SYLVIA PLATH, *Metaphors* 670

GEORGIA DOUGLAS JOHNSON, *Wishes* 670

Responding through Writing 671

Writing about Rhythm and Meter 671

Writing about Connections 672

Writing Research Papers 672

➤ TIPS for Writing about Rhythm and Meter 673

17 Form and Type
Delighting in Design **674**

Reading for Lines 674

GWENDOLYN BROOKS, *We Real Cool* 675

Reading for Stanzas 676

COUNTEE CULLEN, *Incident* 677

Reading Sonnets 679

English (or Shakespearean) Sonnet 679

WILLIAM SHAKESPEARE, *That time of year thou mayst in me behold* 680

Italian (or Petrarchan) Sonnet 681

GERARD MANLEY HOPKINS, *God's Grandeur* 682

Reading Free Verse 684

LESLIE MARMON SILKO, *Prayer to the Pacific* 685

Reading for Internal Form 687

Parallelism 687   Juxtaposition 688   Narrative 688   Logical
Pattern 688   Question-Answer 688   Meditative Movement 688
Association 689   Lists (or Catalogs) and Litanies 689

■ CHECKLIST on Reading for Form and Type 689

Combinations of the Above 690

Further Reading 690

JAMES WRIGHT, *A Blessing* 690

JOY HARJO, *She Had Some Horses* 691

WILLIAM BUTLER YEATS, *The Lake Isle of Innisfree* 693

CLAUDE MCKAY, *If we must die* 694

HELENE JOHNSON, *Sonnet to a Negro in Harlem*   696

E. E. CUMMINGS, *next to of course god america i*   697

DAVID MURA, *Grandfather-in-Law*   698

ELIZABETH BISHOP, *Sestina*   699

JOHN YAU, *Chinese Villanelle*   701

Responding through Writing   703
   Writing about Form and Type   703
➤ **TIPS for Writing about Form and Type   704**
   Writing about Connections   705
   Writing Research Papers   705

18 Writing about Poetry
Applying What You've Learned   **706**

Step 1. Prewriting: Finding a Topic   707   Step 2. Prewriting:
Narrowing the Topic   709   Step 3. Prewriting: Deciding on
an Approach   709   Step 4. Prewriting: Framing a Thesis   711
Step 5. Writing: Developing and Supporting the Thesis   711
➤ **TIPS for Quoting Poetry   712**
   Step 6. Revising, Proofreading, and Formatting   713
Sample Short Paper   714
   Sunkyo Hong's Rough Draft   714   Sunkyo Hong's Final Draft:
   "Experiencing 'First Snow'"   715

19 A Poet in Personal Context — Judith Ortiz Cofer
Two Worlds, One Vision   **720**

The Changeling (poem)   725

The Birthplace (poem)   726

On the Island I Have Seen (poem)   726

The Latin Deli: An Ars Poetica (poem)   727

My Father in the Navy (poem)   728

First Job: The Southern Sweets Sandwich Shop and Bakery (poem)   729

Silent Dancing (memoir)   731

And Are You a Latina Writer? (essay in interview form)   738

RAFAEL OCASIO, *Speaking in Puerto Rican: An Interview with Judith
Ortiz Cofer*   742

MARILYN KALLET, *The Art of Not Forgetting: An Interview with Judith Ortiz Cofer* 744

LORRAINE M. LÓPEZ, *Possibilities for Salsa Music in the Mainstream: An Interview with Judith Ortiz Cofer* 747

BRIDGET KEVANE AND JUANITA HEREDIA, *The Poetic Truth: An Interview with Judith Ortiz Cofer* 751

Responding Through Writing 754
    Papers Using Only the Poetry in the Chapter 754
    Papers Using Both Poetry and Prose in the Chapter 754
    Papers Including Outside Research 755

20 A Collection of Poems
Valuing Various Voices 757

A Dozen Very Short Poems 757
    ANONYMOUS, *Western Wind* 758
    MARGARET ATWOOD, *you fit into me* 758
    LUCILLE CLIFTON, *adam and eve* 758
    COUNTEE CULLEN, *For a Lady I Know* 758
    LANCE HENSON, *song in january* 759
    RANDALL JARRELL, *The Death of the Ball Turret Gunner* 759
    DENISE LEVERTOV, *Leaving Forever* 759
    MARIANNE MOORE, *Poetry* 760
    DOROTHY PARKER, *Résumé* 760
    EZRA POUND, *In a Station of the Metro* 760
    MARY RUEFLE, *Barbarians* 760
    CARL SANDBURG, *Fog* 761

A Variety of Poems for Further Reading 761
    AI, *Why Can't I Leave You?* 761
    AGHA SHAHID ALI, *I Dream It Is Afternoon When I Return to Delhi* 762
    ANONYMOUS, *Sir Patrick Spens* 763

A Pairing of Poems 764
    MARGARET ATWOOD, *True Stories* 764
    RICHARD GARCIA, *Why I Left the Church* 765

    W. H. AUDEN, *Musée des Beaux Arts* 767

JIMMY SANTIAGO BACA, *Family Ties*   768

JIM BARNES, *Return to La Plata, Missouri*   769

ELIZABETH BISHOP, *In the Waiting Room*   770

WILLIAM BLAKE, *The Chimney Sweeper*   772

EAVAN BOLAND, *The Pomegranate*   773

ANNE BRADSTREET, *To My Dear and Loving Husband*   774

OLGA BROUMAS, *Cinderella*   775

STERLING A. BROWN, *Riverbank Blues*   776

ELIZABETH BARRETT BROWNING, *How do I love thee? Let me count the ways*   777

JO CARSON, *I Cannot Remember All the Times . . .*   777

TINA CHANG, *Naming the Light*   779

MARILYN CHIN, *How I Got That Name*   780

LUCILLE CLIFTON, *homage to my hips*   782

SAMUEL TAYLOR COLERIDGE, *Kubla Khan*   783

BILLY COLLINS, *I Chop Some Parsley While Listening to Art Blakey's Version of "Three Blind Mice"*   785

VICTOR HERNÁNDEZ CRUZ, *Problems with Hurricanes*   786

TODD DAVIS, *Accident*   787

TOI DERRICOTTE, *A Note on My Son's Face*   788

EMILY DICKINSON, *I heard a Fly buzz*   790

EMILY DICKINSON, *Because I could not stop for Death*   790

CHITRA BANERJEE DIVAKARUNI, *Nargis' Toilette*   791

JOHN DONNE, *Break of Day*   793

JOHN DONNE, *Death, be not proud*   793

MARK DOTY, *Tiara*   794

RITA DOVE, *Fifth Grade Autobiography*   795

CORNELIUS EADY, *My Mother, If She Had Won Free Dance Lessons*   795

T. S. ELIOT, *The Love Song of J. Alfred Prufrock*   797

GRAY EMERSON, *The Indexer in Love*   800

CAROLYN FORCHÉ, *The Colonel*   801

VIEVEE FRANCIS, *1864, A Pocket Full of Rye*   802

ROBERT FROST, *After Apple-Picking*   803

ROBERT FROST, *Birches*   804

A Pairing of Poems   805

ROBERT FROST, *Design*   805

DAVID HERNANDEZ, *The Butterfly Effect*   806

TESS GALLAGHER, *The Hug*   807

ALLEN GINSBERG, *A Supermarket in California*   808

NIKKI GIOVANNI, *Nikki-Rosa*   809

ARACELIS GIRMAY, *Consider the Hands That Write This Letter*   810

DIANE GLANCY, *Emigrant*   811

RAY GONZÁLEZ, *Praise the Tortilla, Praise Menudo, Praise Chorizo*   811

KIMIKO HAHN, *Mother's Mother*   812

THOMAS HARDY, *The Man He Killed*   814

MICHAEL S. HARPER, *Nightmare Begins Responsibility*   815

TERRANCE HAYES, *Talk*   816

SAMUEL HAZO, *For Fawzi in Jerusalem*   817

GEORGE HERBERT, *The Pulley*   818

ROBERT HERRICK, *To the Virgins, to Make Much of Time*   819

BOB HICOK, *In the loop*   819

JANE HIRSHFIELD, *To Drink*   820

TONY HOAGLAND, *History of Desire*   820

LINDA HOGAN, *Crow Law*   822

GARRETT KAORU HONGO, *Yellow Light*   822

A Pairing of Poems   824

A. E. HOUSMAN, *To an Athlete Dying Young*   824

QUINCY TROUPE, *A Poem For "Magic"*   825

LANGSTON HUGHES, *The Negro Speaks of Rivers*   826

HONORÉE FANONNE JEFFERS, *Unidentified Female Student, Former Slave*   827

BEN JONSON, *On My First Son*   827

A. VAN JORDAN, *From*   828

JOHN KEATS, *Ode on a Grecian Urn*   829

ETHERIDGE KNIGHT, *Hard Rock Returns to Prison from the Hospital for the Criminal Insane*   831

LI-YOUNG LEE, *Visions and Interpretations*   832

DENISE LEVERTOV, *Talking to Grief*   833

PHILIP LEVINE, *What Work Is*   834

LARRY LEVIS, *The Poem You Asked For*   835

AUDRE LORDE, *Hanging Fire*   836

RICHARD LOVELACE, *To Lucasta, Going to the Wars*   837

ROBERT LOWELL, *Skunk Hour*   837

HEATHER MCHUGH, *What He Thought*   839

CHRISTOPHER MARLOWE, *The Passionate Shepherd to His Love*   840

ANDREW MARVELL, *To His Coy Mistress*   841

JOHN MILTON, *When I consider how my light is spent*   843

MARIANNE MOORE, *Poetry*   843

THYLIAS MOSS, *Rush Hour*   844

MARILYN NELSON, *Minor Miracle*   845

LORINE NIEDECKER, *My Life by Water*   846

NAOMI SHIHAB NYE, *The Small Vases from Hebron*   846

SHARON OLDS, *I Go Back to May 1937*   848

SIMON J. ORTIZ, *Speaking*   848

LINDA PASTAN, *love poem*   849

ROBERT PINSKY, *Shirt*   850

SYLVIA PLATH, *Daddy*   851

DUDLEY RANDALL, *Ballad of Birmingham*   853

HENRY REED, *Naming of Parts*   854

ADRIENNE RICH, *Rape*   855

JACK RIDL, *First Cut*   856

ALBERTO RÍOS, *Nani*   857

LUIS J. RODRIGUEZ, *Running to America*   858

WENDY ROSE, *Loo-Wit*   861

WILLIAM SHAKESPEARE, *Shall I compare thee to a summer's day?*   862

A Pairing of Poems   863

PERCY BYSSHE SHELLEY, *Ozymandias*   863

PETER BLUE CLOUD, *Crazy Horse Monument*   863

CHARLES SIMIC, *Classic Ballroom Dances*   864

GARY SOTO, *Moving Away*   865

EDMUND SPENSER, *One day I wrote her name upon the strand*   866

WALLACE STEVENS, *Anecdote of the Jar*   866

MARK STRAND, *Eating Poetry*   867

VIRGIL SUÁREZ, *Tea Leaves, Caracoles, Coffee Beans*   867

MAY SWENSON, *The Shape of Death*   868

ARTHUR SZE, *The Shapes of Leaves*   869

MARY TALLMOUNTAIN, *Matmiya*   870

ALFRED, LORD TENNYSON, *Ulysses*   871

DYLAN THOMAS, *Do not go gentle into that good night*   873

JEAN TOOMER, *Face*   874

JAMES WELCH, *Christmas Comes to Moccasin Flat*   874

PATRICIA JABBEH WESLEY, *There's Nothing You Can Do*   875

ROBERTA HILL WHITEMAN, *The White Land*   876

WALT WHITMAN, From *Song of Myself*   877

RICHARD WILBUR, *Love Calls Us to the Things of This World*   879

NANCY WILLARD, *Questions My Son Asked Me, Answers I Never Gave Him*   881

WILLIAM CARLOS WILLIAMS, *Spring and All*   882

A Pairing of Poems   883

WILLIAM WORDSWORTH, *The world is too much with us*   883

CHERYL SAVAGEAU, *Bones—A City Poem*   883

WILLIAM BUTLER YEATS, *The Second Coming*   885

AL YOUNG, *A Dance for Ma Rainey*   886

RAY A. YOUNG BEAR, *Green Threatening Clouds*   887

PAUL ZIMMER, *Zimmer's Head Thudding against the Blackboard*   888

PART 4   Approaching DRAMA   889

21 Reading Drama
Participating in Serious Play   891

What Is Drama?   891

Why Read Drama?   893

Active Reading: Drama   893

Rereading: Drama   895

22 Character, Conflict, and Dramatic Action
Thinking about Who Does What to Whom and Why   **897**

KELLY STUART, *The New New*   *899*
"It's become stale to say something is NEW. What's the new new?
We need the new NEW."

Reading for Character   904
Reading for Dialogue   905
Reading for Conflict   906
Reading for Dramatic Action   907
■ CHECKLIST on Reading for Character, Conflict, and Dramatic Action   908
Further Reading   908

EDUARDO MACHADO, *Crossing the Border*   *909*
". . . I am trying to teach you something that will get you out of here,
and you don't care."

Responding through Writing   917
Writing about Character, Conflict, and Dramatic Action   917
➤ TIPS for Writing about Character, Conflict, and Dramatic Action   918
Writing about Connections   918
Writing Research Papers   919

23 Setting and Structure
Examining Where, When, and How It Happens   **920**

Reading for Setting   920

SUSAN GLASPELL, *Trifles*   *922*
"'Then why can't I see him?' I asked her, out of patience. ''Cause he's
dead,' says she."

Reading for Structure   934
Compression and Contrast   935
■ CHECKLIST on Reading for Setting and Structure   937
Further Reading   937

DON NIGRO, *Letters from Quebec to Providence in the Rain*   *938*
"You found some letters in an old book. One's likely to stumble upon
anything in the pages of an old book. Flowers. Note cards. Fragments
of human skin."

Responding through Writing   944
Writing about Setting and Structure   944
Writing about Connections   945
➤ TIPS for Writing about Setting and Structure   946
Writing Research Papers   947

24 Writing about Drama
Applying What You've Learned   **948**

Step 1. Prewriting: Finding a Topic   949   Step 2. Prewriting: Narrowing
the Topic   951   Step 3. Prewriting: Deciding on an Approach   951
Step 4. Prewriting: Framing a Thesis and Preparing an Outline   952
Step 5. Writing: Developing and Supporting the Thesis   952
Step 6. Revising, Proofreading, and Formatting   953

➤ **TIPS for Quoting Drama**   **954**

Sample Short Paper   955

Julian Hinson: "Out with the Old, in with the New: The Spin on
Contemporary Values in *The New New*"

25 August Wilson's *Fences* – A Casebook
Wrestling with One Writer's Work   **959**

AUGUST WILSON, *Fences*   963
*"Some people build fences to keep people out . . . and other people build
fences to keep people in. Rose wants to hold on to you all."*

LLOYD RICHARDS, *Introduction*   1018

CLIVE BARNES, *Fiery* Fences: *A Review* (criticism)   1019

FRANK RICH, *Family Ties in Wilson's* Fences: *A Review* (criticism)   1021

BONNIE LYONS, *An Interview with August Wilson*   1023

MILES MARSHALL LEWIS, *Miles Marshall Lewis Talks with
August Wilson*   1027

MISSY DEHN KUBITSCHEK, *August Wilson's Gender Lesson* (criticism)   1029

HARRY J. ELAM, JR., *August Wilson* (criticism)   1034

SUSAN KOPRINCE, *Baseball as History and Myth in August
Wilson's* Fences (criticism)   1038

Responding through Writing   1042

Papers Using No Outside Sources   1042
Papers Using Limited Outside Sources   1043
Papers Involving Further Research   1044

26 A Collection of Plays
Viewing from Various Vantage Points   **1045**

Four Ten-Minute Plays   1045

DAVID IVES, *Sure Thing*   1046
"I was lying. I never really went to college. I just like to party."

MARK LAMBECK, *Intervention* 1055

"We ARE ganging up on him! That's what you do in an intervention."

SUZAN-LORI PARKS, *Father Comes Home from the Wars (Part 1)* 1061

"They should of sent a letter. A letter saying you were coming home."

JOYCE CAROL OATES, *When I Was a Little Girl and My Mother Didn't Want Me* 1062

"My father was killed and I never knew why. Then, I was given away. By my mother."

Two Pairings of Ten-Minute Plays 1066

WOODY ALLEN, *Death Knocks* 1066

"I remind you of Moe Lefkowitz. I'm one of the most terrifying figures you could possibly imagine, and him I remind of Moe Lefkowitz."

DAVID HENRY HWANG, *As the Crow Flies* 1073

"See, I'm really two different folks. You've been knowin' me as Hannah Carter, 'cuz when I'm over here cleanin', that's who I am. But at night, or when I'm outside and stuff, I turn into Sandra Smith."

TENNESSEE WILLIAMS, *This Property Is Condemned* 1083

"The principal used to say there must've been something wrong with my home atmosphere because of the fact that we took in railroad men an' some of 'em slept with my sister."

MARCO RAMIREZ, *I Am Not Batman* 1090

"'Cause all Batman really wants to do is save people and maybe pay Abuela's bills one day and die happy and maybe get like mad famous."

Four Classic Plays 1098

The Impact of Genre and Theater 1098 The Greek Theater 1098

SOPHOCLES, *Antigone* 1103

"I will bury him myself. And even if I die in the act, that death will be a glory."

Elizabethan Drama 1143

WILLIAM SHAKESPEARE, *Othello, the Moor of Venice* 1149

"Then must you speak of one that loved not wisely, but too well."

Post-Elizabethan Theaters 1242

HENRIK IBSEN, *A Doll House* 1245

"How snug and nice our home is, Nora. You're safe here. I'll keep you like a hunted dove I've rescued out of a hawk's claws."

Twentieth-Century Theaters 1298

LORRAINE HANSBERRY, *A Raisin in the Sun* 1300

"Seem like God didn't see fit to give the black man nothing but dreams."

Biographical Sketches   1371

Appendix on Scansion   1422

ALFRED, LORD TENNYSON, From *The Lady of Shalott*   *1424*

SAMUEL TAYLOR COLERIDGE, *Metrical Feet, Lesson for a Boy*   *1425*

EMILY DICKINSON, *I like to see it lap the Miles*   *1425*

Appendix on Reading Critical Essays   1432

SUSAN FARRELL, *Fight vs. Flight: A Re-evaluation of Dee in Alice Walker's "Everyday Use"*   *1436*

Approaching Critical Theory   1445

Glossary of Literary Terms   1469

Index of Authors and Titles   1499

Using This Book

- Terms that are **boldface** in the text are defined in the Glossary of Literary Terms at the end of the book.
- The dates provided for stories indicate their earliest publication; dates for poems give the first publication in a book; dates for plays are for their initial performance. For some poems, when publication was delayed, the probable date of composition is given as well, in *Italics*.
- A rule (——) indicates a space break (in a story) or a stanza break (in a poem) that falls at the bottom or top of a page and otherwise might be undetectable.
- For untitled poems, the first line is often used as a convenient form of reference, though it should not be thought of as a title and thus does not follow the capitalization rules for titles.

PART 1

Approaching LITERATURE

1 Reading Literature 3

2 Writing in Response to Literature 19

3 Writing a Literary Research Paper 55

Overleaf: The novelist, essayist, poet, and children's book author Julia Alvarez was photographed in her home in Vermont, where she has lived and worked since 1988. Alvarez teaches creative writing and is currently the writer-in-residence at Middlebury College. Alvarez and her husband divide their time between their home in Vermont and a cooperative coffee farm—a sustainable farm-literacy center called Alta Gracia—in the Dominican Republic, where Alvarez was raised. When asked why she writes in so many different genres, she says, "I blame my life. Something happens which sends me in a new direction . . . and the telling requires a different form, rhythm, voice." (See p. 1372 for a short biography.)

Reprinted by permission of Cameron Davidson.

I read because it takes me out of myself, it enlarges me. Kathleen Norris

(American Poet and Nonfiction Writer)

Reading Literature
Taking Part in a Process

Why read? Why take the time and possibly even the effort a story, poem, or play requires when we have movies, television, DVDs, and the Internet? Maybe you already love to read and you know why. Maybe you used to read a lot, but something turned you away. Or maybe you never did like to read. If that's the case, we hope that you will consider what so many have discovered: that through reading they learned that they are not alone in what they've experienced. They have had their minds and their worlds opened to include new people and situations different from their own. They have found that the intimate experience of being engaged in reading a book can be personally meaningful and that this form of escape can be an entrance to something richly rewarding. They have found, as they read, that they learn, feel, and think; that they can pause to wonder or reflect; that they feel an inexplicable sense of being alive.

READING TO CONNECT WITH OTHERS   Although reading may seem at first like an individual act, it is by its nature shared and communal. We read what others have written. Reading is not only a source of ideas, challenges, and meanings but it is also an invitation to understanding, empathy, sympathy, judgment, and compassion. Reading enables us to connect with others, to enter the thoughts, feelings, and experiences of those both similar to and different from ourselves. Reading fills a deep yet often unrecognized need, assisting us to become more fully human and more fully humane.

ENTRY POINTS   The following is a personal essay written by Sherman Alexie. An *essay* is a brief discussion, usually in prose, of a limited topic or idea; a *personal essay* deals with a particular part of its author's life and experience. Alexie grew up on the Spokane Indian Reservation in Wellpinit, Washington, where—surprisingly, he says—he found that first reading and then writing became essential to his very being. As you read the essay, pay attention to the way Alexie began reading—not at all a passive taking in, but an active engagement with the work before him. Notice also what goes on as you read the essay, how it requires you also to actively involve yourself in the process.

Sherman Alexie   b. 1966

Superman and Me   [1997]

I learned to read with a *Superman* comic book. Simple enough, I suppose. I cannot recall which particular *Superman* comic book I read, nor can I remember which villain he fought in that issue. I cannot remember the plot, nor the means by which I obtained the comic book. What I can remember is this: I was three years old, a Spokane Indian boy living with his family on the Spokane Indian Reservation in eastern Washington state. We were poor by most standards, but one of my parents usually managed to find some minimum-wage job or another, which made us middle class by reservation standards. I had a brother and three sisters. We lived on a combination of irregular paychecks, hope, fear, and government-surplus food.

APPROACHING THE AUTHOR

Sherman Alexie planned to be a doctor and enrolled in premed courses at Washington State University, but after fainting numerous times in human anatomy class, he realized he needed to change his career path.

For more about him, see page 278.

My father, who is one of the few Indians who went to Catholic school on purpose, was an avid reader of westerns, spy thrillers, murder mysteries, gangster epics, basketball-player biographies, and anything else he could find. He bought his books by the pound at Dutch's Pawn Shop, Goodwill, Salvation Army, and Value Village. When he had extra money, he bought new novels at supermarkets, convenience stores, and hospital gift shops. Our house was filled with books. They were stacked in crazy piles in the bathroom, bedrooms, and living room. In a fit of unemployment-inspired creative energy, my father built a set of bookshelves and soon filled them with a random assortment of books about the Kennedy assassination, Watergate, the Vietnam War, and the entire twenty-three-book series of the Apache westerns. My father loved books, and since I loved my father with an aching devotion, I decided to love books as well.

I can remember picking up my father's books before I could read. The words themselves were mostly foreign, but I still remember the exact moment when I first understood, with a sudden clarity, the purpose of a paragraph. I didn't have the vocabulary to say "paragraph," but I realized that a paragraph was a fence that held words. The words inside a paragraph worked together for a common purpose. They had some specific reason for being inside the same fence. This knowledge delighted me. I began to think of everything in terms of paragraphs. Our reservation was a small paragraph within the United States. My family's house was a paragraph, distinct from the other paragraphs of the LeBrets to the north, the Fords to our south, and the Tribal School to the west. Inside our house, each family member existed as a separate paragraph, but still had genetics and common experiences to link us. Now, using this logic, I can see my changed family as an essay of seven paragraphs: mother, father, older brother, the deceased sister, my younger twin sisters, and our adopted little brother.

At the same time I was seeing the world in paragraphs, I also picked up that *Superman* comic book. Each panel, complete with picture, dialogue, and narrative, was a three-dimensional paragraph. In one panel, Superman breaks through a door. His suit is red, blue, and yellow. The brown door shatters into many pieces. I look at the narrative above the picture. I cannot read the words, but I assume it tells me that Superman is breaking down the door. Aloud, I pretend to read the words and say "Superman is breaking down the door." Words, dialogue, also float out of Superman's mouth. Because he is breaking down the door, I assume he says, "I am breaking down the door." Once again, I pretend to read the words and say aloud, "I am breaking down the door." In this way, I learned to read.

This might be an interesting story all by itself. A little Indian boy teaches   5
himself to read at an early age and advances quickly. He reads *Grapes of Wrath* in kindergarten when other children are struggling through Dick and Jane. If he'd been anything but an Indian boy living on the reservation, he might have been called a prodigy. But he is an Indian boy living on the reservation, and is simply an oddity. He grows into a man who often speaks of his childhood in the third-person, as if it will somehow dull the pain and make him sound more modest about his talents.

A smart Indian is a dangerous person, widely feared and ridiculed by Indians and non-Indians alike. I fought with my classmates on a daily basis. They wanted me to stay quiet when the non-Indian teacher asked for answers, for volunteers, for help. We were Indian children who were expected to be stupid. Most lived up to those expectations inside the classroom, but subverted them on the outside. They struggled with basic reading in school, but could remember how to sing a few dozen powwow songs. They were monosyllabic in front of their non-Indian teachers, but could tell complicated stories and jokes at the dinner table. They submissively ducked their heads when confronted by a non-Indian adult, but would slug it out with the Indian bully who was ten years older. As Indian children, we were expected to fail in the non-Indian world. Those who failed were ceremonially accepted by other Indians and appropriately pitied by non-Indians.

I refused to fail. I was smart. I was arrogant. I was lucky. I read books late into the night, until I could barely keep my eyes open. I read books at recess, then during lunch, and in the few minutes left after I had finished my classroom assignments. I read books in the car when my family traveled to powwows or basketball games. In shopping malls, I ran to the bookstores and read bits and pieces of as many books as I could. I read the books my father brought home from the pawnshops and secondhand stores. I read the books I borrowed from the library. I read the backs of cereal boxes. I read the newspaper. I read the bulletins posted on the walls of the school, the clinic, the tribal offices, the post office. I read junk mail. I read auto-repair manuals. I read magazines. I read anything that had words and paragraphs. I read with equal parts joy and desperation. I loved those books, but I also knew that love had only one purpose. I was trying to save my life.

Despite all the books I read, I am still surprised I became a writer. I was going to be a pediatrician. These days, I write novels, short stories, and poems. I visit schools and teach creative writing to Indian kids. In all my years in the reservation school system, I was never taught how to write poetry, short stories, or novels. I was certainly never taught that Indians wrote poetry, short stories, and novels. Writing was something beyond Indians. I cannot recall a single time that a guest teacher visited the reservation. There must have been visiting teachers. Who were they? Where are they now? Do they exist? I visit the schools as often as possible. The Indian kids crowd the classroom. Many are writing their own poems, short stories, and novels. They have read my books. They have read many other books. They look at me with bright eyes and arrogant wonder. They are trying to save their lives. Then there are the sullen and already defeated Indian kids who sit in the back rows and ignore me with theatrical precision. The pages of their notebooks are empty. They carry neither pencil nor pen. They stare out the window. They refuse and resist. "Books," I say to them. "Books," I say. I throw my weight against their locked doors. The door holds. I am smart. I am arrogant. I am lucky. I am trying to save our lives.

APPROACHING THE READING

1. This chapter opens by giving some reasons people need to read. Which of those reasons do you think apply to Alexie? Why does he need to read?

2. List some things in Alexie's life that made love of reading difficult to sustain, that worked against his learning and growth. Think briefly about your own life. Do you love to read, the way Alexie does? If not, are there factors that work against reading, that make it difficult to do or love?

3. Think about what is involved in the process of reading. How do ideas, feelings, and descriptions get from Alexie's heart and mind to your heart and mind? In what sense are you essential for the communication process to be complete?

READING TO LIVE   Alexie says he read to save his life. He doesn't mean surviving physically, of course. Rather, he realized that his mind and heart and imagination required regular nourishment, which he found could come from books. Without this nourishment, parts of himself, parts essential to his very identity that make him who he really is, would weaken and perhaps eventually starve. If you don't feel that way yourself, we hope this course and this book will lead you to the real value of making reading and writing a vital part of your life, perhaps even change your life. We hope that you will give reading a new chance, will put into reading the attentiveness and receptivity it requires and deserves. If it doesn't *save* your life, at least it certainly will *enrich* it.

THE NATURE OF READING

WHAT IS READING?   If reading is so important, it only makes sense to look more closely at it. Let's start with some very fundamental questions. What *is* reading? What goes on when we read? How do we "read well"? Reading is not just taking in the words on a page and extracting their meaning. That may be the first step for most people as they learn to read, as it was for Sherman Alexie, but reading has to go beyond that. We are not decoding machines like a radio receiving signals and emitting sounds. We are humans engaged in a fairly complex process that involves our whole beings. So, what actually happens when we read?

READING AS SENSE-MAKING   Most reading specialists agree that reading is a sense-*making* activity. It is an interactive encounter between an author, a work, and a reader within a cultural context. The author takes ideas, details, and experiences and puts them into words (often called a "text"). The reader takes in the writer's words, processes them, relates them to what she or he already knows, and constructs pictures, feelings, and meanings. The writer depends on the reader to complete the process, to lift the words off the page and fill them with life and meaning. The way Alexie made sense of paragraphs and related them to his family and tribe is an example of how that process works.

INTERACTING PERSONALLY   Reading as a sense-making activity is inevitably personal and individual. What is written does not convey the same thing to every reader. That doesn't mean, of course, that a text means anything a reader says it means. "It is going to snow" cannot mean "An elephant is doing math," no matter what a particular reader asserts. There *is* a text; there *are* words and sentences on the page that we must look at, take in, and respond to. But *we* both discern what the words mean and fill the words with personal meaning.

ACTIVE READING

COMPLETING WHAT THE AUTHOR STARTED   The stories, poems, and plays in this book are not objects, not just words on a page; rather, they are potential works that are *completed in the reader's mind*. Texts (the words of the writer) are similar to musical scores: The notes on paper are only potential music until a musician brings them to life by performing them. So, too, the reader "performs" a story, poem, or play by bringing it to life in her or his mind through the method of active reading. There can be a text without a reader, but there can't be a living literary work (a story, poem, or play) without a reader (or listener) to complete what the writer began.

RESPONDING INDIVIDUALLY   *Meaning*, then, is the result of an interaction between a piece of writing and an individual reader. Since no two people have the same personality and the same experiences, the story, poem, or play they actualize out of the same text, though perhaps similar, will not be identical. The rooms filled with books that you see in your mind's eye as you read "Superman and Me" may be similar to those someone else imagines, but they won't be the same; we shouldn't gloss over the difference by saying that it is only what they have in common that really matters.

RESPONDING HOLISTICALLY   Your whole being—including your intellect, imagination, emotions, and values—can and should be involved in the reading process. Reading is not a spectator sport: We do not observe words passively from the sidelines. To be good readers, we need to participate, to be actively involved at every moment, with every word. As we read, we draw on our memories and our own understanding of definitions; we create pictures that make sense of the words and phrases we encounter; we anticipate what may be ahead; we revise our earlier anticipation in light of what we find later; we make judgments about what is said and done; and sometimes we need to revise those judgments to come to a satisfactory conclusion.

RESPONDING LITERARILY   All reading is not the same. Actively reading a chemistry book takes different skills from those you use in actively reading a novel; reading an Internet site differs from reading a newspaper. Active reading of literary texts asks you to imagine characters, form mental images, visualize locations and series of actions, and listen for sounds and rhythms. Actively reading literature requires you to pay attention not only to *what* is said but also to *how* it is said, to the techniques a writer uses to develop a work. This book is designed to help you do these things: Its chapters introduce features and techniques that will enrich your reading experience; develop your skills for reading fiction, poetry, and drama; and expand and strengthen your skills in writing about literature.

RESPONDING INTERACTIVELY   Active reading also involves asking questions, wondering "Why? Why? Why?" It includes talking with other readers, talking back to the author or text, underlining words and phrases, jotting notes in the margins, and perhaps writing an outline to clarify the organization of a work. (More is said about these particular reading strategies in Chapter 2.) Active reading is a challenging and an exciting skill, one that leads you to feel dynamically engaged with the work you are reading. You are no longer merely a passive recipient. You are an active participant. We believe this book will encourage you to develop this ability, leading you to find greater and greater pleasure and enrichment from reading literature and from writing about the works you read.

☑ CHECKLIST on Active Reading

❑ Read attentively and alertly—don't put off reading until the last thing at night when it's hard to concentrate.

❑ Adjust to the kind of material you are reading—when reading a chemistry textbook, your mind must be principally involved in studying the material, while literary works in addition to demanding your intellect also require the involvement of your emotions and imagination.

❑ Respond to literature with your whole being—empathize with characters and situations, and let yourself feel a rich complex of emotions when the work calls for it.

❑ Use a pen or pencil—mark up the text if you own and plan to keep the book; take notes if you don't. Jotting things down helps you to concentrate and to remember.

❑ Interrogate the text—ask questions as you read, such as why some things are omitted, why other things are included, why a certain approach or technique is used, and what difference looking at things from another perspective would make.

ENTRY POINTS   Here is a story about the importance reading and writing came to have in the life of a young woman whose family emigrated from the Dominican Republic to New York City. The point is similar to that in "Superman and Me," but notice the difference in form. As an essay, "Superman and Me" explains and discusses personal experiences and their effect on the author. "Daughter of Invention" brings a personal experience to life, telling it as a story, through its characters and a sequence of events. Read it actively: Pay close attention to everything in the text, use your imagination, let yourself feel emotions, think about what happens, visualize, listen, ask questions, underline words and phrases you might want to look at again, and jot notes in the margins.

Julia Alvarez b. 1950

Daughter of Invention   [1988]

She wanted to invent something, my mother. There was a period after we arrived in this country, until five or so years later, when my mother was inventing. They were never pressing, global needs she was addressing with her pencil and pad. She would have said that was for men to do, rockets and engines that ran on gasoline and turned the wheels of the world. She was just fussing with little house things, don't mind her.

She always invented at night, after settling her house down. On his side of the bed my father would be conked out for an hour already, his Spanish newspaper draped over his chest, his glasses, propped up on his bedside table, looking out eerily at the darkened room like a disembodied guard. But in her lighted corner, like some devoted scholar burning the midnight oil, my mother was inventing, sheets pulled to her lap, pillows propped up behind her, her reading glasses riding the bridge of her nose like a schoolmarm's. On her lap lay one of those innumerable pads of paper my father always brought home from his office, compliments of some pharmaceutical company, advertising tranquilizers or antibiotics or skin cream; in her other hand, my mother held a pencil that looked like a pen with a little cylinder of lead inside. She would work on a sketch of something familiar, but drawn at such close range so she could attach a special nozzle or handier handle, the thing looked peculiar. Once, I mistook the spiral of a corkscrew for a nautilus shell, but it could just as well have been a galaxy forming.

It was the only time all day we'd catch her sitting down, for she herself was living proof of the *perpetuum mobile* machine so many inventors had sought over the ages. My sisters and I would seek her out now when she seemed to have a moment to talk to us: We were having trouble at school or we wanted her to persuade my father to give us permission to go into the city or to a shopping mall or a movie — in broad daylight! My mother would wave us out of her room. "The problem with you girls . . ." I can tell you right now what the problem

APPROACHING THE AUTHOR

Julia Alvarez is a vegetarian, though she lives on a farm where her husband, Bill Eichner, not only grows fruits and vegetables but also raises cows, rabbits, and chickens for food.

For more about her, see page 1372.

always boiled down to: We wanted to become Americans and my father—and my mother, at first—would have none of it.

"You girls are going to drive me crazy!" She always threatened if we kept nagging. "When I end up in Bellevue,° you'll be safely sorry!"

She spoke in English when she argued with us, even though, in a matter of months, her daughters were the fluent ones. Her English was much better than my father's, but it was still a mishmash of mixed-up idioms and sayings that showed she was "green behind the ears," as she called it.

If my sisters and I tried to get her to talk in Spanish, she'd snap, "When in Rome, do unto the Romans . . ."

I had become the spokesman for my sisters, and I would stand my ground in that bedroom. "We're not going to that school anymore, Mami!"

"You have to." Her eyes would widen with worry. "In this country, it is against the law not to go to school. You want us to get thrown out?"

"You want us to get killed? Those kids were throwing stones today!"

"Sticks and stones don't break bones . . ." she chanted. I could tell, though, by the look on her face, it was as if one of those stones the kids had aimed at us had hit her. But she always pretended we were at fault. "What did you do to provoke them? It takes two to tangle, you know."

"Thanks, thanks a lot, Mom!" I'd storm out of that room and into mine. I never called her *Mom* except when I wanted her to feel how much she had failed us in this country. She was a good enough Mami, fussing and scolding and giving advice, but a terrible girlfriend parent, a real failure of a Mom.

Back she'd go to her pencil and pad, scribbling and tsking and tearing off paper, finally giving up, and taking up her *New York Times*. Some nights, though, she'd get a good idea, and she'd rush into my room, a flushed look on her face, her tablet of paper in her hand, a cursory knock on the door she'd just thrown open: "Do I have something to show you, Cukita!"

This was my time to myself, after I'd finished my homework, while my sisters were still downstairs watching TV in the basement. Hunched over my small desk, the overhead light turned off, my lamp shining poignantly on my paper, the rest of the room in warm, soft, uncreated darkness, I wrote my secret poems in my new language.

"You're going to ruin your eyes!" My mother would storm into my room, turning on the overly bright overhead light, scaring off whatever shy passion I had just begun coaxing out of a labyrinth of feelings with the blue thread of my writing.

"Oh Mami!" I'd cry out, my eyes blinking up at her. "I'm writing."

"Ay, Cukita." That was her communal pet name for whoever was in her favor. "Cukita, when I make a million, I'll buy you your very own typewriter." (I'd been nagging my mother for one just like the one father had bought her to do his order forms at home.) "Gravy on the turkey" was what she called it when someone was buttering her up. She'd butter and pour. "I'll hire you your very own typist."

Bellevue: Bellevue Psychiatric Hospital, a division of Bellevue Hospital Center in New York City.

Down she'd plop on my bed and hold out her pad to me. "Take a guess, Cukita?" I'd study her rough sketch a moment: soap sprayed from the nozzle head of a shower when you turned the knob a certain way? Coffee with creamer already mixed in? Time-released water capsules for your plants when you were away? A key chain with a timer that would go off when your parking meter was about to expire? (The ticking would help you find your keys easily if you mislaid them.) The famous one, famous only in hindsight, was the stick person dragging a square by a rope—a suitcase with wheels? "Oh, of course," we'd humor her. "What every household needs: a shower like a car wash, keys ticking like a bomb, luggage on a leash!" By now, as you can see, it'd become something of a family joke, our Thomas Edison Mami, our Benjamin Franklin Mom.

Her face would fall. "Come on now! Use your head." One more wrong guess, and she'd tell me, pressing with her pencil point the different highlights of this incredible new wonder. "Remember that time we took the car to Bear Mountain, and we re-ah-lized that we had forgotten to pack an opener with our pick-a-nick?" (We kept correcting her, but she insisted this is how it should be said.) "When we were ready to eat we didn't have any way to open the refreshments cans?" (This before fliptop lids, which she claimed had crossed her mind.) "You know what this is now?" A shake of my head. "Is a car bumper, but see this part is a removable can opener. So simple and yet so necessary, no?"

"Yeah, Mami. You should patent it." I'd shrug. She'd tear off the scratch paper and fold it, carefully, corner to corner, as if she were going to save it. But then, she'd toss it in the wastebasket on her way out of the room and give a little laugh like a disclaimer. "It's half of one or two dozen of another . . ."

I suppose none of her daughters was very encouraging. We resented her 20 spending time on those dumb inventions. Here, we were trying to fit in America among Americans; we needed help figuring out who we were, why these Irish kids whose grandparents were micks two generations ago, why they were calling us spics. Why had we come to the country in the first place? Important, crucial, final things, you see, and here was our own mother, who didn't have a second to help us puzzle any of this out, inventing gadgets to make life easier for American moms. Why, it seemed as if she were arming our own enemy against us!

One time, she did have a moment of triumph. Every night, she liked to read *The New York Times* in bed before turning off her light, to see what the Americans were up to. One night, she let out a yelp to wake up my father beside her, bolt upright, reaching for his glasses which, in his haste, he knocked across the room. "*Que pasa? Que pasa?*" What is wrong? There was terror in his voice, fear she'd seen in his eyes in the Dominican Republic before we left. We were being watched there; he was being followed; he and mother had often exchanged those looks. They could not talk, of course, though they must have whispered to each other in fear at night in the dark bed. Now in America, he was safe, a success even; his Centro Medico in Brooklyn was thronged with the sick and the homesick. But in dreams, he went back to those awful days and long nights, and my mother's screams confirmed his secret fear: We had not gotten away after all; they had come for us at last.

"Ay, Papi, I'm sorry. Go back to sleep, Cukito. It's nothing, nothing really."
My mother held up the *Times* for him to squint at the small print, back page
headline, one hand tapping all over the top of the bedside table for his glasses,
the other rubbing his eyes to wakefulness.

"Remember, remember how I showed you that suitcase with little wheels so
we would not have to carry those heavy bags when we traveled? Someone stole
my idea and made a million!" She shook the paper in his face. She shook the
paper in all our faces that night. "See! See! This man was no *bobo*! He didn't
put all his pokers on a back burner. I kept telling you, one of these days my ship
would pass me by in the night!" She wagged her finger at my sisters and my
father and me, laughing all the while, one of those eerie laughs crazy people in
movies laugh. We had congregated in her room to hear the good news she'd
been yelling down the stairs, and now we eyed her and each other. I suppose we
were all thinking the same thing: Wouldn't it be weird and sad if Mami did end
up in Bellevue as she'd always threatened she might?

"*Ya*, ya! Enough!" She waved us out of her room at last. "There is no use
trying to drink spilt milk, that's for sure."

It was the suitcase rollers that stopped my mother's hand; she had weather 25
vaned a minor brainstorm. She would have to start taking herself seriously. That
blocked the free play of her ingenuity. Besides, she had also begun working at
my father's office, and at night, she was too tired and busy filling in columns
with how much money they had made that day to be fooling with gadgets!

She did take up her pencil and pad one last time to help me out. In ninth
grade, I was chosen by my English teacher, Sister Mary Joseph, to deliver the
teacher's day address at the school assembly. Back in the Dominican Republic,
I was a terrible student. No one could ever get me to sit down to a book. But in
New York, I needed to settle somewhere, and the natives were unfriendly, the
country inhospitable, so I took root in the language. By high school, the nuns
were reading my stories and compositions out loud to my classmates as
examples of imagination at work.

This time my imagination jammed. At first I didn't want and then I
couldn't seem to write that speech. I suppose I should have thought of it as a
"great honor," as my father called it. But I was mortified. I still had a pronounced lilt to my accent, and I did not like to speak in public, subjecting
myself to my classmates' ridicule. Recently, they had begun to warm toward my
sisters and me, and it took no great figuring to see that to deliver a eulogy for a
convent full of crazy, old overweight nuns was no way to endear myself to the
members of my class.

But I didn't know how to get out of it. Week after week, I'd sit down, hoping to polish off some quick, noncommittal little speech. I couldn't get anything down.

The weekend before our Monday morning assembly I went into a panic. My
mother would just have to call in and say I was in the hospital, in a coma. I was
in the Dominican Republic. Yeah, that was it! Recently, my father had been
talking about going back home to live.

My mother tried to calm me down. "Just remember how Mister Lincoln 30 couldn't think of anything to say at the Gettysburg, but then, Bang! 'Four score and once upon a time ago,'" she began reciting. Her version of history was half invention and half truths and whatever else she needed to prove a point. "Something is going to come if you just relax. You'll see, like the Americans say, 'Necessity is the daughter of invention.' I'll help you."

All weekend, she kept coming into my room with help. "Please, Mami, just leave me alone, please," I pleaded with her. But I'd get rid of the goose only to have to contend with the gander. My father kept poking his head in the door just to see if I had "fulfilled my obligations," a phrase he'd used when we were a little younger, and he'd check to see whether we had gone to the bathroom before a car trip. Several times that weekend around the supper table, he'd recite his valedictorian speech from when he graduated from high school. He'd give me pointers on delivery, on the great orators and their tricks. (Humbleness and praise and falling silent with great emotion were his favorites.)

My mother sat across the table, the only one who seemed to be listening to him. My sisters and I were forgetting a lot of our Spanish, and my father's formal, florid diction was even harder to understand. But my mother smiled softly to herself, and turned the Lazy Susan at the center of the table around and around as if it were the prime mover, the first gear of attention.

That Sunday evening, I was reading some poetry to get myself inspired: Whitman in an old book with an engraved cover my father had picked up in a thrift shop next to his office a few weeks back. "I celebrate myself and sing myself . . ." "He most honors my style who learns under it to destroy the teacher." The poet's words shocked and thrilled me. I had gotten used to the nuns, a literature of appropriate sentiments, poems with a message, expurgated texts. But here was a flesh and blood man, belching and laughing and sweating in poems. "Who touches this book touches a man."

That night, at last, I started to write, recklessly, three, five pages, looking up once only to see my father passing by the hall on tiptoe. When I was done, I read over my words, and my eyes filled. I finally sounded like myself in English!

As soon as I had finished that first draft, I called my mother to my room. 35 She listened attentively, as she had to my father's speech, and in the end, her eyes were glistening too. Her face was soft and warm and proud. "That is a beautiful, beautiful speech, Cukita. I want for your father to hear it before he goes to sleep. Then I will type it for you, all right?"

Down the hall we went, the two of us, faces flushed with accomplishment. Into the master bedroom where my father was propped up on his pillows, still awake, reading the Dominican papers, already days old. He had become interested in his country's fate again. The dictatorship had been toppled. The interim government was going to hold the first free elections in thirty years. There was still some question in his mind whether or not we might want to move back. History was in the making, freedom and hope were in the air again! But my mother had gotten used to the life here. She did not want to go back to the old country where she was only a wife and a mother (and a failed one at that, since she had never had the required son). She did not come straight out and disagree with my father's plans. Instead, she fussed with him about reading the papers in bed, soiling those sheets with those poorly printed, foreign tabloids. "*The Times* is not that bad!" she'd claim if my father tried to humor her by saying they shared the same dirty habit.

The minute my father saw my mother and me, filing in, he put his paper down, and his face brightened as if at long last his wife had delivered a son, and that was the news we were bringing him. His teeth were already grinning from the glass of water next to his bedside lamp, so he lisped when he said, "Eh-speech, eh-speech!"

"It is so beautiful, Papi," my mother previewed him, turning the sound off on his TV. She sat down at the foot of the bed. I stood before both of them, blocking their view of the soldiers in helicopters landing amid silenced gun reports and explosions. A few weeks ago it had been the shores of the Dominican Republic. Now it was the jungles of Southeast Asia they were saving. My mother gave me the nod to begin reading.

I didn't need much encouragement. I put my nose to the fire, as my mother would have said, and read from start to finish without looking up. When I was done, I was a little embarrassed at my pride in my own words. I pretended to quibble with a phrase or two I was sure I'd be talked out of changing. I looked questioningly to my mother. Her face was radiant. She turned to share her pride with my father.

But the expression on his face shocked us both. His toothless mouth had   40 collapsed into a dark zero. His eyes glared at me, then shifted to my mother, accusingly. In barely audible Spanish, as if secret microphones or informers were all about, he whispered, "You will permit her to read *that*?"

My mother's eyebrows shot up, her mouth fell open. In the old country, any whisper of a challenge to authority could bring the secret police in their black V.W.'s. But this was America. People could say what they thought. "What is wrong with her speech?" my mother questioned him.

"What ees wrrrong with her eh-speech?" My father wagged his head at her. His anger was always more frightening in his broken English. As if he had mutilated the language in his fury—and now there was nothing to stand between us and his raw, dumb anger. "What is wrong? I will tell you what is wrong. It shows no gratitude. It is boastful. 'I celebrate myself'? 'The best student learns to destroy the teacher'?" He mocked my plagiarized words. "That is insubordinate. It is improper. It is disrespecting of her teachers—" In his anger he had forgotten his fear of lurking spies: Each wrong he voiced was a decibel higher than the last outrage. Finally, he was yelling at me, "As your father, I forbid you to say that eh-speech!"

My mother leapt to her feet, a sign always that she was about to make a speech or deliver an ultimatum. She was a small woman, and she spoke all her pronouncements standing up, either for more protection or as a carry-over from her girlhood in convent schools where one asked for, and literally took, the floor in order to speak. She stood by my side, shoulder to shoulder; we looked down at my father. "That is no tone of voice, Eduardo—" she began.

By now, my father was truly furious. I suppose it was bad enough I was rebelling, but here was my mother joining forces with me. Soon he would be surrounded by a house full of independent American women. He too leapt from his bed, throwing off his covers. The Spanish newspapers flew across the room. He snatched my speech out of my hands, held it before my panicked eyes, a vengeful, mad look in his own, and then once, twice, three, four, countless times, he tore my prize into shreds.

"Are you crazy?" My mother lunged at him. "Have you gone mad? That is her speech for tomorrow you have torn up!"

"Have you gone mad?" He shook her away. "You were going to let her read that . . . that insult to her teachers?"

"Insult to her teachers!" My mother's face had crumpled up like a piece of paper. On it was written a love note to my father. Ever since they had come to this country, their life together was a constant war. "This is America, Papi, America!" she reminded him now. "You are not in a savage country any more!"

I was on my knees, weeping wildly, collecting all the little pieces of my speech, hoping that I could put it back together before the assembly tomorrow morning. But not even a sibyl could have made sense of all those scattered pieces of paper. All hope was lost. "He broke it, he broke it," I moaned as I picked up a handful of pieces.

Probably, if I had thought a moment about it, I would not have done what I did next. I would have realized my father had lost brothers and comrades to the dictator Trujillo.° For the rest of his life, he would be haunted by blood in the streets and late night disappearances. Even after he had been in the states for years, he jumped if a black Volkswagen passed him on the street. He feared anyone in uniform: the meter maid giving out parking tickets, a museum guard approaching to tell him not to touch his favorite Goya at the Metropolitan.

I took a handful of the scraps I had gathered, stood up, and hurled them in his face. "Chapita!"° I said in a low, ugly whisper. "You're just another Chapita!"

It took my father only a moment to register the hated nickname of our dictator, and he was after me. Down the halls we raced, but I was quicker than he and made it to my room just in time to lock the door as my father threw his weight against it. He called down curses on my head, ordered me on his authority as my father to open that door this very instant! He throttled that doorknob, but all to no avail. My mother's love of gadgets saved my hide that night. She had hired a locksmith to install good locks on all the bedroom doors after our house had been broken into while we were away the previous summer. In case burglars broke in again, and we were in the house, they'd have a second round of locks to contend with before they got to us.

"Eduardo," she tried to calm him down. "Don't you ruin my new locks."

Trujillo: Rafael Leónidas Trujillo Molina (1891–1961) was dictator of the Dominican Republic (1930–1961).
Chapita: "Chapita" (Spanish for *bottlecap*) was Trujillo's childhood nickname (one that he hated).

He finally did calm down, his anger spent. I heard their footsteps retreating down the hall. I heard their door close, the clicking of their lock. Then, muffled voices, my mother's peaking in anger, in persuasion, my father's deep murmurs of explanation and of self-defense. At last, the house fell silent, before I heard, far off, the gun blasts and explosions, the serious, self-important voices of newscasters reporting their TV war.

A little while later, there was a quiet knock at my door, followed by a tentative attempt at the doorknob. "Cukita?" my mother whispered. "Open up, Cukita."

"Go away," I wailed, but we both knew I was glad she was there, and I 55 needed only a moment's protest to save face before opening that door.

What we ended up doing that night was putting together a speech at the last moment. Two brief pages of stale compliments and the polite common-places on teachers, wrought by necessity without much invention by mother for daughter late into the night in the basement on the pad of paper and with the same pencil she had once used for her own inventions, for I was too upset to compose the speech myself. After it was drafted, she typed it up while I stood by, correcting her misnomers and mis-sayings.

She was so very proud of herself when I came home the next day with the success story of the assembly. The nuns had been flattered, the audience had stood up and given "our devoted teachers a standing ovation," what my mother had suggested they do at the end of my speech.

She clapped her hands together as I recreated the moment for her. "I stole that from your father's speech, remember? Remember how he put that in at the end?" She quoted him in Spanish, then translated for me into English.

That night, I watched him from the upstairs hall window where I'd retreated the minute I heard his car pull up in front of our house. Slowly, my father came up the driveway, a grim expression on his face as he grappled with a large, heavy cardboard box. At the front door, he set the package down carefully and patted all his pockets for his house keys—precisely why my mother had invented her ticking key chain. I heard the snapping open of the locks downstairs. Heard as he struggled to maneuver the box through the narrow doorway. Then, he called my name several times. But I would not answer him.

"My daughter, your father, he love you very much," he explained from the bot- 60 tom of the stairs. "He just want to protect you." Finally, my mother came up and pleaded with me to go down and reconcile with him. "Your father did not mean to harm. You must pardon him. Always it is better to let bygones be forgotten, no?"

I guess she was right. Downstairs, I found him setting up a brand new electric typewriter on the kitchen table. It was even better than the one I'd been begging to get like my mother's. My father had outdone himself with all the extra features: a plastic carrying case with my initials, in decals, below the handle, a brace to lift the paper upright while I typed, an erase cartridge, an automatic margin tab, a plastic hood like a toaster cover to keep the dust away. Not even my mother, I think, could have invented such a machine!

But her inventing days were over just as mine were starting up with my schoolwide success. That's why I've always thought of that speech my mother wrote for me as her last invention rather than the suitcase rollers everyone else in the family remembers. It was as if she had passed on to me her pencil and pad and said, "Okay, Cukita, here's the buck. You give it a shot."

APPROACHING THE READING

1. Reflect on your experience reading "Daughter of Invention" and be ready to talk about it: What things in the story did you especially like? If there were things you didn't like, talk about why they affected you as they did. Did you learn anything from the story? If the story helped you expand your horizons, enter other people's lives, go places you couldn't go in other ways, consider things you hadn't before, what were these? Talk about the way or ways you were affected.

2. Did you connect with the story imaginatively and emotionally as well as intellectually? Talk about some specific places in the narrative where you made those connections, why you made them, and how the author facilitated them. How do you picture the characters, places, and actions? What emotions did the author get you to feel? At what point in the story did they get evoked? When did you start to care about the main character, to like her (or dislike her)? Explain some of those feelings and how the writing brings them out.

3. Describe the family and family life in this story. Jot down a list of tensions and conflicts among the family members. How is that family and family life similar to or different from your own? If the story made you think about your family and make comparisons to your own life, where in the narrative did that happen? What in the writing triggered your reactions?

4. Some of the conflicts and tensions are the result of the family's relocation from the Dominican Republic to New York. Which ones are created or heightened by relocation? Which would probably exist regardless of whether the family had moved to the United States? Which conflicts, if any, seem similar to ones in your own family and life? Try to offer specific support for your conclusions.

5. Reflect on the last two paragraphs. Why does the father give the speaker the gift that he does? What is he saying through it? What do the final paragraphs suggest about the continuing importance of writing in his daughter's life?

6. Does it seem accurate to say that the speaker in this story reads (and writes) to "save her life"? If so, what does that mean in her case? In what ways is the meaning of reading and writing for the speaker similar to what it means for Sherman Alexie? In what ways are the speakers' situations different? How do those differences make the meaning of reading and writing different for them?

How do I know what I think until I see what I say?

E. M. Forster

(English Novelist, Short Story Writer, Essayist)

Writing in Response to Literature

CHAPTER 2

Entering the Conversation

Responding to literature is like participating in a great, ongoing conversation. It's a lot like posting comments on the most popular Facebook page the world has ever known, one that has postings from the distant past as well as the present and all times in between. Some of this conversation is personal, some public, and the subjects cover an endlessly wide range. Authors read other authors and respond. Scholars and critics publish their ideas and others respond to them. We readers talk about what we're reading with our friends. We talk to ourselves. You have likely found yourself saying, "I really relate to this story" or "Why do we have to read this poem?" when you've been assigned a work. Your conversation might go all the way back to your childhood, if when someone read to you, you kept interrupting to say,"I'm scared of him" or "I love the part where the bear goes in the back door. Read it again!"

In a sense, writing about literature is simply a more thorough explanation of your own thoughtful response. You are truly taking part in this continuing conversation, adding your own two cents' worth to the table talk. Think of this kind of writing as something that will be listened to, considered, and added to by others who love this kind of disussion. This chapter can help you develop confidence in your ability to participate in literary conversations. Learning to do so thoughtfully and skillfully is no different—except in its means for doing so—from being able to talk about any subject—such as basketball, hip-hop, fashion, or cars.

This chapter traces the range of writing about literature through a series of increasingly complex forms:

- Writing in the margins of a book
- Journal writing
- Writing essay examination answers
- Writing short papers

A further form, writing research papers, will be covered in the next chapter.

A basic assumption of this book is that writing is a process: Good writing does not happen in one last-minute, two-hour stage, during which you crank out a first/final draft to turn in to a teacher. Good writing involves a series of stages, from reading to thinking, jotting, outlining, drafting, revising, and checking. This chapter walks you through those steps, to show how they are manageable. Learning to go through the stages attentively is at the heart of what it means to be a writer.

ENTRY POINTS   Throughout this chapter, we draw illustrations from a very short story by African American author Alice Walker, best known for her novel *The Color Purple*. The story shows how a seemingly small event on an ordinary day can turn out to be a life-changing occurrence. Read it twice: once to get a feel for it and a second time to feel more at home with the story and alert to specifics in it.

Alice Walker b. 1944

The Flowers   [1973]

It seemed to Myop as she skipped lightly from hen house to pigpen to smokehouse that the days had never been as beautiful as these. The air held a keenness that made her nose twitch. The harvesting of the corn and cotton, peanuts and squash, made each day a golden surprise that caused excited little tremors to run up her jaws.

Myop carried a short, knobby stick. She struck out at random at chickens she liked, and worked out the beat of a song on the fence around the pigpen. She felt light and good in the warm sun. She was ten, and nothing existed for her but her song, the stick clutched in her dark brown hand, and the tat-de-ta-ta-ta of accompaniment.

Turning her back on the rusty boards of her family's sharecropper cabin, Myop walked along the fence till it ran into the stream made by the spring. Around the spring, where the family got drinking water, silver ferns and wildflowers grew. Along the shallow banks pigs rooted. Myop watched the tiny white bubbles disrupt the thin black scale of soil and the water that silently rose and slid away down the stream.

> **APPROACHING THE AUTHOR**
>
> **Alice Walker**'s parents were sharecroppers who made about $300 a year. Walker would have grown up helping out in the fields, but when she was four years old a schoolteacher noticed her, got her new clothes, and made sure she went to school every day.
>
> For more about her, see page 1417.

She had explored the woods behind the house many times. Often, in late autumn, her mother took her to gather nuts among the fallen leaves. Today she made her own path, bouncing this way and that way, vaguely keeping an eye out for snakes. She found, in addition to various common but pretty ferns and leaves, an armful of strange blue flowers with velvety ridges and a sweetsuds bush full of the brown, fragrant buds.

By twelve o'clock, her arms laden with sprigs of her findings, she was a mile 5 or more from home. She had often been as far before, but the strangeness of the land made it not as pleasant as her usual haunts. It seemed gloomy in the little cove in which she found herself. The air was damp, the silence close and deep.

Myop began to circle back to the house, back to the peacefulness of the morning. It was then she stepped smack into his eyes. Her heel became lodged in the broken ridge between brow and nose, and she reached down quickly, unafraid, to free herself. It was only when she saw his naked grin that she gave a little yelp of surprise.

He had been a tall man. From feet to neck covered a long space. His head lay beside him. When she pushed back the leaves and layers of earth and debris Myop saw that he'd had large white teeth, all of them cracked or broken, long fingers, and very big bones. All his clothes had rotted away except some threads of blue denim from his overalls. The buckles of the overalls had turned green.

Myop gazed around the spot with interest. Very near where she'd stepped into the head was a wild pink rose. As she picked it to add to her bundle she noticed a raised mound, a ring, around the rose's root. It was the rotted remains of a noose, a bit of shredding plowline, now blending benignly into the soil. Around an overhanging limb of a great spreading oak clung another piece. Frayed, rotted, bleached, and frazzled — barely there — but spinning restlessly in the breeze. Myop laid down her flowers.

And the summer was over.

WRITING IN THE MARGINS

Chapter 1 describes reading as an interactive process: The text speaks to the reader, and the reader responds to the text. Your reading should never feel like a one-way "lecture," with you merely taking in the work passively. You, as an active reader, can talk back to the work, agreeing with it, interrogating it, connecting with it, challenging it. One way of doing this is to read with a pencil in hand and jot down your side of the conversation.

MARKING UP THE WORK   If you own the work you are reading, you can jot notes in and around the text itself. If you don't own the work, have paper available, maybe as a bookmark, and use it for keeping notes.

- **Underline or Highlight Key Parts** Underline sentences or phrases that you really like or that strike you as especially important. But don't underline or highlight *everything* — then nothing stands out. Circle words you find particularly noteworthy.
- **Flag Key Sentences in the Text** Put a star, a question mark, or an exclamation point, especially during a first reading, next to passages you might want to return to later to figure out or to think about in light of more information.
- **Talk Back to the Text** Write comments in the margins as you move through a work: "What does this mean?" "Big point!" "Stupid idea!" "Tone shifts."
- **Talk to Yourself about the Text** Jot down thoughts that occur to you as you read — things that remind you of other books you've read, for example, or that connect with a movie or song you like or with something you learned in a biology, history, psychology, or religion course.
- **Write Notes about the Text** Write out definitions and explanations of words and details you had to look up.

This form of "engaged reading," writing in a book, is an ancient and honored tradition. Reading the marginal notes (or *marginalia*) that people centuries ago or very recently wrote in their books can let us know a great deal about the tastes, values, and judgments of some interesting and important people.

MAKING THE WORK YOURS   Personally annotating a work is a way to make it "yours." It now contains your ideas and inquiries as well as the author's. Try it in this book. You might find it interesting to revisit this book years from now, to reread stories, poems, and plays you liked especially and to look again at the notes you wrote about them. You may wonder who that person was who wrote those notes; you might reacquaint yourself with who

you were then; or you might discover how much you have added to your experience with literature since then.

To illustrate what we mean (not to prescribe how it should be done), here in the margins of "The Flowers" is some writing by one of our students, Kortney DeVito (pictured at left). She later used these notes to write a journal entry on the story (see p. 25) and then used the journal entry as the starting point for a paper (see p. 46).

Sample Student Annotations

Alice Walker

The Flowers

interesting name

It seemed to (Myop) as she skipped lightly from hen house to pigpen to smokehouse that the days had never been as beautiful as these. The air held a keenness that made her nose twitch. <u>The harvesting of the corn and cotton, peanuts and squash, made each day a golden surprise that caused excited little tremors to run up her jaws.</u>

Great imagery!

Myop carried a short, knobby stick. She struck out at random at chickens she liked, and worked out the beat of a song on the fence around the pigpen. She felt light and good in the warm sun. She was ten, and nothing existed for her but her song, the stick clutched in her dark brown hand, and the <u>tat-de-ta-ta-ta of accompaniment</u>.

I can nearly hear her sing.

Turning her back on the rusty boards of her family's share-cropper cabin, Myop walked along the fence till it ran into the stream made by the spring. Around the spring, where the family got drinking water, silver ferns and wildflowers grew. Along the shallow banks pigs rooted. <u>Myop watched the tiny white bubbles disrupt the thin black scale of soil and the water that silently rose and slid away down the stream.</u>

I adore this description.

Does Myop see the stream the same way as the narrator?

She had explored the woods behind the house many times. Often, in late autumn, her mother took her to gather nuts among the fallen leaves. Today she made (her own path,) bouncing this way and that way, vaguely keeping an eye out for snakes. She found, in addition to various common but pretty ferns and leaves, an armful of strange blue flowers with velvety ridges and a sweetsuds bush full of the brown, fragrant buds.

growing older, independent

By twelve o'clock, her arms laden with sprigs of her findings, she was a mile or more from home. She had often been as far before, but the strangeness of the land made it not as pleasant as her usual haunts. <u>It seemed gloomy in the little cove in which she found herself. The air was damp, the silence close and deep.</u>

Uh-oh, foreshadowing — sounds creepy.

Yuck!

Myop began to circle back to the house, back to the peaceful-ness of the morning. It was then she stepped smack into his eyes. <u>Her heel became lodged in the broken ridge between brow and nose,</u> and she reached down quickly, unafraid, to free herself. It was only when she saw his naked grin that she gave a little yelp of surprise.

Past tense!

He had been a tall man. From feet to neck covered a long space. His head lay beside him. When she pushed back the leaves and layers of earth and debris Myop saw that he'd had large white teeth, all of them cracked or broken, long fingers, and very big bones. All his clothes had rotted away except some threads of blue denim from his overalls. The buckles of the overalls had turned green.

He had been there for a while.

Most 10-year-olds would have run away!

Gross!!!

Myop gazed around the spot with interest. Very near where she'd stepped into the head was a wild pink rose. As she picked it to add to her bundle she noticed a raised mound, a ring, around the rose's root. It was the rotted remains of a noose, a bit of shred-ding plowline, now blending benignly into the soil. Around an overhanging limb of a great spreading oak clung another piece. Frayed, rotted, bleached, and frazzled—barely there—but spinning restlessly in the breeze. Myop laid down her flowers. And the summer was over.

For the dead man or her childhood and innocence?

JOURNAL WRITING

Journal writing enables you to take the brief notes you jotted in the margins or on paper and extend them into longer responses in which you develop your reactions, insights, and ideas in greater detail. Think of a journal, whether assigned or something you do on your own, as halfway between a diary and a class notebook. It's not intimate or confessional as diaries often are, nor is it as objective, remote, and impersonal as the notebook. A journal is a good place to store information, like characters' names; lines you want to remember; things you were drawn to or put off by. You could regard your journal as a place to reorganize the notes you took in class, perhaps, and to clarify and expand on them (which can be a great help for reviewing later). A journal also provides a place where you can express ideas or emotions stimulated by what you read or by your conversations with other people.

GETTING STARTED   If a journal is assigned for your course or if keeping a journal simply appeals to you, buy a notebook or a memory stick for your computer and begin entering responses to literary works, to chapters of this book, or to discussions and assignments connected with this course. The suggestions for writing at the ends of chapters may stimulate some ideas; your teacher will bring up some; you will think of others yourself. Try to be specific and precise (include brief quotations and page numbers), and date each entry. Keeping journals can help you trace your own development and growth in taste, judgment, and attitudes. As mentioned before, it can be surprising, interesting, and helpful one day to look back at them.

After the Tips box, there is a page from Kortney's journal on "The Flowers." Notice the places where she carries over ideas from her marginal notations and elaborates on or changes them.

TIPS for Effective Journal Writing

- **Choose the right format.** Decide what format (such as notebook, note cards, or computer files) will be most effective, most readily available to you, and most convenient—that is, one that you will actually use and keep up.

- **Don't put it off.** Jot down your notes and reactions directly after you've read the piece, while your thoughts are fresh. Later, add further reflections to what you wrote first.

- **Be honest.** Express your genuine responses and opinions, not what you think a teacher wants you to say or think. Jot down quotations or page references that support your responses and opinions.

- **Make quotations apparent.** Including quotations helps you remember favorite passages and key points and saves you from needing to go back to the work to find them. Be careful to make clear what is quoted and what is summarized or paraphrased (you don't want a paraphrase to appear as if it's a direct quote or vice versa).

- **Include page references.** Check to be sure you include titles and page numbers so you can find the passages you wrote about or quoted. This too can save you valuable time later.

Sample Student Journal Entry

Alice Walker, "The Flowers"

Why the need for a story such as this? Why combine such a beautiful beginning with such a hauntingly grotesque ending? It conveys that throughout life there is death—not just of others but of ourselves. Not one person can stay in one season of his/her life forever. Each season of our lives teaches something special, but at the same time each season becomes obsolete and passes away.

Myop was going through the season known as childhood at the beginning of the story. She thought there was nothing but beauty in the world; each day was a "golden surprise." When she encountered the head of the decaying man, she began to realize the harsh reality that life can possess. It was almost as if she was Eve eating from the Tree of Knowledge in the Garden of Eden—she began to see the horrible truths life is capable of delivering—not just death, but the evil of death by lynching. At the end of the story Myop "laid down her flowers." A question is: where and for whom? Some may say it was to the man whose life was cut short. I believe Myop laid the flowers down for her childhood—the innocence she once possessed was now dead to her.

WRITING ESSAY EXAMINATION ANSWERS

Teachers often include essay questions on examinations to see if you are developing your skill to think through a problem. The question and the answer become a sort of conversation between you and your teacher. Think of it as an opportunity to talk to your teacher one-on-one, to have your teacher's undivided attention for what you want to get across. The object is not just to find out *what* you know but also what you can *do with* what you know—synthesize it, apply it, see it in relation to other things, and respond to its challenges. Here are a few tips for writing essay answers.

Read the Question Carefully

Read the question several times and make sure you understand what it asks you to do. It is crucial to understand what the question is focusing on. Look for two things: a *subject* (the work or character or kind of images or whatever else it asks you to write about) and an *approach* (what it asks you to *do with* that subject, such as explain, compare, contrast, compare and contrast, or discuss).

> Explain [APPROACH] what the final sentence [SUBJECT] of "The Flowers" indicates about the long-term effect of this experience on Myop [SUBJECT].

> Compare and contrast [APPROACH] Myop's experience in "The Flowers" with that of the speaker as a young boy in Countee Cullen's "Incident" [SUBJECT].

Ask for Clarification If Needed

If you need clarification of the subject or approach, ask your teacher for it rather than risk going at the essay incorrectly. If it's an open-book exam (one during which you are allowed to use your book in class), double-check whether and how you may use notes or the marginalia you've jotted in your book.

Organize Your Thoughts

Don't plunge right in. You will actually use your time more effectively if you pause to plan and organize before beginning to write. Reflect on how the approach relates to the material (why was that approach selected for exploring this subject?), and think about what details you need to support what you want to say about the subject.

Make a Point

Your answer should not be a summary of the work or a list of things you noticed or a few comparisons and contrasts; what you say should add up to something, make a point. Jot that point down as your "thesis" and make sure that you state it clearly in your answer — at the beginning, at the end, or both. Sketch an outline of points that will clarify what you mean and will support and illustrate its validity.

Start Writing

The most efficient way to get moving is to state your central point in the first sentence of the answer. As you do, repeat words from the question to indicate that you are answering it directly, meeting it head-on.

Incorporate New Insights

Keep your outline in mind but don't stick to it slavishly. In the process of writing an exam answer, you may get insights and ideas you didn't expect when you began. These often take off in new directions and may even be opposite to what you originally intended to say. There's no time to revise and incorporate such discoveries in a unified way. So, should you ignore the new insight and stick to your outline or should you include it? We think it's better to include it, but you should explain that you're changing directions ("That's the way it looked to me at first, but as I examine the work more closely I see something different in it"). Don't leave the teacher thinking you don't realize that what you are saying now doesn't fit with the way you started.

Divide Your Answer into Paragraphs

Start a new paragraph when you move to a new subpoint, or insert paragraph symbols (¶) to indicate paragraph breaks. This makes the answer clearer and easier for your teacher to read and follow.

Write Clearly

Whatever you do, don't write so fast that your handwriting becomes il-legible—the best ideas in the world are useless if your teacher can't read them.

Proofread Your Answer

Try to leave yourself a couple of minutes to read through your answer. Be sure you have offered support (explanations, details, quotations) for each subpoint. Check spelling and grammar.

The best way to learn how to write better essay answers is to look at examples of ineffective and effective ones. The second of these answers (the effective one) is by Annie Otto (pictured at left). In the first one, we rewrote Annie's answer to make it less effective.

Sample Student Exam Answers, More and Less Effective

LESS EFFECTIVE EXAMPLE   Assignment: Explain the difference in effect if Alice Walker's story had been titled "The Corpse" instead of "The Flowers." (30 minutes)

Opening too broad—not closely related to topic.

Titles have a large influence on a reader. When one reads a title, one expects to read about things that relate to it. When I first saw "The Flowers" I thought of feelings and ideas. I imagined sunshine, fields, joy, beauty. As I started reading Alice Walker's short story, I got everything I expected.

Doesn't respond directly to topic.

If Alice Walker's story had been titled "The Corpse," I would not have been so surprised when Myop ran into the corpse, but as it was, I was shocked. When Myop first started picking the flowers, I expected her to skip back to her family's cabin to put them in a jar for display. I had no idea that they would be used for mourning a man's death.

Not outlined as clearly as it should be.

Myop is ten years old. She feels the sun shining warm rays down to her and she has her very own song to sing. She feels as though she needs to go for a walk and pick wild flowers. Walker includes specific pictures of sunshine, fields, joy, beauty, and a peaceful scene. Then Myop steps into the rotten corpse of a man who was hanged long ago. Whatever my expectations were for Myop, they were not for her to push the debris around to uncover the face of the corpse. Nor did I think that she would "gaze around the spot with interest." Why? Why would a little girl be interested in that?

The cove that Myop found the corpse in gave me a cold feeling, an uncomfortable feeling. When Myop picked that wild pink rose that grew in the center of the rotted noose and added it to her bundle of flowers to lay down by the remains, she paid her respects to the man that used to be. That day she lost her childish innocence.

Includes specific details, but they're not connected to "effect."

The title of a piece of literature prepares readers for specific images. When the story twists so rapidly on us, it is quite unexpected. "The Flowers" ended entirely opposite of what I anticipated.

Never actually addresses assigned topic.

MORE EFFECTIVE EXAMPLE   Assignment: Explain the difference in effect if Alice Walker's story had been titled "The Corpse" instead of "The Flowers." (30 minutes)

The main difference in effect when "The Corpse" is substituted for "The Flowers" in Walker's story is that it wipes out the surprising twist built into the plot construction and lessens the sense of horror the reader experiences.

Clear statement of central point in opening sentence; repeats words from topic.

The title "The Flowers" puts an initial expectation into the reader's mind. Walker tells us of a little girl, Myop, skipping around her yard and enjoying the warm sun's rays. She goes for a walk to pick wildflowers. There is so much life in the story and the descriptions pull the reader into the scene. Walker includes specific pictures of sunshine, fields, joy, beauty, and harmony as seen through the eyes of a child.

Focuses well on "effect."

As I continued to read, I noticed words like "haunts" and "gloomy." I wondered why the author had added some darkness to the story. Myop wanted to turn back to the "peacefulness of the morning," which to me meant that there was a whisper of unrest.

Clear, logical outline throughout.

Then there came a scream of surprise, shock, and horror. That scream was not from the ten-year-old, Myop. It was from me, the twenty-year-old reader. Myop had stepped into the rotten corpse of a man who was hanged long ago. The shock effect was huge, intensified by the contrast between the beauty of nature (the flowers) and the ugliness of a decayed body. I suppose that I tend to react extremely when I get startled as I did when reading this story. I expected that Myop would react similarly and run home screaming, not that she would "gaze around the spot with interest." Why? Why would a little girl be interested in that?

Good example of "effect."

Good use of specific supporting details.

The realization of a person's death is a difficult thing for a child to handle, and death by lynching is an action full of hate. When Myop picked that wild pink rose that grew in the center of the rotted noose and added it to her bundle of flowers to lay down by the remains, she paid her respects to the man that used to be. That day she lost her childish innocence.

Clear contrast to actual title; wraps up discussion nicely.

If the story had been titled "The Corpse," I would have expected a corpse to appear and would not have been so surprised at what Myop found. As it was, I was shocked, and that shock intensified the horror I felt not only at Myop's finding a corpse, but also at the horrible way the man had met his end.

WRITING SHORT PAPERS

Writing papers in college can (perhaps idealistically) be viewed as an opportunity rather than as an obligation. Like essay-exam answers, papers give you a chance to communicate directly with your teacher, to have your teacher's undivided attention for what you want to get across. They also give you the opportunity to think through a topic carefully, develop an idea or a position about it, and express it for others to hear. Because when writing papers on stories, poems, and plays you will need to handle topics and supporting material differently, specific suggestions for writing papers on each genre, and sample papers for each genre, are given at the end of Parts 2, 3, and 4. In this chapter we offer suggestions that apply to literature papers of all kinds.

STEPS IN THE WRITING PROCESS   We said earlier that writing is a process. Most writers proceed through a series of stages that take them from beginning to think about a subject to printing the final draft. As we discuss the process of writing short papers, we will view it in three stages, which we will break down into smaller steps:

- Prewriting
  - finding a topic
  - narrowing that topic
  - deciding on an approach
  - framing a thesis and preparing an outline
- Writing (developing and supporting the thesis)
- Revising, proofreading, and formatting

It's important to realize that writing is an individual act: Everyone does it differently. You as a writer may not follow these steps in this order or may not need to do all of them every time, though you'll need to achieve the result they are aimed at. Also, the steps overlap, so you may be working on more than one at the same time.

In the rest of the chapter, we follow Kortney DeVito as she returns to the marginal notes and journal entry we read earlier (pp. 23–26) and uses them as she moves through the remaining steps toward completing a short paper on "The Flowers."

Step 1. Prewriting: Finding a Topic

GETTING STARTED If you are given a topic, read the assignment carefully several times to make sure you understand the terms being used and what idea the topic is getting at. And keep in mind that although you are being given a topic, you still need to find a thesis that develops a central idea about the topic (see p. 37). If you can choose your own topic, look through your class notes, marginal jottings, and journal entries for works or subjects that got your attention — ones that intrigued you, puzzled you, or opened up new perceptions, insights, or ideas. And check the topics suggested at the end of chapters in this book, in case one might be right for you.

GENERATING IDEAS To get ideas flowing, you might start by reading or rereading the work two or three times so you get a solid feel for it, underlining and annotating as you read. Look for an intriguing theme or issue in the work or an unusual technique or approach or a difficulty you struggled with while you read. Any of these might turn into a worthwhile topic. Look for connections, patterns, focuses, questions, or problems.

A student, Kortney DeVito, on finding a topic: "Before starting to write a paper on 'The Flowers,' I needed to find a topic. Rather than write on a whim, I decided to reread the story and then reread my journal entry on the story to see if I had any 'profound' ideas that might have a foundation for writing a paper. I looked for ideas or sentences that  stuck out to me and could be the catalyst for a thesis. At this point, I was trying to get my ideas down on paper — I knew I would probably not have a polished thesis at this point. I had plenty of opportunity for that in the other writing steps."

ASKING QUESTIONS The most important strategy for generating ideas and getting into a subject is to ask questions. Begin by asking *why*: Why is the speaker's tone this way? Why did the character make that decision? Why does the work end this way? Why was that word used to describe this character? Why does the author bring up that idea? Consider alternatives: Ask how the work's effect would change if it had used a different speaker or different metaphors, been arranged in a different order, or been written in third person instead of first.

FREEWRITING AND CLUSTERING   If ideas don't start coming, try *free-writing*—writing anything that comes to mind about the topic for five minutes, in any order, without stopping, editing, or changing anything. Or try *clustering*: Write down your main point and circle it. Then write points related to the topic in a ring around the main point, circle them, and use lines to connect them to the first circle. For each circle in the ring, write any ideas, examples, facts, and details you think of and use lines to connect them to the points with which they are associated. Below is some clustering that Annie Otto did to pull together her thinking about "The Flowers." Clustering can be very useful for grasping relationships among the various parts of a topic and clarifying what materials are available or needed for developing subtopics.

Step 2. Prewriting: Narrowing the Topic

The process we just described will enable you to generate ideas, which could lead you to an interesting subject area to work with. But it's important to remember that a key aspect of planning a paper involves narrowing and focusing that broad subject area to a clearly defined topic that you can explore in detail within the assigned length. Too large a topic for the length ("Gender and Sexuality in the Novels of Alice Walker") for a five-page paper will prove ineffective because it will skim rather than cover. Too limited a topic ("Lynching in Alice Walker's 'The Flowers'") can leave you without enough to say to fill the needed pages.

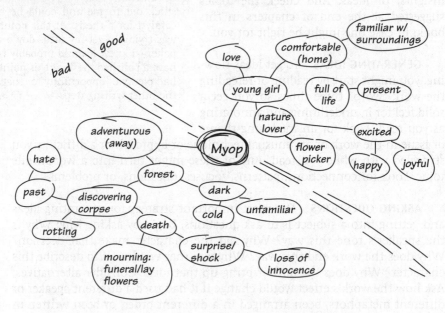

Annie Otto's brainstorm clustering for "The Flowers"

FOCUSING ON A KEY ISSUE   Questions are very useful in narrowing your topic as well as for generating ideas. Try phrasing your topic initially as a question, as Kortney did: "Could Alice Walker have chosen to include contrasting ideas of youth, innocence, and beauty vs. death, decay, and grotesqueness to strengthen the piece and highlight the differences between the lightness of childhood and dark reality of adulthood?" The paper then would be your attempt to answer the question. (Later you will need to convert the question into a statement; your final thesis should not be phrased as a question.)

LIMITING THE SCOPE   You may need to concentrate on one aspect of the issue or make just one point instead of covering everything about it. Limiting the topic in this way enables you to go into depth and achieve some fresh insights about a small slice of the topic. If you attempt to touch on everything at a surface level, both the paper and you will come across as shallow or superficial.

Step 3. Prewriting: Deciding on an Approach

You've decided on a topic and narrowed it to a manageable size. But before you start drafting your paper, take some time to consider the kind of topic you've decided on and how that will affect the way you approach its development.

THREE KINDS OF TOPIC   For papers about literature, topics can be grouped roughly into three categories: those that focus on what goes on *inside* the story, poem, or play (literary analysis), those that focus on what *connects* to the work (comparison-contrast), and those that focus on what infuses the work but also *surrounds* the work (social and cultural criticism). The kind of topic you choose affects the way you frame and carry out your discussion of it. Here we will lay out some general principles. And in Chapters 9, 18, and 24 we will discuss how these principles apply to writing specifically about fiction, poetry, and drama.

LITERARY ANALYSIS PAPERS   One way of writing about literature is to look closely at a work and discuss something going on within it that you find particularly interesting. You might analyze a character, an episode, a theme or an idea, or a technique. Some people feel that literary analysis "tears a story apart." Actually, this is not the case, not any more than telling a friend to notice how well the quarterback is playing tears a football game apart or paying particular attention to the bass player during a concert and talking afterward about that musician's role tears a performance apart. Thinking of literary analysis as tearing apart the work is reductive; we should instead think of literary analysis as expanding the reading experience. Analysis draws our attention to aspects of a work that we may have overlooked and invites us to reflect on them—Kortney's paper is a good example of this. When working with analysis, think of your goal as helping another to see a work with even more insight by focusing on a part and considering the way it relates to and contributes to the whole.

Here are some tips for approaching and organizing a literary analysis paper:

TIPS for Writing Literary Analysis Papers

- **Examine the text closely.** Read with your intellect, imagination, and feelings fully engaged (perhaps reading aloud, at least parts of the selection), paying attention to every image, figure of speech, sentence, even every word, and to the literary technique.

- **Take on a challenge.** Look for something unusual, subtle, or particularly thought-provoking or difficult to initially discover or for what makes the work particularly effective. Actually, what you choose to write about does not have to be what is most central or important to the work: Very strong and interesting papers often focus on the handling of a small detail or minor character.

- **Narrow your scope.** Limit yourself to one or two elements or to one section of the story; don't try to cover too much.

- **Provide ample illustrations.** Back up your analysis with specific examples (including quotations). This grounds and substantiates your conclusions: It shows that you have been attentive to the work and that you can use the work itself to back up your conclusion.

- **Avoid summary.** Retelling a story or summarizing a poem is not literary analysis. Your emphasis needs to be on clarification and explanation. You should work with the *how* and *why* of your subject.

- **Organize topically.** An effective way to guard against putting in too much summary is to avoid using the work itself as the outline for your paper. It's better to organize the paper instead by topics or ideas, a series of techniques, or a series of points about your central idea.

COMPARISON-CONTRAST PAPERS   Another way of writing about literature is to compare and contrast things within a work or to compare and contrast a work with another work. To *compare* things is to point out similarities between or among them; to *contrast* things is to focus on their differences. More often than not a thoughtful paper does both. For your paper to be effective, the things that you choose to compare and contrast must have a good deal in common or share one especially important feature, such as two stories containing characters who are trying to find a first job or who grow up in a difficult family situation. The fact that two poems contain personifications or that two different characters in a play have sisters is in itself probably not significant enough to build a comparison-contrast paper around. These same principles apply to a contrast paper: If two things are totally different, with nothing in common, there's little value in pointing out the differences. It would be as useful as comparing apples with San Diego.

Here are some tips for approaching and organizing a comparison-contrast paper:

TIPS for Writing Comparison-Contrast Papers

- **Watch for meaningful pairings.** As you read, watch for things that pair up: a plot, scene, character, setting, symbol, or technique that reminds you of another in the same work or another work. Especially be alert for comparisons that come from unlikely pairings.

- **Outline similarities and differences.** Make lists and then group related items and select two or three topics to focus on.

- **Spell out comparisons and contrasts.** Don't just list and describe the things you are comparing and contrasting; explain why you think there is a connection and why you think it has significance.

- **Organize effectively.** A paper comparing and contrasting two works, or two aspects of the same work, may use the first half to discuss one work and the second half to bring out similar points about the second. The danger of this approach is that the paper may come across as two separate minipapers on the same topic. A wise alternative is to discuss first the one work and then the other for each point you want to compare and contrast. It is not necessary to give equal space to comparing and to contrasting, nor do you need to give equal time to both items you are discussing.

- **Develop a thesis.** Your paper must not be merely a list of similarities and differences. To be an effective paper, the comparisons and contrasts must add up to something: They need to support and develop a thesis that brings out a point about the significance of the comparisons and contrasts.

SOCIAL AND CULTURAL CRITICISM PAPERS   In addition to literary analysis topics and comparison-contrast topics, papers can examine a work's relation to the cultural and social context that infuses it but that also ties the story to real-world issues that surround us. Such topics involve the use of social and cultural criticism. Usually such papers deal with what a story reveals about social attitudes and relations generally and, more specifically, with issues regarding such things as social background, gender, class, ethnicity, power, and privilege. Authors write works at a specific time, surrounded by specific circumstances and attitudes. Even if the work does not refer directly to events or attitudes contemporary to the writing, those events and attitudes influence the writer and the work, consciously or unconsciously, whether she or he accepts and reflects prevailing attitudes or ignores, rejects, or challenges them. Cultural critics direct our attention to such issues and clarify the relationship between the author and the work and the cultural context in which they exist.

Here are some tips for approaching and organizing a social and cultural criticism paper.

TIPS for Writing Social and Cultural Criticism Papers

- **Read expansively.** Social and cultural critics concentrate on the way the events, ideas, or attitudes in a work are influenced by the economic conditions, political situations, or social conventions that existed when it was written. They can also explore the way a work is a part of a culture and can influence, and perhaps change, the economic conditions, political situations, or social conventions of its time or later times.

- **Plan on doing research.** Social criticism and cultural criticism usually involve information beyond what is found in the text or in common knowledge; it often deals with background information you'll find only by further investigation.

- **Connections are crucial.** Social and cultural criticism usually involve making connections of various kinds: between issues within and outside the text, for example, or between a text and historical or cultural events contemporary with it or between a text and a theoretical text. Social and cultural criticism may, but don't have to, use the comparison-contrast method.

- **Make a point.** Simply describing cultural connections is not enough. A paper has to be coherent, having a significant thesis with developmental points and explanations of their relevance and their implications.

- **Organize topically.** Social criticism and cultural criticism are analytical. Papers using these approaches, much like literary analysis papers, need to be organized stepwise in the development of the topics or ideas being dealt with.

Step 4. Prewriting: Framing a Thesis and Preparing an Outline

Once you've narrowed the topic, you need to sharpen what you want to say about that topic. You need to do more than merely summarize or describe the story or poem or play you're dealing with — that's seldom interesting or valuable for you or your reader. Readers can read the work for themselves. And your teacher certainly has. They can follow the outline and pick out images. But what they can't know in any other way are *your* explanations, interpretations, observations, perceptions, and connections. That's what you need to get across, in as clear, inviting, and accessible a way as possible. You need to develop a central idea that has some insight, interest, and significance. Your job is to persuade readers that your views are sound and convincing.

TOPIC VERSUS THESIS   The central point you want to make should be stated in a *thesis*, a proposition put forward for consideration and usually placed at or near the end of the first paragraph. It's important to notice the difference between a topic and a thesis. A *topic* just names a subject area: "The loss of childhood innocence in 'The Flowers.'" It states a fact. A *thesis* on the other hand adds a *comment* about the subject and turns it into something requiring persuasive support, as in Kortney's final thesis: "I believe Myop laid the flowers down to symbolize the loss of her childhood; the innocence she once possessed is now dead to her." A thesis states an idea that readers may disagree with or reject and that needs to be developed and supported with explanations and evidence.

WORKING THESIS   As you think about your topic and what to say about it, you might start by framing a working *thesis*, a statement of the main idea you think you will develop in the paper. Kortney was able to use the last sentence of her journal entry as her working thesis: That's one of the reasons for taking notes and recording them in a journal. The working thesis often changes or develops as you write—that's natural. But beginning with a tentative point, even if you know it will not be your final version, helps you organize the rest of the paper.

ASSESSING THE THESIS   To develop a convincing paper, you should first examine the thesis to determine what parts of it need to be explained and supported. Kortney revised her working thesis only slightly. Her final thesis, quoted two paragraphs above, implies a series of steps that will develop her ideas. Here is how she analyzed her thesis to identify the points she would need to work on.

> *After revising the working thesis, I reread "The Flowers" looking for examples from the text that support my argument. I looked for examples that support the <u>childhood</u> component of my paper, and for places where Myop is <u>transitioning from childhood to maturity</u>, and for examples of where Myop experiences the <u>death of her childhood</u>. Specifically, I focused particularly on her actions and feelings.*

She had here a potential outline for the body of the paper: a three-part or three-paragraph development. Carefully analyzing the thesis often yields an outline for the paper as well as a better understanding of what it is asserting.

PREPARING AN OUTLINE   Many writers, like Kortney, find it helpful to have an outline—a plan, an advance sketch of the steps the paper will take the reader through.

A student, **Kortney DeVito**, on preparing an outline: "Before starting to write, I often use an outline as a way to organize my thoughts. It is a wonderful way to help guide where I am going with my paper and helps to ensure I won't leave out any of my ideas. My final paper often looks different from the outline I created. I may decide that ideas need rearranging to fit well together. All I want is a road map for guiding me in getting my rough draft down on paper. I can reorganize things later as needed."

Some students write out a detailed, formal outline with roman numerals, letters, and arabic numerals as headings (as Kortney did). Others jot down a list of subtopics. Still others have a clear plan in their heads and don't write it down. Some even write an outline mirroring the finished draft to see if it follows a clear, logical organizational pattern. People work in different ways; you need to find what works best for you.

Kortney's Outline

I. Introduction/Question I am answering: Who does Myop lay the flowers for?
   a. Describe Myop briefly
   b. Touch on the dead man Myop encountered
   c. Thesis: I believe Myop laid the flowers down to symbolize the loss of her childhood; the innocence she once possessed as a child is now dead to her.
II. Childhood—Supporting that Myop is a child at the beginning of the story
   a. Actions
      i. Skipping lightly (para. 1)
      ii. Picking up stick (para. 2)
         1. To hit chickens
         2. To make music—"tat-de-ta-ta-ta"
      iii. Bouncing (para. 4)
      iv. Collecting an armful of flowers (para. 5)
   b. Thoughts
      i. Each day is a "golden surprise" (para. 1)
      ii. All that exists is the present (para. 2)
      iii. No responsibility—she doesn't have to go out to gather nuts like her mother (para. 4)
III. Transition from childhood to maturity
   a. Exploring by herself—no mother or adult around (para. 4)
      i. A mile away from home (para. 5)
   b. "Making her own path" (para. 4)
   c. Feeling uncomfortable with the strange new surroundings (para. 5)
   d. Wants to head back to the peacefulness of morning (para. 6)
IV. Maturity
   a. Suddenly steps into the eyes of the dead man (para. 6)
      i. Heel becomes lodged between nose and brow (para. 6)

b. Myop notices the noose from the lynching while picking up a rose
(para. 6)
   i. Realizes the harsh reality of life. No longer will the childhood
     innocence protect her.
c. Myop laying the flowers for her childhood as soon as she puts
together the events of the man's death
V. Conclusion — Myop loses her childhood innocence
  a. Remind audience of her childish actions at the beginning of the
   story
  b. Discuss the horror Myop sees and how it causes her to grow up
   quickly

Step 5. Writing: Developing and Supporting the Thesis

After all that prewriting, at last you're ready to start writing. But getting started isn't always easy. It's not uncommon for someone to waste an hour or more staring at a blank computer screen, searching for the right words to appear. Don't do that. The key to getting started is to *start*. Don't wait to be "in the right mood." Start writing and, more often than not, you will find yourself getting caught up in your subject. And don't start by spending all evening coming up with a brilliant introduction. The first paragraph you write often gets discarded anyhow. Many writers actually compose the first paragraph after writing the body of the paper because it's often easier to decide on the most effective opening after all the ideas have been articulated.

Some people find that it works best to write a first draft rapidly, getting their ideas down without worrying about neatness, grammar, or spelling. Others need to work more slowly, getting each sentence and each paragraph right before moving on to the next one. There is no single "right" process; discover the one that suits you best.

START WITH IDEA SENTENCES   The way you start the paragraphs in the body of a paper is very important. Just as the thesis of your paper must state an idea, not just a fact, so too should the first sentence — or topic sentence — of each paragraph. The opening sentence of a paragraph is a mini-thesis: It should state briefly the point or idea to be developed in that paragraph. If a paragraph starts with a statement of a fact rather than a statement of an idea, the rest of the paragraph is likely to consist of summary and more factual statements, not to explore an idea or develop an argument.

The second sentence of the paragraph should expand on the point or idea stated briefly in the topic sentence, bringing out its significance and implications, and the rest of the paragraph must develop and support the point or idea. The final draft of Kortney's paper has effective topic sentences (compare them to her rough draft, in which the opening sentences are less effective).

ILLUSTRATE AND EXPLAIN   As you write paragraphs developing the points in your outline, you need to include two things: (1) details from the story and (2) your explanations of them. The two need to go together. Details by themselves do not prove anything. Your explanations are needed to indicate what is important about the details and to tie them in to the whole fabric you are weaving in the paper. Likewise, explanations without supporting details are not specific enough and do not anchor themselves to the work. The key to a successful paper lies in its development and illustration of its ideas: explaining ideas so readers understand them readily and supporting ideas with details so readers have confidence that the points are well-grounded and worth considering.

INCLUDE QUOTATIONS   In any literary paper, some of the supporting evidence must be quotations. Quotations connect your explanations and interpretations directly to the work(s) and show that they are firmly based. Be careful that the phrases or sentences you quote convey what they mean in their context. The way words are selected for quotation must never distort the way they are used in the original text. The final draft of Kortney's paper illustrates effective use of quotations (pp. 47–51).

FOCUS ON KEY PASSAGES   When you write about literature, you may be tempted to start at the beginning of the literary work and follow it on through to the end. Unfortunately, that often leads to summarizing it rather than examining and discussing it. Instead, it's better to organize the paper by topics or ideas—a series of techniques or a series of points about your central idea. One way to be specific and detailed without lapsing into summary is to focus on *key passages*. As we listen to and look at a story, poem, or play, we try to take the whole work into consideration as we seek to grasp its essence. In doing so, we usually find that a particular section—a sentence, a few sentences, a paragraph, a particular scene—seems to shed light on all the other parts of the story.

Teacher and literary critic Benjamin De Mott called such sections "key passages." They are not something writers insert deliberately into a work, as clues to readers; they are simply parts of the work that appear particularly meaningful to an individual reader, in relation to that reader's interpretation. So, instead of trying futilely to discuss every part of a work, you can focus on a key passage in depth, or perhaps two or three key passages, and use it or them to represent, connect with, and illuminate what is occurring in the work as a whole.

WRITE WITH READERS IN MIND   All writers need to be aware of the audience they are addressing. A paper for a literature course should include a larger audience than your teacher alone. In practice, only your teacher may read it, but ideally other people would read it too. And that is how your teacher will read your paper, as if she or he is part of this larger audience.

Blending Quotations into Your Writing

Handling quotations effectively requires you to blend them into your writing smoothly and coherently. Here are some suggestions:

- Avoid long quotations whenever possible. Often the best approach is to combine quotations with summary and to slip quoted extracts into your prose style gracefully, as Kortney does in her paper:

  Myop wanted to experience the feelings of independence so in paragraph four we learn "she made her own path." She left the "rusty boards of her family's sharecropper cabin" to explore her surroundings on a summer morning.

- In some cases, however, it is most effective to introduce a quotation formally, with your sentence coming to a full stop, followed by a colon.

  At the end of paragraph five the once pleasant scenery changes: "It seemed gloomy in the little cove in which she found herself. The air was damp, the silence close and deep." This is a harsh disparity from the summer gaiety Myop experienced at the beginning of the story.

- Quotations can be shortened also by the omission of words or phrases or even sentences. Such omissions must be signaled by the use of ellipses (. . .). For guidelines on handling ellipses, see page 54.
- Don't automatically put commas before and after a quotation: They are needed only if the same words would require commas even if they were not a quotation.
- You should not start a paragraph with a quotation. The paragraph needs an opening topic sentence, setting up the point you want to develop, stated in your own words.
- Don't automatically start a new paragraph after a quotation. Usually each quotation should be followed with an explanation or a comment in your words on the point being illustrated, tying it in to the point the paragraph is developing.

And remember that quotations also require proper punctuation and formatting. For guidelines, see pages 53–54.

In some classes, students read each other's papers to learn from one another, to help each other, to stimulate discussion, and to create a sense that they are writing for the larger conversation we mentioned at the beginning of this chapter.

AVOID SUMMARY When you write a paper for a literature course, address the same group you talk to in class. Visualize your fellow students as well as your teacher as readers. Assume that your audience has read the stories, poems, or plays you are writing about. Thus, you don't need to retell or summarize the work. Take for granted that your audience knows the plot or subject matter, but assume that readers would benefit from help in understanding the work more fully or in seeing all the implications you see. Think of your paper as part of the continuing conversation, helping interested readers by talking clearly about things they would like to think more about.

USE THE "LITERARY PRESENT" When describing, discussing, or introducing specific passages or events from works of literature, use the present tense, even if the work was written in ancient times and even if the work itself uses the past tense. This is referred to as the *literary present* — that is, the action within a literary work continues to happen even if the telling about it looks back from a later point. Thus, if you are writing about Myop's character in Alice Walker's "The Flowers" (p. 23), the story says, "She *was* ten, and nothing *existed* for her but her song," but you should say, "Myop *is* a ten-year-old whose happy songs *demonstrate* the innocent, carefree life she *leads* before encountering the skeleton."

Although you should use the present tense when writing about characters and events in literary works, you should use past tense to relate actual historical facts that are outside of the work itself, as, for example,

Alice Walker first *published* "The Flowers" in 1973.

INTRODUCTIONS Many people find writing introductions and conclusions difficult. There is no easy and sure-fire method we can give you. The opening of a paper should entice a reader to keep reading. It needs to capture your reader's attention immediately, from the first sentence. It can do that by raising an important thought about the subject or by being imaginative in style and wording. It's an opportunity for creativity or wit or a personal touch. As we mentioned before, many writers compose the introduction last. In some cases, the last paragraph you write, the one you planned as the conclusion, can be turned into a good introduction. The final draft of Kortney's paper uses a standard technique by starting with a universal idea about the subject, then narrowing down to the specific case of Myop in "The Flowers."

CONCLUSIONS Your final paragraph should round out the paper and give your readers a sense of finality and resolution. A good conclusion summarizes the central points of the paper, preferably in fresh wording, like Kortney uses in her final draft, and doesn't just repeat the way things were said before. Conclusions often refer back to introductions, giving papers a sense of symmetry and unity by commenting further on something said there or answering a question raised there. Good conclusions are usually brief; don't let yours go on and on.

SELECTING A TITLE   Your paper needs a title. Make sure you create a *title* that indicates the subject of or an idea about your paper (for instance, "Point of View in Alice Walker's 'The Flowers'") and not a heading that is vague (as, for example, "Point of View"). Don't use the title of the literary work as the label for your paper: "The Flowers" is Walker's title; it can't be yours. A title that uses alliteration or wit, one that is catchy or strikingly worded, helps capture the reader's interest and suggests that the rest of the paper will be well written and appealing. Kortney's title, "The Death of Myop's Childhood," is effective because of its personification of childhood: It leads her readers to want to know how a childhood could die and why Myop's does.

Your own title at the top of the paper should not be put in quotation marks (see the sample paper on p. 47).

Step 6. Revising, Proofreading, and Formatting

Once you finish a draft of the paper, the next steps are to revise and then proofread it. Notice that these are separate steps. Revising doesn't mean correcting spelling and grammar errors: That's proofreading, the final step. Revising comes first. The word *revision* derives from the Latin words for *look* and *again*: Revising means examining closely what you've written,

☑ **CHECKLIST for Revising**

❑ **Content:**
- Are your ideas explained and developed fully? Have you included enough solid support so that the points you are making are convincing?
- Have you supplied enough details and examples to show that your points are well-grounded in the work?

❑ **Organization:**
- Are your paragraphs in the most effective order? Do they build from one to the next? Would it be more effective to rearrange them?
- Are the transitions between paragraphs clear and easy to follow?

❑ **Expression:**
- Is your tone serious but not pretentious, warm but not cute or breezy?
- Is there variety in the length and structure of your sentences? Do they read easily, with fluid, appealing rhythms?
- Do the words sound good together? Are there places where a combination of words is too hard to say together or where an unintentional rhyme is distracting? (TIP: Reading a paper aloud is a helpful way to test its style.)

thinking through it again, and trying to find ways to improve its content, organization, and expression. The notes in the margins of Kortney's paper show how she looked again at the content, development, and organization of her paper and made changes to improve them.

REASONS FOR REVISING   Revision is crucial to effective writing: Making your paper the strongest possible usually requires several drafts. You may be able to write one draft and get a C or even a B, but the writing simply won't be as thoughtful and engaging as it would be if you revised. And revision is one of the best ways to learn even more about writing.

GAINING SOME DISTANCE   It's hard to get a fresh look right after you finish writing. You are usually still too close to writing it to come up with different ways to explain, arrange, and express. Revision often works best if you can lay your paper aside for a day or two or even longer before thinking about changes. It also may help to have someone else read the paper, someone whose intelligence will enable her or him to check if the ideas and organization are clear and adequately supported.

CHECKING FOR ERRORS   After revising your paper, proofread and edit it carefully to check for errors in spelling and grammar, for inconsistencies, and for any awkward expressions. If you write your paper on a computer, use its programs to check spelling and grammar. There's no excuse for simple typos when spending a few minutes spell-checking would catch them.

A computer check, of course, doesn't free you from the need to read closely as well. The computer can tell you that it doesn't recognize *thier* and ask if you intended to write *their*, but it won't notice if you wrote *their* when you should have used *there*. Again, distance (coming back after a couple of days) can be helpful because you may have become so familiar with your essay that it is hard to see what should be different. Some writers proofread by starting at the end and reading backward as a way of looking at the words instead of getting caught up in the meaning. Again, having someone read your essay is often useful—if she or he is a good speller and an attentive reader.

Even if you revise and proofread initially on a computer screen, we recommend at least one revision (and the final proofreading and editing) be done from a printed copy. It is helpful to see the sentences and paragraphs the way they will look on paper in the finished product. To save paper, use the back of some scrap paper.

FORMATTING   Papers should be typed (word processed), double-spaced throughout, with one-inch margins all around, and printed in an easily readable 12-point font (e.g., Times New Roman) on 8½ × 11 inch white paper. Use a paper clip to hold pages together, unless your instructor asks that they be stapled. Use Tab to indent the first line of each paragraph a half inch.

IDENTIFICATION AND TITLE   Modern Language Association (MLA) style does not require a title page. Instead, at the top of the first page, against the left margin, on separate double-spaced lines, place your name, your instructor's name, the course number, and the date. Then, double-space and center your title. (See p. 47 for a sample first page.) If your instructor requires a title page, ask for guidelines on formatting it.

PAGINATION   Place the page number (in arabic numerals) preceded by your last name in the upper right-hand corner of each page, a half inch below the top edge (see the sample paper on pp. 47–51).

SAMPLE SHORT PAPER

To allow you to see more of Kortney's writing process, we've printed the rough draft of her paper on the left-hand pages, and the final draft with her comments on the right-hand pages.

Kortney DeVito's Rough Draft

─────────────── ROUGH DRAFT ───────────────

Kortney DeVito
Professor Schakel
Introduction to Literature
7 May 2010

Who did Myop lay the flowers for in Alice Walker's "The Flowers." Was is for the lynched man who lay decaying in the ground next to a wild pink rose? No, I believe Myop laid the flowers down to symbolize the loss of her childhood. There are many seasons we experience throughout our lives; we cannot stay in the same season forever. I believe Myop was forced to grow up very quickly because of her realization.

At the beginning of the story, the reader is meets a curious and energetic ten-year-old girl. Rather than walk, Myop skipped around the farm. Also, Myop carried a stick to tease chickens make a song to carry her along a carefree day. She looked at the beautiful day as a "golden surprise". Through her actions you can tell Myop is a child.

You can tell Myop wanted to experience the feelings of independence when she takes out on an adventure on her own on a summer afternoon. Although she desires to be alone and grown-up on her journey more than a mile away from home, she still exhibits the actions of a child: collecting an armful of wildflowers with no purpose and "bouncing this way and that way". She wants to be grown-up but still acts like a child.

Kortney DeVito's Final Draft with Her Notes

──────── **FINAL DRAFT** ────────

Kortney DeVito
Professor Schakel
Introduction to Literature
20 May 2010

The Death of Myop's Childhood

Childhood is one of the many seasons we experience
throughout life. It is a time filled with wonderment and exploration, merriment and magic, innocence and discovery. Unfortunately, we cannot stay in this season forever. Sometimes we transition through these seasons on our own volition; other times it is
because of circumstances we encounter. In Alice Walker's "The
Flowers," we are introduced to a young girl named Myop whose
childhood departs swiftly because of an awful discovery. After encountering the remains of a lynched man, Myop lays her flowers
down. Some say the flowers are for the lynched man. I believe
Myop lays the flowers down to symbolize the loss of her childhood — the innocence she once possessed is now dead to her.

At the beginning of the story, the narrator introduces an
innocent, energetic, and curious ten-year-old girl. Her actions
exude childlike whimsy. Rather than walking idly in paragraph
one, Myop "skipped lightly" around the farm in a youthful fashion. In paragraph two, Myop "carried a short, knobby stick" selecting chickens to tease and creating a rhythmic song "tat-de-
ta-ta-ta" to carry her along a carefree day — she is in her own
world: "nothing existed for her but her song." She looks at the
beautiful day as a "golden surprise," savoring the succulent
smells of the farm's harvest. The appreciation of simple things
and the actions of Myop paint a picture of a young girl delighting
in the wonders of her childhood.

However charming the morning is, the confines of the
farm become too restricting for Myop; perhaps, the confines of

*My introduction
didn't grab the
audience's at-
tention, so I re-
worked the con-
clusion of my
rough draft to
use it as the
new introduc-
tion.*

*My thesis could
be stronger, so I
added to it.*

*I needed more
support to paint
a picture of
Myop's childish
actions and per-
ceptions. I used
my notes and
referenced the
text to flesh out
this paragraph.*

─────── **ROUGH DRAFT** ───────

DeVito 2

At the end of paragraph five the once pleasant scenery changes: "It seemed gloomy in the little cove in which she found herself. The air was damp, the silence close and deep." This is very different from the beginning of the story. Myop's heel suddenly becomes lodged in between the ridge of a man's brow and nose. The only fear she shows is a "yelp of surprise" when she sees the man's grin. She takes note of his characteristics. Such a haunting situation paired with the bizarre inquisitiveness of the character causes the reader to think Myop still possess a piece of her childhood. That little piece soon vanishes when Myop realizes that the man she discovered did not die by accident. She pieces the execution together. At first, she measures him looks at his decapitated body. Then she stumbles upon the "rotted remains of the noose" in the soil. Still, there is no sign of fear or revulsion from Myop. However, when Myop discovers the other half of the rope on the limb of an oak tree "spinning restlessly in the breeze" she reacts. Myop realizes that this day is no longer "a golden surprise" and that life can be cruel. As suddenly as she stepped in the eyes of the man, Myop lost the gift of innocence childhood provides. "Myop laid down her flowers" to mourn her loss.

DeVito 2

her childhood were becoming restraining as well. Myop wants to experience the feelings of independence, so in paragraph four we learn "she made her own path." She left the "rusty boards of her family's sharecropper cabin" to explore her surroundings on a summer morning. Although she desires to be alone and grown-up on her journey more than a mile away from home, she still exhibits the actions of a child: collecting an armful of wildflowers with no purpose and "bouncing this way and that way." It appears Myop is bordering the great divide of childhood and maturity; in a seemingly juvenile manner, Myop creates a new path for herself in unchartered territory.

> *To engage the reader, I incorporated more sentence variety and lengthened this paragraph. I wrote a more gripping topic sentence and added quotations as support.*

The land along Myop's "own path" exhibits an unpleasantness and "strangeness" in its unfamiliarity. At the end of paragraph five the once pleasant scenery changes: "It seemed gloomy in the little cove in which she found herself. The air was damp, the silence close and deep." This is a harsh disparity from the summer gaiety Myop experiences at the beginning of the story. To magnify this disparity, a grotesque event unexpectedly occurs when "she stepped smack into his eyes." Myop's heel suddenly becomes lodged in between the ridge of his brow and nose. Surprisingly, the curiosity and boldness of her childlike nature allow her to reach down to free her foot. The only fear she shows is a "yelp of surprise" when she sees the man's grin; oddly, however, she continues to investigate the corpse. She takes note of his characteristics: his height, the details of his teeth, the largeness of his bones, even the condition of his clothes. Such a haunting situation paired with the bizarre inquisitiveness of the character cause the reader to think Myop still possesses a piece of her childhood.

> *I wrote a stronger topic sentence.*
>
> *I needed to split my original paragraph into two parts: 1. Discuss time before Myop realizes how the man had died, when a part of her childhood still exists.*

That little piece soon vanishes when Myop realizes that the man she discovers did not die by accident. She pieces the execution together. At first, she measures him "from feet to neck" and sees his head lying beside his body. Then, when reaching down to pick a wild pink rose, she stumbles upon the "rotted remains of the noose" in the soil. Still, there is no sign of fear or

> *2. Discuss when she sees the noose—at which point her childhood is gone.*

ROUGH DRAFT

DeVito 3

Childhood is one of the many seasons we experience throughout life. It is a time filled with wonderment and exploration, innocence. Unfortunately, we cannot stay in this season forever. Sometimes we transition through these seasons on our own; other times it is because of circumstances. In Alice Walker's "The Flowers", we are introduced to a young girl named Myop whose childhood departs swiftly. After encountering the remains of a lynched man, Myop laid her flowers down. Some say the flowers are for the lynched man. I believe Myop laid the flowers down to symbolize the loss of her childhood; the innocence she once possessed is now dead to her.

FINAL DRAFT

DeVito 3

revulsion from Myop. However, when Myop discovers the other half of the rope on the limb of an oak tree "spinning restlessly in the breeze," she reacts. I believe the innocence of the morning is stolen as soon as she pieces together the evidence surrounding her. Myop realizes that this day is no longer "a golden surprise" and that life can be cruel. Gone is the childish innocence of thinking that life will last forever and there is only goodness in humanity — she discovers the hatred and ugliness humanity possesses murdered this man. As suddenly as she stepped in the eyes of the man, Myop lost the gift of innocence childhood provides. "Myop laid down her flowers" to mourn her loss.

I wanted to answer two questions in this paragraph: What causes Myop to lay the flowers down? And why is the loss of her childhood sad?

Within moments during a late summer afternoon, Myop lost something very dear. No longer skipping, bouncing, and making music with a stick, Myop suddenly loses the innocence of childhood — something we all cherish — because of a single encounter. Myop realizes there are more than the sweet smells of harvest, the songs she creates, or the beauty of a flower; there are also hatred, death, and wretchedness. The haunting reality of the world's malice leads Myop to lay the flowers on the forest floor where the lynched man rests. She says goodbye to her season of childhood.

For my new conclusion, I wanted brief highlights of each paragraph and I wanted my last sentence to be simple, to illustrate the solemnity of the story.

TIPS for Writing a Successful Short Paper

The following are five characteristics of a successful short paper.

- **Significant topic.** A successful paper grows out of asking a probing question; it focuses on a specific problem and explores it in some depth.

- **Appropriate approach.** It develops an idea, or an angle, about the problem, selecting an insightful approach to it.

- **Solid preparation.** It shows evidence of careful, perceptive reading and clear critical thinking.

- **Strong development.** It avoids broad generalizations and plot summary but provides precise, pointed explanations and uses details and brief quotations as support and expansion of the idea or interpretation.

- **Good writing.** It is unified and organized coherently and is written in clear, polished prose with correct grammar, spelling, and punctuation.

A CLOSER LOOK AT
Handling Titles

1. Titles of books or long poems (the names of any long work published independently, with its name on the title page) and the names of plays, movies, and TV shows are italicized.

2. Titles of short works (poems, short stories, essays), ones that name a part of a book rather than the whole, are placed within quotation marks.

   "The Flowers" is found in Alice Walker's book *In Love and Trouble: Stories of Black Women.*

   Quotation marks are also used around chapter titles in a book or titles of individual episodes of a TV series.

   The final episode of *Baywatch* in 2001 was entitled "Rescue Me."

3. When the title of a book-length work that would ordinarily be italicized is included in a book title, you may identify the internal title either by not italicizing it or by placing it in quotation marks.

   Solomon, Barbara H., ed. *Critical Essays on Toni Morrison's* Beloved. New York: G. K. Hall, 1998.
   Solomon, Barbara H., ed. *Critical Essays on Toni Morrison's "Beloved."* New York: G. K. Hall, 1998.

A CLOSER LOOK AT

Punctuating and Formatting Quotations

Handling quotations well requires proper punctuation and formatting. Firmly fix the guidelines below in your mind so you get them right automatically, without needing to think about them.

1. Place quotation marks outside commas and periods (." or ,") but inside semicolons and colons ("; or ":). U.S. punctuation conventions never put the period or comma outside quotation marks.

2. Always use double quotation marks ("), except for a quotation within a quotation, which is indicated by single marks ('). However, if an entire quotation consists of dialogue by one speaker and is so introduced, it is not necessary to use the extra single quotation marks.

3. Treat longer passages (more than three lines of poetry or more than four lines of a prose passage) as block quotations, set off from the rest of the text by starting a new line and indenting the passage one inch — sometimes more for poetry — from the left margin. Block quotations should be double-spaced. See Kristina Martinez's paper on page 85 for an example.

4. Treating a passage as a block quotation is the same as putting quotation marks around it. Use quotation marks around an indented passage only if it has quotation marks around it in the source. If, however, the entire quotation consists of dialogue by one speaker and is so introduced, quotation marks are not necessary.

5. The end punctuation of a quotation may be (often should be) dropped and replaced by punctuation appropriate to your sentence; thus, a period ending a quotation may be replaced with a comma if your sentence goes on (you should never have .", or ,". in a paper) or it can be omitted if a parenthetical citation follows: " (**source**). The period or comma is placed *after* a parenthetical citation (as at the end of the previous sentence), not before it. The parenthesis should not be left unattached between two sentences.

6. In all other respects, quotations must be precisely accurate, including original spelling, capitalization, and punctuation. The initial letter of a line of poetry must be capitalized if it is capitalized in the original, even

if the quotation is not indented. Always double-check quotations to make sure they are correct.

7. If you need to insert a word into a quotation (adding a verb to integrate the quotation into your sentence, for example, or changing a pronoun to a noun for clarity), place the inserted word in square brackets [ ], not in parentheses.

8. In some cases, you will want to omit words or punctuation marks to shorten quotations and to make them fit your sentence construction more effectively. Ellipsis points (three periods with a space before and after each: . . .) must be used whenever you omit something from *within* a quotation.

9. Ellipsis points are not used at the beginning or the end of a quotation if what is quoted coincides with the beginning or end of the original sentence or if it is obvious that what is quoted is not a complete sentence in the original (for example, if you quote a brief fragment).

10. If the passage being quoted has ellipsis points in it, square brackets should be placed around your ellipsis to clarify that yours have been added: [. . .].

11. Four dots (a period plus the three ellipsis dots) are needed if you omit (1) the last part of a quoted sentence; (2) the first part of the following sentence; (3) a whole sentence or more; or (4) a whole paragraph or more. If a sentence ends with a question mark or an exclamation point in the original, that punctuation is used instead of the first or fourth period. What precedes and follows the four dots should be grammatically complete sentences, either as quoted or as connected to the text surrounding it.

12. The use of an ellipsis mark must not distort the meaning of the passage being quoted.

The *MLA Handbook for Writers of Research Papers*, 7th edition (New York: Modern Language Association of America, 2009), includes sections providing guidelines on matters of style and punctuation, as does *The Chicago Manual of Style*, 15th edition (Chicago: University of Chicago Press, 2003). Or you can consult the MLA Web site or a college writing handbook, such as Diana Hacker and Nancy Sommers's *A Writer's Reference*, 7th edition (Boston: Bedford/St. Martin's, 2011).

*W*hen you're writing, you're trying to find out something that you don't know.

James Baldwin

(Author of "Sonny's Blues," p. 362)

Writing a Literary Research Paper

CHAPTER 3

Entering the Larger Conversation

When you see a movie you really like, you probably not only want to see it again but also want to find out more about it—what other films an actor has appeared in (and perhaps some details about her or his life), some background on the director and information on the screenwriter, what changes were made from the work on which it was based (if adapted from another source), and what well-informed film critics said about it. When you look for information about these topics in newspapers or magazines or on the Internet, you are, in fact, engaging in research. Research on literary works is much the same: You look to find similar kinds of background information about authors, works, and eras and what well-informed literary critics have said about a particular work. This chapter focuses on how to locate respected literary sources and how to incorporate them as part of your conversation about literature.

THE LARGER CONVERSATION   In Chapter 2, we said that responding to literature is like entering a huge, ongoing conversation. It starts with reading as actively "listening" to a work and "talking back" to it by writing notes in the margins and journalizing. You then may discuss the work in class and perhaps share your enthusiasms, dislikes, and questions with individuals outside class. The conversation expands even more through the work of literary scholars who publish their critical insights about a particular work or era or theme.

It can be interesting and valuable for you, as a student of literature, to be able to enter that larger conversation and use it to expand and deepen your understanding and insights. Literary research involves finding materials, evaluating how sound and reliable they are, keeping track of them, and using them in a paper. Research isn't only for doing research papers—you can use it just to learn more about an author or a work you like. However, our main concern here is to help you improve the way you write research papers for college courses, to increase your confidence and your skills in doing them.

This chapter traces how one writer, Kristina Martinez, a student probably a lot like you, moved through the research process—

- finding materials;
- evaluating sources;
- keeping track of what she read

—and through the steps in writing a research paper:

- finding a topic;
- developing ideas;
- incorporating sources;
- documenting sources;
- revising, proofreading, and double-checking.

THE RESEARCH PROCESS

The Nature of Literary Research

Before we begin following Kristina's progress, we should pause to clarify three main types of literary research: factual research, primary research, and secondary research. Each yields different kinds of information with different uses and draws on different kinds of sources. Since a project often involves more than one type of research, it is important to recognize these types and to consider which will be most applicable in different situations.

Factual Research

The first level of research involves finding pertinent information about the definitions of words, the meaning of details mentioned in a work, the source of allusions, and the biographical and historical context in which the work was written. This sort of investigation, an essential part of engaged, active reading, is usually carried out by consulting sources such as dictionaries, encyclopedias, almanacs, and Internet sites, all of which provide convenient access to ordinary, widely documented information. Such sources do not need to be acknowledged in your paper or included in your bibliography if you use them only to find or verify facts that are readily available, but you must acknowledge them if you quote from them—which generally shouldn't be necessary—or if they provide information that is important to the paper and is not commonly known.

Primary Research

PRIMARY SOURCES   The next, very basic, kind of research involves the reading of literary works and any kind of texts (written, graphic, or oral) contemporary with or earlier than those works, such as letters, diaries, journals, memoirs, and newspapers, even music and works of art of the time. Such texts are referred to as *primary sources*.

THEIR USES   Literary scholars research primary sources to acquire first-hand information about an author's life, times, or culture and to understand literary or artistic influences and traditions that affected an author or helped shape a work. If your subject involves very recent literature, this may be the only kind of research you can do. Since there may be no published studies of the authors or works to make use of, you will need to rely on biographical statements and interviews, and newspapers, magazines, movies, art, advertising, or whatever else might illuminate the writer's ideas and artistry.

DOING PRIMARY RESEARCH   You are doing primary research when, in addition to reading an assigned text, you read other works from the author's time period to discover even more about the text and the author. You might, for example, find reading diaries of women in the nineteenth century both interesting and helpful for understanding the context and implications of Kate Chopin's "The Story of an Hour" (p. 233). Whenever you read personal letters, journals, or newspapers from the time in which the author lived, or look at art or architecture that the author looked at, or listen to music that the author listened to—in essence, study what she or he was influenced by—you are doing primary research.

Secondary Research

SECONDARY SOURCES   The third kind of research we consider involves reading what scholars have written about primary texts and about the life or literary, social, or cultural context of an author or a work, such as biographies of an author and books discussing the events, culture, and ideas of the author's time. Such works are called *secondary sources*—that is, not firsthand works written *by* an author or her or his contemporaries, but secondhand ones written *about* an author or her or his works or era. Secondary sources also include critical books or essays about a work or group of works.

THEIR USES   When literary scholars undertake a project, they do both primary and secondary research. They read as many works as possible by the author and by other scholars who have written about the author or the author's works in order to build on what has been done previously. They also often push further to explore things that earlier scholars over-looked or to arrive at new insights and conclusions. Literary scholars often work alone, but what they do is actually communal and coopera-tive. They listen to and learn from each other's work, modify or correct it when necessary, and extend its range through further exploration of its implications.

DOING SECONDARY RESEARCH   If you are assigned a research paper for this course, you probably will be expected to do secondary research—at least to use some critical books and essays—though on a more limited basis than a professional scholar would. Even if you don't read everything about a work, reading several critical essays adds significantly to your understand-ing and appreciation of it. It's important, however, that you not begin read-ing critical books and essays until you know your primary works well and have reached your own conclusions about them and begun jotting down ideas for possible topics and tentative theses for a paper.

WARNING! A word of caution about one other kind of source. Various types of "study guides" are available, online and in print, for many liter-ary authors and works. They typically offer plot summaries, analyses of characters and themes, and commentaries about key passages. *We recom-mend that you don't use these:* They're an unnecessary substitute for your own careful, attentive reading.

If you do use them, be sure to do so with great care, making sure of their validity. You may want to check with your teacher concerning them. They are seldom written by established literary scholars, and their treat-ment of works is often superficial. Some even contain errors of fact. They tend to present themes as separate from one another and as absolutes (these are *the* themes to find in *Hamlet*), thus reducing the actual com-plexity and richness of the work and misleading unwary readers into thinking the work is not nearly as challenging as it actually is.

If you decide to read one as preparation for writing a paper, *its use must be acknowledged in the bibliography, even if you do not cite it in the paper.* But be forewarned, these are not sources that will enhance the quality of your paper.

FINDING MATERIALS

The development of the Internet, with the many resources available on it, can make it tempting to do all one's research by computer. You may be inclined to start with Google or Yahoo! or AltaVista. Such search engines do have value and we'll come to them later, but they are actually not the best places to start. They make a wealth of information available, but much of it is of marginal value; Internet sources by themselves are not adequate. A good college-level literature research paper needs to include printed sources, such as scholarly books and journals, found in or through your college or university library—usually unavailable at most other public libraries—and the Internet does not provide an adequate substitute for them. We therefore begin with a discussion of library searches. Then we'll move on to Internet searches.

A student, Kristina Martinez, on searching for scholarly books: "The story I enjoyed most, and most wanted to learn more about, was Toni Morrison's 'Recitatif.' After reading 'Recitatif' three times, I decided I wanted to learn more about it. The first thing I did was to go to the library and use the online catalog to look  for books on Morrison. I found several, including an encyclopedia on her (*The Toni Morrison Encyclopedia*, ed. Elizabeth Ann Beaulieu [Westport: Greenwood, 2003])."

Doing Library Searches – for Books

USING AN ONLINE CATALOG   The basic tool for finding library books is the online catalog. It may have a unique, perhaps catchy, tag (the college at which we teach calls it HopeCAT), and the layouts vary, but what is on the page is pretty much standard. You will be given a choice of several ways to search, and often you can select whether to search a specific collection within the library, the entire collection, or the collections of all libraries linked through a particular system.

The basic use of a library catalog is to find the call number and location of a book you already know about so you can look at it or check it out. But the online catalog can also be used as a search engine to find books you don't yet know about. Thus, Kristina could look for other works by Morrison by doing an *author search*; she could look for biographical works and critical studies of Morrison by doing a *subject search*; or she could look for works about race relations by doing a *keyword search*. Keyword is the broadest search category. It calls up all items in which the words you enter appear somewhere in the catalog entry. If the number and variety of items called up is overwhelming, it may help to limit your search: Look on the catalog page for the Advanced Search option or a Help option—or ask a librarian for guidance.

USING REFERENCE BOOKS   In addition to works about your author that turn up in a subject search, some works available in a library's reference section or reference library (and in some cases, for some libraries, online) can provide good background and bibliographical information about many authors. Here are some important ones:

- *Dictionary of Literary Biography*. 360 volumes to date. Detroit: Gale, 1978-. An ongoing series that provides useful biographical and critical introductions to U.S., British, and world authors.
- *Short Story Criticism*. 155 volumes to date. Detroit: Gale, 1988-. Contains biographical sketches of authors of short stories and excerpts of critical essays on their works.
- *Poetry Criticism*. 120 volumes to date. Detroit: Gale, 1953-. Contains biographical sketches of poets and excerpts of critical essays on their works.
- Elliot, Emory, et al. *Columbia Literary History of the United States*. New York: Columbia University Press, 1988. An overview of literary movements and individual writers in the United States.

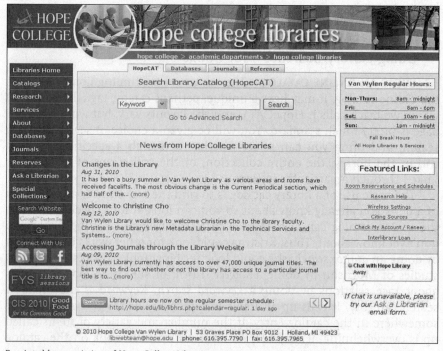

Reprinted by permission of Hope College Libraries.

- *The Oxford History of English Literature.* 13 volumes. Oxford: Oxford University Press, 1945-. Overviews of literary movements and individual writers in England and Great Britain.
- Preminger, Alex, and T. V. F. Brogan, eds. *The New Princeton Encyclopedia of Poetry and Poetics.* Princeton: Princeton University Press, 1993. The most authoritative guide to concepts, terminology, and movements related to poetry.

Reference books may be a good place to start your research, but they should never be the place you stop. And you should never use them as the main sources in a paper.

Doing Library Searches – for Articles

Many of the most valuable studies of particular literary works appear as articles (or essays) in literary journals or in books of collected essays. In most cases such articles do not show up in searches of library catalogs, so locating them requires adding another step in electronic searching.

FINDING ARTICLES IN JOURNALS   Essays about literary topics are usually published as articles in magazines or journals (commonly referred to as *periodicals*, because they are published periodically, at regular intervals—weekly, monthly, or quarterly—rather than once, like a book). For the most part, your search should concentrate on literary journals (edited by and intended for literary scholars) since they are more likely to provide the kind of material you'll need than are general magazines. Articles in scholarly journals are more reliable sources because they are written by literary scholars and they are peer reviewed (see p. 68). The articles Kristina found in *Critical Inquiry* and *Journal of Philosophy,* for example, would be more appropriate for her project than articles in *People* or *Newsweek* would be. You might find personal information, such as interviews with an author, in a general magazine, but not the more thorough critical studies of the kind you need in a college research paper.

> A student, Kristina Martinez, on searching for periodicals: "After looking for books, I searched the *MLA Bibliography* and *JSTOR* to find articles about the story and found several. Then I looked in the notes and bibliographies of the books and articles I had collected to see what those authors used as sources, found some that seemed interesting, and made copies of those."

USING THE *MLA INTERNATIONAL BIBLIOGRAPHY*   The standard resource for finding articles about authors and literary topics is the *MLA International Bibliography of Books and Articles in the Modern Languages and Literature.* It is a complete bibliography, which includes books and Ph.D. dissertations as well as articles. You may find books in the *MLA Bibliography* that are not in your library but you may be able to request them through interlibrary loan. (This may take a week or two—which is another good reason to start your bibliography search early.) But the *MLA Bibliography*'s most important use is for finding journal articles.

The *MLA Bibliography* is available in printed volumes, but most people now use the online version if it's available in their libraries. Look for a link to it on your library's Web site and experiment with ways to focus and restrict your searches: A keyword search for Toni Morrison in the *MLA Bibliography* yields around nineteen hundred hits; adding "Recitatif" to the search reduces the hits to ten. Do a variety of searches, using different terms related to your topic. Try focusing your searches by using connector words ("and," "or," "not"), for example. Ask a librarian for other ways to sharpen your approach.

MLA Bibliography searches, like those in many other databases, also can be limited in various ways: to certain document types (searching only for journal articles, for example, or only for articles in books); to a specific language (searching only for works written in English, for example); to peer

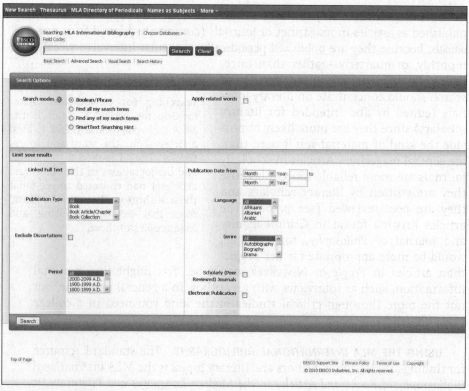

Search screen for the online *MLA Bibliography*.
Reprinted by permission of the Modern Language Association.

reviewing (searching only for materials that have been subject to peer review); to full text (searching only for articles whose full texts are available online in your library); and to available materials (searching only for books or journals held by your library).

FINDING ARTICLES IN BOOKS   Scholarly articles are sometimes published in books of collected essays focused on an author or a topic. The contents may be articles previously published in journals and gathered into a book by an editor to make them more accessible (such as *Women on the Edge: Ethnicity and Gender in Short Stories by American Women*, edited by Corrine H. Dale and J. H. S. Paine, cited in Kristina's paper). Or the book may be made up of essays written especially for the collection and published for the first time in it (for example, *The Toni Morrison Encyclopedia*, edited by Elizabeth Ann Beaulieu, cited in Kristina's paper). The books can be found by searching a library's online catalog, but the essays in the books are indexed in the *MLA Bibliography* among journal articles.

USING *JSTOR* AND *PROJECT MUSE*   In many cases, the full texts of journal articles are now available online, through such databases as *JSTOR* and *Project MUSE*. Most libraries provide a link on their home pages to the list of electronic journals and databases they subscribe to. One way to find articles on your subject is to search these databases for material on your topic. An advantage of searching in them is that, when you find an article

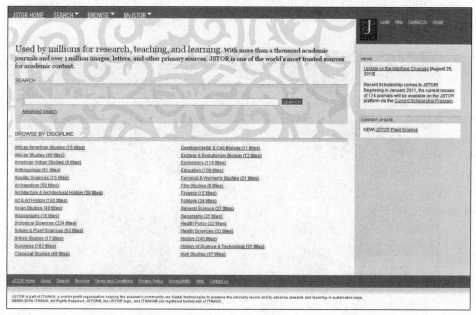

Reprinted courtesy of ITHAKA. © 2010 ITHAKA. All rights reserved.

that looks relevant, the entire article can be called up and you can read it on your computer or print out a hard copy. The disadvantage is that the search will be conducted only in the journals included in that database. It is better, therefore, to start with the *MLA Bibliography*, which will give you the widest possible range of articles.

USING *LITERATURE ONLINE (LION)*   Another valuable resource for literary research available in many libraries is *Literature Online*, better known by the acronym *LION*. (Some libraries have a similar database, *Literature Resource Center;* some have both.) By combining a number of databases, *LION* offers a comprehensive literary Web site. On it you can find biographical information on English and American authors, lists of their works, the full texts of hundreds of poems, novels, and plays (generally those no longer under copyright), lists of critical studies of authors' works (often with links to the full texts), audio readings of selected works, and related Web sites.

LION can be used to search for secondary critical and scholarly materials, but it also can be used to consult or search primary texts (to find the source of a quotation or an allusion, for example). Searches can be restricted and limited in much the same way the *MLA Bibliography* Web site can. For guidance on using *LION*, click on Information Centre, then Getting Started or click on Help at any point—or, as always, consult with a librarian.

USING OTHER BIBLIOGRAPHIC DATABASES   In some cases, your topic may require doing a broader search to include other academic disciplines, beyond what literary databases provide. Many such resources are available. Two of the best-known examples are Gale's *General OneFile* and the OCLC

Search screen for *Literature Online (LION)* database.

FirstSearch databases. These databases cover the humanities, the social sciences, and the sciences. Ask a librarian for the name of particular databases of this type to which your library subscribes (for example, *ProQuest Research Library, Academic Search Premier,* and *Humanities Abstracts*).

In other cases, you may want to conduct searches that include general magazines. Again, many databases for such searches are available, among them *General OneFile* and *LexisNexis*. Look for links to such search engines on your library's Web page, or ask a librarian how to find one. Remember that many of the articles you will find through such databases will not be scholarly or peer reviewed and therefore must be used with care.

USING SPECIALIZED BIBLIOGRAPHIES In addition to indexes for finding articles, book-length bibliographies are available for many well-known authors. These bibliographies list scholarly and critical studies on an author published during a given span of years, in some cases with a brief description or evaluation of the work. Look for such a volume when you do your search of the library catalog. Kristina did not find one for Toni Morrison, but if she had been researching Alice Walker, she might have found this book:

> Banks, Erma Davis, and Keith Byerman. *Alice Walker: An Annotated Bibliography 1968-1986.* New York: Garland, 1989. Print.

It includes a list of primary works by Walker through 1986 as well as reviews and criticism of her works, with a brief description of many items. It is a very convenient way to locate studies of Walker published in those years. For studies since then, you would go to one of the indexes described above. Bibliographies are also available for periods and movements, as, for example:

> Glikin, Ronda. *Black American Women in Literature: A Bibliography, 1976 through 1987.* Jefferson: McFarland, 1989. Print.
>
> Jordan, Casper LeRoy. *A Bibliographical Guide to African-American Women Writers.* Westport: Greenwood, 1993. Print.
>
> Zimmerman, Marc. *U.S. Latino Literature: An Essay and Annotated Bibliography.* Chicago: MARCH/Abrazo, 1992. Print.

To find such volumes, search the library catalog by subject for "African American authors" or "Hispanic American authors" and look for a subheading on "Bibliography."

Doing Searches for Internet Sources

In addition to the print sources discussed above are Web sites and documents posted on the Internet that have not appeared and were never intended to appear in print. You can look for these using search engines like Google,

Yahoo!, or AltaVista. Granted, a great deal of material is available on the Web that is of interest and value to students of literature. However, much of it falls into the category of general sources (enjoyable but unscholarly), but that which is of scholarly significance can fill areas not covered by books and journals.

USING HOME PAGES   Home pages can be found for many authors, some created by fans of the authors, some by academics, some by general readers, or for contemporary writers, by the author her- or himself. Such home pages usually provide a biography and a bibliography, sometimes critical essays, and sometimes—for modern authors—an audio (or video) recording. Home pages can be a useful starting point for learning about an author.

USING OTHER ONLINE RESOURCES   In addition to home pages, myriad other types of online sites can be useful to literature students: reprintings of poems or stories by an author, brief commentaries on literary works, study guides to an author or a work, student papers, odd bits of information (of "The day I met Julia Alvarez" type), collections of photos related to the author, places where books can be purchased, and so forth. Be careful. You can waste a good deal of time clicking on potentially interesting sites only to be disappointed by what comes up.

Home page of Alan Liu's *Voice of the Shuttle* Web site.
Reprinted by permission of Alan Liu, University of California, Santa Barbara.

LIMITING YOUR SEARCH   One way to avoid some of the clutter is to do a more specialized search rather than simply type "Toni Morrison" into Google, Yahoo!, or AltaVista and be confronted by over a million hits. Most search engines have Advanced Search options through which you can restrict or limit your search in ways similar to those described above for databases.

USING LISTS OF RECOMMENDED WEB SITES   As an alternative to relying on Google, Yahoo!, or AltaVista, the English departments at many colleges and universities have assembled lists of recommended literary Web sites — ones that they regard as well organized, reliable, and trustworthy. Such sites are usually linked to their department's or library's home page and are easy to find and access. Or, try one of these two highly regarded Web sites: Jack Lynch's *Literary Resources on the Net* and Alan Liu's *Voice of the Shuttle* (screenshot on opposite page), both of which were created and are maintained by faculty members.

In the end, however, for college-level literary research, the most useful material is found in print sources (in libraries or online) rather than in Internet sources.

RESEARCH ON CONTEMPORARY LITERATURE

If your topic involves very recent literature, doing a research paper will probably present some different challenges and opportunities. For contemporary authors, there often are no published studies to go back to. Therefore, you will need to do the kind of research scholars do, locating background and contextual information, applying it to the author's works, and doing original critical studies of them. You might start by looking for biographical information and interviews; if you find that the author has said certain writers and works have been influential, you could study and draw from them; and you could search for newspapers, magazines, movies, art, television, advertising, reputable online works, or whatever else might clarify the sources of and influences on the writer's ideas and artistry. For some current authors, published book reviews may be available, and these may fill a role similar to that of critical essays.

When published reviews aren't available, look at the unsolicited reviews or comments posted on such sites as Amazon.com or Barnesandnoble.com; remember that these sources must be used with care, but in many cases they are thoughtful and judicious and reflect well how some other readers are responding to a work. Look also at the publishers' summaries and publicity blurbs on those sites; they aren't meant to be objective criticism, but they can provide starting points for getting into a work. More often than not, however, for contemporary authors, you'll need to concentrate on primary sources and what they contribute to a deeper understanding of the authors and works you want to study.

EVALUATING SOURCES

USING THE BEST SOURCES A very important principle of research, in any field, is that "all sources are not equal." And a corollary to this is "research that uses stronger sources is regarded more highly than research that uses weaker sources." One way of assessing a student paper or a book of literary criticism is to look at its bibliography. A bibliography that lists mostly popular magazines or Internet sources or books and articles from the 1960s won't be as strong as a bibliography that lists scholarly articles and includes books written during the past ten to fifteen years. From the beginning of your research project, *be selective* about the sources you decide to consider further.

A student, Kristina Martinez, on evaluating sources: "I began the evaluation process by skimming through books and articles before checking them out or photocopying them. I also looked up where authors got degrees or where they had jobs and checked how much they had published (and where) and if their names appear in footnotes or bibliographies, to see if other people seem to regard them as knowledgeable and reliable."

ASSESSING CAREFULLY As you consider which potential sources to include in your working bibliography, *assess each one carefully*. In reading books, articles, and Internet material, first grasp clearly what is being said. Only then can you decide how valid and valuable the point being made is. Books and essays are not "good" just because they're in print or posted on the Web: Don't use just any source you happen to find. Evaluating the worth of a source is crucial. The quality of your sources affects, even determines, the quality of your paper. To help you evaluate sources, here are five questions to ask.

1. *Who is the author and what are her or his qualifications?* Some people are better informed — are authorities in a field — and better qualified to comment on a work or an author than others are. Kristina followed good steps by checking where the author was educated and when, whether the author had published extensively about the subject, and whether the author had an academic affiliation. Those who have stronger credentials are more likely to qualify as reliable sources. It is often harder to check qualifications for pieces you find on the Web, but you can try to find similar kinds of information about the person who wrote the piece (and if a piece is anonymous, it's generally best not to use it).

2. *Where was the work published?* Articles submitted to scholarly journals and books submitted to well-established presses are carefully screened by experts; this process is known as "peer review." Only works that peer experts regard as accurate and important are accepted for publication. The fact that an article appears in a highly regarded journal or that a book is published by a highly reputable press in most cases can give you confidence

in its quality, though you still have to assess it on its own merits. For material on the Internet, check who hosts the site. Items posted by academic institutions (.edu) are generally more promising than items on commercial sites (.com) and other sites with products for sale. In some cases, the host organization is identified at the bottom of the initial page. Try to find out more about who it is and what it has at stake.

3. *Is the source or its author cited by other scholars?* One way to measure acceptance by other scholars is to note how frequently a scholar's work is favorably commented on or referred to by other scholars or included in their bibliographies. If other scholars rely on a source, you can be fairly sure that its author is respected in the field. Another way is to check reviews of books (*Book Review Digest*, online or in print form in your library, is a good place to start) and, if possible, reviews of articles (some specialized journals offer critiques of articles in their fields).

4. *What is the date of the publication?* In some fields (especially the sciences and social sciences), research more than a decade or two old may be outdated. That tends to be less so in the humanities, but it is still true to some extent. Recent scholarship builds on earlier work, adding to earlier studies and correcting their mistakes, and it draws on current ideas and theoretical approaches. It's acceptable to have some older studies in your bibliography, but in most cases your sources should also include recent, up-to-date studies.

5. *How relevant is it to your topic and argument?* Avoid the temptation to add items to your bibliography or to slip quotations into your paper just because they are written by a leading expert or published by a major press. A source helps your paper only if it fits your topic or relates to your argument and is something you actually can use. Readers are not impressed when your bibliography lists books by several widely known experts but all the citations in your text are to unscholarly Web sites.

KEEPING TRACK OF WHAT YOU'VE READ

USING NOTE CARDS   When doing a research paper, it's important to keep track of what you read. For a short paper, you might get by using your memory and marking up a copy of the primary text; but for a research paper, if it's done well, too much is going on for that tactic to be effective. In the old days, scholars took notes on 3 × 5 or 4 × 6 inch cards (or, earlier, on slips of paper), using one set for bibliographical information and another for summary notes and quotations, cross-referenced to the corresponding bibliography card. This produced excellent results for centuries and is still a good system (it continues to be used in some high school and college writing courses). But it is much less widely used today because of advances in electronic equipment.

A student, Kristina Martinez, on organizing her research: "I photocopied articles that looked good if we had them in the library and printed others where full texts were available online. I then put everything in a three-ring notebook and began reading closely. I was most interested in Twyla, Roberta, and their mothers, and in Maggie and the structure of the story. So I marked in the margins places that referred to any of those. To make it easier to return to these places, I put tabs by them, using sticky notes, a different color for each topic. (When I was writing the paper and used a passage, I removed the tab so I would not go back to the passage again.)"

USING A COPIER   Copiers have changed the need for taking notes and the way many people take notes. For materials available in general areas of a library, many people photocopy pages of books or print whole articles from journals, as Kristina did, instead of copying longhand or typing out passages they might want to use in a paper.[1] In rare-book and special-collection areas, photocopying usually is available only by special arrangement. Photocopies are convenient to use because you can underline important phrases or sentences and jot notes in the margins, something you should never do in a library book or journal. And photocopies have the benefit of accuracy because they reproduce the original exactly. It's easy for errors to slip in when taking notes: Be sure to double-check for accuracy.

USING A COMPUTER   Many scholars still take notes instead of photocopy, especially when using rare-book collections, but they type directly into notebook computers instead of writing on paper. Many libraries are equipped to enable researchers to plug in computers at reading tables and in study carrels. Notes in a computer are easier to use because they can be searched quickly and can be copied and pasted directly into a paper. If you have never tried it before, you might experiment with this form of note taking. Be sure to develop a system for organizing your notes into files—a system that is clear, searchable, and easy to use.

SOME GUIDELINES FOR KEEPING TRACK   No matter what system you use, some principles are the same.

- *Check for completeness.* Be sure to include the author's name and all the information needed for finding the source:
  - published by whom, where, when; page numbers for articles. Put down call numbers for books and articles; they aren't needed in your paper, but having them is convenient in case you have to go back to the sources later. Also note the medium of publication (print, web, etc.).
  - title of Web site, author's name, names of editors and sponsoring organization, database used, date the site was accessed. Keep a record

---

[1] Copyright protection allows photocopying of articles and selected pages from a book when used for personal research but forbids photocopying an entire book or even most of one.

TIP: You will save time later if, as you take notes, you begin preparing the actual Works Cited page for your paper, instead of leaving it to the end, when you're weary and perhaps pressed for time. It is most convenient to create a separate Works Cited file in your computer as you compile your list and to add the list to the end of your paper when it's nearly finished, so the pages will be paginated consecutively with the body of the paper.

of the URL or the pathway you used for reaching the source; it isn't needed in the paper, but having the information is valuable if you have to return to the source later.

Review your notes before moving on to be sure that you have everything down. You certainly don't want to discover — especially the night before a paper is due! — that you forgot to include a date or page number and must to go back to the library (assuming it's not closed for the night) to find it.

- *Check for accuracy.* After you write or type a direct quotation, check that every word and punctuation mark is accurate before you move on. If you leave out a word or phrase or sentence, be sure you indicate that with ellipsis marks (see p. 54). Make sure the bibliographical data you put down is accurate.
- *Check for clarity.* If you're writing or typing notes, indicate clearly what is quoted and what is summary. It's a good idea to write "quote" or "summary" in the margin to make sure you won't mistake one for the other, something that can lead to unfortunate results. Also, add a label indicating what point in your paper the notes apply to. That will make it much easier for you to find and organize your notes when you get ready to use them.

WRITING A RESEARCH PAPER

In nature and form, a research paper is very similar to the papers discussed in Chapter 2, but it is usually longer and broader in scope, going into more depth. Because the basic steps for writing research papers are pretty much the same as those given for writing shorter essays in Chapter 2, we will not repeat them here. Instead we will focus on what is different for research projects.

Finding a Topic

The suggestions on pages 31–32 for finding a topic apply to deciding on a research paper too. It could be helpful to review them. The difference is

A student, Kristina Martinez, on finding a topic and writing a thesis: "The topic that interested me most in 'Recitatif' is the way differences in stories told in 'Recitatif' leave readers feeling ambiguous about race and about Maggie. As I thought about it, I decided it was a topic that was debatable and one that I had seen critics discussing, with differing views. I started trying to come up with a thesis, and after a couple of false starts, decided on this as a working thesis: 'Elements of story are thick throughout this piece. Morrison uses character, point of view, and time to hold readers' attention and leaves them questioning not only race but what really has happened to Maggie.' It was modified slightly in the final version, but most of it was still there in the final draft."

that there has to be something in the topic that needs to be investigated, something you can do research on.

DON'T APPROACH YOUR PAPER AS A REPORT Perhaps the most helpful thing to remember as you think about a topic is that *a research paper is not a report*. A report gives an account of something. Its nature is objective: The writer usually does not interject opinions or interpretations. A research paper sometimes takes the form of a report. For example, for a paper on climate and crops in Papua New Guinea, a student might search for information on the subject and from various sources piece together an account of the climatic conditions, how they affect what can be grown, and how that contributes to the degree of poverty in the country. Often such a paper turns out to be a long string of quotations and paraphrases, with transitional sentences connecting and holding them together. Such is not what this chapter is teaching you to do.

USE AN APPROACH THAT FOCUSES ON A THESIS A report is not what college professors mean by a literary research paper. Like other literary essays, a research paper is unified around a thesis, a central idea that takes a position to be discussed and supported. The most important part of a research paper is what *you* say in it, the development of *your* approach and ideas and interpretations, so your topic needs to be one that invites such an approach.

AIM FOR ORIGINALITY The argument pursued in the paper should be original to you; the thesis should reflect your own thinking. As you carry out your research, however, you may find that someone else has already explored the topic you were planning to focus on, perhaps even argued for the same thesis you had tentatively decided on. That should not be a problem. For a student paper, originality isn't saying something that never has been said before. Recycling a thesis you find in a critical essay is an acceptable way to form the topic for an undergraduate research paper, so long as you acknowledge your source and find different ways to develop and support the argument.

You might bring in your own explanations and examples, ones different from those used before. Or you might approach an issue in a different way. Kristina got an idea from a critic, raised questions about it, and took it in a new direction, which worked well for her. Or you might combine ideas from different fields. Students are in an ideal situation to do this: Try using concepts from your philosophy, sociology, psychology, or political science courses to illuminate works you study in your literature course. Remember, it is essential that the paper embody your own thinking and approach. Don't let it turn into a report on or paraphrase of the earlier article.

As you look for and read sources, it can be tempting to keep only those that agree with your ideas and ignore those that don't. Resist that temptation. Reading different opinions can help sharpen your conclusions and strengthen your arguments, and bringing opposing views into your paper and refuting them can lead to a more thoughtful and thought-provoking paper.

A student, Kristina Martinez, on focusing her thesis: "One of my sources was helpful in setting up the rest of the paper—it showed that Morrison used oral storytelling techniques in writing 'Recitatif.' That led me to wonder about Twyla and Roberta as oral storytellers. Both of them told stories about the same events. I tried to think about both as telling stories in order to lead their listeners (readers) or to mislead them. So I started from an idea in one of my sources, but gave it my own twist. I decided that would be original enough to use as my approach."

Developing Ideas

The steps suggested in Chapter 2 for developing an essay apply equally for a research paper. After deciding on a topic and tentative thesis, you need to think out several subpoints that explore the central point, decide on an outline that organizes the subpoints effectively, and start writing, amplifying the ideas, supplying details and illustrations that support the points you make, and explaining how the ideas and examples support each other in a convincing way. You might want to review the fuller discussion of these steps on pages 36–43.

The main difference from the papers discussed in Chapter 2 is that, as you shape and develop and support your ideas, an additional resource is available to you: the information and ideas found in the sources you've consulted. These can be used as supporting evidence for points you make or as ideas you think need to be expanded or corrected.

A student, Kristina Martinez, on developing an outline: "I wrote an outline of the points I wanted to develop in the paper.

- Narrator—Twyla as primary; Roberta as secondary
- Race—concealing who is white and who is black
- Stories about Maggie and her race
- Both girls identify with Maggie
- First story about Maggie: difference in what they remember
- Second story about Maggie: Did they kick her? Was she black?
- Third story about Maggie: why they *wanted* to kick her
- Conclusion

I wrote the first section in longhand, then typed and printed it, reread it, and revised it. I went on to do the same for the other sections. I wrote by hand because it was easier to put my ideas from head to hand and hand to paper, plus the weather was great and I wrote outside."

Incorporating Sources

The unique aspect in developing a research paper is that additional materials for clarifying ideas and supporting arguments are available from the primary and secondary research you've carried out. Such materials can be incorporated into your paper using four methods:

- citation,
- summary,
- paraphrase, and
- quotation.

A student, Kristina Martinez, on supporting her ideas: "I wrote out what I wanted to say about each point, using summaries and details from the story to support it. Then I went back through my notebook, looking for places where critics' comments could be used to clarify or back up what I was saying. I inserted summaries or quotations where they seemed to fit well."

We illustrate these methods below with examples taken from Kristina's paper (pp. 85–90).

CITATION   In some cases you may want to mention a source that makes a point related to one you are making, though you do not summarize or paraphrase it in developing your ideas. You can do so by making a passing reference to it, or *citing* it, without saying more about it.

> The reader's desire to know is paralleled later in the story by the girls' attempts to determine the race of the servant Maggie (Bennett 212).

Citations often are used to supply additional examples, supporting one that has been described fully.

SUMMARY   In most cases, you will bring sources into your paper by summarizing some information, a key idea, or an overall argument you find valuable. The summary should be a brief restatement of the author's point put in your own words. To avoid accidentally using the author's exact words, summarize from memory, without looking back at the text (close the book or clear the computer screen).

> Race is important to our identities, Anthony Appiah concludes (499), and in that respect it is a central issue in the story.

What you incorporate does not have to summarize the whole book, chapter, or article but may summarize one section or simply one paragraph.

Summary is often used as a way to bring primary texts usefully and efficiently into a paper. Kristina does this repeatedly, as shown in the following example:

Maggie stories emerge also in the last meeting with Roberta that Twyla tells about. The last time they meet in the story is at least a year later when Twyla stops at a downtown diner for coffee after shopping for a Christmas tree and Roberta sits with her for a few minutes. Roberta now backs away from her previous story: She acknowledges that Twyla didn't kick Maggie—neither of them did, only the gar girls did.

PARAPHRASE   A paraphrase, like a summary, is a restatement of an author's point in your own words, but at greater length—usually approximately equal in length to the original passage.

The structure of the story creates ambiguity in racial codes and does not attempt to resolve it. It is too complex to fit the conventional language and stereotypes. Each girl constructed a racial identity for Maggie out of her own cultural and racial context, and we as readers are tempted to do the same (Abel 471–72).

Paraphrase should be used instead of summary when it is important to supply your reader with more detail: if, for example, you want to call specific attention to each step in an argument, perhaps because you want to dispute it step by step. Quoting the passage in such a case might not work as well because a paraphrase allows you to enumerate each step even if the author didn't do so.

QUOTATION   You will probably want to include quotations from secondary sources in your research paper as well as quotations from primary texts. You will encounter passages written so effectively that you won't want to paraphrase them. Be careful, however, not to load your paper with quotations, turning it into a "collage of quotations." The greater danger is not underusing quotations but using too many and using ones that are too long. Quotations must not carry the argument of a paper but must support and illustrate the argument you are presenting in your own words.

The best approach is to combine quotations with summary and to blend brief quoted extracts into your prose style as gracefully as possible. Kristina's paper does this well, as illustrated here.

Robert Stepto points out that many African American authors "choose to see themselves as storytellers instead of storywriters" (qtd. in Goldstein-Shirley 101) because they distrust readers and want people to *listen* to what they have to say. "Recitatif" falls into that category: "Although the text is written," David Goldstein-Shirley notes, "its structure mimics oral storytelling" (101). He goes on to spell out the effect of that form: "The distinctively 'oral' quality of 'Recitatif' also contributes to the

PLAGIARISM ALERT

Plagiarism is the presentation of the work of others as if it were one's own. This is a serious offense. Treating another person's effort and ideas as if they are your own is dishonest. It violates the expectations of trust and honesty in an academic community. In addition, it undercuts the basic purposes of higher education by short-circuiting the processes of inquiry, reflection, and communication that lead to learning.

For examples of plagiarism and ways to avoid it, see pages 91–93.

story's strategy of recruiting the reader in its mission to deconstruct racism" (101).

The guidelines in Chapter 2 for handling quotations effectively are even more important to follow when writing research papers than when writing short papers. You might want to review them (pp. 53–54).

Documenting Sources

The method of citing sources for papers on literature preferred by most teachers is the MLA style, described in detail in the *MLA Handbook for Writers of Research Papers*, 7th ed., by Joseph Gibaldi (New York: Modern Language Association of America, 2009).[2] It is a simple, convenient, two-step system that uses brief parenthetical citations in the text, keyed to an alphabetical list of works at the end of the paper. In the sentence below from Kristina's paper, the name in the parenthesis identifies the source being used. To find information about the location where the source can be found, you would look in the Bs of the Works Cited list for the name "Bennett":

A student, Kristina Martinez, on documenting her sources: "As I photocopied articles or took notes on books or printed out online material, I was careful to write on them all the details about where I found them and double-checked to make sure the details were accurate. I started my Works Cited list as I did my research, typing the information into a separate file, which I copied at the end of my paper when I finished the first draft."

[2]Other methods are preferred in other fields of study: APA (American Psychological Association) style is used in the social sciences; CBE (Council of Biology Editors) style is used in the sciences; and *Chicago* style (*Chicago Manual of Style*) is generally used for history. Each style focuses on the kind of information considered most useful in that discipline and on the format regarded as most convenient.

In-Text Citation

The reader's desire to know is paralleled later in the story by the girls' attempts to determine the race of the servant Maggie (Bennett 212).

Entry in the List of Works Cited

Bennett, Juda. "Toni Morrison and the Burden of the Passing Narrative." *African American Review* 35 (2001): 205-17. *InfoTrac*. Web. 14 Apr. 2010.

In many cases it works well to use an introductory phrase in your sentence leading into your summary, paraphrase, or quotation, giving the source's name and a word or phrase indicating the source's qualifications. Compare the paragraph below to an earlier draft on page 75, and notice how indicating the source's qualifications strengthens Kristina's argument and lends it authority.

> Robert Stepto, professor of African American studies at Yale University, points out that many African American authors "choose to see themselves as storytellers instead of storywriters" (qtd. in Goldstein-Shirley 101) because they distrust readers and want people to *listen* to what they have to say. "Recitatif" falls into that category: "Although the text is written," University of Washington professor David Goldstein-Shirley notes, "its structure mimics oral storytelling" (101). He goes on to spell out the effect of that form: "The distinctively 'oral' quality of 'Recitatif' also contributes to the story's strategy of recruiting the reader in its mission to deconstruct racism" (101).

If you include the name of the source in your sentence, you do not need to repeat it in the parenthetical citation.

In the MLA system, footnotes or endnotes can be used to supply information and comments that do not fit into the text of the paper or that cannot be handled adequately through parenthetical citation, but including notes is not essential.

> You can find additional advice for documenting sources in Diana Hacker's *Research and Documentation Online* at bedfordstmartins.com/rewritinglit.

Step 1. In-Text Citations

The MLA system begins with brief in-text citations. After a quotation or a sentence using facts or opinions drawn from a specific source (wherever a footnote would have been used in earlier documentation systems), one inserts a parenthesis with, ordinarily, the last name of the author and the page or pages on which the information is found, as shown in this sentence from Kristina's paper:

> The result was that, "Without realizing it, however, in hating
> Maggie, they hated themselves and each other" (Furman 110).

This is the most basic form of in-text citation. Notice three formatting conventions followed in it:

1. There is no comma after the author's name and no "page" or "p." preceding the number.
2. The quotation marks come before the parenthesis. The in-text citation identifies the source of the quotation but is not part of the quotation.
3. The punctuation mark closing the sentence follows the parenthetical citation so that the citation is included in the sentence, not left floating unattached between sentences. (An exception is in the case of block quotations, where the period precedes the parenthetical citation.)

MLA In-Text Citations: Variations on the Basic Form

- If the author is named in the text leading up to the quotation (and this is good practice), the name is not repeated in parentheses:

  > As a result, Elizabeth Abel believes, Twyla "feels vulnerable to Roberta's judgment" (473).

- If you use two or more works by the same author, your parenthetical citations should include a short title after the author's name.

  > What this story does is to show how literature can bring readers into a work, "the ways writers . . . tell other stories, fight secret wars, limn out all sorts of debates blanketed in their text" (Morrison, *Playing* 4).

- If the author of the material being cited is unknown, use the title or a shortened form of the title in parentheses, where the author's name would have been. Titles of books and plays should be italicized; titles of stories, poems, and essays should be placed within quotation marks.
- If the work does not have page numbers, omit them from your citation. This is frequently the case for Web sources, except for stable sources such as PDF files, in which case page numbers should be

cited. For electronic sources that number their paragraphs, give those numbers ("Morrison, par. 6").

- If you use two authors with the same last name, include an initial in your parenthetical citation (E. Abel 475), unless the author's full name is given in the text leading up to the quotation.

- If you cite a work you found in an anthology, use the name of the author of the work, not that of the anthology's editor: (Morrison 445), not (Schakel and Ridl 445).

- If you want to quote in your paper something you found quoted by someone else in an essay or a book, the best procedure is to find the original source (that's one of the values of having bibliographical information provided in a work), quote from it directly, and cite it as the source. In case your library does not have the original work or it's checked out, a less desirable but accepted procedure is to copy the quote from the secondary source and use the abbreviation "qtd. in" to indicate that you are doing so.

> Robert Stepto points out that many African American authors "choose to see themselves as storytellers instead of storywriters" (qtd. in Goldstein-Shirley 101).

- If you want to cite two or more sources at once, to indicate that they say much the same thing about a point you are making, you can list them together parenthetically:

> Each girl constructed a racial identity for Maggie out of her own cultural and racial context, and we as readers are tempted to do the same (Abel 471–72; Busia 103; "Toni Morrison" 2).

Step 2. Works Cited Page

The other key part of the MLA system is the bibliography. The *MLA Handbook* recommends that it be a list of Works Cited—that is, a list containing only works referred to within the paper. In some cases, for a student paper, a bibliography of works consulted might be preferred over one of works cited to indicate the range of research, if noncited works are an important part of the context of the paper. Check with your teacher if you think that might apply to your paper.

To find additional advice for preparing a Works Cited page, see Diana Hacker's *Research and Documentation Online* at bedfordstmartins.com/rewritinglit.

BASIC GUIDELINES Here are some basic details about formatting a Works Cited page:

1. Begin on a new page. Continue the pagination begun in the earlier parts of the paper.

2. Center the heading "Works Cited" at the top of the page. Use capitals and lowercase letters, not boldfaced or italicized.
3. Make the first line of each entry flush with the left margin, with subsequent lines, if any, indented a-half inch (learn how to use a "hanging indent," if you don't know already).
4. Double-space the entire list, without extra spaces between entries.
5. Arrange your list alphabetically, by the last name of the author or, for anonymous works, by the first significant word in the title (ignoring an initial *A*, *An*, or *The*). If two authors have the same last name, alphabetize by their first names.
6. To list two or more books by the same author, give the name only in the first entry. For the other entries, substitute three hyphens followed by a period. If the person edited or translated one or more of the books, place a comma after the three hyphens, then the appropriate abbreviation ("ed." or "trans."), then the title. The titles should be in alphabetical order.

Morrison, Toni. *Playing in the Dark: Whiteness and the Literary Imagination*. Cambridge: Harvard UP, 1992. Print.
---. "Recitatif." 1983. *Approaching Literature: Reading + Thinking + Writing*. Ed. Peter Schakel and Jack Ridl. 3rd ed. Boston: Bedford/ St. Martin's, 2011. 445–59. Print.

For an example of a properly formatted Works Cited page, see page 90.

LISTING BOOKS   The most common items on the Works Cited page for a student paper are likely to be entries for books by a single author. Such entries usually have four parts:

Author's name. *Title of the Book*. Publication information. Medium of publication.

This is the way such an entry looks on Kristina's Works Cited page:

Furman, Jan. *Toni Morrison's Fiction*. Columbia: U of South Carolina P, 1996. Print.

Here are some guidelines that clarify these three basic parts:

- **Name of the author,** last name first, followed by a period. If the name ends with an initial, only one period is needed.
- **Title of the book,** italicized, followed by a period. If the book has a subtitle, include it as well, preceded by a colon. For guidelines on handling titles, see page 52.
- **Place of publication,** followed by a colon. If more than one city is listed on the title page of the book, give only the first. Give the name of the

city only, not the state, for places in the United States and well-known cities in other countries. Lesser-known international cities should be identified with a country abbreviation (thus, "Amsterdam:" because it's well-known but "Apeldoorn, Neth.:" because it isn't).

- **Name of the publisher,** shortened ("Macmillan," not "Macmillan Publishing Company, Inc."), followed by a comma. Use abbreviations such as "UP" for "University Press." For books published before 1900, you may omit the publisher's name and put a comma instead of a colon after the city.
- **Year of publication,** followed by a period. If the date of publication is not given on the title page, look for it on the following page (the copyright page). If no date of publication is given there, use the copyright date. (As a last resort, you can look for the publication date in a library catalog.) Sometimes the copyright page includes the dates of successive printings of the book: These are not of interest; the date you use should be that of the first printing, its original appearance.
- **Medium of publication used,** that is, the medium through which you gained access to the information: for example, Print, Web, Radio, Television, CD, Audiocassette, Film, DVD, Performance, Lecture, or PDF file.

Many of the books you use will require additional information to be included. For explanations and examples of these, see pages 94–98.

LISTING SCHOLARLY ARTICLES   Some scholarly articles are published in books of collected essays (see p. 98). But most appear in scholarly journals, usually published several times a year. Each year is designated as a volume, and pages are usually numbered continuously throughout the volume. Works Cited entries for journal articles include four parts:

> Author's name. "Title of the Article." *Title of the Journal* Publication information.

This is the way such an entry looks on Kristina's Works Cited page:

> Abel, Elizabeth. "Black Writing, White Reading: Race and the Politics of Feminist Interpretation." *Critical Inquiry* 19.3 (1993): 470-98. Print.

Here are some guidelines that clarify these four basic parts:

- **Name of the author,** last name first, followed by a period.
- **Title of the article,** enclosed in quotation marks, followed by a period (inside the quotation mark), unless the title ends with a question mark or an exclamation point.
- **Title of the journal,** italicized, no punctuation following it.

- **Volume number of the journal,** using arabic numerals even if roman numerals are used in the journal, followed by a period (no spaces) if an issue number is available.
- **Issue number** (if available), no punctuation following. For journals that number issues without using volume numbers, give the issue number alone: for example, "*Victorian Newsletter* 118 (Fall 2010)."
- **Year of publication,** in parentheses, followed by a colon.
- **Page numbers** (first and last), followed by a period.
- **Medium of publication** (see p. 81), followed by a period.

LISTING MAGAZINE ARTICLES Magazines are usually printed more frequently than scholarly journals (often weekly, biweekly, monthly, or bimonthly) and are paginated by issue. Magazines have volume numbers, but they are not important for locating an issue and are usually left out of Works Cited entries. Works Cited entries for magazine articles use the same four parts and punctuation as journal article entries:

> Author's name. "Title of the Article." *Title of the Magazine* Publication
>   information.

But the information given is different for the last part. Kristina did not use any magazine articles in her paper, but here is what a Works Cited entry for one would look like:

> Kaye, Cheryl Kramer. "Toni Morrison." *Redbook* Dec. 2008: 30. Print.

Here are some guidelines that clarify handling of the fourth part:

- **Date of publication** Day, month (abbreviated, except for May, June, and July), and year (in that order) are given for weekly or biweekly magazines; only month or months and year are given for magazines published monthly or bimonthly. A colon follows, in either case.
- **Page numbers** If the article is longer than one page, give its first and last pages, not just the ones you used, followed by a period. If pagination is not consecutive (for example, the article begins on page 4 and continues on page 8), write only the first page number and a plus sign (4+), with no space between them.

For explanations and examples for listing newspaper stories, book reviews, interviews, letters, and e-mail messages, and republication of any of them in books, see pages 99–101.

LISTING PRINT SOURCES ACCESSED ELECTRONICALLY For Works Cited entries involving the full text of a journal or magazine article accessed through a database such as *JSTOR*, *Project MUSE*, or *InfoTrac*, you must provide the information a reader needs to access the source electronically, as well as the information about its original publication. The basic pattern for such an entry has five parts:

Name of the author. "Title of the Article." Information about print publication. Information about electronic posting. Access information.

This is the way such an entry looks on Kristina's Works Cited page:

Appiah, Anthony. "'But Would That Still Be Me?' Notes on Gender, 'Race,'
Ethnicity, as Sources of 'Identity.'" *Journal of Philosophy* 87.10
(1990): 493-99. *JSTOR*. Web. 3 May 2010.

When the source does not provide all of that information, give as much as you can, following or adapting the following guidelines:

- **Name of the author,** last name first and followed by a period.
- **Title of the article,** enclosed in quotation marks, followed by a period, unless the title ends with a question mark or an exclamation point.
- **As much information about its publication in a journal or magazine as the database makes available,** following the guidelines above for journals and magazines. If no information about print publication is provided, proceed to the next step.
- **Information about where you accessed the article:** Give the name of the database you used (italicized), the medium of publication (Web), and the date you accessed the article.

LISTING INTERNET MATERIALS   For a Web site entry or other Internet source, include as much of the following as possible:

- **Name of the author** of the site or document, if available.
- **The title,** in quotation marks, for separate documents within the site.
- **The name of the site,** italicized. If the site does not have a heading title, give an identifying phrase (not italicized or in quotation marks).
- **The name of the sponsoring organization or institution,** followed by a comma.
- **The date of publication** (day, month, year, as available). If no date is available, insert the abbreviation "n.d." (no date).
- **The medium of publication** (Web).
- **The date you accessed it.**

"The Nobel Prize in Literature 1993: Toni Morrison." *Nobelprize.org*. The
Nobel Foundation, 1993. Web. 20 Aug. 2010.

For explanations and examples of other electronic sources, see pages 101-04.

REVISING, PROOFREADING, AND DOUBLE-CHECKING

Everything we said about revising and proofreading in Chapter 2 applies equally here. Review pages 43–45 and go through the same steps as the final stage in working on your research paper. Add to that list what Kristina talks about: Double-check that your quotations and your Works Cited entries are completely accurate.

A student, Kristina Martinez, on revising and proofreading: "Despite my thorough outline, I ended up writing paragraphs that turned out not to be central to my focus on storytelling. One thing I did in revision was to cut paragraphs—often keeping a sentence I could move to another paragraph and deleting the rest. I also needed to reduce quotations—there were too many at first, and some were too long. I cut a lot. Another revision was to improve the way I led into quotations.

"While revising, I used the Works Cited list I had started earlier as I went through the paper and put a check mark by each item that I actually used in the paper. I checked each for accuracy and deleted the ones I didn't use. Then I checked quotations and corrected a few minor slips. Last, I proofread the whole paper, for spelling, grammar, and sentence style."

SAMPLE RESEARCH PAPER

Here is the final draft of Kristina's paper.

Kristina Martinez
Professor Schakel
English 105-04
3 May 2010

The Structure of Story in Toni Morrison's "Recitatif"

What do stories do? Some are told to entertain, some to inform or instruct, some to mislead. And sometimes the way a story is structured creates ambiguities that make it difficult to tell which of these it is doing. That is the case with Toni Morrison's story "Recitatif." The structure of Twyla's story, and that of Roberta's stories within it, holds a reader's attention and leaves a reader questioning not only race but also what happened to Maggie.

Thesis sentence states central idea.

The structure relates to the kind of story this is. Robert Stepto, professor of African American studies at Yale University, points out that many African American authors "choose to see themselves as storytellers instead of storywriters" (qtd. in Goldstein-Shirley 101) because they distrust readers and want people to *listen* to what they have to say. "Recitatif" falls into that category: "Although the text is written," University of Washington professor David Goldstein-Shirley notes, "its structure mimics oral storytelling" (101). He goes on to spell out the effect of that form: "The distinctively 'oral' quality of 'Recitatif' also contributes to the story's strategy of recruiting the reader in its mission to deconstruct racism" (101).

Use of indirect secondary source (quoted in another source) to set up argument.

The story, in fact, has two storytellers. Twyla is the over-all storyteller. The story begins with her: "My mother danced all night and Roberta's was sick" ("Recitatif" 445). Twyla is a limited narrator, an outsider in her own story, lacking the understanding of things that Roberta possesses from the start ("I liked the way

Clear topic sentences are used throughout the paper.

Secondary source quoted to advance argument, with signal phrase naming author.

she understood things so fast" — "Recitatif" 446). As a result, University of California at Berkeley professor Elizabeth Abel believes, Twyla "feels vulnerable to Roberta's judgment" (473). Twyla's story provides a frame, within which we also hear stories told by Roberta, which often conflict with Twyla's, thus creating tension between the two and forcing the reader to sort out differences and attempt to find the truth.

Primary text quoted to back up assertion.

One of the things readers must grapple with is race. Twyla and Roberta are of different races: "we looked like salt and pepper standing there," Twyla says ("Recitatif" 446). But who is white and who is black is never stated. The reader's desire to know is paralleled later in the story by the girls' attempts to determine the race of the servant Maggie (Bennett 212). Morrison creates a racial ambiguity that, Aimee L. Pozorski of Central Connecticut State University argues, grows out of linguistic ambi-

Secondary source quoted to expand point.

guity: "'Recitatif' becomes an experiment in language, as Morrison considers whether a story can be written without the linguistic shortcuts habitually employed in American literature to categorize and to stereotype its characters" (280). Race is impor-

Secondary source summarized.

tant to our identities, Princeton scholar Anthony Appiah concludes (499), and in that respect it is a central issue in the story. Yet the reader is not allowed to fall back on familiar language and comfortable stereotypes in understanding that issue.

Transition to Part 2.

These discrepancies and ambiguities come to bear especially on their stories about Maggie. Both girls identified to some extent with Maggie. Maggie is, as one critic states, "the lowest

No page number for Web source.

person in the hierarchy" (Holmes). Similarly, Twyla and Roberta were looked down on by other children at the orphanage because "we weren't real orphans with beautiful dead parents in the sky" ("Recitatif" 446). Just as Maggie is mute, so the two girls while at St. Bonny's have no voice. This does not, however, lead them to bond with Maggie. On the contrary, they attempt to separate and distance themselves from her emotionally, Jan Furman, professor at the University of Michigan–Flint, says, because she

Martinez 3

makes them feel inadequate and helpless. The result was that, "Without realizing it, however, in hating Maggie, they hated themselves and each other" (110). That hatred leads them to remember Maggie differently, and thus the stories they tell are different.

Paraphrase and quotation of secondary source to advance argument.

The first story about Maggie occurs when, years after St. Bonny's, they cross paths at the Food Emporium. They have lunch and as they reminisce about the orphanage, Twyla says,

> "I don't remember a hell of a lot from those days, but Lord, St. Bonny's is as clear as daylight. Remember Maggie? The day she fell down and those gar girls laughed at her?"
> Roberta looked up from her salad and stared at me. "Maggie didn't fall," she said.
> "Yes, she did. You remember."
> "No, Twyla. They knocked her down. Those girls pushed her down and tore her clothes. In the orchard."
> "I don't—that's not what happened."
> "Sure it is. In the orchard." ("Recitatif" 453)

Extended block quotation sets up further discussion of Maggie.

The discrepancies bother Twyla ("Roberta had messed up my past somehow with that business about Maggie. I wouldn't forget a thing like that. Would I?"—"Recitatif" 454) and create ambiguity for the reader. Which story is correct, Roberta's or Twyla's (or neither)? Are they remembering details about Maggie differently because one of them is the same race as Maggie and the other not? If so, who is the same?

Series of questions to be explored in rest of paper.

Conflicting stories about Maggie appear again the next time they meet, later that year, outside a school at which Roberta is picketing against busing children to achieve racial balance. They have a bitter exchange about forced integration, in which Roberta blurts out to Twyla, "You're the same little state kid who kicked a poor old black lady when she was down on the ground. You kicked a black lady and you have the nerve to call me a bigot" ("Recitatif" 456). Twyla tells a different story: "Maggie wasn't

Summary of primary text.

Quotations of primary text to highlight crux in story.

black" ("Recitatif" 456), and she hadn't kicked Maggie: "I know I didn't do that, I couldn't do that" ("Recitatif" 457). On further thought, she remains convinced about the kicking, but not about the race: "When I thought about it I actually couldn't be certain" ("Recitatif" 457). The reader is left to figure out why Roberta said this to Twyla, how much of it is true, and how racial difference affects their different memories.

Primary text summarized at length to provide context.

Maggie stories emerge also in the last meeting with Roberta that Twyla tells about. The last time they meet in the story is at least a year later when Twyla stops at a downtown diner for coffee after shopping for a Christmas tree and Roberta sits with her for a few minutes. Roberta now backs away from her previous story: She acknowledges that Twyla didn't kick Maggie— neither of them did, only the gar girls did. The exchange brings out a parallel between Roberta and Twyla: Each had wanted to kick Maggie because each identified Maggie with her mother as well as with herself. For Twyla, "Maggie was my dancing mother. Deaf, I thought, and dumb. Nobody inside. Nobody who would hear you if you cried in the night. Nobody who could tell you

Quotations of primary text to bring out key points.

anything important that you could use" ("Recitatif" 457). Roberta thought Maggie was crazy, like her mother, and had "'been brought up in an institution like my mother was and like I thought I would be too'" (Recitatif 458). Neither girl could ac-cept her own mother, just as neither could accept Maggie: The re-minders of the pain their mothers inflicted were too much to bear (Gillespie 163).

Secondary source summarized.

Citing three sources making a similar point.

The structure of the story creates ambiguity in racial codes and does not attempt to resolve it. It is too complex to fit the conventional language and stereotypes. Each girl constructed a racial identity for Maggie out of her own cultural and racial context, and we as readers are tempted to do the same (Abel 471-72; Busia 103; "Toni Morrison" 2). What this story does is to show how literature can bring readers into a work, "the ways

writers . . . tell other stories, fight secret wars, limn out all sorts
of debates blanketed in their text" (Morrison, *Playing* 4). Readers
are given the language, which takes them through the story and
finally leads them to the point of realizing that this story will not
provide answers to their questions and that acceptance of ambiguity itself answers the need to have answers.

*Title included in
citation because
two works by
Morrison
appear in
Works Cited.*

Works Cited

Abel, Elizabeth. "Black Writing, White Reading: Race and the Politics of
    Feminist Interpretation." *Critical Inquiry* 19.3 (1993): 470-98. Print.

Appiah, Anthony. "'But Would That Still Be Me?' Notes on Gender, 'Race,'
    Ethnicity, as Sources of 'Identity.'" *Journal of Philosophy* 87.10
    (1990): 493-99. *JSTOR*. Web. 14 Apr. 2010.

Ashford, Tomeiko R. "Transfiguring Aesthetics: Conflation, Identity
    Denial, and Transference in 'Passing Texts' of Black Narrative."
    Review of Black Political Economy 33.2 (2005): 89-103. *SpringerLink*.
    Web. 1 May 2010.

Bennett, Juda. "Toni Morrison and the Burden of the Passing Narrative."
    African American Review 35.2 (2001): 205-17. *InfoTrac*. Web. 14
    Apr. 2010.

Busia, Abena P. A. "The Artistic Impulse of Toni Morrison's Shorter
    Works." *The Cambridge Companion to Toni Morrison*. Ed. Justine
    Tally. New York: Cambridge UP, 2007. 101-111. Print.

Furman, Jan. *Toni Morrison's Fiction*. Columbia: U of South Carolina P,
    1996. Print.

Gillespie, Carmen. *A Critical Companion to Toni Morrison: A Literary
    Reference to Her Life and Work*. New York: Facts on File, 2008. Print.

Goldstein-Shirley, David. "Race/[Gender]: Toni Morrison's 'Recitatif.'"
    Journal of the Short Story in English 27 (1996): 83-95. Rpt. in
    *Women on the Edge: Ethnicity and Gender in Short Stories by
    American Women*. Ed. Corrine H. Dale and J. H. E. Paine. New York:
    Garland, 1999. 97-110. Print.

Holmes, Martha Stoddard. "Literature Annotations: Morrison, Toni:
    'Recitatif.'" *Literature, Arts, and Medicine Database*. Web. 20 Apr. 2010.

Morrison, Toni. *Playing in the Dark: Whiteness and the Literary
    Imagination*. Cambridge: Harvard UP, 1992. Print.

---. "Recitatif." 1983. *Approaching Literature: Reading + Thinking +
    Writing*. Ed. Peter Schakel and Jack Ridl. 3rd ed. Boston: Bedford/
    St. Martin's, 2011. 445–59. Print.

Pozorski, Aimee L. "Race." *The Toni Morrison Encyclopedia*. Ed. Elizabeth
    Ann Beaulieu. Westport: Greenwood, 2003. 277-85. Print.

"Toni Morrison." *Short Story Criticism*. Vol. 126. Ed. Jelena Krstović.
    Detroit: Gale, 2010. 1-46. Print. Guide to Gale Literary Criticism Ser.

A CLOSER LOOK AT
Avoiding Plagiarism

WHAT PLAGIARISM IS

The *Oxford English Dictionary* defines *plagiarism* as "The action or practice of taking someone else's work, idea, etc., and passing it off as one's own; literary theft." The word comes from a Latin verb that means "to kidnap." Plagiarism is wrongfully taking someone else's ideas or words and turning them in or publishing them as if they were your own. It is dishonest, because your reader or instructor has a right to believe you did the work yourself unless you acknowledge that you received help drawn from someone else's words, sentences, or ideas. It is shortsighted as well, because only the process of doing work yourself has educational value, not the act of turning in work drawn from the efforts of others.

EXAMPLES OF PLAGIARISM

Some more specific examples of plagiarism clarify that broad description:

- Buying a paper from a commercial source or taking a paper from a classmate, friend, fraternity or sorority file, or anyone else or using parts of such a paper and submitting it as your own—even if you change the introduction or alter some of the wording
- Cutting and pasting material from the Internet into your paper without indicating where it came from
- Using the exact words of another writer in your paper without indicating that they are quoted and providing proper citations for them
- Paraphrasing or summarizing the words of another writer without providing citations that indicate they are rewordings
- Taking important ideas from sources and including them in your paper as if you thought them up, even if the wording is not the same as in the original
- Letting someone else (a friend, classmate, parent, etc.) write parts of your paper for you or correct or edit a paper so extensively that it no longer accurately reflects your work
- Submitting a drawing, painting, musical composition, computer program, or any other kind of material created originally by someone else and claiming or implying that you created it yourself

REUSING A PAPER

One final example of plagiarism often surprises students: Turning in the same paper in different courses is plagiarism, even though all the material is yours. Instructors expect papers to be work done specifically during and for the course for which they were assigned; it's not fair if other students take the time to write a new paper and you just reuse one you wrote in high school or in an earlier college course.

In some cases, you may want to do a research project that involves two courses you are taking at the same time—literature and psychology, for example. In that case, talk to both instructors. They will probably encourage you because making connections between disciplines is a valuable way of learning. But they may require you to do separate papers for each course or allow you to submit the same paper for both courses but require it to be longer than those done by other students.

UNINTENTIONAL PLAGIARISM

Some of the examples above are deliberate cheating. Everyone knows it is unacceptable to buy a paper and turn it in as your own work. Those who do it deserve the severe penalties most instructors and institutions impose. In some cases, however, students stumble into inadvertent plagiarism by not knowing the rules for citation. They may believe, for example, that only direct quotations need to be acknowledged; therefore, they assume that if they totally rephrase a passage and avoid using any words from the original, they don't need to cite a source for it. Not so. You need to give credit to the person who came up with the idea or who did the work of tracing a historical allusion or detail or who thought out the interpretation of a story or poem, even though your phrasing of the material is different. *You are responsible for knowing what plagiarism is and how to avoid it*: Ignorance is not an adequate excuse.

AVOIDING PLAGIARISM

Here are a few guidelines for avoiding plagiarism:

- Put quotation marks around any groups of words (phrases or whole sentences) taken directly from a source.
- Document every direct quotation except phrases that are so common that most people would recognize the source without being told ("Four score and seven years ago," for example).
- Document any idea or information that you attained through your research, except for information that is widely available from many

different sources (even if you looked up the place and date of Alice Walker's birth, you don't need to give a source because that information is readily available in many places).

- Keep in mind that you are taking part in a long-honored tradition: the extension of the ongoing conversation about a literary work of art. Respecting the work of others by acknowledging their contributions is a matter of personal integrity and a standard by which you are welcomed into the community of both established and beginning scholars.

A CLOSER LOOK AT
Preparing a Works Cited Page

Chapter 3 covers the information needed for preparing a Works Cited page in MLA style, focusing on the most basic entries: a book, journal article, or magazine article by a single author. Most Works Cited pages will include entries that go beyond these basic types. The following pages provide instructions for and examples of many other — but not all — types of entries. If you can't find the help you need here, go to the *MLA Handbook for Writers of Research Papers*, 7th Edition, or to Diana Hacker's *Research and Documentation Online* (a link to which can be found by clicking on the Companion Web Site on the *Approaching Literature* home page).

Section 1. Citing Books and Items Included in Books

In Chapter 3, we provide a short list of items that are always included in Works Cited entries for books. Here is an expanded and annotated list that covers other situations. The asterisked items are always included; those without asterisks are included when needed.

- ***Name of the author or editor,** last name first, as it appears on the title page, followed by a period. If this entry ends with an initial, only one period is needed.
- ***Title of the book,** italicized, followed by a period. If the book has a subtitle, include it as well, preceded by a colon (unless the main title ends in a question mark, an exclamation point, or a dash).
- **Name of the editor, translator,** or **compiler,** for a book that has one in addition to an author, preceded by the abbreviation "Ed." or "Trans." or "Comp." (even if there are more than one), and followed by a period.
- **Edition used,** if other than the first, followed by a period ("3rd ed.").
- **Volume used,** for a work that has more than one volume, followed by a period. (See 1g below.)
- **Date of original publication,** for republished books. (See 1e below.)
- ***Place of publication,** followed by a colon. If more than one city is listed on the title page, give only the first one. Give the name of the city only, not the state, for locations in the United States. Identify lesser-known international cities with a country abbreviation ("Amsterdam:" but "Apeldoorn, Neth.:").
- ***Name of the publisher,** shortened ("Macmillan," not "Macmillan Publishing Company, Inc."), followed by a comma. Use abbreviations such as "UP" for "University Press."

- ***Year of publication,** followed by a period. If the date of publication is not given on the title page, look for it on the following page (the copyright page). If no date of publication is given there, use the copyright date. (As a last resort, you can look for the publication date in a library catalog.) Sometimes the copyright page includes the dates of successive printings of the book: These are not of interest; the date you use should be that of its original appearance, or the first printing. For books published before 1900, you may omit the publisher's name and put a comma instead of a colon after the city.
- **Medium of publication** (see p. 81), followed by a period.
- **Series name,** and number (if any), not italicized or enclosed within quotation marks and followed by a period. (See 1d below.)

Here are examples of the most common kinds of entries.

1a. A Book by One Author

Zauditu-Selassie, K. *African Spiritual Traditions in the Novels of Toni Morrison*. Gainesville: UP of Florida, 2009. Print.

1b. A Book by Two or More Authors

To cite a book by more than one author, list the authors' names in the order they appear on the title page; invert only the first author's name, followed by a comma, and list the other name or names in normal order.

Harding, Wendy, and Jacky Martin. *A World of Difference: An Inter-Cultural Study of Toni Morrison's Novels*. Westport: Greenwood, 1994. Print.

For more than three authors, you may give just the first author, followed by "et al." (the abbreviation for the Latin *et alii* or *et aliae,* "and others").

1c. An Edited Collection

To cite a book with chapters by different authors, use the same form as for a book attributed in its entirety to one or more authors, with "ed." or "eds." added after the name(s) of the editor(s), preceded by a comma.

Tally, Justine, ed. *The Cambridge Companion to Toni Morrison*. New York: Cambridge UP, 2007. Print.

To cite a specific chapter from such a collection, see 1j or 2e below.

1d. A Book in a Series

If the book is part of a series (as indicated on the title page or on the copyright page that follows), include the abbreviated series name (not italicized nor in quotation marks) and number, if any, after the medium. Follow it with a period.

> Denard, Carolyn C., ed. *Toni Morrison: Conversations*. Jackson: UP of
> Mississippi, 2008. Print. Literary Conversations Ser.

1e. A Republished Book

To cite a book that has been republished — for example, a paperback reprint of a hardcover book — give the original date of publication, followed by a period, and the publication information for the book you are using. The date of original publication can usually be found on the copyright page of the reprint; if it's not there, you may need to check library catalogs or biographical introductions to the author to find it.

> Morrison, Toni. *The Bluest Eye*. 1970. New York: Vintage, 2007. Print.

1f. An Edited Edition

To cite a work prepared for publication by someone other than the author — by an editor — provide the information you would provide for a republished book, with the name of the editor inserted before the publication information, preceded by "Ed." For a previously published work, if you want to include the original date of publication for clarity, insert the year directly after the title.

> Dunbar, Paul Laurence. *Collected Poetry*. Ed. Joanne M. Bruxton.
> Charlottesville: U of Virginia P, 1993. Print.

Note that although the title page reads *The Collected Poetry of Paul Laurence Dunbar*, repetition can be avoided to make it fit conventional citation form. The following example is not a reprint but the first printing of a collected edition of stories that were originally published separately in several books.

> Hughes, Langston. *The Return of Simple*. Ed. Akiba Sullivan Harper. New
> York: Hill, 1994. Print.

1g. A Multivolume Work

To cite two or more volumes of a multivolume work, give the total number of volumes in the set before the publication information, using an arabic numeral followed by the abbreviation "vols." Parenthetical references in the text will require volume number plus page numbers ("2: 145-47"). For a work in which volumes were published separately, in different years, give the first and last dates at the end of the entry.

David, Arthur P., J. Saunders Redding, and Joyce Ann Joyce, eds. *The New Cavalcade: African American Writing from 1760 to the Present.* 2 vols. Washington: Howard UP, 1991–92. Print.

When you use only one volume of a multivolume work, give its volume number in the bibliographic entry and include publication information for only that volume. In this case, only the page numbers are needed in parenthetical references in the text.

David, Arthur P., J. Saunders Redding, and Joyce Ann Joyce, eds. *The New Cavalcade: African American Writing from 1760 to the Present.* Vol. 2. Washington: Howard UP, 1992. Print.

1h. A Work in a Collection of Stories or Poems

To cite a work from a collection of stories or poems by a single author, insert the title of the story or poem, in quotation marks, between the name of the author and the title of the book, and give the first and last pages on which it appears after the date of publication.

Walker, Alice. "Everyday Use." *In Love and Trouble: Stories of Black Women.* New York: Harcourt, 1973. 47-59. Print.

Citations for additional works from the same collection can be abbreviated:

---. "The Flowers." *In Love and Trouble* 119-20.

You do not need to repeat the medium of publication for subsequent entries.

1i. A Work in an Anthology

When citing a work published in an anthology, give the author's name, the title of the work (in quotation marks for a story, a poem, or an essay; italicized for a play or screenplay), the title of the anthology, the editors, the publication information, and the first and last page numbers on which the work appears. If you want to include the original year of publication for clarity, insert it directly after the title.

Morrison, Toni. "Recitatif." 1983. *Approaching Literature: Reading + Thinking + Writing.* 3rd ed. Ed. Peter Schakel and Jack Ridl. Boston: Bedford/St. Martin's, 2011. 445-59. Print.

If several works from the same anthology are cited in the paper, unnecessary repetition can be avoided by creating a main entry for the anthology and cross-referencing individual works to it. Give the medium only for the complete anthology.

Ríos, Alberto. "Nani." 1982. Schakel and Ridl 857-58.
Schakel, Peter, and Jack Ridl, eds. *Approaching Literature: Reading +
     Thinking + Writing*. 3rd ed. Boston: Bedford/St. Martin's, 2011.
     Print.
Walker, Alice. "The Flowers." 1973. Schakel and Ridl 20-21.

1j. A Scholarly Essay Published for the First Time in a Collection of Essays

Busia, Abena P. A. "The Artistic Impulse of Toni Morrison's Shorter
     Works." *The Cambridge Companion to Toni Morrison*. Ed. Justine Tally.
     New York: Cambridge UP, 2007. 101-11. Print.

Give the first and last pages on which the essay appears. If two or more works from the same volume are cited in the paper, create a main entry for the volume and cross-reference individual works to it, as in 1i above.

1k. An Entry from an Encyclopedia

The citation for an encyclopedia article or dictionary entry follows the pattern for an essay in a collection. When the work has multiple editors, their names usually are not included. If the encyclopedia or dictionary is well-known, publication information can be omitted. If the article is signed, start with the author (sometimes articles in reference books are signed with initials identified elsewhere in the book); if it is anonymous, start with the title of the entry. If entries are arranged alphabetically in the encyclopedia or dictionary, volume and page numbers may be omitted.

"Recitative." *The Oxford English Dictionary Online*. Web. 23 August 2010.
Greenspan, Charlotte. "Recitative." *The New Harvard Dictionary of Music*.
     Ed. Don Michael Randal. Cambridge: Belknap-Harvard UP, 1986.
     Print.

1l. An Entry in a Multivolume Reference Work

Blake, Susan L. "Toni Morrison." *Dictionary of Literary Biography*.
     Vol. 33: *Afro-American Fiction Writers after 1955*. Ed. Thadious M.
     Davis and Trudier Harris. Detroit: Gale, 1984. 187–99. Print.

Section 2. Citing Articles from Journals, Magazines, and Newspapers

2a. An Article Published in a Scholarly Journal

The Works Cited page for a research paper almost always includes entries for articles. Like those for books, such entries usually have four main parts:

> Author's name. "Title of the Article." Publication information. Medium of publication.

In Chapter 3, we provide a short list of items that appear in Works Cited entries for journals and for magazines. We will repeat those lists here, for convenience. All items are to be included, if available:

- **Name of the author,** last name first, followed by a period.
- **Title of the article,** enclosed in quotation marks, followed by a period (inside the quotation mark), unless the title ends with a question mark or an exclamation point.
- **Title of the journal,** italicized, no punctuation following it.
- **Volume number of the journal,** using arabic numerals even if a roman numeral is used in the journal, followed by a period (no spaces) if an issue number is available.
- **Issue number** (if available), with no punctuation following. For journals without volume numbers, give the issue number alone: *Victorian Newsletter* 118 (Fall 2010).
- **Year of publication,** in parentheses, followed by a colon.
- **Page numbers** (first and last), followed by a period.
- **Medium of publication** (see p. 81), followed by a period.

> Abel, Elizabeth. "Black Writing, White Reading: Race and the Politics of Feminist Interpretation." *Critical Inquiry* 19.3 (1993): 470-98. Print.

2b. An Article Published in a Magazine

The name of the author, title of the article, and title of the magazine are handled the same way as for scholarly journal entries. Magazines have volume numbers, but they are not important for locating an issue and are left out of Works Cited entries. Dates and pages are handled differently than for a scholarly journal:

- **Date of publication,** followed by a colon. Day, month (abbreviated except for May, June, and July), and year (in that order) are given for weekly or biweekly magazines; only month or months and year are given for magazines published monthly or bimonthly.

- **Page numbers** (first and last of the whole article, not just the ones you used), followed by a period. If pagination is not consecutive (for example, if an article begins on page 4 and continues on page 8), write only the first page number and a plus sign, with no intervening space.

> Reed, J. R. "Post Feminism Playing for Keeps." *Time* 10 Jan. 1983:
>   60-61. Print.
> Watkins, Mel. "Sexism, Racism and Black Women Writers." *New York*
>   *Times Book Review* 15 June 1986: 4+. Print.

2c. An Article Published in a Newspaper

The format for citing an article in a newspaper is exactly the same as for a weekly magazine, unless the newspaper is published in varied editions (late edition, suburban edition); in that case, the edition is included after the date, separated by a comma. If a newspaper is divided into sections, include the section letter or section number with the page number. If the article is on nonconsecutive pages, give the first page number followed by a plus sign, with no space between them. The title of the newspaper should be given the way it appears on the masthead, but introductory articles should be omitted (*New York Times*, not *The New York Times*).

> Chism, Olin. "American Wins Nobel for Literature: Toni Morrison
>   Renowned for Characterization, Images." *Dallas Morning News* 8 Oct.
>   1993, final home ed.: 1A. Web. *LexisNexis*. 23 Aug. 2010.
> Streitfield, David. "The Novelist's Prism: Toni Morrison Holds Race Up to
>   the Light and Reflects on the Meaning of Color." *Washington Post*
>   6 Jan. 1998, final ed., Style sec.: B1+. Print.

2d. A Review

In citing a review, include the title and author of the work being reviewed after the review title and before the periodical title.

> Atwood, Margaret. "Haunted by Their Nightmares." Rev. of *Beloved*, by
>   Toni Morrison. *New York Times Book Review* 13 Sept. 1987: 1+. Print.
> Ansen, David. "The Ghosts of Slavery." Rev. of *Beloved*, dir. by Jonathan
>   Demme. *Newsweek* 19 Oct. 1998: 76. *General OneFile*. Web.
>   23 Aug. 2010.

2e. A Previously Published Journal Article Reprinted in a Collection

To cite a previously published scholarly article reprinted in a collection, give the complete data for the earlier publication and then add "Rpt. in" (for "Reprinted in"), the title of the collection, and its publication data.

Goldstein-Shirley, David. "Race/[Gender]: Toni Morrison's 'Recitatif.'"
  Journal of the Short Story in English 27 (1996): 83-95. Rpt. in
  *Women on the Edge: Ethnicity and Gender in Short Stories by
  American Women*. Ed. Corrine H. Dale and J. H. E. Paine. New York:
  Garland, 1999. 97-110. Print.

Section 3. Citing Interviews and Other Personal Communications

3a. An Interview

To cite an interview, first give the name of the person being interviewed. If the interview has been published, provide the title (if it has one), in quotation marks, followed by a period and "Interview by," without quotation marks or italics. Add the name of the interviewer if known, pertinent bibliographic information, and the medium of publication.

Morrison, Toni. Interview by Maya Jaggi. *Brick* 76 (2005): 97-103. Print.
Morrison, Toni. "Thinking about a Story." Interview by Jennifer Hoofard.
  Writing on the Edge 17.2 (2007): 87-99. Print.

To cite an interview you conducted personally, give the name of the person interviewed, the kind of interview ("Personal interview," "Telephone interview," "E-mail interview"), and the date or dates, such as the following (which we wish had really taken place):

Morrison, Toni. Personal interview. 7 Sept. 2009.
Morrison, Toni. E-mail interview. 13-15 Oct. 2010.

3b. A Personal Letter or an E-mail

To cite a personal written communication that you received, give the name of the sender, the type of communication, its date, and the form of the material ("MS" for a manuscript, that is, written by hand; "TS" for a typescript, that is, a work prepared by machine).

Morrison, Toni. Letter to the author. 21 Oct. 2007. MS.
Morrison, Toni. E-mail to the author. 28 Oct. 2007. TS.

Section 4. Citing Sources Accessed Electronically

4a. Printed Scholarly Articles Accessed Online

For Works Cited entries involving the full text of a journal or magazine article accessed through a database such as *JSTOR*, *Project MUSE*, or *InfoTrac*, you must provide the information a reader needs to access the source electronically, as well as the information about its original publication. The basic pattern for such an entry is similar to that in 2e above:

> Name of the author. "Title of the Document." Information about print
>   publication. Information about electronic publication. Access
>   information. Medium used.

When the source does not provide all of that information, give as much as you can, following or adapting these guidelines:

- **Name of the author,** last name first and followed by a period.
- **Title of the document,** enclosed in quotation marks, followed by a period (inside the quotation mark), unless the title ends with a question mark or an exclamation point.
- **As much information about its publication in a journal or magazine as the database makes available,** following the guidelines above for journals and magazines. If no information about print publication is provided, proceed to the next step.
- **Information about its electronic reproduction:**
  1. Title of the database or Web site, in italics, followed by a period.
  2. Medium of publication used ("Web"), followed by a period.
  3. Date of access (day, month, year), followed by a period. Abbreviate all months except for May, June, and July.

> Androne, Helane Adams. "Revised Memories and Colliding Identities:
>   Absence and Presence in Morrison's 'Recitatif' and Viramontes's
>   'Tears on My Pillow.'" *MELUS* 32.2 (2007): 133-50. *JSTOR*. Web.
>   22 May 2010.

4b. Texts Accessed through Online Web Sites

Many novels, stories, poems, and plays that are no longer under copyright have been made readily available on the Internet. To list such sources, follow the pattern in 4a, supplying as much information as possible about the original publication, then about its electronic reproduction.

> Douglass, Frederick. "Reconstruction." *Atlantic Monthly* 18 (1866): 761-
>   65. *The Historical Text Archive*. Comp. Donald H. Mabry. 1990-2009.
>   Web. 19 Aug. 2010.
> Johnson, Georgia Douglas. "Sonnet to Those Who See But Darkly."
>   *Bronze*. Boston: Brimmer, 1922. *Literature Online (LION)*. Web. 19
>   Aug. 2010.

4c. A Work in an Online Scholarly Journal

In contrast to 2a above, some scholarly journals exist only in electronic form on the Web, not in print. They are periodicals, appearing on a regular schedule. Thus, to enter a work from such a journal in a Works Cited list, follow the guidelines in 2a as closely as possible, but end with the following items:

- Medium of publication ("Web")
- Date of access (day, month, year), with all months except May, June, and July abbreviated.

An online journal may not have page numbers or may number each item separately. When that is the case, use "n. pag." instead of inclusive page numbers.

> Lessane, Patricia Williams. "Women of Color Facing Feminism—Creating Our Space at Liberation's Table: A Report on the Chicago Foundation for Women's 'F' Series." *Journal of Pan African Studies* 1.7 (2007): 3-10. Web. 3 Aug. 2010.

4d. A Work in an Online Magazine

In contrast to 2b above, some magazines appear, on a regular schedule, only on the Web, not in print. To enter such a work in a Works Cited list, follow the guidelines in Section 2b as closely as possible, but end with the following items:

- Medium of publication used ("Web")
- Date of access (day, month, year), with all months except May, June, and July abbreviated

> Alexie, Sherman. Interview. *Failbetter.com* 31 (2009): n. pag. Web. 19 Aug. 2010.
> Morrison, Toni. Interview by Zia Jaffrey. *Salon.com*. Salon Media Group, 2 Feb. 1998: n. pag. Web. 19 Aug. 2010.

4e. Information on a Web Page

Most Web sites are not periodicals. They are not updated on a regular basis, only as needed or as time permits. Some remain online but are neglected after a promising start, thus possibly reducing their freshness or reliability. Varying amounts and kinds of information are supplied, which makes doing Works Cited entries more challenging. Entries for such sources should contain as much of the following as possible:

- **Name of the author(s) or editor(s)**, if available, followed by a period. If not available, start with the title.

> ## TIPS for Handling Online Sources
>
> MLA style no longer requires the URL at which you found the document because URLs change frequently and because their addresses are so long that it's challenging to type them accurately. It's easier to use a search engine to find the site you need.
>
> Because Internet sites sometimes disappear or move and can't be located again, it is a good idea to print out a copy of the material used for your paper. That way you can still verify information in case the site becomes inaccessible.
>
> Some instructors ask that URLs be included, to make it easier to check use of sources. In that case, enclose the URL in angle brackets (< >) at the end of the Works Cited entry, followed by a period. If you need to divide a URL at the end of a line, break it before a dot or after a slash (do not insert a hyphen).
>
> > Bois, Danuta. "Toni Morrison." *Distinguished Women of Past and*
> > *Present*. N.p. 1996. Web. 19 Aug. 2010. < http://
> > www.distinguishedwomen.com/bio.php?womanid=158 >.

- **Title of the work**, followed by a period. Italicize if this is the title of the entire site; enclose it in quotation marks if the work is part of a larger work.
- **Title of the overall Web site** (italicized, followed by a period), if different from the title of the work being used (see previous entry).
- **Publisher or sponsor of the site**, followed by a period. If the information is not available, use "N.p." (no publisher).
- **Date of publication or posting** (day, month, and year, as available), followed by a period. If no date is indicated, use "n.d." (for no date). Abbreviate all months except May, June, and July.
- **Medium of publication** ("Web"), followed by a period.
- **Date accessed** (day, month, year), followed by a period. Abbreviate all months except May, June, and July.

> "Alice Walker." *Poets.org*. Academy of American Poets, n.d. Web. 19 Aug.
> 2010.
> Bois, Danuta. "Toni Morrison." *Distinguished Women of Past and Present*.
> N.p. 1996. Web. 19 Aug. 2010.

For guidance on handling Works Cited entries for other electronic resources and nonprint media—such as television or radio broadcasts, sound recordings, performances, visual art, and others—see the *MLA Handbook for Writers of Research Papers*, 7th ed. (New York: Modern Language Association, 2009).

PART **2**

Approaching FICTION

4 Reading Fiction 107

5 Plot and Character 112

6 Point of View and Theme 159

7 Setting and Symbol 195

8 Tone, Style, and Irony 232

9 Writing about Fiction 265

10 Sherman Alexie – An Author in Depth 278

11 A Collection of Stories 313

Overleaf: The author James Baldwin in a relaxed portrait of a writer at work, photographed in his New York apartment in 1963. Not yet forty years old when this photograph was taken, Baldwin was already established as a major literary presence with the publication of his semiautographical first novel, Go Tell It on the Mountain *(1953), the essay collection* Notes of a Native Son *(1955), and his second novel,* Giovanni's Room *(1956), among other works. Baldwin's work explores what it meant to be an African American in the twentieth century, and he was a lifelong and fierce defender of racial justice and equality. The responsibility of the writer, Baldwin told an interviewer, "is to excavate the experience of the people who produced him." (See p. 1373 for a short biography.)*

Literary works do not endure as objects but as presences. When you read anything worth remembering, you liberate a human voice; you release into the world again a companion spirit.

Louise Glück

(Pulitzer Prize–winning American poet)

Reading Fiction

CHAPTER 4

Responding to the Real World of Stories

What are your own stories? What books and movies do you love? What television shows do you follow? The stories that you own, that you love, may incline toward realism or science fiction or romance—each of us is different, with individual tastes. But almost all of us are drawn toward stories of some sort. What is it about stories that draws you into their world, that makes you not want to put the book down or miss the show or want to rent the DVD a third and fourth time?

We know that what we are reading or watching is not factual: These are made-up characters doing imaginary things. Yet we become deeply invested in their lives: We begin to think about the characters as if they were real, and we care about what happens to them. Why do we begin to sympathize deeply with a grieving mother or delight in the achievements of a college sophomore, neither of whom actually exists? The answer to these questions must start with the impressive power of imagination—with the way our imaginations respond to the imaginative creations of excellent writers. In the chapters to come, we look closely at such imaginative creations and at the way we use our own imaginations to enter, enjoy, and appreciate them.

WHAT IS FICTION?

STORY   Before we start that closer look, we need to clarify what it is we're talking about. **Story,** considered broadly, is any account of a related series of events in sequential order, usually chronological order (the order in which they happened). Stories did not start out as something to be read:

Long before people read stories or watched them being acted out in plays, they listened to stories being told or sung. From the time ancient peoples gathered around fires in the evening for warmth and safety, they told stories to each other. And although we no longer need campfires for warmth and protection, the storytelling tradition of "stories around the campfire" continues wherever people gather for companionship. Generation after generation of children around the world have said to parents, "Tell me a story."

Story, in this broad sense, includes events that are true or made up—an account of the invading of Normandy in World War II, the planning for the prom during your junior year in high school, or the landing of three-headed cyborgs in an Iowa cornfield. The account can be narrated (told by a storyteller) or dramatized (acted out in drama). It can be told in prose or verse. Chapters 5 to 8 deal only with narrated stories, only with stories in prose, and only with stories that are fictional.

FICTION   **Fiction** refers to narrated stories that are drawn from the imagination or are an imaginative reworking of actual experiences. Incidents and details in a work of fiction can originate in fact, history, or everyday life, but the characters and events as a whole are primarily invented, or altered, in the author's imagination. Imaginative fiction (like movies) varies widely in types, from fast-paced adventures that focus on action to stories that examine characters and ideas in depth; they can be told at great length (**novels** or **epics**) or more briefly (**novellas** or **short stories**).

SHORT STORIES   The works of fiction included in this book are **short stories**, relatively brief fictional narratives in prose that often focus on the essential aspects of a character (instead of showing character development over time, the way a novel can) and on a single event or episode—often a life-changing circumstance. They are characterized by careful, deliberate craftsmanship (in handling of plot, characterization, and point of view).

The short stories included in this book explore the complexities of life and people; they lead us to interact imaginatively with significant human issues; they offer us an opportunity to expand our understanding of ourselves, others, and the multiple cultures we find ourselves living with and within. They are widely respected by other writers, scholars, and general readers for the way they handle the techniques of fiction (ones discussed in Chapters 5 to 8) and for their insights into people, their values, their experiences, and their cultures.

WHY READ FICTION?

ENTERING OTHER LIVES   What is the value of reading such stories? Most important, perhaps, is the way they can take us outside of ourselves and through our imaginations enable us to enter other lives, other selves, other times, places, and cultures, other feelings and experiences. All of us live limited lives. We want to see more, expand our range of experiences, meet people whose lives are different from our own. That's why many people like to travel and why many students want to go away to college. A story enables us, without leaving our chairs, to escape our boundaries and broaden our understanding and vision. Think again of Sherman Alexie (see p. 4) and what reading stories did to "save his life."

ENLARGEMENT OF BEING Author and literary critic C. S. Lewis explained the appeal of story this way: "We seek an enlargement of our being. We want to be more than ourselves.... We want to see with other eyes, to imagine with other imaginations, to feel with other hearts, as well as with our own" (*An Experiment in Criticism* [Cambridge University Press, 1961], 137). Fiction can do that. A story can mirror our own world, take us to a world that is not part of our daily experience, or create a world entirely new to us. To read fiction is to enter a place where you both disappear and find yourself—a place where, when you put the book down and look up, you feel even more yourself than you did before reading.

THE TRUTH OF FICTION You have likely heard someone say, "Fiction? I don't read fiction. I want to read what's true." Fiction is not fact. It may contain facts, but it is still fiction. A literary scholar and a historian who were on a panel together were asked the difference between the two disciplines. The historian spoke about how important it was to get the facts correct in his work. The literary scholar then replied, "Yes. You deal with facts. I deal with truth." What was the literary scholar implying? Not that the historian wasn't searching for the truth within the facts, but that fiction is the embodiment of truth, at times factual truth, but always—if it is a fine work of fiction—the kind of truth that exists within, around, or beyond fact. This is a different kind of truth, the kind of truth that needs story to contain it, the truth of what it is like to live the facts, the kind of truth that exists and comes to life through what the writer "makes up." It is the truth of Captain Ahab's obsession with a white whale, Jane Eyre's dreams, Sherman Alexie's Superman. We need this truth. We need our stories.

ACTIVE READING: Fiction

The more you read, and the more widely you read, the more confident you will become in your ability to follow a story and appreciate what goes in it. The purpose of Chapters 5 to 8 is to help you become a more skilled reader of fiction—more alert to the richness of a work of fiction, to the fascinating variety of good things it has to offer. Most of the things covered in those chapters, however, should not concern you the first time you read a short story or novel. Here are some suggestions for the first time you go through a story with an active imagination.

- *Give the work a fair chance.* Writers generally try to catch a reader's interest immediately, but some short stories and novels start slowly. Don't quit reading after a few paragraphs or pages. Give yourself enough time to get involved in the action and with the characters.

- *Keep going.* Even if some things aren't completely clear, later events probably will clarify them.

- *Watch for what's happening.* As in movies, some stories are filled with action and excitement. Others, often ones that deal with inner struggles, move more deliberately and with less external action.

- *Watch for who it is happening to.* Pay attention to the characters—their appearances, personalities, values, attitudes, struggles, weaknesses, strengths, and so forth.

- *Watch for "why"—why does what happens happen?* What happens that leads to the situations and actions? What causes the action? What motivates the characters?

REREADING: Fiction

Experiencing a story fully requires reading it more than once. The first time through, you primarily concentrate on what's going on. The second and third times through, you begin paying attention to other things—to easily overlooked details and nuances concerning plot and character and to the way the piece is written, the subtlety of techniques the author used.

You probably already do this with movies and music you love. Good movies, ones you really like, you watch twice, or many times, and you listen to favorite CDs over and over. We enjoy experiencing again the things we liked at first, of course; but our follow-up experience is different, richer, because we notice what we didn't notice before. It's the same for reading. Once you get into it, you'll enjoy rereading books or stories for the same reasons you like watching films or listening to music again. Here are some suggestions for rereading.

- *Slow down.* Let yourself absorb the flavor and style; roll the sentences and rhythms around on your tongue; reread paragraphs that aren't fully clear or that you find especially well written and enjoyable; go back to earlier parts to check on details that tie in with later ones.

- *Pay attention to the title.* Often it's significant and revealing, though its significance may not be evident during the first reading. In such cases, as you reread, it's worth reflecting on possible ways the title links to the actions and characters.

- *Look up things that aren't familiar.* Check unfamiliar words in a dictionary. The context often clarifies new words, but in other cases it doesn't, and you can miss something. Do some research on people from history, other literature, or historical events mentioned in the story. Look at a map when real places are used.

- *Pay attention to the first sentence and the first paragraph, especially for short stories.* Authors often embed within them a lot of important indicators about tone, style, setting, and subject. For the same reasons, pay close attention to the last paragraph and last sentence.

- *Pay attention to things that do not seem needed.* What appears insignificant may actually be a subtlety. Reflecting on its part in the whole can open up a deeper understanding of the characters or events.

*W*e are a species that needs and wants to understand who we are. Sheep lice do not seem to share this longing, which is one reason they write so little.

Anne Lamott
(Novelist and Nonfiction Writer)

CHAPTER **5**

Plot and Character
Watching What Happens, to Whom

Often the first thing you notice as you read a story is what happens to whom. Plot and characters: These, the foundation stones of fiction, are worth a closer look. We connect with these probably because they're so basic to life: We care about people (family, friends, enemies, the famous and influential) and about what goes on in their lives. In literature, much the same thing happens: We care, but we care about imaginative constructs. Therefore, as readers of literature, beyond our fascination with what happens to whom, we should be interested in the way plot and character are constructed in order to bring them to life. This chapter focuses on the skills and techniques we should be alert to in the development of both plots and characters.

ENTRY POINTS   Read the following short story, about an unexpected encounter between a young man and a young woman on a street in Los Angeles. After getting a sense of the story from a first reading, read it again. This time see what more you notice in it, especially about the description of what happens and the way the two characters are depicted. Give some thought to how you feel about what happens and how you react to the characters.

112

Dagoberto Gilb b. 1950

Love in L.A. [1993]

Jake slouched in a clot of near motionless traffic, in the peculiar gray of concrete, smog, and early morning beneath the overpass of the Hollywood Freeway on Alvarado Street. He didn't really mind because he knew how much worse it could be trying to make a left onto the onramp. He certainly didn't do that every day of his life, and he'd assure anyone who'd ask that he never would either. A steady occupation had its advantages and he couldn't deny thinking about that too. He needed an FM radio in something better than this '58 Buick he drove. It would have

APPROACHING THE AUTHOR

Dagoberto Gilb says that his most popular story, "Look on the Bright Side," was rejected 125 times before being accepted for publication.

For more about him, see page 1385.

crushed velvet interior with electric controls for the L.A. summer, a nice warm heater and defroster for the winter drives at the beach, a cruise control for those longer trips, mellow speakers front and rear of course, windows that hum closed, snuffing out that nasty exterior noise of freeways. The fact was that he'd probably have to change his whole style. Exotic colognes, plush, dark nightclubs, maitais and daquiris, necklaced ladies in satin gowns, misty and sexy like in a tequila ad. Jake could imagine lots of possibilities when he let himself, but none that ended up with him pressed onto a stalled freeway.

Jake was thinking about this freedom of his so much that when he glimpsed its green light he just went ahead and stared bye bye to the steadily employed. When he turned his head the same direction his windshield faced, it was maybe one second too late. He pounced the brake pedal and steered the front wheels away from the tiny brakelights but the smack was unavoidable. Just one second sooner and it would only have been close. One second more and he'd be crawling up the Toyota's trunk. As it was, it seemed like only a harmless smack, much less solid than the one against his back bumper.

Jake considered driving past the Toyota but was afraid the traffic ahead would make it too difficult. As he pulled up against the curb a few carlengths ahead, it occurred to him that the traffic might have helped him get away too. He slammed the car door twice to make sure it was closed fully and to give himself another second more, then toured front and rear of his Buick for damage on or near the bumpers. Not an impressionable scratch even in the chrome. He perked up. Though the car's beauty was secondary to its ability to start and move, the body and paint were clean except for a few minor dings. This stood out as one of his few clearcut accomplishments over the years.

Before he spoke to the driver of the Toyota, whose looks he could see might present him with an added complication, he signaled to the driver of the car that hit him, still in his car and stopped behind the Toyota, and waved his

hands and shook his head to let the man know there was no problem as far as
he was concerned. The driver waved back and started his engine.

"It didn't even scratch my paint," Jake told her in that way of his. "So   5
how you doin? Any damage to the car? I'm kinda hoping so, just so it takes
a little more time and we can talk some. Or else you can give me your
phone number now and I won't have to lay my regular b.s. on you to get it
later."

He took her smile as a good sign and relaxed. He inhaled her scent like it
was clean air and straightened out his less than new but not unhip clothes.

"You've got Florida plates. You look like you must be Cuban."

"My parents are from Venezuela."

"My name's Jake." He held out his hand.

"Mariana."   10

They shook hands like she'd never done it before in her life.

"I really am sorry about hitting you like that." He sounded genuine. He
fondled the wide dimple near the cracked taillight. "It's amazing how easy it is
to put a dent in these new cars. They're so soft they might replace waterbeds
soon." Jake was confused about how to proceed with this. So much seemed so
unlikely, but there was always possibility. "So maybe we should go out to breakfast somewhere and talk it over."

"I don't eat breakfast."

"Some coffee then."

"Thanks, but I really can't."   15

"You're not married, are you? Not that that would matter that much to me.
I'm an openminded kinda guy."

She was smiling. "I have to get to work."

"That sounds boring."

"I better get your driver's license," she said.

Jake nodded, disappointed. "One little problem," he said. "I didn't bring it.   20
I just forgot it this morning. I'm a musician," he exaggerated greatly, "and, well,
I dunno, I left my wallet in the pants I was wearing last night. If you have some
paper and a pen I'll give you my address and all that."

He followed her to the glove compartment side of her car.

"What if we don't report it to the insurance companies? I'll just get it fixed
for you."

"I don't think my dad would let me do that."

"Your dad? It's not your car?"

"He bought it for me. And I live at home."   25

"Right." She was slipping away from him. He went back around to the back
of her new Toyota and looked over the damage again. There was the trunk lid,
the bumper, a rear panel, a taillight.

"You do have insurance?" she asked, suspicious, as she came around the
back of the car.

"Oh yeah," he lied.

"I guess you better write the name of that down too."

He made up a last name and address and wrote down the name of an 30
insurance company an old girlfriend once belonged to. He considered giving
a real phone number but went against that idea and made one up.

"I act too," he lied to enhance the effect more. "Been in a couple of
movies."

She smiled like a fan.

"So how about your phone number?" He was rebounding maturely.

She gave it to him.

"Mariana, you are beautiful," he said in his most sincere voice. 35

"Call me," she said timidly.

Jake beamed. "We'll see you, Mariana," he said holding out his hand. Her
hand felt so warm and soft he felt like he'd been kissed.

Back in his car he took a moment or two to feel both proud and sad about
his performance. Then he watched the rear view mirror as Mariana pulled up
behind him. She was writing down the license plate numbers on his Buick,
ones that he'd taken off a junk because the ones that belonged to his had
expired so long ago. He turned the ignition key and revved the big engine
and clicked into drive. His sense of freedom swelled as he drove into the now
moving street traffic, though he couldn't stop the thought about that FM stereo
radio and crushed velvet interior and the new car smell that would even make
it better.

APPROACHING THE READING

1. Try sketching out the story, what happens in the order it happens. Reflect
   on the organization of the plot: Why does it start where it does? How
   would the effect be different if it had started at a different point? Why
   does it linger on certain sections and go into great detail? Why does it
   stop where it does and not follow through to the consequences of what
   happens here?

2. Then think about what is left out and what is emphasized in plotting the
   story. Why is what Jake is thinking before his car hits Mariana's important
   to the basic story? If you think it isn't important, explain why the author
   might have included it. What about the exact words Jake and Mariana use
   makes them crucial to the story's impact? Why are they included?

3. Think about what both characters are like. What do you feel about each?
   Do your feelings about either change as the story proceeds? In what way or
   ways?

4. What significance or implications arise out of the decisions about what to
   include, what not to include, and how these details are organized in the
   story? Pick out several specific details and think about their relation to the
   point of the story.

READING FOR PLOT

STORY AND PLOT   Plot, in a literary sense, is the selection and arrangement of events in order to present them most effectively to the reader. Comparing *plot* with *story* can help clarify that. *Story*, as we use the word in Chapter 4, "Reading Fiction," is a straightforward account of everything that happens, in the order it happens. A story is what you would hear if you saw Mariana that evening and she said, "Let me tell you about my day." Story provides the materials (the events, the characters, the outcome) from which a plot is constructed.

PLOT AS STRUCTURE   As an author constructs a story into a plot, she or he makes a decision about who will tell what happens—Jake, Mariana, or a storyteller (we'll come back to this in Chapter 6). The author also decides what to include and what to leave out (things that aren't essential for the effect and emphasis desired) and in what order to tell about what happens (whether to start at the beginning—as "Love in L.A." does—or in the middle or near the end). The author also needs to establish causal connections between the key events. What is interesting about plot is not just what happens but why it happens and the implications or results of what happens. Another way to put it: Plot provides the **structure of a work of fiction, that is, the arrangement of material in it, the ordering of its parts, the design used to draw out and convey its significance.

Starting the Action

**WHERE TO START   A plot usually starts at a point that relates directly and significantly to the series of events being recorded: "Love in L.A." starts at the beginning of the sequence of events the author wanted to focus on, with Jake in his car caught in a traffic jam. But works of fiction don't need to start at the beginning of a sequence of events. Sometimes the first events in the sequence, though necessary to the story, are not the best place to start. Sometimes the most interesting or exciting or important events occur later, and we readers become more quickly and deeply involved when the plot starts there. The background events are set later as needed. "Love in L.A." could have begun in the middle, with Jake's car bumping Mariana's, and then gone back to explain what Jake was daydreaming about instead of paying attention to his driving. If Dagoberto Gilb had wanted to emphasize the accident itself, as a highly dramatic moment, he might have started in the middle. But because he wants readers to focus more on Jake's character than on the accident, he starts with what is going on in Jake's head before the fender bender occurs.

Organizing the Action

STRATEGIES OF ORGANIZATION   Decisions about how to arrange events follow from the decision of where to start. Because "Love in L.A." starts at the sequence's beginning, it is organized in *chronological order*, the order in which the events occur. Stories that don't start at the beginning need different organizational strategies (this way of starting has been used for thousands of years—the Latin phrase ***in medias res*, meaning "into the middle of things," is used to describe it). In this case, the background events are usually filled in through **flashback** (in which earlier events are presented as an inserted narrative or a scene, perhaps with a character *remembering* what happened earlier) or through **exposition** (a nondramatized explanation, often a speech by a character or the narrator, *explaining* what occurred before the initial action of a story or play).

DEVELOPING A CONFLICT   Organizing how the story is told includes incorporating techniques for increasing intensity and holding interest. A crucial technique is to create some kind of **conflict**, some struggle or confrontation between opposing characters or a character and opposing forces. In most cases, at least one side of the struggle involves the main character. Conflict arises in three main forms:

- **Physical conflict.** One basic kind of conflict occurs as a physical struggle or confrontation between a character or group of characters and another character or group of characters: the showdown between a sheriff's posse and a gang of outlaws in an old Western, for example, or a fistfight between two rivals at a high school prom. Physical conflict can also involve humans struggling against nature: a group of sailors, perhaps led by an inexperienced captain, attempting to survive a fierce storm. "Love in L.A." has no physical conflict, but it's easy to imagine how the events could have turned into a road-rage story with physical conflict at its center—read Dave Eggers's brief story "Accident" (p. 315) and notice how it plays around with this possibility.

- **Social conflict.** A second type of conflict involves differences regarding personal or societal relationships or values. This is a common motif in modern fiction. Examples could include a teenager challenging her or his parents, the different gender outlooks a man and a woman might bring to the same situation, or an activist confronting a social injustice. Part of the conflict in "Love in L.A." is the way Jake's lifestyle runs counter to social norms: Society expects drivers to have insurance and accept responsibility for any damage they cause to other people's property; it requires people to carry their driver's licenses and have accurate license plates on their cars. The story gives you as reader the options of identifying with Jake and enjoying the way he flouts social expectations or dismissing him as irresponsible or, perhaps, feeling caught between accepting Jake's laid-back charm and rejecting what he does as illegal and immoral. This is a good example of how conflict can be reflected back to us when we read actively, causing us to internalize the conflict, to reenact the story internally.

- **Internal or psychological conflict.** Another variety of conflict deals with struggles within a character, as she or he wrestles with competing moral claims or a difficult decision. This has always been a central issue for literature. Numerous stories in this book show characters engaged in such inner struggles, often at crucial moments in the characters' lives. For example

- an identity crisis, when an event forces a character to a new or deeper sense of self-knowledge or self-awareness, often a moment of maturation, like Myop's in "The Flowers" (p. 20)
- facing the moment of death, as the grandmother does in "A Good Man Is Hard to Find" (p. 134)
- a belief crisis when something causes a character to reexamine the foundation of what she or he puts faith or trust in, as in "Young Goodman Brown" (p. 337)
- a values crisis when something forces a character to make a moral or an ethical decision, such as Sammy's in "A&P" (p. 552), or sometimes to adhere to standards she or he has held to — or should have adhered to — in the past.

A lack of inner conflict can be equally significant: One of the most revealing things about Jake in "Love in L.A." is his lack of any internal struggle, despite doing some things that would trouble most readers' consciences at least somewhat.

TIP: Focusing on a conflict can be a helpful way to "get into" a story. Usually when you identify a story's conflict or conflicts, you are getting to the center of what's important in the story. That can lead to a valuable discussion about why the conflict is worth taking seriously and how the conflict may serve as a unifying factor in the work.

DEVELOPMENTAL TECHNIQUES In addition to the use of conflict for organizing the action in stories, authors rely on several other techniques that you can enjoy discovering. Be alert to the following, at least when you are rereading:

- **Suspense.** To hold readers' interest, a plot often creates some degree of **suspense**, some uncertainty and concern about how things will turn out, who did what, what the effects on the characters or events will be, or if or when disaster will fall or a rescue occur. The word *suspense* might feel too strong for "Love in L.A.," but the story does make us curious, at least, to find out if Jake gets away with all that he's trying to.
- **Foreshadowing.** The beginning and middle of a story often contain **foreshadowings**, anticipations of things that will happen later. For example, when the mother in "Daughter of Invention" (p. 10) says, "'[W]hen I make a million, I'll buy you your very own typewriter.' (I'd been nagging my mother for one just like the one father had bought her to do his order forms at home)," it foreshadows the ending, where her

father gives her "a brand new electric typewriter . . . even better than the one I'd been begging to get like my mother's" (paras. 16, 61).

- **Repetition.** Repeating a word or an image or a detail can draw attention to especially important aspects of a story. The repeated references to the mother's inventions in "Daughter of Invention," from the title on, set up the key invention later, when mother and daughter together invent a speech to replace the one the father tears up. Similarly, the repetition of "that FM stereo radio and crushed velvet interior" in "Love in L.A." (p. 113) signals what is most important in Jake's value system, and the repeated references to death in Flannery O'Connor's "A Good Man Is Hard to Find" (p. 134) foreshadow what happens at the end of the story.

- **Climax.** The development of a plot holds readers' attention by becoming more complex and more intense (sometimes referred to as **rising action** or **complication**), until it reaches a crisis of some sort, or the **climax**, what the suspense builds toward. This terminology grew out of action-based plots in drama, where the most intense moment is the peak of the physical conflict. The climax of a sci-fi action movie might come when, just before the gelatin-coated cyborg sends an earth-freezing probe into the center of the planet, the kung-fu master heroine shoots a laser into the monster's fifth eye and saves the world. In a story focusing on inner conflict, by contrast, the climax might be a moment of inner realization—the point at which the main character grasps that his gambling is destroying his family and decides to go into rehab.

  It's important for you as a student to remember that picking out a climax is not the same as understanding a work of fiction, nor is it a definite feature all readers identify the same way. There can be differences of opinion about what a story's climax is or even about whether a given story has one. If "Love in L.A." has a climax, it might well come in the next-to-last paragraph when Jake seems not only to have avoided responsibility for the accident but also to have won Mariana's interest in him: "Her hand felt so warm and soft he felt like he'd been kissed" (para. 37).

- **Epiphany.** One particular type of climax is called an **epiphany**, a moment when a character experiences a sudden moment of illumination or revelation, especially as the result of perceiving a commonplace object in a new way or through a new context. Esperanza in "The House on Mango Street" might be said to experience an epiphany when the nun points to her third-floor apartment and says, "You live *there?*" (para. 9). Suddenly she realizes how other people regard her house, what the house says about her and her family, how much she needs to have a "real house" to improve her sense of self-worth and identity.

- **Gaps.** A literary work can't (and shouldn't) include everything that happens during the series of events it is relating—whatever is not significant to the action typically is left out. In "Love in L.A." we hear only about a few minutes in Jake's day. The rest is left out: what time he got up, whether he had breakfast, where he is going. These details may be important in Jake's larger life, but because they are not relevant to his encounter with Mariana, they do not concern readers. For fiction writers, decisions about what to leave out are important to the story's structure, as important as decisions about what to include.

- Some intentional gaps are omissions of insignificant details and occur only to avoid cluttering the story with irrelevancies. For example, we aren't told the circumstances under which the family in "Daughter of Invention" (p. 10) left the Dominican Republic because it is not important to what this story focuses on.

- Some intentional gaps omit significant details and are used as a way of getting readers actively involved. Mystery and detective stories always create gaps (Who did it? Why?) within their structure. Part of the enjoyment of reading stories is using our imaginations to supply missing details or connecting links, anticipating what may be ahead, and revising our earlier anticipations in light of what we find out later.

- Some intentional gaps omit details that could distract us from what is more important. For example, "Daughter of Invention" deliberately does not include the full text of the speech the daughter wrote, not because it is insignificant, but because the author wants the reader to concentrate on the father's reaction. The author gives us enough hints to enable us to imagine what it says, but giving the speech itself would lead us to focus on it instead of on the father.

- Some gaps, however, are unintentional — for example, not including women in a particular story or relegating them to minor roles. Such gaps are significant nonetheless. What the author does *not* think about is part of her or his idea framework, as much as what she or he consciously does think about. Paying attention not just to what is there but also to what is not there requires alert, active involvement in a *process*. Reading this way can feel demanding, but the rewards are well worth the effort.

Concluding the Action

ENDING A STORY   A story must end, of course — it can't go on forever. But it also can't just stop. The difference between just stopping and an effective ending is that the latter gives a sense of wholeness and leaves the reader satisfied or satisfyingly unsatisfied. One of the big differences between fiction and real life is that life carries on after a "big event," while the series of events in a fictional plot reach a terminal point, the conflicts around which it was shaped are resolved (or shown to be unresolvable), and the story ends.

The last paragraph of "Love in L.A," for example, has a feeling of finality: The lives of Jake and Mariana do not end, but nothing that could follow would be relevant to the story of their encounter under the Alvarado Street overpass. You, as an active reader, might imagine Mariana's pained and disappointed reaction and her father's furious response when they find out that all the information Jake gave her was false, which might then form an important part of how you feel about Jake's actions in the final analysis. Jake and Mariana's personal encounter could have touched Jake and made a difference in his life, but the last sentence shows that it didn't. The end takes us back to the beginning and the daydreams he chooses over reality.

DÉNOUEMENT   The French term **dénouement** is often used in discussing the ending of a story. It literally means "unknotting," the untying of the threads that are tangled and knotted, the solution of the mysteries, the explanation of the secrets and misunderstandings. An ending, in addition to unknotting tangles, often ties up the loose ends, leaving us with a sense of finality or a momentary stay against ordinary chaos. That doesn't mean that everything turns out happily—some stories have unresolved, unhappy endings. But it does mean that the questions and problems we have been involved with, if not solved or even resolved, at least are adequately accounted for. We know all that we need to know to comprehend and reflect on the story as a whole.

READING FOR CHARACTER

Important as the events in a story are, however, they cannot be separated from the people involved in the events who carry out the actions. **Characters**, the created persons who appear or are referred to in narratives and dramas (and at times in poems), are in many cases the aspect that is of greatest appeal and interest in the work. Literature offers us the opportunity to learn about, and even imaginatively to enter, the lives of people we would otherwise never get close to, at least not close enough to understand their lives and situations to a significant extent and to sympathize, or even empathize, with them.

When we meet such people in literature, we want to know what they are like, what makes them tick, how they deal with the situations and relationships they encounter. **Characterization** refers to the methods and techniques an author uses to represent people and to enable us to know and relate to them. As we read a work of fiction, we understand characters more fully and accurately if we pay attention to the means by which we attain our knowledge, to the kind of techniques through which they are brought to life in the story.

Techniques of Characterization

Here are some of the most important means of characterization to pay attention to. They can appear individually or in a variety of combinations.

TELLING   In the most direct method of characterization, we are simply told what the characters are like, all at once as they are first introduced or bit by bit as they reappear in the story. A good example of this is Joyce Carol Oates's story "Where Are You Going, Where Have You Been?" (p. 481). The narrator begins by giving us information we need to know about the main character: "Her name was Connie. She was fifteen and she had a quick, nervous giggling habit of craning her neck to glance into mirrors or checking other people's faces to make sure her own was all right." Telling about a character doesn't have to be as direct as that. The narrator of "Love in L.A." doesn't tell us about Jake's character the way Oates's narrator does about Connie, but his choice of words at times can serve the same purpose: The use of *slouched* in the opening sentence and *lied* in paragraph 31, for example, gives us direct insight into Jake's character.

SHOWING   What a character is like can come out through the character's actions, which may be presented without interpretive comment, leaving the reader to draw her or his own conclusions. What Jake does in response to hitting Mariana's car shows the kind of person he is. Aside from suggesting through word choice some reservations about Jake, the narrator does not explicitly evaluate his behavior. We—as active readers—are left to figure out what he is like and decide what we think and feel about him.

DIALOGUE   A great deal can be revealed about a character by what she or he says: **dialogue** (conversation between characters) is an important characterization technique. We gain valuable insights into Jake when he says, "You're not married, are you? Not that that would matter that much to me. I'm an openminded kinda guy" (para. 16) and "I left my wallet in the pants I was wearing last night" (20) and that he'd "[b]een in a couple of movies" (31). What a character is like can also be brought out by having other characters say things about her or him. However, it's important to keep in mind that what characters say depends on how they relate to the characters they are talking about. What is said may need to be taken with a grain or a pound of salt because of a character's bias for or against the character being discussed.

ENTERING A CHARACTER'S MIND   What a character is like can be revealed through her or his thoughts and feelings. The author takes us into a character's mind using techniques such as a partially or wholly omniscient narrator (used in "Love in L.A." to show what goes on in Jake's mind through daydreams, thoughts, and observations), stream of consciousness, and interior monologue. (These techniques will be discussed further in Chapter 6.)

NAMING   In some cases, the names of characters reveal aspects of what they are like. Henry Fielding, one of the first English novelists, names one of his characters Squire Allworthy to reveal how admirable he is in every respect. In other cases, Fielding uses **allusions** to the Bible in naming a character: Parson Abraham Adams, for example, is a man of great faith (like the biblical Abraham) but is also a person as innocent and trusting as the Adam of Genesis chapters 2–3. In many cases, however, names are simply names, yet somehow they invariably sound right (think of David Copperfield or Huckleberry Finn). And the name should fit the character: Would "Love in L.A." have a different feel if the main character were named "Harold" instead of "Jake"?

Categories of Characterization

Our understanding and appreciation of characters in a story are enhanced when we are alert to the varying degrees of their complexity and importance. This analysis is often more intricate but can be very rewarding and can lead to an effective paper if you are asked to write one. Here are some of the ways those varying degrees of character complexity are indicated, along with the terminology widely used for discussing them.

ROUND/FLAT   The novelist E. M. Forster used the terms *flat* and *round* to illustrate differences in complexity.

- **Round characters** are complex and sometimes even challenging to understand. We are offered many sides and facets of their lives and personalities and we may need to reconcile what seem to be incompatible ideas or behaviors. Round characters often are **dynamic**, shown as changing and growing because of what happens to them. But they also can be **static**, not shown as changing, though they may be described in such rich detail that we have a clear sense of how they would, or will, change, even though we don't see it happening. We are shown enough about Henry in "The Red Convertible" (p. 126) for his character to be rounded out; the story shows the changes in him before he goes to Vietnam and after he returns, even though we do not see the changes actually taking place.
- **Flat characters** are generally developed less fully than round, or dynamic, characters. Usually they are static and are represented through only one or two main features or aspects. Unlike round characters, they often can be summed up in a sentence or two. If these one or two traits are developed in considerable detail, the characters may be very interesting. But we can't come to know them as thoroughly and in as much depth as characters who are depicted with more complexity or developed more fully and shown as ones who change and grow throughout the story. Jake and Mariana in "Love in L.A." are flat characters—a thorough-going cad and a rather gullible innocent. That's all they need to be and all that could be expected in such a short, short story.

MAJOR/MINOR   Most major characters in a story or play are round characters, while minor characters are usually flat. Minor characters are at times

stock characters, stereotypes easily recognized by readers or audiences because of their frequent use, such as the absent-minded professor, the evil stepmother, the nerdy computer geek, or the smart but quiet detective or police sergeant. Use of flat characters is not necessarily "bad writing." Some excellent fiction writers create central characters who are flat but are described in such rich detail that they come fully to life. There isn't time in most short stories to develop more than one character in a rounded way, perhaps not even one. Even in a novel or play, the reader might find it too much to handle if every character were rounded out fully.

PROTAGONIST/ANTAGONIST   The terms *protagonist* and *antagonist* are often used to define relationships between characters. The **protagonist** is the central character in a work (the older term **hero** seems less useful because the central character doesn't have to be "heroic"). The **antagonist** is the character, force, or collected forces opposed to the protagonist that give rise to the central conflict of the work—the rival, opponent, or enemy of the protagonist (the older term *villain* works less well because the antagonist isn't always evil and isn't always a person). In the stories included in this chapter, the grandmother is the protagonist of "A Good Man Is Hard to Find"; The Misfit is the antagonist. Henry is the protagonist of "The Red Convertible"; white society and the world outside the reservation are the antagonists.

Qualities of Characterization

MOTIVATED   After you know what the characters are like, you will want to understand why they do the things they do, why they make the kinds of decisions and choices they do. This important aspect of characterization involves **motivation**, conveying the reasons, explanations, or justifications behind a character's behavior. Motivation in fiction usually grows out of a sense of what a character deeply wants or desires and how that leads the character to react in a specific situation. For example, Jake clearly finds Mariana attractive, but his desire to avoid paying the costs of the accident is a stronger motivation than his desire to pursue a relationship with her.

CONSISTENT   A great deal is revealed about characters also by the *way* they handle situations—especially difficult, problematic, or tragic situations or relationships. For characters to be plausible, there must be consistency between their motivations and their actions and consistency in the way they deal with circumstances. If they respond to a situation one way at one time and differently at another, there should be clear reasons for the difference (their inconsistency must be understandable and believable). The fact that Jake has license plates from a junker is

You can further explore plot and characters, including using interactive exercises, with VirtuaLit Fiction at bedfordstmartins.com/rewritinglit.

> ☑ **CHECKLIST on Reading for Plot and Character**
>
> ❏ Notice the structuring of plot:
>
> - its strategies for starting, developing, and ending the action
> - its handling of suspense, foreshadowing, repetition, climax, and in some cases epiphany
> - its decisions about what to include and what to leave out (gaps)
>
> ❏ Look for conflicts — physical, social, internal — and use them as a way to get into the story and to explore its complexity.
>
> ❏ Be attentive to the methods of characterization: Notice what you are told and shown; listen to what characters say and to what other characters say about them; watch what goes on in characters' minds; and consider the way they are named.
>
> ❏ Consider how fully characters are developed: whether they are round or flat, whether they change or stay pretty much the same.

consistent with his giving Mariana false information about insurance, and together they reveal a great deal about him as a character.

FURTHER READING

Below are two stories, both about young persons encountering new situations that change their lives. As you read and then think back on them, try applying what you have learned in this chapter about plot and character.

ENTRY POINTS   The first is a story about two brothers, Lyman and Henry, and a car that comes to epitomize their love for each other. It was written by Louise Erdrich, who grew up near the Turtle Mountain Reservation and is a member of the Turtle Mountain Band of Chippewa. Many of the place names in the story can be found on maps of North and South Dakota.

Pay attention to how the story handles plot — which details the author includes, how these details are arranged, and how they relate to each other and work together to convey a unified effect. Note the story's handling of characters — what they are like and how you come to know them.

Louise Erdrich b. 1954

The Red Convertible   [1984]

I was the first one to drive a convertible on my reservation. And of course it was red, a red Olds. I owned that car along with my brother Henry Junior. We owned it together until his boots filled with water on a windy night and he bought out my share. Now Henry owns the whole car, and his younger brother Lyman (that's myself), Lyman walks everywhere he goes.

How did I earn enough money to buy my share in the first place? My one talent was I could always make money. I had a touch for it, unusual in a Chippewa. From the first I was different that way, and everyone recognized it. I was the only kid they let in the American Legion Hall to shine shoes, for example, and one Christmas I sold spiritual bouquets for the mission door to door. The nuns let me keep a percentage. Once I started, it seemed the more money I made the easier the money came. Everyone encouraged it. When I was fifteen I got a job washing dishes at the Joliet Café, and that was where my first big break happened.

APPROACHING THE AUTHOR

Louise Erdrich held jobs as a lifeguard, waitress, poetry teacher at prisons, truck weigher on the interstate, and construction-flag signaler before she became an editor for the *Circle,* a Boston Indian Council newspaper. For more about her, see page 1383.

It wasn't long before I was promoted to busing tables, and then the short-order cook quit and I was hired to take her place. No sooner than you know it I was managing the Joliet. The rest is history. I went on managing. I soon became part owner, and of course there was no stopping me then. It wasn't long before the whole thing was mine.

After I'd owned the Joliet for one year, it blew over in the worst tornado ever seen around here. The whole operation was smashed to bits. A total loss. The fryalator was up in a tree, the grill torn in half like it was paper. I was only sixteen. I had it all in my mother's name, and I lost it quick, but before I lost it I had every one of my relatives, and their relatives, to dinner, and I also bought that red Olds I mentioned, along with Henry.

The first time we saw it! I'll tell you when we first saw it. We had gotten   5 a ride up to Winnipeg, and both of us had money. Don't ask me why, because we never mentioned a car or anything, we just had all our money. Mine was cash, a big bankroll from the Joliet's insurance. Henry had two checks—a week's extra pay for being laid off, and his regular check from the Jewel Bearing Plant.

We were walking down Portage anyway, seeing the sights, when we saw it. There it was, parked, large as life. Really as *if* it was alive. I thought of the word *repose*, because the car wasn't simply stopped, parked, or whatever. That car reposed, calm and gleaming, a FOR SALE sign in its left front window. Then, before we had thought it over at all, the car belonged to us and our pockets were empty. We had just enough money for gas back home.

We went places in that car, me and Henry. We took off driving all one whole summer. We started off toward the Little Knife River and Mandaree in Fort Berthold and then we found ourselves down in Wakpala somehow, and then suddenly we were over in Montana on the Rocky Boy, and yet the summer was not even half over. Some people hang on to details when they travel, but we didn't let them bother us and just lived our everyday lives here to there.

I do remember this one place with willows. I remember I laid under those trees and it was comfortable. So comfortable. The branches bent down all around me like a tent or a stable. And quiet, it was quiet, even though there was a pow-wow close enough so I could see it going on. The air was not too still, not too windy either. When the dust rises up and hangs in the air around the dancers like that, I feel good. Henry was asleep with his arms thrown wide. Later on, he woke up and we started driving again. We were somewhere in Montana, or maybe on the Blood Reserve — it could have been anywhere. Anyway it was where we met the girl.

All her hair was in buns around her ears, that's the first thing I noticed about her. She was posed alongside the road with her arm out, so we stopped. That girl was short, so short her lumber shirt looked comical on her, like a nightgown. She had jeans on and fancy moccasins and she carried a little suitcase.

"Hop on in," says Henry. So she climbs in between us.   10

"We'll take you home," I says. "Where do you live?"

"Chicken," she says.

"Where the hell's that?" I ask her.

"Alaska."

"Okay," says Henry, and we drive.   15

We got up there and never wanted to leave. The sun doesn't truly set there in summer, and the night is more a soft dusk. You might doze off, sometimes, but before you know it you're up again, like an animal in nature. You never feel like you have to sleep hard or put away the world. And things would grow up there. One day just dirt or moss, the next day flowers and long grass. The girl's name was Susy. Her family really took to us. They fed us and put us up. We had our own tent to live in by their house, and the kids would be in and out of there all day and night. They couldn't get over me and Henry being brothers, we looked so different. We told them we knew we had the same mother, anyway.

One night Susy came in to visit us. We sat around in the tent talking of this and that. The season was changing. It was getting darker by that time, and the cold was even getting just a little mean. I told her it was time for us to go. She stood up on a chair.

"You never seen my hair," Susy said.

That was true. She was standing on a chair, but still, when she unclipped her buns the hair reached all the way to the ground. Our eyes opened. You couldn't tell how much hair she had when it was rolled up so neatly. Then my brother Henry did something funny. He went up to the chair and said, "Jump on my shoulders." So she did that, and her hair reached down past his waist, and he started twirling, this way and that, so her hair was flung out from side to side.

"I always wondered what it was like to have long pretty hair," Henry says.   20 Well we laughed. It was a funny sight, the way he did it. The next morning we got up and took leave of those people.

On to greener pastures, as they say. It was down through Spokane and across Idaho then Montana and very soon we were racing the weather right along under the Canadian border through Columbus, Des Lacs, and then we were in Bottineau County and soon home. We'd made most of the trip, that summer, without putting up the car hood at all. We got home just in time, it turned out, for the army to remember Henry had signed up to join it.

I don't wonder that the army was so glad to get my brother that they turned him into a Marine. He was built like a brick outhouse anyway. We liked to tease him that they really wanted him for his Indian nose. He had a nose big and sharp as a hatchet, like the nose on Red Tomahawk, the Indian who killed Sitting Bull, whose profile is on signs all along the North Dakota highways. Henry went off to training camp, came home once during Christmas, then the next thing you know we got an overseas letter from him. It was 1970, and he said he was stationed up in the northern hill country. Whereabouts I did not know. He wasn't such a hot letter writer, and only got off two before the enemy caught him. I could never keep it straight, which direction those good Vietnam soldiers were from.

I wrote him back several times, even though I didn't know if those letters would get through. I kept him informed all about the car. Most of the time I had it up on blocks in the yard or half taken apart, because that long trip did a hard job on it under the hood.

I always had good luck with numbers, and never worried about the draft myself. I never even had to think about what my number was.° But Henry was never lucky in the same way as me. It was at least three years before Henry came home. By then I guess the whole war was solved in the government's mind, but for him it would keep on going. In those years I'd put his car into almost perfect shape. I always thought of it as his car while he was gone, even though when he left he said, "Now it's yours," and threw me his key.

---

what my number was: A lottery system based on birthdays was used for the military draft from 1970 until 1973. Capsules containing the 365 days of the year were prepared and the days listed in the order drawn. Men like Henry, with birthdays drawn early (approximately the upper third), were certain to be called up for service, while those whose birthdays came in the bottom third (like Lyman) were likely not to be needed. In 1973, the draft ended and the United States converted to an all-volunteer military.

"Thanks for the extra key," I'd said. "I'll put it up in your drawer just in case 25
I need it." He laughed.

When he came home, though, Henry was very different, and I'll say this:
the change was no good. You could hardly expect him to change for the better,
I know. But he was quiet, so quiet, and never comfortable sitting still anywhere
but always up and moving around. I thought back to times we'd sat still for
whole afternoons, never moving a muscle, just shifting our weight along the
ground, talking to whoever sat with us, watching things. He'd always had a joke,
then, too, and now you couldn't get him to laugh, or when he did it was more
the sound of a man choking, a sound that stopped up the throats of other
people around him. They got to leaving him alone most of the time, and I didn't
blame them. It was a fact: Henry was jumpy and mean.

I'd bought a color TV set for my mom and the rest of us while Henry was
away. Money still came very easy. I was sorry I'd ever bought it though, because
of Henry. I was also sorry I'd bought color, because with black-and-white the
pictures seem older and farther away. But what are you going to do? He sat in
front of it, watching it, and that was the only time he was completely still. But
it was the kind of stillness that you see in a rabbit when it freezes and before it
will bolt. He was not easy. He sat in his chair gripping the armrests with all his
might, as if the chair itself was moving at a high speed and if he let go at all he
would rocket forward and maybe crash right through the set.

Once I was in the room watching TV with Henry and I heard his teeth click
at something. I looked over, and he'd bitten through his lip. Blood was going
down his chin. I tell you right then I wanted to smash that tube to pieces. I went
over to it but Henry must have known what I was up to. He rushed from his
chair and shoved me out of the way, against the wall. I told myself he didn't
know what he was doing.

My mom came in, turned the set off real quiet, and told us she had made
something for supper. So we went and sat down. There was still blood going
down Henry's chin, but he didn't notice it and no one said anything, even
though every time he took a bite of his bread his blood fell onto it until he was
eating his own blood mixed in with the food.

While Henry was not around we talked about what was going to happen to 30
him. There were no Indian doctors on the reservation, and my mom couldn't
come around to trusting the old man, Moses Pillager, because he courted her long
ago and was jealous of her husbands. He might take revenge through her son. We
were afraid that if we brought Henry to a regular hospital they would keep him.

"They don't fix them in those places," Mom said; "they just give them drugs."

"We wouldn't get him there in the first place," I agreed, "so let's just forget
about it."

Then I thought about the car.

Henry had not even looked at the car since he'd gotten home, though like
I said, it was in tip-top condition and ready to drive. I thought the car might

bring the old Henry back somehow. So I bided my time and waited for my
chance to interest him in the vehicle.

One night Henry was off somewhere. I took myself a hammer. I went out   35
to that car and I did a number on its underside. Whacked it up. Bent the tail
pipe double. Ripped the muffler loose. By the time I was done with the car it
looked worse than any typical Indian car that has been driven all its life on
reservation roads, which they always say are like government promises—full of
holes. It just about hurt me, I'll tell you that! I threw dirt in the carburetor and
I ripped all the electric tape off the seats. I made it look just as beat up as I
could. Then I sat back and waited for Henry to find it.

Still, it took him over a month. That was all right, because it was just getting
warm enough, not melting, but warm enough to work outside.

"Lyman," he says, walking in one day, "that red car looks like shit."

"Well it's old," I says. "You got to expect that."

"No way!" says Henry. "That car's a classic! But you went and ran the piss
right out of it, Lyman, and you know it don't deserve that. I kept that car in
A-one shape. You don't remember. You're too young. But when I left, that car
was running like a watch. Now I don't even know if I can get it to start again,
let alone get it anywhere near its old condition."

"Well you try," I said, like I was getting mad, "but I say it's a piece of junk."   40

Then I walked out before he could realize I knew he'd strung together more
than six words at once.

After that I thought he'd freeze himself to death working on that car. He
was out there all day, and at night he rigged up a little lamp, ran a cord out the
window, and had himself some light to see by while he worked. He was better
than he had been before, but that's still not saying much. It was easier for him
to do the things the rest of us did. He ate more slowly and didn't jump up and
down during the meal to get this or that or look out the window. I put my hand
in the back of the TV set, I admit, and fiddled around with it good, so that it
was almost impossible now to get a clear picture. He didn't look at it very often
anyway. He was always out with that car or going off to get parts for it. By the
time it was really melting outside, he had it fixed.

I had been feeling down in the dumps about Henry around this time. We had
always been together before. Henry and Lyman. But he was such a loner now that
I didn't know how to take it. So I jumped at the chance one day when Henry seemed
friendly. It's not that he smiled or anything. He just said, "Let's take that old shitbox
for a spin." Just the way he said it made me think he could be coming around.

We went out to the car. It was spring. The sun was shining very bright. My
only sister, Bonita, who was just eleven years old, came out and made us stand
together for a picture. Henry leaned his elbow on the red car's windshield, and he
took his other arm and put it over my shoulder, very carefully, as though it was
heavy for him to lift and he didn't want to bring the weight down all at once.

"Smile," Bonita said, and he did.   45

That picture. I never look at it anymore. A few months ago, I don't know why, I got his picture out and tacked it on the wall. I felt good about Henry at the time, close to him. I felt good having his picture on the wall, until one night when I was looking at television. I was a little drunk and stoned. I looked up at the wall and Henry was staring at me. I don't know what it was, but his smile had changed, or maybe it was gone. All I know is I couldn't stay in the same room with that picture. I was shaking. I got up, closed the door, and went into the kitchen. A little later my friend Ray came over and we both went back into that room. We put the picture in a brown bag, folded the bag over and over tightly, then put it way back in a closet.

I still see that picture now, as if it tugs at me, whenever I pass that closet door. The picture is very clear in my mind. It was so sunny that day Henry had to squint against the glare. Or maybe the camera Bonita held flashed like a mirror, blinding him, before she snapped the picture. My face is right out in the sun, big and round. But he might have drawn back, because the shadows on his face are deep as holes. There are two shadows curved like little hooks around the ends of his smile, as if to frame it and try to keep it there — that one, first smile that looked like it might have hurt his face. He has his field jacket on and the worn-in clothes he'd come back in and kept wearing ever since. After Bonita took the picture, she went into the house and we got into the car. There was a full cooler in the trunk. We started off, east, toward Pembina and the Red River because Henry said he wanted to see the high water.

The trip over there was beautiful. When everything starts changing, drying up, clearing off, you feel like your whole life is starting. Henry felt it, too. The top was down and the car hummed like a top. He'd really put it back in shape, even the tape on the seats was very carefully put down and glued back in layers. It's not that he smiled again or even joked, but his face looked to me as if it was clear, more peaceful. It looked as though he wasn't thinking of anything in particular except the bare fields and windbreaks and houses we were passing.

The river was high and full of winter trash when we got there. The sun was still out, but it was colder by the river. There were still little clumps of dirty snow here and there on the banks. The water hadn't gone over the banks yet, but it would, you could tell. It was just at its limit, hard swollen, glossy like an old gray scar. We made ourselves a fire, and we sat down and watched the current go. As I watched it I felt something squeezing inside me and tightening and trying to let go all at the same time. I knew I was not just feeling it myself; I knew I was feeling what Henry was going through at that moment. Except that I couldn't stand it, the closing and opening. I jumped to my feet. I took Henry by the shoulders and I started shaking him. "Wake up," I says, "wake up, wake up, wake up!" I didn't know what had come over me. I sat down beside him again.

His face was totally white and hard. Then it broke, like stones break all of 50 a sudden when water boils up inside them.

"I know it," he says. "I know it. I can't help it. It's no use."

We start talking. He said he knew what I'd done with the car. It was obvious it had been whacked out of shape and not just neglected. He said he wanted to give the car to me for good now, it was no use. He said he'd fixed it just to give it back and I should take it.

"No way," I says. "I don't want it."

"That's okay," he says, "you take it."

"I don't want it, though," I says back to him, and then to emphasize, just to emphasize, you understand, I touch his shoulder. He slaps my hand off.

"Take that car," he says.

"No," I say. "Make me," I say, and then he grabs my jacket and rips the arm loose. That jacket is a class act, suede with tags and zippers. I push Henry backwards, off the log. He jumps up and bowls me over. We go down in a clinch and come up swinging hard, for all we're worth, with our fists. He socks my jaw so hard I feel like it swings loose. Then I'm at his rib cage and land a good one under his chin so his head snaps back. He's dazzled. He looks at me and I look at him and then his eyes are full of tears and blood and at first I think he's crying. But no, he's laughing. "Ha! Ha!" he says. "Ha! Ha! Take good care of it."

"Okay," I says. "Okay, no problem. Ha! Ha!"

I can't help it, and I start laughing, too. My face feels fat and strange, and after a while I get a beer from the cooler in the trunk, and when I hand it to Henry he takes his shirt and wipes my germs off. "Hoof-and-mouth disease," he says. For some reason this cracks me up, and so we're really laughing for a while, and then we drink all the rest of the beers one by one and throw them in the river and see how far, how fast, the current takes them before they fill up and sink.

"You want to go on back?" I ask after a while. "Maybe we could snag a couple nice Kashpaw girls."

He says nothing. But I can tell his mood is turning again.

"They're all crazy, the girls up here, every damn one of them."

"You're crazy too," I say, to jolly him up. "Crazy Lamartine boys!"

He looks as though he will take this wrong at first. His face twists, then clears, and he jumps up on his feet. "That's right!" he says. "Crazier 'n hell. Crazy Indians!"

I think it's the old Henry again. He throws off his jacket and starts springing his legs up from the knees like a fancy dancer.° He's down doing something between a grass dance and a bunny hop, no kind of dance I ever saw before, but neither has anyone else on all this green growing earth. He's wild. He wants to pitch whoopee! He's up and at me and all over. All this time I'm laughing so hard, so hard my belly is getting tied up in a knot.

"Got to cool me off!" he shouts all of a sudden. Then he runs over to the river and jumps in.

---

fancy dancer: A person performing (often in contests) a style of Native American dance based on traditional and grass dances but done in brilliant costumes, at rapid speeds, with fancy footwork, acrobatic steps, and varied body movements.

There's boards and other things in the current. It's so high. No sound comes from the river after the splash he makes, so I run right over. I look around. It's getting dark. I see he's halfway across the water already, and I know he didn't swim there but the current took him. It's far. I hear his voice, though, very clearly across it.

"My boots are filling," he says.

He says this in a normal voice, like he just noticed and he doesn't know what to think of it. Then he's gone. A branch comes by. Another branch. And I go in.

By the time I get out of the river, off the snag I pulled myself onto, the 70 sun is down. I walk back to the car, turn on the high beams, and drive it up the bank. I put it in first gear and then I take my foot off the clutch. I get out, close the door, and watch it plow softly into the water. The headlights reach in as they go down, searching, still lighted even after the water swirls over the back end. I wait. The wires short out. It is all finally dark. And then there is only the water, the sound of it going and running and going and running and running.

APPROACHING THE READING

1. Outline the plot of "The Red Convertible." Then comment on the way it starts, the way it builds in the middle (what kinds of conflicts appear, how the material is arranged), and the way it ends. What effects are achieved through the way the plot is organized and developed?

2. Think about what is left out and what is added or emphasized in plotting the story. What gaps are left in the story? How do they force you to become actively involved as a reader? What does the inclusion of the episodes about Henry and Lyman's travels—the place under the willows where they rested and taking Susy home to Alaska—contribute to the story? What would be lost if those details were not there?

3. Describe what the main characters are like and how we come to know them (by telling? by showing? by dialogue? by entering their minds? by the significance of their names?). Are they dynamic characters or static ones? To what extent does what we know about Henry depend on what we know about Lyman, and what difference does that make?

4. Why does Henry jump into the river? Does he intend to drown, or is it accidental? In what ways does he change in the story, and what things cause him to change? Why does Lyman roll the car into the river?

ENTRY POINTS   Here is another story that involves cars, but it's a story with a very different style and tone. Flannery O'Connor lived in Georgia and wrote about the South. Her short stories are carefully crafted, with crisp humor. They often focus on unappealing characters who are redeemed by grace, reflecting the influence of her Catholic faith. The first time you read the story, let your emotions get fully involved with what happens. O'Connor is going to take you on an emotional roller coaster.

Flannery O'Connor 1925–1964

A Good Man Is Hard to Find   [1955]

The grandmother didn't want to go to Florida. She wanted to visit some of her connections in east Tennessee and she was seizing at every chance to change Bailey's mind. Bailey was the son she lived with, her only boy. He was sitting on the edge of his chair at the table, bent over the orange sports section of the *Journal*. "Now look here, Bailey," she said, "see here, read this," and she stood with one hand on her thin hip and the other rattling the newspaper at his bald head. "Here this fellow that calls himself The Misfit is aloose from the Federal Pen and headed toward Florida and you read here what it says he did to these people. Just you read it. I wouldn't take my children in any direction with a criminal like that aloose in it. I couldn't answer to my conscience if I did."

> **APPROACHING THE AUTHOR**
>
> When **Flannery O'Connor** was five years old, she taught her pet chicken to walk backward. The Pathe Newsreel Company filmed O'Connor and her chicken and played the reel in movie theaters across the country in 1932.
>
> For more about her, see page 1404.

Bailey didn't look up from his reading so she wheeled around then and faced the children's mother, a young woman in slacks, whose face was as broad and innocent as a cabbage and was tied around with a green head-kerchief that had two points on the top like rabbit's ears. She was sitting on the sofa, feeding the baby his apricots out of a jar. "The children have been to Florida before," the old lady said. "You all ought to take them somewhere else for a change so they would see different parts of the world and be broad. They never have been to east Tennessee."

The children's mother didn't seem to hear her but the eight-year-old boy, John Wesley, a stocky child with glasses, said, "If you don't want to go to Florida, why dontcha stay at home?" He and the little girl, June Star, were reading the funny papers on the floor.

"She wouldn't stay at home to be queen for a day,"° June Star said without raising her yellow head.

Queen for a day: Alluding to the American radio (1945–1957) and television (1956–1964, 1969–1970) show on which several women experiencing difficult circumstances competed, by telling their stories winsomely, to be treated like royalty for a day.

"Yes and what would you do if this fellow, The Misfit, caught you?" the ⁵ grandmother asked.

"I'd smack his face," John Wesley said.

"She wouldn't stay at home for a million bucks," June Star said. "Afraid she'd miss something. She has to go everywhere we go."

"All right, Miss," the grandmother said. "Just remember that the next time you want me to curl your hair."

June Star said her hair was naturally curly.

The next morning the grandmother was the first one in the car, ready to ¹⁰ go. She had her big black valise that looked like the head of a hippopotamus in one corner, and underneath it she was hiding a basket with Pitty Sing, the cat, in it. She didn't intend for the cat to be left alone in the house for three days because he would miss her too much and she was afraid he might brush against one of the gas burners and accidentally asphyxiate himself. Her son, Bailey, didn't like to arrive at a motel with a cat.

She sat in the middle of the back seat with John Wesley and June Star on either side of her. Bailey and the children's mother and the baby sat in front and they left Atlanta at eight forty-five with the mileage on the car at 55890. The grandmother wrote this down because she thought it would be interesting to say how many miles they had been when they got back. It took them twenty minutes to reach the outskirts of the city.

The old lady settled herself comfortably, removing her white cotton gloves and putting them up with her purse on the shelf in front of the back window. The children's mother still had on slacks and still had her head tied up in a green kerchief, but the grandmother had on a navy blue straw sailor hat with a bunch of white violets on the brim and a navy blue dress with a small white dot in the print. Her collars and cuffs were white organdy trimmed with lace and at her neckline she had pinned a purple spray of cloth violets containing a sachet. In case of an accident, anyone seeing her dead on the highway would know at once that she was a lady.

She said she thought it was going to be a good day for driving, neither too hot nor too cold, and she cautioned Bailey that the speed limit was fifty-five miles an hour and that the patrolmen hid themselves behind billboards and small clumps of trees and sped out after you before you had a chance to slow down. She pointed out interesting details of the scenery: Stone Mountain; the blue granite that in some places came up to both sides of the highway; the brilliant red clay banks slightly streaked with purple; and the various crops that made rows of green lace-work on the ground. The trees were full of silver-white sunlight and the meanest of them sparkled. The children were reading comic magazines and their mother had gone back to sleep.

"Let's go through Georgia fast so we won't have to look at it much," John Wesley said.

"If I were a little boy," said the grandmother, "I wouldn't talk about my ¹⁵ native state that way. Tennessee has the mountains and Georgia has the hills."

"Tennessee is just a hillbilly dumping ground," John Wesley said, "and Georgia is a lousy state too."

"You said it," June Star said.

"In my time," said the grandmother, folding her thin veined fingers, "children were more respectful of their native states and their parents and everything else. People did right then. Oh look at the cute little pickaninny!" she said and pointed to a Negro child standing in the door of a shack. "Wouldn't that make a picture, now?" she asked and they all turned and looked at the little Negro out of the back window. He waved.

"He didn't have any britches on," June Star said.

"He probably didn't have any," the grandmother explained. "Little niggers 20 in the country don't have things like we do. If I could paint, I'd paint that picture," she said.

The children exchanged comic books.

The grandmother offered to hold the baby and the children's mother passed him over the front seat to her. She set him on her knee and bounced him and told him about the things they were passing. She rolled her eyes and screwed up her mouth and stuck her leathery thin face into his smooth bland one. Occasionally he gave her a faraway smile. They passed a large cotton field with five or six graves fenced in the middle of it, like a small island. "Look at the graveyard!" the grandmother said, pointing it out. "That was the old family burying ground. That belonged to the plantation."

"Where's the plantation?" John Wesley asked.

"Gone With the Wind,"° said the grandmother. "Ha. Ha."

When the children finished all the comic books they had brought, they 25 opened the lunch and ate it. The grandmother ate a peanut butter sandwich and an olive and would not let the children throw the box and the paper napkins out the window. When there was nothing else to do they played a game by choosing a cloud and making the other two guess what shape it suggested. John Wesley took one the shape of a cow and June Star guessed a cow and John Wesley said, no, an automobile, and June Star said he didn't play fair, and they began to slap each other over the grandmother.

The grandmother said she would tell them a story if they would keep quiet. When she told a story, she rolled her eyes and waved her head and was very dramatic. She said once when she was a maiden lady she had been courted by a Mr. Edgar Atkins Teagarden from Jasper, Georgia. She said he was a very good-looking man and a gentleman and that he brought her a watermelon every Saturday afternoon with his initials cut in it, E. A. T. Well, one Saturday, she said, Mr. Teagarden brought the watermelon and there was nobody at home and he left it on the front porch and returned in his buggy to Jasper, but she never got the watermelon, she said, because a nigger boy ate it when he saw the initials, E. A. T.! This story tickled John Wesley's funny bone and he giggled and

---

Gone With the Wind: The title of the best-selling 1936 novel by Margaret Mitchell dealing with the period of the American Civil War and the Reconstruction, made into an Academy Award–winning film in 1939.

giggled but June Star didn't think it was any good. She said she wouldn't marry a man that just brought her a watermelon on Saturday. The grandmother said she would have done well to marry Mr. Teagarden because he was a gentleman and had bought Coca-Cola stock when it first came out and that he had died only a few years ago, a very wealthy man.

They stopped at The Tower for barbecued sandwiches. The Tower was a part stucco and part wood filling station and dance hall set in a clearing outside of Timothy. A fat man named Red Sammy Butts ran it and there were signs stuck here and there on the building and for miles up and down the highway saying, TRY RED SAMMY'S FAMOUS BARBECUE. NONE LIKE FAMOUS RED SAMMY'S! RED SAM! THE FAT BOY WITH THE HAPPY LAUGH. A VETERAN! RED SAMMY'S YOUR MAN!

Red Sammy was lying on the bare ground outside The Tower with his head under a truck while a gray monkey about a foot high, chained to a small china-berry tree, chattered nearby. The monkey sprang back into the tree and got on the highest limb as soon as he saw the children jump out of the car and run toward him.

Inside, The Tower was a long dark room with a counter at one end and tables at the other and dancing space in the middle. They all sat down at a board table next to the nickelodeon and Red Sam's wife, a tall burnt-brown woman with hair and eyes lighter than her skin, came and took their order. The children's mother put a dime in the machine and played "The Tennessee Waltz," and the grandmother said that tune always made her want to dance. She asked Bailey if he would like to dance but he only glared at her. He didn't have a naturally sunny disposition like she did and trips made him nervous. The grandmother's brown eyes were very bright. She swayed her head from side to side and pretended she was dancing in her chair. June Star said play something she could tap to so the children's mother put in another dime and played a fast number and June Star stepped out onto the dance floor and did her tap routine.

"Ain't she cute?" Red Sam's wife said, leaning over the counter. "Would you   30 like to come be my little girl?"

"No I certainly wouldn't," June Star said. "I wouldn't live in a broken-down place like this for a million bucks!" and she ran back to the table.

"Ain't she cute?" the woman repeated, stretching her mouth politely.

"Aren't you ashamed?" hissed the grandmother.

Red Sam came in and told his wife to quit lounging on the counter and hurry up with these people's order. His khaki trousers reached just to his hip bones and his stomach hung over them like a sack of meal swaying under his shirt. He came over and sat down at a table nearby and let out a combination sigh and yodel. "You can't win," he said. "You can't win," and he wiped his sweating red face off with a gray handkerchief. "These days you don't know who to trust," he said. "Ain't that the truth?"

"People are certainly not nice like they used to be," said the grandmother.   35

"Two fellers come in here last week," Red Sammy said, "driving a Chrysler. It was a old beat-up car but it was a good one and these boys looked all right to me. Said they worked at the mill and you know I let them fellers charge the gas they bought? Now why did I do that?"

"Because you're a good man!" the grandmother said at once.

"Yes'm, I suppose so," Red Sam said as if he were struck with this answer.

His wife brought the orders, carrying the five plates all at once without a tray, two in each hand and one balanced on her arm. "It isn't a soul in this green world of God's that you can trust," she said. "And I don't count nobody out of that, not nobody," she repeated, looking at Red Sammy.

"Did you read about that criminal, The Misfit, that's escaped?" asked the 40 grandmother.

"I wouldn't be a bit surprised if he didn't attact this place right here," said the woman. "If he hears about it being here, I wouldn't be none surprised to see him. If he hears it's two cent in the cash register, I wouldn't be a tall surprised if he . . ."

"That'll do," Red Sam said. "Go bring these people their Co'-Colas," and the woman went off to get the rest of the order.

"A good man is hard to find," Red Sammy said. "Everything is getting terrible. I remember the day you could go off and leave your screen door unlatched. Not no more."

He and the grandmother discussed better times. The old lady said that in her opinion Europe was entirely to blame for the way things were now. She said the way Europe acted you would think we were made of money and Red Sam said it was no use talking about it, she was exactly right. The children ran outside into the white sunlight and looked at the monkey in the lacy chinaberry tree. He was busy catching fleas on himself and biting each one carefully between his teeth as if it were a delicacy.

They drove off again into the hot afternoon. The grandmother took 45 cat naps and woke up every few minutes with her own snoring. Outside of Toombsboro she woke up and recalled an old plantation that she had visited in this neighborhood once when she was a young lady. She said the house had six white columns across the front and that there was an avenue of oaks leading up to it and two little wooden trellis arbors on either side in front where you sat down with your suitor after a stroll in the garden. She recalled exactly which road to turn off to get to it. She knew that Bailey would not be willing to lose any time looking at an old house, but the more she talked about it, the more she wanted to see it once again and find out if the little twin arbors were still standing. "There was a secret panel in this house," she said craftily, not telling the truth but wishing that she were, "and the story went that all the family silver was hidden in it when Sherman came through° but it was never found . . ."

Sherman came through: In November and December 1864, General William Tecumseh Sherman marched with over 60,000 Union soldiers from Atlanta to the Atlantic coast, pillaging and burning towns and farms along the way.

"Hey!" John Wesley said. "Let's go see it! We'll find it! We'll poke all the woodwork and find it! Who lives there? Where do you turn off at? Hey Pop, can't we turn off there?"

"We never have seen a house with a secret panel!" June Star shrieked. "Let's go to the house with the secret panel! Hey Pop, can't we go see the house with the secret panel!"

"It's not far from here, I know," the grandmother said. "It wouldn't take over twenty minutes."

Bailey was looking straight ahead. His jaw was as rigid as a horseshoe. "No," he said.

The children began to yell and scream that they wanted to see the house 50 with the secret panel. John Wesley kicked the back of the front seat and June Star hung over her mother's shoulder and whined desperately into her ear that they never had any fun even on their vacation, that they could never do what THEY wanted to do. The baby began to scream and John Wesley kicked the back of the seat so hard that his father could feel the blows in his kidney.

"All right!" he shouted and drew the car to a stop at the side of the road. "Will you all shut up? Will you all just shut up for one second? If you don't shut up, we won't go anywhere."

"It would be very educational for them," the grandmother murmured.

"All right," Bailey said, "but get this: this is the only time we're going to stop for anything like this. This is the one and only time."

"The dirt road that you have to turn down is about a mile back," the grandmother directed. "I marked it when we passed."

"A dirt road," Bailey groaned.   55

After they had turned around and were headed toward the dirt road, the grandmother recalled other points about the house, the beautiful glass over the front doorway and the candle-lamp in the hall. John Wesley said that the secret panel was probably in the fireplace.

"You can't go inside this house," Bailey said. "You don't know who lives there."

"While you all talk to the people in front, I'll run around behind and get in a window," John Wesley suggested.

"We'll all stay in the car," his mother said.

They turned onto the dirt road and the car raced roughly along in a swirl 60 of pink dust. The grandmother recalled the times when there were no paved roads and thirty miles was a day's journey. The dirt road was hilly and there were sudden washes in it and sharp curves on dangerous embankments. All at once they would be on a hill, looking down over the blue tops of trees for miles around, then the next minute, they would be in a red depression with the dust-coated trees looking down on them.

"This place had better turn up in a minute," Bailey said, "or I'm going to turn around."

The road looked as if no one had traveled on it in months.

"It's not much farther," the grandmother said and just as she said it, a horrible thought came to her. The thought was so embarrassing that she turned red in the face and her eyes dilated and her feet jumped up, upsetting her valise in the corner. The instant the valise moved, the newspaper top she had over the basket under it rose with a snarl and Pitty Sing, the cat, sprang onto Bailey's shoulder.

The children were thrown to the floor and their mother, clutching the baby, was thrown out the door onto the ground; the old lady was thrown into the front seat. The car turned over once and landed right-side-up in a gulch off the side of the road. Bailey remained in the driver's seat with the cat—gray-striped with a broad white face and an orange nose—clinging to his neck like a caterpillar.

As soon as the children saw they could move their arms and legs, they 65
scrambled out of the car, shouting, "We've had an ACCIDENT!" The grandmother was curled up under the dashboard, hoping she was injured so that Bailey's wrath would not come down on her all at once. The horrible thought she had had before the accident was that the house she had remembered so vividly was not in Georgia but in Tennessee.

Bailey removed the cat from his neck with both hands and flung it out the window against the side of a pine tree. Then he got out of the car and started looking for the children's mother. She was sitting against the side of the red gutted ditch, holding the screaming baby, but she only had a cut down her face and a broken shoulder. "We've had an ACCIDENT!" the children screamed in a frenzy of delight.

"But nobody's killed," June Star said with disappointment as the grandmother limped out of the car, her hat still pinned to her head but the broken front brim standing up at a jaunty angle and the violet spray hanging off the side. They all sat down in the ditch, except the children, to recover from the shock. They were all shaking.

"Maybe a car will come along," said the children's mother hoarsely.

"I believe I have injured an organ," said the grandmother, pressing her side, but no one answered her. Bailey's teeth were clattering. He had on a yellow sport shirt with bright blue parrots designed in it and his face was as yellow as the shirt. The grandmother decided that she would not mention that the house was in Tennessee.

The road was about ten feet above and they could see only the tops of the 70
trees on the other side of it. Behind the ditch they were sitting in there were more woods, tall and dark and deep. In a few minutes they saw a car some distance away on top of a hill, coming slowly as if the occupants were watching them. The grandmother stood up and waved both arms dramatically to attract their attention. The car continued to come on slowly, disappeared around a bend and appeared again, moving even slower, on top of the hill they had gone over. It was a big black battered hearse-like automobile. There were three men in it.

It came to a stop just over them and for some minutes, the driver looked down with a steady expressionless gaze to where they were sitting, and didn't speak. Then he turned his head and muttered something to the other two and they got out. One was a fat boy in black trousers and a red sweat shirt with a silver stallion embossed on the front of it. He moved around on the right side of them and stood staring, his mouth partly open in a kind of loose grin. The other had on khaki pants and a blue striped coat and a gray hat pulled down very low, hiding most of his face. He came around slowly on the left side. Neither spoke.

The driver got out of the car and stood by the side of it, looking down at them. He was an older man than the other two. His hair was just beginning to gray and he wore silver-rimmed spectacles that gave him a scholarly look. He had a long creased face and didn't have on any shirt or undershirt. He had on blue jeans that were too tight for him and was holding a black hat and a gun. The two boys also had guns.

"We've had an ACCIDENT!" the children screamed.

The grandmother had the peculiar feeling that the bespectacled man was someone she knew. His face was as familiar to her as if she had known him all her life but she could not recall who he was. He moved away from the car and began to come down the embankment, placing his feet carefully so that he wouldn't slip. He had on tan and white shoes and no socks, and his ankles were red and thin. "Good afternoon," he said. "I see you all had you a little spill."

"We turned over twice!" said the grandmother.   75

"Oncet," he corrected. "We seen it happen. Try their car and see will it run, Hiram," he said quietly to the boy with the gray hat.

"What you got that gun for?" John Wesley asked. "Whatcha gonna do with that gun?"

"Lady," the man said to the children's mother, "would you mind calling them children to sit down by you? Children make me nervous. I want all you all to sit down right together there where you're at."

"What are you telling US what to do for?" June Star asked.

Behind them the line of woods gaped like a dark open mouth. "Come   80
here," said their mother.

"Look here now," Bailey began suddenly, "we're in a predicament! We're in . . ."

The grandmother shrieked. She scrambled to her feet and stood staring. "You're The Misfit!" she said. "I recognized you at once!"

"Yes'm," the man said, smiling slightly as if he were pleased in spite of himself to be known, "but it would have been better for all of you, lady, if you hadn't of reckernized me."

Bailey turned his head sharply and said something to his mother that shocked even the children. The old lady began to cry and The Misfit reddened.

"Lady," he said, "don't you get upset. Sometimes a man says things he don't   85
mean. I don't reckon he meant to talk to you thataway."

"You wouldn't shoot a lady, would you?" the grandmother said and removed a clean handkerchief from her cuff and began to slap at her eyes with it.

The Misfit pointed the toe of his shoe into the ground and made a little hole and then covered it up again. "I would hate to have to," he said.

"Listen," the grandmother almost screamed, "I know you're a good man. You don't look a bit like you have common blood. I know you must come from nice people!"

"Yes mam," he said, "finest people in the world." When he smiled he showed a row of strong white teeth. "God never made a finer woman than my mother and my daddy's heart was pure gold," he said. The boy with the red sweat shirt had come around behind them and was standing with his gun at his hip. The Misfit squatted down on the ground. "Watch them children, Bobby Lee," he said. "You know they make me nervous." He looked at the six of them huddled together in front of him and he seemed to be embarrassed as if he couldn't think of anything to say. "Ain't a cloud in the sky," he remarked, looking up at it. "Don't see no sun but don't see no cloud neither."

"Yes, it's a beautiful day," said the grandmother. "Listen," she said, "you shouldn't call yourself The Misfit because I know you're a good man at heart. I can just look at you and tell." 90

"Hush!" Bailey yelled. "Hush! Everybody shut up and let me handle this!" He was squatting in the position of a runner about to sprint forward but he didn't move.

"I pre-chate that, lady," The Misfit said and drew a little circle in the ground with the butt of his gun.

"It'll take a half a hour to fix this here car," Hiram called, looking over the raised hood of it.

"Well, first you and Bobby Lee get him and that little boy to step over yonder with you," The Misfit said, pointing to Bailey and John Wesley. "The boys want to ast you something," he said to Bailey. "Would you mind stepping back in them woods there with them?"

"Listen," Bailey began, "we're in a terrible predicament! Nobody realizes what this is," and his voice cracked. His eyes were as blue and intense as the parrots in his shirt and he remained perfectly still. 95

The grandmother reached up to adjust her hat brim as if she were going to the woods with him but it came off in her hand. She stood staring at it and after a second she let it fall on the ground. Hiram pulled Bailey up by the arm as if he were assisting an old man. John Wesley caught hold of his father's hand and Bobby Lee followed. They went off toward the woods and just as they reached the dark edge, Bailey turned and supporting himself against a gray naked pine trunk, he shouted, "I'll be back in a minute, Mamma, wait on me!"

"Come back this instant!" his mother shrilled but they all disappeared into the woods.

"Bailey Boy!" the grandmother called in a tragic voice but she found she was looking at The Misfit squatting on the ground in front of her. "I just know you're a good man," she said desperately. "You're not a bit common!"

"Nome, I ain't a good man," The Misfit said after a second as if he had considered her statement carefully, "but I ain't the worst in the world neither.

My daddy said I was a different breed of dog from my brothers and sisters. 'You know,' Daddy said, 'it's some that can live their whole life out without asking about it and it's others has to know why it is, and this boy is one of the latters. He's going to be into everything!'" He put on his black hat and looked up suddenly and then away deep into the woods as if he were embarrassed again. "I'm sorry I don't have on a shirt before you ladies," he said, hunching his shoulders slightly. "We buried our clothes that we had on when we escaped and we're just making do until we can get better. We borrowed these from some folks we met," he explained.

"That's perfectly all right," the grandmother said. "Maybe Bailey has an 100 extra shirt in his suitcase."

"I'll look and see terrectly," The Misfit said.

"Where are they taking him?" the children's mother screamed.

"Daddy was a card himself," The Misfit said. "You couldn't put anything over on him. He never got in trouble with the Authorities though. Just had the knack of handling them."

"You could be honest too if you'd only try," said the grandmother. "Think how wonderful it would be to settle down and live a comfortable life and not have to think about somebody chasing you all the time."

The Misfit kept scratching in the ground with the butt of his gun as if 105 he were thinking about it. "Yes'm, somebody is always after you," he murmured.

The grandmother noticed how thin his shoulder blades were just behind his hat because she was standing up looking down on him. "Do you ever pray?" she asked.

He shook his head. All she saw was the black hat wiggle between his shoulder blades. "Nome," he said.

There was a pistol shot from the woods, followed closely by another. Then silence. The old lady's head jerked around. She could hear the wind move through the tree tops like a long satisfied insuck of breath. "Bailey Boy!" she called.

"I was a gospel singer for a while," The Misfit said. "I been most everything. Been in the arm service, both land and sea, at home and abroad, been twict married, been an undertaker, been with the railroads, plowed Mother Earth, been in a tornado, seen a man burnt alive oncet," and he looked up at the children's mother and the little girl who were sitting close together, their faces white and their eyes glassy; "I even seen a woman flogged," he said.

"Pray, pray," the grandmother began, "pray, pray . . ." 110

"I never was a bad boy that I remember of," The Misfit said in an almost dreamy voice, "but somewheres along the line I done something wrong and got sent to the penitentiary. I was buried alive," and he looked up and held her attention to him by a steady stare.

"That's when you should have started to pray," she said. "What did you do to get sent to the penitentiary that first time?"

"Turn to the right, it was a wall," The Misfit said, looking up again at the cloudless sky. "Turn to the left, it was a wall. Look up it was a ceiling, look down

it was a floor. I forget what I done, lady. I set there and set there, trying to remember what it was I done and I ain't recalled it to this day. Oncet in a while,
I would think it was coming to me, but it never come."

"Maybe they put you in by mistake," the old lady said vaguely.

"Nome," he said. "It wasn't no mistake. They had the papers on me."   115

"You must have stolen something," she said.

The Misfit sneered slightly. "Nobody had nothing I wanted," he said. "It
was a head-doctor at the penitentiary said what I had done was kill my daddy
but I known that for a lie. My daddy died in nineteen ought nineteen of the
epidemic flu° and I never had a thing to do with it. He was buried in the Mount
Hopewell Baptist churchyard and you can go there and see for yourself."

"If you would pray," the old lady said, "Jesus would help you."

"That's right," The Misfit said.

"Well then, why don't you pray?" she asked trembling with delight sud-   120
denly.

"I don't want no hep," he said. "I'm doing all right by myself."

Bobby Lee and Hiram came ambling back from the woods. Bobby Lee was
dragging a yellow shirt with bright blue parrots in it.

"Thow me that shirt, Bobby Lee," The Misfit said. The shirt came flying at
him and landed on his shoulder and he put it on. The grandmother couldn't
name what the shirt reminded her of. "No, lady," The Misfit said while he was
buttoning it up, "I found out the crime don't matter. You can do one thing or
you can do another, kill a man or take a tire off his car, because sooner or later
you're going to forget what it was you done and just be punished for it."

The children's mother had begun to make heaving noises as if she couldn't
get her breath. "Lady," he asked, "would you and that little girl like to step off
yonder with Bobby Lee and Hiram and join your husband?"

"Yes, thank you," the mother said faintly. Her left arm dangled helplessly   125
and she was holding the baby, who had gone to sleep, in the other. "Hep that
lady up, Hiram," The Misfit said as she struggled to climb out of the ditch, "and
Bobby Lee, you hold onto that little girl's hand."

"I don't want to hold hands with him," June Star said. "He reminds me of
a pig."

The fat boy blushed and laughed and caught her by the arm and pulled her
off into the woods after Hiram and her mother.

Alone with The Misfit, the grandmother found that she had lost her voice.
There was not a cloud in the sky nor any sun. There was nothing around her
but woods. She wanted to tell him that he must pray. She opened and closed her
mouth several times before anything came out. Finally she found herself saying,
"Jesus. Jesus," meaning, Jesus will help you, but the way she was saying it, it
sounded as if she might be cursing.

---

epidemic flu: An influenza epidemic in 1918–1919 killed twenty to forty million people worldwide.

"Yes'm," The Misfit said as if he agreed. "Jesus thown everything off balance. It was the same case with Him as with me except He hadn't committed any crime and they could prove I had committed one because they had the papers on me. Of course," he said, "they never shown me my papers. That's why I sign myself now. I said long ago, you get you a signature and sign everything you do and keep a copy of it. Then you'll know what you done and you can hold up the crime to the punishment and see do they match and in the end you'll have something to prove you ain't been treated right. I call myself The Misfit," he said, "because I can't make what all I done wrong fit what all I gone through in punishment."

There was a piercing scream from the woods, followed closely by a pistol 130 report. "Does it seem right to you, lady, that one is punished a heap and another ain't punished at all?"

"Jesus!" the old lady cried. "You've got good blood! I know you wouldn't shoot a lady! I know you come from nice people! Pray! Jesus, you ought not to shoot a lady. I'll give you all the money I've got!"

"Lady," The Misfit said, looking beyond her far into the woods, "there never was a body that give the undertaker a tip."

There were two more pistol reports and the grandmother raised her head like a parched old turkey hen crying for water and called, "Bailey Boy, Bailey Boy!" as if her heart would break.

"Jesus was the only One that ever raised the dead," The Misfit continued, "and He shouldn't have done it. He thrown everything off balance. If He did what He said, then it's nothing for you to do but throw away everything and follow Him, and if He didn't, then it's nothing for you to do but enjoy the few minutes you got left the best way you can—by killing somebody or burning down his house or doing some other meanness to him. No pleasure but meanness," he said and his voice had become almost a snarl.

"Maybe He didn't raise the dead," the old lady mumbled, not knowing what 135 she was saying and feeling so dizzy that she sank down in the ditch with her legs twisted under her.

"I wasn't there so I can't say He didn't," The Misfit said. "I wisht I had of been there," he said, hitting the ground with his fist. "It ain't right I wasn't there because if I had of been there I would of known. Listen lady," he said in a high voice, "if I had of been there I would of known and I wouldn't be like I am now." His voice seemed about to crack and the grandmother's head cleared for an instant. She saw the man's face twisted close to her own as if he were going to cry and she murmured, "Why you're one of my babies. You're one of my own children!" She reached out and touched him on the shoulder. The Misfit sprang back as if a snake had bitten him and shot her three times through the chest. Then he put his gun down on the ground and took off his glasses and began to clean them.

Hiram and Bobby Lee returned from the woods and stood over the ditch, looking down at the grandmother who half sat and half lay in a puddle of blood with her legs crossed under her like a child's and her face smiling up at the cloudless sky.

Without his glasses, The Misfit's eyes were red-rimmed and pale and defenseless-looking. "Take her off and thow her where you thown the others," he said, picking up the cat that was rubbing itself against his leg.

"She was a talker, wasn't she?" Bobby Lee said, sliding down the ditch with a yodel.

"She would of been a good woman," The Misfit said, "if it had been some-body there to shoot her every minute of her life." 140

"Some fun!" Bobby Lee said.

"Shut up, Bobby Lee," The Misfit said. "It's no real pleasure in life."

APPROACHING THE READING

1. Be ready to talk about what you experienced emotionally as you read the story the first time. What did you feel about the characters (minor as well as major characters), and what did you feel about what occurs, especially what happens in the last four or five pages?

2. After reading the story a second time, pick out characterization techniques (pp. 121–25) that O'Connor relies on most. Which ones contribute especially to the story's emotional effects?

3. This story is very carefully organized. Review it and make a brief outline. How does that help you see its structure? Pick out parallels and contrasts in the plot. Look for examples of repetition and foreshadowing. Think about what they contribute to the effect of the story.

4. The "Entry Points" on page 134 explain that O'Connor's stories usually have religious themes, often involving unappealing characters who are un-expectedly offered a "moment of grace," as she put it. Where do you see that happening in this story? Who has a life-changing experience and how does it occur?

APPROACHING GRAPHIC FICTION

AN ANCIENT ART When you think of graphic writing, you might un-derstandably assume that such works go back only to the mid-twentieth century, when most children were told, "Comics are not the same as good literature." And if you are familiar with or a fan of contemporary comics, you may feel that graphic literature is a new, cutting-edge form of literary art. Actually, in one sense graphic communication goes back more than 3,000 years, in the form of pictures and signs for language on Egyptian scrolls. Graphic writing has always been a serious art form. However, in the United States only since the 1980s has it begun to attract fine artists who are also literary storytellers. Today the range of graphic literature spans short story, essay, novel, nonfiction narrative, and memoir. The 1992

Pulitzer Prize for Nonfiction was awarded to *Maus*, a graphic memoir about the Holocaust written by Art Spiegelman (see p. 260), and over the last few years several graphic novels and memoirs have been nominated for and received this country's major literary awards.

HOW GRAPHIC LITERATURE WORKS   It's important to note that graphic literature is not the same as a story with illustrations. In graphic work, there is a dynamic relationship between what is written and what is drawn. Both the written words and the drawings can extend the narrative. At times the words are written as dialogue; at other times, as narration. The artist/author balances the visual impact of film and painting with the intimate "listening" of reading the written word. Graphic literature, by juxtaposing pictorial and written images, invites the reader/viewer to complete the dynamic between the two. And the creation of a deliberate sequence of "panels" separated by "gutters" (both of which will be more fully explained in the paragraphs that follow) leads the reader/viewer to participate by imagining the impact that happens between each depicted moment.

Older adults, accustomed to following lines of words from left to right, then down a page, may find it difficult to read a form that requires shifting from one image to another while taking in both words and visual components. However, a generation that has grown up with television, computers, and video games is readily able to engage with and respond to graphic literature. For that group, graphic literature is an accessible window through which to view our world and to imagine others.

VOCABULARY AND METHODS   For a close look at graphic literature, it is wise to start by understanding some vocabulary and methods unique to the form. Basic to graphic literature are *panels*, the series of individual units containing drawings and words that make up the work. Panels can fill a whole page, or several panels can be presented on the same page. Sometimes they are surrounded by a border, which frames them on the page or separates the various panels. Borders are part of the art and help channel the effect on the reader: A border turns the reader into an outside observer and can create a sense of confinement or restriction within a panel. The space between panels is called a "gutter." Sometimes panels do not have borders but "bleed" out to the edge of the page or into other panels on the same page. A panel without a border can suggest that the reader is being invited into the scene and can increase the reader's involvement; it can give a sense of openness or escape.

READING WORDS AND IMAGES SIMULTANEOUSLY   Active reading is crucial to fully enjoying and appreciating graphic literature. This kind of reading can be compared to watching a film: You must listen to the sounds and absorb the images simultaneously, integrating the two into a single experience. Similarly, in reading graphic literature, you must read the words of the text and read the images simultaneously, as a unified experience: In the hands of the finest graphic-fiction artists, the written words and the drawings are interdependent, forming a seamless whole. They need to happen together. With a bit of practice, reading this way can become as natural as watching and listening to a film.

DEALING WITH FRAGMENTS AND TIME   Active reading is necessary also because of the fragmentary nature of graphic literature: Some words of text are placed here; a cropped image, there. The reader must be able to fill out and connect the fragments in order to understand and experience the story. And active reading is needed in order to follow the passage of time. Graphic literature presents time through the use of space: Time passes as we read words, one following another, and simultaneously we see action happening in the visual images. Arrangement on the page leads to a sense of movement in time, as our eyes move sequentially from frame to frame or are guided from one part of a large frame to another. A series of small panels seems to move rapidly; a larger panel slows down our reading and the passage of time.

LISTENING WITH OUR EYES   Through active reading we imagine sounds—we listen with our eyes. The style, size, and color of the lettering affects what we "hear" in terms of volume and emotional tone. Large or bold lettering often indicates loudness, while small letters can suggest soft speech. Wavy letters may indicate a voice expressing uneasiness or fear, while a rough style of lettering may convey a harsh attitude or cruelty. In some cases words are incorporated directly into the frame; in other cases words are enclosed in balloons that connect them to their speakers. Active reading is required in interpreting the visual aspects of the balloons and the order in which the balloons are to be read.

PLOT AND CHARACTER IN GRAPHIC LITERATURE   In addition to these techniques, graphic literature makes use of the elements of fiction described in Chapters 5–8 of this book, and responding to these elements also requires active reading. Just like other fiction, the plots of graphic fiction involve beginnings, middles, endings, conflicts, foreshadowings, repetitions, gaps, and a sense of wholeness. Depiction of character in graphic fiction includes the same telling, showing, saying, and so forth as in other fiction, but it also requires that the reader be attentive to visual features: facial expressions, gestures, poses, clothes, shading, and lighting, for example. Theme, symbol, style, tone, and irony can be employed to good effect in graphic fiction, just as in other fiction.

POINT OF VIEW IN GRAPHIC LITERATURE   Point of view (discussed in Chapter 6) is vital in graphic literature. It starts with who is telling the story (first-person or third-person narrator) and that person's relation to the story, as in traditional fiction. But in graphic fiction the panel affects viewpoint, establishing perimeters and perspective. The artist can have us look down from above in a detached way, for example, or up from below, which tends to make the reader feel small and at times fearful. Notice how similar this is to filmmaking: The artist, in choosing these frame angles, is like the director of a film. When we watch a movie, we know if we are looking through a person's eyes or not; it's the same with graphic fiction.

SETTING IN GRAPHIC LITERATURE   Setting in a graphic story involves location and time, as in any other story (see Ch. 7), but the graphic work offers visual images to supplement the imagined ones of conventional fiction. The handling of setting varies with the nature and purpose of the writing: The background can be very detailed or sketched out in broad strokes. Often an "establishing shot" is used—with lots of details about the place and the character proportionally very small, all of which will be zoomed in on in later panels. (Notice that here, too, the terminology used in discussing graphic fiction is carried over from the film world.) It can be helpful to remind yourself when reading graphic literature that, as with any visual art, the form of the drawings could take a multiplicity of alternatives. The artist has chosen a particular way of presenting the visual—for a purpose, for an effect, as something you should "read."

READING **GRAPHIC LITERATURE**   *Reading* has become a word that we apply to almost everything. We read faces and places and moods, for example. Graphic literature extends the idea of reading to include both the written and the visual. As an active reader, you are expected to attend to both simultaneously, using your ability to realize implications, nuances, and subtleties in the language and in the visual art. To get the fullest experience from such a work, you must "read" the pictures and the words and understand that "graphic" applies to both the visual and the written.

ENTRY POINTS   As you read the following work of graphic literature the first time, focus on understanding what's going on, what it's about. The second time through, focus on how Lynda Barry uses both words and drawings to advance the plot and to develop and reveal the characters. Notice especially how she uses the gutter between panels. Where does she leave room for you to imagine what leads from one panel to the next? Which panels most directly show the forward movement of the story and which most directly develop the characters?

Lynda Barry b. 1956
Today's Demon: Magic   [2002]

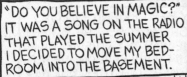

"DO YOU BELIEVE IN MAGIC?" IT WAS A SONG ON THE RADIO THAT PLAYED THE SUMMER I DECIDED TO MOVE MY BEDROOM INTO THE BASEMENT.

I'LL MEETCHA TOMORROW SORTA LATE AT NIGHT

I WAS GROWING MY HAIR OUT AND IT WAS IN AN IN-BETWEEN STAGE THAT DIDN'T MAKE SENSE TO ANYBODY. I'D WANTED LONG HAIR ALL MY LIFE. I WAS WILLING TO LOOK INSANE WHILE I WAITED FOR IT.

DO YOU BELIEVE LIKE I BELIEVE

100

THERE WERE BIG CHANGES GOING ON IN MY HOUSE. GRANDMA MOVED OUT, AND BOTH MY PARENTS WERE "SECRETLY" SEEING OTHER PEOPLE. THEY WERE NEVER AROUND.

HALT! GET OUT OF MY WAY.

NO ONE SAID YOU COULD MOVE TO THE BASEMENT.

BUG OFF.

MAKE ME.

I WAS LEFT TO WATCH MY TWO YOUNGER BROTHERS AND KEEP HOUSE. I WAS SUPPOSED TO STAY AT HOME ALL DAY, EVERY DAY, THE SUMMER THAT SONG PLAYED ON THE RADIO.

WE'RE HUNGRY, MAN! YOU GOTTA MAKE US FOOD, MAN!

CHICKEN POT PIES, OVEN AT 350°.

WE'RE SICK OF CHICKEN POT PIE, MAN!

I'M NOT.

101

102

103

104

105

DID THE SAME THING HAPPEN TO EV? I DON'T KNOW BECAUSE BY THE TIME SHE TURNED 13, WE WERE GHOSTS TO EACH OTHER. I NEVER KNEW HER SONGS AND SHE NEVER KNEW MINE.

FIND IT?

YEAH. THIS IS EV.

THIS IS EV AND ME IN A PHOTO BOOTH.

I REMEMBER CLIMBING ONTO THE ROOF OF THE SCHOOL WITH HER ONCE, LONG BEFORE MY PARENTS WERE DIVORCED, LONG BEFORE HER FATHER LOST HIS JOB. I REMEMBER LAYING DOWN FLAT SO THE COPS WOULDN'T SEE US AND TALKING ABOUT INFINITY.

106

I KNOW NUMBERS CAN GO ON FOREVER. I KNOW EV IS IN HER 40'S NOW. I KNOW ABOUT THE DIFFERENCE BETWEEN THE BASEMENT AND THE ROOF OF THE SCHOOL. WHAT'S INFINITY MINUS 13? MINUS 11?

WHAT'S INFINITY MINUS ALL THE SONGS IN THE WORLD? THE ONES YOU LISTENED TO, THE ONES SHE LISTENED TO, THE ONES YOU SANG TOGETHER THAT DAY. DO YOU BELIEVE IN MAGIC? YES OR NO?

DOWN THE WAY WHERE THE NIGHTS ARE GAY AND THE SUN SHINES DAILY ON THE MOUNTAIN TOP

107

108

APPROACHING THE READING

1. Consider the order of the panels. Try to imagine the choices Lynda Barry made while drawing each panel and offer reasons why you think she chose the approaches that she did.

2. Where do you see Barry revealing the characters more through her drawings? More through her words?

3. How do these drawings define the characters, especially Lynda and Ev? If this were a work of conventional fiction, which drawings would be especially difficult to put into words? Why do you think so?

4. In what ways do you see the drawings advancing the story? Where do you see the words advancing the story?

APPROACHING THE AUTHOR

Lynda Barry started painting monkeys when a friend of hers died. She told herself she'd draw one hundred of them but found that one hundred wasn't enough. Even years later, when she couldn't sleep or felt sad, she'd paint monkeys and feel comforted by the act itself.

For more about her, see page 1374.

RESPONDING THROUGH Writing

WRITING ABOUT PLOT AND CHARACTER

Journal Entries

1. Experiment with the basic principles of plot construction by writing a plot analysis of a TV show or a movie: its beginning, its handling of gaps, its use of flashbacks, its rising action or development (look for conflict, suspense, foreshadowing, and repetitions), and its ending. Write a journal entry summarizing the result and discussing whether, how, and why basic aspects of plot are universal.

2. Choose a crucial event from your past. In a journal entry, outline it as a plot. Consider what you need to include and what you can leave out, what order would be most effective for presenting it, and so on. Add a few sentences pointing out the techniques you bring in and discussing what you learn about plot construction.

You can research the authors in this chapter with LitLinks, or take a quiz on the stories with LitQuiz, at bedfordstmartins.com/rewritinglit.

3. Write an analysis of characterization techniques in a TV show or movie: Look for how telling, showing, dialoguing, conveying a character's thoughts, and naming choices are used to reveal character. Consider which characters are round and which are flat. Write a journal entry summarizing the result and discussing whether, how, and why basic aspects of characterization are similar across different genres.

Literary Analysis Papers

4. Write a paper on the importance and handling of gaps in the plotting of Louise Erdrich's "The Red Convertible" (p. 126).

5. Write a paper examining the relation of plot construction to title in James Baldwin's "Sonny's Blues" (p. 362), James Joyce's "Araby" (p. 242), or Toni Morrison's "Recitatif" (p. 445).

6. Write a paper discussing characterization techniques in Judith Ortiz Cofer's "Nada" (p. 395), Chitra Banerjee Divakaruni's "Clothes" (p. 328), or Katherine Anne Porter's "The Jilting of Granny Weatherall" (p. 533).

Comparison-Contrast Papers

7. Write a paper comparing and contrasting Arnold Friend in Joyce Carol Oates's "Where Are You Going, Where Have You Been?" (p. 481) and The Misfit in Flannery O'Connor's "A Good Man Is Hard to Find" (p. 134).

8. Write a paper comparing the inside view of the Vietnam War presented by the plot of Tim O'Brien's "The Things They Carried" (p. 493) with the outside view found in Louise Erdrich's "The Red Convertible" (p. 126). (You could focus on the handling of gaps in both stories.)

 TIPS for Writing about Plot and Character

- **Explain techniques.** In writing about plot, be sure to *explain* the selection and arrangement of events; don't just summarize what happens in the story.

- **Limit your scope.** In writing about plot, focus on an aspect—or perhaps two or three—that are unique or particularly significant; don't try to deal with everything covered in this chapter.

- **Start with conflicts.** As you select a topic related to plot, look for the key conflict or conflicts in the story, then at how the plot structure makes the conflict stand out. Notice if the story includes an epiphany; if so, notice how it is set up. That can often turn into a valuable topic.

- **Focus on methods.** In writing about character, it's usually best to focus on methods of characterization: Show how aspects of the character are brought out; don't just describe what the character is like. Watch especially for juxtapositions—comparisons and contrasts between characters—in addition to the specific techniques covered in this chapter. Juxtapositions often provide a useful way to get into and organize a paper.

- **Connect to theme.** Plot and character are of most interest as they relate to and bring out theme in the story; try to connect your discussion of plot or character to the overall effect of the story.

WRITING ABOUT CONNECTIONS

One of the most important skills for you to develop is how to make connections between the great variety of things you are learning, things that may at first appear to be unrelated: for example, between things dealt with early in a course and those that come later and between what you have learned in one course or discipline and what you have covered in others. Making connections is also crucial in understanding literature. Throughout this book, this skill is emphasized by pairing elements in chapters, often in unusual combinations, to bring out the connections between them and between all the elements used in writing.

It's valuable and interesting for you to make connections between different works that you read. Doing so can enhance your reading experience and reveal important insights. The connections can be between similar (or contrasting) plots and characters or other techniques and can be thematic. To give you practice and encouragement making connections, each chapter includes "Writing about Connections" prompts. The pairings suggested are for works of the same genre, though equally appropriate pairings could be made across genres. We have selected connections, often between contemporary works and earlier works from the literary canon, that we hope you will find thought provoking and challenging. Here are three such suggestions, which are intended to provide you with a model for coming up with others on your own.

1. "Love and the City": Realizing Relationships in Dagoberto Gilb's "Love in L.A." (p. 113) and Raymond Carver's "What We Talk about When We Talk about Love" (p. 386)

2. "My Brother's Keeper": Supporting Siblings in Louise Erdrich's "The Red Convertible" (p. 126) and James Baldwin's "Sonny's Blues" (p. 362)

3. "Good Men Are Hard to Find": Encounters with Evil in Joyce Carol Oates's "Where Are You Going, Where Have You Been?" (p. 481) and Flannery O'Connor's "A Good Man Is Hard to Find" (p. 134)

WRITING RESEARCH PAPERS

1. In the United States and many other societies, cars carry cultural importance. Research the role cars play in American culture and write a paper on the significance of cars in Dagoberto Gilb's "Love in L.A." (p. 113), Louise Erdrich's "The Red Convertible" (p. 126), Joyce Carol Oates's "Where Are You Going, Where Have You Been?" (p. 481), and your own experience. Consider what types of cars carry various meanings for different cultures. How do cars embody distinctions, and at times conflicts, between cultures? Consider ironies you find in this "car culture."

2. Henry's experiences leaving the reservation to enter basic training and then going to Vietnam for active service are not covered in Louise Erdrich's "The Red Convertible" (p. 126) because of the narrator's limited point of view. But they remain very much a part of the story. Research what Native Americans often encounter when they leave reservations and what military action in Vietnam was like. Then write a paper describing what Henry's experiences probably were like and why he was a changed man when he returned.

Properly speaking, the theme is what is left, like a resonance, in the reader's mind.

R. V. Cassill
(Novelist, Short-Story Writer, Editor, and Artist)

Point of View and Theme

CHAPTER 6

Being Alert to Angles, Open to Insights

This book is about *reading* literature, specifically reading in the interactive manner described in Chapter 1. As we say there, reading literature differs from most other reading: It is often more like listening to someone, more like hearing a voice, than what we usually think of as reading. You've probably heard the phrase "seeing with the mind's eye"; you can also hear with the mind's ear. Responding fully to literature requires training the ear so you can enjoy and benefit from hearing many voices from a variety of places and cultures. This chapter focuses on **voice** in stories and on the way stories give voice to a central idea or **theme**.

ENTRY POINTS   Using your "mind's ear," listen to the following story as if it were being spoken directly to you. It is the first in a series of forty-six connected stories, or a *collective story*, told by a young girl, Esperanza Cordero, growing up in a Latino section of Chicago and seeking both to escape that world and to find herself.

Sandra Cisneros b. 1954

The House on Mango Street   [1983]

We didn't always live on Mango Street. Before that we lived on Loomis on the third floor, and before that we lived on Keeler. Before Keeler it was Paulina, and before that I can't remember. But what I remember most is moving a lot. Each time it seemed there'd be one more of us. By the time we got to Mango Street we were six—Mama, Papa, Carlos, Kiki, my sister Nenny, and me.

The house on Mango Street is ours, and we don't have to pay rent to anybody, or share the yard with the people downstairs, or be careful not to make too much noise, and there isn't a landlord banging on the ceiling with a broom. But even so, it's not the house we'd thought we'd get.

We had to leave the flat on Loomis quick. The water pipes broke and the landlord wouldn't fix them because the house was too old. We had to leave fast. We were using the washroom next door and carrying water over in empty milk gallons. That's why Mama and Papa looked for a house, and that's why we moved into the house on Mango Street, far away, on the other side of town.

They always told us that one day we would move into a house, a real house that would be ours for always so we wouldn't have to move each year. And our house would have running water and pipes that worked. And inside it would have real stairs, not hallway stairs, but stairs inside like the houses on TV. And we'd have a basement and at least three washrooms so when we took a bath we wouldn't have to tell everybody. Our house would be white with trees around it, a great big yard, and grass growing without a fence. This was the house Papa talked about when he held a lottery ticket and this was the house Mama dreamed up in the stories she told us before we went to bed.

But the house on Mango Street is not the way they told it at all. It's small   5 and red with tight steps in front and windows so small you'd think they were holding their breath. Bricks are crumbling in places, and the front door is so swollen you have to push hard to get in. There is no front yard, only four little elms the city planted by the curb. Out back is a small garage for the car we don't own yet and a small yard that looks smaller between the two buildings on either side. There are stairs in our house, but they're ordinary hallway stairs, and the house has only one washroom. Everybody has to share a bedroom—Mama and Papa, Carlos and Kiki, me and Nenny.

Once when we were living on Loomis, a nun from my school passed by and saw me playing out front. The laundromat downstairs had been boarded up because it had been robbed two days before and the owner had painted on the wood YES WE'RE OPEN so as not to lose business.

Where do you live? she asked.

There, I said pointing up to the third floor.

You live *there*?

There. I had to look to where she pointed—the third floor, the paint peeling, 10 wooden bars Papa had nailed on the windows so we wouldn't fall out. You live *there*? The way she said it made me feel like nothing. *There*. I lived *there*. I nodded.

I knew then I had to have a house. A real house. One I could point to. But this isn't it. The house on Mango Street isn't it. For the time being, Mama says. Temporary, says Papa. But I know how those things go.

APPROACHING THE READING

1. Describe the voice you hear in "The House on Mango Street." How old do you imagine the speaker is? What makes you think that? What else can you tell about her from the way she sounds as you listen to her?

2. What is the effect of having the voice and perspective be those of Esperanza? How do you think the story would differ if told by Esperanza's mother? Her father? One of her brothers?

3. Considering the story as a whole, what central point comes through as you listen to what Esperanza says?

READING FOR POINT OF VIEW

As you read a work of fiction, one of the first things to pay attention to is who is telling, or "narrating," the story, whose voice you are listening to as you read. Compare the two very short stories that opened Chapter 5 and Chapter 6. The different techniques used in them reflect differences in the way you view the action in each. "The House on Mango Street" is told by a character who is involved in the story and views the events from the inside. Esperanza uses *I* (the first person) as she tells her story. "Love in L.A." is told by an unnamed, unidentified storyteller (or **narrator**) who is not involved in the story but views it from the outside. The storyteller does not use *I* but refers to characters in the third person ("she" or "he"). The kind of narrator and the way the narrator looks at the things that occur in the story are called the **point of view**. This chapter deals with two questions it is helpful to ask as you read or reflect back on a story: Who tells the story? And, how much does she or he know? Answering those questions can be very helpful in developing your confidence in being able to talk and write about this often-overlooked aspect of a story.

First-Person Narration

When a story is told by a narrator using the first-person pronoun *I*, the story is said to be using a **first-person point of view**. The use of first-person narration can make the story seem more up close and personal, as if the author is relating events from her or his own life. The *I* in any story, however, should *not* be assumed to be the author: The narrator in a work of fiction is always a *narrative construct*, an imagined speaker created by the writer.

It is true that in "The House on Mango Street" many details about Esperanza's life parallel the author's: Cisneros was born in Chicago; was part of a large family (six brothers, no sisters); moved often during her childhood, between Chicago and Mexico, where her father was born; and shared Esperanza's sense of dislocation and a lack of permanence. However, Cisneros did not write an autobiographical essay, the way Sherman Alexie did in "Superman and Me" (p. 4). She clearly drew on her own experiences as she wrote, but she used her imagination to alter the facts of her own life and to invent new ones. She constructed a character for the narrator, one who takes part in, as well as relates, the story. The story's power depends on hearing it from a child's perspective. We, as readers older than Esperanza is, can recognize implications in her story that she is not aware of yet, about poverty, class distinctions, housing patterns, and the power of landlords.

Picking out this point of view is generally straightforward: Just watch for a narrator using *I*. (Occasionally an author uses the first-person plural, *we*, as in "A Rose for Emily," which appears later in this chapter.) But don't stop there. Once again, alert, active reading is essential. Follow up by asking how much the narrator knows as she or he tells the story. First-person narrators can only tell about what they experience, observe, or are told. They cannot look into other characters' minds or feelings, and they may not understand fully the implications of what they see, hear, or experience. Three labels are most often used to indicate the different categories, or different degrees of knowledge, that first-person narrators generally fall into.

NAIVE NARRATOR   The first is the **naive narrator**, a narrator too young or too inexperienced to understand fully the implications of what she or he is talking about. In such cases, active reading is even more important than usual, as you—who understand more than the narrator—must fill in implications the narrator cannot grasp. Such is the case in "The House on Mango Street": Esperanza knows what the family's dream house would be like, and she knows that their present house falls far short of their dreams. But she doesn't understand, until the day the nun sees her playing out front, what the house they live in says about their social situation, and she doesn't realize the kind of economic realities her family is up against. Much of the power of the story comes from our ability, as readers who are older than Esperanza is, to understand the reasons behind her pains and disappointments.

UNRELIABLE NARRATOR   Esperanza's knowledge is limited by her youth and inexperience. Older narrators may have limited knowledge as well or may not reveal all that they know, for various reasons. Similar to a naive narrator is a narrator who does not have the mental capacity to provide a coherent account of events or a narrator who has prejudices (against a race or class or against a particular individual in the story) or a restricted range of experience that the reader perceives even though the narrator is unaware of it. In such cases they are at least partially **unreliable narrators**. We cannot accept in an unquestioning way what they tell us about people and events.

That is the case with Lyman in Louise Erdrich's "The Red Convertible" (p. 126). He is not naive, like Esperanza, and he tells us the truth, as far as he understands it. But the limited range of his experience prevents him from understanding as much as we as readers of the story do. We pick up clues from things that he says, like "I could never keep it straight, which direction those good Vietnam soldiers were from" (para. 22). However, it is important to recognize that it is often the case that we only realize the narrator's limitations at the end of the story. It's probably not until our second reading of "The Red Convertible" that we grasp how Lyman is groping toward an understanding of what we grasp more fully than he is able to.

There are also cases when we can't trust everything the narrator says. The narrator may not tell the whole truth or may distort some things, perhaps deliberately to make them look better or unintentionally because they are too painful to face. In many cases an unreliable narrator's account of what happens is accurate, as in Edgar Allan Poe's "The Cask of Amontillado" (p. 528); but we find that we cannot trust what the narrator tells us about her or his motivation or interpretation of the events. Here, too, you may not realize this until you think back on the story. Sometimes you may start picking up clues earlier, from the tone or style in which the narrator speaks or details the narrator lets slip out. If you think you've picked up such a clue, you'll want to start figuring out what you can take straightforwardly and where you need to make allowances for or corrections in what you are being told.

RELIABLE NARRATOR   First-person narrators often do tell their stories accurately and honestly (as far as they and we can tell). In that case the story is said to have a **reliable narrator**: We can believe or rely on what she or he says, as we do with the narrator in Julia Alvarez's "Daughter of Invention" (p. 10), in Katherine Min's "Courting a Monk" (p. 247), and in Chitra Banerjee Divakaruni's "Clothes" (p. 328). In those stories the narrators give us no reason to doubt or question what they are saying. They don't know everything about everything, of course. But they have a convincing degree of understanding about themselves and what is happening

> **NOTE:** A first-person narrator who seems to speak directly for the author is often referred to as a **persona**: the "character" projected by the author, the *I* of a narrative poem or novel or the speaker whose voice is heard in a lyric poem. Even if a first-person narrator seems to speak directly for the author or is given the author's name, the speaker created by the words of the story or poem is not identical to the real-life author who writes the words.

to them, and we feel trust that as we read we can rely on both their accounts of events and their understandings of what occurred.

Third-Person Narration

Stories told by anonymous or identified outside observers who do not refer to themselves using the pronouns *I* or *we* are said to use **third-person point of view**. "Love in L.A." (p. 113) is such a story. It is told by someone who observes and tells about what happened that morning in L.A. from the outside. We are not told who the narrator is. We might assume that since Dagoberto Gilb is writing the story, he is also its narrator, and in this case that would not be misleading. The narrator and the author do seem very close. But that assumption is not always valid. In some cases a narrator conveys values or positions quite different from the author's. It is well to keep in mind that any narrator, even one who seems very similar to the author, is an imaginative construct, fashioned by the author as a vehicle for telling the story. When you answer the question of who is telling a story, it is safer to refer to the storyteller as a "narrator" instead of as "the author."

The question "What does the narrator know?" applies to third-person point of view as well as to first-person, but the categories for describing the various answers are different. Here are the most important possibilities:

THIRD-PERSON OMNISCIENT POINT OF VIEW   When a story is told by an external narrator who relates actions and conversations but also describes the thoughts or feelings of more than one character, the point of view is referred to as third-person **omniscient** (that is, "having unlimited knowledge"). It's important to keep in mind that omniscient point of view doesn't mean the narrator has to tell the reader everything about a sequence of events or a set of characters; no story can tell everything. Not disclosing everything doesn't mean the narrator is not omniscient. And the fact that the narrator *can* see into every character doesn't mean she or he *will* do so. In Zora Neale Hurston's "Sweat" (p. 421) the third-person narrator shows the flexibility available to an omniscient narrator. The story is told primarily from Delia Jones's perspective, but occasionally the perspective shifts to the men sitting in front of the village store or to Sykes, the husband who abuses Delia. Sometimes the narrator tells what Delia is thinking or feeling (para. 3), and sometimes tells us what her husband is feeling (para. 24) or experiencing (para. 98).

THIRD-PERSON OBJECTIVE POINT OF VIEW   A third-person **objective point of view**, like third-person omniscient, takes an outside view and relates the actions and dialogue; but the narrator is "objective" in the sense of not commenting on what happens and not including inner, personal thoughts or feelings of any of the characters. By describing events only from the outside and not looking into the minds or feelings of characters or explaining why any of the characters do what they do, the narrator leaves it to the reader to draw conclusions from the details and dialogue provided. The invisible narrator in Ernest Hemingway's "Hills Like White Elephants" (p. 196), for example, simply describes where two characters are and what they do and relates what they say to each other, never looking into their thoughts or commenting on or explaining what is going on between them. However, and this is often misunderstood, for a story to be narrated objectively does not necessarily mean that the story is totally objective. The author can convey an attitude or judgment by the way a character is depicted or the choice of words she or he uses, as may be the case in "Hills Like White Elephants."

THIRD-PERSON LIMITED POINT OF VIEW   A third-person limited narrator can look into the mind or feelings of only one character, in contrast to an omniscient narrator, who can see into the minds or feelings of more than one character or all characters. Such a point of view is referred to as **limited omniscient** (that is, partially omniscient). Because the narrator focuses on and follows one character, the narrator generally knows everything that affects that character but does not know about things that occur when that character is not present or about things going on inside other characters. In Flannery O'Connor's "A Good Man Is Hard to Find" (p. 134), for example, the narrator limits description of the actions and dialogue to what is seen and heard by the grandmother, except for the last six paragraphs, when she is dead, and with minor exceptions describes only the thoughts and feelings of the grandmother. The limited point of view is most evident in that we are never taken into the mind or feelings of The Misfit. We know about him only through dialogue and what he does.

Some variants on the category third-person limited are important and often referred to, and thus worth some attention.

Center of Consciousness

The most important of these variants is the **center of consciousness** approach. In it, the narrator relates the story in the third person but tells the story entirely through the consciousness (the experiences, thoughts, feelings, and memories) of one character. This is where "Love in L.A." (p. 113) fits best. We are in Jake's car when the story opens and enter his mind in the second sentence. From there on we experience everything through Jake's perspective. Even all that we know about Mariana comes through his interactions with and impressions of her. The character that the author centers on may be the main character or a minor character; the author may give some third-person description or background information, but it will be a limited amount.

Interior Monologue

A technique sometimes used in presenting center of consciousness is **interior monologue**. A *monologue* in drama is an extended, uninterrupted speech by a single speaker; an *interior monologue* is such a speech occurring within a character's mind, as in Tillie Olsen's "I Stand Here Ironing" (p. 506). It is the representation of unspoken mental activity as if directly overheard by the reader without being selected and organized by a narrator. It can be thoughts, impressions, and memories presented in an associative, disjointed, nonlogical way as they flow through a person's mind. Or it can be a more logical, grammatical flow of thoughts and memories as if they were spoken to an external listener (the way we rehearse in our minds what we plan to say to someone later, but digress along the way, following things we are reminded of before getting back to the topic at hand).

Stream of Consciousness

Authors try sometimes to avoid the seeming artificiality of a narrated, preplanned, organized story by presenting only the continuous flow of whatever passes through the mind (consciousness) of a character. This approach is called **stream of consciousness** and it includes sense perceptions as well as thoughts, memories, and feelings—the total sense of awareness and the mental and emotional response to it. Someone does have to narrate such a stream, but the author usually attempts to make the narrator unnoticeable.

You probably will rarely encounter stream of consciousness and, when you do, will recognize it by its distinctive style. Usually, to capture the fact that much mental activity is nonverbal, stream of consciousness does not use ordinary punctuation or complete sentences; it is associative rather than logical; and it seems disjointed and haphazard. It is at times a chaotic flow of random sense perceptions, mental pictures, sounds, thoughts, and details. Here, for example, is a stream of consciousness passage from James Joyce's novel *Ulysses* (1922), as the main character Leopold Bloom strolls through Dublin, with his mind absorbing impressions and connecting them to random thoughts and memories:

Pineapple rock, lemon platt, butter scotch. A sugar-sticky girl shoveling scoopfuls of creams for a christian brother. Some school great. Bad for their tummies. Lozenge and comfit manufacturer to His Majesty the King. God. Save. Our. Sitting on his throne, sucking red jujubes white.

READING FOR THEME

Along with listening for the voice in a story—who tells the story and how much the storyteller knows—we listen for what the story gives voice to, what it is *about* in the sense of "what it all adds up to." What it all adds up to is usually referred to as the **theme**: the central idea or concept conveyed by a literary work. The *all* in "what it all adds up to" is important—to reach a statement of theme, we must take everything into account, all the different techniques used in telling the story (everything discussed in Chapters 5–8) and all the things that happen to all the characters.

STATING A THEME   A statement of theme should be expressed in two parts: a *subject* and a *predicate* (something about the subject). The subject of "The House on Mango Street," for example, could be said to be a poor immigrant family's search for adequate housing. To turn that into a statement of theme, we would need to add a predicate, perhaps something about how adequate housing involves more than just having a warm, dry place to live. Putting these together—subject and predicate—we might say that a poor immigrant family's need for adequate housing goes beyond comfort and convenience to give the family a sense of respect and self-worth.

LIMITS OF THEME   Theme can never encompass the entire work as a whole; it is always less than the experience of reading the work itself, and even if you are told the theme, knowing it is never an adequate substitute for reading the whole work. Extracting a statement of theme runs the risk of reducing your reading from a holistic and personally rewarding experience, involving the emotions and imagination as well as the intellect, to an intellectual exercise only. It is never an enriching experience to read simply for theme. Articulating a theme is one of the many ways of saying something about a work, but it is never a substitute for fully experiencing the theme itself, let alone the whole work.

VALIDITY OF THEME   Theme is always at least somewhat subjective. Works rarely have a single "right" theme that all readers find and express in the same way. Each of us may find different themes in a rich work of literature, and we may express them in different ways. However, that does not mean that every interpretation is equally valid, or even valid at all. If someone says the theme of "The House on Mango Street" is the importance of mothers in holding families together through

☑ CHECKLIST for Reading about Point of View and Theme

❑ Pay attention to who is telling the story (the narrator) and how much the narrator knows:

- *First-person:* a partially knowing *I* or *we*, sometimes reliable, sometimes naive or unreliable
- *Third-person omniscient:* an all-knowing, often anonymous, reporter of words and actions and the thoughts of more than one character
- *Third-person objective:* a reporter of words and actions, not thoughts or motives
- *Third-person limited:* an observer or participant with partial knowledge

  - Center of consciousness — seeing a story through the consciousness of a particular character
  - Interior monologue — direct presentation of a character's thoughts and memories, without intervention by a narrator
  - Stream of consciousness — the seemingly unstructured perceptions, images, and reflections flowing through a mind

❑ Pay attention to a story's theme, the central idea or concept conveyed in the story:

- Make sure that your statement of theme is complete, that it includes what the story all adds up to.
- Make sure that your statement of theme is firmly grounded in the story.
- Make sure that you have specific details to support the adequacy and importance of your statement of theme.
- Make sure you have found a statement of theme, not just a moral or lesson that can be imposed on the story.

You can further explore point of view and theme, including using interactive exercises, with VirtuaLit Fiction at bedfordstmartins .com/rewritinglit.

difficult circumstances, there would be good reason to object that such an interpretation is not grounded in the story, that it is more an effort to extract a lesson from the story than to draw together what it all adds up to.

Statements of theme must grow out of details in the story, not out of ideas, experiences, or values *we bring to* the story. Stating a theme should not be thought of as finding a moral or lesson in the work; there may be a lesson, but often a literary work is more interested in depicting human behavior than in judging it or drawing lessons from it. We do not need to agree with characters' beliefs or approve of their actions to enjoy and appreciate the work in which they appear.

FURTHER READING

ENTRY POINTS   The following is another story by Alice Walker, who also wrote "The Flowers" (p. 20), which you read in Chapter 2. This one takes us back to the 1960s, when African Americans began turning to Africa in search of their roots and identity, when the adoption of African-influenced clothing, hairstyles, and names in an attempt to connect with one's heritage was new and startling (especially in the old world of the rural South). As you read the story, pay attention to the voice you hear and to the handling of point of view and perspective. Think about the extent to which the way the story "works," the way it achieves its effects, depends on the voice and personality of the narrator.

Alice Walker   b. 1944

Everyday Use   [1973]

for your grandmama

I will wait for her in the yard that Maggie and I made so clean and wavy yesterday afternoon. A yard like this is more comfortable than most people know. It is not just a yard. It is like an extended living room. When the hard clay is swept clean as a floor and the fine sand around the edges lined with tiny, irregular grooves, anyone can come and sit and look up into the elm tree and wait for the breezes that never come inside the house.

Maggie will be nervous until after her sister goes: she will stand hopelessly in corners, homely and ashamed of the burn scars down her arms and legs, eyeing her sister with a mixture of envy and awe. She thinks her sister has held life always in the palm of one hand, that "no" is a word the world never learned to say to her.

APPROACHING THE AUTHOR

One of **Alice Walker**'s brothers accidentally shot her in the eye with a BB gun while playing cowboys and Indians when she was eight years old. She went blind in her right eye. That unfortunate event may  have led to her being able to attend college, as she was granted a rehabilitation scholarship from the state of Georgia.
For more about her, see page 1417.

You've no doubt seen those TV shows where the child who has "made it" is confronted, as a surprise, by her own mother and father, tottering in weakly from backstage. (A pleasant surprise, of course: What would they do if parent and child came on the show only to curse out and insult each other?) On TV mother and child embrace and smile into each other's faces. Sometimes the mother and father weep, the child wraps them in her arms and leans across the table to tell how she would not have made it without their help. I have seen these programs.

Sometimes I dream a dream in which Dee and I are suddenly brought together on a TV program of this sort. Out of a dark and soft-seated limousine I am ushered into a bright room filled with many people. There I meet a smiling, gray, sporty man like Johnny Carson° who shakes my hand and tells me what a fine girl I have. Then we are on the stage and Dee is embracing me with tears in her eyes. She pins on my dress a large orchid, even though she has told me once that she thinks orchids are tacky flowers.

In real life I am a large, big-boned woman with rough, man-working hands. In the winter I wear flannel nightgowns to bed and overalls during the day. I can kill and clean a hog as mercilessly as a man. My fat keeps me hot in zero weather. I can work outside all day, breaking ice to get water for washing; I can eat pork liver cooked over the open fire minutes after it comes steaming from the hog. One winter I knocked a bull calf straight in the brain between the eyes with a sledge hammer and had the meat hung up to chill before nightfall. But of course all this does not show on television. I am the way my daughter would want me to be: a hundred pounds lighter, my skin like an uncooked barley pancake. My hair glistens in the hot bright lights. Johnny Carson has much to do to keep up with my quick and witty tongue.

But that is a mistake. I know even before I wake up. Who ever knew a Johnson with a quick tongue? Who can even imagine me looking a strange white man in the eye? It seems to me I have talked to them always with one foot raised in flight, with my head turned in whichever way is farthest from them. Dee, though. She would always look anyone in the eye. Hesitation was no part of her nature.

"How do I look, Mama?" Maggie says, showing just enough of her thin body enveloped in pink skirt and red blouse for me to know she's there, almost hidden by the door.

"Come out into the yard," I say.

Have you ever seen a lame animal, perhaps a dog run over by some careless person rich enough to own a car, sidle up to someone who is ignorant enough to be kind to him? That is the way my Maggie walks. She has been like this, chin on chest, eyes on ground, feet in shuffle, ever since the fire that burned the other house to the ground.

Dee is lighter than Maggie, with nicer hair and a fuller figure. She's a woman now, though sometimes I forget. How long ago was it that the other house burned? Ten, twelve years? Sometimes I can still hear the flames and feel Maggie's arms sticking to me, her hair smoking and her dress falling off her in little black papery flakes. Her eyes seemed stretched open, blazed open by the

---

Johnny Carson: (1925–2005) U.S. comedian and host of *The Tonight Show Starring Johnny Carson* from 1962 to 1992.

flames reflected in them. And Dee. I see her standing off under the sweet gum tree she used to dig gum out of; a look of concentration on her face as she watched the last dingy gray board of the house fall in toward the red-hot brick chimney. Why don't you do a dance around the ashes? I'd wanted to ask her. She had hated the house that much.

I used to think she hated Maggie, too. But that was before we raised the money, the church and me, to send her to Augusta to school. She used to read to us without pity; forcing words, lies, other folks' habits, whole lives upon us two, sitting trapped and ignorant underneath her voice. She washed us in a river of make-believe, burned us with a lot of knowledge we didn't necessarily need to know. Pressed us to her with the serious way she read, to shove us away at just the moment, like dimwits, we seemed about to understand.

Dee wanted nice things. A yellow organdy dress to wear to her graduation from high school; black pumps to match a green suit she'd made from an old suit somebody gave me. She was determined to stare down any disaster in her efforts. Her eyelids would not flicker for minutes at a time. Often I fought off the temptation to shake her. At sixteen she had a style of her own: and knew what style was.

I never had an education myself. After second grade the school was closed down. Don't ask me why: in 1927 colored asked fewer questions than they do now. Sometimes Maggie reads to me. She stumbles along good-naturedly but can't see well. She knows she is not bright. Like good looks and money, quickness passed her by. She will marry John Thomas (who has mossy teeth in an earnest face) and then I'll be free to sit here and I guess just sing church songs to myself. Although I never was a good singer. Never could carry a tune. I was always better at a man's job. I used to love to milk till I was hooked in the side in '49. Cows are soothing and slow and don't bother you, unless you try to milk them the wrong way.

I have deliberately turned my back on the house. It is three rooms, just like the one that burned, except the roof is tin; they don't make shingle roofs any more. There are no real windows, just some holes cut in the sides, like the port-holes in a ship, but not round and not square, with rawhide holding the shutters up on the outside. This house is in a pasture, too, like the other one. No doubt when Dee sees it she will want to tear it down. She wrote me once that no matter where we "choose" to live, she will manage to come see us. But she will never bring her friends. Maggie and I thought about this and Maggie asked me, "Mama, when did Dee ever *have* any friends?"

She had a few. Furtive boys in pink shirts hanging about on washday after 15 school. Nervous girls who never laughed. Impressed with her they worshiped the well-turned phrase, the cute shape, the scalding humor that erupted like bubbles in lye. She read to them.

When she was courting Jimmy T she didn't have much time to pay to us, but turned all her faultfinding power on him. He *flew* to marry a cheap city girl from a family of ignorant flashy people. She hardly had time to recompose herself.

———————————

When she comes I will meet—but there they are!

Maggie attempts to make a dash for the house, in her shuffling way, but I stay her with my hand. "Come back here," I say. And she stops and tries to dig a well in the sand with her toe.

It is hard to see them clearly through the strong sun. But even the first glimpse of leg out of the car tells me it is Dee. Her feet were always neat-looking, as if God himself had shaped them with a certain style. From the other side of the car comes a short, stocky man. Hair is all over his head a foot long and hanging from his chin like a kinky mule tail. I hear Maggie suck in her breath. "Uhnnnh," is what it sounds like. Like when you see the wriggling end of a snake just in front of your foot on the road. "Uhnnnh."

Dee next. A dress down to the ground, in this hot weather. A dress so loud 20 it hurts my eyes. There are yellows and oranges enough to throw back the light of the sun. I feel my whole face warming from the heat waves it throws out. Earrings gold, too, and hanging down to her shoulders. Bracelets dangling and making noises when she moves her arm up to shake the folds of the dress out of her armpits. The dress is loose and flows, and as she walks closer, I like it. I hear Maggie go "Uhnnnh" again. It is her sister's hair. It stands straight up like the wool on a sheep. It is black as night and around the edges are two long pigtails that rope about like small lizards disappearing behind her ears.

"Wa-su-zo-Tean-o!" she says, coming on in that gliding way the dress makes her move. The short stocky fellow with the hair to his navel is all grin-ning and he follows up with "Asalamalakim, my mother and sister!" He moves to hug Maggie but she falls back, right up against the back of my chair. I feel her trembling there and when I look up I see the perspiration falling off her chin.

"Don't get up," says Dee. Since I am stout it takes something of a push. You can see me trying to move a second or two before I make it. She turns, showing white heels through her sandals, and goes back to the car. Out she peeks next with a Polaroid. She stoops down quickly and lines up picture after picture of me sitting there in front of the house with Maggie cowering behind me. She never takes a shot without making sure the house is included. When a cow comes nibbling around the edge of the yard she snaps it and me and Maggie *and* the house. Then she puts the Polaroid in the back seat of the car, and comes up and kisses me on the forehead.

Meanwhile Asalamalakim is going through motions with Maggie's hand. Maggie's hand is as limp as a fish, and probably as cold, despite the sweat, and she keeps trying to pull it back. It looks like Asalamalakim wants to shake hands but wants to do it fancy. Or maybe he don't know how people shake hands. Anyhow, he soon gives up on Maggie.

"Well," I say. "Dee."

"No, Mama," she says. "Not 'Dee,' Wangero Leewanika Kemanjo!"   25

"What happened to 'Dee'?" I wanted to know.

"She's dead," Wangero said. "I couldn't bear it any longer, being named after the people who oppress me."

"You know as well as me you was named after your aunt Dicie," I said. Dicie is my sister. She named Dee. We called her "Big Dee" after Dee was born.

"But who was *she* named after?" asked Wangero.

"I guess after Grandma Dee," I said.   30

"And who was she named after?" asked Wangero.

"Her mother," I said, and saw Wangero was getting tired. "That's about as far back as I can trace it," I said. Though, in fact, I probably could have carried it back beyond the Civil War through the branches.

"Well," said Asalamalakim, "there you are."

"Uhnnnh," I heard Maggie say.

"There I was not," I said, "before 'Dicie' cropped up in our family, so why 35 should I try to trace it that far back?"

He just stood there grinning, looking down on me like somebody inspecting a Model A car. Every once in a while he and Wangero sent eye signals over my head.

"How do you pronounce this name?" I asked.

"You don't have to call me by it if you don't want to," said Wangero.

"Why shouldn't I?" I asked. "If that's what you want us to call you, we'll call you."

"I know it might sound awkward at first," said Wangero.   40

"I'll get used to it," I said. "Ream it out again."

Well, soon we got the name out of the way. Asalamalakim had a name twice as long and three times as hard. After I tripped over it two or three times he told me to just call him Hakim-a-barber. I wanted to ask him was he a barber, but I didn't really think he was, so I didn't ask.

"You must belong to those beef-cattle peoples down the road," I said. They said "Asalamalakim" when they met you, too, but they didn't shake hands. Always too busy: feeding the cattle, fixing the fences, putting up salt-lick shelters, throwing down hay. When the white folks poisoned some of the herd the men stayed up all night with rifles in their hands. I walked a mile and a half just to see the sight.

Hakim-a-barber said, "I accept some of their doctrines, but farming and raising cattle is not my style." (They didn't tell me, and I didn't ask, whether Wangero (Dee) had really gone and married him.)

We sat down to eat and right away he said he didn't eat collards and pork 45 was unclean. Wangero, though, went on through the chitlins and corn bread, the greens and everything else. She talked a blue streak over the sweet potatoes. Everything delighted her. Even the fact that we still used the benches her daddy made for the table when we couldn't afford to buy chairs.

"Oh, Mama!" she cried. Then turned to Hakim-a-barber. "I never knew how lovely these benches are. You can feel the rump prints," she said, running her hands underneath her and along the bench. Then she gave a sigh and her hand closed over Grandma Dee's butter dish. "That's it!" she said. "I knew there was something I wanted to ask you if I could have." She jumped up from the table and went over in the corner where the churn stood, the milk in it clabber by now. She looked at the churn and looked at it.

"This churn top is what I need," she said. "Didn't Uncle Buddy whittle it out of a tree you all used to have?"

"Yes," I said.

"Uh huh," she said happily. "And I want the dasher, too."

"Uncle Buddy whittle that, too?" asked the barber.

Dee (Wangero) looked up at me.   50

"Aunt Dee's first husband whittled the dash," said Maggie so low you almost couldn't hear her. "His name was Henry, but they called him Stash."

"Maggie's brain is like an elephant's," Wangero said, laughing. "I can use the churn top as a centerpiece for the alcove table," she said, sliding a plate over the churn, "and I'll think of something artistic to do with the dasher."

When she finished wrapping the dasher the handle stuck out. I took it for a moment in my hands. You didn't even have to look close to see where hands pushing the dasher up and down to make butter had left a kind of sink in the wood. In fact, there were a lot of small sinks; you could see where thumbs and fingers had sunk into the wood. It was beautiful light yellow wood, from a tree that grew in the yard where Big Dee and Stash had lived.

After dinner Dee (Wangero) went to the trunk at the foot of my bed and   55 started rifling through it. Maggie hung back in the kitchen over the dishpan. Out came Wangero with two quilts. They had been pieced by Grandma Dee and then Big Dee and me had hung them on the quilt frames on the front porch and quilted them. One was in the Lone Star pattern. The other was Walk Around the Mountain. In both of them were scraps of dresses Grandma Dee had worn fifty and more years ago. Bits and pieces of Grandpa Jarrell's Paisley shirts. And one teeny faded blue piece, about the size of a penny matchbox, that was from Great Grandpa Ezra's uniform that he wore in the Civil War.

"Mama," Wangero said sweet as a bird. "Can I have these old quilts?"

I heard something fall in the kitchen, and a minute later the kitchen door slammed.

"Why don't you take one or two of the others?" I asked. "These old things was just done by me and Big Dee from some tops your grandma pieced before she died."

"No," said Wangero. "I don't want those. They are stitched around the borders by machine."

"That'll make them last better," I said.   60

"That's not the point," said Wangero. "These are all pieces of dresses Grandma used to wear. She did all this stitching by hand. Imagine!" She held the quilts securely in her arms, stroking them.

"Some of the pieces, like those lavender ones, come from old clothes her mother handed down to her," I said, moving up to touch the quilts. Dee (Wangero) moved back just enough so that I couldn't reach the quilts. They already belonged to her.

"Imagine!" she breathed again, clutching them closely to her bosom.

"The truth is," I said, "I promised to give them quilts to Maggie, for when she marries John Thomas."

She gasped like a bee had stung her.   65

"Maggie can't appreciate these quilts!" she said. "She'd probably be backward enough to put them to everyday use."

"I reckon she would," I said. "God knows I been saving 'em for long enough with nobody using 'em. I hope she will!" I didn't want to bring up how I had offered Dee (Wangero) a quilt when she went away to college. Then she had told me they were old-fashioned, out of style.

"But they're *priceless*!" she was saying now, furiously; for she has a temper. "Maggie would put them on the bed and in five years they'd be in rags. Less than that!"

"She can always make some more," I said. "Maggie knows how to quilt."

Dee (Wangero) looked at me with hatred. "You just will not understand.   70 The point is these quilts, *these* quilts!"

"Well," I said, stumped. "What would *you* do with them?"

"Hang them," she said. As if that was the only thing you *could* do with quilts.

Maggie by now was standing in the door. I could almost hear the sound her feet made as they scraped over each other.

"She can have them, Mama," she said, like somebody used to never winning anything, or having anything reserved for her. "I can 'member Grandma Dee without the quilts."

I looked at her hard. She had filled her bottom lip with checkerberry snuff   75 and it gave her face a kind of dopey, hangdog look. It was Grandma Dee and Big Dee who taught her how to quilt herself. She stood there with her scarred hands hidden in the folds of her skirt. She looked at her sister with something like fear but she wasn't mad at her. This was Maggie's portion. This was the way she knew God to work.

When I looked at her like that something hit me in the top of my head and ran down to the soles of my feet. Just like when I'm in church and the spirit of God touches me and I get happy and shout. I did something I never had done before: hugged Maggie to me, then dragged her on into the room, snatched the quilts out of Miss Wangero's hands and dumped them into Maggie's lap. Maggie just sat there on my bed with her mouth open.

"Take one or two of the others," I said to Dee.

But she turned without a word and went out to Hakim-a-barber.

"You just don't understand," she said, as Maggie and I came out to the car.

"What don't I understand?" I wanted to know.   80

"Your heritage," she said. And then she turned to Maggie, kissed her, and said, "You ought to try to make something of yourself, too, Maggie. It's really a new day for us. But from the way you and Mama still live you'd never know it."

She put on some sunglasses that hid everything above the tip of her nose and her chin.

Maggie smiled; maybe at the sunglasses. But a real smile, not scared. After we watched the car dust settle I asked Maggie to bring me a dip of snuff. And then the two of us sat there just enjoying, until it was time to go in the house and go to bed.

APPROACHING THE READING

1. Describe the voice you hear in "Everyday Use." What can you tell about the narrator from the way she sounds as you listen to her? What kind of personality comes through what she says and the way she says it?

2. Identify the point of view used in the story. What is the particular effect of having the narrator address the reader as *you*? In what ways does the effect of the story depend on its voice and perspective?

3. Think about the narrator and decide whether she is totally reliable, partially reliable, or generally unreliable. Explain how you made your decision and be sure to refer to specific places in the story that support your choice.

4. Explain the theme of the story, as you see it. What central point comes through, considering the story as a whole? Point to particular parts of the story that support what you say.

5. Look carefully at the final paragraph of the story. Does it fit well with what you said about voice and theme? Is it an effective and satisfying ending? If so, how and why? If you find it unsatisfying, explain why.

ENTRY POINTS   Like "Everyday Use," the following story is set in the South, but in a white community and earlier in the twentieth century. It tells of a reclusive elderly woman who seems a mystery to the other residents of her small town, especially the younger people with their new attitudes and changing ways of doing things that marginalize her all the more. It is a story that depends heavily on the point of view and perspective from which it is told. Notice them as you read or think back over it.

William Faulkner   1897–1962

A Rose for Emily   [1931]

I

When Miss Emily Grierson died, our whole town went to her funeral: the men through a sort of respectful affection for a fallen monument, the women mostly out of curiosity to see the inside of her house, which no one save an old manservant—a combined gardener and cook—had seen in at least ten years.

It was a big, squarish frame house that had once been white, decorated with cupolas and spires and scrolled balconies in the heavily lightsome style of the seventies, set on what had once been our most select street. But garages and cotton gins had encroached and obliterated even the august names of that neighborhood; only Miss Emily's house was left, lifting its stubborn and coquettish decay above the cotton wagons and the gasoline pumps — an eyesore among eyesores. And now Miss Emily had gone to join the representatives of those august names where they lay in the cedar-bemused cemetery among the ranked and anonymous graves of Union and Confederate soldiers who fell at the battle of Jefferson.

APPROACHING THE AUTHOR

William Faulkner was campus postmaster for two years at the University of Mississippi but was fired because he spent his time reading and working on a novel and people couldn't rely on him to distribute or forward the mail.

For more about him, see page 1383.

Alive, Miss Emily had been a tradition, a duty, and a care; a sort of hereditary obligation upon the town, dating from that day in 1894 when Colonel Sartoris, the mayor — he who fathered the edict that no Negro woman should appear on the streets without an apron — remitted her taxes, the dispensation dating from the death of her father on into perpetuity. Not that Miss Emily would have accepted charity. Colonel Sartoris invented an involved tale to the effect that Miss Emily's father had loaned money to the town, which the town, as a matter of business, preferred this way of repaying. Only a man of Colonel Sartoris' generation and thought could have invented it, and only a woman could have believed it.

When the next generation, with its more modern ideas, became mayors and aldermen, this arrangement created some little dissatisfaction. On the first of the year they mailed her a tax notice. February came, and there was no reply. They wrote her a formal letter, asking her to call at the sheriff's office at her convenience. A week later the mayor wrote her himself, offering to call or to send his car for her, and received in reply a note on paper of an archaic shape, in a thin, flowing calligraphy in faded ink, to the effect that she no longer went out at all. The tax notice was also enclosed, without comment.

They called a special meeting of the Board of Aldermen. A deputation waited upon her, knocked at the door through which no visitor had passed since she ceased giving china-painting lessons eight or ten years earlier. They were admitted by the old Negro into a dim hall from which a stairway mounted into still more shadow. It smelled of dust and disuse — a close, dank smell. The Negro led them into the parlor. It was furnished in heavy, leather-covered furniture. When the Negro opened the blinds of one window, they could see that the leather was cracked; and when they sat down, a faint dust rose sluggishly about their thighs, spinning with slow motes in the single sun-ray. On a tarnished gilt easel before the fireplace stood a crayon portrait of Miss Emily's father.

They rose when she entered—a small, fat woman in black, with a thin gold chain descending to her waist and vanishing into her belt, leaning on an ebony cane with a tarnished gold head. Her skeleton was small and spare; perhaps that was why what would have been merely plumpness in another was obesity in her. She looked bloated, like a body long submerged in motionless water, and of that pallid hue. Her eyes, lost in the fatty ridges of her face, looked like two small pieces of coal pressed into a lump of dough as they moved from one face to another while the visitors stated their errand.

She did not ask them to sit. She just stood in the door and listened quietly until the spokesman came to a stumbling halt. Then they could hear the invisible watch ticking at the end of the gold chain.

Her voice was dry and cold. "I have no taxes in Jefferson. Colonel Sartoris explained it to me. Perhaps one of you can gain access to the city records and satisfy yourselves."

"But we have. We are the city authorities, Miss Emily. Didn't you get a notice from the sheriff, signed by him?"

"I received a paper, yes," Miss Emily said. "Perhaps he considers himself the 10 sheriff . . . I have no taxes in Jefferson."

"But there is nothing on the books to show that, you see. We must go by the—"

"See Colonel Sartoris. I have no taxes in Jefferson."

"But, Miss Emily—"

"See Colonel Sartoris." (Colonel Sartoris had been dead almost ten years.) "I have no taxes in Jefferson. Tobe!" The Negro appeared. "Show these gentlemen out."

II

So she vanquished them, horse and foot, just as she had vanquished their 15 fathers thirty years before about the smell. That was two years after her father's death and a short time after her sweetheart—the one we believed would marry her—had deserted her. After her father's death she went out very little; after her sweetheart went away, people hardly saw her at all. A few of the ladies had the temerity to call, but were not received, and the only sign of life about the place was the Negro man—a young man then—going in and out with a market basket.

"Just as if a man—any man—could keep a kitchen properly," the ladies said; so they were not surprised when the smell developed. It was another link between the gross, teeming world and the high and mighty Griersons.

A neighbor, a woman, complained to the mayor, Judge Stevens, eighty years old.

"But what will you have me do about it, madam?" he said.

"Why, send her word to stop it," the woman said. "Isn't there a law?"

"I'm sure that won't be necessary," Judge Stevens said. "It's probably just a 20 snake or a rat that nigger of hers killed in the yard. I'll speak to him about it."

The next day he received two more complaints, one from a man who came in diffident deprecation. "We really must do something about it, Judge. I'd be

the last one in the world to bother Miss Emily, but we've got to do something."
That night the Board of Aldermen met—three graybeards and one younger man,
a member of the rising generation.

"It's simple enough," he said. "Send her word to have her place cleaned up.
Give her a certain time to do it in, and if she don't . . ."

"Dammit, sir," Judge Stevens said, "will you accuse a lady to her face of
smelling bad?"

So the next night, after midnight, four men crossed Miss Emily's lawn and
slunk about the house like burglars, sniffing along the base of the brickwork
and at the cellar openings while one of them performed a regular sowing
motion with his hand out of a sack slung from his shoulder. They broke open
the cellar door and sprinkled lime there, and in all the outbuildings. As they
recrossed the lawn, a window that had been dark was lighted and Miss Emily
sat in it, the light behind her, and her upright torso motionless as that of an
idol. They crept quietly across the lawn and into the shadow of the locusts that
lined the street. After a week or two the smell went away.

That was when people had begun to feel really sorry for her. People in our 25
town, remembering how old lady Wyatt, her great-aunt, had gone completely
crazy at last, believed that the Griersons held themselves a little too high for
what they really were. None of the young men were quite good enough for
Miss Emily and such. We had long thought of them as a tableau,° Miss Emily
a slender figure in white in the background, her father a spraddled silhouette
in the foreground, his back to her and clutching a horsewhip, the two of them
framed by the back-flung front door. So when she got to be thirty and was still
single, we were not pleased exactly, but vindicated; even with insanity in the
family she wouldn't have turned down all of her chances if they had really
materialized.

When her father died, it got about that the house was all that was left to
her; and in a way, people were glad. At last they could pity Miss Emily. Being
left alone, and a pauper, she had become humanized. Now she too would know
the old thrill and the old despair of a penny more or less.

The day after his death all the ladies prepared to call at the house and offer
condolence and aid, as is our custom. Miss Emily met them at the door, dressed as
usual and with no trace of grief on her face. She told them that her father was not
dead. She did that for three days, with the ministers calling on her, and the doctors,
trying to persuade her to let them dispose of the body. Just as they were about to
resort to law and force, she broke down, and they buried her father quickly.

We did not say she was crazy then. We believed she had to do that. We
remembered all the young men her father had driven away, and we knew that
with nothing left, she would have to cling to that which had robbed her, as
people will.

---

tableau: short for *tableau vivant* (French), "living painting"; a depiction of a scene or picture
by a person or group in costume, posing silently without moving.

III

She was sick for a long time. When we saw her again, her hair was cut short, making her look like a girl, with a vague resemblance to those angels in colored church windows—sort of tragic and serene.

The town had just let the contracts for paving the sidewalks, and in the 30 summer after her father's death they began the work. The construction company came with niggers and mules and machinery, and a foreman named Homer Barron, a Yankee—a big, dark, ready man, with a big voice and eyes lighter than his face. The little boys would follow in groups to hear him cuss the niggers, and the niggers singing in time to the rise and fall of picks. Pretty soon he knew everybody in town. Whenever you heard a lot of laughing anywhere about the square, Homer Barron would be in the center of the group. Presently we began to see him and Miss Emily on Sunday afternoons driving in the yellow-wheeled buggy and the matched team of bays from the livery stable.

At first we were glad that Miss Emily would have an interest, because the ladies all said, "Of course a Grierson would not think seriously of a Northerner, a day laborer." But there were still others, older people, who said that even grief could not cause a real lady to forget *noblesse oblige*°—without calling it *noblesse oblige*. They just said, "Poor Emily. Her kinsfolk should come to her." She had some kin in Alabama; but years ago her father had fallen out with them over the estate of old lady Wyatt, the crazy woman, and there was no communication between the two families. They had not even been represented at the funeral.

And as soon as the old people said, "Poor Emily," the whispering began. "Do you suppose it's really so?" they said to one another. "Of course it is. What else could..." This behind their hands; rustling of craned silk and satin behind jalousies closed upon the sun of Sunday afternoon as the thin, swift clop-clop-clop of the matched team passed: "Poor Emily."

She carried her head high enough—even when we believed that she was fallen. It was as if she demanded more than ever the recognition of her dignity as the last Grierson; as if it had wanted that touch of earthiness to reaffirm her imperviousness. Like when she bought the rat poison, the arsenic. That was over a year after they had begun to say "Poor Emily," and while the two female cousins were visiting her.

"I want some poison," she said to the druggist. She was over thirty then, still a slight woman, though thinner than usual, with cold, haughty black eyes in a face the flesh of which was strained across the temples and about the eye-sockets as you imagine a lighthouse-keeper's face ought to look. "I want some poison," she said.

"Yes, Miss Emily. What kind? For rats and such? I'd recom—"   35

"I want the best you have. I don't care what kind."

---

noblesse oblige: "Nobility obligates" (French); the inferred obligation of people of high rank or social position to behave nobly, generously, and kindly toward others.

The druggist named several. "They'll kill anything up to an elephant. But what you want is—"

"Arsenic," Miss Emily said. "Is that a good one?"

"Is...arsenic? Yes, ma'am. But what you want—"

"I want arsenic."   40

The druggist looked down at her. She looked back at him, erect, her face like a strained flag. "Why, of course," the druggist said. "If that's what you want. But the law requires you to tell what you are going to use it for."

Miss Emily just stared at him, her head tilted back in order to look him eye for eye, until he looked away and went and got the arsenic and wrapped it up. The Negro delivery boy brought her the package; the druggist didn't come back. When she opened the package at home there was written on the box, under the skull and bones: "For rats."

IV

So the next day we all said, "She will kill herself"; and we said it would be the best thing. When she had first begun to be seen with Homer Barron, we had said, "She will marry him." Then we said, "She will persuade him yet," because Homer himself had remarked—he liked men, and it was known that he drank with the younger men in the Elks' Club—that he was not a marrying man. Later we said, "Poor Emily" behind the jalousies as they passed on Sunday afternoon in the glittering buggy, Miss Emily with her head high and Homer Barron with his hat cocked and a cigar in his teeth, reins and whip in a yellow glove.

Then some of the ladies began to say that it was a disgrace to the town and a bad example to the young people. The men did not want to interfere, but at last the ladies forced the Baptist minister—Miss Emily's people were Episcopal—to call upon her. He would never divulge what happened during that interview, but he refused to go back again. The next Sunday they again drove about the streets, and the following day the minister's wife wrote to Miss Emily's relations in Alabama.

So she had blood-kin under her roof again and we sat back to watch   45 developments. At first nothing happened. Then we were sure that they were to be married. We learned that Miss Emily had been to the jeweler's and ordered a man's toilet set in silver, with the letters H. B. on each piece. Two days later we learned that she had bought a complete outfit of men's clothing, including a nightshirt, and we said, "They are married." We were really glad. We were glad because the two female cousins were even more Grierson than Miss Emily had ever been.

So we were not surprised when Homer Barron—the streets had been finished some time since—was gone. We were a little disappointed that there was not a public blowing-off, but we believed that he had gone on to prepare for Miss Emily's coming, or to give her a chance to get rid of the cousins. (By that time it was a cabal, and we were all Miss Emily's allies to help circumvent the

cousins.) Sure enough, after another week they departed. And, as we had expected all along, within three days Homer Barron was back in town. A neighbor
saw the Negro man admit him at the kitchen door at dusk one evening.

And that was the last we saw of Homer Barron. And of Miss Emily for some
time. The Negro man went in and out with the market basket, but the front
door remained closed. Now and then we would see her at a window for a
moment, as the men did that night when they sprinkled the lime, but for
almost six months she did not appear on the streets. Then we knew that this
was to be expected too; as if that quality of her father which had thwarted her
woman's life so many times had been too virulent and too furious to die.

When we next saw Miss Emily, she had grown fat and her hair was turning
gray. During the next few years it grew grayer and grayer until it attained an
even pepper-and-salt iron-gray, when it ceased turning. Up to the day of her
death at seventy-four it was still that vigorous iron-gray, like the hair of an
active man.

From that time on her front door remained closed, save for a period of six
or seven years, when she was about forty, during which she gave lessons in
china-painting. She fitted up a studio in one of the downstairs rooms, where
the daughters and granddaughters of Colonel Sartoris' contemporaries were sent
to her with the same regularity and in the same spirit that they were sent to
church on Sundays with a twenty-five-cent piece for the collection plate.
Meanwhile her taxes had been remitted.

Then the newer generation became the backbone and the spirit of the town,   50
and the painting pupils grew up and fell away and did not send their children
to her with boxes of color and tedious brushes and pictures cut from the ladies'
magazines. The front door closed upon the last one and remained closed for
good. When the town got free postal delivery, Miss Emily alone refused to let
them fasten the metal numbers above her door and attach a mailbox to it. She
would not listen to them.

Daily, monthly, yearly we watched the Negro grow grayer and more stooped,
going in and out with the market basket. Each December we sent her a tax notice, which would be returned by the post office a week later, unclaimed. Now
and then we would see her in one of the downstairs windows—she had evidently shut up the top floor of the house—like the carven torso of an idol in a
niche, looking or not looking at us, we could never tell which. Thus she passed
from generation to generation—dear, inescapable, impervious, tranquil, and
perverse.

And so she died. Fell ill in the house filled with dust and shadows, with only
a doddering Negro man to wait on her. We did not even know she was sick; we
had long since given up trying to get any information from the Negro. He
talked to no one, probably not even to her, for his voice had grown harsh and
rusty, as if from disuse.

She died in one of the downstairs rooms, in a heavy walnut bed with a
curtain, her gray head propped on a pillow yellow and moldy with age and lack
of sunlight.

V

The Negro met the first of the ladies at the front door and let them in, with their hushed, sibilant voices and their quick, curious glances, and then he disappeared. He walked right through the house and out the back and was not seen again.

The two female cousins came at once. They held the funeral on the second 55 day, with the town coming to look at Miss Emily beneath a mass of bought flowers, with the crayon face of her father musing profoundly above the bier and the ladies sibilant and macabre; and the very old men—some in their brushed Confederate uniforms—on the porch and the lawn, talking of Miss Emily as if she had been a contemporary of theirs, believing that they had danced with her and courted her perhaps, confusing time with its mathematical progression, as the old do, to whom all the past is not a diminishing road but, instead, a huge meadow which no winter ever quite touches, divided from them now by the narrow bottle-neck of the most recent decade of years.

Already we knew that there was one room in that region above stairs which no one had seen in forty years, and which would have to be forced. They waited until Miss Emily was decently in the ground before they opened it.

The violence of breaking down the door seemed to fill this room with pervading dust. A thin, acrid pall as of the tomb seemed to lie everywhere upon this room decked and furnished as for a bridal: upon the valance curtains of faded rose color, upon the rose-shaded lights, upon the dressing table, upon the delicate array of crystal and the man's toilet things backed with tarnished silver, silver so tarnished that the monogram was obscured. Among them lay a collar and tie, as if they had just been removed, which, lifted, left upon the surface a pale crescent in the dust. Upon a chair hung the suit, carefully folded; beneath it the two mute shoes and the discarded socks.

The man himself lay in the bed.

For a long while we just stood there, looking down at the profound and fleshless grin. The body had apparently once lain in the attitude of an embrace, but now the long sleep that outlasts love, that conquers even the grimace of love, had cuckolded him. What was left of him, rotted beneath what was left of the nightshirt, had become inextricable from the bed in which he lay; and upon him and upon the pillow beside him lay that even coating of the patient and biding dust.

Then we noticed that in the second pillow was the indentation of a head. 60 One of us lifted something from it, and leaning forward, that faint and invisible dust dry and acrid in the nostrils, we saw a long strand of iron-gray hair.

APPROACHING THE READING

1. Telling a story from a first-person plural point of view is unusual. Who is the narrator? How much does the narrator know? What is the advantage in using the plural? Consider how the effect would be different if in each case "our" was changed to "my" and "we" changed to "I."

2. Do you think the story could have been told effectively from a third-person omniscient point of view? Describe ways it would be different and how its effect would be different.

3. Summarize Miss Emily's character. To what extent is what you know about her shaped and affected by the story's point of view? Would you know her better if the story had used a third-person omniscient point of view? Would that have made the story more effective?

4. What would you say is the central idea (theme) of the story? What does it all add up to? In what ways does the title fit, or relate to, its theme?

ENTRY POINTS   The excerpt on the opposing page is from *Persepolis*, a work that powerfully reveals the horror of war in Iran. As you read it the first time, focus on understanding the powers at war and the impact of the war on the characters. On your second reading, think about the ways the point of view is revealed through the words, the dialogue, the drawings, and the interplay of words and drawings. Notice, too, when the theme is revealed in the drawings, in the words, or in their combination.

APPROACHING THE AUTHOR

Marjane Satrapi cowrote and codirected the animated film version of *Persepolis* which debuted at the 2007 Cannes Film Festival and shared a Special Jury Prize. For more about her, see page 1410.

Marjane Satrapi b. 1969

"The Cigarette" from *Persepolis*   [2003]

THE CIGARETTE

THE WAR HAD BEEN GOING ON FOR TWO YEARS. WE WERE USED TO IT. I WAS GROWING UP AND I EVEN HAD FRIENDS OLDER THAN ME.

YESTERDAY ON THE NEWS THEY SAID WE DESTROYED 13 IRAQI PLANES. RIGHT AFTER ON THE BBC, I HEARD THAT IN FACT THE IRAQIS HAD SHOT DOWN TWO OF OURS.

IT'S PERFECTLY CLEAR. EVERY DAY THEY TELL US THAT WE'VE DESTROYED TEN PLANES AND FIVE TANKS. IF YOU START FROM THE BEGINNING OF THE WAR, THAT MAKES SIX THOUSAND PLANES AND THREE THOUSAND TANKS DESTROYED. EVEN THE AMERICANS DON'T HAVE AN ARMY THIS BIG.

I GET IT. I'M GOING TO TELL MY DAD THAT ONE.

BRINGGG...

HEY, THERE'S THE BELL. DON'T YOU HAVE CLASS?

NO, WE'VE GOT PHYSICAL EDUCATION BUT WE'RE NOT GOING. WE'RE GOING FOR BURGERS.

BURGERS?

THEY ALSO HAVE HOT DOGS.

ALL YOU NEEDED WAS SOME MONEY.

YEAH! AT KANSAS ON JORDAN AVENUE.

DON'T LOOK AT ME LIKE THAT. WE'LL CLIMB THE WALL.

THE WALL??!!

HA HA HA HA! HA HA HA!

IF I WANTED TO BE FRIENDS WITH 14-YEAR-OLDS, I HAD TO DO IT.

I WASN'T CHICKEN, SO I FOLLOWED THEM.

I HAD ALREADY BROKEN THE RULES ONCE BY GOING TO THE DEMONSTRATION IN '79. THIS WAS THE SECOND TIME.

JORDAN AVENUE WAS WHERE THE TEENAGERS FROM NORTH TEHRAN (THE NICE NEIGHBORHOODS) HUNG OUT. KANSAS WAS ITS TEMPLE.

IF SOME PUBLIC PLACES HAD SURVIVED THE REGIME'S REPRESSION, EITHER IT WAS TO LEAVE US A LITTLE FREE SPACE, OR ELSE IT WAS OUT OF IGNORANCE. PERSONALLY, THE LATTER THEORY SOUNDED MORE LIKELY: THEY PROBABLY HADN'T THE SLIGHTEST IDEA WHAT "KANSAS" WAS.

DID YOU SEE HIS HAIR? JUST LIKE ROD STEWART!

YEAH, IF HE GETS CAUGHT, HE'LL GET A BUZZ CUT!

...IN SPITE OF EVERYTHING, KIDS WERE TRYING TO LOOK HIP, EVEN UNDER RISK OF ARREST.

MY FRIENDS WEREN'T ACTUALLY THAT INTERESTED IN THE HAMBURGERS...

WE LET THE BOYS KNOW THAT THEY COULD FOLLOW US BY A FEW SIGNS.

FOLLOW THE OTHERS, I MEAN. I WAS TOO YOUNG TO INTEREST THEM.

WOOOOO

...THE SIRENS WENT OFF.

WHAT THE HELL ARE YOU DOING??

HIT THE DIRT!

?

?

?

WE HAD BEEN TOLD THAT IF WE WERE IN THE STREET DURING A BOMBING, WE SHOULD LIE DOWN IN THE GUTTER FOR SAFETY.

HA! YOU CHICKEN!

THE WONDERFUL DAY WAS SPOILED BY MY MOM.

SO HOW WAS SCHOOL?

OK. WHY?

YOU DARE TO LIE STRAIGHT TO MY FACE?

I'M NOT LYING!

SO MAYBE IT'S ME WHO CUT CLASS?

WHAT CLASS?

YOU TELL ME THE TRUTH RIGHT NOW OR ELSE YOU'LL BE PUNISHED TWICE!

MY MOTHER USED THE SAME TACTICS AS THE TORTURERS.

BUT ALL I HAD WAS RELIGION CLASS!

I DON'T GIVE A DAMN! YOU DON'T CUT CLASS!

AND YOU JUST LIED AGAIN! THE SCHOOL CALLED AND SAID YOU HAD GRAMMAR THIS AFTERNOON!

I HAD SAID RELIGION TO TRY TO MAKE MY MOTHER LESS ANGRY, BUT IT HADN'T WORKED.

THIS TIME I COVERED FOR YOU, BUT IT'S THE LAST TIME! NOW IS THE TIME FOR LEARNING. YOU HAVE YOUR WHOLE LIFE TO HAVE FUN! WHAT ARE YOU GOING TO BE WHEN YOU GROW UP?? IN THIS COUNTRY YOU HAVE TO KNOW EVERYTHING BETTER THAN ANYONE ELSE IF YOU'RE GOING TO SURVIVE!!

DIDN'T YOU MEET DAD WHEN YOU WERE FOURTEEN?

YOU'RE NOT FOURTEEN!

SO? I'M TWELVE!

DICTATOR! YOU ARE THE GUARDIAN OF THE REVOLUTION OF THIS HOUSE!

SOMEWHAT LATER...

THE IRANIAN ARMY HAS RETAKEN KHORRAMSHAHR...

...FOR THE FOURTH TIME THIS MONTH.

EVEN IF IT'S TRUE, WHAT DIFFERENCE DOES IT MAKE TO US?

MAY I GO TO THE BASEMENT, MA'AM?

YES, MISS SATRAPI.

THE BASEMENT WAS MY HIDEAWAY.

CLICK

AS IT TURNED OUT, THEY DID RETAKE KHORRÁMSHAHR. WE ALL THOUGHT THAT THE WAR WOULD FINALLY END.

IN FACT, IRAQ PROPOSED A SETTLEMENT, AND SAUDI ARABIA WAS WILLING TO PAY FOR RECONSTRUCTION, TO RESTORE PEACE TO THE AREA.

BUT OUR GOVERNMENT WAS AGAINST IT.

THEY DECLARED:

WE REFUSE THIS IMPOSED PEACE!

✱ A SHIITE HOLY CITY IN IRAQ

APPROACHING THE READING

1. Think about how a drawing can have what in literature is called a "voice." How would you describe the voice of this piece given that the words and drawings work together?

2. The theme of the work is complex. Think about how you would express that complexity.

3. What do you conclude to be the point of view of the piece? How do the drawings and dialogue support your conclusion?

You can research the authors in this chapter with LitLinks, or take a quiz on the stories with LitQuiz, at bedfordstmartins.com/rewritinglit.

4. What has the most impact on the way Satrapi presents the theme? The drawings? The words? The way they're combined? Where in the narrative does the drawing in the panel enrich the text and deepen your response to the theme? Where does a drawing's portrayal of the theme deepen because of the language?

RESPONDING THROUGH Writing

WRITING ABOUT POINT OF VIEW AND THEME

Journal Entries

1. As a way of getting a hold of point of view in fiction, pay attention to point of view in several TV shows or movies. Notice the perspective from which each is presented: Does it stick to one character or group of characters, or does it switch back and forth between two (or more) characters or groups of characters? Watch the use of the camera as an "eye": From what perspective does it let you see what's happening—only from "outside" and at a distance? Does it ever show just what one character is seeing? Write a journal entry summarizing what you observe and discussing how what you observed might apply to or clarify point of view in fiction.

2. In your journal, rewrite part of a story using a different point of view—Sandra Cisneros's "The House on Mango Street" (p. 160) or John Updike's "A & P" (p. 552) as a third-person instead of first-person narrative, for example.

3. In your journal, rewrite part of a story from a different perspective, for example, from the perspective of the mother in Sandra Cisneros's "The House on Mango Street" (p. 160).

Literary Analysis Papers

4. Write a paper in which you examine how the handling of point of view and time contribute to theme in "The Cigarette" (p. 185).

5. Discussions of point of view usually center on the question of how appropriate and effective the point of view is in terms of the best way to present the action and characters and to develop the story's theme. Write a paper discussing the appropriateness and effectiveness of point of view to presentation and theme in one of the following stories:

   - first-person unreliable in Toni Morrison's "Recitatif" (p. 445)
   - first-person reliable in John Updike's "A & P" (p. 552)
   - third-person omniscient in Zora Neale Hurston's "Sweat" (p. 421)
   - third-person limited in Leslie Marmon Silko's "The Man to Send Rain Clouds" (p. 540)
   - third-person limited and stream of consciousness in Katherine Anne Porter's "The Jilting of Granny Weatherall" (p. 533)
   - interior monologue in Tillie Olsen's "I Stand Here Ironing" (p. 506)

6. Write a paper discussing theme in "Everyday Use" (p. 169). Include a consideration of the title as it applies to Dee (Wangero) and to her mother and sister. Consider what Dee means by, "You just don't understand" (para. 79). What does *Dee* not understand?

Comparison-Contrast Papers

7. Stories about "outsiders" look different depending on the point of view from which they are told. Does a character feel, or is she or he made to feel, like an outsider? Does one character look at another as an outsider? Compare

TIPS for Writing about Point of View and Theme

- **Point out point of view.** Almost every paper about a work of fiction should identify its point of view, usually through a passing reference.

- **Analyze if unusual.** Point of view should be a central focus in a paper only if it is unusual or complex or crucial to the way the story works.

- **Be thorough.** When a paper focuses on point of view, clarify both the person and the perspective precisely, using quotations to illustrate and support what you say. Then explain, with supporting evidence, what is important about how they are handled in the story.

- **Refer to theme regularly.** Because theme is what a story "all adds up to," most papers discussing a story should at least mention its theme and explain how other elements relate to or bring out that theme.

- **Explore complex themes in depth.** When a story is particularly complex or unusual, a paper can be an in-depth exploration of the story's meaning and implications. Be sure that you do more than summarize what the story is about or restate what is obvious in it.

and contrast both perspectives in a story dealing with an outsider—Esperanza in Sandra Cisneros's "The House on Mango Street" (p. 160), or Henry in Louise Erdrich's "The Red Convertible" (p. 126), Arnold in Joyce Carol Oates's "Where Are You Going, Where Have You Been?" (p. 481), or the narrator in Ralph Ellison's "Battle Royal" (p. 402).

8. Write a paper that compares and contrasts the handling of parent-child conflict in two of the following stories: Alice Walker's "Everyday Use" (p. 169), Tillie Olsen's "I Stand Here Ironing" (p. 506), or Amy Tan's "Two Kinds" (p. 543).

WRITING ABOUT CONNECTIONS

Points of view and themes, by the way they work in a story, connect us with the complexities, both joyful and disappointing, of our own and others' lives.

Such connections often yield even richer and more nuanced experiences and insights when stories are paired with each other, especially when two stories from different cultures or different time periods are brought together. Here are just a few examples to consider:

1. "Staring Out Front Windows": Seeking Escape in Sandra Cisneros's "The House on Mango Street" (p. 160) and James Joyce's "Araby" (p. 242)

2. "Can You Come Home Again?": The Difficulty of Returning in Alice Walker's "Everyday Use" (p. 169) and James Baldwin's "Sonny's Blues" (p. 362)

3. "Tales of Entrapment": Lives Lacking Fulfillment in David Means's "The Secret Goldfish" (p. 215) and John Steinbeck's "The Chrysanthemums" (p. 320)

WRITING RESEARCH PAPERS

1. Conduct research into the cultural meaning of houses—of owning one's own place, of the type of house one owns and its location. In what ways does the house one lives in affect one's self and life, have power, and lead to acceptance or conflict or rejection? Write a paper on this topic, focusing on Sandra Cisneros's "The House on Mango Street" (p. 160) and Alice Walker's "Everyday Use" (p. 169) as starting points.

2. Explore the importance of quilts as cultural artifacts. In what ways are they important beyond providing warmth? What do they reveal about the people who make them and the society that values them? Write a paper applying what you find to Alice Walker's "Everyday Use" (p. 169), showing how a deeper knowledge of quilts adds more meaning to the story.

Remember in your story that setting is the other character. It is as important to your story as the people in it.

Rob Parnell

(*Author of* The Easy Way to Write a Novel)

Setting and Symbol
Meeting Meaning in Places and Objects

Of all the memories we look back on, those involving places often carry particularly important emotional weight. We may have special memories of a grandmother's house or a good friend's apartment; a street corner or a park down the street; a gymnasium or playground across town—or even nightmarish memories of an abandoned house in the country, a cemetery, or a back alley. Reflect for a moment on some significant places in your own life. What specific details come back to mind?

Place (or setting) is very important in stories as well, as the area and context in which the characters live and where the events occur. Place may be the key locale of a story, or in addition it may convey symbolic meaning, taking on an expanding significance beyond that of the location of the action. This chapter explores setting and symbol to help you realize more fully what these two contribute to a story and how they sometimes interrelate.

READING FOR SETTING

ENTRY POINTS The **setting** of a story, poem, or play is its overall context—where, when, and in what circumstances the action occurs. In the following story, the setting plays an important role. Two characters, a young woman named Jig and her male companion, are waiting for a train. As you read about them, listen for a major conflict in their relationship and what their discussion of it reveals about their characters. Focus also on where they are (the country, the part of the country, the specific building and its surroundings) and on how the place is described. Look for connections between where they are and what they are talking about.

Ernest Hemingway 1899–1961

Hills Like White Elephants   [1927]

The hills across the valley of the Ebro were long and white. On this side there was no shade and no trees and the station was between two lines of rails in the sun. Close against the side of the station there was the warm shadow of the building and a curtain, made of strings of bamboo beads, hung across the open door into the bar, to keep out flies. The American and the girl with him sat at a table in the shade, outside the building. It was very hot and the express from Barcelona would come in forty minutes. It stopped at this junction for two minutes and went on to Madrid.

"What should we drink?" the girl asked. She had taken off her hat and put it on the table.

"It's pretty hot," the man said.

"Let's drink beer."

"Dos cervezas,"° the man said into   5
the curtain.

"Big ones?" a woman asked from the doorway.

"Yes. Two big ones."

The woman brought two glasses of beer and two felt pads. She put the felt pads and the beer glasses on the table and looked at the man and the girl. The girl was looking off at the line of hills. They were white in the sun and the country was brown and dry.

"They look like white elephants," she said.

"I've never seen one," the man drank his beer.   10

"No, you wouldn't have."

"I might have," the man said. "Just because you say I wouldn't have doesn't prove anything."

The girl looked at the bead curtain. "They've painted something on it," she said. "What does it say?"

Dos cervezas: Two beers (Spanish).

"Anis del Toro. It's a drink."

"Could we try it?"

The man called "Listen" through the curtain. The woman came out from the bar.

"Four reales."

"We want two Anis del Toro."

"With water?"

"Do you want it with water?"

"I don't know," the girl said. "Is it good with water?"

"It's all right."

"You want them with water?" asked the woman.

"Yes, with water."

"It tastes like licorice," the girl said and put the glass down.

"That's the way with everything."

"Yes," said the girl. "Everything tastes of licorice. Especially all the things you've waited so long for, like absinthe."

"Oh, cut it out."

"You started it," the girl said. "I was being amused. I was having a fine time."

"Well, let's try and have a fine time."

"All right. I was trying. I said the mountains looked like white elephants. Wasn't that bright?"

"That was bright."

"I wanted to try this new drink. That's all we do, isn't it — look at things and try new drinks?"

"I guess so."

The girl looked across at the hills.

"They're lovely hills," she said. "They don't really look like white elephants. I just meant the coloring of their skin through the trees."

"Should we have another drink?"

"All right."

The warm wind blew the bead curtain against the table.

"The beer's nice and cool," the man said.

"It's lovely," the girl said.

"It's really an awfully simple operation, Jig," the man said. "It's not really an operation at all."

The girl looked at the ground the table legs rested on.

"I know you wouldn't mind it, Jig. It's really not anything. It's just to let the air in."

The girl did not say anything.

"I'll go with you and I'll stay with you all the time. They just let the air in and then it's all perfectly natural."

"Then what will we do afterward?"

"We'll be fine afterward. Just like we were before."

"What makes you think so?"

"That's the only thing that bothers us. It's the only thing that's made us unhappy."

The girl looked at the bead curtain, put her hand out and took hold of two of the strings of beads.

"And you think then we'll be all right and be happy."

"I know we will. You don't have to be afraid. I've known lots of people that have done it."

"So have I," said the girl. "And afterward they were all so happy."

"Well," the man said, "if you don't want to you don't have to. I wouldn't 55 have you do it if you didn't want to. But I know it's perfectly simple."

"And you really want to?"

"I think it's the best thing to do. But I don't want you to do it if you don't really want to."

"And if I do it you'll be happy and things will be like they were and you'll love me?"

"I love you now. You know I love you."

"I know. But if I do it, then it will be nice again if I say things are like white 60 elephants, and you'll like it?"

"I'll love it. I love it now but I just can't think about it. You know how I get when I worry."

"If I do it you won't ever worry?"

"I won't worry about that because it's perfectly simple."

"Then I'll do it. Because I don't care about me."

"What do you mean?"   65

"I don't care about me."

"Well, I care about you."

"Oh, yes. But I don't care about me. And I'll do it and then everything will be fine."

"I don't want you to do it if you feel that way."

The girl stood up and walked to the end of the station. Across, on the other 70 side, were fields of grain and trees along the banks of the Ebro. Far away, beyond the river, were mountains. The shadow of a cloud moved across the field of grain and she saw the river through the trees.

"And we could have all this," she said. "And we could have everything and every day we make it more impossible."

"What did you say?"

"I said we could have everything."

"We can have everything."

"No, we can't."   75

"We can have the whole world."

"No, we can't."

"We can go everywhere."

"No, we can't. It isn't ours any more."

"It's ours."

"No, it isn't. And once they take it away, you never get it back."   80

"But they haven't taken it away."

"We'll wait and see."

"Come on back in the shade," he said. "You mustn't feel that way."

"I don't feel any way," the girl said. "I just know things."   85

"I don't want you to do anything that you don't want to do—"

"Nor that isn't good for me," she said. "I know. Could we have another beer?"

"All right. But you've got to realize—"

"I realize," the girl said. "Can't we maybe stop talking?"

They sat down at the table and the girl looked across at the hills on the dry   90
side of the valley and the man looked at her and at the table.

"You've got to realize," he said, "that I don't want you to do it if you don't want to. I'm perfectly willing to go through with it if it means anything to you."

"Doesn't it mean anything to you? We could get along."

"Of course it does. But I don't want anybody but you. I don't want any one else. And I know it's perfectly simple."

"Yes, you know it's perfectly simple."

"It's all right for you to say that, but I do know it."   95

"Would you do something for me now?"

"I'd do anything for you."

"Would you please please please please please please please stop talking?"

He did not say anything but looked at the bags against the wall of the station. There were labels on them from all the hotels where they had spent nights.

"But I don't want you to," he said, "I don't care anything about it."   100

"I'll scream," the girl said.

The woman came out through the curtains with two glasses of beer and put them down on the damp felt pads. "The train comes in five minutes," she said.

"What did she say?" asked the girl.

"That the train is coming in five minutes."

The girl smiled brightly at the woman, to thank her.   105

"I'd better take the bags over to the other side of the station," the man said. She smiled at him.

"All right. Then come back and we'll finish the beer."

He picked up the two heavy bags and carried them around the station to the other tracks. He looked up the tracks but could not see the train. Coming back, he walked through the barroom, where people waiting for the train were drinking. He drank an Anis at the bar and looked at the people. They were all waiting reasonably for the train. He went out through the bead curtain. She was sitting at the table and smiled at him.

"Do you feel better?" he asked.

"I feel fine," she said. "There's nothing wrong with me. I feel fine."   110

APPROACHING THE READING

1. Think first about what you saw as you read the story. References to Barcelona, Madrid, and the Ebro broadly identify the place where the scene happens as Spain. You might look at a map to identify where these places

are and find a book with pictures of that area so you can visualize the scene more precisely. How does it affect you to have the story occur in Europe? How might the effect differ if it had occurred in the United States?

2. Think about the immediate location—a train junction out in the middle of nowhere. What is the effect of the rural train junction? How would it be different if the American and Jig were in a big train station in Madrid? Sitting in a coffee shop in Paris or New York or a small town in the United States?

3. White elephants are mentioned in the title and several times in the story. Jig says she is referring to elephants that are white. Could there be more to the words than that? Look "white elephant" up in a dictionary. Think about why the words have a symbolic significance.

4. Consider possible connections between white elephants and the conflict, or conflicts, between the main characters. What do you think is the operation the man is urging on Jig? What details from the story support your answer? Is the operation their only conflict?

5. "We'll be fine afterward. Just like we were before," the American says to Jig (para. 48). This line opens an enormous gap—their future—for you to fill in. Where do you think they would go if the story continued? What would happen? How does ending where it does indicate what is important in the story? How do you respond to Jig's concluding lines?

Setting as Place

INDICATING PLACE   Basic to a story's context is place, or locale—the physical environment. We need to know the locale in a broad sense: Where does the action take place? What country? What city or region of that country? We also need to know the locale in a specific, narrower sense: What kind of place—downtown, suburban neighborhood, rural area, or highway? What specific street, house, farm, or junction? Physical setting—whether an apartment, a factory, a train station, or a prison camp—can be presented through vibrant, specific details, or it can be sketched broadly with a few, quick strokes. The setting of "Hills Like White Elephants" is indicated in the first paragraph: the broad setting—eastern Spain, about a third of the way from Barcelona to Madrid—and the specific setting—a hot day at a rural train station, a junction where two lines meet in the middle of nowhere.

SIGNIFICANCE OF PLACE   The description of a setting often evokes its significance, what it conveys and suggests. Reflect, for example, on the significance of the principal setting in "The Red Convertible" (p. 126) being a reservation. Ask yourself how the story would be different if Lyman and Henry lived in Chicago. Think about the locale of "Hills Like White Elephants," how by creating a sense of isolation, the story focuses our attention on the two people and their problem. There are other people in the bar, but we see no one else except the waitress — the other people are just there, like the chairs and tables.

The location includes only a railway junction: No town or city is indicated, which increases the sense of isolation. There is no community to support or affect them in what they face or decide (especially in what Jig faces and must decide) — just two individuals, making an individual decision as if it affects no one but themselves (at least that's how the man views it). Using a train station as locale also creates a sense of transience — no roots, no home, no ties. And placing the story at a junction suggests that the characters are facing a decision about the direction in which they should go.

Setting as Time

Setting also includes the time in which the events occur, time in all its dimensions: the century, the year, the season, the day, the hour, maybe even the exact second. In some cases, a specific time is not indicated: The events are universal and could as well have occurred a minute or a millennium ago. Often, however, a specific or approximate time is either assumed (the time may seem the same as when the story was written or published) or indicated — perhaps by giving a date in the story, by mentioning historical events that were going on at the time of the story, or by describing the way people talk, act, or dress. In those cases, the specific time may be significant, and knowing something about that time period may help you understand what is going on or the significance of what occurs.

HISTORICAL EVENTS   Assessing the significance of a specific time may require asking questions and then doing some investigating — in an encyclopedia, or on the Internet, or through more specialized books, depending on the time period involved and the way the story uses its setting.

Consider, for example, "Hills Like White Elephants." The action is probably contemporaneous with when it was written, in the mid-1920s. To decide if that time setting is significant to the story, ask what was going on at that time, what was significant or noteworthy. You might check a time line of world or European historical events. You'll notice that the story takes place less than ten years after the end of World War I (1914–1918).

To gain the full impact of the story's setting in time, you might need to do some reading about the war and its aftermath (an encyclopedia entry on the war probably would suffice). The war caused immense loss of life, physical suffering, and psychological and emotional damage from trench warfare and the use of nerve gas. It is estimated that 8.5 million military personnel died (a high percentage of a whole generation's young men), along with 10 million civilians. Although the corresponding numbers in World War II were much greater, at the time the number of deaths and amount of devastation were unprecedented. It was called the Great War with good reason.

SOCIAL MILIEU   Your investigation might include the social environment of the era, especially the social changes that took place during and after the war. Information from an encyclopedia, books, or Internet articles might help clarify what was going on in the background of "Hills Like White Elephants," if you find yourself interested enough to explore at another level. (The more you dig, the more you'll find and the richer your reading of the story will become.) In broad terms, the war shattered the optimistic outlook held by much of the population in Western Europe and the United States. After the war ended, many people reacted by deciding to enjoy life fully in the present, since the war showed that life can end so quickly, and by rejecting older values (including prevailing sexual mores) and traditional roles (especially for women). The war led to changes in gender roles: With young men away in the military, young women had to work in factories instead of in homes, schools, or offices.

The war also led to changes in family and community life. Having seen large cities and other countries, young people found it difficult to return to the sheltered, conservative communities in which they grew up. A large number of writers, artists, and socialites — Ernest Hemingway among them — moved from the United States to Europe, which they considered more sophisticated. The American man in "Hills Like White Elephants" seems to be one of them and to reflect the sense of restlessness and desire to see new places and have new experiences. "That's all we do, isn't it," Jig says, "look at things and try new drinks?" (para. 33).

Setting as Cultural Context

SOCIAL CIRCUMSTANCES   Setting also involves the social circumstances of the time and place. Here too, active reading may require some research. Beyond the historical events at the time, try to find what attitudes people held about what was going on. What social and political problems were people facing? How were people below the poverty line treated, and what were the attitudes of the economically secure? What kinds of social change were occurring?

Such social and cultural contexts are closely related to the kind of historical events we discussed above — actually, all aspects of setting are interrelated and inseparable. So, for example, to understand "The Red Convertible" fully it helps to know something about the Vietnam War and attitudes toward it. Notice also how it involves transplanting a young Native American from his familiar, traditional culture to a strikingly different military culture and then to a strange foreign culture.

CULTURAL TRANSPLANTATION   Like "The Red Convertible," "Hills Like White Elephants" involves cultural transplantation: an American writer, Ernest Hemingway, living in Paris, writing in English (thus mainly for an American audience), about an American traveling in Spain (a conservative, predominantly Catholic country) with a companion (to whom he does not seem to be married) from an unspecified country. The fact that he is called "the American" suggests that Jig is not American; she apparently is not from Spain since she cannot converse with the waitress (we are supposed to assume the man is talking to the waitress in Spanish, even though his words and hers are written in English). Such details economically and efficiently convey a mixture of cultures and values, as well as a cosmopolitan outlook.

The Effects of Setting

Setting, thus, provides a "world" for the story to take place in, a location and a background for the events. But as you pay even closer attention to setting, you'll see that it usually does more. Again, you need to ask questions, especially about further implications of when and where the events happen. Ask yourself what the setting reveals about characters. What is suggested by where a person lives (the kind of house and furniture) or the place in which we encounter her or him (a bar, a gym, a library, the woods)? Does the setting help clarify what she or he is like?

Setting and Atmosphere

Ask yourself also how the setting affects the way you feel about the characters and events. Setting can be important in evoking **atmosphere** — that is, the mood or emotional quality that surrounds and permeates a literary work. Part of the effect in the **gothic story** "A Rose for Emily" (p. 176) is created by the eerie atmosphere of the house in which Miss Emily secludes herself for much of her life. In other stories the emotional aura may be less dramatic, but it is always there and affects how you respond to the work as a whole.

READING FOR SYMBOLS

Works of literature not only help us see things in fresh and meaningful ways, but can also lead us to see deeply *into* and *beyond* things through the use of symbolism. A **symbol** in literature is an object, an event, or a person that suggests more than its literal meaning. Every day you encounter symbols. You send flowers to someone important to you. The flowers are an object, something that can be touched and smelled. But of course you hope that the recipient will recognize them as more than just objects, that they will know the flowers suggest your love, concern, and support and therefore will respond to their *symbolic* implications.

Note that *implications* in the previous sentence is plural. Symbols usually convey a cluster of possible meanings; they are rich, suggestive, and evocative. It's crucial that we never reduce them to a single, definite meaning: The verb *suggests* may be safer to use than the verb *symbolizes* because it conveys better a sense of a symbol's openness, inclusivity, and plurality, as in our sentence about the flowers above.

Recognizing Symbols

Even though almost anything can take on symbolic significance, not every object, character, or act in a literary work should be labeled a symbol. Symbols draw their power from standing out, and they don't stand out if we call everything a symbol. A prudent way to proceed is to assume that objects, characters, and actions are always themselves and are not meant to be taken as symbols *unless* a further sense of meaning forces itself on us. If you miss something others regard as a symbol, don't worry. Symbols add to a work's meaning, but a work usually doesn't depend on your recognizing them. It's better to miss a symbolic meaning than to impose one and reduce a work to a string of abstractions.

PROMINENCE OR WEIGHTINESS   How, then, do you recognize a symbol? The key signal is *prominence*: Objects that are mentioned repeatedly, described in detail, or appear in noticeable or strategic positions (at the beginning or end, in the title, at a crucial moment, in the climactic lines) may point toward a meaning beyond themselves. The red convertible in Louise Erdrich's story (p. 126) certainly meets all these criteria. Signals, however, are not always structural. Another signal can be a sense of *weightiness* or *significance*: Sometimes you may notice that an image, character, or action differs from others, that it is beginning to embody an idea related to an area of major concern in the work. In such a case, it might be a symbol.

IMAGE COMES FIRST   Be careful, however, not to undermine the use of concrete details by dismissing their crucial part in the work because you see them as symbols. Their literal role always comes first. A symbol is first an image, and its representation of an actual thing plays a key role in a work even if it also becomes a symbol. The quilts in "Everyday Use" (p. 169) come to symbolize the Johnson family's culture and heritage, but first and foremost they are actual quilts. At the end of the story, the narrator gives Maggie coverings she can put on a bed, not some abstract "heritage" (though the bed coverings carry that sense of heritage with them). To separate the symbolic meaning from the literal diminishes the richness of both. The warmth of the Johnsons' heritage comes alive in the warmth provided by the quilts.

Be careful also not to turn an abstraction into a symbol. A rose can be a symbol of love, but love (an abstraction) can never be a symbol of something else. And be sure that the symbolic meaning seems plausible: Its connection to the image, character, or action must seem likely and convincing within the context of the story. To claim that the red convertible is a symbol of Lyman's Marxist leanings (since red was associated with communism during the Cold War) has no relevance to the context of the story.

Literary Symbols

A *literary symbol* is an object, character, or action that is part of the literal story in a literary work—it can be seen, touched, smelled, heard, tasted, encountered, or experienced by people in the work—*and* suggests abstract meanings beyond itself. The red convertible is a real object in Erdrich's story: Lyman and Henry buy a car, fix it up, and drive around in it. But beyond being an object the brothers own, the car also represents their friendship and the bond they share. It suggests carefreeness, spontaneity, and freedom (think of the difference if the car was a tan minivan); perhaps it even reflects Henry's life and soul. When Lyman rolls the car into the river, the red convertible becomes part of a symbolic act. He isn't just getting rid of the car; he is giving it to Henry, evidence of his love for and close connection to his brother.

The red convertible is a literary symbol because it derives its meanings from the context of the literary work itself. Red convertibles traditionally carry cultural status in society—they're sexy. But they do not carry the particular symbolic meanings that are relied on in Erdrich's story. The car in "The Red Convertible" develops its meanings from its specific associations with Lyman and Henry and their situation. It is a "story-specific" symbol, one that receives its significance from the work and may not have the same significance outside of that work. If you see a red convertible on the street, it may remind you of this story and its symbolic significance in the story, but it won't suggest the same significance for someone who hasn't read the story.

Symbols in "Hills Like White Elephants"

WHITE ELEPHANTS AS IMAGE   Some traditional symbols can bring into a literary work the clusters of meaning they already possess outside the work. For us to respond to them depends on our having, or our learning about, the shared background and experiences they depend on. No actual white elephants appear in the setting of Hemingway's story: They are the imaginative half of a simile. The title itself should make us begin asking in what ways hills are like white elephants. We should start with the physical, with the hills as images: In the story, Jig is looking at the line of hills, white in the sun, and says "They look like white elephants" (para. 9). She surely is talking about physical appearance: The hills are rounded and lumpy (not with sharp peaks and points), so they look sort of, a little bit, like the bodies of elephants. Jig says later, "They don't really look like white elephants. I just meant the coloring of their skin through the trees" (para. 36), but by then most readers probably have a visual image of their shape as well.

PROMINENCE OF WHITE ELEPHANTS   If that was the only time the phrase was used in the story, it would simply be a part of the description of the setting. But it is repeated three times, as well as being the title phrase. Dwelling on it this way suggests there is more to it than an imaginative description of setting. And if Jig had said only that the hills are like elephants, the phrase probably wouldn't get beyond the physical. But she says they are like *white* elephants. That takes us further, probably requiring us to explore what white elephants are. The *Oxford English Dictionary* gives the following definitions for *white elephant* (all current when Hemingway was writing):

> a. A rare albino variety of elephant which is highly venerated in some Asian countries. b. *fig.* A burdensome or costly possession (from the story that the kings of Siam were accustomed to make a present of one of these animals to courtiers who had rendered themselves obnoxious, in order to ruin the recipient by the cost of its maintenance). Also, an object, scheme, etc., considered to be without use or value.

White elephants have taken on traditional symbolic significance in Eastern cultures and, to some extent, Western societies. Some of that traditional symbolic significance is carried into "Hills Like White Elephants" through the repeated references to, and resulting prominence of, white elephants in the story.

SIGNIFICANCE OF WHITE ELEPHANTS   The story implies that Jig, unlike the man, has seen white elephants:

> "They look like white elephants," she said.
> "I've never seen one," the man drank his beer.
> "No, you wouldn't have." (paras. 9–11)

If she has, she probably knows that they are both rare and venerated and (figuratively) a burdensome or useless possession. Their conversation goes from "all the things you've waited so long for" to "white elephants" to the operation: the "simple operation" that is "not really an operation at all." It's left to the reader to decide what the operation is. One possibility is an abortion (see if that fits the way they talk about it). In that case, her use of *white elephant* suggests an ambiguity—whether she intends the application or not—between pregnancy and new life as, on the one hand, a highly valued treasure and, on the other, a burden or an object without value. In addition, the story implies that, if Jig stays pregnant, the man may soon think of her as a burdensome and unwanted possession.

Symbols are powerful and understanding them is among the most evocative experiences for an active reader. If read undiscerningly, they can turn a literary work into a hunt for "hidden meaning." But when read with thoughtful common sense, they add a rich, suggestive aura and depth to a work and help us realize that meanings are not hidden but embodied and revealed, suggested, or evoked.

READING FOR ALLEGORY

Closely related to symbol is **allegory**: a form or manner, usually narrative, in which objects, persons, and actions literally present in a story are equated in a sustained, obvious, one-to-one way with meanings that lie outside the story, usually indicated by names or characteristics ascribed to them. Those meanings, in allegory, often seem or are of more importance to the work than the literal story. A classic example of allegory is John Bunyan's *Pilgrim's Progress* (1678), an allegorical dream vision in which a character named Christian undertakes a journey through the wilderness of this world, passing through such places as the Slough (swamp) of Despair and a carnival called Vanity Fair on his way to the Celestial City (heaven).

A CAUTION ABOUT READING ALLEGORICALLY   Be careful not to impose an allegorical reading (looking for representational meaning everywhere) on works that are not allegorical. This happens especially when readers are taught to search for "deeper meanings" in literary works and to ask, for almost every character, object, and event, "What does it stand for?" That may appear to be active reading, but it's not. Active readers wisely refrain from trying to find meanings everywhere, "hidden" below the surface. Rather, they seek to engage actively with what is right there on the surface. It is vitally important to get to know characters, actions, and objects as themselves, to understand them as thoroughly as possible—which in some cases includes their representational significance but in most cases does not.

> You can further explore setting and symbol, including interactive exercises, with VirtuaLit Fiction at bedfordstmartins.com/ rewritinglit.

✓ CHECKLIST on Reading for Setting and Symbol

❑ Be attentive to setting in a literary work:
  • setting in terms of place, in its broad sense and in its sense of narrower, individual places
  • setting in time
  • setting as historical, social, and cultural context

❑ Be aware of different effects setting can have in a work—revealing character, conveying atmosphere, reinforcing meaning, serving as a symbol or occasionally almost as a character.

❑ Be able to explain the difference between an image or an action or a character that is only itself and one used as a symbol (an image or an action or a character that also embodies an idea).

(continued)

❏ Know the formal devices commonly used for indicating that an image, an action, or a character may be a symbol: repetition, description, prominent placement (title, beginning, ending, climactic scene), or a sense of weightiness or significance beyond the literal function in the work. Be able to use those signals to perceive when a work is using symbols.

❏ Be alert to the ways symbols can enrich the meaning and effect of a literary work.

❏ Be able to recognize allegory (a sustained equating of objects, persons, or actions in a story with a pattern of abstract meaning outside the story, which is often more important than the literal story), and be able to differentiate that from symbol.

❏ Be comfortable with allowing details to be details.

FURTHER READING

ENTRY POINTS   In the following story, setting plays a very important role. Sylvia, a young African American girl growing up in Harlem, goes on a field trip to Midtown Manhattan to visit F.A.O. Schwarz, one of the most famous (and expensive) toy stores in the world. The experience expands her horizons in several dynamic ways. Also very important in this story is the presentation of character and its effect. After your first reading, notice and reflect on the point of view and what Sylvia is like and how you get to know her. Then read the story again, this time asking yourself where in the story Sylvia changes and how setting contributes to her development.

Toni Cade Bambara   1939–1995

The Lesson   [1972]

Back in the days when everyone was old and stupid or young and foolish and me and Sugar were the only ones just right, this lady moved on our block with nappy hair and proper speech and no make-up. And quite naturally we laughed at her, laughed the way we did at the junk man who went about his business like he was some big-time president and his sorry-ass horse his secretary. And we kinda hated her too, hated the way we did the winos who cluttered up our parks and pissed on our handball walls and stank up our hallways and

APPROACHING THE AUTHOR

Toni Cade Bambara was born Miltona Mirkin Cade and changed her name to Toni Cade while in kindergarten. In 1970 she adopted the name Bambara, which she discovered as a signature on a sketchbook in her great-grandmother's trunk.

For more about her, see page 1373.

stairs so you couldn't halfway play hide-and-seek without a goddamn gas mask.
Miss Moore was her name. The only woman on the block with no first name.
And she was black as hell, cept for her feet, which were fish-white and spooky.
And she was always planning these boring-ass things for us to do, us being my
cousin, mostly, who lived on the block cause we all moved North the same time
and to the same apartment then spread out gradual to breathe. And our parents
would yank our heads into some kinda shape and crisp up our clothes so we'd
be presentable for travel with Miss Moore, who always looked like she was going
to church, though she never did. Which is just one of the things the grownups
talked about when they talked behind her back like a dog. But when she came
calling with some sachet she'd sewed up or some gingerbread she'd made or
some book, why then they'd all be too embarrassed to turn her down and we'd
get handed over all spruced up. She'd been to college and said it was only right
that she should take responsibility for the young ones' education, and she not
even related by marriage or blood. So they'd go for it. Specially Aunt Gretchen.
She was the main gofer in the family. You got some ole dumb shit foolishness
you want somebody to go for, you send for Aunt Gretchen. She been screwed
into the go-along for so long, it's a blood-deep natural thing with her. Which is
how she got saddled with me and Sugar and Junior in the first place while our
mothers were in a la-de-da apartment up the block having a good ole time.

So this one day Miss Moore rounds us all up at the mailbox and it's puredee
hot and she's knockin herself out about arithmetic. And school suppose to let
up in summer I heard, but she don't never let up. And the starch in my pinafore
scratching the shit outta me and I'm really hating this nappy-head bitch and
her goddamn college degree. I'd much rather go to the pool or to the show
where it's cool. So me and Sugar leaning on the mailbox being surly, which is a
Miss Moore word. And Flyboy checking out what everybody brought for lunch.
And Fat Butt already wasting his peanut-butter-and-jelly sandwich like the pig
he is. And Junebug punchin on Q.T.'s arm for potato chips. And Rosie Giraffe
shifting from one hip to the other waiting for somebody to step on her foot or
ask her if she from Georgia so she can kick ass, preferably Mercedes'. And Miss
Moore asking us do we know what money is, like we a bunch of retards. I mean
real money, she say, like it's only poker chips or monopoly papers we lay on the
grocer. So right away I'm tired of this and say so. And would much rather snatch
Sugar and go to the Sunset and terrorize the West Indian kids and take their
hair ribbons and their money too. And Miss Moore files that remark away for
next week's lesson on brotherhood, I can tell. And finally I say we oughta get to
the subway cause it's cooler and besides we might meet some cute boys. Sugar
done swiped her mama's lipstick, so we ready.

So we heading down the street and she's boring us silly about what things
cost and what our parents make and how much goes for rent and how money
ain't divided up right in this country. And then she gets to the part about we all
poor and live in the slums, which I don't feature. And I'm ready to speak on that,
but she steps out in the street and hails two cabs just like that. Then she hustles
half the crew in with her and hands me a five-dollar bill and tells me to calculate

10 percent tip for the driver. And we're off. Me and Sugar and Junebug and Flyboy hangin out the window and hollering to everybody, putting lipstick on each other cause Flyboy a faggot anyway, and making farts with our sweaty armpits. But I'm mostly trying to figure how to spend this money. But they all fascinated with the meter ticking and Junebug starts laying bets as to how much it'll read when Flyboy can't hold his breath no more. Then Sugar lays bets as to how much it'll be when we get there. So I'm stuck. Don't nobody want to go for my plan, which is to jump out at the next light and run off to the first bar-b-que we can find. Then the driver tells us to get the hell out cause we there already. And the meter reads eighty-five cents. And I'm stalling to figure out the tip and Sugar say give him a dime. And I decide he don't need it bad as I do, so later for him. But then he tries to take off with Junebug foot still in the door so we talk about his mama something ferocious. Then we check out that we on Fifth Avenue and everybody dressed up in stockings. One lady in a fur coat, hot as it is. White folks crazy.

"This is the place," Miss Moore say, presenting it to us in the voice she uses at the museum. "Let's look in the windows before we go in."

"Can we steal?" Sugar asks very serious like she's getting the ground rules squared away before she plays. "I beg your pardon," say Miss Moore, and we fall out. So she leads us around the windows of the toy store and me and Sugar screamin, "This is mine, that's mine, I gotta have that, that was made for me, I was born for that," till Big Butt drowns us out.

"Hey, I'm goin to buy that there."

"That there? You don't even know what it is, stupid."

"I do so," he say punchin on Rosie Giraffe. "It's a microscope."

"Whatcha gonna do with a microscope, fool?"

"Look at things." 10

"Like what, Ronald?" ask Miss Moore. And Big Butt ain't got the first notion. So here go Miss Moore gabbing about the thousands of bacteria in a drop of water and the somethinorother in a speck of blood and the million and one living things in the air around us is invisible to the naked eye. And what she say that for? Junebug go to town on that "naked" and we rolling. Then Miss Moore ask what it cost. So we all jam into the window smudgin it up and the price tag say $300. So then she ask how long'd take for Big Butt and Junebug to save up their allowances. "Too long," I say. "Yeh," adds Sugar, "outgrown it by that time." And Miss Moore say no, you never outgrow learning instruments. "Why, even medical students and interns and," blah, blah, blah. And we ready to choke Big Butt for bringing it up in the first damn place.

"This here costs four hundred eighty dollars," say Rosie Giraffe. So we pile up all over her to see what she pointin out. My eyes tell me it's a chunk of glass cracked with something heavy, and different-color inks dripped into the splits, then the whole thing put into a oven or something. But for $480 it don't make sense.

"That's a paperweight made of semi-precious stones fused together under tremendous pressure," she explains slowly, with her hands doing the mining and all the factory work.

"So what's a paperweight?" asks Rosie Giraffe.

"To weigh paper with, dumbbell," say Flyboy, the wise man from the East.   15

"Not exactly," say Miss Moore, which is what she say when you warm or way off too. "It's to weigh paper down so it won't scatter and make your desk untidy." So right away me and Sugar curtsy to each other and then to Mercedes who is more the tidy type.

"We don't keep paper on top of the desk in my class," say Junebug, figuring Miss Moore crazy or lyin one.

"At home, then," she say. "Don't you have a calendar and a pencil case and a blotter and a letter-opener on your desk at home where you do your home-work?" And she know damn well what our homes look like cause she nosys around in them every chance she gets.

"I don't even have a desk," say Junebug. "Do we?"

"No. And I don't get no homework neither," say Big Butt.   20

"And I don't even have a home," say Flyboy like he do at school to keep the white folks off his back and sorry for him. Send this poor kid to camp posters, is his specialty.

"I do," says Mercedes. "I have a box of stationery on my desk and a picture of my cat. My godmother bought the stationery and the desk. There's a big rose on each sheet and the envelopes smell like roses."

"Who wants to know about your smelly-ass stationery," say Rosie Giraffe fore I can get my two cents in.

"It's important to have a work area all your own so that . . ."

"Will you look at this sailboat, please," say Flyboy, cuttin her off and poin-   25
tin to the thing like it was his. So once again we tumble all over each other to gaze at this magnificent thing in the toy store which is just big enough to maybe sail two kittens across the pond if you strap them to the posts tight. We all start reciting the price tag like we in assembly. "Handcrafted sailboat of fiberglass at one thousand one hundred ninety-five dollars."

"Unbelievable," I hear myself say and am really stunned. I read it again for myself just in case the group recitation put me in a trance. Same thing. For some reason this pisses me off. We look at Miss Moore and she lookin at us, waiting for I dunno what.

"Who'd pay all that when you can buy a sailboat set for a quarter at Pop's, a tube of glue for a dime, and a ball of string for eight cents? It must have a motor and a whole lot else besides," I say. "My sailboat cost me about fifty cents."

"But will it take water?" say Mercedes with her smart ass.

"Took mine to Alley Pond Park once," say Flyboy. "String broke. Lost it. Pity."

"Sailed mine in Central Park and it keeled over and sank. Had to ask my   30
father for another dollar."

"And you got the strap," laugh Big Butt. "The jerk didn't even have a string on it. My old man wailed on his behind."

Little Q.T. was staring hard at the sailboat and you could see he wanted it bad. But he too little and somebody'd just take it from him. So what the hell. "This boat for kids, Miss Moore?"

"Parents silly to buy something like that just to get all broke up," say Rosie Giraffe.

"That much money it should last forever," I figure.

"My father'd buy it for me if I wanted it."   35

"Your father, my ass," say Rosie Giraffe getting a chance to finally push Mercedes.

"Must be rich people shop here," say Q.T.

"You are a very bright boy," say Flyboy. "What was your first clue?" And he rap him on the head with the back of his knuckles, since Q.T. the only one he could get away with. Though Q.T. liable to come up behind you years later and get his licks in when you half expect it.

"What I want to know is," I says to Miss Moore though I never talk to her, I wouldn't give the bitch that satisfaction, "is how much a real boat costs? I figure a thousand'd get you a yacht any day."

"Why don't you check that out," she says, "and report back to the group?"   40 Which really pains my ass. If you gonna mess up a perfectly good swim day least you could do is have some answers. "Let's go in," she say like she got something up her sleeve. Only she don't lead the way. So me and Sugar turn the corner to where the entrance is, but when we get there I kinda hang back. Not that I'm scared, what's there to be afraid of, just a toy store. But I feel funny, shame. But what I got to be shamed about? Got as much right to go in as anybody. But somehow I can't seem to get hold of the door, so I step away for Sugar to lead. But she hangs back too. And I look at her and she looks at me and this is ridiculous. I mean, damn, I have never ever been shy about doing nothing or going nowhere. But then Mercedes steps up and then Rosie Giraffe and Big Butt crowd in behind and shove, and next thing we all stuffed into the doorway with only Mercedes squeezing past us, smoothing out her jumper and walking right down the aisle. Then the rest of us tumble in like a glued-together jigsaw done all wrong. And people lookin at us. And it's like the time me and Sugar crashed into the Catholic church on a dare. But once we got in there and everything so hushed and holy and the candles and the bowin and the handkerchiefs on all the drooping heads, I just couldn't go through with the plan. Which was for me to run up to the altar and do a tap dance while Sugar played the nose flute and messed around in the holy water. And Sugar kept givin me the elbow. Then later teased me so bad I tied her up in the shower and turned it on and locked her in. And she'd be there till this day if Aunt Gretchen hadn't finally figured I was lyin about the boarder takin a shower.

Same thing in the store. We all walkin on tiptoe and hardly touchin the games and puzzles and things. And I watched Miss Moore who is steady watchin us like she waitin for a sign. Like Mama Drewery watches the sky and sniffs the air and takes note of just how much slant is in the bird formation. Then me and Sugar bump smack into each other, so busy gazing at the toys, 'specially the sailboat. But we don't laugh and go into our fat-lady bump-stomach routine. We just stare at that price tag. Then Sugar run a finger over the whole boat. And I'm jealous and want to hit her. Maybe not her, but I sure want to punch somebody in the mouth.

"Watcha bring us here for, Miss Moore?"

"You sound angry, Sylvia. Are you mad about something?" Givin me one of them grins like she tellin a grown-up joke that never turns out to be funny. And she's lookin very closely at me like maybe she plannin to do my portrait from memory. I'm mad, but I won't give her that satisfaction. So I slouch around the store bein very bored and say, "Let's go."

Me and Sugar at the back of the train watchin the tracks whizzin by large then small then gettin gobbled up in the dark. I'm thinkin about this tricky toy I saw in the store. A clown that somersaults on a bar then does chin-ups just cause you yank lightly at his leg. Cost $35. I could see me askin my mother for a $35 birthday clown. "You wanna who that costs what?" she'd say, cocking her head to the side to get a better view of the hole in my head. Thirty-five dollars could buy new bunk beds for Junior and Gretchen's boy. Thirty-five dollars and the whole household could go visit Granddaddy Nelson in the country. Thirty-five dollars would pay for the rent and the piano bill too. Who are these people that spend that much for performing clowns and $1,000 for toy sailboats? What kinda work they do and how they live and how come we ain't in on it? Where we are is who we are, Miss Moore always pointin out. But it don't necessarily have to be that way, she always adds then waits for somebody to say that poor people have to wake up and demand their share of the pie and don't none of us know what kind of pie she talkin about in the first damn place. But she ain't so smart cause I still got her four dollars from the taxi and she sure ain't gettin it. Messin up my day with this shit. Sugar nudges me in my pocket and winks.

Miss Moore lines us up in front of the mailbox where we started from, seem like years ago, and I got a headache for thinkin so hard. And we lean all over each other so we can hold up under the draggy-ass lecture she always finishes us off with at the end before we thank her for borin us to tears. But she just looks at us like she readin tea leaves. Finally she say, "Well, what did you think of F.A.O. Schwarz?"

Rosie Giraffe mumbles, "White folks crazy."

"I'd like to go there again when I get my birthday money," says Mercedes, and we shove her out the pack so she has to lean on the mailbox by herself.

"I'd like a shower. Tiring day," say Flyboy.

Then Sugar surprises me by sayin, "You know, Miss Moore, I don't think all of us here put together eat in a year what that sailboat costs." And Miss Moore lights up like somebody goosed her. "And?" she say, urging Sugar on. Only I'm standin on her foot so she don't continue.

"Imagine for a minute what kind of society it is in which some people can spend on a toy what it would cost to feed a family of six or seven. What do you think?"

"I think," say Sugar pushing me off her feet like she never done before, cause I whip her ass in a minute, "that this is not much of a democracy if you ask me. Equal chance to pursue happiness means an equal crack at the dough, don't it?" Miss Moore is besides herself and I am disgusted with Sugar's treachery. So I stand on her foot one more time to see if she'll shove me. She shuts up, and Miss Moore looks at me, sorrowfully I'm thinkin. And somethin weird is goin on, I can feel it in my chest.

45

50

"Anybody else learn anything today?" lookin dead at me. I walk away and Sugar has to run to catch up and don't even seem to notice when I shrug her arm off my shoulder.

"Well, we got four dollars anyway," she says.

"Uh hunh."

"We could go to Hascombs and get half a chocolate layer and then go to 55 the Sunset and still have plenty money for potato chips and ice-cream sodas."

"Uh hunh."

"Race you to Hascombs," she say.

We start down the block and she gets ahead which is O.K. by me cause I'm goin to the West End and then over to the Drive to think this day through. She can run if she want to and even run faster. But ain't nobody gonna beat me at nuthin.

APPROACHING THE READING

1. If you're not familiar with New York City and the F.A.O. Schwarz store there, do some research that will help bring the setting to life for you. Go online or to the library to find a map of New York City. Locate Harlem, find some photographs of it, and then read about its distinctive culture both in the past and present. Then find Fifth Avenue at West 58th Street, where F.A.O. Schwarz is located, on the map and look at Web sites that describe and include photos of the New York F.A.O. Schwarz store.

2. Consider the effect setting has on the characters in this story. Be ready to discuss the attitude Sylvia has toward Miss Moore, the other children, white people, and the world in general. How does where she lives help shape her attitude? Describe the ways Sylvia's horizons are expanded.

3. What is Sylvia, the narrator of the story, like? Try sketching her character. In what ways does the "voice" you hear as she tells the story help develop her character? How did you feel about her on your first reading of the story? While rereading the story, or as you thought back over it, did your feelings about her change or become more complex? Do you notice specific evidence that Sylvia herself changes? If so, point out the particular things that in your eyes both reveal and lead to a change.

4. In what ways is the point of view important to the effect of the story? How would the story change if it had a different point of view? How would you describe the author's attitude toward Sylvia? What is it about the use of the first-person point of view that enables this attitude to come through?

5. Does Miss Moore have a teaching plan? What lessons do the children learn that day? In what ways do you think they are or are not the ones Miss Moore intended them to learn? Why do you think so? It seems clear that Sugar is affected by what she experiences. Do you think that Sylvia is

similarly affected, or do you think that she successfully resists? Try describing the kind of person you predict Sylvia will be when she reaches college age, if the story were to follow her life further.

ENTRY POINTS   The following story, in contrast to the previous one, takes place in an expensive house in a fashionable neighborhood. From the outside, it appears calm and cozy, but the situation inside turns murky both for its human inhabitants and the pet goldfish. After you read the story and become acquainted with the characters and conflicts developed in it, reread it and consider what specifics about the setting contribute to the effect of the story. Then ask yourself if any objects, events, or characters take on symbolic significance.

David Means   b. 1961

The Secret Goldfish   [2004]

He had a weird growth along his dorsal fin, and that gape-mouth grimace you see in older fish. Way too big for his tank, too, having outgrown the standard goldfish age limit. Which is what? About one month? He was six years old — outlandishly old for a fish. One afternoon, Teddy, as he was called then, now just Ted, took notice of the condition of Fish's tank: a wedge of sunlight plunged through the window of his bedroom and struck the water's surface, disappearing. The water was so clotted it had become a solid mass, a putty within which Fish was presumably swimming, or

> **APPROACHING THE AUTHOR**
>
> **David Means**'s class was studying Edgar Allan Poe on 11 September 2001, the day of the attack on the Twin Towers in New York City. He says that was hard on them all because "the apocalyptic landscape we were studying was actually happening around us."
> For more about him, see page 1400.

dead. Most likely dead. Where's Fish? Where's Fish? Teddy yelled to his mom. She came into his room, caught sight of the tank, and gave a small yelp. Once again, a fish had been neglected.

Everyone knows the story. The kids beg and plead: Please, please get us a fish (or a dog), we'll feed it, we will, honest, we'll take care of it and you won't have to do a single thing. We'll clean the tank walls with the brush and make sure the filter charcoal is replaced regularly and refill the water when it evaporates. Please, please, we can handle it, we're old enough now, we are, it'll be so much fun, it will, so much fun. But in the end they don't. They dump too much food in no matter how often they're told to be careful, to use just a pinch, and even after they've read biblical-sounding fables about the fish who ate too much and grew too large for its bowl, shattering the sides, they watch gleefully while he consumes like mad, unable to stop. It's fun to watch him eat, to witness the physical manifestation of a fact: The level of Fish's hunger is permanently set to high. In the metaphysics of the fish universe, gluttony is not a sin. The delicate wafers of food fall lightly onto the water, linger on the surface tension, and are broken apart on infinitely eager lips. She overfeeds, too (on the days when she's pretty sure the kids haven't fed him). Her shaking mechanics are sloppy. The light flakes become moist, collude, collect their inertia, and all too often fall out of the can in a large clump. Really, she hasn't neglected the poor fish. "Neglect" seems a word too heavy with submerged intent. Something was bound to slip to the side amid the chaos of the domestic arena. But Fish has sustained himself in terrible conditions. He is the king of all goldfish survivors.

Her own childhood goldfish—named Fred—ended his days in Grayling Pond, a hole near her house in northern Michigan, dug out by the state D.N.R.° on a pond-production grant. (Why the Great Lakes state needed more ponds is anyone's guess.) Garnished with a wide band of lily pads, the water a pale yellow, speckled with skeeter-bug ripples, the pond was close to becoming a marsh. Hope you survive, Fred, her father had said as he slopped the fish out of the pail and into the pond. She did not forget the sight of her beloved fish as he slipped from the lip of the bucket and rode the glassine tube of water into the pond. The rest of the summer she imagined his orange form—brilliantly bright and fluorescent against the glimmer of water—in a kind of slow-motion replay. Dumbest animals on earth, she remembered her father adding. Nothing dumber than a carp. Except maybe a catfish, or your goddam mother.

Not long after that afternoon at Grayling Pond, her father left the house in a fit of rage. Gone for good, her mother said. Thank Christ. Then, a few months later, he was killed in a freak accident, crushed between hunks of ice and the hull of a container ship in Duluth. Superior's slush ice was temperamental that winter, chewing up the coastline, damaging bulkheads. Her father had signed on as one of the men who went down with poles and gave furtive pokes and prods, in the tradition of those Michigan rivermen who had once dislodged logjams with their peaveys and pike poles, standing atop the timber in their spiked boots, sparring with magnificent forces. Accounts varied, but the basic story was that the ice shifted, some kind of crevasse formed, and he slipped in. Then the lake gave a heave and his legs were crushed, clamped in the jaw of God's stupid justice. As she liked to imagine it, he had just enough time to piece together a little prayer asking for forgiveness for being a failure of a father ("Dear Heavenly Father, forgive me for my huge failings as a father to my dear

---

D.N.R.: Department of Natural Resources.

daughter and even more for my gaping failure as a husband to my wife") and for dumping Fred ("and for getting rid of that fish my daughter loved more than me"), and then to watch as the pale winter sun slipped quickly away while the other men urged him to remain calm and told him that he'd be fine and they'd have him out in a minute or so, while knowing for certain that they wouldn't.

Long after her father was gone, she imagined Fred lurking in the lower reaches 5 of Grayling Pond, in the coolest pockets, trying to conserve his energy. Sometimes, when she was cleaning upstairs and dusting Teddy's room, she would pause in the deep, warm, silent heart of a suburban afternoon and watch Fish as he dangled asleep, wide-eyed, unmoving, just fluffing his fins softly on occasion. One time she even tried it herself, standing still, suspended in the dense fluid of an unending array of demanding tasks—cleaning, cooking, washing, grocery shopping, snack-getting—while outside the birds chirped and the traffic hissed past on the parkway.

The marriage had fallen apart abruptly. Her husband—who worked in the city as a corporate banker and left the house each morning at dawn with the *Times*, still wrapped in its bright-blue delivery bag, tucked beneath his arm—had betrayed his vows. One evening, he'd arrived home from work with what seemed to be a new face: His teeth were abnormally white. He'd had them bleached in the city. (In retrospect, she saw that his bright teeth were the first hint of his infidelity.) He had found a dentist on Park Avenue. Soon he was coming home late on some nights and not at all on others, under the vague pretense of work obligations. In Japan, he explained, people sleep overnight in town as a sign of their dedication to business; they rent cubicles just wide enough for a body, like coffins, he said, and for days when he did not return she thought of those small compartments and she chose to believe him. (Of course I know about the Japanese, she had said, emphatically.) Then one night she found him in the bathroom with a bar of soap, rubbing it gently against his wedding ring. It's too tight, he said. I'm just trying to loosen it. When others were perplexed by the fact that she had not deduced his infidelity, picked up on the clues, during those fall months, she felt compelled (though she never did) to describe the marriage in all of its long complexity—fifteen years—starting with the honeymoon in Spain: the parador in Chinchón, outside Madrid, that had once been a monastery, standing naked with him at the balcony door in the dusky night air listening to the sounds of the village and the splash of the pool. She had given up her career for the relationship, for the family. She had given up plenty in order to stay home for Teddy's and Annie's formative years, to make sure those brain synapses formed correctly, to be assured that the right connections were fused. (Because studies had made it clear that a kid's success depends on the first few years. It was important to develop the fine motor skills, to have the appropriate hand play, not to mention critical reasoning skills, before the age of four!) So, yes, she guessed the whole decision to give herself over to the domestic job had been an act of free will, but now it felt as though the act itself had been carried out in the conditions of betrayal that would eventually unfold before her.

Fish had come into the family fold in a plastic Baggie of water, bulging dangerously, knotted at the top, with a mate, Sammy, who would end up a floater two days later. Pet Universe had given free goldfish to all the kids on a preschool field trip. In less than a year, Fish had grown too big for his starter bowl and begun to tighten his spiralled laps, restricted in his movements by his gathering bulk and the glass walls of the bowl. Then he graduated to a classic five-gallon bowl, where, in the course of the next few years, he grew, until one afternoon, still deep in what seemed to be a stable domestic situation, with the kids off at school, she went out to Pet Universe and found a large tank and some water-prep drops and a filter unit, one that sat on the rim and produced a sleek, fountainlike curl of water, and some turquoise gravel and a small figurine to keep the fish company: a cartoonish pirate galleon—a combination of Mark Twain riverboat and man-of-war—with an exaggerated bow and an orange plastic paddle wheel that spun around in the tank's currents until it gobbed up and stuck. The figurine, which was meant to please the eyes of children, had that confused mix of design that put commercial viability ahead of the truth. Teddy and Annie hated it. Ultimately, the figure served one purpose. It rearranged the conceptual space of the tank and gave the illusion that Fish now had something to do, something to work around, during his languorous afternoon laps, and she found herself going in to watch him, giving deep philosophical consideration to his actions: Did Fish remember that he had passed that way before? Was he aware of his eternal hell, caught in the tank's glass grip? Or did he feel wondrously free, swimming—for all he knew—in Lake Superior, an abundant, wide field of water, with some glass obstructions here and there? Was he basically free of wants, needs, and everything else? Did he wonder at the food miraculously appearing atop the surface tension, food to be approached with parted lips?

One evening, after observing Fish, when she was at the sink looking out the window at the yard, she saw her husband there, along the south side, holding his phone to his ear and lifting his free hand up and down from his waist in a slight flapping gesture that she knew indicated that he was emotionally agitated.

Shortly after that, the tank began to murk up. Through the dim months of January and February, the filter clotted, the flow stopped, and stringy green silk grew on the lip of the waterfall. The murk thickened. In the center of the darkness, Fish swam in random patterns and became a sad, hopeless entity curled into his plight. He was no longer fooled by his short-term memory into thinking that he was eternally free. Nor was he bored by the repetitive nature of his laps, going around the stupid ship figurine, sinking down into the gravel, picking—typical bottom-feeder—for scraps. Instead, he was lost in the eternal roar of an isotropic universe, flinging himself wildly within the expanding big bang of tank murk. On occasion, he found his way to the light and rubbed his eye against the glass, peering out in a judgmental way. But no one was there to see him. No one seemed available to witness these outward glances. Until the day when Teddy, now just Ted, noticed and said, Mom, Mom, the tank, and she went and cleaned it, but only after she had knocked her knuckle a few times on the glass and seen that he was alive, consumed in the dark but moving and seemingly healthy. Then she felt awe at the fact that life was sustainable even under the most abhorrent conditions. She felt a fleeting connection between this awe and the possibility that God exists. But then she reminded herself that it was only Fish. Just frickin' Fish, she thought. Here I am so weepy and sad, trying to make sense of my horrible situation, that something like this will give me hope. Of course, she was probably also thinking back to that afternoon, watching her father sluice Fred down into the warm waters of the shallow pond in Michigan. Her memory of it was profoundly clear. The vision of the fish itself—pristine and orange—travelling through the water as it spilled from the bucket was exact and perfect.

She set to work scooping out the water with an old Tupperware bowl, 10 replacing it in increments so the chlorine would evaporate, driving to Pet Universe to get another cotton filter, some water-clarifying drops, and a pound sack of activated charcoal nuggets. She disassembled the pump mechanism—a small magnet attached to a ring of plastic that hovered, embraced by a larger magnet. Somehow the larger magnet cooperated with the magnet on the plastic device and used physical laws of some sort to suck the water up and through the filter, where it cascaded over the wide lip and twisted as it approached the surface. It seemed to her as her fingers cleaned the device that it was not only a thing of great simplicity and beauty but also something much deeper, a tool meant to sustain Fish's life and, in turn, his place in the family. The afternoon was clear, blue-skied, wintry bright—and out the kitchen window she saw the uncut lawn, dark straw brown, matted down in van Gogh swirls, frosted with cold. Past the lawn, the woods, through which she could see the cars moving on the parkway, stood stark and brittle in the direct implications of the winter light. It was a fine scene, embarrassingly suburban, but certainly fine. Back upstairs, she saw Fish swimming jauntily in his new conditions and she was pretty sure that he was delighted, moving with swift strokes from one end of the tank to the other, skirting the figurine professionally, wagging his back fin—what was that called? was it the caudal fin?—fashionably, like a cabaret dancer working her fan. A beautiful tail, unfurling in a windswept motion in the clearing water. When she leaned down for a closer look, it became apparent that the fin was much, much larger than it seemed when it was in action and twining in on itself. When Fish paused, it swayed open beautifully—a fine, healthy, wide carp tail. Along his sides, he had the usual scars of an abused fish, a wound or two, a missing scale, a new, smaller growth of some kind down near his anal fin. But otherwise he seemed big, brutally healthy, still blinking off the shock of the sudden glare.

Then the tank fell back into its murk, got worse, stank up, and became, well, completely, utterly, fantastically murky. Here one might note tangentially: If, as Aristotle claims, poetry is something of graver import than history—partly because of the naturalness of its statements—then Fish was more important than any domestic history, because Fish was poetic, in that he had succumbed to the darkness that had formed around him, and yet he was unwilling to die—or, rather, he *did not* die. He kept himself alive. He kept at it. Somehow he gathered enough oxygen from the water—perhaps by staying directly under the trickle that made its way over the lip of the filter. Of course, by nature he was a bottom-feeder, a mud-fish, accustomed to slime and algae and to an environment that, for other fish, would be insufferable. No trout could sustain itself in these conditions. Not even close. A good brookie would've gone belly up long ago. A brookie would want cool pockets of a fast-moving stream, sweet riffles, bubbling swirls, to live a good life. But Fish stood in his cave of slime, graver than the history of the household into which his glass enclave had been placed: Dad packing his suitcases, folding and refolding his trousers and taking his ties off the electric tie rack and carefully fold-ing them inside sheets of tissue, and then taking his shoes and putting each pair, highly glossed oxfords (he was one of the few to make regular use of the shoeshine stand at Grand Central), into cotton drawstring sacks, and then emptying his top dresser drawer, taking his cufflinks, his old wallets, and a few other items. All of this stuff, the history of the house, the legal papers signed and sealed and the at-tendant separation agreement and, of course, the divorce that left her the house—all this historical material was transpiring outside the gist of Fish. He could chart his course and touch each corner of the tank and still not know shit. But he understood something. That much was clear. The world is a mucky mess. It gets clotted up, submerged in its own gunk. End of story.

He brushed softly against the beard of algae that hung from the filter device, worked his way over to the figurine, leaned his flank against her side, and felt the shift of temperature as night fell—Teddy liked to sleep with the window cracked a bit—and the oxygen content increased slightly as the water cooled. During the day, the sun cranked through the window, the tank grew warm, and he didn't move at all, unless someone came into the room and knocked on the tank or the floor, and then he jerked forward slightly before quickly settling down. A few times the downstairs door slammed hard enough to jolt him awake. Or there was a smashing sound from the kitchen. Or voices. "What in the world should we do?" "I would most certainly like this to be amicable, for the sake of the kids." Or a shoe striking the wall in the adjacent master bedroom. At times he felt a kinship with the figurine, as if another carp were there alongside him, waiting, hovering. Other times he felt a slight kinship with the sides of the tank, which touched his gill flaps when he went in search of light. God, if only he knew that he, Fish, was at the very center of the domestic arena, holding court with his own desire to live. He might have died happily right there! But he was not a symbolic fish. He seemed to have no desire to stand as the tragic hero in this drama.

Sent out, told to stay out, the kids were playing together down in the yard so that, inside, the two central figures, Dad and Mom, might have one final talk. The kids were standing by the playhouse—which itself was falling to decrepitude, dark-gray smears of mildew growing on its fake logs—pretending to be a mom and a dad themselves, although they were a bit too old and self-conscious for playacting. Perhaps they were old enough to know that they were faking it on two levels, regressing to a secondary level of playacting they'd pretty much rejected but playing Mom and Dad anyway, Teddy saying, I'm gonna call my lawyer if you don't settle with me, and Annie responding, in her high sweet voice, I knew you'd lawyer up on me, I just knew it, and then both kids giggling in that secretive, all-knowing way they have. Overhead, the tree branches were fuzzed with the first buds of spring, but it was still a bit cold, and words hovered in vapor from their mouths and darkness was falling fast over the trees, and beyond the trees the commuter traffic hissed unnoticed.

If you were heading south on the Merritt Parkway on the afternoon of April 3rd, and you happened to look to your right through the trees after Exit 35, you might've seen them, back beyond the old stone piles, the farm fences that no longer held significance except maybe as a reminder of the Robert Frost poem about good fences and good neighbors and all of that: two kids leaning against an old play-house while the house behind them appeared cozy, warm, and, clearly, expensive. A fleeting tableau without much meaning to the commuting folk aside from the formulaic economics of the matter: near the parkway = reduced value, but an ex-pensive area + buffer of stone walls + old trees + trendiness of area = more value.

There is something romantic and heartening about seeing those homes through 15 the trees from the vantage of the parkway—those safe, confided Connecticut lives. Inside the house, the secret goldfish is going about his deeply moving predicament, holding his life close to the gills, subdued by the dark but unwilling to relinquish his cellular activities, the Krebs cycle still spinning its carbohydrate breakdown. The secret goldfish draws close to the center of the cosmos. In the black hole of familial carelessness, he awaits the graceful moment when the mother, spurred on by Teddy, will give yet another soft shriek. She'll lean close to the glass and put her eye there to search for Fish. Fish will be there, of course, hiding in the core of the murk near the figurine, playing possum, so that she will, when she sees him, feel the pitiful sinking in her gut—remembering the preschool field trip to Pet Universe—and a sorrow so deep it will send her to her knees to weep. She'll think of the sad little pet funeral she hoped to perform when Fish died (when Fish's sidekick died, Dad flushed him away): a small but deeply meaningful moment in the back yard, with the trowel, digging a shoebox-size hole, putting the fish in, performing a small rite ("Dear Lord, dear Heavenly Father, dear Fish God, God of Fish, in Fish's name we gather here to put our dear fish to rest"), and then placing atop the burial mound a big rock painted with the word "FISH." It would be a moment designed to teach the children the ways of loss, and the soft intricacies of seeing something that was once alive now dead, and to clarify that sharp defining difference, to smooth it over a bit, so that they will remember the moment and know, later, recalling it, that she was a good mother, the kind who would hold pet funerals.

But Fish is alive. His big old carp gills clutch and lick every tiny trace of oxygen from the froth of depravity in the inexplicably determinate manner that only animals have. He will have nothing to do with this household. And later that evening, once Dad is gone, they'll hold a small party to celebrate his resur-rection, because they had assumed—as was natural in these circumstances—that he was dead, or near enough death to be called dead, having near-death visions, as the dead are wont: that small pinpoint of light at the end of the tunnel and visions of an existence as a fish in some other ethery world, a better world for a fish, with fresh clear water bursting with oxygen and other carp large and small in communal bliss and just enough muck and mud for good pickings. After the celebration, before bedtime, they'll cover the top of the clean tank in plastic wrap and, working together, moving slowly with the unison of pallbearers, being careful not to slosh the water, carry it down the stairs to the family room, where with a soft patter of congratulatory applause they'll present Fish with a new home, right next to the television set.

APPROACHING THE READING

1. Describe the way the plot is structured—notice how what we are told is arranged, the way the story progresses, and the way it uses flashbacks, parallels, and contrasts. Point out specific passages that illustrate and support what you say.

2. Consider the point of view in the story and its role in the story's structure. Pick out specific illustrative passages and be ready to talk about how they clarify what the point of view is and how the point of view contributes to the development of the story.

3. Consider the setting of the story: Where, when, and in what social/cultural context do the events take place? How does location affect the meaning of the story? How would the story be different if it took place in a city, for example? How would it be different if it took place fifty years ago?

4. Explain the theme or themes of the story, what it all adds up to. Pick out specific illustrative passages to show that what you say is grounded firmly in the story. In particular, consider how setting contributes to the story's theme and effect.

5. Which objects, actions, or persons in the story might be regarded as symbolic? What about them could lead a reader to conclude that they have the prominence or weightiness to justify calling them symbols? If you, too, are convinced that they are symbols, what do they contribute to the effect of the story?

ENTRY POINTS The following selection, "Here" is a strange, even bizarre, work of graphic literature. Read it once to grasp what is going on. Try to determine its theme and get a solid feel for the characters. Then on a second reading, take time to explore the setting (place and time) in each panel. Richard McGuire expects you to notice both obvious and subtle things going on with the interrelationships within a panel. After attending to these aspects, go through the work to see if anything in the drawings carries the characteristics of symbol as discussed in this chapter.

Richard McGuire b. 1957

Here

[1989]

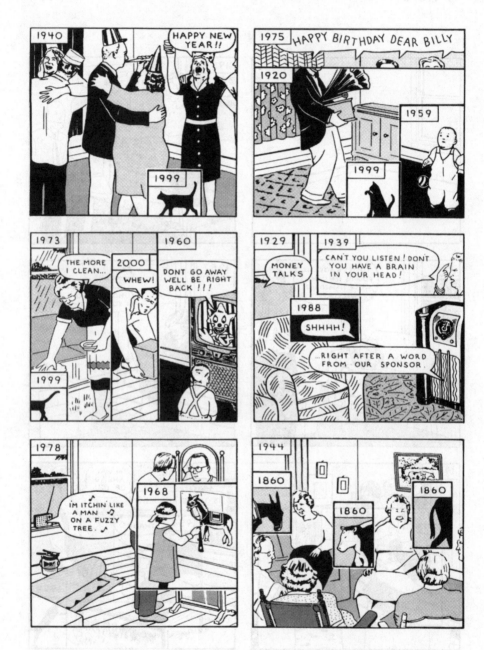

APPROACHING THE READING

1. How would you describe your initial responses to "Here"? Did they change at all the second or third time you read the selection? If so, to what extent and in what ways?

2. A symbol, as you learned in this chapter, is first of all an image. The storyteller of a graphic work can create images with both words and drawings. Where in the selection do you notice either language or drawings that might be experienced as symbols? Think back to the way the chapter suggested you discern when something is a symbol and support your conclusions.

> **APPROACHING THE AUTHOR**
>
> In addition to **Richard McGuire**'s success as a graphic artist and illustrator, he is the bassist for the influential New York City post-punk/post-disco band Liquid Liquid. For more about him, see page 1399.

3. What particular challenges would a writer have creating this piece with words only? Would it even be possible to do so?

4. This piece focuses on the same angle of the setting in each panel. Think about the options the graphic storyteller has in depicting a setting. Pick out some panels where Richard McGuire has dressed the scene to help you understand shifts in time and its effects on the characters. How would you describe what makes this effective?

5. In "Here," McGuire broke new ground by depicting various time periods within a single panel format. The piece requires you to realize the impact of the gaps in time. How would you describe your experience engaging a work in this way?

RESPONDING THROUGH Writing

WRITING ABOUT SETTING AND SYMBOL

Journal Entries

1. Focus on the way settings are handled in two or three TV shows or movies. Pay attention to what was discussed in this chapter: setting as place broadly and specifically, setting in time, setting in social and cultural context. Consider uses and effects of setting: for atmosphere, characterization, symbol, and meaning. Then write a journal entry discussing ways that what you found can enhance your grasp of setting in literature.

> You can research the authors in this chapter with LitLinks, or take a quiz on the stories with LitQuiz, at bedfordstmartins.com/rewritinglit.

2. Read Tim O'Brien's "The Things They Carried" (p. 493) and find ways to deepen your visual sense of what being a soldier in Vietnam was like for the

characters. Find a book of photographs on the Vietnam War and/or watch films such as *Platoon*; *Good Morning, Vietnam*; or *Apocalypse Now*. Write a journal entry in which you describe how these visual texts affect the way you imagine the setting and action of the story. Does it make a significant difference? Think about why it does or does not in light of the power of literary description.

3. Write a journal entry discussing the use of setting and symbol in Ann Beattie's "Snow" (p. 314)

Literary Analysis Papers

4. Write a paper discussing the importance of the setting in Flannery O'Connor's "A Good Man Is Hard to Find" (p. 134), John Updike's "A & P" (p. 552), or Isabel Allende's "And of Clay Are We Created" (p. 355).

5. Write a paper discussing the relationship between setting, symbol, and character in Ralph Ellison's "Battle Royal" (p. 402), Richard McGuire's "Here" (p. 223), John Steinbeck's "The Chrysanthemums" (p. 320), or another story of your choice.

6. Write a paper on the literal and symbolic uses of music in Joyce Carol Oates's "Where Are You Going, Where Have You Been?" (p. 481) or James Baldwin's "Sonny's Blues" (p. 362).

Comparison-Contrast Papers

7. Compare and contrast the use and significance of setting in Alice Walker's "Everyday Use" (p. 169) and ZZ Packer's "Brownies" (p. 512).

TIPS for Writing about Setting and Symbol

- **Include setting when it's important.** Setting ordinarily is brought into a paper only if it stands out or has special significance. Discuss its effect in the story precisely and specifically.

- **Cover setting completely.** When writing about setting, be sure to cover place in whatever dimension is important (a room, a building, a city, a country, another planet or world) and to treat time and social milieu, when relevant.

- **Show; don't just say, "It's a symbol."** When you write about a symbol, be sure to explain the features that justify calling it so (as we do, for example, on pp. 205–06); don't assume your reader will agree automatically that the item is symbolic.

- **Look for meanings, not *a* meaning.** Remember that usually a rich symbol does not have one definite meaning that you must find, but rather it is the focal point of a central aspect in the story.

- **Avoid using *symbolize*.** In discussing symbols, it is preferable to use a verb like *suggests* or *conveys*, rather than *symbolizes* or *means*.

8. Compare and contrast the use of darkness as a symbol in James Baldwin's "Sonny's Blues" (p. 362) and Ralph Ellison's "Battle Royal" (p. 402).

WRITING ABOUT CONNECTIONS

Setting and symbol are all about connections. We connect with people by being in the same place and time as they are, and symbols by their nature connect an image with an abstract quality closely associated with it. Thus, any paper you write on setting or symbol will inevitably deal with connections. Along with those connections are thematic connections between stories with similar (or contrasting) settings and symbols. These often can lead to interesting and illuminating papers. Here are a few possibilities:

1. "Secrets of the Heart": Keeping Hope Alive in Ernest Hemingway's "Hills Like White Elephants" (p. 196) and David Means's "The Secret Goldfish" (p. 215)
2. "Dealing with Death": Struggles with Grief in Judith Ortiz Cofer's "Nada" (p. 395), Chitra Banerjee Divakaruni's "Clothes" (p. 328), and/or Bharati Mukherjee's "The Management of Grief" (p. 459).
3. "'A Good Man Is Hard to Find'": Depictions of Men in William Faulkner's "A Rose for Emily" (p. 176) and Zora Neale Hurston's "Sweat" (p. 421).

WRITING RESEARCH PAPERS

1. Find and read several stories about the war in Vietnam by authors other than Tim O'Brien, and do research on the climate and topography of the country. Write a research paper exploring the way O'Brien in "The Things They Carried" (p. 493) and two or three other writers depict the setting and use it in a meaningful way in their stories.

2. Do some research into Yoknapatawpha County, the imaginary county in Mississippi in which most of William Faulkner's stories take place. Using "A Rose for Emily" (p. 176) and perhaps other stories by Faulkner, write a paper exploring how the locale he created becomes as real and meaningful as an actual one as a setting for his stories.

I like short sentences. They are forceful and can get you out of big trouble.

Annie Dillard

(Nonfiction Writer, Novelist, and Poet)

CHAPTER **8**

Tone, Style, and Irony
Attending to Expression and Attitude

The way things are said, their tone and style, matters — a lot. The way you phrase what you say and the tone of voice you use to express yourself can affect the meaning of your words and decidedly alter the message. "Nice shirt!" can mean you love it or you hate it, depending on how you say it. This chapter focuses on some of the key elements that create tone and style and attends specifically to the tone of irony, in order to give you confidence as you encounter these elements in literary works.

ENTRY POINTS As you read the following short story the first time, you'll probably focus more on what's happening than on the tone and style. Most of us pay attention to such techniques on a second reading. So the second time, pay close attention to the way things are expressed — to particular word choices, for example, and to the way sentences are constructed. Recognize that using different words and sentence constructions would definitely alter the effect of what's said. Think about why the style seems appropriate and effective in conveying what happens to the central character and the feelings she experiences on hearing that her husband has died.

Kate Chopin 1851–1904

The Story of an Hour   [1894]

Knowing that Mrs. Mallard was afflicted with a heart trouble, great care was taken to break to her as gently as possible the news of her husband's death.

It was her sister Josephine who told her, in broken sentences; veiled hints that revealed in half concealing. Her husband's friend Richards was there, too, near her. It was he who had been in the newspaper office when intelligence of the railroad disaster was received, with Brently Mallard's name leading the list of "killed." He had only taken the time to assure himself of its truth by a second telegram, and had hastened to forestall any less careful, less tender friend in bearing the sad message.

She did not hear the story as many women have heard the same, with a paralyzed inability to accept its significance. She wept at once, with sudden, wild abandonment, in her sister's arms. When the storm of grief had spent itself she went away to her room alone. She would have no one follow her.

There stood, facing the open window, a comfortable, roomy armchair. Into this she sank, pressed down by a physical exhaustion that haunted her body and seemed to reach into her soul.

She could see in the open square before her house the tops of trees that   5 were all aquiver with the new spring life. The delicious breath of rain was in the air. In the street below a peddler was crying his wares. The notes of a distant song which some one was singing reached her faintly, and countless sparrows were twittering in the eaves.

There were patches of blue sky showing here and there through the clouds that had met and piled one above the other in the west facing her window.

She sat with her head thrown back upon the cushion of the chair, quite motionless, except when a sob came up into her throat and shook her, as a child who has cried itself to sleep continues to sob in its dreams.

She was young, with a fair, calm face, whose lines bespoke repression and even a certain strength. But now there was a dull stare in her eyes, whose gaze was fixed away off yonder on one of those patches of blue sky. It was not a glance of reflection, but rather indicated a suspension of intelligent thought.

There was something coming to her and she was waiting for it, fearfully. What was it? She did not know; it was too subtle and elusive to name. But she felt it, creeping out of the sky, reaching toward her through the sounds, the scents, the color that filled the air.

Now her bosom rose and fell tumultuously. She was beginning to recognize 10 this thing that was approaching to possess her, and she was striving to beat it back with her will—as powerless as her two white slender hands would have been.

When she abandoned herself a little whispered word escaped her slightly parted lips. She said it over and over under her breath: "free, free, free!" The vacant stare and the look of terror that had followed it went from her eyes. They stayed keen and bright. Her pulses beat fast, and the coursing blood warmed and relaxed every inch of her body.

She did not stop to ask if it were or were not a monstrous joy that held her. A clear and exalted perception enabled her to dismiss the suggestion as trivial.

She knew that she would weep again when she saw the kind, tender hands folded in death; the face that had never looked save with love upon her, fixed and gray and dead. But she saw beyond that bitter moment a long procession of years to come that would belong to her absolutely. And she opened and spread her arms out to them in welcome.

There would be no one to live for her during those coming years; she would live for herself. There would be no powerful will bending hers in that blind persistence with which men and women believe they have a right to impose a private will upon a fellow-creature. A kind intention or a cruel intention made the act seem no less a crime as she looked upon it in that brief moment of illumination.

And yet she had loved him—sometimes. Often she had not. What did it mat- 15
ter! What could love, the unsolved mystery, count for in face of this possession of self-assertion which she suddenly recognized as the strongest impulse of her being!

"Free! Body and soul free!" she kept whispering.

Josephine was kneeling before the closed door with her lips to the keyhole, imploring for admission. "Louise, open the door! I beg; open the door—you will make yourself ill. What are you doing, Louise? For heaven's sake open the door."

"Go away. I am not making myself ill." No; she was drinking in a very elixir of life through that open window.

Her fancy was running riot along those days ahead of her. Spring days, and summer days, and all sorts of days that would be her own. She breathed a quick prayer that life might be long. It was only yesterday she had thought with a shudder that life might be long.

She arose at length and opened the door to her sister's importunities. There 20
was a feverish triumph in her eyes, and she carried herself unwittingly like a goddess of Victory. She clasped her sister's waist, and together they descended the stairs. Richards stood waiting for them at the bottom.

Some one was opening the front door with a latchkey. It was Brently Mallard who entered, a little travel-stained, composedly carrying his grip-sack and umbrella. He had been far from the scene of accident, and did not even know there had been one. He stood amazed at Josephine's piercing cry; at Richards' quick motion to screen him from the view of his wife.

But Richards was too late.

When the doctors came they said she had died of heart disease—of joy that kills.

APPROACHING THE READING

1. A story about the tragic death of a husband would of course be serious in the "tone of voice" in which it is narrated. Consider how the tone is established in the first few paragraphs by the style the narrator uses in telling it. Consider the effect of the long sentences and short paragraphs, as well as the effect of word choice. The narrator's language may sound a bit formal. Even in the 1890s, words such as *afflicted, intelligence, forestall, bespoke,* and *fancy,* although part of an educated person's vocabulary, were seldom used in everyday speech. How would the depiction of Mrs. Mallard's situation feel different if the words and sentences seemed more conversational, like those in Alice Walker's "Everyday Use" (p. 169)?

You can explore this author and story in depth, including images and cultural documents, with VirtuaLit Fiction at bedfordstmartins .com/rewritinglit.

2. Reflect on the character of Mrs. Mallard. What is she like? In what ways does the style suit or contribute to her character and the way we respond to her?

3. Do your feelings about her change as she begins to consider how her life will be different? How does the narrator's tone lead you to sympathize with her? Where do you find dramatic irony in the story? Do you think it is effective?

4. Consider the two single-sentence paragraphs at the end. Ask yourself what would be different if the two sentences were combined into a single paragraph. What is the effect of the very short next-to-last paragraph?

READING FOR TONE

Tone (that is, "tone of voice") is a significant aspect of all communication: It can add to, modify, or even invert the meaning of the words expressed. If someone says, "Please close the door behind you," it makes a big difference if the words are spoken as a simple reminder or as an angry demand. Therefore, when you listen to a story, it's important to pay attention to its tone. Tone in a literary work gets in, around, and behind the words to indicate the attitude the work takes toward the characters, setting, subject, or issues or the attitude a character reveals toward an issue, situation, setting, or another character.

TONE IN PROSE WRITING   When we talk, our own tone is conveyed by the inflections in our voice. For a writer, spoken inflections, obviously, are not available, so tone must usually be created through style: Word choice, ways of phrasing, and kinds of comparisons all can convey an attitude (serious, sober, solemn, playful, excited, impassioned, and a host of other possibilities) toward what is being described or discussed. For example, as the mother in "Everyday Use" describes the way Dee used to read to her and Maggie, the word choice creates a tone that is not objective or positive, but rather bitter, almost angry: "She used to read to us *without pity*; *forcing* words, *lies*, other folks' habits, whole lives upon us two, sitting *trapped* and *ignorant* underneath her voice" [italics added] (para. 11).

COMPLEXITY IN TONE   A work can have a single tone, but more often it is mixed, with two or more tones juxtaposed or mingled or played off each other. And tone, especially when it is complex, can be challenging to determine. When Jig in "Hills Like White Elephants" says, "Everything tastes of licorice. Especially all the things you've waited so long for" (para. 27), the tone is difficult to assess: Is it wistful? Angry? Bitter? Tone rarely can be summed up in a word or two. It needs to be described and discussed in a way that does justice to its full complexity.

TONE AND EFFECT   How tone is handled can make a significant difference in the effect or meaning of a story. In "The Story of an Hour," our sympathy for Mrs. Mallard is aroused through the tone of the first two paragraphs, as she receives news of the sudden death of her husband. That tone and our sympathy continue in the following paragraphs, where she appears devastated by what she has heard. Then comes the twist: She isn't devastated, she's elated. At that point the story risks losing our sympathy. If the unexpectedness of her line "free, free, free!" would cause readers to laugh or even smile, the effect of the story would be destroyed. But the formal, dignified style prevents us from laughing, makes us sustain our serious response to her husband's death, as well as the death itself.

RESPONDING ACTIVELY TO TONE   "The Story of an Hour" goes on to say that, kind and loving though her husband had been toward her, his personality dominated their relationship, and she felt trapped. Instead of looking forward to her future, she dreaded what lay ahead. Our sympathy, thus, can turn to being happy for her when she spreads out her arms to welcome the "long procession of years to come that would belong to her absolutely." Readers who respond actively to the tone, as it changes along the way, will experience the full effect of the surprise ending: sadness and regret that she doesn't get to enjoy the new life she briefly glimpses.

READING FOR STYLE

If your teacher asks you to discuss the **style** of a work, she or he wants you to describe or explain the way the author handles words and sentences. Discussion of style is valuable for its own sake, but it is also very important for the way it affects the tone of the work, as we've suggested above. In the paragraphs that follow, we explore the handling of words and sentences in more detail.

Word Choice

Central to style is an author's **diction**, or word choice. A writer can employ any of several types of diction, and the kind selected by a published author, or by you as a student writer, affects the feel and impact of the writing. Style is the *way* the work presents its subject, which always needs to be appropriate to the occasion in which it is being used.

FORMAL DICTION   The most striking thing about the diction in "The Story of an Hour" is its formality, the use of words such as *afflicted* in the first sentence and "had *hastened* to *forestall* any less careful, less tender friend in *bearing* the sad message" in the second pararaph. Try substituting more casual and common words and you'll feel the difference: "*hurried* to *get there first before* any less careful, less tender friend *brings* the sad message." The subject announced in the first sentence, "her husband's death," must be treated seriously, so a formal style is appropriate. The fact that the narrator refers to her as Mrs. Mallard rather than as Louise maintains a sense of dignity and respect — but perhaps a bit of stiffness as well, which seems to fit her traits as a character.

OTHER KINDS OF DICTION   Another type of diction can be characterized by its use of *concrete, everyday words*, like the diction in the first sentence of "Everyday Use": "I will wait for her in the yard that Maggie and I made so clean and wavy yesterday afternoon" (p. 169). Everyday language usually names things you can see and touch, such as "the *hard clay* is *swept* clean as a *floor* and the *fine sand* around the *edges* lined with *tiny, irregular grooves*" ("Everyday Use," para. 1). Concrete language is essential for vivid descriptions (words that attend to particulars are often referred to as **images**). In contrast is **abstract language**, words that convey concepts rather than things. Note Dee's parting words of advice in "Everyday Use": "You just don't understand . . . Your *heritage* . . . make *something* of yourself . . . *a new day*" [italics added] (paras. 79–81). Words like *something* and *a new day* are vague, as if Dee can't express what they mean specifically. They suggest that it is she, not her mother or sister, who lacks the deeper understanding. Kinds of diction range much further, from the technical terminology used by experts in many fields all the way to slang and informal colloquialisms (*gonna, kinda*). Be alert for various levels of language and to the different effects they create.

Sentence Structure

The way phrases and sentences are put together is crucial in creating an effective style. Writers can work with sentences of various lengths. They can craft them tightly or structure them in a loose, ambling way. They can use formal sentences or casual sentences. Here, too, appropriateness is key: suitability to the speakers—both the narrator and the characters in dialogue—and to the occasion and the impact of events, settings, and moments.

RHYTHM   An important ingredient of prose style is **rhythm**, the pattern and cadences in the flow and movement of sentences created by the arrangement of words and phrases. Thus we say that the rhythms in a piece of prose are, for example, fast, slow, syncopated, disjointed, smooth, halting, graceful, rough, deliberate, and so on. Listen for the smooth, graceful, almost wavelike rhythm in the following sentence from the opening paragraph of "Sonny's Blues": "I stared at it in the swinging lights of the subway car, and in the faces and bodies of the people, and in my own face, trapped in the darkness which roared outside" (p. 362). Notice the difference between that rhythm and the edgy, staccato rhythm of this sentence from "Where Are You Going, Where Have You Been?": "Her mother, who noticed everything and knew everything and who hadn't much reason any longer to look at her own face, always scolded Connie about it" (p. 481).

CONTRASTING SENTENCE STYLES   Paying attention to differences in language and sentence structure helps you develop your ear, enabling you to hear and feel on another level as you read, sensing what is often called the musicality of fine writing. Listen first to a sentence from William Faulkner's "A Rose for Emily" as an example of writing that is formal in its diction and **syntax** (sentence style):

> Alive, Miss Emily had been a tradition, a duty, and a care; a sort of hereditary obligation upon the town, dating from that day in 1894 when Colonel Sartoris, the mayor—he who fathered the edict that no Negro woman should appear on the streets without an apron—remitted her taxes, the dispensation dating from the death of her father on into perpetuity. (p. 177)

Writers' stylistic features are recognizable to readers who know their works well. Several things in the sentence above are typical of Faulkner's writing: the educated, exact diction; the long, languid sentences; phrases interjected into sentences; and the use of extra words ("a tradition, a duty, and a care") to get a point or feeling or image exactly right.

Contrast Faulkner's style with that of Ernest Hemingway, as in the opening paragraph of "Hills Like White Elephants":

> The hills across the valley of the Ebro were long and white. On this side there was no shade and no trees and the station was between two lines of rails in the sun. Close against the side of the station there was the warm shadow of the building and a curtain, made of strings of bamboo beads, hung across the open door into the bar, to keep out flies. The American and the girl with him sat at a table in the shade, outside the building. It was very hot and the express from Barcelona would come in forty minutes. It stopped at this junction for two minutes and went on to Madrid. (p. 196)

This passage is typical of Hemingway, with its ordinary, largely concrete, diction and its combinations of short, concise, tightly knit sentences, with cumulative longer sentences made up of short phrases connected by *and* or a comma.

APPROPRIATENESS Appropriateness is key with sentence construction, as it pertains to suitability of language to the speaker and the occasion. As with word choice, the sentences used in the narrative parts of a story must suit the narrator, and those used in dialogue must be appropriate for the characters using them and the contexts.

READING FOR IRONY

Style is particularly important for the more complex tone of **irony**: expression in which the writer or speaker creates a discrepancy or incongruity between what seems to be (appearance) and what is (reality). Because words used ironically don't mean what they literally say, readers have to be active in recognizing the difference between what is said and what is meant, and they need stylistic signals as a guide. Irony appears in a variety of forms. The paragraphs that follow describe the most important types of irony and indicate what to listen for to discern each type.

VERBAL IRONY To notice **verbal irony**, be alert for when what is said is the opposite of what is meant ("Beautiful day!" when the weather is miserable). In "Where Are You Going, Where Have You Been?" (p. 481), the name *Arnold Friend* is an example. Arnold is anything but a friend to Connie. Verbal irony needs stylistic indicators that what is said is not to be taken in a straightforward way — listen for exaggerated and contradictory word choice, for example, or the sheer absurdity of what is said (it can't be straightforwardly true) or the cutting tone in which a word or phrase seems intended to be spoken.

SARCASM   **Sarcasm** is an especially harsh, bitter, often hurtful form of irony. ("Oh, no, these eggs are fine. I *prefer* them black and fused to the plate.") Most sarcasm is like verbal irony, in that the words say the opposite of what is meant; but not all verbal irony is sarcasm. Much verbal irony is more humorous, less personal and cutting than sarcasm is. The narrator's put-down of Sonny's friend, in "Sonny's Blues," "And how about you? You're pretty goddamn smart, I bet" (para. 21), is sarcastic. If we miss such signals, we risk misreading the work.

DRAMATIC IRONY   To notice dramatic irony, watch for when a character says or does something that a reader or audience realizes has a meaning opposite to what the character intends. You can detect dramatic irony by watching for when characters don't realize the full implications of what they are saying or of what happens to them and you see and understand more about it than they do. The last line of "The Story of an Hour" (p. 233) depends on dramatic irony: We know the doctors are wrong — Mrs. Mallard isn't killed by joy at seeing her husband alive and well but dies from shock and disappointment.

SITUATIONAL IRONY   To notice **situational irony**, watch for when a result or situation turns out very differently from what was expected or hoped for. Look for reversals — when something changes from what it used to be, what was expected, what was desired. In many cases, such a reversal is not only ironic in itself but also has ironic implications. In "Everyday Use," for example, as Dee insists on being given the quilts her grandmother made, Mama recalls how she "offered Dee (Wangero) a quilt when she went away to college. Then she had told me they were old-fashioned, out of style" (para. 67). Irony arises out of the altered situation, the change in Dee's attitude toward her heritage. And it's ironic when Dee accuses Mama of not appreciating her heritage when the situation clearly implies that it's Dee who lacks such understanding.

You can further explore tone, style, and irony, including using interactive exercises, with VirtuaLit Fiction at bedfordstmartins .com/rewritinglit.

☑ CHECKLIST on Reading for Tone, Style, and Irony

❑ Listen for tone, the attitude toward the subject implied in a literary work, the "tone of voice" that indicates how what is said should be taken — seriously, ironically, sympathetically, condescendingly, and so on. Does the tone convey humor, affection, anger, frustration, horror, grief, concern, scorn, bitterness (to name only a few possibilities)?

❑ Be especially attentive to style — word selection, sentence construction, sentence rhythms — for its own sake and its effect on tone.

❑ Consider the effectiveness (appropriateness) of a story's narrative style and the style used in characters' dialogue and thoughts. When applicable, think about how style differs in various parts of a story.

❑ Be alert for irony, an expression involving a discrepancy between appearance and reality, between what is said and what is intended. Identify the kind of irony being employed:

  • *Verbal irony:* a discrepancy between what is said and what is intended; saying the opposite of what is actually meant.
  • *Dramatic irony:* a discrepancy between what a reader or audience knows and what is known by a speaker or character; usually the reader or audience knows more than the speaker or character or recognizes implications the speaker or character is not aware of.
  • *Situational irony:* a discrepancy between what is expected or what should be and what actually occurs; in it, a result or situation turns out very differently from what was anticipated or hoped for.

FURTHER READING

ENTRY POINTS   The following is a story about growing up, an initiation tale. As you read it, be sure to pay attention to the narrator's inner world of romantic dreams and longings that contrast with the drab, mundane external world of twentieth-century Dublin. On a second or third reading, listen just for the style, noticing Joyce's word choice, sentence structure and length, and rhythm.

James Joyce 1882–1941

Araby [1914]

North Richmond Street, being blind, was a quiet street except at the hour when the Christian Brothers' School set the boys free. An uninhabited house of two storeys stood at the blind end, detached from its neighbors in a square ground. The other houses of the street, conscious of decent lives within them, gazed at one another with brown imperturbable faces.

The former tenant of our house, a priest, had died in the back drawing-room. Air, musty from having been long enclosed, hung in all the rooms, and the waste room behind the kitchen was littered with old useless papers. Among these I found a few paper-covered books, the pages of which were curled and damp: *The Abbot*, by Walter Scott, *The Devout Communicant*, and *The Memoirs of Vidocq*. I liked the last best because its leaves were yellow. The wild garden behind the house contained a central apple-tree and a few straggling bushes under one of which I found the late tenant's rusty bicycle-pump. He had been a very charitable priest; in his will he had left all his money to institutions and the furniture of his house to his sister.

When the short days of winter came dusk fell before we had well eaten our dinners. When we met in the street the houses had grown somber. The space of sky above us was the color of ever-changing violet and towards it the lamps of the street lifted their feeble lanterns. The cold air stung us and we played till our bodies glowed. Our shouts echoed in the silent street. The career of our play brought us through the dark muddy lanes behind the houses where we ran the gauntlet of the rough tribes from the cottages, to the back doors of the dark dripping gardens where odors arose from the ashpits, to the dark odorous stables where a coachman smoothed and combed the horse or shook music from the buckled harness. When we returned to the street light from the kitchen windows had filled the areas. If my uncle was seen turning the corner we hid in the shadow until we had seen him safely housed. Or if Mangan's sister came out on the doorstep to call her brother in to his tea we watched her from our shadow peer up and down the street. We waited to see whether she would remain or go in and, if she remained, we left our shadow and walked up to Mangan's steps resignedly. She was waiting for us, her figure defined by the light from the half-opened door. Her brother always teased her before he obeyed and I stood by the railings looking at her. Her dress swung as she moved her body and the soft rope of her hair tossed from side to side.

Every morning I lay on the floor in the front parlor watching her door. The blind was pulled down to within an inch of the sash so that I could not be seen. When she came out on the doorstep my heart leaped. I ran to the hall, seized my books, and followed her. I kept her brown figure always in my eye and, when we came near the point at which our ways diverged, I quickened my pace and passed her. This happened morning after morning. I had never spoken to her, except for a few casual words, and yet her name was like a summons to all my foolish blood.

Her image accompanied me even in places the most hostile to romance. On 5 Saturday evenings when my aunt went marketing I had to go to carry some of the parcels. We walked through the flaring streets, jostled by drunken men and bargaining women, amid the curses of laborers, the shrill litanies of shop-boys who stood on guard by the barrel of pigs' cheeks, the nasal chanting of street-singers, who sang a *come-all-you* about O'Donovan Rossa, or a ballad about the troubles in our native land. These noises converged in a single sensation of life for me: I imagined that I bore my chalice safely through a throng of foes. Her name sprang to my lips at moments in strange prayers and praises which I myself did not understand. My eyes were often full of tears (I could not tell why) and at times a flood from my heart seemed to pour itself out into my bosom. I thought little of the future. I did not know whether I would ever speak to her or not or, if I spoke to her, how I could tell her of my confused adoration. But my body was like a harp and her words and gestures were like fingers running upon the wires.

One evening I went into the back drawing-room in which the priest had died. It was a dark rainy evening and there was no sound in the house. Through one of the broken panes I heard the rain impinge upon the earth, the fine incessant needles of water playing in the sodden beds. Some distant lamp or lighted window gleamed below me. I was thankful that I could see so little. All my senses seemed to desire to veil themselves and, feeling that I was about to slip from them, I pressed the palms of my hands together until they trembled, murmuring: *"O love! O love!"* many times.

At last she spoke to me. When she addressed the first words to me I was so confused that I did not know what to answer. She asked me was I going to *Araby*. I forgot whether I answered yes or no. It would be a splendid bazaar, she said she would love to go.

"And why can't you?" I asked.

While she spoke she turned a silver bracelet round and round her wrist. She could not go, she said, because there would be a retreat that week in her convent. Her brother and two other boys were fighting for their caps and I was alone at the railings. She held one of the spikes, bowing her head towards me. The light from the lamp opposite our door caught the white curve of her neck, lit up her hair that rested there and, falling, lit up the hand upon the railing. It fell over one side of her dress and caught the white border of a petticoat, just visible as she stood at ease.

"It's well for you," she said.   10

"If I go," I said, "I will bring you something."

What innumerable follies laid waste my waking and sleeping thoughts after that evening! I wished to annihilate the tedious intervening days. I chafed against the work of school. At night in my bedroom and by day in the classroom her image came between me and the page I strove to read. The syllables of the word *Araby* were called to me through the silence in which my soul luxuriated and cast an Eastern enchantment over me. I asked for leave to go to the bazaar on Saturday night. My aunt was surprised and hoped it was not some Freemason affair. I answered few questions in class. I watched my master's face pass from amiability to sternness; he hoped I was not beginning to idle. I could not call my wandering thoughts together. I had hardly any patience with the serious work of life which, now that it stood between me and my desire, seemed to me child's play, ugly monotonous child's play.

On Saturday morning I reminded my uncle that I wished to go to the bazaar in the evening. He was fussing at the hallstand, looking for the hat-brush, and answered me curtly:

"Yes, boy, I know."

As he was in the hall I could not go into the front parlor and lie at the 15 window. I left the house in bad humor and walked slowly towards the school. The air was pitilessly raw and already my heart misgave me.

When I came home to dinner my uncle had not yet been home. Still it was early. I sat staring at the clock for some time and, when its ticking began to irritate me, I left the room. I mounted the staircase and gained the upper part of the house. The high cold empty gloomy rooms liberated me and I went from room to room singing. From the front window I saw my companions playing below in the street. Their cries reached me weakened and indistinct and, leaning my forehead against the cool glass, I looked over at the dark house where she lived. I may have stood there for an hour, seeing nothing but the brown-clad figure cast by my imagination, touched discreetly by the lamplight at the curved neck, at the hand upon the railings and at the border below the dress.

When I came downstairs again I found Mrs. Mercer sitting at the fire. She was an old garrulous woman, a pawnbroker's widow, who collected used stamps for some pious purpose. I had to endure the gossip of the tea-table. The meal was prolonged beyond an hour and still my uncle did not come. Mrs. Mercer stood up to go: she was sorry she couldn't wait any longer, but it was after eight o'clock and she did not like to be out late, as the night air was bad for her. When she had gone I began to walk up and down the room, clenching my fists. My aunt said:

"I'm afraid you may put off your bazaar for this night of Our Lord."

At nine o'clock I heard my uncle's latchkey in the halldoor. I heard him talking to himself and heard the hallstand rocking when it had received the weight of his overcoat. I could interpret these signs. When he was midway through his dinner I asked him to give me the money to go to the bazaar. He had forgotten.

"The people are in bed and after their first sleep now," he said.   20

I did not smile. My aunt said to him energetically:

"Can't you give him the money and let him go? You've kept him late enough as it is."

My uncle said he was very sorry he had forgotten. He said he believed in the old saying: "All work and no play makes Jack a dull boy." He asked me where I was going and, when I had told him a second time he asked me did I know *The Arab's Farewell to his Steed*. When I left the kitchen he was about to recite the opening lines of the piece to my aunt.

I held a florin tightly in my hand as I strode down Buckingham Street towards the station. The sight of the streets thronged with buyers and glaring with gas recalled to me the purpose of my journey. I took my seat in a third-class carriage of a deserted train. After an intolerable delay the train moved out of the station slowly. It crept onward among ruinous houses and over the twinkling river. At Westland Row Station a crowd of people pressed to the carriage doors; but the porters moved them back, saying that it was a special train for the bazaar. I remained alone in the bare carriage. In a few minutes the train drew up beside an improvised wooden platform. I passed out on to the road and saw by the lighted dial of a clock that it was ten minutes to ten. In front of me was a large building which displayed the magical name.

I could not find any sixpenny entrance and, fearing that the bazaar would   25 be closed, I passed in quickly through a turnstile, handing a shilling to a weary-looking man. I found myself in a big hall girdled at half its height by a gallery. Nearly all the stalls were closed and the greater part of the hall was in darkness. I recognized a silence like that which pervades a church after a service. I walked into the center of the bazaar timidly. A few people were gathered about the stalls which were still open. Before a curtain, over which the words *Café Chantant* were written in colored lamps, two men were counting money on a salver. I listened to the fall of the coins.

Remembering with difficulty why I had come I went over to one of the stalls and examined porcelain vases and flowered tea-sets. At the door of the stall a young lady was talking and laughing with two young gentlemen. I remarked their English accents and listened vaguely to their conversation.

"O, I never said such a thing!"

"O, but you did!"

"O, but I didn't!"

"Didn't she say that?"   30

"Yes. I heard her."

"O, there's a . . . fib!"

Observing me the young lady came over and asked me did I wish to buy anything. The tone of her voice was not encouraging; she seemed to have spoken to me out of a sense of duty. I looked humbly at the great jars that stood like eastern guards at either side of the dark entrance to the stall and murmured:

"No, thank you."

The young lady changed the position of one of the vases and went back to 35
the two young men. They began to talk of the same subject. Once or twice the
young lady glanced at me over her shoulder.

I lingered before her stall, though I knew my stay was useless, to make
my interest in her wares seem the more real. Then I turned away slowly and
walked down the middle of the bazaar. I allowed the two pennies to fall
against the sixpence in my pocket. I heard a voice call from one end of
the gallery that the light was out. The upper part of the hall was now completely dark.

Gazing up into the darkness I saw myself as a creature driven and derided
by vanity; and my eyes burned with anguish and anger.

APPROACHING THE READING

1. Above we called "Araby" a story about growing up, an initiation tale. How
   would you describe the main character as a young boy? What was it about
   the bazaar (a temporary, fancy fair in imitation of a Middle Eastern market) that so strongly appealed to him? Should the bazaar be viewed literally
   (meaning only itself), figuratively (meaning other than itself), or symboli-
   cally (meaning more than itself)?

2. The narrator is an older man looking back at a crucial event early in his life.
   What is the effect of telling the story with this narrative approach? Pick out
   contrasts and ironies that are evident to the adult narrator but probably
   were not to the young boy he once was.

3. Joyce generally had his stories culminate in an **epiphany**, a moment of
   illumination in which the essential nature of a person, a situation, or
   an object is suddenly perceived. Where do you see an epiphany in
   "Araby"? Be ready to discuss what it is that the narrator perceives at that
   moment and what implications that perception presumably has on the
   narrator's life.

4. The story develops the setting carefully, both the immediate setting of
   North Richmond Street and the wider setting of Dublin. The story was
   originally published in 1914 in Joyce's collection entitled *Dubliners*,
   which depicts Irish middle-class life in Dublin in the early twentieth
   century. What impression of Dublin does the story convey? Consider
   how the images of confinement, decay, and darkness are affected by the
   narrative approach, by having a now older narrator look back on the
   city. How would you describe the effect the city seems to have had on
   his life?

5. The story has a richly textured prose style, laced with images, imaginative
   comparisons, and allusions. Try listening to yourself or someone else read
   a paragraph aloud (perhaps paragraph 3, 5, or 25). How does hearing the

language help you notice distinctive qualities of the writing? Be prepared to point out the precise diction, apt and fresh figurative language, variations in sentence length and structures, and effective use of rhythm and sounds.

ENTRY POINTS   Here is another story about personal growth, narrated by a character named Gina who doesn't seem to want to learn more about herself. In this story, too, style plays an important role. The narrator says that words were not her father's medium, but they were hers: "I pursued words. English words. . . . It was important to get it right, every word, every nuance" (para. 21). As you reread, focus on word choice, sentence constructions, and rhythms, as you did for the previous story, and see if you think Gina gets it right. Also, be sure to pay close attention to tone, watching particularly for uses of irony.

Katherine Min   b. 1959

Courting a Monk   [1996]

When I first saw my husband he was sitting cross-legged under a tree on the quad, his hair as short as peach fuzz, large blue eyes staring upward, the smile on his face so wide and undirected as to seem moronic. I went flying by him every minute or two, guarding man-to-man, or chasing down a pass, and out of the corner of my eye I would see him watching and smiling. What I noticed about him most was his tremendous capacity for stillness. His hands were like still-life objects resting on his knees; his posture was impeccable. He looked so rooted there, like some cheerful, exotic mushroom, that I began to feel awkward in my exertion. Sweat funneled into the valley of my back, cooling and sticking when I stopped, hands on knees, to regain my breath. I tried to stop my gape-mouthed panting, refashioned my ponytail, and wiped my hands on the soft front of my sweatpants.

APPROACHING THE AUTHOR

Katherine Min says she was an incorrigible liar as a child. "And the lies I told were literally unbelievable, like that I was really Swedish but had had some sort of operation to disguise myself. From such ignoble beginnings, one has no choice but to become a fiction writer — or a felon, I suppose."

For more about her, see page 1401.

He was still there two plays later when my team was down by one. Sully stole a pass and flipped to Graham. Graham threw me a long bomb that sailed wide and I leapt for it, sailing with the Frisbee for a moment in a parallel line—floating, flying, reaching—before coming down whap! against the ground. I groaned. I'd taken a tree root in the solar plexus. The wind was knocked out of me. I lay there, the taste of dry leaves in my mouth.

"Sorry, Gina. Lousy pass," Graham said, coming over. "You O.K.?"

"Fine," I gasped, fingering my ribs. "Just let me sit out for a while."

I sat down in the leaves, breathing carefully as I watched them play. The day   5 was growing dark and the Frisbee was hard to see. Everyone was tired and played in a sloppy rhythm of errant throws and dropped passes.

Beside me on the grass crept the guy from under the tree. I had forgotten about him. He crouched shyly next to me, leaves cracking under his feet, and, when I looked up, he whispered, "You were magnificent," and walked away smiling.

I spotted him the next day in the vegetarian dining hall. I was passing through with my plate of veal cordon bleu when I saw him sitting by himself next to the window. He took a pair of wooden chopsticks out of the breast pocket of his shirt and poked halfheartedly at his tofu and wilted mung beans. I sat down across from him and demanded his life story.

It turned out he wanted to be a monk. Not the Chaucerian kind, bald-pated and stout, with a hooded robe, ribald humor, and penchant for wine. Something even more baffling—a Buddhist. He had just returned from a semester in Nepal, studying in a monastery in the Himalayas. His hair was coming back in in soft spikes across his head and he had a watchful manner—not cautious but receptive, waiting.

He was from King of Prussia, off the Philadelphia Main Line, and this made me mistrust the depth of his beliefs. I have discovered that a fascination for the East is often a prelude to a pass, a romantic overture set in motion by an "I think Oriental girls are so beautiful," and a viselike grip on the upper thigh. But Micah was different. He understood I was not impressed by his belief, and he did not aim to impress.

"My father was raised Buddhist," I told him. "But he's a scientist now."   10

"Oh," said Micah. "So, he's not spiritual."

"Spirit's insubstantial," I said. "He doesn't hold with intangibility."

"Well, you can't hold atoms in your hand," Micah pointed out.

"Ah," I said, smiling, "but you can count them."

———————

I told Micah my father was a man of science, and this was true. He was a   15 man, also, of silence. Unlike Micah, whose reticence seemed calming, so undisturbed, like a pool of light on still water, my father's silence was like the lid on a pot, sealing off some steaming, inner pressure.

Words were not my father's medium. "Language," my father liked to say, "is an imprecise instrument." (For though he said little, when he hit upon a phrase he liked, he said it many times.) He was fond of Greek letters and numerals set together in intricate equations, symbolizing a certain physical law or experimental hypothesis. He filled yellow legal pads in a strong, vertical hand, writing these beauties down in black, indelible felt-tip pen. I think it was a source of tremendous irritation to him that he could not communicate with other people in so ordered a fashion, that he could not simply draw an equals sign after something he'd said, have them solve for *x* or *y*.

That my father's English was not fluent was only part of it. He was not a garrulous man, even in Korean, among visiting relatives, or alone with my mother. And with me, his only child—who could speak neither of his preferred languages, Korean or science—my father had conspicuously little to say. "Pick up this mess," he would tell me, returning from work in the evening. "Homework finished?" he would inquire, raising an eyebrow over his rice bowl as I excused myself to go watch television.

He limited himself to the imperative mood, the realm of injunction and command; the kinds of statement that required no answer, that left no opening for discussion or rejoinder. These communications were my father's verbal equivalent to his neat numerical equations. They were hermetically sealed.

When I went away to college, my father's parting words constituted one of the longest speeches I'd heard him make. Surrounded by station wagons packed with suitcases, crates of books, and study lamps, amid the excited chattering and calling out of students, among the adults with their nervous, parental surveillance of the scene, my father leaned awkwardly forward with his hands in his pockets, looking at me intently. He said, "Study hard. Go to bed early. Do not goof off. And do not let the American boys take advantages."

This was the same campus my father had set foot on twenty years before, 20 when he was a young veteran of the Korean War, with fifty dollars in his pocket and about that many words of English. Stories of his college years constituted family legend and, growing up, I had heard them so often they were as vivid and dreamlike as my own memories. My father in the dorm bathroom over Christmas, vainly trying to hard-boil an egg in a sock by running it under hot water; his triumph in the physics lab where his ability with the new language did not impede him, and where his maturity and keen scientific mind garnered him highest marks and the top physics prize in his senior year—these were events I felt I'd witnessed, like some obscure, envious ghost.

In the shadow of my father's achievements then, on the same campus where he had first bowed his head to a microscope, lost in a chalk-dust mathematical dream, I pursued words. English words. I committed myself to expertise. I studied Shakespeare and Eliot, Hardy and Conrad, Joyce and Lawrence and Hemingway and Fitzgerald. It was important to get it right, every word, every nuance, to fill in my father's immigrant silences, the gaps he had left for me.

Other gaps he'd left. Staying up late and studying little, I did things my father would have been too shocked to merely disapprove. As for American boys, I heeded my father's advice and did not let them take advantage. Instead I took advantage of them, of their proximity, their good looks, and the amiable way they would fall into bed with you if you gave them the slightest encouragement. I liked the way they moved in proud possession of their bodies, the rough feel of their unshaven cheeks, their shoulders and smooth, hairless chests, the curve of their backs like burnished wood. I liked the way I could look up at them, or down, feeling their shuddering climax like a distant earthquake; I could make it happen, moving in undulant circles from above or below, watching them, holding them, making them happy. I collected boys like baubles, like objects not particularly valued, which you stash away in the back of some drawer. It was the pleasant interchangeability of their bodies I liked. They were all white boys.

Micah refused to have sex with me. It became a matter of intellectual disagreement between us. "Sex saps the will," he said.

"Not necessarily," I argued. "Just reroutes it."

"There are higher forms of union," he said.   25

"Not with your clothes off," I replied.

"Gina," he said, looking at me with kindness, a concern that made me flush with anger. "What need do you have that sex must fill?"

"Fuck you, Micah," I said. "Be a monk, not a psychologist."

He laughed. His laughter was always a surprise to me, like a small disturbance to the universe. I wanted to seduce him, this was true. I considered Micah the only real challenge among an easy field. But more than seduction, I wanted to rattle him, to get under that sense of peace, that inward contentment. No one my age, I reasoned, had the right to such self-possession.

We went for walks in the bird sanctuary, rustling along the paths slowly,   30
discussing Emily Dickinson or maple-syrup-making, but always I brought the subject around.

"What a waste of a life," I said once. "Such indulgence. All that monkly devotion and quest for inner peace. Big deal. It's selfish. Not only is it selfish, it's a cop-out. An escape from this world and its messes."

Micah listened, a narrow smile on his lips, shaking his head regretfully. "You're so wonderfully passionate, Gina, so alive and in the world. I can't make you see. Maybe it is a cop-out, as you say, but Buddhism makes no distinction between the world outside or the world within the monastery. And historically, monks have been in the middle of political protest and persecution. Look at Tibet."

"I was thinking about, ahem, something more basic," I said.

Micah laughed. "Of course," he said. "You don't seem to understand, Gina, Buddhism is all about the renunciation of desire."

I sniffed. "What's wrong with desire? Without desire, you might as well not   35
be alive."

The truth was that I was fascinated by this idea, the renunciation of desire. My life was fueled by longing, by vast and clamorous desires; a striving toward things I did not have and, perhaps, had no hope of having. I could vaguely imagine an end, some point past desiring, of satiety, but I could not fathom the laying down of desire, walking away in full appetite.

"The desire to renounce desire," I said now, "is still desire, isn't it?"

Micah sunk his hands into his pockets and smiled. "It's not," he said, walking ahead of me. "It's a conscious choice."

We came to a pond, sun-dappled in a clearing, bordered by white birch and maples with the bright leaves of mid-autumn. A fluttering of leaves blew from the trees, landing on the water as gently as if they'd been placed. The color of the pond was a deep canvas green; glints of light snapped like sparks above the surface. There was the lyric coo of a mourning dove, the chitter-chitter of late-season insects. Micah's capacity for appreciation was vast. Whether this had anything to do with Buddhism, I didn't know, but watching him stand on the edge of the pond, his head thrown back, his eyes eagerly taking in the light, I felt his peace and also his sense of wonder. He stood motionless for a long time.

I pulled at ferns, weaved their narrow leaves in irregular samplers, braided   40
tendrils together, while Micah sat on a large rock and, taking his chopsticks from his breast pocket, began to tap them lightly against one another in a solemn rhythm.

"Every morning in the monastery," he said, "we woke to the prayer drum. Four o'clock and the sky would be dark and you'd hear the hollow wooden sound—plock, plock, plock—summoning you to meditation." He smiled dreamily. The chopsticks made a somewhat less effectual sound, a sort of ta ta ta. I imagined sunrise across a Himalayan valley—the wisps of pink-tinged cloud on a cold spring morning, the austerity of a monk's chamber.

Micah had his eyes closed, face to the sun. He continued to tap the chopsticks together slowly. He looked singular and new, sitting on that rock, like an advance scout for some new tribe, with his crest of hair and calm, and the attentiveness of his body to his surroundings.

I think it was then I fell in love with him, or, it was in that moment that my longing for him became so great that it was no longer a matter of simple gratification. I needed his response. I understood what desire was then, the disturbance of a perfect moment in anticipation of another.

"Wake-up call," I said. I peeled off my turtleneck and sweater in one clever motion and tossed them at Micah's feet. Micah opened his eyes. I pulled my pants off and my underwear and stood naked. "Plock, plock, who's there?"

Micah did not turn away. He looked at me, his chopsticks poised in the air.   45
He raised one toward me and held it, as though he were an artist with a paintbrush raised for a proportion, or a conductor ready to lead an orchestra. He held the chopstick suspended in the space between us, and it was as though I couldn't move for as long as he held it. His eyes were fathomless blue. My nipples constricted with the cold. Around us leaves fell in shimmering lights to the water, making a soft rustling sound like the rub of stiff fabric. He brought his hand down and I was released. I turned and leapt into the water.

A few nights later I bought a bottle of cheap wine and goaded Micah into drinking it with me. We started out on the steps of the library after it had closed for the night, taking sloppy swigs from a brown paper bag. The lights of the Holyoke range blinked in the distance, across the velvet black of the freshman quad. From there we wandered the campus, sprawling on the tennis courts, bracing a stiff wind from the terrace of the science center, sedately rolling down Memorial Hill like a pair of tumbleweeds.

"J'a know what a koan is?" he asked me, when we were perched at the top of the bleachers behind home plate. We unsteadily contemplated the steep drop off the back side.

"You mean like ice cream?" I said.

"No, a ko-an. In Buddhism."

"Nope." 50

"It's a question that has no answer, sort of like a riddle. You know, like 'What is the sound of one hand clapping?' Or 'What was your face before you were born?'"

"'What was my face before it was born?' That makes no sense."

"Exactly. You're supposed to contemplate the koan until you achieve a greater awareness."

"Of what?"

"Of life, of meaning." 55

"Oh, O.K.," I said. "I've got it." I was facing backwards, the bag with the bottle in both my hands. "How 'bout, 'What's the sound of one cheek farting?'"

He laughed for a long time, then retched off the side of the bleachers. I got him home and put him to bed; his forehead was feverish, his eyes glassy with sickness.

"Sorry," I said. "I'm a bad influence." I kissed him. His lips were hot and slack.

"Don't mind," he murmured, half-asleep.

The next night we slept in the same bed together for the first time. He kept 60 his underwear on and his hands pressed firmly to his sides, like Gandhi° among his young virgins. I was determined to make it difficult for him. I kept brushing my naked body against him, draping a leg across his waist, stroking his narrow chest with my fingertips. He wiggled and pushed away, feigning sleep. When I woke in the morning, he was gone and the *Ode to Joy* was blasting from my stereo.

Graham said he missed me. We'd slept together a few times before I met Micah, enjoying the warm, healthful feeling we got from running or playing Ultimate, taking a quick sauna, and falling into bed. He was good-looking, dark and broad, with sinewy arms and a tight chest. He made love to a woman like he was lifting Nautilus, all grim purpose and timing. It was hard to believe that had ever been appealing. I told him I was seeing someone else.

"Not the guy with the crew cut?" he said. "The one who looks like a baby seal?"

Gandhi: Mahatma Gandhi (1869–1948), leader of the independence movement in India, is reputed to have slept next to naked virgins as a way of testing his vow of *brahmacharya*, or total chastity in thought and deed.

I shrugged.

Graham looked at me skeptically. "He doesn't seem like your type," he said.

"No," I agreed. "But at least he's not yours."   65

Meanwhile I stepped up my attack. I asked endless questions about Buddhist teaching. Micah talked about *dukkha*; the four noble truths; the five aggregates of attachment; the noble eightfold path to enlightenment. I listened dutifully, willing to acknowledge that it all sounded nice, that the goal of perfect awareness and peace seemed worth attaining. While he talked, I stretched my feet out until my toes touched his thigh; I slid my hand along his back; or leaned way over so he could see down my loose, barely-buttoned blouse.

"Too bad you aren't Tantric,"° I said. I'd been doing research.

Micah scoffed. "Hollywood Buddhism," he said. "Heavy breathing and theatrics."

"They believe in physical desire," I said. "They have sex."

"Buddha believes in physical desire," Micah said. "It's impermanent, that's   70 all. Something to get beyond."

"To get beyond it," I said petulantly, "you have to do it."

Micah sighed. "Gina," he said, "you are beautiful, but I can't. There are a lot of guys who will."

"A lot of them do."

He smiled a bit sadly. "Well, then . . ."

I leaned down to undo his shoelaces. I tied them together in double knots.   75 "But I want you," I said.

My parents lived thirty miles from campus and my mother frequently asked me to come home for dinner. I went only once that year, and that was with Micah. My parents were not the kind of people who enjoyed the company of strangers. They were insular people who did not like to socialize much or go out — or anyway, my father was that way, and my mother accommodated herself to his preferences.

My mother had set the table in the dining room with blue linen. There were crystal wine glasses and silver utensils in floral patterns. She had made some dry baked chicken with overcooked peas and carrots — the meal she reserved for when Americans came to dinner. When it came to Korean cooking, my mother was a master. She made fabulous marinated short ribs and sautéed transparent bean noodles with vegetables and beef, pork dumplings and batter-fried shrimp, and cucumber and turnip kimchis which she made herself and fermented in brown earthenware jars. But American cuisine eluded her; it bored her. I think she thought it was meant to be tasteless.

"Just make Korean," I had urged her on the phone. "He'll like that."

Tantric: A variant in several Indian religions that reveres the body as a temple, instead of rejecting it, and includes sexual rituals as one of its ways to seek ultimate reality.

My mother was skeptical. "Too spicy," she said. "I know what Americans like."

"Not the chicken dish," I pleaded. "He's a vegetarian."   80

"We'll see," said my mother, conceding nothing.

Micah stared down at his plate. My mother smiled serenely. Micah nodded. He ate a forkful of vegetables, took a bite of bread. His Adam's apple seemed to be doing a lot of work. My father, too, was busy chewing, his Adam's apple moving up and down his throat like the ratchets of a tire jack. No one had said a thing since my father had uncorked the Chardonnay and read to us the description from his well-creased paperback edition of *The New York Times Guide to Wine.*

The sound of silverware scraping on ceramic plates seemed amplified. I was aware of my own prolonged chewing. My father cleared his throat. My mother looked at him expectantly. He coughed.

"Micah studied Buddhism in Nepal," I offered into the silence.

"Oh!" my mother exclaimed. She giggled.   85

My father kept eating. He swallowed exaggeratedly and looked up. "That so?" he said, sounding almost interested.

Micah nodded. "I was only there four months," he said. "Gina tells me you were brought up Buddhist."

My father grunted. "Well, of course," he said, "in Korea in those days, our families were all Buddhist. I do not consider myself a Buddhist now."

Micah and I exchanged a look.

"It's become quite fashionable, I understand," my father went on. "With 90 you American college kids. Buddhism has become fad."

I saw Micah wince.

"I think it is wonderful, Hi Joon," my mother interceded, "for Americans to learn about Asian religion and philosophy. I was a philosophy major in college, Micah. I studied Whitehead, American pragmatism."

My father leaned back in his chair and watched, frowning, while my mother and Micah talked. It was like he was trying to analyze Micah, not as a psychiatrist analyzes — my father held a dim view of psychology — but as a chemist would, breaking him down to his basic elements, the simple chemical formula that would define his makeup.

Micah was talking about the aggregates of matter, sensation, perception, mental formations, and consciousness that comprise being in Buddhist teaching. "It's a different sense of self than in Christian religions," he explained, looking at my mother.

"Nonsense," my father interrupted. "There is no self in Buddhist 95 doctrine. . . ."

My mother and I watched helplessly as they launched into discussion. I was surprised that my father seemed to know so much about it, and by how much he was carrying forth. I was surprised also by Micah's deference. He seemed to have lost all his sureness, the walls of his conviction. He kept nodding and conceding to my father certain points that he had rigorously defended to me before. "I guess I don't know as much about it," he said more than once, and "Yes, I see what you mean" several times, with a sickening air of humility.

I turned from my father's glinting, pitiless intelligence, to Micah's respectfulness, his timid manner, and felt a rising irritation I could not place, anger at my father's belligerence, at Micah's backing down, at my own strange motives for having brought them together. Had I really expected them to get along? And yet, my father was concentrating on Micah with such an intensity—almost as though he were a rival—in a way in which he never focused on me.

When the dialogue lapsed, and after we had consumed as much of the food as we deemed polite, my mother took the dishes away and brought in a bowl of rice with kimchi for my father. Micah's eyes lit up. "May I have some of that, too, Mrs. Kim?"

My mother looked doubtful. "Too spicy," she said.

"Oh, I love spicy food," Micah assured her. My mother went to get him a   100 bowl.

"You can use chopsticks?" my mother said, as Micah began eating with them.

"Mom, it's no big deal," I said.

My father looked up from his bowl. Together, my parents watched while Micah ate a large piece of cabbage kimchi.

"Hah!" my father said, suddenly smiling. "Gina doesn't like kimchi," he said. He looked at me. "Gina," he said. "This boy more Korean than you."

"Doesn't take much," I said.   105

My father ignored me. "Gina always want to be American," he told Micah. "Since she was little girl, she want blue eyes, yellow hair." He stabbed a chopstick toward Micah's face. "Like yours."

"If I had hair," said Micah, grinning, rubbing a hand across his head.

My father stared into his bowl. "She doesn't want to be Korean girl. She thinks she can be 100 percent American, but she cannot. She has Korean blood—100 percent. Doesn't matter where you grow up—blood is most important. What is in the blood." He gave Micah a severe look. "You think you can become Buddhist. Same way. But it is not in your blood. You cannot know real Buddha's teaching. You should study Bible."

"God, Dad!" I said. "You sound like a Nazi!"

"Gina!" my mother warned.   110

"You're embarrassing me," I said. "Being rude to my guest. Discussing me as if I wasn't here. You can say what you want, Dad, I'm American whether you like it or not. Blood's got nothing to do with it. It's what's up here." I tapped my finger to my temple.

"It's not Nazi," my father said. "Is fact! What you have here," he pointed to his forehead, "is all from blood, from genetics. You got from me!"

"Heaven help me," I said.

"Gina!" my mother implored.

"Mr. Kim —" Micah began.   115

"You just like American girl in one thing," my father shouted. "You have no respect for father. In Korea, daughters do not talk back to their parents, is big shame!"

"In Korea, girls are supposed to be submissive doormats for fathers to wipe their feet on!" I shouted back.

"What do you know about Korea? You went there only once when you were six years old."

"It's in my blood," I said. I stood up. "I'm not going to stay here for this. Come on, Micah."

Micah looked at me uncertainly, then turned to my father.   120

My father was eating again, slowly levering rice to his mouth with his chopsticks. He paused. "She was always this way," he said, seeming to address the table. "So angry. Even as a little girl."

"Mr. Kim," Micah said, "Um, thank you very much. We're . . . I think we're heading out now."

My father chewed ruminatively. "I should never have left Korea," he said quietly, with utter conviction.

"Gina," my mother said. "Sit down. Hi Joon, please!"

"Micah," I said. "You coming?"   125

We left my father alone at the dining-room table.

"I should have sent you to live with Auntie Soo!" he called after me.

My mother followed us out to the driveway with a Tupperware container of chicken Micah hadn't eaten.

———————

On the way home we stopped for ice cream. Koans, I told Micah. "What is the sound of Swiss chocolate almond melting?" I asked him. "What was the vanilla before it was born?"

Inside the ice-cream parlor the light was too strong, a ticking fluorescence   130
bleaching everything bone-white. Micah leaned down to survey the cardboard barrels of ice cream in their plastic cases. He looked shrunken, subdued. He ordered a scoop of mint chocolate chip and one of black cherry on a sugar cone and ate it with the long, regretful licks of a child who'd spent the last nickel of his allowance. There was a ruefulness to his movements, a sense of apology. He had lost his monklike stillness and seemed suddenly adrift.

The cold of the ice cream gave me a headache, all the blood vessels in my temples seemed strung out and tight. I shivered and the cold was like fury, spreading through me with the chill.

Micah rubbed my back.

"You're hard on your father," he said. "He's not a bad guy."

"Forget it," I said. "Let's go."

———————

We walked from the dorm parking lot in silence. There were lights 135
going on across the quad and music spilling from the windows out into the
cool air. What few stars there were seemed too distant to wage a constant
light.

Back in my room, I put on the Rolling Stones at full blast. Mick Jagger's
voice was taunting and cruel. I turned out the lights and lit a red candle.

"O.K., this is going to stop," I said. I felt myself trembling. I pushed Micah
back on the bed. I was furious. He had ruined it for me, the lightness, the skimming quality of my life. It had seemed easy, with the boys, the glib words and
feelings, the simple heat and surface pleasures. It was like the sensation of flying, leaping for the Frisbee and sailing through the air. For a moment you lose
a feeling for gravity, for the consciousness of your own skin or species. For a
moment you are free.

I started to dance, fast, swinging and swaying in front of the bed. I closed
my eyes and twirled wildly, bouncing off the walls like a pinball, stumbling on
my own stockings. I danced so hard the stereo skipped, Jagger forced to stutter
in throaty monosyllables, gulping repetitions. I whirled and circled, threw my
head from side to side until I could feel the baffled blood, brought my hair up
off my neck and held it with both hands.

Micah watched me dance. His body made an inverted-S upon my bed, his
head propped by the pillar of his own arm. The expression on his face was the
same as he'd had talking with my father, that look of deference, of fawn-eyed
yielding. But I could see there was something hidden.

With white-knuckled fingers, I undid the buttons of my sweater and ripped 140
my shirt lifting it off my head. I danced out of my skirt and underthings, kicking them into the corner, danced until the song was over, until I was soaked
with sweat and burning—and then I jumped him.

It was like the taste of food after a day's starvation—unexpectedly
strong and substantial. Micah responded to my fury, met it with his own
mysterious passion; it was like a brawl, a fight, with something at stake
that neither of us wanted to lose. Afterward we sat up in bed and listened
to *Ode to Joy* while Micah, who had a surplus supply of chopsticks lying
around the room, did his Leonard Bernstein impersonation. Later, we went
out for a late-night snack to All-Star Dairy and Micah admitted to me that
he was in love.

My father refused to attend the wedding. He liked Micah, but he did
not want me to marry a Caucasian. It became a joke I would tell people.
Korean custom, I said, to give the bride away four months before the
ceremony.

Micah became a high-school biology teacher. I am an associate dean of
students at the local college. We have two children. When Micah tells the story

of our courtship, he tells it with great self-deprecation and humor. He makes it sound as though he were crazy to ever consider becoming a monk. "Think of it," he tells our kids. "Your dad."

Lately I've taken to reading books about Buddhism. Siddhartha Gotama° was thirty-five years old when he sat under the Bodhi-tree on the bank of the river Neranjara and gained Enlightenment. Sometimes, when I see my husband looking at me across the breakfast table, or walking toward me from the other side of a room, I catch a look of distress on his face, a blinking confusion, as though he cannot remember who I am. I have happened on him a few times, on a Sunday when he has disappeared from the house, sitting on a bench with the newspaper in his lap staring across the town common, so immersed in his thoughts that he is not roused by my calling of his name.

I remember the first time I saw him, that tremendous stillness he carried, 145 the contentment in his face. I remember how he looked on the rocks by that pond, like a pioneer in a new land, and I wonder if he regrets, as I do, the loss of his implausible faith. Does he miss the sound of the prayer drum, the call to an inner life without the configuration of desire? I think of my father, running a sock under heated water thousands of miles from home, as yet unaware of the daughter he will raise with the same hopeful, determined, and ultimately futile, effort. I remember the way I used to play around with koans, and I wonder, "What is the sound of a life not lived?"

Siddhartha Gotama: Born in India some 2,500 years ago, he is the one to whom Theravada Buddhists generally are referring when they speak of "the Buddha."

APPROACHING THE READING

1. Pick out words—make a list—that characterize or describe the narrator's tone. Study the list and reflect on why you think these are appropriate for the attitude of the narrator and for the themes in the story. Which words are ironic when applied to the narrator and the story? In what ways? What makes the ironies appropriate, fitting?

2. Notice how Katherine Min varies her sentence structures. Look, for example, at the second paragraph. Reflect on the effect of this style and consider what you might say to someone to help her or him realize that style creates an impact on the reader. Find other examples where style creates an impact.

3. Recall the three types of irony. Where do you see them at play in the story? What particular cultural ironies does the story bring out? Are there moments of irony that the characters themselves are unaware of?

4. Where and how does Min change the tone in the story? Think about the ways characters speak, the shifts in tone from one paragraph or section to another, as well as shifts in sentence structure, word choice, intensity of verbs, and descriptions.

5. Notice the ways Gina and Micah change in the story, and then reflect on why those changes occur. Be ready to discuss what they seem to think about how they've changed, and what you think about it. What do the final two paragraphs contribute to that discussion and to "what the story all adds up to"?

ENTRY POINTS   *Maus*, a book-length graphic work about the Holocaust, is especially unsettling. As you read the following excerpt the first time, in addition to getting a solid sense of what is going on, think about why the use of animals, and these particular animals, is so powerful in dealing with the Holocaust. We have been discussing style in this chapter. With graphic literature, when you consider the style, you need to do so in terms of both the language and the way the artist draws the panels. On your second reading, think about how you would describe the style of drawing and the style of writing and the way they complement one another. Also, in what ways is the tone of the work brought out in the words of the narrator? In what ways is the tone created by the artwork? The piece is rich in irony. Pick out the types and be ready to support your conclusions using examples from both the language and the drawings.

Art Spiegelman b. 1948

From *Maus*   [1986]

I TELL YOU, THERE'S A POGROM GOING ON IN GERMANY TODAY!

ONE FELLOW TOLD US OF HIS COUSIN WHAT WAS LIVING IN GERMANY...

...HE HAD TO SELL HIS BUSINESS TO A GERMAN AND RUN OUT FROM THE COUNTRY WITHOUT EVEN THE MONEY.

I AM A FILTHY JEW

IT WAS VERY HARD THERE FOR THE JEWS—TERRIBLE!

ANOTHER FELLOW TOLD US OF A RELATIVE IN BRANDENBERG—THE POLICE CAME TO HIS HOUSE AND NO ONE HEARD AGAIN FROM HIM.

This town is Jew Free

IT WAS MANY, MANY SUCH STORIES—SYNAGOGUES BURNED, JEWS BEATEN WITH NO REASON, WHOLE TOWNS PUSHING OUT ALL JEWS—EACH STORY WORSE THAN THE OTHER.

LET'S HOPE THOSE NAZI GANGSTERS GET THROWN OUT OF POWER!

JUST PRAY THAT THEY DON'T START A WAR!!

APPROACHING THE READING

1. Reflect on and describe what makes Art Spiegelman's daring way of depicting the characters effective and appropriate.

2. How would you describe Spiegelman's style? Think about his use of dialogue, dialect, style of drawing, and choices of what to depict.

APPROACHING THE AUTHOR

Art Spiegelman's parents wanted him to be a dentist. Instead, when he went to Harpur College (now a part of Binghamton University), he majored in art and philosophy. He never graduated, but thirty years later, the university presented him with an honorary doctorate.

For more about him, see page 1413.

3. Pick out several panels and talk about how they depict and evoke the tone of the work. Considering how tone can reveal the attitude of the characters and of the creator, what would you conclude to be the attitude of the father, the son, and Spiegelman toward the Holocaust and its consequences? Make sure you don't think it is as simple as "against it"!

4. The work is rich in ironies. Pick out some of the more obvious ones and some of the more subtle ones and note the type of irony and how the drawings and the language support your conclusions. Where do you discover an ironic interplay between what is being said and what is drawn? Think about what makes this juxtaposition powerful.

5. Think about how you would describe the distinctions in style, both verbal and visual, among the four works of graphic literature presented in this book. Lynda Barry's "Today's Demon: Magic" (p. 150), the excerpt from Marjane Satrapi's *Persepolis* (p. 185), Richard McGuire's "Here" (p. 223), and the excerpt from Art Spiegelman's *Maus* in this chapter.

RESPONDING THROUGH Writing

WRITING ABOUT TONE, STYLE, AND IRONY

Journal Entries

1. In the course of a day, listen and watch for the word *style* in regard to anything — music, clothes, sports, and so on. Pay attention to radio voices, TV shows, advertisements, what you say, what you overhear other people saying, and so forth. Write a journal entry describing several styles you discover. How can the ways words are used elsewhere help clarify their uses in literature?

2. Analyze a recording star or television host in terms of style. Think about everything that goes into the making of the person's image, or style. Write a journal entry summarizing your conclusions and commenting on how doing

this exercise can help illuminate or help someone recognize what style is and how it contributes to effect in literature.

You can further research the authors in this chapter with LitLinks, or take a quiz on the stories with LitQuiz, at bedfordstmartins.com/rewritinglit.

3. In your journal, list instances of irony that you notice during a day. Discuss how and why verbal irony in particular was used and how it affected the people at whom it was directed.

Literary Analysis Papers

4. Choose a paragraph from one of the stories in this chapter and rewrite it in the style of a different author. Then write a short paper explaining why you chose the authors you did and in what ways the changes in style changed the nature and effect of the story as a whole.

5. Write a paper analyzing the relation of style, tone, and theme in David Means's "The Secret Goldfish" (p. 215), Jamaica Kincaid's "Girl" (p. 317), Ralph Ellison's "Battle Royal" (p. 402), or Ha Jin's "Saboteur" (p. 347).

6. Write a paper discussing the importance of irony in Flannery O'Connor's "A Good Man Is Hard to Find" (p. 134), Joyce Carol Oates's "Where Are You Going, Where Have You Been?" (p. 481), or ZZ Packer's "Brownies" (p. 512).

Comparison-Contrast Papers

7. Write a paper exploring how Katherine Min's use of comparisons and contrasts in "Courting a Monk" (p. 247) — between Gina and her father, for example, or Micah and Gina's father, or Gina and Micah — contribute to its richness of tone and theme.

8. Write a paper in which you compare and contrast style, tone, and theme in Ernest Hemingway's "Hills Like White Elephants" (p. 196) and Raymond Carver's "What We Talk about When We Talk about Love" (p. 386).

WRITING ABOUT CONNECTIONS

Tone, style, and irony are used by writers not only for the story itself but also to connect with readers, to help shape the effect a story has on people as they read it. Looking at the way tone, style, and/or irony are handled in two stories, and the ways they can connect the two stories' themes, can be an interesting and valuable paper topic. The results can be especially revealing when the stories come from different eras or cultures. Here are a few possibilities:

1. "Tales of Survival": Katherine Anne Porter's "The Jilting of Granny Weatherall" (p. 533) and Chitra Banerjee Divakaruni's "Clothes" (p. 328)
2. "Learning out of School": Personal Maturity in Toni Cade Bambara's "The Lesson" (p. 208) and John Updike's "A & P" (p. 552)

3. "'Gather Ye Rosebuds'": Looking for Love in William Faulkner's "A Rose for Emily" (p. 176) and Katherine Min's "Courting a Monk" (p. 247)

TIPS for Writing about Tone, Style, and Irony

- **Concentrating on tone.** Tone can be the central topic of a paper if it is a crucial element in achieving the effect of a story or novel. The outline for such an analysis might include two or three aspects or techniques used to create tone(s) or two or three points about how tone alters or shifts in significant ways in the work.

- **Including style.** Prose style is one of the most challenging and rewarding topics to write about, requiring close, careful analysis and precise, detailed explanations. Include it in a paper only when the style is unusual or important, perhaps bringing it up in passing or treating it in one paragraph, as an aspect contributing to a broader analysis of the story. Be sure to discuss its effect in the story and its connections to other elements.

- **Centering on style.** In some cases, when style is unusually complex or distinctive, it can be the subject of an entire paper. In that case, three or four stylistic features become the outline of the paper.

- **Pointing out irony.** When irony plays an important role in a story, it is essential at least to point it out in a paper and explain its role in creating the story's effect.

- **Focusing on irony.** If irony plays a major part in a story's approach and effect, analyzing the techniques through which it is established or the way it shapes meaning can form the topic for a whole paper. Be sure to ground your discussion in specific details and examples.

WRITING RESEARCH PAPERS

1. A full understanding of and appreciation for Katherine Min's "Courting a Monk" (p. 247) requires some knowledge of Buddhism. Research Buddhism and write a research paper in which you clarify and illuminate parts of the text that could benefit from such explanation and explicate the reversal of roles at the end of the story.

2. The idea of achieving the American dream has had a profound impact on many people. This concept distinctively affected many minorities. Do some research into that idea—what it means, how it arose, how realistic its attainment has been and can be. Write a research paper using what you learn as you compare and contrast ways that theme is embodied (and the tone in which it is handled) in Katherine Min's "Courting a Monk" (p. 247) and James Baldwin's "Sonny's Blues" (p. 362).

When you write you invite a reader to look in through a
window on everything.

William Stafford

(American Poet; see p. 639)

Writing about Fiction

CHAPTER **9**

Applying What You've Learned

Writing papers about fiction is one way of participating in the ongoing conversation about literature described in Chapter 2. There's a natural progression from asking a friend or classmate about what happened in a story (Did the narrator really bury Fortunato alive? Did I get that right?) to discussing the story in class (What sort of person could do that, could have that attitude about revenge?) to writing a paper on the disturbed personality of the narrator in Edgar Allan Poe's "The Cask of Amontillado" (p. 528).

The information in Chapters 5–8 helps equip you to read fiction actively and confidently. At the same time, it prepares you to write about fiction effectively and with assurance. These chapters provide you ways to "enter" a short story or novel and be able not only to understand what is involved within a piece of fiction but also to talk and write about what makes it work, how its effects are achieved. The section "Writing Short Papers" in Chapter 2 (pp. 30–45) provides you with general guidance for writing a short literary paper. We suggest that you review parts of that section as you move through the steps in the writing process. Instead of repeating in this chapter what we say there, we will focus on tips for writing specifically about fiction.

We asked students in one of our introduction to literature classes to write an analytical paper on Dagoberto Gilb's "Love in L.A." (p. 113). If you don't remember the story, rereading it will make this chapter easier to apply to your own work. The assignment was to "Write a two- to three-page paper analyzing the way one of the techniques for fiction covered in Chapters 5–8 is handled in 'Love in L.A.'" This chapter will follow one of our students, Alicia Abood, through the writing process in completing that assignment, using her own words as she retraces her steps.

Step 1. Prewriting: Finding a Topic

When looking for a topic, look first for a story you enjoy reading and thinking about. You will write best when you have a topic you enjoy. Read the story two or three times. In the second or third reading, notice what catches your interest. Reflect on the characters, what they are like and what they do. You might decide to write on one or two characters in a character-analysis paper. Pay attention to the way the author handles such things as plot, point of view, setting, symbols, style, tone, irony; notice which play a particularly important role in the story. Perhaps you could focus on one or more of these in a paper analyzing literary techniques. Do you find the ideas explored in the story appealing or challenging? In that case you might do a thematic analysis. See if juxtapositions have a significant place in the story, or if connections between the story and another work seem meaningful enough to study and write about. Consider if the social or cultural context has a significant impact on the story. If so, might that be something meaningful to examine and write about?

A student, Alicia Abood, on finding a topic: "In reading 'Love in L.A.,' I felt very challenged by the main character, Jake. Even after reading the story a handful of times, I felt like I still hadn't figured Jake out. He made me feel unsettled, in less than three pages! This made me think Jake's character might work for my essay. Perhaps exploring my questions about his character would allow me to feel more confident with my thoughts on this complex individual."

Keep asking questions: Why? How? What if? Alicia asked these questions as she looked for a topic she wanted to write about.

We provide suggestions for paper topics at the end of Chapters 5, 6, 7, and 8. If you're still looking for a topic, you might look at those again (pp. 156, 192, 229, and 262). Here are a dozen additional possibilities:

1. The interconnectedness of plot, point of view, and theme in Bharati Mukherjee's "The Management of Grief" (p. 459) or Haruki Murakami's "Birthday Girl" (p. 471)
2. The handling of time in William Faulkner's "A Rose for Emily" (p. 176), Kate Chopin's "The Story of an Hour" (p. 233), Helena María Viramontes's "The Moths" (p. 557), or another story of your choice. Try focusing on the way short stories frequently include an unusual moment in which time moves in a different way—faster or slower than usual—or stops briefly, forcing a character to a point of crisis or to make a crucial decision.

3. Struggles with questions of personal/ethnic identity and cultural borders in Louise Erdrich's "The Red Convertible" (p. 126), Alice Walker's "Everyday Use" (p. 169), Katherine Min's "Courting a Monk" (p. 247), or James Baldwin's "Sonny's Blues" (p. 362)
4. The relevance of the title in Toni Morrison's "Recitatif" (p. 445)
5. An examination of how two stories about brothers, Louise Erdrich's "The Red Convertible" (p. 126) and James Baldwin's "Sonny's Blues" (p. 362), use setting and symbol to bring out the differences between the characters
6. Character, symbol, and theme in John Steinbeck's "The Chrysanthemums" (p. 320)
7. A consideration of the effects of memory in ZZ Packer's "Brownies" (p. 512) and Toni Morrison's "Recitatif" (p. 445)
8. An analysis of what love means in two or more of the following: Raymond Carver's "What We Talk about When We Talk about Love" (p. 386), Tillie Olsen's "I Stand Here Ironing" (p. 506), and Katherine Anne Porter's "The Jilting of Granny Weatherall" (p. 533)
9. The effect houses have on the people who live in them. Start by doing some reading on the social and economic implications of adequate housing; then apply what you find to two or all the following stories: Sandra Cisneros's "The House on Mango Street" (p. 160), Alice Walker's "Everyday Use" (p. 169), Richard McGuire's "Here" (p. 223), and Zora Neale Hurston's "Sweat" (p. 421)
10. Racial stereotypes and racial tensions in Toni Morrison's "Recitatif" (p. 445)
11. John Updike's "A&P" (p. 552) examined from a feminist approach (see p. 1458)
12. The weight, in various senses, of everything U.S. military personnel in Vietnam carried in Tim O'Brien's "The Things They Carried" (p. 493)

Step 2. Prewriting: Narrowing the Topic

You can't write about everything in a story. Even a story as short as "Love in L.A." is too complex for that to be possible. You need to narrow your focus to what is especially pertinent to or valuable for your topic, as Alicia had to do for her paper. Marking up a text as you reread can be a helpful way to pick out parts you'll want to focus on. Return to page 40 and read again

A student, Alicia Abood, on narrowing her topic: "Once I decided that I wanted to write a character analysis on Jake, I did a 'freewriting' journal entry of sorts. I basically 'thought aloud' on paper so that I could get everything I was thinking down in one place. Since I was having a difficult time pinpointing exactly how I'd examine Jake's character in an articulate manner, this was very helpful. I even wrote down questions about Jake, such as 'Is Jake the jerk we're led to believe that he is?' or 'Why hasn't he been able to achieve any of his dreams?' or 'What does Gilb want us to think about Jake?' Though these questions sound sort of obvious, it was helpful for me to write the questions down on paper, so that they were staring back at me—asking me to process my thoughts more clearly."

about Benjamin De Mott's idea of focusing on "key passages." Then reread your story watching for and marking what may be key passages. As you go over passages you've marked and notes you've written, check if some of them connect with each other. That could point you toward a way of limiting or narrowing the topic from the whole story to parts that relate to each other.

Step 3. Prewriting: Deciding on an Approach

We say in Chapter 2 that there are several major categories of approaches you might take in a paper about literature: literary analysis, comparison-contrast, social and cultural analysis, or a combination of these (see pp. 33–36). Sometimes, of course, the topic you select has an approach built in, as, for example, if you decide to write a paper comparing and contrasting Lyman with Henry in "The Red Convertible." But other times part of the process of focusing your topic and preparing to frame a thesis, and then deciding how to develop it, involves figuring out what approach the topic requires, as Alicia needed to do in selecting an approach to fit her topic.

The best way to start is to notice whether the topic focuses on what goes on *inside* the story (literary analysis), focuses on *connections* within the story or between your story and another one (comparison-contrast), or focuses on what infuses the work but also *surrounds* the work (social and cultural criticism). For example, think about this as a possible topic: Discuss the characters of Sonny and his brother in James Baldwin's "Sonny's Blues" (p. 362). It concentrates on what goes on inside the story. It would definitely require character analysis. It could also involve comparisons and contrasts between the two brothers. In that case, the two could be examined separately, in the first and second halves of the paper. But it would probably be more interesting to do some comparing and contrasting, without separating them, because the story seems to invite looking at them as foils to each other.

Consider another possibility: Discuss the motif of women and work in Zora Neale Hurston's "Sweat" (p. 421), Tillie Olsen's "I Stand Here Ironing" (p. 506), and Katherine Anne Porter's "The Jilting of Granny Weatherall" (p. 533). The topic focuses on how women and work are treated within the story, perhaps involving

> **A student, Alicia Abood, on deciding on an approach:** "As I considered my options on how to formally respond to 'Love in L.A.,' I tried to focus on what spoke to me most in the reading and rereading process. I knew pretty early on that Jake's character was one of the greatest complexities — at least in my mind — of this short story, but I still had a lot of questions about why I couldn't put my finger on what type of person Jake was and decided to do an in-depth discussion. Although I explore some of the social implications surrounding Jake's character, I chose to do a literary analysis because I wanted to examine how Jake's character is portrayed through the inner workings of the story."

comparison and contrast, but perhaps showing how the stories connect in developing the same point or idea. Since the topic of women and work has a large cultural and social interest, the paper might be strengthened by bringing in some information about the subject from outside sources.

Here's one more possibility: The different effects of mixing fantasy with techniques of realism in two of the following stories: Helena María Viramontes's "The Moths" (p. 557), Gabriel García Márquez's "A Very Old Man with Enormous Wings" (p. 413), or Haruki Murakami's "Birthday Girl" (p. 471). The starting point for work on this topic would almost surely be finding good definitions of *fantasy* and *realism*. Then you might apply those definitions to the two stories you choose for your paper. The word *different* in the topic indicates that you will need to do some contrasting—but keep in mind that comparisons could also add to your paper's effectiveness.

Step 4. Prewriting: Framing a Thesis

Chapter 2 explains that an effective paper on literature needs a thesis, a central idea that it must develop and support in a convincing way. Your job as a writer is to persuade your readers that your point is sound and worth considering seriously. Review pages 36–37 on ways of making sure you have a thesis. In writing about fiction, some students slip into writing plot summary. If a story is challenging and a student struggles to figure out the plot, she or he may feel that writing a summary is sufficient because it demonstrates success in understanding the story. But grasping what happens in a story is only the first step. A literary paper must go further. It must illuminate or clarify the story in some way, presenting ideas with convincing support, not just as statements of fact. Alicia's comment illustrates the careful consideration framing a thesis requires.

> A student, Alicia Abood, on turning her topic into a thesis: "I had a difficult time coming up with a thesis statement that I found challenging enough—my thoughts on Jake felt very straightforward, like 'Jake isn't necessarily the jerk we all think he is at first.' This led me to think about first impressions and society, and from there I tried coming up with something that had more meat to it. Also, I didn't want to sound *too* assuming in my thesis. Though I was able to find some sympathy for Jake's character, I didn't want to argue too strongly for this because he obviously has some serious character flaws. Between the working draft and the final draft, I was able to state my central idea in a way that felt right."

Step 5. Writing: Developing and Supporting the Thesis

How to develop and support the ideas in a literature paper is discussed fully in Chapter 2. It might be good for you to go back and reread the sections "Illustrate and Explain," "Include Quotations," "Focus on Key Passages," "Write with Readers in Mind," and "Avoid Summary" (see pp. 40–42). Reviewing the section "Use the 'Literary Present'" (p. 42) would be especially helpful for writing about fiction. Your development and support of the arguments you advance will be the heart of your paper. The most amazing ideas in the world are of little value if they are not supported convincingly. Alicia shows awareness of that in what she says about development and support:

A student, Alicia Abood, on developing and supporting her thesis: "In the journal entry I wrote, I had included a couple of the quotes that stood out to me the most on my final readings, including the quote in which Jake tells Mariana that he is a musician. I figured that the quotes that still stood out to me in my final readings would be some of the most valuable to work with.

"When I began writing the actual essay, I used my journal notes to develop a very bare-bones outline so that I had a basic understanding of the body of the essay. Whenever I felt stuck during the writing process, I would reread the story again or look through the notes to help trigger more thoughts. I was able to focus my thoughts and get ideas for filling out points from writing the journal prompt.

"For the first draft, I started by working to get at least some form of a workable essay down on paper. I wrote the introduction and body paragraphs in one sitting—incorporating only a couple of quotes. I wrote the conclusion, added and deleted some quotes, and continued to tweak the introduction as I revised the first draft."

Step 6. Revising, Proofreading, and Formatting

Chapter 2 covers the importance of careful revision and editing (proofreading) and gives tips for doing it well. We suggest that you review them before you proceed with this step (pp. 43–45). Alicia comments on how she went about it on page 271.

Here's a demonstration of how Alicia's second paragraph changed from her first draft to the final draft (deletions are struck through; additions are in bold):

At the beginning of the story, we discover that Jake's dreams are perhaps less idealistic than most. While Jake ~~sat~~ **sits** in ~~his car,~~ the "clot of near motionless traffic," he ~~dreamt of things~~ **dreams of an FM radio for his "'58 Buick" along with "crushed velvet interior," among other luxuries,** to help spruce up his current, less satisfying, vehicle. His desire to make his car better appears to be a youthful, frivolous dream. Here, Gilb gives us a taste of how lost Jake is—by painting him immediately with a more superficial dream in mind. As readers, we're left to wonder about **the integrity of** Jake's dreams. Do they extend beyond improving his dumpy vehicle? An update such as an ~~f.m.~~ **FM** radio might bring Jake a temporary satisfaction, but we don't hear of anything of true substance. **Also, throughout the story, there is no mention of his family, nor external support of any kind to motivate him to do better. We're left with the sense that he is out on his own in the world—without a real driver's license or car insurance.** While we're never given an age for Jake, his dreams of a more fashionable car ask me to picture him as a teenager or young adult. We don't know where Jake ~~was~~ **is** headed when the story starts on the Hollywood ~~freeway~~ **Freeway**. Given the youthfulness of Jake's dreams, and his uncertain route, we're left to believe that Jake has yet to grow up—to discover what his dreams truly are.

A student, Alicia Abood, on revising and proofreading: "In the early stages of revision I gave my paper to a friend and she generously looked it over. While she mainly made editing notes, she also helped the paper to become more succinct. She asked me to take out some unnecessary lines (which I did) and asked me to clarify on moments that were unclear. In looking at an earlier draft of my paper compared to the final draft, I can definitely appreciate the revision process. Having concrete feedback from one of my peers allowed me to notice errors and brought attention to added fluff that really interfered with the clarity that I wanted to achieve in the paper. After I made some editing changes that my friend provided, I took a break from the paper before going back and making more significant content changes. Since I spend a lot of time at the computer, my brain can easily turn to mush after a while, and I don't think as clearly as I need to. Furthermore, taking time to *not* think about the story allowed me to come back with a fresher and clearer perspective as I was trying to figure out what I needed to make the essay click."

SAMPLE SHORT PAPER

Here are the rough draft and the final draft of Alicia's paper, with comments on the changes from the earlier version to the later one. To allow you to see more of Alicia's writing process, we've printed the rough draft of her paper on the left-hand pages and the final draft on the right-hand pages, with our comments on both versions.

Alicia Abood's Rough Draft with Notes about Weaknesses

ROUGH DRAFT

Rather flat opening sentence.

For many, first impressions go a long way, but they do run the danger of being inaccurate or unfair. In Dagoberto Gilb's short story "Love in L.A.," the first impression of the main character, Jake, is a troublesome one. While at first Jake came across as egotistical and selfish, more time spent examining his actions and behaviors allow us to feel sympathy, or perhaps at least a more clarified understanding, toward him. Through examining the way Jake dreams and presents himself to the other character in the story, Mariana, the complexities of Jake's identity come to the surface. Gilb provides his audience with just enough information about Jake to force his readers to question Jake's true identity, or lack thereof.

Working thesis; will need reworking.

Weak paragraph opening: states a fact, not an idea.

While Jake sat in his car, he dreamt of things to help spruce up his current, less satisfying, vehicle. His desire to make his car better appears to be a youthful, frivolous dream. Here, Gilb indicates how lost Jake is—by painting him immediately with a more superficial dream in mind. As readers, we're left to wonder about Jake's dreams. Do they extend beyond improving his dumpy vehicle? An update such as an f.m. radio might bring Jake a temporary satisfaction, but we don't hear of anything of true substance. While we're never given an age for Jake, his dreams of a more fashionable car ask me to picture him as a teenager or young adult. We don't know where Jake was headed when the story starts on the Hollywood freeway. Given the

Needs quotations to back up statements.

Alicia Abood's Final Draft with Notes about Revisions

——————— **FINAL DRAFT** ———————

Alicia Abood
Professor Schakel
Introduction to Literature
13 April 2010

A Lost Identity: Taking a Deeper Look at Jake in "Love in L.A."

First impressions go a long way for many people, and in Dagoberto Gilb's short story "Love in L.A.," the first impression of the main character, Jake, is a troublesome one. Gilb provides his audience with just enough information about Jake to force his readers to question Jake's true identity, or lack thereof. Through examining the way Jake dreams and presents himself to the other character in the story, Mariana, the complexities of Jake's identity come to the surface. While initially Jake comes across as egotistical and selfish, spending more time examining his actions and behaviors allows us to feel a bit of sympathy, or perhaps at least a more clarified understanding, toward him.

At the beginning of the story, we discover that Jake's dreams are perhaps less idealistic than most. While Jake sits in the "clot of near motionless traffic," he dreams of an FM radio for his "'58 Buick" along with "crushed velvet interior," among other luxuries, to help spruce up his current, less satisfying vehicle. His desire to make his car better appears to be youthful and frivolous. Here, Gilb gives us a taste of how lost Jake is—by painting him immediately with superficial goals in mind. As readers, we're left to wonder about the integrity of Jake's dreams. Do they extend beyond improving his dumpy vehicle? An update such as an FM radio might bring Jake a temporary satisfaction, but we don't hear of anything of true substance. Also, throughout the story, there is no mention of his family or of external support of any other kind that might motivate him to do better. We're left with the sense that he is out on his own in the world—without a real driver's license or car insurance. While we're never given an age for Jake, his dreams

Title suggests central topic.

Opening sentence more inviting than the one in the rough draft.

Thesis sentence is clearer and stronger.

Topic sentence now focuses on an idea.

Quotations blended nicely into sentences.

Improved paragraph development.

——— **ROUGH DRAFT** ———

Abood 2

youthfulness of Jake's dreams, and his uncertain route, we're left to believe that Jake has yet to grow up—to discover what his dreams truly are.

Again, statement of fact, not of idea.

While Jake was daydreaming on the freeway, he hit Mariana's car. Before Jake even spoke to Mariana, he first took time to check out his vehicle and approaches her by saying "It didn't even scratch my paint" (114). This should turn us off to Jake immediately. Then he proceeds to flirt with her and tries to distract her from the situation at hand. While Jake tried to smooth talk Mariana, his naïveté becomes evident. Jake approached Mariana in a sleazy way, and he seems unashamed of the tone of his approach. Toward the end of the story, Gilb describes the interaction when Jake and Mariana shake hands: Jake's youthfulness and lack of experience is shown in the world shines through.

Too many short sentences together.

This paragraph needs an idea sentence.

When Mariana asks Jake to show her his driver's license, he makes up a lie. Gilb describes Jake's description of himself as a musician as a great exaggeration, and to the reader, Jake's lost sense of identity became even a bit heartbreaking. Jake was hiding under a mask of someone that he perhaps hopes to be, but isn't. Jake proceeds to lie—about his car insurance and his phone number, and he thinks he pulled off yet another lie. Then he looks in his rearview mirror and sees Mariana writing down his license plate numbers. We discover that even these numbers aren't real, because he pulled them off of an old vehicle after his expired.

Paragraph needs clarification and support.

Abood 2

of a more fashionable car lead me to picture him as a teenager or young adult. We don't know where Jake is headed when the story starts on the Hollywood Freeway. Given the youthfulness of his dreams, and his uncertain route, we're left to believe that Jake has yet to grow up—to discover what his dreams truly are.

Jake's character is primarily shown as he interacts with Mariana—the young, innocent girl who owns the Toyota Jake hits. Before Jake even speaks to Mariana, he takes time to check out his vehicle and approaches her by saying, "It didn't even scratch my paint" (114). That his first thought is of his own car probably turns off most readers immediately. If that's not enough, he proceeds to say:

Improved transition and topic sentence.

> So how you doin? Any damage to the car? I'm kinda hoping
> so, just so it takes a little more time and we can talk some.
> Or else you can give me your phone number now and I won't
> have to lay my regular b.s. on you to get it later. (114)

Use of a block quotation.

As Jake tries to smooth talk Mariana, his naïveté becomes pressingly obvious. He approaches her in a sleazy way, and he seems unashamed—and almost unaware—of the tone of his approach. While Jake knows he is smooth talking Mariana, he does not seem aware of the person he is becoming. Toward the end of the story, Gilb describes the interaction when Jake and Mariana shake hands: "Her hand felt so warm and soft he felt like he'd been kissed" (115). Again, Jake's lack of experience and youthfulness shine through. Jake's response to this simple handshake shows that Jake hasn't interacted with that many women before and that he still gets a thrill out of playful flirtation.

Greater precision in word choice and greater fluency in sentences.

Quotation introduced formally with a colon.

Most importantly, the persona that Jake presents to Mariana shows that Jake is still very uncertain of who he is. When Mariana asks Jake to show her his driver's license, he makes up a lie: "'I didn't bring it. I just forgot it this morning. I'm a musician,' he exaggerated greatly, 'and, well, I dunno, I left

Improved transition and topic sentence.

─────────── **ROUGH DRAFT** ───────────

Abood 3

Even though Jake is unsure of who he is, it also becomes clear that he is unsure of the weight of his dishonesty. It's as if he is mind is completely murky—totally unaware of his decisions. Because of his apparent youth and lack of support, Jake is able to live without a true sense of self. While Mariana seems far more innocent than Jake, his naïveté and confusion with the world still stand up against Mariana's innocence. Truthfully—Mariana's sharpness shines through at the end of the story, when she has the sense to write down Jake's license plate numbers, albeit false ones. As Mariana's apparent lack of trust is right in front of Jake's eyes, he still sits in his car and dreams of his FM radio. This lack of awareness and selfishness evokes sympathy, or at least an understanding, for Jake's character and his place in the world. While Jake's shameless actions don't give us a solid first impression of who he is, we sympathize with his character and understand him better, and hope that one day he can live up to the identity he tries to dream of for himself.

Repetition.

FINAL DRAFT

Abood 3

my wallet in the pants I was wearing last night'" (114). When
Gilb points out that Jake's description of himself as a musician is
a great exaggeration, Jake's lost sense of identity could seem sad
for a reader. Jake is hiding under a mask of someone that he perhaps hopes to be, but isn't. Everything about him is a lie—even
his car insurance and his phone number. After they say goodbye,
Jake returns to his car to feel both "proud and sad about his performance" (115). All that he was doing was acting—it seems a
bit sad that there apparently was nothing genuine going on at
all. Then he looks in his rearview mirror and notices Mariana writing down his license plate numbers. But even these numbers
aren't real—he took them "off a junk because the ones that belonged to his had expired so long ago" (115). Jake is able to
move along with these lies, it seems, because he is young and
the effects of such actions haven't caught up with him yet.

Better develop-
ment of points
and precision in
expression.

     Even though Jake is unsure of who he is, it also becomes
clear that he is unsure of the weight of his dishonesty. Because
of his apparent youth and lack of support, Jake is able to live
without a true sense of self. While Mariana seems far more innocent than Jake, his naïveté and confusion with the world still
make an impression alongside Mariana's innocence. Mariana's
sharpness is crystalized at the end of the story, when she has
the sense to write down Jake's license plate numbers, albeit false
ones. Although Mariana's apparent lack of trust is right in front
of Jake's eyes, he still sits in his car and dreams of his FM radio.
While Jake's selfishness and lack of awareness at first might initiate a disgusted response, further analysis might call on us to
sympathize, or at least begin to attempt to understand his character, and hope that one day he can live up to the identity he
tries to dream of for himself.

Improved topic
sentence and
expansion of
the idea.

Closing summa-
ry; ties back to
introduction.

I don't want to write books that provide [entertainment and a form of escape]. I want books that challenge, anger, and possibly offend.

Sherman Alexie

CHAPTER **10** **Sherman Alexie—
An Author in Depth**

"I've always had crazy dreams"

Sherman Alexie was born in 1966 in Wellpinit, a tiny town on the 150,000-acre Spokane Indian Reservation in eastern Washington, about fifty miles northeast of Spokane. His father is Coeur d'Alene Indian and his mother is Spokane Indian. When he was six months old, he was diagnosed with hydrocephalus, an abnormal buildup of fluid creating too much pressure on the brain, and underwent surgery. It was expected that he would not survive or, if he survived, that he would be left mentally retarded. But he did survive, without retardation, though he suffered seizures and uncontrollable bed-wetting well into childhood.

Alexie learned to read by age three, and his love of reading as he grew up created barriers between him and his peers: He describes himself as a geek during his school years. His parents decided to have him attend high school in nearby Reardan, where he could receive a better education than he could on the reservation. He was the only Native American in the school. Throughout his time there, he was an excellent student and a star basketball player. He attended Gonzaga University in Spokane for two years, then Washington State University in Pullman, from which

Sherman Alexie
Reprinted by permission of
Rob Casey.© Rob Casey.

A still from Sherman Alexie's movie Smoke Signals, *with Adam Beach (left) as Victor Joseph and Evan Adams as Thomas Builds-the-Fire.*
© Miramax Films/Jill Sabella/Everett Collection. Reprinted by permission.

he graduated in 1991. He started out as a premed student, but a human anatomy class on the one hand and a poetry workshop on the other changed his direction. He discovered he loved writing, and was good at it, and didn't love human anatomy. Writing soon became the center of his life.

His early efforts as a poet were supported by a Washington State Arts Commission Poetry Fellowship in 1991 and a National Endowment for the Arts Poetry Fellowship in 1992. He wrote prolifically and found success immediately, publishing two poetry collections — *The Business of Fancydancing* (1992) and *I Would Steal Horses* (1993). His first collection of short stories, *The Lone Ranger and Tonto Fistfight in Heaven* (1993), was equally successful, receiving a PEN/Hemingway Award and the Great Lakes Colleges Association Award for best first book of fiction, and a Lila Wallace-Reader's Digest Writers' Award. His first novel, *Reservation Blues* (1995), won the Before Columbus Foundation's American Book Award and the Murray Morgan Prize, and he was named one of *Granta*'s Best of Young American Novelists. His second novel, *Indian Killer* (1996), was selected as a *New York Times* Notable Book. In June 1999, Alexie was featured in the *New Yorker*'s Summer Fiction Edition, "20 Writers for the 21st Century." In 2010 he was honored with the Native Writers' Circle of the Americas Lifetime Achievement Award.

Sherman Alexie accepts the National Book Award for Young People's Literature for his book The Absolutely True Diary of a Part-Time Indian *at the 58th National Book Awards in New York, Wednesday, Nov. 14, 2007.*

AP/Wide World Photos/Seth Wenig.

In 1997 he began work on a screenplay based on "This Is What It Means to Say Phoenix, Arizona," a short story from *The Lone Ranger and Tonto Fistfight in Heaven*. Written in collaboration with Chris Eyre, a Cheyenne/Arapaho Indian who also directed, the film was produced by Shadow Catcher Entertainment as *Smoke Signals*. Released at the Sundance Film Festival in January 1998, it won two awards, the Audience Award and the Filmmakers Trophy, and was subsequently distributed by Miramax Films. *Smoke Signals* was the first feature film distributed in the United States that was written, directed, and produced entirely by Native Americans. It received a Christopher Award, presented to the creators of artistic works "which affirm the highest values of the human spirit." Alexie was also nominated for the Independent Feature Project/West 1999 Independent Spirit Award for Best First Screenplay.

Alexie wrote another screenplay, *The Business of Fancydancing*, which he directed and produced in 2002 as a low-budget, independent film production filmed on digital video, thus freeing him from the artistic constraints imposed by commercial filmmakers. His most recent books are a collection of poetry, *Face* (2009); a collection of stories, *War Dances* (2009) — winner of the 2010 PEN/Faulkner Award for Fiction; a novel, *Flight* (2007); and a young adult novel, *The Absolutely True Diary of a Part-Time Indian* (2007), winner of many awards including the 2007 National Book Award for Young People's Literature.

Alexie does occasional reading and stand-up performances with musician Jim Boyd, a Colville Indian. They recorded an album, *Reservation Blues*, made up of songs from Alexie's novel by that name. Alexie made his debut as a stand-up comedian at the Foolproof Northwest Comedy Festival in Seattle in April 1999 and was the featured performer at the Vancouver International Comedy Festival's opening night gala in July 1999. Alexie continues making public appearances as an author and writing in several genres from his home in Seattle, where he lives with his wife and two sons.

There are three ways of using the material in this chapter for writing assignments. The first is to write a paper on one or both of the stories without reading the interviews with Alexie or the critical articles on him. In this case, you would think of the two stories as if they were included in the "Collection of Stories" and do a paper without outside sources. If you choose this option, remember that if you do read the interviews or critical essays, or any part of them, you must acknowledge that by including them in a bibliography, even if you don't quote from them or refer to them.

In a second way of using this chapter, your instructor might ask you to write a paper using outside sources but limit you to what is included in this chapter. Such a paper provides practice incorporating ideas from secondary materials, selecting passages to quote and blending quotations into your writing, and constructing a Works Cited page. But it isn't actually a research paper since you aren't going out to find the materials to use in the paper. The reasons an instructor might select this option are that it doesn't require as much time as a full-blown research project does and it allows the instructor to evaluate your use of sources knowledgeably, since you are using only sources she or he is familiar with. We have included the original publication data and page numbers for the stories, interviews, and critical essays, so you can use that data on the Works Cited page instead of having all references be to this textbook. For such a paper, you should review the guidelines for handling quotations (pp. 53–54); and you should read the appendix, "Reading Critical Essays," and the sections on incorporating sources, documenting sources, and preparing a Works Cited page and avoiding plagiarism in Chapter 3 (pp. 74–83 and 91–93).

A third way to use this chapter is as a starting point for an actual research paper. That is, after reading the stories and essays in this chapter, you would begin searching for additional sources—perhaps only in the library or perhaps also using electronic sources, as your instructor prefers. You might read more primary works by Alexie; you surely will be expected to read and use additional biographical or critical works about his thoughts and works. For such a project, in addition to reviewing the guidelines for handling quotations (pp. 53–54) and reading the appendix, "Reading Critical Essays," you should read all of Chapter 3, "Writing a Literary Research Paper."

This Is What It Means to Say Phoenix, Arizona°   [1993]

Just after Victor lost his job at the BIA, he also found out that his father had died of a heart attack in Phoenix, Arizona. Victor hadn't seen his father in a few years, only talked to him on the telephone once or twice, but there still was a genetic pain, which was soon to be pain as real and immediate as a broken bone.

Victor didn't have any money. Who does have money on a reservation, except the cigarette and fireworks salespeople? His father had a savings account waiting to be claimed, but Victor needed to find a way to get to Phoenix. Victor's mother [p. 59]° was just as poor as he was, and the rest of his family didn't have any use at all for him. So Victor called the Tribal Council.

"Listen," Victor said. "My father just died. I need some money to get to Phoenix to make arrangements."

"Now, Victor," the council said. "You know we're having a difficult time financially."

"But I thought the council had special funds set aside for stuff like this."   5

"Now, Victor, we do have some money available for the proper return of tribal members' bodies. But I don't think we have enough to bring your father all the way back from Phoenix."

"Well," Victor said. "It ain't going to cost all that much. He had to be cremated. Things were kind of ugly. He died of a heart attack in his trailer and nobody found him for a week. It was really hot, too. You get the picture."

"Now, Victor, we're sorry for your loss and the circumstances. But we can really only afford to give you one hundred dollars."

"That's not even enough for a plane ticket."

"Well, you might consider driving down to Phoenix."   10

"I don't have a car. Besides, I was going to drive my father's pickup back up here."

"Now, Victor," the council said. "We're sure there is somebody who could drive you to Phoenix. Or is there somebody who could lend you the rest of the money?"

"You know there ain't nobody around with that kind of money."

"Well, we're sorry, Victor, but that's the best we can do." [p. 60]

Victor accepted the Tribal Council's offer. What else could he do? So he   15 signed the proper papers, picked up his check, and walked over to the Trading Post to cash it.

While Victor stood in line, he watched Thomas Builds-the-Fire standing near the magazine rack, talking to himself. Like he always did. Thomas was a storyteller that nobody wanted to listen to. That's like being a dentist in a town where everybody has false teeth.

Alexie, Sherman. "This Is What It Means to Say Phoenix, Arizona." *The Lone Ranger and Tonto Fistfight in Heaven.* New York: HarperPerennial, 1993. 59–75. Print.
(Page citations in square brackets refer to the original publication.)

Victor and Thomas Builds-the-Fire were the same age, had grown up and played in the dirt together. Ever since Victor could remember, it was Thomas who always had something to say.

Once, when they were seven years old, when Victor's father still lived with the family, Thomas closed his eyes and told Victor this story: "Your father's heart is weak. He is afraid of his own family. He is afraid of you. Late at night he sits in the dark. Watches the television until there's nothing but that white noise. Sometimes he feels like he wants to buy a motorcycle and ride away. He wants to run and hide. He doesn't want to be found."

Thomas Builds-the-Fire had known that Victor's father was going to leave, knew it before anyone. Now Victor stood in the Trading Post with a one-hundred-dollar check in his hand, wondering if Thomas knew that Victor's father was dead, if he knew what was going to happen next.

Just then Thomas looked at Victor, smiled, and walked over to him.   20

"Victor, I'm sorry about your father," Thomas said.

"How did you know about it?" Victor asked.

"I heard it on the wind. I heard it from the birds. I felt it in the sunlight. Also, your mother was just in here crying." [p. 61]

"Oh," Victor said and looked around the Trading Post. All the other Indians stared, surprised that Victor was even talking to Thomas. Nobody talked to Thomas anymore because he told the same damn stories over and over again. Victor was embarrassed, but he thought that Thomas might be able to help him. Victor felt a sudden need for tradition.

"I can lend you the money you need," Thomas said suddenly. "But you have   25 to take me with you."

"I can't take your money," Victor said. "I mean, I haven't hardly talked to you in years. We're not really friends anymore."

"I didn't say we were friends. I said you had to take me with you."

"Let me think about it."

Victor went home with his one hundred dollars and sat at the kitchen table. He held his head in his hands and thought about Thomas Builds-the-Fire, remembered little details, tears and scars, the bicycle they shared for a summer, so many stories.

Thomas Builds-the-Fire sat on the bicycle, waited in Victor's yard. He   30 was ten years old and skinny. His hair was dirty because it was the Fourth of July.

"Victor," Thomas yelled. "Hurry up. We're going to miss the fireworks."

After a few minutes, Victor ran out of his house, jumped the porch railing, and landed gracefully on the sidewalk.

"And the judges award him a 9.95, the highest score of the summer," Thomas said, clapped, laughed. [p. 62]

"That was perfect, cousin," Victor said. "And it's my turn to ride the bike."

Thomas gave up the bike and they headed for the fairgrounds. It was   35 nearly dark and the fireworks were about to start.

"You know," Thomas said. "It's strange how us Indians celebrate the Fourth of July. It ain't like it was *our* independence everybody was fighting for."

"You think about things too much," Victor said. "It's just supposed to be fun. Maybe Junior will be there."

"Which Junior? Everybody on this reservation is named Junior."

And they both laughed.

The fireworks were small, hardly more than a few bottle rockets and a foun- 40
tain. But it was enough for two Indian boys. Years later, they would need much more.

Afterwards, sitting in the dark, fighting off mosquitoes, Victor turned to Thomas Builds-the-Fire.

"Hey," Victor said. "Tell me a story."

Thomas closed his eyes and told this story: "There were these two Indian boys who wanted to be warriors. But it was too late to be warriors in the old way. All the horses were gone. So the two Indian boys stole a car and drove to the city. They parked the stolen car in front of the police station and then hitch-hiked back home to the reservation. When they got back, all their friends cheered and their parents' eyes shone with pride. *You were very brave*, everybody said to the two Indian boys. *Very brave.*"

"Ya-hey," Victor said. "That's a good one. I wish I could be a warrior." [p. 63]

"Me too," Thomas said. 45

They went home together in the dark, Thomas on the bike now, Victor on foot. They walked through shadows and light from streetlamps.

"We've come a long ways," Thomas said. "We have outdoor lighting."

"All I need is the stars," Victor said. "And besides, you still think about things too much."

They separated then, each headed for home, both laughing all the way.

Victor sat at his kitchen table. He counted his one hundred dollars again 50
and again. He knew he needed more to make it to Phoenix and back. He knew he needed Thomas Builds-the-Fire. So he put his money in his wallet and opened the front door to find Thomas on the porch.

"Ya-hey, Victor," Thomas said. "I knew you'd call me."

Thomas walked into the living room and sat down on Victor's favorite chair.

"I've got some money saved up," Thomas said. "It's enough to get us down there, but you have to get us back."

"I've got this hundred dollars," Victor said. "And my dad had a savings ac-count I'm going to claim."

"How much in your dad's account?" 55

"Enough. A few hundred."

"Sounds good. When we leaving?" [p. 64]

When they were fifteen and had long since stopped being friends, Victor and Thomas got into a fistfight. That is, Victor was really drunk and beat

Thomas up for no reason at all. All the other Indian boys stood around and watched it happen. Junior was there and so were Lester, Seymour, and a lot of others. The beating might have gone on until Thomas was dead if Norma Many Horses hadn't come along and stopped it.

"Hey, you boys," Norma yelled and jumped out of her car. "Leave him alone."

If it had been someone else, even another man, the Indian boys would've 60 just ignored the warnings. But Norma was a warrior. She was powerful. She could have picked up any two of the boys and smashed their skulls together. But worse than that, she would have dragged them all over to some tipi and made them listen to some elder tell a dusty old story.

The Indian boys scattered, and Norma walked over to Thomas and picked him up.

"Hey, little man, are you okay?" she asked.

Thomas gave her a thumbs up.

"Why they always picking on you?"

Thomas shook his head, closed his eyes, but no stories came to him, no 65 words or music. He just wanted to go home, to lie in his bed and let his dreams tell his stories for him.

Thomas Builds-the-Fire and Victor sat next to each other in the airplane, coach section. A tiny white woman had the window seat. She was busy twisting her body into pretzels. She was flexible. [p. 65]

"I have to ask," Thomas said, and Victor closed his eyes in embarrassment.

"Don't," Victor said.

"Excuse me, miss," Thomas asked. "Are you a gymnast or something?"

"There's no something about it," she said. "I was first alternate on the 1980 70 Olympic team."

"Really?" Thomas asked.

"Really."

"I mean, you used to be a world-class athlete?" Thomas asked.

"My husband still thinks I am."

Thomas Builds-the-Fire smiled. She was a mental gymnast, too. She pulled 75 her leg straight up against her body so that she could've kissed her kneecap.

"I wish I could do that," Thomas said.

Victor was ready to jump out of the plane. Thomas, that crazy Indian storyteller with ratty old braids and broken teeth, was flirting with a beautiful Olympic gymnast. Nobody back home on the reservation would ever believe it.

"Well," the gymnast said. "It's easy. Try it."

Thomas grabbed at his leg and tried to pull it up into the same position as the gymnast. He couldn't even come close, which made Victor and the gymnast laugh.

"Hey," she asked. "You two are Indian, right?"   80

"Full-blood," Victor said.

"Not me," Thomas said. "I'm half magician on my mother's side and half clown on my father's."

They all laughed.

"What are your names?" she asked. [p. 66]

"Victor and Thomas."

"Mine is Cathy. Pleased to meet you all."

The three of them talked for the duration of the flight. Cathy the gymnast complained about the government, how they screwed the 1980 Olympic team by boycotting.

"Sounds like you all got a lot in common with Indians," Thomas said.

Nobody laughed.

After the plane landed in Phoenix and they had all found their way to the terminal, Cathy the gymnast smiled and waved good-bye.

"She was really nice," Thomas said.

"Yeah, but everybody talks to everybody on airplanes," Victor said. "It's too bad we can't always be that way."

"You always used to tell me I think too much," Thomas said. "Now it sounds like you do."

"Maybe I caught it from you."

"Yeah."

Thomas and Victor rode in a taxi to the trailer where Victor's father died.

"Listen," Victor said as they stopped in front of the trailer. "I never told you I was sorry for beating you up that time."

"Oh, it was nothing. We were just kids and you were drunk."

"Yeah, but I'm still sorry."

"That's all right."

Victor paid for the taxi and the two of them stood in the hot Phoenix summer. They could smell the trailer.

"This ain't going to be nice," Victor said. "You don't have to go in." [p. 67]

"You're going to need help."

Victor walked to the front door and opened it. The stink rolled out and made them both gag. Victor's father had lain in that trailer for a week in hundred-degree temperatures before anyone found him. And the only reason anyone found him was because of the smell. They needed dental records to identify him. That's exactly what the coroner said. They needed dental records.

"Oh, man," Victor said. "I don't know if I can do this."

"Well, then don't."

"But there might be something valuable in there."

"I thought his money was in the bank."

"It is. I was talking about pictures and letters and stuff like that."

"Oh," Thomas said as he held his breath and followed Victor into the trailer.

When Victor was twelve, he stepped into an underground wasp nest. His foot was caught in the hole, and no matter how hard he struggled, Victor couldn't pull free. He might have died there, stung a thousand times, if Thomas Builds-the-Fire had not come by.

"Run," Thomas yelled and pulled Victor's foot from the hole. They ran then, hard as they ever had, faster than Billy Mills,° faster than Jim Thorpe,° faster than the wasps could fly.

Victor and Thomas ran until they couldn't breathe, ran until it was cold and dark outside, ran until they were lost and it took hours to find their way home. All the way back, Victor counted his stings.

"Seven," Victor said. "My lucky number." [p. 68]

Victor didn't find much to keep in the trailer. Only a photo album and a   115
stereo. Everything else had that smell stuck in it or was useless anyway.

"I guess this is all," Victor said. "It ain't much."

"Better than nothing," Thomas said.

"Yeah, and I do have the pickup."

"Yeah," Thomas said. "It's in good shape."

"Dad was good about that stuff."   120

"Yeah, I remember your dad."

"Really?" Victor asked. "What do you remember?"

Thomas Builds-the-Fire closed his eyes and told this story: "I remember when I had this dream that told me to go to Spokane, to stand by the Falls in the middle of the city and wait for a sign. I knew I had to go there but I didn't have a car. Didn't have a license. I was only thirteen. So I walked all the way, took me all day, and I finally made it to the Falls. I stood there for an hour waiting. Then your dad came walking up. *What the hell are you doing here?* he asked me. I said, *Waiting for a vision.* Then your father said, *All you're going to get here is mugged.* So he drove me over to Denny's, bought me dinner, and then drove me home to the reservation. For a long time I was mad because I thought my dreams had lied to me. But they didn't. Your dad was my vision. *Take care of each other* is what my dreams were saying. *Take care of each other.*"

Victor was quiet for a long time. He searched his mind for memories of his father, found the good ones, found a few bad ones, added it all up, and smiled.

"My father never told me about finding you in Spokane," Victor said. [p. 69]   125

"He said he wouldn't tell anybody. Didn't want me to get in trouble. But he said I had to watch out for you as part of the deal."

"Really?"

"Really. Your father said you would need the help. He was right."

Billy Mills: An Oglala Sioux from Pine Ridge, South Dakota, Mills (b. 1938) won the 10,000-meter race at the 1964 summer Olympic games in Tokyo, Japan, and went on to set several other records in distance running.   **Jim Thorpe:** Of mixed descent but raised as a Sac and Fox, Thorpe (1888–1953) won the decathlon and the pentathlon at the 1912 summer Olympics in Stockholm, Sweden, and went on to play professional baseball, football, and basketball. In 1950 he was named by the Associated Press the greatest athlete of the first half of the twentieth century, and in 1999 he ranked third on the Associated Press list of athletes of the century.

"That's why you came down here with me, isn't it?" Victor asked.

"I came because of your father."   130

Victor and Thomas climbed into the pickup, drove over to the bank, and claimed the three hundred dollars in the savings account.

Thomas Builds-the-Fire could fly.

Once, he jumped off the roof of the tribal school and flapped his arms like a crazy eagle. And he flew. For a second, he hovered, suspended above all the other Indian boys who were too smart or too scared to jump.

"He's flying," Junior yelled, and Seymour was busy looking for the trick wires or mirrors. But it was real. As real as the dirt when Thomas lost altitude and crashed to the ground.

He broke his arm in two places.   135

"He broke his wing," Victor chanted, and the other Indian boys joined in, made it a tribal song.

"He broke his wing, he broke his wing, he broke his wing," all the Indian boys chanted as they ran off, flapping their wings, wishing they could fly, too. They hated Thomas for his courage, his brief moment as a bird. Everybody has dreams about flying. Thomas flew. [p. 70]

One of his dreams came true for just a second, just enough to make it real.

Victor's father, his ashes, fit in one wooden box with enough left over to fill a cardboard box.

"He always was a big man," Thomas said.   140

Victor carried part of his father and Thomas carried the rest out to the pickup. They set him down carefully behind the seats, put a cowboy hat on the wooden box and a Dodgers cap on the cardboard box. That's the way it was supposed to be.

"Ready to head back home," Victor asked.

"It's going to be a long drive."

"Yeah, take a couple days, maybe."

"We can take turns," Thomas said.   145

"Okay," Victor said, but they didn't take turns. Victor drove for sixteen hours straight north, made it halfway up Nevada toward home before he finally pulled over.

"Hey, Thomas," Victor said. "You got to drive for a while."

"Okay."

Thomas Builds-the-Fire slid behind the wheel and started off down the road. All through Nevada, Thomas and Victor had been amazed at the lack of animal life, at the absence of water, of movement.

"Where is everything?" Victor had asked more than once.   150

Now when Thomas was finally driving they saw the first animal, maybe the only animal in Nevada. It was a long-eared jackrabbit. [p. 71]

"Look," Victor yelled. "It's alive."

Thomas and Victor were busy congratulating themselves on their discovery when the jackrabbit darted out into the road and under the wheels of the pickup.

"Stop the goddamn car," Victor yelled, and Thomas did stop, backed the pickup off the dead jackrabbit.

"Oh, man, he's dead," Victor said as he looked at the squashed animal.   155
"Really dead."

"The only thing alive in this whole state and we just killed it."

"I don't know," Thomas said. "I think it was suicide."

Victor looked around the desert, sniffed the air, felt the emptiness and loneliness, and nodded his head.

"Yeah," Victor said. "It had to be suicide."   160

"I can't believe this," Thomas said. "You drive for a thousand miles and there ain't even any bugs smashed on the windshield. I drive for ten seconds and kill the only living thing in Nevada."

"Yeah," Victor said. "Maybe I should drive."

"Maybe you should."

Thomas Builds-the-Fire walked through the corridors of the tribal school by himself. Nobody wanted to be anywhere near him because of all those stories. Story after story.

Thomas closed his eyes and this story came to him: "We are all given one thing   165
by which our lives are measured, one determination. Mine are the stories which can change or not change the world. It doesn't matter which as long as I continue
[p. 72] to tell the stories. My father, he died on Okinawa in World War II, died fighting for this country, which had tried to kill him for years. My mother, she died giving birth to me, died while I was still inside her. She pushed me out into the world with her last breath. I have no brothers or sisters. I have only my stories which came to me before I even had the words to speak. I learned a thousand stories before I took my first thousand steps. They are all I have. It's all I can do."

Thomas Builds-the-Fire told his stories to all those who would stop and listen. He kept telling them long after people had stopped listening.

Victor and Thomas made it back to the reservation just as the sun was rising. It was the beginning of a new day on earth, but the same old shit on the reservation.

"Good morning," Thomas said.

"Good morning."

The tribe was waking up, ready for work, eating breakfast, reading the news-   170
paper, just like everybody else does. Willene LeBret was out in her garden wearing a bathrobe. She waved when Thomas and Victor drove by.

"Crazy Indians made it," she said to herself and went back to her roses.

Victor stopped the pickup in front of Thomas Builds-the-Fire's HUD house. They both yawned, stretched a little, shook dust from their bodies.

"I'm tired," Victor said.

"Of everything," Thomas added.

They both searched for words to end the journey. Victor [p. 73] needed to   175
thank Thomas for his help, for the money, and make the promise to pay it all back.

"Don't worry about the money," Thomas said. "It don't make any difference anyhow."

"Probably not, enit?"

"Nope."

Victor knew that Thomas would remain the crazy storyteller who talked to
dogs and cars, who listened to the wind and pine trees. Victor knew that he
couldn't really be friends with Thomas, even after all that had happened. It was
cruel but it was real. As real as the ashes, as Victor's father, sitting behind the
seats.

"I know how it is," Thomas said. "I know you ain't going to treat me any   180
better than you did before. I know your friends would give you too much shit
about it."

Victor was ashamed of himself. Whatever happened to the tribal ties, the
sense of community? The only real thing he shared with anybody was a bottle
and broken dreams. He owed Thomas something, anything.

"Listen," Victor said and handed Thomas the cardboard box which contained half of his father. "I want you to have this."

Thomas took the ashes and smiled, closed his eyes, and told this story: "I'm
going to travel to Spokane Falls one last time and toss these ashes into the
water. And your father will rise like a salmon, leap over the bridge, over me, and
find his way home. It will be beautiful. His teeth will shine like silver, like a
rainbow. He will rise, Victor, he will rise."

Victor smiled.

"I was planning on doing the same thing with my half," [p. 74] Victor said.   185
"But I didn't imagine my father looking anything like a salmon. I thought it'd
be like cleaning the attic or something. Like letting things go after they've
stopped having any use."

"Nothing stops, cousin," Thomas said. "Nothing stops."

Thomas Builds-the-Fire got out of the pickup and walked up his driveway.
Victor started the pickup and began the drive home.

"Wait," Thomas yelled suddenly from his porch. "I just got to ask one favor."

Victor stopped the pickup, leaned out the window, and shouted back.
"What do you want?"

"Just one time when I'm telling a story somewhere, why don't you stop and   190
listen?" Thomas asked.

"Just once?"

"Just once."

Victor waved his arms to let Thomas know that the deal was good. It was a
fair trade, and that was all Victor had ever wanted from his whole life. So Victor
drove his father's pickup toward home while Thomas went into his house,
closed the door behind him, and heard a new story come to him in the silence
afterwards. [p. 75]

The Lone Ranger and Tonto Fistfight in Heaven° [1993]

Too hot to sleep so I walked down to the Third Avenue 7-11 for a Creamsicle and the company of a graveyard-shift cashier. I know that game. I worked graveyard for a Seattle 7-11 and got robbed once too often. The last time the bastard locked me in the cooler. He even took my money and basketball shoes.

The graveyard-shift worker in the Third Avenue 7-11 looked like they all do. Acne scars and a bad haircut, work pants that showed off his white socks, and those cheap black shoes that have no support. My arches still ache from my year at the Seattle 7-11. [p. 181]°

"Hello," he asked when I walked into his store. "How you doing?"

I gave him a half-wave as I headed back to the freezer. He looked me over so he could describe me to the police later. I knew the look. One of my old girlfriends said I started to look at her that way, too. She left me not long after that. No, I left her and don't blame her for anything. That's how it happened. When one person starts to look at another like a criminal, then the love is over. It's logical.

"I don't trust you," she said to me. "You get too angry."   5

She was white and I lived with her in Seattle. Some nights we fought so bad that I would just get in my car and drive all night, only stop to fill up on gas. In fact, I worked the graveyard shift to spend as much time away from her as possible. But I learned all about Seattle that way, driving its back ways and dirty alleys.

Sometimes, though, I would forget where I was and get lost. I'd drive for hours, searching for something familiar. Seems like I'd spent my whole life that way, looking for anything I recognized. Once, I ended up in a nice residential neighborhood and somebody must have been worried because the police showed up and pulled me over.

"What are you doing out here?" the police officer asked me, as he looked over my license and registration.

"I'm lost."

"Well, where are you supposed to be?" he asked me, and I knew there were   10
plenty of places I wanted to be, but none where I was supposed to be. [p. 182]

"I got in a fight with my girlfriend," I said. "I was just driving around, blowing off steam, you know?"

"Well, you should be more careful where you drive," the officer said. "You're making people nervous. You don't fit the profile of the neighborhood."

I wanted to tell him that I didn't really fit the profile of the country but I knew it would just get me into trouble.

Alexie, Sherman. "The Lone Ranger and Tonto Fistfight in Heaven." *The Lone Ranger and Tonto Fistfight in Heaven*. New York: HarperPerennial, 1993. 181–90. Print.
(Page citations in square brackets refer to the original publication.)

"Can I help you?" the 7-11 clerk asked me loudly, searching for some response that would reassure him that I wasn't an armed robber. He knew this dark skin and long, black hair of mine was dangerous. I had potential.

"Just getting a Creamsicle," I said after a long interval. It was a sick twist to 15 pull on the guy, but it was late and I was bored. I grabbed my Creamsicle and walked back to the counter slowly, scanned the aisles for effect. I wanted to whistle low and menacingly but I never learned to whistle.

"Pretty hot out tonight?" he asked, that old rhetorical weather bullshit question designed to put us both at ease.

"Hot enough to make you go crazy," I said and smiled. He swallowed hard like a white man does in those situations. I looked him over. Same old green, red, and white 7-11 jacket and thick glasses. But he wasn't ugly, just misplaced and marked by loneliness. If he wasn't working there that night, he'd be at home alone, flipping through channels and wishing he could afford HBO or Showtime.

"Will this be all?" he asked me, in that company effort to make me do some impulse shopping. Like adding a clause onto a treaty. *We'll take Washington and Oregon and you get six* [p. 183] *pine trees and a brand-new Chrysler Cordoba.* I knew how to make and break promises.

"No," I said and paused. "Give me a Cherry Slushie, too."

"What size?" he asked, relieved.   20

"Large," I said, and he turned his back to me to make the drink. He realized his mistake but it was too late. He stiffened, ready for the gunshot or the blow behind the ear. When it didn't come, he turned back to me.

"I'm sorry," he said. "What size did you say?"

"Small," I said and changed the story.

"But I thought you said large."

"If you knew I wanted a large, then why did you ask me again?" I asked him 25 and laughed. He looked at me, couldn't decide if I was giving him serious shit or just goofing. There was something about him I liked, even if it was three in the morning and he was white.

"Hey," I said. "Forget the Slushie. What I want to know is if you know all the words to the theme from 'The Brady Bunch'?"

He looked at me, confused at first, then laughed.

"Shit," he said. "I was hoping you weren't crazy. You were scaring me."

"Well, I'm going to get crazy if you don't know the words."

He laughed loudly then, told me to take the Creamsicle for free. He was the 30 graveyard-shift manager and those little demonstrations of power tickled him. All seventy-five cents of it. I knew how much everything cost.

"Thanks," I said to him and walked out the door. I took [p. 184] my time walking home, let the heat of the night melt the Creamsicle all over my hand. At three in the morning I could act just as young as I wanted to act. There was no one around to ask me to grow up.

In Seattle, I broke lamps. She and I would argue and I'd break a lamp, just pick it up and throw it down. At first she'd buy replacement lamps, expensive and beautiful. But after a while she'd buy lamps from Goodwill or garage sales. Then she just gave up the idea entirely and we'd argue in the dark.

"You're just like your brother," she'd yell. "Drunk all the time and stupid."

"My brother don't drink that much."

She and I never tried to hurt each other physically. I did love her, after all, 35 and she loved me. But those arguments were just as damaging as a fist. Words can be like that, you know? Whenever I get into arguments now, I remember her and I also remember Muhammad Ali. He knew the power of his fists but, more importantly, he knew the power of his words, too. Even though he only had an IQ of 80 or so, Ali was a genius. And she was a genius, too. She knew exactly what to say to cause me the most pain.

But don't get me wrong. I walked through that relationship with an executioner's hood. Or more appropriately, with war paint and sharp arrows. She was a kindergarten teacher and I continually insulted her for that.

"Hey, schoolmarm," I asked. "Did your kids teach you anything new today?"

And I always had crazy dreams. I always have had them, but it seemed they became nightmares more often in Seattle. [p. 185]

In one dream, she was a missionary's wife and I was a minor war chief. We fell in love and tried to keep it secret. But the missionary caught us fucking in the barn and shot me. As I lay dying, my tribe learned of the shooting and attacked the whites all across the reservation. I died and my soul drifted above the reservation.

Disembodied, I could see everything that was happening. Whites killing 40 Indians and Indians killing whites. At first it was small, just my tribe and the few whites who lived there. But my dream grew, intensified. Other tribes arrived on horseback to continue the slaughter of whites, and the United States Cavalry rode into battle.

The most vivid image of that dream stays with me. Three mounted soldiers played polo with a dead Indian woman's head. When I first dreamed it, I thought it was just a product of my anger and imagination. But since then, I've read similar accounts of that kind of evil in the old West. Even more terrifying, though, is the fact that those kinds of brutal things are happening today in places like El Salvador.

All I know for sure, though, is that I woke from that dream in terror, packed up all my possessions, and left Seattle in the middle of the night.

"I love you," she said as I left her. "And don't ever come back."

I drove through the night, over the Cascades, down into the plains of central Washington, and back home to the Spokane Indian Reservation. [p. 186]

When I finished the Creamsicle that the 7-11 clerk gave me, I held the 45 wooden stick up into the air and shouted out very loudly. A couple lights flashed on in windows and a police car cruised by me a few minutes later. I waved to the men in blue and they waved back accidentally. When I got home it was still too hot to sleep so I picked up a week-old newspaper from the floor and read.

There was another civil war, another terrorist bomb exploded, and one more plane crashed and all aboard were presumed dead. The crime rate was rising in every city with populations larger than 100,000, and a farmer in Iowa shot his banker after foreclosure on his 1,000 acres.

A kid from Spokane won the local spelling bee by spelling the word *rhinoceros*.

When I got back to the reservation, my family wasn't surprised to see me. They'd been expecting me back since the day I left for Seattle. There's an old Indian poet who said that Indians can reside in the city, but they can never live there. That's as close to truth as any of us can get.

Mostly I watched television. For weeks I flipped through channels, searched for answers in the game shows and soap operas. My mother would circle the want ads in red and hand the paper to me.

"What are you going to do with the rest of your life?" she asked.   50

"Don't know," I said, and normally, for almost any other Indian in the country, that would have been a perfectly fine [p. 187] answer. But I was special, a former college student, a smart kid. I was one of those Indians who was supposed to make it, to rise above the rest of the reservation like a fucking eagle or something. I was the new kind of warrior.

For a few months I didn't even look at the want ads my mother circled, just left the newspaper where she had set it down. After a while, though, I got tired of television and started to play basketball again. I'd been a good player in high school, nearly great, and almost played at the college I attended for a couple years. But I'd been too out of shape from drinking and sadness to ever be good again. Still, I liked the way the ball felt in my hands and the way my feet felt inside my shoes.

At first I just shot baskets by myself. It was selfish, and I also wanted to learn the game again before I played against anybody else. Since I had been good before and embarrassed fellow tribal members, I knew they would want to take revenge on me. Forget about the cowboys versus Indians business. The most intense competition on any reservation is Indians versus Indians.

But on the night I was ready to play for real, there was this white guy at the gym, playing with all the Indians.

"Who is that?" I asked Jimmy Seyler.   55

"He's the new BIA chief's kid."

"Can he play?"

"Oh, yeah."

And he could play. He played Indian ball, fast and loose, better than all the Indians there.

"How long's he been playing here?" I asked.   60

"Long enough."

I stretched my muscles, and everybody watched me. All [p. 188] these Indians watched one of their old and dusty heroes. Even though I had played most of my ball at the white high school I went to, I was still all Indian, you know? I was Indian when it counted, and this BIA kid needed to be beaten by an Indian, any Indian.

I jumped into the game and played well for a little while. It felt good. I hit a few shots, grabbed a rebound or two, played enough defense to keep the other team honest. Then that white kid took over the game. He was too good. Later, he'd play college ball back East and would nearly make the Knicks team a couple years on. But we didn't know any of that would happen. We just knew he was better that day and every other day.

The next morning I woke up tired and hungry, so I grabbed the want ads, found a job I wanted, and drove to Spokane to get it. I've been working at the high school exchange program ever since, typing and answering phones. Sometimes I wonder if the people on the other end of the line know that I'm Indian and if their voices would change if they did know.

One day I picked up the phone and it was her, calling from Seattle.   65

"I got your number from your mom," she said. "I'm glad you're working."

"Yeah, nothing like a regular paycheck."

"Are you drinking?"

"No, I've been on the wagon for almost a year."

"Good."   70

The connection was good. I could hear her breathing in the spaces between our words. How do you talk to the real person whose ghost has haunted you? How do you tell the difference between the two? [p. 189]

"Listen," I said. "I'm sorry for everything."

"Me, too."

"What's going to happen to us?" I asked her and wished I had the answer for myself.

"I don't know," she said. "I want to change the world."   75

These days, living alone in Spokane, I wish I lived closer to the river, to the falls where ghosts of salmon jump. I wish I could sleep. I put down my paper or book and turn off all the lights, lie quietly in the dark. It may take hours, even years, for me to sleep again. There's nothing surprising or disappointing in that.

I know how all my dreams end anyway. [p. 190]

Tomson Highway

Interview with Sherman Alexie°   [1998]

Tomson Highway: *When did you start writing?*

Sherman Alexie: I started writing because I kept fainting in human anatomy class and needed a career change. The only class that fit where the human anatomy class had been was a poetry writing workshop. I always liked poetry.

Highway, Tomson. "Interview with Sherman Alexie." *boston.sidewalk.com.* 1 July 1998, n. pag. Web. 1 July 1998.

I'd never heard of, or nobody'd ever showed me, a book written by a First Nations person, ever. I got into the class, and my professor, Alex Kwo, gave me an anthology of contemporary Native American poetry called *Songs from This Earth on Turtle's Back*. I opened it up and—oh my gosh—I saw my life in poems and stories for the very first time.

T.H.: *Who were some of the writers in the book?*

S.A.: Linda Hogan, Simon Ortiz, Joy Harjo, James Welch, Adrian Louis. There were poems about reservation life: fry bread, bannock, 49's, fried baloney, government food, and terrible housing. But there was also joy and happiness.

There's a line by a Paiute poet named Adrian Louis that says, "Oh, Uncle Adrian, I'm in the reservation of my mind." I thought, "Oh my God, somebody understands me!" At that moment I realized, "I can do this!" That's when I started writing—in 1989.

T.H.: *The poetry that you would have studied in American Studies, for instance, the poetry of Wallace Stevens or e. e. cummings or Emily Dickinson never influenced you at all?*

S.A.: Of course it did. I loved that stuff. I still love it. Walt Whitman and Emily Dickinson are two of my favorites. Wallace Stevens leaves me kind of dry, but the other poets, they're still a primary influence. I always tell people my literary influences are Stephen King, John Steinbeck, my mother, my grandfather, and the Brady Bunch.

T.H.: *Then you moved on to short stories.*

S.A.: I'd written a couple of them in college. After my first book of poems, *The Business of Fancydancing*, was published by Hanging Loose Press in Brooklyn, New York, I got a great *New York Times* book review. The review called me "one of the major lyric voices of our time." I was a twenty-five-year-old Spokane Indian guy working as a secretary at a high school exchange program in Spokane, Washington, when my poetry editor faxed that review to me. I pulled it out of the fax machine beside my desk and read, "one of the major lyric voices of our time." I thought, "Great! Where do I go from here!?" After that, the agents started calling *me*.

T.H.: *Where did that book of poetry come from?*

S.A.: It was my first semester poetry manuscript. Part of the assignment was to submit to literary magazines. The one I liked in the Washington State library was *Hanging Loose* magazine. I liked that it started the same year I was born. The magazine, the press, and I are the same age. Over the next year and a half they kept taking poems of mine to publish. Then they asked if I had a manuscript. I said, "Yes!" and sent it in.

It was a *thousand* copies. I figured I'd sell a hundred and fifty to my family. My mom would buy a hundred herself and that would be about it. But, it took off. I never expected it. Sometimes I think it would have been nicer if it had not been as big, because my career has been a rocket ride. There's a lot of pressure.

Åse Nygren

A World of Story-Smoke:
A Conversation with Sherman Alexie°   [2005]

Åse Nygren: What are some of the inspirations and motivations behind your writing? Are they autobiographical, political, or historical?

Sherman Alexie: Like we were saying just before we turned the tape on, people in Scandinavia don't really know about Indian writers or know that there even are Indian writers. I didn't know either. Even though I was growing up on a reservation, and going to reservation schools, I had never really been shown Indian literature before. So it wasn't even a possibility growing up. I loved reading but I hadn't thought of a career as a writer. I hadn't thought about books as a career in any form. I took a class in creative writing because I couldn't handle human anatomy lab and it was the only class that fit my schedule. This was the first time anyone had shown me contemporary poetry. The most contemporary poem I had read before was "The Waste Land." I had no idea you could write about NOW. I read Allen Ginsberg's "Howl" for the first time. Even Langston Hughes felt new to me. And I fell in love with it immediately. Over night, I knew I was going to be a writer.

ÅN: Were there any Indian writers on the reading list for the poetry class you took?

SA: The poetry teacher gave me a book called *Songs from This Earth on Turtle's Back*, an anthology on Native literature by Joseph Bruchac. Before I read that book I had no idea that you could write about Indian life with powwows, ceremonies, broken [151]° down cars, cheap motels; all this stuff that was my life as I was growing up on the reservation. I remember in particular one line by Adrian Louis, a Paiute poet: "Adrian, I'm in the reservation of my mind!" It captured for me the way I felt about myself, at least then. It was nothing I'd ever had before. I thought to myself: I want to write like this! So that's where it began. The beginning was accidental. But I got very serious about it quickly. I went through the college library looking at poetry journals trying to figure out what was going on in the world, trying to catch up, essentially, for a lifetime of not reading.

ÅN: Did you read all different kinds of poetry, or did you focus on works by American Indians?

SA: Any poetry. Anything and everything. I pulled books off the shelves randomly because I liked the title, or the cover, or the author photo. I read hundreds of poems over a year or so to catch up. As I sat there in the poetry stacks in the library a whole new world opened to me. Before, I had always thought that I was a freak in the way I saw and felt about the world. As I started reading the works of all these poets I realized that I, at least, wasn't the

---

Nygren, Åse. "A World of Story-Smoke: A Conversation with Sherman Alexie." *MELUS* 30.4 (Winter 2005): 149–69. Print.
(Page citations in square brackets refer to the original interview.)

only freak! [Laughs] I think we belong to a lot of tribes; culturally, ethnically, and racially. I'm a poet and this is the world in which I belong.

ÅN: So your ambitions and motivations weren't political to begin with?

SA: No. My writing was very personal and autobiographical. I was simply finding out who I was and who I wanted to be. As I started writing I became more political, much because of people's reactions to me. I was writing against so many ideas of what I was supposed to be writing. So even though much of my early work deals with alcohol and alcoholism because of personal experiences, I got a lot of criticism because alcoholism is such a loaded topic for Indians. People thought I was writing about stereotypes, but more than anything I was writing about my own life. As an Indian, you don't have the luxury of being called an autobiographical writer often. You end up writing for the whole race. At the beginning [p. 152] of my career I was twenty-one years old, and I didn't have any defense against that. So I became political because people viewed me politically. I got political to fight people's ideas about me. It is only in the last few years that my politics has found a way into my work that feels natural. Part of the reason is because you grow older. The way I think about it is that I used to spend more time looking inside myself, looking internally. Now I look at more of the world and a wider range of people. . . . [p. 153]

ÅN: One important concern among American Indian writers has been the question of how one deals with a painful past, such as the one shared by the Indian peoples of the United States, without [p. 155] falling into the trap of victimization. How important is this issue for you when you write your fiction?

SA: I write autobiographically, so when you talk about surviving pain and trauma and getting out of it—I did, I have! But the people I know have not. So what do I do in my literature? Do I portray the Indian world as I see it? And I do see it as doomed, and that you have to get lucky to escape that. Should I write the literature of hope no matter how I feel? No! I'm not hopeful. So how do you avoid victimization? We can't. We are victims. . . .

ÅN: I find the concept of "collective trauma" particularly useful concerning the suffering that many of your characters are experiencing. Many of them suffer from not only personal losses and grievances—absent fathers, poverty, unemployment, alcoholism, etc.—but also from a cultural loss and a collective trauma, which include experiences of racism and stereotyping. Their losses [p. 156] and grievances affect their behavior and their lives on many levels. In my view, your fiction explores how such trauma both damages and creates community and identity alike. Both identity and community are, of course, condemned to ongoing dysfunction. Do you think that suffering is part of what constitutes Indianness? Perhaps in a somewhat comparable way by which we have come to associate African American identity with slavery, or Jewish identity with the Holocaust? If so, how does this relation differ from, e.g., the relation between African Americans and suffering, or Jews and suffering?

SA: Yes! The phrase I've also used is "blood memory." I think the strongest parallel in my mind has always been the Jewish people and the Holocaust. Certainly, their oppression has been constant for 1900 years longer, but the fact is that you cannot separate our identity from our pain. At some point it becomes primarily our identity. The whole idea of authenticity—"How Indian are you?"—is the most direct result of the fact that we don't know what an American Indian identity is. There is no measure anymore. There is no way of knowing, except perhaps through our pain. And so, we're lost. We're always wandering. . . . [p. 157]

ÅN: Although the subject matters in your texts are morally and ethically engaging, the same texts are often ironic, satiric, and full of humor. I read your ironic and satiric rethinking, even defamiliarization, of a painful past, in alignment with writer Art Spiegelman and filmmaker Roberto Benigni. Spiegelman's two books in cartoon form, entitled *Maus: A Survivor's Tale I* and *II*, and Benigni's film *Life Is Beautiful* both deal with the Jewish Holocaust in the comic mode, and have, consequently, shocked readers/viewers out of any lingering sense of familiarity with the historic events described. Would you like your books to have a similar effect on your readers? What are some of the gains? Dangers?

SA: Well, I'm a big fan of graphic novels. I like their immediacy. Automatically when you look at a graphic novel, or when you look [p. 159] at a cartoon, there is always an ironical, satirical edge and an underlying humor. So yes, I aim to be funny, and I aim for my humor to be very political. But I think more along the lines of political stand-up comedians like Richard Pryor and Lenny Bruce than I do about other writers.

ÅN: What might be some of the gains and dangers?

SA: Dangers? Playing to the audience. Reacting completely to the audience rather than generating it from yourself, so that you're reflexive and you're performing rather than dealing with something on an emotional level. I think I have a tendency in my work to lapse into performance mode. Rather than something out of my heart, it ends up being something on the surface designed for effect. One of the great things is that through that immediacy of performance and humor you can reach people who otherwise might not be listening. I think being funny breaks down barriers between people. I can get up in front of any crowd, and if I make them laugh first I can say almost anything to them. . . . [p. 160]

ÅN: Are you ever afraid that the comical element will subvert attention from the gravitas of your writing?

SA: Yes, it happens all the time. People assume that you're not being serious because you're being funny. By and large I figure that people who say those sort of things aren't funny. And being funny is just how I am. I can't just stop . . . [Laughs]. But it's also a personal defense, of course. When I don't want to talk about something, or when I'm uncomfortable. It's not all good, humor, but it's always serious. [p. 161]

Joseph L. Coulombe

The Approximate Size of His Favorite Humor: Sherman Alexie's Comic Connections and Disconnections in *The Lone Ranger and Tonto Fistfight in Heaven*°   [2002]

In this essay I will argue that Alexie's humor is central to a constructive social and moral purpose evident throughout his fiction but particularly in his collection of short stories, *The Lone Ranger and Tonto Fistfight in Heaven*. He uses humor—or his characters use humor—to reveal injustice, protect self-esteem, heal wounds, and create bonds. The function of humor changes from scene to scene, shifting to serve these myriad goals. In *Indi'n Humor* Kenneth Lincoln explains the many different roles of humor within Indian communities. He describes "the contrary powers of Indian humor" as "[t]he powers to heal and to hurt, to bond and to exorcize, to renew and to purge" (5). Like the legendary Trickster figure, humor in Indian communities embodies shifting meanings and serves conflicting ends. However, rather than a sign of his "hip" [p. 94]° irreverence for all things Indian, Alexie's sophisticated use of humor unsettles conventional ways of thinking and compels reevaluation and growth, which ultimately allows Indian characters to connect to their heritage in novel ways and forces non-Indian readers to reconsider simplistic generalizations.

In his best work to date, *The Lone Ranger and Tonto Fistfight in Heaven*, humor allows his characters to display strengths and hide weaknesses, to expose prejudices and avoid realities, and to create bonds and construct barricades. These "contrary powers" often coexist simultaneously, requiring the characters and readers to position and then reposition themselves within shifting personal and cultural contexts. Alexie's cross-cultural humor alternately engages readers—creating positive connections between individuals of diverse backgrounds—and disrupts communities (both Indian and white), erecting barriers that make constructive communication difficult. Here lies its principal challenge for readers. Alexie's shifting treatment of humor serves as a means of connection as well as an instrument of separation. However, it is precisely this complexity and plasticity that allow him to negotiate successfully the differences between Indian communities and mainstream American society, while simultaneously instigating crucial dialogue about social and moral issues especially important to Indian communities. . . .

I contend that Alexie's brand of humor, more than others perhaps, is "that trickster at the heart of the Native American imagination." As such, it embodies the potential for facilitating mutual understanding and respect between diverse

Coulombe, Joseph L. "The Approximate Size of His Favorite Humor: Sherman Alexie's Comic Connections and Disconnections in *The Lone Ranger and Tonto Fistfight in Heaven*." *American Indian Quarterly* 30.1 (Winter 2002): 94–115. Print.
(Page citations in square brackets refer to the original article.)

peoples. By exploding expectations and compelling dialogue, humor teaches self-knowledge and social awareness, much like Trickster. Alexie's use of humor encourages readers to think anew by creating a space of shared inquiry and reciprocal empathy. . . . Alexie's humor [p. 95] . . . provides an emotional and intellectual meeting ground for his readers to reconsider reductive stereotypes and expectations. . . . Alexie challenges readers of diverse backgrounds to join together to reevaluate past and present ideologies. Humor generates a freely occupied space in which readers can begin sorting through the myriad connections and disconnections that face us all today. Stephen Evans, in an evaluation of Alexie's refashioning of stereotypes (particularly that of the "drunken Indian"), correctly notes how satire compels "the collaborative making of meaning between Alexie and his readers" (54). Readers are not passive receptacles; they engage, question, resist, learn, and grow during the reading process. They join Alexie . . . to hash out interpretations of the past, responses to the present, and prospects for the future. This delicate alliance between author and audience—facilitated in large part by humor—promises to be more effective than purely logical, historical, or traditional efforts to promote understanding. With its shifting layers and elaborate surprises, Alexie's humor disrupts readers' complacency and necessitates analysis, clarification, and, ultimately, identification. [p. 96]

Works Cited

Alexie, Sherman. *The Lone Ranger and Tonto Fistfight in Heaven*. New York: Harper Perennial, 1993. Print.

Evans, Stephen F. "'Open Containers': Sherman Alexie's Drunken Indians." *American Indian Quarterly* 25.1 (Winter 2001): 46–72. Print.

Lincoln, Kenneth. *Indi'n Humor: Bicultural Play in Native America*. New York: Oxford UP, 1993. Print.

Jerome DeNuccio

Slow Dancing with Skeletons: Sherman Alexie's *The Lone Ranger and Tonto Fistfight in Heaven*°

[2002]

The Spokane Indian characters in Sherman Alexie's short story collection *The Lone Ranger and Tonto Fistfight in Heaven* wage daily battle against small humiliations and perennial hurts. Situated on a reservation where the Department of Housing and Urban Development (HUD) houses, the Bureau of Indian Affairs (BIA) trucks, and commodity foods continually mirror paternalism and dependency, and where "tribal ties" and a cohesive "sense of community" (74) have waned, Alexie's characters confront the dilemma of how to be "real Indians," of how to find "their true names, their adult names" (20), of how to

DeNuccio, Jerome. "Slow Dancing with Skeletons: Sherman Alexie's *The Lone Ranger and Tonto Fistfight in Heaven*." *Critique: Studies in Contemporary Fiction* 44.1 (Fall 2002): 86–96. Print.

find a warrior dignity and courage when it is "too late to be warriors in the old way" (63), of how to ameliorate what Adrian C. Louis has termed "the ghost-pain of history" (35)—that haunting sense of personal and cultural loss that generates a paralyzing sense of ineffectuality. They struggle to cope with passivity, cynicism, and despair to find healing for the pain that turns into self-pity and the anger that turns into self-loathing.

One of Alexie's characters, Thomas Builds-the-Fire, a Spokane storyteller, articulates a useful image for understanding the distress and anguish these characters experience: *"There are things you should learn,"* he tells Victor and Junior, two young Spokanes who either narrate or are featured in eighteen of the collection's twenty-two stories. "Your past is a skeleton walking one step behind you, and your future is a skeleton walking one step in front of you." Indians, thus, are always *"trapped in the now."* But the skeletons are "not necessarily evil, unless you let them be." Because "these skeletons are made of memories, dreams, and voices," and because they are "wrapped up in the now," it becomes imperative to "keep moving, [p. 86]° keep walking, in step with your skeletons." To stop or slow down, to "slow dance" with one's skeletons, risks being caught "in the in-between, between touching and becoming," the immediately felt and the potentially experienced. Such a situation severs the necessary relation between the structure of experience that at any one moment has shaped each life and the structure of ongoing time to which that life must continuously adapt and in which it develops. Keeping in step is not easy, however, for "your skeletons will talk to you, tell you to sit down and take a rest, . . . make you promises, tell you all the things you want to hear." They can "dress up" as seductive women, as a best friend offering a drink, as parents offering gifts. But, "no matter what they do," Thomas warns, "keep walking, keep moving" (21–22).

Thomas's image of the skeletons suggests that Indian subjectivity is dislogic, an interplay of perspectives and points of view that Bakhtin describes as "a plurality of unmerged consciousness" (Bakhtin, *Art and Answerability* 26). The self is positioned in a social space replete with memories, dreams, and voices that invite attention and response, that must be accommodated and negotiated if the self as an individual and a tribal subject is to emerge. Such negotiation, although paramount, is never easy. Memories, dreams, and voices form a dense network of social significations. They bear traces, are mediated by social relations and cultural dynamics, are inflected by family, friends, lovers, traditions, mass media, history. The term *Indian* names a subject position traversed by competing claims, saturated by multiple insinuations, the confusion or mastering force of which can induce a capitulation that Thomas identifies as failing to keep "in step with your skeletons." Such capitulation forecloses choice, and the result is often self-sabotage. Commenting on what appears to a white state trooper as an unmotivated suicide by a successful tribal member, Junior notes that "when we look in the mirror, see the history of our tribe in our eyes, taste failure in the tap water, and shake with old tears, we understand completely" (178). To "keep moving,

---

(Page citations in square brackets refer to the original article.)

keep walking, in step with your skeletons," then, suggests the necessity of listening to *and answering* the multiple voices that clamor for attention, a process of accommodation *and negotiation* that resists totalization and keeps the self "unconsummated" and "yet-to-be" (Bakhtin, *Art and Answerability* 13), moving always toward "becoming" rather than trapped "between touching and becoming," moving so that some coherent story of the self can be discovered. Thomas's image of the skeletons resonates throughout the collection's twenty-two stories, precisely because so many characters have fallen out of step and, thus, are suspended, passively and destructively, in a seemingly incoherent present.

Appropriately enough, the collection's opening story, "Every Little Hurricane," displays the provenance of those elements that problematize Indian subjectivity. Significantly, Alexie sets the story at a New Year's Eve party ushering in 1976, the bicentennial year. Nine-year-old Victor, whose parents are hosting the party, awakens to what he thinks is a hurricane but is really a metaphor Alexie uses to represent Victor's experience of the intensifying anger and painful [p. 87] memories, unleashed by alcohol, that circulate among the Indian partygoers. Victor's father, for instance, remembers his father being spit on at a Spokane bus stop; his mother remembers being involuntarily sterilized by an Indian Health Service (IHS) doctor after Victor's birth; his uncles Adolph and Arnold fight savagely because each reminds the other of childhood poverty so great that they hid crackers in their bedroom so they wouldn't have to go to bed hungry. Lying in his basement bedroom, Victor thinks he sees the ceiling lower "with the weight of each Indian's pain, until it was just inches from [his] nose" (8). As the adults' drunken rage fills the house, it blends with and feeds Victor's own nightmare fears of drowning in the rain, of alcoholic "fluids swallowing him," for at the age of five he had witnessed at a powwow an Indian man drown after passing out and falling "facedown into the water collected in a tire track." "Even at five," the narrator notes, "Victor understood what that meant, how it defined nearly everything" (7). Seeking the comfort of physical connection, he lies between his unconscious parents, and, putting a hand on each of their stomachs, feels "enough hunger in both, enough movement, enough geography and history, enough of everything to destroy the reservations" (10–11). As this image suggests, the confluence of past currents of suffering meet in Victor.

Given the intensity of the pain that presses upon Indian subjectivity, it is not surprising that the adults and their children get caught "in the in-between, between touching and becoming." The now of felt experience becomes ceaseless repetition of what has been. Without a viable counterbalance of Spokane culture—a point Alexie implies by setting his opening story on the eve of America's bicentennial festivities—the self appears finalized, unmodifiable because personal history appears consumed by the totalizing narrative of History. There is no sense of particularity, of difference that prevents the self from being absorbed into the larger culture's dominant narrative, no way to position the self so that its story unfolds within, not into, ongoing time, no "outsidedness" (Bakhtin, *Speech Genres* 7) where the choice to keep moving in step with one's skeletons keeps the impinging or "touching" now provisionally open to "becoming." . . . [p. 88]

Alexie's Indian characters are caught, as Bakhtin puts it, in the "framework of *other people's* words" about them, a framework that can "finalize and deaden" the self. But Alexie also demonstrates that in his characters "there is always something that only [they themselves] can reveal, in a free act of self-consciousness and discourse, something that does not submit to an externalizing second-hand definition" (Bakhtin, *Problems* 59, 58). And Alexie again uses the Spokane storyteller Thomas Builds-the-Fire to explain this resistant something. [p. 91]

> We are all given one thing by which our lives are measured, one determination. Mine are the stories which can change or not change the world. It doesn't matter which as long as I continue to tell the stories. . . . They are all I have. It's all I can do. (72–73)

Thomas's "one determination" posits subjectivity as both determined and particular, given, and its own measure of value. There is a personal narrative that unfolds within the larger culture's master narrative, which situates an individual subjectivity within the cultural topography and keeps it in step with the skeletons of past and future. For Thomas, only recognizing and choosing to follow that "one determination" matters. Thomas himself is widely ignored by his tribe, yet he tells his stories, stories that he does not author but that come to him from the culturally specific ground to which he is connected and which his storytelling articulates. What Thomas transmits, then, is the persistence and adaptability of Spokane signifying practices. . . . [p. 92]

Stories, then, teach survival. They *re*-member, bridging the rupture created by "what we have lost" (143), reconnecting time to aspect, past and present to progressive and perfective. Talking stories yields something "aboriginal and recognizable," something, as Thomas says, "by which our lives are measured." In the story "Family Portrait," Junior, contemplating his hands, is led to an acute realization of cultural loss:

> Years ago, the hands might have held the spear that held the salmon that held the dream of the tribe. Years ago, the hands might have touched the hands of the dark-skinned men who touched medicine and the magic of ordinary gods. (196)

He then recalls a story his father told about "the first television he ever saw." It had "just one channel and all it showed was a woman sitting on top of the same television. Over and over until it hurt your eyes and head" (197). That image, persistently reflexive, depicts the kind of storytelling Alexie himself enacts: an unsparing examination of what is gone and what remains. That, Junior declares, is "how we find our history." And repossess it, too, for although such storytelling [p. 95] must, of necessity, measure "heartbreak" and "fear," it also becomes the means "by which we measure the beginning of all our lives," the means "by which we measure all our stories, until we understand that one story"—the official historiography—"can never be all" (197). Like the television that continuously frames the image it continuously represents, broadcasting in the present its backward gaze, Alexie's storytelling links "now" with "then," Indian lives with "five hundred years of convenient lies" (150), repeatedly, for though "it hurt[s] your eyes and head," it speaks survival. [p. 96]

Works Cited

Alexie, Sherman. *The Lone Ranger and Tonto Fistfight in Heaven.* New York: HarperCollins, 1993. Print.

Bakhtin, Mikhail. *Art and Answerability: Early Philosophical Essays.* Eds. Michael Holquist and Vadim Liapunov. Trans. Vadim Liapunov. Austin: U of Texas P, 1990. Print.

——. *Problems of Dostoevsky's Poetics.* Ed. and trans. Caryl Emerson. Minneapolis: U of Minnesota P, 1984. Print.

——. *Speech Genres and Other Late Essays.* Eds. Caryl Emerson and Michael Holquist. Trans. Vern W. McGee. Austin: U of Texas P, 1986. Print.

Louis, Adrian C. *Skins.* New York: Crown, 1995. Print.

James Cox

Muting White Noise: The Subversion of Popular Culture Narratives of Conquest in Sherman Alexie's Fiction°   [1997]

> "Partisan writers have chronicled the story of conquest, and political stranglers see to it that the public is kept blinded to actual conditions."
> —*Cogewea in* Cogewea: The Half-Blood,
> *by Mourning Dove (Hum-Ishu-Ma)*

Scholars from many academic disciplines have considered in detail the history of European and Euro-American (mis)representation of Native American peoples. In *Savagism and Civilization* (1953), American literature professor Roy Harvey Pearce considered the misrepresentations the result of the culturally sanctioned European belief in a binary of civilized and savage, of god-fearing and godless. Historian Robert Berkhofer Jr. entitles his study of misrepresentation *The White Man's Indian* (1978), and in *God Is Red* (1994), lawyer, political activist, and Native American studies professor Vine Deloria Jr. calls the stereotypical images "The Indians of the American Imagination." Native American novelists are also interested in this history of misrepresentation defined by written and visual ethnocentric narratives that tell a story of the European conquest of North America. These authors and their characters are involved in a narrative construction or reconstruction of a Native American–identified self that counters a racist historical context and the conquest narratives that are often sustained by the ubiquitous white man's Indian. Whether in brief critique, as in Louise

Cox, James. "Muting White Noise: The Subversion of Popular Culture Narratives of Conquest in Sherman Alexie's Fiction." *Studies in American Indian Literatures* 9.4 (Winter 1997): 52–70. Print.

Erdrich's, Louis Owens's, and James Welch's novels, or in full-scale revision and subversion, as in Sherman Alexie's work, Native American authors write new narratives of self-representation that critically question and often radically revise and [p. 52]° subvert the dominant culture's conquest narratives and mass-produced misrepresentations of Native Americans. . . . [p. 53]

In *The Lone Ranger and Tonto Fistfight in Heaven*, Sherman Alexie's critical response to popular culture differs from Owens's, Erdrich's, and Welch's; rather than exclusively offering critiques of the conquest narratives the dominant culture produces and consumes, he illustrates the damage these narratives engender in his Native American characters, then rewrites or revises and subverts them. The radio and television program *The Lone Ranger* is a conquest narrative in that the American Indian, Tonto, is present only to serve the white hero/master, the Lone Ranger.[1] In Alexie's eight-word revision, Tonto refuses to be the loyal companion, a twentieth-century incarnation of the noble savage, literally a white man's (the Lone Ranger's) Indian. Tonto engages the Lone Ranger in a fistfight, and thereby refuses to occupy the subordinate social space defined and assigned to him by the Lone Ranger, the iconographic [p. 55] Western hero and the representative of the dominant culture. The subversive title is a guide to the short stories that follow. Alexie's characters are engaged in the same metaphorical fistfight as the titular Tonto: They struggle for self-definition and self-representation against the oppressive technological narratives that define Native Americans as a conquered people, as decontextualized, romanticized, subservient Tontos, and Native America as a conquered landscape.

A white noise infiltrates the fictionalized Spokane Reservation in several stories in Alexie's collection. White noise is the static on a television after a station plays "The Star-Spangled Banner," then ends its broadcasting day. Alexie uses the static to signify a broad historical context in which European and Euro-American culture has attempted to assimilate and destroy the Spokane. The white noise is, literally, the oppressive noise of white mass-produced culture, the loud demand to abandon all that is Indian and conform to the dictates of the invader's cultural belief system or be destroyed. As the source of the white noise, television is an instrument of late-twentieth-century colonialism. In Alexie's fiction, conquest narratives disseminated by the technological tools of the dominant culture, such as television, have a pervasive, destructive influence on Native America. Cumulative references to television's destructive presence on Alexie's fictionalized reservation indicate this Euro-American technology is an iconographic evil against which the Spokane must struggle.[2]

Alexie composes "All I Wanted to Do Was Dance" of several narrative threads in the life of the primary character, Victor. In the episode that begins the story, Victor drinks at a bar and dances with Indian women as his "compensation, his confession, largest sin, and penance" for having fallen in love with a white woman who left him (83). After Victor shouts, "I started World War I . . . I shot

---

(Page citations in square brackets refer to the original publication.)

Lincoln," Alexie writes, "He was underwater drunk, staring up at the faces of his past. He recognized Neil Armstrong and Christopher Columbus, his mother and father, James Dean, Sal Mineo, Natalie Wood" (84). Victor's desperate shout to be acknowledged is an attempt to inscribe himself into a history the dominant culture privileges, a history of great wars and great white men. In the catalog of the "faces of his past," Victor's image of his parents is trapped between a Euro-American and European cultural hero and the actors who play heroes of white middle-class rebellion in Nicholas Ray's 1955 film *Rebel Without a Cause*. He searches for an identity in a past confused and distorted by historical and popular culture narratives from which he has been excluded. . . . [p. 56]

Confused, distracted, and literally colonized by the omnipresent white noise permeating the reservation, Alexie's characters ignore Thomas Builds-the-Fire, the Spokane's best storyteller. Alexie introduces Thomas in *The Business of Fancydancing* in "Special Delivery," in which Thomas explains his friend Simon's definition of truth: "If there's a tree in the distance and you run to get there, run across the grass with all your heart, and you make it and touch the tree, press your face against the bark, then it's all true. But if you stumble and fall, lose your way, move to the city and buy a VCR and watch cowboy movies all the time, then nothing is true" (47). While truth cannot emerge from Hollywood's Westerns, Thomas's imagination produces truths when his ideas manifest as powerful images to other characters. In "Special Delivery," he commits a crime for which he is on trial in "The Trial of Thomas Builds-the-Fire" in *The Lone Ranger and Tonto Fistfight in Heaven*. A BIA agent explains Thomas is dangerous because of "[a] storytelling fetish accompanied by an extreme need to tell the truth" (93), and Alexie adds, "Thomas was in the holding cell because he had once held the reservation postmaster hostage for eight hours with the *idea* of a gun and had also threatened to make significant changes in the tribal vision" (93; emphasis mine). Thomas's ideas are powerful enough to hold people captive, to make them listen, and with a receptive audience, he threatens a reservation power structure defined by a tribal vision that readers know has been distorted and corrupted by dominant media culture.

At his trial, Thomas decides "to represent himself," an act with a specific legal meaning, but one that also suggests Thomas will construct an image of himself and tell his own story as a defense (95). He refuses to have his narrative diffused through another medium; Thomas, like the Tonto of the title, will fight to speak for himself. As part of his self-representation, Thomas inserts himself as a character in Spokane tribal history. In the first story, he is a horse in a Spokane herd that Colonel Wright of the U.S. Army slaughtered in 1858.[3] Thomas writes his own escape into the story: "They could not break me. Some may have wanted to kill me for my arrogance, but others respected my anger, my refusal to admit defeat. I lived that day, even escaped Colonel Wright, and galloped into other histories" (98). Thomas establishes himself as a transhistorical and mythological figure who creates victories for his tribe out of defeats. He writes a narrative of survival that subverts any narratives about a "vanishing race" and repopulates the landscape with Native Americans. [p. 59]

In his second story, Thomas speaks of himself as Qualchan, the son of an Upper Yakima chief who fought against the U.S. Army. Thomas does not revise this historical event because the "point" of the story, which the judge demands, is, "The City of Spokane is now building a golf course named after me, Qualchan, located in the valley where I was hanged" (99).[4] Qualchan transcends time and his physical death to voice his grievances against the abuse of his name; Thomas invokes Spokane tribal history to protest how Euro-American culture commercializes and consumes Native America. In "The Only Traffic Signal on the Reservation Doesn't Flash Red Anymore," Victor says, "Indians need heroes to help them learn how to survive" (49). Thomas creates the hero that Victor says the Spokane need. After this story, "[t]he courtroom burst into motion and emotion" (99); Thomas's story successfully elicits activity from people numbed by past and present defeat and popular culture narratives that assume the defeat was absolute.

The judge, who sentences Thomas to "two concurrent life terms in the Walla Walla State Penitentiary," is the representative of the dominant culture, and his judicial decision implies his investment in the image of Native America as presented in the conventional Lone Ranger narrative (102). But the newspaper clipping that reports the end of the trial notes Thomas was "transported away from this story and into the next" (103). Thomas is the physical manifestation of a living Spokane history, and his transhistorical, mythological identity makes imprisonment impossible. Alexie suggests Thomas is present in the margins or between the lines of the other stories, though the characters do not see him. Thomas's active storytelling benefits the tribe by offering an alternative to Euro-American popular culture's definitions of what it means to be Native American. As a mythological figure, Thomas exists beyond the boundaries of the visual and written ethnocentric stories of European conquest; he cannot be commercialized and commodified. In addition, Thomas is a more powerful hero than the Lone Ranger, whose actions are restricted by the static generic constraints of his narrative.

In "The Only Traffic Signal on the Reservation Doesn't Flash Red Anymore," Victor explains the significance of Tonto's uprising in the title of Alexie's short story collection. He says, "It's the small things that hurt the most. The white waitress who wouldn't take an order, Tonto, the Washington Redskins" (49). The story of Tonto's rebellion, briefly encapsulated in the title, is Alexie's revision and subversion of the legend of the Lone Ranger and, concomitantly, an attempt at Indian self-representation and an effort to alleviate the hurt of characters like Victor. Thomas Builds-the-Fire, like Alexie, is a storyteller who subverts the [p. 60] image of Tonto constructed by the dominant culture. Thomas revisits and enlivens Spokane history in his search for answers to what being Native American in the twentieth century means; he does not seek answers in the popular culture propaganda that, like an omnipresent white noise, silences all other narratives. In his essay "White Men Can't Drum," Alexie writes, "What does it mean to be a man? What does it mean to be Indian? What does it mean to be an Indian man? I press the mute button on the remote control so that everyone can hear the answer" (31). Thomas, who mutes the white noise that infects the reservation in order to speak his stories, is the source of this answer in *The Lone Ranger and Tonto Fistfight in Heaven*. . . . [p. 61]

The difference between subverting popular culture narratives and revising Spokane tribal history is that a larger, non-Spokane audience has access to the source of his popular culture allusions. Alexie exploits this accessibility. With a superficial foundation constructed around a fanciful cultural ideal, mass-produced reductive narratives of white culture, such as the small-town middle-class story depicted in *Leave It to Beaver*, are vulnerable to mockery and subversion. In addition, the dominant culture distributes self-defining narratives in a large public arena with technology that disconnects the authors from the stories, thereby relinquishing control of audience interpretation. By intervening in a media the dominant culture privileges, Alexie claims an authoritative place from which to speak. Once he occupies an authoritative space, his narrative subversions enliven the voices the dominant culture's stories of conquest silence and exposes the absurd incongruities between the European and Euro-American narratives and what Cogewea in Mourning Dove's novel calls "actual conditions."

The cumulative effect of Alexie's attention to the practice of storytelling is to privilege the narrative power to create perception and, therefore, a culturally sanctioned version of reality. European and Euro-American writers had presented their uncontested version of history for hundreds of years. As Louis Owens states in *Other Destinies: Understanding the American Indian Novel*, "Native cultures — their voices systematically silenced — had no part in the ongoing discourse that evolved over several centuries to define the utterance 'Indian' in the language of the invaders" (*Other* 7). Alexie revises the narratives from the perspective of the invaded, and the cultural conflict becomes a battle of stories, or, more precisely, a battle between storytellers. By telling the same stories over and over again, Euro-Americans make the stories one-dimensional, static, and vulnerable to parodic revision. Alexie exploits this weakness by intervening in the narratives, exposing their destructive cultural biases and ideologies, and re-visioning them to tell new tales of Native American resistance. [p. 66]

Notes

[1]See Terrace, *The Complete Encyclopedia of Television Programs: 1947-1979*, 575-76. *The Lone Ranger* ran for 221 episodes between September 15, 1949, and September 4, 1965. An additional 26 episodes of an animated version ran between September 10, 1966, and September 6, 1969. A radio program of *The Lone Ranger* preceded the television and subsequent cinematic incarnations.

[2]In her article "Reservation Home Movies: Sherman Alexie's Poetry," Jennifer Gillan discusses how Alexie, in his poetry and several short stories from *The Lone Ranger and Tonto Fistfight in Heaven*, confronts and attempts to resist the dominant culture's technology and the ubiquitous, destructive images disseminated by that technology.

[3]Robert H. Ruby and John A. Brown have written two histories of the Spokane, *The Spokane Indians: Children of the Sun* and *Half-Sun on the Columbia: A Biography of Chief Moses*. For their account of the massacre of the Spokane's horses, see *The Spokane Indians*, 136-37. Alexie includes *The Spokane Indians: Children of the Sun* on the "Acknowledgments" page of *Reservation Blues*.

[4]For an account of Qualchan's hanging, see Ruby and Brown, *The Spokane Indians: Children of the Sun*, 139–40. [p. 67]

Works Cited

Alexie, Sherman. *The Business of Fancydancing*. Brooklyn, NY: Hanging Loose, 1992. Print.

——. *The Lone Ranger and Tonto Fistfight in Heaven*. New York: Harper, 1994. Print.

——. "White Men Can't Drum." *New York Times Magazine* 4 Oct. 1992: 30–31. Print.

Berkhofer, Robert F., Jr. *The White Man's Indian: Images of the American Indian from Columbus to the Present*. New York: Vintage, 1978. Print.

Deloria, Vine, Jr. *God Is Red: A Native View of Religion*. 1972. Golden, CO: Fulcrum, 1994. Print.

Erdrich, Louise. *Love Medicine*. New and Expanded Edition. New York: Harper, 1993. Print.

Gillan, Jennifer. "Reservation Home Movies: Sherman Alexie's Poetry." *American Literature* 68.1 (1996): 91–110. Print.

Owens, Louis. *Bone Game: A Novel*. Norman: U of Oklahoma P, 1994. Print.

——. *Other Destinies: Understanding the American Indian Novel*. Norman: U of Oklahoma P, 1992. Print.

Pearce, Roy Harvey. *Savagism and Civilization: A Study of the Indian and the American Mind*. 1967. Berkeley: U of California P, 1988. Print.

Ruby, Robert H., and John A. Brown. *Half-Sun on the Columbia: A Biography of Chief Moses*. Norman: U of Oklahoma P, 1965. Print.

——. *The Spokane Indians: Children of the Sun*. Norman: U of Oklahoma P, 1970. Print.

Terrace, Vincent. *The Complete Encyclopedia of Television Programs: 1947–1979*. Volume 1, A–L. New York: AS Barnes, 1979. Print.

Welch, James. *Winter in the Blood*. New York: Penguin, 1974. Print.

RESPONDING THROUGH Writing

Here are some suggestions for writing on Sherman Alexie, but for a chapter like this one, you should not limit yourself to these topics. An important purpose behind it is learning how to find good topics on your own.

PAPERS USING NO OUTSIDE SOURCES

Literary Analysis Papers

1. Write an analytical paper discussing the narrators, and the effect of their use, in "This Is What It Means to Say Phoenix, Arizona" (p. 282) and "The Lone Ranger and Tonto Fistfight in Heaven" (p. 291).

2. Write a paper on the complexity of love and trust in "This Is What It Means to Say Phoenix, Arizona" (p. 282) and "The Lone Ranger and Tonto Fistfight in Heaven" (p. 291).

Comparison-Contrast Papers

3. Write a paper comparing and contrasting Thomas and Victor in "This Is What It Means to Say Phoenix, Arizona" (p. 282) and explaining what Sherman Alexie is bringing out by juxtaposing them in the story.

4. Write a paper comparing and contrasting the narrative techniques and their effects in "This Is What It Means to Say Phoenix, Arizona" (p. 282) and "The Lone Ranger and Tonto Fistfight in Heaven" (p. 291).

Cultural Studies Papers

5. Write a paper analyzing the thematic use of allusions to aspects of mainstream popular culture in "The Lone Ranger and Tonto Fistfight in Heaven" (p. 291).

6. Write a paper on the theme of "outsiders" in "This Is What It Means to Say Phoenix, Arizona" (p. 282) and "The Lone Ranger and Tonto Fistfight in Heaven" (p. 291).

PAPERS USING LIMITED OUTSIDE SOURCES

Literary Analysis Papers

1. Joseph L. Coulombe says that "[r]eaders are not passive receptacles; they engage, question, resist, learn, and grow during the reading process" (p. 301). Write a paper discussing techniques Sherman Alexie uses to engage readers in his fiction and examining the effects of such reader engagement.

2. Write a paper on the importance of "memories, dreams, and voices" (DeNuccio, p. 302) in "This Is What It Means to Say Phoenix, Arizona" (p. 282) and "The Lone Ranger and Tonto Fistfight in Heaven" (p. 291).

Comparison-Contrast Papers

3. Write a paper comparing and contrasting the types of humor and its uses and effects in "This Is What It Means to Say Phoenix, Arizona" (p. 282) and "The Lone Ranger and Tonto Fistfight in Heaven" (p. 291).

4. In "Superman and Me" (p. 4), Sherman Alexie says he read "to save [his] life." Write a paper comparing and contrasting what Alexie *says* there, in a nonfiction essay, and in the interview with Åse Nygren, with what he *does* in "This Is What It Means to Say Phoenix, Arizona" (p. 282) and "The Lone Ranger and Tonto Fistfight in Heaven" (p. 291). In the fiction, is he also *writing* to save his life?

Cultural Studies Papers

5. Write a paper that examines "This Is What It Means to Say Phoenix, Arizona" (p. 282) and "The Lone Ranger and Tonto Fistfight in Heaven" (p. 291) as tales of Native American resistance (Cox, p. 305).

6. In his interview with Åse Nygren, Sherman Alexie says Native Americans are "lost. We're always wandering" (p. 299). Write a paper that explores a motif of wandering in "This Is What It Means to Say Phoenix, Arizona" (p. 282) and "The Lone Ranger and Tonto Fistfight in Heaven" (p. 291).

PAPERS INVOLVING FURTHER RESEARCH

Literary Analysis Paper

1. Write a research paper on the archetypal Trickster figure in Native American mythology and literature, focusing particularly on how it is adapted and used in selected works by Sherman Alexie.

2. Write a research paper on a recurring symbol (such as salmon, dancing, 7-11 stores, or many others) in Sherman Alexie's works, both fiction and poetry, and its effect or importance in his thinking or writing.

Comparison-Contrast Papers

3. Write a paper comparing and contrasting how action, characters, and details are handled in "This Is What It Means to Say Phoenix, Arizona" (p. 282) and the movie or screenplay of *Smoke Signals*. You might, for example, focus on what such a comparison shows about differences between writing fiction and screenwriting.

4. Do research on the depiction of Native Americans in popular culture (especially in films, some before 1960 and some after), and use what you find to write a paper in which you compare and contrast those stereotypes with how Sherman Alexie depicts his characters.

Cultural Studies Papers

5. Write a paper on Sherman Alexie's use of baseball and basketball in his writings, focusing on the importance of sports in mainstream culture and Native American culture. Doing so will require reading some of his poetry and more of his fiction and reading literary critics who have worked on this topic.

6. Write a paper on the importance of story in Sherman Alexie's thought and works. Doing so will require reading some of his poetry and more of his fiction and reading literary critics who have explored this topic.

A Collection of Stories

CHAPTER 11

Investigating Various Vistas

FLASH FICTION

There is a fascinating and popular fiction genre that packs an entire short story into a neatly delivered page or two, a few paragraphs, or even a smattering of sentences. Although it's known variously as flash fiction, the short-short, sudden fiction, or Blaster, we use the term *flash fiction* in this book. You may wonder how such a form can even be called a story. That is certainly one of the challenges to the author: how to create a story in such a confined structure. The reader has to be plunged immediately into the heart of the work and moved to its conclusion at a pace that, while propelling her or him along to a direct ending, also allows for an interval for pausing to reflect.

Suffice it to say that what is left out of the story is often as important as what is present on the page. Flash fiction, though compressed, is never over before it begins. If anything, it begins after it's over. You may wonder what happened, how something so brief hit you so hard. So, what then is this form? How can we define it? Well, it's one that slips between the cracks of categorization. It's not a prose poem, not an anecdote, not a sketch or fragment, not a joke, quick take, or summary. Perhaps its only clear characteristic is its protean nature. Its very limitations of scale lead each writer to define the form by the story itself. Try defining it yourself as you read these examples. (For more information about the authors included here, see their listings in "Biographical Sketches," p. 1371.)

Ann Beattie b. 1947

Snow [1986]

I remember the cold night you brought in a pile of logs and a chipmunk jumped off as you lowered your arms. "What do you think *you're* doing in here?" you said, as it ran through the living room. It went through the library and stopped at the front door as though it knew the house well. This would be difficult for anyone to believe, except perhaps as the subject of a poem. Our first week in the house was spent scraping, finding some of the house's secrets, like wallpaper underneath wallpaper. In the kitchen, a pattern of white-gold trellises supported purple grapes as big and round as Ping-Pong balls. When we painted the walls yellow, I thought of the bits of grape that remained underneath and imagined the vine popping through, the way some plants can tenaciously push through anything. The day of the big snow, when you had to shovel the walk and couldn't find your cap and asked me how to wind a towel so that it would stay on your head — you, in the white towel turban, like a crazy king of the snow. People liked the idea of our being together, leaving the city for the country. So many people visited, and the fireplace made all of them want to tell amazing stories: the child who happened to be standing on the right corner when the door of the ice-cream truck came open and hundreds of Popsicles cascaded out; the man standing on the beach, sand sparkling in the sun, one bit glinting more than the rest, stooping to find a diamond ring. Did they talk about amazing things because they thought we'd turn into one of them? Now I think they probably guessed it wouldn't work. It was as hopeless as giving a child a matched cup and saucer. Remember the night, out on the lawn, knee-deep in snow, chins pointed at the sky as the wind whirled down all that whiteness? It seemed that the world had been turned upside down, and we were looking into an enormous field of Queen Anne's lace. Later, headlights off, our car was the first to ride through the newly fallen snow. The world outside the car looked solarized.

You remember it differently. You remember that the cold settled in stages, that a small curve of light was shaved from the moon night after night, until you were no longer surprised the sky was black, that the chipmunk ran to hide in the dark, not simply to a door that led to its escape. Our visitors told the same stories people always tell. One night, giving me a lesson in storytelling, you said, "Any life will seem dramatic if you omit mention of most of it."

This, then, for drama: I drove back to that house not long ago. It was April, and Allen had died. In spite of all the visitors, Allen, next door, had been the good friend in bad times. I sat with his wife in their living room, looking out the glass doors to the backyard, and there was Allen's pool, still covered with black plastic that had been stretched across it for winter. It had rained, and as the rain fell, the cover collected more and more water until it finally spilled onto the concrete. When I left that day, I drove past what had been our house. Three or four crocus were blooming in the front — just a few dots of white, no field of snow. I felt embarrassed for them. They couldn't compete.

This is a story, told the way you say stories should be told: Somebody grew up, fell in love, and spent a winter with her lover in the country. This, of course, is the barest outline, and futile to discuss. It's as pointless as throwing birdseed on the ground while snow still falls fast. Who expects small things to survive when even the largest get lost? People forget years and remember moments. Seconds and symbols are left to sum things up: the black shroud over the pool. Love, in its shortest form, becomes a word. What I remember about all that time is one winter. The snow. Even now, saying "snow," my lips move so that they kiss the air.

No mention has been made of the snowplow that seemed always to be   5 there, scraping snow off our narrow road — an artery cleared, though neither of us could have said where the heart was.

Lydia Davis b. 1947

What She Knew   [1986]

People did not know what she knew, that she was not really a woman but a man, often a fat man, but more often, probably, an old man. The fact that she was an old man made it hard for her to be a young woman. It was hard for her to talk to a young man, for instance, though the young man was clearly interested in her. She had to ask herself, Why is this young man flirting with this old man?

Dave Eggers b. 1970

Accident   [2005]

You all get out of your cars. You are alone in yours, and there are three teenagers in theirs, an older Camaro in new condition. The accident was your fault, and you walk over to tell them this.

Walking over to their car, which you have ruined, it occurs to you that if the three teenagers are angry teenagers, this encounter could be very unpleasant. You pulled into an intersection, obstructing them, and their car hit yours. They have every right to be upset, or livid, or even violence-contemplating.

As you approach, you see that their driver's side door won't open. The driver pushes against it, and you are reminded of scenes where drivers are stuck in submerged cars. Soon they all exit through the passenger side door and walk around the Camaro, inspecting the damage. None of them is hurt, but the car is wrecked. "Just bought this today," the driver says. He is 18, blond, average in all ways. "Today?" you ask.

You are a bad person, you think. You also think: what a dorky car for a teenager to buy in 2005. "Yeah, today," he says, then sighs. You tell him that you are sorry. That you are so, so sorry. That it was your fault and that you will cover all costs.

You exchange insurance information, and you find yourself, minute by 5 minute, ever more thankful that none of these teenagers has punched you, or even made a remark about your being drunk, which you are not, or being stupid, which you are, often. You become more friendly with all of them, and you realize that you are much more connected to them, particularly to the driver, than possible in perhaps any other way.

You have done him and his friends harm, in a way, and you jeopardized their health, and now you are so close you feel like you share a heart. He knows your name and you know his, and you almost killed him and, because you got so close to doing so but didn't, you want to fall on him, weeping, because you are so lonely, so lonely always, and all contact is contact, and all contact makes us so grateful we want to cry and dance and cry and cry.

In a moment of clarity, you finally understand why boxers, who want so badly to hurt each other, can rest their heads on the shoulders of their opponents, can lean against one another like tired lovers, so thankful for a moment of peace.

Ray Gonzalez   b. 1952

The Jalapeño Contest   [2001]

Freddy and his brother Tesoro have not seen each other in five years, and they sit at the kitchen table in Freddy's house and have a jalapeño contest. A large bowl of big green and orange jalapeño peppers sits between the two brothers. A salt shaker and two small glasses of beer accompany this feast. When Tesoro nods his head, the two men begin to eat the raw jalapeños. The contest is to see which man can eat more peppers. It is a ritual from their father, but the two brothers tried it only once, years ago. Both quit after two peppers and laughed it off. This time, things are different. They are older and have to prove a point. Freddy eats his first one more slowly than Tesoro, who takes two bites to finish his and is now on his second. Neither says anything, though a close study of each man's face would tell you that the sudden burst of jalapeño energy does not waste time in changing the eater's perception of reality. Freddy works on his second as Tesoro rips into his fourth. Freddy is already sweating from his head and is surprised to see that Tesoro's fat face has not changed its steady, consuming look. Tesoro's long black hair is neatly combed, and not one bead of sweat has popped out. He is the first to sip from the beer before hitting his fifth jalapeño. Freddy leans back as the table begins to sway in his damp vision. He coughs, and a sharp pain rips through his chest. Tesoro attempts to laugh at his brother, but Freddy sees it is something else. As Freddy finishes his third jalapeño, Tesoro begins to breathe faster upon swallowing his sixth. The contest momentarily stops as both brothers shift in their seats and the sweat pours down their faces. Freddy clutches his stomach as he reaches for a fourth delight. Tesoro has not taken his seventh, and it is clear to Freddy that his brother is suffering big-time. There is a bright blue bird sitting on Tesoro's head, and Tesoro is struggling to laugh because Freddy has a huge red spider crawling on top of his head. Freddy wipes the sweat from his eyes and finishes his fourth pepper. Tesoro sips more beer, sprinkles salt on the tip of his jalapeño, and bites it down to the stem. Freddy, who has not touched his beer, stares in amazement as two Tesoros sit in front of him. They both rise hastily, their beer guts pushing the table against Freddy, who leans back as the two Tesoros waver in the kitchen light. Freddy hears a tremendous fart erupt from his brother, who sits down again. Freddy holds his fifth jalapeño and can't breathe. Tesoro's face is purple, but the blue bird has been replaced by a burning flame of light that weaves over Tesoro's shiny head. Freddy is convinced that he is having a heart attack as he watches his brother fight for breath. Freddy bites into his fifth as Tesoro flips his eighth jalapeño into his mouth, stem and all. This is it. Freddy goes into convulsions and drops to the floor as he tries to reach for his glass of beer. He shakes on the dirty floor as the huge animal that is Tesoro pitches forward and throws up millions of jalapeño seeds all over the table. The last thing Freddy sees before he passes out is his brother's body levitating above the table as an angel, dressed in green jalapeño robes, floats into the room, extends a hand to Tesoro, and floats away with him. When Freddy wakes minutes later, he gets up and makes it to the bathroom before his body lets go through his pants. As he reaches the bathroom door, he turns and gazes upon the jalapeño plants growing healthy and large on the kitchen table, thick peppers hanging under their leaves, their branches immersed in the largest pile of yellow jalapeño seeds Freddy has ever seen.

Jamaica Kincaid   b. 1949

Girl   [1978]

Wash the white clothes on Monday and put them on the stone heap; wash the color clothes on Tuesday and put them on the clothesline to dry; don't walk barehead in the hot sun; cook pumpkin fritters in very hot sweet oil; soak your little cloths right after you take them off; when buying cotton to make yourself a nice blouse, be sure that it doesn't have gum on it, because that way it won't hold up well after a wash; soak salt fish overnight before you cook it; is it true that you sing benna° in Sunday school?; always eat your food in such a way that it won't turn someone else's stomach; on Sundays try to walk like a lady and not like the slut you are so bent on becoming; don't sing benna in Sunday school; you mustn't speak to wharf-rat boys, not even to give directions; don't eat fruits on the street — flies will follow you; *but I don't sing benna on Sundays at all and never in Sunday school*; this is how to sew on a button; this is how to make a buttonhole for the button you have just sewed on; this is how to hem a dress when you see the hem coming down and so to prevent yourself from looking like the slut I know you are so bent on becoming; this is how you iron your father's khaki shirt so that it doesn't have a crease; this is how you iron your father's khaki pants so that they don't have a crease; this is how you grow okra — far from the house, because okra tree harbors red ants; when you are growing dasheen,° make sure it gets plenty of water or else it makes your throat itch when you are eating it; this is how you sweep a corner; this is how you sweep a whole house; this is how you sweep a yard; this is how you smile to someone you don't like too much; this is how you smile to someone you don't like at all; this is how you smile to someone you like completely; this is how you set a table for tea; this is how you set a table for dinner; this is how you set a table for dinner with an important guest; this is how you set a table for lunch; this is how you set a table for breakfast; this is how to behave in the presence of men who don't know you very well, and this way they won't recognize immediately the slut I have warned you against becoming; be sure to wash every day, even if it is with your own spit; don't squat down to play marbles — you are not a boy, you know; don't pick people's flowers — you might catch something; don't throw stones at blackbirds, because it might not be a blackbird at all; this

You can explore Jamaica Kincaid and "Girl" in depth, including images and cultural documents, with VirtuaLit Fiction at bedfordstmartins.com/rewritinglit.

is how to make a bread pudding; this is how to make doukona;° this is how to make pepper pot; this is how to make a good medicine for a cold; this is how to make a good medicine to throw away a child before it even becomes a child; this is how to catch a fish; this is how to throw back a fish you don't like, and that way something bad won't fall on you; this is how to bully a man; this is how a man bullies you; this is how to love a man, and if this doesn't work there are other ways, and if they don't work don't feel too bad about giving up; this is how to spit up in the air if you feel like it, and this is how to move quick so that it doesn't fall on you; this is how to make ends meet; always squeeze bread to make sure it's fresh; *but what if the baker won't let me feel the bread?*; you mean to say that after all you are really going to be the kind of woman who the baker won't let near the bread?

---

benna: Calypso music.   **dasheen:** Caribbean herb.   **doukona:** A spicy Caribbean pudding.

Michael Oppenheimer b. 1943

The Paring Knife   [1982]

I found a knife under the refrigerator while the woman I love and I were cleaning our house. It was a small paring knife that we lost many years before and had
since forgotten about. I showed the knife to the woman I love and she said, "Oh.
Where did you find it?" After I told her, she put the knife on the table and then
went into the next room and continued to clean. While I cleaned the kitchen floor,
I remembered something that happened four years before that explained how the
knife had gotten under the refrigerator.

We had eaten a large dinner and had drunk many glasses of wine. We
turned all the lights out, took our clothing off, and went to bed. We thought
we would make love, but something happened and we had an argument while
making love. We had never experienced such a thing. We both became extremely angry. I said some very hurtful things to the woman I love. She kicked
at me in bed and I got out and went into the kitchen. I fumbled for a chair and
sat down. I wanted to rest my arms on the table and then rest my head in my
arms, but I felt the dirty dishes on the table and they were in the way. I became
incensed. I swept everything that was on the table onto the floor. The noise was
tremendous, but then the room was very quiet and I suddenly felt sad. I thought
I had destroyed everything. I began to cry. The woman I love came into the
kitchen and asked if I was all right. I said, "Yes." She turned the light on and
we looked at the kitchen floor. Nothing much was broken, but the floor was
very messy. We both laughed and then went back to bed and made love. The
next morning we cleaned up the mess, but obviously overlooked the knife.

I was about to ask the woman I love if she remembered that incident when
she came in from the next room and without saying a word, picked up the knife
from the table and slid it back under the refrigerator.

TWO SHORT STORY PAIRINGS

As we note on page 157, making connections between things is an important part of reading, and of learning generally. Connections within stories
are important (see p. 157 on juxtapositions, for example) as is connecting
stories with related stories. In Chapters 11, 20, and 26 — the collections
of additional short stories, poems, and plays — we include pairings of
works that can be interesting and illuminating to consider together. Below
are two pairs of stories that in some ways are very different but also connect with each other in ways that might be surprising. With both pairings
think about what connections there are across ethnic and cultural contexts. Compare and contrast the ways these distinct voices deal with their
subjects. Consider also the differences and similarities in stories written

(continued on next page)

during time periods quite distant from one another. Think about how the author of each story in both pairings works with stylistic elements, images, tone, setting, and point of view. Where do you notice particular connections? In what ways do they differ in their handling? Imagine a conversation between the two paired writers. What would they ask one another? What would they say about one another's work? When paired, what in each story comes to the foreground when you think about it in the context of the other story?

ENTRY POINTS   Both of the following stories are set in California and deal with the relationship between husbands (good men who want the best for their wives) and their wives, each of whom is seeking an identity that goes beyond the one society has assigned her. However, the times and the cultural contexts are different. As you read the stories and reflect on them, consider the ways the authors deal with a situation common to many time periods and societies. Do you feel the times and cultures influence the characters' responses? If so, how? If not, why? Do you think that certain situations and responses to them can be the same across time and cultures? Why or why not?

John Steinbeck   1902–1968

The Chrysanthemums   [1937]

The high grey-flannel fog of winter closed off the Salinas Valley from the sky and from all the rest of the world. On every side it sat like a lid on the mountains and made of the great valley a closed pot. On the broad, level land floor the gang plows bit deep and left the black earth shining like metal where the shares had cut. On the foothill ranches across the Salinas River, the yellow stubble fields seemed to be bathed in pale cold sunshine, but there was no sunshine in the valley now in December. The thick willow scrub along the river flamed with sharp and positive yellow leaves.

It was a time of quiet and of waiting. The air was cold and tender. A light wind blew up from the southwest so that the farmers were mildly hopeful of a good rain before long; but fog and rain do not go together.

Across the river, on Henry Allen's foothill ranch there was little work to be done, for the hay was cut and stored and the orchards were plowed up to receive the rain deeply when it should come. The cattle on the higher slopes were becoming shaggy and rough-coated.

Elisa Allen, working in her flower garden, looked down across the yard and saw Henry, her husband, talking to two men in business suits. The three of them stood by the tractor shed, each man with one foot on the side of the little Fordson. They smoked cigarettes and studied the machine as they talked.

Elisa watched them for a moment and then went back to her work. She was   5 thirty-five. Her face was lean and strong and her eyes were as clear as water. Her figure looked blocked and heavy in her gardening costume, a man's black hat pulled low down over her eyes, clod-hopper shoes, a figured print dress almost completely covered by a big corduroy apron with four big pockets to hold the snips, the trowel and scratcher, the seeds and the knife she worked with. She wore heavy leather gloves to protect her hands while she worked.

She was cutting down the old year's chrysanthemum stalks with a pair of short and powerful scissors. She looked down toward the men by the tractor shed now and then. Her face was eager and mature and handsome; even her work with the scissors was over-eager, over-powerful. The chrysanthemum stems seemed too small and easy for her energy.

She brushed a cloud of hair out of her eyes with the back of her glove, and left a smudge of earth on her cheek in doing it. Behind her stood the neat white farm house with red geraniums close-banked around it as high as the windows. It was a hard-swept looking little house, with hard-polished windows, and a clean mud-mat on the front steps.

Elisa cast another glance toward the tractor shed. The strangers were getting into their Ford coupe. She took off a glove and put her strong fingers down into the forest of new green chrysanthemum sprouts that were growing around the old roots. She spread the leaves and looked down among the close-growing stems. No aphids were there, no sowbugs or snails or cutworms. Her terrier fingers destroyed such pests before they could get started.

Elisa started at the sound of her husband's voice. He had come near quietly, and he leaned over the wire fence that protected her flower garden from cattle and dogs and chickens.

"At it again," he said. "You've got a strong new crop coming."   10

Elisa straightened her back and pulled on the gardening glove again. "Yes. They'll be strong this coming year." In her tone and on her face there was a little smugness.

"You've got a gift with things," Henry observed. "Some of those yellow chrysanthemums you had this year were ten inches across. I wish you'd work out in the orchard and raise some apples that big."

Her eyes sharpened. "Maybe I could do it, too. I've a gift with things, all right. My mother had it. She could stick anything in the ground and make it grow. She said it was having planters' hands that knew how to do it."

"Well, it sure works with flowers," he said.

"Henry, who were those men you were talking to?"   15

"Why, sure, that's what I came to tell you. They were from the Western Meat Company. I sold those thirty head of three-year-old steers. Got nearly my own price, too."

"Good," she said. "Good for you."

"And I thought," he continued, "I thought how it's Saturday afternoon, and we might go into Salinas for dinner at a restaurant, and then to a picture show—to celebrate, you see."

"Good," she repeated. "Oh, yes. That will be good."

Henry put on his joking tone. "There's fights tonight. How'd you like to go   20 to the fights?"

"Oh, no," she said breathlessly. "No, I wouldn't like fights."

"Just fooling, Elisa. We'll go to a movie. Let's see. It's two now. I'm going to take Scotty and bring down those steers from the hill. It'll take us maybe two hours. We'll go in town about five and have dinner at the Cominos Hotel. Like that?"

"Of course I'll like it. It's good to eat away from home."

"All right, then. I'll go get up a couple of horses."

She said, "I'll have plenty of time to transplant some of these sets, I   25 guess."

She heard her husband calling Scotty down by the barn. And a little later she saw the two men ride up the pale yellow hillside in search of the steers.

There was a little square sandy bed kept for rooting the chrysanthemums. With her trowel she turned the soil over and over, and smoothed it and patted it firm. Then she dug ten parallel trenches to receive the sets. Back at the chrysanthemum bed she pulled out the little crisp shoots, trimmed off the leaves of each one with her scissors and laid it on a small orderly pile.

A squeak of wheels and plod of hoofs came from the road. Elisa looked up. The country road ran along the dense bank of willows and cottonwoods that bordered the river, and up this road came a curious vehicle, curiously drawn. It was an old spring-wagon, with a round canvas top on it like the cover of a prairie schooner. It was drawn by an old bay horse and a little grey-and-white burro. A big stubble-bearded man sat between the cover flaps and drove the crawling team. Underneath the wagon, between the hind wheels, a lean and rangy mongrel dog walked sedately. Words were painted on the canvas, in clumsy, crooked letters. "Pots, pans, knives, sisors, lawn mores, Fixed." Two rows of articles, and the triumphantly definitive "Fixed" below. The black paint had run down in little sharp points beneath each letter.

Elisa, squatting on the ground, watched to see the crazy, loose-jointed wagon pass by. But it didn't pass. It turned into the farm road in front of her house, crooked old wheels skirling and squeaking. The rangy dog darted from between the wheels and ran ahead. Instantly the two ranch shepherds flew out at him. Then all three stopped, and with stiff and quivering tails, with taut straight legs, with ambassadorial dignity, they slowly circled, sniffing daintily. The caravan pulled up to Elisa's wire fence and stopped. Now the newcomer dog, feeling out-numbered, lowered his tail and retired under the wagon with raised hackles and bared teeth.

The man on the wagon seat called out, "That's a bad dog in a fight when he gets started." 30

Elisa laughed. "I see he is. How soon does he generally get started?"

The man caught up her laughter and echoed it heartily. "Sometimes not for weeks and weeks," he said. He climbed stiffly down, over the wheel. The horse and the donkey drooped like unwatered flowers.

Elisa saw that he was a very big man. Although his hair and beard were greying, he did not look old. His worn black suit was wrinkled and spotted with grease. The laughter had disappeared from his face and eyes the moment his laughing voice ceased. His eyes were dark, and they were full of the brooding that gets in the eyes of teamsters and of sailors. The calloused hands he rested on the wire fence were cracked, and every crack was a black line. He took off his battered hat.

"I'm off my general road, ma'am," he said. "Does this dirt road cut over across the river to the Los Angeles highway?"

Elisa stood up and shoved the thick scissors in her apron pocket. "Well, yes, 35 it does, but it winds around and then fords the river. I don't think your team could pull through the sand."

He replied with some asperity, "It might surprise you what them beasts can pull through."

"When they get started?" she asked.

He smiled for a second. "Yes. When they get started."

"Well," said Elisa, "I think you'll save time if you go back to the Salinas road and pick up the highway there."

He drew a big finger down the chicken wire and made it sing. "I ain't in any 40 hurry, ma'am. I go from Seattle to San Diego and back every year. Takes all my time. About six months each way. I aim to follow nice weather."

Elisa took off her gloves and stuffed them in the apron pocket with the scissors. She touched the under edge of her man's hat, searching for fugitive hairs. "That sounds like a nice kind of a way to live," she said.

He leaned confidentially over the fence. "Maybe you noticed the writing on my wagon. I mend pots and sharpen knives and scissors. You got any of them things to do?"

"Oh, no," she said quickly. "Nothing like that." Her eyes hardened with resistance.

"Scissors is the worst thing," he explained. "Most people just ruin scissors trying to sharpen 'em, but I know how. I got a special tool. It's a little bobbit kind of thing, and patented. But it sure does the trick."

"No. My scissors are all sharp." 45

"All right, then. Take a pot," he continued earnestly, "a bent pot, or a pot with a hole. I can make it like new so you don't have to buy no new ones. That's a saving for you."

"No," she said shortly. "I tell you I have nothing like that for you to do."

His face fell to an exaggerated sadness. His voice took on a whining under-tone. "I ain't had a thing to do today. Maybe I won't have no supper tonight. You see I'm off my regular road. I know folks on the highway clear from Seattle to San Diego. They save their things for me to sharpen up because they know I do it so good and save them money."

"I'm sorry," Elisa said irritably. "I haven't anything for you to do."

His eyes left her face and fell to searching the ground. They roamed about   50
until they came to the chrysanthemum bed where she had been working. "What's them plants, ma'am?"

The irritation and resistance melted from Elisa's face. "Oh, those are chry-santhemums, giant whites and yellows. I raise them every year, bigger than anybody around here."

"Kind of a long-stemmed flower? Looks like a quick puff of colored smoke?" he asked.

"That's it. What a nice way to describe them."

"They smell kind of nasty till you get used to them," he said.

"Its a good bitter smell," she retorted, "not nasty at all."   55

He changed his tone quickly. "I like the smell myself."

"I had ten-inch blooms this year," she said.

The man leaned farther over the fence. "Look. I know a lady down the road a piece, has got the nicest garden you ever seen. Got nearly every kind of flower but no chrysantheums. Last time I was mending a copper-bottom washtub for her (that's a hard job but I do it good), she said to me, 'If you ever run acrost some nice chrysantheums I wish you'd try to get me a few seeds.' That's what she told me."

Elisa's eyes grew alert and eager. "She couldn't have known much about chrysanthemums. You *can* raise them from seed, but it's much easier to root the little sprouts you see here."

"Oh," he said. "I s'pose I can't take none to her, then."   60

"Why yes you can," Elisa cried. "I can put some in damp sand, and you can carry them right along with you. They'll take root in the pot if you keep them damp. And then she can transplant them."

"She'd sure like to have some, ma'am. You say they're nice ones?"

"Beautiful," she said. "Oh, beautiful." Her eyes shone. She tore off the bat-tered hat and shook out her dark pretty hair. "I'll put them in a flower pot, and you can take them right with you. Come into the yard."

While the man came through the picket gate Elisa ran excitedly along the geranium-bordered path to the back of the house. And she returned carrying a big red flower pot. The gloves were forgotten now. She kneeled on the ground by the starting bed and dug up the sandy soil with her fingers and scooped it into the bright new flower pot. Then she picked up the little pile of shoots she had prepared. With her strong fingers she pressed them into the sand and tamped around them with her knuckles. The man stood over her. "I'll tell you what to do," she said. "You remember so you can tell the lady."

"Yes, I'll try to remember."   65

"Well, look. These will take root in about a month. Then she must set them out, about a foot apart in good rich earth like this, see?" She lifted a handful of dark soil for him to look at. "They'll grow fast and tall. Now remember this: In July tell her to cut them down, about eight inches from the ground."

"Before they bloom?" he asked.

"Yes, before they bloom." Her face was tight with eagerness. "They'll grow right up again. About the last of September the buds will start."

She stopped and seemed perplexed. "It's the budding that takes the most care," she said hesitantly. "I don't know how to tell you." She looked deep into his eyes, searchingly. Her mouth opened a little, and she seemed to be listening. "I'll try to tell you," she said "Did you ever hear of planting hands?"

"Can't say I have, ma'am."   70

"Well, I can only tell you what it feels like. It's when you're picking off the buds you don't want. Everything goes right down into your fingertips. You watch your fingers work. They do it themselves. You can feel how it is. They pick and pick the buds. They never make a mistake. They're with the plant. Do you see? Your fingers and the plant. You can feel that, right up your arm. They know. They never make a mistake. You can feel it. When you're like that you can't do anything wrong. Do you see that? Can you understand that?"

She was kneeling on the ground looking up at him. Her breast swelled passionately.

The man's eyes narrowed. He looked away self-consciously. "Maybe I know," he said. "Sometimes in the night in the wagon there—"

Elisa's voice grew husky. She broke in on him, "I've never lived as you do, but I know what you mean. When the night is dark—why, the stars are sharp-pointed, and there's quiet. Why, you rise up and up! Every pointed star gets driven into your body. It's like that. Hot and sharp and—lovely."

Kneeling there, her hand went out toward his legs in the greasy black trou-   75 sers. Her hesitant fingers almost touched the cloth. Then her hand dropped to the ground. She crouched low like a fawning dog.

He said, "It's nice, just like you say. Only when you don't have no dinner, it ain't."

She stood up then, very straight, and her face was ashamed. She held the flower pot out to him and placed it gently in his arms. "Here. Put it in your wagon, on the seat, where you can watch it. Maybe I can find something for you to do."

At the back of the house she dug in the can pile and found two old and battered aluminum saucepans. She carried them back and gave them to him. "Here, maybe you can fix these."

His manner changed. He became professional. "Good as new I can fix them." At the back of his wagon he set a little anvil, and out of an oily tool box dug a small machine hammer. Elisa came through the gate to watch him while he pounded out the dents in the kettles. His mouth grew sure and knowing. At a difficult part of the work he sucked his under-lip.

"You sleep right in the wagon?" Elisa asked.   80

"Right in the wagon, ma'am. Rain or shine I'm dry as a cow in there."

"It must be nice," she said. "It must be very nice. I wish women could do such things."

"It ain't the right kind of a life for a woman."

Her upper lip raised a little, showing her teeth. "How do you know? How can you tell?" she said.

"I don't know, ma'am," he protested. "Of course I don't know. Now here's your kettles, done. You don't have to buy no new ones." 85

"How much?"

"Oh, fifty cents'll do. I keep my prices down and my work good. That's why I have all them satisfied customers up and down the highway."

Elisa brought him a fifty-cent piece from the house and dropped it in his hand. "You might be surprised to have a rival some time. I can sharpen scissors, too. And I can beat the dents out of little pots. I could show you what a woman might do."

He put his hammer back in the oily box and shoved the little anvil out of sight. "It would be a lonely life for a woman, ma'am, and a scarey life, too, with animals creeping under the wagon all night." He climbed over the singletree, steadying himself with a hand on the burro's white rump. He settled himself in the seat, picked up the lines. "Thank you kindly, ma'am," he said. "I'll do like you told me; I'll go back and catch the Salinas road."

"Mind," she called, "if you're long in getting there, keep the sand damp." 90

"Sand, ma'am? . . . Sand? Oh, sure. You mean around the chrysantheums. Sure I will." He clucked his tongue. The beasts leaned luxuriously into their collars. The mongrel dog took his place between the back wheels. The wagon turned and crawled out the entrance road and back the way it had come, along the river.

Elisa stood in front of her wire fence watching the slow progress of the caravan. Her shoulders were straight, her head thrown back, her eyes half-closed, so that the scene came vaguely into them. Her lips moved silently, forming the words "Good-bye—good-bye." Then she whispered, "That's a bright direction. There's a glowing there." The sound of her whisper startled her. She shook herself free and looked about to see whether anyone had been listening. Only the dogs had heard. They lifted their heads toward her from their sleeping in the dust, and then stretched out their chins and settled asleep again. Elisa turned and ran hurriedly into the house.

In the kitchen she reached behind the stove and felt the water tank. It was full of hot water from the noonday cooking. In the bathroom she tore off her soiled clothes and flung them into the corner. And then she scrubbed herself with a little block of pumice, legs and thighs, loins and chest and arms, until her skin was scratched and red. When she had dried herself she stood in front of a mirror in her bedroom and looked at her body. She tightened her stomach and threw out her chest. She turned and looked over her shoulder at her back.

After a while she began to dress, slowly. She put on her newest under-clothing and her nicest stockings and the dress which was the symbol of her prettiness. She worked carefully on her hair, penciled her eyebrows and rouged her lips.

Before she was finished she heard the little thunder of hoofs and the shouts   95 of Henry and his helper as they drove the red steers into the corral. She heard the gate bang shut and set herself for Henry's arrival.

His step sounded on the porch. He entered the house calling, "Elisa, where are you?"

"In my room, dressing. I'm not ready. There's hot water for your bath. Hurry up. It's getting late."

When she heard him splashing in the tub, Elisa laid his dark suit on the bed, and shirt and socks and tie beside it. She stood his polished shoes on the floor beside the bed. Then she went to the porch and sat primly and stiffly down. She looked toward the river road where the willow-line was still yellow with frosted leaves so that under the high grey fog they seemed a thin band of sunshine. This was the only color in the grey afternoon. She sat unmoving for a long time. Her eyes blinked rarely.

Henry came banging out of the door, shoving his tie inside his vest as he came. Elisa stiffened and her face grew tight. Henry stopped short and looked at her. "Why—why, Elisa. You look so nice!"

"Nice? You think I look nice? What do you mean by 'nice'?"   100

Henry blundered on. "I don't know. I mean you look different, strong and happy."

"I am strong? Yes, strong. What do you mean 'strong'?"

He looked bewildered. "You're playing some kind of game," he said helplessly. "It's a kind of a play. You look strong enough to break a calf over your knee, happy enough to eat it like a watermelon."

For a second she lost her rigidity. "Henry! Don't talk like that. You didn't know what you said." She grew complete again. "I'm strong," she boasted. "I never knew before how strong."

Henry looked down toward the tractor shed, and when he brought his eyes   105 back to her, they were his own again. "I'll get out the car. You can put on your coat while I'm starting."

Elisa went into the house. She heard him drive to the gate and idle down his motor, and then she took a long time to put on her hat. She pulled it here and pressed it there. When Henry turned the motor off she slipped into her coat and went out.

The little roadster bounced along on the dirt road by the river, raising the birds and driving the rabbits into the brush. Two cranes flapped heavily over the willow-line and dropped into the river-bed.

Far ahead on the road Elisa saw a dark speck. She knew.

She tried not to look as they passed it, but her eyes would not obey. She whispered to herself sadly, "He might have thrown them off the road. That wouldn't have been much trouble, not very much. But he kept the pot," she explained. "He had to keep the pot. That's why he couldn't get them off the road."

The roadster turned a bend and she saw the caravan ahead. She swung full 110
around toward her husband so she could not see the little covered wagon and
the mismatched team as the car passed them.

In a moment it was over. The thing was done. She did not look back.

She said loudly, to be heard above the motor, "It will be good, tonight, a
good dinner."

"Now you're changed again," Henry complained. He took one hand from
the wheel and patted her knee. "I ought to take you in to dinner oftener. It
would be good for both of us. We get so heavy out on the ranch."

"Henry," she asked, "could we have wine at dinner?"

"Sure we could. Say! That will be fine." 115

She was silent for a while; then she said, "Henry, at those prize fights, do
the men hurt each other very much?"

"Sometimes a little, not often. Why?"

"Well, I've read how they break noses, and blood runs down their chests.
I've read how the fighting gloves get heavy and soggy with blood."

He looked around at her. "What's the matter, Elisa? I didn't know you read
things like that." He brought the car to a stop, then turned to the right over the
Salinas River bridge.

"Do any women ever go to the fights?" she asked. 120

"Oh, sure, some. What's the matter, Elisa? Do you want to go? I don't
think you'd like it, but I'll take you if you really want to go."

She relaxed limply in the seat. "Oh, no. No. I don't want to go. I'm sure I
don't." Her face was turned away from him. "It will be enough if we can have
wine. It will be plenty." She turned up her coat collar so he could not see that
she was crying weakly—like an old woman.

Chitra Banerjee Divakaruni b. 1956

Clothes [1995]

APPROACHING THE AUTHOR

To earn money for her education after coming to the United States in 1976, **Chitra Banerjee Divakaruni** held many odd jobs: selling merchandise in an Indian boutique, slicing bread in a bakery, and washing instruments in a science lab.

For more about her, see page 1380.

The water of the women's lake laps against my breasts, cool, calming. I can
feel it beginning to wash the hot nervousness away from my body. The little
waves tickle my armpits, make my sari float up around me, wet and yellow, like a sunflower after rain. I close my eyes and smell the sweet brown odor of the *ritha* pulp my friends Deepali and Radha are working into my hair so it will glisten with little lights this evening. They scrub with more vigor than usual and wash it out more carefully, because today is a special day. It is the day of my bride-viewing.

"Ei, Sumita! Mita! Are you deaf?" Radha says. "This is the third time I've asked you the same question."

"Look at her, already dreaming about her husband, and she hasn't even seen him yet!" Deepali jokes. Then she adds, the envy in her voice only half hidden, "Who cares about friends from a little Indian village when you're about to go live in America?"

I want to deny it, to say that I will always love them and all the things we did together through my growing-up years—visiting the *charak* fair where we always ate too many sweets, raiding the neighbor's guava tree summer afternoons while the grown-ups slept, telling fairy tales while we braided each other's hair in elaborate patterns we'd invented. *And she married the handsome prince who took her to his kingdom beyond the seven seas.* But already the activities of our girlhood seem to be far in my past, the colors leached out of them, like old sepia photographs.

His name is Somesh Sen, the man who is coming to our house with his   5 parents today and who will be my husband "if I'm lucky enough to be chosen," as my aunt says. He is coming all the way from California. Father showed it to me yesterday, on the metal globe that sits on his desk, a chunky pink wedge on the side of a multicolored slab marked *Untd. Sts. of America.* I touched it and felt the excitement leap all the way up my arm like an electric shock. Then it died away, leaving only a beaten-metal coldness against my fingertips.

For the first time it occurred to me that if things worked out the way everyone was hoping, I'd be going halfway around the world to live with a man I hadn't even met. Would I ever see my parents again? *Don't send me so far away,* I wanted to cry, but of course I didn't. It would be ungrateful. Father had worked so hard to find this match for me. Besides, wasn't it every woman's destiny, as Mother was always telling me, to leave the known for the unknown? She had done it, and her mother before her. *A married woman belongs to her husband, her in-laws.* Hot seeds of tears pricked my eyelids at the unfairness of it.

"Mita Moni, little jewel," Father said, calling me by my childhood name. He put out his hand as though he wanted to touch my face, then let it fall to his side. "He's a good man. Comes from a fine family. He will be kind to you." He was silent for a while. Finally he said, "Come, let me show you the special sari I bought in Calcutta for you to wear at the bride-viewing."

"Are you nervous?" Radha asks as she wraps my hair in a soft cotton towel. Her parents are also trying to arrange a marriage for her. So far three families have come to see her, but no one has chosen her because her skin-color is considered too dark. "Isn't it terrible, not knowing what's going to happen?"

I nod because I don't want to disagree, don't want to make her feel bad by saying that sometimes it's worse when you know what's coming, like I do. I knew it as soon as Father unlocked his mahogany *almirah* and took out the sari.

It was the most expensive sari I had ever seen, and surely the most beauti-   10 ful. Its body was a pale pink, like the dawn sky over the women's lake. The color of transition. Embroidered all over it were tiny stars made out of real gold *zari* thread.

"Here, hold it," said Father.

The sari was unexpectedly heavy in my hands, silk-slippery, a sari to walk carefully in. A sari that could change one's life. I stood there holding it, wanting to weep. I knew that when I wore it, it would hang in perfect pleats to my feet and shimmer in the light of the evening lamps. It would dazzle Somesh and his parents and they would choose me to be his bride.

When the plane takes off, I try to stay calm, to take deep, slow breaths like Father does when he practices yoga. But my hands clench themselves on to the folds of my sari and when I force them open, after the *fasten seat belt* and *no smoking* signs have blinked off, I see they have left damp blotches on the delicate crushed fabric.

We had some arguments about this sari. I wanted a blue one for the journey, because blue is the color of possibility, the color of the sky through which I would be traveling. But Mother said there must be red in it because red is the color of luck for married women. Finally, Father found one to satisfy us both: midnight-blue with a thin red border the same color as the marriage mark I'm wearing on my forehead.

It is hard for me to think of myself as a married woman. I whisper my new 15 name to myself, Mrs. Sumita Sen, but the syllables rustle uneasily in my mouth like a stiff satin that's never been worn.

Somesh had to leave for America just a week after the wedding. He had to get back to the store, he explained to me. He had promised his partner. The store. It seems more real to me than Somesh—perhaps because I know more about it. It was what we had mostly talked about the night after the wedding, the first night we were together alone. It stayed open twenty-four hours, yes, all night, every night, not like the Indian stores which closed at dinnertime and sometimes in the hottest part of the afternoon. That's why his partner needed him back.

The store was called *7-Eleven*. I thought it a strange name, exotic, risky. All the stores I knew were piously named after gods and goddesses—*Ganesh Sweet House, Lakshmi Vastralaya for Fine Saris*—to bring the owners luck.

The store sold all kinds of amazing things—apple juice in cardboard cartons that never leaked; American bread that came in cellophane packages, already cut up; canisters of potato chips, each large grainy flake curved exactly like the next. The large refrigerator with see-through glass doors held beer and wine, which Somesh said were the most popular items.

"That's where the money comes from, especially in the neighborhood where our store is," said Somesh, smiling at the shocked look on my face. (The only places I knew of that sold alcohol were the village toddy shops, "dark, stinking dens of vice," Father called them.) "A lot of Americans drink, you know. It's a part of their culture, not considered immoral, like it is here. And really, there's nothing wrong with it." He touched my lips lightly with his finger. "When you come to California, I'll get you some sweet white wine and you'll see how good it makes you feel. . . ." Now his fingers were stroking my cheeks, my throat, moving downward. I closed my eyes and tried not to jerk away because after all it was my wifely duty.

"It helps if you can think about something else," my friend Madhavi had 20 said when she warned me about what most husbands demanded on the very first night. Two years married, she already had one child and was pregnant with a second one.

I tried to think of the women's lake, the dark cloudy green of the *shapla* leaves that float on the water, but his lips were hot against my skin, his fingers fumbling with buttons, pulling at the cotton night-sari I wore. I couldn't breathe.

"Bite hard on your tongue," Madhavi had advised. "The pain will keep your mind off what's going on down there."

But when I bit down, it hurt so much that I cried out. I couldn't help it although I was ashamed. Somesh lifted his head. I don't know what he saw on my face, but he stopped right away. "Shhh," he said, although I had made myself silent already. "It's OK, we'll wait until you feel like it." I tried to apologize but he smiled it away and started telling me some more about the store.

And that's how it was the rest of the week until he left. We would lie side by side on the big white bridal pillow I had embroidered with a pair of doves for married harmony, and Somesh would describe how the store's front windows were decorated with a flashing neon Dewar's sign and a lighted Budweiser waterfall *this big*. I would watch his hands moving excitedly through the dim air of the bedroom and think that Father had been right, he was a good man, my husband, a kind, patient man. And so handsome, too, I would add, stealing a quick look at the strong curve of his jaw, feeling luckier than I had any right to be.

The night before he left, Somesh confessed that the store wasn't making 25 much money yet. "I'm not worried, I'm sure it soon will," he added, his fingers pleating the edge of my sari. "But I just don't want to give you the wrong impression, don't want you to be disappointed."

In the half dark I could see he had turned toward me. His face, with two vertical lines between the brows, looked young, apprehensive, in need of protection. I'd never seen that on a man's face before. Something rose in me like a wave.

"It's all right," I said, as though to a child, and pulled his head down to my breast. His hair smelled faintly of the American cigarettes he smoked. "I won't be disappointed. I'll help you." And a sudden happiness filled me.

That night I dreamed I was at the store. Soft American music floated in the background as I moved between shelves stocked high with brightly colored cans and elegant-necked bottles, turning their labels carefully to the front, polishing them until they shone.

Now, sitting inside this metal shell that is hurtling through emptiness, I try to remember other things about my husband: how gentle his hands had been, and his lips, surprisingly soft, like a woman's. How I've longed for them through those drawn-out nights while I waited for my visa to arrive. He will be standing at the customs gate, and when I reach him, he will lower his face to mine. We will kiss in front of everyone, not caring, like Americans, then pull back, look each other in the eye, and smile.

But suddenly, as I am thinking this, I realize I cannot recall Somesh's face. 30 I try and try until my head hurts, but I can only visualize the black air swirling outside the plane, too thin for breathing. My own breath grows ragged with panic as I think of it and my mouth fills with sour fluid the way it does just before I throw up.

I grope for something to hold on to, something beautiful and talismanic from my old life. And then I remember. Somewhere down under me, low in the belly of the plane, inside my new brown case which is stacked in the dark with a hundred others, are my saris. Thick Kanjeepuram silks in solid purples and golden yellows, the thin hand-woven cottons of the Bengal countryside, green as a young banana plant, gray as the women's lake on a monsoon morning. Already I can feel my shoulders loosening up, my breath steadying. My wedding Benarasi, flame-orange, with a wide *palloo* of gold-embroidered dancing pea-cocks. Fold upon fold of Dhakais so fine they can be pulled through a ring. Into each fold my mother has tucked a small sachet of sandalwood powder to protect the saris from the unknown insects of America. Little silk sachets, made from *her* old saris—I can smell their calm fragrance as I watch the American air host-ess wheeling the dinner cart toward my seat. It is the smell of my mother's hands.

I know then that everything will be all right. And when the air hostess bends her curly golden head to ask me what I would like to eat, I understand every word in spite of her strange accent and answer her without stumbling even once over the unfamiliar English phrases.

Late at night I stand in front of our bedroom mirror trying on the clothes Somesh has bought for me and smuggled in past his parents. I model each one for him, walking back and forth, clasping my hands behind my head, lips pouted, left hip thrust out just like the models on TV, while he whispers ap-plause. I'm breathless with suppressed laughter (Father and Mother Sen must not hear us) and my cheeks are hot with the delicious excitement of conspiracy. We've stuffed a towel at the bottom of the door so no light will shine through.

I'm wearing a pair of jeans now, marveling at the curves of my hips and thighs, which have always been hidden under the flowing lines of my saris. I love the color, the same pale blue as the *nayantara* flowers that grow in my parents' garden. The solid comforting weight. The jeans come with a close-fitting T-shirt which outlines my breasts.

I scold Somesh to hide my embarrassed pleasure. He shouldn't have been 35 so extravagant. We can't afford it. He just smiles.

The T-shirt is sunrise-orange—the color, I decide, of joy, of my new American life. Across its middle, in large black letters, is written *Great America*. I was sure the letters referred to the country, but Somesh told me it is the name of an amusement park, a place where people go to have fun. I think it a wonderful concept, novel. Above the letters is the picture of a train. Only it's not a train, Somesh tells me, it's a roller coaster. He tries to explain how it moves, the insane speed, the dizzy ground falling away, then gives up. "I'll take you there, Mita sweetheart," he says, "as soon as we move into our own place."

That's our dream (mine more than his, I suspect) — moving out of this two-room apartment where it seems to me if we all breathed in at once, there would be no air left. Where I must cover my head with the edge of my Japan nylon sari (my expensive Indian ones are to be saved for special occasions — trips to the temple, Bengali New Year) and serve tea to the old women that come to visit Mother Sen, where like a good Indian wife I must never address my husband by his name. Where even in our bed we kiss guiltily, uneasily, listening for the giveaway creak of springs. Sometimes I laugh to myself, thinking how ironic it is that after all my fears about America, my life has turned out to be no different from Deepali's or Radha's. But at other times I feel caught in a world where everything is frozen in place, like a scene inside a glass paperweight. It is a world so small that if I were to stretch out my arms, I would touch its cold unyielding edges. I stand inside this glass world, watching helplessly as America rushes by, wanting to scream. Then I'm ashamed. Mita, I tell myself, you're growing westernized. Back home you'd never have felt this way.

We must be patient. I know that. Tactful, loving children. That is the Indian way. "I'm their life," Somesh tells me as we lie beside each other, lazy from lovemaking. He's not boasting, merely stating a fact. "They've always been there when I needed them. I could never abandon them at some old people's home." For a moment I feel rage. You're constantly thinking of them, I want to scream. But what about me? Then I remember my own parents, Mother's hands cool on my sweat-drenched body through nights of fever, Father teaching me to read, his finger moving along the crisp black angles of the alphabet, transforming them magically into things I knew, water, dog, mango tree. I beat back my unreasonable desire and nod agreement.

Somesh has bought me a cream blouse with a long brown skirt. They match beautifully, like the inside and outside of an almond. "For when you begin working," he says. But first he wants me to start college. Get a degree, perhaps in teaching. I picture myself in front of a classroom of girls with blond pigtails and blue uniforms, like a scene out of an English movie I saw long ago in Calcutta. They raise their hands respectfully when I ask a question. "Do you really think I can?" I ask. "Of course," he replies.

I am gratified he has such confidence in me. But I have another plan, a secret 40 that I will divulge to him once we move. What I really want is to work in the store. I want to stand behind the counter in the cream-and-brown skirt set (color of earth, color of seeds) and ring up purchases. The register drawer will glide open. Confident, I will count out green dollars and silver quarters. Gleaming copper pennies. I will dust the jars of gilt-wrapped chocolates on the counter. Will straighten, on the far wall, posters of smiling young men raising their beer mugs to toast scantily clad redheads with huge spiky eyelashes. (I have never visited the store — my in-laws don't consider it proper for a wife — but of course I know exactly what it looks like.) I will charm the customers with my smile, so that they will return again and again just to hear me telling them to have a nice day.

Meanwhile, I will the store to make money for us. Quickly. Because when we move, we'll be paying for two households. But so far it hasn't worked. They're running at a loss, Somesh tells me. They had to let the hired help go. This means most nights Somesh has to take the graveyard shift (that horrible word, like a cold hand up my spine) because his partner refuses to.

"The bastard!" Somesh spat out once. "Just because he put in more money he thinks he can order me around. I'll show him!" I was frightened by the vicious twist of his mouth. Somehow I'd never imagined that he could be angry.

Often Somesh leaves as soon as he has dinner and doesn't get back till after I've made morning tea for Father and Mother Sen. I lie mostly awake those nights, picturing masked intruders crouching in the shadowed back of the store, like I've seen on the police shows that Father Sen sometimes watches. But Somesh insists there's nothing to worry about, they have bars on the windows and a burglar alarm. "And remember," he says, "the extra cash will help us move out that much quicker."

I'm wearing a nightie now, my very first one. It's black and lacy, with a bit of a shine to it, and it glides over my hips to stop outrageously at mid-thigh. My mouth is an O of surprise in the mirror, my legs long and pale and sleek from the hair remover I asked Somesh to buy me last week. The legs of a movie star. Somesh laughs at the look on my face, then says, "You're beautiful." His voice starts a flutter low in my belly.

"Do you really think so," I ask, mostly because I want to hear him say it 45 again. No one has called me beautiful before. My father would have thought it inappropriate, my mother that it would make me vain.

Somesh draws me close. "Very beautiful," he whispers. "The most beautiful woman in the whole world." His eyes are not joking as they usually are. I want to turn off the light, but "Please," he says, "I want to keep seeing your face." His fingers are taking the pins from my hair, undoing my braids. The escaped strands fall on his face like dark rain. We have already decided where we will hide my new American clothes—the jeans and T-shirt camouflaged on a hanger among Somesh's pants, the skirt set and nightie at the bottom of my suitcase, a sandalwood sachet tucked between them, waiting.

I stand in the middle of our empty bedroom, my hair still wet from the purification bath, my back to the stripped bed I can't bear to look at. I hold in my hands the plain white sari I'm supposed to wear. I must hurry. Any minute now there'll be a knock at the door. They are afraid to leave me alone too long, afraid I might do something to myself.

The sari, a thick voile that will bunch around the waist when worn, is borrowed. White. Widow's color, color of endings. I try to tuck it into the top of the petticoat, but my fingers are numb, disobedient. It spills through them and there are waves and waves of white around my feet. I kick out in sudden rage, but the sari is too soft, it gives too easily. I grab up an edge, clamp down with my teeth and pull, feeling a fierce, bitter satisfaction when I hear it rip.

There's a cut, still stinging, on the side of my right arm, halfway to the elbow. It is from the bangle-breaking ceremony. Old Mrs. Ghosh performed the ritual, since she's a widow, too. She took my hands in hers and brought them down hard on the bedpost, so that the glass bangles I was wearing shattered and multicolored shards flew out in every direction. Some landed on the body that was on the bed, covered with a sheet. I can't call it Somesh. He was gone already. She took an edge of the sheet and rubbed the red marriage mark off my forehead. She was crying. All the women in the room were crying except me. I watched them as though from the far end of a tunnel. Their flared nostrils, their red-veined eyes, the runnels of tears, salt-corrosive, down their cheeks.

It happened last night. He was at the store. "It isn't too bad," he would tell me on the days when he was in a good mood. "Not too many customers. I can put up my feet and watch MTV all night. I can sing along with Michael Jackson as loud as I want." He had a good voice, Somesh. Sometimes he would sing softly at night, lying in bed, holding me. Hindi songs of love, *Mere Sapnon Ki Rani,* queen of my dreams. (He would not sing American songs at home out of respect for his parents, who thought they were decadent.) I would feel his warm breath on my hair as I fell asleep.

Someone came into the store last night. He took all the money, even the little rolls of pennies I had helped Somesh make up. Before he left he emptied the bullets from his gun into my husband's chest.

"Only thing is," Somesh would say about the night shifts, "I really miss you. I sit there and think of you asleep in bed. Do you know that when you sleep you make your hands into fists, like a baby? When we move out, will you come along some nights to keep me company?"

My in-laws are good people, kind. They made sure the body was covered before they let me into the room. When someone asked if my hair should be cut off, as they sometimes do with widows back home, they said no. They said I could stay at the apartment with Mrs. Ghosh if I didn't want to go to the crematorium. They asked Dr. Das to give me something to calm me down when I couldn't stop shivering. They didn't say, even once, as people would surely have in the village, that it was my bad luck that brought death to their son so soon after his marriage.

They will probably go back to India now. There's nothing here for them anymore. They will want me to go with them. You're like our daughter, they will say. Your home is with us, for as long as you want. For the rest of your life. *The rest of my life.* I can't think about that yet. It makes me dizzy. Fragments are flying about my head, multicolored and piercing sharp like bits of bangle glass.

I want you to go to college. Choose a career. I stand in front of a classroom of smiling children who love me in my cream-and-brown American dress. A faceless parade straggles across my eyelids: all those customers at the store that I will never meet. The lace nightie, fragrant with sandalwood, waiting in its blackness inside my suitcase. The savings book where we have $3605.33. *Four thousand and we can move out, maybe next month.* The name of the panty hose I'd asked him to buy me for my birthday: sheer golden-beige. His lips, unexpectedly soft, woman-smooth. Elegant-necked wine bottles swept off shelves, shattering on the floor.

I know Somesh would not have tried to stop the gunman. I can picture his silhouette against the lighted Dewar's sign, hands raised. He is trying to find the right expression to put on his face, calm, reassuring, reasonable. *OK, take the money. No, I won't call the police.* His hands tremble just a little. His eyes darken with disbelief as his fingers touch his chest and come away wet.

I yanked away the cover. I had to see. *Great America, a place where people go to have fun.* My breath roller-coasting through my body, my unlived life gathering itself into a scream. I'd expected blood, a lot of blood, the deep red-black of it crusting his chest. But they must have cleaned him up at the hospital. He was dressed in his silk wedding *kurta.* Against its warm ivory his face appeared remote, stern. The musky aroma of his aftershave lotion that someone must have sprinkled on the body. It didn't quite hide that other smell, thin, sour, metallic. The smell of death. The floor shifted under me, tilting like a wave.

I'm lying on the floor now, on the spilled white sari. I feel sleepy. Or perhaps it is some other feeling I don't have a word for. The sari is seductive-soft, drawing me into its folds.

Sometimes, bathing at the lake, I would move away from my friends, their endless chatter. I'd swim toward the middle of the water with a lazy backstroke, gazing at the sky, its enormous blueness drawing me up until I felt weightless and dizzy. Once in a while there would be a plane, a small silver needle drawn through the clouds, in and out, until it disappeared. Sometimes the thought came to me, as I floated in the middle of the lake with the sun beating down on my closed eyelids, that it would be so easy to let go, to drop into the dim brown world of mud, of water weeds fine as hair.

Once I almost did it. I curled my body inward, tight as a fist, and felt it start   60 to sink. The sun grew pale and shapeless; the water, suddenly cold, licked at the insides of my ears in welcome. But in the end I couldn't.

They are knocking on the door now, calling my name. I push myself off the floor, my body almost too heavy to lift up, as when one climbs out after a long swim. I'm surprised at how vividly it comes to me, this memory I haven't called up in years: the desperate flailing of arms and legs as I fought my way upward; the press of the water on me, heavy as terror; the wild animal trapped inside my chest, clawing at my lungs. The day returning to me as searing air, the way I drew it in, in, in, as though I would never have enough of it.

That's when I know I cannot go back. I don't know yet how I'll manage, here in this new, dangerous land. I only know I must. Because all over India, at this very moment, widows in white saris are bowing their veiled heads, serving tea to in-laws. Doves with cut-off wings.

I am standing in front of the mirror now, gathering up the sari. I tuck in the ripped end so it lies next to my skin, my secret. I make myself think of the store, although it hurts. Inside the refrigerated unit, blue milk cartons neatly lined up by Somesh's hands. The exotic smell of Hills Brothers coffee brewed black and strong, the glisten of sugar-glazed donuts nestled in tissue. The neon Budweiser emblem winking on and off like a risky invitation.

I straighten my shoulders and stand taller, take a deep breath. Air fills me — the same air that traveled through Somesh's lungs a little while ago. The thought is like an unexpected, intimate gift. I tilt my chin, readying myself for the arguments of the coming weeks, the remonstrations. In the mirror a woman holds my gaze, her eyes apprehensive yet steady. She wears a blouse and skirt the color of almonds.

ENTRY POINTS   Here are two stories about newlyweds, both of whom encounter situations that radically change their lives. Both men are separated from their wives — one willingly, the other not. Both men encounter evil: one of a religious nature, the other of a sociopolitical nature. Both undergo transformations from what they experience. As you reflect on both stories, think about the characters' transformations and consider the similarities and differences in their experiences, especially in the kind of evils they are forced to deal with. Think about what in their personalities and lives leads each to respond and change as he does.

Nathaniel Hawthorne   1804–1864

Young Goodman Brown   [1835]

Young Goodman° Brown came forth, at sunset, into the street of Salem village,° but put his head back, after crossing the threshold, to exchange a parting kiss with his young wife. And Faith, as the wife was aptly named, thrust her own pretty head into the street, letting the wind play with the pink ribbons of her cap, while she called to Goodman Brown.

"Dearest heart," whispered she, softly and rather sadly, when her lips were close to his ear, "pr'y thee, put off your journey until sunrise, and sleep in your own bed to-night. A lone woman is troubled with such dreams and such thoughts, that she's afeard

---

Goodman: A man of ordinary status who was head of a household.   Salem village: Village in the Massachusetts Bay Colony.

of herself, sometimes. Pray, tarry with me this night, dear husband, of all nights in the year!"

"My love and my Faith," replied young Goodman Brown, "of all nights in the year, this one night must I tarry away from thee. My journey, as thou callest it, forth and back again, must needs be done 'twixt now and sunrise. What, my sweet, pretty wife, dost thou doubt me already, and we but three months married!"

"Then, God bless you!" said Faith, with the pink ribbons, "and may you find all well when you come back."

"Amen!" cried Goodman Brown. "Say thy prayers, dear Faith, and go to bed   5
at dusk, and no harm will come to thee."

So they parted; and the young man pursued his way, until, being about to turn the corner by the meeting-house, he looked back, and saw the head of Faith still peeping after him, with a melancholy air, in spite of her pink ribbons.

"Poor little Faith!" thought he, for his heart smote him. "What a wretch am I, to leave her on such an errand! She talks of dreams, too. Methought, as she spoke, there was trouble in her face, as if a dream had warned her what work is to be done to-night. But, no, no! 'twould kill her to think it. Well; she's a blessed angel on earth; and after this one night, I'll cling to her skirts and follow her to Heaven."

With this excellent resolve for the future, Goodman Brown felt himself justified in making more haste on his present evil purpose. He had taken a dreary road, darkened by all the gloomiest trees of the forest, which barely stood aside to let the narrow path creep through, and closed immediately behind. It was all as lonely as could be; and there is this peculiarity in such a solitude, that the traveller knows not who may be concealed by the innumerable trunks and the thick boughs overhead; so that, with lonely footsteps, he may yet be passing through an unseen multitude.

"There may be a devilish Indian behind every tree," said Goodman Brown, to himself; and he glanced fearfully behind him, as he added, "What if the devil himself should be at my very elbow!"

His head being turned back, he passed a crook of the road, and looking   10
forward again, beheld the figure of a man, in grave and decent attire, seated at the foot of an old tree. He arose, at Goodman Brown's approach, and walked onward, side by side with him.

"You are late, Goodman Brown," said he. "The clock of the Old South was striking as I came through Boston; and that is full fifteen minutes agone."°

"Faith kept me back awhile," replied the young man, with a tremor in his voice, caused by the sudden appearance of his companion, though not wholly unexpected.

It was now deep dusk in the forest, and deepest in that part of it where these two were journeying. As nearly as could be discerned, the second traveller was

---

full fifteen minutes agone: This mysterious figure apparently traveled the sixteen miles from Old South Church in Boston to woods outside Salem in a quarter of an hour.

about fifty years old, apparently in the same rank of life as Goodman Brown, and bearing a considerable resemblance to him, though perhaps more in expression than features. Still, they might have been taken for father and son. And yet, though the elder person was as simply clad as the younger, and as simple in manner too, he had an indescribable air of one who knew the world, and would not have felt abashed at the governor's dinnertable, or in King William's court,° were it possible that his affairs should call him thither. But the only thing about him, that could be fixed upon as remarkable, was his staff, which bore the likeness of a great black snake, so curiously wrought, that it might almost be seen to twist and wriggle itself, like a living serpent. This, of course, must have been an ocular deception, assisted by the uncertain light.

"Come, Goodman Brown!" cried his fellow-traveller, "this is a dull pace for the beginning of a journey. Take my staff, if you are so soon weary."

"Friend," said the other, exchanging his slow pace for a full stop, "having 15 kept covenant by meeting thee here, it is my purpose now to return whence I came. I have scruples, touching the matter thou wot'st° of."

"Sayest thou so?" replied he of the serpent, smiling apart. "Let us walk on, nevertheless, reasoning as we go, and if I convince thee not, thou shalt turn back. We are but a little way in the forest, yet."

"Too far, too far!" exclaimed the goodman, unconsciously resuming his walk. "My father never went into the woods on such an errand, nor his father before him. We have been a race of honest men and good Christians, since the days of the martyrs.° And shall I be the first of the name of Brown, that ever took this path, and kept—"

"Such company, thou wouldst say," observed the elder person, interpreting his pause. "Well said, Goodman Brown! I have been as well acquainted with your family as with ever a one among the Puritans; and that's no trifle to say. I helped your grandfather, the constable, when he lashed the Quaker woman so smartly through the streets of Salem. And it was I that brought your father a pitch-pine knot, kindled at my own hearth, to set fire to an Indian village, in King Philip's war.° They were my good friends, both; and many a pleasant walk have we had along this path, and returned merrily after midnight. I would fain be friends with you, for their sake."

"If it be as thou sayest," replied Goodman Brown, "I marvel they never spoke of these matters. Or, verily, I marvel not, seeing that the least rumor of the sort would have driven them from New-England. We are a people of prayer, and good works, to boot, and abide no such wickedness."

King William's court: William III was king of England from 1689 to 1702, ruling jointly with his wife Mary II until her death in 1694. **wot'st:** Know. **days of the martyrs:** Period in England during the rule of a Catholic monarch, Mary I (1553–1558), when Protestants were persecuted and many ancestors of the New England Pilgrims lost their lives for their religious faith. **King Philip's war:** A bitter conflict (1675–1676) between the colonists and several New England tribes led by Metacomet, chief of the Wampanoag Indians, who was called King Philip by the colonists.

"Wickedness or not," said the traveller with the twisted staff, "I have a very 20
general acquaintance here in New-England. The deacons of many a church have
drunk the communion wine with me; the selectmen, of divers towns, make me
their chairman; and a majority of the Great and General Court° are firm sup-
porters of my interest. The governor and I, too—but these are state-secrets."

"Can this be so!" cried Goodman Brown, with a stare of amazement at his
undisturbed companion. "Howbeit, I have nothing to do with the governor and
council; they have their own ways, and are no rule for a simple husbandman,°
like me. But, were I to go on with thee, how should I meet the eye of that good
old man, our minister, at Salem village? Oh, his voice would make me tremble,
both Sabbath-day and lecture-day!"°

Thus far, the elder traveller had listened with due gravity, but now burst
into a fit of irrepressible mirth, shaking himself so violently, that his snake-like
staff actually seemed to wriggle in sympathy.

"Ha! ha! ha!" shouted he, again and again; then composing himself, "Well,
go on, Goodman Brown, go on; but pr'y thee, don't kill me with laughing!"

"Well, then, to end the matter at once," said Goodman Brown, considerably nettled, "there is my wife, Faith. It would break her dear little heart; and
I'd rather break my own!"

"Nay, if that be the case," answered the other, "e'en go thy ways, Goodman 25
Brown. I would not, for twenty old women like the one hobbling before us, that
Faith should come to any harm."

As he spoke, he pointed his staff at a female figure on the path, in whom
Goodman Brown recognized a very pious and exemplary dame, who had taught
him his catechism, in youth, and was still his moral and spiritual adviser,
jointly with the minister and Deacon Gookin.

"A marvel, truly, that Goody° Cloyse should be so far in the wilderness, at
night-fall!" said he. "But, with your leave, friend, I shall take a cut through the
woods, until we have left this Christian woman behind. Being a stranger to you,
she might ask whom I was consorting with, and whither I was going."

"Be it so," said his fellow-traveller. "Betake you to the woods, and let me
keep the path."

Accordingly, the young man turned aside, but took care to watch his companion, who advanced softly along the road, until he had come within a staff's
length of the old dame. She, meanwhile, was making the best of her way, with
singular speed for so aged a woman, and mumbling some indistinct words, a
prayer, doubtless, as she went. The traveller put forth his staff, and touched her
withered neck with what seemed the serpent's tail.

"The devil!" screamed the pious old lady. 30

Great and General Court: Colonial legislature. husbandman: Farmer. lecture-day: A
weekday church service with a sermon. Goody: Short for Goodwife, a married woman of
ordinary status (cf. "goodman"). Goody Cloyse and Goody Cory, along with Martha Carrier,
were sentenced to death at the Salem witchcraft trials of 1692, at which Hawthorne's great-
grandfather was a judge.

"Then Goody Cloyse knows her old friend?" observed the traveller, confronting her, and leaning on his writhing stick.

"Ah, forsooth, and is it your worship, indeed?" cried the good dame. "Yea, truly is it, and in the very image of my old gossip,° Goodman Brown, the grandfather of the silly fellow that now is. But—would your worship believe it?—my broomstick hath strangely disappeared, stolen, as I suspect, by that unhanged witch, Goody Cory, and that, too, when I was all anointed with the juice of smallage and cinque-foil and wolf's-bane—"°

"Mingled with fine wheat and the fat of a new-born babe," said the shape of old Goodman Brown.

"Ah, your worship knows the receipt," cried the old lady, cackling aloud. "So, as I was saying, being all ready for the meeting, and no horse to ride on, I made up my mind to foot it; for they tell me, there is a nice young man to be taken into communion to-night. But now your good worship will lend me your arm, and we shall be there in a twinkling."

"That can hardly be," answered her friend. "I may not spare you my arm, Goody Cloyse, but here is my staff, if you will."   35

So saying, he threw it down at her feet, where, perhaps, it assumed life, being one of the rods which its owner had formerly lent to the Egyptian Magi.° Of this fact, however, Goodman Brown could not take cognizance. He had cast up his eyes in astonishment, and looking down again, beheld neither Goody Cloyse nor the serpentine staff, but his fellow-traveller alone, who waited for him as calmly as if nothing had happened.

"That old woman taught me my catechism!" said the young man; and there was a world of meaning in this simple comment.

They continued to walk onward, while the elder traveller exhorted his companion to make good speed and persevere in the path, discoursing so aptly, that his arguments seemed rather to spring up in the bosom of his auditor, than to be suggested by himself. As they went, he plucked a branch of maple, to serve for a walking-stick, and began to strip it of the twigs and little boughs, which were wet with evening dew. The moment his fingers touched them, they became strangely withered and dried up, as with a week's sunshine. Thus the pair proceeded, at a good free pace, until suddenly, in a gloomy hollow of the road, Goodman Brown sat himself down on the stump of a tree, and refused to go any farther.

"Friend," said he, stubbornly, "my mind is made up. Not another step will I budge on this errand. What if a wretched old woman do choose to go to the devil, when I thought she was going to Heaven! Is that any reason why I should quit my dear Faith, and go after her?"

---

gossip: Godfather or godmother, sponsor at a baptism. **smallage . . . bane:** "Smallage" is wild celery or water parsley; "cinque-foil" is a type of rose; "wolf's-bane" is aconite or monkshood. All are ingredients in a witch's brew. **Egyptian Magi:** Egyptian magicians who were able, like Aaron in the biblical account, to turn rods into serpents. See Exodus 7:11–12.

"You will think better of this, by-and-by," said his acquaintance, compos-   40
edly. "Sit here and rest yourself awhile; and when you feel like moving again,
there is my staff to help you along."

Without more words, he threw his companion the maple stick, and was as
speedily out of sight, as if he had vanished into the deepening gloom. The young
man sat a few moments, by the road-side, applauding himself greatly, and thinking with how clear a conscience he should meet the minister, in his morning-
walk, nor shrink from the eye of good old Deacon Gookin. And what calm sleep
would be his, that very night, which was to have been spent so wickedly, but
purely and sweetly now, in the arms of Faith! Amidst these pleasant and praise-
worthy meditations, Goodman Brown heard the tramp of horses along the
road, and deemed it advisable to conceal himself within the verge of the forest,
conscious of the guilty purpose that had brought him thither, though now so
happily turned from it.

On came the hoof-tramps and the voices of the riders, two grave old voices,
conversing soberly as they drew near. These mingled sounds appeared to pass
along the road, within a few yards of the young man's hiding-place; but owing,
doubtless, to the depth of the gloom, at that particular spot, neither the travel-
lers nor their steeds were visible. Though their figures brushed the small boughs
by the way-side, it could not be seen that they intercepted, even for a moment,
the faint gleam from the strip of bright sky, athwart which they must have
passed. Goodman Brown alternately crouched and stood on tip-toe, pulling
aside the branches, and thrusting forth his head as far as he durst, without
discerning so much as a shadow. It vexed him the more, because he could have
sworn, were such a thing possible, that he recognized the voices of the minister
and Deacon Gookin, jogging along quietly, as they were wont to do, when
bound to some ordination or ecclesiastical council. While yet within hearing,
one of the riders stopped to pluck a switch.

"Of the two, reverend Sir," said the voice like the deacon's, "I had rather
miss an ordination-dinner than to-night's meeting. They tell me that some of
our community are to be here from Falmouth and beyond, and others from
Connecticut and Rhode-Island; besides several of the Indian powows,° who,
after their fashion, know almost as much deviltry as the best of us. Moreover,
there is a goodly young woman to be taken into communion."

"Mighty well, Deacon Gookin!" replied the solemn old tones of the minister. "Spur up, or we shall be late. Nothing can be done, you know, until I get on
the ground."

The hoofs clattered again, and the voices, talking so strangely in the empty   45
air, passed on through the forest, where no church had ever been gathered, nor
solitary Christian prayed. Whither, then, could these holy men be journeying,
so deep into the heathen wilderness? Young Goodman Brown caught hold of a
tree, for support, being ready to sink down on the ground, faint and overbur-
thened with the heavy sickness of his heart. He looked up to the sky, doubting

---

powows: Medicine men.

whether there really was a Heaven above him. Yet, there was the blue arch, and the stars brightening in it.

"With Heaven above, and Faith below, I will yet stand firm against the devil!" cried Goodman Brown.

While he still gazed upward, into the deep arch of the firmament, and had lifted his hands to pray, a cloud, though no wind was stirring, hurried across the zenith, and hid the brightening stars. The blue sky was still visible, except directly overhead, where this black mass of cloud was sweeping swiftly northward. Aloft in the air, as if from the depths of the cloud, came a confused and doubtful sound of voices. Once, the listener fancied that he could distinguish the accents of town's-people of his own, men and women, both pious and ungodly, many of whom he had met at the communion-table, and had seen others rioting at the tavern. The next moment, so indistinct were the sounds, he doubted whether he had heard aught but the murmur of the old forest, whispering without a wind. Then came a stronger swell of those familiar tones, heard daily in the sunshine, at Salem village, but never, until now, from a cloud of night. There was one voice, of a young woman, uttering lamentations, yet with an uncertain sorrow, and entreating for some favor, which, perhaps, it would grieve her to obtain. And all the unseen multitude, both saints and sinners, seemed to encourage her onward.

"Faith!" shouted Goodman Brown, in a voice of agony and desperation; and the echoes of the forest mocked him, crying—"Faith! Faith!" as if bewildered wretches were seeking her, all through the wilderness.

The cry of grief, rage, and terror, was yet piercing the night, when the unhappy husband held his breath for a response. There was a scream, drowned immediately in a louder murmur of voices, fading into far-off laughter, as the dark cloud swept away, leaving the clear and silent sky above Goodman Brown. But something fluttered lightly down through the air, and caught on the branch of a tree. The young man seized it, and beheld a pink ribbon.

"My Faith is gone!" cried he, after one stupefied moment. "There is no good 50 on earth; and sin is but a name. Come, devil! for to thee is this world given."

And maddened with despair, so that he laughed loud and long, did Goodman Brown grasp his staff and set forth again, at such a rate, that he seemed to fly along the forest-path, rather than to walk or run. The road grew wilder and drearier, and more faintly traced, and vanished at length, leaving him in the heart of the dark wilderness, still rushing onward, with the instinct that guides mortal man to evil. The whole forest was peopled with frightful sounds; the creaking of the trees, the howling of wild beasts, and the yell of Indians; while, sometimes, the wind tolled like a distant church-bell, and sometimes gave a broad roar around the traveller, as if all Nature were laughing him to scorn. But he was himself the chief horror of the scene, and shrank not from its other horrors.

"Ha! ha! ha!" roared Goodman Brown, when the wind laughed at him. "Let us hear which will laugh loudest! Think not to frighten me with your deviltry! Come witch, come wizard, come Indian powow, come devil himself! and here comes Goodman Brown. You may as well fear him as he fear you!"

In truth, all through the haunted forest, there could be nothing more frightful than the figure of Goodman Brown. On he flew, among the black pines, brandishing his staff with frenzied gestures, now giving vent to an inspiration of horrid blasphemy, and now shouting forth such laughter, as set all the echoes of the forest laughing like demons around him. The fiend in his own shape is less hideous, than when he rages in the breast of man. Thus sped the demoniac on his course, until, quivering among the trees, he saw a red light before him, as when the felled trunks and branches of a clearing have been set on fire, and throw up their lurid blaze against the sky, at the hour of midnight. He paused, in a lull of the tempest that had driven him onward, and heard the swell of what seemed a hymn, rolling solemnly from a distance, with the weight of many voices. He knew the tune; it was a familiar one in the choir of the village meetinghouse. The verse died heavily away, and was lengthened by a chorus, not of human voices, but of all the sounds of the benighted wilderness, pealing in awful harmony together. Goodman Brown cried out; and his cry was lost to his own ear, by its unison with the cry of the desert.

In the interval of silence, he stole forward, until the light glared full upon his eyes. At one extremity of an open space, hemmed in by the dark wall of the forest, arose a rock, bearing some rude, natural resemblance either to an altar or a pulpit, and surrounded by four blazing pines, their tops aflame, their stems untouched, like candles at an evening meeting. The mass of foliage, that had overgrown the summit of the rock, was all on fire, blazing high into the night, and fitfully illuminating the whole field. Each pendent twig and leafy festoon was in a blaze. As the red light arose and fell, a numerous congregation alternately shone forth, then disappeared in shadow, and again grew, as it were, out of the darkness, peopling the heart of the solitary woods at once.

"A grave and dark-clad company!" quoth Goodman Brown.   55

In truth, they were such. Among them, quivering to-and-fro, between gloom and splendor, appeared faces that would be seen, next day, at the council-board of the province, and others which, Sabbath after Sabbath, looked devoutly heavenward, and benignantly over the crowded pews, from the holiest pulpits in the land. Some affirm, that the lady of the governor was there. At least, there were high dames well known to her, and wives of honored husbands, and widows, a great multitude, and ancient maidens, all of excellent repute, and fair young girls, who trembled, lest their mothers should espy them. Either the sudden gleams of light, flashing over the obscure field, bedazzled Goodman Brown, or he recognized a score of the church-members of Salem village, famous for their especial sanctity. Good old Deacon Gookin had arrived, and waited at the skirts of that venerable saint, his revered pastor. But, irreverently consorting with these grave, reputable, and pious people, these elders of the church, these chaste dames and dewy virgins, there were men of dissolute lives and women of spotted fame, wretches given over to all mean and filthy vice, and suspected even of horrid crimes. It was strange to see, that the good shrank not from the wicked, nor were the sinners abashed by the saints. Scattered, also, among their pale-faced enemies, were the Indian priests, or

powows, who had often scared their native forest with more hideous incanta-
tions than any known to English witchcraft.

"But, where is Faith?" thought Goodman Brown; and, as hope came into
his heart, he trembled.

Another verse of the hymn arose, a slow and mournful strain, such as the
pious love, but joined to words which expressed all that our nature can conceive
of sin, and darkly hinted at far more. Unfathomable to mere mortals is the lore
of fiends. Verse after verse was sung, and still the chorus of the desert swelled
between, like the deepest tone of a mighty organ. And, with the final peal of
that dreadful anthem, there came a sound, as if the roaring wind, the rushing
streams, the howling beasts, and every other voice of the unconverted wilderness, were mingling and according with the voice of guilty man, in homage to
the prince of all. The four blazing pines threw up a loftier flame, and obscurely
discovered shapes and visages of horror on the smoke-wreaths, above the impi-
ous assembly. At the same moment, the fire on the rock shot redly forth, and
formed a glowing arch above its base, where now appeared a figure. With reverence be it spoken, the figure bore no slight similitude, both in garb and manner,
to some grave divine of the New-England churches.

"Bring forth the converts!" cried a voice, that echoed through the field and
rolled into the forest.

At the word, Goodman Brown stept forth from the shadow of the trees, and   60
approached the congregation, with whom he felt a loathful brotherhood, by the
sympathy of all that was wicked in his heart. He could have well nigh sworn,
that the shape of his own dead father beckoned him to advance, looking downward from a smoke-wreath, while a woman, with dim features of despair, threw
out her hand to warn him back. Was it his mother? But he had no power to
retreat one step, nor to resist, even in thought, when the minister and good old
Deacon Gookin seized his arms, and led him to the blazing rock. Thither came
also the slender form of a veiled female, led between Goody Cloyse, that pious
teacher of the catechism, and Martha Carrier, who had received the devil's
promise to be queen of hell. A rampant hag was she! And there stood the pros-
elytes, beneath the canopy of fire.

"Welcome, my children," said the dark figure, "to the communion of your
race! Ye have found, thus young, your nature and your destiny. My children,
look behind you!"

They turned; and flashing forth, as it were, in a sheet of flame, the fiend-
worshippers were seen; the smile of welcome gleamed darkly on every visage.

"There," resumed the sable form, "are all whom ye have reverenced from
youth. Ye deemed them holier than yourselves, and shrank from your own sin,
contrasting it with their lives of righteousness, and prayerful aspirations heavenward. Yet, here are they all, in my worshipping assembly! This night it shall
be granted you to know their secret deeds; how hoary-bearded elders of the
church have whispered wanton words to the young maids of their households;
how many a woman, eager for widow's weeds, has given her husband a drink at
bed-time, and let him sleep his last sleep in her bosom; how beardless youths

have made haste to inherit their fathers' wealth; and how fair damsels — blush not, sweet ones! — have dug little graves in the garden, and bidden me, the sole guest, to an infant's funeral. By the sympathy of your human hearts for sin, ye shall scent out all the places — whether in church, bed-chamber, street, field, or forest — where crime has been committed, and shall exult to behold the whole earth one stain of guilt, one mighty bloodspot. Far more than this! It shall be yours to penetrate, in every bosom, the deep mystery of sin, the fountain of all wicked arts, and which inexhaustibly supplies more evil impulses than human power — than my power, at its utmost! — can make manifest in deeds. And now, my children, look upon each other."

They did so; and, by the blaze of the hell-kindled torches, the wretched man beheld his Faith, and the wife her husband, trembling before that unhallowed altar.

"Lo! there ye stand, my children," said the figure, in a deep and solemn 65 tone, almost sad, with its despairing awfulness, as if his once angelic nature could yet mourn for our miserable race. "Depending upon one another's hearts, ye had still hoped, that virtue were not all a dream. Now are ye undeceived! Evil is the nature of mankind. Evil must be your only happiness. Welcome, again, my children, to the communion of your race!"

"Welcome!" repeated the fiend-worshippers, in one cry of despair and triumph.

And there they stood, the only pair, as it seemed, who were yet hesitating on the verge of wickedness, in this dark world. A basin was hollowed, naturally, in the rock. Did it contain water, reddened by the lurid light? or was it blood? or, perchance, a liquid flame? Herein did the Shape of Evil dip his hand, and prepare to lay the mark of baptism upon their foreheads, that they might be partakers of the mystery of sin, more conscious of the secret guilt of others, both in deed and thought, than they could now be of their own. The husband cast one look at his pale wife, and Faith at him. What polluted wretches would the next glance shew them to each other, shuddering alike at what they disclosed and what they saw!

"Faith! Faith!" cried the husband. "Look up to Heaven, and resist the Wicked One!"

Whether Faith obeyed, he knew not. Hardly had he spoken, when he found himself amid calm night and solitude, listening to a roar of the wind, which died heavily away through the forest. He staggered against the rock and felt it chill and damp, while a hanging twig, that had been all on fire, besprinkled his cheek with the coldest dew.

The next morning, young Goodman Brown came slowly into the street of 70 Salem village, staring around him like a bewildered man. The good old minister was taking a walk along the grave-yard, to get an appetite for breakfast and meditate his sermon, and bestowed a blessing, as he passed, on Goodman Brown. He shrank from the venerable saint, as if to avoid an anathema.° Old

---

anathema: A thing accursed or consigned to damnation by an official decree of the church.

Deacon Gookin was at domestic worship, and the holy words of his prayer were heard through the open window. "What God doth the wizard pray to?" quoth Goodman Brown. Goody Cloyse, that excellent old Christian, stood in the early sunshine, at her own lattice, catechising a little girl, who had brought her a pint of morning's milk. Goodman Brown snatched away the child, as from the grasp of the fiend himself. Turning the corner by the meeting-house, he spied the head of Faith, with the pink ribbons, gazing anxiously forth, and bursting into such joy at sight of him, that she skipt along the street, and almost kissed her husband before the whole village. But, Goodman Brown looked sternly and sadly into her face, and passed on without a greeting.

Had Goodman Brown fallen asleep in the forest, and only dreamed a wild dream of a witch-meeting?

Be it so, if you will. But, alas! it was a dream of evil omen for young Goodman Brown. A stern, a sad, a darkly meditative, a distrustful, if not a desperate man, did he become, from the night of that fearful dream. On the Sabbath-day, when the congregation were singing a holy psalm, he could not listen, because an anthem of sin rushed loudly upon his ear, and drowned all the blessed strain. When the minister spoke from the pulpit, with power and fervid eloquence, and, with his hand on the open Bible, of the sacred truths of our religion, and of saint-like lives and triumphant deaths, and of future bliss or misery unutterable, then did Goodman Brown turn pale, dreading, lest the roof should thunder down upon the gray blasphemer and his hearers. Often, awakening suddenly at midnight, he shrank from the bosom of Faith, and at morning or eventide, when the family knelt down at prayer, he scowled, and muttered to himself, and gazed sternly at his wife, and turned away. And when he had lived long, and was borne to his grave, a hoary corpse, followed by Faith, an aged woman, and children and grandchildren, a goodly procession, besides neighbors, not a few, they carved no hopeful verse upon his tomb-stone; for his dying hour was gloom.

You can explore Nathaniel Hawthorne and "Young Goodman Brown" in depth, including images and cultural documents, with VirtuaLit Fiction at bedfordstmartins.com/rewritinglit.

Ha Jin b. 1956

Saboteur   [2000]

Mr. Chiu and his bride were having lunch in the square before Muji Train Station. On the table between them were two bottles of soda spewing out brown foam and two paper boxes of rice and sautéed cucumber and pork. "Let's eat," he said to her, and broke the connected ends of the chopsticks. He picked up a slice of streaky

APPROACHING THE AUTHOR

Ha Jin intended to return to China after completing his dissertation at Brandeis University. After watching televised coverage of the Tiananmen Square massacre, however, he decided to stay in the United States with his wife and young son and be a teacher. When he couldn't find a teaching job, he turned to writing instead.

For more about him, see page 1387 or 1393.

pork and put it into his mouth. As he was chewing, a few crinkles appeared on his thin jaw.

To his right, at another table, two railroad policemen were drinking tea and laughing; it seemed that the stout, middle-aged man was telling a joke to his young comrade, who was tall and of athletic build. Now and again they would steal a glance at Mr. Chiu's table.

The air smelled of rotten melon. A few flies kept buzzing above the couple's lunch. Hundreds of people were rushing around to get on the platform or to catch buses to downtown. Food and fruit vendors were crying for customers in lazy voices. About a dozen young women, representing the local hotels, held up placards which displayed the daily prices and words as large as a palm, like FREE MEALS, AIR-CONDITIONING, and ON THE RIVER. In the center of the square stood a concrete statue of Chairman Mao, at whose feet peasants were napping, their backs on the warm granite and their faces toward the sunny sky. A flock of pigeons perched on the Chairman's raised hand and forearm.

The rice and cucumber tasted good, and Mr. Chiu was eating unhurriedly. His sallow face showed exhaustion. He was glad that the honeymoon was finally over and that he and his bride were heading back for Harbin. During the two weeks' vacation, he had been worried about his liver, because three months ago he had suffered from acute hepatitis; he was afraid he might have a relapse. But he had had no severe symptoms, despite his liver being still big and tender. On the whole he was pleased with his health, which could endure even the strain of a honeymoon; indeed, he was on the course of recovery. He looked at his bride, who took off her wire glasses, kneading the root of her nose with her fingertips. Beads of sweat coated her pale cheeks.

"Are you all right, sweetheart?" he asked.   5

"I have a headache. I didn't sleep well last night."

"Take an aspirin, will you?"

"It's not that serious. Tomorrow is Sunday and I can sleep in. Don't worry."

As they were talking, the stout policeman at the next table stood up and threw a bowl of tea in their direction. Both Mr. Chiu's and his bride's sandals were wet instantly.

"Hooligan!" she said in a low voice.   10

Mr. Chiu got to his feet and said out loud, "Comrade Policeman, why did you do this?" He stretched out his right foot to show the wet sandal.

"Do what?" the stout man asked huskily, glaring at Mr. Chiu while the young fellow was whistling.

"See, you dumped tea on our feet."

"You're lying. You wet your shoes yourself."

"Comrade Policeman, your duty is to keep order, but you purposely tortured   15
us common citizens. Why violate the law you are supposed to enforce?" As Mr. Chiu was speaking, dozens of people began gathering around.

With a wave of his hand, the man said to the young fellow, "Let's get hold of him!"

They grabbed Mr. Chiu and clamped handcuffs around his wrists. He cried, "You can't do this to me. This is utterly unreasonable."

"Shut up!" The man pulled out his pistol. "You can use your tongue at our headquarters."

The young fellow added, "You're a saboteur, you know that? You're disrupting public order."

The bride was too petrified to say anything coherent. She was a recent college graduate, had majored in fine arts, and had never seen the police make an arrest. All she could say was, "Oh, please, please!"   20

The policemen were pulling Mr. Chiu, but he refused to go with them, holding the corner of the table and shouting, "We have a train to catch. We already bought the tickets."

The stout man punched him in the chest. "Shut up. Let your ticket expire." With the pistol butt he chopped Mr. Chiu's hands, which at once released the table. Together the two men were dragging him away to the police station.

Realizing he had to go with them, Mr. Chiu turned his head and shouted to his bride, "Don't wait for me here. Take the train. If I'm not back by tomorrow morning, send someone over to get me out"

She nodded, covering her sobbing mouth with her palm.

After removing his belt, they locked Mr. Chiu into a cell in the back of the   25
Railroad Police Station. The single window in the room was blocked by six steel bars; it faced a spacious yard, in which stood a few pines. Beyond the trees, two swings hung from an iron frame, swaying gently in the breeze. Somewhere in the building a cleaver was chopping rhythmically. There must be a kitchen upstairs, Mr. Chiu thought.

He was too exhausted to worry about what they would do to him, so he lay down on the narrow bed and shut his eyes. He wasn't afraid. The Cultural Revolution was over already, and recently the Party had been propagating the idea that all citizens were equal before the law. The police ought to be a law-abiding model for common people. As long as he remained coolheaded and reasoned with them, they probably wouldn't harm him.

Late in the afternoon he was taken to the Interrogation Bureau on the second floor. On his way there, in the stairwell, he ran into the middle-aged policeman who had manhandled him. The man grinned, rolling his bulgy eyes and pointing his fingers at him as if firing a pistol. Egg of a tortoise! Mr. Chiu cursed mentally.

The moment he sat down in the office, he burped, his palm shielding his mouth. In front of him, across a long desk, sat the chief of the bureau and a donkey-faced man. On the glass desktop was a folder containing information on his case. He felt it bizarre that in just a matter of hours they had accumulated a small pile of writing about him. On second thought he began to wonder whether they had kept a file on him all the time. How could this have happened? He lived and worked in Harbin, more than three hundred miles away, and this was his first time in Muji City.

The chief of the bureau was a thin, bald man who looked serene and intelligent. His slim hands handled the written pages in the folder in the manner of a lecturing scholar. To Mr. Chiu's left sat a young scribe, with a clipboard on his knee and a black fountain pen in his hand.

"Your name?" the chief asked, apparently reading out the question from a form. 30

"Chiu Maguang."

"Age?"

"Thirty-four."

"Profession?"

"Lecturer." 35

"Work unit?"

"Harbin University."

"Political status?"

"Communist Party member."

The chief put down the paper and began to speak. "Your crime is sabotage, 40 although it hasn't induced serious consequences yet. Because you are a Party member, you should be punished more. You have failed to be a model for the masses and you—"

"Excuse me, sir," Mr. Chiu cut him off.

"What?"

"I didn't do anything. Your men are the saboteurs of our social order. They threw hot tea on my feet and on my wife's feet. Logically speaking, you should criticize them, if not punish them."

"That statement is groundless. You have no witness. Why should I believe you?" the chief said matter-of-factly.

"This is my evidence." He raised his right hand. "Your man hit my fingers 45 with a pistol."

"That doesn't prove how your feet got wet. Besides, you could have hurt your fingers yourself."

"But I am telling the truth!" Anger flared up in Mr. Chiu. "Your police station owes me an apology. My train ticket has expired, my new leather sandals are ruined, and I am late for a conference in the provincial capital. You must compensate me for the damage and losses. Don't mistake me for a common citizen who would tremble when you sneeze. I'm a scholar, a philosopher, and an expert in dialectical materialism. If necessary, we will argue about this in *The Northeastern Daily*, or we will go to the highest People's Court in Beijing. Tell me, what's your name?" He got carried away with his harangue, which was by no means trivial and had worked to his advantage on numerous occasions.

"Stop bluffing us," the donkey-faced man broke in. "We have seen a lot of your kind. We can easily prove you are guilty. Here are some of the statements given by eyewitnesses." He pushed a few sheets of paper toward Mr. Chiu.

Mr. Chiu was dazed to see the different handwritings, which all stated that he had shouted in the square to attract attention and refused to obey the police. One of the witnesses had identified herself as a purchasing agent from a shipyard in Shanghai. Something stirred in Mr. Chiu's stomach, a pain rising to his rib. He gave out a faint moan.

"Now you have to admit you are guilty," the chief said. "Although it's a serious crime, we won't punish you severely, provided you write out a self-criticism and promise that you won't disrupt the public order again. In other words, your release will depend on your attitude toward this crime."

"You're daydreaming," Mr. Chiu cried. "I won't write a word, because I'm innocent. I demand that you provide me with a letter of apology so I can explain to my university why I'm late."

Both the interrogators smiled contemptuously. "Well, we've never done that," said the chief, taking a puff at his cigarette.

"Then make this a precedent."

"That's unnecessary. We are pretty certain that you will comply with our wishes." The chief blew a column of smoke toward Mr. Chiu's face.

At the tilt of the chief's head, two guards stepped forward and grabbed the criminal by the arms. Mr. Chiu meanwhile went on saying, "I shall report you to the Provincial Administration. You'll have to pay for this! You are worse than the Japanese military police."

They dragged him out of the room.

After dinner, which consisted of a bowl of millet porridge, a corn bun, and a piece of pickled turnip, Mr. Chiu began to have a fever, shaking with a chill and sweating profusely. He knew that the fire of anger had gotten into his liver and that he was probably having a relapse. No medicine was available, because his briefcase had been left with his bride. At home it would have been time for him to sit in front of their color TV, drinking jasmine tea and watching the evening news. It was so lonesome in here. The orange bulb above the single bed was the only source of light, which enabled the guards to keep him under surveillance at night. A moment ago he had asked them for a newspaper or a magazine to read, but they turned him down.

Through the small opening on the door noises came in. It seemed that the police on duty were playing cards or chess in a nearby office; shouts and laughter could be heard now and then. Meanwhile, an accordion kept coughing from a remote corner in the building. Looking at the ballpoint and the letter paper left for him by the guards when they took him back from the Interrogation Bureau, Mr. Chiu remembered the old saying, "When a scholar runs into soldiers, the more he argues, the muddier his point becomes." How ridiculous this whole thing was. He ruffled his thick hair with his fingers.

He felt miserable, massaging his stomach continually. To tell the truth, he was more upset than frightened, because he would have to catch up with his work once he was back home—a paper that was due at the printers next week, and two dozen books he ought to read for the courses he was going to teach in the fall.

A human shadow flitted across the opening. Mr. Chiu rushed to the door and shouted through the hole, "Comrade Guard, Comrade Guard!"

"What do you want?" a voice rasped.

"I want you to inform your leaders that I'm very sick. I have heart disease and hepatitis. I may die here if you keep me like this without medication."

"No leader is on duty on the weekend. You have to wait till Monday."

"What? You mean I'll stay in here tomorrow?"

"Yes."   65

"Your station will be held responsible if anything happens to me."

"We know that. Take it easy, you won't die."

It seemed illogical that Mr. Chiu slept quite well that night, though the light above his head had been on all the time and the straw mattress was hard and infested with fleas. He was afraid of ticks, mosquitoes, cockroaches — any kind of insect but fleas and bedbugs. Once, in the countryside, where his school's faculty and staff had helped the peasants harvest crops for a week, his colleagues had joked about his flesh, which they said must have tasted nonhuman to fleas. Except for him, they were all afflicted with hundreds of bites.

More amazing now, he didn't miss his bride a lot. He even enjoyed sleeping alone, perhaps because the honeymoon had tired him out and he needed more rest.

The backyard was quiet on Sunday morning. Pale sunlight streamed   70
through the pine branches. A few sparrows were jumping on the ground, catching caterpillars and ladybugs. Holding the steel bars, Mr. Chiu inhaled the morning air, which smelled meaty. There must have been an eatery or a cooked-meat stand nearby. He reminded himself that he should take this detention with ease. A sentence that Chairman Mao had written to a hospitalized friend rose in his mind: "Since you are already in here, you may as well stay and make the best of it."

His desire for peace of mind originated in his fear that his hepatitis might get worse. He tried to remain unperturbed. However, he was sure that his liver was swelling up, since the fever still persisted. For a whole day he lay in bed, thinking about his paper on the nature of contradictions. Time and again he was overwhelmed by anger, cursing aloud, "A bunch of thugs!" He swore that once he was out, he would write an article about this experience. He had better find out some of the policemen's names.

It turned out to be a restful day for the most part; he was certain that his university would send somebody to his rescue. All he should do now was remain calm and wait patiently. Sooner or later the police would have to release him, although they had no idea that he might refuse to leave unless they wrote him an apology. Damn those hoodlums, they had ordered more than they could eat!

When he woke up on Monday morning, it was already light. Somewhere a man was moaning; the sound came from the backyard. After a long yawn, and kicking off the tattered blanket, Mr. Chiu climbed out of bed and went to the window. In the middle of the yard, a young man was fastened to a pine, his wrists handcuffed around the trunk from behind. He was wriggling and swearing loudly, but there was no sight of anyone else in the yard. He looked familiar to Mr. Chiu.

Mr. Chiu squinted his eyes to see who it was. To his astonishment, he recognized the man, who was Fenjin, a recent graduate from the Law Department at Harbin University. Two years ago Mr. Chiu had taught a course in Marxist materialism, in which Fenjin had enrolled. Now, how on earth had this young devil landed here?

Then it dawned on him that Fenjin must have been sent over by his bride. 75 What a stupid woman! A bookworm, who only knew how to read foreign novels! He had expected that she would contact the school's Security Section, which would for sure send a cadre here. Fenjin held no official position; he merely worked in a private law firm that had just two lawyers; in fact, they had little business except for some detective work for men and women who suspected their spouses of having extramarital affairs. Mr. Chiu was overcome with a wave of nausea.

Should he call out to let his student know he was nearby? He decided not to, because he didn't know what had happened. Fenjin must have quarreled with the police to incur such a punishment. Yet this could never have occurred if Fenjin hadn't come to his rescue. So no matter what, Mr. Chiu had to do something. But what could he do?

It was going to be a scorcher. He could see purple steam shimmering and rising from the ground among the pines. Poor devil, he thought, as he raised a bowl of corn glue to his mouth, sipped, and took a bite of a piece of salted celery.

When a guard came to collect the bowl and the chopsticks, Mr. Chiu asked him what had happened to the man in the backyard. "He called our boss 'bandit,'" the guard said. "He claimed he was a lawyer or something. An arrogant son of a rabbit."

Now it was obvious to Mr. Chiu that he had to do something to help his rescuer. Before he could figure out a way, a scream broke out in the backyard. He rushed to the window and saw a tall policeman standing before Fenjin, an iron bucket on the ground. It was the same young fellow who had arrested Mr. Chiu in the square two days before. The man pinched Fenjin's nose, then raised his hand, which stayed in the air for a few seconds, then slapped the lawyer across the face. As Fenjin was groaning, the man lifted up the bucket and poured water on his head.

"This will keep you from getting sunstroke, boy. I'll give you some more 80 every hour," the man said loudly.

Fenjin kept his eyes shut, yet his wry face showed that he was struggling to hold back from cursing the policeman, or, more likely, that he was sobbing in silence. He sneezed, then raised his face and shouted, "Let me go take a piss."

"Oh yeah?" the man bawled. "Pee in your pants."

Still Mr. Chiu didn't make any noise, gripping the steel bars with both hands, his fingers white. The policeman turned and glanced at the cell's window; his pistol, partly holstered, glittered in the sun. With a snort he spat his cigarette butt to the ground and stamped it into the dust.

Then the door opened and the guards motioned Mr. Chiu to come out. Again they took him upstairs to the Interrogation Bureau.

The same men were in the office, though this time the scribe was sitting   85
there empty-handed. At the sight of Mr. Chiu the chief said, "Ah, here you are.
Please be seated."

After Mr. Chiu sat down, the chief waved a white silk fan and said to him,
"You may have seen your lawyer. He's a young man without manners, so our
director had him taught a crash course in the backyard."

"It's illegal to do that. Aren't you afraid to appear in a newspaper?"

"No, we are not, not even on TV. What else can you do? We are not afraid
of any story you make up. We call it fiction. What we do care about is that you
cooperate with us. That is to say, you must admit your crime."

"What if I refuse to cooperate?"

"Then your lawyer will continue his education in the sunshine."   90

A swoon swayed Mr. Chiu, and he held the arms of the chair to steady
himself. A numb pain stung him in the upper stomach and nauseated him, and
his head was throbbing. He was sure that the hepatitis was finally attacking
him. Anger was flaming up in his chest; his throat was tight and clogged.

The chief resumed, "As a matter of fact, you don't even have to write out
your self-criticism. We have your crime described clearly here. All we need is
your signature."

Holding back his rage, Mr. Chiu said, "Let me look at that."

With a smirk the donkey-faced man handed him a sheet, which carried
these words:

> I hereby admit that on July 13 I disrupted public order at Muji Train Station,
> and that I refused to listen to reason when the railroad police issued their
> warning. Thus I myself am responsible for my arrest. After two days' deten-
> tion, I have realized the reactionary nature of my crime. From now on,
> I shall continue to educate myself with all my effort and shall never commit
> this kind of crime again.

A voice started screaming in Mr. Chiu's ears, "Lie, lie!" But he shook his   95
head and forced the voice away. He asked the chief, "If I sign this, will you release both my lawyer and me?"

"Of course, we'll do that." The chief was drumming his fingers on the blue
folder—their file on him.

Mr. Chiu signed his name and put his thumbprint under his signature.

"Now you are free to go," the chief said with a smile, and handed him a
piece of paper to wipe his thumb with.

Mr. Chiu was so sick that he couldn't stand up from the chair at first try.
Then he doubled his effort and rose to his feet. He staggered out of the building
to meet his lawyer in the backyard, having forgotten to ask for his belt back. In
his chest he felt as though there were a bomb. If he were able to, he would have
razed the entire police station and eliminated all their families. Though he knew
he could do nothing like that, he made up his mind to do something.

"I'm sorry about this torture, Fenjin," Mr. Chiu said when they met.   100

"It doesn't matter. They are savages." The lawyer brushed a patch of dirt off his jacket with trembling fingers. Water was still dribbling from the bottoms of his trouser legs.

"Let's go now," the teacher said.

The moment they came out of the police station, Mr. Chiu caught sight of a tea stand. He grabbed Fenjin's arm and walked over to the old woman at the table. "Two bowls of black tea," he said and handed her a one-yuan note.

After the first bowl, they each had another one. Then they set out for the train station. But before they walked fifty yards, Mr. Chiu insisted on eating a bowl of tree-ear soup at a food stand. Fenjin agreed. He told his teacher, "You mustn't treat me like a guest."

"No, I want to eat something myself."

105

As if dying of hunger, Mr. Chiu dragged his lawyer from restaurant to restaurant near the police station, but at each place he ordered no more than two bowls of food. Fenjin wondered why his teacher wouldn't stay at one place and eat his fill.

Mr. Chiu bought noodles, wonton, eight-grain porridge, and chicken soup, respectively, at four restaurants. While eating, he kept saying through his teeth, "If only I could kill all the bastards!" At the last place he merely took a few sips of the soup without tasting the chicken cubes and mushrooms.

Fenjin was baffled by his teacher, who looked ferocious and muttered to himself mysteriously, and whose jaundiced face was covered with dark puckers. For the first time Fenjin thought of Mr. Chiu as an ugly man.

Within a month over eight hundred people contracted acute hepatitis in Muji. Six died of the disease, including two children. Nobody knew how the epidemic had started.

STORIES FOR FURTHER READING

Isabel Allende   Chile, b. 1942

And of Clay Are We Created   [1984]

Translated by Margaret Sayers Peden

They discovered the girl's head protruding from the mudpit, eyes wide open, calling soundlessly. She had a First Communion name, Azucena. Lily. In that vast cemetery where the odor of death was already attracting vultures from far away, and where the weeping of orphans and wails of the injured filled the air, the little girl obstinately clinging to life became the symbol of the tragedy. The television cameras transmitted so often the unbearable image of the head budding like a black squash from the clay that there was no one who did not recognize her and know her name. And every time we saw her on the screen, right behind her was Rolf Carlé, who had gone there on assignment, never suspecting that he would find a fragment of his past, lost thirty years before.

First a subterranean sob rocked the cotton fields, curling them like waves of foam. Geologists had set up their seismographs weeks before and knew that the mountain had awakened again. For some time they had predicted that the heat of the eruption could detach the eternal ice from the slopes of the volcano, but no one heeded their warnings; they sounded like the tales of frightened old women. The towns in the valley went about their daily life, deaf to the moaning of the earth, until that fateful Wednesday night in November when a prolonged roar announced the end of the world, and walls of snow broke loose, rolling in an avalanche of clay, stones, and water that descended on the villages and buried them beneath unfathomable meters of telluric vomit. As soon as the survivors emerged from the paralysis of that first awful terror, they could see that houses, plazas, churches, white cotton plantations, dark coffee forests, cattle pastures — all had disappeared. Much later, after soldiers and volunteers had arrived to rescue the living and try to assess the magnitude of the cataclysm, it was calculated that beneath the mud lay more than twenty thousand human beings and an indefinite number of animals putrefying in a viscous soup. Forests and rivers had also been swept away, and there was nothing to be seen but an immense desert of mire.

When the station called before dawn, Rolf Carlé and I were together. I crawled out of bed, dazed with sleep, and went to prepare coffee while he hurriedly dressed. He stuffed his gear in the green canvas backpack he always carried, and we said goodbye, as we had so many times before. I had no presentiments. I sat in the kitchen, sipping my coffee and planning the long hours without him, sure that he would be back the next day.

He was one of the first to reach the scene, because while other reporters were fighting their way to the edges of that morass in jeeps, bicycles, or on foot, each getting there however he could, Rolf Carlé had the advantage of the television helicopter, which flew him over the avalanche. We watched on our screens the footage captured by his assistant's camera, in which he was up to his knees in muck, a microphone in his hand, in the midst of a bedlam of lost children, wounded survivors, corpses, and devastation. The story came to us in his calm voice. For years he had been a familiar figure in newscasts, reporting live at the scene of battles and catastrophes with awesome tenacity. Nothing could stop him, and I was always amazed at his equanimity in the face of danger and suffering; it seemed as if nothing could shake his fortitude or deter his curiosity. Fear seemed never to touch him, although he had confessed to me that he was not a courageous man, far from it. I believe that the lens of the camera had a strange effect on him; it was as if it transported him to a different time from which he could watch events without actually participating in them. When I knew him better, I came to realize that this fictive distance seemed to protect him from his own emotions.

Rolf Carlé was in on the story of Azucena from the beginning. He filmed 5
the volunteers who discovered her, and the first persons who tried to reach her;
his camera zoomed in on the girl, her dark face, her large desolate eyes, the
plastered-down tangle of her hair. The mud was like quicksand around her, and
anyone attempting to reach her was in danger of sinking. They threw a rope to
her that she made no effort to grasp until they shouted to her to catch it; then
she pulled a hand from the mire and tried to move, but immediately sank a little
deeper. Rolf threw down his knapsack and the rest of his equipment and waded
into the quagmire, commenting for his assistant's microphone that it was cold
and that one could begin to smell the stench of corpses.

"What's your name?" he asked the girl, and she told him her flower name.
"Don't move, Azucena," Rolf Carlé directed, and kept talking to her, without a
thought for what he was saying, just to distract her, while slowly he worked his
way forward in mud up to his waist. The air around him seemed as murky as
the mud.

It was impossible to reach her from the approach he was attempting, so he
retreated and circled around where there seemed to be firmer footing. When
finally he was close enough, he took the rope and tied it beneath her arms, so
they could pull her out. He smiled at her with that smile that crinkles his eyes
and makes him look like a little boy; he told her that everything was fine, that
he was here with her now, that soon they would have her out. He signaled the
others to pull, but as soon as the cord tensed, the girl screamed. They tried
again, and her shoulders and arms appeared, but they could move her no farther; she was trapped. Someone suggested that her legs might be caught in the
collapsed walls of her house, but she said it was not just rubble, that she was
also held by the bodies of her brothers and sisters clinging to her legs.

"Don't worry, we'll get you out of here," Rolf promised. Despite the quality
of the transmission, I could hear his voice break, and I loved him more than
ever. Azucena looked at him, but said nothing.

During those first hours Rolf Carlé exhausted all the resources of his ingenuity to rescue her. He struggled with poles and ropes, but every tug was an
intolerable torture for the imprisoned girl. It occurred to him to use one of the
poles as a lever but got no result and had to abandon the idea. He talked a
couple of soldiers into working with him for a while, but they had to leave because so many other victims were calling for help. The girl could not move, she
barely could breathe, but she did not seem desperate, as if an ancestral resignation allowed her to accept her fate. The reporter, on the other hand, was determined to snatch her from death. Someone brought him a tire, which he placed
beneath her arms like a life buoy, and then laid a plank near the hole to hold
his weight and allow him to stay closer to her. As it was impossible to remove
the rubble blindly, he tried once or twice to dive toward her feet, but emerged
frustrated, covered with mud, and spitting gravel. He concluded that he would
have to have a pump to drain the water, and radioed a request for one, but received in return a message that there was no available transport and it could
not be sent until the next morning.

"We can't wait that long!" Rolf Carlé shouted, but in the pandemonium no   10
one stopped to commiserate. Many more hours would go by before he accepted
that time had stagnated and reality had been irreparably distorted.

A military doctor came to examine the girl, and observed that her heart was
functioning well and that if she did not get too cold she could survive the night.

"Hang on, Azucena, we'll have the pump tomorrow," Rolf Carlé tried to
console her.

"Don't leave me alone," she begged.

"No, of course I won't leave you."

Someone brought him coffee, and he helped the girl drink it, sip by sip. The   15
warm liquid revived her and she began telling him about her small life, about
her family and her school, about how things were in that little bit of world
before the volcano had erupted. She was thirteen, and she had never been outside her village. Rolf Carlé, buoyed by a premature optimism, was convinced
that everything would end well: the pump would arrive, they would drain the
water, move the rubble, and Azucena would be transported by helicopter to a
hospital where she would recover rapidly and where he could visit her and bring
her gifts. He thought, She's already too old for dolls, and I don't know what
would please her; maybe a dress. I don't know much about women, he concluded, amused, reflecting that although he had known many women in his
lifetime, none had taught him these details. To pass the hours he began to tell
Azucena about his travels and adventures as a newshound, and when he exhausted his memory, he called upon imagination, inventing things he thought
might entertain her. From time to time she dozed, but he kept talking in the
darkness, to assure her that he was still there and to overcome the menace of
uncertainty.

That was a long night.

Many miles away, I watched Rolf Carlé and the girl on a television screen.
I could not bear the wait at home, so I went to National Television, where I
often spent entire nights with Rolf editing programs. There, I was near his
world, and I could at least get a feeling of what he lived through during those
three decisive days. I called all the important people in the city, senators, com-
manders of the armed forces, the North American ambassador, and the president of National Petroleum, begging them for a pump to remove the silt, but
obtained only vague promises. I began to ask for urgent help on radio and television, to see if there wasn't *someone* who could help us. Between calls I would
run to the newsroom to monitor the satellite transmissions that periodically
brought new details of the catastrophe. While reporters selected scenes with
most impact for the news report, I searched for footage that featured Azucena's
mudpit. The screen reduced the disaster to a single plane and accentuated the
tremendous distance that separated me from Rolf Carlé; nonetheless, I was
there with him. The child's every suffering hurt me as it did him; I felt his frustration, his impotence. Faced with the impossibility of communicating with
him, the fantastic idea came to me that if I tried, I could reach him by force of
mind and in that way give him encouragement. I concentrated until I was

dizzy — a frenzied and futile activity. At times I would be overcome with compassion and burst out crying; at other times, I was so drained I felt as if I were staring through a telescope at the light of a star dead for a million years.

I watched that hell on the first morning broadcast, cadavers of people and animals awash in the current of new rivers formed overnight from the melted snow. Above the mud rose the tops of trees and the bell towers of a church where several people had taken refuge and were patiently awaiting rescue teams. Hundreds of soldiers and volunteers from the Civil Defense were clawing through rubble searching for survivors, while long rows of ragged specters awaited their turn for a cup of hot broth. Radio networks announced that their phones were jammed with calls from families offering shelter to orphaned children. Drinking water was in scarce supply, along with gasoline and food. Doctors, resigned to amputating arms and legs without anesthesia, pled that at least they be sent serum and painkillers and antibiotics; most of the roads, however, were impassable, and worse were the bureaucratic obstacles that stood in the way. To top it all, the clay contaminated by decomposing bodies threatened the living with an outbreak of epidemics.

Azucena was shivering inside the tire that held her above the surface. Immobility and tension had greatly weakened her, but she was conscious and could still be heard when a microphone was held out to her. Her tone was humble, as if apologizing for all the fuss. Rolf Carlé had a growth of beard, and dark circles beneath his eyes; he looked near exhaustion. Even from that enormous distance I could sense the quality of his weariness, so different from the fatigue of other adventures. He had completely forgotten the camera; he could not look at the girl through a lens any longer. The pictures we were receiving were not his assistant's but those of other reporters who had appropriated Azucena, bestowing on her the pathetic responsibility of embodying the horror of what had happened in that place. With the first light Rolf tried again to dislodge the obstacles that held the girl in her tomb, but he had only his hands to work with; he did not dare use a tool for fear of injuring her. He fed Azucena a cup of the cornmeal mush and bananas the Army was distributing, but she immediately vomited it up. A doctor stated that she had a fever, but added that there was little he could do: antibiotics were being reserved for cases of gangrene. A priest also passed by and blessed her, hanging a medal of the Virgin around her neck. By evening a gentle, persistent drizzle began to fall.

"The sky is weeping," Azucena murmured, and she, too, began to cry.   20

"Don't be afraid," Rolf begged. "You have to keep your strength up and be calm. Everything will be fine. I'm with you, and I'll get you out somehow."

Reporters returned to photograph Azucena and ask her the same questions, which she no longer tried to answer. In the meanwhile, more television and movie teams arrived with spools of cable, tapes, film, videos, precision lenses, recorders, sound consoles, lights, reflecting screens, auxiliary motors, cartons of supplies, electricians, sound technicians, and cameramen: Azucena's face was beamed to millions of screens around the world. And all the while Rolf Carlé kept pleading for a pump. The improved technical facilities bore results, and National Television began receiving sharper pictures and clearer sound; the distance seemed suddenly compressed, and I had the horrible sensation that Azucena and Rolf were by my side, separated from me by impenetrable glass. I was able to follow events hour by hour; I knew everything my love did to wrest the girl from her prison and help her endure her suffering; I overheard fragments of what they said to one another and could guess the rest; I was present when she taught Rolf to pray, and when he distracted her with the stories I had told him in a thousand and one nights beneath the white mosquito netting of our bed.

When darkness came on the second day, Rolf tried to sing Azucena to sleep with old Austrian folk songs he had learned from his mother, but she was far beyond sleep. They spent most of the night talking, each in a stupor of exhaustion and hunger, and shaking with cold. That night, imperceptibly, the unyielding floodgates that had contained Rolf Carlé's past for so many years began to open, and the torrent of all that had lain hidden in the deepest and most secret layers of memory poured out, leveling before it the obstacles that had blocked his consciousness for so long. He could not tell it all to Azucena; she perhaps did not know there was a world beyond the sea or time previous to her own; she was not capable of imagining Europe in the years of the war. So he could not tell her of defeat, nor of the afternoon the Russians had led them to the concentration camp to bury prisoners dead from starvation. Why should he describe to her how the naked bodies piled like a mountain of firewood resembled fragile china? How could he tell this dying child about ovens and gallows? Nor did he mention the night that he had seen his mother naked, shod in stiletto-heeled red boots, sobbing with humiliation. There was much he did not tell, but in those hours he relived for the first time all the things his mind had tried to erase. Azucena had surrendered her fear to him and so, without wishing it, had obliged Rolf to confront his own. There, beside that hellhole of mud, it was impossible for Rolf to flee from himself any longer, and the visceral terror he had lived as a boy suddenly invaded him. He reverted to the years when he was the age of Azucena, and younger, and, like her, found himself trapped in a pit without escape, buried in life, his head barely above ground; he saw before his eyes the boots and legs of his father, who had removed his belt and was whipping it in the air with the never-forgotten hiss of a viper coiled to strike. Sorrow flooded through him, intact and precise, as if it had lain always in his mind, waiting. He was once again in the armoire where his father locked him to punish him for imagined misbehavior, there where for eternal hours he had crouched with his eyes closed, not to see the darkness, with his hands over his ears, to shut out the beating of his heart, trembling, huddled like a cornered animal. Wandering in the mist of his memories he found his sister Katharina, a sweet, retarded child who spent her life hiding, with the hope that her father would forget the disgrace of her having been born. With Katharina, Rolf crawled beneath the dining room table, and with her hid there under the long white tablecloth, two children forever embraced, alert to footsteps and voices. Katharina's scent melded with his own sweat, with aromas of cooking, garlic, soup, freshly baked bread, and the unexpected odor of putrescent clay. His sister's hand in his, her frightened breathing, her silk hair against his cheek, the candid gaze of her eyes. Katharina . . . Katharina materialized before him, floating on the air like a flag, clothed in the white tablecloth, now a winding sheet, and at last he could weep for her death and for the guilt of having abandoned her. He understood then that all his exploits as a reporter, the feats that had won him such recognition and fame, were merely an attempt to keep his most ancient fears at bay, a stratagem for taking refuge behind a lens to test whether reality was more tolerable from that perspective. He took excessive risks as an exercise of courage, training by day to conquer the monsters that tormented him by night. But he had come face to face with the moment of truth; he could not continue to escape his past. He *was* Azucena; he was buried in the clayey mud; his terror was not the distant emotion of an almost forgotten childhood, it was a claw sunk in his throat. In the flush of his tears he saw his mother, dressed in black and clutching her imitation-crocodile pocketbook to her bosom, just as he had last seen her on the dock when she had come to put him on the boat to South America. She had not come to dry his tears, but to tell him to pick up a shovel: the war was over and now they must bury the dead.

"Don't cry. I don't hurt anymore. I'm fine," Azucena said when dawn came.

"I'm not crying for you," Rolf Carlé smiled. "I'm crying for myself. I hurt   25
all over."

The third day in the valley of the cataclysm began with a pale light filtering through storm clouds. The President of the Republic visited the area in his tailored safari jacket to confirm that this was the worst catastrophe of the century; the country was in mourning; sister nations had offered aid; he had ordered a state of siege; the Armed Forces would be merciless, anyone caught stealing or committing other offenses would be shot on sight. He added that it was impossible to remove all the corpses or count the thousands who had disappeared; the entire valley would be declared holy ground, and bishops would come to celebrate a solemn mass for the souls of the victims. He went to the Army field tents to offer relief in the form of vague promises to crowds of the rescued, then to the improvised hospital to offer a word of encouragement to doctors and nurses worn down from so many hours of tribulations. Then he asked to be taken to see Azucena, the little girl the whole world had seen. He waved to her with a limp statesman's hand, and microphones recorded his emotional voice and paternal tone as he told her that her courage had served as an example to the nation. Rolf Carlé interrupted to ask for a pump, and the President assured him that he personally would attend to the matter. I caught a glimpse of Rolf for a few seconds kneeling beside the mudpit. On the evening news broadcast, he was still in the same position; and I, glued to the screen like a fortuneteller to her crystal ball, could tell that something fundamental had changed in him. I knew somehow that during the night his defenses had crumbled and he had given in to grief; finally he was vulnerable. The girl had touched a part of him that he himself had no access to, a part he had never shared with me. Rolf had wanted to console her, but it was Azucena who had given him consolation.

I recognized the precise moment at which Rolf gave up the fight and surrendered to the torture of watching the girl die. I was with them, three days and two nights, spying on them from the other side of life. I was there when she told him that in all her thirteen years no boy had ever loved her and that it was a pity to leave this world without knowing love. Rolf assured her that he loved her more than he could ever love anyone, more than he loved his mother, more than his sister, more than all the women who had slept in his arms, more than he loved me, his life companion, who would have given anything to be trapped in that well in her place, who would have exchanged her life for Azucena's, and I watched as he leaned down to kiss her poor forehead, consumed by a sweet, sad emotion he could not name. I felt how in that instant both were saved from despair, how they were freed from the clay, how they rose above the vultures and helicopters, how together they flew above the vast swamp of corruption and laments. How, finally, they were able to accept death. Rolf Carlé prayed in silence that she would die quickly, because such pain cannot be borne.

By then I had obtained a pump and was in touch with a general who had agreed to ship it the next morning on a military cargo plane. But on the night of that third day, beneath the unblinking focus of quartz lamps and the lens of a hundred cameras, Azucena gave up, her eyes locked with those of the friend who had sustained her to the end. Rolf Carlé removed the life buoy, closed her eyelids, held her to his chest for a few moments, and then let her go. She sank slowly, a flower in the mud.

You are back with me, but you are not the same man. I often accompany you to the station and we watch the videos of Azucena again; you study them intently, looking for something you could have done to save her, something you did not think of in time. Or maybe you study them to see yourself as if in a mirror, naked. Your cameras lie forgotten in a closet; you do not write or sing; you sit long hours before the window, staring at the mountains. Beside you, I wait for you to complete the voyage into yourself, for the old wounds to heal. I know that when you return from your nightmares, we shall again walk hand in hand, as before.

James Baldwin   1924–1987

Sonny's Blues   [1957]

I read about it in the paper, in the subway, on my way to work. I read it, and I couldn't believe it, and I read it again. Then perhaps I just stared at it, at the newsprint spelling out his name, spelling out the story. I stared at it in the swinging lights of the subway car, and in the faces and bodies of the people, and in my own face, trapped in the darkness which roared outside.

It was not to be believed and I kept telling myself that, as I walked from the subway station to the high school. And at the same time

APPROACHING THE AUTHOR

James Baldwin published his first story in a church newspaper when he was twelve and became a preacher at the small Fireside Pentecostal Church in Harlem when he was fourteen.

For more about him, see page 1373.

I couldn't doubt it. I was scared, scared for Sonny. He became real to me again. A great block of ice got settled in my belly and kept melting there slowly all day long, while I taught my classes algebra. It was a special kind of ice. It kept melting, sending trickles of ice water all up and down my veins, but it never got less. Sometimes it hardened and seemed to expand until I felt my guts were going to come spilling out or that I was going to choke or scream. This would always be at a moment when I was remembering some specific thing Sonny had once said or done.

When he was about as old as the boys in my classes his face had been bright and open, there was a lot of copper in it; and he'd had wonderfully direct brown eyes, and great gentleness and privacy. I wondered what he looked like now. He had been picked up, the evening before, in a raid on an apartment downtown, for peddling and using heroin.

I couldn't believe it: but what I mean by that is that I couldn't find any room for it anywhere inside me. I had kept it outside me for a long time. I hadn't wanted to know. I had had suspicions, but I didn't name them, I kept putting them away. I told myself that Sonny was wild, but he wasn't crazy. And he'd always been a good boy, he hadn't ever turned hard or evil or disrespectful, the way kids can, so quick, so quick, especially in Harlem. I didn't want to believe that I'd ever see my brother going down, coming to nothing, all that light in his face gone out, in the condition I'd already seen so many others. Yet it had happened and here I was, talking about algebra to a lot of boys who might, every one of them for all I knew, be popping off needles every time they went to the head. Maybe it did more for them than algebra could.

I was sure that the first time Sonny had ever had horse, he couldn't have   5
been much older than these boys were now. These boys, now, were living as we'd been living then, they were growing up with a rush and their heads bumped abruptly against the low ceiling of their actual possibilities. They were filled with rage. All they really knew were two darknesses, the darkness of their lives, which was now closing in on them, and the darkness of the movies, which had blinded them to that other darkness, and in which they now, vindictively, dreamed, at once more together than they were at any other time, and more alone.

When the last bell rang, the last class ended, I let out my breath. It seemed I'd been holding it for all that time. My clothes were wet—I may have looked as though I'd been sitting in a steam bath, all dressed up, all afternoon. I sat alone in the classroom a long time. I listened to the boys outside, downstairs, shouting and cursing and laughing. Their laughter struck me for perhaps the first time. It was not the joyous laughter which—God knows why—one associates with children. It was mocking and insular, its intent to denigrate. It was disenchanted, and in this, also, lay the authority of their curses. Perhaps I was listening to them because I was thinking about my brother and in them I heard my brother. And myself.

One boy was whistling a tune, at once very complicated and very simple, it seemed to be pouring out of him as though he were a bird, and it sounded very cool and moving through all that harsh, bright air, only just holding its own through all those other sounds.

I stood up and walked over to the window and looked down into the court-yard. It was the beginning of the spring and the sap was rising in the boys. A teacher passed through them every now and again, quickly, as though he or she couldn't wait to get out of that courtyard, to get those boys out of their sight and off their minds. I started collecting my stuff. I thought I'd better get home and talk to Isabel.

The courtyard was almost deserted by the time I got downstairs. I saw this boy standing in the shadow of a doorway, looking just like Sonny. I almost called his name. Then I saw that it wasn't Sonny, but somebody we used to know, a boy from around our block. He'd been Sonny's friend. He'd never been mine, having been too young for me, and, anyway, I'd never liked him. And now, even though he was a grown-up man, he still hung around that block, still spent hours on the street corners, was always high and raggy. I used to run into him from time to time and he'd often work around to asking me for a quarter or fifty cents. He always had some real good excuse, too, and I always gave it to him, I don't know why.

But now, abruptly, I hated him. I couldn't stand the way he looked at me, partly like a dog, partly like a cunning child. I wanted to ask him what the hell he was doing in the school courtyard. 10

He sort of shuffled over to me, and he said, "I see you got the papers. So you already know about it."

"You mean about Sonny? Yes, I already know about it. How come they didn't get you?"

He grinned. It made him repulsive and it also brought to mind what he'd looked like as a kid. "I wasn't there. I stay away from them people."

"Good for you." I offered him a cigarette and I watched him through the smoke. "You come all the way down here just to tell me about Sonny?"

"That's right." He was sort of shaking his head and his eyes looked strange, as though they were about to cross. The bright sun deadened his damp dark brown skin and it made his eyes look yellow and showed up the dirt in his kinked hair. He smelled funky. I moved a little away from him and I said, "Well, thanks. But I already know about it and I got to get home." 15

"I'll walk you a little ways," he said. We started walking. There were a couple of kids still loitering in the courtyard and one of them said goodnight to me and looked strangely at the boy beside me.

"What're you going to do?" he asked me. "I mean, about Sonny?"

"Look. I haven't seen Sonny for over a year, I'm not sure I'm going to do anything. Anyway, what the hell *can* I do?"

"That's right," he said quickly, "ain't nothing you can do. Can't much help old Sonny no more, I guess."

It was what I was thinking and so it seemed to me he had no right to say it. 20

"I'm surprised at Sonny, though," he went on — he had a funny way of talk-ing, he looked straight ahead as though he were talking to himself — "I thought Sonny was a smart boy, I thought he was too smart to get hung."

"I guess he thought so too," I said sharply, "and that's how he got hung. And how about you? You're pretty goddamn smart, I bet."

Then he looked directly at me, just for a minute. "I ain't smart," he said. "If I was smart, I'd have reached for a pistol a long time ago."

"Look. Don't tell *me* your sad story, if it was up to me, I'd give you one." Then I felt guilty—guilty, probably, for never having supposed that the poor bastard *had* a story of his own, much less a sad one, and I asked, quickly, "What's going to happen to him now?"

He didn't answer this. He was off by himself some place. "Funny thing," he 25 said, and from his tone we might have been discussing the quickest way to get to Brooklyn, "when I saw the papers this morning, the first thing I asked myself was if I had anything to do with it. I felt sort of responsible."

I began to listen more carefully. The subway station was on the corner, just before us, and I stopped. He stopped, too. We were in front of a bar and he ducked lightly, peering in, but whoever he was looking for didn't seem to be there. The juke box was blasting away with something black and bouncy and I half watched the barmaid as she danced her way from the juke box to her place behind the bar. And I watched her face as she laughingly responded to something someone said to her, still keeping time to the music. When she smiled one saw the little girl, one sensed the doomed, still-struggling woman beneath the battered face of the semi-whore.

"I never *give* Sonny nothing," the boy said finally, "but a long time ago I come to school high and Sonny asked me how it felt." He paused, I couldn't bear to watch him, I watched the barmaid, and I listened to the music which seemed to be causing the pavement to shake. "I told him it felt great." The music stopped, the barmaid paused and watched the juke box until the music began again. "It did."

All this was carrying me some place I didn't want to go. I certainly didn't want to know how it felt. It filled everything, the people, the houses, the music, the dark, quicksilver barmaid, with menace; and this menace was their reality.

"What's going to happen to him now?" I asked again.

"They'll send him away some place and they'll try to cure him." He shook 30 his head. "Maybe he'll even think he's kicked the habit. Then they'll let him loose"—he gestured, throwing his cigarette into the gutter. "That's all."

"What do you mean, that's *all*?"

But I knew what he meant.

"I *mean*, that's *all*." He turned his head and looked at me, pulling down the corners of his mouth. "Don't you know what I mean?" he asked, softly.

"How the hell *would* I know what you mean?" I almost whispered it, I don't know why.

"That's right," he said to the air, "how would *he* know what I mean?" He 35 turned toward me again, patient and calm, and yet I somehow felt him shaking, shaking as though he were going to fall apart. I felt that ice in my guts again, the dread I'd felt all afternoon; and again I watched the barmaid, moving about the bar, washing glasses, and singing. "Listen. They'll let him out and then it'll just start all over again. That's what I mean."

"You mean—they'll let him out. And then he'll just start working his way back in again. You mean he'll never kick the habit. Is that what you mean?"

"That's right," he said, cheerfully. "*You* see what I mean."

"Tell me," I said at last, "why does he want to die? He must want to die, he's killing himself, why does he want to die?"

He looked at me in surprise. He licked his lips. "He don't want to die. He wants to live. Don't nobody want to die, ever."

Then I wanted to ask him—too many things. He could not have answered, 40 or if he had, I could not have borne the answers. I started walking. "Well, I guess it's none of my business."

"It's going to be rough on old Sonny," he said. We reached the subway station. "This is your station?" he asked. I nodded. I took one step down. "Damn!" he said, suddenly. I looked up at him. He grinned again. "Damn it if I didn't leave all my money home. You ain't got a dollar on you, have you? Just for a couple of days, is all."

All at once something inside gave and threatened to come pouring out of me. I didn't hate him any more. I felt that in another moment I'd start crying like a child.

"Sure," I said. "Don't sweat." I looked in my wallet and didn't have a dollar, I only had a five. "Here," I said. "That hold you?"

He didn't look at it—he didn't want to look at it. A terrible closed look came over his face, as though he were keeping the number on the bill a secret from him and me. "Thanks," he said, and now he was dying to see me go. "Don't worry about Sonny. Maybe I'll write him or something."

"Sure," I said. "You do that. So long." 45

"Be seeing you," he said. I went on down the steps.

And I didn't write Sonny or send him anything for a long time. When I finally did, it was just after my little girl died, he wrote me back a letter which made me feel like a bastard.

Here's what he said:

Dear brother,

You don't know how much I needed to hear from you. I wanted to write you many a time but I dug how much I must have hurt you and so I didn't write. But now I feel like a man who's been trying to climb up out of some deep, real deep and funky hole and just saw the sun up there, outside. I got to get outside.

I can't tell you much about how I got here. I mean I don't know how to tell you. I guess I was afraid of something or I was trying to escape from something and you know I have never been very strong in the head (smile). I'm glad Mama and Daddy are dead and can't see what's happened to their son and I swear if I'd known what I was doing I would never have hurt you so, you and a lot of other fine people who were nice to me and who believed in me.

I don't want you to think it had anything to do with me being a musician. It's more than that. Or maybe less than that. I can't get anything straight in my head down here and I try not to think about what's going to happen to me when I get outside again. Sometime I think I'm going to flip and *never* get outside and sometime I think I'll come straight back. I tell you one thing, though, I'd rather blow my brains out than go through this again. But that's what they all say, so they tell me. If I tell you when I'm coming to New York and if you could meet me, I sure would appreciate it. Give my love to Isabel and the kids and I was sure sorry to hear about little Gracie. I wish I could be like Mama and say the Lord's will be done, but I don't know it seems to me that trouble is the one thing that never does get stopped and I don't know what good it does to blame it on the Lord. But maybe it does some good if you believe it.

Your brother,
Sonny

Then I kept in constant touch with him and I sent him whatever I could and I went to meet him when he came back to New York. When I saw him many things I thought I had forgotten came flooding back to me. This was because I had begun, finally, to wonder about Sonny, about the life that Sonny lived inside. This life, whatever it was, had made him older and thinner and it had deepened the distant stillness in which he had always moved. He looked very unlike my baby brother. Yet, when he smiled, when we shook hands, the baby brother I'd never known looked out from the depths of his private life, like an animal waiting to be coaxed into the light.

"How you been keeping?" he asked me.   50

"All right. And you?"

"Just fine." He was smiling all over his face. "It's good to see you again."

"It's good to see you."

The seven years' difference in our ages lay between us like a chasm: I wondered if these years would ever operate between us as a bridge. I was remembering, and it made it hard to catch my breath, that I had been there when he was born; and I had heard the first words he had ever spoken. When he started to walk, he walked from our mother straight to me. I caught him just before he fell when he took the first steps he ever took in this world.

"How's Isabel?"   55

"Just fine. She's dying to see you."

"And the boys?"

"They're fine, too. They're anxious to see their uncle."

"Oh, come on. You know they don't remember me."

"Are you kidding? Of course they remember you."   60

He grinned again. We got into a taxi. We had a lot to say to each other, far too much to know how to begin.

As the taxi began to move, I asked, "You still want to go to India?"

He laughed. "You still remember that. Hell, no. This place is Indian enough for me."

"It used to belong to them," I said.

And he laughed again. "They damn sure knew what they were doing when   65 they got rid of it."

Years ago, when he was around fourteen, he'd been all hipped on the idea of going to India. He read books about people sitting on rocks, naked, in all kinds of weather, but mostly bad, naturally, and walking barefoot through hot coals and arriving at wisdom. I used to say that it sounded to me as though they were getting away from wisdom as fast as they could. I think he sort of looked down on me for that.

"Do you mind," he asked, "if we have the driver drive alongside the park? On the west side—I haven't seen the city in so long."

"Of course not," I said. I was afraid that I might sound as though I were humoring him, but I hoped he wouldn't take it that way.

So we drove along, between the green of the park and the stony, lifeless elegance of hotels and apartment buildings, toward the vivid, killing streets of our childhood. These streets hadn't changed, though housing projects jutted up out of them now like rocks in the middle of a boiling sea. Most of the houses in which we had grown up had vanished, as had the stores from which we had stolen, the basements in which we had first tried sex, the rooftops from which we had hurled tin cans and bricks. But houses exactly like the houses of our past yet dominated the landscape, boys exactly like the boys we once had been found themselves smothering in these houses, came down into the streets for light and air and found themselves encircled by disaster. Some escaped the trap, most didn't. Those who got out always left something of themselves behind, as some animals amputate a leg and leave it in the trap. It might be said, perhaps, that I had escaped, after all, I was a school teacher; or that Sonny had, he hadn't lived in Harlem for years. Yet, as the cab moved uptown through streets which seemed, with a rush, to darken with dark people, and as I covertly studied Sonny's face, it came to me that what we both were seeking through our separate cab windows was that part of ourselves which had been left behind. It's always at the hour of trouble and confrontation that the missing member aches.

We hit 110th Street and started rolling up Lenox Avenue. And I'd known   70 this avenue all my life, but it seemed to me again, as it had seemed on the day I'd first heard about Sonny's trouble, filled with a hidden menace which was its very breath of life.

"We almost there," said Sonny.

"Almost." We were both too nervous to say anything more.

We live in a housing project. It hasn't been up long. A few days after it was up it seemed uninhabitably new, now, of course, it's already rundown. It looks like a parody of the good, clean, faceless life—God knows the people who live in it do their best to make it a parody. The beat-looking grass lying around isn't enough to make their lives green, the hedges will never hold out the streets, and they know it. The big windows fool no one, they aren't big enough to make space out of no space. They don't bother with the windows, they watch the TV screen instead. The playground is most popular with the children who don't play at jacks, or skip rope, or roller skate, or swing, and they can be found in it after dark. We moved in partly because it's not too far from where I teach, and partly for the kids; but it's really just like the houses in which Sonny and I grew up. The same things happen, they'll have the same things to remember. The moment Sonny and I started into the house I had the feeling that I was simply bringing him back into the danger he had almost died trying to escape.

Sonny has never been talkative. So I don't know why I was sure he'd be dying to talk to me when supper was over the first night. Everything went fine, the oldest boy remembered him, and the youngest boy liked him, and Sonny had remembered to bring something for each of them; and Isabel, who is really much nicer than I am, more open and giving, had gone to a lot of trouble about dinner and was genuinely glad to see him. And she's always been able to tease Sonny in a way that I haven't. It was nice to see her face so vivid again and to hear her laugh and watch her make Sonny laugh. She wasn't, or, anyway, she didn't seem to be, at all uneasy or embarrassed. She chatted as though there were no subject which had to be avoided and she got Sonny past his first, faint stiffness. And thank God she was there, for I was filled with that icy dread again. Everything I did seemed awkward to me, and everything I said sounded freighted with hidden meaning. I was trying to remember everything I'd heard about dope addiction and I couldn't help watching Sonny for signs. I wasn't doing it out of malice. I was trying to find out something about my brother. I was dying to hear him tell me he was safe.

"Safe!" my father grunted, whenever Mama suggested trying to move to a   75 neighborhood which might be safer for children. "Safe, hell! Ain't no place safe for kids, nor nobody."

He always went on like this, but he wasn't, ever, really as bad as he sounded, not even on weekends, when he got drunk. As a matter of fact, he was always on the lookout for "something a little better," but he died before he found it. He died suddenly, during a drunken weekend in the middle of the war, when Sonny was fifteen. He and Sonny hadn't ever got on too well. And this was partly because Sonny was the apple of his father's eye. It was because he loved Sonny so much and was frightened for him, that he was always fighting with him. It doesn't do any good to fight with Sonny. Sonny just moves back, inside himself, where he can't be reached. But the principal reason that they never hit it off is that they were so much alike. Daddy was big and rough and loud-talking, just the opposite of Sonny, but they both had—that same privacy.

Mama tried to tell me something about this, just after Daddy died. I was home on leave from the army.

This was the last time I ever saw my mother alive. Just the same, this picture gets all mixed up in my mind with pictures I had of her when she was younger. The way I always see her is the way she used to be on a Sunday afternoon, say, when the old folks were talking after the big Sunday dinner. I always see her wearing pale blue. She'd be sitting on the sofa. And my father would be sitting in the easy chair, not far from her. And the living room would be full of church folks and relatives. There they sit, in chairs all around the living room, and the night is creeping up outside, but nobody knows it yet. You can see the darkness growing against the windowpanes and you hear the street noises every now and again, or maybe the jangling beat of a tambourine from one of the churches close by, but it's real quiet in the room. For a moment nobody's talking, but every face looks darkening, like the sky outside. And my mother rocks a little from the waist, and my father's eyes are closed. Everyone is looking at something a child can't see. For a minute they've forgotten the children. Maybe a kid is lying on the rug, half asleep. Maybe somebody's got a kid in his lap and is absent-mindedly stroking the kid's head. Maybe there's a kid, quiet and big-eyed, curled up in a big chair in the corner. The silence, the darkness coming, and the darkness in the faces frightens the child obscurely. He hopes that the hand which strokes his forehead will never stop—will never die. He hopes that there will never come a time when the old folks won't be sitting around the living room, talking about where they've come from, and what they've seen, and what's happened to them and their kinfolk.

But something deep and watchful in the child knows that this is bound to end, is already ending. In a moment someone will get up and turn on the light. Then the old folks will remember the children and they won't talk any more that day. And when light fills the room, the child is filled with darkness. He knows that everytime this happens he's moved just a little closer to that darkness outside. The darkness outside is what the old folks have been talking about. It's what they've come from. It's what they endure. The child knows that they won't talk any more because if he knows too much about what's happened to *them*, he'll know too much too soon, about what's going to happen to *him*.

The last time I talked to my mother, I remember I was restless. I wanted to get out and see Isabel. We weren't married then and we had a lot to straighten out between us.

There Mama sat, in black, by the window. She was humming an old church song, *Lord, you brought me from a long ways off.* Sonny was out somewhere. Mama kept watching the streets.

"I don't know," she said, "if I'll ever see you again, after you go off from here. But I hope you'll remember the things I tried to teach you."

"Don't talk like that," I said, and smiled. "You'll be here a long time yet."

She smiled, too, but she said nothing. She was quiet for a long time. And I said, "Mama, don't you worry about nothing. I'll be writing all the time, and you be getting the checks. . . ."

"I want to talk to you about your brother," she said, suddenly. "If anything happens to me he ain't going to have nobody to look out for him."

"Mama," I said, "ain't nothing going to happen to you *or* Sonny. Sonny's all right. He's a good boy and he's got good sense."

"It ain't a question of his being a good boy," Mama said, "nor of his having good sense. It ain't only the bad ones, nor yet the dumb ones that gets sucked under." She stopped, looking at me. "Your Daddy once had a brother," she said, and she smiled in a way that made me feel she was in pain. "You didn't never know that, did you?"

"No," I said, "I never knew that," and I watched her face.

"Oh, yes," she said, "your Daddy had a brother." She looked out of the window again. "I know you never saw your Daddy cry. But *I* did—many a time, through all these years."

I asked her, "What happened to his brother? How come nobody's ever 90 talked about him?"

This was the first time I ever saw my mother look old.

"His brother got killed," she said, "when he was just a little younger than you are now. I knew him. He was a fine boy. He was maybe a little full of the devil, but he didn't mean nobody no harm."

Then she stopped and the room was silent, exactly as it had sometimes been on those Sunday afternoons. Mama kept looking out into the streets.

"He used to have a job in the mill," she said, "and, like all young folks, he just liked to perform on Saturday nights. Saturday nights, him and your father would drift around to different places, go to dances and things like that, or just sit around with people they knew, and your father's brother would sing, he had a fine voice, and play along with himself on his guitar. Well, this particular Saturday night, him and your father was coming home from some place, and they were both a little drunk and there was a moon that night, it was bright like day. Your father's brother was feeling kind of good, and he was whistling to himself, and he had his guitar slung over his shoulder. They was coming down a hill and beneath them was a road that turned off from the highway. Well, your father's brother, being always kind of frisky, decided to run down this hill, and he did, with that guitar banging and clanging behind him, and he ran across the road, and he was making water behind a tree. And your father was sort of amused at him and he was still coming down the hill, kind of slow. Then he heard a car motor and that same minute his brother stepped from behind the tree, into the road, in the moonlight. And he started to cross the road. And your father started to run down the hill, he says he don't know why. This car was full of white men. They was all drunk, and when they seen your father's brother they let out a great whoop and holler and they aimed the car straight at him. They was having fun, they just wanted to scare him, the way they do some-times, you know. But they was drunk. And I guess the boy, being drunk, too, and scared, kind of lost his head. By the time he jumped it was too late. Your father says he heard his brother scream when the car rolled over him, and he heard the wood of that guitar when it give, and he heard them strings go flying, and he heard them white men shouting, and the car kept on a-going and it ain't stopped till this day. And, time your father got down the hill, his brother weren't nothing but blood and pulp."

Tears were gleaming on my mother's face. There wasn't anything I 95 could say.

"He never mentioned it," she said, "because I never let him mention it before you children. Your Daddy was like a crazy man that night and for many a night thereafter. He says he never in his life seen anything as dark as that road after the lights of that car had gone away. Weren't nothing, weren't nobody on that road, just your Daddy and his brother and that busted guitar. Oh, yes. Your Daddy never did really get right again. Till the day he died he weren't sure but that every white man he saw was the man that killed his brother."

She stopped and took out her handkerchief and dried her eyes and looked at me.

"I ain't telling you all this," she said, "to make you scared or bitter or to make you hate nobody. I'm telling you this because you got a brother. And the world ain't changed."

I guess I didn't want to believe this. I guess she saw this in my face. She turned away from me, toward the window again, searching those streets.

"But I praise my Redeemer," she said at last, "that He called your Daddy   100
home before me. I ain't saying it to throw no flowers at myself, but, I declare, it keeps me from feeling too cast down to know I helped your father get safely through this world. Your father always acted like he was the roughest, strongest man on earth. And everybody took him to be like that. But if he hadn't had *me* there — to see his tears!"

She was crying again. Still, I couldn't move. I said, "Lord, Lord, Mama, I didn't know it was like that."

"Oh, honey," she said, "there's a lot that you don't know. But you are going to find it out." She stood up from the window and came over to me. "You got to hold on to your brother," she said, "and don't let him fall, no matter what it looks like is happening to him and no matter how evil you gets with him. You going to be evil with him many a time. But don't you forget what I told you, you hear?"

"I won't forget," I said. "Don't you worry, I won't forget. I won't let nothing happen to Sonny."

My mother smiled as though she were amused at something she saw in my face. Then, "You may not be able to stop nothing from happening. But you got to let him know you's *there*."

Two days later I was married, and then I was gone. And I had a lot of things   105
on my mind and I pretty well forgot my promise to Mama until I got shipped home on a special furlough for her funeral.

And, after the funeral, with just Sonny and me alone in the empty kitchen, I tried to find out something about him.

"What do you want to do?" I asked him.

"I'm going to be a musician," he said.

For he had graduated, in the time I had been away, from dancing to the juke box to finding out who was playing what, and what they were doing with it, and he had bought himself a set of drums.

"You mean, you want to be a drummer?" I somehow had the feeling that   110
being a drummer might be all right for other people but not for my brother Sonny.

"I don't think," he said, looking at me very gravely, "that I'll ever be a good drummer. But I think I can play a piano."

I frowned. I'd never played the role of the older brother quite so seriously before, had scarcely ever, in fact, *asked* Sonny a damn thing. I sensed myself in the presence of something I didn't really know how to handle, didn't understand. So I made my frown a little deeper as I asked: "What kind of musician do you want to be?"

He grinned. "How many kinds do you think there are?"

"Be *serious*," I said.

He laughed, throwing his head back, and then looked at me. "I *am* serious."   115

"Well, then, for Christ's sake, stop kidding around and answer a serious question. I mean, do you want to be a concert pianist, you want to play classical music and all that, or — or what?" Long before I finished he was laughing again. "For Christ's *sake*, Sonny!"

He sobered, but with difficulty. "I'm sorry. But you sound so — *scared!*" and he was off again.

"Well, you may think it's funny now, baby, but it's not going to be so funny when you have to make your living at it, let me tell you *that*. I was furious because I knew he was laughing at me and I didn't know why.

"No," he said, very sober now, and afraid, perhaps, that he'd hurt me, "I don't want to be a classical pianist. That isn't what interests me. I mean" — he paused, looking hard at me, as though his eyes would help me to understand, and then gestured helplessly, as though perhaps his hand would help — "I mean, I'll have a lot of studying to do, and I'll have to study *everything*, but, I mean, I want to play *with* — jazz musicians." He stopped. "I want to play jazz," he said.

Well, the word had never before sounded as heavy, as real, as it sounded   120 that afternoon in Sonny's mouth. I just looked at him and I was probably frowning a real frown by this time. I simply couldn't see why on earth he'd want to spend his time hanging around nightclubs, clowning around on bandstands, while people pushed each other around a dance floor. It seemed — beneath him, somehow. I had never thought about it before, had never been forced to, but I suppose I had always put jazz musicians in a class with what Daddy called "good-time people."

"Are you *serious*?"

"Hell, *yes*, I'm serious."

He looked more helpless than ever, and annoyed, and deeply hurt.

I suggested, helpfully: "You mean — like Louis Armstrong?"

His face closed as though I'd struck him. "No. I'm not talking about none   125 of that old-time, down home crap."

"Well, look, Sonny, I'm sorry, don't get mad. I just don't altogether get it, that's all. Name somebody — you know, a jazz musician you admire."

"Bird."

"Who?"

"Bird! Charlie Parker!° Don't they teach you nothing in the goddamn army?"

I lit a cigarette. I was surprised and then a little amused to discover that I   130
was trembling. "I've been out of touch," I said. "You'll have to be patient with
me. Now. Who's this Parker character?"

"He's just one of the greatest jazz musicians alive," said Sonny, sullenly, his
hands in his pockets, his back to me. "Maybe *the* greatest," he added, bitterly,
"that's probably why you never heard of him."

"All right," I said, "I'm ignorant. I'm sorry. I'll go out and buy all the cat's
records right away, all right?"

"It don't," said Sonny, with dignity, "make any difference to me. I don't
care what you listen to. Don't do me no favors."

I was beginning to realize that I'd never seen him so upset before. With
another part of my mind I was thinking that this would probably turn out to be
one of those things kids go through and that I shouldn't make it seem important by pushing it too hard. Still, I didn't think it would do any harm to ask:
"Doesn't all this take a lot of time? Can you make a living at it?"

He turned back to me and half leaned, half sat, on the kitchen table.   135
"Everything takes time," he said, "and—well, yes, sure, I can make a living at it.
But what I don't seem to be able to make you understand is that it's the only
thing I want to do."

"Well, Sonny," I said, gently, "you know people can't always do exactly
what they *want* to do—"

"*No*, I don't know that," said Sonny, surprising me. "I think people *ought*
to do what they want to do, what else are they alive for?"

"You getting to be a big boy," I said desperately, "it's time you started thinking about your future."

"I'm thinking about my future," said Sonny, grimly. "I think about it all the
time."

I gave up. I decided, if he didn't change his mind, that we could always talk   140
about it later. "In the meantime," I said, "you got to finish school." We had
already decided that he'd have to move in with Isabel and her folks. I knew this
wasn't the ideal arrangement because Isabel's folks are inclined to be dicty and
they hadn't especially wanted Isabel to marry me. But I didn't know what else
to do. "And we have to get you fixed up at Isabel's."

There was a long silence. He moved from the kitchen table to the window.
"That's a terrible idea. You know it yourself."

"Do you have a *better* idea?"

He just walked up and down the kitchen for a minute. He was as tall as I
was. He had started to shave. I suddenly had the feeling that I didn't know him
at all.

Charlie Parker: Parker (1920–1955), saxophonist and composer, is widely regarded as one of
the greatest jazz musicians. His original nickname "Yardbird" (of disputed origin) was later
shortened to "Bird."

He stopped at the kitchen table and picked up my cigarettes. Looking at me with a kind of mocking, amused defiance, he put one between his lips. "You mind?"

"You smoking already?"   145

He lit the cigarette and nodded, watching me through the smoke. "I just wanted to see if I'd have the courage to smoke in front of you." He grinned and blew a great cloud of smoke to the ceiling. "It was easy." He looked at my face. "Come on, now. I bet you was smoking at my age, tell the truth."

I didn't say anything but the truth was on my face, and he laughed. But now there was something very strained in his laugh. "Sure. And I bet that ain't all you was doing."

He was frightening me a little. "Cut the crap," I said. "We already decided that you was going to go and live at Isabel's. Now what's got into you all of a sudden?"

"*You* decided it," he pointed out. "*I* didn't decide nothing." He stopped in front of me, leaning against the stove, arms loosely folded. "Look, brother. I don't want to stay in Harlem no more, I really don't." He was very earnest. He looked at me, then over toward the kitchen window. There was something in his eyes I'd never seen before, some thoughtfulness, some worry all his own. He rubbed the muscle of one arm. "It's time I was getting out of here."

"Where do you want to *go*, Sonny?"   150

"I want to join the army. Or the navy, I don't care. If I say I'm old enough, they'll believe me."

Then I got mad. It was because I was so scared. "You must be crazy. You goddamn fool, what the hell do you want to go and join the *army* for?"

"I just told you. To get out of Harlem."

"Sonny, you haven't even finished *school*. And if you really want to be a musician, how do you expect to study if you're in the *army*?"

He looked at me, trapped, and in anguish. "There's ways. I might be able to 155
work out some kind of deal. Anyway, I'll have the G.I. Bill when I come out."

"*If* you come out." We stared at each other. "Sonny, please. Be reasonable. I know the setup is far from perfect. But we got to do the best we can."

"I ain't learning nothing in school," he said. "Even when I go." He turned away from me and opened the window and threw his cigarette out into the narrow alley. I watched his back. "At least, I ain't learning nothing you'd want me to learn." He slammed the window so hard I thought the glass would fly out, and turned back to me. "And I'm sick of the stink of these garbage cans!"

"Sonny," I said, "I know how you feel. But if you don't finish school now, you're going to be sorry later that you didn't." I grabbed him by the shoulders. "And you only got another year. It ain't so bad. And I'll come back and I swear I'll help you do *whatever* you want to do. Just try to put up with it till I come back. Will you please do that? For me?"

He didn't answer and he wouldn't look at me.

"Sonny. You hear me?"   160

He pulled away. "I hear you. But you never hear anything *I* say."

I didn't know what to say to that. He looked out of the window and then back at me. "OK," he said, and sighed. "I'll try."

Then I said, trying to cheer him up a little, "They got a piano at Isabel's. You can practice on it."

And as a matter of fact, it did cheer him up for a minute. "That's right," he said to himself. "I forgot that." His face relaxed a little. But the worry, the thoughtfulness, played on it still, the way shadows play on a face which is staring into the fire.

But I thought I'd never hear the end of that piano. At first, Isabel would write me, saying how nice it was that Sonny was so serious about his music and how, as soon as he came in from school, or wherever he had been when he was supposed to be at school, he went straight to that piano and stayed there until suppertime. And, after supper, he went back to that piano and stayed there until everybody went to bed. He was at the piano all day Saturday and all day Sunday. Then he bought a record player and started playing records. He'd play one record over and over again, all day long sometimes, and he'd improvise along with it on the piano. Or he'd play one section of the record, one chord, one change, one progression, then he'd do it on the piano. Then back to the record. Then back to the piano.

Well, I really don't know how they stood it. Isabel finally confessed that it wasn't like living with a person at all, it was like living with sound. And the sound didn't make any sense to her, didn't make any sense to any of them — naturally. They began, in a way, to be afflicted by this presence that was living in their home. It was as though Sonny were some sort of god, or monster. He moved in an atmosphere which wasn't like theirs at all. They fed him and he ate, he washed himself, he walked in and out of their door; he certainly wasn't nasty or unpleasant or rude, Sonny isn't any of those things; but it was as though he were all wrapped up in some cloud, some fire, some vision all his own; and there wasn't any way to reach him.

At the same time, he wasn't really a man yet, he was still a child, and they had to watch out for him in all kinds of ways. They certainly couldn't throw him out. Neither did they dare to make a great scene about that piano because even they dimly sensed, as I sensed, from so many thousands of miles away, that Sonny was at that piano playing for his life.

But he hadn't been going to school. One day a letter came from the school board and Isabel's mother got it — there had, apparently, been other letters but Sonny had torn them up. This day, when Sonny came in, Isabel's mother showed him the letter and asked where he'd been spending his time. And she finally got it out of him that he'd been down in Greenwich Village, with musicians and other characters, in a white girl's apartment. And this scared her and she started to scream at him and what came up, once she began — though she denies it to this day — was what sacrifices they were making to give Sonny a decent home and how little he appreciated it.

Sonny didn't play the piano that day. By evening, Isabel's mother had calmed down but then there was the old man to deal with, and Isabel herself. Isabel says she did her best to be calm but she broke down and started crying. She says she just watched Sonny's face. She could tell, by watching him, what was happening with him. And what was happening was that they penetrated his cloud, they had reached him. Even if their fingers had been a thousand times more gentle than human fingers ever are, he could hardly help feeling that they had stripped him naked and were spitting on that nakedness. For he also had to see that his presence, that music, which was life or death to him, had been torture for them and that they had endured it, not at all for his sake, but only for mine. And Sonny couldn't take that. He can take it a little better today than he could then but he's still not very good at it and, frankly, I don't know any-body who is.

The silence of the next few days must have been louder than the sound of   170 all the music ever played since time began. One morning, before she went to work, Isabel was in his room for something and she suddenly realized that all of his records were gone. And she knew for certain that he was gone. And he was. He went as far as the navy would carry him. He finally sent me a postcard from some place in Greece and that was the first I knew that Sonny was still alive. I didn't see him any more until we were both back in New York and the war had long been over.

He was a man by then, of course, but I wasn't willing to see it. He came by the house from time to time, but we fought almost every time we met. I didn't like the way he carried himself, loose and dreamlike all the time, and I didn't like his friends, and his music seemed to be merely an excuse for the life he led. It sounded just that weird and disordered.

Then we had a fight, a pretty awful fight, and I didn't see him for months. By and by I looked him up, where he was living, in a furnished room in the Village, and I tried to make it up. But there were lots of people in the room and Sonny just lay on his bed, and he wouldn't come downstairs with me, and he treated these other people as though they were his family and I weren't. So I got mad and then he got mad, and then I told him that he might just as well be dead as live the way he was living. Then he stood up and he told me not to worry about him any more in life, that he *was* dead as far as I was concerned. Then he pushed me to the door and the other people looked on as though nothing were happening, and he slammed the door behind me. I stood in the hallway, staring at the door. I heard somebody laugh in the room and then the tears came to my eyes. I started down the steps, whistling to keep from crying, I kept whistling to myself, *You going to need me, baby, one of these cold, rainy days.*

I read about Sonny's trouble in the spring. Little Grace died in the fall. She was a beautiful little girl. But she only lived a little over two years. She died of polio and she suffered. She had a slight fever for a couple of days, but it didn't seem like anything and we just kept her in bed. And we would certainly have called the doctor, but the fever dropped, she seemed to be all right. So we thought it had just been a cold. Then, one day, she was up, playing, Isabel was in the kitchen fixing lunch for the two boys when they'd come in from school, and she heard Grace fall down in the living room. When you have a lot of children you don't always start running when one of them falls, unless they start screaming or something. And, this time, Grace was quiet. Yet, Isabel says that when she heard that *thump* and then that silence, something happened in her to make her afraid. And she ran to the living room and there was little Grace on the floor, all twisted up, and the reason she hadn't screamed was that she couldn't get her breath. And when she did scream, it was the worst sound, Isabel says, that she'd ever heard in all her life, and she still hears it sometimes in her dreams. Isabel will sometimes wake me up with a low, moaning, strangled sound and I have to be quick to awaken her and hold her to me and where Isabel is weeping against me seems a mortal wound.

I think I may have written Sonny the very day that little Grace was buried. I was sitting in the living room in the dark, by myself, and I suddenly thought of Sonny. My trouble made his real.

One Saturday afternoon, when Sonny had been living with us, or, anyway, 175 been in our house, for nearly two weeks, I found myself wandering aimlessly about the living room, drinking from a can of beer, and trying to work up the courage to search Sonny's room. He was out, he was usually out whenever I was home, and Isabel had taken the children to see their grandparents. Suddenly I was standing still in front of the living room window, watching Seventh Avenue. The idea of searching Sonny's room made me still. I scarcely dared to admit to myself what I'd be searching for. I didn't know what I'd do if I found it. Or if I didn't.

On the sidewalk across from me, near the entrance to a barbecue joint, some people were holding an old-fashioned revival meeting. The barbecue cook, wearing a dirty white apron, his conked hair reddish and metallic in the pale sun, and a cigarette between his lips, stood in the doorway, watching them. Kids and older people paused in their errands and stood there, along with some older men and a couple of very tough-looking women who watched everything that happened on the avenue, as though they owned it, or were maybe owned by it. Well, they were watching this, too. The revival was being carried on by three sisters in black, and a brother. All they had were their voices and their Bibles and a tambourine. The brother was testifying and while he testified two of the sisters stood together, seeming to say, amen, and the third sister walked around with the tambourine outstretched and a couple of people dropped coins into it. Then the brother's testimony ended and the sister who had been taking up the collection dumped the coins into her palm and transferred them to the pocket of her long black robe. Then she raised both hands, striking the tambourine against the air, and then against one hand, and she started to sing. And the two other sisters and the brother joined in.

It was strange, suddenly, to watch, though I had been seeing these street meetings all my life. So, of course, had everybody else down there. Yet, they paused and watched and listened and I stood still at the window. *"Tis the old ship of Zion,"* they sang, and the sister with the tambourine kept a steady, jangling beat, *"it has rescued many a thousand!"* Not a soul under the sound of their voices was hearing this song for the first time, not one of them had been rescued. Nor had they seen much in the way of rescue work being done around them. Neither did they especially believe in the holiness of the three sisters and the brother, they knew too much about them, knew where they lived, and how. The woman with the tambourine, whose voice dominated the air, whose face was bright with joy, was divided by very little from the woman who stood watching her, a cigarette between her heavy, chapped lips, her hair a cuckoo's nest, her face scarred and swollen from many beatings, and her black eyes glittering like coal. Perhaps they both knew this, which was why, when, as rarely, they addressed each other, they addressed each other as Sister. As the singing filled the air the watching, listening faces underwent a change, the eyes focusing on something within; the music seemed to soothe a poison out of them; and time seemed, nearly, to fall away from the sullen, belligerent, battered faces, as though they were fleeing back to their first condition, while dreaming of their last. The barbecue cook half shook his head and smiled, and dropped his cigarette and disappeared into his joint. A man fumbled in his pockets for change and stood holding it in his hand impatiently, as though he had just remembered a pressing appointment further up the avenue. He looked furious. Then I saw Sonny, standing on the edge of the crowd. He was carrying a wide, flat notebook with a green cover, and it made him look, from where I was standing, almost like a schoolboy. The coppery sun brought out the copper in his skin, he was very faintly smiling, standing very still. Then the singing stopped, the tambourine turned into a collection plate again. The furious man dropped in his coins and vanished, so did a couple of the women, and Sonny dropped some change in the plate, looking directly at the woman with a little smile. He started across the avenue, toward the house. He has a slow, loping walk something like the way Harlem hipsters walk, only he's imposed on this his own half-beat. I had never really noticed it before.

I stayed at the window, both relieved and apprehensive. As Sonny disappeared from my sight, they began singing again. And they were still singing when his key turned in the lock.

"Hey," he said.

"Hey, yourself. You want some beer?"   180

"No. Well, maybe." But he came up to the window and stood beside me, looking out. "What a warm voice," he said.

They were singing *If I could only hear my mother pray again!*

"Yes," I said, "and she can sure beat that tambourine."

"But what a terrible song," he said, and laughed. He dropped his notebook on the sofa and disappeared into the kitchen. "Where's Isabel and the kids?"

"I think they went to see their grandparents. You hungry?"   185

"No." He came back into the living room with his can of beer. "You want to come some place with me tonight?"

I sensed, I don't know how, that I couldn't possibly say no. "Sure. Where?"

He sat down on the sofa and picked up his notebook and started leafing through it. "I'm going to sit in with some fellows in a joint in the Village."

"You mean, you're going to play, tonight?"

"That's right." He took a swallow of his beer and moved back to the window. He gave me a sidelong look. "If you can stand it."

"I'll try," I said.

He smiled to himself and we both watched as the meeting across the way broke up. The three sisters and the brother, heads bowed, were singing *God be with you till we meet again*. The faces around them were very quiet. Then the song ended. The small crowd dispersed. We watched the three women and the lone man walk slowly up the avenue.

"When she was singing before," said Sonny, abruptly, "her voice reminded me for a minute of what heroin feels like sometimes—when it's in your veins. It makes you feel sort of warm and cool at the same time. And distant. And—and sure." He sipped his beer, very deliberately not looking at me. I watched his face. "It makes you feel—in control. Sometimes you've got to have that feeling."

"Do you?" I sat down slowly in the easy chair.

"Sometimes." He went to the sofa and picked up his notebook again. "Some people do."

"In order," I asked, "to play?" And my voice was very ugly, full of contempt and anger.

"Well"—he looked at me with great, troubled eyes, as though, in fact, he hoped his eyes would tell me things he could never otherwise say—"they *think* so. And *if* they think so—!"

"And what do *you* think?" I asked.

He sat on the sofa and put his can of beer on the floor. "I don't know," he said, and I couldn't be sure if he were answering my question or pursuing his thoughts. His face didn't tell me. "It's not so much to *play*. It's to *stand* it, to be able to make it at all. On any level." He frowned and smiled: "In order to keep from shaking to pieces."

"But these friends of yours," I said, "they seem to shake themselves to pieces pretty goddamn fast."

"Maybe." He played with the notebook. And something told me that I should curb my tongue, that Sonny was doing his best to talk, that I should listen. "But of course you only know the ones that've gone to pieces. Some don't—or at least they haven't *yet* and that's just about all *any* of us can say." He paused. "And then there are some who just live, really, in hell, and they know it and they see what's happening and they go right on. I don't know." He sighed, dropped the notebook, folded his arms. "Some guys, you can tell from the way they play, they on something *all* the time. And you can see that, well, it makes something real for them. But of course," he picked up his beer from the floor and sipped it and put the can down again, "they want to, too, you've got to see that. Even some of them that say they don't—*some*, not all."

"And what about you?" I asked—I couldn't help it. "What about you? Do *you* want to?"

He stood up and walked to the window and remained silent for a long time. Then he sighed. "Me," he said. Then: "While I was downstairs before, on my way here, listening to that woman sing, it struck me all of a sudden how much suffering she must have had to go through—to sing like that. It's *repulsive* to think you have to suffer that much."

I said: "But there's no way not to suffer—is there, Sonny?"

"I believe not," he said and smiled, "but that's never stopped anyone from 205 trying." He looked at me. "Has it?" I realized, with this mocking look, that there stood between us, forever, beyond the power of time or forgiveness, the fact that I had held silence—so long!—when he had needed human speech to help him. He turned back to the window. "No, there's no way not to suffer. But you try all kinds of ways to keep from drowning in it, to keep on top of it, and to make it seem—well, like *you*. Like you did something, all right, and now you're suffering for it. You know?" I said nothing. "Well you know," he said, impatiently, "why *do* people suffer? Maybe it's better to do something to give it a reason, *any* reason."

"But we just agreed," I said, "that there's no way not to suffer. Isn't it better, then, just to—take it?"

"But nobody just takes it," Sonny cried, "that's what I'm telling you! *Everybody* tries not to. You're just hung up on the *way* some people try—it's not *your* way!"

The hair on my face began to itch, my face felt wet. "That's not true," I said, "that's not true. I don't give a damn what other people do, I don't even care how they suffer. I just care how *you* suffer." And he looked at me. "Please believe me," I said, "I don't want to see you—die—trying not to suffer."

"I won't," he said, flatly, "die trying not to suffer. At least, not any faster than anybody else."

"But there's no need," I said, trying to laugh, "is there? in killing yourself." 210

I wanted to say more, but I couldn't. I wanted to talk about will power and how life could be—well, beautiful. I wanted to say that it was all within; but was it? or, rather, wasn't that exactly the trouble? And I wanted to promise that I would never fail him again. But it would all have sounded—empty words and lies.

So I made the promise to myself and prayed that I would keep it.

"It's terrible sometimes, inside," he said, "that's what's the trouble. You walk these streets, black and funky and cold, and there's not really a living ass to talk to, and there's nothing shaking, and there's no way of getting it out—that storm inside. You can't talk it and you can't make love with it, and when you finally try to get with it and play it, you realize *nobody's* listening. So *you've* got to listen. You got to find a way to listen."

And then he walked away from the window and sat on the sofa again, as though all the wind had suddenly been knocked out of him. "Sometimes you'll do *anything* to play, even cut your mother's throat." He laughed and looked at me. "Or your brother's." Then he sobered. "Or your own." Then: "Don't worry. I'm all right now and I think I'll *be* all right. But I can't forget—where I've been. I don't mean just the physical place I've been, I mean where I've *been*. And *what* I've been."

"What have you been, Sonny?" I asked.

He smiled—but sat sideways on the sofa, his elbow resting on the back his fingers playing with his mouth and chin, not looking at me. "I've been something I didn't recognize, didn't know I could be. Didn't know anybody could be." He stopped, looking inward, looking helplessly young, looking old. "I'm not talking about it now because I feel *guilty* or anything like that—maybe it would be better if I did, I don't know. Anyway, I can't really talk about it. Not to you, not to anybody," and now he turned and faced me. "Sometimes, you know, and it was actually when I was most *out* of the world, I felt that I was in it, that I was *with* it, really, and I could play or I didn't really have to *play*, it just came out of me, it was there. And I don't know how I played, thinking about it now, but I know I did awful things, those times, sometimes, to people. Or it wasn't that I *did* anything to them—it was that they weren't real." He picked up the beer can; it was empty; he rolled it between his palms: "And other times—well, I needed a fix, I needed to find a place to lean, I needed to clear a space to *listen*—and I couldn't find it, and I—went crazy, I did terrible things to *me*, I was terrible *for* me." He began pressing the beer can between his hands, I watched the metal begin to give. It glittered, as he played with it, like a knife, and I was afraid he would cut himself, but I said nothing. "Oh well. I can never tell you. I was all by myself at the bottom of something, stinking and sweating and crying and shaking, and I smelled it, you know? *my* stink, and I thought I'd die if I couldn't get away from it and yet, all the same, I knew that everything I was doing was just locking me in with it. And I didn't know," he paused, still flattening the beer can, "I didn't know, I still *don't* know, something kept telling me that maybe it was good to smell your own stink, but I didn't think that *that* was what I'd been trying to do—and—who can stand it?" and he abruptly dropped the ruined beer can, looking at me with a small, still smile, and then rose, walking to the window as though it were the lodestone rock. I watched his face, he watched the avenue. "I couldn't tell you when Mama died—but the reason I wanted to leave Harlem so bad was to get away from drugs. And then, when I ran away, that's what I was running from—really. When I came back, nothing had changed, *I* hadn't changed, I was just—older." And he stopped, drumming with his fingers on the windowpane. The sun had vanished, soon darkness would fall. I watched his face. "It can come again," he said, almost as though speaking to himself. Then he turned to me. "It can come again," he repeated. "I just want you to know that."

"All right," I said, at last. "So it can come again. All right."

He smiled, but the smile was sorrowful. "I had to try to tell you," he said.

"Yes," I said. "I understand that."

"You're my brother," he said, looking straight at me, and not smiling at all.

"Yes," I repeated, "yes. I understand that."

He turned back to the window, looking out. "All that hatred down there," he said, "all that hatred and misery and love. It's a wonder it doesn't blow the avenue apart."

———————

We went to the only nightclub on a short, dark street, downtown. We squeezed through the narrow, chattering, jam-packed bar to the entrance of the big room, where the bandstand was. And we stood there for a moment, for the lights were very dim in this room and we couldn't see. Then, "Hello, boy," said a voice and an enormous black man, much older than Sonny or myself, erupted out of all that atmospheric lighting and put an arm around Sonny's shoulder. "I been sitting right here," he said, "waiting for you."

He had a big voice, too, and heads in the darkness turned toward us.

Sonny grinned and pulled a little away, and said, "Creole, this is my brother. 225 I told you about him."

Creole shook my hand. "I'm glad to meet you, son," he said, and it was clear that he was glad to meet me *there*, for Sonny's sake. And he smiled, "You got a real musician in *your* family," and he took his arm from Sonny's shoulder and slapped him, lightly, affectionately, with the back of his hand.

"Well. Now I've heard it all," said a voice behind us. This was another musician, and a friend of Sonny's, a coal-black cheerful-looking man, built close to the ground. He immediately began confiding to me, at the top of his lungs, the most terrible things about Sonny, his teeth gleaming like a lighthouse and his laugh coming up out of him like the beginning of an earthquake. And it turned out that everyone at the bar knew Sonny, or almost everyone; some were musicians, working there, or nearby, or not working, some were simply hangers-on, and some were there to hear Sonny play. I was introduced to all of them and they were all very polite to me. Yet, it was clear that, for them, I was only Sonny's brother. Here, I was in Sonny's world. Or, rather: his kingdom. Here, it was not even a question that his veins bore royal blood.

They were going to play soon and Creole installed me, by myself, at a table in a dark corner. Then I watched them, Creole, and the little black man, and Sonny, and the others, while they horsed around, standing just below the bandstand. The light from the bandstand spilled just a little short of them and, watching them laughing and gesturing and moving about, I had the feeling that they, nevertheless, were being most careful not to step into that circle of light too suddenly: that if they moved into the light too suddenly, without thinking, they would perish in flame. Then, while I watched, one of them, the small, black man, moved into the light and crossed the bandstand and started fooling around with his drums. Then—being funny and being, also, extremely ceremonious—Creole took Sonny by the arm and led him to the piano. A woman's voice called Sonny's name and a few hands started clapping. And Sonny, also being funny and being ceremonious, and so touched, I think, that he could have cried, but neither hiding it nor showing it, riding it like a man, grinned, and put both hands to his heart and bowed from the waist.

Creole then went to the bass fiddle and a lean, very bright-skinned brown man jumped up on the bandstand and picked up his horn. So there they were, and the atmosphere on the bandstand and in the room began to change and tighten. Someone stepped up to the microphone and announced them. Then there were all kinds of murmurs. Some people at the bar shushed others. The waitress ran around, frantically getting in the last orders, guys and chicks got closer to each other, and the lights on the bandstand, on the quartet, turned to a kind of indigo. Then they all looked different there. Creole looked about him for the last time, as though he were making certain that all his chickens were in the coop, and then he—jumped and struck the fiddle. And there they were.

All I know about music is that not many people ever really hear it. And even then, on the rare occasions when something opens within, and the music enters, what we mainly hear, or hear corroborated, are personal, private, vanishing evocations. But the man who creates the music is hearing something else, is dealing with the roar rising from the void and imposing order on it as it hits the air. What is evoked in him, then, is of another order, more terrible because it has no words, and triumphant, too, for that same reason. And his triumph, when he triumphs, is ours. I just watched Sonny's face. His face was troubled, he was working hard, but he wasn't with it. And I had the feeling that, in a way, everyone on the bandstand was waiting for him, both waiting for him and pushing him along. But as I began to watch Creole, I realized that it was Creole who held them all back. He had them on a short rein. Up there, keeping the beat with his whole body, wailing on the fiddle, with his eyes half closed, he was listening to everything, but he was listening to Sonny. He was having a dialogue with Sonny. He wanted Sonny to leave the shoreline and strike out for the deep water. He was Sonny's witness that deep water and drowning were not the same thing—he had been there, and he knew. And he wanted Sonny to know. He was waiting for Sonny to do the things on the keys which would let Creole know that Sonny was in the water.

And, while Creole listened, Sonny moved, deep within, exactly like someone in torment. I had never before thought of how awful the relationship must be between the musician and his instrument. He has to fill it, this instrument, with the breath of life, his own. He has to make it do what he wants it to do. And a piano is just a piano. It's made out of so much wood and wires and little hammers and big ones, and ivory. While there's only so much you can do with it, the only way to find this out is to try; to try and make it do everything.

And Sonny hadn't been near a piano for over a year. And he wasn't on much better terms with his life, not the life that stretched before him now. He and the piano stammered, started one way, got scared, stopped; started another way, panicked, marked time, started again; then seemed to have found a direction, panicked again, got stuck. And the face I saw on Sonny I'd never seen before. Everything had been burned out of it, and, at the same time, things usually hidden were being burned in, by the fire and fury of the battle which was occurring in him up there.

Yet, watching Creole's face as they neared the end of the first set, I had the feeling that something had happened, something I hadn't heard. Then they finished, there was scattered applause, and then, without an instant's warning, Creole started into something else, it was almost sardonic, it was *Am I Blue*. And, as though he commanded, Sonny began to play. Something began to happen.

And Creole let out the reins. The dry, low, black man said something awful on the drums, Creole answered, and the drums talked back. Then the horn insisted, sweet and high, slightly detached perhaps, and Creole listened, commenting now and then, dry, and driving, beautiful and calm and old. Then they all came together again, and Sonny was part of the family again. I could tell this from his face. He seemed to have found, right there beneath his fingers, a damn brand-new piano. It seemed that he couldn't get over it. Then, for awhile, just being happy with Sonny, they seemed to be agreeing with him that brand-new pianos certainly were a gas.

Then Creole stepped forward to remind them that what they were playing was the blues. He hit something in all of them, he hit something in me, myself, and the music tightened and deepened, apprehension began to beat the air. Creole began to tell us what the blues were all about. They were not about anything very new. He and his boys up there were keeping it new, at the risk of ruin, destruction, madness, and death, in order to find new ways to make us listen. For, while the tale of how we suffer, and how we are delighted, and how we may triumph is never new, it always must be heard. There isn't any other tale to tell, it's the only light we've got in all this darkness.

And this tale, according to that face, that body, those strong hands on those strings, has another aspect in every country, and a new depth in every generation. Listen, Creole seemed to be saying, listen. Now these are Sonny's blues. He made the little black man on the drums know it, and the bright, brown man on the horn. Creole wasn't trying any longer to get Sonny in the water. He was wishing him Godspeed. Then he stepped back, very slowly, filling the air with the immense suggestion that Sonny speak for himself.

Then they all gathered around Sonny and Sonny played. Every now and again one of them seemed to say, amen. Sonny's fingers filled the air with life, his life. But that life contained so many others. And Sonny went all the way back, he really began with the spare, flat statement of the opening phrase of the song. Then he began to make it his. It was very beautiful because it wasn't hurried and it was no longer a lament. I seemed to hear with what burning he had made it his, with what burning we had yet to make it ours, how we could cease lamenting. Freedom lurked around us and I understood, at last, that he could help us to be free if we would listen, that he would never be free until we did. Yet, there was no battle in his face now. I heard what he had gone through, and would continue to go through until he came to rest in earth. He had made it his: that long line, of which we knew only Mama and Daddy. And he was giving it back, as everything must be given back, so that, passing through death, it can live forever. I saw my mother's face again, and felt, for the first time, how the stones of the road she had walked on must have bruised her feet. I saw the moonlit road where my father's brother died. And it brought something else back to me, and carried me past it. I saw my little girl again and felt Isabel's tears again, and I felt my own tears begin to rise. And I was yet aware that this was only a moment, that the world waited outside, as hungry as a tiger, and that trouble stretched above us, longer than the sky.

Then it was over. Creole and Sonny let out their breath, both soaking wet, and grinning. There was a lot of applause and some of it was real. In the dark, the girl came by and I asked her to take drinks to the bandstand. There was a long pause, while they talked up there in the indigo light and after awhile I saw the girl put a Scotch and milk on top of the piano for Sonny. He didn't seem to notice it, but just before they started playing again, he sipped from it and looked toward me, and nodded. Then he put it back on top of the piano. For me, then, as they began to play again, it glowed and shook above my brother's head like the very cup of trembling.

Raymond Carver   1938–1988

What We Talk about When We Talk about Love   [1981]

My friend Mel McGinnis was talking. Mel McGinnis is a cardiologist, and sometimes that gives him the right.

The four of us were sitting around his kitchen table drinking gin. Sunlight filled the kitchen from the big window behind the sink. There were Mel and me and his second wife, Teresa—Terri, we called her—and my wife, Laura. We lived in Albuquerque then. But we were all from somewhere else.

There was an ice bucket on the table. The gin and the tonic water kept going around, and we somehow got on the subject of love. Mel thought real love was nothing less than spiritual love. He said he'd spent five years in a seminary before quitting to go to medical school. He said he still looked back on those years in the seminary as the most important years in his life.

Terri said the man she lived with before she lived with Mel loved her so much he tried to kill her. Then Terri said, "He beat me up one night. He dragged me around the living room by my ankles. He kept saying, 'I love you, I love you, you bitch.' He went on dragging me around the living room. My head kept knocking on things." Terri looked around the table. "What do you do with love like that?"

She was a bone-thin woman with a pretty face, dark eyes, and brown hair   5 that hung down her back. She liked necklaces made of turquoise, and long pendant earrings.

"My God, don't be silly. That's not love, and you know it," Mel said. "I don't know what you'd call it, but I sure know you wouldn't call it love."

"Say what you want to, but I know it was," Terri said. "It may sound crazy to you, but it's true just the same. People are different, Mel. Sure, sometimes he may have acted crazy. Okay. But he loved me. In his own way maybe, but he loved me. There was love there, Mel. Don't say there wasn't."

Mel let out his breath. He held his glass and turned to Laura and me. "The man threatened to kill me," Mel said. He finished his drink and reached for the gin bottle. "Terri's a romantic. Terri's of the kick-me-so-I'll-know-you-love-me school. Terri, hon, don't look that way." Mel reached across the table and touched Terri's cheek with his fingers. He grinned at her.

"Now he wants to make up," Terri said.

"Make up what?" Mel said. "What is there to make up? I know what I 10 know. That's all."

"How'd we get started on this subject, anyway?" Terri said. She raised her glass and drank from it. "Mel always has love on his mind," she said. "Don't you, honey?" She smiled, and I thought that was the last of it.

"I just wouldn't call Ed's behavior love. That's all I'm saying, honey," Mel said. "What about you guys?" Mel said to Laura and me. "Does that sound like love to you?"

"I'm the wrong person to ask," I said. "I didn't even know the man. I've only heard his name mentioned in passing. I wouldn't know. You'd have to know the particulars. But I think what you're saying is that love is an absolute."

Mel said, "The kind of love I'm talking about is. The kind of love I'm talking about, you don't try to kill people."

Laura said, "I don't know anything about Ed, or anything about the situa- 15 tion. But who can judge anyone else's situation?"

I touched the back of Laura's hand. She gave me a quick smile. I picked up Laura's hand. It was warm, the nails polished, perfectly manicured. I encircled the broad wrist with my fingers, and I held her.

"When I left, he drank rat poison," Terri said. She clasped her arms with her hands. "They took him to the hospital in Santa Fe. That's where we lived then, about ten miles out. They saved his life. But his gums went crazy from it. I mean they pulled away from his teeth. After that, his teeth stood out like fangs. My God," Terri said. She waited a minute, then let go of her arms and picked up her glass.

"What people won't do!" Laura said.

"He's out of the action now," Mel said. "He's dead."

Mel handed me the saucer of limes. I took a section, squeezed it over my 20 drink, and stirred the ice cubes with my finger.

"It gets worse," Terri said. "He shot himself in the mouth. But he bungled that too. Poor Ed," she said. Terri shook her head.

"Poor Ed nothing," Mel said. "He was dangerous."

Mel was forty-five years old. He was tall and rangy with curly soft hair. His face and arms were brown from the tennis he played. When he was sober, his gestures, all his movements, were precise, very careful.

"He did love me though, Mel. Grant me that," Terri said. "That's all I'm asking. He didn't love me the way you love me. I'm not saying that. But he loved me. You can grant me that, can't you?"

"What do you mean, he bungled it?" I said. 25

Laura leaned forward with her glass. She put her elbows on the table and held her glass in both hands. She glanced from Mel to Terri and waited with a look of bewilderment on her open face, as if amazed that such things happened to people you were friendly with.

"How'd he bungle it when he killed himself?" I said.

"I'll tell you what happened," Mel said. "He took this twenty-two pistol he'd bought to threaten Terri and me with. Oh, I'm serious, the man was always threatening. You should have seen the way we lived in those days. Like fugitives. I even bought a gun myself. Can you believe it? A guy like me? But I did. I bought one for self-defense and carried it in the glove compartment. Sometimes I'd have to leave the apartment in the middle of the night. To go to the hospital, you know? Terri and I weren't married then, and my first wife had the house and kids, the dog, everything, and Terri and I were living in this apartment here. Sometimes, as I say, I'd get a call in the middle of the night and have to go in to the hospital at two or three in the morning. It'd be dark out there in the parking lot, and I'd break into a sweat before I could even get to my car. I never knew if he was going to come up out of the shrubbery or from behind a car and start shooting. I mean, the man was crazy. He was capable of wiring a bomb, anything. He used to call my service at all hours and say he needed to talk to the doctor, and when I'd return the call, he'd say, 'Son of a bitch, your days are numbered.' Little things like that. It was scary, I'm telling you."

"I still feel sorry for him," Terri said.

"It sounds like a nightmare," Laura said. "But what exactly happened after   30 he shot himself?"

Laura is a legal secretary. We'd met in a professional capacity. Before we knew it, it was a courtship. She's thirty-five, three years younger than I am. In addition to being in love, we like each other and enjoy one another's company. She's easy to be with.

"What happened?" Laura said.

Mel said, "He shot himself in the mouth in his room. Someone heard the shot and told the manager. They came in with a passkey, saw what had happened, and called an ambulance. I happened to be there when they brought him in, alive but past recall. The man lived for three days. His head swelled up to twice the size of a normal head. I'd never seen anything like it, and I hope I never do again. Terri wanted to go in and sit with him when she found out about it. We had a fight over it. I didn't think she should see him like that. I didn't think she should see him, and I still don't."

"Who won the fight?" Laura said.

"I was in the room with him when he died," Terri said. "He never came out   35 of it. But I sat with him. He didn't have anyone else."

"He was dangerous," Mel said. "If you call that love, you can have it."

"It was love," Terri said. "Sure, it's abnormal in most people's eyes. But he was willing to die for it. He did die for it."

"I sure as hell wouldn't call it love," Mel said. "I mean, no one knows what he did it for. I've seen a lot of suicides, and I couldn't say anyone ever knew what they did it for."

Mel put his hands behind his neck and tilted his chair back. "I'm not interested in that kind of love," he said. "If that's love, you can have it."

Terri said, "We were afraid. Mel even made a will out and wrote to his   40
brother in California who used to be a Green Beret. Mel told him who to look
for if something happened to him."

Terri drank from her glass. She said, "But Mel's right—we lived like fugitives. We were afraid. Mel was, weren't you, honey? I even called the police at
one point, but they were no help. They said they couldn't do anything until Ed
actually did something. Isn't that a laugh?" Terri said.

She poured the last of the gin into her glass and waggled the bottle. Mel got
up from the table and went to the cupboard. He took down another bottle.

"Well, Nick and I know what love is," Laura said. "For us, I mean," Laura
said. She bumped my knee with her knee. "You're supposed to say something
now," Laura said, and turned her smile on me.

For an answer, I took Laura's hand and raised it to my lips. I made a big
production out of kissing her hand. Everyone was amused.

"We're lucky," I said.   45

"You guys," Terri said. "Stop that now. You're making me sick. You're still
on the honeymoon, for God's sake. You're still gaga, for crying out loud. Just
wait. How long have you been together now? How long has it been? A year?
Longer than a year?"

"Going on a year and a half," Laura said, flushed and smiling.

"Oh, now," Terri said. "Wait awhile."

She held her drink and gazed at Laura.

"I'm only kidding," Terri said.   50

Mel opened the gin and went around the table with the bottle.

"Here, you guys," he said. "Let's have a toast. I want to propose a toast. A
toast to love. To true love," Mel said.

We touched glasses.

"To love," we said.

Outside in the backyard, one of the dogs began to bark. The leaves of   55
the aspen that leaned past the window ticked against the glass. The afternoon
sun was like a presence in this room, the spacious light of ease and generosity.
We could have been anywhere, somewhere enchanted. We raised our glasses
again and grinned at each other like children who had agreed on something
forbidden.

"I'll tell you what real love is," Mel said. "I mean, I'll give you a good
example. And then you can draw your own conclusions." He poured more gin
into his glass. He added an ice cube and a sliver of lime. We waited and sipped
our drinks. Laura and I touched knees again. I put a hand on her warm thigh
and left it there.

"What do any of us really know about love?" Mel said. "It seems to me
we're just beginners at love. We say we love each other and we do, I don't doubt
it. I love Terri and Terri loves me, and you guys love each other too. You know

the kind of love I'm talking about now. Physical love, that impulse that drives you to someone special, as well as love of the other person's being, his or her essence, as it were. Carnal love and, well, call it sentimental love, the day-to-day caring about the other person. But sometimes I have a hard time accounting for the fact that I must have loved my first wife too. But I did, I know I did. So I suppose I am like Terri in that regard. Terri and Ed." He thought about it and then he went on. "There was a time when I thought I loved my first wife more than life itself. But now I hate her guts. I do. How do you explain that? What happened to that love? What happened to it, is what I'd like to know. I wish someone could tell me. Then there's Ed. Okay, we're back to Ed. He loves Terri so much he tries to kill her and he winds up killing himself." Mel stopped talking and swallowed from his glass. "You guys have been together eighteen months and you love each other. It shows all over you. You glow with it. But you both loved other people before you met each other. You've both been married before, just like us. And you probably loved other people before that too, even. Terri and I have been together five years, been married for four. And the terrible thing, the terrible thing is, but the good thing too, the saving grace, you might say, is that if something happened to one of us—excuse me for saying this—but if something happened to one of us tomorrow, I think the other one, the other person, would grieve for a while, you know, but then the surviving party would go out and love again, have someone else soon enough. All this, all of this love we're talking about, it would just be a memory. Maybe not even a memory. Am I wrong? Am I way off base? Because I want you to set me straight if you think I'm wrong. I want to know. I mean, I don't know anything, and I'm the first one to admit it."

"Mel, for God's sake," Terri said. She reached out and took hold of his wrist. "Are you getting drunk? Honey? Are you drunk?"

"Honey, I'm just talking," Mel said. "All right? I don't have to be drunk to say what I think. I mean, we're all just talking, right?" Mel said. He fixed his eyes on her.

"Sweetie, I'm not criticizing," Terri said.   60

She picked up her glass.

"I'm not on call today," Mel said. "Let me remind you of that. I am not on call," he said.

"Mel, we love you," Laura said.

Mel looked at Laura. He looked at her as if he could not place her, as if she was not the woman she was.

"Love you too, Laura," Mel said. "And you, Nick, love you too. You know   65
something?" Mel said. "You guys are our pals," Mel said.

He picked up his glass.

Mel said, "I was going to tell you about something. I mean, I was going to prove a point. You see, this happened a few months ago, but it's still going on right now, and it ought to make us feel ashamed when we talk like we know what we're talking about when we talk about love."

"Come on now," Terri said. "Don't talk like you're drunk if you're not drunk."

"Just shut up for once in your life," Mel said very quietly. "Will you do me a favor and do that for a minute? So as I was saying, there's this old couple who had this car wreck out on the interstate. A kid hit them and they were all torn to shit and nobody was giving them much chance to pull through."

Terri looked at us and then back at Mel. She seemed anxious, or maybe   70
that's too strong a word.

Mel was handing the bottle around the table.

"I was on call that night," Mel said. "It was May or maybe it was June. Terri and I had just sat down to dinner when the hospital called. There'd been this thing out on the interstate. Drunk kid, teenager, plowed his dad's pickup into this camper with this old couple in it. They were up in their mid-seventies, that couple. The kid — eighteen, nineteen, something — he was DOA. Taken the steering wheel through his sternum. The old couple, they were alive, you understand. I mean, just barely. But they had everything. Multiple fractures, internal injuries, hemorrhaging, contusions, lacerations, the works, and they each of them had themselves concussions. They were in a bad way, believe me. And, of course, their age was two strikes against them. I'd say she was worse off than he was. Ruptured spleen along with everything else. Both kneecaps broken. But they'd been wearing their seatbelts and, God knows, that's what saved them for the time being."

"Folks, this is an advertisement for the National Safety Council," Terri said. "This is your spokesman, Dr. Melvin R. McGinnis, talking." Terri laughed. "Mel," she said, "sometimes you're just too much. But I love you, hon," she said.

"Honey, I love you," Mel said.

He leaned across the table. Terri met him halfway. They kissed.   75

"Terri's right," Mel said as he settled himself again. "Get those seatbelts on. But seriously, they were in some shape, those oldsters. By the time I got down there, the kid was dead, as I said. He was off in a corner, laid out on a gurney. I took one look at the old couple and told the ER nurse to get me a neurologist and an orthopedic man and a couple of surgeons down there right way."

He drank from his glass. "I'll try to keep this short," he said. "So we took the two of them up to the OR and worked like fuck on them most of the night. They had these incredible reserves, those two. You see that once in a while. So we did everything that could be done, and toward morning we're giving them a fifty-fifty chance, maybe less than that for her. So here they are, still alive the next morning. So, okay, we move them into the ICU, which is where they both kept plugging away at it for two weeks, hitting it better and better on all the scopes. So we transfer them out to their own room."

Mel stopped talking. "Here," he said, "let's drink this cheapo gin the hell up. Then we're going to dinner, right? Terri and I know a new place. That's where we'll go, to this new place we know about. But we're not going until we finish up this cut-rate, lousy gin."

Terri said, "We haven't actually eaten there yet. But it looks good. From the outside, you know."

"I like food," Mel said. "If I had it to do all over again, I'd be a chef, you know? Right, Terri?" Mel said. ₈₀

He laughed. He fingered the ice in his glass.

"Terri knows," he said. "Terri can tell you. But let me say this. If I could come back again in a different life, a different time and all, you know what? I'd like to come back as a knight. You were pretty safe wearing all that armor. It was all right being a knight until gunpowder and muskets and pistols came along."

"Mel would like to ride a horse and carry a lance," Terri said.

"Carry a woman's scarf with you everywhere," Laura said.

"Or just a woman," Mel said. ₈₅

"Shame on you," Laura said.

Terri said, "Suppose you came back as a serf. The serfs didn't have it so good in those days," Terri said.

"The serfs never had it good," Mel said. "But I guess even the knights were vessels to someone. Isn't that the way it worked? But then everyone is always a vessel to someone. Isn't that right? Terri? But what I liked about knights, besides their ladies, was that they had that suit of armor, you know, and they couldn't get hurt very easy. No cars in those days, you know? No drunk teenagers to tear into your ass."

"Vassals," Terri said.

"What?" Mel said. ₉₀

"Vassals," Terri said. "They were called vassals, not vessels."

"Vassals, vessels," Mel said, "what the fuck's the difference? You knew what I meant anyway. All right," Mel said. "So I'm not educated. I learned my stuff. I'm a heart surgeon, sure, but I'm just a mechanic. I go in and I fuck around and I fix things. Shit," Mel said.

"Modesty doesn't become you," Terri said.

"He's just a humble sawbones," I said. "But sometimes they suffocated in all that armor, Mel. They'd even have heart attacks if it got too hot and they were too tired and worn out. I read somewhere that they'd fall off their horses and not be able to get up because they were too tired to stand with all that armor on them. They got trampled by their own horses sometimes."

"That's terrible," Mel said. "That's a terrible thing, Nicky. I guess they'd just ₉₅ lay there and wait until somebody came along and made a shish kebab out of them."

"Some other vessel," Terri said.

"That's right," Mel said. "Some vassal would come along and spear the bastard in the name of love. Or whatever the fuck it was they fought over in those days."

"Same things we fight over these days," Terri said.

Laura said, "Nothing's changed."

The color was still high in Laura's cheeks. Her eyes were bright. She brought   100
her glass to her lips.

Mel poured himself another drink. He looked at the label closely as if study-ing a long row of numbers. Then he slowly put the bottle down on the table and slowly reached for the tonic water.

"What about the old couple?" Laura said. "You didn't finish that story you started."

Laura was having a hard time lighting her cigarette. Her matches kept going out.

The sunshine inside the room was different now, changing, getting thinner. But the leaves outside the window were still shimmering, and I stared at the pattern they made on the panes and on the Formica counter. They weren't the same patterns, of course.

"What about the old couple?" I said.   105

"Older but wiser," Terri said.

Mel stared at her.

Terri said, "Go on with your story, hon. I was only kidding. Then what hap-pened?"

"Terri, sometimes," Mel said.

"Please, Mel," Terri said. "Don't always be so serious, sweetie. Can't you   110
take a joke?"

"Where's the joke?" Mel said.

He held his glass and gazed steadily at his wife.

"What happened?" Laura said.

Mel fastened his eyes on Laura. He said, "Laura, if I didn't have Terri and if I didn't love her so much, and if Nick wasn't my best friend, I'd fall in love with you. I'd carry you off, honey," he said.

"Tell your story," Terri said. "Then we'll go to that new place, okay?"   115

"Okay," Mel said. "Where was I?" he said. He stared at the table and then he began again.

"I dropped in to see each of them every day, sometimes twice a day if I was up doing other calls anyway. Casts and bandages, head to foot, the both of them. You know, you've seen it in the movies. That's just the way they looked, just like in the movies. Little eye-holes and nose holes and mouth-holes. And she had to have her legs slung up on top of it. Well, the husband was very depressed for the longest while. Even after he found out that his wife was going to pull through, he was still very depressed. Not about the accident, though. I mean, the accident was one thing, but it wasn't everything. I'd get up to his mouth-hole, you know, and he'd say no, it wasn't the accident exactly but it was because he couldn't see her through his eye-holes. He said that was what was making him feel so bad. Can you imagine? I'm telling you, the man's heart was breaking because he couldn't turn his goddamn head and *see* his goddamn wife."

Mel looked around the table and shook his head at what he was going to say.

"I mean, it was killing the old fart just because he couldn't *look* at the fucking woman."

We all looked at Mel.   120

"Do you see what I'm saying?" he said.

Maybe we were a little drunk by then. I know it was hard keeping things in focus. The light was draining out of the room, going back through the window where it had come from. Yet nobody made a move to get up from the table to turn on the overhead light.

"Listen," Mel said. "Let's finish this fucking gin. There's about enough left here for one shooter all around. Then let's go eat. Let's go to the new place."

"He's depressed," Terri said. "Mel, why don't you take a pill?"

Mel shook his head. "I've taken everything there is."   125

"We all need a pill now and then," I said.

"Some people are born needing them," Terri said.

She was using her finger to rub at something on the table. Then she stopped rubbing.

"I think I want to call my kids," Mel said. "Is that all right with everybody? I'll call my kids," he said.

Terri said, "What if Marjorie answers the phone? You guys, you've heard us   130 on the subject of Marjorie? Honey, you know you don't want to talk to Marjorie. It'll make you feel even worse."

"I don't want to talk to Marjorie," Mel said. "But I want to talk to my kids."

"There isn't a day goes by that Mel doesn't say he wishes she'd get married again. Or else die," Terri said. "For one thing," Terri said, "she's bankrupting us. Mel says it's just to spite him that she won't get married again. She has a boyfriend who lives with her and the kids, so Mel is supporting the boyfriend too."

"She's allergic to bees," Mel said. "If I'm not praying she'll get married again, I'm praying she'll get herself stung to death by a swarm of fucking bees."

"Shame on you," Laura said.

"Bzzzzzzz," Mel said, turning his fingers into bees and buzzing them at   135 Terri's throat. Then he let his hands drop all the way to his sides.

"She's vicious," Mel said. "Sometimes I think I'll go up there dressed like a beekeeper. You know, that hat that's like a helmet with the plate that comes down over your face, the big gloves, and the padded coat? I'll knock on the door and let loose a hive of bees in the house. But first I'd make sure the kids were out, of course."

He crossed one leg over the other. It seemed to take him a lot of time to do it. Then he put both feet on the floor and leaned forward, elbows on the table, his chin cupped in his hands.

"Maybe I won't call the kids, after all. Maybe it isn't such a hot idea. Maybe we'll just go eat. How does that sound?"

"Sounds fine to me," I said. "Eat or not eat. Or keep drinking. I could head right on out into the sunset."

"What does that mean, honey?" Laura said.   140

"It just means what I said," I said. "It means I could just keep going. That's all it means."

"I could eat something myself," Laura said. "I don't think I've ever been so hungry in my life. Is there something to nibble on?"

"I'll put out some cheese and crackers," Terri said.

But Terri just sat there. She did not get up to get anything.

Mel turned his glass over. He spilled it out on the table.   145

"Gin's gone," Mel said.

Terri said, "Now what?"

I could hear my heart beating. I could hear everyone's heart. I could hear the human noise we sat there making, not one of us moving, not even when the room went dark.

Judith Ortiz Cofer b. 1952

Nada°   [1993]

Almost as soon as Doña Ernestina got the telegram about her son's having been killed in Vietnam, she started giving her possessions away. At first we didn't realize what she was doing. By the time we did, it was too late.

The army people had comforted Doña Ernestina with the news that her son's "remains" would have to be "collected and shipped" back to New Jersey at some later date, since other "personnel" had also been lost on the same day. In other words, she would have to wait until Tony's body could be processed.

Processed. Doña Ernestina spoke that word like a curse when she told us. We were all down in El Basement — that's what we called the cellar of our apartment building: no windows for light, boilers making such a racket that you could scream and almost no one would hear you. Some of us had started meeting here on Saturday mornings — as much to talk as to wash our clothes — and over the years it became a sort of women's club where we could catch up on a week's worth of gossip. That Saturday, however, I had dreaded going down the cement steps. All of us had just heard the news about Tony the night before.

I should have known the minute I saw her, holding court in her widow's costume, that something had cracked inside Doña Ernestina. She was in full luto — black from head to toe, including a mantilla. In contrast, Lydia and Isabelita were both in rollers and bathrobes: our customary uniform for these Saturday morning gatherings — maybe our way of saying "No Men Allowed." As I approached them, Lydia stared at me with a scared-rabbit look in her eyes.

Doña Ernestina simply waited for me to join the other two leaning against 5 the machines before she continued explaining what had happened when the news of Tony had arrived at her door the day before. She spoke calmly, a haughty

---

Nada: Nothing (Spanish).

expression on her face, looking like an offended duchess in her beautiful black dress. She was pale, pale, but she had a wild look in her eyes. The officer had told her that—when the time came—they would bury Tony with "full military honors"; for now they were sending her the medal and a flag. But she had said, "No, *gracias,*" to the funeral, and she sent the flag and medals back marked *Ya no vive aquí*: Does not live here anymore. "Tell the Mr. President of the United States what I say: No, gracias."

Then she waited for our response.

Lydia shook her head, indicating that she was speechless. And Elenita looked pointedly at me, forcing me to be the one to speak the words of sympathy for all of us, to reassure Doña Ernestina that she had done exactly what any of us would have done in her place: yes, we would have all said *No, gracias,* to any president who had actually tried to pay for a son's life with a few trinkets and a folded flag.

Doña Ernestina nodded gravely. Then she picked up the stack of neatly folded men's shirts from the sofa (a discard we had salvaged from the sidewalk) and walked regally out of El Basement.

Lydia, who had gone to high school with Tony, burst into tears as soon as Doña Ernestina was out of sight. Elenita and I sat her down between us on the sofa and held her until she had let most of it out. Lydia is still young—a woman who has not yet been visited too often by *la muerte.*° Her husband of six months has just gotten his draft notice, and they have been trying for a baby—trying very hard. The walls of El Building are thin enough so that it has become a secret joke (kept only from Lydia and Roberto) that he is far more likely to escape the draft due to acute exhaustion than by becoming a father.

"Doesn't Doña Ernestina feel *anything?*" Lydia asked in between sobs. "Did 10 you see her, dressed up like an actress in a play—and not one tear for her son?"

"We all have different ways of grieving," I said, though I couldn't help thinking that there *was* a strangeness to Doña Ernestina and that Lydia was right when she said that the woman seemed to be acting out a part. "I think we should wait and see what she is going to do."

"Maybe," said Elenita. "Did you get a visit from *el padre*° yesterday?"

We nodded, not surprised to learn that all of us had gotten personal calls from Padre Álvaro, our painfully shy priest, after Doña Ernestina had frightened him away. Apparently el padre had come to her apartment immediately after hearing about Tony, expecting to comfort the woman as he had when Don Antonio died suddenly a year ago. Her grief then had been understandable in its immensity, for she had been burying not only her husband but also the dream shared by many of the barrio women her age—that of returning with her man to the Island after retirement, of buying a *casita*° in the old pueblo, and of being buried on native ground alongside *la familia.* People *my* age—those of us born or raised here—have had our mothers drill this fantasy into our brains

---

muerte: Death (here, personified). **padre:** Father (here, priest). **casita:** Little house.

all of our lives. So when Don Antonio dropped his head on the domino table, scattering the ivory pieces of the best game of the year, and when he was laid out in his best black suit at Ramírez's Funeral Home, all of us knew how to talk to the grieving widow.

That was the last time we saw both her men. Tony was there, too — home on a two-day pass from basic training — and he cried like a little boy over his father's handsome face, calling him Papi, Papi. Doña Ernestina had had a full mother's duty then, taking care of the hysterical boy. It was a normal chain of grief, the strongest taking care of the weakest. We buried Don Antonio at Garden State Memorial Park, where there are probably more Puerto Ricans than on the Island. Padre Álvaro said his sermon in a soft, trembling voice that was barely audible over the cries of the boy being supported on one side by his mother, impressive in her quiet strength and dignity, and on the other by Cheo, owner of the bodega where Don Antonio had played dominoes with other barrio men of his age for over twenty years.

Just about everyone from El Building had attended that funeral, and it had 15 been done right. Doña Ernestina had sent her son off to fight for America and then had started collecting her widow's pension. Some of us asked Doña Iris (who knew how to read cards) about Doña Ernestina's future, and Doña Iris had said: "A long journey within a year" — which fit with what we had thought would happen next: Doña Ernestina would move back to the Island and wait with her relatives for Tony to come home from the war. Some older women actually went home when they started collecting social security or pensions, but that was rare. Usually, it seemed to me, somebody had to die before the island dream would come true for women like Doña Ernestina. As for my friends and me, we talked about "vacations" in the Caribbean. But we knew that if life was hard for us in this barrio, it would be worse in a pueblo where no one knew us (and had maybe only heard of our parents before they came to *Los Estados Unidos de América,* where most of us had been brought as children).

When Padre Álvaro had knocked softly on my door, I had yanked it open, thinking it was that ex-husband of mine asking for a second chance again. (That's just the way Miguel knocks when he's sorry for leaving me — about once a week — when he wants a loan.) So I was wearing my go-to-hell face when I threw open the door, and the poor priest nearly jumped out of his skin. I saw him take a couple of deep breaths before he asked me in his slow way — he tries to hide his stutter by dragging out his words — if I knew whether or not Doña Ernestina was ill. After I said, "No, not that I know," Padre Álvaro just stood there, looking pitiful, until I asked him if he cared to come in. I had been sleeping on the sofa and watching TV all afternoon, and I really didn't want him to see the mess, but I had nothing to fear. The poor man actually took one step back at my invitation. No, he was in a hurry, he had a few other parishioners to visit, etc. These were difficult times, he said, so-so-so many young people lost to drugs or dying in the wa-wa-war. I asked him if *he* thought Doña Ernestina was sick, but he just shook his head. The man looked like an orphan at my door with those sad, brown eyes. He was actually appealing in a homely way: that long nose nearly touched the tip of his chin when he smiled, and his big crooked teeth broke my heart.

"She does not want to speak to me," Padre Álvaro said as he caressed a large silver crucifix that hung on a thick chain around his neck. He seemed to be dragged down by its weight, stoop-shouldered and skinny as he was.

I felt a strong impulse to feed him some of my chicken soup, still warm on the stove from my supper. Contrary to what Lydia says about me behind my back, I like living by myself. And I could not have been happier to have that mama's boy Miguel back where he belonged—with his mother, who thought that he was still her baby. But this scraggly thing at my door needed home cooking and maybe even something more than a hot meal to bring a little spark into his life. (I mentally asked God to forgive me for having thoughts like these about one of his priests. *Ay bendito,*° but they too are made of flesh and blood.)

"Maybe she just needs a little more time, Padre," I said in as comforting a voice as I could manage. Unlike the other women in El Building, I am not convinced that priests are truly necessary—or even much help—in times of crisis.

"Sí, Hija, perhaps you're right," he muttered sadly—calling me "daughter"   20
even though I'm pretty sure I'm five or six years older. (Padre Álvaro seems so "untouched" that it's hard to tell his age. I mean, when you live, it shows. He looks hungry for love, starving himself by choice.) I promised him that I would look in on Doña Ernestina. Without another word, he made the sign of the cross in the air between us and turned away. As I heard his slow steps descending the creaky stairs, I asked myself: what do priests dream about?

When el padre's name came up again during that Saturday meeting in El Basement, I asked my friends what *they* thought a priest dreamed about. It was a fertile subject, so much so that we spent the rest of our laundry time coming up with scenarios. Before the last dryer stopped, we all agreed that we could not receive communion the next day at mass unless we went to confession that afternoon and told another priest, not Álvaro, about our "unclean thoughts."

As for Doña Ernestina's situation, we agreed that we should be there for her if she called, but the decent thing to do, we decided, was give her a little more time alone. Lydia kept repeating, in that childish way of hers, "Something is wrong with the woman," but she didn't volunteer to go see what it was that was making Doña Ernestina act so strangely. Instead she complained that she and Roberto had heard pots and pans banging and things being moved around for hours in 4-D last night—they had hardly been able to sleep. Isabelita winked at me behind Lydia's back. Lydia and Roberto still had not caught on: if they could hear what was going on in 4-D, the rest of us could also get an earful of what went on in 4-A. They were just kids who thought they had invented sex: I tell you, a telenovela could be made from the stories in El Building.

On Sunday Doña Ernestina was not at the Spanish mass and I avoided Padre Álvaro so he would not ask me about her. But I was worried. Doña Ernestina was

---

Ay bendito: Oh my goodness, or Oh my.

a church cucaracha—a devout Catholic who, like many of us, did not always do what the priests and the Pope ordered but who knew where God lived. Only a serious illness or tragedy could keep her from attending mass, so afterward I went straight to her apartment and knocked on her door. There was no answer, although I had heard scraping and dragging noises, like furniture being moved around. At least she was on her feet and active. Maybe housework was what she needed to snap out of her shock. I decided to try again the next day.

As I went by Lydia's apartment, the young woman opened her door—I knew she had been watching me through the peephole—to tell me about more noises from across the hall during the night. Lydia was in her baby-doll pajamas. Although she stuck only her nose out, I could see Roberto in his jockey underwear doing something in the kitchen. I couldn't help thinking about Miguel and me when we had first gotten together. We were an explosive combination. After a night of passionate lovemaking, I would walk around thinking: Do not light cigarettes around me. No open flames. Highly combustible materials being transported. But when his mama showed up at our door, the man of fire turned into a heap of ashes at her feet.

"Let's wait and see what happens," I told Lydia again.   25

We did not have to wait for long. On Monday Doña Ernestina called to invite us to a wake for Tony, a *velorio*, in her apartment. The word spread fast. Everyone wanted to do something for her. Cheo donated fresh chickens and island produce of all kinds. Several of us got together and made arroz con pollo, also flan for dessert. And Doña Iris made two dozen *pasteles*° and wrapped the meat pies in banana leaves that she had been saving in her freezer for her famous Christmas parties. We women carried in our steaming plates, while the men brought in their bottles of Palo Viejo rum for themselves and candy-sweet Manischewitz wine for us. We came ready to spend the night saying our rosaries and praying for Tony's soul.

Doña Ernestina met us at the door and led us into her living room, where the lights were off. A photograph of Tony and one of her deceased husband Don Antonio were sitting on top of a table, surrounded by at least a dozen candles. It was a spooky sight that caused several of the older women to cross themselves. Doña Ernestina had arranged folding chairs in front of this table and told us to sit down. She did not ask us to take our food and drinks to the kitchen. She just looked at each of us individually, as if she were taking attendance in a class, and then said: "I have asked you here to say good-bye to my husband Antonio and my son Tony. You have been my friends and neighbors for twenty years, but they were my life. Now that they are gone, I have nada. Nada. Nada."

I tell you, that word is like a drain that sucks everything down. Hearing her say *nada* over and over made me feel as if I were being yanked into a dark pit. I could feel the others getting nervous around me too, but here was a woman

---

pasteles: Traditional food, similar to tamales.

deep into her pain: We had to give her a little space. She looked around the room, then walked out without saying another word.

As we sat there in silence, stealing looks at each other, we began to hear the sounds of things being moved around in other rooms. One of the older women took charge then, and soon the drinks were poured, the food served—all this while the strange sounds kept coming from different rooms in the apartment. Nobody said much, except once when we heard something like a dish fall and break. Doña Iris pointed her index finger at her ear and made a couple of circles—and out of nervousness, I guess, some of us giggled like schoolchildren.

It was a long while before Doña Ernestina came back out to us. By then we   30
were gathering our dishes and purses, having come to the conclusion that it was time to leave. Holding two huge Sears shopping bags, one in each hand, Doña Ernestina took her place at the front door as if she were a society hostess in a receiving line. Some of us women hung back to see what was going on. But Tito, the building's super, had had enough and tried to get past her. She took his hand, putting in it a small ceramic poodle with a gold chain around its neck. Tito gave the poodle a funny look, then glanced at Doña Ernestina as though he were scared and hurried away with the dog in his hand.

We were let out of her place one by one but not until she had forced one of her possessions on each of us. She grabbed without looking from her bags. Out came her prized *miniaturas,* knickknacks that take a woman a lifetime to collect. Out came ceramic and porcelain items of all kinds, including vases and ashtrays; out came kitchen utensils, dishes, forks, knives, spoons; out came old calendars and every small item that she had touched or been touched by in the last twenty years. Out came a bronzed baby shoe—and I got that.

As we left the apartment, Doña Iris said "Psst" to some of us, so we followed her down the hallway. "Doña Ernestina's faculties are temporarily out of order," she said very seriously. "It is due to the shock of her son's death."

We all said "Sí" and nodded our heads.

"But what can we do?" Lydia said, her voice cracking a little. "What should I do with this?" She was holding one of Tony's baseball trophies in her hand: 1968 Most Valuable Player, for the Pocos Locos, our barrio's team.

Doña Iris said, "Let us keep her things safe for her until she recovers her   35
senses. And let her mourn in peace. These things take time. If she needs us, she will call us." Doña Iris shrugged her shoulders. *"Así es la vida, hijas:* that's the way life is."

As I passed Tito on the stairs, he shook his head while looking up at Doña Ernestina's door: "I say she needs a shrink. I think somebody should call the social worker." He did not look at me when he mumbled these things. By "somebody" he meant one of us women. He didn't want trouble in his building, and he expected one of us to get rid of the problems. I just ignored him.

In my bed I prayed to the Holy Mother that she would find peace for Doña Ernestina's troubled spirit, but things got worse. All that week Lydia saw strange things happening through the peephole on her door. Every time people came to Doña Ernestina's apartment—to deliver flowers, or telegrams from the Island, or anything—the woman would force something on them. She pleaded with them to take this or that; if they hesitated, she commanded them with those tragic eyes to accept a token of her life.

And they did, walking out of our apartment building, carrying cushions, lamps, doilies, clothing, shoes, umbrellas, wastebaskets, schoolbooks, and notebooks: things of value and things of no worth at all to anyone but the person who had owned them. Eventually winos and street people got the news of the great giveaway in 4-D, and soon there was a line down the stairs and out the door. Nobody went home empty-handed; it was like a soup kitchen. Lydia was afraid to step out of her place because of all the dangerous-looking characters hanging out on that floor. And the smell! Entering our building was like coming into a cheap bar and public urinal combined.

Isabelita, living alone with her two little children and fearing for their safety, was the one who finally called a meeting of the residents. Only the women attended, since the men were truly afraid of Doña Ernestina. It isn't unusual for men to be frightened when they see a woman go crazy. If they are not the cause of her madness, then they act as if they don't understand it and usually leave us alone to deal with our "woman's problems." This is just as well.

Maybe I *am* just bitter because of Miguel—I know what is said behind my 40 back. But this is a fact: When a woman is in trouble, a man calls in her mama, her sisters, or her friends, and then he makes himself scarce until it's all over. This happens again and again. At how many bedsides of women have I sat? How many times have I made the doctor's appointment, taken care of the children, and fed the husbands of my friends in the barrio? It is not that the men can't do these things; it's just that they know how much women help each other. Maybe the men even suspect that we know one another better than they know their own wives. As I said, it is just as well that they stay out of our way when there is trouble. It makes things simpler for us.

At the meeting, Isabelita said right away that we should go up to 4-D and try to reason with *la pobre*° Doña Ernestina. Maybe we could get her to give us a relative's address in Puerto Rico—the woman obviously needed to be taken care of. What she was doing was putting us all in a very difficult situation. There were no dissenters this time. We voted to go as a group to talk to Doña Ernestina the next morning.

But that night we were all awakened by crashing noises on the street. In the light of the full moon, I could see that the air was raining household goods: kitchen chairs, stools, a small TV, a nightstand, pieces of a bed frame. Everything was splintering as it landed on the pavement. People were running for cover and yelling up at our building. The problem, I knew instantly, was in apartment 4-D.

Putting on my bathrobe and slippers, I stepped out into the hallway. Lydia and Roberto were rushing down the stairs, but on the flight above my landing,

---

pobre: poor one (expressing sympathy).

I caught up with Doña Iris and Isabelita, heading toward 4-D. Out of breath, we stood in the fourth-floor hallway, listening to police sirens approaching our building in front. We could hear the slamming of car doors and yelling—in both Spanish and English. Then we tried the door to 4-D. It was unlocked.

We came into a room virtually empty. Even the pictures had been taken down from the walls; all that was left were the nail holes and the lighter places on the paint where the framed photographs had been for years. We took a few seconds to spot Doña Ernestina: She was curled up in the farthest corner of the living room, naked.

"Cómo salió a este mundo,"° said Doña Iris, crossing herself.   45

Just as she had come into the world. Wearing nothing. Nothing around her except a clean, empty room. Nada. She had left nothing behind—except the bottles of pills, the ones the doctors give to ease the pain, to numb you, to make you feel nothing when someone dies.

The bottles were empty too, and the policemen took them. But we didn't let them take Doña Ernestina until we each had brought up some of our own best clothes and dressed her like the decent woman that she was. *La decencia.* Nothing can ever change that—not even la muerte. This is the way life is. *Así es la vida.*

"Cómo . . . mundo": "How she/he came into this world."

Ralph Ellison 1914–1994

Battle Royal   [1952]

It goes a long way back, some twenty years. All my life I had been looking for something, and everywhere I turned someone tried to tell me what it was. I accepted their answers too, though they were often in contradiction and even self-contradictory. I was naive. I was looking for myself and asking everyone except myself questions which I, and only I, could answer. It took me a long time and much painful boomeranging of my expectations to achieve a realization everyone else appears to have been born with: That I am nobody but myself. But first I had to discover that I am an invisible man!

And yet I am no freak of nature, nor of history. I was in the cards, other things having been equal (or unequal) eighty-five years ago. I am not ashamed of my grandparents for having been slaves. I am only ashamed of myself for having at one time been ashamed. About eighty-five years ago they were told that they were free, united with others of our country in everything pertaining to the common good, and, in everything social, separate like the fingers of the hand. And they believed it. They exulted in it. They stayed in their place, worked hard, and brought up my father to do the same. But my grandfather is the one. He was an odd old guy, my grandfather, and I am told I take after him. It was he who caused the trouble. On his deathbed he called my father to him and said, "Son, after I'm gone I want you to keep up the good fight. I never told you, but our life is a war and I have been a traitor all my born days, a spy in the enemy's country ever since I give up my gun back in the Reconstruction. Live with your head in the lion's mouth. I want you to overcome 'em with yeses, undermine 'em with grins, agree 'em to death and destruction, let 'em swoller you till they vomit or bust wide open." They thought the old man had gone out of his mind. He had been the meekest of men. The younger children were rushed from the room, the shades drawn and the flame of the lamp turned so low that it sputtered on the wick like the old man's breathing. "Learn it to the younguns," he whispered fiercely; then he died.

But my folks were more alarmed over his last words than over his dying. It was as though he had not died at all, his words caused so much anxiety. I was warned emphatically to forget what he had said and, indeed, this is the first time it has been mentioned outside the family circle. It had a tremendous effect upon me, however. I could never be sure of what he meant. Grandfather had been a quiet old man who never made any trouble, yet on his deathbed he had called himself a traitor and a spy, and he had spoken of his meekness as a dangerous activity. It became a constant puzzle which lay unanswered in the back of my mind. And whenever things went well for me I remembered my grandfather and felt guilty and uncomfortable. It was as though I was carrying out his advice in spite of myself. And to make it worse, everyone loved me for it. I was praised by the most lily-white men of the town. I was considered an example of desirable conduct—just as my grandfather had been. And what puzzled me was that the old man had defined it as *treachery*. When I was praised for my conduct I felt a guilt that in some way I was doing something that was really against the wishes of the white folks, that if they had understood they would have desired me to act just the opposite, that I should have been sulky and mean, and that that really would have been what they wanted, even though they were fooled and thought they wanted me to act as I did. It made me afraid that some day they would look upon me as a traitor and I would be lost. Still I was more afraid to act any other way because they didn't like that at all. The old man's words were like a curse. On my graduation day I delivered an oration in which I showed that humility was the secret, indeed, the very essence of progress. (Not that I believed this—how could I, remembering my grandfather?—I only believed that it worked.) It was a great success. Everyone praised me and I was invited to give the speech at a gathering of the town's leading white citizens. It was a triumph for our whole community.

It was in the main ballroom of the leading hotel. When I got there I discovered that it was on the occasion of a smoker, and I was told that since I was to be there anyway I might as well take part in the battle royal to be fought by some of my schoolmates as part of the entertainment. The battle royal came first.

All of the town's big shots were there in their tuxedoes, wolfing down the 5 buffet foods, drinking beer and whiskey and smoking black cigars. It was a large room with a high ceiling. Chairs were arranged in neat rows around three sides of a portable boxing ring. The fourth side was clear, revealing a gleaming space of polished floor. I had some misgivings over the battle royal, by the way. Not from a distaste for fighting, but because I didn't care too much for the other fellows who were to take part. They were tough guys who seemed to have no grandfather's curse worrying their minds. No one could mistake their tough-ness. And besides, I suspected that fighting a battle royal might detract from the dignity of my speech. In those pre-invisible days I visualized myself as a poten-tial Booker T. Washington.° But the other fellows didn't care too much for me either, and there were nine of them. I felt superior to them in my way, and I didn't like the manner in which we were all crowded together into the servants' elevator. Nor did they like my being there. In fact, as the warmly lighted floors flashed past the elevator we had words over the fact that I, by taking part in the fight, had knocked one of their friends out of a night's work.

We were led out of the elevator through a rococo hall into an anteroom and told to get into our fighting togs. Each of us was issued a pair of boxing gloves and ushered out into the big mirrored hall, which we entered looking cau-tiously about us and whispering, lest we might accidentally be heard above the noise of the room. It was foggy with cigar smoke. And already the whiskey was taking effect. I was shocked to see some of the most important men of the town quite tipsy. They were all there—bankers, lawyers, judges, doctors, fire chiefs, teachers, merchants. Even one of the more fashionable pastors. Something we could not see was going on up front. A clarinet was vibrating sensuously and the men were standing up and moving eagerly forward. We were a small tight group, clustered together, our bare upper bodies touching and shining with anticipatory sweat; while up front the big shots were becoming increasingly excited over something we still could not see. Suddenly I heard the school su-perintendent, who had told me to come, yell, "Bring up the shines, gentlemen! Bring up the little shines!"

We were rushed up to the front of the ballroom, where it smelled even more strongly of tobacco and whiskey. Then we were pushed into place. I almost wet my pants. A sea of faces, some hostile, some amused, ringed around us, and in the center, facing us, stood a magnificent blonde—stark naked. There was dead silence. I felt a blast of cold air chill me. I tried to back away, but they were behind me and around me. Some of the boys stood with lowered heads, trem-bling. I felt a wave of irrational guilt and fear. My teeth chattered, my skin

---

Booker T. Washington: (1856–1915), African American educator, author, orator, and politi-cal leader; he advocated working with supportive whites, instead of taking a confrontational approach toward whites.

turned to goose flesh, my knees knocked. Yet I was strongly attracted and looked in spite of myself. Had the price of looking been blindness, I would have looked. The hair was yellow like that of a circus kewpie doll, the face heavily powdered and rouged, as though to form an abstract mask, the eyes hollow and smeared a cool blue, the color of a baboon's butt. I felt a desire to spit upon her as my eyes brushed slowly over her body. Her breasts were firm and round as the domes of East Indian temples, and I stood so close as to see the fine skin texture and beads of pearly perspiration glistening like dew around the pink and erected buds of her nipples. I wanted at one and the same time to run from the room, to sink through the floor, or go to her and cover her from my eyes and the eyes of the others with my body; to feel the soft thighs, to caress her and destroy her, to love her and murder her, to hide from her, and yet to stroke where below the small American flag tattooed upon her belly her thighs formed a capital V. I had a notion that of all in the room she saw only me with her impersonal eyes.

And then she began to dance, a slow sensuous movement; the smoke of a hundred cigars clinging to her like the thinnest of veils. She seemed like a fair bird-girl girdled in veils calling to me from the angry surface of some gray and threatening sea. I was transported. Then I became aware of the clarinet playing and the big shots yelling at us. Some threatened us if we looked and others if we did not. On my right I saw one boy faint. And now a man grabbed a silver pitcher from a table and stepped close as he dashed ice water upon him and stood him up and forced two of us to support him as his head hung and moans issued from his thick bluish lips. Another boy began to plead to go home. He was the largest of the group, wearing dark red fighting trunks much too small to conceal the erection which projected from him as though in answer to the insinuating low-registered moaning of the clarinet. He tried to hide himself with his boxing gloves.

And all the while the blonde continued dancing, smiling faintly at the big shots who watched her with fascination, and faintly smiling at our fear. I noticed a certain merchant who followed her hungrily, his lips loose and drooling. He was a large man who wore diamond studs in a shirtfront which swelled with the ample paunch underneath, and each time the blonde swayed her undulating hips he ran his hand through the thin hair of his bald head and, with his arms upheld, his posture clumsy like that of an intoxicated panda, wound his belly in a slow and obscene grind. This creature was completely hypnotized. The music had quickened. As the dancer flung herself about with a detached expression on her face, the men began reaching out to touch her. I could see their beefy fingers sink into the soft flesh. Some of the others tried to stop them and she began to move around the floor in graceful circles, as they gave chase, slipping and sliding over the polished floor. It was mad. Chairs went crashing, drinks were spilt, as they ran laughing and howling after her. They caught her just as she reached a door, raised her from the floor, and tossed her as college boys are tossed at a hazing, and above her red, fixed-smiling lips I saw the terror and disgust in her eyes, almost like my own terror and that which I saw in some of the other boys. As I watched, they tossed her twice and her soft breasts seemed to flatten against the air and her legs flung wildly as she spun. Some of the more sober ones helped her to escape. And I started off the floor, heading for the anteroom with the rest of the boys.

Some were still crying and in hysteria. But as we tried to leave we were 10 stopped and ordered to get into the ring. There was nothing to do but what we were told. All ten of us climbed under the ropes and allowed ourselves to be blindfolded with broad bands of white cloth. One of the men seemed to feel a bit sympathetic and tried to cheer us up as we stood with our backs against the ropes. Some of us tried to grin. "See that boy over there?" one of the men said. "I want you to run across at the bell and give it to him right in the belly. If you don't get him, I'm going to get you. I don't like his looks." Each of us was told the same. The blindfolds were put on. Yet even then I had been going over my speech. In my mind each word was as bright as flame. I felt the cloth pressed into place, and frowned so that it would be loosened when I relaxed.

But now I felt a sudden fit of blind terror. I was unused to darkness. It was as though I had suddenly found myself in a dark room filled with poisonous cottonmouths. I could hear the bleary voices yelling insistently for the battle royal to begin.

"Get going in there!"

"Let me at that big nigger!"

I strained to pick up the school superintendent's voice, as though to squeeze some security out of that slightly more familiar sound.

"Let me at those black sonsabitches!" someone yelled.   15

"No, Jackson, no!" another voice yelled. "Here, somebody, help me hold Jack."

"I want to get at that ginger-colored nigger. Tear him limb from limb," the first voice yelled.

I stood against the ropes trembling. For in those days I was what they called ginger-colored, and he sounded as though he might crunch me between his teeth like a crisp ginger cookie.

Quite a struggle was going on. Chairs were being kicked about and I could hear voices grunting as with a terrific effort. I wanted to see, to see more desperately than ever before. But the blindfold was tight as a thick skin-puckering scab and when I raised my gloved hands to push the layers of white aside a voice yelled, "Oh, no you don't, black bastard! Leave that alone!"

"Ring the bell before Jackson kills him a coon!" someone boomed in the 20 sudden silence. And I heard the bell clang and the sound of the feet scuffling forward.

A glove smacked against my head. I pivoted, striking out stiffly as someone went past, and felt the jar ripple along the length of my arm to my shoulder. Then it seemed as though all nine of the boys had turned upon me at once. Blows pounded me from all sides while I struck out as best I could. So many blows landed upon me that I wondered if I were not the only blindfolded fighter in the ring, or if the man called Jackson hadn't succeeded in getting me after all.

Blindfolded, I could no longer control my motions. I had no dignity. I stumbled about like a baby or a drunken man. The smoke had become thicker and with each new blow it seemed to sear and further restrict my lungs. My saliva became like hot bitter glue. A glove connected with my head, filling my mouth with warm blood. It was everywhere. I could not tell if the moisture I felt upon my body was sweat or blood. A blow landed hard against the nape of my neck. I felt myself going over, my head hitting the floor. Streaks of blue light filled the black world behind the blindfold. I lay prone, pretending that I was knocked out, but felt myself seized by hands and yanked to my feet. "Get going, black boy! Mix it up!" My arms were like lead, my head smarting from blows. I managed to feel my way to the ropes and held on, trying to catch my breath. A glove landed in my mid-section and I went over again, feeling as though the smoke had become a knife jabbed into my guts. Pushed this way and that by the legs milling around me, I finally pulled erect and discovered that I could see the black, sweat-washed forms weaving in the smoky-blue atmosphere like drunken dancers weaving to the rapid drum-like thuds of blows.

Everyone fought hysterically. It was complete anarchy. Everybody fought everybody else. No group fought together for long. Two, three, four, fought one, then turned to fight each other, were themselves attacked. Blows landed below the belt and in the kidney, with the gloves open as well as closed, and with my eye partly opened now there was not so much terror. I moved carefully, avoiding blows, although not too many to attract attention, fighting from group to group. The boys groped about like blind, cautious crabs crouching to protect their mid-sections, their heads pulled in short against their shoulders, their arms stretched nervously before them, with their fists testing the smoke-filled air like the knobbed feelers of hyper-sensitive snails. In one corner I glimpsed a boy violently punching the air and heard him scream in pain as he smashed his hand against a ring post. For a second I saw him bent over holding his hand, then going down as a blow caught his unprotected head. I played one group against the other, slipping in and throwing a punch then stepping out of range while pushing the others into the melee to take the blows blindly aimed at me. The smoke was agonizing and there were no rounds, no bells at three minute intervals to relieve our exhaustion. The room spun round me, a swirl of lights, smoke, sweating bodies surrounded by tense white faces. I bled from both nose and mouth, the blood spattering upon my chest.

The men kept yelling, "Slug him, black boy! Knock his guts out!"

"Uppercut him! Kill him! Kill that big boy!"   25

Taking a fake fall, I saw a boy going down heavily beside me as though we were felled by a single blow, saw a sneaker-clad foot shoot into his groin as the two who had knocked him down stumbled upon him. I rolled out of range, feeling a twinge of nausea.

The harder we fought the more threatening the men became. And yet, I had begun to worry about my speech again. How would it go? Would they recognize my ability? What would they give me?

I was fighting automatically when suddenly I noticed that one after another of the boys was leaving the ring. I was surprised, filled with panic, as though I had been left alone with an unknown danger. Then I understood. The boys had arranged it among themselves. It was the custom for the two men left in the ring to slug it out for the winner's prize. I discovered this too late. When the bell sounded two men in tuxedoes leaped into the ring and removed the blindfold. I found myself facing Tatlock, the biggest of the gang. I felt sick at my stomach. Hardly had the bell stopped ringing in my ears than it clanged again and I saw him moving swiftly toward me. Thinking of nothing else to do I hit him smash on the nose. He kept coming, bringing the rank sharp violence of stale sweat. His face was a black blank of a face, only his eyes alive — with hate of me and aglow with a feverish terror from what had happened to us all. I became anxious. I wanted to deliver my speech and he came at me as though he meant to beat it out of me. I smashed him again and again, taking his blows as they came. Then on a sudden impulse I struck him lightly and as we clinched, I whispered, "Fake like I knocked you out, you can have the prize."

"I'll break your behind," he whispered hoarsely.

"For *them?*"   30

"For *me*, sonofabitch!"

They were yelling for us to break it up and Tatlock spun me half around with a blow, and as a joggled camera sweeps in a reeling scene, I saw the howling red faces crouching tense beneath the cloud of blue-gray smoke. For a moment the world wavered, unraveled, flowed, then my head cleared and Tatlock bounced before me. That fluttering shadow before my eyes was his jabbing left hand. Then falling forward, my head against his damp shoulder, I whispered,

"I'll make it five dollars more."

"Go to hell!"

But his muscles relaxed a trifle beneath my pressure and I breathed, "Seven?"   35

"Give it to your ma," he said, ripping me beneath the heart.

And while I still held him I butted him and moved away. I felt myself bombarded with punches. I fought back with hopeless desperation. I wanted to deliver my speech more than anything else in the world, because I felt that only these men could judge truly my ability, and now this stupid clown was ruining my chances. I began fighting carefully now, moving in to punch him and out again with my greater speed. A lucky blow to his chin and I had him going too — until I heard a loud voice yell, "I got my money on the big boy."

Hearing this, I almost dropped my guard. I was confused: Should I try to win against the voice out there? Would not this go against my speech, and was not this a moment for humility, for nonresistance? A blow to my head as I danced about sent my right eye popping like a jack-in-the-box and settled my dilemma. The room went red as I fell. It was a dream fall, my body languid and fastidious as to where to land, until the floor became impatient and smashed up to meet me. A moment later I came to. An hypnotic voice said FIVE emphatically. And I lay there, hazily watching a dark red spot of my own blood shaping itself into a butterfly, glistening and soaking into the soiled gray world of the canvas.

When the voice drawled TEN I was lifted up and dragged to a chair. I sat dazed. My eye pained and swelled with each throb of my pounding heart and I wondered if now I would be allowed to speak. I was wringing wet, my mouth still bleeding. We were grouped along the wall now. The other boys ignored me as they congratulated Tatlock and speculated as to how much they would be paid. One boy whimpered over his smashed hand. Looking up front, I saw attendants in white jackets rolling the portable ring away and placing a small square rug in the vacant space surrounded by chairs. Perhaps, I thought, I will stand on the rug to deliver my speech.

Then the M.C. called to us, "Come on up here boys and get your money."   40

We ran forward to where the men laughed and talked in their chairs, waiting. Everyone seemed friendly now.

"There it is on the rug," the man said. I saw the rug covered with coins of all dimensions and a few crumpled bills. But what excited me, scattered here and there, were the gold pieces.

"Boys, it's all yours," the man said. "You get all you grab."

"That's right, Sambo," a blond man said, winking at me confidentially.

I trembled with excitement, forgetting my pain. I would get the gold and   45
the bills, I thought. I would use both hands. I would throw my body against the boys nearest me to block them from the gold.

"Get down around the rug now," the man commanded, "and don't anyone touch it until I give the signal."

"This ought to be good," I heard.

As told, we got around the square rug on our knees. Slowly the man raised his freckled hand as we followed it upward with our eyes.

I heard, "These niggers look like they're about to pray!"

Then, "Ready," the man said. "Go!"   50

I lunged for a yellow coin lying on the blue design of the carpet, touching it and sending a surprised shriek to join those rising around me. I tried frantically to remove my hand but could not let go. A hot, violent force tore through my body, shaking me like a wet rat. The rug was electrified. The hair bristled up on my head as I shook myself free. My muscles jumped, my nerves jangled, writhed. But I saw that this was not stopping the other boys. Laughing in fear and embarrassment, some were holding back and scooping up the coins knocked off by the painful contortions of the others. The men roared above us as we struggled.

"Pick it up, goddamnit, pick it up!" someone called like a bass-voiced parrot. "Go on, get it!"

I crawled rapidly around the floor, picking up the coins, trying to avoid the coppers and to get greenbacks and the gold. Ignoring the shock by laughing, as I brushed the coins off quickly, I discovered that I could contain the electricity—a contradiction, but it works. Then the men began to push us onto the rug. Laughing embarrassedly, we struggled out of their hands and kept after the coins. We were all wet and slippery and hard to hold. Suddenly I saw a boy lifted into the air, glistening with sweat like a circus seal, and dropped, his wet back landing flush upon the charged rug, heard him yell and saw him literally dance upon his back, his elbows beating a frenzied tattoo upon the floor, his muscles twitching like the flesh of a horse stung by many flies. When he finally rolled off, his face was gray and no one stopped him when he ran from the floor amid booming laughter.

"Get the money," the M.C. called. "That's good hard American cash!"

And we snatched and grabbed, snatched and grabbed. I was careful not to   55
come too close to the rug now, and when I felt the hot whiskey breath descend upon me like a cloud of foul air I reached out and grabbed the leg of a chair. It was occupied and I held on desperately.

"Leggo, nigger! Leggo!"

The huge face wavered down to mine as he tried to push me free. But my body was slippery and he was too drunk. It was Mr. Colcord, who owned a chain of movie houses and "entertainment palaces." Each time he grabbed me I slipped out of his hands. It became a real struggle. I feared the rug more than I did the drunk, so I held on, surprising myself for a moment by trying to topple *him* upon the rug. It was such an enormous idea that I found myself actually carrying it out. I tried not to be obvious, yet when I grabbed his leg, trying to tumble him out of the chair, he raised up roaring with laughter, and, looking at me with soberness dead in the eye, kicked me viciously in the chest. The chair leg flew out of my hand and I felt myself going and rolled. It was as though I had rolled through a bed of hot coals. It seemed a whole century would pass before I would roll free, a century in which I was seared through the deepest levels of my body to the fearful breath within me and the breath seared and heated to the point of explosion. It'll all be over in a flash, I thought as I rolled clear. It'll all be over in a flash.

But not yet, the men on the other side were waiting, red faces swollen as though from apoplexy as they bent forward in their chairs. Seeing their fingers coming toward me I rolled away as a fumbled football rolls off the receiver's fingertips, back into the coals. That time I luckily sent the rug sliding out of place and heard the coins ringing against the floor and the boys scuffling to pick them up and the M.C. calling, "All right, boys, that's all. Go get dressed and get your money."

I was limp as a dish rag. My back felt as though it had been beaten with wires.

When we had dressed the M.C. came in and gave us each five dollars, ex-   60
cept Tatlock, who got ten for being last in the ring. Then he told us to leave. I was not to get a chance to deliver my speech, I thought. I was going out into the dim alley in despair when I was stopped and told to go back. I returned to the ballroom, where the men were pushing back their chairs and gathering in groups to talk.

The M.C. knocked on a table for quiet. "Gentlemen," he said, "we almost forgot an important part of the program. A most serious part, gentlemen. This boy was brought here to deliver a speech which he made at his graduation yesterday . . ."

"Bravo!"

"I'm told that he is the smartest boy we've got out there in Greenwood. I'm told that he knows more big words than a pocket-sized dictionary."

Much applause and laughter.

"So now, gentlemen, I want you to give him your attention."   65

There was still laughter as I faced them, my mouth dry, my eye throbbing. I began slowly, but evidently my throat was tense, because they began shouting, "Louder! Louder!"

"We of the younger generation extol the wisdom of that great leader and educator," I shouted, "who first spoke these flaming words of wisdom: 'A ship lost at sea for many days suddenly sighted a friendly vessel. From the mast of the unfortunate vessel was seen a signal: "Water, water; we die of thirst!" The answer from the friendly vessel came back: "Cast down your bucket where you are." The captain of the distressed vessel, at last heeding the injunction, cast down his bucket, and it came up full of fresh sparkling water from the mouth of the Amazon River.' And like him I say, and in his words, 'To those of my race who depend upon bettering their condition in a foreign land, or who underestimate the importance of cultivating friendly relations with the Southern white man, who is his next-door neighbor, I would say: "Cast down your bucket where you are" — cast it down in making friends in every manly way of the people of all races by whom we are surrounded . . .'"

I spoke automatically and with such fervor that I did not realize that the men were still talking and laughing until my dry mouth, filling up with blood from the cut, almost strangled me. I coughed, wanting to stop and go to one of the tall brass, sand-filled spittoons to relieve myself, but a few of the men, especially the superintendent, were listening and I was afraid. So I gulped it down, blood, saliva and all, and continued. (What powers of endurance I had during those days! What enthusiasm! What a belief in the rightness of things!) I spoke even louder in spite of the pain. But still they talked and still they laughed, as though deaf with cotton in dirty ears. So I spoke with greater emotional emphasis. I closed my ears and swallowed blood until I was nauseated. The speech seemed a hundred times as long as before, but I could not leave out a single word. All had to be said, each memorized nuance considered, rendered. Nor was that all. Whenever I uttered a word of three or more syllables a group of voices would yell for me to repeat it. I used the phrase "social responsibility" and they yelled:

"What's that word you say, boy?"

"Social responsibility," I said.   70

"What?"

"Social . . ."

"Louder."

". . . responsibility."

"More!"   75

"Respon —"

"Repeat!"

" — sibility."

The room filled with the uproar of laughter until, no doubt distracted by having to gulp down my blood, I made a mistake and yelled a phrase I had often seen denounced in newspaper editorials, heard debated in private.

"Social . . ."   80

"What?" they yelled.

". . . equality—"

The laughter hung smokelike in the sudden stillness. I opened my eyes, puzzled. Sounds of displeasure filled the room. The M.C. rushed forward. They shouted hostile phrases at me. But I did not understand.

A small dry mustached man in the front row blared out, "Say that slowly, son!"

"What, sir?"   85

"What you just said!"

"Social responsibility, sir," I said.

"You weren't being smart, were you, boy?" he said, not unkindly.

"No, sir!"

"You sure that about 'equality' was a mistake?"   90

"Oh, yes, sir," I said. "I was swallowing blood."

"Well, you had better speak more slowly so we can understand. We mean to do right by you, but you've got to know your place at all times. All right, now, go on with your speech."

I was afraid. I wanted to leave but I wanted also to speak and I was afraid they'd snatch me down.

"Thank you, sir," I said, beginning where I had left off, and having them ignore me as before.

Yet when I finished there was a thunderous applause. I was surprised to see   95
the superintendent come forth with a package wrapped in white tissue paper, and, gesturing for quiet, address the men.

"Gentlemen, you see that I did not overpraise this boy. He makes a good speech and some day he'll lead his people in the proper paths. And I don't have to tell you that that is important in these days and times. This is a good, smart boy, and so to encourage him in the right direction, in the name of the Board of Education I wish to present him a prize in the form of this . . ."

He paused, removing the tissue paper and revealing a gleaming calfskin brief case.

". . . in the form of this first-class article from Shad Whitmore's shop."

"Boy," he said, addressing me, "take this prize and keep it well. Consider it a badge of office. Prize it. Keep developing as you are and some day it will be filled with important papers that will help shape the destiny of your people."

I was so moved that I could hardly express my thanks. A rope of bloody   100
saliva forming a shape like an undiscovered continent drooled upon the leather and I wiped it quickly away. I felt an importance that I had never dreamed.

"Open it and see what's inside," I was told.

My fingers a-tremble, I complied, smelling the fresh leather and finding an official-looking document inside. It was a scholarship to the state college for Negroes. My eyes filled with tears and I ran awkwardly off the floor.

I was overjoyed; I did not even mind when I discovered that the gold pieces I had scrambled for were brass pocket tokens advertising a certain make of automobile.

When I reached home everyone was excited. Next day the neighbors came to congratulate me. I even felt safe from grandfather, whose deathbed curse usually spoiled my triumphs. I stood beneath his photograph with my brief case in hand and smiled triumphantly into his stolid black peasant's face. It was a face that fascinated me. The eyes seemed to follow everywhere I went.

That night I dreamed I was at a circus with him and that he refused 105 to laugh at the clowns no matter what they did. Then later he told me to open my brief case and read what was inside and I did, finding an official envelope stamped with the state seal; and inside the envelope I found another and another, endlessly, and I thought I would fall of weariness. "Them's years," he said. "Now open that one." And I did and in it I found an engraved document containing a short message in letters of gold. "Read it," my grandfather said. "Out loud!"

"To Whom It May Concern," I intoned. "Keep This Nigger-Boy Running."

I awoke with the old man's laughter ringing in my ears.

(It was a dream I was to remember and dream again for many years after. But at that time I had no insight into its meaning. First I had to attend college.)

Gabriel García Márquez   Colombia, b. 1928

A Very Old Man with Enormous Wings   [1955]
A Tale for Children

Translated by Gregory Rabassa

On the third day of rain they had killed so many crabs inside the house that Pelayo had to cross his drenched courtyard and throw them into the sea, because the newborn child had a temperature all night and they thought it was due to the stench. The world had been sad since Tuesday. Sea and sky were a single ash-gray thing and the sands of the beach, which on March nights glimmered like powdered light, had become a stew of mud and rotten shellfish. The light was so weak at noon that when Pelayo was coming back to the house after throwing away the crabs, it was hard for him to see what it was that was moving and groaning in the rear of the courtyard. He had to go very close to see that it was an old man, a very old man, lying face down in the mud, who, in spite of his tremendous efforts, couldn't get up, impeded by his enormous wings.

Frightened by that nightmare, Pelayo ran to get Elisenda, his wife, who was putting compresses on the sick child, and he took her to the rear of the courtyard. They both looked at the fallen body with mute stupor. He was dressed like a ragpicker. There were only a few faded hairs left on his bald skull and very few teeth in his mouth, and his pitiful condition of a drenched great-grandfather had taken away any sense of grandeur he might have had. His huge buzzard wings, dirty and half-plucked, were forever entangled in the mud. They looked at him so long and so closely that Pelayo and Elisenda very soon overcame their surprise and in the end found him familiar. Then they dared speak to him, and he answered in an incomprehensible dialect with a strong sailor's voice. That was how they skipped over the inconvenience of the wings and quite intelligently concluded that he was a lonely castaway from some foreign ship wrecked by the storm. And yet, they called in a neighbor woman who knew everything about life and death to see him, and all she needed was one look to show them their mistake.

"He's an angel," she told them. "He must have been coming for the child, but the poor fellow is so old that the rain knocked him down."

On the following day everyone knew that a flesh-and-blood angel was held captive in Pelayo's house. Against the judgment of the wise neighbor woman, for whom angels in those times were the fugitive survivors of a celestial conspiracy, they did not have the heart to club him to death. Pelayo watched over him all afternoon from the kitchen, armed with his bailiff's club, and before going to bed he dragged him out of the mud and locked him up with the hens in the wire chicken coop. In the middle of the night, when the rain stopped, Pelayo and Elisenda were still killing crabs. A short time afterward the child woke up without a fever and with a desire to eat. Then they felt magnanimous and decided to put the angel on a raft with fresh water and provisions for three days and leave him to his fate on the high seas. But when they went out into the courtyard with the first light of dawn, they found the whole neighborhood in front of the chicken coop having fun with the angel, without the slightest reverence, tossing him things to eat through the openings in the wire as if he weren't a supernatural creature but a circus animal.

Father Gonzaga arrived before seven o'clock, alarmed at the strange news. 5 By that time onlookers less frivolous than those at dawn had already arrived and they were making all kinds of conjectures concerning the captive's future. The simplest among them thought that he should be named mayor of the world. Others of sterner mind felt that he should be promoted to the rank of five-star general in order to win all wars. Some visionaries hoped that he could be put to stud in order to implant on earth a race of winged wise men who could take charge of the universe. But Father Gonzaga, before becoming a priest, had been a robust woodcutter. Standing by the wire, he reviewed his catechism in an instant and asked them to open the door so that he could take a close look at that pitiful man who looked more like a huge decrepit hen among the fascinated chickens. He was lying in a corner drying his open wings in the sunlight among the fruit peels and breakfast leftovers that the early risers had thrown him. Alien to the impertinences of the world, he only lifted his antiquarian eyes and murmured something in his dialect when Father Gonzaga went into the chicken coop and said good morning to him in Latin. The parish priest had his first suspicion of an imposter when he saw that he did not understand the language of God or know how to greet His ministers. Then he noticed that seen close up he was much too human: he had an unbearable smell of the outdoors, the back side of his wings was strewn with parasites and his main feathers had been mistreated by terrestrial winds, and nothing about him measured up to the proud dignity of angels. Then he came out of the chicken coop and in a brief sermon warned the curious against the risks of being ingenuous. He reminded them that the devil had the bad habit of making use of carnival tricks in order to confuse the unwary. He argued that if wings were not the essential element in determining the difference between a hawk and an airplane, they were even less so in the recognition of angels. Nevertheless, he promised to write a letter to his bishop so that the latter would write to his primate so that the latter would write to the Supreme Pontiff in order to get the final verdict from the highest courts.

His prudence fell on sterile hearts. The news of the captive angel spread with such rapidity that after a few hours the courtyard had the bustle of a marketplace and they had to call in troops with fixed bayonets to disperse the mob that was about to knock the house down. Elisenda, her spine all twisted from sweeping up so much marketplace trash, then got the idea of fencing in the yard and charging five cents admission to see the angel.

The curious came from far away. A traveling carnival arrived with a flying acrobat who buzzed over the crowd several times, but no one paid any attention to him because his wings were not those of an angel but, rather, those of a sidereal° bat. The most unfortunate invalids on earth came in search of health: a poor woman who since childhood had been counting her heartbeats and had run out of numbers; a Portuguese man who couldn't sleep because the noise of the stars disturbed him; a sleepwalker who got up at night to undo the things he had done while awake; and many others with less serious ailments. In the midst of that shipwreck disorder that made the earth tremble, Pelayo and Elisenda were happy with fatigue, for in less than a week they had crammed their rooms with money and the line of pilgrims waiting their turn to enter still reached beyond the horizon.

The angel was the only one who took no part in his own act. He spent his time trying to get comfortable in his borrowed nest, befuddled by the hellish heat of the oil lamps and sacramental candles that had been placed along the wire. At first they tried to make him eat some mothballs, which, according to the wisdom of the wise neighbor woman, were the food prescribed for angels. But he turned them down, just as he turned down the papal lunches that the penitents brought him, and they never found out whether it was because he was an angel or because he was an old man that in the end he ate nothing but eggplant mush. His only supernatural virtue seemed to be patience. Especially during the first days, when the hens pecked at him, searching for the stellar parasites that proliferated in his wings, and the cripples pulled out feathers to touch their defective

---

sidereal: Coming from the stars.

parts with, and even the most merciful threw stones at him, trying to get him to rise so they could see him standing. The only time they succeeded in arousing him was when they burned his side with an iron for branding steers, for he had been motionless for so many hours that they thought he was dead. He awoke with a start, ranting in his hermetic language and with tears in his eyes, and he flapped his wings a couple of times, which brought on a whirlwind of chicken dung and lunar dust and a gale of panic that did not seem to be of this world. Although many thought that his reaction had been one not of rage but of pain, from then on they were careful not to annoy him, because the majority understood that his passivity was not that of a hero taking his ease but that of a cataclysm in repose.

Father Gonzaga held back the crowd's frivolity with formulas of maidservant inspiration while awaiting the arrival of a final judgment on the nature of the captive. But the mail from Rome showed no sense of urgency. They spent their time finding out if the prisoner had a navel, if his dialect had any connection with Aramaic, how many times he could fit on the head of a pin, or whether he wasn't just a Norwegian with wings. Those meager letters might have come and gone until the end of time if a providential event had not put an end to the priest's tribulations.

It so happened that during those days, among so many other carnival attractions, there arrived in town the traveling show of the woman who had been changed into a spider for having disobeyed her parents. The admission to see her was not only less than the admission to see the angel, but people were permitted to ask her all manner of questions about her absurd state and to examine her up and down so that no one would ever doubt the truth of her horror. She was a frightful tarantula the size of a ram and with the head of a sad maiden. What was most heartrending, however, was not her outlandish shape but the sincere affliction with which she recounted the details of her misfortune. While still practically a child she had sneaked out of her parents' house to go to a dance, and while she was coming back through the woods after having danced all night without permission, a fearful thunderclap rent the sky in two and through the crack came the lightning bolt of brimstone that changed her into a spider. Her only nourishment came from the meatballs that charitable souls chose to toss into her mouth. A spectacle like that, full of so much human truth and with such a fearful lesson, was bound to defeat without even trying that of a haughty angel who scarcely deigned to look at mortals. Besides, the few miracles attributed to the angel showed a certain mental disorder, like the blind man who didn't recover his sight but grew three new teeth, or the paralytic who didn't get to walk but almost won the lottery, and the leper whose sores sprouted sunflowers. Those consolation miracles, which were more like mocking fun, had already ruined the angel's reputation when the woman who had been changed into a spider finally crushed him completely. That was how Father Gonzaga was cured forever of his insomnia and Pelayo's courtyard went back to being as empty as during the time it had rained for three days and crabs walked through the bedrooms.

10

The owners of the house had no reason to lament. With the money they saved they built a two-story mansion with balconies and gardens and high net-ting so that crabs wouldn't get in during the winter, and with iron bars on the windows so that angels wouldn't get in. Pelayo also set up a rabbit warren close to town and gave up his job as bailiff for good, and Elisenda bought some satin pumps with high heels and many dresses of iridescent silk, the kind worn on Sunday by the most desirable women in those times. The chicken coop was the only thing that didn't receive any attention. If they washed it down with creolin and burned tears of myrrh inside it every so often, it was not in homage to the angel but to drive away the dungheap stench that still hung everywhere like a ghost and was turning the new house into an old one. At first, when the child learned to walk, they were careful that he not get too close to the chicken coop. But then they began to lose their fears and got used to the smell, and before the child got his second teeth he'd gone inside the chicken coop to play, where the wires were falling apart. The angel was no less standoffish with him than with other mortals, but he tolerated the most ingenious infamies with the patience of a dog who had no illusions. They both came down with chicken pox at the same time. The doctor who took care of the child couldn't resist the temptation to listen to the angel's heart, and he found so much whistling in the heart and so many sounds in his kidneys that it seemed impossible for him to be alive. What surprised him most, however, was the logic of his wings. They seemed so natural on that completely human organism that he couldn't understand why other men didn't have them too.

When the child began school it had been some time since the sun and rain had caused the collapse of the chicken coop. The angel went dragging himself about here and there like a stray dying man. They would drive him out of the bedroom with a broom and a moment later find him in the kitchen. He seemed to be in so many places at the same time that they grew to think that he'd been duplicated, that he was reproducing himself all through the house, and the exasperated and unhinged Elisenda shouted that it was awful living in that hell full of angels. He could scarcely eat and his antiquarian eyes had also become so foggy that he went about bumping into posts. All he had left were the bare cannulae° of his last feathers. Pelayo threw a blanket over him and extended him the charity of letting him sleep in the shed, and only then did they notice that he had a temperature at night, and was delirious with the tongue twisters of an old Norwegian. That was one of the few times they became alarmed, for they thought he was going to die and not even the wise neighbor woman had been able to tell them what to do with dead angels.

And yet he not only survived his worst winter, but seemed improved with the first sunny days. He remained motionless for several days in the farthest corner of the courtyard, where no one would see him, and at the beginning of December some large, stiff feathers began to grow on his wings, the feathers of

---

cannulae: The tubelike quills by which feathers are attached to a body.

a scarecrow, which looked more like another misfortune of decrepitude. But he must have known the reason for those changes, for he was quite careful that no one should notice them, that no one should hear the sea chanteys that he sometimes sang under the stars. One morning Elisenda was cutting some bunches of onions for lunch when a wind that seemed to come from the high seas blew into the kitchen. Then she went to the window and caught the angel in his first attempts at flight. They were so clumsy that his fingernails opened a furrow in the vegetable patch and he was on the point of knocking the shed down with the ungainly flapping that slipped on the light and couldn't get a grip on the air. But he did manage to gain altitude. Elisenda let out a sigh of relief, for herself and for him, when she saw him pass over the last houses, holding himself up in some way with the risky flapping of a senile vulture. She kept watching him even when she was through cutting the onions and she kept on watching until it was no longer possible for her to see him, because then he was no longer an annoyance in her life but an imaginary dot on the horizon of the sea.

Langston Hughes   1902–1967

Thank You, M'am   [1950]

She was a large woman with a large purse that had everything in it but hammer and nails. It had a long strap and she carried it slung across her shoulder. It was about eleven o'clock at night, and she was walking alone, when a boy ran up behind her and tried to snatch her purse. The strap broke with the single tug the boy gave it from behind. But the boy's weight, and the weight of the purse combined caused him to lose his balance so, instead of taking off full blast as he had hoped, the boy fell on his back on the sidewalk, and his legs flew up. The large woman simply turned around and kicked him right square in his blue jeaned sitter. Then she reached down, picked the boy up by his shirt front, and shook him until his teeth rattled.

After that the woman said, "Pick up my pocketbook, boy, and give it here."

She still held him. But she bent down enough to permit him to stoop and pick up her purse. Then she said, "Now ain't you ashamed of yourself?"

Firmly gripped by his shirt front, the boy said, "Yes'm."

The woman said, "What did you want to do it for?"   5

The boy said, "I didn't aim to."

She said, "You a lie!"

By that time two or three people passed, stopped, turned to look, and some stood watching.

"If I turn you loose, will you run?" asked the woman.

"Yes'm," said the boy.   10

"Then I won't turn you loose," said the woman. She did not release him.

"I'm very sorry, lady, I'm sorry," whispered the boy.

"Um-hum! And your face is dirty. I got a great mind to wash your face for you. Ain't you got nobody home to tell you to wash your face?"

"No'm," said the boy.

"Then it will get washed this evening," said the large woman starting up the street, dragging the frightened boy behind her.   15

He looked as if he were fourteen or fifteen, frail and willow-wild, in tennis shoes and blue jeans.

The woman said, "You ought to be my son. I would teach you right from wrong. Least I can do right now is to wash your face. Are you hungry?"

"No'm," said the being-dragged boy. "I just want you to turn me loose."

"Was I bothering *you* when I turned that corner?" asked the woman.

"No'm."   20

"But you put yourself in contact with *me*," said the woman. "If you think that that contact is not going to last awhile, you got another thought coming. When I get through with you, sir, you are going to remember Mrs. Luella Bates Washington Jones."

Sweat popped out on the boy's face and he began to struggle. Mrs. Jones stopped, jerked him around in front of her, put a half-nelson about his neck, and continued to drag him up the street. When she got to her door, she dragged the boy inside, down a hall, and into a large kitchenette-furnished room at the rear of the house. She switched on the light and left the door open. The boy could hear other roomers laughing and talking in the large house. Some of their doors were open, too, so he knew he and the woman were not alone. The woman still had him by the neck in the middle of her room.

She said, "What is your name?"

"Roger," answered the boy.

"Then, Roger, you go to that sink and wash your face," said the woman, whereupon she turned him loose—at last. Roger looked at the door—looked at the woman—looked at the door—*and went to the sink.*   25

"Let the water run until it gets warm," she said. "Here's a clean towel."

"You gonna take me to jail?" asked the boy, bending over the sink.

"Not with that face, I would not take you nowhere," said the woman. "Here I am trying to get home to cook me a bite to eat and you snatch my pocketbook! Maybe you ain't been to your supper either, late as it be. Have you?"

"There's nobody home at my house," said the boy.

"Then we'll eat," said the woman. "I believe you're hungry—or been hungry—to try to snatch my pocketbook."   30

"I wanted a pair of blue suede shoes," said the boy.

"Well, you didn't have to snatch *my* pocketbook to get some suede shoes," said Mrs. Luella Bates Washington Jones. "You could of asked me."

"M'am?"

The water dripping from his face, the boy looked at her. There was a long pause. A very long pause. After he had dried his face and not knowing what else to do dried it again, the boy turned around, wondering what next. The door was open. He could make a dash for it down the hall. He could run, run, run, run, *run!*

The woman was sitting on the day-bed. After awhile she said, "I were young 35 once and I wanted things I could not get."

There was another long pause. The boy's mouth opened. Then he frowned, but not knowing he frowned.

The woman said, "Um-hum! You thought I was going to say *but*, didn't you? You thought I was going to say, *but I didn't snatch people's pocketbooks.* Well, I wasn't going to say that." Pause. Silence. "I have done things, too, which I would not tell you, son—neither tell God, if he didn't already know. So you set down while I fix us something to eat. You might run that comb through your hair so you will look presentable."

In another corner of the room behind a screen was a gas plate and an ice-box. Mrs. Jones got up and went behind the screen. The woman did not watch the boy to see if he was going to run now, nor did she watch her purse which she left behind her on the day-bed. But the boy took care to sit on the far side of the room where he thought she could easily see him out of the corner of her eye, if she wanted to. He did not trust the woman *not* to trust him. And he did not want to be mistrusted now.

"Do you need somebody to go to the store," asked the boy, "maybe to get some milk or something?"

"Don't believe I do," said the woman, "unless you just want sweet milk 40 yourself. I was going to make cocoa out of this canned milk I got here."

"That will be fine," said the boy.

She heated some lima beans and ham she had in the icebox, made the cocoa, and set the table. The woman did not ask the boy anything about where he lived, or his folks, or anything else that would embarrass him. Instead, as they ate, she told him about her job in a hotel beauty-shop that stayed open late, what the work was like, and how all kinds of women came in and out, blondes, red-heads, and Spanish. Then she cut him a half of her ten-cent cake.

"Eat some more, son," she said.

When they were finished eating she got up and said, "Now, here, take this ten dollars and buy yourself some blue suede shoes. And next time, do not make the mistake of latching onto *my* pocketbook *nor nobody else's*—because shoes come by devilish like that will burn your feet. I got to get my rest now. But I wish you would behave yourself, son, from here on in."

She led him down the hall to the front door and opened it. "Goodnight! 45 Behave yourself, boy!" she said, looking out into the street.

The boy wanted to say something else other than, "Thank you, m'am," to Mrs. Luella Bates Washington Jones, but he couldn't do so as he turned at the barren stoop and looked back at the large woman in the door. He barely managed to say, "Thank you," before she shut the door. And he never saw her again.

Zora Neale Hurston 1891–1960

Sweat   [1926]

It was eleven o'clock of a Spring night in Florida. It was Sunday. Any other night, Delia Jones would have been in bed for two hours by this time. But she was a washwoman, and Monday morning meant a great deal to her. So she collected the soiled clothes on Saturday when she returned the clean things. Sunday night after church, she sorted them and put the white things to soak. It saved her almost a half day's start. A great hamper in the bedroom held the clothes that she brought home. It was so much neater than a number of bundles lying around.

She squatted on the kitchen floor beside the great pile of clothes, sorting them into small heaps according to color, and humming a song in a mournful key, but wondering through it all where Sykes, her husband, had gone with her horse and buckboard.

Just then something long, round, limp and black fell upon her shoulders and slithered to the floor beside her. A great terror took hold of her. It softened her knees and dried her mouth so that it was a full minute before she could cry out or move. Then she saw that it was the big bull whip her husband liked to carry when he drove.

She lifted her eyes to the door and saw him standing there bent over with laughter at her fright. She screamed at him.

"Sykes, what you throw dat whip on me like dat? You know it would skeer   5
me — looks just like a snake, an' you knows how skeered Ah is of snakes."

"Course Ah knowed it! That's how come Ah done it." He slapped his leg with his hand and almost rolled on the ground in his mirth. "If you such a big fool dat you got to have a fit over a earth worm or a string, Ah don't keer how bad Ah skeer you."

"You aint got no business doing it. Gawd knows it's a sin. Some day Ah'm gointuh drop dead from some of yo' foolishness. 'Nother thing, where you been wid mah rig? Ah feeds dat pony. He aint fuh you to be drivin' wid no bull whip."

"You sho is one aggravatin' nigger woman!" he declared and stepped into the room. She resumed her work and did not answer him at once. "Ah done tole you time and again to keep them white folks' clothes outa dis house."

He picked up the whip and glared down at her. Delia went on with her work. She went out into the yard and returned with a galvanized tub and sat it on the washbench. She saw that Sykes had kicked all of the clothes together again, and now stood in her way truculently, his whole manner hoping, *praying,* for an argument. But she walked calmly around him and commenced to re-sort the things.

"Next time, Ah'm gointer kick 'em outdoors," he threatened as he struck a 10 match along the leg of his corduroy breeches.

Delia never looked up from her work, and her thin, stooped shoulders sagged further.

"Ah aint for no fuss t'night, Sykes. Ah just come from taking sacrament at the church house."

He snorted scornfully. "Yeah, you just come from de church house on a Sunday night, but heah you is gone to work on them clothes. You ain't nothing but a hypocrite. One of them amen-corner Christians — sing, whoop, and shout, then come home and wash white folks clothes on the Sabbath."

He stepped roughly upon the whitest pile of things, kicking them helter-skelter as he crossed the room. His wife gave a little scream of dismay, and quickly gathered them together again.

"Sykes, you quit grindin' dirt into these clothes! How can Ah git through 15 by Sat'day if Ah don't start on Sunday?"

"Ah don't keer if you never git through. Anyhow, Ah done promised Gawd and a couple of other men, Ah aint gointer have it in mah house. Don't gimme no lip neither, else Ah'll throw 'em out and put mah fist up side yo' head to boot."

Delia's habitual meekness seemed to slip from her shoulders like a blown scarf. She was on her feet; her poor little body, her bare knuckly hands bravely defying the strapping hulk before her.

"Looka heah, Sykes, you done gone too fur. Ah been married to you fur fifteen years, and Ah been takin' in washin' fur fifteen years. Sweat, sweat, sweat! Work and sweat, cry and sweat, pray and sweat!"

"What's that got to do with me?" he asked brutally.

"What's it got to do with you, Sykes? Mah tub of suds is filled yo' belly with 20 vittles more times than yo' hands is filled it. Mah sweat is done paid for this house and Ah reckon Ah kin keep on sweatin' in it."

She seized the iron skillet from the stove and struck a defensive pose, which act surprised him greatly, coming from her. It cowed him and he did not strike her as he usually did.

"Naw you won't," she panted, "that ole snaggle-toothed black woman you runnin' with aint comin' heah to pile up on *mah* sweat and blood. You aint paid for nothin' on this place, and Ah'm gointer stay right heah till Ah'm toted out foot foremost."

"Well, you better quit gittin' me riled up, else they'll be totin' you out sooner than you expect. Ah'm so tired of you Ah don't know whut to do. Gawd! how Ah hates skinny wimmen!"

A little awed by this new Delia, he sidled out of the door and slammed the back gate after him. He did not say where he had gone, but she knew too well. She knew very well that he would not return until nearly daybreak also. Her work over, she went on to bed but not to sleep at once. Things had come to a pretty pass!

She lay awake, gazing upon the debris that cluttered their matrimonial trail. 25
Not an image left standing along the way. Anything like flowers had long ago
been drowned in the salty stream that had been pressed from her heart. Her
tears, her sweat, her blood. She had brought love to the union and he had
brought a longing after the flesh. Two months after the wedding, he had given
her the first brutal beating. She had the memory of his numerous trips to
Orlando with all of his wages when he had returned to her penniless, even
before the first year had passed. She was young and soft then, but now she
thought of her knotty, muscled limbs, her harsh knuckly hands, and drew herself up into an unhappy little ball in the middle of the big feather bed. Too late
now to hope for love, even if it were not Bertha it would be someone else. This
case differed from the others only in that she was bolder than the others. Too
late for everything except her little home. She had built it for her old days, and
planted one by one the trees and flowers there. It was lovely to her, lovely.

Somehow, before sleep came, she found herself saying aloud: "Oh well,
whatever goes over the Devil's back, is got to come under his belly. Sometime or
ruther, Sykes, like everybody else, is gointer reap his sowing." After that she was
able to build a spiritual earthworks against her husband. His shells could no
longer reach her. *Amen*. She went to sleep and slept until he announced his presence in bed by kicking her feet and rudely snatching the cover away.

"Gimme some kivah heah, an' git yo' damn foots over on yo' own side! Ah
oughter mash you in yo' mouf fuh drawing dat skillet on me."

Delia went clear to the rail without answering him. A triumphant indifference to all that he was or did.

The week was as full of work for Delia as all other weeks, and Saturday
found her behind her little pony, collecting and delivering clothes.

It was a hot, hot day near the end of July. The village men on Joe Clarke's 30
porch even chewed cane listlessly. They did not hurl the cane-knots as usual.
They let them dribble over the edge of the porch. Even conversation had collapsed under the heat.

"Heah come Delia Jones," Jim Merchant said, as the shaggy pony came
'round the bend of the road toward them. The rusty buckboard was heaped with
baskets of crisp, clean laundry.

"Yep," Joe Lindsay agreed. "Hot or col', rain or shine, jes ez reg'lar ez de
weeks roll roun' Delia carries 'em an' fetches 'em on Sat'day."

"She better if she wanter eat," said Moss. "Sykes Jones aint wuth de shot
an' powder hit would tek tuh kill 'em. Not to *huh* he aint."

"He sho' aint," Walter Thomas chimed in. "It's too bad, too, cause she wuz
a right pritty li'l trick when he got huh. Ah'd uh mah'ied huh mahseff if he
hadnter beat me to it."

Delia nodded briefly at the men as she drove past. 35

"Too much knockin' will ruin *any* 'oman. He done beat huh 'nough tuh kill
three women, let 'lone change they looks," said Elijah Moseley. "How Sykes kin
stommuck dat big black greasy Mogul he's layin' roun' wid, gits me. Ah swear

dat eight-rock couldn't kiss a sardine can Ah done thowed out de back do' 'way las' yeah."

"Aw, she's fat, thass how come. He's allus been crazy 'bout fat women," put in Merchant. "He'd a' been tied up wid one long time ago if he could a' found one tuh have him. Did Ah tell yuh 'bout him come sidlin' roun' *mah* wife—bringin' her a basket uh pee-cans outa his yard fuh a present? Yessir, mah wife! She tol' him tuh take 'em right straight back home, cause Delia works so hard ovah dat washtub she reckon everything on de place taste lak sweat an' soap-suds. Ah jus' wisht Ah'd a' caught 'im 'roun' dere! Ah'd a' made his hips ketch on fiah down dat shell road."

"Ah know he done it, too. Ah sees 'im grinnin' at every 'oman dat passes," Walter Thomas said. "But even so, he useter eat some mighty big hunks uh humble pie tuh git dat lil' 'oman he got. She wuz ez pritty ez a speckled pup! Dat wuz fifteen yeahs ago. He useter be so skeered uh losin' huh, she could make him do some parts of a husband's duty. Dey never wuz de same in de mind."

"There oughter be a law about him," said Lindsay. "He aint fit tuh carry guts tuh a bear."

Clarke spoke for the first time. "Taint no law on earth dat kin make a man 40
be decent if it aint in 'im. There's plenty men dat takes a wife lak dey do a joint uh sugar-cane. It's round, juicy an' sweet when dey gits it. But dey squeeze an' grind, squeeze an' grind an' wring tell dey wring every drop uh pleasure dat's in 'em out. When dey's satisfied dat dey is wrung dry, dey treats 'em jes lak dey do a cane-chew. Dey thows 'em away. Dey knows whut dey is doin' while dey is at it, an' hates theirselves fuh it but they keeps on hangin' after huh tell she's empty. Den dey hates huh fuh bein' a cane-chew an' in de way."

"We oughter take Sykes an' dat stray 'oman uh his'n down in Lake Howell swamp an' lay on de rawhide till they cain't say 'Lawd a' mussy.' He allus wuz uh ovahbearin' niggah, but since dat white 'oman from up north done teached 'im how to run a automobile, he done got too biggety to live—an' we oughter kill 'im," Old Man Anderson advised.

A grunt of approval went around the porch. But the heat was melting their civic virtue and Elijah Moseley began to bait Joe Clarke.

"Come on, Joe, git a melon outa dere an' slice it up for yo' customers. We'se all sufferin' wid de heat. De bear's done got *me*!"

"Thass right, Joe, a watermelon is jes' whut Ah needs tuh cure de eppizu-dicks." Walter Thomas joined forces with Moseley. "Come on dere, Joe. We all is steady customers an' you aint set us up in a long time. Ah chooses dat long, bowlegged Floridy favorite."

"A god, an' be dough. You all gimme twenty cents and slice away," Clarke 45
retorted. "Ah needs a col' slice m'self. Heah, everybody chip in. Ah'll lend y'all mah meat knife."

The money was quickly subscribed and the huge melon brought forth. At that moment, Sykes and Bertha arrived. A determined silence fell on the porch and the melon was put away again.

Merchant snapped down the blade of his jack-knife and moved toward the store door.

"Come on in, Joe, an' gimme a slab uh sow belly an' uh pound uh coffee — almost fuhgot 'twas Sat'day. Got to git on home." Most of the men left also.

Just then Delia drove past on her way home, as Sykes was ordering magnificently for Bertha. It pleased him for Delia to see.

"Git whutsoever yo' heart desires, Honey. Wait a minute, Joe. Give huh two   50
bottles uh strawberry soda-water, uh quart uh parched ground-peas, an a block uh chewin' gum."

With all this they left the store, with Sykes reminding Bertha that this was his town and she could have it if she wanted it.

The men returned soon after they left, and held their watermelon feast.

"Where did Sykes Jones git dat 'oman from nohow?" Lindsay asked.

"Ovah Apopka. Guess dey musta been cleanin' out de town when she lef'. She don't look lak a thing but a hunk uh liver wid hair on it."

"Well, she sho' kin squall," Dave Carter contributed. "When she gits ready   55
tuh laff, she jes' opens huh mouf an' latches it back tuh de las' notch. No ole grandpa alligator down in Lake Bell aint got nothin' on huh."

Bertha had been in town three months now. Sykes was still paying her room rent at Della Lewis' — the only house in town that would have taken her in. Sykes took her frequently to Winter Park to "stomps." He still assured her that he was the swellest man in the state.

"Sho' you kin have dat lil' ole house soon's Ah kin git dat 'oman outa dere. Everything b'longs tuh me an' you sho' kin have it. Ah sho' 'bominates uh skinny 'oman. Lawdy, you sho' is got one portly shape on you! You kin git *anything* you wants. Dis is *mah* town an' you sho' kin have it."

Delia's work-worn knees crawled over the earth in Gethsemane° and up the rocks of Calvary many, many times during these months. She avoided the villagers and meeting places in her efforts to be blind and deaf. But Bertha nullified this to a degree, by coming to Delia's house to call Sykes out to her at the gate.

Delia and Sykes fought all the time now with no peaceful interludes. They slept and ate in silence. Two or three times Delia had attempted a timid friendliness, but she was repulsed each time. It was plain that the breaches must remain agape.

The sun had burned July to August. The heat streamed down like a million hot   60
arrows, smiting all things living upon the earth. Grass withered, leaves browned, snakes went blind in shedding and men and dogs went mad. Dog days!

Gethsemane: The garden in which Jesus agonized and prayed (Matthew 26:36–46) before being taken prisoner and crucified on a hill called Calvary (Luke 23:33).

Delia came home one day and found Sykes there before her. She wondered, but started to go on into the house without speaking, even though he was standing in the kitchen door and she must either stoop under his arm or ask him to move. He made no room for her. She noticed a soap box beside the steps, but paid no particular attention to it, knowing that he must have brought it there. As she was stooping to pass under his outstretched arm, he suddenly pushed her backward, laughingly.

"Look in de box dere Delia, Ah done brung yuh somethin'!"

She nearly fell upon the box in her stumbling, and when she saw what it held, she all but fainted outright.

"Sykes! Sykes, mah Gawd! You take dat rattlesnake 'way from heah! You *gottuh*. Oh, Jesus, have mussy!"

"Ah aint gut tuh do nuthin' uh de kin'—fact is Ah aint got tuh do nothin' 65 but die. Taint no use uh you puttin' on airs makin' out lak you skeered uh dat snake—he's gointer stay right heah tell he die. He wouldn't bite me cause Ah knows how tuh handle 'im. Nohow he wouldn't risk breakin' out his fangs 'gin yo' skinny laigs."

"Naw, now Sykes, don't keep dat thing 'roun' heah tuh skeer me tuh death. You knows Ah'm even feared uh earth worms. Thass de biggest snake Ah evah did see. Kill 'im Sykes, please."

"Doan ast me tuh do nothin' fuh yuh. Goin' 'roun' tryin' tuh be so damn astorperious. Naw, Ah aint gonna kill it. Ah think uh damn sight mo' uh him dan you! Dat's a nice snake an' anybody doan lak 'im kin jes' hit de grit."

The village soon heard that Sykes had the snake, and came to see and ask questions.

"How de hen-fire did you ketch dat six-foot rattler, Sykes?" Thomas asked.

"He's full uh frogs so he caint hardly move, thass how Ah eased up on 'm. 70 But Ah'm a snake charmer an' knows how tuh handle 'em. Shux, dat aint nothin'. Ah could ketch one eve'y day if Ah so wanted tuh."

"Whut he needs is a heavy hick'ry club leaned real heavy on his head. Dat's de bes 'way tuh charm a rattlesnake."

"Naw, Walt, y'all jes' don't understand dese diamon' backs lak Ah do," said Sykes in a superior tone of voice.

The village agreed with Walter, but the snake stayed on. His box remained by the kitchen door with its screen wire covering. Two or three days later it had digested its meal of frogs and literally came to life. It rattled at every movement in the kitchen or the yard. One day as Delia came down the kitchen steps she saw his chalky-white fangs curved like scimitars hung in the wire meshes. This time she did not run away with averted eyes as usual. She stood for a long time in the doorway in a red fury that grew bloodier for every second that she regarded the creature that was her torment.

That night she broached the subject as soon as Sykes sat down to the table.

"Sykes, Ah wants you tuh take dat snake 'way fum heah. You done starved 75 me an' Ah put up widcher, you done beat me an Ah took dat, but you done kilt all mah insides bringin' dat varmint heah."

Sykes poured out a saucer full of coffee and drank it deliberately before he answered her.

"A whole lot Ah keer 'bout how you feels inside uh out. Dat snake aint goin' no damn wheah till Ah gits ready fuh 'im tuh go. So fur as beatin' is concerned, yuh aint took near all dat you gointer take ef yuh stay 'roun' *me*."

Delia pushed back her plate and got up from the table. "Ah hates you, Sykes," she said calmly. "Ah hates you tuh de same degree dat Ah useter love yuh. Ah done took an' took till mah belly is full up tuh mah neck. Dat's de reason Ah got mah letter fum de church an' moved mah membership tuh Woodbridge — so Ah don't haftuh take no sacrament wid yuh. Ah don't wantuh see yuh 'roun' me a-tall. Lay 'roun' wid dat 'oman all yuh wants tuh, but gwan 'way fum me an' mah house. Ah hates yuh lak uh suck-egg dog."

Sykes almost let the huge wad of corn bread and collard greens he was chewing fall out of his mouth in amazement. He had a hard time whipping himself up to the proper fury to try to answer Delia.

"Well, Ah'm glad you does hate me. Ah'm sho' tiahed uh you hangin'   80 ontuh me. Ah don't want yuh. Look at yuh stringey ole neck! Yo' rawbony laigs an' arms is enough tuh cut uh man tuh death. You looks jes' lak de devvul's doll-baby tuh *me*. You cain't hate me no worse dan Ah hates you. Ah been hatin' *you* fuh years."

"Yo' ole black hide don't look lak nothin' tuh me, but uh passel uh wrinkled up rubber, wid yo' big ole yeahs flappin' on each side lak uh paih uh buzzard wings. Don't think Ah'm gointuh be run 'way fum mah house. Ah'm goin' tuh de white folks bout *you*, mah young man, de very nex' time you lay yo' han's on me. Mah cup is done run ovah." Delia said this with no signs of fear and Sykes departed from the house, threatening her, but made not the slightest move to carry out any of them.

That night he did not return at all, and the next day being Sunday, Delia was glad that she did not have to quarrel before she hitched up her pony and drove the four miles to Woodbridge.

She stayed to the night service — "love feast" — which was very warm and full of spirit. In the emotional winds her domestic trials were borne far and wide so that she sang as she drove homeward,

Jurden water, black an' col'
Chills de body, not de soul
An' Ah wantah cross Jurden in uh calm time.

She came from the barn to the kitchen door and stopped.

"Whut's de mattah, ol' satan, you aint kickin' up yo' racket?" She addressed   85 the snake's box. Complete silence. She went on into the house with a new hope in its birth struggles. Perhaps her threat to go to the white folks had frightened Sykes! Perhaps he was sorry! Fifteen years of misery and suppression had brought Delia to the place where she would hope *anything* that looked towards a way over or through her wall of inhibitions.

She felt in the match safe behind the stove at once for a match. There was only one there.

"Dat niggah wouldn't fetch nothin' heah tuh save his rotten neck, but he kin run thew whut Ah brings quick enough. Now he done toted off nigh on tuh haff uh box uh matches. He done had dat 'oman heah in mah house, too."

Nobody but a woman could tell how she knew this even before she struck the match. But she did and it put her into a new fury.

Presently she brought in the tubs to put the white things to soak. This time she decided she need not bring the hamper out of the bedroom; she would go in there and do the sorting. She picked up the pot-bellied lamp and went in. The room was small and the hamper stood hard by the foot of the white iron bed. She could sit and reach through the bedposts—resting as she worked.

"Ah wantah cross Jurden in uh calm time." She was singing again. The mood of the "love feast" had returned. She threw back the lid of the basket almost gaily. Then, moved by both horror and terror, she sprung back toward the door. *There lay the snake in the basket!* He moved sluggishly at first, but even as she turned round and round, jumped up and down in an insanity of fear, he began to stir vigorously. She saw him pouring his awful beauty from the basket upon the bed, then she seized the lamp and ran as fast as she could to the kitchen. The wind from the open door blew out the light and the darkness added to her terror. She sped to the darkness of the yard, slamming the door after her before she thought to set down the lamp. She did not feel safe even on the ground, so she climbed up in the hay barn.

There for an hour or more she lay sprawled upon the hay a gibbering wreck.

Finally she grew quiet, and after that, coherent thought. With this, stalked through her a cold, bloody rage. Hours of this. A period of introspection, a space of retrospection, then a mixture of both. Out of this an awful calm.

"Well, Ah done de bes' Ah could. If things aint right, Gawd knows taint mah fault."

She went to sleep—a twitchy sleep—and woke up to a faint gray sky. There was a loud hollow sound below. She peered out. Sykes was at the wood-pile, demolishing a wire-covered box.

He hurried to the kitchen door, but hung outside there some minutes before he entered, and stood some minutes more inside before he closed it after him.

The gray in the sky was spreading. Delia descended without fear now, and crouched beneath the low bedroom window. The drawn shade shut out the dawn, shut in the night. But the thin walls held back no sound.

"Dat ol' scratch is woke up now!" She mused at the tremendous whirr inside, which every woodsman knows, is one of the sound illusions. The rattler is a ventriloquist. His whirr sounds to the right, to the left, straight ahead, behind, close under foot—everywhere but where it is. Woe to him who guesses wrong unless he is prepared to hold up his end of the argument! Sometimes he strikes without rattling at all.

Inside, Sykes heard nothing until he knocked a pot lid off the stove while trying to reach the match safe in the dark. He had emptied his pockets at Bertha's.

The snake seemed to wake up under the stove and Sykes made a quick leap
into the bedroom. In spite of the gin he had had, his head was clearing now.

"Mah Gawd!" he chattered, "ef Ah could on'y strack uh light!"   100

The rattling ceased for a moment as he stood paralyzed. He waited. It
seemed that the snake waited also.

"Oh fuh de light! Ah thought he'd be too sick" — Sykes was muttering to
himself when the whirr began again, closer, right underfoot this time. Long
before this, Sykes' ability to think had been flattened down to primitive instinct
and he leaped — onto the bed.

Outside Delia heard a cry that might have come from a maddened chim-
panzee, a stricken gorilla. All the terror, all the horror, all the rage that man
possibly could express, without a recognizable human sound.

A tremendous stir inside there, another series of animal screams, the intermittent whirr of the reptile. The shade torn violently down from the window,
letting in the red dawn, a huge brown hand seizing the window stick, great dull
blows upon the wooden floor punctuating the gibberish of sound long after the
rattle of the snake had abruptly subsided. All this Delia could see and hear from
her place beneath the window, and it made her ill. She crept over to the four-
o'clocks and stretched herself on the cool earth to recover.

She lay there. "Delia, Delia!" She could hear Sykes calling in a most de-   105
spairing tone as one who expected no answer. The sun crept on up, and he
called. Delia could not move — her legs were gone flabby. She never moved, he
called, and the sun kept rising.

"Mah Gawd!" she heard him moan. "Mah Gawd fum Heben!" She heard
him stumbling about and got up from her flower-bed. The sun was growing
warm. As she approached the door she heard him call out hopefully, "Delia, is
dat you Ah heah?"

She saw him on his hands and knees as soon as she reached the door. He
crept an inch or two toward her — all that he was able, and she saw his horribly
swollen neck and his one open eye shining with hope. A surge of pity too strong
to support bore her away from that eye that must, could not, fail to see the tubs.
He would see the lamp. Orlando with its doctors was too far. She could scarcely reach the Chinaberry tree, where she waited in the growing heat while inside
she knew the cold river was creeping up and up to extinguish that eye which
must know by now that she knew.

Bel Kaufman   b. 1911

Sunday in the Park   [1985]

It was still warm in the late-afternoon sun, and the city noises came muffled through the trees in the park. She put her book down on the bench, removed her sunglasses, and sighed contentedly. Morton was reading the *Times
Magazine* section, one arm flung around her shoulder; their three-year-old son,

Larry, was playing in the sandbox; a faint breeze fanned her hair softly against her cheek. It was five-thirty of a Sunday afternoon, and the small playground, tucked away in a corner of the park, was all but deserted. The swings and see-saws stood motionless and abandoned, the slides were empty, and only in the sandbox two little boys squatted diligently side by side. *How good this is,* she thought, and almost smiled at her sense of well-being. They must go out in the sun more often; Morton was so city-pale, cooped up all week inside the gray factorylike university. She squeezed his arm affectionately and glanced at Larry, delighting in the pointed little face frowning in concentration over the tunnel he was digging. The other boy suddenly stood up and with a quick, deliberate swing of his chubby arm threw a spadeful of sand at Larry. It just missed his head. Larry continued digging; the boy remained standing, shovel raised, stolid and impassive.

"No, no, little boy." She shook her finger at him, her eyes searching for the child's mother or nurse. "We mustn't throw sand. It may get in some-one's eyes and hurt. We must play nicely in the nice sandbox." The boy looked at her in unblinking expectancy. He was about Larry's age but per-haps ten pounds heavier, a husky little boy with none of Larry's quickness and sensitivity in his face. Where was his mother? The only other people left in the playground were two women and a little girl on roller skates leaving now through the gate, and a man on a bench a few feet away. He was a big man, and he seemed to be taking up the whole bench as he held the Sunday comics close to his face. She supposed he was the child's father. He did not look up from his comics, but spat once deftly out of the corner of his mouth. She turned her eyes away.

At that moment, as swiftly as before, the fat little boy threw another spade-ful of sand at Larry. This time some of it landed on his hair and forehead. Larry looked up at his mother, his mouth tentative; her expression would tell him whether to cry or not.

Her first instinct was to rush to her son, brush the sand out of his hair, and punish the other child, but she controlled it. She always said that she wanted Larry to learn to fight his own battles.

"Don't *do* that, little boy," she said sharply, leaning forward on the bench. "You mustn't throw sand!"

The man on the bench moved his mouth as if to spit again, but instead he spoke. He did not look at her, but at the boy only.

"You go right ahead, Joe," he said loudly. "Throw all you want. This here is a *public* sandbox."

She felt a sudden weakness in her knees as she glanced at Morton. He had become aware of what was happening. He put his *Times* down carefully on his lap and turned his fine, lean face toward the man, smiling the shy, apologetic smile he might have offered a student in pointing out an error in his thinking. When he spoke to the man, it was with his usual reasonableness.

"You're quite right," he said pleasantly, "but just because this is a public place . . ."

The man lowered his funnies and looked at Morton. He looked at him from   10
head to foot, slowly and deliberately. "Yeah?" His insolent voice was edged with
menace. "My kid's got just as good right here as yours, and if he feels like throwing sand, he'll throw it, and if you don't like it, you can take your kid the hell
out of here."

The children were listening, their eyes and mouths wide open, their spades
forgotten in small fists. She noticed the muscle in Morton's jaw tighten. He was
rarely angry; he seldom lost his temper. She was suffused with a tenderness for
her husband and an impotent rage against the man for involving him in a situation so alien and so distasteful to him.

"Now, just a minute," Morton said courteously, "you must realize . . ."

"Aw, shut up," said the man.

Her heart began to pound. Morton half rose; the *Times* slid to the ground.
Slowly the other man stood up. He took a couple of steps toward Morton, then
stopped. He flexed his great arms, waiting. She pressed her trembling knees
together. Would there be violence, fighting? How dreadful, how incredible . . .
She must do something, stop them, call for help. She wanted to put her hand
on her husband's sleeve, to pull him down, but for some reason she didn't.

Morton adjusted his glasses. He was very pale. "This is ridiculous," he said   15
unevenly. "I must ask you . . ."

"Oh, yeah?" said the man. He stood with his legs spread apart, rocking a
little, looking at Morton with utter scorn. "You and who else?"

For a moment the two men looked at each other nakedly. Then Morton
turned his back on the man and said quietly, "Come on, let's get out of here."
He walked awkwardly, almost limping with self-consciousness, to the sandbox.
He stooped and lifted Larry and his shovel out.

At once Larry came to life; his face lost its rapt expression and he began
to kick and cry. "I don't *want* to go home, I want to play better, I don't *want*
any supper, I don't *like* supper . . ." It became a chant as they walked, pulling
their child between them, his feet dragging on the ground. In order to get to
the exit gate they had to pass the bench where the man sat sprawling again.
She was careful not to look at him. With all the dignity she could summon,
she pulled Larry's sandy, perspiring little hand, while Morton pulled the
other. Slowly and with head high she walked with her husband and child out
of the playground.

Her first feeling was one of relief that a fight had been avoided, that no one
was hurt. Yet beneath it there was a layer of something else, something heavy
and inescapable. She sensed that it was more than just an unpleasant incident,
more than defeat of reason by force. She felt dimly it had something to do with
her and Morton, something acutely personal, familiar and important.

Suddenly Morton spoke. "It wouldn't have proved anything."   20

"What?" she asked.

"A fight. It wouldn't have proved anything beyond the fact that he's bigger
than I am."

"Of course," she said.

"The only possible outcome," he continued reasonably, "would have been—what? My glasses broken, perhaps a tooth or two replaced, a couple of days' work missed—and for what? For justice? For truth?"

"Of course," she repeated. She quickened her step. She wanted only to get   25 home and to busy herself with her familiar tasks; perhaps then the feeling, glued like heavy plaster on her heart, would be gone. *Of all the stupid, despicable bullies*, she thought, pulling harder on Larry's hand. The child was still crying. Always before she had felt a tender pity for his defenseless little body, the frail arms, the narrow shoulders with sharp, winglike shoulder blades, the thin and unsure legs, but now her mouth tightened in resentment.

"Stop crying," she said sharply. "I'm ashamed of you!" She felt as if all three of them were tracking mud along the street. The child cried louder.

If there had been an issue involved, she thought, *if there had been something to fight for . . . But what else could he possibly have done? Allow himself to be beaten? Attempt to educate the man? Call a policeman? "Officer, there's a man in the park who won't stop his child from throwing sand on mine. . . ."* The whole thing was as silly as that, and not worth thinking about.

"Can't you keep him quiet, for Pete's sake?" Morton asked irritably.

"What do you suppose I've been trying to do?" she said.

Larry pulled back, dragging his feet.   30

"If you can't discipline this child, I will," Morton snapped, making a move toward the boy.

But her voice stopped him. She was shocked to hear it, thin and cold and penetrating with contempt. "Indeed?" she heard herself say. "You and who else?"

Yiyun Li b. 1972

The Princess of Nebraska   [2005]

Sasha looked at Boshen in the waiting line for a moment before turning her eyes to the window. She wished that she would never have to see Boshen again after this trip. She had run to the bathroom the moment they entered the McDonald's, leaving him to order for them both. He had suggested a good meal in Chinatown, and she had refused. She wanted to see downtown Chicago before going to the clinic at Planned Parenthood the next morning. It was the only reason for her to ride the Greyhound bus all day from Nebraska. Kansas City would have been a wiser choice, closer, cheaper, but there was nothing to see there—the trip was not meant for sightseeing, but Sasha hoped to get at least something out of it. She did not want to spend all her money only to remember a drugged sleep in a dreary motel in the middle of nowhere. Sasha had grown up in a small town in Inner Mongolia; vast and empty landscapes depressed her.

"You must be tired," Boshen said as he pushed the tray of food to Sasha, who had taken a table by the window. She looked tiny in the oversized sweatshirt.

Her face was slightly swollen, and the way she checked out the customers in the store, her eyes staying on each face a moment too long, moved him. She was twenty-one, a child still.

"I got a fish sandwich for you," Boshen said when Sasha did not answer him.

"I haven't seen one happy face since arriving," Sasha said. "What's the other one?"

"Chicken."

Sasha threw the fish sandwich across the table and grabbed the chicken sandwich from Boshen's tray. "I hate fish," she said.

"It's good for you now," Boshen said.

"Now will be over soon," Sasha said. She looked forward to the moment when she was ready to move on. "Moving on" was a phrase she just learned, an American concept that suited her well. It was such a wonderful phrase that Sasha could almost see herself stapling her Chinese life, one staple after another around the pages until they became one solid block that nobody would be able to open and read. She would have a fresh page then, for her American life. She was four months late already.

Boshen said nothing and unwrapped the fish sandwich. It was a change — sitting at a table and having an ordered meal — after months of eating in the kitchen of the Chinese restaurant where he worked as a helper to the Sichuan chef. Boshen had come to America via a false marriage to a friend five months earlier, when he had been put under house arrest for his correspondence with a Western reporter regarding a potential AIDS epidemic in a central province. He had had to publish a written confession of his wrongdoing to earn his freedom. A lesbian friend, a newly naturalized American citizen herself, had offered to marry him out of China. Before that, he had lived an openly gay life in Beijing, madly in love with Yang, an eighteen-year-old boy. Boshen had tried different ways to contact Yang since he had arrived in America, but the boy never responded. The checks Boshen sent him were not cashed, either.

They ate without speaking. Sasha swallowed her food fast, and waited for Boshen to finish his. Outside the window, more and more people appeared, all moving toward downtown, red reindeer's antlers on the heads of children who sat astride their fathers' shoulders. Boshen saw the question in Sasha's eyes and told her that there was a parade that evening, and all the trees on Michigan Avenue would light up for the coming Thanksgiving and Christmas holidays. "Do you want to stay for it?" he asked halfheartedly, hoping that she would choose instead to rest after the long bus ride.

"Why not?" Sasha said, and put on her coat.

Boshen folded the sandwich wrapper like a freshly ironed napkin. "I wonder if we could talk for a few minutes here," he said.

Sasha sighed. She never liked Boshen, whom she had met only once and who had struck her as the type of man as fussy as an old hen. She had not hesitated, however, to call him and ask for help when she had found out his number through an acquaintance. She had spoken in a dry, matter-of-fact way about her pregnancy, which had gone too long for an abortion in the state of

Nebraska. Yang had fathered the baby; she had told Boshen this first in their phone call. She had had no intention of sparing Boshen the truth; in a way, she felt Boshen was responsible for her misfortune, too.

"Have you, uh, made up your mind about the operation?" Boshen asked.

"What do you think I'm here for?" Sasha said. Over the past week Boshen   15 had called her twice, bringing up the possibility of keeping the baby. Both times she had hung up right away. Whatever interest he had in the baby was stupid and selfish, Sasha had decided.

The easiest solution may not be the best one in life, Boshen thought of telling Sasha, but then, what right did he have to talk about options, when the decisions he had made for his life were all compromises? At thirty-eight, Boshen felt he had achieved less than he had failed. He was a mediocre doctor before he was asked politely to leave the hospital for establishing the first counseling hotline for homosexuals in the small Chinese city where he lived. He moved to Beijing and took on a part-time job at a private clinic while working as an activist for gay rights. After a few visits from the secret police, however, he realized that, in the post-Tiananmen era, talk of any kind of human rights was dangerous. He decided to go into a less extreme and more practical area, advocating for AIDS awareness, but even that he had to give up after pressure from the secret police and his family. He was in love with a boy twenty years younger, and he thought he could make a difference in the boy's life. In the end, he was the one to marry a woman and leave. Boshen had thought of adopting the baby—half of her blood came from Yang, after all—but Sasha's eyes, sharp and unrelenting, chilled him. He smiled weakly and said, "I just wanted to make sure."

Sasha wrapped her head in a shawl and stood up. Boshen did not move, and when she asked him if he was leaving, he said, "I've heard from my friends that Yang is prostituting again."

Not a surprise, Sasha thought, but the man at the table, too old for a role as a heartbroken lover and too serious for it, was pitiful. In a kinder voice she said, "Then we'll have to live with that, no?"

Boshen was not the first man to have fallen in love with Yang, but he believed, for a long time, that he was the only one to have seen and touched the boy's soul. Since the age of seven, Yang had been trained as a *Nan Dan*—a male actor who plays female roles on stage in the Peking Opera—and had lived his life in the opera school. At seventeen, when he was discovered going out with a male lover, he was expelled. Boshen had written several articles about the incident, but he had not met Yang until he had become a *money boy*. Yang could've easily enticed a willing man to keep him for a good price, but rumors were that the boy was interested only in selling after his first lover abandoned him.

The day Boshen heard about Yang's falling into prostitution, he went to the   20 park where men paid for such services. It was near dusk when he arrived, and men of all ages slipped into the park like silent fish. Soon night fell; beneath the lampposts, transactions started in whispers, familiar scenarios for Boshen, but standing in the shade of a tree—a customer instead of researcher—made him tremble. It was not difficult to recognize Yang in the moon-white-colored silk shirt and pants he was reputed to wear every day to the park. Boshen looked at the boy, too beautiful for the grimy underground, a white lotus blossom untouched by the surrounding mud.

After watching the boy for several days, Boshen finally offered to pay Yang's asking price. The night Yang came home with Boshen, he became drunk on his own words. For a long time he talked about his work, his dream of bringing an end to injustice and building a more tolerant world; Yang huddled on the couch and listened. Boshen thought of shutting up, but the more he talked, the more he despaired at the beautiful and impassive face of Yang—in the boy's eyes he must be the same as all the other men, so full of themselves. Finally Boshen said, "Someday I'll make you go back to the stage."

"*An empty promise of a man keeps a woman's heart full,*" Yang recited in a low voice.

"But this," Boshen said, pointing to the pile of paperwork on his desk. "This is the work that will make it illegal for them to take you away from the stage because of who you are."

Yang's face softened. Boshen watched the unmistakable hope in the boy's eyes. Yang was too young to hide his pain, despite years of wearing female masks and portraying others' tragedies onstage. Boshen wanted to save him from his suffering. After a few weeks of pursuing, Boshen convinced Yang to try a new life. Boshen redecorated the apartment with expensive hand-painted curtains that featured the costumes of the Peking Opera and huge paper lanterns bearing the Peking Opera masks. He sold a few pieces of furniture to make space, and borrowed a rug from a friend for Yang to practice on. Yang fit into the quiet life like the most virtuous woman he had played on stage. He got up early every morning, stretching his body into unbelievable positions, and dancing the most intricate choreography. He trained his voice, too, in the shower so that the neighbors would not hear him. Always Boshen stood outside and listened, Yang's voice splitting the waterfall, the bath curtain, the door, and the rest of the dull world like a silver knife. At those moments Boshen was overwhelmed by gratitude—he was not the only one to have been touched by the boy's beauty, but he was the one to guard and nurture it. That alone lifted him above his mundane, disappointing life.

When Boshen was at work, Yang practiced painting and calligraphy. 25 Sometimes they went out to parties, but most evenings they stayed home. Yang never performed for Boshen, and he dared not ask him to. Yang was an angel falling out of the heavens, and every day Boshen dreaded that he would not be able to return the boy to where he belonged.

Such a fear, as it turned out, was not unfounded. Two months into the relationship, Yang started to show signs of restlessness. During the day he went out more than before, and he totally abandoned painting and calligraphy. Boshen wondered if the boy was suffocated by the stillness of their life.

One day shortly before Boshen was expelled from Beijing and put under house arrest in his hometown, Yang asked him casually how his work was going. Fine, Boshen said, feeling uneasy. Yang had never asked him anything about his work; it was part of the ugly world that Boshen had wanted to shelter Yang from.

"What are you working on?" Yang asked.

"Why, the usual stuff," Boshen said.

"I heard you were working on AIDS," Yang said. "What has that to do with   30
you?"

Stunned, Boshen tried to find an explanation. Finally he said, "You don't understand, Yang."

"I'm not a child," Yang said. "Why are you concerned with that dirty disease? The more you work on it, the more people will connect it with gay people. What good does it do for me?"

"I'm trying to help more people," Boshen said.

"But you've promised to help me get back to the stage," Yang said. "If you insist on working on something irrelevant, you'll never fulfill your promise."

Boshen could not answer Yang. Afterward, Yang started to go out more   35
often, and a few days later, he did not come home for the first time in their relationship. Boshen thought of all the predators waiting to set their fangs and claws on Yang, and he did not sleep that night.

"There's nothing for you to worry about," Yang said with a strange smile when Boshen confronted him. "You're not as endangered as you imagine."

"At least you should've let me know where you were," Boshen said.

"I was with a girl," Yang said, and mentioned the name Sasha, which sounded slightly familiar to Boshen. They had met her at a party, Yang reminded Boshen, but he did not remember who she was; he did not understand why Yang was going out with her, either.

"Why? What a silly question," Yang said. "You do things when you feel like it, no?"

The first time Sasha met Yang, at a party, she felt that she was looking into   40
a mirror that reflected not her own face, but that of someone she could never become. She watched the ballet of his long fingers across the table while he listened absentmindedly to the conversation of others around the table. She looked at the innocent half-moons on his fingernails; her own fingers were plump and blunt. His cream-colored face, his delicate nose and mouth reminded her of an exquisite china doll. Later, when they sat closer, she saw the melancholy in his eyes and decided that he was more like a statue of Kuanyin, the male Buddha in a female body, the goddess who listened and responded to the prayers of suffering women and children. Sitting next to him, Sasha felt like a mass-produced rubber doll.

The uneasy feeling lasted only for a moment. Sasha had heard of his stories, and was glad to see him finally in person. She leaned toward him and asked, as if picking up from a conversation they had dropped somewhere, "What do you think of girls, then?"

He looked up at her, and she saw a strange light in his eyes. They reminded her of a wounded sparrow she had once kept during a cold Mongolian winter.

Sparrows were an obstinate species that would never eat and drink once they were caged, her mother told her. Sasha did not believe it. She locked up the bird for days, and it kept bumping into the cage until its head started to go bald. Still she refused to release it, mesmerized by its eyes, wild but helplessly tender, too. She nudged the little bowl of soaked millet closer to the sparrow, but the bird was blind to her hospitality. Cheap birds, a neighbor told her; only cheap birds would be so stubborn. Have a canary, the neighbor said, and she would be singing for you every morning by now.

The boy lowered his eyes at Sasha's scrutiny, and she felt the urge to chase the beautiful eyes, a huntress of that strange light. "You must have known some girls, no?" she said. "When you went to the opera school, were there girls in the school?"

"Yes," the boy said, his voice reminding her of a satin dress.

"So?"   45

"We didn't talk. They played handmaids and nannies, background roles."

"So you were the princess, huh?" Sasha laughed and saw the boy blush, with anger perhaps, but it made her more curious and insistent in cornering him. "What's your name?" she said.

"Which name?"

"How many names do you have?"

"Two. One given by my parents. One given by the opera school."   50

"What are they?"

He dipped one finger into a glass of orange juice and wrote on the dark marble tabletop. She followed the wet trace of his finger. It was Yang, a common boy's name with the character for the sun, the masculine principle of nature, the opposite of Yin.

"A so-so name. What's your opera name?"

"Sumeng," he said. A serene and pure dreamer, it meant.

"Worse. Sounds like a weepy name from a romance novel," Sasha said.   55 "You need a better name. I'll have to think of one for you."

In the end she did not use either name, and did not find a better one for him. She called him "my little *Nan Dan*," and that was what he was to her, a boy destined to play a woman's part. She paged him often, and invited him to movies and walks in the park. She made decisions for them both, and he let her. She tried to pry him open with questions — she was so curious about him — and slowly he started to talk, about the man he had loved and men who loved him. He never said anything about the opera school or his stage life, and she learned not to push him. He was so vain, Sasha thought when he spent a long time fixing his hair or when he put on an expression of aloofness at the slightest attention of a stranger; she teased him, and then felt tender and guilty when he did not defend himself. She made fun of the other people in Yang's life, too: his lover, Boshen, whom she believed to be a useless dreamer, and the men who boldly asked him for his number. She believed she was the first person in his life who did not worship him in any way, and he must be following her around because of that. It pleased her.

Was she dating the boy? Sasha's classmates asked when they saw her with Yang more than once. Of course not, she said. In a month, Sasha was to go to America for graduate school, and it was pointless to start a relationship now. Besides, how smart was it to date a boy who loved no one but himself?

Even the wind could not cut through the warm bodies lined up on both sides of Michigan Avenue. Sasha pushed through the crowd. They looked so young and carefree, these Americans, happy as a group of pupils on a field trip. She envied these people, who would stand in a long line in front of a popcorn shop waiting for a bag of fresh popcorn, lovers leaning into each other, children hanging on to their parents. They were born to be themselves, naive and contented with their naivety.

"I would trade my place with any one of them," Sasha said to Boshen, but when he raised his voice and asked her to repeat her words, she shook her head. If only there were a law in America binding her to where her baby belonged so that the baby would have a reason to live!

Sasha herself had once been used by the law to trap her mother in the grassland. One of the thousands of high school students sent down from Beijing to Inner Mongolia for labor reeducation, her mother, in order to join the Party, married a Mongolian herdsman, one of the model interracial marriages that were broadcast across the grassland. Five years later, at the end of the Cultural Revolution, all of the students were allowed to return to Beijing. Sasha's mother, however, was forced to stay, even after she divorced her Mongolian husband. Their two daughters, born in the grassland, did not have legal residency in Beijing, and the mother had to stay where the children belonged.

Sasha pushed forward, looking at every store window. Silky scarves curved around the mannequins' necks with soft obedience. Diamonds glistened on dark velvet. At a street corner, children gathered and watched the animated story displayed in the windows of Marshall Field's. If only her baby were a visa that would admit her into this prosperity, Sasha thought, saddened by the memories of Nebraska and Inner Mongolia, the night skies of both places black with lonely, lifeless stars.

"There's an open spot there," Boshen said. "Do you want to stand there?"

Sasha nodded, and Boshen followed her. Apart from the brief encounter at the party in Beijing and a few phone calls, he did not know her. He had thought about her often after she had called him about the pregnancy. What kind of girl, he had wondered, would've made Yang a father? He had imagined a mature and understanding girl. Beautiful, too. He had made up a perfect woman for Yang and for his own peace of mind, but Sasha had disappointed him. When they settled along the curb, he said, "So, what's your plan after the operation?"

Sasha stood on tiptoe like a child, and looked in the direction where the parade would start. Boshen regretted right away speaking with such animosity. Seeing nothing, she turned to him and said, "What's *your* plan in America? Where's your new wife, anyway?"

Boshen frowned. He had told Yang that the marriage would be used as a   65
cover, and his departure was meant only to be a temporary one. He had promised Yang other things, too, money he would send, help he would seek in the
overseas Chinese community for Yang's return to the stage. Not a day since he
had arrived did he forget his promises, but Sasha's words stung him. His marriage must have been an unforgivable betrayal, in Sasha's and Yang's eyes alike.
"I can't defend myself," Boshen said finally.

"Of course not. You were the one sending him back to the street," Sasha
said.

"It's been a troubled time," Boshen said, struggling over the words. "It's
been difficult for all of us. But we certainly should try to help him out."

Sasha turned to look at Boshen with an amused smile. "You speak like the
worst kind of politician," she said. "Show me the solution."

"I am thinking." Boshen hesitated, and said, "I've been thinking — if we can
tell him that he'll be able to perform in America, maybe he would want to leave
Beijing?"

"And then?"   70

"We will try here. There's a *Nan Dan* master in New York. Maybe we can
contact him and ask for his help. But the first thing we do is to get Yang out of
the country."

"Does that 'we' include me?"

"If you could marry Yang, he would be here in no time. I know him. If
there's one percent chance to go back to the stage, he'll try."

"A very nice plan, Boshen," Sasha said. "But why should I agree to the pro-
posal? What's in it for me?"

Boshen looked away from Sasha and watched a couple kiss at the other side   75
of the street. After a long moment, he turned to Sasha and tried to look into
her eyes. "You must have loved him at least once, Sasha," he said, his voice
trembling.

Sasha had not planned for love, or even an affair. The friendship was out of
whimsy, a convenience for the empty days immediately before graduating from
college. The movie they watched one night in July was not planned, either. It was
ten o'clock when Sasha purchased the tickets, at the last minute. Yang looked at
the clock in the ticket booth and wondered aloud if it was too late, and Sasha
laughed, asking him if he was a child and if his lover had a curfew for him.

The movie was *Pretty Woman*, with almost unreadable Chinese subtitles.
When they came out to the midnight street, Sasha said, "Don't you just love
Julia Roberts?"

"What's to love about her?" Yang said.

Sasha glanced at Yang. He was quiet throughout the movie — he did not
understand English, but Sasha thought at least he could've enjoyed the beautiful
actress. "She's pretty, and funny, and so — American," Sasha said. "America is a
good place. Everything could happen there. A prostitute becomes a princess; a
crow turns into a swan overnight."

"A prostitute never becomes a princess," Yang said.   80

"How do you know?" Sasha said. "If only you could come with me to America and take a look at it yourself."

After a long moment, Yang said, "Every place is a good place. Only time goes wrong."

Sasha said nothing. She did not want to spend the night philosophizing. When they walked past a small hotel, she asked Yang if he wanted to come in with her. Just for the fun of staying out for a night, she said; he needn't have to report to his lover anyway, she added. Yang hesitated, and she grabbed his hand and pulled him into the foyer with her. A middle-aged woman at the reception opened the window and said, "What do you want?"

"Comrade, do you have a single room for two persons?" Sasha said.

The woman threw out a pad for registration and shut the window. Sasha   85 filled in the form. The woman scanned the pad. "Your ID?" she asked.

Sasha handed her ID to the woman. The woman looked at it for a long time, and pointed to Yang with her chin. "His ID?"

"He's my cousin from Inner Mongolia," Sasha said in a cheerful voice. "He forgot to bring his ID with him."

"Then there's no room tonight." The woman threw out Sasha's ID and closed the window.

"Comrade." Sasha tapped on the glass.

The woman opened the window. "Go away," she said. "Your cousin? Let me   90 tell you — either you have a marriage license and I will give you a room, or you go out and do that shameless thing in the street and let the cops arrest you. Don't you think I don't know girls like you?"

Sasha dragged Yang out the door, his lips quavering. "I don't believe I can't find a room for us," Sasha said finally.

Yang looked at Sasha with a baffled look. "Why do we have to do this?" he said.

"Ha, you're afraid now. Go ahead if you don't want to come," Sasha said, and started to walk. Yang followed Sasha to an even smaller hotel at the end of a narrow lane. An old man was sitting behind a desk, playing poker with himself. "Grandpapa," Sasha said, handing her ID to the old man. "Do you have a single room for my brother and me?"

The old man looked at Sasha and then Yang. "He's not fifteen yet so he doesn't have an ID," Sasha said, and Yang smiled shyly at the old man, his white teeth flashing in the dark.

The old man nodded and handed a registration pad to Sasha. Five minutes   95 later they were granted a key. It was a small room on the second floor, with two single beds, a rusty basin stand with two basins, and a window that did not have a curtain. Roaches scurried to find a hiding place when Sasha turned on the light. They stood just inside the door, and all of a sudden she did not know what the excitement was of spending a night together in a filthy hotel. "Why don't we just go home?" Yang said behind her.

"Where's the place you call home?" Sasha snapped. She turned off the light and lay down on a bed without undressing. "Go back to the man who keeps you if this is not a place for a princess like you," she said.

Yang stood for a long moment before he got into the other bed. Sasha waited for him to speak, and when he did not, she became angry with him, and with herself.

The next morning, when the city stirred to life, they both lay awake in their own beds. The homing pigeons flew across the sky, the small brass whistles bound to their tails humming in a harmonious low tone. Not far away, Tao music played on a tape recorder, calling for the early risers to join the practice of tai chi. Old men, the fans of Peking Opera, sang their favorite parts of the opera, their voices cracking at high notes. Then the doors down the lane creaked open, releasing the shouting children headed to school, and adults to work, their bicycle bells clanking.

Later, someone turned on a record player and music blasted across the alley. Sasha sat up and looked out the window. A young man was setting up a newspaper stand at the end of the alley, making theatrical movements along with a song in which a rock singer was yelling, "Oh, Genghis Khan,° Genghis Khan, he's a powerful old man. He's rich, he's strong, and I want to marry him."

Sasha listened to the song repeat and said, "I don't understand why these people think they have the right to trash Genghis Khan." 100

"Their ears are dead to real music," Yang said.

"When I was little, my father taught me a song about Genghis Khan. It's the only Mongolian song I remember now," Sasha said, and opened her mouth to sing the song. The melody was in her mind, but no words came to her tongue. She had forgotten almost all of the Mongolian words she had learned, after her parents' divorce; she had not seen her father for fifteen years. "Well, I don't remember it anymore."

"*The broken pillars, the slanted roof, they once saw the banqueting days; the dying trees, the withering peonies, they once danced in the heavenly music. The young girls dreamed of their lovers who were enlisted to fight the Huns. They did not know the loved ones had become white bones glistening in the moonlight,*" Yang chanted in a low voice to the ceiling. "Our masters say that real arts never die. Real arts are about remembrance."

"What's the point of remembering the song anyway? I don't even remember what my father looked like." Sasha thought about her father, one of the offspring of Genghis Khan. Genghis Khan was turned into a clown in the pop song. Mongolia was once the biggest empire in the world, and now it was a piece of meat, sandwiched by China and Russia.

"We live in a wrong time," Yang said. 105

Genghis Khan: (c. 1162–1227), the founder and ruler of the Mongol Empire, which became the largest contiguous empire in the history of the world.

Sasha turned to look at Yang. He lay on his hands and stared at the ceiling, his face taking on the resigned look of an old man. It hurt her, and scared her too, to glimpse a world beneath his empty beauty. "We were born into a wrong place, is what our problem is," she said, trying to cheer him and herself up. "Why don't you come to America with me, Yang?"

Yang smiled. "Who am I to follow you?"

"A husband, a lover, a brother, I don't care. Why don't you get out of Beijing and have a new life in America?" The words, once said, hung in the room like heavy fog, and Sasha wondered if Yang, too, had difficulty breathing. Outside the window, a vendor was sharpening a chopper with a whetstone, the strange sound making their mouths water unpleasantly. Then the vendor started to sing in a drawn-out voice about his tasty pig heads.

"Sasha," Yang said finally. "Is Sasha a Mongolian name?"

"Not really. It's Russian, a name of my mom's favorite heroine in a Soviet 110
war novel."

"That's why it doesn't sound Chinese. I would rather it is a Mongolian name," Yang said. "Sasha, the princess of Mongolia."

Sasha walked barefoot to Yang's bed and knelt beside him. He did not move, and let Sasha hold his face with both hands. "Come to America with me," she said. "We'll be the prince and the princess of Nebraska."

"I was not trained to play a prince," Yang said.

"The script is changed," Sasha said. "From today on."

Yang turned to look at Sasha. She tried to kiss him, but he pushed her away 115
gently. *"A beautiful body is only a bag of bones,"* he sang in a low voice.

Sasha had never seen Yang perform, and could not imagine him onstage; he had played princesses and prostitutes, but he did not have to live with the painted mask and the silk costume. "The Peking Opera is dead," she said. "Why don't you give it up?"

"Who are you to say that about the Peking Opera?" Yang said, his face turning suddenly stern.

Sasha saw the iciness in Yang's eyes and let the topic drop. Afterward, neither mentioned anything about the stay in the hotel. A week later, when Boshen was escorted away from Beijing, Sasha was relieved and scared. There was, all of a sudden, time for them to fill. To her relief and disappointment, Yang seemed to have forgotten the moment when they were close, so close that they were almost in love.

The parade started with music and laughter, colorful floats moving past, on which happy people waved to the happy audience. Boshen looked at Sasha's face, lit up by curiosity, and sighed. Despite her willfulness and unfriendliness, the thought of the baby—Yang's baby—made him eager to forgive her. "Do you still not want to tell Yang about the baby?" he said.

"You've asked this the hundredth time," Sasha said. "Why should I?" 120

"He might want to come to the U.S. if he learned about the baby," Boshen said.

"There'll be no baby after tomorrow," Sasha said. She had tried Yang's phone number when she had learned of the pregnancy; she had tried his pager, too. At first it was measured by hours and days, and then it became weeks since she had left the message on his pager. He might be living in another apartment with a new telephone number. The pager might no longer belong to him. She knew he had every reason for not getting her message, but she could not forgive his silence. In the meantime, her body changed. She felt the growth inside her and she was disgusted by it. Sometimes she hated it from morning till night, hoping that it would finally go away, somehow, surrendering to the strength of her resentment. Other times she kept her mind away for as long as she could, thinking that it would disappear as if it had never existed. Still, in the end, it required her action. In the end, she thought, it was just a chunk of flesh and blood.

"But why was there a baby in the first place?" Boshen said. Why and how it happened were the questions that had been haunting him since he had heard from Sasha. He wanted to ask her if she, too, had been dazzled by the boy's body, smooth, lithe, perfectly shaped. He wanted to know if she had loved him as he had, but in that case, how could she have the heart to discard what had been left with her?

Sasha turned to Boshen. For the first time, she studied the man with curiosity. Not handsome or ugly, he had a candid face that Sasha thought she could not fall in love with but nonetheless could trust. A man like Boshen should have an ordinary life, boring and comfortable, yet his craze for Yang made him a more interesting man than he deserved to be. But that must be what was Yang's value—he made people fall in love with him, and the love led them astray, willingly, from their otherwise tedious paths. Yang had been the one to bring up the idea of spending a night together again, and Sasha the one to ask a friend for the use of her rented room, a few days before Sasha's flight. It was one of the soggiest summer evenings. After their lovemaking, sweet and short and uneventful, they stayed on the floor, on top of the blanket Sasha had brought for the purpose, an arm's length between them, each too warm to touch the other. Outside, the landlady's family and two other neighbor families were sitting in the courtyard and watching a TV program, their voices mixed with the claps of their hands killing the mosquitoes. Sasha turned to look at Yang, who was lying with his back to her. The little pack of condoms she had bought was tucked underneath the blanket, unopened. She had suggested it and he had refused. A rubber was for people who touched without loving each other, Yang had said; his words had made her hopeful again. "Do you want to come to America with me now?" she asked, tracing his back with one finger.

"What am I going to do in America? Be kept as a canary by you?" Yang said 125 and moved farther away from her finger.

"You can spend some time learning English, and get a useful degree in America."

"Useful? Don't you already know that I am useless? Besides, nothing humiliates a man more than living as a parasite on his woman," Yang said, and reached for a silk robe he had packed with him. Before Sasha had the time to stop him, he walked out the door. Sasha jumped to her feet and watched from behind the curtain; Yang walked with a calculated laziness, not looking at the people who turned their eyes away from the television to stare at him. When he reached the brick sink in the middle of the courtyard, he sat on the edge and raised his bare legs to the tap. The water had run for a long moment before the landlady recovered from her shock and said, "Hey, the water costs me money."

Yang smiled. "It's so hot," he said in a pleasant voice.

"Indeed," the landlady agreed.

Yang turned off the tap and walked back to the room, with the same grace   130 and idleness, knowing that the people in the courtyard were all watching him, his willowy body wrapped in the moon white robe. Sasha stood by the window, cold with disappointment. She became his audience, one of the most difficult to capture, perhaps, but he succeeded after all.

A Disney float approached the corner where Sasha and Boshen stood. "Look," Sasha said and pointed at a giant glove of Mickey Mouse moving ahead of the float. "There're only four fingers."

"I didn't know that," Boshen said.

"Yang needs us no more than that glove needs us for our admiration," Sasha said.

"But our love is the only thing to protect him, and to save him, too."

Sasha turned and looked into Boshen's eyes. "It's people like us who have   135 destroyed him, isn't it? Why was there *Nan Dan* in the Peking Opera in the first place? *Men loved him because he was playing a woman; women loved him because he was a man playing*," she said.

"That's totally wrong."

"Why else do you want so much to put him back on the stage? Don't think I'm happy to see him fall. Believe me, I wanted to help him as much as you do. He didn't have to be a man playing a woman—I thought I would make him understand. But what did I end up with? You're not the one who has a baby inside; he's not the one having an abortion," Sasha said, and started to cry.

Boshen held out his hand and touched Sasha's shoulder hesitantly. If only she could love the boy one more time. Yang could choose to live with either of them; he could choose not to love them at all but their love would keep him safe and intact; they could—the three of them—bring up the baby together. Yang would remain the princess, exiled, yes, but a true princess, beautiful in a foreign land. If only he knew how to make Sasha love Yang again, Boshen thought.

Sasha did not move away when Boshen put an arm around her shoulder. They must look like the most ordinary couple to strangers, a nervous husband comforting his moody wife after an argument. They might as well be a couple, out of love, he caring only for the baby inside her, she having no feeling left for anything, her unborn child included.

As if responding, the baby moved. A tap, and then another one, gentle and   140 tentative, the first greeting that Sasha had wished she would never have to answer, but it seemed impossible, once it happened, not to hope for more. After a long moment, people in the street shouted, and children screamed out of excitement. Sasha looked up—the lights were lit up in the trees, thousands of stars forming a constellation. She thought about the small Mongolian town where her mother lived alone now, her long shadow trailing behind her as she walked home along the dimly lit alley. Her mother had been born into a wrong time, lived all her adult life in a wrong place, yet she had never regretted the births of her two daughters. Sasha held her breath and waited for more of the baby's messages. America was a good country, she thought, a right place to be born into, even though the baby had come at a wrong time. Everything was possible in America, she thought, and imagined a baby possessing the beauty of her father but happier, and luckier. Sasha smiled, but then when the baby moved again, she burst into tears. Being a mother must be the saddest yet the most hopeful thing in the world, falling into a love that, once started, would never end.

Toni Morrison b. 1931

Recitatif   [1983]

My mother danced all night and Roberta's was sick. That's why we were taken to St. Bonny's. People want to put their arms around you when you tell them you were in a shelter, but it really wasn't bad. No big long room with one hundred beds like Bellevue. There were four to a room, and when Roberta and me came, there was a shortage of state kids, so we were the only ones assigned to 406 and could go from bed to bed if we wanted to. And we wanted to, too. We changed beds every night and for the whole four months we were there we never picked one out as our own permanent bed.

It didn't start out that way. The minute I walked in and the Big Bozo introduced us, I got sick to my stomach. It was one thing to be taken out of your own bed early in the morning—it was something else to be stuck in a strange place with a girl from a whole other race. And Mary, that's my mother, she was right. Every now and then she would stop dancing long enough to tell me something important and one of the things she said was that they never washed their hair and they smelled funny. Roberta sure did. Smell funny, I mean. So when the Big Bozo (nobody ever called her Mrs. Itkin, just like nobody ever said St. Bonaventure)—when she said, "Twyla, this is Roberta. Roberta, this is Twyla. Make each other welcome." I said, "My mother won't like you putting me in here."

"Good," said Bozo. "Maybe then she'll come and take you home."

How's that for mean? If Roberta had laughed I would have killed her, but she didn't. She just walked over to the window and stood with her back to us.

"Turn around," said the Bozo. "Don't be rude. Now Twyla. Roberta. When   5
you hear a loud buzzer, that's the call for dinner. Come down to the first floor. Any fights and no movie." And then, just to make sure we knew what we would be missing, "*The Wizard of Oz.*"

Roberta must have thought I meant that my mother would be mad about my being put in the shelter. Not about rooming with her, because as soon as Bozo left she came over to me and said, "Is your mother sick too?"

"No," I said. "She just likes to dance all night."

"Oh," she nodded her head and I liked the way she understood things so fast. So for the moment it didn't matter that we looked like salt and pepper standing there and that's what the other kids called us sometimes. We were eight years old and got F's all the time. Me because I couldn't remember what I read or what the teacher said. And Roberta because she couldn't read at all and didn't even listen to the teacher. She wasn't good at anything except jacks, at which she was a killer: pow scoop pow scoop pow scoop.

We didn't like each other all that much at first, but nobody else wanted to play with us because we weren't real orphans with beautiful dead parents in the sky. We were dumped. Even the New York City Puerto Ricans and the upstate Indians ignored us. All kinds of kids were in there, black ones, white ones, even two Koreans. The food was good, though. At least I thought so. Roberta hated it and left whole pieces of things on her plate: Spam, Salisbury steak—even jello with fruit cocktail in it, and she didn't care if I ate what she wouldn't. Mary's idea of supper was popcorn and a can of Yoo-Hoo. Hot mashed potatoes and two weenies was like Thanksgiving for me.

It really wasn't bad, St. Bonny's. The big girls on the second floor pushed us around now and then. But that was all. They wore lipstick and eyebrow pencil and wobbled their knees while they watched TV. Fifteen, sixteen, even, some of them were. They were put-out girls, scared runaways most of them. Poor little girls who fought their uncles off but looked tough to us, and mean. God did they look mean. The staff tried to keep them separate from the younger children, but sometimes they caught us watching them in the orchard where they played radios and danced with each other. They'd light out after us and pull our hair or twist our arms. We were scared of them, Roberta and me, but neither of us wanted the other one to know it. So we got a good list of dirty names we could shout back when we ran from them through the orchard. I used to dream a lot and almost always the orchard was there. Two acres, four maybe, of these little apple trees. Hundreds of them. Empty and crooked like beggar women when I first came to St. Bonny's but fat with flowers when I left. I don't know why I dreamt about that orchard so much. Nothing really happened there. Nothing all that important, I mean. Just the big girls dancing and playing the radio. Roberta and me watching. Maggie fell down there once. The kitchen woman with legs like parentheses. And the big girls laughed at her. We should have helped her up, I know, but we were scared of those girls with lipstick and eyebrow pencil. Maggie couldn't talk. The kids said she had her tongue cut out, but I think she was just born that way: mute. She was old and sandy-colored and she worked in the kitchen. I don't know if she was nice or not. I just remember her legs like parentheses and how she rocked when she walked. She worked from early in the morning till two o'clock, and if she was late, if she had too much cleaning and didn't get out till two-fifteen or so, she'd cut through

10

the orchard so she wouldn't miss her bus and have to wait another hour. She wore this really stupid little hat—a kid's hat with ear flaps—and she wasn't much taller than we were. A really awful little hat. Even for a mute, it was dumb—dressing like a kid and never saying anything at all.

"But what about if somebody tries to kill her?" I used to wonder about that. "Or what if she wants to cry? Can she cry?"

"Sure," Roberta said. "But just tears. No sounds come out."

"She can't scream?"

"Nope. Nothing."

"Can she hear?"   15

"I guess."

"Let's call her," I said. And we did.

"Dummy! Dummy!" She never turned her head.

"Bow legs! Bow legs!" Nothing. She just rocked on, the chin straps of her baby-boy hat swaying from side to side. I think we were wrong. I think she could hear and didn't let on. And it shames me even now to think there was somebody in there after all who heard us call her those names and couldn't tell on us.

We got along all right, Roberta and me. Changed beds every night, got F's   20 in civics and communication skills and gym. The Bozo was disappointed in us, she said. Out of 130 of us state cases, 90 were under twelve. Almost all were real orphans with beautiful dead parents in the sky. We were the only ones dumped and the only ones with F's in three classes including gym. So we got along—what with her leaving whole pieces of things on her plate and being nice about not asking questions.

I think it was the day before Maggie fell down that we found out our mothers were coming to visit us on the same Sunday. We had been at the shelter twenty-eight days (Roberta twenty-eight and a half) and this was their first visit with us. Our mothers would come at ten o'clock in time for chapel, then lunch with us in the teachers' lounge. I thought if my dancing mother met her sick mother it might be good for her. And Roberta thought her sick mother would get a big bang out of a dancing one. We got excited about it and curled each other's hair. After breakfast we sat on the bed watching the road from the window. Roberta's socks were still wet. She washed them the night before and put them on the radiator to dry. They hadn't, but she put them on anyway because their tops were so pretty—scalloped in pink. Each of us had a purple construction-paper basket that we had made in craft class. Mine had a yellow crayon rabbit on it. Roberta's had eggs with wiggly lines of color. Inside were cellophane grass and just the jelly beans because I'd eaten the two marshmallow eggs they gave us. The Big Bozo came herself to get us. Smiling she told us we looked very nice and to come downstairs. We were so surprised by the smile we'd never seen before, neither of us moved.

"Don't you want to see your mommies?"

I stood up first and spilled the jelly beans all over the floor. Bozo's smile disappeared while we scrambled to get the candy up off the floor and put it back in the grass.

She escorted us downstairs to the first floor, where the other girls were lining up to file into the chapel. A bunch of grown-ups stood to one side. Viewers mostly. The old biddies who wanted servants and the fags who wanted company looking for children they might want to adopt. Once in a while a grandmother. Almost never anybody young or anybody whose face wouldn't scare you in the night. Because if any of the real orphans had young relatives they wouldn't be real orphans. I saw Mary right away. She had on those green slacks I hated and hated even more now because didn't she know we were going to chapel? And that fur jacket with the pocket linings so ripped she had to pull to get her hands out of them. But her face was pretty—like always, and she smiled and waved like she was the little girl looking for her mother—not me.

I walked slowly, trying not to drop the jelly beans and hoping the paper   25 handle would hold. I had to use my last Chiclet because by the time I finished cutting everything out, all the Elmer's was gone. I am left-handed and the scissors never worked for me. It didn't matter, though; I might just as well have chewed the gum. Mary dropped to her knees and grabbed me, mashing the basket, the jelly beans, and the grass into her ratty fur jacket.

"Twyla, baby. Twyla, baby!"

I could have killed her. Already I heard the big girls in the orchard the next time saying, "Twyyyyyla, baby!" But I couldn't stay mad at Mary while she was smiling and hugging me and smelling of Lady Esther dusting powder. I wanted to stay buried in her fur all day.

To tell the truth I forgot about Roberta. Mary and I got in line for the traipse into chapel and I was feeling proud because she looked so beautiful even in those ugly green slacks that made her behind stick out. A pretty mother on earth is better than a beautiful dead one in the sky even if she did leave you all alone to go dancing.

I felt a tap on my shoulder, turned, and saw Roberta smiling. I smiled back, but not too much lest somebody think this visit was the biggest thing that ever happened in my life. Then Roberta said, "Mother, I want you to meet my roommate, Twyla. And that's Twyla's mother."

I looked up it seemed for miles. She was big. Bigger than any man and on   30 her chest was the biggest cross I'd ever seen. I swear it was six inches long each way. And in the crook of her arm was the biggest Bible ever made.

Mary, simple-minded as ever, grinned and tried to yank her hand out of the pocket with the raggedy lining—to shake hands, I guess. Roberta's mother looked down at me and then looked down at Mary too. She didn't say anything, just grabbed Roberta with her Bible-free hand and stepped out of line, walking quickly to the rear of it. Mary was still grinning because she's not too swift when it comes to what's really going on. Then this light bulb goes off in her head and she says "That bitch!" really loud and us almost in the chapel now. Organ music whining; the Bonny Angels singing sweetly. Everybody in the world turned around to look. And Mary would have kept it up—kept calling names if I hadn't squeezed her hand as hard as I could. That helped a little, but she still twitched and crossed and uncrossed her legs all through service. Even groaned a couple of times. Why did I think she would come there and act right? Slacks. No hat like the grandmothers and viewers, and groaning all the while. When we stood for hymns she kept her mouth shut. Wouldn't even look at the words on the page. She actually reached in her purse for a mirror to check her lipstick. All I could think of was that she really needed to be killed. The sermon lasted a year, and I knew the real orphans were looking smug again.

We were supposed to have lunch in the teachers' lounge, but Mary didn't bring anything, so we picked fur and cellophane grass off the mashed jelly beans and ate them. I could have killed her. I sneaked a look at Roberta. Her mother had brought chicken legs and ham sandwiches and oranges and a whole box of chocolate-covered grahams. Roberta drank milk from a thermos while her mother read the Bible to her.

Things are not right. The wrong food is always with the wrong people. Maybe that's why I got into waitress work later—to match up the right people with the right food. Roberta just let those chicken legs sit there, but she did bring a stack of grahams up to me later when the visit was over. I think she was sorry that her mother would not shake my mother's hand. And I liked that and I liked the fact that she didn't say a word about Mary groaning all the way through the service and not bringing any lunch.

Roberta left in May when the apple trees were heavy and white. On her last day we went to the orchard to watch the big girls smoke and dance by the radio. It didn't matter that they said, "Twyyyyyla, baby." We sat on the ground and breathed. Lady Esther. Apple blossoms. I still go soft when I smell one or the other. Roberta was going home. The big cross and the big Bible was coming to get her and she seemed sort of glad and sort of not. I thought I would die in that room of four beds without her and I knew Bozo had plans to move some other dumped kid in there with me. Roberta promised to write every day, which was really sweet of her because she couldn't read a lick so how could she write anybody. I would have drawn pictures and sent them to her but she never gave me her address. Little by little she faded. Her wet socks with the pink scalloped tops and her big serious-looking eyes—that's all I could catch when I tried to bring her to mind.

I was working behind the counter at the Howard Johnson's on the Thruway 35 just before the Kingston exit. Not a bad job. Kind of a long ride from Newburgh, but okay once I got there. Mine was the second night shift—eleven to seven. Very light until a Greyhound checked in for breakfast around six-thirty. At that hour the sun was all the way clear of the hills behind the restaurant. The place looked better at night—more like shelter—but I loved it when the sun broke in, even if it did show all the cracks in the vinyl and the speckled floor looked dirty no matter what the mop boy did.

It was August and a bus crowd was just unloading. They would stand around a long while: going to the john, and looking at gifts and junk-for-sale machines, reluctant to sit down so soon. Even to eat. I was trying to fill the coffee pots and get them all situated on the electric burners when I saw her. She was sitting in a booth smoking a cigarette with two guys smothered in head and facial hair. Her own hair was so big and wild I could hardly see her face. But the eyes. I would know them anywhere. She had on a powder-blue halter and shorts outfit and earrings the size of bracelets. Talk about lipstick and eyebrow pencil. She made the big girls look like nuns. I couldn't get off the counter until seven o'clock, but I kept watching the booth in case they got up to leave before that. My replacement was on time for a change, so I counted and stacked my receipts as fast as I could and signed off. I walked over to the booth, smiling and wondering if she would remember me. Or even if she wanted to remember me. Maybe she didn't want to be reminded of St. Bonny's or to have anybody know she was ever there. I know I never talked about it to anybody.

I put my hands in my apron pockets and leaned against the back of the booth facing them.

"Roberta? Roberta Fisk?"

She looked up. "Yeah?"

"Twyla." 40

She squinted for a second and then said, "Wow."

"Remember me?"

"Sure. Hey. Wow."

"It's been a while," I said, and gave a smile to the two hairy guys.

"Yeah. Wow. You work here?" 45

"Yeah," I said. "I live in Newburgh."

"Newburgh? No kidding?" She laughed then a private laugh that included the guys but only the guys, and they laughed with her. What could I do but laugh too and wonder why I was standing there with my knees showing out from under that uniform. Without looking I could see the blue and white triangle on my head, my hair shapeless in a net, my ankles thick in white oxfords. Nothing could have been less sheer than my stockings. There was this silence that came down right after I laughed. A silence it was her turn to fill up. With introductions, maybe, to her boyfriends or an invitation to sit down and have a Coke. Instead she lit a cigarette off the one she'd just finished and said, "We're on our way to the Coast. He's got an appointment with Hendrix." She gestured casually toward the boy next to her.

"Hendrix? Fantastic," I said. "Really fantastic. What's she doing now?"

Roberta coughed on her cigarette and the two guys rolled their eyes up at the ceiling.

"Hendrix. Jimi Hendrix, asshole. He's only the biggest—Oh, wow. Forget it." 50

I was dismissed without anyone saying goodbye, so I thought I would do it for her.

"How's your mother?" I asked. Her grin cracked her whole face. She swallowed. "Fine," she said. "How's yours?"

"Pretty as a picture," I said and turned away. The backs of my knees were damp. Howard Johnson's really was a dump in the sunlight.

James is as comfortable as a house slipper. He liked my cooking and I liked his big loud family. They have lived in Newburgh all of their lives and talk about it the way people do who have always known a home. His grandmother has a porch swing older than his father and when they talk about streets and avenues and buildings they call them names they no longer have. They still call the A & P Rico's because it stands on property once a mom and pop store owned by Mr. Rico. And they call the new community college Town Hall because it once was. My mother-in-law puts up jelly and cucumbers and buys butter wrapped in cloth from a dairy. James and his father talk about fishing and baseball and I can see them all together on the Hudson in a raggedy skiff. Half the population of Newburgh is on welfare now, but to my husband's family it was still some upstate paradise of a time long past. A time of ice houses and vegetable wagons, coal furnaces and children weeding gardens. When our son was born my mother-in-law gave me the crib blanket that had been hers.

But the town they remembered had changed. Something quick was in the 55 air. Magnificent old houses, so ruined they had become shelter for squatters and rent risks, were bought and renovated. Smart IBM people moved out of their suburbs back into the city and put shutters up and herb gardens in their backyards. A brochure came in the mail announcing the opening of a Food Emporium. Gourmet food it said—and listed items the rich IBM crowd would want. It was located in a new mall at the edge of town and I drove out to shop there one day—just to see. It was late in June. After the tulips were gone and the Queen Elizabeth roses were open everywhere. I trailed my cart along the aisle tossing in smoked oysters and Robert's sauce and things I knew would sit in my cupboard for years. Only when I found some Klondike ice cream bars did I feel less guilty about spending James's fireman's salary so foolishly. My father-in-law ate them with the same gusto little Joseph did.

Waiting in the check-out line I heard a voice say, "Twyla!"

The classical music piped over the aisles had affected me and the woman leaning toward me was dressed to kill. Diamonds on her hand, a smart white summer dress. "I'm Mrs. Benson," I said.

"Ho. Ho. The Big Bozo," she sang.

For a split second I didn't know what she was talking about. She had a bunch of asparagus and two cartons of fancy water.

"Roberta!"   60

"Right."

"For heaven's sake. Roberta."

"You look great," she said.

"So do you. Where are you? Here? In Newburgh?"

"Yes. Over in Annandale."   65

I was opening my mouth to say more when the cashier called my attention to her empty counter.

"Meet you outside." Roberta pointed her finger and went into the express line.

I placed the groceries and kept myself from glancing around to check Roberta's progress. I remembered Howard Johnson's and looking for a chance to speak only to be greeted with a stingy "wow." But she was waiting for me and her huge hair was sleek now, smooth around a small, nicely shaped head. Shoes, dress, everything lovely and summery and rich. I was dying to know what happened to her, how she got from Jimi Hendrix to Annandale, a neighborhood full of doctors and IBM executives. Easy, I thought. Everything is so easy for them. They think they own the world.

"How long," I asked her. "How long have you been here?"

"A year. I got married to a man who lives here. And you, you're married too, right? Benson, you said."

"Yeah. James Benson."

"And is he nice?"

"Oh, is he nice?"

"Well, is he?" Roberta's eyes were steady as though she really meant the question and wanted an answer.

"He's wonderful, Roberta. Wonderful."

"So you're happy."

"Very."

"That's good," she said and nodded her head. "I always hoped you'd be happy. Any kids? I know you have kids."

"One. A boy. How about you?"

"Four."

"Four?"

She laughed. "Step kids. He's a widower."

"Oh."

"Got a minute? Let's have a coffee."

I thought about the Klondikes melting and the inconvenience of going all the way to my car and putting the bags in the trunk. Served me right for buying all that stuff I didn't need. Roberta was ahead of me.

"Put them in my car. It's right here."

And then I saw the dark blue limousine.

"You married a Chinaman?"

"No," she laughed. "He's the driver."

"Oh, my. If the Big Bozo could see you now."

We both giggled. Really giggled. Suddenly, in just a pulse beat, twenty years disappeared and all of it came rushing back. The big girls (whom we called gar girls—Roberta's misheard word for the evil stone faces described in a civics class) there dancing in the orchard, the ploppy mashed potatoes, the double weenies, the Spam with pineapple. We went into the coffee shop holding on to one another and I tried to think why we were glad to see each other this time and not before. Once, twelve years ago, we passed like strangers. A black girl and a white girl meeting in a Howard Johnson's on the road and having nothing to say. One in a blue and white triangle waitress hat—the other on her way to see Hendrix. Now we were behaving like sisters separated for much too long. Those four short months were nothing in time. Maybe it was the thing itself. Just being there, together. Two little girls who knew what nobody else in the world knew—how not to ask questions. How to believe what had to be believed. There was politeness in that reluctance and generosity as well. Is your mother sick too? No, she dances all night. Oh—and an understanding nod.

We sat in a booth by the window and fell into recollection like veterans.

"Did you ever learn to read?"

"Watch." She picked up the menu. "Special of the day. Cream of corn soup. Entrées. Two dots and a wriggly line. Quiche. Chef salad, scallops . . ."

I was laughing and applauding when the waitress came up.   95

"Remember the Easter baskets?"

"And how we tried to *introduce* them?"

"Your mother with that cross like two telephone poles."

"And yours with those tight slacks."

We laughed so loudly heads turned and made the laughter harder to suppress.   100

"What happened to the Jimi Hendrix date?"

Roberta made a blow-out sound with her lips.

"When he died I thought about you."

"Oh, you heard about him finally?"

"Finally. Come on, I was a small-town country waitress."   105

"And I was a small-town country dropout. God, were we wild. I still don't know how I got out of there alive."

"But you did."

"I did. I really did. Now I'm Mrs. Kenneth Norton."

"Sounds like a mouthful."

"It is."   110

"Servants and all?"

Roberta held up two fingers.

"Ow! What does he do?"

"Computers and stuff. What do I know?"

"I don't remember a hell of a lot from those days, but Lord, St. Bonny's is   115 as clear as daylight. Remember Maggie? The day she fell down and those gar girls laughed at her?"

Roberta looked up from her salad and stared at me. "Maggie didn't fall," she said.

"Yes, she did. You remember."

"No, Twyla. They knocked her down. Those girls pushed her down and tore her clothes. In the orchard."

"I don't—that's not what happened."

"Sure it is. In the orchard. Remember how scared we were?"   120

"Wait a minute. I don't remember any of that."

"And Bozo was fired."

"You're crazy. She was there when I left. You left before me."

"I went back. You weren't there when they fired Bozo."

"What?"   125

"Twice. Once for a year when I was about ten, another for two months when I was fourteen. That's when I ran away."

"You ran away from St. Bonny's?"

"I had to. What do you want? Me dancing in that orchard?"

"Are you sure about Maggie?"

"Of course I'm sure. You've blocked it, Twyla. It happened. Those girls had   130
behavior problems, you know."

"Didn't they, though. But why can't I remember the Maggie thing?"

"Believe me. It happened. And we were there."

"Who did you room with when you went back?" I asked her as if I would
know her. The Maggie thing was troubling me.

"Creeps. They tickled themselves in the night."

My ears were itching and I wanted to go home suddenly. This was all very   135
well but she couldn't just comb her hair, wash her face and pretend everything
was hunky-dory. After the Howard Johnson's snub. And no apology. Nothing.

"Were you on dope or what that time at Howard Johnson's?" I tried to
make my voice sound friendlier than I felt.

"Maybe, a little. I never did drugs much. Why?"

"I don't know; you acted sort of like you didn't want to know me then."

"Oh, Twyla, you know how it was in those days: black—white. You know
how everything was."

But I didn't know. I thought it was just the opposite. Busloads of blacks and   140
whites came into Howard Johnson's together. They roamed together then: students, musicians, lovers, protesters. You got to see everything at Howard
Johnson's and blacks were very friendly with whites in those days. But sitting
there with nothing on my plate but two hard tomato wedges wondering about
the melting Klondikes it seemed childish remembering the slight. We went to
her car, and with the help of the driver, got my stuff into my station wagon.

"We'll keep in touch this time," she said.

"Sure," I said. "Sure. Give me a call."

"I will," she said, and then just as I was sliding behind the wheel, she leaned
into the window. "By the way. Your mother. Did she ever stop dancing?"

I shook my head. "No. Never."

Roberta nodded.   145

"And yours? Did she ever get well?"

She smiled a tiny sad smile. "No. She never did. Look, call me, okay?"

"Okay," I said, but I knew I wouldn't. Roberta had messed up my past somehow with that business about Maggie. I wouldn't forget a thing like that. Would I?

Strife came to us that fall. At least that's what the paper called it. Strife.
Racial strife. The word made me think of a bird—a big shrieking bird out of
1,000,000,000 B.C. Flapping its wings and cawing. Its eye with no lid always
bearing down on you. All day it screeched and at night it slept on the rooftops.
It woke you in the morning and from the *Today* show to the eleven o'clock news
it kept you an awful company. I couldn't figure it out from one day to the next.
I knew I was supposed to feel something strong, but I didn't know what, and
James wasn't any help. Joseph was on the list of kids to be transferred from the

junior high school to another one at some far-out-of-the-way place and I thought it was a good thing until I heard it was a bad thing. I mean I didn't know. All the schools seemed dumps to me, and the fact that one was nicer looking didn't hold much weight. But the papers were full of it and then the kids began to get jumpy. In August, mind you. Schools weren't even open yet. I thought Joseph might be frightened to go over there, but he didn't seem scared so I forgot about it, until I found myself driving along Hudson Street out there by the school they were trying to integrate and saw a line of women marching. And who do you suppose was in line, big as life, holding a sign in front of her bigger than her mother's cross? MOTHERS HAVE RIGHTS TOO! — it said.

I drove on, and then changed my mind. I circled the block, slowed down, 150 and honked my horn.

Roberta looked over and when she saw me she waved. I didn't wave back, but I didn't move either. She handed her sign to another woman and came over to where I was parked.

"Hi."

"What are you doing?"

"Picketing. What's it look like?"

"What for?"   155

"What do you mean, 'What for?' They want to take my kids and send them out of the neighborhood. They don't want to go."

"So what if they go to another school? My boy's being bussed too, and I don't mind. Why should you?"

"It's not about us, Twyla. Me and you. It's about our kids."

"What's more *us* than that?"

"Well, it is a free country."   160

"Not yet, but it will be."

"What the hell does that mean? I'm not doing anything to you."

"You really think that?"

"I know it."

"I wonder what made me think you were different."   165

"I wonder what made me think you were different."

"Look at them," I said. "Just look. Who do they think they are? Swarming all over the place like they own it. And now they think they can decide where my child goes to school. Look at them, Roberta. They're Bozos."

Roberta turned around and looked at the women. Almost all of them were standing still now, waiting. Some were even edging toward us. Roberta looked at me out of some refrigerator behind her eyes. "No, they're not. They're just mothers."

"And what am I? Swiss cheese?"

"I used to curl your hair."   170

"I hated your hands in my hair."

The women were moving. Our faces looked mean to them of course and they looked as though they could not wait to throw themselves in front of a police car, or better yet, into my car and drag me away by my ankles. Now they surrounded my car and gently, gently began to rock it. I swayed back and forth like a sideways yo-yo. Automatically I reached for Roberta, like the old days in the orchard when they saw us watching them and we had to get out of there, and if one of us fell the other pulled her up and if one of us was caught the other stayed to kick and scratch, and neither would leave the other behind. My arm shot out of the car window but no receiving hand was there. Roberta was looking at me sway from side to side in the car and her face was still. My purse slid from the car seat down under the dashboard. The four policemen who had been drinking Tab in their car finally got the message and strolled over, forcing their way through the women. Quietly, firmly they spoke. "Okay, ladies. Back in line or off the streets."

Some of them went away willingly; others had to be urged away from the car doors and the hood. Roberta didn't move. She was looking steadily at me. I was fumbling to turn on the ignition, which wouldn't catch because the gearshift was still in drive. The seats of the car were a mess because the swaying had thrown my grocery coupons all over it and my purse was sprawled on the floor.

"Maybe I am different now, Twyla. But you're not. You're the same little state kid who kicked a poor old black lady when she was down on the ground. You kicked a black lady and you have the nerve to call me a bigot."

The coupons were everywhere and the guts of my purse were bunched 175 under the dashboard. What was she saying? Black? Maggie wasn't black.

"She wasn't black," I said.

"Like hell she wasn't, and you kicked her. We both did. You kicked a black lady who couldn't even scream."

"Liar!"

"You're the liar! Why don't you just go on home and leave us alone, huh?"

She turned away and I skidded away from the curb.   180

The next morning I went into the garage and cut the side out of the carton our portable TV had come in. It wasn't nearly big enough, but after a while I had a decent sign: red spray-painted letters on a white background — AND SO DO CHILDREN****. I meant just to go down to the school and tack it up somewhere so those cows on the picket line across the street could see it, but when I got there, some ten or so others had already assembled — protesting the cows across the street. Police permits and everything. I got in line and we strutted in time on our side while Roberta's group strutted on theirs. That first day we were all dignified, pretending the other side didn't exist. The second day there was name calling and finger gestures. But that was about all. People changed signs from time to time, but Roberta never did and neither did I. Actually my sign didn't make sense without Roberta's. "And so do children what?" one of the women on my side asked me. Have rights, I said, as though it was obvious.

Roberta didn't acknowledge my presence in any way and I got to thinking maybe she didn't know I was there. I began to pace myself in the line, jostling people one minute and lagging behind the next, so Roberta and I could reach the end of our respective lines at the same time and there would be a moment in our turn when we would face each other. Still, I couldn't tell whether she saw me and knew my sign was for her. The next day I went early before we were scheduled to assemble. I waited until she got there before I exposed my new creation. As soon as she hoisted her MOTHERS HAVE RIGHTS TOO I began to wave my new one, which said, HOW WOULD YOU KNOW? I know she saw that one, but I had gotten addicted now. My signs got crazier each day, and the women on my side decided that I was a kook. They couldn't make heads or tails out of my brilliant screaming posters.

I brought a painted sign in queenly red with huge black letters that said, IS YOUR MOTHER WELL? Roberta took her lunch break and didn't come back for the rest of the day or any day after. Two days later I stopped going too and couldn't have been missed because nobody understood my signs anyway.

It was a nasty six weeks. Classes were suspended and Joseph didn't go to anybody's school until October. The children—everybody's children—soon got bored with that extended vacation they thought was going to be so great. They looked at TV until their eyes flattened. I spent a couple of mornings tutoring my son, as the other mothers said we should. Twice I opened a text from last year that he had never turned in. Twice he yawned in my face. Other mothers organized living room sessions so the kids would keep up. None of the kids could concentrate so they drifted back to *The Price Is Right* and *The Brady Bunch*. When the school finally opened there were fights once or twice and some sirens roared through the streets every once in a while. There were a lot of photographers from Albany. And just when ABC was about to send up a news crew, the kids settled down like nothing in the world had happened. Joseph hung my HOW WOULD YOU KNOW? sign in his bedroom. I don't know what became of AND SO DO CHILDREN****. I think my father-in-law cleaned some fish on it. He was always puttering around in our garage. Each of his five children lived in Newburgh and he acted as though he had five extra homes.

I couldn't help looking for Roberta when Joseph graduated from high 185 school, but I didn't see her. It didn't trouble me much what she had said to me in the car. I mean the kicking part. I know I didn't do that, I couldn't do that. But I was puzzled by her telling me Maggie was black. When I thought about it I actually couldn't be certain. She wasn't pitch-black, I knew, or I would have remembered that. What I remember was the kiddie hat, and the semicircle legs. I tried to reassure myself about the race thing for a long time until it dawned on me that the truth was already there, and Roberta knew it. I didn't kick her; I didn't join in with the gar girls and kick that lady, but I sure did want to. We watched and never tried to help her and never called for help. Maggie was my dancing mother. Deaf, I thought, and dumb. Nobody inside. Nobody who would hear you if you cried in the night. Nobody who could tell you anything important that you could use. Rocking, dancing, swaying as she walked. And when the gar girls pushed her down, and started roughhousing, I knew she wouldn't scream, couldn't—just like me—and I was glad about that.

We decided not to have a tree, because Christmas would be at my mother-in-law's house, so why have a tree at both places? Joseph was at SUNY

New Paltz and we had to economize, we said. But at the last minute, I changed
my mind. Nothing could be that bad. So I rushed around town looking for a
tree, something small but wide. By the time I found a place, it was snowing and
very late. I dawdled like it was the most important purchase in the world and
the tree man was fed up with me. Finally I chose one and had it tied onto the
trunk of the car. I drove away slowly because the sand trucks were not out yet
and the streets could be murder at the beginning of a snowfall. Downtown the
streets were wide and rather empty except for a cluster of people coming out of
the Newburgh Hotel. The one hotel in town that wasn't built out of cardboard
and Plexiglas. A party, probably. The men huddled in the snow were dressed in
tails and the women had on furs. Shiny things glittered from underneath their
coats. It made me tired to look at them. Tired, tired, tired. On the next corner
was a small diner with loops and loops of paper bells in the window. I stopped
the car and went in. Just for a cup of coffee and twenty minutes of peace before
I went home and tried to finish everything before Christmas Eve.

"Twyla?"

There she was. In a silvery evening gown and dark fur coat. A man and
another woman were with her, the man fumbling for change to put in the
cigarette machine. The woman was humming and tapping on the counter with
her fingernails. They all looked a little bit drunk.

"Well. It's you."

"How are you?"   190

I shrugged. "Pretty good. Frazzled. Christmas and all."

"Regular?" called the woman from the counter.

"Fine," Roberta called back and then, "Wait for me in the car."

She slipped into the booth beside me. "I have to tell you something, Twyla.
I made up my mind if I ever saw you again, I'd tell you."

"I'd just as soon not hear anything, Roberta. It doesn't matter now,   195
anyway."

"No," she said. "Not about that."

"Don't be long," said the woman. She carried two regulars to go and the
man peeled his cigarette pack as they left.

"It's about St. Bonny's and Maggie."

"Oh, please."

"Listen to me. I really did think she was black. I didn't make that up. I   200
really thought so. But now I can't be sure. I just remember her as old, so old.
And because she couldn't talk—well, you know, I thought she was crazy. She'd
been brought up in an institution like my mother was and like I thought I would
be too. And you were right. We didn't kick her. It was the gar girls. Only them.
But, well, I wanted to. I really wanted them to hurt her. I said we did it, too. You
and me, but that's not true. And I don't want you to carry that around. It was
just that I wanted to do it so bad that day—wanting to is doing it."

Her eyes were watery from the drinks she'd had, I guess. I know it's that
way with me. One glass of wine and I start bawling over the littlest thing.

"We were kids, Roberta."

"Yeah. Yeah. I know, just kids."

"Eight."

"Eight."   205

"And lonely."

"Scared, too."

She wiped her cheeks with the heel of her hand and smiled. "Well, that's all I wanted to say."

I nodded and couldn't think of any way to fill the silence that went from the diner past the paper bells on out into the snow. It was heavy now. I thought I'd better wait for the sand trucks before starting home.

"Thanks, Roberta."   210

"Sure."

"Did I tell you? My mother, she never did stop dancing."

"Yes. You told me. And mine, she never got well." Roberta lifted her hands from the tabletop and covered her face with her palms. When she took them away she really was crying. "Oh shit, Twyla. Shit, shit, shit. What the hell happened to Maggie?"

Bharati Mukherjee   b. 1940

The Management of Grief   [1988]

A woman I don't know is boiling tea the Indian way in my kitchen. There are a lot of women I don't know in my kitchen, whispering, and moving tactfully. They open doors, rummage through the pantry, and try not to ask me where things are kept. They remind me of when my sons were small, on Mother's Day or when Vikram and I were tired, and they would make big, sloppy omelets. I would lie in bed pretending I didn't hear them.

Dr. Sharma, the treasurer of the Indo-Canada Society, pulls me into the hallway. He wants to know if I am worried about money. His wife, who has just come up from the basement with a tray of empty cups and glasses, scolds him. "Don't bother Mrs. Bhave with mundane details." She looks so monstrously pregnant her baby must be days overdue. I tell her she shouldn't be carrying heavy things. "Shaila," she says, smiling, "this is the fifth." Then she grabs a teenager by his shirttails. He slips his Walkman off his head. He has to be one of her four children, they have the same domed and dented foreheads. "What's the official word now?" she demands. The boy slips the headphones back on. "They're acting evasive, Ma. They're saying it could be an accident or a terrorist bomb."

All morning, the boys have been muttering, Sikh Bomb, Sikh Bomb. The men, not using the word, bow their heads in agreement. Mrs. Sharma touches her forehead at such a word. At least they've stopped talking about space debris and Russian lasers.

Two radios are going in the dining room. They are tuned to different stations. Someone must have brought the radios down from my boys' bedrooms. I haven't gone into their rooms since Kusum came running across the front lawn in her bathrobe. She looked so funny, I was laughing when I opened the door.

The big TV in the den is being whizzed through American networks and   5
cable channels.

"Damn!" some man swears bitterly. "How can these preachers carry on like nothing's happened?" I want to tell him we're not that important. You look at the audience, and at the preacher in his blue robe with his beautiful white hair, the potted palm trees under a blue sky, and you know they care about nothing.

The phone rings and rings. Dr. Sharma's taken charge. "We're with her," he keeps saying. "Yes, yes, the doctor has given calming pills. Yes, yes, pills are having necessary effect." I wonder if pills alone explain this calm. Not peace, just a deadening quiet. I was always controlled, but never repressed. Sound can reach me, but my body is tensed, ready to scream. I hear their voices all around me. I hear my boys and Vikram cry, "Mommy, Shaila!" and their screams insulate me, like headphones.

The woman boiling water tells her story again and again. "I got the news first. My cousin called from Halifax before six A.M., can you imagine? He'd gotten up for prayers and his son was studying for medical exams and he heard on a rock channel that something had happened to a plane. They said first it had disappeared from the radar, like a giant eraser just reached out. His father called me, so I said to him, what do you mean, 'something bad'? You mean a hijacking? And he said, *behn*, there is no confirmation of anything yet, but check with your neighbors because a lot of them must be on that plane. So I called poor Kusum straightaway. I knew Kusum's husband and daughter were booked to go yesterday."

Kusum lives across the street from me. She and Satish had moved in less than a month ago. They said they needed a bigger place. All these people, the Sharmas and friends from the Indo-Canada Society, had been there for the housewarming. Satish and Kusum made homemade tandoori on their big gas grill and even the white neighbors piled their plates high with that luridly red, charred, juicy chicken. Their younger daughter had danced, and even our boys had broken away from the Stanley Cup telecast to put in a reluctant appearance. Everyone took pictures for their albums and for the community newspapers—another of our families had made it big in Toronto—and now I wonder how many of those happy faces are gone. "Why does God give us so much if all along He intends to take it away?" Kusum asks me.

I nod. We sit on carpeted stairs, holding hands like children. "I never   10
once told him that I loved him," I say. I was too much the well brought up woman. I was so well brought up I never felt comfortable calling my husband by his first name.

"It's all right," Kusum says. "He knew. My husband knew. They felt it. Modern young girls have to say it because what they feel is fake."

Kusum's daughter, Pam, runs in with an overnight case. Pam's in her McDonald's uniform. "Mummy! You have to get dressed!" Panic makes her cranky. "A reporter's on his way here."

"Why?"

"You want to talk to him in your bathrobe?" She starts to brush her mother's long hair. She's the daughter who's always in trouble. She dates Canadian boys and hangs out in the mall, shopping for tight sweaters. The younger one, the goody-goody one according to Pam, the one with a voice so sweet that when she sang *bhajans*° for Ethiopian relief even a frugal man like my husband wrote out a hundred dollar check, *she* was on that plane. *She* was going to spend July and August with grandparents because Pam wouldn't go. Pam said she'd rather waitress at McDonald's. "If it's a choice between Bombay and Wonderland, I'm picking Wonderland," she'd said.

"Leave me alone," Kusum yells. "You know what I want to do? If I didn't   15 have to look after you now, I'd hang myself."

Pam's young face goes blotchy with pain. "Thanks," she says, "don't let me stop you."

"Hush," pregnant Mrs. Sharma scolds Pam. "Leave your mother alone. Mr. Sharma will tackle the reporters and fill out the forms. He'll say what has to be said."

Pam stands her ground. "You think I don't know what Mummy's thinking? *Why her?* that's what. That's sick! Mummy wishes my little sister were alive and I were dead."

Kusum's hand in mine is trembly hot. We continue to sit on the stairs.

She calls before she arrives, wondering if there's anything I need. Her name   20 is Judith Templeton and she's an appointee of the provincial government. "Multiculturalism?" I ask, and she says, "partially," but that her mandate is bigger. "I've been told you knew many of the people on the flight," she says. "Perhaps if you'd agree to help us reach the others . . . ?"

She gives me time at least to put on tea water and pick up the mess in the front room. I have a few *samosas* from Kusum's housewarming that I could fry up, but then I think, Why prolong this visit?

Judith Templeton is much younger than she sounded. She wears a blue suit with a white blouse and a polka dot tie. Her blond hair is cut short, her only jewelry is pearl drop earrings. Her briefcase is new and expensive looking, a gleaming cordovan leather. She sits with it across her lap. When she looks out the front windows onto the street, her contact lenses seem to float in front of her light blue eyes.

"What sort of help do you want from me?" I ask. She has refused the tea, out of politeness, but I insist, along with some slightly stale biscuits.

---

bhajans: Indian devotional songs.

"I have no experience," she admits. "That is, I have an MSW and I've worked in liaison with accident victims, but I mean I have no experience with a tragedy of this scale—"

"Who could?" I ask.   25

"—and with the complications of culture, language, and customs. Someone mentioned that Mrs. Bhave is a pillar—because you've taken it more calmly."

At this, perhaps, I frown, for she reaches forward, almost to take my hand. "I hope you understand my meaning, Mrs. Bhave. There are hundreds of people in Metro directly affected, like you, and some of them speak no English. There are some widows who've never handled money or gone on a bus, and there are old parents who still haven't eaten or gone outside their bedrooms. Some houses and apartments have been looted. Some wives are still hysterical. Some husbands are in shock and profound depression. We want to help, but our hands are tied in so many ways. We have to distribute money to some people, and there are legal documents—these things can be done. We have interpreters, but we don't always have the human touch, or maybe the right human touch. We don't want to make mistakes, Mrs. Bhave, and that's why we'd like to ask you to help us."

"More mistakes, you mean," I say.

"Police matters are not in my hands," she answers.

"Nothing I can do will make any difference," I say. "We must all grieve in   30 our own way."

"But you are coping very well. All the people said, Mrs. Bhave is the strongest person of all. Perhaps if the others could see you, talk with you, it would help them."

"By the standards of the people you call hysterical, I am behaving very oddly and very badly, Miss Templeton." I want to say to her, *I wish I could scream, starve, walk into Lake Ontario, jump from a bridge.* "They would not see me as a model. I do not see myself as a model."

I am a freak. No one who has ever known me would think of me reacting this way. This terrible calm will not go away.

She asks me if she may call again, after I get back from a long trip that we all must make. "Of course," I say. "Feel free to call, anytime."

Four days later, I find Kusum squatting on a rock overlooking a bay in   35 Ireland. It isn't a big rock, but it juts sharply out over water. This is as close as we'll ever get to them. June breezes balloon out her sari and unpin her knee-length hair. She has the bewildered look of a sea creature whom the tides have stranded.

It's been one hundred hours since Kusum came stumbling and screaming across my lawn. Waiting around the hospital, we've heard many stories. The police, the diplomats, they tell us things thinking that we're strong, that knowledge is helpful to the grieving, and maybe it is. Some, I know, prefer ignorance, or their own versions. The plane broke into two, they say. Unconsciousness was instantaneous. No one suffered. My boys must have just finished their breakfasts.

They loved eating on planes, they loved the smallness of plates, knives, and forks. Last year they saved the airline salt and pepper shakers. Half an hour more and they would have made it to Heathrow.

Kusum says that we can't escape our fate. She says that all those people — our husbands, my boys, her girl with the nightingale voice, all those Hindus, Christians, Sikhs, Muslims, Parsis, and atheists on that plane — were fated to die together off this beautiful bay. She learned this from a swami in Toronto.

I have my Valium.

Six of us "relatives" — two widows and four widowers — choose to spend the day today by the waters instead of sitting in a hospital room and scanning photographs of the dead. That's what they call us now: relatives. I've looked through twenty-seven photos in two days. They're very kind to us, the Irish are very understanding. Sometimes understanding means freeing a tourist bus for this trip to the bay, so we can pretend to spy our loved ones through the glassiness of waves or in sun-speckled cloud shapes.

I could die here, too, and be content. 40

"What is that, out there?" She's standing and flapping her hands and for a moment I see a head shape bobbing in the waves. She's standing in the water, I, on the boulder. The tide is low, and a round, black, head-sized rock has just risen from the waves. She returns, her sari end dripping and ruined and her face is a twisted remnant of hope, the way mine was a hundred hours ago, still laughing but inwardly knowing that nothing but the ultimate tragedy could bring two women together at six o'clock on a Sunday morning. I watch her face sag into blankness.

"That water felt warm, Shaila," she says at length.

"You can't," I say. "We have to wait for our turn to come."

I haven't eaten in four days, haven't brushed my teeth.

"I know," she says. "I tell myself I have no right to grieve. They are in a 45 better place than we are. My swami says I should be thrilled for them. My swami says depression is a sign of our selfishness."

Maybe I'm selfish. Selfishly I break away from Kusum and run, sandals slapping against stones, to the water's edge. What if my boys aren't lying pinned under the debris? What if they aren't stuck a mile below that innocent blue chop? What if, given the strong currents. . . .

Now I've ruined my sari, one of my best. Kusum has joined me, knee-deep in water that feels to me like a swimming pool. I could settle in the water, and my husband would take my hand and the boys would slap water in my face just to see me scream.

"Do you remember what good swimmers my boys were, Kusum?"

"I saw the medals," she says.

One of the widowers, Dr. Ranganathan from Montreal, walks out to us, 50 carrying his shoes in one hand. He's an electrical engineer. Someone at the hotel mentioned his work is famous around the world, something about the place where physics and electricity come together. He has lost a huge family, something indescribable. "With some luck," Dr. Ranganathan suggests to me, "a good swimmer could make it safely to some island. It is quite possible that there may be many, many microscopic islets scattered around."

"You're not just saying that?" I tell Dr. Ranganathan about Vinod, my elder son. Last year he took diving as well.

"It's a parent's duty to hope," he says. "It is foolish to rule out possibilities that have not been tested. I myself have not surrendered hope."

Kusum is sobbing once again. "Dear lady," he says, laying his free hand on her arm, and she calms down.

"Vinod is how old?" he asks me. He's very careful, as we all are. *Is*, not was.

"Fourteen. Yesterday he was fourteen. His father and uncle were going to   55
take him down to the Taj and give him a big birthday party. I couldn't go with them because I couldn't get two weeks off from my stupid job in June." I process bills for a travel agent. June is a big travel month.

Dr. Ranganathan whips the pockets of his suit jacket inside out. Squashed roses, in darkening shades of pink, float on the water. He tore the roses off creepers in somebody's garden. He didn't ask anyone if he could pluck the roses, but now there's been an article about it in the local papers. When you see an Indian person, it says, please give him or her flowers.

"A strong youth of fourteen," he says, "can very likely pull to safety a younger one."

My sons, though four years apart, were very close. Vinod wouldn't let Mithun drown. *Electrical engineering,* I think, foolishly perhaps: this man knows important secrets of the universe, things closed to me. Relief spins me lightheaded. No wonder my boys' photographs haven't turned up in the gallery of photos of the recovered dead. "Such pretty roses," I say.

"My wife loved pink roses. Every Friday I had to bring a bunch home. I used to say, Why? After twenty odd years of marriage you're still needing proof positive of my love?" He has identified his wife and three of his children. Then others from Montreal, the lucky ones, intact families with no survivors. He chuckles as he wades back to shore. Then he swings around to ask me a question. "Mrs. Bhave, you are wanting to throw in some roses for your loved ones? I have two big ones left."

But I have other things to float: Vinod's pocket calculator; a half-painted   60
model B-52 for my Mithun. They'd want them on their island. And for my husband? For him I let fall into the calm, glassy waters a poem I wrote in the hospital yesterday. Finally he'll know my feelings for him.

"Don't tumble, the rocks are slippery," Dr. Ranganathan cautions. He holds out a hand for me to grab.

Then it's time to get back on the bus, time to rush back to our waiting posts on hospital benches.

Kusum is one of the lucky ones. The lucky ones flew here, identified in multiplicate their loved ones, then will fly to India with the bodies for proper ceremonies. Satish is one of the few males who surfaced. The photos of faces we saw on the walls in an office at Heathrow and here in the hospital are mostly of women. Women have more body fat, a nun said to me matter-of-factly. They float better.

Today I was stopped by a young sailor on the street. He had loaded bodies, he'd gone into the water when—he checks my face for signs of strength—when the sharks were first spotted. I don't blush, and he breaks down. "It's all right," I say. "Thank you." I had heard about the sharks from Dr. Ranganathan. In his orderly mind, science brings understanding, it holds no terror. It is the shark's duty. For every deer there is a hunter, for every fish a fisherman.

The Irish are not shy; they rush to me and give me hugs and some are cry- 65
ing. I cannot imagine reactions like that on the streets of Toronto. Just strangers, and I am touched. Some carry flowers with them and give them to any Indian they see.

After lunch, a policeman I have gotten to know quite well catches hold of me. He says he thinks he has a match for Vinod. I explain what a good swimmer Vinod is.

"You want me with you when you look at photos?" Dr. Ranganathan walks ahead of me into the picture gallery. In these matters, he is a scientist, and I am grateful. It is a new perspective. "They have performed miracles," he says. "We are indebted to them."

The first day or two the policemen showed us relatives only one picture at a time; now they're in a hurry, they're eager to lay out the possibles, and even the probables.

The face on the photo is of a boy much like Vinod; the same intelligent eyes, the same thick brows dipping into a V. But this boy's features, even his cheeks, are puffier, wider, mushier.

"No." My gaze is pulled by other pictures. There are five other boys who 70
look like Vinod.

The nun assigned to console me rubs the first picture with a fingertip. "When they've been in the water for a while, love, they look a little heavier." The bones under the skin are broken, they said on the first day—try to adjust your memories. It's important.

"It's not him. I'm his mother. I'd know."

"I know this one!" Dr. Ranganathan cries out suddenly from the back of the gallery. "And this one!" I think he senses that I don't want to find my boys. "They are the Kutty brothers. They were also from Montreal." I don't mean to be crying. On the contrary, I am ecstatic. My suitcase in the hotel is packed heavy with dry clothes for my boys.

The policeman starts to cry. "I am so sorry, I am so sorry, ma'am. I really thought we had a match."

With the nun ahead of us and the policeman behind, we, the unlucky ones 75
without our children's bodies, file out of the makeshift gallery.

From Ireland most of us go on to India. Kusum and I take the same direct flight to Bombay, so I can help her clear customs quickly. But we have to argue with a man in uniform. He has large boils on his face. The boils swell and glow with sweat as we argue with him. He wants Kusum to wait in line and he refuses to take authority because his boss is on a tea break. But Kusum won't let her coffins out of sight, and I shan't desert her though I know that my parents, elderly and diabetic, must be waiting in a stuffy car in a scorching lot.

"You bastard!" I scream at the man with the popping boils. Other passengers press closer. "You think we're smuggling contraband in those coffins!"

Once upon a time we were well brought up women; we were dutiful wives who kept our heads veiled, our voices shy and sweet.

In India, I become, once again, an only child of rich, ailing parents. Old friends of the family come to pay their respects. Some are Sikh, and inwardly, involuntarily, I cringe. My parents are progressive people; they do not blame communities for a few individuals.

In Canada it is a different story now.   80

"Stay longer," my mother pleads. "Canada is a cold place. Why would you want to be all by yourself?" I stay.

Three months pass. Then another.

"Vikram wouldn't have wanted you to give up things!" they protest. They call my husband by the name he was born with. In Toronto he'd changed to Vik so the men he worked with at his office would find his name as easy as Rod or Chris. "You know, the dead aren't cut off from us!"

My grandmother, the spoiled daughter of a rich *zamindar*,° shaved her head with rusty razor blades when she was widowed at sixteen. My grandfather died of childhood diabetes when he was nineteen, and she saw herself as the harbinger of bad luck. My mother grew up without parents, raised indifferently by an uncle, while her true mother slept in a hut behind the main estate house and took her food with the servants. She grew up a rationalist. My parents abhor mindless mortification.

The zamindar's daughter kept stubborn faith in Vedic rituals; my parents   85
rebelled. I am trapped between two modes of knowledge. At thirty-six, I am too old to start over and too young to give up. Like my husband's spirit, I flutter between worlds.

Courting aphasia, we travel. We travel with our phalanx of servants and poor relatives. To hill stations and to beach resorts. We play contract bridge in dusty gymkhana clubs. We ride stubby ponies up crumbly mountain trails. At tea dances, we let ourselves be twirled twice round the ballroom. We hit the holy spots we hadn't made time for before. In Varanasi, Kalighat, Rishikesh, Hardwar, astrologers and palmists seek me out and for a fee offer me cosmic consolations.

Already the widowers among us are being shown new bride candidates. They cannot resist the call of custom, the authority of their parents and older brothers. They must marry; it is the duty of a man to look after a wife. The new wives will be young widows with children, destitute but of good family. They will

---

zamindar: Hereditary aristocrat holding great tracts of land and pursuing a lavish lifestyle.

make loving wives, but the men will shun them. I've had calls from the men over crackling Indian telephone lines. "Save me," they say, these substantial, educated, successful men of forty. "My parents are arranging a marriage for me." In a month they will have buried one family and returned to Canada with a new bride and partial family.

I am comparatively lucky. No one here thinks of arranging a husband for an unlucky widow.

Then, on the third day of the sixth month into this odyssey, in an abandoned temple in a tiny Himalayan village, as I make my offering of flowers and sweetmeats to the god of a tribe of animists, my husband descends to me. He is squatting next to a scrawny *sadhu°* in moth-eaten robes. Vikram wears the vanilla suit he wore the last time I hugged him. The *sadhu* tosses petals on a butter-fed flame, reciting Sanskrit mantras and sweeps his face of flies. My husband takes my hands in his.

You're beautiful, he starts. Then, *What are you doing here?*   90

Shall I stay? I ask. He only smiles, but already the image is fading. *You must finish alone what we started together.* No seaweed wreathes his mouth. He speaks too fast just as he used to when we were an envied family in our pink splitlevel. He is gone.

In the windowless altar room, smoky with joss sticks and clarified butter lamps, a sweaty hand gropes for my blouse. I do not shriek. The *sadhu* arranges his robe. The lamps hiss and sputter out.

When we come out of the temple, my mother says, "Did you feel something weird in there?"

My mother has no patience with ghosts, prophetic dreams, holy men, and cults. "No," I lie. "Nothing."   95

But she knows that she's lost me. She knows that in days I shall be leaving.

Kusum's put her house up for sale. She wants to live in an ashram in Hardwar. Moving to Hardwar was her swami's idea. Her swami runs two ashrams, the one in Hardwar and another here in Toronto.

"Don't run away," I tell her.

"I'm not running away," she says. "I'm pursuing inner peace. You think you or that Ranganathan fellow are better off?"

Pam's left for California. She wants to do some modeling, she says. She says   100 when she comes into her share of the insurance money she'll open a yoga-cumaerobics studio in Hollywood. She sends me postcards so naughty I daren't leave them on the coffee table. Her mother has withdrawn from her and the world.

The rest of us don't lose touch, that's the point. Talk is all we have, says Dr. Ranganathan, who has also resisted his relatives and returned to Montreal and to his job, alone. He says, whom better to talk with than other relatives? We've been melted down and recast as a new tribe.

---

sadhu: A wandering ascetic Hindu monk or holy man.

He calls me twice a week from Montreal. Every Wednesday night and every Saturday afternoon. He is changing jobs, going to Ottawa. But Ottawa is over a hundred miles away, and he is forced to drive two hundred and twenty miles a day. He can't bring himself to sell his house. The house is a temple, he says; the king-sized bed in the master bedroom is a shrine. He sleeps on a folding cot. A devotee.

There are still some hysterical relatives. Judith Templeton's list of those needing help and those who've "accepted" is in nearly perfect balance. Acceptance means you speak of your family in the past tense and you make active plans for moving ahead with your life. There are courses at Seneca and Ryerson we could be taking. Her gleaming leather briefcase is full of college catalogues and lists of cultural societies that need our help. She has done impressive work, I tell her.

"In the textbooks on grief management," she replies—I am her confidante, I realize, one of the few whose grief has not sprung bizarre obsessions—"there are stages to pass through: rejection, depression, acceptance, reconstruction." She has compiled a chart and finds that six months after the tragedy, none of us still reject reality, but only a handful are reconstructing. "Depressed Acceptance" is the plateau we've reached. Remarriage is a major step in reconstruction (though she's a little surprised, even shocked, over *how* quickly some of the men have taken on new families). Selling one's house and changing jobs and cities is healthy.

How do I tell Judith Templeton that my family surrounds me, and that like 105 creatures in epics, they've changed shapes? She sees me as calm and accepting but worries that I have no job, no career. My closest friends are worse off than I. I cannot tell her my days, even my nights, are thrilling.

She asks me to help with families she can't reach at all. An elderly couple in Agincourt whose sons were killed just weeks after they had brought their parents over from a village in Punjab. From their names, I know they are Sikh. Judith Templeton and a translator have visited them twice with offers of money for airfare to Ireland, with bank forms, power-of-attorney forms, but they have refused to sign, or to leave their tiny apartment. Their sons' money is frozen in the bank. Their sons' investment apartments have been trashed by tenants, the furnishings sold off. The parents fear that anything they sign or any money they receive will end the company's or the country's obligations to them. They fear they are selling their sons for two airline tickets to a place they've never seen.

The high-rise apartment is a tower of Indians and West Indians, with a sprinkling of Orientals. The nearest bus stop kiosk is lined with women in saris. Boys practice cricket in the parking lot. Inside the building, even I wince a bit from the ferocity of onion fumes, the distinctive and immediate Indianness of frying *ghee*, but Judith Templeton maintains a steady flow of information. These poor old people are in imminent danger of losing their place and all their services.

I say to her, "They are Sikh. They will not open up to a Hindu woman." And what I want to add is, as much as I try not to, I stiffen now at the sight of beards and turbans. I remember a time when we all trusted each other in this new country, it was only the new country we worried about.

The two rooms are dark and stuffy. The lights are off, and an oil lamp sput-
ters on the coffee table. The bent old lady has let us in, and her husband is
wrapping a white turban over his oiled, hip-length hair. She immediately goes
to the kitchen, and I hear the most familiar sound of an Indian home, tap water
hitting and filling a teapot.

They have not paid their utility bills, out of fear and the inability to write a   110
check. The telephone is gone; electricity and gas and water are soon to follow.
They have told Judith their sons will provide. They are good boys, and they have
always earned and looked after their parents.

We converse a bit in Hindi. They do not ask about the crash and I wonder
if I should bring it up. If they think I am here merely as a translator, then they
may feel insulted. There are thousands of Punjabi-speakers, Sikhs, in Toronto to
do a better job. And so I say to the old lady, "I too have lost my sons, and my
husband, in the crash."

Her eyes immediately fill with tears. The man mutters a few words which
sound like a blessing. "God provides and God takes away," he says.

I want to say, But only men destroy and give back nothing. "My boys and
my husband are not coming back," I say. "We have to understand that."

Now the old woman responds. "But who is to say? Man alone does not
decide these things." To this her husband adds his agreement.

Judith asks about the bank papers, the release forms. With a stroke of the   115
pen, they will have a provincial trustee to pay their bills, invest their money,
send them a monthly pension.

"Do you know this woman?" I ask them.

The man raises his hand from the table, turns it over and seems to regard each
finger separately before he answers. "This young lady is always coming here, we
make tea for her and she leaves papers for us to sign." His eyes scan a pile of papers
in the corner of the room. "Soon we will be out of tea, then will she go away?"

The old lady adds, "I have asked my neighbors and no one else gets *angrezi*°
visitors. What have we done?"

"It's her job," I try to explain. "The government is worried. Soon you will
have no place to stay, no lights, no gas, no water."

"Government will get its money. Tell her not to worry, we are honorable   120
people."

I try to explain the government wishes to give money, not take. He raises his
hand. "Let them take," he says. "We are accustomed to that. That is no problem."

"We are strong people," says the wife. "Tell her that."

"Who needs all this machinery?" demands the husband. "It is unhealthy,
the bright lights, the cold air on a hot day, the cold food, the four gas rings. God
will provide, not government."

"When our boys return," the mother says. Her husband sucks his teeth.
"Enough talk," he says.

Angrezi: English or Anglo.

Judith breaks in. "Have you convinced them?" The snaps on her cordovan   125
briefcase go off like firecrackers in that quiet apartment. She lays the sheaf of
legal papers on the coffee table. "If they can't write their names, an X will
do—I've told them that."

Now the old lady has shuffled to the kitchen and soon emerges with a pot
of tea and two cups. "I think my bladder will go first on a job like this," Judith
says to me, smiling. "If only there was some way of reaching them. Please thank
her for the tea. Tell her she's very kind."

I nod in Judith's direction and tell them in Hindi, "She thanks you for the
tea. She thinks you are being very hospitable but she doesn't have the slightest
idea what it means."

I want to say, Humor her. I want to say, My boys and my husband are with
me too, more than ever. I look in the old man's eyes and I can read his stubborn, peasant's message: *I have protected this woman as best I can. She is the only
person I have left. Give to me or take from me what you will, but I will not sign for
it. I will not pretend that I accept.*

In the car, Judith says, "You see what I'm up against? I'm sure they're
lovely people, but their stubbornness and ignorance are driving me crazy. They
think signing a paper is signing their sons' death warrants, don't they?"

I am looking out the window. I want to say, *In our culture, it is a parent's*   130
duty to hope.

"Now Shaila, this next woman is a real mess. She cries day and night, and
she refuses all medical help. We may have to—"

"—Let me out at the subway," I say.

"I beg your pardon?" I can feel those blue eyes staring at me.

It would not be like her to disobey. She merely disapproves, and slows at a corner
to let me out. Her voice is plaintive. "Is there anything I said? Anything I did?"

I could answer her suddenly in a dozen ways, but I choose not to. "Shaila?   135
Let's talk about it," I hear, then slam the door.

A wife and mother begins her new life in a new country, and that life is cut
short. Yet her husband tells her: Complete what we have started. We who stayed
out of politics and came halfway around the world to avoid religious and political feuding have been the first in the New World to die from it. I no longer know
what we started, nor how to complete it. I write letters to the editors of local
papers and to members of Parliament. Now at least they admit it was a bomb.
One MP answers back, with sympathy, but with a challenge. You want to make
a difference? Work on a campaign. Work on mine. Politicize the Indian voter.

My husband's old lawyer helps me set up a trust. Vikram was a saver and a
careful investor. He had saved the boys' boarding school and college fees. I sell
the pink house at four times what we paid for it and take a small apartment
downtown. I am looking for a charity to support.

We are deep in the Toronto winter, gray skies, icy pavements. I stay indoors,
watching television. I have tried to assess my situation, how best to live my life, to
complete what we began so many years ago. Kusum has written me from Hardwar

that her life is now serene. She has seen Satish and has heard her daughter sing again. Kusum was on a pilgrimage, passing through a village when she heard a young girl's voice, singing one of her daughter's favorite *bhajans*. She followed the music through the squalor of a Himalayan village, to a hut where a young girl, an exact replica of her daughter, was fanning coals under the kitchen fire. When she appeared, the girl cried out, "Ma!" and ran away. What did I think of that?

I think I can only envy her.

Pam didn't make it to California, but writes me from Vancouver. She works 140
in a department store, giving make-up hints to Indian and Oriental girls. Dr. Ranganathan has given up his commute, given up his house and job, and accepted an academic position in Texas where no one knows his story and he has vowed not to tell it. He calls me now once a week.

I wait, I listen, and I pray, but Vikram has not returned to me. The voices and the shapes and the nights filled with visions ended abruptly several weeks ago.

I take it as a sign.

One rare, beautiful, sunny day last week, returning from a small errand on Yonge Street, I was walking through the park from the subway to my apartment. I live equidistant from the Ontario House of Parliament and the University of Toronto. The day was not cold, but something in the bare trees caught my attention. I looked up from the gravel, into the branches and the clear blue sky beyond. I thought I heard the rustling of larger forms, and I waited a moment for voices. Nothing.

"What?" I asked.

Then as I stood in the path looking north to Queen's Park and west to the 145
university, I heard the voices of my family one last time. *Your time has come*, they said. *Go, be brave.*

I do not know where this voyage I have begun will end. I do not know which direction I will take. I dropped the package on a park bench and started walking.

Haruki Murakami Japan, b. 1949

Birthday Girl [2004]

Translated by Jay Rubin

She waited on tables as usual that day, her twentieth birthday. She always worked on Fridays, but if things had gone according to plan that particular Friday, she would have had the night off. The other part-time girl had agreed to switch shifts with her as a matter of course: being screamed at by an angry chef while lugging pumpkin gnocchi and seafood fritto misto to customers' tables

APPROACHING THE AUTHOR

Haruki Murakami is a keen marathon runner and triathlete, although he did not start running until he was thirty-three years old. On June 23, 1996, he completed his first ultramarathon, a 100-kilometer race around Lake Saroma in Hokkaido, Japan.

For more about him, see page 1402.

was no way to spend one's twentieth birthday. But the other girl had aggravated a cold and gone to bed with unstoppable diarrhea and a fever of 104, so she ended up working after all on short notice.

She found herself trying to comfort the sick girl, who had called to apologize. "Don't worry about it," she said. "I wasn't going to do anything special anyway, even if it is my twentieth birthday."°

And in fact she was not all that disappointed. One reason was the terrible argument she had had a few days earlier with the boyfriend who was supposed to be with her that night. They had been going together since high school. The argument had started from nothing much but it had taken an unexpected turn for the worse until it became a long and bitter shouting match — one bad enough, she was pretty sure, to have snapped their long-standing ties once and for all. Something inside her had turned rock-hard and died. He had not called her since the blowup, and she was not about to call him.

Her workplace was one of the better-known Italian restaurants in the tony Roppongi district of Tokyo. It had been in business since the late sixties, and while its cuisine was hardly cutting edge, its high reputation was fully justified. It had many repeat customers and they were never disappointed. The dining room had a calm, relaxed atmosphere without a hint of pushiness. Rather than a young crowd, the restaurant drew an older clientele that included some famous stage people and writers.

The two full-time waiters worked six days a week. She and the other part-time   5 waitress were students who took turns working three days each. In addition there was one floor manager and, at the register, a skinny middle-aged woman who supposedly had been there since the restaurant opened — literally sitting in the one place, it seemed, like some gloomy old character from *Little Dorrit*.° She had exactly two functions: to accept payment from the customers and to answer the phone. She spoke only when necessary and always wore the same black dress. There was something cold and hard about her: if you set her afloat on the night-time sea, she would probably sink any boat that happened to ram her.

The floor manager was perhaps in his late forties. Tall and broad-shouldered, his build suggested that he had been a sportsman in his youth, but excess flesh was now beginning to accumulate on his belly and chin. His short, stiff hair was thinning at the crown, and a special aging bachelor smell clung to him — like newsprint that had been stored in a drawer with cough drops. She had a bachelor uncle who smelled like that.

The manager always wore a black suit, white shirt, and bow tie — not a clip-on bow tie, but the real thing, tied by hand. It was a point of pride for him that he could tie it perfectly without looking in the mirror. He performed his duties adroitly day after day. They consisted of checking the arrival and departure of guests, keeping abreast of the reservation schedule, knowing the names of regular

---

twentieth birthday: In Japan, the "coming of age" year, the beginning of adulthood. **Little Dorrit:** Satiric novel by Charles Dickens (1812–1870), published serially from 1855–1857.

customers, greeting them with a smile, lending a respectful ear to any complaints that might arise, giving expert advice on wines, and overseeing the work of the waiters and waitresses. It was also his special task to deliver dinner to the room of the restaurant's owner.

———————

"The owner had his own room on the sixth floor of the same building where the restaurant was," she said. "An apartment, or office or something."

Somehow she and I had gotten on to the subject of our twentieth birthdays — what sort of day it had been for each of us. Most people remember the day they turned twenty. Hers had happened more than ten years earlier.

"He never, ever showed his face in the restaurant, though. The only one who saw him was the manager. It was strictly *his* job to deliver the owner's dinner to him. None of the other employees knew what he looked like."

"So basically, the owner was getting home delivery from his own restaurant."

"Right," she said. "Every night at eight, the manager had to bring dinner to the owner's room. It was the restaurant's busiest time, so having the manager disappear just then was always a problem for us, but there was no way around it because that was the way it had always been done. They'd load the dinner onto one of those carts that hotels use for room service, the manager would push it into the elevator wearing a respectful look on his face, and fifteen minutes later he'd come back empty-handed. Then, an hour later, he'd go up again and bring down the cart with empty plates and glasses. Every day, like clockwork. I thought it was really weird the first time I saw it happen. It was like some kind of religious ritual, you know? But after a while I got used to it, and never gave it a second thought."

The owner always had chicken. The recipe and the vegetable sides were a little different every day, but the main dish was always chicken. A young chef once told her that he had tried sending up the same exact roast chicken every day for a week just to see what would happen, but there was never any complaint. A chef wants to try different ways of preparing things, of course, and each new chef would challenge himself with every technique for chicken that he could think of. They'd make elegant sauces, they'd try chickens from different suppliers, but none of their efforts had any effect: they might just as well have been throwing pebbles into an empty cave. In the end, every one of them gave up and sent the owner some run-of-the-mill chicken dish every day. That's all that was ever asked of them.

Work started as usual on her twentieth birthday, November 17. It had been raining on and off since the afternoon, and pouring since early evening. At five o'clock the manager gathered the employees together to explain the day's specials. Servers were required to memorize them word for word and not use crib sheets: veal Milanese, pasta topped with sardines and cabbage, chestnut mousse. Sometimes the manager would play the role of a customer and test them with questions. Then came the employees' meal: waiters in *this* restaurant were not going to have growling stomachs as they took their customers' orders!

The restaurant opened its doors at six o'clock, but guests were slow to arrive 15 because of the downpour, and several reservations were simply canceled. Women didn't want their dresses ruined by the rain. The manager walked around tight-lipped, and the waiters killed time polishing the salt and pepper shakers or chatting with the chef about cooking. She surveyed the dining room with its single couple at table and listened to the harpsichord music flowing discreetly from ceiling speakers. A deep smell of late autumn rain worked its way into the restaurant.

It was after seven thirty when the manager started feeling sick. He stumbled over to a chair and sat there for a while pressing his stomach, as if he had just been shot. A greasy sweat clung to his forehead. "I think I'd better go to the hospital," he muttered. For him to be taken ill was a most unusual occurrence: he had never missed a day since he started working in the restaurant over ten years earlier. It was another point of pride for him that he had never been out with illness or injury, but his painful grimace made it clear that he was in very bad shape.

She stepped outside with an umbrella and hailed a cab. One of the waiters held the manager steady and climbed into the car with him to take him to a nearby hospital. Before ducking into the cab, the manager said to her hoarsely, "I want you to take a dinner up to room 604 at eight o'clock. All you have to do is ring the bell, say 'Your dinner is here,' and leave it."

"That's room 604, right?" she said.

"At eight o'clock," he repeated. "On the dot." He grimaced again, climbed in, and the taxi took him away.

———————

The rain showed no signs of letting up after the manager had left, and cus- 20 tomers arrived at long intervals. No more than one or two tables were occupied at a time, so if the manager and one waiter had to be absent, this was a good time for it to happen. Things could get so busy that it was not unusual even for the full staff to have trouble coping.

When the owner's meal was ready at eight o'clock, she pushed the room service cart into the elevator and rode up to the sixth floor. It was the standard meal for him: a half bottle of red wine with the cork loosened, a thermal pot of coffee, a chicken entree with steamed vegetables, rolls and butter. The heavy aroma of cooked chicken quickly filled the little elevator. It mingled with the smell of the rain. Water droplets dotted the elevator floor, suggesting that someone with a wet umbrella had recently been aboard.

She pushed the cart down the corridor, bringing it to a stop in front of the door marked "604." She double-checked her memory: 604. That was it. She cleared her throat and pressed the doorbell.

There was no answer. She stood there for a good twenty seconds. Just as she was thinking of pressing the bell again, the door opened inward and a skinny old man appeared. He was shorter than she was, by some four or five inches.

He had on a dark suit and a necktie. Against his white shirt, the tie stood out distinctly, its brownish yellow coloring like withered leaves. He made a very clean impression, his clothes perfectly pressed, his white hair smoothed down: he looked as though he were about to go out for the night to some sort of gathering. The deep wrinkles that creased his brow made her think of ravines in an aerial photograph.

"Your dinner, sir," she said in a husky voice, then quietly cleared her throat again. Her voice grew husky whenever she was tense.

"Dinner?"   25

"Yes, sir. The manager suddenly took sick. I had to take his place today. Your meal, sir."

"Oh, I see," the old man said, almost as if talking to himself, his hand still perched on the doorknob. "Took sick, eh? You don't say."

"His stomach started to hurt him all of a sudden. He went to the hospital. He thinks he might have appendicitis."

"Oh, that's not good," the old man said, running his fingers along the wrinkles of his forehead. "Not good at all."

She cleared her throat again. "Shall I bring your meal in, sir?" she asked.   30

"Ah yes, of course," the old man said. "Yes, of course, if you wish. That's fine with me."

If I wish? she thought. What a strange way to put it. What am I supposed to wish?

The old man opened the door the rest of the way, and she wheeled the cart inside. The floor had short gray carpeting with no area for removing shoes. The first room was a large study, as though the apartment was more a workplace than a residence. The window looked out on the nearby Tokyo Tower, its steel skeleton outlined in lights. A large desk stood by the window, and beside the desk was a compact sofa and love seat. The old man pointed to the plastic laminate coffee table in front of the sofa. She arranged his meal on the table: white napkin and silverware, coffeepot and cup, wine and wineglass, bread and butter, and the plate of chicken and vegetables.

"If you would be kind enough to set the dishes in the hall as usual, sir, I'll come to get them in an hour."

Her words seemed to snap him out of an appreciative contemplation of his   35
dinner. "Oh yes, of course. I'll put them in the hall. On the cart. In an hour. If you wish."

Yes, she replied inwardly, for the moment that is exactly what I wish. "Is there anything else I can do for you, sir?"

"No, I don't think so," he said after a moment's consideration. He was wearing black shoes polished to a high sheen. They were small and chic. He's a stylish dresser, she thought. And he stands very straight for his age.

"Well, then, sir, I'll be getting back to work."

"No, wait just a moment," he said.

"Sir?"   40

"Do you think it might be possible for you to give me five minutes of your time, miss? I have something I'd like to say to you."

He was so polite in his request that it made her blush. "I . . . think it should be all right," she said "I mean, if it really is just five minutes." He was her employer, after all. He was paying her by the hour. It was not a question of her giving or his taking her time. And this old man did not look like a person who would do anything bad to her.

"By the way, how old are you?" the old man asked, standing by the table with arms folded and looking directly into her eyes.

"I'm twenty now," she said.

"Twenty *now*," he repeated, narrowing his eyes as if peering through some   45 kind of crack. "Twenty *now*. As of when?"

"Well, I just turned twenty," she said. After a moment's hesitation, she added, "Today is my birthday, sir."

"I *see*," he said, rubbing his chin as if this explained a great deal for him. "Today, is it? Today is your twentieth birthday?"

She nodded.

"Your life in this world began exactly twenty years ago today."

"Yes, sir," she said, "that is true."   50

"I see, I see," he said. "That's wonderful. Well, then, happy birthday."

"Thank you very much," she said, and then it dawned on her that this was the very first time all day that anyone had wished her a happy birthday. Of course, if her parents had called from Oita, she might find a message from them on her answering machine when she got home from work.

"Well, well, this is certainly a cause for celebration," he said. "How about a little toast? We can drink this red wine."

"Thank you, sir, but I couldn't, I'm working now."

"Oh, what's the harm in a little sip? No one's going to blame you if I say   55 it's all right. Just a token drink to celebrate."

The old man slid the cork from the bottle and dribbled a little wine into his glass for her. Then he took an ordinary drinking glass from a glass-doored cabinet and poured some wine for himself.

"Happy birthday," he said. "May you live a rich and fruitful life, and may there be nothing to cast dark shadows on it."

They clinked glasses.

May there be nothing to cast dark shadows on it: she silently repeated his remark to herself. Why had he chosen such unusual words for her birthday toast?

"Your twentieth birthday comes only once in a lifetime, miss. It's an irre-   60 placeable day."

"Yes, sir, I know," she said, taking one cautious sip of wine.

"And here, on your special day, you have taken the trouble to deliver my dinner to me like a kindhearted fairy."

"Just doing my job, sir."

"But still," the old man said with a few quick shakes of the head. "But still, lovely young miss."

The old man sat down in the leather chair by his desk and motioned her   65 to the sofa. She lowered herself gingerly onto the edge of the seat, with the wineglass still in her hand. Knees aligned, she tugged at her skirt, clearing her throat again. She saw raindrops tracing lines down the windowpane. The room was strangely quiet.

"Today just happens to be your twentieth birthday, and on top of that you have brought me this wonderful warm meal," the old man said as if reconfirming the situation. Then he set his glass on the desktop with a little thump. "This has to be some kind of special convergence, don't you think?"

Not quite convinced, she managed a nod.

"Which is why," he said, touching the knot of his withered-leaf-colored necktie, "I feel it is important for me to give you a birthday present. A special birthday calls for a special commemorative gift."

Flustered, she shook her head and said, "No, please, sir, don't give it a second thought. All I did was bring your meal the way they ordered me to."

The old man raised both hands, palms toward her. "No, miss, don't *you* give   70
it a second thought. The kind of 'present' I have in mind is not something tangible, not something with a price tag. To put it simply"—he placed his hands on the desk and took one long, slow breath—"what I would like to do for a lovely young fairy such as you is to grant a wish you might have, to make your wish come true. Anything. Anything at all that you wish for—assuming that you *do* have such a wish."

"A wish?" she asked, her throat dry.

"Something you would like to have happen, miss. If you have a wish—one wish, I'll make it come true. That is the kind of birthday present I can give you. But you had better think about it very carefully because I can grant you only one." He raised a finger. "Just one. You can't change your mind afterward and take it back."

She was at a loss for words. One wish? Whipped by the wind, raindrops tapped unevenly at the windowpane. As long as she remained silent, the old man looked into her eyes, saying nothing. Time marked its irregular pulse in her ears.

"I have to wish for something, and it will be granted?"

Instead of answering her question, the old man—hands still side by side on   75
the desk—just smiled. He did it in the most natural and amiable way.

"Do you *have* a wish, miss—or not?" he asked gently.

———————

"This really did happen," she said, looking straight at me. "I'm not making it up."

"Of course not," I said. She was not the sort of person to invent some goofy story out of thin air. "So did you make a wish?"

She went on looking at me for a while, then released a tiny sigh. "Don't get me wrong," she said. "I wasn't taking him one hundred percent seriously myself. I mean, at twenty you're not exactly living in a fairy-tale world anymore. If this was his idea of a joke, though, I had to hand it to him for coming up with it on the spot. He was a dapper old fellow with a twinkle in his eye, so I decided to play along with him. It *was* my twentieth birthday, after all: I figured I ought to have *something* not-so-ordinary happen to me that day. It wasn't a question of believing or not believing."

I nodded without saying anything. 80

"You can understand how I felt, I'm sure. My twentieth birthday was coming to an end without anything special happening, nobody wishing me a happy birthday, and all I'm doing is carrying tortellini with anchovy sauce to people's tables."

I nodded again. "Don't worry," I said. "I understand."

"So I made a wish."

The old man kept his gaze fixed on her, saying nothing, hands still on the desk. Also on the desk were several thick folders that might have been account books, plus writing implements, a calendar, and a lamp with a green shade. Lying among them, his small hands looked like another set of desktop furnishings. The rain continued to beat against the window, the lights of Tokyo Tower filtering through the shattered drops.

The wrinkles on the old man's forehead deepened slightly. "That is your 85 wish?"

"Yes," she said. "That is my wish."

"A bit unusual for a girl your age," he said. "I was expecting something different."

"If it's no good, I'll wish for something else," she said, clearing her throat. "I don't mind. I'll think of something else."

"No, no," the old man said, raising his hands and waving them like flags. "There's nothing wrong with it, not at all. It's just a little surprising, miss. Don't you have something else? Like, say, you want to be prettier, or smarter, or rich: you're OK with not wishing for something like that—something an ordinary girl would ask for?"

She took some moments to search for the right words. The old man just 90 waited, saying nothing, his hands at rest together on the desk again.

"Of course I'd like to be prettier or smarter or rich. But I really can't imagine what would happen to me if any of those things came true. They might be more than I could handle. I still don't really know what life is all about. I don't know how it *works*."

"I see," the old man said, intertwining his fingers and separating them again. "I see."

"So, is my wish OK?"

"Of course," he said. "Of course. It's no trouble at all for me."

The old man suddenly fixed his eyes on a spot in the air. The wrinkles of his 95 forehead deepened: they might have been the wrinkles of his brain itself as it concentrated on his thoughts. He seemed to be staring at something—perhaps all-but-invisible bits of down—floating in the air. He opened his arms wide, lifted himself slightly from his chair, and whipped his palms together with a dry smack. Settling in the chair again, he slowly ran his fingertips along the wrinkles of his brow as if to soften them, and then turned to her with a gentle smile.

"That did it," he said. "Your wish has been granted."

"Already?"

"Yes, it was no trouble at all. Your wish has been granted, lovely miss. Happy birthday. You may go back to work now. Don't worry, I'll put the cart in the hall."

She took the elevator down to the restaurant. Empty-handed now, she felt almost disturbingly light, as though she were walking on some kind of mysterious fluff.

"Are you OK? You look spaced out," the younger waiter said to her.   100

She gave him an ambiguous smile and shook her head. "Oh, really? No, I'm fine."

"Tell me about the owner. What's he like?"

"I dunno, I didn't get a very good look at him," she said, cutting the conversation short.

An hour later she went to bring the cart down. It was out in the hall, utensils in place. She lifted the lid to find the chicken and vegetables gone. The wine bottle and coffeepot were empty. The door to room 604 stood there, closed and expressionless. She stared at it for a time, feeling it might open at any moment, but it did not open. She brought the cart down in the elevator and wheeled it in to the dishwasher. The chef looked blankly at the plate: empty as always.

———————

"I never saw the owner again," she said. "Not once. The manager turned   105
out to have just an ordinary stomachache and went back to delivering the owner's meal again himself the next day. I quit the job after New Year's, and I've never been back to the place. I don't know, I just felt it was better not to go near there, kind of like a premonition."

She toyed with a paper coaster, thinking her own thoughts. "Sometimes I get the feeling that everything that happened to me on my twentieth birthday was some kind of illusion. It's as though something happened to make me think that things happened that never really happened at all. But I know for sure that they *did* happen. I can still bring back vivid images of every piece of furniture and every knickknack in room 604. What happened to me in there really happened, and it had an important meaning for me, too."

The two of us kept silent, drinking our drinks and thinking our separate thoughts.

"Do you mind if I ask you one thing?" I asked. "Or, more precisely, *two* things."

"Go right ahead," she said. "I imagine you're going to ask me what I wished for that time. That's the first thing you want to know."

"But it looks as though you don't want to talk about that."   110

"Does it?"

I nodded.

She put the coaster down and narrowed her eyes as if staring at something in the distance. "You're not supposed to tell anybody what you wished for, you know."

"I won't try to drag it out of you," I said. "I *would* like to know whether or not it came true, though. And also—whatever the wish itself might have been—whether or not you later came to regret what it was you chose to wish for. Were you ever sorry you didn't wish for something else?"

"The answer to the first question is yes and also no. I still have a lot of living left to do, probably. I haven't seen how things are going to work out to the end." 115

"So it was a wish that takes time to come true?"

"You could say that. Time is going to play an important role."

"Like in cooking certain dishes."

She nodded.

I thought about that for a moment, but the only thing that came to mind 120 was the image of a gigantic pie cooking slowly in an oven at low heat.

"And the answer to my second question?"

"What was that again?"

"Whether you ever regretted your choice of what to wish for."

A moment of silence followed. The eyes she turned on me seemed to lack any depth. The desiccated shadow of a smile flickered at the corners of her mouth, suggesting a kind of hushed sense of resignation.

"I'm married now," she said. "To a CPA three years older than me. And I 125 have two children, a boy and a girl. We have an Irish setter. I drive an Audi, and I play tennis with my girlfriends twice a week. That's the life I'm living now."

"Sounds pretty good to me," I said.

"Even if the Audi's bumper has two dents?"

"Hey, bumpers are *made* for denting."

"That would make a great bumper sticker," she said. "'Bumpers are for denting.'"

I looked at her mouth when she said that. 130

"What I'm trying to tell you is this," she said more softly, scratching an earlobe. It was a beautifully shaped earlobe. "No matter what they wish for, no matter how far they go, people can never be anything but themselves. That's all."

"There's another good bumper sticker," I said. "'No matter how far they go, people can never be anything but themselves.'"

She laughed aloud, with a real show of pleasure, and the shadow was gone.

She rested her elbow on the bar and looked at me. "Tell me," she said. "What would you have wished for if you had been in my position?"

"On the night of my twentieth birthday, you mean?"

"Uh-huh." 135

I took some time to think about that, but I couldn't come up with a single wish.

"I can't think of anything," I confessed. "I'm too far away now from my twentieth birthday."

"You really can't think of anything?"

I nodded.

"Not one thing?"

"Not one thing."

She looked into my eyes again — straight in — and said, "That's because you've already *made* your wish."

"But you had better think about it very carefully, my lovely young fairy, because I can grant you only one." In the darkness somewhere, an old man wearing a withered-leaf-colored tie raises a finger. "Just one. You can't change your mind afterward and take it back."

Joyce Carol Oates b. 1938

Where Are You Going, Where Have You Been?   [1966]

For Bob Dylan

Her name was Connie. She was fifteen and she had a quick, nervous giggling habit of craning her neck to glance into mirrors or checking other people's faces to make sure her own was all right. Her mother, who noticed everything and knew everything and who hadn't much reason any longer to look at her own face, always scolded Connie about it. "Stop gawking at yourself. Who are you? You think you're so pretty?" she would say. Connie would raise her eyebrows at these familiar old complaints and look right through her mother, into a shadowy vision of herself as she was right at that moment: she knew she

was pretty and that was everything. Her mother had been pretty once too, if you could believe those old snapshots in the album, but now her looks were gone and that was why she was always after Connie.

"Why don't you keep your room clean like your sister? How've you got your hair fixed — what the hell stinks? Hair spray? You don't see your sister using that junk."

Her sister June was twenty-four and still lived at home. She was a secretary in the high school Connie attended, and if that wasn't bad enough — with her in the same building — she was so plain and chunky and steady that Connie had to hear her praised all the time by her mother and her mother's sisters. June did this, June did that, she saved money and helped clean the house and cooked and Connie couldn't do a thing, her mind was all filled with trashy daydreams.

140

Their father was away at work most of the time and when he came home he wanted supper and he read the newspaper at supper and after supper he went to bed. He didn't bother talking much to them, but around his bent head Connie's mother kept picking at her until Connie wished her mother was dead and she herself was dead and it was all over. "She makes me want to throw up sometimes," she complained to her friends. She had a high, breathless, amused voice that made everything she said sound a little forced, whether it was sincere or not.

There was one good thing: June went places with girl friends of hers, girls who were just as plain and steady as she, and so when Connie wanted to do that her mother had no objections. The father of Connie's best girl friend drove the girls the three miles to town and left them at a shopping plaza so they could walk through the stores or go to a movie, and when he came to pick them up again at eleven he never bothered to ask what they had done.

They must have been familiar sights, walking around the shopping plaza in   5 their shorts and flat ballerina slippers that always scuffed the sidewalk, with charm bracelets jingling on their thin wrists; they would lean together to whisper and laugh secretly if someone passed who amused or interested them. Connie had long dark blond hair that drew anyone's eye to it, and she wore part of it pulled up on her head and puffed out and the rest of it she let fall down her back. She wore a pullover jersey blouse that looked one way when she was at home and another way when she was away from home. Everything about her had two sides to it, one for home and one for anywhere that was not home: her walk, which could be childlike and bobbing, or languid enough to make anyone think she was hearing music in her head; her mouth, which was pale and smirking most of the time, but bright and pink on these evenings out; her laugh, which was cynical and drawling at home — "Ha, ha, very funny" — but high-pitched and nervous anywhere else, like the jingling of the charms on her bracelet.

Sometimes they did go shopping or to a movie, but sometimes they went across the highway, ducking fast across the busy road, to a drive-in restaurant where older kids hung out. The restaurant was shaped like a big bottle, though squatter than a real bottle, and on its cap was a revolving figure of a grinning boy holding a hamburger aloft. One night in midsummer they ran across, breathless with daring, and right away someone leaned out a car window and invited them over, but it was just a boy from high school they didn't like. It made them feel good to be able to ignore him. They went up through the maze of parked and cruising cars to the bright-lit, fly-infested restaurant, their faces pleased and expectant as if they were entering a sacred building that loomed up out of the night to give them what haven and blessing they yearned for. They sat at the counter and crossed their legs at the ankles, their thin shoulders rigid with excitement, and listened to the music that made everything so good: the music was always in the background, like music at a church service; it was something to depend upon.

A boy named Eddie came in to talk with them. He sat backwards on his stool, turning himself jerkily around in semicircles and then stopping and

turning back again, and after a while he asked Connie if she would like something to eat. She said she would and so she tapped her friend's arm on her way
out — her friend pulled her face up into a brave, droll look — and Connie said she
would meet her at eleven, across the way. "I just hate to leave her like that,"
Connie said earnestly, but the boy said that she wouldn't be alone for long. So
they went out to his car, and on the way Connie couldn't help but let her eyes
wander over the windshields and faces all around her, her face gleaming with a
joy that had nothing to do with Eddie or even this place; it might have been the
music. She drew her shoulders up and sucked in her breath with the pure pleasure of being alive, and just at that moment she happened to glance at a face
just a few feet from hers. It was a boy with shaggy black hair, in a convertible
jalopy painted gold. He stared at her and then his lips widened into a grin.
Connie slit her eyes at him and turned away, but she couldn't help glancing
back and there he was, still watching her. He wagged a finger and laughed and
said, "Gonna get you, baby," and Connie turned away again without Eddie
noticing anything.

She spent three hours with him, at the restaurant where they ate hamburgers and drank Cokes in wax cups that were always sweating, and then down an
alley a mile or so away, and when he left her off at five to eleven only the movie
house was still open at the plaza. Her girl friend was there, talking with a boy.
When Connie came up, the two girls smiled at each other and Connie said,
"How was the movie?" and the girl said, "*You* should know." They rode off with
the girl's father, sleepy and pleased, and Connie couldn't help but look back at
the darkened shopping plaza with its big empty parking lot and its signs that
were faded and ghostly now, and over at the drive-in restaurant where cars were
still circling tirelessly. She couldn't hear the music at this distance.

Next morning June asked her how the movie was and Connie said, "So-so."

She and that girl and occasionally another girl went out several times   10
a week, and the rest of the time Connie spent around the house — it was summer vacation — getting in her mother's way and thinking, dreaming about the
boys she met. But all the boys fell back and dissolved into a single face that was
not even a face but an idea, a feeling, mixed up with the urgent insistent pounding of the music and the humid night of July. Connie's mother kept dragging
her back to the daylight by finding things for her to do or saying suddenly,
"What's this about the Pettinger girl?"

And Connie would say nervously, "Oh, her. That dope." She always drew
thick clear lines between herself and such girls, and her mother was simple and
kind enough to believe it. Her mother was so simple, Connie thought, that it
was maybe cruel to fool her so much. Her mother went scuffling around the
house in old bedroom slippers and complained over the telephone to one sister
about the other, then the other called up and the two of them complained
about the third one. If June's name was mentioned her mother's tone was approving, and if Connie's name was mentioned it was disapproving. This did not
really mean she disliked Connie, and actually Connie thought that her mother
preferred her to June just because she was prettier, but the two of them kept up

a pretense of exasperation, a sense that they were tugging and struggling over something of little value to either of them. Sometimes, over coffee, they were almost friends, but something would come up—some vexation that was like a fly buzzing suddenly around their heads—and their faces went hard with contempt.

One Sunday Connie got up at eleven—none of them bothered with church—and washed her hair so that it could dry all day long in the sun. Her parents and sister were going to a barbecue at an aunt's house and Connie said no, she wasn't interested, rolling her eyes to let her mother know just what she thought of it. "Stay home alone then," her mother said sharply. Connie sat out back in a lawn chair and watched them drive away, her father quiet and bald, hunched around so that he could back the car out, her mother with a look that was still angry and not at all softened through the windshield, and in the back seat poor old June, all dressed up as if she didn't know what a barbecue was, with all the running yelling kids and the flies. Connie sat with her eyes closed in the sun, dreaming and dazed with the warmth about her as if this were a kind of love, the caresses of love, and her mind slipped over onto thoughts of the boy she had been with the night before and how nice he had been, how sweet it always was, not the way someone like June would suppose but sweet, gentle, the way it was in movies and promised in songs; and when she opened her eyes she hardly knew where she was, the back yard ran off into weeds and a fence-like line of trees and behind it the sky was perfectly blue and still. The asbestos "ranch house" that was now three years old startled her—it looked small. She shook her head as if to get awake.

It was too hot. She went inside the house and turned on the radio to drown out the quiet. She sat on the edge of her bed, barefoot, and listened for an hour and a half to a program called XYZ Sunday Jamboree, record after record of hard, fast, shrieking songs she sang along with, interspersed by exclamations from "Bobby King": "An' look here, you girls at Napoleon's—Son and Charley want you to pay real close attention to this song coming up!"

And Connie paid close attention herself, bathed in a glow of slow-pulsed joy that seemed to rise mysteriously out of the music itself and lay languidly about the airless little room, breathed in and breathed out with each gentle rise and fall of her chest.

After a while she heard a car coming up the drive. She sat up at once, 15 startled, because it couldn't be her father so soon. The gravel kept crunching all the way in from the road—the driveway was long—and Connie ran to the window. It was a car she didn't know. It was an open jalopy, painted a bright gold that caught the sunlight opaquely. Her heart began to pound and her fingers snatched at her hair, checking it, and she whispered, "Christ, Christ," wondering how bad she looked. The car came to a stop at the side door and the horn sounded four short taps, as if this were a signal Connie knew.

She went into the kitchen and approached the door slowly, then hung out the screen door, her bare toes curling down off the step. There were two boys in the car and now she recognized the driver: he had shaggy, shabby black hair that looked crazy as a wig and he was grinning at her.

"I ain't late, am I?" he said.

"Who the hell do you think you are?" Connie said.

"Toldja I'd be out, didn't I?"

"I don't even know who you are."   20

She spoke sullenly, careful to show no interest or pleasure, and he spoke in a fast, bright monotone. Connie looked past him to the other boy, taking her time. He had fair brown hair, with a lock that fell onto his forehead. His sideburns gave him a fierce, embarrassed look, but so far he hadn't even bothered to glance at her. Both boys wore sunglasses. The driver's glasses were metallic and mirrored everything in miniature.

"You wanta come for a ride?" he said.

Connie smirked and let her hair fall loose over one shoulder.

"Don'tcha like my car? New paint job," he said. "Hey."

"What?"   25

"You're cute."

She pretended to fidget, chasing flies away from the door.

"Don'tcha believe me, or what?" he said.

"Look, I don't even know who you are," Connie said in disgust.

"Hey, Ellie's got a radio, see. Mine broke down." He lifted his friend's arm and 30
showed her the little transistor radio the boy was holding, and now Connie began to hear the music. It was the same program that was playing inside the house.

"Bobby King?" she said.

"I listen to him all the time. I think he's great."

"He's kind of great," Connie said reluctantly.

"Listen, that guy's *great*. He knows where the action is."

Connie blushed a little, because the glasses made it impossible for her to 35
see just what this boy was looking at. She couldn't decide if she liked him or if he was just a jerk, and so she dawdled in the doorway and wouldn't come down or go back inside. She said, "What's all that stuff painted on your car?"

"Can'tcha read it?" He opened the door very carefully, as if he were afraid it might fall off. He slid out just as carefully, planting his feet firmly on the ground, the tiny metallic world in his glasses slowing down like gelatine hardening, and in the midst of it Connie's bright green blouse. "This here is my name, to begin with," he said. ARNOLD FRIEND was written in tarlike black letters on the side, with a drawing of a round, grinning face that reminded Connie of a pumpkin, except it wore sunglasses. "I wanta introduce myself, I'm Arnold Friend and that's my real name and I'm gonna be your friend, honey, and inside the car's Ellie Oscar, he's kinda shy." Ellie brought his transistor radio up to his shoulder and balanced it there. "Now, these numbers are a secret code, honey," Arnold Friend explained. He read off the numbers 33, 19, 17 and raised his eyebrows at her to see what she thought of that, but she didn't think much of it. The left rear fender had been smashed and around it was written, on the gleaming gold background: DONE BY CRAZY WOMAN DRIVER. Connie had to laugh at that. Arnold Friend was pleased at her laughter and looked up at her. "Around the other side's a lot more—you wanta come and seem them?"

"No."

"Why not?"

"Why should I?"

"Don'tcha wanta see what's on the car? Don'tcha wanta go for a ride?"   40

"I don't know."

"Why not?"

"I got things to do."

"Like what?"

"Things."   45

He laughed as if she had said something funny. He slapped his thighs. He was standing in a strange way, leaning back against the car as if he were balancing himself. He wasn't tall, only an inch or so taller than she would be if she came down to him. Connie liked the way he was dressed, which was the way all of them dressed: tight faded jeans stuffed into black, scuffed boots, a belt that pulled his waist in and showed how lean he was, and a white pullover shirt that was a little soiled and showed the hard small muscles of his arms and shoulders. He looked as if he probably did hard work, lifting and carrying things. Even his neck looked muscular. And his face was a familiar face, somehow: the jaw and chin and cheeks slightly darkened because he hadn't shaved for a day or two, and the nose long and hawklike, sniffing as if she were a treat he was going to gobble up and it was all a joke.

"Connie, you ain't telling the truth. This is your day set aside for a ride with me and you know it," he said, still laughing. The way he straightened and recovered from his fit of laughing showed that it had been all fake.

"How do you know what my name is?" she said suspiciously.

"It's Connie."

"Maybe and maybe not."   50

"I know my Connie," he said, wagging his finger. Now she remembered him even better, back at the restaurant, and her cheeks warmed at the thought of how she had sucked in her breath just at the moment she passed him—how she must have looked to him. And he had remembered her. "Ellie and I come out here especially for you," he said. "Ellie can sit in back. How about it?"

"Where?"

"Where what?"

"Where're we going?"

He looked at her. He took off the sunglasses and she saw how pale the skin   55 around his eyes was, like holes that were not in shadow but instead in light. His eyes were like chips of broken glass that catch the light in an amiable way. He smiled. It was as if the idea of going for a ride somewhere, to someplace, was a new idea to him.

"Just for a ride, Connie sweetheart."

"I never said my name was Connie," she said.

"But I know what it is. I know your name and all about you, lots of things," Arnold Friend said. He had not moved yet but stood still leaning back against the side of his jalopy. "I took a special interest in you, such a pretty girl, and

found out all about you—like I know your parents and sister are gone somewheres and I know where and how long they're going to be gone, and I know
who you were with last night, and your best girl friend's name is Betty. Right?"

He spoke in a simple lilting voice, exactly as if he were reciting the words
to a song. His smile assured her that everything was fine. In the car Ellie turned
up the volume on his radio and did not bother to look around at them.

"Ellie can sit in the back seat," Arnold Friend said. He indicated his friend   60
with a casual jerk of his chin, as if Ellie did not count and she should not
bother with him.

"How'd you find out all that stuff?" Connie said.

"Listen: Betty Schultz and Tony Fitch and Jimmy Pettinger and Nancy
Pettinger," he said in a chant. "Raymond Stanley and Bob Hutter—"

"Do you know all those kids?"

"I know everybody."

"Look, you're kidding. You're not from around here."   65

"Sure."

"But—how come we never saw you before?"

"Sure you saw me before," he said. He looked down at his boots, as if he
were a little offended. "You just don't remember."

"I guess I'd remember you," Connie said.

"Yeah?" He looked up at this, beaming. He was pleased. He began to mark   70
time with the music from Ellie's radio, tapping his fists lightly together. Connie
looked away from his smile to the car, which was painted so bright it almost hurt
her eyes to look at it. She looked at that name, ARNOLD FRIEND. And up at the front
fender was an expression that was familiar—MAN THE FLYING SAUCERS. It was an
expression kids had used the year before but didn't use this year. She looked at it
for a while as if the words meant something to her that she did not yet know.

"What're you thinking about? Huh?" Arnold Friend demanded. "Not worried about your hair blowing around in the car, are you?"

"No."

"Think I maybe can't drive good?"

"How do I know?"

"You're a hard girl to handle. How come?" he said. "Don't you know I'm   75
your friend? Didn't you see me put my sign in the air when you walked by?"

"What sign?"

"My sign." And he drew an X in the air, leaning out toward her. They were
maybe ten feet apart. After his hand fell back to his side the X was still in the
air, almost visible. Connie let the screen door close and stood perfectly still
inside it, listening to the music from her radio and the boy's blend together. She
stared at Arnold Friend. He stood there so stiffly relaxed, pretending to be relaxed, with one hand idly on the door handle as if he were keeping himself up
that way and had no intention of ever moving again. She recognized most
things about him, the tight jeans that showed his thighs and buttocks and the
greasy leather boots and the tight shirt, and even that slippery friendly smile of
his, that sleepy dreamy smile that all the boys used to get across ideas they

didn't want to put into words. She recognized all this and also the singsong way he talked, slightly mocking, kidding, but serious and a little melancholy, and she recognized the way he tapped one fist against the other in homage to the perpetual music behind him. But all these things did not come together.

She said suddenly, "Hey, how old are you?"

His smile faded. She could see then that he wasn't a kid, he was much older—thirty, maybe more. At this knowledge her heart began to pound faster.

"That's a crazy thing to ask. Can'tcha see I'm your own age?" 80

"Like hell you are."

"Or maybe a coupla years older. I'm eighteen."

"Eighteen?" she said doubtfully.

He grinned to reassure her and lines appeared at the corners of his mouth. His teeth were big and white. He grinned so broadly his eyes became slits and she saw how thick the lashes were, thick and black as if painted with a black tarlike material. Then, abruptly, he seemed to become embarrassed and looked over his shoulder at Ellie. "*Him*, he's crazy," he said. "Ain't he a riot? He's a nut, a real character." Ellie was still listening to the music. His sunglasses told nothing about what he was thinking. He wore a bright orange shirt unbuttoned halfway to show his chest, which was a pale, bluish chest and not muscular like Arnold Friend's. His shirt collar was turned up all around and the very tips of the collar pointed out past his chin as if they were protecting him. He was pressing the transistor radio up against his ear and sat there in a kind of daze, right in the sun.

"He's kinda strange," Connie said. 85

"Hey, she says you're kinda strange! Kinda strange!" Arnold Friend cried. He pounded on the car to get Ellie's attention. Ellie turned for the first time and Connie saw with shock that he wasn't a kid either—he had a fair, hairless face, cheeks reddened slightly as if the veins grew too close to the surface of his skin, the face of a forty-year-old baby. Connie felt a wave of dizziness rise in her at this sight and she stared at him as if waiting for something to change the shock of the moment, make it all right again. Ellie's lips kept shaping words, mumbling along with the words blasting in his ear.

"Maybe you two better go away," Connie said faintly.

"What? How come?" Arnold Friend cried. "We come out here to take you for a ride. It's Sunday." He had the voice of the man on the radio now. It was the same voice, Connie thought. "Don'tcha know it's Sunday all day? And honey, no matter who you were with last night, today you're with Arnold Friend and don't you forget it! Maybe you better step out here," he said, and this last was in a different voice. It was a little flatter, as if the heat was finally getting to him.

"No. I got things to do."

"Hey." 90

"You two better leave."

"We ain't leaving until you come with us."

"Like hell I am—"

"Connie, don't fool around with me. I mean—I mean, don't fool *around*," he said, shaking his head. He laughed incredulously. He placed his sunglasses on top of his head, carefully, as if he were indeed wearing a wig, and brought the stems down behind his ears. Connie stared at him, another wave of dizziness and fear rising in her so that for a moment he wasn't even in focus but was just a blur standing there against his gold car, and she had the idea that he had driven up the driveway all right but had come from nowhere before that and belonged nowhere and that everything about him and even about the music that was so familiar to her was only half real.

"If my father comes and sees you—"   95

"He ain't coming. He's at a barbecue."

"How do you know that?"

"Aunt Tillie's. Right now they're—uh—they're drinking. Sitting around," he said vaguely, squinting as if he were staring all the way to town and over to Aunt Tillie's back yard. Then the vision seemed to get clear and he nodded energetically. "Yeah. Sitting around. There's your sister in a blue dress, huh? And high heels, the poor sad bitch—nothing like you, sweetheart! And your mother's helping some fat woman with the corn, they're cleaning the corn—husking the corn—"

"What fat woman?" Connie cried.

"How do I know what fat woman, I don't know every goddamn fat woman   100 in the world!" Arnold Friend laughed.

"Oh, that's Mrs. Hornsby. . . . Who invited her?" Connie said. She felt a little lightheaded. Her breath was coming quickly.

"She's too fat. I don't like them fat. I like them the way you are, honey," he said, smiling sleepily at her. They stared at each other for a while through the screen door. He said softly, "Now, what you're going to do is this: you're going to come out that door. You're going to sit up front with me and Ellie's going to sit in the back, the hell with Ellie, right? This isn't Ellie's date. You're my date. I'm your lover, honey."

"What? You're crazy—"

"Yes, I'm your lover. You don't know what that is but you will," he said. "I know that too. I know all about you. But look: it's real nice and you couldn't ask for nobody better than me, or more polite. I always keep my word. I'll tell you how it is, I'm always nice at first, the first time. I'll hold you so tight you won't think you have to try to get away or pretend anything because you'll know you can't. And I'll come inside you where it's all secret and you'll give in to me and you'll love me—"

"Shut up! You're crazy!" Connie said. She backed away from the door. She   105 put her hands up against her ears as if she'd heard something terrible, something not meant for her. "People don't talk like that, you're crazy," she muttered. Her heart was almost too big now for her chest and its pumping made sweat break out all over her. She looked out to see Arnold Friend pause and then take a step toward the porch, lurching. He almost fell. But, like a clever drunken man, he managed to catch his balance. He wobbled in his high boots and grabbed hold of one of the porch posts.

"Honey?" he said. "You still listening?"

"Get the hell out of here!"

"Be nice, honey. Listen."

"I'm going to call the police—"

He wobbled again and out of the side of his mouth came a fast spat curse,   110
an aside not meant for her to hear. But even this "Christ!" sounded forced.
Then he began to smile again. She watched this smile come, awkward as if he
were smiling from inside a mask. His whole face was a mask, she thought
wildly, tanned down to his throat but then running out as if he had plastered
makeup on his face but had forgotten about his throat.

"Honey—? Listen, here's how it is. I always tell the truth and I promise you
this: I ain't coming in that house after you."

"You better not! I'm going to call the police if you—if you don't—"

"Honey," he said, talking right through her voice, "honey, I'm not coming
in there but you are coming out here. You know why?"

She was panting. The kitchen looked like a place she had never seen before,
some room she had run inside but that wasn't good enough, wasn't going to
help her. The kitchen window had never had a curtain, after three years, and
there were dishes in the sink for her to do—probably—and if you ran your hand
across the table you'd probably feel something sticky there.

"You listening, honey? Hey?"   115

"—going to call the police—"

"Soon as you touch the phone I don't need to keep my promise and can
come inside. You won't want that."

She rushed forward and tried to lock the door. Her fingers were shaking.
"But why lock it," Arnold Friend said gently, talking right into her face. "It's just
a screen door. It's just nothing." One of his boots was at a strange angle, as if
his foot wasn't in it. It pointed out to the left, bent at the ankle. "I mean, anybody can break through a screen door and glass and wood and iron or anything
else if he needs to, anybody at all, and specially Arnold Friend. If the place got
lit up with a fire, honey, you'd come runnin' out into my arms, right into my
arms an' safe at home—like you knew I was your lover and'd stopped fooling
around." Part of those words were spoken with a slight rhythmic lilt, and
Connie somehow recognized them—the echo of a song from last year, about a
girl rushing into her boy friend's arms and coming home again—

Connie stood barefoot on the linoleum floor, staring at him. "What do you
want?" she whispered.

"I want you," he said.   120

"What?"

"Seen you that night and thought, that's the one, yes sir. I never needed to
look anymore."

"But my father's coming back. He's coming to get me. I had to wash
my hair first—" She spoke in a dry, rapid voice, hardly raising it for him to hear.

"No, your daddy is not coming and yes, you had to wash your hair and you
washed it for me. It's nice and shining and all for me. I thank you sweetheart,"
he said with a mock bow, but again he almost lost his balance. He had to bend
and adjust his boots. Evidently his feet did not go all the way down; the boots

must have been stuffed with something so that he would seem taller. Connie stared out at him and behind him at Ellie in the car, who seemed to be looking off toward Connie's right, into nothing. This Ellie said, pulling the words out of the air one after another as if he were just discovering them, "You want me to pull out the phone?"

"Shut your mouth and keep it shut," Arnold Friend said, his face red from 125 bending over or maybe from embarrassment because Connie had seen his boots. "This ain't none of your business."

"What — what are you doing? What do you want?" Connie said. "If I call the police they'll get you, they'll arrest you — "

"Promise was not to come in unless you touch that phone, and I'll keep that promise," he said. He resumed his erect position and tried to force his shoulders back. He sounded like a hero in a movie, declaring something important. But he spoke too loudly and it was as if he were speaking to someone behind Connie. "I ain't made plans for coming in that house where I don't belong but just for you to come out to me, the way you should. Don't you know who I am?"

"You're crazy," she whispered. She backed away from the door but did not want to go into another part of the house, as if this would give him permission to come through the door. "What do you . . . you're crazy, you. . . ."

"Huh? What're you saying, honey?"

Her eyes darted everywhere in the kitchen. She could not remember what 130 it was, this room.

"This is how it is, honey: you come out and we'll drive away, have a nice ride. But if you don't come out we're gonna wait till your people come home and then they're all going to get it."

"You want that telephone pulled out?" Ellie said. He held the radio away from his ear and grimaced, as if without the radio the air was too much for him.

"I toldja shut up, Ellie," Arnold Friend said, "you're deaf, get a hearing aid, right? Fix yourself up. This little girl's no trouble and's gonna be nice to me, so Ellie keep to yourself, this ain't your date — right? Don't hem in on me, don't hog, don't crush, don't bird dog, don't trail me," he said in a rapid, meaningless voice, as if he were running through all the expressions he'd learned but was no longer sure which of them was in style, then rushing on to new ones, making them up with his eyes closed. "Don't crawl under my fence, don't squeeze in my chipmunk hole, don't sniff my glue, suck my popsicle, keep your own greasy fingers on yourself!" He shaded his eyes and peered in at Connie, who was backed against the kitchen table. "Don't mind him, honey, he's just a creep. He's a dope. Right? I'm the boy for you and like I said, you come out here nice like a lady and give me your hand, and nobody else gets hurt, I mean, your nice old bald-headed daddy and your mummy and your sister in her high heels. Because listen: why bring them in this?"

"Leave me alone," Connie whispered.

"Hey, you know that old woman down the road, the one with the chickens 135 and stuff — you know her?"

"She's dead!"

"Dead? What? You know her?" Arnold Friend said.

"She's dead —"

"Don't you like her?"

"She's dead — she's — she isn't here any more —" 140

"But don't you like her, I mean, you got something against her? Some grudge or something?" Then his voice dipped as if he were conscious of a rudeness. He touched the sunglasses perched up on top of his head as if to make sure they were still there. "Now, you be a good girl."

"What are you going to do?"

"Just two things, or maybe three," Arnold Friend said. "But I promise it won't last long and you'll like me the way you get to like people you're close to. You will. It's all over for you here, so come on out. You don't want your people in any trouble, do you?"

She turned and bumped against a chair or something, hurting her leg, but she ran into the back room and picked up the telephone. Something roared in her ear, a tiny roaring, and she was so sick with fear that she could do nothing but listen to it — the telephone was clammy and very heavy and her fingers groped down to the dial but were too weak to touch it. She began to scream into the phone, into the roaring. She cried out, she cried for her mother, she felt her breath start jerking back and forth in her lungs as if it were something Arnold Friend was stabbing her with again and again with no tenderness. A noisy sorrowful wailing rose all about her and she was locked inside it the way she was locked inside this house.

After a while she could hear again. She was sitting on the floor with her wet 145 back against the wall.

Arnold Friend was saying from the door, "That's a good girl. Put the phone back."

She kicked the phone away from her.

"No, honey. Pick it up. Put it back right."

She picked it up and put it back. The dial tone stopped.

"That's a good girl. Now, you come outside." 150

She was hollow with what had been fear but what was now just an emptiness. All that screaming had blasted it out of her. She sat, one leg cramped under her, and deep inside her brain was something like a pinpoint of light that kept going and would not let her relax. She thought, I'm not going to see my mother again. She thought, I'm not going to sleep in my bed again. Her bright green blouse was all wet.

Arnold Friend said, in a gentle-loud voice that was like a stage voice, "The place where you came from ain't there any more, and where you had in mind to go is cancelled out. This place you are now — inside your daddy's house — is nothing but a cardboard box I can knock down any time. You know that and always did know it. You hear me?"

She thought, I have got to think. I have got to know what to do.

"We'll go out to a nice field, out in the country here where it smells so nice and it's sunny," Arnold Friend said. "I'll have my arms tight around you so you won't need to try to get away and I'll show you what love is like, what it does.

The hell with this house! It looks solid all right," he said. He ran a fingernail down the screen and the noise did not make Connie shiver, as it would have the day before. "Now, put your hand on your heart, honey. Feel that? That feels solid too but we know better. Be nice to me, be sweet like you can because what else is there for a girl like you but to be sweet and pretty and give in? — and get away before her people come back?"

She felt her pounding heart. Her hand seemed to enclose it. She thought for 155 the first time in her life that it was nothing that was hers, that belonged to her, but just a pounding, living thing inside this body that wasn't really hers either.

"You don't want them to get hurt," Arnold Friend went on. "Now, get up, honey. Get up all by yourself."

She stood.

"Now, turn this way. That's right. Come over here to me. — Ellie, put that away, didn't I tell you? You dope. You miserable creepy dope," Arnold Friend said. His words were not angry but only part of an incantation. The incantation was kindly. "Now, come out through the kitchen to me, honey, and let's see a smile, try it, you're a brave, sweet little girl and now they're eating corn and hot dogs cooked to bursting over an outdoor fire, and they don't know one thing about you and never did and honey, you're better than them because not a one of them would have done this for you."

Connie felt the linoleum under her feet; it was cool. She brushed her hair back out of her eyes. Arnold Friend let go of the post tentatively and opened his arms for her, his elbows pointing in toward each other and his wrists limp, to show that this was an embarrassed embrace and a little mocking, he didn't want to make her self-conscious.

She put out her hand against the screen. She watched herself push the door 160 slowly open as if she were back safe somewhere in the other doorway, watching this body and this head of long hair moving out into the sunlight where Arnold Friend waited.

"My sweet little blue-eyed girl," he said in a half-sung sigh that had nothing to do with her brown eyes but was taken up just the same by the vast sunlit reaches of the land behind him and on all sides of him — so much land that Connie had never seen before and did not recognize except to know that she was going to it.

Tim O'Brien b. 1946

The Things They Carried   [1986]

First Lieutenant Jimmy Cross carried letters from a girl named Martha, a junior at Mount Sebastian College in New Jersey. They were not love letters, but Lieutenant Cross was hoping, so he kept them folded in plastic at the bottom of his rucksack. In the late afternoon, after a day's march, he would dig his foxhole, wash his hands under a canteen, unwrap the letters, hold them with the tips of his fingers, and spend the last hour of light pretending. He would imagine romantic camping trips into the White Mountains in New Hampshire. He would sometimes taste the envelope flaps, knowing her tongue had been there. More than anything, he wanted Martha to love him as he loved her, but the letters were mostly chatty, elusive on the matter of love. She was a virgin, he was almost sure. She was an English major at Mount Sebastian, and she wrote beautifully about her professors and roommates and midterm exams, about her respect for Chaucer and her great affection for Virginia Woolf. She often quoted lines of poetry; she never mentioned the war, except to say, Jimmy, take care of yourself. The letters weighed 10 ounces. They were signed Love, Martha, but Lieutenant Cross understood that Love was only a way of signing and did not mean what he sometimes pretended it meant. At dusk, he would carefully return the letters to his rucksack. Slowly, a bit distracted, he would get up and move among his men, checking the perimeter, then at full dark he would return to his hole and watch the night and wonder if Martha was a virgin.

The things they carried were largely determined by necessity. Among the necessities or near-necessities were P-38 can openers, pocket knives, heat tabs, wristwatches, dog tags, mosquito repellent, chewing gum, candy, cigarettes, salt tablets, packets of Kool-Aid, lighters, matches, sewing kits, Military Payment Certificates, C rations, and two or three canteens of water. Together, these items weighed between 15 and 20 pounds, depending upon a man's habits or rate of metabolism. Henry Dobbins, who was a big man, carried extra rations; he was especially fond of canned peaches in heavy syrup over pound cake. Dave Jensen, who practiced field hygiene, carried a toothbrush, dental floss, and several hotel-sized bars of soap he'd stolen on R&R° in Sydney, Australia. Ted Lavender, who was scared, carried tranquilizers until he was shot in the head outside the village of Than Khe in mid-April. By necessity, and because it was SOP,° they all carried steel helmets that weighed 5 pounds including the liner and camouflage cover. They carried the standard fatigue jackets and trousers. Very few carried under-wear. On their feet they carried jungle boots — 2.1 pounds — and Dave Jensen carried three pairs of socks and a can of Dr. Scholl's foot powder as a precaution against trench foot. Until he was shot, Ted Lavender carried six or seven ounces of premium dope, which for him was a necessity. Mitchell Sanders, the RTO,° carried condoms. Norman Bowker carried a diary. Rat Kiley carried comic books. Kiowa, a devout Baptist, carried an illustrated New Testament that had been pre-sented to him by his father, who taught Sunday school in Oklahoma City, Oklahoma. As a hedge against bad times, however, Kiowa also carried his grand-mother's distrust of the white man, his grandfather's old hunting hatchet. Necessity dictated. Because the land was mined and booby-trapped, it was SOP for each man to carry a steel-centered, nylon-covered flak jacket, which weighed

---

R&R: Rest and recreation; a brief getaway from active service.   SOP: Standard operating procedure.   RTO: Radio and telephone operator.

6.7 pounds, but which on hot days seemed much heavier. Because you could die so quickly, each man carried at least one large compress bandage, usually in the helmet band for easy access. Because the nights were cold, and because the monsoons were wet, each carried a green plastic poncho that could be used as a raincoat or groundsheet or makeshift tent. With its quilted liner, the poncho weighed almost two pounds, but it was worth every ounce. In April, for instance, when Ted Lavender was shot, they used his poncho to wrap him up, then to carry him across the paddy, then to lift him into the chopper that took him away.

They were called legs or grunts.

To carry something was to hump it, as when Lieutenant Jimmy Cross humped his love for Martha up the hills and through the swamps. In its intransitive form, to hump meant to walk, or to march, but it implied burdens far beyond the intransitive.

Almost everyone humped photographs. In his wallet, Lieutenant Cross carried two photographs of Martha. The first was a Kodacolor snapshot signed Love, though he knew better. She stood against a brick wall. Her eyes were gray and neutral, her lips slightly open as she stared straight-on at the camera. At night, sometimes, Lieutenant Cross wondered who had taken the picture, because he knew she had boyfriends, because he loved her so much, and because he could see the shadow of the picture-taker spreading out against the brick wall. The second photograph had been clipped from the 1968 Mount Sebastian yearbook. It was an action shot—women's volleyball—and Martha was bent horizontal to the floor, reaching, the palms of her hands in sharp focus, the tongue taut, the expression frank and competitive. There was no visible sweat. She wore white gym shorts. Her legs, he thought, were almost certainly the legs of a virgin, dry and without hair, the left knee cocked and carrying her entire weight, which was just over one hundred pounds. Lieutenant Cross remembered touching that left knee. A dark theater, he remembered, and the movie was *Bonnie and Clyde*, and Martha wore a tweed skirt, and during the final scene, when he touched her knee, she turned and looked at him in a sad, sober way that made him pull his hand back, but he would always remember the feel of the tweed skirt and the knee beneath it and the sound of the gunfire that killed Bonnie and Clyde, how embarrassing it was, how slow and oppressive. He remembered kissing her good night at the dorm door. Right then, he thought, he should've done something brave. He should've carried her up the stairs to her room and tied her to the bed and touched that left knee all night long. He should've risked it. Whenever he looked at the photographs, he thought of new things he should've done.

What they carried was partly a function of rank, partly of field specialty.

As a first lieutenant and platoon leader, Jimmy Cross carried a compass, maps, code books, binoculars, and a .45-caliber pistol that weighed 2.9 pounds fully loaded. He carried a strobe light and the responsibility for the lives of his men.

As an RTO, Mitchell Sanders carried the PRC-25 radio, a killer, 26 pounds with its battery.

As a medic, Rat Kiley carried a canvas satchel filled with morphine and plasma and malaria tablets and surgical tape and comic books and all the things a medic must carry, including M&M's° for especially bad wounds, for a total weight of nearly 20 pounds.

As a big man, therefore a machine gunner, Henry Dobbins carried the   10 M-60, which weighed 23 pounds unloaded, but which was almost always loaded. In addition, Dobbins carried between 10 and 15 pounds of ammunition draped in belts across his chest and shoulders.

As PFCs or Spec 4s, most of them were common grunts and carried the standard M-16 gas-operated assault rifle. The weapon weighed 7.5 pounds un-loaded, 8.2 pounds with its full 20-round magazine. Depending on numerous factors, such as topography and psychology, the riflemen carried anywhere from 12 to 20 magazines, usually in cloth bandoliers, adding on another 8.4 pounds at minimum, 14 pounds at maximum. When it was available, they also carried M-16 maintenance gear—rods and steel brushes and swabs and tubes of LSA oil—all of which weighed about a pound. Among the grunts, some carried the M-79 grenade launcher, 5.9 pounds unloaded, a reasonably light weapon except for the ammunition, which was heavy. A single round weighed 10 ounces. The typical load was 25 rounds. But Ted Lavender, who was scared, carried 34 rounds when he was shot and killed outside Than Khe, and he went down under an exceptional burden, more than 20 pounds of ammunition, plus the flak jacket and helmet and rations and water and toilet paper and tranquilizers and all the rest, plus the unweighed fear. He was dead weight. There was no twitch-ing or flopping. Kiowa, who saw it happen, said it was like watching a rock fall, or a big sandbag or something—just boom, then down—not like the movies where the dead guy rolls around and does fancy spins and goes ass over teakettle—not like that, Kiowa said, the poor bastard just flat-fuck fell. Boom. Down. Nothing else. It was a bright morning in mid-April. Lieutenant Cross felt the pain. He blamed himself. They stripped off Lavender's canteens and ammo, all the heavy things, and Rat Kiley said the obvious, the guy's dead, and Mitchell Sanders used his radio to report one U.S. KIA° and to request a chopper. Then they wrapped Lavender in his poncho. They carried him out to a dry paddy, established security, and sat smoking the dead man's dope until the chopper came. Lieutenant Cross kept to himself. He pictured Martha's smooth young face, thinking he loved her more than anything, more than his men, and now Ted Lavender was dead because he loved her so much and could not stop think-ing about her. When the dustoff arrived, they carried Lavender aboard. Afterward they burned Than Khe. They marched until dusk, then dug their holes, and that night Kiowa kept explaining how you had to be there, how fast it was, how the poor guy just dropped like so much concrete. Boom-down, he said. Like cement.

M&M's: Medical supplies.   **KIA:** Killed in action.

In addition to the three standard weapons—the M-60, M-16, and M-79—they carried whatever presented itself, or whatever seemed appropriate as a means of killing or staying alive. They carried catch-as-catch-can. At various times, in various situations, they carried M-14s and CAR-15s and Swedish Ks and grease guns and captured AK-47s and Chi-Coms and RPGs and Simonov carbines and black market Uzis and .38-caliber Smith & Wesson handguns and 66 mm LAWs and shotguns and silencers and blackjacks and bayonets and C-4 plastic explosives. Lee Strunk carried a slingshot; a weapon of last resort, he called it. Mitchell Sanders carried brass knuckles. Kiowa carried his grandfather's feathered hatchet. Every third or fourth man carried a Claymore antipersonnel mine—3.5 pounds with its firing device. They all carried fragmentation grenades—14 ounces each. They all carried at least one M-18 colored smoke grenade—24 ounces. Some carried CS or tear gas grenades. Some carried white phosphorus grenades. They carried all they could bear, and then some, including a silent awe for the terrible power of the things they carried.

In the first week of April, before Lavender died, Lieutenant Jimmy Cross received a good-luck charm from Martha. It was a simple pebble, an ounce at most. Smooth to the touch, it was a milky white color with flecks of orange and violet, oval-shaped, like a miniature egg. In the accompanying letter, Martha wrote that she had found the pebble on the Jersey shoreline, precisely where the land touched water at high tide, where things came together but also separated. It was this separate-but-together quality, she wrote, that had inspired her to pick up the pebble and to carry it in her breast pocket for several days, where it seemed weightless, and then to send it through the mail, by air, as a token of her truest feelings for him. Lieutenant Cross found this romantic. But he wondered what her truest feelings were, exactly, and what she meant by separate-but-together. He wondered how the tides and waves had come into play on that afternoon along the Jersey shoreline when Martha saw the pebble and bent down to rescue it from geology. He imagined bare feet. Martha was a poet, with the poet's sensibilities, and her feet would be brown and bare, the toenails unpainted, the eyes chilly and somber like the ocean in March, and though it was painful, he wondered who had been with her that afternoon. He imagined a pair of shadows moving along the strip of sand where things came together but also separated. It was phantom jealousy, he knew, but he couldn't help himself. He loved her so much. On the march, through the hot days of early April, he carried the pebble in his mouth, turning it with his tongue, tasting sea salt and moisture. His mind wandered. He had difficulty keeping his attention on the war. On occasion he would yell at his men to spread out the column, to keep their eyes open, but then he would slip away into daydreams, just pretending, walking barefoot along the Jersey shore, with Martha, carrying nothing. He would feel himself rising. Sun and waves and gentle winds, all love and lightness.

What they carried varied by mission.

When a mission took them to the mountains, they carried mosquito netting, machetes, canvas tarps, and extra bug juice.   15

If a mission seemed especially hazardous, or if it involved a place they knew to be bad, they carried everything they could. In certain heavily mined AOs,° where the land was dense with Toe Poppers and Bouncing Betties, they took turns humping a 28-pound mine detector. With its headphones and big sensing plate, the equipment was a stress on the lower back and shoulders, awkward to handle, often useless because of the shrapnel in the earth, but they carried it anyway, partly for safety, partly for the illusion of safety.

On ambush, or other night missions, they carried peculiar little odds and ends. Kiowa always took along his New Testament and a pair of moccasins for silence. Dave Jensen carried night-sight vitamins high in carotene. Lee Strunk carried his slingshot; ammo, he claimed, would never be a problem. Rat Kiley carried brandy and M&M's candy. Until he was shot, Ted Lavender carried the starlight scope, which weighed 6.3 pounds with its aluminum carrying case. Henry Dobbins carried his girlfriend's pantyhose wrapped around his neck as a comforter. They all carried ghosts. When dark came, they would move out single file across the meadows and paddies to their ambush coordinates, where they would quietly set up the Claymores and lie down and spend the night waiting.

Other missions were more complicated and required special equipment. In mid-April, it was their mission to search out and destroy the elaborate tunnel complexes in the Than Khe area south of Chu Lai. To blow the tunnels, they carried one-pound blocks of pentrite high explosives, four blocks to a man, 68 pounds in all. They carried wiring, detonators, and battery-powered clackers. Dave Jensen carried earplugs. Most often, before blowing the tunnels, they were ordered by higher command to search them, which was considered bad news,° but by and large they just shrugged and carried out orders. Because he was a big man, Henry Dobbins was excused from tunnel duty. The others would draw numbers. Before Lavender died there were 17 men in the platoon, and whoever drew the number 17 would strip off his gear and crawl in headfirst with a flashlight and Lieutenant Cross's .45-caliber pistol. The rest of them would fan out as security. They would sit down or kneel, not facing the hole, listening to the ground beneath them, imagining cobwebs and ghosts, whatever was down there—the tunnel walls squeezing in—how the flashlight seemed impossibly heavy in the hand and how it was tunnel vision in the very strictest sense, compression in all ways, even time, and how you had to wiggle in—ass and elbows—a swallowed-up feeling—and how you found yourself worrying about odd things: Will your flashlight go dead? Do rats carry rabies? If you screamed, how far would the sound carry? Would your buddies hear it? Would they have the courage to drag you out? In some respects, though not many, the waiting was worse than the tunnel itself. Imagination was a killer.

On April 16, when Lee Strunk drew the number 17, he laughed and muttered something and went down quickly. The morning was hot and very still. Not good, Kiowa said. He looked at the tunnel opening, then out across a dry paddy toward the village of Than Khe. Nothing moved. No clouds or birds or

---

AOs: Areas of operations.

people. As they waited, the men smoked and drank Kool-Aid, not talking much, feeling sympathy for Lee Strunk but also feeling the luck of the draw. You win some, you lose some, said Mitchell Sanders, and sometimes you settle for a rain check. It was a tired line and no one laughed.

Henry Dobbins ate a tropical chocolate bar. Ted Lavender popped a tran- 20 quilizer and went off to pee.

After five minutes, Lieutenant Jimmy Cross moved to the tunnel, leaned down, and examined the darkness. Trouble, he thought — a cave-in maybe. And then suddenly, without willing it, he was thinking about Martha. The stresses and fractures, the quick collapse, the two of them buried alive under all that weight. Dense, crushing love. Kneeling, watching the hole, he tried to concentrate on Lee Strunk and the war, all the dangers, but his love was too much for him, he felt paralyzed, he wanted to sleep inside her lungs and breathe her blood and be smothered. He wanted her to be a virgin and not a virgin, all at once. He wanted to know her. Intimate secrets: Why poetry? Why so sad? Why that grayness in her eyes? Why so alone? Not lonely, just alone — riding her bike across campus or sitting off by herself in the cafeteria — even dancing, she danced alone — and it was the aloneness that filled him with love. He remembered telling her that one evening. How she nodded and looked away. And how, later, when he kissed her, she received the kiss without returning it, her eyes wide open, not afraid, not a virgin's eyes, just flat and uninvolved.

Lieutenant Cross gazed at the tunnel. But he was not there. He was buried with Martha under the white sand at the Jersey shore. They were pressed together, and the pebble in his mouth was her tongue. He was smiling. Vaguely, he was aware of how quiet the day was, the sullen paddies, yet he could not bring himself to worry about matters of security. He was beyond that. He was just a kid at war, in love. He was twenty-four years old. He couldn't help it.

A few moments later Lee Strunk crawled out of the tunnel. He came up grinning, filthy but alive. Lieutenant Cross nodded and closed his eyes while the others clapped Strunk on the back and made jokes about rising from the dead.

Worms, Rat Kiley said. Right out of the grave. Fuckin' zombie.

The men laughed. They all felt great relief.   25

Spook city, said Mitchell Sanders.

Lee Strunk made a funny ghost sound, a kind of moaning, yet very happy, and right then, when Strunk made that high happy moaning sound, when he went *Ahhooooo*, right then Ted Lavender was shot in the head on his way back from peeing. He lay with his mouth open. The teeth were broken. There was a swollen black bruise under his left eye. The cheekbone was gone. Oh shit, Rat Kiley said, the guy's dead. The guy's dead, he kept saying, which seemed profound — the guy's dead. I mean really.

The things they carried were determined to some extent by superstition. Lieutenant Cross carried his good-luck pebble. Dave Jensen carried a rabbit's foot. Norman Bowker, otherwise a very gentle person, carried a thumb that had been presented to him as a gift by Mitchell Sanders. The thumb was dark brown, rubbery to the touch, and weighed four ounces at most. It had been cut from a VC corpse, a boy of fifteen or sixteen. They'd found him at the bottom of an irrigation ditch, badly burned, flies in his mouth and eyes. The boy wore black shorts and sandals. At the time of his death he had been carrying a pouch of rice, a rifle, and three magazines of ammunition.

You want my opinion, Mitchell Sanders said, there's a definite moral here.

He put his hand on the dead boy's wrist. He was quiet for a time, as if 30 counting a pulse, then he patted the stomach, almost affectionately, and used Kiowa's hunting hatchet to remove the thumb.

Henry Dobbins asked what the moral was.

Moral?

You know. *Moral.*

Sanders wrapped the thumb in toilet paper and handed it across to Norman Bowker. There was no blood. Smiling, he kicked the boy's head, watched the flies scatter, and said, It's like with that old TV show—Paladin. Have gun, will travel.

Henry Dobbins thought about it.   35

Yeah, well, he finally said. I don't see no moral.

There it *is*, man.

Fuck off.

They carried USO° stationery and pencils and pens. They carried Sterno, safety pins, trip flares, signal flares, spools of wire, razor blades, chewing tobacco, liberated joss sticks and statuettes of the smiling Buddha, candles, grease pencils, *The Stars and Stripes*, fingernail clippers, Psy Ops° leaflets, bush hats, bolos, and much more. Twice a week, when the resupply choppers came in, they carried hot chow in green mermite cans and large canvas bags filled with iced beer and soda pop. They carried plastic water containers, each with a two-gallon capacity. Mitchell Sanders carried a set of starched tiger fatigues for special occasions. Henry Dobbins carried Black Flag insecticide. Dave Jensen carried empty sandbags that could be filled at night for added protection. Lee Strunk carried tanning lotion. Some things they carried in common. Taking turns, they carried the big PRC-77 scrambler radio, which weighed 30 pounds with its battery. They shared the weight of memory. They took up what others could no longer bear. Often, they carried each other, the wounded or weak. They carried infections. They carried chess sets, basketballs, Vietnamese-English dictionaries, insignia of rank, Bronze Stars and Purple Hearts, plastic cards imprinted with the Code of Conduct. They carried diseases, among them malaria and dysentery. They carried lice and ringworm and leeches and paddy algae and various rots and molds. They carried the land itself—Vietnam, the place, the soil—a powdery orange-red dust that covered their boots and fatigues and faces. They carried the sky. The whole atmosphere, they carried it, the humidity, the monsoons, the stink of fungus and decay, all of it, they carried gravity. They moved like mules. By daylight they took sniper fire, at night they were mortared,

---

USO: United Service Organization.   **Psy Ops:** Psychological operations.

but it was not battle, it was just the endless march, village to village, without purpose, nothing won or lost. They marched for the sake of the march. They plodded along slowly, dumbly, leaning forward against the heat, unthinking, all blood and bone, simple grunts, soldiering with their legs, toiling up the hills and down into the paddies and across the rivers and up again and down, just humping, one step and then the next and then another, but no volition, no will, because it was automatic, it was anatomy, and the war was entirely a matter of posture and carriage, the hump was everything, a kind of inertia, a kind of emptiness, a dullness of desire and intellect and conscience and hope and human sensibility. Their principles were in their feet. Their calculations were biological. They had no sense of strategy or mission. They searched the villages without knowing what to look for, not caring, kicking over jars of rice, frisking children and old men, blowing tunnels, sometimes setting fires and sometimes not, then forming up and moving on to the next village, then other villages, where it would always be the same. They carried their own lives. The pressures were enormous. In the heat of early afternoon, they would remove their helmets and flak jackets, walking bare, which was dangerous but which helped ease the strain. They would often discard things along the route of march. Purely for comfort, they would throw away rations, blow their Claymores and grenades, no matter because by nightfall the resupply choppers would arrive with more of the same, then a day or two later still more, fresh watermelons and crates of ammunition and sunglasses and woolen sweaters—the resources were stunning—sparklers for the Fourth of July, colored eggs for Easter—it was the great American war chest—the fruits of science, the smokestacks, the canneries, the arsenals at Hartford, the Minnesota forests, the machine shops, the vast fields of corn and wheat—they carried like freight trains; they carried it on their backs and shoulders—and for all the ambiguities of Vietnam, all the mysteries and unknowns, there was at least the single abiding certainty that they would never be at a loss for things to carry.

After the chopper took Lavender away, Lieutenant Jimmy Cross led his men   40
into the village of Than Khe. They burned everything. They shot chickens and dogs, they trashed the village well, they called in artillery and watched the wreckage, then they marched for several hours through the hot afternoon, and then at dusk, while Kiowa explained how Lavender died, Lieutenant Cross found himself trembling.

He tried not to cry. With his entrenching tool, which weighed five pounds, he began digging a hole in the earth.

He felt shame. He hated himself. He had loved Martha more than his men, and as a consequence Lavender was now dead, and this was something he would have to carry like a stone in his stomach for the rest of the war.

All he could do was dig. He used his entrenching tool like an ax, slashing, feeling both love and hate, and then later, when it was full dark, he sat at the bottom of his foxhole and wept. It went on for a long while. In part, he was grieving for Ted Lavender, but mostly it was for Martha, and for himself, because she belonged to another world, which was not quite real, and because she was a junior at Mount Sebastian College in New Jersey, a poet and a virgin and uninvolved, and because he realized she did not love him and never would.

Like cement, Kiowa whispered in the dark. I swear to God—boom, down. Not a word.

I've heard this, said Norman Bowker.   45

A pisser, you know? Still zipping himself up. Zapped while zipping.

All right, fine. That's enough.

Yeah, but you had to see it, the guy just—

I *heard*, man. Cement. So why not shut the fuck *up?*

Kiowa shook his head sadly and glanced over at the hole where Lieutenant   50
Jimmy Cross sat watching the night. The air was thick and wet. A warm dense fog had settled over the paddies and there was the stillness that precedes rain.

After a time Kiowa sighed.

One thing for sure, he said. The lieutenant's in some deep hurt. I mean that crying jag—the way he was carrying on—it wasn't fake or anything, it was real heavy-duty hurt. The man cares.

Sure, Norman Bowker said.

Say what you want, the man does care.

We all got problems.   55

Not Lavender.

No, I guess not, Bowker said. Do me a favor, though.

Shut up?

That's a smart Indian. Shut up.

Shrugging, Kiowa pulled off his boots. He wanted to say more, just to   60
lighten up his sleep, but instead he opened his New Testament and arranged it beneath his head as a pillow. The fog made things seem hollow and unattached. He tried not to think about Ted Lavender, but then he was thinking how fast it was, no drama, down and dead, and how it was hard to feel anything except surprise. It seemed unchristian. He wished he could find some great sadness, or even anger, but the emotion wasn't there and he couldn't make it happen. Mostly he felt pleased to be alive. He liked the smell of the New Testament under his cheek, the leather and ink and paper and glue, whatever the chemicals were. He liked hearing the sounds of night. Even his fatigue, it felt fine, the stiff muscles and the prickly awareness of his own body, a floating feeling. He enjoyed not being dead. Lying there, Kiowa admired Lieutenant Jimmy Cross's capacity for grief. He wanted to share the man's pain, he wanted to care as Jimmy Cross cared. And yet when he closed his eyes, all he could think was Boom-down, and all he could feel was the pleasure of having his boots off and the fog curling in around him and the damp soil and the Bible smells and the plush comfort of night.

After a moment Norman Bowker sat up in the dark.

What the hell, he said. You want to talk, *talk*. Tell it to me.

Forget it.

No, man, go on. One thing I hate, it's a silent Indian.

———

For the most part they carried themselves with poise, a kind of dignity. Now 65 and then, however, there were times of panic, when they squealed or wanted to squeal but couldn't, when they twitched and made moaning sounds and covered their heads and said Dear Jesus and flopped around on the earth and fired their weapons blindly and cringed and sobbed and begged for the noise to stop and went wild and made stupid promises to themselves and to God and to their mothers and fathers, hoping not to die. In different ways, it happened to all of them. Afterward, when the firing ended, they would blink and peek up. They would touch their bodies, feeling shame, then quickly hiding it. They would force themselves to stand. As if in slow motion, frame by frame, the world would take on the old logic—absolute silence, then the wind, then sunlight, then voices. It was the burden of being alive. Awkwardly, the men would reassemble themselves, first in private, then in groups, becoming soldiers again. They would repair the leaks in their eyes. They would check for casualties, call in dustoffs, light cigarettes, try to smile, clear their throats and spit and begin cleaning their weapons. After a time someone would shake his head and say, No lie, I almost shit my pants, and someone else would laugh, which meant it was bad, yes, but the guy had obviously not shit his pants, it wasn't that bad, and in any case nobody would ever do such a thing and then go ahead and talk about it. They would squint into the dense, oppressive sunlight. For a few moments, perhaps, they would fall silent, lighting a joint and tracking its passage from man to man, inhaling, holding in the humiliation. Scary stuff, one of them might say. But then someone else would grin or flick his eyebrows and say, Roger-dodger, almost cut me a new asshole, *almost.*

There were numerous such poses. Some carried themselves with a sort of wistful resignation, others with pride or stiff soldierly discipline or good humor or macho zeal. They were afraid of dying but they were even more afraid to show it.

They found jokes to tell.

They used a hard vocabulary to contain the terrible softness. *Greased* they'd say. *Offed, lit up, zapped while zipping.* It wasn't cruelty, just stage presence. They were actors. When someone died, it wasn't quite dying, because in a curious way it seemed scripted, and because they had their lines mostly memorized, irony mixed with tragedy, and because they called it by other names, as if to encyst and destroy the reality of death itself. They kicked corpses. They cut off thumbs. They talked grunt lingo. They told stories about Ted Lavender's supply of tranquilizers, how the poor guy didn't feel a thing, how incredibly tranquil he was.

There's a moral here, said Mitchell Sanders.

They were waiting for Lavender's chopper, smoking the dead man's dope. 70

The moral's pretty obvious, Sanders said, and winked. Stay away from drugs. No joke, they'll ruin your day every time.

Cute, said Henry Dobbins.

Mind blower, get it? Talk about wiggy. Nothing left, just blood and brains.

They made themselves laugh.

There it is, they'd say. Over and over—there it is, my friend, there it is—as   75
if the repetition itself were an act of poise, a balance between crazy and almost
crazy, knowing without going, there it is, which meant be cool, let it ride, because Oh yeah, man, you can't change what can't be changed, there it is, there
it absolutely and positively and fucking well *is*.

They were tough.

They carried all the emotional baggage of men who might die. Grief, terror,
love, longing—these were intangibles, but the intangibles had their own mass and
specific gravity, they had tangible weight. They carried shameful memories. They
carried the common secret of cowardice barely restrained, the instinct to run or
freeze or hide, and in many respects this was the heaviest burden of all, for it could
never be put down, it required perfect balance and perfect posture. They carried their
reputations. They carried the soldier's greatest fear, which was the fear of blushing.
Men killed, and died, because they were embarrassed not to. It was what had
brought them to the war in the first place, nothing positive, no dreams of glory or
honor, just to avoid the blush of dishonor. They died so as not to die of embarrassment. They crawled into tunnels and walked point and advanced under fire. Each
morning, despite the unknowns, they made their legs move. They endured. They
kept humping. They did not submit to the obvious alternative, which was simply to
close the eyes and fall. So easy, really. Go limp and tumble to the ground and let the
muscles unwind and not speak and not budge until your buddies picked you up and
lifted you into the chopper that would roar and dip its nose and carry you off to the
world. A mere matter of falling, yet no one ever fell. It was not courage, exactly; the
object was not valor. Rather, they were too frightened to be cowards.

By and large they carried these things inside, maintaining the masks of
composure. They sneered at sick call. They spoke bitterly about guys who had
found release by shooting off their own toes or fingers. Pussies, they'd say.
Candyasses. It was fierce, mocking talk, with only a trace of envy or awe, but
even so the image played itself out behind their eyes.

They imagined the muzzle against flesh. So easy: squeeze the trigger and
blow away a toe. They imagined it. They imagined the quick, sweet pain, then the
evacuation to Japan, then a hospital with warm beds and cute geisha nurses.

And they dreamed of freedom birds.   80

At night, on guard, staring into the dark, they were carried away by jumbo
jets. They felt the rush of takeoff. *Gone!* they yelled. And then velocity—wings
and engines—a smiling stewardess—but it was more than a plane, it was a real
bird, a big sleek silver bird with feathers and talons and high screeching. They
were flying. The weights fell off; there was nothing to bear. They laughed and
held on tight, feeling the cold slap of wind and altitude, soaring, thinking *It's
over, I'm gone!*—they were naked, they were light and free—it was all lightness,
bright and fast and buoyant, light as light, a helium buzz in the brain, a giddy
bubbling in the lungs as they were taken up over the clouds and the war, beyond
duty, beyond gravity and mortification and global entanglements—*Sin loi!*° they

---

Sin loi: Vietnamese for "sorry."

yelled. *I'm sorry, motherfuckers, but I'm out of it, I'm goofed, I'm on a space cruise, I'm gone!* — and it was a restful, unencumbered sensation, just riding the light waves, sailing that big silver freedom bird over the mountains and oceans, over America, over the farms and great sleeping cities and cemeteries and highways and the golden arches of McDonald's, it was flight, a kind of fleeing, a kind of falling, falling higher and higher, spinning off the edge of the earth and beyond the sun and through the vast, silent vacuum where there were no burdens and where everything weighed exactly nothing — *Gone!* they screamed. *I'm sorry but I'm gone!* — and so at night, not quite dreaming, they gave themselves over to lightness, they were carried, they were purely borne.

On the morning after Ted Lavender died, First Lieutenant Jimmy Cross crouched at the bottom of his foxhole and burned Martha's letters. Then he burned the two photographs. There was a steady rain falling, which made it difficult, but he used heat tabs and Sterno to build a small fire, screening it with his body, holding the photographs over the tight blue flame with the tips of his fingers.

He realized it was only a gesture. Stupid, he thought. Sentimental, too, but mostly just stupid.

Lavender was dead. You couldn't burn the blame.

Besides, the letters were in his head. And even now, without photographs, Lieutenant Cross could see Martha playing volleyball in her white gym shorts and yellow T-shirt. He could see her moving in the rain.   85

When the fire died out, Lieutenant Cross pulled his poncho over his shoulders and ate breakfast from a can.

There was no great mystery, he decided.

In those burned letters Martha had never mentioned the war, except to say, Jimmy, take care of yourself. She wasn't involved. She signed the letters Love, but it wasn't love, and all the fine lines and technicalities did not matter. Virginity was no longer an issue. He hated her. Yes, he did. He hated her. Love, too, but it was a hard, hating kind of love.

The morning came up wet and blurry. Everything seemed part of everything else, the fog and Martha and the deepening rain.

He was a soldier, after all.   90

Half smiling, Lieutenant Jimmy Cross took out his maps. He shook his head hard, as if to clear it, then bent forward and began planning the day's march. In ten minutes, or maybe twenty, he would rouse the men and they would pack up and head west, where the maps showed the country to be green and inviting. They would do what they had always done. The rain might add some weight, but otherwise it would be one more day layered upon all the other days.

He was realistic about it. There was that new hardness in his stomach. He loved her but he hated her.

No more fantasies, he told himself.

Henceforth, when he thought about Martha, it would be only to think that she belonged elsewhere. He would shut down the daydreams. This was not Mount Sebastian, it was another world, where there were no pretty poems or mid-term exams, a place where men died because of carelessness and gross stupidity. Kiowa was right. Boom-down, and you were dead, never partly dead.

Briefly, in the rain, Lieutenant Cross saw Martha's gray eyes gazing back at him. 95 He understood.

It was very sad, he thought. The things men carried inside. The things men did or felt they had to do.

He almost nodded at her, but didn't.

Instead he went back to his maps. He was now determined to perform his duties firmly and without negligence. It wouldn't help Lavender, he knew that, but from this point on he would comport himself as an officer. He would dispose of his good-luck pebble. Swallow it, maybe, or use Lee Strunk's slingshot, or just drop it along the trail. On the march he would impose strict field discipline. He would be careful to send out flank security, to prevent straggling or bunching up, to keep his troops moving at the proper pace and at the proper interval. He would insist on clean weapons. He would confiscate the remainder of Lavender's dope. Later in the day, perhaps, he would call the men together and speak to them plainly. He would accept the blame for what had happened to Ted Lavender. He would be a man about it. He would look them in the eyes, keeping his chin level, and he would issue the new SOPs in a calm, impersonal tone of voice, a lieutenant's voice, leaving no room for argument or discussion. Commencing immediately, he'd tell them, they would no longer abandon equipment along the route of march. They would police up their acts. They would get their shit together, and keep it together, and maintain it neatly and in good working order.

He would not tolerate laxity. He would show strength, distancing himself. 100

Among the men there would be grumbling, of course, and maybe worse, because their days would seem longer and their loads heavier, but Lieutenant Jimmy Cross reminded himself that his obligation was not to be loved but to lead. He would dispense with love; it was not now a factor. And if anyone quarreled or complained, he would simply tighten his lips and arrange his shoulders in the correct command posture. He might give a curt little nod. Or he might not. He might just shrug and say, Carry on, then they would saddle up and form into a column and move out toward the villages west of Than Khe.

Tillie Olsen   (1912–2007)

I Stand Here Ironing   [1961]

APPROACHING THE AUTHOR

Tillie Olsen was determined to read all the fiction in the Omaha Public Library. She would pick up a book, read a few pages, and, if she did not like it, move on to the next.
For more about her, see page 1405.

I stand here ironing, and what you asked me moves tormented back and forth with the iron.

"I wish you would manage the time to come in and talk with me about your daughter. I'm sure you can help me understand her. She's a youngster who needs help and whom I'm deeply interested in helping."

"Who needs help." . . . Even if I came, what good would it do? You think because I am her mother I have a key, or that in some way you could use me as a key? She has lived for nineteen years. There is all that life that has happened outside of me, beyond me.

And when is there time to remember, to sift, to weigh, to estimate, to total? I will start and there will be an interruption and I will have to gather it all together again. Or I will become engulfed with all I did or did not do, with what should have been and what cannot be helped.

She was a beautiful baby. The first and only one of our five that was beautiful at birth. You do not guess how new and uneasy her tenancy in her now-loveliness. You did not know her all those years she was thought homely, or see her poring over her baby pictures, making me tell her over and over how beautiful she had been—and would be, I would tell her—and was now, to the seeing eye. But the seeing eyes were few or nonexistent. Including mine.

I nursed her. They feel that's important nowadays. I nursed all the children, but with her, with all the fierce rigidity of first motherhood, I did like the books then said. Though her cries battered me to trembling and my breasts ached with swollenness, I waited till the clock decreed.

Why do I put that first? I do not even know if it matters, or if it explains anything.

She was a beautiful baby. She blew shining bubbles of sound. She loved motion, loved light, loved color and music and textures. She would lie on the floor in her blue overalls patting the surface so hard in ecstasy her hands and feet would blur. She was a miracle to me, but when she was eight months old I had to leave her daytimes with the woman downstairs to whom she was no miracle at all, for I worked or looked for work and for Emily's father, who "could no longer endure" (he wrote in his good-bye note) "sharing want with us."

I was nineteen. It was the pre-relief, pre-WPA world of the depression. I would start running as soon as I got off the streetcar, running up the stairs, the place smelling sour, and awake or asleep to startle awake, when she saw me she would break into a clogged weeping that could not be comforted, a weeping I can hear yet.

After a while I found a job hashing at night so I could be with her days, and it was better. But it came to where I had to bring her to his family and leave her.

It took a long time to raise the money for her fare back. Then she got chicken pox and I had to wait longer. When she finally came, I hardly knew her, walking quick and nervous like her father, looking like her father, thin, and dressed in a shoddy red that yellowed her skin and glared at the pockmarks. All the baby loveliness gone.

She was two. Old enough for nursery school they said, and I did not know then what I know now—the fatigue of the long day, and the lacerations of group life in the kinds of nurseries that are only parking places for children.

Except that it would have made no difference if I had known. It was the only place there was. It was the only way we could be together, the only way I could hold a job.

And even without knowing, I knew. I knew the teacher that was evil because all these years it has curdled into my memory, the little boy hunched in the corner, her rasp, "why aren't you outside, because Alvin hits you? that's no reason, go out, scaredy." I knew Emily hated it even if she did not clutch and implore "don't go Mommy" like the other children, mornings.

She always had a reason why we should stay home. Momma, you look sick. 15 Momma, I feel sick. Momma, the teachers aren't there today, they're sick. Momma, we can't go, there was a fire there last night. Momma, it's a holiday today, no school, they told me.

But never a direct protest, never rebellion. I think of our others in their three-, four-year-oldness—the explosions, the tempers, the denunciations, the demands—and I feel suddenly ill. I put the iron down. What in me demanded that goodness in her? And what was the cost to her of such goodness?

The old man living in the back once said in his gentle way: "You should smile at Emily more when you look at her." What *was* in my face when I looked at her? I loved her. There were all the acts of love.

It was only with the others I remembered what he said, and it was the face of joy, and not of care or tightness or worry I turned to them—too late for Emily. She does not smile easily, let alone almost always as her brothers and sisters do. Her face is closed and somber, but when she wants, how fluid. You must have seen it in her pantomimes, you spoke of her rare gift for comedy on the stage that rouses a laughter out of the audience so dear they applaud and applaud and do not want to let her go.

Where does it come from, that comedy? There was none of it in her when she came back to me that second time, after I had had to send her away again. She had a new daddy now to learn to love, and I think perhaps it was a better time.

Except when we left her alone nights, telling ourselves she was old enough. 20 "Can't you go some other time, Mommy, like tomorrow?" she would ask. "Will it be just a little while you'll be gone? Do you promise?"

The time we came back, the front door open, the clock on the floor in the hall. She rigid awake. "It wasn't just a little while. I didn't cry. Three times I called you, just three times, and then I ran downstairs to open the door so you could come faster. The clock talked loud. I threw it away, it scared me what it talked."

She said the clock talked loud again that night I went to the hospital to have Susan. She was delirious with the fever that comes before red measles, but she was fully conscious all the week I was gone and the week after we were home when she could not come near the new baby or me.

She did not get well. She stayed skeleton thin, not wanting to eat, and night after night she had nightmares. She would call for me, and I would rouse from exhaustion to sleepily call back: "You're all right, darling, go to sleep, it's just a dream," and if she still called, in a sterner voice, "now go to sleep, Emily, there's nothing to hurt you." Twice, only twice, when I had to get up for Susan anyhow, I went in to sit with her.

Now when it is too late (as if she would let me hold and comfort her like I 25 do the others) I get up and go to her at once at her moan or restless stirring. "Are you awake, Emily? Can I get you something?" And the answer is always the same: "No, I'm all right, go back to sleep, Mother."

They persuaded me at the clinic to send her away to a convalescent home in the country where "she can have the kind of food and care you can't manage for her, and you'll be free to concentrate on the new baby." They still send children to that place. I see pictures on the society page of sleek young women planning affairs to raise money for it, or dancing at the affairs, or decorating Easter eggs or filling Christmas stockings for the children.

They never have a picture of the children so I do not know if the girls still wear those gigantic red bows and the ravaged looks on the every other Sunday when parents can come to visit "unless otherwise notified" — as we were notified the first six weeks.

Oh it is a handsome place, green lawns and tall trees and fluted flower beds. High up on the balconies of each cottage the children stand, the girls in their red bows and white dresses, the boys in white suits and giant red ties. The parents stand below shrieking up to be heard and the children shriek down to be heard, and between them the invisible wall "Not To Be Contaminated by Parental Germs or Physical Affection."

There was a tiny girl who always stood hand in hand with Emily. Her parents never came. One visit she was gone. "They moved her to Rose Cottage" Emily shouted in explanation. "They don't like you to love anybody here."

She wrote once a week, the labored writing of a seven-year-old. "I am fine. 30 How is the baby. If I write my leter nicly I will have a star. Love." There never was a star. We wrote every other day, letters she could never hold or keep but only hear read — once. "We simply do not have room for children to keep any personal possessions," they patiently explained when we pieced one Sunday's shrieking together to plead how much it would mean to Emily, who loved so to keep things, to be allowed to keep her letters and cards.

Each visit she looked frailer. "She isn't eating," they told us.

(They had runny eggs for breakfast or mush with lumps, Emily said later, I'd hold it in my mouth and not swallow. Nothing ever tasted good, just when they had chicken.)

It took us eight months to get her released home, and only the fact that she gained back so little of her seven lost pounds convinced the social worker.

I used to try to hold and love her after she came back, but her body would stay stiff, and after a while she'd push away. She ate little. Food sickened her, and I think much of life too. Oh she had physical lightness and brightness, twinkling by on skates, bouncing like a ball up and down up and down over the jump rope, skimming over the hill; but these were momentary.

She fretted about her appearance, thin and dark and foreign-looking at a 35 time when every little girl was supposed to look or thought she should look a chubby blonde replica of Shirley Temple. The doorbell sometimes rang for her, but no one seemed to come and play in the house or be a best friend. Maybe because we moved so much.

There was a boy she loved painfully through two school semesters. Months later she told me how she had taken pennies from my purse to buy him candy. "Licorice was his favorite and I brought him some every day, but he still liked Jennifer better'n me. Why, Mommy?" The kind of question for which there is no answer.

School was a worry to her. She was not glib or quick in a world where glibness and quickness were easily confused with ability to learn. To her overworked and exasperated teachers she was an overconscientious "slow learner" who kept trying to catch up and was absent entirely too often.

I let her be absent, though sometimes the illness was imaginary. How different from my now-strictness about attendance with the others. I wasn't working. We had a new baby, I was home anyhow. Sometimes, after Susan grew old enough, I would keep her home from school, too, to have them all together.

Mostly Emily had asthma, and her breathing, harsh and labored, would fill the house with a curiously tranquil sound. I would bring the two old dresser mirrors and her boxes of collections to her bed. She would select beads and single earrings, bottle tops and shells, dried flowers and pebbles, old postcards and scraps, all sorts of oddments; then she and Susan would play Kingdom, setting up landscapes and furniture, peopling them with action.

Those were the only times of peaceful companionship between her and 40 Susan. I have edged away from it, that poisonous feeling between them, that terrible balancing of hurts and needs I had to do between the two, and did so badly, those earlier years.

Oh there are conflicts between the others too, each one human, needing, demanding, hurting, taking—but only between Emily and Susan, no, Emily toward Susan that corroding resentment. It seems so obvious on the surface, yet it is not obvious. Susan, the second child, Susan, golden- and curly-haired and chubby, quick and articulate and assured, everything in appearance and manner Emily was not; Susan, not able to resist Emily's precious things, losing or sometimes clumsily breaking them; Susan telling jokes and riddles to company for applause while Emily sat silent (to say to me later: that was *my* riddle, Mother, I told it to Susan); Susan, who for all the five years' difference in age was just a year behind Emily in developing physically.

I am glad for that slow physical development that widened the difference between her and her contemporaries, though she suffered over it. She was too vulnerable for that terrible world of youthful competition, of preening and parading, of constant measuring of yourself against every other, of envy, "If I had that copper hair," "If I had that skin. . . ." She tormented herself enough about not looking like the others, there was enough of the unsureness, the having to be conscious of words before you speak, the constant caring—what are they thinking of me? without having it all magnified by the merciless physical drives.

Ronnie is calling. He is wet and I change him. It is rare there is such a cry now. That time of motherhood is almost behind me when the ear is not one's own but must always be racked and listening for the child cry, the child call. We sit for a while and I hold him, looking out over the city spread in charcoal with its soft aisles of light. "Shoogily," he breathes and curls closer. I carry him back to bed, asleep. *Shoogily.* A funny word, a family word, inherited from Emily, invented by her to say: *comfort.*

In this and other ways she leaves her seal, I say aloud. And startle at my saying it. What do I mean? What did I start to gather together, to try and make coherent? I was at the terrible, growing years. War years. I do not remember them well. I was working, there were four smaller ones now, there was not time for her. She had to help be a mother, and housekeeper, and shopper. She had to set her seal. Mornings of crisis and near hysteria trying to get lunches packed, hair combed, coats and shoes found, everyone to school or Child Care on time, the baby ready for transportation. And always the paper scribbled on by a smaller one, the book looked at by Susan then mislaid, the homework not done. Running out to that huge school where she was one, she was lost, she was a drop; suffering over the unpreparedness, stammering and unsure in her classes.

There was so little time left at night after the kids were bedded down. She   45 would struggle over books, always eating (it was in those years she developed her enormous appetite that is legendary in our family) and I would be ironing, or preparing food for the next day, or writing V-mail to Bill, or tending the baby. Sometimes, to make me laugh, or out of her despair, she would imitate happenings or types at school.

I think I said once: "Why don't you do something like this in the school amateur show?" One morning she phoned me at work, hardly understandable through the weeping: "Mother, I did it. I won, I won; they gave me first prize; they clapped and clapped and wouldn't let me go."

Now suddenly she was Somebody, and as imprisoned in her difference as she had been in anonymity.

She began to be asked to perform at other high schools, even in colleges, then at city and statewide affairs. The first one we went to, I only recognized her that first moment when thin, shy, she almost drowned herself into the curtains. Then: Was this Emily? The control, the command, the convulsing and deadly clowning, the spell, then the roaring, stamping audience, unwilling to let this rare and precious laughter out of their lives.

Afterwards: You ought to do something about her with a gift like that—but without money or knowing how, what does one do? We have left it all to her, and the gift has as often eddied inside, clogged and clotted, as been used and growing.

She is coming. She runs up the stairs two at a time with her light graceful   50 step, and I know she is happy tonight. Whatever it was that occasioned your call did not happen today.

"Aren't you ever going to finish the ironing, Mother? Whistler painted his mother in a rocker. I'd have to paint mine standing over an ironing board." This is one of her communicative nights and she tells me everything and nothing as she fixes herself a plate of food out of the icebox.

She is so lovely. Why did you want me to come in at all? Why were you concerned? She will find her way.

She starts up the stairs to bed. "Don't get me up with the rest in the morning." "But I thought you were having midterms." "Oh, those," she comes back in, kisses me, and says quite lightly, "in a couple of years when we'll all be atom-dead they won't matter a bit."

She has said it before. She *believes* it. But because I have been dredging the past, and all that compounds a human being is so heavy and meaningful in me, I cannot endure it tonight.

I will never total it all. I will never come in to say: She was a child sel-   55
dom smiled at. Her father left me before she was a year old. I had to work her first six years when there was work, or I sent her home and to his relatives. There were years she had care she hated. She was dark and thin and foreign-looking in a world where the prestige went to blondeness and curly hair and dimples, she was slow where glibness was prized. She was a child of anxious, not proud, love. We were poor and could not afford for her the soil of easy growth. I was a young mother, I was a distracted mother. There were the other children pushing up, demanding. Her younger sister seemed all that she was not. There were years she did not want me to touch her. She kept too much in herself, her life was such she had to keep too much in herself. My wisdom came too late. She has much to her and probably nothing will come of it. She is a child of her age, of depression, of war, of fear.

Let her be. So all that is in her will not bloom — but in how many does it? There is still enough left to live by. Only help her to know — help make it so there is cause for her to know — that she is more than this dress on the ironing board, helpless before the iron.

ZZ Packer b. 1973

Brownies   [2003]

By our second day at Camp Crescendo, the girls in my Brownie troop had decided to kick the asses of each and every girl in Brownie Troop 909. Troop 909 was doomed from the first day of camp; they were white girls, their complexions a blend of ice cream: strawberry, vanilla. They turtled out from their bus in pairs, their rolled-up sleeping bags chromatized with Disney characters: Sleeping Beauty, Snow White, Mickey Mouse; or the generic ones cheap parents bought: washed-out rainbows, unicorns, curly-eyelashed frogs. Some clutched Igloo coolers and still others held on to stuffed toys like pacifiers, looking all around them like tourists determined to be dazzled.

Our troop was wending its way past their bus, past the ranger station, past the colorful trail guide drawn like a treasure map, locked behind glass.

"Man, did you smell them?" Arnetta said, giving the girls a slow once-over, "They smell like Chihuahuas. *Wet* Chihuahuas." Their troop was still at the entrance, and though we had passed them by yards, Arnetta raised her nose in the air and grimaced.

Arnetta said this from the very rear of the line, far away from Mrs. Margolin, who always strung our troop behind her like a brood of obedient ducklings. Mrs. Margolin even looked like a mother duck — she had hair cropped close to a small ball of a head, almost no neck, and huge, miraculous breasts. She wore enormous belts that looked like the kind that weightlifters wear, except hers would be cheap metallic gold or rabbit fur or covered with gigantic fake sunflowers, and often these belts would become nature lessons in and of themselves. "See," Mrs. Margolin once said to us, pointing to her belt, "this one's made entirely from the feathers of baby pigeons."

The belt layered with feathers was uncanny enough, but I was more dis-   5
turbed by the realization that I had never actually *seen* a baby pigeon. I searched weeks for one, in vain — scampering after pigeons whenever I was downtown with my father.

But nature lessons were not Mrs. Margolin's top priority. She saw the position of troop leader as an evangelical post. Back at the A.M.E.° church where our Brownie meetings were held, Mrs. Margolin was especially fond of imparting religious aphorisms by means of acrostics — "Satan" was the "Serpent Always Tempting and Noisome"; she'd refer to the "Bible" as "Basic Instructions Before Leaving Earth." Whenever she quizzed us on these, expecting to hear the acrostics parroted back to her, only Arnetta's correct replies soared over our vague mumblings. "Jesus?" Mrs. Margolin might ask expectantly, and Arnetta alone would dutifully answer, "Jehovah's Example, Saving Us Sinners."

Arnetta always made a point of listening to Mrs. Margolin's religious talk and giving her what she wanted to hear. Because of this, Arnetta could have blared through a megaphone that the white girls of Troop 909 were "wet Chihuahuas" without so much as a blink from Mrs. Margolin. Once, Arnetta killed the troop goldfish by feeding it a french fry covered in ketchup, and when Mrs. Margolin demanded that she explain what had happened, claimed the goldfish had been eyeing her meal for *hours,* then the fish — giving in to temptation — had leapt up and snatched a whole golden fry from her fingertips.

"*Serious* Chihuahua," Octavia added, and though neither Arnetta nor Octavia could *spell* "Chihuahua," had ever *seen* a Chihuahua, trisyllabic words had gained a sort of exoticism within our fourth-grade set at Woodrow Wilson Elementary. Arnetta and Octavia would flip through the dictionary, determined to work the vulgar-sounding ones like "Djibouti" and "asinine" into conversation.

"*Caucasian* Chihuahuas," Arnetta said.

That did it. The girls in my troop turned elastic: Drema and Elise doubled   10
up on one another like inextricably entwined kites; Octavia slapped her belly;

A.M.E.: African Methodist Episcopal.

Janice jumped straight up in the air, then did it again, as if to slam-dunk her own head. They could not stop laughing. No one had laughed so hard since a boy named Martez had stuck a pencil in the electric socket and spent the whole day with a strange grin on his face.

"Girls, girls," said our parent helper, Mrs. Hedy. Mrs. Hedy was Octavia's mother, and she wagged her index finger perfunctorily, like a windshield wiper. "Stop it, now. Be good." She said this loud enough to be heard, but lazily, bereft of any feeling or indication that she meant to be obeyed, as though she could say these words again at the exact same pitch if a button somewhere on her were pressed.

But the rest of the girls didn't stop; they only laughed louder. It was the word "Caucasian" that got them all going. One day at school, about a month before the Brownie camping trip, Arnetta turned to a boy wearing impossibly high-ankled floodwater jeans and said, "What are you? *Caucasian?*" The word took off from there, and soon everything was Caucasian. If you ate too fast you ate like a Caucasian, if you ate too slow you ate like a Caucasian. The biggest feat anyone at Woodrow Wilson could do was to jump off the swing in midair, at the highest point in its arc, and if you fell (as I had, more than once) instead of landing on your feet, knees bent Olympic gymnast–style, Arnetta and Octavia were prepared to comment. They'd look at each other with the silence of passengers who'd narrowly escaped an accident, then nod their heads, whispering with solemn horror, "*Caucasian.*"

Even the only white kid in our school, Dennis, got in on the Caucasian act. That time when Martez stuck a pencil in the socket, Dennis had pointed and yelled, "That was *so* Caucasian!"

When you lived in the south suburbs of Atlanta, it was easy to forget about whites. Whites were like those baby pigeons: real and existing, but rarely seen or thought about. Everyone had been to Rich's to go clothes shopping, everyone had seen white girls and their mothers coo-cooing over dresses; everyone had gone to the downtown library and seen white businessmen swish by importantly, wrists flexed in front of them to check the time as though they would change from Clark Kent into Superman at any second. But those images were as fleeting as cards shuffled in a deck, whereas the ten white girls behind us — *invaders*, Arnetta would later call them — were instantly real and memorable, with their long, shampoo-commercial hair, straight as spaghetti from the box. This alone was reason for envy and hatred. The only black girl most of us had ever seen with hair that long was Octavia, whose hair hung past her butt like a Hawaiian hula dancer's. The sight of Octavia's mane prompted other girls to listen to her reverentially, as though whatever she had to say would somehow activate their own follicles. For example, when, on the first day of camp, Octavia made as if to speak, and everyone fell silent. "Nobody," Octavia said, "calls us niggers."

At the end of that first day, when half of our troop made their way back to   15
the cabin after tag-team restroom visits, Arnetta said she'd heard one of the

Troop 909 girls call Daphne a nigger. The other half of the girls and I were helping Mrs. Margolin clean up the pots and pans from the campfire ravioli dinner.
When we made our way to the restrooms to wash up and brush our teeth, we
met up with Arnetta midway.

"Man, I completely heard the girl," Arnetta reported. "Right, Daphne?"

Daphne hardly ever spoke, but when she did, her voice was petite and tinkly,
the voice one might expect from a shiny new earring. She'd written a poem
once, for Langston Hughes Day, a poem brimming with all the teacher-winning
ingredients — trees and oceans, sunsets and moons — but what cinched the poem
for the grown-ups, snatching the win from Octavia's musical ode to Grandmaster
Flash and the Furious Five, were Daphne's last lines:

> You are my father, the veteran
> When you cry in the dark
> It rains and rains and rains in my heart

She'd always worn clean, though faded, jumpers and dresses when Chic
jeans were the fashion, but when she went up to the dais to receive her prize
journal, pages trimmed in gold, she wore a new dress with a velveteen bodice
and a taffeta skirt as wide as an umbrella. All the kids clapped, though none of
them understood the poem. I'd read encyclopedias the way others read comics,
and I didn't get it. But those last lines pricked me, they were so eerie, and as my
father and I ate cereal, I'd whisper over my Froot Loops, like a mantra, *"You are
my father, the veteran. You are my father, the veteran, the veteran, the veteran,"*
until my father, who acted in plays as Caliban and Othello and was not a veteran, marched me up to my teacher one morning and said, "Can you tell me
what's wrong with this kid?"

I thought Daphne and I might become friends, but I think she grew
spooked by me whispering those lines to her, begging her to tell me what they
meant, and I soon understood that two quiet people like us were better off quiet
alone.

"Daphne? Didn't you hear them call you a nigger?" Arnetta asked, giving 20
Daphne a nudge.

The sun was setting behind the trees, and their leafy tops formed a canopy
of black lace for the flame of the sun to pass through. Daphne shrugged her
shoulders at first, then slowly nodded her head when Arnetta gave her a hard
look.

Twenty minutes later, when my restroom group returned to the cabin,
Arnetta was still talking about Troop 909. My restroom group had passed by
some of the 909 girls. For the most part, they deferred to us, waving us into the
restrooms, letting us go even though they'd gotten there first.

We'd seen them, but from afar, never within their orbit enough to see
whether their faces were the way all white girls appeared on TV — ponytailed and
full of energy, bubbling over with love and money. All I could see was that some
of them rapidly fanned their faces with their hands, though the heat of the day

had long passed. A few seemed to be lolling their heads in slow circles, half purposefully, as if exercising the muscles of their necks, half ecstatically, like Stevie Wonder.

"We can't let them get away with that," Arnetta said, dropping her voice to a laryngitic whisper. "We can't let them get away with calling us niggers. I say we teach them a lesson." She sat down cross-legged on a sleeping bag, an embittered Buddha, eyes glimmering acrylic-black. "We can't go telling Mrs. Margolin, either. Mrs. Margolin'll say something about doing unto others and the path of righteousness and all. Forget that shit." She let her eyes flutter irreverently till they half closed, as though ignoring an insult not worth returning. We could all hear Mrs. Margolin outside, gathering the last of the metal campware.

Nobody said anything for a while. Usually people were quiet after Arnetta   25 spoke. Her tone had an upholstered confidence that was somehow both regal and vulgar at once. It demanded a few moments of silence in its wake, like the ringing of a church bell or the playing of taps. Sometimes Octavia would ditto or dissent to whatever Arnetta had said, and this was the signal that others could speak. But this time Octavia just swirled a long cord of hair into pretzel shapes.

"Well?" Arnetta said. She looked as if she had discerned the hidden severity of the situation and was waiting for the rest of us to catch up. Everyone looked from Arnetta to Daphne. It was, after all, Daphne who had supposedly been called the name, but Daphne sat on the bare cabin floor, flipping through the pages of the Girl Scout handbook, eyebrows arched in mock wonder, as if the handbook were a catalogue full of bright and startling foreign costumes. Janice broke the silence. She clapped her hands to broach her idea of a plan.

"They gone be sleeping," she whispered conspiratorially, "then we gone sneak into they cabin, then we'll put daddy longlegs in they sleeping bags. Then they'll wake up. Then we gone beat 'em up till they're as flat as frying pans!" She jammed her fist into the palm of her hand, then made a sizzling sound.

Janice's country accent was laughable, her looks homely, her jumpy acrobatics embarrassing to behold. Arnetta and Octavia volleyed amused, arrogant smiles whenever Janice opened her mouth, but Janice never caught the hint, spoke whenever she wanted, fluttered around Arnetta and Octavia futilely offering her opinions to their departing backs. Whenever Arnetta and Octavia shooed her away, Janice loitered until the two would finally sigh and ask, "What is it, Miss Caucausoid? What do you want?"

"Shut up, Janice," Octavia said, letting a fingered loop of hair fall to her waist as though just the sound of Janice's voice had ruined the fun of her hair twisting.

Janice obeyed, her mouth hung open in a loose grin, unflappable, unhurt.   30

"All right," Arnetta said, standing up. "We're going to have a secret meeting and talk about what we're going to do."

Everyone gravely nodded her head. The word "secret" had a built-in importance, the modifier form of the word carried more clout than the noun. A secret meant nothing; it was like gossip: just a bit of unpleasant knowledge about someone who happened to be someone other than yourself. A secret *meeting,* or a secret *club* was entirely different.

That was when Arnetta turned to me as though she knew that doing so was both a compliment and a charity.

"Snot, you're not going to be a bitch and tell Mrs. Margolin, are you?"

I had been called "Snot" ever since first grade, when I'd sneezed in class and 35 two long ropes of mucus had splattered a nearby girl.

"Hey," I said. "Maybe you didn't hear them right — I mean —"

"Are you gonna tell on us or not?" was all Arnetta wanted to know, and by the time the question was asked, the rest of our Brownie troop looked at me as though they'd already decided their course of action, me being the only impediment.

Camp Crescendo used to double as a high-school-band and field hockey camp until an arcing field hockey ball landed on the clasp of a girl's metal barrette, knifing a skull nerve and paralyzing the right side of her body. The camp closed down for a few years and the girl's teammates built a memorial, filling the spot on which the girl fell with hockey balls, on which they had painted — all in nail polish — get-well tidings, flowers, and hearts. The balls were still stacked there, like a shrine of ostrich eggs embedded in the ground.

On the second day of camp, Troop 909 was dancing around the mound of hockey balls, their limbs jangling awkwardly, their cries like the constant summer squeal of an amusement park. There was a stream that bordered the field hockey lawn, and the girls from my troop settled next to it, scarfing down the last of lunch: sandwiches made from salami and slices of tomato that had gotten waterlogged from the melting ice in the cooler. From the stream bank, Arnetta eyed the Troop 909 girls, scrutinizing their movements to glean inspiration for battle.

"Man," Arnetta said, "we could bumrush them right now if that damn lady 40 would *leave.*"

The 909 troop leader was a white woman with the severe pageboy hairdo of an ancient Egyptian. She lay on a picnic blanket, sphinxlike, eating a banana, sometimes holding it out in front of her like a microphone. Beside her sat a girl slowly flapping one hand like a bird with a broken wing. Occasionally, the leader would call out the names of girls who'd attempted leapfrogs and flips, or of girls who yelled too loudly or strayed far from the circle.

"I'm just glad Big Fat Mama's not following us here," Octavia said. "At least we don't have to worry about her." Mrs. Margolin, Octavia assured us, was having her Afternoon Devotional, shrouded in mosquito netting, in a clearing she'd found. Mrs. Hedy was cleaning mud from her espadrilles in the cabin.

"I handled them." Arnetta sucked on her teeth and proudly grinned. "I told her we was going to gather leaves."

"Gather leaves," Octavia said, nodding respectfully. "That's a good one. Especially since they're so mad-crazy about this camping thing." She looked from ground to sky, sky to ground. Her hair hung down her back in two braids like a squaw's. "I mean, I really don't know why it's even called *camping* — all we

ever do with Nature is find some twigs and say something like, 'Wow, this fell
from a tree.'" She then studied her sandwich. With two disdainful fingers, she
picked out a slice of dripping tomato, the sections congealed with red slime. She
pitched it into the stream embrowned with dead leaves and the murky effigies
of other dead things, but in the opaque water, a group of small silver-brown fish
appeared. They surrounded the tomato and nibbled.

"Look!" Janice cried. "Fishes! Fishes!" As she scrambled to the edge of the   45
stream to watch, a covey of insects threw up tantrums from the wheatgrass and
nettle, a throng of tiny electric machines, all going at once. Octavia sneaked up
behind Janice as if to push her in. Daphne and I exchanged terrified looks. It
seemed as though only we knew that Octavia was close enough—and bold
enough—to actually push Janice into the stream. Janice turned around quickly,
but Octavia was already staring serenely into the still water as though she was
gathering some sort of courage from it. "What's so funny?" Janice said, eyeing
them all suspiciously.

Elise began humming the tune to "Karma Chameleon," all the girls joining
in, their hums light and facile. Janice also began to hum, against everyone else,
the high-octane opening chords of "Beat It."

"I love me some Michael Jackson," Janice said when she'd finished humming, smacking her lips as though Michael Jackson were a favorite meal. "I *will*
marry Michael Jackson."

Before anyone had a chance to impress upon Janice the impossibility of
this, Arnetta suddenly rose, made a sun visor of her hand, and watched Troop
909 leave the field hockey lawn.

"Dammit!" she said. "We've got to get them *alone.*"

"They won't ever be alone," I said. All the rest of the girls looked at me, for   50
I usually kept quiet. If I spoke even a word, I could count on someone calling
me Snot. Everyone seemed to think that we could beat up these girls; no one
entertained the thought that they might fight *back.* "The only time they'll be
unsupervised is in the bathroom."

"Oh shut up, Snot," Octavia said.

But Arnetta slowly nodded her head. "The bathroom," she said. "The bathroom," she said, again and again. "The bathroom! The bathroom!"

According to Octavia's watch, it took us five minutes to hike to the restrooms, which were midway between our cabin and Troop 909's. Inside, the
mirrors above the sinks returned only the vaguest of reflections, as though
someone had taken a scouring pad to their surfaces to obscure the shine. Pine
needles, leaves, and dirty, flattened wads of chewing gum covered the floor like
a mosaic. Webs of hair matted the drain in the middle of the floor. Above the
sinks and below the mirrors, stacks of folded white paper towels lay on a long
metal counter. Shaggy white balls of paper towels sat on the sinktops in a line
like corsages on display. A thread of floss snaked from a wad of tissues dotted
with the faint red-pink of blood. One of those white girls, I thought, had just
lost a tooth.

Though the restroom looked almost the same as it had the night before, it   55
somehow seemed stranger now. We hadn't noticed the wooden rafters coming
together in great V's. We were, it seemed, inside a whale, viewing the ribs of the
roof of its mouth.

"Wow. It's a mess," Elise said.

"You can say that again."

Arnetta leaned against the doorjamb of a restroom stall. "This is where
they'll be again," she said. Just seeing the place, just having a plan seemed to
satisfy her. "We'll go in and talk to them. You know, 'How you doing? How
long'll you be here?' That sort of thing. Then Octavia and I are gonna tell them
what happens when they call any one of us a nigger."

"I'm going to say something, too," Janice said.

Arnetta considered this. "Sure," she said. "Of course. Whatever you want."   60

Janice pointed her finger like a gun at Octavia and rehearsed the line she'd
thought up, "'We're gonna teach you a *lesson!*' That's what I'm going to say."
She narrowed her eyes like a TV mobster. "'We're gonna teach you little girls a
lesson!'"

With the back of her hand, Octavia brushed Janice's finger away. "You
couldn't teach me to shit in a toilet."

"But," I said, "what if they say, 'We didn't say that? We didn't call anyone
an N-I-G-G-E-R.'"

"Snot," Arnetta said, and then sighed. "Don't think. Just fight. If you even
know how."

Everyone laughed except Daphne. Arnetta gently laid her hand on Daphne's   65
shoulder. "Daphne. You don't have to fight. We're doing this for you."

Daphne walked to the counter, took a clean paper towel, and carefully unfolded it like a map. With it, she began to pick up the trash all around. Everyone
watched.

"C'mon," Arnetta said to everyone. "Let's beat it." We all ambled toward
the doorway, where the sunshine made one large white rectangle of light. We
were immediately blinded, and we shielded our eyes with our hands and our
forearms.

"Daphne?" Arnetta asked. "Are you coming?"

We all looked back at the bending girl, the thin of her back hunched like
the back of a custodian sweeping a stage, caught in limelight. Stray strands of
her hair were lit near-transparent, thin fiber-optic threads. She did not nod yes
to the question, nor did she shake her head no. She abided, bent. Then she
began again, picking up leaves, wads of paper, the cotton fluff innards from a
torn stuffed toy. She did it so methodically, so exquisitely, so humbly, she must
have been trained. I thought of those dresses she wore, faded and old, yet so
pressed and clean. I then saw the poverty in them; I then could imagine her
mother, cleaning the houses of others, returning home, weary.

"I guess she's not coming."   70

We left her and headed back to our cabin, over pine needles and leaves,
taking the path full of shade.

"What about our secret meeting?" Elise asked.

Arnetta enunciated her words in a way that defied contradiction: "We just had it."

It was nearing our bedtime, but the sun had not yet set.

"Hey, your mama's coming," Arnetta said to Octavia when she saw Mrs. 75
Hedy walk toward the cabin, sniffling. When Octavia's mother wasn't giving bored, parochial orders, she sniffled continuously, mourning an imminent divorce from her husband. She might begin a sentence, "I don't know what Robert will do when Octavia and I are gone. Who'll buy him cigarettes?" and Octavia would hotly whisper, *"Mama,"* in a way that meant: Please don't talk about our problems in front of everyone. Please shut up.

But when Mrs. Hedy began talking about her husband, thinking about her husband, seeing clouds shaped like the head of her husband, she couldn't be quiet, and no one could dislodge her from the comfort of her own woe. Only one thing could perk her up — Brownie songs. If the girls were quiet, and Mrs. Hedy was in her dopey, sorrowful mood, she would say, "Y'all know I like those songs, girls. Why don't you sing one?" Everyone would groan, except me and Daphne. I, for one, liked some of the songs.

"C'mon, everybody," Octavia said drearily. "She likes the Brownie song best."

We sang, loud enough to reach Mrs. Hedy:

"I've got something in my pocket;
It belongs across my face.
And I keep it very close at hand
   in a most convenient place.
I'm sure you couldn't guess it
If you guessed a long, long while.
So I'll take it out and put it on —
it's a great big Brownie smile!"

The Brownie song was supposed to be sung cheerfully, as though we were elves in a workshop, singing as we merrily cobbled shoes, but everyone except me hated the song so much that they sang it like a maudlin record, played on the most sluggish of rpms.°

"That was good," Mrs. Hedy said, closing the cabin door behind her. 80
"Wasn't that nice, Linda?"

"Praise God," Mrs. Margolin answered without raising her head from the chore of counting out Popsicle sticks for the next day's craft session.

"Sing another one," Mrs. Hedy said. She said it with a sort of joyful aggression, like a drunk I'd once seen who'd refused to leave a Korean grocery.

"God, Mama, get over it," Octavia whispered in a voice meant only for Arnetta, but Mrs. Hedy heard it and started to leave the cabin.

---

rpms: Revolutions per minute. Here, phonograph playing sluggishly at 33½, 45, or 78 rpms.

"Don't go," Arnetta said. She ran after Mrs. Hedy and held her by the arm. "We haven't finished singing." She nudged us with a single look. "Let's sing the 'Friends Song.' For Mrs. Hedy."

Although I liked some of the songs, I hated this one: 85

Make new friends
But keep the o-old,
One is silver
And the other gold.

If most of the girls in the troop could be any type of metal, they'd be bunched-up wads of tinfoil, maybe, or rusty iron nails you had to get tetanus shots for.

"No, no, no," Mrs. Margolin said before anyone could start in on the "Friends Song." "An uplifting song. Something to lift her up and take her mind off all these earthly burdens."

Arnetta and Octavia rolled their eyes. Everyone knew what song Mrs. Margolin was talking about, and no one, no one, wanted to sing it.

"Please, no," a voice called out. "Not 'The Doughnut Song.'"

"Please not 'The Doughnut Song,'" Octavia pleaded.   90

"I'll brush my teeth two times if I don't have to sing 'The Doughnut—'"

"Sing!" Mrs. Margolin demanded.

We sang:

"Life without Jesus is like a do-ough-nut!
Like a do-ooough-nut!
Like a do-ooough-nut!
Life without Jesus is like a do-ough-nut!
There's a hole in the middle of my soul!"

There were other verses, involving other pastries, but we stopped after the first one and cast glances toward Mrs. Margolin to see if we could gain a reprieve. Mrs. Margolin's eyes fluttered blissfully. She was half asleep.

"Awww," Mrs. Hedy said, as though giant Mrs. Margolin were a cute baby,   95
"Mrs. Margolin's had a long day."

"Yes indeed," Mrs. Margolin answered. "If you don't mind, I might just go to the lodge where the beds are. I haven't been the same since the operation."

I had not heard of this operation, or when it had occurred, since Mrs. Margolin had never missed the once-a-week Brownie meetings, but I could see from Daphne's face that she was concerned, and I could see that the other girls had decided that Mrs. Margolin's operation must have happened long ago in some remote time unconnected to our own. Nevertheless, they put on sad faces. We had all been taught that adulthood was full of sorrow and pain, taxes and bills, dreaded work and dealings with whites, sickness and death. I tried to do what the others did. I tried to look silent.

"Go right ahead, Linda," Mrs. Hedy said. "I'll watch the girls." Mrs. Hedy seemed to forget about divorce for a moment; she looked at us with dewy eyes, as if we were mysterious, furry creatures. Meanwhile, Mrs. Margolin walked through the maze of sleeping bags until she found her own. She gathered a neat stack of clothes and pajamas slowly, as though doing so was almost painful. She took her toothbrush, her toothpaste, her pillow. "All right!" Mrs. Margolin said, addressing us all from the threshold of the cabin. "Be in bed by nine." She said it with a twinkle in her voice, letting us know she was allowing us to be naughty and stay up till nine-fifteen.

"C'mon everybody," Arnetta said after Mrs. Margolin left. "Time for us to wash up."

Everyone watched Mrs. Hedy closely, wondering whether she would insist   100
on coming with us since it was night, making a fight with Troop 909 nearly impossible. Troop 909 would soon be in the bathroom, washing their faces, brushing their teeth — completely unsuspecting of our ambush.

"We won't be long," Arnetta said. "We're old enough to go to the restrooms by ourselves."

Ms. Hedy pursed her lips at this dilemma. "Well, I guess you Brownies are almost Girl Scouts, right?"

"Right!"

"Just one more badge," Drema said.

"And about," Octavia droned, "a million more cookies to sell." Octavia   105
looked at all of us, *Now's our chance,* her face seemed to say, but our chance to do *what,* I didn't exactly know.

Finally, Mrs. Hedy walked to the doorway where Octavia stood dutifully waiting to say goodbye but looking bored doing it. Mrs. Hedy held Octavia's chin. "You'll be good?"

"Yes, Mama."

"And remember to pray for me and your father? If I'm asleep when you get back?"

"Yes, Mama."

When the other girls had finished getting their toothbrushes and wash-   110
cloths and flashlights for the group restroom trip, I was drawing pictures of tiny birds with too many feathers. Daphne was sitting on her sleeping bag, reading.

"You're not going to come?" Octavia asked.

Daphne shook her head.

"I'm gonna stay, too," I said. "I'll go to the restroom when Daphne and Mrs. Hedy go."

Arnetta leaned down toward me and whispered so that Mrs. Hedy, who'd taken over Mrs. Margolin's task of counting Popsicle sticks, couldn't hear. "No, Snot. If we get in trouble, you're going to get in trouble with the rest of us."

We made our way through the darkness by flashlight. The tree branches   115
that had shaded us just hours earlier, along the same path, now looked like

arms sprouting menacing hands. The stars sprinkled the sky like spilled salt. They seemed fastened to the darkness, high up and holy, their places fixed and definite as we stirred beneath them.

Some, like me, were quiet because we were afraid of the dark; others were talking like crazy for the same reason.

"Wow!" Drema said, looking up. "Why are all the stars out here? I never see stars back on Oneida Street."

"It's a camping trip, that's why," Octavia said. "You're supposed to see stars on camping trips."

Janice said, "This place smells like my mother's air freshener."

"These woods are *pine*," Elise said. "Your mother probably uses *pine* air   120
freshener."

Janice mouthed an exaggerated "Oh," nodding her head as though she just then understood one of the world's great secrets.

No one talked about fighting. Everyone was afraid enough just walking through the infinite deep of the woods. Even though I didn't fight to fight, was afraid of fighting, I felt I was part of the rest of the troop; like I was defending something. We trudged against the slight incline of the path, Arnetta leading the way.

"You know," I said, "their leader will be there. Or they won't even be there. It's dark already. Last night the sun was still in the sky. I'm sure they're already finished."

Arnetta acted as if she hadn't heard me. I followed her gaze with my flashlight, and that's when I saw the squares of light in the darkness. The bathroom was just ahead.

But the girls were there. We could hear them before we could see them.   125

"Octavia and I will go in first so they'll think there's just two of us, then wait till I say, 'We're gonna teach you a lesson,'" Arnetta said. "Then, bust in. That'll surprise them."

"That's what I was supposed to say," Janice said.

Arnetta went inside, Octavia next to her. Janice followed, and the rest of us waited outside.

They were in there for what seemed like whole minutes, but something was wrong. Arnetta hadn't given the signal yet. I was with the girls outside when I heard one of the Troop 909 girls say, "NO. That did NOT happen!"

That was to be expected, that they'd deny the whole thing. What I hadn't   130
expected was *the voice* in which the denial was said. The girl sounded as though her tongue were caught in her mouth. "That's a BAD word!" the girl continued. "We don't say BAD words!"

"Let's go in," Elise said.

"No," Drema said, "I don't want to. What if we get beat up?"

"Snot?" Elise turned to me, her flashlight blinding. It was the first time anyone had asked my opinion, though I knew they were just asking because they were afraid.

"I say we go inside, just to see what's going on."

"But Arnetta didn't give us the signal," Drema said. "She's supposed to say, 135
'We're gonna teach you a lesson,' and I didn't hear her say it."

"C'mon," I said. "Let's just go in."

We went inside. There we found the white girls—about five girls huddled
up next to one big girl. I instantly knew she was the owner of the voice we'd
heard. Arnetta and Octavia inched toward us as soon as we entered.

"Where's Janice?" Elise asked, then we heard a flush. "Oh."

"I think," Octavia said, whispering to Elise, "they're retarded."

"We ARE NOT retarded!" the big girl said, though it was obvious that she 140
was. That they all were. The girls around her began to whimper.

"They're just pretending," Arnetta said, trying to convince herself. "I know
they are."

Octavia turned to Arnetta. "Arnetta. Let's just leave."

Janice came out of a stall, happy and relieved, then she suddenly remembered her line, pointed to the big girl, and said, "We're gonna teach you a
lesson."

"Shut up, Janice," Octavia said, but her heart was not in it. Arnetta's face
was set in a lost, deep scowl. Octavia turned to the big girl and said loudly,
slowly, as if they were all deaf, "We're going to leave. It was nice meeting you,
O.K.? You don't have to tell anyone that we were here. O.K.?"

"Why not?" said the big girl, like a taunt. When she spoke, her lips did not 145
meet, her mouth did not close. Her tongue grazed the roof of her mouth, like a
little pink fish. "You'll get in trouble. I know. *I* know."

Arnetta got back her old cunning. "If you said anything, then you'd be a
tattletale."

The girl looked sad for a moment, then perked up quickly. A flash of genius
crossed her face. "I *like* tattletale."

"It's all right, girls. It's gonna be all right!" the 909 troop leader said. All of
Troop 909 burst into tears. It was as though someone had instructed them all
to cry at once. The troop leader had girls under her arm, and all the rest of the
girls crowded about her. It reminded me of a hog I'd seen on a field trip, where
all the little hogs gathered about the mother at feeding time, latching onto her
teats. The 909 troop leader had come into the bathroom, shortly after the big
girl had threatened to tell. Then the ranger came, then, once the ranger had
radioed the station, Mrs. Margolin arrived with Daphne in tow.

The ranger had left the restroom area, but everyone else was huddled just
outside, swatting mosquitoes.

"Oh. They *will* apologize," Mrs. Margolin said to the 909 troop leader, but 150
she said this so angrily, I knew she was speaking more to us than to the other
troop leader. "When their parents find out, every one a them will be on punishment."

"It's all right, it's all right," the 909 troop leader reassured Mrs. Margolin.
Her voice lilted in the same way it had when addressing the girls. She smiled the

whole time she talked. She was like one of those TV-cooking-show women who talk and dice onions and smile all at the same time.

"See. It could have happened. I'm not calling your girls fibbers or anything." She shook her head ferociously from side to side, her Egyptian-style pageboy flapping against her cheeks like heavy drapes. "It *could* have happened. See. Our girls are *not* retarded. They are *delayed* learners." She said this in a syrupy instructional voice, as though our troop might be delayed learners as well. "We're from the Decatur Children's Academy. Many of them just have special needs."

"Now we won't be able to walk to the bathroom by ourselves!" the big girl said.

"Yes you will," the troop leader said, "but maybe we'll wait till we get back to Decatur—"

"I don't want to wait!" the girl said. "I want my Independence badge!"   155

The girls in my troop were entirely speechless. Arnetta looked stoic, as though she were soon to be tortured but was determined not to appear weak. Mrs. Margolin pursed her lips solemnly and said, "Bless them, Lord. Bless them."

In contrast, the Troop 909 leader was full of words and energy. "Some of our girls are echolalic—" She smiled and happily presented one of the girls hanging onto her, but the girl widened her eyes in horror, and violently withdrew herself from the center of attention, sensing she was being sacrificed for the village sins. "Echolalic," the troop leader continued. "That means they will say whatever they hear, like an echo—that's where the word comes from. It comes from 'echo.'" She ducked her head apologetically, "I mean, not all of them have the most *progressive* of parents, so if they heard a bad word, they might have repeated it. But I guarantee it would not have been *intentional*."

Arnetta spoke. "I saw her say the word. I heard her." She pointed to a small girl, smaller than any of us, wearing an oversized T-shirt that read: "Eat Bertha's Mussels."

The troop leader shook her head and smiled, "That's impossible. She doesn't speak. She can, but she doesn't."

Arnetta furrowed her brow. "No. It wasn't her. That's right. It was *her*."   160

The girl Arnetta pointed to grinned as though she'd been paid a compliment. She was the only one from either troop actually wearing a full uniform: the mocha-colored A-line shift, the orange ascot, the sash covered with badges, though all the same one—the Try-It patch. She took a few steps toward Arnetta and made a grand sweeping gesture toward the sash. "See," she said, full of self-importance, "I'm a Brownie." I had a hard time imagining this girl calling anyone a "nigger"; the girl looked perpetually delighted, as though she would have cuddled up with a grizzly if someone had let her.

On the fourth morning, we boarded the bus to go home.

The previous day had been spent building miniature churches from Popsicle sticks. We hardly left the cabin. Mrs. Margolin and Mrs. Hedy guarded us so closely, almost no one talked for the entire day.

Even on the day of departure from Camp Crescendo, all was serious and silent. The bus ride began quietly enough. Arnetta had to sit beside Mrs. Margolin; Octavia had to sit beside her mother. I sat beside Daphne, who gave me her prize journal without a word of explanation.

"You don't want it?"   165

She shook her head no. It was empty.

Then Mrs. Hedy began to weep. "Octavia," Mrs. Hedy said to her daughter without looking at her, "I'm going to sit with Mrs. Margolin. All right?"

Arnetta exchanged seats with Mrs. Hedy. With the two women up front, Elise felt it safe to speak. "Hey," she said, then she set her face into a placid, vacant stare, trying to imitate that of a Troop 909 girl. Emboldened, Arnetta made a gesture of mock pride toward an imaginary sash, the way the girl in full uniform had done. Then they all made a game of it, trying to do the most exaggerated imitations of the Troop 909 girls, all without speaking, all without laughing loud enough to catch the women's attention.

Daphne looked down at her shoes, white with sneaker polish. I opened the journal she'd given me. I looked out the window, trying to decide what to write, searching for lines, but nothing could compare with what Daphne had written, *"My father, the veteran,"* my favorite line of all time. It replayed itself in my head, and I gave up trying to write.

By then, it seemed that the rest of the troop had given up making fun of   170 the girls in Troop 909. They were now quietly gossiping about who had passed notes to whom in school. For a moment the gossiping fell off, and all I heard was the hum of the bus as we sped down the road and the muffled sounds of Mrs. Hedy and Mrs. Margolin talking about serious things.

"You know," Octavia whispered, "why did *we* have to be stuck at a camp with retarded girls? You know?"

"*You* know why," Arnetta answered. She narrowed her eyes like a cat. "My mama and I were in the mall in Buckhead, and this white lady just kept looking at us. I mean, like we were foreign or something. Like we were from China."

"What did the woman say?" Elise asked.

"Nothing," Arnetta said. "She didn't say nothing."

A few girls quietly nodded their heads.   175

"There was this time," I said, "when my father and I were in the mall and—"

"Oh shut up, Snot," Octavia said.

I stared at Octavia, then rolled my eyes from her to the window. As I watched the trees blur, I wanted nothing more than to be through with it all: the bus ride, the troop, school—all of it. But we were going home. I'd see the same girls in school the next day. We were on a bus, and there was nowhere else to go.

"Go on, Laurel," Daphne said to me. It seemed like the first time she'd spoken the whole trip, and she'd said my name. I turned to her and smiled weakly so as not to cry, hoping she'd remember when I'd tried to be her friend, thinking maybe that her gift of the journal was an invitation of friendship. But she didn't smile back. All she said was, "What happened?"

I studied the girls, waiting for Octavia to tell me to shut up again before I 180 even had a chance to utter another word, but everyone was amazed that Daphne had spoken. The bus was silent. I gathered my voice. "Well," I said. "My father and I were in this mall, but I was the one doing the staring." I stopped and glanced from face to face. I continued. "There were these white people dressed like Puritans or something, but they weren't Puritans. They were Mennonites. They're these people who, if you ask them to do a favor, like paint your porch or something, they have to do it. It's in their rules."

"That sucks," someone said.

"C'mon," Arnetta said. "You're lying."

"I am not."

"How do you know that's not just some story someone made up?" Elise asked, her head cocked full of daring. "I mean, who's gonna do whatever you ask?"

"It's not made up. I know because when I was looking at them, my father 185 said, 'See those people? If you ask them to do something, they'll do it. Anything you want.'"

No one would call anyone's father a liar—then they'd have to fight the person. But Drema parsed her words carefully. "How does your *father* know that's not just some story? Huh?"

"Because," I said, "he went up to the man and asked him would he paint our porch, and the man said yes. It's their religion."

"Man, I'm glad I'm a Baptist," Elise said, shaking her head in sympathy for the Mennonites.

"So did the guy do it?" Drema asked, scooting closer to hear if the story got juicy.

"Yeah," I said. "His whole family was with him. My dad drove them to our 190 house. They all painted our porch. The woman and girl were in bonnets and long, long skirts with buttons up to their necks. The guy wore this weird hat and these huge suspenders."

"Why," Arnetta asked archly, as though she didn't believe a word, "would someone pick a *porch*? If they'll do anything, why not make them paint the whole *house*? Why not ask for a hundred bucks?"

I thought about it, and then remembered the words my father had said about them painting our porch, though I had never seemed to think about his words after he'd said them.

"He said," I began, only then understanding the words as they uncoiled from my mouth, "it was the only time he'd have a white man on his knees doing something for a black man for free."

I now understood what he meant, and why he did it, though I didn't like it. When you've been made to feel bad for so long, you jump at the chance to do it to others. I remembered the Mennonites bending the way Daphne had bent when she was cleaning the restroom. I remembered the dark blue of their bonnets, the black of their shoes. They painted the porch as though scrubbing a floor. I was already trembling before Daphne asked quietly, "Did he thank them?"

I looked out the window. I could not tell which were the thoughts and 195
which were the trees. "No," I said, and suddenly knew there was something
mean in the world that I could not stop.

Arnetta laughed. "If I asked them to take off their long skirts and bonnets
and put on some jeans, would they do it?"

And Daphne's voice, quiet, steady: "Maybe they would. Just to be nice."

Edgar Allan Poe 1809–1849

The Cask of Amontillado   [1846]

The thousand injuries of Fortunato I had borne as I best could; but when
he ventured upon insult, I vowed revenge. You, who so well know the nature of
my soul, will not suppose, however, that I gave utterance to a threat. *At length*
I would be avenged; this was a point definitively settled—but the very defini-
tiveness with which it was resolved precluded the idea of risk. I must not only
punish, but punish with impunity. A wrong is unredressed when retribution
overtakes its redresser. It is equally unredressed when the avenger fails to make
himself felt as such to him who has done the wrong.

It must be understood that neither by word nor deed had I given
Fortunato cause to doubt my good will. I continued, as was my wont, to smile
in his face, and he did not perceive that my smile *now* was at the thought of
his immolation.

He had a weak point—this Fortunato—although in other regards he was a
man to be respected and even feared. He prided himself on his connoisseurship
in wine. Few Italians have the true virtuoso spirit. For the most part their enthusiasm is adopted to suit the time and opportunity—to practice imposture
upon the British and Austrian *millionaires*. In painting and gemmary Fortunato,
like his countrymen, was a quack—but in the matter of old wines he was sincere. In this respect I did not differ from him materially; I was skilful in the
Italian vintages myself, and bought largely whenever I could.

It was about dusk, one evening during the supreme madness of the carnival
season, that I encountered my friend. He accosted me with excessive warmth,
for he had been drinking much. The man wore motley. He had on a tight-fitting
parti-striped dress, and his head was surmounted by the conical cap and bells.
I was so pleased to see him that I thought I should never have done wringing
his hand.

I said to him—"My dear Fortunato, you are luckily met. How remarkably 5
well you are looking to-day! But I have received a pipe° of what passes for
Amontillado, and I have my doubts."

---

pipe: A large keg or cask.

"How?" said he. "Amontillado? A pipe? Impossible! And in the middle of the carnival!"

"I have my doubts," I replied; "and I was silly enough to pay the full Amontillado price without consulting you in the matter. You were not to be found, and I was fearful of losing a bargain."

"Amontillado!"

"I have my doubts."

"Amontillado!"   10

"And I must satisfy them."

"Amontillado!"

"As you are engaged, I am on my way to Luchesi. If any one has a critical turn, it is he. He will tell me—"

"Luchesi cannot tell Amontillado from Sherry."

"And yet some fools will have it that his taste is a match for your own."   15

"Come, let us go."

"Whither?"

"To your vaults."

"My friend, no; I will not impose upon your good nature. I perceive you have an engagement. Luchesi—"

"I have no engagement;—come."   20

"My friend, no. It is not the engagement, but the severe cold with which I perceive you are afflicted. The vaults are insufferably damp. They are encrusted with nitre."

"Let us go, nevertheless. The cold is merely nothing. Amontillado! You have been imposed upon. And as for Luchesi, he cannot distinguish Sherry from Amontillado."

Thus speaking, Fortunato possessed himself of my arm. Putting on a mask of black silk, and drawing a *roquelaire*° closely about my person, I suffered him to hurry me to my palazzo.

There were no attendants at home; they had absconded to make merry in honor of the time. I had told them that I should not return until the morning, and had given them explicit orders not to stir from the house. These orders were sufficient, I well knew, to insure their immediate disappearance, one and all, as soon as my back was turned.

I took from their sconces two flambeaux, and giving one to Fortunato,   25 bowed him through several suites of rooms to the archway that led into the vaults. I passed down a long and winding staircase, requesting him to be cautious as he followed. We came at length to the foot of the descent, and stood together on the damp ground of the catacombs of the Montresors.

The gait of my friend was unsteady, and the bells upon his cap jingled as he strode.

"The pipe," said he.

---

roquelaire: A short cloak.

"It is farther on," said I; "but observe the white web-work which gleams from these cavern walls."

He turned towards me, and looked into my eyes with two filmy orbs that distilled the rheum of intoxication.

"Nitre?" he asked, at length.   30

"Nitre," I replied. "How long have you had that cough?"

"Ugh! ugh! ugh! — ugh! ugh! ugh! — ugh! ugh! ugh! — ugh! ugh! ugh! — ugh! ugh! ugh!"

My poor friend found it impossible to reply for many minutes.

"It is nothing," he said, at last.

"Come," I said, with decision, "we will go back; your health is precious. You   35
are rich, respected, admired, beloved; you are happy, as once I was. You are a man to be missed. For me it is no matter. We will go back; you will be ill, and I cannot be responsible. Besides, there is Luchesi—"

"Enough," he said; "the cough is a mere nothing; it will not kill me. I shall not die of a cough."

"True—true," I replied; "and, indeed, I had no intention of alarming you unnecessarily—but you should use all proper caution. A draught of this Medoc will defend us from the damps."

Here I knocked off the neck of a bottle which I drew from a long row of its fellows that lay upon the mould.

"Drink," I said, presenting him the wine.

He raised it to his lips with a leer. He paused and nodded to me familiarly,   40
while his bells jingled.

"I drink," he said, "to the buried that repose around us."

"And I to your long life."

He again took my arm, and we proceeded.

"These vaults," he said, "are extensive."

"The Montresors," I replied, "were a great and numerous family."   45

"I forget your arms."

"A huge human foot d'or,° in a field azure; the foot crushes a serpent rampant whose fangs are imbedded in the heel."

"And the motto?"

"Nemo me impune lacessit."°

"Good!" he said.   50

The wine sparkled in his eyes and the bells jingled. My own fancy grew warm with the Medoc. We had passed through walls of piled bones, with casks and puncheons intermingling, into the inmost recesses of the catacombs. I paused again, and this time I made bold to seize Fortunato by an arm above the elbow.

"The nitre!" I said; "see, it increases. It hangs like moss upon the vaults. We are below the river's bed. The drops of moisture trickle among the bones. Come, we will go back ere it is too late. Your cough—"

---

d'or: Of gold. *Nemo me impune lacessit:* No one provokes me with impunity (Latin; the motto of the Order of the Thistle in Scotland and the national motto of Scotland).

"It is nothing," he said; "let us go on. But first, another draught of the Medoc."

I broke and reached him a flaçon of De Grâve. He emptied it at a breath. His eyes flashed with a fierce light. He laughed and threw the bottle upwards with a gesticulation I did not understand.

I looked at him in surprise. He repeated the movement—a grotesque one. 55

"You do not comprehend?" he said.

"Not I," I replied.

"Then you are not of the brotherhood."

"How?"

"You are not of the masons." 60

"Yes, yes," I said, "yes, yes."

"You? Impossible! A mason?"

"A mason," I replied.

"A sign," he said.

"It is this," I answered, producing a trowel from beneath the folds of my 65 *roquelaire*.

"You jest," he exclaimed, recoiling a few paces. "But let us proceed to the Amontillado."

"Be it so," I said, replacing the tool beneath the cloak, and again offering him my arm. He leaned upon it heavily. We continued our route in search of the Amontillado. We passed through a range of low arches, descended, passed on, and descending again, arrived at a deep crypt, in which the foulness of the air caused our flambeaux rather to glow than flame.

At the most remote end of the crypt there appeared another less spacious. Its walls had been lined with human remains, piled to the vault overhead, in the fashion of the great catacombs of Paris. Three sides of this interior crypt were still ornamented in this manner. From the fourth the bones had been thrown down, and lay promiscuously upon the earth, forming at one point a mound of some size. Within the wall thus exposed by the displacing of the bones, we perceived a still interior recess, in depth about four feet, in width three, in height six or seven. It seemed to have been constructed for no especial use within itself, but formed merely the interval between two of the colossal supports of the roof of the catacombs, and was backed by one of their circum-scribing walls of solid granite.

It was in vain that Fortunato, uplifting his dull torch, endeavored to pry into the depth of the recess. Its termination the feeble light did not enable us to see.

"Proceed," I said; "herein is the Amontillado. As for Luchesi—" 70

"He is an ignoramus," interrupted my friend, as he stepped unsteadily forward, while I followed immediately at his heels. In an instant he had reached the extremity of the niche, and finding his progress arrested by the rock, stood stupidly bewildered. A moment more and I had fettered him to the granite. In its surface were two iron staples, distant from each other about two feet, horizontally. From one of these depended a short chain, from the other a padlock. Throwing the links about his waist, it was but the work of a few seconds to

secure it. He was too much astounded to resist. Withdrawing the key I stepped
back from the recess.

"Pass your hand," I said, "over the wall; you cannot help feeling the nitre.
Indeed it is *very* damp. Once more let me *implore* you to return. No? Then I
must positively leave you. But I must first render you all the little attentions in
my power."

"The Amontillado!" ejaculated my friend, not yet recovered from his
astonishment.

"True," I replied; "the Amontillado."

As I said these words I busied myself among the pile of bones of which I   75
have before spoken. Throwing them aside, I soon uncovered a quantity of building stone and mortar. With these materials and with the aid of my trowel, I
began vigorously to wall up the entrance of the niche.

I had scarcely laid the first tier of the masonry when I discovered that the
intoxication of Fortunato had in a great measure worn off. The earliest indication
I had of this was a low moaning cry from the depth of the recess. It was *not* the
cry of a drunken man. There was then a long and obstinate silence. I laid the
second tier, and the third, and the fourth; and then I heard the furious vibrations
of the chain. The noise lasted for several minutes, during which, that I might
hearken to it with the more satisfaction, I ceased my labors and sat down upon
the bones. When at last the clanking subsided, I resumed the trowel, and finished
without interruption the fifth, the sixth, and the seventh tier. The wall was now
nearly upon a level with my breast. I again paused, and holding the flambeaux
over the mason-work, threw a few feeble rays upon the figure within.

A succession of loud and shrill screams, bursting suddenly from the throat
of the chained form, seemed to thrust me violently back. For a brief moment I
hesitated—I trembled. Unsheathing my rapier, I began to grope with it about
the recess: but the thought of an instant reassured me. I placed my hand upon
the solid fabric of the catacombs, and felt satisfied. I reapproached the wall. I
replied to the yells of him who clamored. I re-echoed—I aided—I surpassed
them in volume and in strength. I did this, and the clamorer grew still.

It was now midnight, and my task was drawing to a close. I had completed
the eighth, the ninth, and the tenth tier. I had finished a portion of the last and
the eleventh; there remained but a single stone to be fitted and plastered in. I
struggled with its weight; I placed it partially in its destined position. But now
there came from out the niche a low laugh that erected the hairs upon my head.
It was succeeded by a sad voice, which I had difficulty in recognizing as that of
the noble Fortunato. The voice said—

"Ha! ha! ha!—he! he!—a very good joke indeed—an excellent jest. We will
have many a rich laugh about it at the palazzo—he! he! he!—over our wine—he!
he! he!"

"The Amontillado!" I said.   80

"He! he! he!—he! he! he!—yes, the Amontillado. But is it not getting late?
Will not they be awaiting us at the palazzo, the Lady Fortunato and the rest? Let
us be gone."

"Yes," I said, "let us be gone."

"*For the love of God, Montresor!*"

"Yes," I said, "for the love of God!"

But to these words I hearkened in vain for a reply. I grew impatient. I called 85
aloud—

"Fortunato!"

No answer. I called again—

"Fortunato!"

No answer still. I thrust a torch through the remaining aperture and let it fall within. There came forth in return only a jingling of the bells. My heart grew sick—on account of the dampness of the catacombs. I hastened to make an end of my labor. I forced the last stone into its position; I plastered it up. Against the new masonry I re-erected the old rampart of bones. For the half of a century no mortal has disturbed them. *In páce requiescat!*°

In páce requiescat!: May he rest in peace!

Katherine Anne Porter 1890–1980

The Jilting of Granny Weatherall   [1929]

She flicked her wrist neatly out of Doctor Harry's pudgy careful fingers and pulled the sheet up to her chin. The brat ought to be in knee breeches. Doctoring around the country with spectacles on his nose! "Get along now, take your schoolbooks and go. There's nothing wrong with me."

Doctor Harry spread a warm paw like a cushion on her forehead where the forked green vein danced and made her eyelids twitch. "Now, now, be a good girl, and we'll have you up in no time."

"That's no way to speak to a woman nearly eighty years old just because she's down. I'd have you respect your elders, young man."

"Well, Missy, excuse me." Doctor Harry patted her cheek. "But I've got to warn you, haven't I? You're a marvel, but you must be careful or you're going to be good and sorry."

"Don't tell me what I'm going to be. I'm on my feet now, morally speaking. 5 It's Cornelia. I had to go to bed to get rid of her."

Her bones felt loose, and floated around in her skin, and Doctor Harry floated like a balloon around the foot of the bed. He floated and pulled down his waistcoat and swung his glasses on a cord. "Well, stay where you are, it certainly can't hurt you."

"Get along and doctor your sick," said Granny Weatherall. "Leave a well woman alone. I'll call for you when I want you. . . . Where were you forty years ago when I pulled through milk-leg and double pneumonia? You weren't even born. Don't let Cornelia lead you on," she shouted, because Doctor Harry appeared to float up to the ceiling and out. "I pay my own bills, and I don't throw my money away on nonsense!"

She meant to wave good-by, but it was too much trouble. Her eyes closed of themselves, it was like a dark curtain drawn around the bed. The pillow rose and floated under her, pleasant as a hammock in a light wind. She listened to the leaves rustling outside the window. No, somebody was swishing newspapers: no, Cornelia and Doctor Harry were whispering together. She leaped broad awake, thinking they whispered in her ear.

"She was never like this, *never* like this!" "Well, what can we expect?" "Yes, eighty years old. . . ."

Well, and what if she was? She still had ears. It was like Cornelia to whisper 10 around doors. She always kept things secret in such a public way. She was always being tactful and kind. Cornelia was dutiful; that was the trouble with her. Dutiful and good: "So good and dutiful," said Granny, "that I'd like to spank her." She saw herself spanking Cornelia and making a fine job of it.

"What'd you say, Mother?"

Granny felt her face tying up in hard knots.

"Can't a body think, I'd like to know?"

"I thought you might want something."

"I do. I want a lot of things. First off, go away and don't whisper."   15

She lay and drowsed, hoping in her sleep that the children would keep out and let her rest a minute. It had been a long day. Not that she was tired. It was always pleasant to snatch a minute now and then. There was always so much to be done, let me see: tomorrow.

Tomorrow was far away and there was nothing to trouble about. Things were finished somehow when the time came; thank God there was always a little margin over for peace: then a person could spread out the plan of life and tuck in the edges orderly. It was good to have everything clean and folded away, with the hair brushes and tonic bottles sitting straight on the white embroidered linen: the day started without fuss and the pantry shelves laid out with rows of jelly glasses and brown jugs and white stone-china jars with blue whirligigs and words painted on them: coffee, tea, sugar, ginger, cinnamon, allspice: and the bronze clock with the lion on top nicely dusted off. The dust that lion could collect in twenty-four hours! The box in the attic with all those letters tied up, well, she'd have to go through that tomorrow. All those letters—George's letters and John's letters and her letters to them both—lying around for the children to find afterwards made her uneasy. Yes, that would be tomorrow's business. No use to let them know how silly she had been once.

While she was rummaging around she found death in her mind and it felt clammy and unfamiliar. She had spent so much time preparing for death there was no need for bringing it up again. Let it take care of itself now. When she was sixty she had felt very old, finished, and went around making farewell trips to see her children and grandchildren, with a secret in her mind: This is the very last of your mother, children! Then she made her will and came down with a long fever. That was all just a notion like a lot of other things, but it was lucky too, for she had once for all got over the idea of dying for a long time. Now she couldn't be worried. She hoped she had better sense now. Her father had lived to be one hundred and two years old and had drunk a noggin of strong hot toddy on his last birthday. He told the reporters it was his daily habit, and he owed his long life to that. He had made quite a scandal and was very pleased about it. She believed she'd just plague Cornelia a little.

"Cornelia! Cornelia!" No footsteps, but a sudden hand on her cheek. "Bless you, where have you been?"

"Here, Mother."   20

"Well, Cornelia, I want a noggin of hot toddy."

"Are you cold, darling?"

"I'm chilly, Cornelia. Lying in bed stops the circulation. I must have told you that a thousand times."

Well, she could just hear Cornelia telling her husband that Mother was getting a little childish and they'd have to humor her. The thing that most annoyed her was that Cornelia thought she was deaf, dumb, and blind. Little hasty glances and tiny gestures tossed around her and over her head saying, "Don't cross her, let her have her way, she's eighty years old," and she sitting there as if she lived in a thin glass cage. Sometimes Granny almost made up her mind to pack up and move back to her own house where nobody could remind her every minute that she was old. Wait, wait, Cornelia, till your own children whisper behind your back!

In her day she had kept a better house and had got more work done. She 25 wasn't too old yet for Lydia to be driving eighty miles for advice when one of the children jumped the track, and Jimmy still dropped in and talked things over: "Now, Mammy, you've a good business head, I want to know what you think of this? . . ." Old. Cornelia couldn't change the furniture around without asking. Little things, little things! They had been so sweet when they were little. Granny wished the old days were back again with the children young and everything to be done over. It had been a hard pull, but not too much for her. When she thought of all the food she had cooked, and all the clothes she had cut and sewed, and all the gardens she had made—well, the children showed it. There they were, made out of her, and they couldn't get away from that. Sometimes she wanted to see John again and point to them and say, Well, I didn't do so badly, did I? But that would have to wait. That was for tomorrow. She used to think of him as a man, but now all the children were older than their father, and he would be a child beside her if she saw him now. It seemed strange and there was something wrong in the idea. Why, he couldn't possibly recognize her. She had fenced in a hundred acres once, digging the post holes herself and clamping the wires with just a negro boy to help. That changed a woman. John would be looking for a young woman with the peaked Spanish comb in her hair and the painted fan. Digging post holes changed a woman. Riding country roads in the winter when women had their babies was another thing: sitting up nights with sick horses and sick negroes and sick children and hardly ever losing one. John, I hardly ever lost one of them! John would see that in a minute, that would be something he could understand, she wouldn't have to explain anything!

It made her feel like rolling up her sleeves and putting the whole place to rights again. No matter if Cornelia was determined to be everywhere at once, there were a great many things left undone on this place. She would start to-morrow and do them. It was good to be strong enough for everything, even if all you made melted and changed and slipped under your hands, so that by the time you finished you almost forgot what you were working for. What was it I set out to do? she asked herself intently, but she could not remember. A fog rose over the valley, she saw it marching across the creek swallowing the trees and moving up the hill like an army of ghosts. Soon it would be at the near edge of the orchard, and then it was time to go in and light the lamps. Come in, chil-dren, don't stay out in the night air.

Lighting the lamps had been beautiful. The children huddled up to her and breathed like little calves waiting at the bars in the twilight. Their eyes followed the match and watched the flame rise and settle in a blue curve, then they moved away from her. The lamp was lit, they didn't have to be scared and hang on to mother any more. Never, never, never more. God, for all my life I thank Thee. Without Thee, my God, I could never have done it. Hail, Mary, full of grace.

I want you to pick all the fruit this year and see that nothing is wasted. There's always someone who can use it. Don't let good things rot for want of using. You waste life when you waste good food. Don't let things get lost. It's bitter to lose things. Now, don't let me get to thinking, not when I am tired and taking a little nap before supper. . . .

The pillow rose about her shoulders and pressed against her heart and the memory was being squeezed out of it: oh, push down the pillow, somebody: it would smother her if she tried to hold it. Such a fresh breeze blowing and such a green day with no threats in it. But he had not come, just the same. What does a woman do when she has put on the white veil and set out the white cake for a man and he doesn't come? She tried to remember. No, I swear he never harmed me but in that. He never harmed me but in that . . . and what if he did? There was the day, the day, but a whirl of dark smoke rose and covered it, crept up and over into the bright field where everything was planted so carefully in orderly rows. That was hell, she knew hell when she saw it. For sixty years she had prayed against remembering him and against losing her soul in the deep pit of hell, and now the two things were mingled in one and the thought of him was a smoky cloud from hell that moved and crept in her head when she had just got rid of Doctor Harry and was trying to rest a minute. Wounded vanity, Ellen, said a sharp voice in the top of her mind. Don't let your wounded vanity get the upper hand of you. Plenty of girls get jilted. You were jilted, weren't you? Then stand up to it. Her eyelids wavered and let in streamers of blue-gray light like tissue paper over her eyes. She must get up and pull the shades down or she'd never sleep. She was in bed again and the shades were not down. How could that happen? Better turn over, hide from the light, sleeping in the light gave you nightmares. "Mother, how do you feel now?" and a stinging wetness on her forehead. But I don't like having my face washed in cold water!

Hapsy? George? Lydia? Jimmy? No, Cornelia, and her features were swollen   30 and full of little puddles. "They're coming, darling, they'll all be here soon." Go wash your face, child, you look funny.

Instead of obeying, Cornelia knelt down and put her head on the pillow. She seemed to be talking but there was no sound. "Well, are you tongue-tied? Whose birthday is it? Are you going to give a party?"

Cornelia's mouth moved urgently in strange shapes. "Don't do that, you bother me, daughter."

"Oh, no, Mother. Oh, no. . . ."

Nonsense. It was strange about children. They disputed your every word. "No what, Cornelia?"

"Here's Doctor Harry."   35

"I won't see that boy again. He just left five minutes ago."

"That was this morning, Mother. It's night now. Here's the nurse."

"This is Doctor Harry, Mrs. Weatherall. I never saw you look so young and happy!"

"Ah, I'll never be young again — but I'd be happy if they'd let me lie in peace and get rested."

She thought she spoke up loudly, but no one answered. A warm weight on   40 her forehead, a warm bracelet on her wrist, and a breeze went on whispering, trying to tell her something. A shuffle of leaves in the everlasting hand of God, He blew on them and they danced and rattled. "Mother, don't mind, we're going to give you a little hypodermic." "Look here, daughter, how do ants get in this bed? I saw sugar ants yesterday." Did you send for Hapsy too?

It was Hapsy she really wanted. She had to go a long way back through a great many rooms to find Hapsy standing with a baby on her arm. She seemed to herself to be Hapsy also, and the baby on Hapsy's arm was Hapsy and himself and herself, all at once, and there was no surprise in the meeting. Then Hapsy melted from within and turned flimsy as gray gauze and the baby was a gauzy shadow, and Hapsy came up close and said, "I thought you'd never come," and looked at her very searchingly and said, "You haven't changed a bit!" They leaned forward to kiss, when Cornelia began whispering from a long way off, "Oh, is there anything you want to tell me? Is there anything I can do for you?"

Yes, she had changed her mind after sixty years and she would like to see George. I want you to find George. Find him and be sure to tell him I forgot him. I want him to know I had my husband just the same and my children and my house like any other woman. A good house too and a good husband that I loved and fine children out of him. Better than I hoped for even. Tell him I was given back everything he took away and more. Oh, no, oh, God, no, there was something else besides the house and the man and the children. Oh, surely they were not all? What was it? Something not given back. . . . Her breath crowded down under her ribs and grew into a monstrous frightening shape with cutting edges; it bored up into her head, and the agony was unbelievable: Yes, John, get the Doctor now, no more talk, my time has come.

When this one was born it should be the last. The last. It should have been born first, for it was the one she had truly wanted. Everything came in good time. Nothing left out, left over. She was strong, in three days she would be as well as ever. Better. A woman needed milk in her to have her full health.

"Mother, do you hear me?"

"I've been telling you—"   45

"Mother, Father Connolly's here."

"I went to Holy Communion only last week. Tell him I'm not so sinful as all that."

"Father just wants to speak to you."

He could speak as much as he pleased. It was like him to drop in and inquire about her soul as if it were a teething baby, and then stay on for a cup of tea and a round of cards and gossip. He always had a funny story of some sort, usually about an Irishman who made his little mistakes and confessed them, and the point lay in some absurd thing he would blurt out in the confessional showing his struggles between native piety and original sin. Granny felt easy about her soul. Cornelia, where are your manners? Give Father Connolly a chair. She had her secret comfortable understanding with a few favorite saints who cleared a straight road to God for her. All as surely signed and sealed as the papers for the new Forty Acres. Forever . . . heirs and assigns forever. Since the day the wedding cake was not cut, but thrown out and wasted. The whole bottom dropped out of the world, and there she was blind and sweating with nothing under her feet and the walls falling away. His hand had caught her under the breast, she had not fallen, there was the freshly polished floor with the green rug on it, just as before. He had cursed like a sailor's parrot and said, "I'll kill him for you." Don't lay a hand on him, for my sake leave something to God. "Now, Ellen, you must believe what I tell you. . . ."

So there was nothing, nothing to worry about any more, except sometimes 50 in the night one of the children screamed in a nightmare, and they both hustled out shaking and hunting for the matches and calling, "There, wait a minute, here we are!" John, get the doctor now, Hapsy's time has come. But there was Hapsy standing by the bed in a white cap. "Cornelia, tell Hapsy to take off her cap. I can't see her plain."

Her eyes opened very wide and the room stood out like a picture she had seen somewhere. Dark colors with the shadows rising towards the ceiling in long angles. The tall black dresser gleamed with nothing on it but John's picture, enlarged from a little one, with John's eyes very black when they should have been blue. You never saw him, so how do you know how he looked? But the man insisted the copy was perfect, it was very rich and handsome. For a picture, yes, but it's not my husband. The table by the bed had a linen cover and a candle and a crucifix. The light was blue from Cornelia's silk lampshades. No sort of light at all, just frippery. You had to live forty years with kerosene lamps to appreciate honest electricity. She felt very strong and she saw Doctor Harry with a rosy nimbus around him.

"You look like a saint, Doctor Harry, and I vow that's as near as you'll ever come to it."

"She's saying something."

"I heard you, Cornelia. What's all this carrying-on?"

"Father Connolly's saying—"

Cornelia's voice staggered and bumped like a cart in a bad road. It rounded corners and turned back again and arrived nowhere. Granny stepped up in the cart very lightly and reached for the reins, but a man sat beside her and she knew him by his hands, driving the cart. She did not look in his face, for she knew without seeing, but looked instead down the road where the trees leaned over and bowed to each other and a thousand birds were singing a Mass. She felt like singing too, but she put her hand in the bosom of her dress and pulled out a rosary, and Father Connolly murmured Latin in a very solemn voice and tickled her feet. My God, will you stop that nonsense? I'm a married woman. What if he did run away and leave me to face the priest by myself? I found another a whole world better. I wouldn't have exchanged my husband for anybody except St. Michael himself, and you may tell him that for me with a thank you in the bargain.

Light flashed on her closed eyelids, and a deep roaring shook her. Cornelia, is that lightning? I hear thunder. There's going to be a storm. Close all the windows. Call the children in. . . . "Mother, here we are, all of us." "Is that you, Hapsy?" "Oh, no, I'm Lydia. We drove as fast as we could." Their faces drifted above her, drifted away. The rosary fell out of her hands and Lydia put it back. Jimmy tried to help, their hands fumbled together, and Granny closed two fingers around Jimmy's thumb. Beads wouldn't do, it must be something alive. She was so amazed her thoughts ran round and round. So, my dear Lord, this is my death and I wasn't even thinking about it. My children have come to see me die. But I can't, it's not time. Oh, I always hated surprises. I wanted to give Cornelia the amethyst set—Cornelia, you're to have the amethyst set, but Hapsy's to wear it when she wants, and, Doctor Harry, do shut up. Nobody sent for you. Oh, my dear Lord, do wait a minute. I meant to do something about the Forty Acres, Jimmy doesn't need it and Lydia will later on, with that worthless husband of hers. I meant to finish the altar cloth and send six bottles of wine to Sister Borgia for her dyspepsia. I want to send six bottles of wine to Sister Borgia, Father Connolly, now don't let me forget.

Cornelia's voice made short turns and tilted over and crashed. "Oh, Mother, oh, Mother, oh, Mother. . . ."

"I'm not going, Cornelia. I'm taken by surprise. I can't go."

You'll see Hapsy again. What about her? "I thought you'd never come." Granny made a long journey outward, looking for Hapsy. What if I don't find her? What then? Her heart sank down and down, there was no bottom to death, she couldn't come to the end of it. The blue light from Cornelia's lampshade drew into a tiny point in the center of her brain, it flickered and winked like an eye, quietly it fluttered and dwindled. Granny lay curled down within herself, amazed and watchful, staring at the point of light that was herself; her body was now only a deeper mass of shadow in an endless darkness and this darkness would curl around the light and swallow it up. God, give a sign!

For the second time there was no sign. Again no bridegroom and the priest in the house. She could not remember any other sorrow because this grief wiped them all away. Oh, no, there's nothing more cruel than this — I'll never forgive it. She stretched herself with a deep breath and blew out the light.

Leslie Marmon Silko   b. 1948

The Man to Send Rain Clouds   [1981]

They found him under a big cottonwood tree. His Levi jacket and pants were faded light blue so that he had been easy to find. The big cottonwood tree stood apart from a small grove of winterbare cottonwoods which grew in the wide, sandy arroyo. He had been dead for a day or more, and the sheep had wandered and scattered up and down the arroyo. Leon and his brother-in-law, Ken, gathered the sheep and left them in the pen at the sheep camp before they returned to the cottonwood tree. Leon waited under the tree while Ken drove the truck through the deep sand to the edge of the arroyo. He squinted up at the sun and unzipped his jacket — it sure was hot for this time of year. But high and northwest the blue mountains were still in snow. Ken came sliding down the low, crumbling bank about fifty yards down, and he was bringing the red blanket.

APPROACHING THE AUTHOR

Leslie Marmon Silko is of mixed ancestry — Laguna Pueblo, Mexican, and white — but grew up in Laguna society. At school she was prohibited from speaking the Keresan language that her Laguna aunts and grandmothers used in storytelling. However, she learned the traditional Laguna stories from them and as a result always identified most strongly with the native part of her ancestry.

For more about her, see page 1411.

Before they wrapped the old man, Leon took a piece of string out of his pocket and tied a small gray feather in the old man's long white hair. Ken gave him the paint. Across the brown wrinkled forehead he drew a streak of white and along the high cheekbones he drew a strip of blue paint. He paused and watched Ken throw pinches of corn meal and pollen into the wind that fluttered the small gray feather. Then Leon painted with yellow under the old man's broad nose, and finally, when he had painted green across the chin, he smiled.

"Send us rain clouds, Grandfather." They laid the bundle in the back of the pickup and covered it with a heavy tarp before they started back to the pueblo.

They turned off the highway onto the sandy pueblo road. Not long after they passed the store and post office they saw Father Paul's car coming toward them. When he recognized their faces he slowed his car and waved for them to stop. The young priest rolled down the car window.

"Did you find old Teofilo?" he asked loudly.   5

Leon stopped the truck. "Good morning, Father. We were just out to the sheep camp. Everything is O.K. now."

"Thank God for that. Teofilo is a very old man. You really shouldn't allow him to stay at the sheep camp alone."

"No, he won't do that any more now."

"Well, I'm glad you understand. I hope I'll be seeing you at Mass this week—we missed you last Sunday. See if you can get old Teofilo to come with you." The priest smiled and waved at them as they drove away.

Louise and Teresa were waiting. The table was set for lunch, and the coffee   10
was boiling on the black iron stove. Leon looked at Louise and then at Teresa.

"We found him under a cottonwood tree in the big arroyo near sheep camp. I guess he sat down to rest in the shade and never got up again." Leon walked toward the old man's bed. The red plaid shawl had been shaken and spread carefully over the bed, and a new brown flannel shirt and pair of stiff new Levi's were arranged neatly beside the pillow. Louise held the screen door open while Leon and Ken carried in the red blanket. He looked small and shriveled, and after they dressed him in the new shirt and pants he seemed more shrunken.

It was noontime now because the church bells rang the Angelus. They ate the beans with hot bread, and nobody said anything until after Teresa poured the coffee.

Ken stood up and put on his jacket. "I'll see about the gravediggers. Only the top layer of soil is frozen. I think it can be ready before dark."

Leon nodded his head and finished his coffee. After Ken had been gone for a while, the neighbors and clanspeople came quietly to embrace Teofilo's family and to leave food on the table because the gravediggers would come to eat when they were finished.

The sky in the west was full of pale yellow light. Louise stood outside with   15
her hands in the pockets of Leon's green army jacket that was too big for her. The funeral was over, and the old men had taken their candles and medicine bags and were gone. She waited until the body was laid into the pickup before she said anything to Leon. She touched his arm, and he noticed that her hands were still dusty from the corn meal that she had sprinkled around the old man. When she spoke, Leon could not hear her.

"What did you say? I didn't hear you."

"I said that I had been thinking about something."

"About what?"

"About the priest sprinkling holy water for Grandpa. So he won't be thirsty."

Leon stared at the new moccasins that Teofilo had made for the ceremo-   20
nial dances in the summer. They were nearly hidden by the red blanket. It was getting colder, and the wind pushed gray dust down the narrow pueblo road. The sun was approaching the long mesa where it disappeared during the winter.

Louise stood there shivering and watching his face. Then he zipped up his jacket and opened the truck door. "I'll see if he's there."

Ken stopped the pickup at the church, and Leon got out; and then Ken drove down the hill to the graveyard where people were waiting. Leon knocked at the old carved door with its symbols of the Lamb. While he waited he looked up at the twin bells from the king of Spain with the last sunlight pouring around them in their tower.

The priest opened the door and smiled when he saw who it was. "Come in! What brings you here this evening?"

The priest walked toward the kitchen, and Leon stood with his cap in his hand, playing with the earflaps and examining the living room—the brown sofa, the green armchair, and the brass lamp that hung down from the ceiling by links of chain. The priest dragged a chair out of the kitchen and offered it to Leon.

"No thank you, Father. I only came to ask you if you would bring your holy water to the graveyard."

The priest turned away from Leon and looked out the window at the patio 25 full of shadows and the dining-room windows of the nuns' cloister across the patio. The curtains were heavy, and the light from within faintly penetrated; it was impossible to see the nuns inside eating supper. "Why didn't you tell me he was dead? I could have brought the Last Rites anyway."

Leon smiled. "It wasn't necessary, Father."

The priest stared down at his scuffed brown loafers and the worn hem of his cassock. "For a Christian burial it was necessary."

His voice was distant, and Leon thought that his blue eyes looked tired.

"It's O.K. Father, we just want him to have plenty of water."

The priest sank down into the green chair and picked up a glossy missionary 30 magazine. He turned the colored pages full of lepers and pagans without looking at them.

"You know I can't do that, Leon. There should have been the Last Rites and a funeral Mass at the very least."

Leon put on his green cap and pulled the flaps down over his ears. "It's getting late, Father. I've got to go."

When Leon opened the door Father Paul stood up and said, "Wait." He left the room and came back wearing a long brown overcoat. He followed Leon out the door and across the dim churchyard to the adobe steps in front of the church. They both stooped to fit through the low adobe entrance. And when they started down the hill to the graveyard only half of the sun was visible above the mesa.

The priest approached the grave slowly, wondering how they had managed to dig into the frozen ground; and then he remembered that this was New Mexico, and saw the pile of cold loose sand beside the hole. The people stood close to each other with little clouds of steam puffing from their faces. The priest looked at them and saw a pile of jackets, gloves, and scarves in the yellow, dry tumbleweeds that grew in the graveyard. He looked at the red blanket, not sure that Teofilo was so small, wondering if it wasn't some perverse Indian trick—something they did in March to ensure a good harvest—wondering if maybe old Teofilo was actually at sheep camp corraling the sheep for the night. But there he was, facing into a cold dry wind and squinting at the last sunlight, ready to bury a red wool blanket while the faces of his parishioners were in shadow with the last warmth of the sun on their backs.

His fingers were stiff, and it took him a long time to twist the lid off the 35 holy water. Drops of water fell on the red blanket and soaked into dark icy spots. He sprinkled the grave and the water disappeared almost before it touched the dim, cold sand; it reminded him of something—he tried to remember what it was, because he thought if he could remember he might understand this. He sprinkled more water; he shook the container until it was empty, and the water fell through the light from sundown like August rain that fell while the sun was still shining, almost evaporating before it touched the wilted squash flowers.

The wind pulled at the priest's brown Franciscan robe and swirled away the corn meal and pollen that had been sprinkled on the blanket. They lowered the bundle into the ground, and they didn't bother to untie the stiff pieces of new rope that were tied around the ends of the blanket. The sun was gone, and over on the highway the eastbound lane was full of headlights. The priest walked away slowly. Leon watched him climb the hill, and when he had disappeared within the tall, thick walls, Leon turned to look up at the high blue mountains in the deep snow that reflected a faint red light from the west. He felt good because it was finished, and he was happy about the sprinkling of the holy water; now the old man could send them big thunderclouds for sure.

Amy Tan b. 1952

Two Kinds [1989]

My mother believed you could be anything you wanted to be in America. You could open a restaurant. You could work for the government and get good retirement. You could buy a house with almost no money down. You could become rich. You could become instantly famous.

"Of course you can be prodigy, too," my mother told me when I was nine. "You can be best anything. What does Auntie Lindo know? Her daughter, she is only best tricky."

America was where all my mother's hopes lay. She had come here in 1949 after losing everything in China: her mother and

> **APPROACHING THE AUTHOR**
>
> When **Amy Tan** began her career by writing business manuals and speeches for executives, she felt pressured to write under an American-sounding pseudonym, so she chose "May Brown"—she rearranged *Amy* to get *May*, and *Brown* is a synonym for *Tan*. For more about her, see page 1415.

father, her family home, her first husband, and two daughters, twin baby girls. But she never looked back with regret. There were so many ways for things to get better.

We didn't immediately pick the right kind of prodigy. At first my mother thought I could be a Chinese Shirley Temple. We'd watch Shirley's old movies on TV as though they were training films. My mother would poke my arm and say, *"Ni kan"* — You watch. And I would see Shirley tapping her feet, or singing a sailor song, or pursing her lips into a very round O while saying, "Oh my goodness."

"Ni kan," said my mother as Shirley's eyes flooded with tears. "You already know how. Don't need talent for crying!"   5

Soon after my mother got this idea about Shirley Temple, she took me to a beauty training school in the Mission district and put me in the hands of a student who could barely hold the scissors without shaking. Instead of getting big fat curls, I emerged with an uneven mass of crinkly black fuzz. My mother dragged me off to the bathroom and tried to wet down my hair.

"You look like Negro Chinese," she lamented, as if I had done this on purpose.

The instructor of the beauty training school had to lop off these soggy clumps to make my hair even again. "Peter Pan is very popular these days," the instructor assured my mother. I now had hair the length of a boy's, with straight-across bangs that hung at a slant two inches above my eyebrows. I liked the haircut and it made me actually look forward to my future fame.

In fact, in the beginning, I was just as excited as my mother, maybe even more so. I pictured this prodigy part of me as many different images, trying each one on for size. I was a dainty ballerina girl standing by the curtains, waiting to hear the right music that would send me floating on my tiptoes. I was like the Christ child lifted out of the straw manger, crying with holy indignity. I was Cinderella stepping from her pumpkin carriage with sparkly cartoon music filling the air.

In all of my imaginings, I was filled with a sense that I would soon become   10 *perfect*. My mother and father would adore me. I would be beyond reproach. I would never feel the need to sulk for anything.

But sometimes the prodigy in me became impatient. "If you don't hurry up and get me out of here, I'm disappearing for good," it warned. "And then you'll always be nothing."

Every night after dinner, my mother and I would sit at the Formica kitchen table. She would present new tests, taking her examples from stories of amazing children she had read in *Ripley's Believe It or Not*, or *Good Housekeeping*, *Reader's Digest*, and a dozen other magazines she kept in a pile in our bathroom. My mother got these magazines from people whose houses she cleaned. And since she cleaned many houses each week, we had a great assortment. She would look through them all, searching for stories about remarkable children.

The first night she brought out a story about a three-year-old boy who knew the capitals of all the states and even most of the European countries. A teacher was quoted as saying the little boy could also pronounce the names of the foreign cities correctly.

"What's the capital of Finland?" my mother asked me, looking at the magazine story.

All I knew was the capital of California, because Sacramento was the name   15
of the street we lived on in Chinatown. "Nairobi!" I guessed, saying the most foreign word I could think of. She checked to see if that was possibly one way to pronounce "Helsinki" before showing me the answer.

The tests got harder—multiplying numbers in my head, finding the queen of hearts in a deck of cards, trying to stand on my head without using my hands, predicting the daily temperatures in Los Angeles, New York, and London.

One night I had to look at a page from the Bible for three minutes and then report everything I could remember. "Now Jehoshaphat had riches and honor in abundance and . . . that's all I remember, Ma," I said.

And after seeing my mother's disappointed face once again, something inside of me began to die. I hated the tests, the raised hopes and failed expectations. Before going to bed that night, I looked in the mirror above the bathroom sink and when I saw only my face staring back—and that it would always be this ordinary face—I began to cry. Such a sad, ugly girl! I made high-pitched noises like a crazed animal, trying to scratch out the face in the mirror.

And then I saw what seemed to be the prodigy side of me—because I had never seen that face before. I looked at my reflection, blinking so I could see more clearly. The girl staring back at me was angry, powerful. This girl and I were the same. I had new thoughts, willful thoughts, or rather thoughts filled with lots of won'ts. I won't let her change me, I promised myself. I won't be what I'm not.

So now on nights when my mother presented her tests, I performed list-   20
lessly, my head propped on one arm. I pretended to be bored. And I was. I got so bored I started counting the bellows of the foghorns out on the bay while my mother drilled me in other areas. The sound was comforting and reminded me of the cow jumping over the moon. And the next day, I played a game with myself, seeing if my mother would give up on me before eight bellows. After a while I usually counted only one, maybe two bellows at most. At last she was beginning to give up hope.

Two or three months had gone by without any mention of my being a prodigy again. And then one day my mother was watching *The Ed Sullivan Show* on TV. The TV was old and the sound kept shorting out. Every time my mother got halfway up from the sofa to adjust the set, the sound would go back on and Ed would be talking. As soon as she sat down, Ed would go silent again. She got up, the TV broke into loud piano music. She sat down. Silence. Up and down, back and forth, quiet and loud. It was like a stiff embraceless dance between her and the TV set. Finally she stood by the set with her hand on the sound dial.

She seemed entranced by the music, a little frenzied piano piece with this mesmerizing quality, sort of quick passages and then teasing lilting ones before it returned to the quick playful parts.

"*Ni kan*," my mother said, calling me over with hurried hand gestures, "Look here."

I could see why my mother was fascinated by the music. It was being pounded out by a little Chinese girl, about nine years old, with a Peter Pan haircut. The girl had the sauciness of a Shirley Temple. She was proudly modest like a proper Chinese child. And she also did this fancy sweep of a curtsy, so that the fluffy skirt of her white dress cascaded slowly to the floor like the petals of a large carnation.

In spite of these warning signs, I wasn't worried. Our family had no piano   25 and we couldn't afford to buy one, let alone reams of sheet music and piano lessons. So I could be generous in my comments when my mother bad-mouthed the little girl on TV.

"Play note right, but doesn't sound good! No singing sound," complained my mother.

"What are you picking on her for?" I said carelessly. "She's pretty good. Maybe she's not the best, but she's trying hard." I knew almost immediately I would be sorry I said that.

"Just like you," she said. "Not the best. Because you not trying." She gave a little huff as she let go of the sound dial and sat down on the sofa.

The little Chinese girl sat down also to play an encore of "Anitra's Dance" by Grieg. I remember the song, because later on I had to learn how to play it.

Three days after watching *The Ed Sullivan Show,* my mother told me what   30 my schedule would be for piano lessons and piano practice. She had talked to Mr. Chong, who lived on the first floor of our apartment building. Mr. Chong was a retired piano teacher and my mother had traded housecleaning services for weekly lessons and a piano for me to practice on every day, two hours a day, from four until six.

When my mother told me this, I felt as though I had been sent to hell. I whined and then kicked my foot a little when I couldn't stand it anymore.

"Why don't you like me the way I am? I'm *not* a genius! I can't play the piano. And even if I could, I wouldn't go on TV if you paid me a million dollars!" I cried.

My mother slapped me. "Who ask you be genius?" she shouted. "Only ask you be your best. For you sake. You think I want you be genius? Hnnh! What for! Who ask you!"

"So ungrateful," I heard her mutter in Chinese. "If she had as much talent as she has temper, she would be famous now."

Mr. Chong, whom I secretly nicknamed Old Chong, was very strange, al-   35 ways tapping his fingers to the silent music of an invisible orchestra. He looked ancient in my eyes. He had lost most of the hair on top of his head and he wore thick glasses and had eyes that always looked tired and sleepy. But he must have been younger than I thought, since he lived with his mother and was not yet married.

I met Old Lady Chong once and that was enough. She had this peculiar smell like a baby that had done something in its pants. And her fingers felt like a dead person's, like an old peach I once found in the back of the refrigerator; the skin just slid off the meat when I picked it up.

I soon found out why Old Chong had retired from teaching piano. He was deaf. "Like Beethoven!" he shouted to me. "We're both listening only in our head!" And he would start to conduct his frantic silent sonatas.

Our lessons went like this. He would open the book and point to different things, explaining their purpose: "Key! Treble! Bass! No sharps or flats! So this is C major! Listen now and play after me!"

And then he would play the C scale a few times, a simple chord, and then, as if inspired by an old, unreachable itch, he gradually added more notes and running trills and a pounding bass until the music was really something quite grand.

I would play after him, the simple scale, the simple chord, and then I just 40 played some nonsense that sounded like a cat running up and down on top of garbage cans. Old Chong smiled and applauded and then said, "Very good! But now you must learn to keep time!"

So that's how I discovered that Old Chong's eyes were too slow to keep up with the wrong notes I was playing. He went through the motions in half-time. To help me keep rhythm, he stood behind me, pushing down on my right shoulder for every beat. He balanced pennies on top of my wrists so I would keep them still as I slowly played scales and arpeggios. He had me curve my hand around an apple and keep that shape when playing chords. He marched stiffly to show me how to make each finger dance up and down, staccato like an obedient little soldier.

He taught me all these things, and that was how I also learned I could be lazy and get away with mistakes, lots of mistakes. If I hit the wrong notes because I hadn't practiced enough, I never corrected myself. I just kept playing in rhythm. And Old Chong kept conducting his own private reverie.

So maybe I never really gave myself a fair chance. I did pick up the basics pretty quickly, and I might have become a good pianist at that young age. But I was so determined not to try, not to be anybody different that I learned to play only the most ear-splitting preludes, the most discordant hymns.

Over the next year, I practiced like this, dutifully in my own way. And then one day I heard my mother and her friend Lindo Jong both talking in a loud bragging tone of voice so others could hear. It was after church, and I was leaning against the brick wall wearing a dress with stiff white petticoats. Auntie Lindo's daughter, Waverly, who was about my age, was standing farther down the wall about five feet away. We had grown up together and shared all the closeness of two sisters squabbling over crayons and dolls. In other words, for the most part, we hated each other. I thought she was snotty. Waverly Jong had gained a certain amount of fame as "Chinatown's Littlest Chinese Chess Champion."

"She bring home too many trophy," lamented Auntie Lindo that Sunday. 45 "All day she play chess. All day I have no time do nothing but dust off her winnings." She threw a scolding look at Waverly, who pretended not to see her.

"You lucky you don't have this problem," said Auntie Lindo with a sigh to my mother.

And my mother squared her shoulders and bragged: "Our problem worser than yours. If we ask Jing-mei wash dish, she hear nothing but music. It's like you can't stop this natural talent."

And right then, I was determined to put a stop to her foolish pride.

A few weeks later, Old Chong and my mother conspired to have me play in a talent show which would be held in the church hall. By then, my parents had saved up enough to buy me a secondhand piano, a black Wurlitzer spinet with a scarred bench. It was the showpiece of our living room.

For the talent show, I was to play a piece called "Pleading Child" from 50 Schumann's *Scenes from Childhood*. It was a simple, moody piece that sounded more difficult than it was. I was supposed to memorize the whole thing, playing the repeat parts twice to make the piece sound longer. But I dawdled over it, playing a few bars and then cheating, looking up to see what notes followed. I never really listened to what I was playing. I daydreamed about being somewhere else, about being someone else.

The part I liked to practice best was the fancy curtsy: right foot out, touch the rose on the carpet with a pointed foot, sweep to the side, left leg bends, look up and smile.

My parents invited all the couples from the Joy Luck Club to witness my debut. Auntie Lindo and Uncle Tin were there. Waverly and her two older brothers had also come. The first two rows were filled with children both younger and older than I was. The littlest ones got to go first. They recited simple nursery rhymes, squawked out tunes on miniature violins, twirled Hula Hoops, pranced in pink ballet tutus, and when they bowed or curtsied, the audience would sigh in unison, "Awww," and then clap enthusiastically.

When my turn came, I was very confident. I remember my childish excitement. It was as if I knew, without a doubt, that the prodigy side of me really did exist. I had no fear whatsoever, no nervousness. I remember thinking to myself, This is it! This is it! I looked out over the audience, at my mother's blank face, my father's yawn, Auntie Lindo's stiff-lipped smile, Waverly's sulky expression. I had on a white dress layered with sheets of lace, and a pink bow in my Peter Pan haircut. As I sat down I envisioned people jumping to their feet and Ed Sullivan rushing up to introduce me to everyone on TV.

And I started to play. It was so beautiful. I was so caught up in how lovely I looked that at first I didn't worry how I would sound. So it was a surprise to me when I hit the first wrong note and I realized something didn't sound quite right. And then I hit another and another followed that. A chill started at the top of my head and began to trickle down. Yet I couldn't stop playing, as though my hands were bewitched. I kept thinking my fingers would adjust themselves back, like a train switching to the right track. I played this strange jumble through two repeats, the sour notes staying with me all the way to the end.

When I stood up, I discovered my legs were shaking. Maybe I had just been 55 nervous and the audience, like Old Chong, had seen me go through the right motions and had not heard anything wrong at all. I swept my right foot out, went down on my knee, looked up and smiled. The room was quiet, except for Old Chong, who was beaming and shouting, "Bravo! Bravo! Well done!" But then I saw my mother's face, her stricken face. The audience clapped weakly, and as I walked back to my chair, with my whole face quivering as I tried not to cry, I heard a little boy whisper loudly to his mother, "That was awful," and the mother whispered back, "Well, she certainly tried."

And now I realized how many people were in the audience, the whole world it seemed. I was aware of eyes burning into my back. I felt the shame of my mother and father as they sat stiffly throughout the rest of the show.

We could have escaped during intermission. Pride and some strange sense of honor must have anchored my parents to their chairs. And so we watched it all: the eighteen-year-old boy with a fake mustache who did a magic show and juggled flaming hoops while riding a unicycle. The breasted girl with white makeup who sang from *Madama Butterfly* and got honorable mention. And the eleven-year-old boy who won first prize playing a tricky violin song that sounded like a busy bee.

After the show, the Hsus, the Jongs, and the St. Clairs from the Joy Luck Club came up to my mother and father.

"Lots of talented kids," Auntie Lindo said vaguely, smiling broadly.

"That was somethin' else," said my father, and I wondered if he was refer- 60 ring to me in a humorous way, or whether he even remembered what I had done.

Waverly looked at me and shrugged her shoulders. "You aren't a genius like me," she said matter-of-factly. And if I hadn't felt so bad, I would have pulled her braids and punched her stomach.

But my mother's expression was what devastated me: a quiet, blank look that said she had lost everything. I felt the same way, and it seemed as if everybody were now coming up, like gawkers at the scene of an accident, to see what parts were actually missing. When we got on the bus to go home, my father was humming the busy-bee tune and my mother was silent. I kept thinking she wanted to wait until we got home before shouting at me. But when my father unlocked the door to our apartment, my mother walked in and then went to the back, into the bedroom. No accusations. No blame. And in a way, I felt disappointed. I had been waiting for her to start shouting, so I could shout back and cry and blame her for all my misery.

I assumed my talent-show fiasco meant I never had to play the piano again. But two days later, after school, my mother came out of the kitchen and saw me watching TV.

"Four clock," she reminded me as if it were any other day. I was stunned, as though she were asking me to go through the talent-show torture again. I wedged myself more tightly in front of the TV.

"Turn off TV," she called from the kitchen five minutes later.   65

I didn't budge. And then I decided. I didn't have to do what my mother said anymore. I wasn't her slave. This wasn't China. I had listened to her before and look what happened. She was the stupid one.

She came out from the kitchen and stood in the arched entryway of the living room. "Four clock," she said once again, louder.

"I'm not going to play anymore," I said nonchalantly. "Why should I? I'm not a genius."

She walked over and stood in front of the TV. I saw her chest was heaving up and down in an angry way.

"No!" I said, and I now felt stronger, as if my true self had finally emerged.   70 So this was what had been inside me all along.

"No! I won't!" I screamed.

She yanked me by the arm, pulled me off the floor, snapped off the TV. She was frighteningly strong, half pulling, half carrying me toward the piano as I kicked the throw rugs under my feet. She lifted me up and onto the hard bench. I was sobbing by now, looking at her bitterly. Her chest was heaving even more and her mouth was open, smiling crazily as if she were pleased I was crying.

"You want me to be someone that I'm not!" I sobbed. "I'll never be the kind of daughter you want me to be!"

"Only two kinds of daughters," she shouted in Chinese. "Those who are obedient and those who follow their own mind! Only one kind of daughter can live in this house. Obedient daughter!"

"Then I wish I wasn't your daughter. I wish you weren't my mother," I   75 shouted. As I said these things I got scared. It felt like worms and toads and slimy things crawling out of my chest, but it also felt good, as if this awful side of me had surfaced, at last.

"Too late change this," said my mother shrilly.

And I could sense her anger rising to its breaking point. I wanted to see it spill over. And that's when I remembered the babies she had lost in China, the ones we never talked about. "Then I wish I'd never been born!" I shouted. "I wish I were dead! Like them."

It was as if I had said the magic words. Alakazam! — and her face went blank, her mouth closed, her arms went slack, and she backed out of the room, stunned, as if she were blowing away like a small brown leaf, thin, brittle, lifeless.

It was not the only disappointment my mother felt in me. In the years that followed, I failed her so many times, each time asserting my own will, my right to fall short of expectations. I didn't get straight As. I didn't become class president. I didn't get into Stanford. I dropped out of college.

For unlike my mother, I did not believe I could be anything I wanted to be.   80 I could only be me.

And for all those years, we never talked about the disaster at the recital or my terrible accusations afterward at the piano bench. All that remained unchecked, like a betrayal that was now unspeakable. So I never found a way to ask her why she had hoped for something so large that failure was inevitable.

And even worse, I never asked her what frightened me the most: Why had she given up hope?

For after our struggle at the piano, she never mentioned my playing again. The lessons stopped. The lid to the piano was closed, shutting out the dust, my misery, and her dreams.

So she surprised me. A few years ago, she offered to give me the piano, for my thirtieth birthday. I had not played in all those years. I saw the offer as a sign of forgiveness, a tremendous burden removed.

"Are you sure?" I asked shyly. "I mean, won't you and Dad miss it?"   85

"No, this your piano," she said firmly. "Always your piano. You only one can play."

"Well, I probably can't play anymore," I said. "It's been years."

"You pick up fast," said my mother, as if she knew this was certain. "You have natural talent. You could been genius if you want to."

"No I couldn't."

"You just not trying," said my mother. And she was neither angry nor sad.   90
She said it as if to announce a fact that could never be disproved. "Take it," she said.

But I didn't at first. It was enough that she had offered it to me. And after that, every time I saw it in my parents' living room, standing in front of the bay windows, it made me feel proud, as if it were a shiny trophy I had won back.

Last week I sent a tuner over to my parents' apartment and had the piano reconditioned, for purely sentimental reasons. My mother had died a few months before and I had been getting things in order for my father, a little bit at a time. I put the jewelry in special silk pouches. The sweaters she had knitted in yellow, pink, bright orange—all the colors I hated—I put those in moth-proof boxes. I found some old Chinese silk dresses, the kind with little slits up the sides. I rubbed the old silk against my skin, then wrapped them in tissue and decided to take them home with me.

After I had the piano tuned, I opened the lid and touched the keys. It sounded even richer than I remembered. Really, it was a very good piano. Inside the bench were the same exercise notes with handwritten scales, the same secondhand music books with their covers held together with yellow tape.

I opened up the Schumann book to the dark little piece I had played at the recital. It was on the left-hand side of the page, "Pleading Child." It looked more difficult than I remembered. I played a few bars, surprised at how easily the notes came back to me.

And for the first time, or so it seemed, I noticed the piece on the right-hand   95
side. It was called "Perfectly Contented." I tried to play this one as well. It had

a lighter melody but the same flowing rhythm and turned out to be quite easy. "Pleading Child" was shorter but slower; "Perfectly Contented" was longer, but faster. And after I played them both a few times, I realized they were two halves of the same song.

John Updike   1932–2009

A & P°   [1961]

In walks these three girls in nothing but bathing suits. I'm in the third checkout slot, with my back to the door, so I don't see them until they're over by the bread. The one that caught my eye first was the one in the plaid green two-piece. She was a chunky kid, with a good tan and a sweet broad soft-looking can with those two crescents of white just under it, where the sun never seems to hit, at the top of the backs of her legs. I stood there with my hand on a box of HiHo crackers trying to remember if I rang it up or not. I ring it up again and the customer starts giving me hell. She's one of these cash-register-watchers, a witch about fifty with rouge on her cheekbones and no eyebrows, and I know it made her day to trip me up. She'd been watching cash registers for fifty years and probably never seen a mistake before.

By the time I got her feathers smoothed and her goodies into a bag—she gives me a little snort in passing, if she'd been born at the right time they would have burned her over in Salem—by the time I get her on her way the girls had circled around the bread and were coming back, without a pushcart, back my way along the counters, in the aisle between the checkouts and the Special bins. They didn't even have shoes on. There was this chunky one, with the two-piece—it was bright green and the seams on the bra were still sharp and her belly was still pretty pale so I guessed she just got it (the suit)—there was this one, with one of those chubby berry-faces, the lips all bunched together under her nose, this one, and a tall one, with black hair that hadn't quite frizzed right, and one of these sunburns right across under the eyes, and a chin that was too long—you know, the kind of girl other girls think is very "striking" and "attractive" but never quite makes it, as they very well know, which is why they like her so much—and then the third one, that wasn't quite so tall. She was the queen. She kind of led them, the other two peeking around and making their shoulders round. She didn't look around, not this queen, she just walked straight on slowly, on these long white prima-donna legs. She came down a little hard on her heels, as if she didn't walk in her bare feet that much, putting down her heels and then letting the weight move along to her toes as if she was testing the floor with every step, putting a little deliberate extra action into it.

A & P: Grocery stores operated by the Great Atlantic & Pacific Tea Company, which was founded in New York City in 1859 and is currently headquartered in Montvale, New Jersey.

You never know for sure how girls' minds work (do you really think it's a mind in there or just a little buzz like a bee in a glass jar?) but you got the idea she had talked the other two into coming in here with her, and now she was showing them how to do it, walk slow and hold yourself straight.

She had on a kind of dirty-pink—beige maybe, I don't know—bathing suit with a little nubble all over it and, what got me, the straps were down. They were off her shoulders looped loose around the cool tops of her arms, and I guess as a result the suit had slipped a little on her, so all around the top of the cloth there was this shining rim. If it hadn't been there you wouldn't have known there could have been anything whiter than those shoulders. With the straps pushed off, there was nothing between the top of the suit and the top of her head except just *her*, this clean bare plane of the top of her chest down from the shoulder bones like a dented sheet of metal tilted in the light. I mean, it was more than pretty.

She had sort of oaky hair that the sun and salt had bleached, done up in a bun that was unravelling, and a kind of prim face. Walking into the A & P with your straps down, I suppose it's the only kind of face you *can* have. She held her head so high her neck, coming up out of those white shoulders, looked kind of stretched, but I didn't mind. The longer her neck was, the more of her there was.

She must have felt in the corner of her eye me and over my shoulder 5 Stokesie in the second slot watching, but she didn't tip. Not this queen. She kept her eyes moving across the racks, and stopped, and turned so slow it made my stomach rub the inside of my apron, and buzzed to the other two, who kind of huddled against her for relief, and then they all three of them went up the cat-and-dog-food-breakfast-cereal-macaroni-rice-raisins-seasonings-spreads-spaghetti-soft-drinks-crackers-and-cookies aisle. From the third slot I look straight up this aisle to the meat counter, and I watched them all the way. The fat one with the tan sort of fumbled with the cookies, but on second thought she put the package back. The sheep pushing their carts down the aisle—the girls were walking against the usual traffic (not that we have one-way signs or anything)—were pretty hilarious. You could see them, when Queenie's white shoulders dawned on them, kind of jerk, or hop, or hiccup, but their eyes snapped back to their own baskets and on they pushed. I bet you could set off dynamite in an A & P and the people would by and large keep reaching and checking oatmeal off their lists and muttering "Let me see, there was a third thing, began with A, asparagus, no, ah, yes, applesauce!" or whatever it is they do mutter. But there was no doubt, this jiggled them. A few houseslaves in pin curlers even looked around after pushing their carts past to make sure what they had seen was correct.

You know, it's one thing to have a girl in a bathing suit down on the beach, where what with the glare nobody can look at each other much anyway, and another thing in the cool of the A & P, under the fluorescent lights, against all those stacked packages, with her feet paddling along naked over our checkerboard green-and-cream rubber-tile floor.

"Oh Daddy," Stokesie said beside me. "I feel so faint."

"Darling," I said. "Hold me tight." Stokesie's married, with two babies chalked up on his fuselage already, but as far as I can tell that's the only difference. He's twenty-two, and I was nineteen this April.

"Is it done?" he asks, the responsible married man finding his voice. I forgot to say he thinks he's going to be manager some sunny day, maybe in 1990 when it's called the Great Alexandrov and Petrooshki Tea Company or something.

What he meant was, our town is five miles from a beach, with a big sum- 10 mer colony out on the Point, but we're right in the middle of town, and the women generally put on a shirt or shorts or something before they get out of the car into the street. And anyway these are usually women with six children and varicose veins mapping their legs and nobody, including them, could care less. As I say, we're right in the middle of town, and if you stand at our front doors you can see two banks and the Congregational church and the newspaper store and three real-estate offices and about twenty-seven old freeloaders tearing up Central Street because the sewer broke again. It's not as if we're on the Cape; we're north of Boston and there's people in this town haven't seen the ocean for twenty years.

The girls had reached the meat counter and were asking McMahon something. He pointed, they pointed, and they shuffled out of sight behind a pyramid of Diet Delight peaches. All that was left for us to see was old McMahon patting his mouth and looking after them sizing up their joints. Poor kids, I began to feel sorry for them, they couldn't help it.

Now here comes the sad part of the story, at least my family says it's sad, but I don't think it's so sad myself. The store's pretty empty, it being Thursday afternoon, so there was nothing much to do except lean on the register and wait for the girls to show up again. The whole store was like a pinball machine and I didn't know which tunnel they'd come out of. After a while they come around out of the far aisle, around the light bulbs, records at discount of the Caribbean Six or Tony Martin Sings or some such gunk you wonder they waste the wax on, sixpacks of candy bars, and plastic toys done up in cellophane that fall apart when a kid looks at them anyway. Around they come, Queenie still leading the way, and holding a little gray jar in her hand. Slots Three through Seven are unmanned and I could see her wondering between Stokes and me, but Stokesie with his usual luck draws an old party in baggy gray pants who stumbles up with four giant cans of pineapple juice (what do these bums *do* with all that pineapple juice? I've often asked myself) so the girls come to me. Queenie puts down the jar and I take it into my fingers icy cold. Kingfish Fancy Herring Snacks in Pure Sour Cream: 49¢. Now her hands are empty, not a ring or a bracelet, bare as God made them, and I wonder where the money's coming from. Still with that prim look she lifts a folded dollar bill out of the hollow at the center of her nubbled pink top. The jar went heavy in my hand. Really, I thought that was so cute.

Then everybody's luck begins to run out. Lengel comes in from haggling with a truck full of cabbages on the lot and is about to scuttle into that door marked MANAGER behind which he hides all day when the girls touch his eye. Lengel's pretty dreary, teaches Sunday school and the rest, but he doesn't miss that much. He comes over and says, "Girls, this isn't the beach."

Queenie blushes, though maybe it's just a brush of sunburn I was noticing for the first time, now that she was so close. "My mother asked me to pick up a jar of herring snacks." Her voice kind of startled me, the way voices do when you see the people first, coming out so flat and dumb yet kind of tony, too, the way it ticked over "pick up" and "snacks." All of a sudden I slid right down her voice into her living room. Her father and the other men were standing around in ice-cream coats and bow ties and the women were in sandals picking up herring snacks on toothpicks off a big glass plate and they were all holding drinks the color of water with olives and sprigs of mint in them. When my parents have somebody over they get lemonade and if it's a real racy affair Schlitz in tall glasses with "They'll Do It Every Time" cartoons stencilled on.

"That's all right," Lengel said. "But this isn't the beach." His repeating this   15 struck me as funny, as if it had just occurred to him, and he had been thinking all these years the A & P was a great big dune and he was the head lifeguard. He didn't like my smiling — as I say he doesn't miss much — but he concentrates on giving the girls that sad Sunday-school-superintendent stare.

Queenie's blush is no sunburn now, and the plump one in plaid, that I liked better from the back — a really sweet can — pipes up, "We weren't doing any shopping. We just came in for the one thing."

"That makes no difference," Lengel tells her, and I could see from the way his eyes went that he hadn't noticed she was wearing a two-piece before. "We want you decently dressed when you come in here."

"We *are* decent," Queenie says suddenly, her lower lip pushing, getting sore now that she remembers her place, a place from which the crowd that runs the A & P must look pretty crummy. Fancy Herring Snacks flashed in her very blue eyes.

"Girls, I don't want to argue with you. After this come in here with your shoulders covered. It's our policy." He turns his back. That's policy for you. Policy is what the kingpins want. What the others want is juvenile delinquency.

All this while, the customers had been showing up with their carts but, you   20 know, sheep, seeing a scene, they had all bunched up on Stokesie, who shook open a paper bag as gently as peeling a peach, not wanting to miss a word. I could feel in the silence everybody getting nervous, most of all Lengel, who asks me, "Sammy, have you rung up their purchase?"

I thought and said "No" but it wasn't about that I was thinking. I go through the punches, 4, 9, GROC, TOT — it's more complicated than you think, and after you do it often enough, it begins to make a little song, that you hear words to, in my case "Hello (*bing*) there, you (*gung*) hap-py *pee*-pul (*splat*)!" — the *splat* being the drawer flying out. I uncrease the bill, tenderly as you may imagine, it just having come from between the two smoothest scoops of vanilla I had ever known were there, and pass a half and a penny into her narrow pink palm, and nestle the herrings in a bag and twist its neck and hand it over, all the time thinking.

The girls, and who'd blame them, are in a hurry to get out, so I say "I quit" to Lengel quick enough for them to hear, hoping they'll stop and watch me, their unsuspected hero. They keep right on going, into the electric eye; the door flies open and they flicker across the lot to their car, Queenie and Plaid and Big Tall Goony-Goony (not that as raw material she was so bad), leaving me with Lengel and a kink in his eyebrow.

"Did you say something, Sammy?"

"I said I quit."

"I thought you did."   25

"You didn't have to embarrass them."

"It was they who were embarrassing us."

I started to say something that came out "Fiddle-de-doo." It's a saying of my grandmother's, and I know she would have been pleased.

"I don't think you know what you're saying," Lengel said.

"I know you don't," I said. "But I do." I pull the bow at the back of my   30
apron and start shrugging it off my shoulders. A couple customers that had been heading for my slot begin to knock against each other, like scared pigs in a chute.

Lengel sighs and begins to look very patient and old and gray. He's been a friend of my parents for years. "Sammy, you don't want to do this to your Mom and Dad," he tells me. It's true, I don't. But it seems to me that once you begin a gesture it's fatal not to go through with it. I fold the apron, "Sammy" stitched in red on the pocket, and put it on the counter, and drop the bow tie on top of it. The bow tie is theirs, if you've ever wondered. "You'll feel this for the rest of your life," Lengel says, and I know that's true, too, but remembering how he made that pretty girl blush makes me so scrunchy inside I punch the No Sale tab and the machine whirs "pee-pul" and the drawer splats out. One advantage to this scene taking place in summer, I can follow this up with a clean exit, there's no fumbling around getting your coat and galoshes, I just saunter into the electric eye in my white shirt that my mother ironed the night before, and the door heaves itself open, and outside the sunshine is skating around on the asphalt.

I look around for my girls, but they're gone, of course. There wasn't anybody but some young married screaming with her children about some candy they didn't get by the door of a powder-blue Falcon station wagon. Looking back in the big windows, over the bags of peat moss and aluminum lawn furniture stacked on the pavement, I could see Lengel in my place in the slot, checking the sheep through. His face was dark gray and his back stiff, as if he'd just had an injection of iron, and my stomach kind of fell as I felt how hard the world was going to be to me hereafter.

Helena María Viramontes b. 1954

The Moths   [1985]

I was fourteen years old when Abuelita requested my help. And it seemed
only fair. Abuelita° had pulled me through the rages of scarlet fever by placing,
removing and replacing potato slices on the temples of my forehead; she had
seen me through several whippings, an arm
broken by a dare jump off Tío Enrique's
toolshed, puberty, and my first lie. Really, I
told Amá, it was only fair.

Not that I was her favorite granddaughter or anything special. I wasn't even pretty
or nice like my older sisters and I just
couldn't do the girl things they could do.
My hands were too big to handle the finer-
ies of crocheting or embroidery and I always
pricked my fingers or knotted my colored
threads time and time again while my sis-

APPROACHING THE AUTHOR

Helena María Viramontes began writing in
college in the early 1970s, first poetry and
then fiction. Her stories soon began to be
published and recognized. In 1977, she won
first prize in a literary contest sponsored by
Statement magazine for her story "Requiem
for the Poor."

For more about her, see page 1417.

ters laughed and called me bull hands with their cute waterlike voices. So I
began keeping a piece of jagged brick in my sock to bash my sisters or anyone
who called me bull hands. Once, while we all sat in the bedroom, I hit Teresa
on the forehead, right above her eyebrow and she ran to Amá with her mouth
open, her hand over her eye while blood seeped between her fingers. I was used
to the whippings by then.

I wasn't respectful either. I even went so far as to doubt the power of
Abuelita's slices, the slices she said absorbed my fever. "You're still alive, aren't
you?" Abuelita snapped back, her pasty gray eye beaming at me and burning
holes in my suspicions. Regretful that I had let secret questions drop out of my
mouth, I couldn't look into her eyes. My hands began to fan out, grow like a
liar's nose until they hung by my side like low weights. Abuelita made a balm
out of dried moth wings and Vicks and rubbed my hands, shaped them back to
size and it was the strangest feeling. Like bones melting. Like sun shining
through the darkness of your eyelids. I didn't mind helping Abuelita after that,
so Amá would always send me over to her.

In the early afternoon Amá would push her hair back, hand me my sweater and shoes, and tell me to go to Mama Luna's. This was to avoid another fight
and another whipping, I knew. I would deliver one last direct shot on Marisela's
arm and jump out of our house, the slam of the screen door burying her cries
of anger, and I'd gladly go help Abuelita plant her wild lilies or jasmine or he-
liotrope or cilantro or hierbabuena in red Hills Brothers coffee cans. Abuelita

------

Abuelita: Grandmother (Spanish).

would wait for me at the top step of her porch holding a hammer and nail and empty coffee cans. And although we hardly spoke, hardly looked at each other as we worked over root transplants, I always felt her gray eye on me. It made me feel, in a strange sort of way, safe and guarded and not alone. Like God was supposed to make you feel.

On Abuelita's porch, I would puncture holes in the bottom of the coffee   5 cans with a nail and a precise hit of a hammer. This completed, my job was to fill them with red clay mud from beneath her rose bushes, packing it softly, then making a perfect hole, four fingers round, to nest a sprouting avocado pit, or the spidery sweet potatoes that Abuelita rooted in mayonnaise jars with toothpicks and daily water, or prickly chayotes that produced vines that twisted and wound all over her porch pillars, crawling to the roof, up and over the roof, and down the other side, making her small brick house look like it was cradled within the vines that grew pear-shaped squashes ready for the pick, ready to be steamed with onions and cheese and butter. The roots would burst out of the rusted coffee cans and search for a place to connect. I would then feed the seedlings with water.

But this was a different kind of help, Amá said, because Abuelita was dying. Looking into her gray eye, then into her brown one, the doctor said it was just a matter of days. And so it seemed only fair that these hands she had melted and formed found use in rubbing her caving body with alcohol and marihuana, rubbing her arms and legs, turning her face to the window so that she could watch the Bird of Paradise blooming or smell the scent of clove in the air. I toweled her face frequently and held her hand for hours. Her gray wiry hair hung over the mattress. Since I could remember, she'd kept her long hair in braids. Her mouth was vacant and when she slept, her eyelids never closed all the way. Up close, you could see her gray eye beaming out the window, staring hard as if to remember everything. I never kissed her. I left the window open when I went to the market.

Across the street from Jay's Market there was a chapel. I never knew its denomination, but I went in just the same to search for candles. I sat down on one of the pews because there were none. After I cleaned my fingernails, I looked up at the high ceiling. I had forgotten the vastness of these places, the coolness of the marble pillars and the frozen statues with blank eyes. I was alone. I knew why I had never returned.

That was one of Apá's biggest complaints. He would pound his hands on the table, rocking the sugar dish or spilling a cup of coffee and scream that if I didn't go to mass every Sunday to save my goddamn sinning soul, then I had no reason to go out of the house, period. Punto final. He would grab my arm and dig his nails into me to make sure I understood the importance of cate-chism. Did he make himself clear? Then he strategically directed his anger at Amá for her lousy ways of bringing up daughters, being disrespectful and unbe-lieving, and my older sisters would pull me aside and tell me if I didn't get to mass right this minute, they were all going to kick the holy shit out of me. Why am I so selfish? Can't you see what it's doing to Amá, you idiot? So I would wash my feet and stuff them in my black Easter shoes that shone with Vaseline, grab a missal and veil, and wave good-bye to Amá.

I would walk slowly down Lorena to First to Evergreen, counting the cracks on the cement. On Evergreen I would turn left and walk to Abuelita's. I liked her porch because it was shielded by the vines of the chayotes and I could get a good look at the people and car traffic on Evergreen without them knowing. I would jump up the porch steps, knock on the screen door as I wiped my feet and call Abuelita? mi Abuelita? As I opened the door and stuck my head in, I would catch the gagging scent of toasting chile on the placa.° When I entered the sala,° she would greet me from the kitchen, wringing her hands in her apron. I'd sit at the corner of the table to keep from being in her way. The chiles made my eyes water. Am I crying? No, Mama Luna, I'm sure not crying. I don't like going to mass, but my eyes watered anyway, the tears dropping on the tablecloth like candle wax. Abuelita lifted the burnt chiles from the fire and sprinkled water on them until the skins began to separate. Placing them in front of me, she turned to check the menudo.° I peeled the skins off and put the flimsy, limp looking green and yellow chiles in the molcajete° and began to crush and crush and twist and crush the heart out of the tomato, the clove of garlic, the stupid chiles that made me cry, crushed them until they turned into liquid under my bull hand. With a wooden spoon, I scraped hard to destroy the guilt, and my tears were gone. I put the bowl of chile next to a vase filled with freshly cut roses. Abuelita touched my hand and pointed to the bowl of menudo that steamed in front of me. I spooned some chile into the menudo and rolled a corn tortilla thin with the palms of my hands. As I ate, a fine Sunday breeze entered the kitchen and a rose petal calmly feathered down to the table.

I left the chapel without blessing myself and walked to Jay's. Most of the time Jay didn't have much of anything. The tomatoes were always soft and the cans of Campbell soups had rusted spots on them. There was dust on the tops of cereal boxes. I picked up what I needed: rubbing alcohol, five cans of chicken broth, a big bottle of Pine Sol. At first Jay got mad because I thought I had forgotten the money. But it was there all the time, in my back pocket. 10

When I returned from the market, I heard Amá crying in Abuelita's kitchen. She looked up at me with puffy eyes. I placed the bags of groceries on the table and began putting the cans of soup away. Amá sobbed quietly. I never kissed her. After a while, I patted her on the back for comfort. Finally: "¿Y mi Amá?"° she asked in a whisper, then choked again and cried into her apron.

Abuelita fell off the bed twice yesterday, I said, knowing that I shouldn't have said it and wondering why I wanted to say it because it only made Amá cry harder. I guess I became angry and just so tired of the quarrels and beatings and unanswered prayers and my hands just there hanging helplessly by my side. Amá looked at me again, confused, angry, and her eyes were filled with sorrow.

---

placa: Plate. **sala:** Living room. **menudo:** Traditional Mexican soup made with tripe. **molcajete:** Stone bowl for grinding spices and chiles with a pestle (tejolote). **"¿Y mi Amá?":** "And my Mama?"

I went outside and sat on the porch swing and watched the people pass. I sat there until she left. I dozed off repeating the words to myself like rosary prayers: when do you stop giving when do you start giving when do you . . . and when my hands fell from my lap, I awoke to catch them. The sun was setting, an orange glow, and I knew Abuelita was hungry.

There comes a time when the sun is defiant. Just about the time when moods change, inevitable seasons of a day, transitions from one color to another, that hour or minute or second when the sun is finally defeated, finally sinks into the realization that it cannot with all its power to heal or burn, exist forever, there comes an illumination where the sun and earth meet, a final burst of burning red orange fury reminding us that although endings are inevitable, they are necessary for rebirths, and when that time came, just when I switched on the light in the kitchen to open Abuelita's can of soup, it was probably then that she died.

The room smelled of Pine Sol and vomit and Abuelita had defecated the remains of her cancerous stomach. She had turned to the window and tried to speak, but her mouth remained open and speechless. I heard you, Abuelita, I said, stroking her cheek, I heard you. I opened the windows of the house and let the soup simmer and overboil on the stove. I turned the stove off and poured the soup down the sink. From the cabinet I got a tin basin, filled it with lukewarm water and carried it carefully to the room. I went to the linen closet and took out some modest bleached white towels. With the sacredness of a priest preparing his vestments, I unfolded the towels one by one on my shoulders. I removed the sheets and blankets from her bed and peeled off her thick flannel nightgown. I toweled her puzzled face, stretching out the wrinkles, removing the coils of her neck, toweled her shoulders and breasts. Then I changed the water. I returned to towel the creases of her stretch-marked stomach, her sporadic vaginal hairs, and her sagging thighs. I removed the lint from between her toes and noticed a mapped birthmark on the fold of her buttock. The scars on her back which were as thin as the life lines on the palms of her hands made me realize how little I really knew of Abuelita. I covered her with a thin blanket and went into the bathroom. I washed my hands, and turned on the tub faucets and watched the water pour into the tub with vitality and steam. When it was full, I turned off the water and undressed. Then, I went to get Abuelita.

She was not as heavy as I thought and when I carried her in my arms, her body 15 fell into a V, and yet my legs were tired, shaky, and I felt as if the distance between the bedroom and bathroom was miles and years away. Amá, where are you?

I stepped into the bathtub one leg first, then the other. I bent my knees slowly to descend into the water slowly so I wouldn't scald her skin. There, there, Abuelita, I said, cradling her, smoothing her as we descended, I heard you. Her hair fell back and spread across the water like eagle's wings. The water in the tub overflowed and poured onto the tile of the floor. Then the moths came. Small, gray ones that came from her soul and out through her mouth fluttering to light, circling the single dull light bulb of the bathroom. Dying is lonely and I wanted to go to where the moths were, stay with her and plant chayotes whose vines would crawl up her fingers and into the clouds; I wanted to rest my head on her chest with her stroking my hair, telling me about the moths that lay within the soul and slowly eat the spirit up; I wanted to return to the waters of the womb with her so that we would never be alone again. I wanted. I wanted my Amá. I removed a few strands of hair from Abuelita's face and held her small light head within the hollow of my neck. The bathroom was filled with moths, and for the first time in a long time I cried, rocking us, crying for her, for me, for Amá, the sobs emerging from the depths of anguish, the misery of feeling half born, sobbing until finally the sobs rippled into circles and circles of sadness and relief. There, there, I said to Abuelita, rocking us gently, there, there.

PART 3

Approaching POETRY

12 Reading Poetry   565

13 Words and Images   570

14 Voice, Tone, and Sound   595

15 Figurative Language   627

16 Rhythm and Meter   652

17 Form and Type   674

18 Writing about Poetry   706

19 A Poet in Personal Context –
Judith Ortiz Cofer   720

20 A Collection of Poems   757

Overleaf: Naomi Shihab Nye, who refers to herself as "a wandering poet," is shown here in a photo that captures her welcoming stance toward the world. Throughout her life, Nye has been an ambassador for peace, bringing people together through poetry. Long an advocate of multicultural exchange, she herself is the daughter of an American mother and a Palestinian father. She has authored multiple collections of poetry, works of fiction and nonfiction, and books for children and young adults. She has edited anthologies for adults, children, and young adults, an example of which is The Same Sky, *a collection of 129 poems from 68 poets from around the world. Nye is also a singer-songwriter with several albums to her credit. In 2009, she was named one of PeaceByPeace.com's first peace heroes. (See p. 846 for her poem "The Small Vases from Hebron" and p. 1403 for a short biography.)*

Photo reprinted by permission of Ha Lam.

Poetry is a conversation with the world; poetry is a conversation with the words on the page in which you allow those words to speak back to you; and poetry is a conversation with yourself.

Naomi Shihab Nye

(Author of "The Small Vases from Hebron," p. 846)

Reading Poetry

Realizing the Richness in Poems

Why would a person feel suddenly compelled to write a poem? After the events of September 11, 2001, thousands of poems were written, sent, stored away, stuck in a wallet or purse, pasted in a scrapbook. Students took time out from their usual classroom studies and wrote poems. Parents sent their poems to their children away at school or gone from the nest. Poems expressed by "nonpoets" showed up on Web sites and subway walls, in newsletters, within in-house publications, during school announcements, and in memos, letters, and e-mails. People from every walk of life wrote and expressed their reactions, what they were feeling. Very few if any of us who are not fiction writers or playwrights decide one day to sit down and write a novel or a play. And yet time and time again, people who do not consider themselves poets write poems. Why? And what might that say about the nature and value of poetry—about what poetry is and what poetry does?

WHAT IS POETRY?

We can usually tell someone what a novel, a play, or an essay is, but a poem can be baffling to explain. It can't be defined as writing that has meter: A lot of poetry is nonmetrical. It's not confined to writing that rhymes, for many poems do not use rhyme. Though most poetry is written in lines, prose poems don't have line divisions. Much poetry uses figurative language and is intense and emotional—but the same is true for powerful prose. Whatever characteristics one tries to apply are never typical of all poetry or exclusive to poetry alone. So, what is this thing we call poetry?

Those we would think ought to know usually offer personal responses: E. E. Cummings said that poetry is "dancing on your own grave." Ezra Pound purportedly said it is "what poets write." Emily Dickinson described poetry by its effect: "If I read a book [and] it makes my whole body so cold no fire ever can warm me, I know THAT is poetry. If I feel physically as if the top of my head were taken off, I know THAT is poetry. These are the only ways I know it. Is there any other way?"

What Does Poetry Do?

POETRY SAYS "AH-H-H"   Maybe a better way to approach the question "What is poetry?" is to ask "What does poetry do?" Poetry often comes from some deep impulse or an idea that the writer needs or wants to express; no other form of expression is sufficient under the circumstances. Lucille Clifton once said, "Poetry began when somebody walked off a savanna or out of a cave and looked up at the sky with wonder and said, 'Ah-h-h!' *That* was the first poem. The urge toward 'Ah-h-h' is very human, it's in everybody."

POETRY CROSSES BOUNDARIES   Poetry that has an emotional edge often crosses, or even eliminates, boundaries. We are all citizens in the culture of joy, pain, anger, love, fear, despair, hope. Every one of us carries the emotions of every other one of us. Our situations and stories and conflicts may differ, but the news from the heart comes to each of us. And though we can't claim "I know just how you feel," we can say with confidence, "I, too, have known that feeling."

POETRY GIVES VOICE   And poetry gives voice. For many of us in our day-to-day lives, voices come at us — from the news media, sales pitches, movies, and general information overload. It often seems our own voices can't be heard. Poetry offers a chance to speak, and speak from a valued part of ourselves. The words are our words, the rhythms are our rhythms, the clumsiness and sophistication of phrasings are ours, the sounds, the tones, the attempts to be artful are ours.

POETRY IS PART OF OUR LIVES   Former poet laureate Rita Dove has stated, "[I want] to help people see that poetry is not something above them or somehow distant; it's part of their very lives. I would like to remind people that we *have* an interior life — even if we don't talk about it because it's not expedient, because it's not cool, because it's potentially embarrassing — and without that interior life, we are shells, we are nothing." Is that also why, under a sense of urgency, many feel the impulse to express themselves in poetry? Do they suddenly experience that connection to their inner lives? Do thoughts and feelings rise up and ask, even demand, to be expressed, and expressed in their own voice?

WHY READ POETRY?

EFFECTS OF POETRY   Poetry gives the poet a voice, but why do others read poetry? There are several reasons. Some people read poetry to hear that what they themselves are moved by and want to express is something others do too. Some read poetry to relish an artist's craftsmanship; to experience the beauty of the words and sounds and pictures through which a poem expresses emotions and ideas or tells a story. Others feel life with greater intensity through a particular poem and open themselves to wider and more inclusive experiences. Many people read poetry to be challenged, to be shaken, to be comforted.

TYPES OF POETRY   Traditionally poetry has been classified in three major types: *narrative*, poems that follow a sequence of events; *dramatic*, plays written in verse or poems that use techniques from drama, such as rising action, climax, and dialogue; and *lyric*, usually shorter poems focusing on a specific subject and characterized by melody and intensity of feelings. A number of the poems in this book tell stories. Many of the rest are lyric poems or combine narrative with lyric.

Some poems and some kinds of poetry you will like better than others, but we hope that you give them all a chance and remain open to the variety of cultures and experiences they embody.

ACTIVE READING: Poetry

The essence of poetry is elusive. There is no one way to pin it down. Although that may be intimidating, it is also part of the appeal, part of the seductiveness of poetry. We enter the world of a poem, every poem, not really knowing what to expect. And whenever we enter something new — whether an unfamiliar city, or a new job, or a new relationship — we tend to feel uncertain. We have to look around. We have to be attentive. Here are some suggestions for reading poetry with an active imagination.

- *Read straight through.* Go straight through a poem the first time you read it. If you wonder about a word or want to savor a line, stop only briefly. Then keep going. Get a feel for the poem without worrying about what you don't know or understand.

- *Look and listen.* Be attentive to everything in and about the poem. Start with its shape, the way the poem appears on the page. Listen to its sounds — the way it sounds when it's read aloud, the rhythms, the word sounds, and the combinations of sounds. Look for what it helps you see — the mental pictures called up by some of the words.

- *Watch the words.* After noting shape and sounds, start paying attention to what the words say—not what the whole poem means, but what the words say. Don't be overly eager to figure out what a poem "means," especially some deep, "hidden" meaning. When you walk through a wood, you don't keep saying, "What does that tree mean?" or "What does that stone mean?" You accept them for what they are. So it should be with poetry: Look at the words, listen for what they say, and understand them as best you can. And if at first you don't understand all that much, don't worry—there are many things in a poem that you can experience even before you "understand" it.

- *Interact with the work.* Reading a poem differs from reading a newspaper or an e-mail message or a textbook. You usually read those to glean some information or ideas. Many poems, of course, also contain information and ideas. But they can do other things: They can lead us to feel intensely, to experience deeply, to perceive freshly, to extend our understanding of experiences different from our own, and to affirm our own ideas, feelings, and experiences.

- *Take in what is happening.* Consider what the speaker or primary character in the poem is experiencing, dealing with, going through, or feeling, much as you would with a character in a work of fiction or drama.

REREADING: Poetry

Rereading is just as important for poetry as for fiction, perhaps more so. Reread until you've internalized parts of the poem. Focus on something different each time you go back. If you're open to the poem, it will give and give. Here are some suggestions for rereading.

- *Slow down.* You have to slow down to read a poem. You can't speed-read a poem any more than you can speed-listen to your favorite recordings. So slow down and listen: Listen for, and to, the poem.

- *Read aloud.* Many poems are meant to be heard. Their sounds and rhythms need to be read aloud. In poet Robert Pinsky's phrase, you should "say the poem" so the poem comes out from within you as you vocalize the poem and feel the words, phrases, and rhythms in your mouth, the way you did as a kid when you kept saying certain words over and over just because they felt good. Hide if you are worried that someone will laugh at you.

- *Hear the "music."* Poems work with what is often called the musicality of language, by blending the sounds and rhythms of words and word connections. It's not unlike a song lyric together with its music, but in this case the poem is aspiring to music through the sounds and rhythms of language.

- *Focus on what catches your attention.* You might be drawn to a particular image, how it alters your usual perception of something. Maybe you like the sounds of the language or the way the rhythm shifts or remains regular in every line. Maybe the poem is funny or poignant or both. You don't have to have a masterful grasp of the whole poem to notice things within it or wonder about it or begin talking about it. Paying passionate attention to what is actually in a poem is a wise way to start.

- *Follow the sentences.* The sentences in the poem may be broken up into lines, but they are still sentences. Get their sense correct. If the order of words in a sentence is inverted, it's important to pay attention to cues that identify what is subject and what is object. If a poet uses incomplete sentences, "fragments," try to figure out the purpose behind them. After working out where sentences start and stop, focus on the lines: Begin noticing what the line divisions and line breaks add to the experience of the sentence.

- *Ask questions.* You can, of course, ask what a poem means, but you don't need to start with that question. Try instead asking questions such as, What is going on in this poem? What is this poem doing? Why am I drawn to that phrase or line? What is the poem connecting me with or challenging me about? How is the poem shifting my usual way of perceiving things and leading me to reconsider the ways I've thought and felt?

The imagery of one line exudes a sparkling fountain of energy that fills your spirit.

Jimmy Santiago Baca

(Author of "Family Ties," p. 768)

13 Words and Images
Seizing on Sense and Sight

Perhaps you are hesitant about your ability to understand a poem or even have the feeling that a poem is in some code you have to break. Or perhaps you think that poetry can "just mean anything." With prose, we usually gain our understanding by reading whole units of focused meaning (sentences and paragraphs). But poems are often not written that way. Maybe that's a reason why we feel poems are difficult to grasp. Poems ask us to look both at and within lines and sentences, to focus our attention on particular words and particular images in them.

POETS RELY ON WORDS To comprehend a poem, then, requires attention to its words. That's obvious enough. But when you read poetry, you not only have to look at words but also need to pay closer attention than you usually would. **Diction**, the choice and arrangement of words, is an important aspect of style, whether in prose (see pp. 237–38) or poetry. This chapter's aim is to enable you to enjoy and appreciate poetry by developing confidence in your ability to work with the rewarding complexities of words and images.

POETS ARE FASCINATED BY WORDS Like most writers, poets are fascinated by words—their look, their sounds, their textures, the associations clustered around them, what they evoke, their power. Poets roll words around on their tongues and in their minds, experimenting with different combinations, playing with them, listening to the results. They care about their meanings, and the uses and abuses of those meanings. They look for ways to put everything into exactly the right words.

POETS CREATE WITH WORDS Poets, just like fiction writers, work with words in three ways: to report ("There's a dog at the back door"), to describe

("There's a wet old dog at the back door"), and to provide a new or fresh way of perceiving ("There's a dog at the back door that looks as if it's been dragged through a car wash"). All three are found in the opening lines of Robert Hayden's "Those Winter Sundays" (p. 572). The speaker reports: "Sundays too my father got up early." He describes: "cracked hands that ached / from labor in the weekday weather." And he gives us a fresh way of perceiving: "hear the cold splintering, breaking." Watching for those uses as you continue reading poetry can help you be alert to and responsive to the ways words work.

READING FOR DENOTATION

WHAT WORDS MEAN   In focusing attention on words, it's important to realize that words have two dimensions, denotation and connotation. **Denotation** refers to what words mean, to their dictionary definitions. It may seem obvious that, in reading, we need to pay attention to what the words mean; but sometimes it takes effort, and at times you will probably need to use different dictionaries. In other kinds of reading, the context may convey adequately the general meaning of an unfamiliar word, but in reading poetry, approximate meanings can lead to a misreading. And sometimes in poetry the secondary, less familiar meanings of a word may be as important as, or more important than, the first meaning.

EARLIER MEANINGS   Denotations pose a bigger problem when you read poems from the past or from a culture different from your own. You already know you need to look up unfamiliar words. Much trickier are words that look familiar but seem unusual in the context of the poem. In some cases, often in poems written several centuries ago, word meanings have changed or previous meanings are no longer used. A desk dictionary may indicate such changes, but a better resource is the *Oxford English Dictionary*, often called the *OED*. It is a historical dictionary found in most libraries and online through many libraries. It gives you what words meant in earlier times as well as now, and it uses illustrative quotations to show when each meaning was in use and, if it is no longer current, when that usage ceased.

Consider the following lines from Shakespeare's *Julius Caesar*, where Portia asks Brutus what has been bothering him.

> Is Brutus sick? And is it physical
> To walk unbraced and suck up the humors
> Of the dank morning? (2.1.262)

Both *physical* and *humor* are familiar words, but none of our current uses seems to fit these lines. Looking in an ordinary desk dictionary won't help, but using the *OED* does. If you look up *physical*, under definition 5b, you find, "Beneficial to health; curative, remedial" (if this seems odd, think of the word *physician*). The line from *Julius Caesar* is quoted as an illustration of this definition. If you look up *humor* (it appears under the British spelling *humour*), the first entry fits — "Moisture; damp exhalation; vapour." The last example cited for this usage is from 1697 — this is the latest example of this usage that has been found in print. By then that meaning may already have disappeared from spoken language, or it may have lingered in speech a bit longer; in any case, it died out completely around 1700, so present-day dictionaries do not bother to include it (not even as an "archaic" usage).

ENTRY POINTS   The denotations of words in the following poem probably seem straightforward and clear, even from your first reading. But spend some time looking up words that you're unfamiliar with or that look important and perhaps might mean more than the context conveys (perhaps the words *banked*, *chronic*, *austere*, and *offices*; and what about *blueblack*?). Remember too that denotation involves not just the meaning of individual words but the meaning of words combined with other words: Think about the meaning of "chronic angers" and "love's austere and lonely offices."

APPROACHING THE AUTHOR

Robert Hayden had severe vision problems as a child, preventing him from participating in activities like sports. He compensated by reading voraciously and developing his talents as a writer.
  For more about him, see page 1388.

Robert Hayden   1913–1980

Those Winter Sundays   [1962]

Sundays too my father got up early
and put his clothes on in the blueblack cold,
then with cracked hands that ached
from labor in the weekday weather made
banked fires blaze. No one ever thanked him.   5

I'd wake and hear the cold splintering, breaking.
When the rooms were warm, he'd call,
and slowly I would rise and dress,
fearing the chronic angers of that house,

Speaking indifferently to him,   10
who had driven out the cold
and polished my good shoes as well.
What did I know, what did I know
of love's austere and lonely offices?

APPROACHING THE READING

1. In addition to "important" words such as *banked, chronic, austere, offices,* and *blueblack,* pay attention to easily overlooked "little" words such as *those* in the title and *too* in line 1. Why do they matter? Discuss their effect and impact.

2. What is suggested in line 9 by the phrase "chronic angers of that house"? Why did the son speak "indifferently" to his father? What does word choice indicate about relationships in the family?

3. What do you make of the last five words of the poem? Explain why you think they are effective or ineffective as the ending of this poem.

4. What is the effect of the repetition in line 13? How is what the speaker now knows different from what he thought as a child?

One could readily argue that the success of this poem in all its elements and effects is the result of Hayden's accomplished use of diction. Notice the beautifully muted combinations of words, each of which reveals a profound intelligence quietly coming to life-changing realizations throughout the poem: "Sundays too" rather than "Even on Sunday"; "the blueblack cold" — the words and order mysteriously convey both how the cold felt to the father and how the son came to recognize the depth and continuity of the father's responsibility; "banked" starts the fifth line and rhymes with "thanked" later in the line, gently emphasizing the contrast between duty fulfilled and a lack of gratitude. "Chronic angers" (line 9) is striking in combining a technical word, *chronic,* with a common one, *angers.* The result leads us to realize and imagine the atmosphere the speaker grew up within. And the unusual combination of the word *love* with *austere, lonely,* and *offices* provokes us to reflect on and reconsider what real love is.

READING FOR CONNOTATION

WHAT WORDS IMPLY   Of course, words are more than their dictionary definitions. Words also have **connotations**, the shared or communal implications and associations they carry in addition to their dictionary meanings. Two words may have almost the same denotation but very different connotations; the associations a reader connects with them could make one suitable and the other unsuitable in a certain situation. For example, in "Those Winter Sundays," "working in the weekday weather" means almost the same thing, denotatively, as "labor in the weekday weather." But Hayden uses *labor* in line 4 probably because its connotations suggest work of a harder and more fatiguing kind than *working* does, and that's what Hayden wants to say about his father.

ENTRY POINTS   Poets search for the right word and then depend on you as reader to weigh its denotations and connotations carefully. As you read the following poem about an elderly couple, pay particular attention to the words—to what the denotations of familiar and unfamiliar words and the connotations of simple, ordinary words contribute to the poem and to your experience of it.

APPROACHING THE AUTHOR

When **Gwendolyn Brooks**'s parents discovered her talent for writing poetry, they provided her with a desk and bookshelves and began excusing her from many household chores. Their support proved beneficial: By age sixteen, Brooks had published nearly seventy-five poems.

For more about her, see page 1375.

Gwendolyn Brooks 1917–2000

The Bean Eaters   [1960]

They eat beans mostly, this old yellow pair.
Dinner is a casual affair.
Plain chipware on a plain and creaking wood,
Tin flatware.

Two who are Mostly Good.   5
Two who have lived their day,
But keep on putting on their clothes
And putting things away.

And remembering . . .
Remembering, with twinklings and twinges,   10
As they lean over the beans in their rented back room that is full of beads
    and receipts and dolls and cloths, tobacco crumbs, vases and fringes.

APPROACHING THE READING

1. Look up any words whose denotations are not clear to you. What words are particularly important for their connotations?

2. Brooks chose the words she did for both denotations and connotations. Consider why they are appropriate for this couple, their daily lives, the setting, and their circumstances. Pick out some uses of diction that seem particularly striking or important and explain why you feel that they are.

The denotations of words in "The Bean Eaters" are likely clear to you, but maybe not *flatware* (utensils, such as knives, forks, and spoons) or *chipware* (you are not likely to find it in a dictionary; it appears to be a term Brooks coined for beat-up china). You can probably figure out most of the words, including *chipware*, from the context. More important are the words' connotations.

WORDS CARRY ASSOCIATIONS   What beans are, denotatively, is not the crucial thing; what they suggest and what we associate them with are. The feeling or association generated by a word depends to some extent on the background and experiences of the readers. Brooks probably expects that readers will associate beans with being inexpensive and ordinary. Given those connotations, it seems safe to conclude that this couple's eating beans *mostly* suggests that they are poor. *Yellow* may factually, denotatively, describe the color of their skin, but equally important are the feelings of age, health, and fragility that many people associate with the word *yellow*. The facts of what chipware and tin flatware are do not solely create their effect as words in the poem; the way we perceive them as inexpensive, utilitarian products does.

Denotatively, "rented back room" simply states that the room the couple lives in is not in the front of the building and is owned by someone else. But the connotations are meaningful. Back rooms are cheaper (and less desirable) than front rooms. Presumably, Brooks's couple is renting a back room because they cannot afford even to rent a front room, let alone buy their own home.

WORDS CONVEY FEELINGS   Finally, the things listed in the last line are more important to the couple — and to us — for the feelings they evoke than for what they are in and of themselves. This old pair lives more in the past than in the present, and memories cluster with "twinklings and twinges" around the objects that fill the room. Perhaps you have more — or other — connotations for the words in the poem. Bring them into the reading of it and discuss how they differ from those we present here. Also, think about what part your background plays in your response to the poem.

READING FOR IMAGES

Our earliest knowledge of the world comes through the senses. Babies become acquainted with objects by looking at them, touching them, putting them in their mouths; everything to them is wonderfully sensate and interesting. As poet W. S. Merwin has said, "A child picks up a fallen leaf and doesn't say, what is it good for? To the child, a leaf is what it is." The senses remain crucial sources of knowledge for us as adults as well, but as we get older, we become accustomed to the things we encounter. One of the beauties of poetry is that it often reconnects us to the world of our senses and thus to a world of wonder.

LITERARY IMAGES In literature, an **image** is a word or group of words that evokes in our imagination a representation of an object or action that can be known by one or more of the senses — sight, hearing, touch, smell, taste. Poetry relies heavily on images. To comprehend and *experience* what is going on in poems, being attentive to images is vital.

ENTRY POINTS Focus on literary images in the following poem, which describes the sights and sounds of night at a lakeshore cottage and is full of sensory detail. By letting yourself enter the scene fully, you will notice how your imagination converts words to rich images.

APPROACHING THE AUTHOR

Maxine Kumin and her husband live on a two-hundred-acre farm in New Hampshire, where they breed Arabian and quarter horses. When she was seventy-three, she suffered an accident while preparing a horse for competition and broke her neck. She survived and regained mobility (contrary to doctors' predictions) and went on to write about her recovery in a memoir called *Inside the Halo and Beyond* (2000).

For more about her, see page 1397.

Maxine Kumin b. 1925

The Sound of Night   [1961]

And now the dark comes on, all full of chitter noise.
Birds huggermugger crowd the trees,
the air thick with their vesper cries,
and bats, snub seven-pointed kites,
skitter across the lake, swing out,   5
squeak, chirp, dip, and skim on skates
of air, and the fat frogs wake and prink
wide-lipped, noisy as ducks, drunk
on the boozy black, gloating chink-chunk.

And now on the narrow beach we defend ourselves from dark.   10
The cooking done, we build our firework
bright and hot and less for outlook
than for magic, and lie in our blankets
while night nickers around us. Crickets
chorus hallelujahs; paws, quiet   15
and quick as raindrops, play on the stones
expertly soft, run past and are gone;
fish pulse in the lake; the frogs hoarsen.

Now every voice of the hour — the known, the supposed, the strange,
the mindless, the witted, the never seen —   20

sing, thrum, impinge, and rearrange
endlessly; and debarred from sleep we wait
for the birds, importantly silent,
for the crease of first eye-licking light,
for the sun, lost long ago and sweet.   25
By the lake, locked black away and tight,
we lie, day creatures, overhearing night.

APPROACHING THE READING

1. This poet clearly loves to explore the possibilities of language. Pick out examples of unusual uses of language and consider why they are effective. Look up words that aren't familiar. Why is each right for the place it's used?

2. Notice examples of active, energetic verbs. Consider why they are effective in creating mental images.

3. Pick out words and phrases that create mental images of the way things look, sound, and feel.

The diction of this poem aims to bring to life a scene for readers to recall or create in their imaginations. Its emphasis is not on an intellectual meaning or an abstract idea, but on evoking what you see at the lake and especially what you hear. In describing sounds, the poem emphasizes verbs, such as "skitter," "squeak, chirp," and "prink" in the first stanza. Look for other examples in stanzas two and three. Notice also that the verbs are present tense, giving the scene immediacy. This is not a scene from the past, which is over and gone, but a scene that continues in the memory of the speaker, and now in you the reader. Having memories come to life is one of the remarkable powers of images, of imagistic language.

ENTRY POINTS   The power of concrete detail is at the heart of William Carlos Williams's short and much-discussed poem, "The Red Wheelbarrow." Focus on the mental picture the words of the poem evoke for you, and reflect on whether that picture is what the poem is about or whether it is also the starting point for something more abstract.

APPROACHING THE AUTHOR

William Carlos Williams decided in college that he wanted to be both a physician and a writer. He went on to study pediatrics in Germany and set up private practice in his hometown of Rutherford, New Jersey, where he worked on his writing between seeing patients and after hours.

For more about him, see page 1419.

William Carlos Williams   1883–1963

The Red Wheelbarrow   [1923]

so much depends
upon

a red wheel
barrow

glazed with rain   5
water

beside the white
chickens.

APPROACHING THE READING

1. Pick out words in the poem that help create sensory impressions in your mind (its images). How many of the words are imagistic?

2. Try sketching the scene on paper or visualizing it clearly in your mind. Consider what it would look like as a still-life painting in an art gallery. Even though this poem is highly visual, why might a sketch or painting fail to "capture" the poem?

3. What do you think is the "so much" that "depends" (line 1)? Why does it "depend"?

Some readers distrust or overlook the literal effects of Williams's images and search for "deeper meanings." The opening line of "The Red Wheelbarrow" seems to invite digging for deeper meaning—if "so much depends" on the objects mentioned, we had better figure out what they *really* mean. But the line more likely asserts the importance of images as themselves: So much depends on sensuously experiencing and respecting and realizing the value of things as themselves, on experiencing the world with our senses alert and sensitive.

You can further explore words and images, including interactive exercises, with VirtuaLit Poetry at bedfordstmartins.com/rewritinglit.

VISUALIZING SPECIFIC DETAILS Writers usually work with specific details and precise images that use concrete language rather than abstract language (see p. 237). If you hear, "Think of an animal," you may visualize whatever you choose. However, if you hear, "Don't imagine an elephant," such is the power of images that, even though you're told not to, you can't help visualizing one.

TRUSTING THE LITERAL   Some people are convinced that all poetry is indirect and symbolic — even a "code." They think that reading poetry means finding hidden meanings, as if poets think of meanings and then hide them. But an image is, first and foremost, simply itself. Poems do use symbols, and much of what was said about symbols in fiction (pp. 203-07) applies as well to poetry: A symbol is initially "an image that is exactly what it is." True, an image may suggest further meanings, but it doesn't "turn into" something else. It is always itself. And it always retains its literal meaning. Because imagery is so rich a part of poetry, one starting point in reading poems is to look at — and trust — the literal, to realize, appreciate, and enjoy the images for what they are and for what they do.

☑ CHECKLIST on Reading for Words and Images

❏ Pay careful attention to denotations — the pertinent dictionary definitions of words in a poem.

❏ Use a desk dictionary and specialized dictionaries (such as the *Oxford English Dictionary*) for finding useful and sometimes surprising denotations.

❏ Be open to the connotations of words in poetry — the overtones or associations that become connected with a word through repeated uses.

❏ Respond with your senses, intellect, and emotions to images (words representing sensory experience or objects that can be known by one or more of the senses) and to sense images (mental representations of sensory experience) in a poem.

FURTHER READING

ENTRY POINTS   Because language is important to all of us, it's not surprising that poets frequently write about it. The following two poems take a lighthearted look at words and at looking words up. You might need to do some looking up yourself in order to catch the humor in both. For the first poem, you might review what was said about the *OED* on page 571.

APPROACHING THE AUTHOR

Richard Jones says he doesn't work from inspiration: "But even were I an inspired poet, I'd still probably find inspiration to be a very small part of the artistic process, a divine instant followed by years of labor. I think of poetry more as working in a salt mine than standing atop Mount Parnassus."

For more about him, see page 1394.

Richard Jones b. 1953

OED   [2010]

In the dictionary one finds the word
lucubrate, meaning "to study
by artificial light late at night
that one might express oneself
in writing," on the heels of *luctiferous* —   5
"bringing sorrow" — and this immediately
preceded by *lucrous*, which, of course, is
"pertaining to lucre" and suggests "avaricious."

To the right of *lucubrate* is *ludibrious* —
"subject of mockery" —   10
and the familiar *ludicrous* —
all that which is "laughably absurd."

And in the far-right column, variations
on two small words, *luff* and *lug*,
"to bring the head of a ship   15
nearer the wind,"
and "to pull and tug heavily and slowly,"
two tiny words that describe
what I am doing
writing at my desk late at night,   20
turning the pages of the dictionary to find
the correct spelling and exact meaning
of *lugubrious*.

APPROACHING THE READING

1. Think about how the poem creates the experience of what it's like to get lost
   in the *OED* or, perhaps, any dictionary.

2. How does the poem support the chapter's emphasis on how a poet feels
   about words?

3. Think about the closing of the poem in relation to what it reveals about the
   work of the poet. What is surprising about the poem's last word and what
   might it imply about the speaker?

ENTRY POINTS   As you read the following poem, be ready to have your
perceptions about some very common things affected, changed, or expanded.
Listen for the two different voices: that of the questioner and that of the one
who responds.

APPROACHING THE AUTHOR

Now living in southern California, **Ron Koertge** grew up in an agricultural area where he "learned to drive a tractor and buck hay bales, which are clearly useful skills in Los Angeles."

For more about him, see page 1396.

Ron Koertge   b. 1940

Q and A   [2000]

What exactly is a thesaurus?

> A thesaurus is like a thousand family
> reunions, all in the same hotel, but each
> one in a separate ballroom. A dictionary,
> on the other hand, is like the Army where   5
> everyone lines up for roll call.

Do words have feelings?

> Absolutely. One picture can burden a
> thousand words with low self-esteem.

How can I have a large vocabulary?   10

> Exercise. Start with *air, leaf, inch*. Then
> increase slowly. Be patient and careful.
> The first time you try *incarnadine*,
> have someone spot you.

Do words die?   15

> Of course. I remember the funeral
> of *a go-go*. She looked completely natural
> in her black boots, miniskirt, and fringed
> blouse.

How can I remember the parts of speech?   20

> Picture a fancy restaurant: An adjective
> lights the cigarette of a noun. Two adverbs
> accompany a verb to the rest room. An
> article holds the door; a preposition hands
> the verb a warm hand towel.   25

APPROACHING THE READING

1. As suggested in the chapter, one way a poet uses words and images might be to create fresh perceptions. That is certainly an aim of this poem.

What struck you as a new way of looking at and thinking about each question?

2. Be ready to talk about any serious considerations this lighthearted poem raises for you.

3. Consider insights the poem gives you into the dynamics of language and the ways it works. Which ones hit home? Why?

ENTRY POINTS   A culture is deeply embedded in its language. You learned about your own culture partly through its words. To begin to learn about a different culture, a key step would be to learn its language. Words are important to your individual identity as well: To some extent, you are the kinds of words you use. Look for what the following poem says about words and for the way it uses words and sounds to consider the effect of language on culture and on relationships between different ethnic groups.

APPROACHING THE AUTHOR

As a child, **Allison Joseph** found inspiration in the poems of Gwendolyn Brooks, which she said taught her that "you don't have to write about Mount Olympus. You can write about your neighborhood — what's happening on the corner."

For more about her, see page 1395.

Allison Joseph   b. 1967

On Being Told I Don't Speak
Like a Black Person   [1999]

Emphasize the "h," you hignorant ass,
was what my mother was told
when colonial-minded teachers
slapped her open palm with a ruler
in that Jamaican schoolroom.   5
Trained in England, they tried
to force their pupils to speak
like Eliza Doolittle° after
her transformation, fancying themselves
British as Henry Higgins,°   10

8–10. Eliza Doolittle . . . Henry Higgins: Flower-girl with a strong Cockney (working-class) accent in George Bernard Shaw's play *Pygmalion* and the musical based on it, *My Fair Lady*. Henry Higgins, a linguistics professor, takes on the challenge of teaching her how to speak (and act and dress) like a proper British lady.

despite dark, sun-ripened skin.
Mother never lost her accent,
though, the music of her voice
charming everyone, an infectious lilt
I can imitate, not duplicate.   15
No one in the States told her
to eliminate the accent,
my high school friends adoring
the way her voice would lift
when she called me to the phone—   20
A-ll-i-son, it's friend Cathy.
Why don't you sound like her,
they'd ask. I didn't sound
like anyone or anything,
no grating New Yorker nasality,   25
no fastidious British mannerisms
like the ones my father affected
when he wanted to sell someone
something. And I didn't sound
like a Black American,   30
college acquaintances observed,
sure they knew what a black person
was supposed to sound like.
Was I supposed to sound lazy,
dropping syllables here and there   35
not finishing words but
slurring their final letters
so each sentence joined
the next, sliding past the listener?
Were certain words off limits,   40
too erudite for someone whose skin
came with a natural tan?
I asked them what they meant
and they stuttered, blushed,
said *you know, Black English,*   45
applying a term from that
semester's text. *Does everyone*
in your family speak alike,
I'd ask, and they'd say *don't*
take this the wrong way,   50
nothing personal.

Now I realize there's nothing
more personal than speech,
that I don't have to defend

how I speak, how any person,   55
black, white, chooses to speak.
Let us speak. Let us talk
with the sounds of our mothers
and fathers still reverberating
in our minds, wherever our mothers   60
or fathers come from:
Arkansas, Belize, Alabama,
Brazil, Aruba, Arizona.
Let us simply speak
to one another,   65
listen and prize the inflections,
never assuming how any person will sound
until his mouth opens, until her
mouth opens, greetings welcome
in any language.   70

APPROACHING THE READING

1. Most of the language of the poem is straightforward. Look up any words you aren't familiar with. Pick out a few phrases you reacted to, those with especially effective or interesting diction, and be prepared to explain why they struck you.

2. The speaker mentions that her acquaintances seemed sure they knew what a black person is supposed to sound like. What does she mean by that? Reflect on the cultural assumptions that lie behind such certainty.

3. The speaker says in lines 52–55 that "there's nothing / more personal than speech, / that I don't have to defend / how I speak." Think about your own speech. In what ways is it yours? When do you feel you have to defend your speech or even abandon or change or modify it?

ENTRY POINTS As you read this poem, try to use your imagination to feel the surroundings, especially the tactile experiences created. Notice how Trethewey mixes together many senses, not simply attending to one and then on to another. The poem allows you to feel the changes in time periods and the changes in values and attitudes that have taken place between those times. You may want to look into the history that lies behind this history lesson.

Natasha Trethewey b. 1966

History Lesson

[2000]

I am four in this photograph, standing
on a wide strip of Mississippi beach,
my hands on the flowered hips

of a bright bikini. My toes dig in,
curl around wet sand. The sun cuts   5
the rippling Gulf in flashes with each

tidal rush. Minnows dart at my feet
glinting like switchblades. I am alone
except for my grandmother, other side

of the camera, telling me how to pose.   10
It is 1970, two years after they opened
the rest of this beach to us,

forty years since the photograph
where she stood on a narrow plot
of sand marked *colored*, smiling,   15

her hands on the flowered hips
of a cotton meal-sack dress.

APPROACHING THE READING

1. This is a powerful poem that uses a commonplace experience to reveal extraordinary changes. Pick out the places where the images and particular words lead you to feel the changes and their impact.

2. What *is* the history lesson? Who learns it or is meant to learn it?

3. Think back to the poems used to show how important a single word or a particularly well-chosen image can be. Where do you see a similar impact in this poem? How did that impact affect you?

4. What do you think the speaker is going through as she looks closely at the photograph?

ENTRY POINTS   Nature is important in the next two poems. The focus in the first is on the strong friendship between two young, hurting, vulnerable girls — one who is blind, the other who misses her father. Consider how denotations, connotations, and images create an impact in it.

APPROACHING THE AUTHOR

Anita Endrezze is an artist as well as a poet. Her paintings have been exhibited in Wales, England, Sweden, Denmark, and the United States. Several of her paintings appear on anthology covers as well as on her own books.

For more about her, see page 1382.

Anita Endrezze   b. 1952

The Girl Who Loved the Sky   [1992]

Outside the second grade room,
the jacaranda tree blossomed
into purple lanterns, the papery petals
drifted, darkening the windows.
Inside, the room smelled like glue.   5
The desks were made of yellowed wood,
the tops littered with eraser rubbings,
rulers, and big fat pencils.
Colored chalk meant special days.
The walls were covered with precise   10
bright tulips and charts with shiny stars
by certain names. There, I learned
how to make butter by shaking a jar
until the pale cream clotted
into one sweet mass. There, I learned   15
that numbers were fractious beasts
with dens like dim zeros. And there,
I met a blind girl who thought the sky
tasted like cold metal when it rained
and whose eyes were always covered   20
with the bruised petals of her lids.

She loved the formless sky, defined
only by sounds, or the cool umbrellas
of clouds. On hot, still days
we listened to the sky falling   25
like chalk dust. We heard the noon

whistle of the pig-mash factory,
smelled the sourness of home-bound men.

I had no father; she had no eyes;
we were best friends. The other girls   30
drew shaky hopscotch squares
on the dusty asphalt, talked about
pajama parties, weekend cookouts,
and parents who bought sleek-finned cars.
Alone, we sat in the canvas swings,   35
our shoes digging into the sand, then pushing,
until we flew high over their heads,
our hands streaked with red rust
from the chains that kept us safe.

I was born blind, she said, an act of nature. 40
Sure, I thought, like birds born
without wings, trees without roots.
I didn't understand. The day she moved
I saw the world clearly: the sky
backed away from me like a departing father.   45
I sat under the jacaranda, catching
the petals in my palm, enclosing them
until my fist was another lantern
hiding a small and bitter flame.

APPROACHING THE READING

1. Notice the rich sensory texture of this poem. Find examples of words that evoke each of the five senses—sight, hearing, smell, taste, and touch. Why is sensory imagery so important to the impact of this poem?

2. If you have never seen a jacaranda tree or its blossoms, look at pictures of them in an encyclopedia or plant book or online. How do those pictures help sharpen the way you visualize lines 1–4, 20–21, and 46–49?

3. We get to know the speaker and her friend partly through the poem's images, through the kinds of things they notice and experience. Describe what both girls are like, grounding your response in the poem's details.

4. Discuss the nature of the girls' friendship. What makes it solid, touching, vulnerable? How do certain images help convey friendship?

5. Reread the final stanza of the poem on the effect of the experience on the narrator. Explain how images help get her points across. How fully did the speaker understand the experience then? What indication is there that the poet, in looking back, has a different understanding of it now?

ENTRY POINTS   Nature is important as well in the following poem. Here the narrator describes how connecting with "wild things" leads him to get in touch with a different side of himself. Watch how words and images create and convey a sense of peacefulness and reveal the contrast between the worlds in which he lives.

APPROACHING THE AUTHOR

In 1965 **Wendell Berry** and his wife moved to a farm in Kentucky and began small-scale farming, using horses to work the land and employing organic methods of fertilization and pest control. Perhaps in keeping with his farming lifestyle, Berry does not use a computer.

For more about him, see page 1374.

Wendell Berry   b. 1934

The Peace of Wild Things   [1968]

When despair for the world grows in me
and I wake in the night at the least sound
in fear of what my life and my children's lives may be,
I go and lie down where the wood drake
rests in his beauty on the water, and the great heron feeds.   5
I come into the peace of wild things
who do not tax their lives with forethought
of grief. I come into the presence of still water.
And I feel above me the day-blind stars
waiting with their light. For a time   10
I rest in the grace of the world, and am free.

APPROACHING THE READING

1. This poem is direct in what it presents through denotations. Are there any words or images that also carry connotations for you? Which ones? What are their connotations? Pick out some images, word choices, and moments that you feel yourself. Why do you think that they struck you as they did?

2. The poem is less about altering perceptions than it is about revealing how the speaker depends on the natural world. What is it about the natural world that brings renewal to the speaker? What words and images has the poet used to convey this?

3. There are some "little," "common" words and phrases in this poem that carry great importance and are used in unusual ways. Take a closer look at *for* in the phrase "for the world" (l. 1), at *in* in "the wood drake / rests in his beauty"(ll. 4–5), at *come into* in "I come into the presence of still water" (8),

and *with* in "the day-blind stars / waiting with their light" (9–10). How would you describe the experience these unassuming words create?

ENTRY POINTS   As you read this poem that movingly depicts the impact of dislocation on a culture, try to picture each moment frame by frame as you would watch a movie. Move from image to image, moment to moment, reflection to reflection. See the figures from each generation. Imagine the landscapes portrayed. Do your best to enter into the full experience of the poem, which is lush with images and feeling.

APPROACHING THE AUTHOR

Cathy Song credits her family's frequent travels — her father was a pilot — for inspiring her to become a writer. "I guess I was around nine years old when I decided I wanted to be the family chronicler," she says.

For more about her, see page 1412.

Cathy Song   b. 1955

Heaven   [1988]

He thinks when we die we'll go to China.
Think of it — a Chinese heaven
where, except for his blond hair,
the part that belongs to his father,
everyone will look like him.   5
China, that blue flower on the map,
bluer than the sea
his hand must span like a bridge
to reach it.
An octave away.   10

I've never seen it.
It's as if I can't sing that far.
But look —
on the map, this black dot.
Here is where we live,   15
on the pancake plains
just east of the Rockies,
on the other side of the clouds.
A mile above the sea,
the air is so thin, you can starve on it.   20
No bamboo trees

but the alpine equivalent,
reedy aspen with light, fluttering leaves.
Did a boy in Guangzhou° dream of this
as his last stop?   25

I've heard the trains at night
whistling past our yards,
what we've come to own,
the broken fences, the whiny dog, the rattletrap cars.
It's still the wild west,   30
mean and grubby,
the shootouts and fistfights in the back alley.
With my son the dreamer
and my daughter, who is too young to walk,
I've sat in this spot   35
and wondered why here?
Why in this short life,
this town, this creek they call a river?

He had never planned to stay,
the boy who helped to build   40
the railroads° for a dollar a day.
He had always meant to go back.
When did he finally know
that each mile of track led him further away,
that he would die in his sleep,   45
dispossessed,
having seen Gold Mountain,°
the icy wind tunneling through it,
these landlocked, makeshift ghost towns?

It must be in the blood,   50
this notion of returning.
It skipped two generations, lay fallow,
the garden an unmarked grave.
On a spring sweater day
it's as if we remember him.   55
I call to the children.
We can see the mountains
shimmering blue above the air.

---

24. **Guangzhou:** Also known as Canton, a large seaport city in southeastern China.   **40–41
build . . . railroads:**   The Central Pacific Railroad used mostly Chinese immigrant laborers to
lay the western section of tracks for the first transcontinental railroad.   **47. Gold
Mountain:** Name given by the Chinese to California and British Columbia during the gold
rush of the nineteenth century.

If you look really hard
says my son the dreamer,
leaning out from the laundry's rigging,
the work shirts fluttering like sails,
you can see all the way to heaven.

60

APPROACHING THE READING

1. Song uses vivid words and images to combine tough, realistic experience with deep, complex emotional and spiritual experience. Pick out some moments and talk about why you were moved by them. Be ready to describe how the images and words create the power and poignancy in the poem.

2. Think about the word *heaven*, its denotations and connotations, and about various images you have come across for heaven. How do denotation, connotation, and images of heaven play a role in the poem? How do they influence the people in, as well as your own experience of, the poem?

3. The poem is a powerful portrayal of hope, loss, dislocation, despair, courage, and dreams. Pick one of these ideas and discuss how the poet's images, words, and phrases evoke that experience. What has the poet done to make you share the experience? Compare the poem's creation of this experience to a so-called objective report on such a circumstance. What are crucial differences between the two? Which do you think would have the most impact on you? Why?

4. The speaker says, "I've sat on this spot / and wondered why here?" (lines 35–36). What is she referring to? When have you thought something similar? Talk about what it was like for you to wonder "why here?"

RESPONDING THROUGH Writing

WRITING ABOUT WORDS AND IMAGES

Journal Entries

1. As an exercise on language, write in your journal lists of words that you notice during an entire day: unfamiliar words, moving words, words that sound beautiful, words that look good, and so on. At the end of the day and a few days later, look back over the list and run through the words using your memory and imagination. Jot some notes about experiences, feelings,

You can research the authors in this chapter with Litlinks at bedfordstmartins.com/ rewritinglit.

and associations some of the words bring back to you: It may give you a new sense of the power and importance words have.

2. Choose a nonpoetic text—a letter, an advertisement, a magazine article, or an editorial, for example—and look closely at its handling of language. Discuss in your journal how the denotations and connotations of the words are or are not manipulated.

3. Images—visual and verbal—are enormously important for the advertising industry. In your journal, list some examples of how advertisers use words and pictures to imprint images in your mind and to stimulate your imagination, to get you to notice and remember their products. Write some reflections on some ways advertisers use the same techniques as poets, though with a different purpose.

Literary Analysis Papers

4. Write a paper that examines the diction in Maxine Kumin's "The Sound of Night" (p. 576), especially how its mixing of ordinary, everyday words with

TIPS for Writing about Words and Images

- **Read words attentively.** Assume that every word a poet chooses is used deliberately, and pay careful attention to each one. Of course you can't write about all the words, even in a short poem, so it's a good idea to focus on diction that is unusual, unexpected, striking, or especially significant.

- **Use a dictionary.** Make ample use of a good dictionary when you're writing about diction or imagery. Pay attention to etymologies as well as various definitions. Remember that a poet may want you to use more than one definition for a word, that doing so will add even more to the poem.

- **Look for patterns.** As you study a poem, watch for patterns, connections, or relationships among the words and images. Also, notice how poetic images sometimes change our usual ways of perceiving things. These often can result in insightful paper topics.

- **Avoid the general.** Don't just give lists of images or tell your reader what she or he already knows, like "The image of the stabbing was violent" or "the 'splintering cold' helps a reader feel how cold it was in the room" (you might instead focus on how "splintering" changes our usual way of thinking about coldness).

- **Relate to effect or theme.** Whenever you write about words and images, as the topic of an entire paper or as passing comments within a larger topic, your comments need to be used to help clarify the way words or images contribute to the overall effect or theme of the poem.

evocatively lush language creates a portrait that changes our usual perceptions of the world of the country.

5. Write a paper discussing the imagery of Anita Endrezze's "The Girl Who Loved the Sky" (p. 586) or another poem by thinking of it in terms of cinematography. See the poem as film. Note where in the poem you would use crucial camera angles, shots, close-ups, pans, and so forth. Help your reader see the poem as a film. Explain why you decided to film it as you did.

6. Write a paper on the use of imagery in capturing and conveying the atmosphere of a season: autumn, for example, in T. S. Eliot's "The Love Song of J. Alfred Prufrock" (p. 796), or winter in Mary Oliver's "First Snow" (p. 644), or spring in William Carlos Williams's "Spring and All" (p. 882).

Comparison-Contrast Papers

7. Write a paper comparing and contrasting what two or more poems about words say about language (perhaps including the cultural implications of language) and the diction they use to communicate it. Some poems you might consider are Kimiko Hahn's "Mother's Mother" (p. 812), Allison Joseph's "On Being Told I Don't Speak Like a Black Person" (p. 582), Gary Miranda's "Love Poem" (p. 668), and Alberto Ríos's "Nani" (p. 857).

8. Write a paper comparing and contrasting the expressions of love in Elizabeth Barrett Browning's "How do I love thee? Let me count the ways" (p. 777) and Gary Miranda's "Love Poem" (p. 668). Consider the extent to which each relies on images and how the effect of each differs.

WRITING ABOUT CONNECTIONS

Words and images are the key vehicles through which writers connect with readers, through which they convey what they hope readers will respond to. Examining a poet's choices and handling of diction and imagery in a poem can be an effective paper topic. Another way to deal with words and images in a paper is to look for thematic connections between two poems that use similar or contrasting diction and/or imagery, especially a contemporary poem and a poem from an earlier period. Here are a few examples of such topic possibilities.

1. "The Road Taken": Making Life Choices in Robert Frost's "The Road Not Taken" (p. 666) and Cathy Song's "Heaven" (p. 589)

2. "Seeing the City": The Contrasting Perspectives of Jonathan Swift's "A Description of the Morning" (available online) and Cheryl Savageau's "Bones — A City Poem" (p. 883)

3. "Impermanence's Permanence": Anita Endrezze's "The Girl Who Loved the Sky" (p. 586) and Edmund Spenser's "One day I wrote her name upon the strand" (p. 866)

WRITING RESEARCH PAPERS

1. Research the way the British taught the English language in their colonies, and reflect on what might have been the effects and consequences of doing so. In what ways do your research findings compare and contrast with the issues raised by today's controversies over bilingual education? Also look into Ebonics, or "black English." Use what you find to illuminate Allison Joseph's "On Being Told I Don't Speak Like a Black Person" (p. 582), especially what the poem suggests about the teaching or learning of language.

2. Select a poem of political protest, such as Pat Mora's "La Migra" (p. 617), Carolyn Forché's "The Colonel" (p. 801), Luis J. Rodriguez's "Running to America" (p. 858), or Peter Blue Cloud's "Crazy Horse Monument" (p. 863). Research the historical and social/political/economic backgrounds of the poem. Write a paper showing how awareness of this contextual knowledge helps clarify the meaning and impact of the poem and how the poem's use of diction and images reflects the background, helping to present the situation in a powerful way.

P oetic speech is a way of sounding in order to hear that voice. And once you hear it, everything else is like dishwater.

Li-Young Lee

(Author of "Eating Alone," p. 596)

Voice, Tone, and Sound

CHAPTER **14**

Hearing How Sense Is Said

In Chapter 4 we said that stories originally were not something to be read: People listened to stories being told long before they read them. The same is true of poems. Even today, when poems are written down, most are meant not only to be read but also to be heard. In narrative poetry, you listen with your mind's ear to a storyteller, a first- or third-person narrator. In nonnarrative poetry, you hear the imagined voice of a **speaker**, of someone "speaking" the poem, either the poet directly or a character. This chapter aims to develop your ability to listen for the voice of the speaker (or narrator), and to help you hear the sounds and rhythms that create poetry's musicality.

READING FOR VOICE

In a first-person poem, a key question to ask is whether the *I* speaking is a voice very similar to that of the author or is a character different from the author. Just as you should not assume that the *I* in a story is identical to the author, you shouldn't automatically assume that the *I* in a poem is the author. Thomas Hardy, for example, wrote a poem in which the *I* is a soldier (p. 814); Gerald Stern wrote a poem in which the *I* is a dead dog (p. 614).

ENTRY POINTS In the following poem, pay attention to the speaker as he recalls his father and expresses his love for what is now lost. Watch for indications of what the *I* is like—character traits and attitudes. And listen for indications of whether the voice you hear represents that of the author or of a character separate and different from the author.

APPROACHING THE AUTHOR

Paul Elledge Photography.

Believing that poetry was interfering with his pursuits in activism, **Li-Young Lee** decided to stop writing. Soon after, he developed severe insomnia. Convinced his inability to sleep was the result of his having given up creating poetry, he quickly began writing again and hasn't stopped since.

    For more about him, see page 1397.

Li-Young Lee b. 1957

Eating Alone   [1986]

I've pulled the last of the year's young onions.
The garden is bare now. The ground is cold,
brown and old. What is left of the day flames
in the maples at the corner of my
eye. I turn, a cardinal vanishes.   5
By the cellar door, I wash the onions,
then drink from the icy metal spigot.

Once, years back, I walked beside my father
among the windfall pears. I can't recall
our words. We may have strolled in silence. But   10
I still see him bend that way—left hand braced
on knee, creaky—to lift and hold to my
eye a rotten pear. In it, a hornet
spun crazily, glazed in slow, glistening juice.

It was my father I saw this morning   15
waving to me from the trees. I almost
called to him, until I came close enough
to see the shovel, leaning where I had
left it, in the flickering, deep green shade.

White rice steaming, almost done. Sweet green peas   20
fried in onions. Shrimp braised in sesame
oil and garlic. And my own loneliness.
What more could I, a young man, want.

APPROACHING THE READING

1. How does the last stanza of the poem relate to the previous three stanzas? What do you make of the final line?

2. Describe the voice you hear as you listen to the poem. What personal qualities and attributes come through what is said? How does the title affect your sense of the voice of the poem?

3. Describe how hearing the poem's voice enriches your experience of the poem. What would be lost if you did not hear the voice?

In the text of "Eating Alone," there seems to be no reason for thinking the *I* is significantly different from the author, and biographical information about the author (including the biographical sketch on p. 1398) confirms basic similarities between the speaker and the poem. The voice we hear appears to be Li-Young Lee's voice. Or, perhaps we should say, his voice as a poet in this poem. What we really mean when we talk about **voice** is authorial presence not as a biographical personality but as the sense conveyed by a poem of an intelligence and sensibility that has invented, arranged, and expressed the elements and ideas in a particular manner.

CONVEYING VOICE DIRECTLY   From the beginning of "Eating Alone," the person speaking seems low-keyed, quiet, with muted emotions. He is observant, in touch with his surroundings, someone who notices the appearance of the now-barren earth, the brilliant sunset shining through the leaves of a maple tree, the flight of a cardinal. The voice in the second stanza sounds soft, sensitive, perhaps pensive, as he recalls a particular moment, years ago, with his father, who seems no longer to be living. The moment was memorable not for what they said to each other but for the particular way his father bent over to pick up a rotting pear and showed him a hornet circling drunkenly in its hollowed-out center. From his father's influence, it seems, the speaker learned the attentiveness to nature demonstrated in the first stanza.

CONVEYING VOICE INDIRECTLY   The third stanza makes clear that the speaker felt a great deal of emotion when he thought he saw his father, but then realized what he saw was actually a shovel in flickering light. But the voice we hear restrains that deep emotion, understates it, which may end up making it sound all the stronger. The understated emotion is carried over to the final stanza, in the details of an excellent meal, fit for a festive, shared occasion, in striking contrast to the speaker's "loneliness."

COMPLEXITY OF VOICE   The word *loneliness* and the final line raise key questions about voice, questions of the kind that each reader must think through. What kind of voice says the words "my own loneliness"? Is it a depressing, isolated loneliness brought on by his feeling lost without his father? Is it an accepted loneliness, in which he misses his father's physical presence but is consoled by a sense of the father's continuing presence in his memories? Could it be a mixture of the two, or something else?

Similarly, what kind of voice says the last line, "What more could I, a young man, want"? Is the voice heavy with irony? (There's a lot more I could want, starting with having my father back!) Does it express the genuine consolations that are found in good food and the flood of memories associated with the food and with other experiences? The title brings those questions about the voice into focus: Is eating alone a sad, solitary activity for the speaker? Does he actually feel lonely as he eats alone? When do being alone and not being lonely coincide? When do they not?

It is important when working with a poem to assume complexity of emotion. Our feelings are always "mixed," meaning complex, even contradictory. A poem—an effective, honest poem—is never emotionally simplistic.

ENTRY POINTS   The following poem is about a father-son relationship rather different from that in "Eating Alone." This one is a narrative poem, describing the father-son interactions in story form. As you read and reread it, pay attention to the *I* telling the story. Notice and then try to describe the character traits of the speaker and the father.

APPROACHING THE AUTHOR

Charles Bukowski worked an odd array of jobs to support his writing: He was employed at a dog-biscuit factory, at a slaughterhouse, and at a cake and cookie factory and also was a dishwasher, a truck driver, a mail carrier, a gas-station attendant, a parking-lot attendant, an elevator operator, and a poster hanger in New York City subways.

For more about him, see page 1376.

Charles Bukowski 1920–1994

my old man   [1977]

16 years old
during the depression
I'd come home drunk
and all my clothing—
shorts, shirts, stockings—   5
suitcase, and pages of
short stories
would be thrown out on the
front lawn and about the
street.   10

my mother would be
waiting behind a tree:
"Henry, Henry, don't

go in . . . he'll
kill you, he's read   15
your stories . . ."

"I can whip his
ass . . ."

"Henry, please take
this . . . and   20
find yourself a room."

but it worried him
that I might not
finish high school
so I'd be back   25
again.

one evening he walked in
with the pages of
one of my short stories
(which I had never submitted   30
to him)
and he said, "this is
a great short story."
I said, "o.k.,"
and he handed it to me   35
and I read it.
it was a story about
a rich man
who had a fight with
his wife and had   40
gone out into the night
for a cup of coffee
and had observed
the waitress and the spoons
and forks and the   45
salt and pepper shakers
and the neon sign
in the window
and then had gone back
to his stable   50
to see and touch his
favorite horse
who then
kicked him in the head
and killed him.   55

somehow
the story held
meaning for him
though
when I had written it   60
I had no idea
of what I was
writing about.

so I told him,
"o.k., old man, you can   65
have it."
and he took it
and walked out
and closed the door.
I guess that's   70
as close
as we ever got.

APPROACHING THE READING

1. Describe the voice you hear in the poem. Do you think it is the voice of the poet directly, or of a character distinct from the poet? What would you use from the poem to support your opinion?

2. How would you characterize the father? The son? Do you sympathize with either? Why or why not?

3. Why do you think the father likes the story?

4. Why do you think Henry wrote the story? He says he had no idea of what he was writing about.

5. Why do you think the poet included the story? How does it fit the voice of the poem?

This is a first-person narrative, which may have autobiographical overtones. Bukowski's given name was Heinrich Karl (Henry Charles) and he did have a tempestuous relationship with his father. But the poem does not have to be read as autobiographical: It can stand on its own as a narrative poem with complex, interesting characterizations. Try reading it both ways, and see if the voice and the effect of the poem differ depending on how you approach it.

VOICE AND POINT OF VIEW   In this poem, thinking in terms of point of view (see p. 161) helps. We hear everything from Henry's perspective. What happens and what is said would sound quite different from the father's vantage point.

Some books use the term **persona** for the first-person narrator through whom an author speaks or the speaker whose voice is heard in a lyric poem. They assume that one can never hear the author directly in a written work, even when she or he uses *I*, that the author always, inevitably talks through a mask the way actors did in Greek plays (which is where the term *persona* came from). This book does not make that assumption, though it stresses that an *I* should never automatically be equated with the author.

READING A DRAMATIC MONOLOGUE

One poetic form in which the *I* is definitely a character is the **dramatic monologue**. In dramatic monologues, there is only one speaker, a character overheard in a dramatic moment, usually addressing another character or characters who do not speak. The speaker's words reveal what is going on in the scene and bring out significant aspects of what the speaker is like. You can, therefore, figure out who is speaking, to whom, and on what occasion, and the substance and tone of what she or he is saying. See, for example, Robert Browning's "My Last Duchess" (p. 622). (If the character is speaking to her- or himself, the poem is using interior monologue—see p. 166; that is probably the case in T. S. Eliot's "The Love Song of J. Alfred Prufrock"—p. 796.)

READING FOR TONE

When you hear a voice, an important aspect of what you are hearing is its tone. **Tone** was defined in Chapter 8 (p. 232) as the attitude or "stance" toward the subject and toward the reader or audience implied in a work. Tone is as important in poems as it is in stories. Poems can have a single tone, but usually the tone is complex rather than straightforward; it cannot be summed up in a word or two. More often two or more tones mix and play off or with each other. In "my old man" (p. 598), for example, one needs to consider Henry's tone—his attitude toward his father and perhaps toward life in general—and the tone the poem takes toward Henry.

ENTRY POINTS Here is another poem about a son's memories of his father. Listen carefully for its voice and tone. Pay attention to the diction, connotations, and images. Compare the father-son relationship to that of "Eating Alone" or that of "my old man."

APPROACHING THE AUTHOR

As a child, **Theodore Roethke** spent much time in the greenhouse owned by his father and uncle. His impressions of the natural world contained there would later profoundly influence the subjects and imagery of his verse.

For more about him, see page 1410.

Theodore Roethke   1908–1963

My Papa's Waltz   [1948]

The whiskey on your breath
Could make a small boy dizzy;
But I hung on like death:
Such waltzing was not easy.

We romped until the pans   5
Slid from the kitchen shelf;
My mother's countenance
Could not unfrown itself.

The hand that held my wrist
Was battered on one knuckle;   10
At every step you missed
My right ear scraped a buckle.

You beat time on my head
With a palm caked hard by dirt,
Then waltzed me off to bed   15
Still clinging to your shirt.

APPROACHING THE READING

You can explore this author and poem in depth, including images and cultural documents, with VirtuaLit Poetry at bedfordstmartins .com/rewritinglit.

1. Consider the voice in the poem. Do you think the *I* is a character narrating the episode or the voice of the poet?

2. Unlike "Eating Alone" (p. 596) and "my old man" (p. 598), which address the reader, this poem addresses *you*, the father. How does that affect the voice of the poem? Try changing *you* and *your* to *he* and *his*. What effect does that have on the voice? How would you explain the difference?

3. Be ready to discuss the age of the speaker whose voice we hear—his age now and at the time of the event—and what you think he felt then and feels now. What difference does it make to the way you hear the voice whether the father is living or has died?

4. Discuss the effect of the word *papa* on the tone of the poem. Substitute *daddy* or *father* or *old man*. What happens?

5. Discuss the effect of the word *Waltz* in the title on the tone of the poem. Substitute *Drinking* or *Rowdiness*. What happens?

A DARK TONE? "My Papa's Waltz" affects readers in different ways. For some the poem describes a troubled relationship or dysfunctional home. The word *whiskey* suggests for them that the father has a drinking problem; the mother's disapproval suggests that the father and mother have a difficult relationship. *Battered* indicates that the father abuses his son and perhaps his wife. The simile "I hung on like death" in line 3 suggests a home in which fear pervades the atmosphere. For these readers, the poem has a dark tone, perhaps a tragic one, as a little boy—too young to be aware of what he's doing—puts up with his father's frightening romps because he is forced to physically and tries desperately to gain his father's love and approval.

OR A JOYFUL TONE?   Other readers discern a different tone in the poem. For them words such as *waltz* and *romped* convey a lighter tone—a waltz is a graceful, flowing, lyrical dance that suggests joy and celebration (though, of course, the poet could be using the word ironically). The father described is a physical laborer (his hands are battered and caked with dirt) who has a couple of drinks with his buddies after work on a Friday. Feeling good, he frolics with his son, more wildly than he probably should, creating disorder in the kitchen, and more roughly than he should, thus scraping the boy's ear and tapping on his head enthusiastically. The romp is scary for the small boy ("dizzy," "like death," "clinging")—but excitingly scary. For these readers, the poem describes a speaker looking back at his childhood, recalling a happy memory, a memory that evinces his father's affection (people generally waltz with people they love) and his own positive response to his father (one can cling out of love as well as fear).

COMPLEXITY OF TONE   Assessing tone is a central part of the total interpretation of a literary work. As in all interpretation, it's not simple or straightforward. Every aspect of the work can come to bear on tone. It's important always to be alert for indicators of tone. Some are the same as in fiction—word choice, ways of phrasing, repetitions, understatement, overstatement, a particular figure of speech. Others—such as the handling of sounds and rhythm, lines, and line breaks—are more particular to poetry. And as "My Papa's Waltz" makes clear, tone is not an objective detail on which all readers must agree. Readers can read tones differently, and discussions about tone often form a vital part of conversations about literature, with each side pointing to aspects that lead them to respond to the work the way they do.

READING FOR IRONY

As you read a poem, be alert for signals that what is said is not to be taken in a literal way: word choice, the sheer absurdity of what is said, the way a thought is phrased, the sounds and rhythms in which it is expressed. Recognition of irony is crucial to reading well.

ENTRY POINTS   Irony is as important in poetry as it is in stories. Review the discussion of irony in Chapter 8 (pp. 239–41), especially—for poetry—the sections on verbal irony and sarcasm. Then try out your ear for irony as you read the following poem. Pay attention especially to word choice, exaggerations, and incongruities.

Marge Piercy   b. 1936

Barbie Doll   [1973]

This girlchild was born as usual
and presented dolls that did pee-pee
and miniature GE stoves and irons
and wee lipsticks the color of cherry candy.
Then in the magic of puberty, a classmate said: 5
You have a great big nose and fat legs.

She was healthy, tested intelligent,
possessed strong arms and back,
abundant sexual drive and manual dexterity.
She went to and fro apologizing.   10
Everyone saw a fat nose on thick legs.

She was advised to play coy,
exhorted to come on hearty,
exercise, diet, smile and wheedle.
Her good nature wore out   15
like a fan belt.
So she cut off her nose and her legs
and offered them up.

In the casket displayed on satin she lay
with the undertaker's cosmetics painted on,   20
a turned-up putty nose,
dressed in a pink and white nightie.
Doesn't she look pretty? everyone said.
Consummation at last.
To every woman a happy ending.   25

APPROACHING THE READING

1. What effect on tone do words such as *girlchild*, *pee-pee*, *wee*, and *cherry candy* have? How did they strike you the first time you read them?

2. What do you think the speaker means by the "magic" of puberty in line 5? How does the wording of line 6 connect with it? How would you describe the tone the two lines convey?

3. At what point in your reading did you realize this poem critiques prevailing social attitudes?

4. Point out several examples of irony in the poem.

THE VOICE This poem is narrated by an unidentified, third-person observer, not the poet in first person and not a character involved in the action. It has a heavily ironic tone. In such cases, of course, it is important to distinguish between the voice of the speaker (who seems to say the events have a happy ending) and the voice of the poem (which means the opposite).

THE IRONIES The title and opening lines can seem straightforward initially, with words such as "girlchild" and "did pee-pee" creating a child-like simplicity. Then, a deeper seriousness begins to emerge in line 6: "You have a great big nose and fat legs." The middle stanzas develop the contrast between what this young woman was and the Barbie Doll and supermodel expectations society imposes on women. Phrasings such as "went to and fro apologizing" (l. 10) and "a fat nose on thick legs" (l. 11) and the comparison "wore out / like a fan belt" (ll. 15–16) signal that the voice is not to be heard as straightforward. Line 17 is certainly not straightforward: "So she cut off her nose and her legs" is the speaker's ironic way of saying that, unable to cope with what she perceived as society's expectations, she committed suicide.

THE EFFECTS The ironies intensify in the final paragraph. In her coffin, thanks to the undertakers' skills, she looks like a Barbie doll and everyone now, when she can't hear them, says how pretty she looks. The poem's voice continues to intensify in the final lines: "Consummation at last" (l. 24) is highly ironic in that her consummation — completion, fulfillment, perfection — is found only after death. The most common use of *consummation* — the completion of a marriage by sexual intercourse — makes the irony even stronger since she did not feel sexually attractive when she was living, and perhaps did not seem so to young men, with their society-shaped expectations. In the final line — "To every woman a happy ending" — the ironic voice turns sarcastic.

The rest of this chapter, along with the chapters that follow, goes on to discuss specific techniques and elements poets draw from when they compose a poem. As we focus on sounds, metaphors, rhythm, and form, however, it is important that you continue to listen for, and to, the voices in poems. Listen to the variety of voices, from different times, different experiences, and different backgrounds. Listen for and to the variety of things they give voice to in their poems. *Hear* the poems and *hear* what the poems are saying.

READING FOR SOUND

Fine writers have "good ears." They attend to sounds of words as well as combinations of sounds, listening for the way sound and rhythm work together to create the poem's "music," all of which contribute to the voice of a poem. Rhythm is treated later in the book, in Chapter 16. Here we focus on the effects of repeating or contrasting syllable sounds, vowel sounds, and consonant sounds. To gain the full experience of effective writing, a reader needs to hear not only the words but also the repetitions, connections, contrasts, and combinations of vowels, consonants, and syllables that form the words.

  TIPS for Reading Poems Aloud

Because of the importance of voice and sounds, it can be helpful to read poems aloud at least once, if not several times, and to listen to someone else read them. Attending to the sounds and rhythms will bring out aspects of the poem that you otherwise might overlook. Here are some suggestions for reading aloud:

- **Don't rush.** Reading too fast distorts the rhythms and blurs the words and sounds.

- **Pay attention to punctuation.** Take a full stop at a period or semicolon and a brief pause at a comma, both within lines and at the ends of lines.

- **Read with expression.** Your voice needs to convey what the sentences are saying, which means you need to understand the content and tone. But be careful not to overdramatize.

- **Read to communicate.** Even if you are reading to yourself, pretend that you have an audience and that you are trying hard to help them receive and appreciate the poem fully.

Reading aloud might feel uncomfortable at first, but soon you may find yourself enjoying what can happen when you do. It can also influence your silent reading, making you more attentive to your mental voice.

ENTRY POINTS   The following poem is about an African American driver being stopped by a police officer. Listen for the sounds made by the words and phrases—repetitions of words, parallel constructions, felicitous phrasings, echoes of vowel and consonant sounds, and rhyming words as well as the sound of the speaker's voice. Think about the ways that the sounds help create the impact of the experience.

Sekou Sundiata   1948–2007

Blink Your Eyes   [1995]

Remembering Sterling A. Brown°

I was on my way to see my woman
but the Law said I was on my way
thru a red light red light red light
and if you saw my woman
you could understand,   5
I was just being a man
It wasn't about no light
it was about my ride
and if you saw my ride
you could dig that too, you dig?   10
Sunroof stereo radio black leather
bucket seats sit low you know,
the body's cool, but the tires are worn.
Ride when the hard time come, ride
when they're gone, in other words   15
the light was green.

I could wake up in the morning
without a warning
and my world could change:
blink your eyes.   20
All depends, all depends on the skin,
all depends on the skin you're living in.

Up to the window comes the Law
with his hand on his gun
what's up? what's happening?   25
I said I guess
that's when I really broke the law.

APPROACHING THE AUTHOR

When **Sekou Sundiata** discovered there was poetry in "the language we speak," he realized we could, as he put it, make poetry out of what we say all the time. He often gave readings with a group of jazz musicians, fusing his poetry with their music.

For more about him, see page 1414.

Sterling A. Brown: Brown (1901–1989) was an African American poet and a longtime professor at Howard University. See his poem "Riverbank Blues" (p. 776) and biographical sketch (p. 1415).

He said *a routine, step out the car*
a routine, assume the position.
Put your hands up in the air   30
you know the routine, like you just don't care.
License and registration.
Deep was the night and the light
from the North Star on the car door, déjà vu
we've been through this before,   35
why did you stop me?
Somebody had to stop you.
I watch the news, you always lose.
You're unreliable, that's undeniable.
This is serious, you could be dangerous.   40

I could wake up in the morning
without a warning
and my world could change:
blink your eyes.
All depends, all depends on the skin,   45
all depends on the skin you're living in.

New York City, they got laws
Can't no bruthas drive outdoors,
in certain neighborhoods, on particular streets
near and around certain types of people.   50
They got laws.
All depends, all depends on the skin,
all depends on the skin you're living in.

APPROACHING THE READING

1. As you listen to the *I* in this poem, does it seem like you are hearing the voice of the author directly, a character speaking for the author, or a character different from the author? What would you use to support your conclusion?

2. Is there an overall tone in the poem, or do different types of tone appear in different parts? Or would you say that both are true? How would you describe the tone of the repeated phrase "all depends on the skin you're living in"?

3. Read the first stanza of the poem aloud. Pay close attention to the sounds of the syllables, words, and phrases in those lines (not sounds they describe, but the sounds you hear as you say them aloud). Find examples of repeated consonant sounds and vowel sounds, of words repeated rhythmically, of words that rhyme. Reflect on the "feel" and tone the sounds create.

4. Do an online search for "Sundiata Blink Your Eyes." You should be able to find video or audio of Sundiata performing the poem. As you watch or listen, compare his reading with the one you just did, and consider if listening to him adds to your impression of the poem and to its effectiveness.

A significant portion of the effect of "Blink Your Eyes" arises from the sounds — the rhymes, the repetitions, the echoes of vowels and consonants that create an aura and reinforce the poem's ironies.

The poem describes an experience of racial profiling: Encountering such racism has the potential to change one's world in the blink of an eye. Even though the speaker voices the poem as an event in his past, he is still able to remember the innocence of his excited anticipation of driving to see his lover. We can feel that throughout the poem's opening section with its vivid picture of how "cool" his car was, as conveyed by the images, and how hip he was, as conveyed by the sounds and rhythms of the words he uses.

Then he is accused of running a red light and everything changes. He realizes there are two different worlds with two different ways of enforcing the law, that it "all depends on the skin you're living in." The subject turns more serious after line 23, but the use of rhyme, the repetition of phrases, and the echoes of vowels and consonants continue, creating a spirit of positive defiance in the face of injustice.

Close examination of techniques of sound can become technical and abstract and risks making you want to back away. Yet, only by looking closely can we see exactly how the effects we appreciate are created. We ask you to focus on just four important types of sound technique — alliteration, assonance, repetition, and rhyme — with examples from "Blink Your Eyes" to illustrate them.

Alliteration

One kind of sound, **alliteration**, is the repetition of identical consonant sounds in words relatively near one another (in the same line or adjacent lines usually). Alliteration is most common at the beginnings of words or syllables, especially the beginnings of stressed syllables ("*green* as *grass*"), though it sometimes can occur within words and syllables as well ("*golden baggage*"). Throughout this chapter, the pronunciation is what matters, not the letters. "Call the *k*id in the *c*enter" does alliterate (Call/kid), but "Call" and "center" do not. Notice the alliterative *s*, *r*, *b*, and *l* sounds in these lines:

Sunroof stereo radio black leather
bucket seats sit low you know.

Alliteration should be used meaningfully, not just to "show off" an ability. It can call attention to words, giving them greater emphasis, linking words together to get us to connect their meanings, and making phrases more memorable. And it can evoke the feeling of an experience, can elicit emotion, can intensify tone.

> A variant on alliteration is **consonance**, the use of words whose consonant sounds are the same but whose vowels are different. In perfect examples, all the consonants are alike: *live, love; chitter, chatter; reader, rider;* or, in Romeo's words, "I'll *look* to *like*, if *looking liking* move" (*Romeo and Juliet* 1.4.98). The more usual examples of consonance are words in which the consonants following the main vowels are identical: *dive, love; swatter, chitter; sound, bond.* Line 5 of "Blink Your Eyes" (p. 607) employs consonance: "you could understand"; likewise, lines 7–8: "It wasn't about no light / it was about my ride."
>
> Thus, alliteration is the repetition of *initial* consonant sounds; consonance is the repetition of *final* consonant sounds.

Assonance

Another kind of sound, **assonance**, is the repetition of identical vowel sounds in words whose consonants differ. It too can be initial ("*under* the *umbrella*"), though internal is more usual ("*tree* by *leaf*," "*tree* and *treat*"). Its strongest effect is a subtle musical quality that often reinforces the tone of a poem, adds gradations to its feel, and contributes to levels of meaning by making connections and adding emphasis. Listen for the assonance in lines 14–16 from "Blink Your Eyes." Then reread them, thinking about its effects.

> Ride when the hard time come, ride
> when they're gone, in other words
> the light was green.

Repetition

Repetition is the reuse of a word, group of words, line, or lines later in the same poem, but close enough so you remember the earlier use. You may hear the later use as an echo or as a contrast created by a shift in intensity or implication. The lines "All depends, all depends on the skin, / all depends on the skin you're living in" repeat "all depends" and "all depends on the skin" for rhythmic effect, for emphasis, and to build up to the climactic key phrase "on the skin you're living in." These two lines are repeated three times in the poem, increasing the intensity of their emphasis.

Rhyme

You are probably familiar with rhyme. Rhyme, often thought of, wrongly, as a defining characteristic of poetry, is, in fact, only one of many kinds of sound that can appear in a poem. Many poems do not rhyme. **Rhyme** is the repetition of the final vowel sound and all following consonant sounds in two or more words that have differing consonant sounds preceding the vowel, as in the words *air* and *care* in lines 30–31 from "Blink Your Eyes":

> *Put your hands up in the* air
> *you know the routine, like you just don't* care.

Rhyme leads to various effects. In the lines above, the rhymes become a bitter comic device, used to ridicule the officer who has stopped and racially profiled the speaker. In other situations, rhyme emphasizes important words; it creates a connection or a bonding; it tightens the organization and strengthens unity; it contains meaning; it provides a sense of completion, or termination, to lines, stanzas, and whole poems; and it pleases the ear through its musicality and expectation or surprise. If well written — and well read — rhyme does not distract us from the poem itself but blends with everything else in the poem. When reading a poem aloud, make sure to say the rhyming words in a way that enables a listener to hear the rhymes as echoes of sound, without letting them "steal the show."

Rhyme is described according to several categories: exact or approximate, end or internal, single or double.

EXACT OR APPROXIMATE   The definition given above is for **exact rhyme**, in which the vowel and the consonant sounds following the vowel are the same: br*ight* and n*ight*, *art* and h*eart*, "*I watch the* news, *you always* lose."

Approximate rhyme, or **slant rhyme**, is a form of rhyme in which words contain similar sounds but do not rhyme perfectly (usually involving assonance or, more frequently, consonance): d*eep* and f*eet*; rhyme and wr*ithe*; g*ate* and m*at*; *all* and st*ole*, w*ill*, or h*ale*.

END OR INTERNAL   **End rhyme** involves rhyming words that occur at the ends of lines, such as *air* and *care*:

> *Put your hands up in the* air
> *you know the routine, like you just don't* care.

In **internal rhyme**, two or more words within a line, or within lines near each other, rhyme with each other, or words within lines rhyme with words at the ends:

> *I watch the* news, *you always* lose.
> *You're* unreliable, *that's* undeniable.

SINGLE OR DOUBLE   Single rhyme involves only the final, stressed syllable in rhyming words: *west* and *vest*, *away* and *today*.

> All depends, all depends on the *skin*,
> all depends on the *skin* you're living *in*.

In **double rhyme** the accented, rhyming syllable is followed by one or more identical, unstressed syllables: *thrilling* and *killing*, *marry* and *tarry*, *unreliable* and *undeniable*.

> I could wake up in the *morning*
> without a *warning*.

Unless specified otherwise, the word *rhyme* used alone means exact, end, single rhyme.

Single rhyme used to be called **masculine rhyme** (because it was considered "strong" and "forceful"), and double rhyme was called **feminine rhyme** (because it was regarded as "weaker" than single rhyme). These labels generally are no longer used because of their sexist overtones.

The pattern of end rhymes in a poem or stanza, that is, its recurring sequence, is called its **rhyme scheme**. The pattern is usually described by assigning a letter to each word sound, the same word sounds having the same letter. For poems in stanzas, the pattern is usually the same for each stanza. In that case, you need to mark the rhyme scheme only once. Thus the rhyme scheme of Samuel Hazo's "For Fawzi in Jerusalem" (p. 817) is *abcba*.

ONOMATOPOEIA   In some cases sounds seem to suggest meaning. This is particularly true in **onomatopoeia**, words whose pronunciation suggests their meaning. Samuel Johnson, in the eighteenth century, described it this way: "Every language has some words framed to exhibit the noises which they express, as *thump, rattle, growl, hiss*." Onomatopoeia, at its best, involves not just individual words but entire passages that carry their meaning in their sounds. Listen to these lines from "The Princess" by Alfred, Lord Tennyson: "The moan of doves in immemorial elms, / And murmuring of innumerable bees." Reread Maxine Kumin's "The Sound of Night" (p. 576) and notice her effective use of onomatopoetic language such as "chitter noise," "huggermugger crowd," "skitter across," and "squeak, chirp, dip, and skim."

SOUNDS FITTING MEANING   The important thing to notice is that sounds in a poem do generally seem to fit the meanings being expressed. Alexander Pope illustrated that point in his poem "An Essay on Criticism" (1711) by suggesting differences in the sounds of the words used to describe a gentle breeze and a fierce storm: "Soft is the strain when Zephyr gently blows" and "The hoarse, rough verse shou'd like the Torrent roar." For an active reader of poetry, therefore, listening attentively to the sounds of words and syllables can enrich your understanding of the meaning those words are creating.

> You can further explore voice, tone, and sound, including using interactive exercises, with VirtuaLit Poetry at bedfordstmartins .com/rewritinglit.

☑ CHECKLIST on Reading for Voice, Tone, and Sound

❑ Listen for the voice of the speaker, if the speaker and poet are almost the same, or for the voice of the speaker and the voice of the poem if they are different. In either case, listen for the intelligence and sensibility that has invented, arranged, and expressed the elements and ideas in a particular manner.

❑ Listen for the tone: the tone of voice or attitude toward the subject or situation in the poem (playful, serious, ironic, cheerful, pessimistic, sorrowful, and so forth).

❑ Listen for irony: an expression involving a discrepancy or incongruity between appearance and reality, between what is said and what is intended. In poetry, verbal irony (saying what is nearly opposite of what is meant) is used most often, though situational irony (things turning out not as hoped or expected) is frequent as well.

❑ Listen for and respond to patterns of sound, such as alliteration (repetition of initial consonant sounds), consonance (repetition of all consonant sounds or of final consonant sounds), assonance (repetition of identical vowel sounds), rhyme (repetition of the accented vowel sound of a word and all succeeding sounds), onomatopoeia (words whose pronunciation suggests their meaning), and repetitions (of words, phrases, or lines).

FURTHER READING

ENTRY POINTS   Here's a poem in which voice and tone are very important. You will probably need one reading just to get oriented to and used to the voice, that of a dead dog. On your next readings, pay attention to the tone, especially to irony.

> **APPROACHING THE AUTHOR**
>
> **Gerald Stern** grew up in Pittsburgh in a house with no books. It wasn't
> that becoming a writer was discouraged, he says; it just wasn't consid-
> ered something that anyone in his family would aspire to.
>   For more about him, see page 1413.

Gerald Stern b. 1925

The Dog   [1987]

What I was doing with my white teeth exposed
like that on the side of the road I don't know,
and I don't know why I lay beside the sewer
so that lover of dead things could come back
with his pencil sharpened and his piece of white paper.   5
I was there for a good two hours whistling
dirges, shrieking a little, terrifying
hearts with my whimpering cries before I died
by pulling the one leg up and stiffening.
There is a look we have with the hair of the chin   10
curled in mid-air, there is a look with the belly
stopped in the midst of its greed. The lover of dead things
stoops to feel me, his hand is shaking. I know
his mouth is open and his glasses are slipping.
I think his pencil must be jerking and the terror   15
of smell — and sight — is overtaking him;
I know he has that terrified faraway look
that death brings — he is contemplating. I want him
to touch my forehead once and rub my muzzle
before he lifts me up and throws me into   20
that little valley. I hope he doesn't use
his shoe for fear of touching me; I know,
or used to know, the grasses down there; I think
I knew a hundred smells. I hope the dog's way
doesn't overtake him, one quick push,   25
barely that, and the mind freed, something else,
some other thing, to take its place. Great heart,
great human heart, keep loving me as you lift me,
give me your tears, great loving stranger, remember
the death of dogs, forgive the yapping, forgive   30
the shitting, let there be pity, give me your pity.
How could there be enough? I have given

my life for this, emotion has ruined me, oh lover,
I have exchanged my wildness — little tricks
with the mouth and feet, with the tail, my tongue is a parrot's,   35
I am a rampant horse, I am a lion,
I wait for the cookie, I snap my teeth —
as you have taught me, oh distant and brilliant and lonely.

APPROACHING THE READING

1. It isn't uncommon for someone's tone to shift while talking about a subject. Where do you see such tonal shifts in the dog's voice? What do these shifts say about what the dog feels and about the dog's attitude toward the person it is talking about?

2. The dog talks about a poet. What makes this especially ironic?

3. Why does the dog address the poet as the "lover of dead things" (lines 4, 12)? Make sure that you consider the tone when thinking about your response.

4. The poem begins moving toward a crescendo at line 27, with the sentence that begins "Great heart." How did you find yourself reacting to this buildup through to the closing line? Why do you think the dog refers to itself as a "rampant horse" and a "lion" (line 36)? Why does it say, "my tongue is a parrot's" (35)? The poem is constructed of specific images until the very last line. What do you make of the shift in diction as well as tone in "oh distant and brilliant and lonely"?

ENTRY POINTS   Poetry provides many people — whether they are published or unpublished authors — a way to "give voice to" what is otherwise very difficult to express or to express adequately. In each of the next four poems, consider what the poet is giving voice to and why poetry is an appropriate vehicle for that expression.

As you read the following poem the first time, get a feel for what the speaker felt as a child and what she feels now. On a second reading, listen especially to the way words and combinations of words create what the chapter earlier referred to as "musicality."

APPROACHING THE AUTHOR

Jane Kenyon spent the last two decades of her short life at her farm in New Hampshire where she wrote powerfully and without a note of self-pity of her experiences with depression. In addition to her own work, she translated poetry and encouraged all poets to translate poems. Cameron Diaz read Kenyon's poetry in the film *In Her Shoes*.

For more about her, see page 1396.

Jane Kenyon   1947–1995

A Boy Goes into the World   [1990]

My brother rode off on his bike
into the summer afternoon, but
Mother called me back
from the end of the sandy drive:
"It's different for girls."   5

He'd be gone for hours, come back
with things: a cocoon, gray-brown
and papery around a stick;
a puff ball, ripe, wrinkled,
and exuding spores; owl pellets—   10
bits of undigested bone and fur;
and pieces of moss that might
have made toupees for preposterous
green men, but went instead
into a wide-necked jar for a terrarium.   15

He mounted his plunder on poster
board, gluing and naming
each piece. He has long since
forgotten those days and things, but
I at last can claim them as my own.   20

APPROACHING THE READING

1. From the title of the poem until the last line, you are invited to realize the
   implications of what *is* talked about and what *is not*. "It's different for girls"
   (line 5). Discuss the different attitudes toward boys and girls in the poem.
   How you think the speaker felt then? How do you think she feels now?

2. How would you describe the voice of the poem? Is there a dominant tone?
   Be careful to discern gradations in the tone.

3. Pick out various sound elements. How do they contribute to the impact of
   the poem?

4. Discuss the gender issues the poem addresses. How have they changed since
   the speaker's childhood? In what ways have they not changed?

ENTRY POINTS   Voice plays an important role in the following poem. The first time you read it, listen for who is speaking and in what context. As you reread it, consider how the complex handling of voice intensifies the impact of the concerns the poem is giving voice to.

Pat Mora   b. 1942

La Migra   [1995]

1

Let's play La Migra.°
I'll be the Border Patrol.
You be the Mexican maid.
I get the badge and sunglasses.
You can hide and run,
but you can't get away
because I have a jeep.
I can take you wherever
I want, but don't ask
questions because
I don't speak Spanish.
I can touch you wherever
I want but don't complain
too much because I've got
boots and kick—if I have to,   15
and I have handcuffs.
Oh, and a gun.
Get ready, get set, run.

2

Let's play La Migra.
You be the Border Patrol.   20
I'll be the Mexican woman.
Your jeep has a flat,
and you have been spotted
by the sun.
All you have is heavy: hat,   25
glasses, badge, shoes, gun.
I know this desert,

APPROACHING THE AUTHOR

Pat Mora's grandparents moved to the United States during the Mexican Revolution. They settled in El Paso, Texas, where Mora's mother grew up in a Spanish-speaking household while attending a school where English was spoken and often played translator between these two worlds. One generation later, Mora grew up in a bilingual home and attended a school where English was spoken.

For more about her, see page 1401.

---

1. **La Migra** (Spanish): Border patrol agents

where to rest,
where to drink.
Oh, I am not alone.   30
You hear us singing
and laughing with the wind,
Agua dulce brota aquí, aquí, aquí,°
but since you can't speak Spanish,
you do not understand.   35
Get ready.

---

33. **Agua...aquí** (Spanish): Sweet water springs, here, here, here.

APPROACHING THE READING

1. Discuss what leads the opening line — "Let's play La Migra" — to have an impact on all that follows. Consider the poet's choices of voice and tone. Describe how these intensify the experience in the poem and on the reader.

2. Think about the differences in stanzas 1 and 2. Who is the speaker? What is the impact of the pronoun change in line 2 of each stanza? Look at the last line of each stanza. What is implied by the differences between the two lines? What do you make of the very last line, "Get ready"?

3. Notice the way the lines are written: short, direct, even at times blunt. What is the impact of this line length? How do the lines help characterize the speaker? The speaker's knowledge and attitude? What the speaker is saying about the Border Patrol?

4. What might be suggested by "All you have is heavy" (line 25)?

5. Discuss the poem in relation to its subject as you hear it currently discussed.

ENTRY POINTS   As you read the poems below, in addition to paying attention to voice and sounds, listen for and keep in mind what the poet is giving voice to. In the following two poems, former soldiers wrestle with their feelings about War, the first dealing with World War I, the second with the Vietnam War.

APPROACHING THE AUTHOR

Wilfred Owen was killed in the Battle of the Sambre a week before the end of World War I. The telegram informing his mother of his death was delivered as her town's church bells were ringing in celebration of the armistice.

For more about him, see page 1405.

Wilfred Owen 1893–1918

Dulce et Decorum Est   [1920]

Bent double, like old beggars under sacks,
Knock-kneed, coughing like hags, we cursed through sludge,
Till on the haunting flares we turned our backs
And towards our distant rest began to trudge.
Men marched asleep. Many had lost their boots   5
But limped on, blood-shod. All went lame; all blind;
Drunk with fatigue; deaf even to the hoots
Of tired, outstripped Five-Nines° that dropped behind.

Gas! GAS! Quick, boys! — An ecstasy of fumbling,
Fitting the clumsy helmets just in time;   10
But someone still was yelling out and stumbling
And flound'ring like a man in fire or lime...
Dim, through the misty panes° and thick green light,
As under a green sea, I saw him drowning.

In all my dreams, before my helpless sight,   15
He plunges at me, guttering, choking, drowning.

If in some smothering dreams you too could pace
Behind the wagon that we flung him in,
And watch the white eyes writhing in his face,
His hanging face, like a devil's sick of sin;   20
If you could hear, at every jolt, the blood
Come gargling from the froth-corrupted lungs,
Obscene as cancer, bitter as the cud
Of vile, incurable sores on innocent tongues, —
My friend, you would not tell with such high zest   25
To children ardent for some desperate glory,
The old Lie: Dulce et decorum est
Pro patria mori.°

---

8. Five-Nines: 5.9-inch caliber shells.   **13. misty panes:** Of a gas mask.   **27–28. Dulce...
mori** (Latin): It is sweet and fitting / to die for one's country (Horace, *Odes* 3.12.13).

APPROACHING THE READING

1. Describe the speaker/voice of the poem. The poem looks back at the incident it describes. What is the effect of having it told from a later point? How
   do you think the distance in time has affected the speaker?

2. Consider the speaker's use of second person beginning in line 17. On the original draft of the poem, a dedication "To Jessie Pope" is scratched out and replaced with "To a certain Poetess." Jessie Pope published patriotic poems in a popular London newspaper during World War I. Neither dedication was included in published versions of "Dulce et Decorum Est." How does knowledge of the dedication affect your reading of the poem? How would your reading be affected if "you" and "My friend" were limited to Jessie Pope?

3. Pick out alliteration, assonance, and rhyme. What do such sound techniques contribute to the effect of the poem? How would you describe the tone achieved by rhyming "glory" with the Latin word for "to die"?

APPROACHING THE AUTHOR

Yusef Komunyakaa was profoundly influenced by growing up in Bogalusa, Louisiana, which at the time was a center of Ku Klux Klan activity and later became a focal point for the Civil Rights movement. During the Vietnam War he served as a war correspondent, which has also influenced his poetry.

For more about him, see page 1397.

Yusef Komunyakaa b. 1947

Facing It   [1988]

My black face fades,
hiding inside the black granite.
I said I wouldn't,
dammit: No tears.
I'm stone. I'm flesh.   5
My clouded reflection eyes me
like a bird of prey, the profile of night
slanted against morning. I turn
this way—the stone lets me go.
I turn that way—I'm inside   10
the Vietnam Veterans Memorial
again, depending on the light
to make a difference.
I go down the 58,022 names,
half-expecting to find   15
my own in letters like smoke.
I touch the name Andrew Johnson;
I see the booby trap's white flash.
Names shimmer on a woman's blouse
but when she walks away   20
the names stay on the wall.

Brushstrokes flash, a red bird's
wings cutting across my stare.
The sky. A plane in the sky.
A white vet's image floats   25
closer to me, then his pale eyes
look through mine. I'm a window.
He's lost his right arm
inside the stone. In the black mirror
a woman's trying to erase names: 30
No, she's brushing a boy's hair.

APPROACHING THE READING

1. Characterize the speaker of the voice you hear in the poem. What can you
   tell about the speaker's experiences and feelings?

2. How does the title fit the poem and the speaker? How does the last line fit?

3. Discuss the tone of the poem and point to specific details or techniques that
   help shape it.

4. If you have not visited the Vietnam Veterans Memorial in Washington,
   D.C., look at pictures of it and read about it (you can do both on the Web or
   in books). Talk to someone who has seen it, if you can. Reflect on how all
   this affects the way you visualize and experience the poem.

5. Pick out examples of sound techniques such as alliteration, assonance,
   rhyme. What do such sound techniques contribute to the effect of the poem?

ENTRY POINTS   The following poem is a dramatic monologue (p. 601)
based on events that occurred in the life of Alfonso II, Duke of Ferrara in
sixteenth-century northern Italy. The speaker is the duke. He is giving a guest
a personal guided tour of his palace and pauses to show him a portrait of his
previous wife painted by a fictitious but supposedly famous painter, Frà (that
is, "brother," or monk) Pandolf. Ferrara's first wife, Lucrezia, died in 1561 at
age seventeen after three years of marriage. We overhear what he says about
the painting and about her. From that we are left to determine what he is like,
what she was like, who the guest is, and why the duke says what he does.

APPROACHING THE AUTHOR

Robert Browning was able to read and write by age five and by fourteen
was fluent in Latin, Greek, Italian, and French. He attended University
College London for one year but said later in life that "Italy was my university," for he lived there many years and its art and atmosphere had a
deep influence on him.

   For more about him, see page 1376.

Robert Browning 1812–1889

My Last Duchess   [1842]

Ferrara

That's my last Duchess painted on the wall,
Looking as if she were alive. I call
That piece a wonder, now: Frà Pandolf's hands
Worked busily a day, and there she stands.
Will't please you sit and look at her? I said   5
"Frà Pandolf" by design, for never read
Strangers like you that pictured countenance,
The depth and passion of its earnest glance,
But to myself they turned (since none puts by
The curtain I have drawn for you, but I)   10
And seemed as they would ask me, if they durst,
How such a glance came there; so, not the first
Are you to turn and ask thus. Sir, 'twas not
Her husband's presence only, called that spot
Of joy into the Duchess' cheek: perhaps   15
Frà Pandolf chanced to say "Her mantle laps
Over my lady's wrist too much," or "Paint
Must never hope to reproduce the faint
Half-flush that dies along her throat": such stuff
Was courtesy, she thought, and cause enough   20
For calling up that spot of joy. She had
A heart—how shall I say?—too soon made glad,
Too easily impressed; she liked whate'er
She looked on, and her looks went everywhere.
Sir, 'twas all one! My favour at her breast,   25
The dropping of the daylight in the West,
The bough of cherries some officious fool
Broke in the orchard for her, the white mule
She rode with round the terrace—all and each
Would draw from her alike the approving speech,   30
Or blush, at least. She thanked men,—good! but thanked
Somehow—I know not how—as if she ranked
My gift of a nine-hundred-year-old name
With anybody's gift. Who'd stoop to blame
This sort of trifling? Even had you skill   35
In speech—(which I have not)—to make your will
Quite clear to such an one, and say, "Just this
Or that in you disgusts me; here you miss,

Or there exceed the mark" — and if she let
Herself be lessoned so, nor plainly set   40
Her wits to yours, forsooth, and made excuse,
— E'en then would be some stooping; and I choose
Never to stoop. Oh sir, she smiled, no doubt,
Whene'er I passed her; but who passed without
Much the same smile? This grew; I gave commands;   45
Then all smiles stopped together. There she stands
As if alive. Will't please you rise? We'll meet
The company below, then. I repeat,
The Count your master's known munificence
Is ample warrant that no just pretence   50
Of mine for dowry will be disallowed;
Though his fair daughter's self, as I avowed
At starting, is my object. Nay, we'll go
Together down, sir. Notice Neptune, though,
Taming a sea-horse, thought a rarity,   55
Which Claus of Innsbruck° cast in bronze for me!

---

56. **Claus of Innsbruck:** A fictional sculptor.

APPROACHING THE READING

1. The point of a dramatic monologue is that the speaker's voice and what it says reveal his or her character. What sort of person is the duke? Point out the details that lead you to your conclusions about him.

2. In a dramatic monologue, you listen to the voice of a character speaking in a setting and situation. What are the setting and situation in this poem? Whom is the duke talking to? Try thinking in terms of "a person who..."

3. What the duke says also reveals all that we can know about the duchess. What sort of person was she? What happened to her?

4. Consider tone in the poem. What is the duke's attitude toward the duchess? What is the poem's attitude toward the duke?

5. This is a useful poem for reviewing the techniques of sound. Look for examples of alliteration and assonance; think about what they contribute to the effect of the poem. The poem is written in couplets, two consecutive lines of poetry with the same end rhyme, though the rhyme is not so obvious because of the use of run-on lines (see p. 653). What does the rhyme add to the poem? How would its effect be different if it did not rhyme or if the rhyme was more obvious?

RESPONDING THROUGH Writing

WRITING ABOUT VOICE, TONE, AND SOUND

Journal Entries

1. During an average day, we're bombarded with voices: from radios or TVs, at home, on the street, on a bus, in class. The list could go on and on. To some we give close attention; others we pretty much ignore. In your journal, write a list of voices you notice during a morning or even an hour. Note which ones you pay attention to and which you don't. Of the ones you do pay attention to, reflect on what matters about the quality of each voice — whether it's interesting, engaging, honest, pleasant, appealing, and so on.

You can research the authors in this chapter with LitLinks at bedfordstmartins.com/rewritinglit.

2. The same techniques for word sounds discussed in this chapter are also very important in the world of advertising. As you read or hear advertisements during a day or a few hours, keep track of techniques you notice (alliteration, assonance, repetition, rhyme, and so forth). Jot notes describing the effects the techniques achieve.

3. Take a poem and change some of the diction (words) to alter the tone. Write a journal entry describing what you did and the ways the effect of the poem now is different.

Literary Analysis Papers

4. Write a paper on the voice and tone, or shifts in them, in Robert Hayden's "Those Winter Sundays" (p. 572), Agha Shahid Ali's "I Dream It Is Afternoon When I Return to Delhi" (p. 762), Elizabeth Bishop's "In the Waiting Room" (p. 770), Eavan Boland's "The Pomegranate" (p. 773), or another poem of your choice.

5. Write a paper discussing techniques of sound and their effect in Robert Browning's "My Last Duchess" (p. 622), Leslie Marmon Silko's "Prayer to the Pacific" (p. 685), Samuel Taylor Coleridge's "Kubla Khan" (p. 783), Samuel Hazo's "For Fawzi in Jerusalem" (p. 817), Alberto Ríos's "Nani" (p. 857), or another poem of your choice.

6. Write a paper discussing the character of the speaker in T. S. Eliot's "The Love Song of J. Alfred Prufrock" (p. 796). The poem is usually regarded as a dramatic monologue, but readers differ on whether it uses interior monologue. If you think it does, show how that contributes to characterization and the effect of the poem.

Comparison-Contrast Papers

7. Write a paper on Wilfred Owen's "Dulce et Decorum Est" (p. 619) and Richard Lovelace's "To Lucasta, Going to the Wars" (p. 837), exploring what you discover about similarities and differences in what they say about war and in how they express their ideas through voice, tone, and sound.

8. Write a paper in which you compare and contrast the way Olga Broumas's "Cinderella" (p. 775) and Jo Carson's "I Cannot Remember All the Times" (p. 777) deal with the mistreatment of women, comparing and contrasting how each uses voice, tone, and sound to convey a similar message to different audiences.

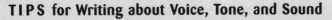

TIPS for Writing about Voice, Tone, and Sound

- **Hear the poem.** Poems often are meant to be heard. As part of your preparation for writing, read the poem aloud several times, listening for its voice, tone, and sound dimensions; then listen while someone else reads it aloud to you.

- **Focus on tone.** Tone can be an interesting topic especially when the tone is unusual or complex or one that changes or shifts in intensity as you move through the poem.

- **Sounds' effects.** The use of sounds (alliteration, assonance, repetition, rhyme) can be a challenging paper topic, especially for poems that make prominent use of such devices — but even their absence can be worth attention as a topic or subtopic in a paper. In addition to describing what devices are used, your paper should consider how they are used, to what degree, and in what contexts and discuss in what ways they are appropriate for what the poem is dealing with.

- **Illustrations and explanations.** A paper on voice, tone, or sound must include quotations that illustrate the relevant points you are making. You also will want to explain how the effects of voice, tone, or sound are achieved, what goes into creating those effects.

- **Relationship to effect or theme.** A crucial part in any paper on voice, tone, or sound must be a discussion of how that element contributes to the effect, theme, or significance of the poem.

WRITING ABOUT CONNECTIONS

Although this chapter focuses particularly on poems' use of voice, tone, and sound, those aspects can also be useful in exploring poems thematically. Interesting paper topics that lead to fresh insights can result from making connections between poems, especially ones from different eras. Here are a few possibilities:

1. "All the Comforts of Home": Contrasting Voices of Adventure in Luis J. Rodriguez's "Running to America" (p. 858) and Alfred, Lord Tennyson's "Ulysses" (p. 871)
2. "Arms and the Man": War without Glory in Wilfred Owen's "Dulce et Decorum Est" (p. 619) and Vievee Francis's "1864, A Pocket Full of Rye" (p. 802)
3. "Dancing with the Dark": Movement and Memory in Theodore Roethke's "My Papa's Waltz" (p. 602) and Cornelius Eady's "My Mother, If She Had Won Free Dance Lessons" (p. 795)

WRITING RESEARCH PAPERS

1. Research racial profiling and, if possible, talk to people who have experienced it. Write a paper discussing Sekou Sundiata's "Blink Your Eyes" (p. 607) in light of what you discover.

2. Conduct interviews with at least two war veterans. Listen to the way they talk about their experiences as well as to what they say. Write a paper discussing similarities and/or differences between their ways of "voicing" their experiences and that in Wilfred Owen's "Dulce et Decorum Est" (p. 619) or Yusef Komunyakaa's "Facing It" (p. 620).

Metaphor has interested me more as a way of knowledge, a way of grasping something. I like to . . . use the metaphor as a way to discover something about the nature of reality. Charles Simic

(Author of "Classic Ballroom Dances," p. 864)

Figurative Language

Wondering What This Has to Do with That

When Romeo says, "But, soft, what light through yonder window breaks? / It is the east, and Juliet is the sun," the hearer or reader of Shakespeare's *Romeo and Juliet* knows perfectly well that Romeo doesn't think Juliet actually is the sun. He may be lovesick, but he's not loony. The ability almost all of us have to process language lets us understand, almost instantaneously, that Romeo is comparing Juliet to, or identifying her with, the sun. Romeo is making imaginative, not logical, sense. He is using a **figure of speech** or **figurative language**, that is, a shift from standard or customary usage of words to achieve a special effect or particular meaning. He is trying to pack lots of meaning into a few words: that Juliet's beauty dazzles like the sun, that Juliet is the center of his life the way the sun is the center of our solar system. An important part of comprehending poetry is being able to recognize when language is to be taken "figuratively" instead of at face value and what its figurativeness conveys.

From the dozens of specific types of figurative language available to writers, it is valuable for you to know and recognize only five. Some people grimace when asked to learn the particular vocabulary of poetry. But think about it. When you are talking about a sound system, you might use the terms *bass* or *amplifier*. If you can assume that your listener understands these terms, you don't need to take the time to explain

627

them. Similarly, knowing the names of figures provides a useful, shared shorthand when talking about a poem. Equally or even more important, however, than using the correct label is being able to describe what the figure creates in the poem and how it affects your reading. That is the focus in this chapter.

READING FOR SIMILE

To help someone understand something — how you felt on the first day of the new school year, for example — you might use a *comparison*: "When I walked into my first class, my mind seemed as blank as the paper in my notebook." You would be using **simile**, an expression of a direct similarity, using words such as *like*, *as*, or *than*, between two things that would ordinarily be regarded as dissimilar.

Such figurative (that is, unexpected and imaginative) comparisons occur when we discover that two things we assumed were entirely dissimilar actually have attributes in common or when the comparison leads us to a new way of perceiving or considering something. The comparison stretches our ideas about perception and about experiences of the things compared ("I've never thought about or seen it that way before"). The following poem may do this for you.

APPROACHING THE AUTHOR

Martín Espada worked as a salesperson, clerk, telephone solicitor, gas-station attendant, bouncer, bartender, printing-plant bindery worker, tenant lawyer, and supervisor of a legal services program before becoming a professor of creative writing.

For more about him, see page 1383.

Martín Espada   b. 1957

Latin Night at the Pawnshop   [1990]

Chelsea, Massachusetts,
Christmas, 1987

The apparition of a salsa band
gleaming in the Liberty Loan
pawnshop window:

Golden trumpet,
silver trombone,   5
congas, maracas, tambourine,
all with price tags dangling
like the city morgue ticket
on a dead man's toe.

APPROACHING THE READING

1. Consider the simile. What makes it such a surprise in this poem? After thinking about the simile and its relation to the rest of the poem, talk about its effect and what makes it, surprising as it is, appropriate. What does it suggest?

2. The simile at the very end of the poem affects all that comes before. Discuss how that final simile affected your perceptions of and feelings about what came prior to it. Describe the difference in effect if the simile had come at the start of the poem.

3. Discuss the role of the title and why it is an integral part of the poem.

At first the poem can be seen as a vivid description of a collection of instruments in a pawnshop window. But when we encounter the word *apparition*, we realize that the instruments are a ghostly appearance of the band in which they were played. And then we notice the surprising simile that turns the instruments into corpses of unidentified victims in the city morgue. The simile brings out another layer of meaning: In desperation the musicians sold their instruments, leading to the death of the music they loved and, perhaps, to the death of their dreams.

FIGURES STRETCH OUR IMAGINATIONS   Reread Anita Endrezze's poem "The Girl Who Loved the Sky" (p. 586). Endrezze uses comparisons to get across how a blind girl experiences the world, especially how she conceives the sky she cannot see: "I met a blind girl who thought the sky / tasted like cold metal when it rained." What is the taste of cold metal? Is its taste different in the rain? How can the sky have taste at all? The blind girl uses her imagination to grasp what the sky is like since she can't see it. Endrezze helps us experience that imaginative process by giving us language that stretches our imaginations to a point where our rational minds can't grasp or put into logical terms what the words are expressing. And yet we intuitively understand it.

FIGURES IN EVERYDAY LANGUAGE   Actually, figurative language isn't limited to literary writers. All of us use it all the time: "I worked like a dog," "tough as nails." In fact, much of language by its very nature is figurative. Almost all of the words we use, except ones that identify concrete objects or actions such as *cup* or *kick*, involve figures. Often the figures go unnoticed. You are reading this section to comprehend it. *Comprehend*, in that context, is figurative: Its root is the Latin word *hendere*, "to grasp or hold with the thumb." That physical action has been extended imaginatively to include "grasping" or "taking hold of" an idea or concept.

We don't even notice or react to most of the figures we use in everyday language. Some originally inventive figures (a river bed, a table leg) have been absorbed into the language to such an extent that, though they still are figures, we seldom think of them as figurative. And yet even these, when you look at them as figures, may surprise you.

DIRECT, SURPRISING COMPARISONS   Direct comparisons, or similes, are usually the easiest figures to notice because they carry the signal word with them. But only surprising, unexpected comparisons are similes. The comparison discussed above from Anita Endrezze's "The Girl Who Loved the Sky" was a simile. So is this, a few lines further: "On hot, still days / we listened to the sky falling / like chalk dust." The comparison is surprising: It would take keen hearing to catch the sound of chalk dust falling; one would have to be even more alert to hear the sound of the sky falling. Similes appear again later in the poem:

> I was born blind, she said, an act of nature.
> Sure, I thought, like birds born
> without wings, trees without roots.

Here the speaker's comparisons bring out her anger at her friend's fate, but also her failure to understand that her friend, though she cannot see physically, is not rendered helpless the way a bird without wings would be. Also,

> The day she moved
> I saw the world clearly: the sky
> backed away from me like a departing father.

The simile connects two great losses in the speaker's world — her father's absence and her friend's departure — and those losses, at this point anyhow, come to define the way she views her world.

NONFIGURATIVE COMPARISONS   On the other hand, Endrezze's line "the room smells like glue" is not a simile: It is not surprising and not imaginative (the room smells the way glue smells or smells of glue because glue is used in the room). Comparisons between similar things (squid tastes like chicken; his eyes are like his father's) are straightforward analogies, not similes and not figurative.

ENTRY POINTS   The following poem uses a series of six comparisons to suggest the effect of having the attainment of one's hopes and aspirations delayed indefinitely. Watch for them as you read and notice how the sixth is different from the first five.

APPROACHING THE AUTHOR

Langston Hughes thought attending Columbia University would allow him to jump-start his career in poetry, but he actually got his first big break after dropping out and working odd jobs. It was while Hughes was working as a busboy at a hotel in Washington, D.C., that the famous poet Vachel Lindsay, a guest there, discovered Hughes's poems and publicized them.

For more about him, see page 1392.

Langston Hughes   1902–1967

Harlem   [1951]

What happens to a dream deferred?

   Does it dry up
   like a raisin in the sun?
   Or fester like a sore—
   And then run?   5
   Does it stink like rotten meat?
   Or crust and sugar over—
   like a syrupy sweet?

   Maybe it just sags
   like a heavy load.   10

   Or does it explode?

APPROACHING THE READING

1. How would you explain why each of the comparisons is effective and
   meaningful?

2. How is the comparison in the final line different from the other five? How
   does that difference increase its power as well as the impact of the whole
   poem?

3. The poem refers to any dreams, but especially to the "American dream." If
   you are not familiar with the term, look it up. Relate it to the title of the
   poem and consider the bitter ironies that reading evokes.

In response to the question raised in the opening line, Hughes's poem
poses further questions, suggesting a number of possible answers. These
follow-up questions rely on similes to intensify their points. Read the lines
without the similes and notice what happens: "What happens to a dream
deferred? Does it dry up or fester? Does it stink, or crust and sugar over?
Maybe it just sags." The points make sense. Dreams can dry up if their fulfillment keeps getting put off and the dreamer loses hope of ever achieving
or receiving what she or he dreams about. But the points by themselves lack
emotional intensity and they certainly aren't memorable.

READING FOR METAPHOR

"All the world is like a stage." "All the world is a stage." Sense the difference? The former is a simile; the latter is a **metaphor**, a figure of speech in which two things usually thought to be dissimilar are treated as if they were the same, the same because they have characteristics in common. The word *metaphor* is derived from the Greek *metaphora*, "carry (*phor*) across (*meta*)." In a metaphor, characteristics of one thing are "carried across" to another, from the thing used to illustrate ("stage") to the subject being illustrated ("world").

NOT "LIKE" BUT "THE SAME AS" Metaphors are basic to poetry and are widely used in fiction and drama as well. Shakespeare's character Jaques asserts, "All the world's a stage," in the comedy *As You Like It*. Without even thinking about it, we may treat this as a comparison ("the world is *like* a stage," with people playing roles, making entrances and exits, and so on). The line, however, does not say that the world is *like* a stage, but that it *is* a stage. Common sense and logic, of course, claim that the world is not part of a theater. But the figure says it is. Here metaphor opens our minds, enabling us to see what we may not have seen before. A metaphor can break down a barrier and carry us into a world in which, through our imaginations, we discover transformations and uncommon relationships, sometimes even new "realities" and ways of experiencing.

NOT EXPLICIT BUT IMPLIED Metaphors are easiest to recognize when the comparison is explicit, when *is* or *are* or some other linking word is present, as in "All the world is a stage." More difficult to recognize and explain are **implied metaphors**, in which the *to be* verb is omitted and the comparison may be implied, or "buried," rather than stated directly. "A car thief is a dirty dog" is direct metaphor. "Some dirty dog stole my car" contains an implied metaphor: The key term ("car thief") is implied, and you must supply it to complete the equation involved. Look again at "Harlem." Notice how it relies on a shift from similes in lines 2–10 to the implied metaphor of line 11: *"Or does it explode?"* The reader must supply the object that describes the ultimate effect of having dreams deferred: the possibility of frustration exploding into riot? defeat? revolution? despair? The fact that the poem doesn't use the word it refers to but has the reader think of it makes the conclusion more interactive and its impact all the stronger.

EMOTIVE AS WELL AS INFORMATIVE In "The Girl Who Loved the Sky" (p. 586), Endrezze uses both explicit and implied metaphors. "I learned / that numbers were fractious beasts" is an explicit metaphor: Math is equated with a threateningly wild beast. The comparison conveys her feelings vividly. "The bruised petals of her lids" is implied, or buried, metaphor: The blind girl's eyelids apparently are dark, and this line compares them, even equates them, to the purple petals of the jacaranda tree outside the classroom. Similarly, the final lines of the poem also use metaphor: "until my fist was another lantern / hiding a small and bitter flame." Her fist is not a lantern, but the figure equates it with one; and her fist, like her heart, holds not a literal flame but petals and memories that remind her how the world takes those she loves from her, leaving her lonely and angry.

ENTRY POINTS   Read the following poem in which the speaker reflects on a southern African city at night and expresses his affection for it, despite its many problems. The poem is rich with figurative language, especially similes and implied metaphors. Watch for the way the figures pack the poem with meaning, beyond what literal equivalents could convey.

APPROACHING THE AUTHOR

Dennis Brutus led the fight to use sports as a weapon against the apartheid policies of South Africa. As a result, he was exiled, shot in the back, and imprisoned, in a cell next to Nelson Mandela's on Robben Island, the notorious prison colony.

For more about him, see page 1376.

Dennis Brutus   1924–2009

Nightsong: City   [1963]

Sleep well, my love, sleep well:
the harbour lights glaze over restless docks,
police cars cockroach through the tunnel streets;

from the shanties creaking iron-sheets
violence like a bug-infested rag is tossed   5
and fear is immanent as sound in the wind-swung bell;

the long day's anger pants from sand and rocks;
but for this breathing night at least,
my land, my love, sleep well.

APPROACHING THE READING

1. The poem starts off as if it were a love poem addressed to a person. At what point do you realize that line 1 is figurative and the "love" it refers to is the city the speaker calls home? What leads you to that realization?

2. In line 3, the author uses a noun (*cockroach*) as a verb and turns it into a vivid metaphor. Explain how it works figuratively and why you think it is effective.

3. Line 4 takes us to a shantytown and helps us see houses with sheet-metal walls and roofs and hear the sounds as they creak in the wind. The following two lines use similes to convey the violence and fear that pervade the area. Explain the comparisons and discuss their effectiveness.

4. Pick out the metaphors in lines 7 and 8 and, after reading the next section, the personification in line 9, and explain what each contributes to the poem.

The poem starts out with "Sleep well, my love." The title might suggest that a city is the setting for a night song to someone. It might be only after reading it a second time or looking back from the end of the poem that you realize that "my love" is the city the speaker loves. Saying that a city can sleep compares it to, or identifies it with, a living creature — an animal (metaphor) or a human being (see the next section on personification). The latter seems to fit best: The words of the first line sound like ones the speaker would offer at night to someone cherished. It may come as a surprise that the words are spoken to a city, but of course that shows how much he cares about it.

In this poem, the figurative comparisons add distinctness and vivid immediacy to the appearance of the city at night (harbor lights make the docks look shiny, the way a glaze does when applied to pottery or china; police cars dart around between rows of high-rise buildings with the quickness and agility of cockroaches). And they intensify the emotional impact of the descriptions of life in the city: Violence pervades the shantytowns the way bugs infest a rag, fear is as present through the city as the sound of a bell, and the anger that fills the days "pants" everywhere like a fierce animal. But for the moment, the speaker wants to forget all that. For this one living, "breathing" night, he hopes his beloved city rests quietly and sleeps well.

READING FOR PERSONIFICATION

Personification is a figure of speech in which something nonhuman is given attributes of a person or is treated as if it has human characteristics or takes human actions. Sometimes abstract qualities are treated as if they are human: In the line "Death, be not proud," from a sonnet by John Donne (p. 793), for example, death is treated as if it is human and could have the human attribute of pride. In other cases, concrete things are given human characteristics: In the lines "the sky / backed away from me like a departing father," from "The Girl Who Loved the Sky" (p. 586), the sky is made human for a moment, able to walk away from the speaker the way her father did.

Personification is sometimes defined incorrectly as treating something not living in terms of just being alive rather than specifically being human. For example, in Shakespeare's *Romeo and Juliet*, Juliet, fearful of being drugged and buried in a vault, expresses fear of the tomb's "foul mouth [that] no healthsome air breathes in" (4.3.34). "Mouth" here is metaphor, not personification, since animals as well as humans have mouths and breathe through them.

A particular type of personification is **apostrophe**, that is, addressing someone not present or something ordinarily not spoken to as if present or capable of understanding, as when Macbeth says "Time, thou anticipatest my dread exploits" (4.1.144). Dennis Brutus uses apostrophe as well when his speaker in "Nightsong: City" talks to the city as if it could hear and understand.

ENTRY POINTS   The following poem uses figurative language in describing a scene in nature. Watch for places where a nonliving thing is spoken of as if living. Then decide which of these exemplify personification and consider what such personifications contribute to the effect of the poem.

APPROACHING THE AUTHOR

Angelina Weld Grimké wrote her three-act play *Rachel* to protest lynching and other racial violence. First performed in Washington, D.C., in 1916 by an all-black cast, it was a response to the highly controversial 1915 silent film *The Birth of a Nation*, which depicts the Ku Klux Klan as heroes and southern blacks as villains.

For more about her, see page 1386.

Angelina Weld Grimké   1880–1958

A Winter Twilight   [1923]

A silence slipping around like death,
Yet chased by a whisper, a sigh, a breath;
One group of trees, lean, naked and cold,
Inking their crest 'gainst a sky green-gold;
One path that knows where the corn flowers were;   5
Lonely, apart, unyielding, one fir;
And over it softly leaning down,
One star that I loved ere the fields went brown.

APPROACHING THE READING

1. What examples do you find of nonliving things treated as if alive? Point out ones that are personification—where the living attributes apply only to

humans — and ones that are metaphors — where the connection could also apply to animals.

2. Consider the effect of personifications in the poem. What do they contribute that a comparison to something nonhuman wouldn't?

You may have heard someone speak of how a painting "brings a scene to life." That could be said of "A Winter Twilight" as well. The poem creates a picture, almost a verbal landscape painting. And, as with a painting, it slows everything to a stop, arrests this one moment, suspending it in time so that we can more deeply experience it. Actual life experiences go by so fast that we can't experience them fully. We need the arts to give us the chance to stop and really take in what otherwise goes by and is lost.

This poet wants not only to see the scene — she also wants to bring alive its feeling and aura. She does so through metaphors and personifications comparing landscape features to living things. That this is a quiet scene is evoked by the way silence "slips around" in it, as an animal or a person would, and the way it is "chased by a whisper." For the trees to be "naked" treats them as living beings, specifically as persons, since that word generally is applied only to humans. Similarly, the path comes alive through personification (since it "knows" where the corn flowers are), as does the "lonely" fir tree (a word usually reserved for a human conscious reaction to feeling cut off from what matters).

A winter scene can seem dead and lifeless, and the poem is acutely aware of death, mentioning it in the opening line; but that very awareness heightens the way the figures of speech bring out the life present even in a "barren" landscape. The poem closes with a sense of the intimacy of life and death: The star is given the living attribute of "leaning down," but this is a star the speaker loved (past tense — does she or he no longer love it?) before the fields "went brown" (died? lost their appeal and desirability?).

READING FOR METONYMY AND SYNECDOCHE

SUBSTITUTING SOMETHING CLOSELY ASSOCIATED   Another figure of speech that, like metaphor, talks about one thing in terms of another is **metonymy**, a figure of speech in which the name of one thing is substituted for that of something closely associated with it. Like similes and metaphors, metonymies are used every day. When you hear a news reporter say, "The White House announced today . . . ," you've encountered a metonymy: "White House" invites you to visualize a familiar image closely associated with the president that substitutes for the staff members who issued the announcement. When the speaker in "The Girl Who Loved the Sky" (p. 586) says her friend "had no eyes," she does not mean that the girl's eye sockets were empty; she substitutes "eyes" for what is closely associated with eyes, "sight," because the word *eyes* is more concrete and vivid than the abstract word *sight*.

SUBSTITUTING A PART FOR THE WHOLE   A subset of metonymy is **synec-doche**, a special kind of metonymy in which a part of a thing is substituted for the whole of which it is a part. When someone says to you, "Give me a hand," she or he actually wants help not just from your hands but also from the rest of you. Likewise, the familiar phrases "many mouths to feed" or "let's count noses" use synecdoche. When the two girls in "The Girl Who Loved the Sky" (p. 586) are swinging and flying (note the metaphor—riding in a swing is something like flying) high over the other girls' heads, "heads" is synecdoche, a part substituted for the whole because it is the highest part of their bodies.

THE IMPORTANCE OF LITTLE THINGS   Recognizing metonymies and synecdoches helps you appreciate the way little things can have greater importance than they seem to at first. Robert Frost said, "If I must be classified as a poet, I might be called a Synecdochist, for I prefer the synecdoche in poetry," that figure of speech in which "a little thing touches a larger thing." Instead of starting with huge, complex themes and issues, Frost often uses local, everyday experiences as subjects, trusting our minds will be led to "a larger thing." Read his poem "Design" (p. 805) and think about how it embodies Frost's idea.

ENTRY POINTS   Look in the following poem, about the life of a wealthy man everyone envies, for examples of nonliteral expression, figures of various sorts, including metonymy and synecdoche. Consider how the figures work (what is compared to what or what is substituted for what), and why the use of figures is effective and contributes to the poem's overall effect.

APPROACHING THE AUTHOR

Because **Edwin Arlington Robinson**'s parents wanted a girl, they hadn't decided on a boy's name before he was born. When they visited a holiday resort with their still-unnamed six-month-old, the other vacationers decided that he should have a name. They selected a man from Arlington, Massachusetts, to draw one out of a hat.

For more about him, see page 1409.

Edwin Arlington Robinson   1869–1935

Richard Cory   [1897]

Whenever Richard Cory went down town,
We people on the pavement looked at him:
He was a gentleman from sole to crown,
Clean favored, and imperially slim.

And he was always quietly arrayed,   5
And he was always human when he talked;

But still he fluttered pulses when he said,
"Good-morning," and he glittered when he walked.

And he was rich—yes, richer than a king—
And admirably schooled in every grace: 10
In fine, we thought that he was everything
To make us wish that we were in his place.

So on we worked, and waited for the light,
And went without the meat, and cursed the bread;
And Richard Cory, one calm summer night,   15
Went home and put a bullet through his head.

APPROACHING THE READING

1. Pick out examples of metonymy and synecdoche and explain how they
   work (what is being substituted for what). What do they contribute to the
   effect of the poem?

Here are three other figures of speech that you will frequently encounter:

- **Paradox:** A figure of speech in which a statement initially seeming
  self-contradictory or absurd turns out to make good sense when
  seen in another light. In Shakespeare's *Much Ado about Nothing*, for
  example, when the Friar says to Hero, "Come, lady, die to live"
  (4.1.252), he is using paradox. By pretending to die, she may regain
  the reputation she has lost through false slander. A subset of paradox is **oxymoron**, a self-contradictory combination of words or
  phrases, such as "O brawling love! O loving hate! . . . Feather of
  lead, bright smoke, cold fire, sick health!" in Shakespeare's *Romeo
  and Juliet* (1.1).
- **Hyperbole:** Exaggeration, or overstatement; a figure of speech in
  which something is stated more strongly than is warranted.
  Hyperbole is often used to make a point emphatically, as when
  Hamlet protests that he loved Ophelia much more than her brother
  did: "Forty thousand brothers / Could not with all their quantity of
  love / Make up my sum" (5.1.272-74).
- **Understatement:** A figure of speech that expresses something in an
  unexpectedly restrained way. Paradoxically, to deemphasize through
  understatement can be a way of emphasizing, of making people react
  with "there must be more to it than that." When Mercutio in *Romeo
  and Juliet*, after being stabbed by Tybalt, calls his wound "a scratch, a
  scratch" (3.1.92), he is understating, for the wound is serious. He
  calls for a doctor in the next line and dies a few minutes later.

2. Describe the speaker. What is the effect of using *we* for the speaker instead of *I*? Could one say that "We people on the pavement" is a kind of synecdoche? Explain.

3. Pick out examples of other figures of speech and explain how they work and what they bring to the poem. Also point out examples of irony (see p. 603). Consider how both figures and irony bring out the "point" of the poem.

Robinson's poem seems a good example of Frost's point about being a synecdochist: The poem has lots of little things that touch larger things. One person speaks the poem but uses the pronoun *we*, thus attempting to suggest that what he felt was true for the whole population of the town. The poem focuses on "little" details — the way Richard Cory dresses, walks, and talks (even the way he says so little a thing as "Good-morning" makes hearts beat faster). The townspeople long for any little thing to improve their lives, "light" substituting for "better days" because they see only dark despair around them and get by on almost nothing ("bread" substituted for "bare essentials") because they can't afford anything more ("meat" substituted for luxuries of any sort). Robinson could have told the story without figures of speech, but the use of synecdoches especially, with their emphasis on parts and small aspects, seems right for a poem that contrasts having a lot and having very little.

TWO OTHER OBSERVATIONS ABOUT FIGURES

No sharp lines divide figures of speech from one another. Read the following poem about a driver coming upon a deer that an earlier driver had struck and killed. Watch for the way it relies on images and figures for its effect and for the way some figures could be labeled and explained in different ways.

William Stafford   1914–1993

Traveling through the Dark   [1962]

Traveling through the dark I found a deer
dead on the edge of the Wilson River road.
It is usually best to roll them into the canyon:
that road is narrow; to swerve might make more dead.

By glow of the tail-light I stumbled back of the car   5
and stood by the heap, a doe, a recent killing;
she had stiffened already, almost cold.
I dragged her off; she was large in the belly.

My fingers touching her side brought me the reason—
her side was warm; her fawn lay there waiting,   10
alive, still, never to be born.
Beside that mountain road I hesitated.

The car aimed ahead its lowered parking lights;
under the hood purred the steady engine.
I stood in the glare of the warm exhaust turning red;   15
around our group I could hear the wilderness listen.

I thought hard for us all—my only swerving—
then pushed her over the edge into the river.

APPROACHING THE AUTHOR

William Stafford began publishing his poetry late in life, his first major collection appearing when he was forty-eight years old. He kept a daily journal for fifty years and composed nearly 22,000 poems, of which roughly 3,000 were published.

For more about him, see page 1413.

APPROACHING THE READING

1. Pick out several figures of speech, identify them, and explain how they work. Which ones could be labeled as more than one type of figure? Explain why or how. Consider why images seem appropriate in the first twelve lines and figures in the last six.

2. The figures supply a large part of the poetic impact of the poem. However, there are other poetic aspects that come through the use of alliteration and assonance, along with some slant rhyme (see pp. 609–12). Mark examples of such sound techniques. Think about how they cooperate with the figurative language to develop the theme of the poem.

The first twelve lines of the poem are narrative, describing what happened. They rely on images, without any figures. Lines 13–18 reflect on the experience and use a good deal of figurative language, such as bringing the car to life by having it purr like a harmless cat (though ironically it was a similar car that killed the deer) and making the wilderness not just a living thing but one that listens and presumably understands. And the word *swerve*, which is used in a literal sense in line 4, comes back in a figurative sense in line 17 as the speaker momentarily avoids doing what he must before proceeding to do it.

ALTERNATIVE WAYS OF EXPLAINING FIGURES The poem illustrates two important characteristics of figurative language. First, a figure often fits into more than one category. "I could hear the wilderness listen," for example, stands either as metonymy ("wilderness" being substituted for the creatures and the natural habitat in it) or as personification ("wilderness" given humanlike ability to understand, not just hear). In this and most cases, applying labels to figures is a means to an end: It alerts you to their presence, helps you talk and write about them, and helps clarify the nature of the imaginative action you experience as you read them.

POEMS ARE NOT FIGURES   In addition to being aware that figures overlap with each other, keep in mind that figures of speech occur *within* poems, not *as* poems. Some people attempt to treat entire poems as figures of speech. After reading "Traveling through the Dark," they may say, "On the surface it's about a man finding a deer on the road, but what it's *really* about is our journey through life and the difficult decisions we face along the way." They substitute an abstract "meaning" for the concrete images of the poem. The poem is *really* about a deer on the road, though it may *also* (as opposed to *really*) be about life's journey. This book discusses images before figures because of the importance of grounding the experience in images and of letting the action or description be first and always itself.

> You can further explore figurative language, including using interactive exercises, with VirtuaLit Poetry at bedfordstmartins.com/rewritinglit.

☑ CHECKLIST on Reading for Figurative Language

❏ Notice any figurative language and the way it works imaginatively, especially these five types:

- Simile: the expression of a direct similarity, using words such as *like*, *as*, or *than*, between two things usually regarded as dissimilar
- Metaphor: treating two things usually thought to be dissimilar as if they are the same and have characteristics in common
- Personification: treating something nonhuman as if it has human characteristics or takes human actions
- Metonymy: substituting the name of one thing for that of something closely associated with it
- Synecdoche: substituting a part of something for the whole of it

❏ Consider how the choice of a figure affects the concept being developed.

FURTHER READING

ENTRY POINTS   The following two short poems use figurative language to enable us to see an eagle and a student from a fresh perspective. Read each, and then reread them, focusing on their imaginative uses of language. Pick out figures of speech and be ready to explain what is figurative about them and how they contribute to the effect of the poem.

APPROACHING THE AUTHOR

Alfred, Lord Tennyson was so shortsighted that he couldn't see to eat without wearing his monocle. It also made reading and writing difficult, so he composed much of his poetry in his head and often didn't write poems down until friends insisted or did it for him.

For more about him, see page 1415.

Alfred, Lord Tennyson 1809–1892

The Eagle   [1851]

He clasps the crag with crookèd hands;
Close to the sun in lonely lands,
Ringed with the azure world, he stands.

The wrinkled sea beneath him crawls;
He watches from his mountain walls,   5
And like a thunderbolt he falls.

APPROACHING THE READING

1. Pick out particulars that gave you a fresh perspective on the eagle that differed from the more common ways of seeing and describing it.

2. Notice how the poet set things up for the last line, not unlike the way the punch line in a joke is set up. What makes the last line effective? What would make it, as with a bad joke, fall flat?

3. Think about the sounds in the poem. What do they create? What makes them strikingly appropriate for the subject? Would the poem's impact be different if it were written in something other than three-line stanzas? If it were written without stanzas?

4. The simile at the end is certainly crucial to the impact of the poem. By now, this image has become rather commonplace. Is it still effective for you? If so, why? If not, why not?

Ted Kooser b. 1939

Student   [2004]

The green shell of his backpack makes him lean
into wave after wave of responsibility,
and he swings his stiff arms and cupped hands,

paddling ahead. He has extended his neck
to its full length, and his chin, hard as a beak,   5
breaks the cold surf. He's got his baseball cap on

backward as up he crawls, out of the froth
of a hangover and onto the sand of the future,
and lumbers, heavy with hope, into the library.

APPROACHING THE AUTHOR

In addition to his career as a poet, **Ted Kooser** worked as vice president
of a life-insurance company in Lincoln, Nebraska. He would write in the
morning before going to work, and he'd show his secretary what he'd
written. He'd ask if the poem made sense to her; if it didn't, he knew he
had to keep working on it.

For more about him, see page 1397.

APPROACHING THE READING

1. Pick out the different uses of figurative language in the poem and describe
   what they create, what their effect is, and how they strike you.

2. Do you think the poem is about a particular student? Do you think it is a
   generalization? What do you make of the tone in light of what it reveals
   about the attitude of the speaker or the poet?

3. What makes the use of water and sand appropriate for the subject? What is
   implied by their usage?

ENTRY POINTS   The two poems that follow offer fresh, unusual, striking
ways of experiencing and reflecting on a snowstorm. After reading both,
reread them and consider how their unique depiction of snow is achieved
through images and figures of speech. Be ready to discuss what is similar
about their approaches to the subject and what is different.

APPROACHING THE AUTHOR

Emily Dickinson wrote nearly eighteen hundred poems during her lifetime, but only
about a dozen were published. After her death, her younger sister found forty small,
carefully ordered, sewn booklets full of nearly eight hundred of her poems. It took over
fifty years for all of her poems to be published in their original form.

For more about her, see page 1380.

Emily Dickinson   1830–1886

It sifts from Leaden Sieves   [c. *1862*; 1891]

It sifts from Leaden Sieves—
It powders all the Wood.
It fills with Alabaster Wool
The Wrinkles of the Road—

It makes an Even Face 5
Of Mountain, and of Plain —
Unbroken Forehead from the East
Unto the East again —

It reaches to the Fence —
It wraps it Rail by Rail 10
Till it is lost in Fleeces —
It deals Celestial Vail

To Stump, and Stack — and Stem —
A Summer's empty Room —
Acres of Joints, where Harvests were, 15
Recordless, but for them —

It Ruffles Wrists of Posts
As Ankles of a Queen —
Then stills its Artisans — like Ghosts —
Denying they have been — 20

APPROACHING THE READING

1. Note as many metaphors in the poem as you can. Which are implied? If
   you hadn't been told that the poem focuses on snow, what might you find
   in the poem that would lead you to conclude that was its subject?

2. Pick out two figures of speech that particularly strike you and talk about why.

3. Is the snow personified? If you think it is, what in the poem supports your
   conclusion? If you think it is not, explain.

4. Is the snow itself a figure? Explain why you think it is or why you think it
   should not be considered a figure.

Mary Oliver b. 1935

First Snow [1983]

The snow
began here
this morning and all day
continued, its white
rhetoric everywhere 5
calling us back to *why, how,*
whence such beauty and *what*

the meaning; such
an oracular fever! flowing
past windows, an energy it seemed   10
would never ebb, never settle
less than lovely! and only now,
deep into night,
it has finally ended.
The silence   15
is immense,
and the heavens still hold
a million candles; nowhere
the familiar things:
stars, the moon,   20
the darkness we expect
and nightly turn from. Trees
glitter like castles
of ribbons, the broad fields
smolder with light, a passing   25
creekbed lies
heaped with shining hills;
and though the questions
that have assailed us all day
remain — not a single   30
answer has been found —
walking out now
into the silence and the light
under the trees,
and through the fields,   35
feels like one.

APPROACHING THE AUTHOR

Mary Oliver draws much of her poetry from
the natural landscape of Cape Cod where
she lives. She once found herself lost in the
woods and deeply inspired, but without pen
and paper. She soon returned and hid pencils in the trees so she would never find
herself in the same situation again.
   For more about her, see page 1404.

APPROACHING THE READING

1. The poem begins with a narrative account of the snow falling all day, using several figures that invite readers to reflect and wonder. For a couple of them, you may need to look up words ("white *rhetoric*," "*oracular* fever"); be ready to explain them, as well as the use of *flowing* and *ebb*.

2. About halfway through, the figures turn visual. Pick out several examples and be able to describe the effect of that change. How do the images and figures in the first half relate to those in the second half?

3. Think back to the discussion of the meaningful use of form. How has Mary Oliver used form to evoke the feeling and meaning?

4. What do you think the speaker implies by saying that walking out into the snowfall feels like an "answer"?

ENTRY POINTS   The following poem, like the previous two, is about snow, but unlike them it connects snow and winter to death. This is a familiar, archetypal association (see p. 681), but as you will see, this poem uses it in an unusual and striking way.

Judith Ortiz Cofer   b. 1952

Cold as Heaven   [1995]

Before there is a breeze again
before the cooling days of Lent, she may be gone.
My grandmother asks me to tell her
again about the snow.
We sit on her white bed   5
in this white room, while outside
the Caribbean sun winds up the world
like an old alarm clock. I tell her
about the enveloping blizzard I lived through
that made everything and everyone the same;   10
how we lost ourselves in drifts so tall
we fell through our own footprints;
how wrapped like mummies in layers of wool
that almost immobilized us, we could only
take hesitant steps like toddlers   15
toward food, warmth, shelter.
I talk winter real for her,
as she would once conjure for me to dream
at sweltering siesta time,
cool stone castles in lands far north.   20
Her eyes wander to the window,
to the teeming scene of children
pouring out of a yellow bus, then to the bottle
dripping minutes through a tube
into her veins. When her eyes return to me,   25
I can see she's waiting to hear more
about the purifying nature of ice,
how snow makes way for a body,
how you can make yourself an angel
by just lying down and waving your arms   30
as you do when you say
good-bye.

APPROACHING THE READING

1. Consider weather in the poem. How does literal weather fit in the poem? In what ways is weather metaphorical? Why are both essential for the poem to have the deepest impact?

2. Pick out uses of simile, metaphor, metonymy, and synecdoche. What do they add to the poem's meaning and effect?

3. Discuss the relationship between the granddaughter and grandmother. How would you describe the tone (attitude of the speaker toward her grandmother's death and toward herself)? Point out figures that express what both are feeling.

4. How would you explain the implications of the simile in the poem's title? Consider the contrasts between cold and heat. What does snow convey in the poem? What do you think the speaker means in line 17 by saying, "I talk winter real for her"?

ENTRY POINTS The following poem, like the previous, deals with mortality, but in this case with a young girl learning about death as she watches a television news program. Thus, in a sense, it is a poem about losing one's innocence, about growing up and learning that the adult world can be threatening. As you reread the poem, watch for ways that the images and figures of speech incorporate and convey what the speaker is learning.

Julia Alvarez b. 1950

How I Learned to Sweep   [1996]

My mother never taught me sweeping.
One afternoon she found me watching
t.v. She eyed the dusty floor
boldly, and put a broom before
me, and said she'd like to be able   5
to eat her dinner off that table,
and nodded at my feet, then left.
I knew right off what she expected
and went at it. I stepped and swept;
the t.v. blared the news; I kept   10

my mind on what I had to do,
until in minutes, I was through.
Her floor was as immaculate
as a just-washed dinner plate.
I waited for her to return   15
and turned to watch the President,
live from the White House, talk of war:
in the Far East our soldiers were
landing in their helicopters
into jungles their propellers   20
swept like weeds seen underwater
while perplexing shots were fired
from those beautiful green gardens
into which these dragonflies
filled with little men descended.   25
I got up and swept again
as they fell out of the sky.
I swept all the harder when
I watched a dozen of them die —
as if their dust fell through the screen   30
upon the floor I had just cleaned.
She came back and turned the dial;
the screen went dark. *That's beautiful,*
she said, and ran her clean hand through
my hair, and on, over the window-   35
sill, coffee table, rocker, desk,
and held it up — I held my breath —
That's beautiful, she said, impressed,
she hadn't found a speck of death.

APPROACHING THE READING

1. Explain what is going on in lines 1–14, 15–25, and 26–39, and how the
   three sections relate to each other. Pick out similes, metaphors, and metonymies that clarify each section. What does the occasional use of rhyme
   contribute to the poem?

2. How would you explain the title itself as a metonymy? What is the mother
   teaching the speaker? What is the speaker learning?

3. Look again at the last line. One expects to read "speck of dust," or "dirt." In
   what ways is the substitution of "death" meaningful?

RESPONDING THROUGH Writing

WRITING ABOUT FIGURATIVE LANGUAGE

Journal Entries

1. Look for similes as you read your favorite magazine; look at advertisements in magazines online, or on billboards; or watch commercials on TV. List several examples in your journal and comment on why advertisement writers often use similes.

You can research the authors in this chapter with LitLinks at bedfordstmartins.com/rewritinglit.

2. As a journal entry, finish this line: "Waiting for you is like _____." Come up with three different similes, each having the effect of "stretching your reader's perception." Try to push each one further than the one before. For example:

   like waiting for summer

   like listening to a scratched CD

   like Thursday

   Then, choose a subject and write several different figures for it. For example:

   Love is like _____.

   Love is _____.

   Love _____.

   Write a paragraph in which you discuss the varied effects the different figures create.

3. Watch and/or listen to several comedians. Write a journal entry discussing their uses of paradox, overstatement, and understatement.

Literary Analysis Papers

4. Select a poem with striking use of figures, such as Larry Levis's "The Poem You Asked For" (p. 835), Jean Toomer's "Face" (p. 874), or Andrew Marvell's "To His Coy Mistress" (p. 841). Write a paper in which you discuss what the poem's figures suggest, what they help you realize, and how they affect your perceptions.

5. Go back to one of the poems in chapters 13–14 that relies heavily on figurative language, such as Robert Hayden's "Those Winter Sundays" (p. 572) or Yusef Komunyakaa's "Facing It" (p. 620). Write a paper discussing the effect of figurative language in the poem.

6. Write a paper discussing the use of figures and archetypes in A. E. Housman's "To an Athlete Dying Young" (p. 824). Consider how the poem's ideas relate to the present-day emphasis on superstar athletes and athletics.

Comparison-Contrast Papers

7. Write a paper comparing and contrasting two poems about the death of a child — Michael S. Harper's "Nightmare Begins Responsibility" (p. 815) and Ben Jonson's "On My First Son" (p. 827) — including the differences in their choice and handling of figurative language.

8. Write a paper comparing and contrasting what Margaret Atwood in "True Stories" (p. 764) and Li-Young Lee in "Visions and Interpretations" (p. 832) say about seeking or knowing the truth, focusing particularly on the way they use figures of speech to explore the subject.

WRITING ABOUT CONNECTIONS

Figures of speech by their nature make connections, and many of the topics suggested above involve discussions of the surprising and meaningful comparisons, equations, and substitutions that establish such imaginative connections.

TIPS for Writing about Figurative Language

- **Main topic or subtopic** As with most elements of poetry, you can concentrate on figurative language as the main subject of a paper or include it as a subtopic in a paper that concentrates on other aspects of the poem.

- **How it works and what it achieves** When writing about figurative language, you should both explain how the figure works (what is compared to what or equated with what or substituted for what) and discuss the effect, role, or meaning the imaginative language contributes to the poem.

- **Focusing on altered perceptions** Figurative language often alters the ways we perceive things. For example, it may lead readers to see an image in a fresh, unusual, even challenging way. Explaining in detail how that occurs can turn into an engaging topic for a paper or a section of a paper.

- **Focusing on figurative patterns** A discussion of the imagery of a poem or group of poems, in the sense of a related pattern of imaginative comparisons and allusions running through an entire literary work or a portion of one (see p. 1477), can be an illuminating topic for a paper.

- **Using correct labels** For a paper dealing specifically with figurative language, it is wise to use the traditional terminology (simile, metaphor, implied metaphor, personification, metonymy, synecdoche, and paradox) and to use it precisely.

The same kind of imaginative thinking can be used in noticing surprising and meaningful thematic connections between poems and turning them into interesting paper topics. Here are a few possibilities to illustrate:

1. "Innocence and Experience": Confrontations with Evil in Julia Alvarez's "How I Learned to Sweep" (p. 647) and William Blake's "The Chimney Sweeper" (p. 772)
2. "A Joyful Melancholy": Nature and Beauty in Mary Oliver's "First Snow" (p. 644) and Angelina Weld Grimké's "A Winter Twilight" (p. 635)
3. "Knowing Deep the Seasons": Antitheses of Life in William Shakespeare's "That time of year thou mayst in me behold" (p. 680) and William Carlos Williams's "Spring and All" (p. 882)

WRITING RESEARCH PAPERS

1. Research the history and controversies surrounding the Crazy Horse Memorial in the Black Hills of South Dakota and use what you find to illuminate Peter Blue Cloud's poem "Crazy Horse Monument" (p. 863).

2. Conduct research into the problem of spouse or partner abuse and into poems related to the subject, such as Jo Carson's "I Cannot Remember All the Times" (p. 777) or poems in Mary Marecek's book *Breaking Free from Partner Abuse: Voices of Battered Women Caught in the Cycle of Domestic Violence* (1993) or another similar book. Write a paper on how poetry has been and can be used as a way of dealing with the problem or communicating to others about the problem.

There's poetry in the language I speak. There's poetry,
therefore, in my culture, and in this place. Sekou Sundiata

(Author of "Blink Your Eyes," page 607)

16 Rhythm and Meter

Feeling the Beat, the Flux, and the Flow

Our lives are rich with rhythms: the regular rhythms of sunrise and sunset, the change of seasons, the waves on the shore, the beats of our heart, even the routines in our lives—holidays, trash days, final exam week, income tax time. Life also has irregular rhythms that are, paradoxically, rhythmical: the syncopations of the city, the stutter step of a basketball player, the anxious cadence of our speech under stress and uncertainty, people dropping by, and the infamous pop quiz. We need rhythms and live by them, regardless of whether we are aware of them. The same can be said of poetry: Every poem has rhythm, and experiencing a poem fully requires being attentive to its rhythms. This chapter focuses on the ways rhythms, regular and irregular, contribute to a poem's impact and meanings and on ways to help you hear and feel these rhythms more accurately and more intensely.

READING FOR RHYTHM

All dynamic writing has **rhythm**, the patterned "movement" created by words and their arrangement. Poetry in particular emphasizes it. Rhythm is somewhat difficult to describe. Because no set of precise descriptive labels is available, we turn to metaphorical language. We say that rhythm is, for example, fast, slow, syncopated, disjointed, smooth, halting, graceful, rough, deliberate, frenzied, or a mixture of any of these. The differing rhythms result from different ways of handling a variety of formal structures in the poems.

Line Length

Short lines can have one effect, long lines another, though the effect varies from poem to poem. Usually short lines create a faster rhythm and longer lines a slower rhythm, but that's not always the case. Compare the rapid rhythms in the short lines of Charles Bukowski's "my old man" (p. 598) with the slower ones of Elizabeth Bishop's "In the Waiting Room" (p. 770), and the fairly rapid long lines of David Mura's "Grandfather-in-Law" (p. 698) with the slower ones of Gerard Manley Hopkins's "God's Grandeur" (p. 682).

Phrasings

The combinations of short and longer groups of words into phrases affect a poem's rhythm, creating cadences, especially the regularity or irregularity of movement across and down the page. See, for example, how phrasings contribute to Leslie Marmon Silko's "Prayer to the Pacific" (p. 685).

Line Endings

Lines without end punctuation are said to "run on" into the next line (**run-on lines**; also called **enjambment**), which tends toward a faster, smoother pace from line to line. Lines with end punctuation, especially periods and semicolons (**end-stopped lines**), often slow down. Notice the difference in rhythm between lines 1–2 (end-stopped) and lines 3–4 (run-on) of the third stanza of Edwin Arlington Robinson's, "Richard Cory" (p. 637):

> And he was rich—yes, richer than a king—
> And admirably schooled in every grace:
> In fine, we thought that he was everything
> To make us wish that we were in his place.

Lines broken at unexpected or irregular places create a jolt and break up the rhythmic flow; line breaks at expected or "natural" places create a gentle shift carrying the rhythm along gracefully.

Pauses

Pauses (or lack of them) within lines can affect their pace and smoothness. A **pause**, called a **caesura** and usually indicated by punctuation, tends to break up the flow of a line, slow it down a bit, sometimes even make it "jagged" or "halting." Compare the first three lines, broken by pauses, with the unbroken last line of the final stanza of "Richard Cory" (p. 637):

> So on we worked, and waited for the light,
> And went without the meat, and cursed the bread;

And Richard Cory, one calm summer night,
Went home and put a bullet through his head.

How would placing a comma after "home" in the last line change the effect?

Spaces

Leaving gaps within, at the beginning or end of, or between lines can slow up the movement, even stop it altogether, or indicate which words to group together; crowding things together can speed up a rhythm. (Note the various uses of spacing in "Buffalo Bill 's" on the next page.)

Word Choice and Combinations of Sounds

Words that are easy to say together can create a steady, smooth, harmonious pace in a line; those hard to say can make it "jagged" or "harsh" or "tired" or simply slow and deliberate. Notice the difference between the way sounds slide into each other and are easy to say in the line "And he was always human when he talked," from the second stanza of "Richard Cory," and the way the words in the last line, "Went home and put a bullet through his head," force us to enunciate each separately and distinctly. The sounds don't flow together but come from different parts of the mouth, which takes longer to get them out.

It is important to realize that different rhythms may be appropriate for the same experience. For example, a frantic or a calm rhythm may be appropriate for a poem about a traffic accident, depending on what the poet wants you to experience.

ENTRY POINTS The following poem celebrates a hero of the old American West. As you read it, notice the effects of line lengths, line endings, pauses within lines (or lack of them), spaces, word choices, and combinations of sounds.

APPROACHING THE AUTHOR

E. E. Cummings wrote his first of some eventual 2,900 poems when he was only three years old. It read, "Oh, the pretty birdie, 0; / with his little toe, toe, toe!"

For more about him, see page 1379.

E. E. Cummings   1894–1962

Buffalo Bill 's   [1923]

Buffalo Bill 's
defunct
     who used to
       ride a watersmooth-silver
             stallion   5
and break onetwothreefourfive pigeonsjustlikethat
                      Jesus

   he was a handsome man
             and what i want to know is
how do you like your blueeyed boy   10
Mister Death

APPROACHING THE READING

1. Try reading the poem aloud, respecting line divisions by pausing briefly at the ends of lines (but without letting your voice drop the way it does at the end of a sentence) and reading "onetwothreefourfive" as nearly like one word as possible. Listen for how all this affects pace and rhythm.

2. Then read for meaning. What is the effect on meaning to put individual words on separate lines, to break lines and situate words at unexpected places, and to jam several words together? Write a brief statement of your interpretation of the poem's theme.

To help focus on the effect of gaps, spaces, line divisions, and line groupings, listen to the poem the way it could have been written — in six lines, using conventional punctuation, and a fairly regular beat:

> Buffalo Bill's defunct, who used to ride
> A water-smooth silver stallion and break
> One, two, three, four, five pigeons, just like that.
> Jesus, he was a handsome man.
> And what I want to know is,
> How do you like your blue-eyed boy, Mister Death?

Notice how Cummings's form of the poem creates a rhythm entirely different from this version written in six conventional lines. The rhythm definitely affects the meaning.

- A line break invites you to pause briefly after "Buffalo Bill 's," to linger on the name and give it emphasis as well as creating a moment of anticipation. Without the line break, the emphasis would fall on "defunct," instead of each line receiving emphasis.

- The pause in the middle of the infinitive "to ride" shifts meaning from "used to *ride*" to "who *used to*," which reinforces the meaning of "defunct" (used to, but does so no more). This break simultaneously sets up anticipation and emphasizes the loss.
- Emphasis falls next on "a watersmooth-silver" and on "stallion," a single-word line emphatic in both rhythm and meaning.
- Jamming the words "onetwothreefourfive" and "pigeonsjustlikethat" together creates a quick staccato rhythm that echoes the rapid firing of a revolver.
- The rhythm slows with "Jesus" set off in a line of its own far to the right: Its position far to the right requires a pause, not unlike the exhaled sigh one expresses when saying "Jesus" in this manner, but so does the extra space between it and the next line of text.
- The next three phrases also are slower and more reflective. Their similarity in length (six, seven, and eight syllables) creates a rhythmical similarity that makes the short, abrupt last line surprising in rhythm as well as in meaning and tone.

After saying all this about rhythmic strategies in "Buffalo Bill 's," it is important to emphasize that rhythm is not fixed. Your involvement as a reader is crucial. How long a word is to be "held," how much stress is to be put on a syllable, how short a short line is and how long a long line is, and how much pause there is in a pause are effects you create or decide on.

READING FOR METER

As part of their rhythm, poems can have a regular "beat." You're already familiar with beat: When you listen to certain types of music, you are probably struck by or react to the beat. You may say or hear someone else say, "I love the beat of that song."

STRESSED AND UNSTRESSED SYLLABLES A beat in poetry arises from the contrast of emphasized (stressed or accented) and muted (unstressed or unaccented) syllables. Poetry with a steady beat, or measured pulse, is said to have **meter**, a regularized beat created by a repeating pattern of accents, syllables, or both. The most widely used type of meter in English (called *accentual-syllabic*) takes into account both the number of stresses and the number of syllables per line. If you're unsure about syllables and accents for a particular word, check a dictionary: It divides each word into syllables and indicates where the stress falls as you pronounce it.

The process of picking out a poem's meter by marking stressed and unstressed syllables is called **scansion**. For a fuller and more technical discussion of meter and scansion, see the appendix on scansion (pp. 1422–31).

POETIC FEET   The basis of accentual-syllabic meter is the repetition of metrical "feet." A **foot** is a two- or three-syllable metrical unit made up (usually) of one stressed and one or two unstressed syllables. As these combinations of stressed plus unstressed syllables (*da DA*, or *da da DA*) are repeated, a regular pattern or beat (*da DA da DA da DA*, or *da da DA da da DA*) becomes established in your ear; you unconsciously expect to continue to hear it, and you notice variations from the "norm."

IAMBIC METER   There are terms, or names, for these feet. The *da DA* feet, called **iambs**, create iambic meter. Listen for it in this line:

i AM bic ME ter GOES like THIS.

Now listen for it in the opening lines of Alfred, Lord Tennyson's "Ulysses" (p. 871):

it LITtle PROfits THAT an I-dle KING
by THIS STILL HEARTH, aMONG these BARren CRAGS,
MATCHED with an A-ged WIFE, i METE and DOLE
unEqual LAWS unTO a SAvage RACE,
that HOARD, and SLEEP, and FEED, and KNOW not ME

Iambic is by far the most frequently used foot. The other feet are often used for variation in mostly iambic poems, though sometimes they are found as the dominant foot in an entire poem.

TROCHAIC METER   The inversion of the iambic foot is the **trochee** (*DA da*), which forms a trochaic meter (again, listen for it):

TRO chees PUT the AC cent FIRST.

In the third line quoted above from "Ulysses," "MATCHED with" is a trochaic foot, used as a **substitution** (a different kind of foot put in place of the one normally demanded by the meter). Substitutions add variety, emphasize the dominant foot by contrasting with it, and often coincide with a switch in meaning. Here the substitution makes "MATCHED with" more emphatic and foregrounds its meaning.

Listen for trochaic feet in this stanza from the introduction to William Blake's (mostly cheerful) *Songs of Innocence*:

> PIPing DOWN the VALleys WILD,
> PIPing SONGS of PLEASant GLEE,
> ON a CLOUD i SAW a CHILD,
> AND he LAUGHing SAID to ME:
>
> "PIPE a SONG aBOUT a LAMB."
> SO i PIPED with MERry CHEER.

Stresses are never equally strong; that is one way of attaining rhythmic variety even in lines that are metrically regular. Thus, in the third line, CLOUD and CHILD get more stress than ON and SAW. Some syllables (AND in the fourth line, SO in line 6) are given a light stress mainly because we expect, from the pattern established, that they *should* be stressed. You may have noticed that these lines have four stressed syllables but only three unstressed syllables; the fourth trochee in each line is incomplete, lacking its unstressed syllable, which is replaced by a mandatory pause: All the lines are end-stopped. This is another way to do something unusual with, and add variety to, a metrical poem.

ANAPESTIC AND DACTYLIC METERS   Two other feet add an unstressed syllable to the feet described above: an **anapest** adds one to an iamb (*da da DA*), and a **dactyl** adds one to a trochee (*DA da da*). Whole poems in these meters are unusual; they are typically used for substitutions in predominantly iambic or trochaic poems. Here, however, are the final lines from a poem mostly in anapestic meter, also by William Blake, "The Chimney Sweeper" (p. 772), which appeared in his more pessimistic *Songs of Experience*. The poem describes the awful lives of small boys forced to climb up chimneys and clean out the soot. The lilting anapests create a sharply ironic contrast with the content, as Tom receives comfort from a dream about heaven he had the night before:

> Though the MORNing was COLD, Tom was HAPpy and WARM;
> So if ALL do their DUty, they NEED not fear HARM.

SPONDEE   One other important foot, the **spondee**, has two stressed syllables (*DA DA*), with no unstressed syllables, as in GOOD NIGHT and RAGE, RAGE in these lines from a poem by Dylan Thomas pleading to his father not to accept death passively and quietly (p. 873):

> Do NOT go GENtle INto THAT GOOD NIGHT.
> RAGE, RAGE aGAINST the DYing OF the LIGHT.

Many other feet have been given names, but knowing these five (iamb, trochee, anapest, dactyl, spondee) will enable you to describe the basic meter and variations from it in most poems — and describing them will help you hear them more clearly.

LINE LENGTHS   The other thing to notice in poems in traditional meters involves the length of the lines. Line lengths are measured by the number of feet in each line and are labeled with names derived from Greek roots; for example,

> **monometer** = a line with one foot
>
> **dimeter** = a line with two feet
>
> **trimeter** = a line with three feet
>
> **tetrameter** = a line with four feet
>
> **pentameter** = a line with five feet
>
> **hexameter** = a line with six feet (and so on)

The line we used above ("iAMbic MEter GOES like THIS") is *iambic tetrameter*. The description identifies the predominant foot (here, iamb) and the predominant line length (four feet) in a poem — that is, the ones used the majority of the time.

ENTRY POINTS   The following poem by a late-nineteenth-century African American poet expresses the conflict experienced for persons of color forced to conform to societal expectations of behavior and attitude. Try picking out the meter in the poem by noting the syllables stressed in each line.

APPROACHING THE AUTHOR

Although he excelled in school, **Paul Laurence Dunbar** was forced to take a job as an elevator operator because of his race. He frequently wrote poetry during slow hours, earning him the moniker "elevator boy poet."
    For more about him, see page 1381.

Paul Laurence Dunbar 1872–1906

We Wear the Mask   [1896]

We wear the mask that grins and lies,
It hides our cheeks and shades our eyes, —
This debt we pay to human guile;
With torn and bleeding hearts we smile,
And mouth with myriad subtleties.   5

Why should the world be over-wise,
In counting all our tears and sighs?
Nay, let them only see us, while
    We wear the mask.

We smile, but, O great Christ, our cries   10
To thee from tortured souls arise.
We sing, but oh the clay is vile
Beneath our feet, and long the mile;
But let the world dream otherwise,
    We wear the mask!   15

APPROACHING THE READING

1. Hearing a regular beat in the first few lines should be fairly easy: All the words have one syllable, and important words alternate with less important ones. Label the predominant meter and the predominant line length. Do you find any variations (substitutions) from the predominant feet? If so, point them out.

2. Label the metrical feet and length of lines 9 and 15. What is the effect of changing from the longer lines to which our ears have become accustomed to a shorter line?

3. Notice the interplay between rhythmic devices and meter. The meter provides a very regular beat, but pauses and variance in line endings break up the rhythm and keep the beat from dominating the poem. Point out examples, especially from lines 8–15.

4. In what sense could writing a poem on this topic in a traditional meter be thought of as an example of wearing a mask?

In this poem, the meter stands out; it is almost glaringly regular. Here and there a spondee may be substituted for one of the predominant iambs, depending on where a reader decides to place particular emphasis. "We" might well be stressed equally with the verb following it in lines 1, 9, 10, 12, and 15, in order to emphasize the *people* who are forced to present a false image to others while hiding their authentic self: "WE WEAR," "WE SMILE," "WE SING." A poem that calls attention to the mask also lifts it off, enabling us to realize that it is a mask, that it is a lie (line 1), and, ironically, that it is a form of resistance at the same time it is a mark of servitude.

One could even ask, in that regard, if the use of meter in Dunbar's poem serves also as a mask. In the late nineteenth century, meter was still expected in poetry. Only a few poets, such as Walt Whitman, wrote nonmetrical poems, and Whitman was regarded warily as a radical. An African American poet had to use meter to have her or his work be read widely and not be dismissed as unskilled. But it must have created some tension to write in the cadences of white educated society instead of the cadences and rhythms sung by workers in the fields or when they gathered in the evenings. So Dunbar wrote in meter, probably to have his verse accepted but also perhaps because its strict, almost excessive regularity might suggest that the metrical form is a mask, a lie, a form not freely chosen but forced on him.

What does paying attention to meter gain you? It can help you hear more clearly a central rhythmic feature in a metrical poem, its regular beat and the irregular alterations in that beat. Poems written in meter usually have a dominant foot, that is, one used the majority of the time. Once you get accustomed to the meter, your ear becomes attuned to that foot, begins to expect it, and notices when a different foot is substituted and alters the "sameness." Such substitution is an important means of controlling emphasis as well as adding variety.

> You can further explore rhythm and meter, including using interactive exercises, with VirtuaLit Poetry at bedfordstmartins.com/rewritinglit.

☑ CHECKLIST on Reading for Rhythm and Meter

❏ Listen for and respond to the rhythms of poems.

❏ Note formal structures that affect rhythm (such as line length, line endings, pauses, word choice, combinations of sound).

❏ Listen for the difference between poems with metrical verse (written in meter with a regular beat, such as "Richard Cory" — p. 637) and non-metrical verse (such as "Cold as Heaven" — p. 646).

❏ Listen for the recurring beat in metrical poems and be able to identify the most important traditional metrical feet: iamb (*da DA*), trochee (*DA da*), anapest (*da da DA*), dactyl (*DA da da*), and spondee (*DA DA*).

FURTHER READING

ENTRY POINTS Here are two poems about remembrance — one about whether people are remembered after their deaths for what they have been and done, the second about the desire to go home again and the difficulty of doing so. The first poem reflects on a visit to a southern plantation and on what the tour guide points out (and doesn't point out). In the second, the speaker returns to the urban scene she once wanted to get away from, with the hope that by going there she will get in touch with a part of her identity. Listen for rhythm in each — how the handling of lines, line endings and groupings, combinations of words and sounds and pauses all lead you to speed up, slow down, pause, and adjust your timing.

Lucille Clifton   1936–2010

at the cemetery, walnut grove plantation, south carolina, 1989   [1991]

among the rocks
at walnut grove
your silence drumming
in my bones,
tell me your names.   5

nobody mentioned slaves
and yet the curious tools
shine with your fingerprints.
nobody mentioned slaves
but somebody did this work   10
who had no guide, no stone,
who moulders under rock.

tell me your names,
tell me your bashful names
and i will testify.   15

the inventory lists ten slaves
but only men were recognized.

among the rocks
at walnut grove
some of these honored dead   20
were dark
some of these dark
were slaves
some of these slaves
were women   25
some of them did this
honored work.
tell me your names

foremothers, brothers,
tell me your dishonored names.   30
here lies
here lies
here lies
here lies
hear   35

APPROACHING THE READING

1. This begins as a poem of address. Consider how the rhythms of the poem
   fit the way the speaker addresses the dead slaves.

2. Select groups of two or three lines anywhere in the poem and mark the
   stressed syllables (see the appendix on scansion [pp. 1422–31] for the traditional method of doing so). Is there a regular beat all the time, or some of
   the time, or never? If there is a regular beat at all, comment on how it contributes to the rhythm and effect of the poem.

3. Describe the rhythm of the last five lines. What makes it effective? What is
   the effect of the serious pun as the last line?

4. "[T]ell me your names," the speaker says, "and i will testify" (ll. 13, 15). What
   does "testify" denote and connote here? In what sense is the poem itself a
   testimony? In what sense does it have the rhythms of testimony? Why can the
   speaker testify even though she receives no response to her request in line 13?

Lorna Dee Cervantes   b. 1954

Freeway 280   [1981]

Las casitas° near the gray cannery,	*little houses*
nestled amid wild abrazos° of climbing roses	*hugs*
and man-high red geraniums	
are gone now. The freeway conceals it	
all beneath a raised scar. 5	

But under the fake windsounds of the open lanes,	
in the abandoned lots below, new grasses sprout,	
wild mustard remembers, old gardens	
come back stronger than they were,	
trees have been left standing in their yards. 10	
Albaricoqueros, cerezos, nogales° . . .	*apricot, cherry, walnut trees*
Viejitas° come here with paper bags to gather greens.	*old women*
Espinaca, verdolagas, yerbabuena° . . .	*spinach, purslane, mint*

I scramble over the wire fence
that would have kept me out.   15

Once, I wanted out, wanted the rigid lanes
to take me to a place without sun,
without the smell of tomatoes burning
on swing shift in the greasy summer air.

Maybe it's here   20
en los campos extraños de esta ciudad°   *in the strange fields of this city*
where I'll find it, that part of me
mown under
like a corpse
or a loose seed.   25

APPROACHING THE AUTHOR

Lorna Dee Cervantes's parents allowed her and her brother to speak only English at home, to avoid the racism present in her community at that time. The resulting inability to fully identify with her heritage fueled her later poetry.

For more about her, see page 1377.

APPROACHING THE READING

1. The poem starts with description of a scene, juxtaposing the way it was before, as the speaker looks back, and the way it is now. Listen to the rhythms in the first two sections of the poem. How do they fit the subject and tone? Why do you think the speaker uses Spanish words part of the time? In what ways do they fit the subject and tone? The rhythm?

2. Listen to the rhythm of each line in stanzas 3 and 4, as well as the rhythm of the whole poem. The speaker says that in the past she "wanted out" (l. 16). Why? What is the speaker's attitude now? What was it before? How does the rhythm fit and reinforce what she is saying?

3. Where does this poem have meter? Be ready to talk about how the meter interacts with, or becomes a part of, the rhythm, and how the meter shapes or contributes to intensity, emphasis, meaning, and implications.

4. Consider the comparisons to " a corpse / or a loose seed" in the short closing lines. Why does the speaker see the comparison differently now? How does the rhythm of the three short concluding lines fit the poem?

5. How does the title fit the poem? Why that as title?

ENTRY POINTS   Here is another remembrance poem, one that connects us with a profound experience of loss. As you read, notice how the poem, with great restraint, slowly and quietly builds to its poignant closing. Try to imagine the entire scene, recognizing how rich and emotionally complex it is.

> **APPROACHING THE AUTHOR**
>
> As a young country boy growing up in quiet County Derry, Ireland, **Seamus Heaney** watched American soldiers in nearby fields drill in preparation for the Normandy invasion. He says impressions like this one solidified his conception of himself as a poet poised between the poles of "history and ignorance."
>   For more about him, see page 1389.

Seamus Heaney   b. 1939

Mid-Term Break   [1966]

I sat all morning in the college sick bay
Counting bells knelling classes to a close.
At two o'clock our neighbours drove me home.

In the porch I met my father crying—
He had always taken funerals in his stride—   5
And Big Jim Evans saying it was a hard blow.

The baby cooed and laughed and rocked the pram
When I came in, and I was embarrassed
By old men standing up to shake my hand

And tell me they were "sorry for my trouble,"   10
Whispers informed strangers I was the eldest,
Away at school, as my mother held my hand

In hers and coughed out angry tearless sighs.
At ten o'clock the ambulance arrived
With the corpse, stanched and bandaged by the nurses.   15

Next morning I went up into the room. Snowdrops
And candles soothed the bedside; I saw him
For the first time in six weeks. Paler now,

Wearing a poppy bruise on his left temple,
He lay in the four foot box as in his cot.   20
No gaudy scars, the bumper knocked him clear.

A four foot box, a foot for every year.

APPROACHING THE READING

1. Notice how clearly and directly the speaker tells the story. At the same time, pick out particular words and images that moved you, and that made you see the scene in remarkably precise ways. Be ready to discuss this complex

combination of a speaker being clear and direct while at the same time sharing a profoundly emotional experience.

2. Think about the form and the rhythm and meter. What is the primary meter? Why might the poet have added irregular beats to what otherwise appears to be regular meter? Some argue that three-line stanzas create a subtle sense of incompleteness. What do you think? Explain your response. What do you make of the closing being a single line?

3. We never are told what the speaker is feeling or what anyone else is feeling. And yet, you likely know, and you probably also feel for the speaker and others in the poem. How does the poem achieve that effect?

4. The speaker has been away at school. He says directly, "I saw him / For the first time in six weeks" (ll. 17–18). Describe what you think he might be feeling and reflecting on even though it remains unsaid.

ENTRY POINTS   The following poem is also a memory poem, as the speaker thinks back on a decision, a turning point she or he will long remember and reflect on. Unlike the previous poems, this one is metrical throughout. Read the poem, emphasizing the meter. Then reread it, concentrating on words and expression, feeling the meter as you would a bass guitar behind a rhythm guitar. Think about how meter contributes in significant ways to the poem's rhythm.

APPROACHING THE AUTHOR

Robert Frost never worked at a desk or in a designated writing room. He preferred sitting in an armless chair with a writing board. "I use all sorts of things," he once said. "Write on the sole of my shoe."
For more about him, see page 1384.

Robert Frost 1874–1963

The Road Not Taken   [1916]

Two roads diverged in a yellow wood,
And sorry I could not travel both
And be one traveler, long I stood
And looked down one as far as I could
To where it bent in the undergrowth;   5

Then took the other, as just as fair,
And having perhaps the better claim,
Because it was grassy and wanted wear;
Though as for that, the passing there
Had worn them really about the same,   10

And both that morning equally lay
In leaves no step had trodden black.
Oh, I kept the first for another day!
Yet knowing how way leads on to way,
I doubted if I should ever come back.   15

I shall be telling this with a sigh
Somewhere ages and ages hence:
Two roads diverged in a wood, and I—
I took the one less traveled by,
And that has made all the difference.   20

APPROACHING THE READING

1. This poem is often read as a poem about not conforming to the majority, taking the road that most do *not* take. However, Robert Frost was hesitant about advocating that reading. What other reading or readings could you give to the poem? Think about a choice you made in your life and what you found yourself thinking about it afterward.

2. Frost called himself a "Synecdochist" because he preferred poetry in which "a little thing touches a larger thing" (see p. 637 for the quote and pp. 636–37 for **synecdoche**). What does this suggest about the choice the speaker made and about the poem as a whole? What does it suggest about details in the poem? Consider the little word *by* in line 19. What different ways can you read that line based on the meanings of the word?

3. Frost commented that his poems often say one thing in order to mean another. Where do you see possible instances of that in this poem? For example, what do you make of the word *sigh* (l. 16)? Think about some of its connotations.

4. Mark the stressed and unstressed syllables in the poem and try dividing them into poetic feet. What foot is predominant? Label it and the line length. Note instances that vary from the predominant foot and consider how such variations affect the way you read the poem.

5. Describe the poem's rhythm and point out techniques that shape the rhythm. Be ready to comment on how meter contributes to the overall rhythm.

6. Why would a poet as intelligent and crafty as Frost end this famous poem with a cliché, with something so trite?

ENTRY POINTS   The following poem, like the four previous ones, is a memory poem, or at least culminates as a memory poem. Unlike the others, it is a love poem, albeit an unusual one since it approaches its subject indirectly. Notice rhythms, as you read and reread it: The poem talks about rhythm ("slow motion," music, dancing) as well as employs it. Reflect on how the poem's rhythm fits with and contributes to its meaning and effect.

APPROACHING THE AUTHOR

Gary Miranda stopped writing poetry when he became a father, feeling that he couldn't do justice to both callings. He turned to writing screenplays instead and has completed six so far.

For more about him, see page 1401.

Gary Miranda   b. 1938

Love Poem   [1978]

A kind of slant: the way a ball will glance
off the end of a bat when you swing for the fence
and miss — that is, if you could watch that once,
up close and in slow motion; or the chance
meanings, not even remotely intended, that dance   5
at the edge of words, like sparks. Bats bounce
just so off the edges of the dark at a moment's
notice, as swallows do off sunlight. Slants

like these have something to do with why *angle*
is one of my favorite words, whenever it chances   10
to be a verb; and with why the music I single
out tonight — eighteenth-century dances —
made me think just now of you untangling
blueberries, carefully, from their dense branches.

APPROACHING THE READING

1. Miranda brings together a group of things that one would not expect to go together, let alone in a love poem: a foul ball when the batter swings for a home run, the music of eighteenth-century dances, untangling blueberry branches, his love of the word "angle" when used as a verb, bats and swallows, dense branches. What do you make of this combination, and what do you think these things have to do with love?

2. Notice as you read how the rhythms of the lines fit what the poem is saying. Think about how you would describe that.

3. Look for where there is a regular beat (a metrical beat) and where you find that breaking down or becoming more of a syncopated rhythm. Consider what makes this appropriate, effective for what the poem is working with.

4. How would you describe the speaker and the speaker's attitude toward love?

ENTRY POINTS   Each of the following four poems deals with the theme of identity. Decide which of them is/are written in meter and which is/are nonmetrical. Watch for how their handling of rhythm, metrical or nonmetrical, contributes to the effect and meaning of each poem.

A. K. Ramanujan 1929–1993

Self-Portrait   [1966]

I resemble everyone
but myself, and sometimes see
in shop-windows,
    despite the well-known laws
    of optics,   5
the portrait of a stranger,
date unknown,
often signed in a corner
by my father.

Emily Dickinson 1830–1886

I'm Nobody! Who are you?   [c. *1861;* 1891]

I'm Nobody! Who are you?
Are you — Nobody — Too?
Then there's a pair of us?
Don't tell! they'd advertise — you know!

How dreary — to be — Somebody!   5
How public — like a Frog —
To tell one's name — the livelong June —
To an admiring Bog!

Sylvia Plath 1932–1963

Metaphors   [1960]

I'm a riddle in nine syllables,
An elephant, a ponderous house,
A melon strolling on two tendrils.
O red fruit, ivory, fine timbers!
This loaf's big with its yeasty rising.   5
Money's new-minted in this fat purse.
I'm a means, a stage, a cow in calf.
I've eaten a bag of green apples,
Boarded the train there's no getting off.

Georgia Douglas Johnson 1880–1966

Wishes   [1927]

I'm tired of pacing the petty round of the ring of the thing I know—
I want to stand on the daylight's edge and see where the sunsets go.

I want to sail on a swallow's tail and peep through the sky's blue glass.
I want to see if the dreams in me shall perish or come to pass.

I want to look through the moon's pale crook and gaze on the moon-
        man's face.   5
I want to keep all the tears I weep and sail to some unknown place.

APPROACHING THE READING

1. Read each poem aloud. Listen for a regular beat or look for a regular pattern; if you find one, mark syllables in several lines to help decide if the
   poem is metrical.

2. If the lines are metrical, label the metrical form and listen for how the meter
   interacts with and becomes a part of the rhythm. Consider how the meter
   shapes or contributes to intensity, emphasis, meaning, and implications.

3. If the lines are not metrical, consider how the rhythm seems appropriate to
   and helps develop the subject, tone, and theme.

4. For each poem, write a brief statement of theme and a brief explanation of
   how rhythm contributes to the way the poem deals with its themes.

RESPONDING THROUGH Writing

WRITING ABOUT RHYTHM AND METER

Journal Entries

1. Review the discussion of prose rhythms in Chapter 8 (p. 238). Then read a poem written in long, prose-like lines, such as David Mura's "Grandfather-in-Law" (p. 698), Allen Ginsberg's "A Supermarket in California" (p. 808), and Etheridge Knight's "Hard Rock Returns to Prison from the Hospital for the Criminal Insane" (p. 831). In your journal, discuss ways rhythms in prose and rhythms in poetry are similar and different (and are created in similar and different ways).

2. Fill in the following sentence: I got up this morning and _____, then I _____, and then I _____. Now break it into rhythmic units, writing each unit as a line of poetry. Try dividing it in other places. In your journal, discuss how rhythm and emphasis change as a result of different breaks, and reflect on the kinds of aesthetic decisions a writer has to make about where to divide lines.

You can research the authors in this chapter with LitLinks at bedfordstmartins.com/rewritinglit.

3. Nursery rhymes and children's poetry are often written in meter. Choose two or three examples, write a few lines of each in your journal, mark the stressed syllables, and label the metric foot and line length. Then perhaps write a paper examining the handling of meter in a nursery rhyme or children's poem—or more than one of them—and discussing why meter is an effective technique in verse for children.

Literary Analysis Papers

4. Write a paper on the effect of sound and rhythm on the characterization of the speaker and the development of theme in T. S. Eliot's "The Love Song of J. Alfred Prufrock" (p. 796).

5. Rhythm is important in poems that are about or draw upon music. Write a paper discussing the relation of rhythm to what is being said in one of the following poems, or one not in this book: Sterling A. Brown's "Riverbank Blues" (p. 776), Walt Whitman's *Song of Myself* (p. 877), or Al Young's "A Dance for Ma Rainey" (p. 886).

6. Write a paper discussing the interaction of meter and rhythm in Wilfred Owen's "Dulce et Decorum Est" (p. 619), Samuel Taylor Coleridge's "Kubla Khan" (p. 783), Andrew Marvell's "To His Coy Mistress" (p. 841), Dudley Randall's "Ballad of Birmingham" (p. 853), or Dylan Thomas's "Do not go gentle into that good night" (p. 873).

Comparison-Contrast Papers

7. Write a paper comparing and contrasting the role and handling of rhythm in two poems about rivers: Langston Hughes's "The Negro Speaks of Rivers" (p. 826) and Lorine Niedecker's "My Life by Water" (p. 846).

8. Rhythm is important in poems about dance, often to theme as well as technique. Write a paper comparing and contrasting the presence of rhythm in two or more of the following poems: Theodore Roethke's "My Papa's Waltz" (p. 602), Cornelius Eady's "My Mother, If She Had Won Free Dance Lessons" (p. 795), Charles Simic's "Classic Ballroom Dances" (p. 864), Al Young's "A Dance for Ma Rainey" (p. 886).

WRITING ABOUT CONNECTIONS

There is a tendency to think in terms of relating metrical poems to other metrical poems and nonmetrical poems to nonmetrical ones, but that overlooks other significant linkages. Valuable thematic connections can occur from pairing two poems that have similar subjects but that handle rhythm quite differently. Here are some possibilities:

1. "Remembering the Unremembered": The Language of Preservation in Lucille Clifton's "at the cemetery, walnut grove plantation, south carolina, 1989" (p. 662) and Thomas Gray's "Elegy Written in a Country Churchyard" (available online)

2. "On the Road Again": The Search for Self in Lorna Dee Cervantes's "Freeway 280" (p. 665) and Alfred, Lord Tennyson's "Ulysses" (p. 871)

3. "Grief beyond Grief": Dealing with Death in Ben Jonson's "On My First Son" (p. 827) and Michael S. Harper's "Nightmare Begins Responsibility" (p. 815)

WRITING RESEARCH PAPERS

1. Olga Broumas's "Cinderella" (p. 775) retells the Cinderella story in terms of the social and cultural context of the 1970s, a time of significant raising of awareness about issues affecting women. It was a time when changes were both worked for and resisted. More women pursued careers, challenging many implanted ideas about men and women in the workplace. There were real gains and some changes that only seemed to be gains. Do research on women and work in the 1970s and use what you find to write a paper on the ambivalence the poem's speaker expresses about what is and isn't happening at the time, and the way tone, figurative language, and rhythm contribute effectively to the issues the poem explores.

TIPS for Writing about Rhythm and Meter

- **Deciding about rhythm and meter.** If rhythm and meter are integral to the discussion of your topic, it is essential to include them, even as a subtopic. Be sure to use specific examples (including quotations) and thorough explanations. Otherwise, making them a part of your paper is seldom crucial in the way it might be for diction, tone, or figurative language. However, finding a way to refer to them could enrich your paper and add more sophistication to it.

- **Focusing on rhythm.** When working with a poem's rhythm as the main subject of a paper, it is important to make sure that you choose a poem or poems in which the rhythm plays a key role, is distinctive, carries meaning and/or feeling, creates an impact, or is handled in an otherwise especially subtle or distinctive way. Such a paper will need to include a careful analysis of the techniques used to achieve the poem's rhythmic effects and of the way they contribute to its theme or significance.

- **Focusing on appropriateness.** An interesting approach to a paper about rhythm can be one in which you examine how the rhythm of a poem is appropriate for the speaker or the speaker's tone and voice in dealing with the poem's subject or some combination thereof.

- **Focusing on form and rhythm in free verse.** For free verse, writing about the relationship between form and rhythm, especially how form often results from decisions about rhythm, can be a fruitful topic for a paper or a subtopic in a paper focusing on other aspects of the poem.

- **Focusing on meter.** For an example of how to write a paper focused on meter and its effect on rhythm, see the appendix on scansion (pp. 1422–31). Working with such a topic turns out best when an author uses meter in especially meaningful, integrated, or unusual ways. A metrical poem that is almost entirely regular and predictable won't give you much to talk about unless there is particular significance, accomplishment, or irony in its regularity.

2. Write a paper on William Blake's critique of the social and/or economic situation in early nineteenth-century England, especially the neglect and exploitation of children. Do research on the topic and read several poems by Blake that deal with the subject, including one in this book ("The Chimney Sweeper," p. 772) and others from Blake's *Songs of Experience*, such as "Holy Thursday" and "London." Consider as part of your analysis the appropriateness of Blake's use of form, meter, rhythm, and rhyme in developing his themes.

That's something which is not always recognized, the freeing effect of a lot of traditional techniques. Richard Wilbur

(Author of "Love Calls Us to the Things of This World," p. 879)

17 Form and Type
Delighting in Design

Think of the effect when a well-designed Internet site appears on the screen—how it can catch your eye, grab your attention, and make you want to explore the site further. We notice such effective uses of shape or layout every day all around us. The impact of visual design, along with internal design, is often part of poetry's appeal. **Form** can refer to external structure, the way the poem looks on the page—which may relate to the type of poem it is (to its "genre") and to what the poem is dealing with. It can refer also to the inner structure that arranges, organizes, or connects the various elements in a work. Every poem has form, in both senses. This chapter will help you appreciate the formal constructs of poems. It will discuss the role of form and of poetic types, as well as what form can mean, embody, express, or reveal.

In some cases, poets start out with an external form in mind. It may be an "inherited" form—perhaps a haiku or a sonnet or a villanelle. In other cases, instead of starting with a form in mind, poets begin with an image, feeling, experience, or idea, or with a few words or lines. The writing itself leads to or creates the form, both the inner arrangement and the external shape. The form, therefore, is a result of working with the other elements of poetry.

READING FOR LINES

Most poems are written in **lines**, and each line normally focuses our attention and holds something of significance to the whole poem. In prose, the layout on the page is controlled by margins. Poets, however, control the beginnings and ends of lines, giving them additional opportunities for added attention, anticipation, and emphasis. Each line also creates a rhythm, what Ezra Pound called "the musical phrase."

Lines can also become units of rhythm discovered or decided on within a sentence. As you read line by line, feel the musicality with each. At the same time you need to read "past" the lines to follow the meaning of the sentences. This superimposing of lines on sentences can also direct our attention to words that might otherwise get passed over. Watch for this in the following poem.

APPROACHING THE AUTHOR

In 1950 **Gwendolyn Brooks** became the first African American to win a Pulitzer Prize.

For more about her, see page 1375.

Gwendolyn Brooks 1917–2000

We Real Cool   [1960]

The Pool Players.
Seven at the Golden Shovel.

We real cool. We
Left school. We

Lurk late. We
Strike straight. We

Sing sin. We   5
Thin gin. We

Jazz June. We
Die soon.

APPROACHING THE READING

1. Read the poem aloud, pausing at the end of each line by emphasizing the *We*. Don't let your voice drop, since the sentence continues in the next line.

2. What is the effect of dividing the sentences into two lines?

3. What is the effect of starting each new sentence at the end of each line?

4. Notice the cumulative effect of the various things the pool players at the Golden Shovel boast about doing. What poetic devices are used to unify and build the intensity of the lines?

5. What is the effect of having a deliberate rhyme scheme (see p. 612), even a typical end rhyme format? How is it affected by the addition of the repeated *We* at the line's end?

6. Notice the last line, lacking the *We* and the third beat. What effect does this create?

Not all poems are separated into lines: **Prose poems** are a notable exception. The prose poem works with all the elements of poetry except line. It is often written in common paragraph form. It is a hybrid form, drawing together some of the best aspects of both prose and poetry, creating new possibilities out of the challenges presented by the way it fuses the two forms. For examples of prose poems, see Carolyn Forché's "The Colonel" (p. 801) and A. Van Jordan's "From" (p. 828).

The unusual line breaks create anticipation and a jazzlike rhythm; they place emphasis on both the subjects and predicates of the sentences; and they lead to the isolated and unsettling last line. Test the effect of the poem's line breaks and the importance of its form by reading it this way:

> We real cool.
> We left school.
>
> We lurk late.
> We strike straight.
>
> We sing sin.
> We thin gin.
>
> We jazz June.
> We die soon.

The words are the same, but it is not the same poem. Changing the form of a poem gives it a different effect and makes it a different work.

Part of the pleasure for us as readers is that we can respond to the rhythms of lines, can notice and feel how certain words get emphasized by their position in the line, can appreciate the interplay between line and sentence, and can recognize and experience the role of each line in the life of a poem. Notice and feel the rhythms and emphases in the lines as they are used in varying ways throughout the rest of this chapter.

READING FOR STANZAS

The word *stanza* derives from the Italian word for "room," so one could say that stanzas are "rooms" into which some poems are divided. A **stanza** is a grouping of poetic lines into a section, set off by a space, either according to a given form—each section having the same number of lines and the same arrangement of line lengths, meter, and rhyme—or according to shifts in thought, moment, setting, effect, voice, time, and so on.

INVENTED STANZA FORMS   Stanza shapes can be *invented*, that is, individually created, unique to a particular poem. The poet may plan out such a stanza form before beginning to write or may create it in the process of writing. Look again at "We Real Cool" (p. 675). Probably no other poem in existence has stanzas just like these. Perhaps the first stanza found its own form, without conscious attention to it; perhaps Brooks initially wrote

> We real cool.
> We left school.

and then realized the powerful effect of ending the lines with *We*. If so, at that point Brooks began consciously thinking about the form and making the other stanzas fit the form she had "found" for the first one.

INHERITED STANZA FORMS   Many stanza patterns, however, are not invented but *inherited*: handed down through the centuries, from one generation of poets to another, often with a prescribed meter and sometimes a set rhyme scheme. The most frequently used inherited stanza forms, in the past and today, are four-line stanzas called **quatrains**. One variety of quatrain, the **ballad stanza**, has a long history, used in traditional ballads for many centuries. The ballad stanza is a simple but easily adaptable form — four-line stanzas rhyming *abcb* with eight syllables in the first and third lines, six in the second and fourth. Perhaps it is easier to visualize in diagram form (each square equals one syllable):

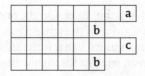

Look for that structure in the following poem (in some of its lines you will find an extra syllable — that's typical of the form).

Countee Cullen   1903–1946

Incident   [1925]

for Eric Walrond°

Once riding in old Baltimore,
   Heart-filled, head-filled with glee,

Eric Walrond: Walrond (1898–1966) was a writer and activist in the New York literary community from the early 1920s.

I saw a Baltimorean
  Keep looking straight at me.

Now I was eight and very small,   5
  And he was no whit bigger,
And so I smiled, but he poked out
  His tongue, and called me, "Nigger."

I saw the whole of Baltimore
  From May until December;   10
Of all the things that happened there
  That's all that I remember.

APPROACHING THE AUTHOR

Countee Cullen was born 30 March 1903, but scholars don't know where (Louisville? Baltimore? New York City?) nor with whom he spent the earliest years of his childhood.
  For more about him, see page 1379.

APPROACHING THE READING

1. Notice that each stanza is made up of one sentence. What is the effect of the spaces after lines 4 and 8 that divide the poem into three stanzas? How would the poem read differently if it were a single unit of twelve lines, without stanza breaks? Explain.

2. Each sentence is divided into four lines. On the one hand, we need to read past the lines and grasp the meaning of the sentence as a whole. But we also should give attention to the lines as units. What is the effect of the division into lines? What is lost when you read straight through without such divisions?

Traditionally, ballad stanzas were used for narrative poems, often tragic stories with a melancholy tone. Cullen's use of the form seems appropriate: Like the early folk ballads, it tells a sad story, with a distinctly melancholy tone. A great deal of the poem's emotional power is generated by its form. The stanzas divide the incident into three distinct segments, each building to a climax. The lines help control the rhythm, leading us to pause after each line and focus on each statement individually, letting its point sink in. And the words at the end of the second and fourth lines in each stanza receive strong emphasis, from their position in the stanzas and from the rhyme. The poem opens with an "old world" sense of decorum conveying the child's natural excitement, void of any apprehension. Then comes the "incident" and we move to the speaker's later realization: that no matter how much positive experience he accumulates, it is cruelty's impact that he remembers. The word *incident* usually carries a connotation of inconsequence. The irony of Cullen's title is certainly bitter.

Other stanza forms are used less frequently. Some well-known inherited examples are described in the glossary (pp. 1469–88). Look, for example, at **Chaucerian stanza**, **ottava rima**, **Spenserian stanza**, and **terza rima**.

INHERITED POETIC TYPES   A poet may plan from the beginning to use an inherited form, perhaps setting out to write a poem in a preset pattern such as a sestina or a sonnet. The poet may feel the traditional form is most appropriate for the subject. Or the poet may want to participate in a centuries-old poetic tradition, to refresh an inherited form, to embody meaning within the form, or to meet the challenge of working within the form's requirements. The opportunities offered by a prescribed form can lead a writer's imagination to come up with something it likely would not have without the "pressure" of the form.

Or the poet may think about an inherited form while writing—may start with a subject or images but no particular form in mind, and then discover that an effective way the poem can develop is as a sonnet, as a sestina, as couplets, or as a variation on a particular form. In such cases, the poet discovers that the material "needs" or perhaps even "demands" that form, or the poet may realize that the form may be the perfect "fit" for that poem.

READING SONNETS

The inherited form you likely encounter most often is the **sonnet**. These fourteen-line poems originally were lyrical love poems, but they came to be used also for meditations on death and nature. Poets now use the sonnet form for all subjects. In English, they are usually written in iambic pentameter (see pp. 656–59). You can visualize a typical sonnet as a grid of 140 squares in fourteen lines, each line containing ten squares. The poet must fit one syllable into each square, with those in the even-numbered squares usually being stressed, those in the odd-numbered ones unstressed, and the final syllables fitting a given rhyme scheme. Sonnets in English typically fall into two types, differentiated by the structure of their development and their rhyme schemes.

English (or Shakespearean) Sonnet

The **English sonnet** is formed of three quatrains (four-line units, typically rhyming *abab cdcd efef*) and a couplet (two rhyming lines), as in the following diagram:

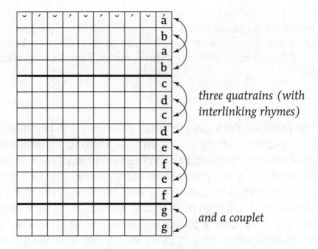

three quatrains (with interlinking rhymes)

and a couplet

Usually the subject is introduced in the first quatrain, expanded or restated in different terms in the second, and expanded further or restated again in the third; the couplet adds a logical, sometimes pithy conclusion or a surprising twist.

ENTRY POINTS   See, for example, this sonnet by William Shakespeare. Often sonnets celebrate young love. This one is uncommon in that it celebrates love between an older couple. Watch how it uses different metaphors to describe getting older and then makes a strong assertion about old age and love.

APPROACHING THE AUTHOR

In addition to composing sonnets and dramas, **William Shakespeare** acted in plays, both his own and others'. He is rumored to have enjoyed playing the part of the ghost in *Macbeth*.

For more about him, see page 1411.

William Shakespeare   1564–1616

That time of year thou mayst in me behold   [1609]

That time of year thou mayst in me behold
When yellow leaves, or none, or few, do hang
Upon those boughs which shake against the cold,

Bare ruined choirs,° where late° the sweet birds sang. *choirstalls; lately*
In me thou seest the twilight of such day   5
As after sunset fadeth in the west,
Which by and by black night doth take away,
Death's second self, that seals up all in rest.
In me thou seest the glowing of such fire
That on the ashes of his youth doth lie,   10
As the deathbed whereon it must expire,
Consumed with that which it was nourished by.
  This thou perceiv'st, which makes thy love more strong,
  To love that well which thou must leave ere long.

APPROACHING THE READING

1. Outline the poem by summarizing the ideas developed in the quatrains and explain how they relate to each other.

2. Explain the relationship between lines 1–12 and the concluding couplet.

3. Consider how the subject matter of the poem seems appropriate to the traditional uses of the sonnet form.

  In this case, the three quatrains express essentially the same idea—that the speaker is getting older, approaching death—but they use different **archetypes** to convey it: that is, symbols, characters, or plot lines that have been used again and again through the centuries and carry a nearly universal significance. The first four lines describe old age in terms of late autumn, with few leaves left on the branches; lines 5–8 describe the approach of death in terms of twilight, with darkness—which closely resembles death—approaching; and lines 9–12 compare the speaker's stage in life to a bed of coals, what is left of a fire that earlier had burned brightly, consuming the firewood that nourished it. The pithy conclusion in lines 13–14 clarifies that the "thou" is not us, the readers, but someone who cares about the speaker and who loves him not less as he grows older and less "lovely" but loves him more because it is clear that they do not have all that much time left together.

Italian (or Petrarchan) Sonnet

  The **Italian sonnet** is composed of an **octave** (an eight-line unit), rhyming *abbaabba*, and a **sestet** (a six-line unit), often rhyming *cdecde* or *cdcdcd*, though variations are frequent. The octave usually develops an idea or question or problem; then the poem pauses or "turns," and the sestet

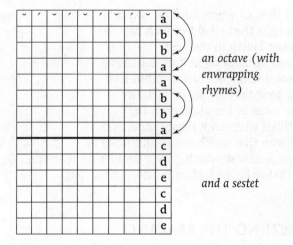

an octave (with
enwrapping
rhymes)

and a sestet

completes the idea, answers the question, or resolves the difficulty. See, for example, Gary Miranda's "Love Poem" (p. 668) and the following poem.

ENTRY POINTS   In 1877, Gerard Manley Hopkins was ordained a Catholic priest. Almost all of the poetry he wrote after becoming a Catholic was, though seldom dogmatic, deeply religious. The octave of "God's Grandeur" declares that the beauty of the world is a reflection of God's glory and expresses profound concern that humankind has not respected and taken adequate care of that world. The sestet then affirms that, despite such neglect, God continues to love and nurture it.

Gerard Manley Hopkins   1844–1889

God's Grandeur   [1877; 1918]

The world is charged with the grandeur of God.
  It will flame out, like shining from shook foil;°   shaken gold foil
  It gathers to a greatness, like the ooze of oil°   from olives
Crushed. Why do men then now not reck° his rod?°   recognize; discipline
Generations have trod, have trod, have trod;   5
  And all is seared with trade; bleared, smeared with toil;
  And wears man's smudge and shares man's smell: the soil
Is bare now, nor can foot feel, being shod.

And, for° all this, nature is never spent;   *despite*
    There lives the dearest freshness deep down things;   10
And though the last lights off the black West went
    Oh, morning, at the brown brink eastward, springs—
Because the Holy Ghost over the bent
    World broods with warm breast and with ah! bright wings.

APPROACHING THE AUTHOR

After his conversion to Roman Catholicism, **Gerard Manley Hopkins**
burned all the poetry he had written up to that point and did not write
poems again until his superiors in the church encouraged him to do so
seven years later.
    For more about him, see page 1391.

APPROACHING THE READING

1. Summarize the idea developed in lines 1–4 and 5–8 and clarify the connection between the two quatrains.

2. Explain the relationship between lines 1–8 and the concluding sestet.

3. Consider the difference in effect between a Shakespearean division of lines 1–12 and 13–14 and the Italian division of lines 1–8 and 9–14.

The opening quatrain affirms that the natural world, in its great beauty, is filled with—loaded to capacity with—God's glory. It should be unmissable—it should flash in our eyes the way sunlight shines off a piece of gold foil; it collects around us the way olive oil emerges as olives are crushed. Yet, people ignore God by neglecting their responsibility to the world God created. The second quatrain images that neglect: For generations people have focused on trade, industry, and self-advancement. That they are out of touch with nature is signaled by shoes: No longer do we feel the soil and thus care about its condition.

The sestet is set off by a space, as if the speaker pauses to draw a big breath and then give vent to an outburst of praise and affirmation: No matter what human beings do to the earth, they will never eliminate God from it. Even if they destroy all human life, put out the "last lights," and leave the planet in darkness, God's presence will be there still, arising as the light of a new day. The poem concludes by comparing God's constant, caring presence to a mother bird brooding over her newborn chicks, but with the bright wings of an angel.

The tight, orderly traditional form of the sonnet seems fitting for a poem conveying a sense of orderliness—that God has a plan for the world

There are many other inherited types of poem. Here are two illustrated later in this chapter:

- **Sestina** A lyric poem consisting of six six-line stanzas and a three-line concluding stanza (or "envoy"). The six end-words of the first stanza must be used as the end-words of the other five stanzas, in a prescribed pattern. Read Elizabeth Bishop's "Sestina" (p. 699) and try to pick out the pattern on your own; then check the results by looking in the glossary (p. 1484).
- **Villanelle** A nineteen-line lyric poem divided into five tercets and a final four-line stanza, with a prescribed rhyme scheme and some lines repeated in a set pattern. Try to pick out the formal patterns in John Yau's "Chinese Villanelle" (p. 701) or Dylan Thomas's "Do not go gentle into that good night" (p. 873), or look it up in the glossary (p. 1488).

Some other well-known types are described in the glossary (p. 1469–88). Look, for example, at **epic**, **ballad**, **epigram**, and **haiku**.

There are also inherited patterns for nonstanzaic verse. Two important ones are

- **Blank verse** Lines of unrhymed iambic pentameter. This is the most widely used verse form in English poetry, the one found in many Shakespearean plays, Milton's *Paradise Lost* and *Paradise Regained*, Wordsworth's *Prelude*, and countless other long poems. For an example in this book, see Alfred, Lord Tennyson's "Ulysses" (p. 871).
- **Couplet** A unit consisting of two consecutive lines of poetry with the same end rhyme. Couplets can be grouped into stanzas (as in A. E. Housman's "To an Athlete Dying Young," p. 824), but more often they are strung out in extended, nonstanzaic poems or passages: see, for example, Robert Browning's "My Last Duchess" (p. 622) and Gwendolyn Brooks's "We Real Cool" (p. 675).

itself that humans should not violate. The rhythms and sounds are intensified by their confinement in a compressed space: The energy of the poem seems to burst out as the reader opens the poem.

READING FREE VERSE

Many modern and contemporary poets do not use inherited or pre-planned forms, preferring to work without a blueprint for a poem's form. They allow the entire poem to "find" its own shape. The poem may emerge from the poet's imagination and skillful intuition in the form that it needs, or the form may develop in the process of writing and revising. In either case, the poet's attention is focused primarily on other things—on images, sounds, rhythms — and the poet allows the form to develop, either con- sciously shaping it as it is discovered or letting it result from attention to line, line break, rhythm, and so forth.

Such poems traditionally have been called **free verse** because they are free of predetermined metrical and stanzaic patterns. The term *free verse* is mislead- ing, however, if it is interpreted to mean "anything goes," that form and the other elements don't matter. Some books use the term **open form** to avoid such misunderstanding. Either term is usually acceptable. Just remember that no matter how "free" a poem appears, it *does have form*. Every poem does.

Unlike metrical or stanzaic poetry, free verse does not rely on organized structural repetition (like those of meter, rhyme, stanza, or identical syllable counts) to achieve form and coherence. Instead, it relies on connected images and sounds, parallelism in phrasing, and handlings of lines, spaces, rhythms, indentations, gaps, and timing. For the beginning poet, writing in open form may look easier than writing in inherited forms. However, each approach requires an ability to work with the elements of poetry. Each is challenging when one is aware of the complexities of writing any poem well. Each is easy only if done carelessly.

ENTRY POINTS   In the following poem, the speaker stands at the shore of the Pacific and offers thanks to the ocean for carrying her people to this land and for continuing to provide them with the gift of rain. Obviously, the poem is not written in traditional Anglo-European meter and stanza patterns; how- ever, it is certainly influenced by tradition and an understanding of form. Reflect on how its form contributes to the effect of what it is saying.

APPROACHING THE AUTHOR

Leslie Marmon Silko grew up in a prominent mixed-blood family on the Laguna Pueblo reservation and struggled to be fully accepted by both the Laguna tribe and whites. Nonetheless, she eventually learned to identify with her tribal culture and says she considers herself first and foremost Laguna.

For more about her, see page 1411.

Leslie Marmon Silko   b. 1948

Prayer to the Pacific   [1981]

> I traveled to the ocean
>   distant
>   from my southwest land of sandrock
>   to the moving blue water
>   Big as the myth of origin.   5

Pale
pale water in the yellow-white light of
                sun   floating west
                        to China
          where ocean herself was born.   10
Clouds that blow across the sand are wet.

Squat in the wet sand and speak to the Ocean:
       I return to you   turquoise   the red coral you sent us,
              sister spirit of Earth.
Four round stones in my pocket   I carry back the ocean   15
            to suck and to taste.

Thirty thousand years ago
            Indians came riding across the ocean
            carried by giant sea turtles.

Waves were high that day   20
          great sea turtles waded   slowly out
                from the gray sundown sea.

Grandfather Turtle rolled in the sand   four times
          and disappeared
                swimming into the sun.   25
And so   from that time
        immemorial,
            as the old people say,
rain clouds drift from the west
                gift from the ocean.   30

Green leaves in the wind
Wet earth on my feet
       swallowing raindrops
           clear from China.

APPROACHING THE READING

1. Examine the form of the poem carefully, focusing on its visual appearance. Consider how the structure affects your reading of the poem, how the lines' placement creates a kind of choreography of movement for your eyes. How is this structure essential to the timing, energy, and rhythm within the poem?

2. Follow the way sentences run through several lines. Discuss what the juxtaposition of lines with sentences adds to the effect of the poem.

3. In what ways is the form appropriate to the speaker and to the prayer being offered?

A striking formal feature of this poem is the attractiveness of its layout on the page. To look at the poem is like observing a work of visual art, with its clear attention to composition, design, and proportion. There is a kinetic sense to Silko's poem. As we follow the movement of the lines, we can feel in our bodies the energy, oceanic rhythm, and "flow" of the poem.

Along with such visual appeal, the poem's division into lines and its arrangement on the page indicate how it should be read—which lines go together, where pauses amplify its impact, what particular words should be emphasized. The poem describes the speaker's journey to the seaside to offer a prayer to the ocean—by dropping four round stones into its waters. It is a prayer of gratitude for the gift in the past of the ocean carrying the speaker's ancestors to these shores on giant turtles and for the gift in the present of carrying clouds with much-needed rain across the waters to the land the speaker inhabits.

The use of open, seemingly organic, form to evoke a trust in the natural world feels appropriate to the Native American stories it recounts, certainly more appropriate than using an inherited verse form from another culture, such as those discussed earlier in this chapter.

READING FOR INTERNAL FORM

In addition to shape, or external form, a poem also has an *internal form*, the inner arrangement or organization of its parts and content. The variety of techniques and arrangements used by poets is extensive; we list here some of the most important ones.

Parallelism

Parallelism can be considered in two ways: (1) When elements of equal weight within phrases, sentences, or paragraphs are expressed in a similar grammatical order and structure. It can appear within a line or pair of lines: "And he was always quietly arrayed, / And he was always human when he talked"—Edwin Arlington Robinson's "Richard Cory" (p. 637); or, more noticeably, it can appear as a series of parallel items, as in Langston Hughes's "Harlem" (p. 631). (2) When two consecutive lines in open form are related by the second line's repeating, expanding on, or contrasting with the idea of the first, as, for example, in the poetry of Walt Whitman (p. 877).

Juxtaposition

Juxtaposition is the placement of things (often very different things) side by side or close together for comparison or contrast or to create something new from the union, without necessarily making them grammatically parallel. See, for example, how Victor Hernández Cruz's "Problems with Hurricanes" (p. 785) juxtaposes the seriousness of death during a hurricane (drowning or being hurled by the wind against a mountain) with the ludicrous danger of dying from being smashed by a mango, banana, or plantain.

Narrative

One of the most basic approaches to structure is **narrative**, a poet recounting an event as a sequence of actions and details, as in Jimmy Santiago Baca's "Family Ties" (p. 768) or Heather McHugh's "What He Thought" (p. 839). There are also *long* narrative poems, stories cast in poetic form, from Homer on down to the present.

Logical Pattern

Material can be arranged in a logical pattern of development. This could be in the form of a logical argument, like the three-part attempt at persuasion in Andrew Marvell's "To His Coy Mistress" (p. 841), or of logical explanation, like the "wonderings" in Cornelius Eady's "My Mother, If She Had Won Free Dance Lessons" (p. 795), or of raising a problem and offering a solution or a response, as in John Milton's "When I consider how my light is spent" (p. 843).

Question-Answer

Poems can raise a question (explicitly or implicitly) and work toward an answer (which also can be stated or implied). Emily Dickinson's "I'm Nobody! Who are you?" (p. 669) raises and explores a deep, perennial question. Langston Hughes's "Harlem" (p. 631) is a series of questions with an implied answer phrased as a final question, and the title of Ai's "Why Can't I Leave You?" (p. 761) raises a question that the rest of the poem seeks to answer.

Meditative Movement

Some poems are arranged as meditations, often moving from a reflection on a physical place or object or a scene to personal or spiritual perceptions, as in James Wright's "A Blessing" (p. 690) or Lucille Clifton's "at the cemetery, walnut grove plantation, south carolina, 1989" (p. 662).

Association

Poems can be arranged by moving from one word, image, idea, or other element to another word, image, idea, or other element on the basis of associations, as in Tina Chang's "Naming the Light" (p. 779), Aracelis Girmay's "Consider the Hands That Write This Letter" (p. 810), and Charles Simic's "Classic Ballroom Dances" (p. 864).

Lists (or Catalogs) and Litanies

Lists and litanies are a common use of form (we all construct them). Lists can create range, rhythm, intensity, and texture. A poem structured as a litany uses a series of invocations and repeated responses — see, for example, Joy Harjo's "She Had Some Horses" (p. 691). Catalogs also can structure parts of a poem, as in the last line of Gwendolyn Brooks's "The Bean Eaters" (p. 574).

> You can further explore form and type, including using interactive exercises, with VirtuaLit Poetry at bedfordstmartins.com/rewritinglit.

☑ CHECKLIST on Reading for Form and Type

❑ Notice the role form plays in a poem and the effect it has on your experience of reading the poem.

❑ Watch for the handlings of lines and consider the various ways they affect a poem's appearance, rhythm, and emphasis, and the way they interact with sentences.

❑ Be aware of both a poem's external form (the way the poem looks on the page) and its inner form (the artistic design or structure that arranges, organizes, or connects the various elements).

❑ For poems in stanzas, consider the effectiveness and appropriateness of the form selected for the poem. If the poet introduces a variation in the form once established, consider what the changes convey in meaning, tone, and effect.

❑ Watch for inherited forms (such as the English sonnet, the Italian sonnet, ballad stanza, couplets, and blank verse) and consider the kind of creativity and imaginativeness that writing such poetry entails.

❑ Watch for poetry written as free verse (lacking such repeated features as rhyme, meter, or stanza, but using unity of pattern, such as visual structures, parallelism, or rhythm) and consider the kind of creativity and craft that writing such poetry requires.

Combinations of the Above

Almost any of the structures described above can be used in combination with another or others. See what combinations you can find in, for example, Nikki Giovanni's "Nikka-Rosa" (p. 809) and Heather McHugh's "What He Thought" (p. 839).

FURTHER READING

ENTRY POINTS   Consider form in the following poems, asking such questions as: How would you describe the structuring of the poem? Is it an inherited form or free verse? In what ways is the form appropriate for the poem? In what ways does the form itself carry, add to, or intensify the meaning or effect of the poem? In what ways is the form aesthetically satisfying?

The first two poems have a common subject, horses, but are very different in form, content, and effect.

APPROACHING THE AUTHOR

James Wright and his son Franz Wright are the only parent-child pair to have won a Pulitzer Prize in the same category (both are poets).
    For more about him, see page 1419.

James Wright   1927–1980

A Blessing   [1963]

Just off the highway to Rochester, Minnesota,
Twilight bounds softly forth on the grass.
And the eyes of those two Indian ponies
Darken with kindness.
They have come gladly out of the willows   5
To welcome my friend and me.
We step over the barbed wire into the pasture
Where they have been grazing all day, alone.
They ripple tensely, they can hardly contain their happiness
That we have come.   10
They bow shyly as wet swans. They love each other.
There is no loneliness like theirs.
At home once more,
They begin munching the young tufts of spring in the darkness.
I would like to hold the slenderer one in my arms,   15
For she has walked over to me
And nuzzled my left hand.
She is black and white,

Her mane falls wild on her forehead,
And the light breeze moves me to caress her long ear   20
That is delicate as the skin over a girl's wrist.
Suddenly I realize
That if I stepped out of my body I would break
Into blossom.

APPROACHING THE READING

1. The form of the poem relies on lineation. Consider the effects of the longer and shorter lines and of the variation between longer and shorter.

2. What techniques of inner arrangement do you find in the poem? What effects do they create?

3. What mood is evoked by the images throughout the poem?

4. Why do you think the speaker refers to this experience as a blessing? What are the denotations and connotations of *blessing*? Do any of them fit this poem?

5. Explain what is suggested by the last three lines.

APPROACHING THE AUTHOR

Joy Harjo performs her poetry and plays saxophone with her band, Poetic Justice. You can hear some of her music on her Web site.
For more about her, see page 1388.

Joy Harjo   b. 1951

She Had Some Horses   [1983]

She had some horses.

She had horses who were bodies of sand.
She had horses who were maps drawn of blood.
She had horses who were skins of ocean water.
She had horses who were the blue air of sky.   5
She had horses who were fur and teeth.
She had horses who were clay and would break.
She had horses who were splintered red cliff.

She had some horses.

She had horses with long, pointed breasts.   10
She had horses with full, brown thighs.
She had horses who laughed too much.

She had horses who threw rocks at glass houses.
She had horses who licked razor blades.

She had some horses.   15

She had horses who danced in their mothers' arms.
She had horses who thought they were the sun and their
bodies shone and burned like stars.
She had horses who waltzed nightly on the moon.
She had horses who were much too shy, and kept quiet   20
in stalls of their own making.

She had some horses.

She had horses who liked Creek Stomp Dance songs.
She had horses who cried in their beer.
She had horses who spit at male queens who made   25
them afraid of themselves.
She had horses who said they weren't afraid.
She had horses who lied.
She had horses who told the truth, who were stripped
bare of their tongues.   30

She had some horses.

She had horses who called themselves, "horse."
She had horses who called themselves, "spirit," and kept
their voices secret and to themselves.
She had horses who had no names.   35
She had horses who had books of names.

She had some horses.

She had horses who whispered in the dark, who were afraid to speak.
She had horses who screamed out of fear of the silence, who
carried knives to protect themselves from ghosts.   40
She had horses who waited for destruction.
She had horses who waited for resurrection.

She had some horses.

She had horses who got down on their knees for any saviour.
She had horses who thought their high price had saved them.   45
She had horses who tried to save her, who climbed in her
bed at night and prayed as they raped her.

She had some horses.

She had some horses she loved.
She had some horses she hated.   50

These were the same horses.

APPROACHING THE READING

1. This poem is composed using one of the oldest of forms, the litany. Read it aloud, feeling the rhythms of its lines and inner arrangement. Consider what the rhythm and repetition of litany contribute to the impact, effect, and power of the poem.

2. The poem uses other techniques for inner arrangement along with the list or litany. Pick out at least three and describe what each contributes to the poem's effectiveness.

3. What do you make of the last three lines?

4. Harjo has said that she has been asked the most about this poem and has the least to say about it. Speculate on why you think each is the case.

ENTRY POINTS   The following poem is about nature and ways it relates or speaks to human life. As you read and reread it, think about why the stanzaic form is appropriate for the poem; ways the form carries, adds to, or intensifies meaning; ways the form is aesthetically satisfying; and ways the form affects your reading.

APPROACHING THE AUTHOR

William Butler Yeats was tone-deaf. Ironically, in hopes of reviving the bardic tradition in Ireland, he fiercely advocated that his poems be sung or intoned while accompanied by the psaltery, a stringed instrument.
   For more about him, see page 1420.

William Butler Yeats 1865–1939

The Lake Isle of Innisfree   [1892]

I will arise and go now, and go to Innisfree,
And a small cabin build there, of clay and wattles made:
Nine bean-rows will I have there, a hive for the honey-bee,
And live alone in the bee-loud glade.

And I shall have some peace there, for peace comes dropping slow,   5
Dropping from the veils of the morning to where the cricket sings;
There midnight's all a glimmer, and noon a purple glow,
And evening full of the linnet's wings.

I will arise and go now, for always night and day
I hear lake water lapping with low sounds by the shore;   10
While I stand on the roadway, or on the pavements grey,
I hear it in the deep heart's core.

APPROACHING THE READING

1. Remember that *stanza* is derived from the Italian word for *room*. In what ways do the stanzas fulfill the idea of different "rooms" in the poem?

2. Notice that each stanza is a single sentence, with phrases arranged within the sentence to create a lyrical musicality. Read the poem again, paying attention to the phrasing and how it makes you feel. What makes this use of phrasing especially appropriate for the poem's subject?

3. The poem is rich with sounds. Read the poem aloud, listening for them, and point out a number of the techniques you notice. What do they create in the poem and in what ways are they appropriate? Notice, too, how Yeats uses words that create sounds in keeping with the images. Pick out some and describe their effect.

4. Describe the speaker. What is the speaker feeling? What does the speaker want? Think about the last line. What do you think the speaker means by, "I hear it in the deep heart's core"? Notice that it says "the deep heart's core" not "the heart's deep core." What for you is the difference?

ENTRY POINTS   The following three poems are sonnets, each quite different in content. The first was written in response to a summer of antiblack violence in several cities, particularly Chicago. The author said later that the poem did not refer directly to blacks and whites.

APPROACHING THE AUTHOR

Claude McKay was attracted to communism in his early life, but after a visit to the Soviet Union, he decided that communism was too disciplined and confining.

For more about him, see page 1400.

Claude McKay   1890–1948

If we must die   [1919]

If we must die, let it not be like hogs
Hunted and penned in an inglorious spot,
While round us bark the mad and hungry dogs,

Making their mock at our accursed lot.
If we must die, O let us nobly die,   5
So that our precious blood may not be shed
In vain; then even the monsters we defy
Shall be constrained to honor us though dead!
O kinsmen! we must meet the common foe!
Though far outnumbered let us show us brave,   10
And for their thousand blows deal one deathblow!
What though before us lies the open grave?
Like men we'll face the murderous, cowardly pack,
Pressed to the wall, dying, but fighting back!

APPROACHING THE READING

1. Outline the movement of the poem quatrain by quatrain. Note the way sentences are used to structure the four sections of the poem.

2. Consider the appropriateness of using a traditional sonnet for the poem's subject. Why is it effective to use a prescribed form for such an emotional situation?

3. Imagine the poem without meter, rhyme, and these specific line breaks. In what ways does its actual form contribute to its effect? What things might it lose if it were written in a freer form?

4. What ironies are suggested by having an African American voice speak within this most Anglo of poetic forms?

ENTRY POINTS   This sonnet celebrates beauty in the world, but beauty of a specific kind. It is a paean of appreciation for the appearance and demeanor of a man who, while standing on a street in Harlem, arrests the attention of the speaker. Consider how the sonnet form contributes to the poem's power and intensity.

APPROACHING THE AUTHOR

Helene Johnson, praised as one of the most-talented voices of the Harlem Renaissance, was often compared in form and style to Langston Hughes. Although she published only thirty-four poems and stopped publishing after 1937, she continued to write for herself, composing a poem a day for the rest of her life.

For more about her, see page 1394.

Helene Johnson 1906–1995

Sonnet to a Negro in Harlem   [1927]

You are disdainful and magnificent—
Your perfect body and your pompous gait,
Your dark eyes flashing solemnly with hate,
Small wonder that you are incompetent
To imitate those whom you so despise—   5
Your shoulders towering high above the throng,
Your head thrown back in rich, barbaric song,
Palm trees and mangoes stretched before your eyes.
Let others toil and sweat for labor's sake
And wring from grasping hands their meed° of gold.   *reward*   10
Why urge ahead your supercilious feet?
Scorn will efface each footprint that you make.
I love your laughter arrogant and bold.
You are too splendid for this city street.

APPROACHING THE READING

1. Notice the way the subject is adapted to the structure, with its turn after the octave. Summarize what is said in lines 1–8, in 9–12, and then in 13–14. In what ways are the form and its handling appropriate and effective?

2. In this sonnet, sentences do not coincide with the quatrains—the poem seems to be playing off against the form as well as adopting it. What makes that appropriate and effective for the content?

3. Like McKay in the previous poem, Johnson employs a form from the white literary tradition. What ironies do you see in that? It could be said she is claiming the form for her race as well as her purposes. Does anything in the poem support saying that?

ENTRY POINTS   As you read this poem, ride along as it roars ahead, feel its energy, and listen to the voice. Do your best to get a sense of the speaker's tone, which is key to experiencing this poem. Remember that tone usually reveals an attitude. Think about how casually the speaker "tosses out" one thing after another. What do you make of that?

APPROACHING THE AUTHOR

At the time of his death in 1962, **E. E. Cummings** was the most widely read poet in the United States, after Robert Frost.

For more about him, see page 1379.

E. E. Cummings 1894–1962

"next to of course god america i   [1926]

"next to of course god america i
love you land of the pilgrims' and so forth oh
say can you see by the dawn's early my
country 'tis of centuries come and go
and are no more what of it we should worry   5
in every language even deafanddumb
thy sons acclaim your glorious name by gorry
by jingo by gee by gosh by gum
why talk of beauty what could be more beaut-
iful than these heroic happy dead   10
who rushed like lions to the roaring slaughter
they did not stop to think they died instead
then shall the voice of liberty be mute?"

He spoke.   And drank rapidly a glass of water

APPROACHING THE READING

1. Talk about E. E. Cummings's juxtaposition of a formal, traditional, inherited sonnet structure with wildly inventive diction and syntax, an earthy speaker, and subversive content. What are the effects of this approach?

2. Do you think the poem is being critical? If so, of what? Of whom? Do you think the poem is affirming? If so, of what? Of whom?

3. Look closely at the internal form. What types of construction of the inner form do you notice? How do they contribute to the impact of the poem?

4. Discuss the tone of the poem. Be ready to talk about why the tone is especially important here and why it could be misunderstood. What do you make of the major shift from the next to last line to the isolated last line?

ENTRY POINTS   The following two poems are about grandparents and grandchildren, thus about generational separation, or even distance. In form they are very different: One is written in almost prose-like lines, the other is in a set, complicated, repetitive pattern. As you read and reflect on the two poems, think about the appropriateness of each form to its subject, how each form contributes to meaning, ways the form is aesthetically satisfying, and ways the form affects the way you read the poem.

APPROACHING THE AUTHOR

In addition to his poetry, **David Mura** creates performance and theater pieces and is founder of the Asian-American Renaissance, an arts organization in Minneapolis.

For more about him, see page 1402.

David Mura   b. 1952

Grandfather-in-Law   [1989]

It's nothing really, and really, it could have been worse, and of course,
    he's now several years dead,
and his widow, well, if oftentimes she's somewhat distracted, overly
    cautious when we visit—
after all, Boston isn't New York—she seems, for some reason, enormously
    proud that there's now a writer in the family,
and periodically, sends me clippings about the poet laureate, Thoreau,
    Anne Sexton's daughter, Lowell, New England literary lore—
in which I fit, if I fit at all, simply because I write in English—as if
    color of skin didn't matter anymore.   5
Still, years ago, during my first visit to Boston, when we were all
    asleep,
he, who used to require that my wife memorize lines of Longfellow or Poe
    and recite them on the phone,
so that, every time he called, she ran outdoors and had to be coaxed back,
    sometimes with threats, to talk to Pops
(though she remembers too his sly imitations of Lincoln, ice cream at
    Brighams, burgers and fries, all the usual grandfatherly treats),
he, who for some reason was prejudiced against Albanians—where on
    earth did he find them I wondered—   10
who, in the thirties, would vanish to New York, catch a show, buy a suit,
    while up north,
the gas and water bills pounded the front door (his spendthrift ways
    startled me with my grandfather's resemblance),
who for over forty years came down each morning, "How's the old goat?"
    with a tie only his wife could knot circling his neck,

he slipped into my wife's room — we were unmarried at the time — and
    whispered so softly she thought
he almost believed she was really asleep, and was saying this like a wish
    or spell, some bohunk miscalculated Boston sense of duty: 15
"Don't make a mistake with your life, Susie. Don't make a
    mistake . . ."
Well. The thing that gets me now, despite the dangling rantings I've let
    go, is that, at least at that time,
he was right: There was, inside me, some pressing, raw unpeeled persis-
    tence, some libidinous desire for dominance
that, in the scribbled first drafts of my life, seemed to mark me as wastrel
    and rageful, bound to be unfaithful,
to destroy, in some powerful, nuclear need, fissioned both by childhood
    and racism, whatever came near —   20
And I can't help but feel, forgiving him now, that if she had listened, if
    she had been awake,
if this flourishing solace, this muscled-for-happiness, shared by us now,
    had never awakened,
he would have become for me a symbol of my rage and self-destruction,
    another raw, never healing wound,
and not this silenced grandfatherly presence, a crank and scoundrel, red-
    necked Yankee who created the delicate seed of my wife, my child.

APPROACHING THE READING

1. The most notable formal feature of the poem is the use of long, prose-like
   lines. What effect do they create — in terms of the speaker, the overall situation, the tone, your role as reader?

2. Give some attention to the interplay of lines and sentences. What is the
   effect of the long, rambling sentences — on character, on tone, on rhythm?

3. Consider the inner arrangement of the poem. How does it bring out the
   conflicts between generations and their resolution? How does the idea of
   forgiveness in line 21 fit in?

Elizabeth Bishop 1911–1979

Sestina   [1965]

September rain falls on the house.
In the failing light, the old grandmother
sits in the kitchen with the child
beside the Little Marvel Stove,

reading the jokes from the almanac,   5
laughing and talking to hide her tears.

She thinks that her equinoctial tears
and the rain that beats on the roof of the house
were both foretold by the almanac,
but only known to a grandmother.   10
The iron kettle sings on the stove.
She cuts some bread and says to the child,

It's time for tea now; but the child
is watching the teakettle's small hard tears
dance like mad on the hot black stove,   15
the way the rain must dance on the house.
Tidying up, the old grandmother
hangs up the clever almanac

on its string. Birdlike, the almanac
hovers half open above the child,   20
hovers above the old grandmother
and her teacup full of dark brown tears.
She shivers and says she thinks the house
feels chilly, and puts more wood in the stove.

It was to be, says the Marvel Stove.   25
I know what I know, says the almanac.
With crayons the child draws a rigid house
and a winding pathway. Then the child
puts in a man with buttons like tears
and shows it proudly to the grandmother.   30

But secretly, while the grandmother
busies herself about the stove,
the little moons fall down like tears
from between the pages of the almanac
into the flower bed the child   35
has carefully placed in the front of the house.

Time to plant tears, says the almanac.
The grandmother sings to the marvellous stove
and the child draws another inscrutable house.

APPROACHING THE READING

1. Summarize what the poem is about, what's going on in it. What gives the
   poem a kind of folktale or children's story or fable feel? What do you make of
   the juxtaposition of that feeling with the "adultness" of the subject material?

2. Look up *sestina* in the glossary (p. 1484) and go through the poem, checking how it meets the specifications of the form. Consider the choice of repeated words and the effects created by repetition. In what ways does the repetition affect your reading?

3. In what ways does the sestina form add to the feel, the impact, of the poem? How does the form fit the subject? How does the form take part in creating the atmosphere of the poem?

4. Think about the speaker and the way the speaker uses language and syntax. How would you describe the speaker and the speaker's tone?

5. A nineteenth-century poet, the Comte de Gramont, described the sestina as "a reverie in which the same ideas, the same objects, occur to the mind in a succession of different aspects, which nonetheless resemble one another, fluid and changing shape like the clouds in the sky." Bishop's sestina has often been praised as one of the finest sestinas ever written. In light of Gramont's description, why do you think it has received that commendation?

ENTRY POINTS   As you read "Chinese Villanelle" for the first time, don't let its complexity intimidate you. Even on a first reading you can sense the intensity in the speaker's voice and the choice of words. Pay attention to the "you" that is addressed and think about what the speaker's feelings are toward that person. Notice also how the impact, and perhaps the meaning, of the repeated lines change. Also notice and consider the shift from reflecting on the past to acknowledging the present at the closing.

> **APPROACHING THE AUTHOR**
>
> Although **John Yau**'s parents spoke Chinese to each other, they refused to teach it to their children. As a result, Yau felt alienated from his Chinese heritage. This sense of cultural dislocation has influenced Yau's poetry throughout his career.
>   For more about him, see page 1420.

John Yau b. 1950

Chinese Villanelle   [1979]

I have been with you, and I have thought of you
Once the air was dry and drenched with light
I was like a lute filling the room with description

We watched glum clouds reject their shape
We dawdled near a fountain, and listened   5
I have been with you, and I have thought of you

Like a river worthy of its gown
And like a mountain worthy of its insolence . . .
Why am I like a lute left with only description

How does one cut an axe handle with an axe   10
What shall I do to tell you all my thoughts
When I have been with you, and thought of you

A pelican sits on a dam, while a duck
Folds its wings again; the song does not melt
I remember you looking at me without description   15

Perhaps a king's business is never finished,
Though "perhaps" implies a different beginning
I have been with you, and I have thought of you
Now I am a lute filled with this wandering description

APPROACHING THE READING

1. The villanelle is one of the strictest forms. In what ways do you think this
   form is appropriate for the subject of the poem? Think about what the
   repetition of lines may reveal about the speaker. Think about the repeated
   lines' changes in diction as well as the subtle ways they change in meaning
   and intensity depending on the lines that precede them.

2. Imagine you are the "you" in the poem. How would you respond to the
   speaker?

3. Notice the comparisons in the poem. Talk about how they affect the way
   you think of the speaker and the relationship between the speaker and the
   one addressed. In what ways do the comparisons lead you to see things in a
   new way?

4. Some would argue that there is a revealing juxtaposition between what is
   said and this highly formalized structure. If you agree, what do you think
   is revealed? Be ready to support your conclusion. If you disagree, explain
   why.

RESPONDING THROUGH Writing

WRITING ABOUT FORM AND TYPE

Journal Entries

1. Choose a poem and change the way it is divided into lines. Then write in your journal about what you discovered from these changes.

2. Be on the lookout for **found poetry**, that is, prose found in newspapers, magazines, advertisements, textbooks, or elsewhere in everyday life that contains elements of poetry, such as effective rhythm, phrasings that can be divided into lines, meter, imaginative uses of language and sound, and so on. Collect several examples for your journal, dividing them carefully into poetic lines. Comment briefly on what this revealed to you about choices poets make about line divisions and about their effect.

You can research the authors in this chapter with LitLinks at bedfordstmartins.com/ rewritinglit.

3. In your journal, describe and discuss briefly the inner arrangements for two of the following poems: Richard Lovelace's "To Lucasta, Going to the Wars" (p. 837), Henry Reed's "Naming of Parts" (p. 854), Cheryl Savageau's "Bones — A City Poem" (p. 883), Charles Simic's "Classic Ballroom Dances" (p. 864), or Mark Strand's "Eating Poetry" (p. 867).

Literary Analysis Papers

4. For one of the following poems, write a paper describing its form and discussing the effectiveness and appropriateness of its distinctive handling of lines: Charles Bukowski's "my old man" (p. 598), Allen Ginsberg's "A Supermarket in California" (p. 808), Jane Hirshfield's "To Drink" (p. 820), Wendy Rose's "Loo-Wit" (p. 861), or Nancy Willard's "Questions My Son Asked Me, Answers I Never Gave Him" (p. 880).

5. The form of May Swenson's "The Shape of Death" (p. 868), with its two parallel columns, makes unusual demands of a reader. Write a paper discussing what is going on in the poem and how form contributes to its effectiveness.

6. Write a paper explicating a sonnet with emphasis on the way its structure fits and brings out its subject and theme. Use a traditional sonnet such as John Milton's "When I consider how my light is spent" (p. 843) or Edmund Spenser's "One day I wrote her name upon the strand" (p. 866), or use a poem that seems surprising to see in sonnet form, such as Gary Miranda's "Love Poem" (p. 668).

Comparison-Contrast Papers

7. Write a paper on two or more poems that focus on what poetry is and does, as for example Heather McHugh's "What He Thought" (p. 839), Marianne Moore's "Poetry" (p. 843), and Mark Strand's "Eating Poetry" (p. 867). Compare and contrast their ideas and the way form and type contribute to what the poems say and do.

8. Write a paper comparing the free verse form used in two of the following poems and discussing for each how the invented form fits and accentuates the poem's subject and theme: Cornelius Eady's "My Mother, If She Had Won Free Dance Lessons" (p. 795), Linda Hogan's "Crow Law" (p. 822),

TIPS for Writing about Form and Type

- **Look for the unusual.** When a poem's form is quite unusual, or when it contributes in a significant way to effect or meaning, it can make a revealing topic for a paper. Handling it successfully requires describing the form in detail and explaining carefully how and why it creates the effects it does. But even when you are writing about other elements in a poem, it can be helpful to include a brief description of the poem's form or type (for example, mentioning that it's in blank verse or a variation on the Italian sonnet or free verse).

- **Look for juxtapositions.** Even when writing about other elements, it is wise to watch for juxtapositions. They can highlight the importance of particular images or the speaker's vision or point of view, or how a poem takes a common way of seeing and turns it into a fresh way. They can be an important structural feature, often emphasizing how things that ordinarily are not associated with one another create a dynamic experience when placed together. A single juxtaposition can sometimes make an entire poem cohere.

- **Consider what to cover.** A paper dealing with form doesn't have to cover all aspects. Good papers can result from focusing on one aspect, such as handling of line breaks, line lengths, meter, stanza structures, collage, or shape.

- **Consider form in free verse.** Form can lead to a perceptive paper (or part of a topic) on free-verse poetry, especially when the form is strikingly apt for the poem's subject. Such a paper must go beyond describing the form and include discussion of the form's appropriateness, its effects, its possible meaningfulness, and the ways it embodies the artistry of the poem as a whole.

- **Consider the effect of using a traditional type.** For poems written in traditional types (such as sonnet, sestina, or villanelle), you might discuss why the choice of type is fitting and why it is effective. This can make for a whole paper or a segment of a broader one.

Gary Soto's "Moving Away" (p. 865), or Quincy Troupe's "A Poem for 'Magic'" (p. 825).

WRITING ABOUT CONNECTIONS

Obviously connections occur between poems using the same inherited form, and several of the topics above involve looking at how two or more poets handle sonnets and sestinas. One can also find connections between free-verse poems through formal strategies or techniques. In addition to formal connections, thematic connections can be found between poems in the same form and across forms, between poets writing in the same century or different centuries. Here are a few topic possibilities:

1. "Amazing Grace": Being Blessed from Within and from Without in Mary Oliver's "First Snow" (p. 644) and James Wright's "A Blessing" (p. 690)
2. "'Which thou must leave ere long'": Confronting Separation in Elizabeth Bishop's "Sestina" (p. 699) and William Shakespeare's "That time of year thou mayst in me behold" (p. 680)
3. "The Solace of Solitude": Place and Peace in Wendell Berry's "The Peace of Wild Things" (p. 588) and Henry Reed's "Naming of Parts" (p. 854)

WRITING RESEARCH PAPERS

1. Research the significance of turtles (especially Grandfather Turtle) in Native American legends and use what you find to illuminate the Father Turtle story in Leslie Marmon Silko's "Prayer to the Pacific" (p. 685).

2. Research the history, use, and development of the villanelle as a form, and write a paper in which you discuss how a villanelle "works" (how it affects and appeals to poets and to readers), illustrating it with examples from at least two villanelles, perhaps the ones in this book—Dylan Thomas's "Do not go gentle into that good night" (p. 873) and John Yau's "Chinese Villanelle" (p. 701)—or others that you find.

CHAPTER 18 **Writing about Poetry**
Applying What You've Learned

We write about poetry for the same reasons we write about fiction—to participate in an ongoing conversation about things that interest, provoke, excite, or puzzle us about the literary works we read. After asking a friend or classmate about the meaning of a line (What's the point behind Marge Piercy's "Barbie Doll" cutting off her nose and legs and "offer[ing] them up"?) and participating in class discussion of the poem (What does it show about attitudes toward women that she was "advised to play coy, / exhorted to come on hearty, / exercise, diet, smile and wheedle"? Would men be told things like that?), you might decide to write a paper on "Marge Piercy's Critique of Social Attitudes toward Women in 'Barbie Doll.'"

Chapters 12–17 helped prepare you to read poetry with increasing sensitivity, alertness and confidence and also prepared you to write about poetry. Each chapter provides ways to move into a poem and to enlarge your experience of the variety of things happening in it: in terms of subject matter, formal elements, range of effects, and techniques through which effects are achieved. The section on short papers in Chapter 2 (pp. 30–43) provides you with general guidance for writing essays on literature. This chapter examines the particular challenges posed by writing about poetry.

We gave students in one of our introduction to literature classes the following assignment: Write a two- to three-page paper discussing how one of the following poems explores an author's experience with nature—James Wright's "A Blessing" (p. 690), William Stafford's "Traveling through the Dark" (p. 639), or Mary Oliver's "First Snow" (p. 644). One of our students, Sunkyo Hong, chose to write on "First Snow." This chapter follows Sunkyo through the writing process in completing that assignment, using

706

his own words as he retraces his steps. Reading or rereading "First Snow" will make this chapter easier to follow and to apply to your own work.

Step 1. Prewriting: Finding a Topic

When looking for a topic, look first for a poem you enjoy reading and thinking about. Usually you will write best when you deal with a work you enjoy. It's wise to spread a dozen or more readings of the poem over at least a week. Coming back to a poem every day leads you to see things that reading it several times in one sitting won't. Sometimes read the poem aloud; sometimes — if you can arrange it — listen to someone else read it. Each time you read the poem, focus on a different aspect — one time on the speaker and voice, another time on images, another time on rhythm, and so on. Photocopy the poem and mark it up; jot notes that you can come back to later. When you do this, the poem becomes part of you (to the point that you'll probably even be able to recite parts or all of it from memory).

Poetry often involves transforming an experience into words. One topic might focus on such an experience and why the poet might have wanted to express something about it. Another kind of topic might involve what techniques the poet uses. For this kind of paper, you might pay attention to what stands out and seems important in the way the poem is handled or focus on things that might escape immediate notice but turn out to be very significant in shaping the poem's effect. The way a poem handles voice or images or figures of speech or line endings or rhythm may become the entire focus of a literary analysis paper. Another paper might focus on ideas explored in the poem. Be sure to pick topics that appeal to or challenge you enough that you can discuss them in detail in a thematic analysis paper. You might also consider whether social or cultural context influences the poem significantly. If so, that might be meaningful to examine and write about. To generate ideas, keep asking questions: What is the poem revealing? What is the poem doing? Why is this or that handled the way it is? What is the effect or impact of the poet's use of particular elements? What if it were done differently?

Sunkyo got started by first getting a clear understanding of the assignment and then deciding to do an analytic paper on themes and techniques in "First Snow."

> A student, Sunkyo Hong, on finding a topic: "When I was given the assignment, I read the three poems several times each, looking for possible meanings, alternative interpretations, and structural clues. I liked all of the choices, but I was drawn to 'First Snow' because I felt I could relate to it,  since I like snow, and because the poem does a great job of conveying wonder with pictures and comparisons. Having decided on a poem, I had my topic: the author's experience with nature in Mary Oliver's 'First Snow.'"

We have provided suggestions for paper topics at the ends of Chapters 13, 14, 15, 16, and 17. If you're still looking for a topic, you might look at those again (pp. 591, 624, 649, 671, and 703). Here are a dozen additional possibilities:

1. An analysis of the interaction of form and feeling in Li-Young Lee's "Visions and Interpretations" (p. 832)
2. Similarities and differences in tone, technique, and theme in Lucille Clifton's "at the cemetery, walnut grove plantation, south carolina, 1989" (p. 662) and Thomas Gray's "Elegy Written in a Country Churchyard" (available online)
3. An exploration of cultural stereotypes in Olga Broumas's "Cinderella" (p. 775)
4. An explication dealing with diction and meaning in Michael S. Harper's "Nightmare Begins Responsibility" (p. 815)
5. The handling of the loss of innocence or "coming of age" theme in Elizabeth Bishop's "In the Waiting Room" (p. 770) and Julia Alvarez's "How I Learned to Sweep" (p. 647)
6. Cultural misunderstandings and tensions in Samuel Hazo's "For Fawzi in Jerusalem" (p. 817), Luis J. Rodriguez's "Running to America" (p. 858), or James Welch's "Christmas Comes to Moccasin Flat" (p. 874)
7. A consideration of two of the following poems about fathers: Li-Young Lee's "Eating Alone" (p. 596), Charles Bukowski's "my old man" (p. 598), Judith Ortiz Cofer's "My Father in the Navy" (p. 728), and Sylvia Plath's "Daddy" (p. 851)
8. The theme of searching for truth in Margaret Atwood's "True Stories" (p. 764) and Li-Young Lee's "Visions and Interpretations" (p. 832)
9. An analysis of how Dudley Randall's "Ballad of Birmingham" (p. 853) follows and adapts the ballad tradition, bringing in "Sir Patrick Spens" (p. 763) as an example of the traditional ballad
10. An explication focused on the role of personification and metaphor in Emily Dickinson's "Because I could not stop for Death" (p. 790)
11. The use of one or more of the following poems in exploring war and peace: Wilfred Owen's "Dulce et Decorum Est" (p. 619), Thomas Hardy's "The Man He Killed" (p. 814), Henry Reed's "Naming of Parts" (p. 854), and/or May Swenson's "The Shape of Death" (p. 868)
12. The relation of language to cultural separation and acceptance in such poems as Allison Joseph's "On Being Told I Don't Speak Like a Black Person" (p. 582), Marilyn Chin's "How I Got That Name" (p. 779), Terrance Hayes's "Talk" (p. 816), and/or James Welch's "Christmas Comes to Moccasin Flat" (p. 874). Include some discussion of why poetry is an appropriate form for exploring this topic.

Step 2. Prewriting: Narrowing the Topic

Although most poems are shorter than most stories and plays, you can't write about everything in them. There's simply too much going on in terms of techniques and themes. You need to focus on what interests you and is particularly significant or valuable to your topic. For discussing poems as well as stories and plays, Benjamin De Mott's technique of focusing on "key passages" (see p. 40) often works well. Reread the poem, marking it up further and jotting more notes to yourself. Then look for connections between what you've marked or jotted. Such connections will likely point you toward a way of limiting the topic. See the box to the right for details on how Sunkyo narrowed his topic.

> **A student, Sunkyo Hong, on narrowing his topic:** "Limiting my topic came about mostly through taking notes as I worked through the poem intensively. I started outlining the main topics dealt with in the poem: It snows all day, it stops snowing at night, the speaker walks out in the snow, the speaker describes not just the snow but the way the snow makes her feel. I decided to try focusing my topic on wonder, in two of its senses, as a noun (a sense of amazement or admiration) and as a verb (to be curious about, to question)."

Step 3. Prewriting: Deciding on an Approach

We say in Chapter 2 that there are four major categories of approaches you can take in a paper about literature: literary analysis, comparison-contrast, social and cultural analysis, or a combination of these (see pp. 34–36). Sometimes, of course, the topic you select or the assignment you are given tells you the approach to take. But other times part of the process of focusing your topic and preparing to frame a thesis, and then deciding how to develop it, involves figuring out what approach the topic needs.

CHECKING ALTERNATIVES   If indeed you do need to figure out what approach to take, the best way to start is to notice whether the topic focuses on what goes on *inside* the poem, in theme or technique (literary analysis), focuses on *connections* between your poem and another one (comparison-contrast), or focuses on what infuses the poem but also *surrounds* the poem (social and cultural criticism). For example, looking at some of the topics listed under Step 1 above, topic 4 (An explication dealing with diction and meaning in Michael S. Harper's "Nightmare Begins Responsibility") clearly involves literary analysis. It concentrates on what goes on inside the poem. On the other hand, if you want to work on topic 8 (The theme of searching for truth in Margaret Atwood's "True Stories" and Li-Young Lee's "Visions and Interpretations"), it will require you to compare and contrast the kinds of questions about truth or reality each is asking (and perhaps answering). Topic 3, on exploring cultural stereotypes in Olga Broumas's "Cinderella," will involve social or cultural analysis. Unless you're already well versed in gender stereotypes, you'll need to do some exploring on the Internet or in the library and bring what you find to bear on the topic. You might also want to look into the background of the poem, to see, for example, what gender relationships were like when the poem was written in the 1970s.

EXPLICATING A POEM   We want to focus for a moment on the first of the alternative approaches above, literary analysis. Analysis of a poem often takes the form of **explication**. Explication involves looking closely at a poem, opening it up line by line, clarifying how diction, images, figurative language, symbols, sounds, rhythm, form, and allusions contribute to shaping what the poem says or depicts or reveals and to its effect. Such analysis should never isolate a single feature from the rest of the work; instead, it must always look closely at how the feature contributes to seeing the entire poem more clearly and fully. Explication often focuses on ambiguities, complexities, gaps, and the interrelationships within a text. It requires you to be especially attentive to specific words and phrases, considering their effects, discussing the impact and implications of ambiguities and subtleties, and explaining how these elements work together toward a particular purpose or theme. For longer poems, you may need to explicate only a key passage and relate it to the whole poem.

ORGANIZING AN EXPLICATION   An explication paper can be organized by going through the poem from beginning to end, line by line (or section by section), clarifying how techniques and features in the lines create their meaning or effect. This is the way Sunkyo organized his paper. If you use this approach, make sure your paper has a unifying principle and a central idea (thesis), as Sunkyo's does.

An explication paper also can be organized topically. That is, one paragraph might discuss the poem's use of images, another its use of figures, and others its tone, use of sound techniques, and rhythm. Each paragraph should include examples from different parts of the poem, chosen so that somewhere in the paper nearly every line or combination of lines is discussed (though not necessarily in the order they appear in the poem). Each paragraph needs to explain how the element it covers contributes to building the total effect of the poem. An advantage of this approach is that it usually runs less risk of sliding into a mere summary of the poem than the line-by-line approach does.

The shaded box to the left contains what Sunkyo said about the approach his topic needed.

A student, Sunkyo Hong, on choosing an approach: "The assignment pretty much prescribed the approach for my paper. When the assignment says, 'discuss how one of the following poems explores an author's experience with nature,' it is telling me to do an analysis, to look closely at and into the poem. My challenge is not deciding on an approach but deciding on what kind of analysis, of themes or techniques or both. I decided on both."

Step 4. Prewriting: Framing a Thesis

Chapter 2 explains that an effective paper on literature needs a thesis, a central idea that is developed and supported. Your job as a writer is to convince your readers that your idea is sound and helpful, worth considering seriously. You might want to review pages 36–39 on ways of making sure you have an idea-based thesis. Sometimes students feel so good about having figured out what a poem is about that they want to demonstrate what they know by summarizing it. If you are given an assignment asking you to summarize or paraphrase a poem, explaining what the poem is about is acceptable. But a summary is never enough if you are asked to write a paper; you must go further. Such a paper must clarify or explain things about the poem, perhaps about how it's written, what is significant about what it says or does, how it relates to another poem, or what cultural or social issues are connected to it, to the author's experiences, or to your own. See box to the right for what Sunkyo says about framing his thesis.

Step 5. Writing: Developing and Supporting the Thesis

Methods of developing and supporting the ideas in a literature paper are discussed fully in Chapter 2. It might be good for you to go back and reread the sections on how to explain and illustrate, include quotations, focus on key passages, and avoid summary (see pp. 39–42). The development and support of the arguments you advance will be the heart of your paper. The most brilliant insights are of little value if they can't be supported convincingly.

A student, Sunkyo Hong, on turning his topic into a thesis: "I started with this as an elaboration of my topic: 'Mary Oliver's poem "First Snow" is about a time when it snowed and what the experience was like for the author. The author found the snow wonderful and beautiful. When she stepped out into the snow, she felt that an "answer [had] been found" (line 31).' I then worked further on the poem to gain a thorough in-depth knowledge of it. I looked up words, for example, *rhetoric* (with its phrase 'white rhetoric') and *oracular*. Then I focused on the questions raised by the speaker in the poem: 'its white / rhetoric everywhere / calling us back to *why, how,* / *whence* such beauty and *what* / the meaning.' I spent a lot of time pondering those lines and rereading the poem to see how they fit in, how they relate to 'oracular.' What kind of divinely inspired pronouncement was the snow making? Eventually I came up with the following as a tentative thesis: 'Watching the snow from inside, the author had felt wonder at the sight. Now being in it, she feels a part of it. It might be that questions cannot continue to be uttered in the profound silence, and the light feels enlightening, so in a way, the author has found the answer to her questions through experiencing the snow.'"

A strong argument includes evidence from the poem: quotations that bolster your view. Handling poetry quotations involves some unique conventions. It is important that you follow the tips on the following page.

TIPS for Quoting Poetry

Because of the line divisions in poetry, some conventions for dealing with quotations are unique to poetry. Here are four tips on handling poetry quotations:

- **Fewer than four lines of poetry.** Blend them into your sentence, using a slash, with a space before and after, to indicate line divisions:

  My favorite part of Gary Miranda's "Love Poem" is, "or the chance / meanings, not even remotely intended, that dance / at the edge of words, like sparks" (lines 4–6).

- **Four or more lines of poetry.** Type them into the paper as a block quotation with each line on a separate line. Indent the passage an inch and a half or two inches from the left. The passage should look the same way it looks in the source, with the same indentations and spacing. If you begin the quotation in the middle of a poetic line, place the first word approximately where it occurs in the line, not at the left-hand margin. (See, for example, Sunkyo Hong's paper, p. 717.)

- **Citations.** Cite line numbers in parentheses at the end of the passage for lines quoted or cited. For the first reference, include the word "line" (not abbreviated); for later references, give the numbers alone. Page numbers will be included on the Works Cited page.

- **Omissions.** If you omit words, indicate that by including an ellipsis (see p. 54). If you omit a complete line or more than one line, indicate this by a row of spaced periods as long as a line of the poem.

Here's what Sunkyo says about how he developed and supported his thesis:

A student, Sunkyo Hong, on developing and supporting his thesis: "Once I had a working thesis, the first challenge in developing it was deciding how to organize the steps in my discussion of the poem, how to divide it up. I decided to go through the poem from beginning to end, dividing it into three sections: lines 1–12, on the speaker looking back on how the snow fell all day; lines 12–27, that night as the speaker shifts to present tense and reflects on how everything looks and feels different now; and lines 28–36, which shift from description to participation, as the speaker goes out into the snow and seems to find answers to the questions asked in section one. Each section has a crux to deal with—a group of lines that I needed to study carefully, looking up words and figuring out what was going on in them. For each section I chose lines to quote and discuss in detail, trying as I did so to unify the paper by relating parts to each other. With all this sketched out, I just started writing a first draft."

Step 6. Revising, Proofreading, and Formatting

Chapter 2 covers the importance of careful revision and editing (proofreading) and offers tips for doing it well. We suggest that you review them (pp. 43–45) before you proceed with this step. Here's the way Sunkyo revised and edited his first draft.

A student, Sunkyo Hong, on revising and proofreading: "I don't like working with technically clumsy drafts, so I like to make technical corrections and adjustments before I revise content and structure. For example, I deleted the word 'line' from all the citations in parentheses following quotations except the first one, to follow MLA practice—that the rest also refer to line numbers can be inferred. I put *oracular* and *fever* in italics in the third paragraph of the draft because that is the convention when looking at words as words. And I caught a few mistakes in punctuation. I changed the quotation in draft paragraph 4 to an indented quotation because in the final paper it is more than three lines long.

In regard to content, there were four major things I felt I should work on:

(1) I needed a better title, one that was not just a heading but that reflected the central idea in the paper.

(2) I needed a better opening paragraph. The original one is short and thin, only vaguely touching on what the paper will discuss. I want the beginning to be more appealing and inviting, and I want to give readers help in following the movement of the paper. After experimenting with a couple of openings, I decided to preface the essay with a personal anecdote because the experience described in the poem is personal.

(3) The fourth paragraph needs refocusing: Elsewhere I describe the author's experiences; here I get caught up in what the candles are and are not. I can get to focusing on the experience by putting the word pictures back into the context of the grand scene, since the choice of words used to describe a scene reveals how the writer experiences that scene.

(4) The ending needs to be improved. It feels a bit abrupt, and somehow doesn't seem to convey a satisfying conclusive touch. I had to do a lot of experimenting to find a solution that felt right to me."

SAMPLE SHORT PAPER

Here is the first draft of Sunkyo's paper. To allow you to see more of Sunkyo's writing process, we've printed the rough draft of his paper on the left-hand pages, and the final draft on the right-hand pages.

ROUGH DRAFT

Mary Oliver's "First Snow"

Mary Oliver's poem "First Snow" is about a time when it snowed, and what that experience was like for the author. In the poem, the author finds snow wonderful and beautiful. When she steps out into the snow, she feels that an "answer has been found" (line 31).

The poem begins with the author describing how the snow began: "The snow / began here / this morning" (lines 1–3). With this opening, the author gives the reader a natural starting place. This opening is similar to the common story opening, i.e., "Once upon a time in such and such a place."

The poem then proceeds to say that the snow kept falling throughout the day (lines 3–4) and describes how the snow fell and what it seemed like. The snow falling had "white / rhetoric everywhere" (lines 4–5). Rhetoric is persuasive speaking or writing. The next lines say what the snow's white rhetoric was doing: "calling us back to *why, how, / whence* such beauty and *what / the meaning*" (lines 6–8). The rhetoric was persuading the author to wonder, in the literal sense, about the beauty and meaning of the snow and wonder at it in the sense of amazement also. The questions of "why, how, whence such beauty" and "what the

Here is the revised, final draft of Sunkyo's paper.

FINAL DRAFT

Sunkyo Hong
Professor Ridl
English 248
15 May 2010

Experiencing "First Snow"

I had seen snow before coming to college in Michigan, but never like this. I woke up one December morning to find yesterday's green lawns a continuous, smooth, white expanse. The indifferent ground of the day before now noticed my shoe soles and kept their shape as I took a few experimental steps outside the doorway. Another time, as I walked through the pine grove in the center of campus during a large-flaked snowfall, I could not see a single campus building or a single person. I felt that I had somehow stepped into a gentle winter world without time. It was calming how the falling of a million flaky water-drops could transform a landscape and absorb my attention.

Mary Oliver's poem "First Snow" recalls a similar experience. In the poem, Oliver describes the snowfall, from the morning, when it began, to the night, when it ended. Her chronological tracing of the event allows us to experience the same wonder and admiration she feels in watching the snow and its effects.

The poem begins with the author describing how the snow began: "The snow / began here / this morning" (lines 1–3). With this opening, the author gives the reader a natural starting place. The opening is similar to the common story opening, that is, "Once upon a time in such and such a place."

The poem continues with Oliver describing how the snow fell throughout the day and what it was like. The snow falling had "white / rhetoric everywhere" (4–5). Rhetoric is persuasive speaking or writing. The next lines say what the snow's "white rhetoric"

ROUGH DRAFT
---

meaning" indicate that the author is dumbfounded. Her sense of amazement continues into the next line, where she exclaims "such / an oracular fever!" (lines 8–9). "Oracular" means of an oracle, and therefore inspired, authoritative, or sent from above. "Fever" can mean having a high body temperature or a state of excitement or activity. Since there is no indication in the poem that the author is ill, "fever" describes how the snow is moving and the excitement the author is feeling. Thus, the oracular fever is both the swirling flurry of snow the author sees and the inspired, giddy feeling she gets from watching it.

Until now, the poem has been about how the snow has fallen throughout the day and has been told in the past tense. For the rest of the poem, the author focuses on the present, describing how the scene is now, blanketed by snow. By line 13, it is night, and the snow has stopped falling. The author can feel the silence because it is "immense" (lines 15–16). And although it is night, the sky still brims with light as if lit by "a million candles" (line 18). At first, it seems like the million candles are stars, but lines 18–20 show that there are no stars: "nowhere / the familiar things: / stars." Whatever the candles are is not obvious, but it is clear that they convey the sense of brightness, which is further developed by the details of smoldering fields (lines 24–25), "shining hills" (line 27), and "light / under the trees" (lines 33–34). Light is there in abundance and changes the appearance of things. It obscures the stars, the moon, and the darkness (lines 20–21). It allows the trees to "glitter like castles / of ribbons" (lines 22–24).

was doing: "calling us back to *why, how, / whence* such beauty and *what* / the meaning" (6–8). The rhetoric was persuading the author to wonder, in the literal sense, about the beauty and meaning of the snow and wonder at it in the sense of amazement also. The questions of *"why, how, / whence* such beauty" and *"what* / the meaning" indicate that the author is dumbfounded. Her sense of amazement continues into the next line, where she exclaims "such / an oracular fever!" (8–9). *Oracular* means pertaining to an oracle, thus a prophetic utterance, often enigmatic or mysterious. Since there is no indication of illness in the poem, *fever* describes how the snow is moving and the excitement the author is feeling. Thus, the "oracular fever" is both the swirling flurry of snow the author sees and the inspired feeling of awe and mystery she gets from watching it. We share her marvel as we witness the snow-white energy "[flow] / past [the] windows" (9–10) and show no sign of waning or becoming "less than lovely" (12).

Until now, the poem has been about how the snow has fallen throughout the day, and it has been told in the past tense. For the rest of the poem, Oliver focuses on the present, describing how the scene is now blanketed by snow. By line 13 it is night, and the snow has stopped falling. The author can feel the silence because it is "immense" (15–16). Although it is night, the sky still brims with light as if lit by "a million candles" (18). At first, it seems as if the million candles are stars, but lines 18–22 show that the skyscape has been transformed so much because of the snow that the stars are not visible:

> nowhere
> the familiar things:
> stars, the moon,
> the darkness we expect
> and nightly turn from.

─── **ROUGH DRAFT** ───

In the final part of the poem, the author steps out into the snow. She has observed the snow falling all day, so the questions that have "assailed" (line 29) her are none other than "*why, how, / whence* such beauty and *what /* the meaning" (lines 6–8) in the snowfall. The author says in the final line that walking out into the snow — "into the silence and the light / under the trees, / and through the fields" (lines 33–35) — "feels like" an answer (line 36). Watching the snow from inside, the author had felt wonder at the sight. Now being in it, she feels a part of it. It might be that questions cannot continue to be uttered in the profound silence and the light feels enlightening, so in a way, the author has found the answer to her questions in experiencing the snow.

Hong 3

The heavens are bright, with "broad fields / smolder[ing] with light" (24–25) and "a passing / creekbed ... / heaped with shining hills" (25–27). There is "light / under the trees" (33–34). The "broad fields" and "shining hills" indicate that the landscape has also changed. In this burning landscape, trees glitter with frost "like castles / of ribbons" (22–24), reminding us of some romantic fantasyland.

 The final section of the poem shifts from a description of the snow-covered scene to participation in it. Oliver and her companions—let us imagine we are they—walk out into the snow and feel that an answer has been found: "[T]he questions / that have assailed us all day / remain" (28–30) — *why, how, / whence* such beauty and *what* / the meaning" (6–8) — and "not a single / answer has been found" (30–31). We had been wondering at the sight all day. Now, trooping "into the silence and the light / under the trees, / and through the fields" (33–35) — in short, immersing ourselves in the snow that made us wonder — "feels like [an answer]" (36). This is because walking out into the snow places us in the wonder itself, and that experience somehow satisfies our wonder without diminishing it. Thus, the answer is the experience.

 "First Snow" presents an impressionistic account of a snowfall. The poem unfolds chronologically, and this ordering enables us to follow Oliver's experience vicariously with ease. The author witnesses the seemingly infinite falling of the snow throughout the day, observes the transformed landscape after the snow has stopped falling, and feels the immense silence when walking out into the snow. We share her wonder at each step, and at the end of the poem we share the answer of stepping out into the snow with our imaginations. This experiential answer is what makes every snowfall a "first snow."

All I know is that I'm a writer, period, writing about the one thing that defines me as a human being — my biculturalism.

Judith Ortiz Cofer

Judith Ortiz Cofer

CHAPTER 19 **A Poet in Personal Context — Judith Ortiz Cofer**

Two Worlds, One Vision

Judith Ortiz Cofer° was born in 1952 in Hormigueros, a small city at the western end of Puerto Rico. Her family moved to Paterson, New Jersey, in 1955, when her father, after joining the U.S. Navy, was assigned to the Brooklyn shipyard in New York City. For the next decade, whenever her father went on a lengthy sea tour, he sent his wife and children to Puerto Rico because he regarded Paterson as a place unsafe for a woman and her children to be alone. As a result, Ortiz Cofer° grew up moving between two very different worlds, something that later highly influenced her writing. Her works draw their power and vision from that bifurcation, from a search for stability and a sense of belonging in very different places, but not finding them fully in either.

That sense of bifurcation was accentuated by the differences between her father and mother. Her father, quiet and intellectual, sought always to escape Puerto Rico and the limitations he felt it imposed on him. He joined the navy, moved to New Jersey, made it a goal to move outside the barrio,° and made sure his children mastered English and received good educations. His wife, on the other hand, loved Puerto Rico and longed for it whenever

---

Ortiz Cofer: Although we use *Ortiz Cofer* in referring to her in the text, in alphabetizing we will follow the Library of Congress practice of placing the author's name with the Cs.   **the barrio:** The Puerto Rican neighborhood.

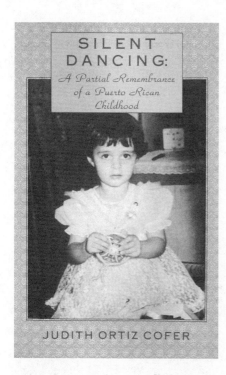

JUDITH ORTIZ COFER

Judith Ortiz Cofer's well-received collection of essays and poems, Silent Dancing, *was published in 1991 with an image of Ortiz Cofer as a young girl on the cover.*

she was on the mainland. She never learned English because she thought of her life in New Jersey as an "exile" and a temporary stay. She made every attempt to surround herself with a Puerto Rican environment: She served only Puerto Rican foods bought at Puerto Rican shops, listened to Puerto Rican music, and told stories of life in Puerto Rico.

Ortiz Cofer and her brother did their best to deal with a new language and culture on the mainland but, at the same time, felt torn between their parents' conflicting outlooks. As a result, Ortiz Cofer turned inward and found solace and companionship in books. As she put it in the chapter entitled "Casa" in her memoir *Silent Dancing*, "Being the outsiders . . . turned my brother and me into cultural chameleons, developing early the ability to blend into a crowd, to sit and read quietly in a fifth story apartment building for days and days when it was too bitterly cold to play outside" (17–18).

When Ortiz Cofer was in high school, her father retired from the navy and the family moved to Augusta, Georgia, adding even more complexity to the issues that result from having a diverse cultural background. The South was so overwhelmingly different from New Jersey that in *The Latin Deli* Ortiz Cofer compares it to "moving from one planet to another." In a high school of almost two thousand students, she was the only Puerto Rican. Her academic life was very successful, but her social life was all but nonexistent.

A recent portrait of Judith Ortiz Cofer
Reprinted by permission of University of Georgia,
Peter Frey.

She received a scholarship from Augusta College, and soon after her graduation in 1971, she married and had a daughter. After completing a graduate degree, she began teaching English. But, she says, something was missing from her life: She realized that she needed to write. The problem was finding time, so she began getting up at 5:00 A.M. to give herself two hours for writing, a ritual she refined and continues today. She describes her routine in *The Latin Deli*: "I get up at five and put on a pot of coffee. Then I sit in my rocking chair and read what I did the previous day until the coffee is ready. I take fifteen minutes to drink two cups of coffee . . . [and] when I'm ready, I write." This decision, she goes on, "to get up early and to work every day, forced me to come to terms with the discipline of art. I wrote my poems in this manner for nearly ten years before my first book was published. When I decided to give my storytelling impulse full rein and write a novel, I divided my two hours: the first hour for poetry, the second for fiction: two pages minimum per day."

Her first book of poetry, *Reaching for the Mainland*, was published in 1987, followed by *Terms of Survival* (1989) and *A Love Story Beginning in Spanish* (2005). *The Latin Deli: Prose and Poetry* (1993) received the Anisfield Wolf Book Award, and *The Year of Our Revolution: New and Selected Stories and Poems* (1998) received the Paterson Book Prize given by the Poetry Center at Passaic County Community College. In addition to poetry and stories, Ortiz Cofer has published two novels, *The Line of the Sun* (1989) and *The Meaning of Consuelo* (2003); a memoir, *Silent Dancing: A Partial*

Remembrance of a Puerto Rican Childhood (1990); a book about writing, *Woman in Front of the Sun: On Becoming a Writer* (2000); and two young adult novels, *Call Me Maria* (2004) and *If I Could Fly* (2011). Her young adult book *An Island Like You: Stories of the Barrio* (1996) was awarded the American Library Association Reforma Pura Belpre Medal and the Fanfare Best Book of the Year award. She is Regents' and Franklin Professor of English and Creative Writing at the University of Georgia and lives with her husband on the family farm near Louisville, Georgia.

As the preceding paragraph indicates, Ortiz Cofer writes successfully in a wide variety of genres, even combining them in the same collection. She started with and remains centered in poetry—admitting, "Poetry is [her] obsession"—and has added to that corpus short stories, adolescent fiction, novels, creative nonfiction, and memoir. She looks on the different genres as being closely related, in craft as well as themes and imagery: "Poetry fine tunes my writing. When I go from working on my poetry to working on a novel, the demands of language are already established." In her prose, she seeks the same economy, concentration, and intensity of style that she seeks in her poetry. For Ortiz Cofer, prose and poetry are less different than they are for many writers. She works in each genre not because she feels they are distinctive in effect but to explore each form and to challenge her writing with the demands of each. To achieve a deeper understanding and appreciation of Ortiz Cofer as a writer, you will want to read her work in all the genres she writes in and to read not just a single poem or story but a range of her poetry, fiction, and nonfiction.

This chapter can assist you in that endeavor: We have included in it, and in earlier chapters, examples of Ortiz Cofer's writing from several different genres. Before continuing, it might be helpful to read or reread Ortiz Cofer's story "Nada" (p. 395) and her poem "Cold as Heaven" (p. 646). The rest of this chapter contains more of her poems; a chapter from *Silent Dancing*; an essay, "And Are You a Latina Writer?" written in the form of an interview; and several actual interviews, focusing especially on the issues that arise from being regarded not only as a writer but also as an ethnic writer. As you read the selections, be alert for the literary elements that you worked with in the fiction and poetry sections of this book. Think critically as you read to notice the influence of poetry on her prose and to discover how her exploration of genres results in a variety of effects. Think about what would be different if Ortiz Cofer had written a prose piece as poetry or a poem as a work of prose.

As with most writers, particular themes, techniques, and images appear repeatedly in Ortiz Cofer's work. One of the rewards of reading a writer in depth, especially one who is comfortable working in multiple genres, is to trace such recurring motifs and make connections between works and between genres. As you read this chapter, watch for such repeated elements. Notice, for example, the way the importance of place and its accompanying images is a continuing motif in many of Ortiz Cofer's works. We seek to identify people, perhaps even to categorize them, by asking, "Where are you from?" That is a complicated question for Ortiz Cofer. Should she answer Puerto Rico? New Jersey? Georgia? Works such as "The Birthplace," "The Latin Deli," and "Silent Dancing" explore her sense of having two homes — the island of Puerto Rico and the mainland United States — while feeling an outsider in both.

Another recurring theme is the importance of story. In "Speaking in Puerto Rican," Ortiz Cofer says, "Most of the stories in my work date back to the times when I would sit around at my grandmother's house and listen to the women telling their stories" (p. 743). In that light, consider the meanings of *story*, how it is emphasized and the ways it is treated in "The Changeling," "Silent Dancing," and "And Are You a Latina Writer?" The importance of mothers and grandmothers in Ortiz Cofer's life is another theme, as evidenced in such works as "And Are You a Latina Writer?" and "Speaking in Puerto Rican." These are a few examples of the kinds of themes that recur throughout Ortiz Cofer's work. Be alert for others. Looking for such themes can lead you to interesting and valuable realizations when you read and explore one writer in depth.

There are three ways of using the material in this chapter for writing assignments. The first is to write a paper on one or more of the poems without reading the prose material that follows them. In that case you would think of the poems as if they were included in the "Collection of Poems," and do a paper without outside sources. When choosing this option, remember that if you do read the prose works or interviews, or any part of them, you must acknowledge it by including them in a bibliography, even if you don't quote from or refer to them.

As a second way of utilizing the material in this chapter, your instructor might ask you to write a paper using both the poems and the prose pieces but no additional outside sources. Such a paper provides you practice working with and incorporating other primary sources, selecting passages to quote and blending quotations into your writing, and constructing a Works Cited page. But it isn't a full research paper because you aren't going out to find materials to use in the paper and aren't using critical books and essays. The reason an instructor might select this method is that it doesn't require the amount of time a full-blown research project does. You and your instructor will be working with material you are both familiar with. For such a paper, you should review the guidelines for handling quotations on pages 53–54 and the sections on incorporating sources, documenting sources, and preparing a Works Cited page in Chapter 3 (pp. 76–83). We have included original publication information and page references, which you can use for your in-text citations and Works Cited page, as if you had access to the actual books and periodicals.

A third way to use this chapter is as a starting point for an actual research paper. That is, after reading the poems, essays, and interviews in this chapter, you would search—perhaps only in the library, perhaps also using electronic resources—to locate additional material by or about Ortiz Cofer. You might read more primary works by her, and you will definitely be expected to read and use critical studies of her thought and works. For such a project, in addition to reviewing the guidelines for handling quotations on pages 53–54 and reading the appendix "Reading Critical Essays," you should read or review Chapter 3, "Writing a Literary Research Paper."

The Changeling°

[1993]

As a young girl
vying for my father's attention,
I invented a game that made him look up
from his reading and shake his head
as if both baffled and amused.   5

In my brother's closet, I'd change
into his dungarees—the rough material
molding me into boy shape; hide
my long hair under an army helmet
he'd been given by Father, and emerge   10
transformed into the legendary Che
of grown-up talk.

Strutting around the room,
I'd tell of life in the mountains,
of carnage and rivers of blood,   15
and of manly feasts with rum and music
to celebrate victories *para la libertad.*°   *for freedom*
He would listen with a smile
to my tales of battles and brotherhood
until Mother called us to dinner.   20

She was not amused
by my transformations, sternly forbidding me
from sitting down with them as a man.
She'd order me back to the dark cubicle
that smelled of adventure, to shed   25
my costume, to braid my hair furiously
with blind hands, and to return invisible,
as myself,
to the real world of her kitchen.

Ortiz Cofer, Judith. "The Changeling." *The Latin Deli: Prose and Poetry.* Athens: Georgia UP, 1993. 38. Print.

The Birthplace°   [1987]

There is no danger now
that these featureless hills
will hold me.
That church
sitting on the highest one   5
like a great hen
spreading her marble wings
over the penitent houses
does not beckon to me.
This dusty road under my feet   10
is like any other road
I have traveled,
it leads only
to other roads.
Towns everywhere are the same   15
when shadows thicken.
Yet, each window
casting a square of light,
that grassy plain under a weighted sky
turning to plum,   20
tell me
that as surely as my dreams are mine,
I must be home.

Ortiz Cofer, Judith. "The Birthplace." *Reaching for the Mainland and Selected New Poems.* Tempe:
Bilingual Press/Editorial Bilingüe, 1995. 21. Print.

On the Island I Have Seen°   [1987]

Men cutting cane under a sun relentless
as an overseer with a quota,
measuring their days
with each swing of their machetes,
mixing their sweat with the sugar   5
destined to sweeten half a continent's coffee.

Old men playing dominoes in the plazas
cooled by the flutter of palms,
divining from the ivory pieces
that clack like their bones, the future   10
of the children who pass by on their way to school,

ducklings following the bobbing beak
of the starched nun who leads them in silence.

Women in black dresses keeping all the holy days,
asking the priest in dark confessionals   15
what to do about the anger in their sons' eyes.
Sometimes their prayers are answered
and the young men take their places
atop the stacked wedding cakes.
The ones who are lost to God and mothers   20
may take to the fields, the dry fields,
where a man learns the danger of words,
where even a curse can start a fire.

Ortiz Cofer, Judith. "On the Island I Have Seen." *Reaching for the Mainland and Selected New Poems*. Tempe: Bilingual Press/Editorial Bilingüe, 1995. 9. Print.

The Latin Deli: An Ars Poetica°   [1993]

Presiding over a formica counter,
plastic Mother and Child magnetized
to the top of an ancient register,
the heady mix of smells from the open bins
of dried codfish, the green plantains   5
hanging in stalks like votive offerings,
she is the Patroness of Exiles,
a woman of no-age who was never pretty,
who spends her days selling canned memories
while listening to the Puerto Ricans complain   10
that it would be cheaper to fly to San Juan
than to buy a pound of Bustelo coffee here,
and to Cubans perfecting their speech
of a "glorious return" to Havana—where no one
has been allowed to die and nothing to change until then;   15
to Mexicans who pass through, talking lyrically
of *dólares* to be made in El Norte—
                              all wanting the comfort
of spoken Spanish, to gaze upon the family portrait
of her plain wide face, her ample bosom   20
resting on her plump arms, her look of maternal interest
as they speak to her and each other
of their dreams and their disillusions—
how she smiles understanding,
when they walk down the narrow aisles of her store   25

reading the labels of packages aloud, as if
they were the names of lost lovers: *Suspiros*,
Merengues, the stale candy of everyone's childhood.

                                                        She spends her days
slicing *jamón y queso* and wrapping it in wax paper   30
tied with string: plain ham and cheese
that would cost less at the A&P, but it would not satisfy
the hunger of the fragile old man lost in the folds
of his winter coat, who brings her lists of items
that he reads to her like poetry, or the others,   35
whose needs she must divine, conjuring up products
from places that now exist only in their hearts —
closed ports she must trade with.

Ortiz Cofer, Judith. "The Latin Deli: An Ars Poetica." *The Latin Deli: Prose and Poetry*. Athens:
Georgia UP, 1993. 3–4. Print.

My Father in the Navy°   [1990]

Stiff and immaculate
in the white cloth of his uniform
and a round cap on his head like a halo,
he was an apparition on leave from a shadow-world
and only flesh and blood when he rose from below   5
the waterline where he kept watch over the engines
and dials making sure the ship parted the waters
on a straight course.
Mother, brother and I kept vigil
on the nights and dawns of his arrival,   10
watching the corner beyond the neon sign of a quasar
for the flash of white, our father like an angel
heralding a new day.
His homecomings were the verses
we composed over the years making up   15
the siren's song that kept him coming back
from the bellies of iron whales
and into our nights
like the evening prayer.

Ortiz Cofer, Judith. "My Father in the Navy." *Silent Dancing: A Partial Remembrance of a Puerto
Rican Childhood*. Houston: Arte Publico Press, 1990. 100. Print.

First Job: The Southern Sweets Sandwich Shop and Bakery°

[2005]

Lillie Mae glows, she hates the word sweat,
as she balances a platter of baked sweets over her head,
showing me how to walk with grace
even under the weight of minimum wage
and a mountain of cookies,   5
turnovers, and tarts, which she blames
for her "voluptuous" figure. She calls me
"shuggah," and is teaching me the job.
We are both employed by Mr. Raymond, who keeps her
in a little house outside of town.   10

I'm fifteen, living my first year
in the strange country called Georgia.
Lillie Mae hired me for my long black hair
she couldn't wait to braid, and for my gift
of tongues, which she witnessed as I turned   15
my mother's desire for a sugar bubble
she called a merengue into something nearly equal
behind the glass wall.
"Shuggah," she will on occasion call me
out front, "talk foreign for my friend."   20
And I will say whatever comes into my head,
"You're a pig, Mr. Jones, I see your hand
under the table stroking her thigh." If they're impressed
with my verbal prowess, I may suggest something tasty
from our menu; if they presume I am Pocahontas   25
at the palace, there only to amuse their royal selves,
I tell them, smiling sweetly, to try the mierda,°
which is especially good that day. Soon I can make
anything sound appetizing in Spanish.

Lillie Mae carries her silver-plated tray   30
to Mr. Raymond for inspection, looking seductive
as a plump Salomé° in her fitted white nylon uniform.

He is a rotund King Herod asking for the divinity
though he knows it is on its way. She sorts her delicacies,

Ortiz Cofer, Judith. "First Job: The Southern Sweets Sandwich Shop and Bakery." *A Love Story Beginning in Spanish: Poems.* Athens: Georgia UP, 2005. 25–27. Print.
27. mierda: Shit (Spanish). **32. Salomé:** New Testament daughter of Herodias who danced before King Herod (Matthew 14:3–11). Oscar Wilde's play *Salomé* (1891) portrays her as a seductive beauty.

pointing out the sugar-coated wedding cookies with the tips   35
of her pink glue-on nails she is so proud of.

"Because, Shuggah, a woman's hands should always
be soft and beautiful; never mind you scrubbed, waxed
pushed, pulled, and carried all blessed day.
That's what a man expects."   40

I watch them as they talk shop and lock eyes,
but cannot quite imagine the carnival of their couplings.
Instead, I see them licking their chops over strudel,
consuming passion while ensconced in her edible house
with peppermint stick columns and gingerbread walls.   45

In the kitchen of the Southern Sweets the black cook,
Margaret, worships at the altar of her Zenith radio. Hank Aaron°
is working his way to heaven. She is bone-sticking thin,
despises sweets, loves only her man Hank, Otis Redding,°
and a smoke. She winks at me when he connects,   50
dares to ignore Mr. Raymond when Aaron is up. Mysteriously
the boss-man understands the priority of home runs,
and the sacrilege of speaking ordinary words like my
"triple decker club on a bun with fries" frozen at tongue-tip
when Margaret holds up one bony finger at us, demanding   55
a little respect for the man at the plate.

That windowless kitchen, with its soul-melting
hot floors and greasy walls, had to disappear for her,
like a magician's trick at the sweet snap of the ball and bat
that sent her into orbit, her eyes rolling back in ecstasy,   60
mouth circling the O in wonder as if she had seen the glory.

At closing, Lillie Mae fluffs her boot-black curls,
heads home to entertain her sugar daddy or to be alone,
glue on new nails, pin-curl her hair, and practice walking
gracefully under heavy trays.   65

I have homework to do, words to add to my arsenal
of sweet-sounding missiles for mañana.
My father waits for me in his old brown Galaxy.
He is wary of these slow-talking tall Southerners, another race

he must avoid or face; tired of navigating his life,   70
which is a highway crowded with strangers sealed in their vehicles,

---

47. Hank Aaron: Henry Louis Aaron (b. 1934), Major League baseball star (1954–1976), who set a MLB record for most career home runs (755).   **49. Otis Redding:** Otis Ray Redding Jr. (1941–1967), American soul singer, popularly known as the "King of Soul."

and badly marked with signs that he will never fully understand.
I offer him a day-old doughnut, but no, at least from me
he does not have to accept second-best anything.

We drive by the back lot, where Margaret stands   75
puffing small perfect clouds, her eyes fixed to a piece of sky
between the twin smokestacks of Continental Can, and beyond
what I can see from where I am. Still tracking Aaron's message
hovering above us all in the airwaves?
Her lips move and I can read the drawled-out "shee-it"   80
followed by that characteristic shake of her head
that meant, Girl, in this old world,
some things are still possible.

Silent Dancing°   [1990]

*We have a home movie of this party. Several times my mother and I have
watched it together, and I have asked questions about the silent revellers coming in
and out of focus. It is grainy and of short duration but a great visual aid to my first
memory of life in Paterson at that time. And it is in color — the only complete scene
in color I can recall from those years.*

We lived in Puerto Rico until my brother was born in 1954. Soon after,
because of economic pressures on our growing family, my father joined the
United States Navy. He was assigned to duty on a ship in Brooklyn Yard, New
York City — a place of cement and steel that was to be his home base in the
States until his retirement more than twenty years later.

He left the Island first, tracking down his uncle who lived with his family
across the Hudson River, in Paterson, New Jersey. There he found a tiny apartment in a huge apartment building that had once housed Jewish families and
was just being transformed into a tenement by Puerto Ricans overflowing from
New York City. In 1955 he sent for us. My mother was only twenty years old, I
was not quite three, and my brother was a toddler when we arrived at *El
Building*, as the place had been christened by its new residents.

My memories of life in Paterson during those first few years are in shades
of gray. Maybe I was too young [p. 87]° to absorb vivid colors and details, or to
discriminate between the slate blue of the winter sky and the darker hues of the
snow-bearing clouds, but the single color washes over the whole period. The
building we lived in was gray, the streets were gray with slush the first few
months of my life there, the coat my father had bought for me was dark in color
and too big. It sat heavily on my thin frame.

Ortiz Cofer, Judith. "Silent Dancing." *Silent Dancing: A Partial Remembrance of a Puerto Rican
Childhood.* Houston: Arte Publico Press, 1990. 87–98.   (Page citations in square brackets refer
to the original publication.)

I do remember the way the heater pipes banged and rattled, startling all of 5
us out of sleep until we got so used to the sound that we automatically either
shut it out or raised our voices above the racket. The hiss from the valve punctuated my sleep, which has always been fitful, like a nonhuman presence in the
room — the dragon sleeping at the entrance of my childhood. But the pipes were
a connection to all the other lives being lived around us. Having come from a
house made for a single family back in Puerto Rico — my mother's extended-
family home — it was curious to know that strangers lived under our floor and
above our heads, and that the heater pipe went through everyone's apartments.
(My first spanking in Paterson came as a result of playing tunes on the pipes in
my room to see if there would be an answer.) My mother was as new to this
concept of beehive life as I was, but had been given strict orders by my father to
keep the doors locked, the noise down, ourselves to ourselves.

It seems that Father had learned some painful lessons about prejudice while
searching for an apartment in Paterson. Not until years later did I hear how
much resistance he had encountered with landlords who were panicking at the
influx of Latinos into a neighborhood that had been Jewish for a couple of
generations. But it was the American phenomenon of ethnic turnover that was
changing the urban core of Paterson, and the [p. 88] human flood could not
be held back with an accusing finger.

"You Cuban?" the man had asked my father, pointing a finger at his name
tag on the Navy uniform — even though my father had the fair skin and light
brown hair of his northern Spanish family background and our name is as common in Puerto Rico as Johnson is in the U.S.

"No," my father had answered looking past the finger into his adversary's
angry eyes "I'm Puerto Rican."

"Same shit." And the door closed. My father could have passed as European,
but we couldn't. My brother and I both have our mother's black hair and olive
skin, and so we lived in El Building and visited our great-uncle and his fair
children on the next block. It was their private joke that they were the German
branch of the family. Not many years later that area too would be mainly Puerto
Rican. It was as if the heart of the city map were being gradually colored in
brown — *café-con-leche* brown. Our color.

The movie opens with a sweep of the living room. It is "typical" immigrant 10
Puerto Rican decor for the time: The sofa and chairs are square and hard-looking,
upholstered in bright colors (blue and yellow in this instance, and covered in the
transparent plastic) that furniture salesmen then were adept at making women buy.
The linoleum on the floor is light blue, and if it was subjected to the spike heels as it
was in most places, there were dime-sized identations all over it that cannot be seen
in this movie. The room is full of people dressed in mainly two colors: dark suits for
the men, red dresses for the women. I have asked my mother why most of the women
are in red that night, and she shrugs, "I don't remember. Just a coincidence." She
doesn't have my obsession for assigning symbolism to everything. [p. 89]

The three women in red sitting on the couch are my mother, my eighteen-year-
old cousin, and her brother's girlfriend. The "novia" is just up from the Island,

which is apparent in her body language. She sits up formally, and her dress is carefully pulled over her knees. She is a pretty girl but her posture makes her look insecure, lost in her full skirted red dress which she has carefully tucked around her to make room for my gorgeous cousin, her future sister-in-law. My cousin has grown up in Paterson and is in her last year of high school. She doesn't have a trace of what Puerto Ricans call "la mancha" (literally, the stain: the mark of the new immigrant — something about the posture, the voice, or the humble demeanor making it obvious to everyone that that person has just arrived on the mainland; has not yet acquired the polished look of the city dweller). My cousin is wearing a tight red-sequined cocktail dress. Her brown hair has been lightened with peroxide around the bangs, and she is holding a cigarette very expertly between her fingers, bringing it up to her mouth in a sensuous arc of her arm to her as she talks animatedly with my mother, who has come to sit between the two women, both only a few years younger than herself. My mother is somewhere halfway between the poles they represent in our culture.

It became my father's obsession to get out of the barrio, and thus we were never permitted to form bonds with the place or with the people who lived there. Yet the building was a comfort to my mother, who never got over yearning for *la isla.* She felt surrounded by her language: The walls were thin, and voices speaking and arguing in Spanish could be heard all day. *Salsas* blasted out of radios turned on early in the morning and left on for company. Women seemed to cook rice and beans perpetually — the strong aroma of red kidney beans boiling permeated the hallways. [p. 90]

Though Father preferred that we do our grocery shopping at the supermarket when he came home on weekend leaves, my mother insisted that she could cook only with products whose labels she could read, and so, during the week, I accompanied her and my little brother to *La Bodega* — a hole-in-the-wall grocery store across the street from *El Building.* There we squeezed down three narrow aisles jammed with various products. Goya and Libby's — those were the trademarks trusted by her Mamá, and so my mother bought cans of Goya beans, soups and condiments. She bought little cans of Libby's fruit juices for us. And she bought Colgate toothpaste and Palmolive soap. (The final *e* is pronounced in both those products in Spanish, and for many years I believed that they were manufactured on the Island. I remember my surprise at first hearing a commercial on television for the toothpaste in which Colgate rhymed with "ate.")

We would linger at La Bodega, for it was there that mother breathed best, taking in the familiar aromas of the foods she knew from Mamá's kitchen, and it was also there that she got to speak to the other women of El Building without violating outright Father's dictates against fraternizing with our neighbors.

But he did his best to make our "assimilation" painless. I can still see him carrying a Christmas tree up several flights of stairs to our apartment, leaving a trail of aromatic pine. He carried it formally, as if it were a flag in a parade. We were the only ones in El Building that I knew of who got presents on both Christmas Day and on *Día de Reyes,* the day when the Three Kings brought gifts to Christ and to Hispanic children.

Our greatest luxury in El Building was having our own television set. It must have been a result of Father's guilt feelings over the isolation he had imposed [p. 91] on us, but we were one of the first families in the barrio to have one. My brother quickly became an avid watcher of Captain Kangaroo and Jungle Jim. I loved all the family series, and by the time I started first grade in school, I could have drawn a map of Middle America as exemplified by the lives of characters in *Father Knows Best*, *The Donna Reed Show*, *Leave It to Beaver*, *My Three Sons*, and (my favorite) *Bachelor Father*, where John Forsythe treated his adopted teenage daughter like a princess because he was rich and had a Chinese houseboy to do everything for him. Compared to our neighbors in El Building, we were rich. My father's Navy check provided us with financial security and a standard of life that the factory workers envied. The only thing his money could not buy us was a place to live away from the barrio—his greatest wish and Mother's greatest fear.

In the home movie the men are shown next, sitting around a card table set up in one corner of the living room, playing dominoes. The clack of the ivory pieces is a familiar sound. I heard it in many houses on the Island and in many apartments in Paterson. In Leave It to Beaver, *the Cleavers played bridge in every other episode; in my childhood, the men started every social occasion with a hotly debated round of dominoes: The women would sit around and watch, but they never participated in the games.*

Here and there you can see a small child. Children were always brought to parties and, whenever they got sleepy, put to bed in the host's bedrooms. Babysitting was a concept unrecognized by the Puerto Rican women I knew: A responsible mother did not leave her children with any stranger. And in a culture where children are not considered intrusive, there is no need to leave the children at home. We went where our mother went. [p. 92]

Of my pre-school years I have only impressions: the sharp bite of the wind in December as we walked with our parents towards the brightly lit stores downtown, how I felt like a stuffed doll in my heavy coat, boots and mittens; how good it was to walk into the five-and-dime and sit at the counter drinking hot chocolate.

On Saturdays our whole family would walk downtown to shop at the big 20 department stores on Broadway. Mother bought all our clothes at Penney's and Sears, and she liked to buy her dresses at the women's specialty shops like Lerner's and Diana's. At some point we would go into Woolworth's and sit at the soda fountain to eat.

We never ran into other Latinos at these stores or eating out, and it became clear to me only years later that the women from El Building shopped mainly at other places—stores owned either by other Puerto Ricans, or by Jewish merchants who had philosophically accepted our presence in the city and decided to make us their good customers, if not neighbors and friends. These establishments were located not downtown, but in the blocks around our street, and they were referred to generically as *La Tienda, El Bazar, La*

Bodega, La Botánica. Everyone knew what was meant. These were the stores where your face did not turn a clerk to stone, where your money was as green as anyone else's.

On New Year's Eve we were dressed up like child models in the Sears catalogue — my brother in a miniature man's suit and bow tie, and I in black patent leather shoes and a frilly dress with several layers of crinolines underneath. My mother wore a bright red dress that night, I remember, and spike heels; her long black hair hung to her waist. Father, who usually wore his Navy uniform during his short visits home, had put on a dark civilian suit for the occasion: We had been invited [p. 93] to his uncle's house for a big celebration. Everyone was excited because my mother's brother, Hernán — a bachelor who could indulge himself in such luxuries — had bought a movie camera which he would be trying out that night.

Even the home movie cannot fill in the sensory details such a gathering left imprinted in a child's brain. The thick sweetness of women's perfume mixing with the ever-present smells of food cooking in the kitchen: meat and plantain *pasteles*, the ubiquitous rice dish made special with pigeon peas — *gandules* — and seasoned with the precious *sofrito* sent up from the island by somebody's mother or smuggled in by a recent traveler. *Sofrito* was one of the items that women hoarded, since it was hardly ever in stock at La Bodega. It was the flavor of Puerto Rico.

The men drank Palo Viejo rum and some of the younger ones got weepy. The first time I saw a grown man cry was at a New Year's Eve party. He had been reminded of his mother by the smells in the kitchen. But what I remember most were the boiled *pasteles* — the plantain or yucca rectangles stuffed with corned beef or other meats, olives, and many other savory ingredients, all wrapped in banana leaves. Everyone had to fish one out with a fork. There was always a "trick" pastel — one without stuffing — and whoever got that one was the "New Year's Fool."

There was also the music. Long-playing albums were treated like precious 25 china in these homes. Mexican recordings were popular, but the songs that brought tears to my mother's eyes were sung by the melancholic Daniel Santos, whose life as a drug addict was the stuff of legend. Felipe Rodríguez was a particular favorite of couples. He sang about faithless women and broken-hearted men. There is a snatch of a lyric that has stuck [p. 94] in my mind like a needle on a worn groove: "De piedra ha de ser mi cama, de piedra la cabecera . . . la mujer que a mi me quiera . . . ha de quererme de veras. Ay, Ay, corazón, ¿por qué no amas . . . ?"° I must have heard it a thousand times since the idea of a bed made of stone, and its connection to love, first troubled me with its disturbing images.

"**De piedra . . . no amas . . . ?**": "Of stone must be the bed, of stone the head board . . . the woman who loves me . . . has to truly love me. Ay, ay, [my] heart, why do you not love?" Lyrics from a familiar song by Cuco Sanchez (1921–2000), popular Mexican singer and songwriter.

The five-minute home movie ends with people dancing in a circle. The creative filmmaker must have asked them to do that so that they could file past him. It is both comical and sad to watch silent dancing. Since there is no justification for the absurd movements that music provides for some of us, people appear frantic, their faces embarrassingly intense. It's as if you were watching sex. Yet for years, I've had dreams in the form of this home movie. In a recurring scene, familiar faces push themselves forward into my mind's eye, plastering their features into distorted close-ups. And I'm asking them: "Who is she? Who is the woman I don't recognize? Is she an aunt? Somebody's wife? Tell me who she is. Tell me who these people are."

"No, see the beauty mark on her cheek as big as a hill on the lunar landscape of her face—well, that runs in the family. The women on your father's side of the family wrinkle early; it's the price they pay for that fair skin. The young girl with the green stain on her wedding dress is *La Novia*°—just up from the island. See, she lowers her eyes as she approaches the camera like she's supposed to. Decent girls never look you directly in the face. *Humilde*, humble, a girl should express humility in all her actions. She will make a good wife for your cousin. He should consider himself lucky to have met her only weeks after she arrived here. If he marries her quickly, she will make him a good Puerto Rican–style wife; but if he waits too long, she will be corrupted by [p. 95] the city, just like your cousin there."

"She means me. I do what I want. This is not some primitive island I live on. Do they expect me to wear a black *mantilla*° on my head and go to mass every day? Not me. I'm an American woman and I will do as I please. I can type faster than anyone in my senior class at Central High, and I'm going to be a secretary to a lawyer when I graduate. I can pass for an American girl anywhere—I've tried it—at least for Italian, anyway. I never speak Spanish in public. I hate these parties, but I wanted the dress. I look better than any of these *humildes*° here. My life is going to be different. I have an American boyfriend. He is older and has a car. My parents don't know it, but I sneak out of the house late at night sometimes to be with him. If I marry him, even my name will be American. I hate rice and beans. It's what makes these women fat."

"Your *prima*° is pregnant by that man she's been sneaking around with. Would I lie to you? I'm your great-uncle's common-law wife—the one he abandoned on the island to marry your cousin's mother. I was not invited to this party, but I came anyway. I came to tell you that story about your cousin that you've always wanted to hear. Remember that comment your mother made to a neighbor that has always haunted you? The only thing you heard was your cousin's name and then you saw your mother pick up your doll from the couch and say: 'It was as big as this doll when they flushed it down the toilet.' This image has bothered you for years, hasn't it? You had nightmares about babies being flushed down the toilet, and you wondered why anyone would do such a

---

La Novia: The girlfriend.   *mantilla*: Black veil.   *humildes*: Here, poor people.   *prima*: Cousin.

horrible thing. You didn't dare ask your mother about it. She would only tell you that you had not heard her right and yell at you for listening to adult conversations.   But later, when [p. 96] you were old enough to know about abortions, you suspected. I am here to tell you that you were right. Your cousin was growing an *Americanito* in her belly when this movie was made. Soon after she put something long and pointy into her pretty self, thinking maybe she could get rid of the problem before breakfast and still make it to her first class at the high school. Well, *Niña*, her screams could be heard downtown. Your aunt, her Mamá, who had been a midwife on the Island, managed to pull the little thing out. Yes, they probably flushed it down the toilet, what else could they do with it — give it a Christian burial in a little white casket with blue bows and ribbons? Nobody wanted that baby — least of all the father, a teacher at her school with a house in West Paterson that he was filling with real children, and a wife who was a natural blond.

"Girl, the scandal sent your uncle back to the bottle. And guess where   30 your cousin ended up? Irony of ironies. She was sent to a village in Puerto Rico to live with a relative on her mother's side: a place so far away from civilization that you have to ride a mule to reach it. A real change in scenery. She found a man there. Women like that cannot live without male company. But believe me, the men in Puerto Rico know how to put a saddle on a woman like her. *La Gringa*,° they call her. Ha, ha, ha. *La Gringa* is what she always wanted to be . . ."

The old woman's mouth becomes a cavernous black hole I fall into. And as I fall, I can feel the reverberations of her laughter. I hear the echoes of her last mocking words: *La Gringa, La Gringa!* And the conga line keeps moving silently past me. There is no music in my dream for the dancers.

When Odysseus visits Hades asking to see the spirit of his mother, he makes an offering of sacrificial blood, but since all of the souls crave an audience with the [p. 97] living, he has to listen to many of them before he can ask questions.° I, too, have to hear the dead and the forgotten speak in my dream. Those who are still part of my life remain silent, going around and around in their dance. The others keep pressing their faces forward to say things about the past.

My father's uncle is last in line. He is dying of alcoholism, shrunken and shriveled like a monkey, his face is a mass of wrinkles and broken arteries. As he comes closer I realize that in his features I can see my whole family. If you were to stretch that rubbery flesh, you could find my father's face, and deep within *that* face — mine. I don't want to look into those eyes ringed in purple. In a few years he will retreat into silence, and take a long, long time to die. *Move back, Tío,* I tell him. *I don't want to hear what you have to say. Give the dancers room to move, soon it will be midnight. Who is the New Year's Fool this time?* [p. 98]

La Gringa: The white woman.   **Odysseus . . . ask questions:** See Homer, *The Odyssey,* book 11.

And Are You a Latina Writer?°   [2000]

Back in 1978, having just finished graduate school and feeling somewhat inhibited by having read and dissected the major works of great, dead men of letters, I thought I'd be glad if someday someone referred to me simply as a "writer." Now I find myself not just a writer, but bearing the added responsibility of being a *Latina* writer. What is a Latina writer, and how did I become one? My case as a developing Latina writer is somewhat different from others in that, except for the years during my childhood when my family lived in Puerto Rico and in a Puerto Rican neighborhood in Paterson, New Jersey, I have lived in relative geographical isolation from the Latino communities of the United States.

I stress the word *geographical* because, in my mind, I have never abandoned the island of my birth, or perhaps that obsession called "the Island" has never left me. It is the subject [p. 105]° of much of my writing. However, I am not a scholar in the field of Latino literature, but rather a writer of books written in English whose main subjects and settings often reflect the author's emigrant background and issues pertaining to her ethnicity. I would like to reiterate some of the questions that have been put to me by persons trying to determine whether I am a Puerto Rican writer:

Why don't you write in Spanish? Isn't writing in English a selling out to the mainstream culture on your part?

My choice of languages is not a political statement: English is my literary language, the language I learned in the schools of the country where my parents brought me to live as a child. Spanish is my familial language, the tongue I speak with my blood relatives, that I dream in, that lies between the lines of my English sentences. The Puerto Rican American writer Nicholasa Mohr summed it up best when she stated in an essay about her work, "Because I am a daughter of the Puerto Rican Diaspora, English is the language that gives life to my work, the characters I create, and that stimulates me as a writer."* [p. 106]

Isn't the barrio what you write about? Don't you need a sense of place and com- 5
munity for your art? What are you doing in Georgia?

These are the questions I am often asked by people who cannot imagine what a *puertorriqueña* is doing in the Deep South. Once I heard that a Puerto Rican writer had asked where I lived; on hearing the answer, she had said, "No wonder she's mad." At first, offended, I took that "mad" to mean "crazy," but I decided that a benevolent interpretation would be better: What my colleague

---

Ortiz Cofer, Judith. "And Are You a Latina Writer?" *Woman in Front of the Sun: On Becoming a Writer.* Athens: Georgia UP, 2000. 105–15. Print.   (Page citations in square brackets refer to the original publication.)
*"Puerto Rican Writers in the U.S., Puerto Rican Writers in Puerto Rico: A Separation Beyond Language," in *Breaking Boundaries: Latina Writing and Critical Readings*, edited by Asunsion Horno-Delgado, Eliana Ortega, Nina M. Scott, and Nancy Saporta Sternback (Amherst: University of Massachusetts Press, 1989), 12. Print.

had obviously meant was that my isolation from others like her, like myself by extension, had not prevented me from being a part of what Las Vasquez has referred to as the phenomenon of the Latina as "the angry storyteller." I choose to believe that my fellow writer, my *compañera* in art, meant that living in the piney woods has not dissipated the passion of my art. Because my literary universe exists within me, and although admitting the need for "community" where the free exchange of ideas can be stimulating, I write in isolation and anywhere that I can find a room of my own. [p. 107]

In the isolation of my art I find a significant relation to the separateness that is an inherent component of my psyche as the child of emigrants. In his Nobel lecture, Octavio Paz spoke of "this consciousness of being separate [as a] constant feature of our [Latino] spiritual history." He also proposed that our divided souls may be the genesis for our most powerful artistic expression: "[Our isolation creates] an anguished awareness that invites self-examination, at other times it appears as a challenge, a spur to action, to go forth and encounter others and the outside world." His conclusion is that, although he speaks as a Mexican writer, out of his particular experiences and worldview, aloneness is the condition of humankind, and as artists our goal is to build the bridges "to overcome the separation and reunite us with the world and our fellow beings."

In the 1960s, growing up in two confusing and increasingly fragmented cultures, I absorbed literature, both the spoken *cuentos* I heard the women in my family tell and the books I buried my head in as if I were a creature who consumed paper and ink for sustenance. As a young college student I first majored in sociology, hoping to find a way to change the world. With the Vietnam War on my TV screen daily and the other ongoing attacks on my political naïveté, it was not long before [p. 108] the spell of innocence was broken. For the spiritual sustenance I craved I returned to my first love, literature. Although the world was tearing itself asunder, each author I read put it back together for me, giving order to chaos, however fleetingly. While I was visiting the realm of its creator, the poem, the story, or the novel made sense of things for me. I decided that words were my medium; language could be tamed. I could make it perform for me, if I could only hold back the madness outside with my pen. In other words, I had to believe that my work was important to my being. My mission as an emerging writer became to use my art as a bridge, so that I would not be like my parents, who precariously straddled cultures, always fearing the fall, anxious as to which side they really belonged to; I would be crossing the bridge of my design and construction, at will, not abandoning either side, but traveling back and forth without fear and confusion as to where I belonged — I belong to both.

This is what it means to me to be a Puerto Rican American writer: to claim my heritage — to drink from the life-giving waters of my own backyard well, to eat the mango fruit of knowledge of good and evil that grows in Borinquen, the tropical island of my grandmother's tales, as well as to acknowledge the [p. 109] troubled, real country of Puerto Rico I can travel back to any time I desire — and also to claim the language of my education, English, the culture and literature of the country I was brought to as a child. I claim both. I plant my little writer's flag on both shores. There are exclusivists who would have me choose sides: I do not find such a choice necessary, any more than Isaac Bashevis Singer gave up being Jewish when he wrote his universal tales, any more than Alice Walker denies her African American roots and Deep South beginnings to write her American novels. It is neither necessary nor beneficial to me as a writer and an individual to give up anything that makes me a whole person.

Where does your work belong in the American literature canon?   10

I am glad to have to consider this question at all. I feel that I risk hubris in addressing it. I believe that the work of Latina writers, myself included, belongs, if it is judged worthy enough, alongside the work of other American writers whose work reflects the concerns of people experiencing our time. There common ground is found, at the level of our obsessions. In an important essay that defines Latina writing, the editors of *Breaking Boundaries: Latina Writings and Critical Readings* [p. 110] have stated, "the Latina writer will often prioritize the lives of women who have, like themselves, carved an existence within a woman's space. More specifically, their recognition and celebration of what we call 'a matriarchal heritage' can be expressed in remarks such as Ana Castillo's: 'We all have our *abuelita* (little grandmother) poems.' It is not infrequent in Latina discourse to pay tribute to a long line of female ancestors" (12).

I had no idea when I wrote the following early poem about my grandmother that I was falling into the category of Latina writer. The only major woman writer I had heard "speak" directly to me from the canon I was following in graduate school was Virginia Woolf, and it would be many years later that I would read her "A Room of One's Own" in which she stated: "A Woman Writing thinks back through her mothers."

Claims

Last time I saw her, Grandmother
had grown seamed as a Bedouin tent.
She had claimed the right
to sleep alone, to own [p. 111]
her nights, to never bear
the weight of sex again, nor to accept
its gift of comfort, for the luxury
of stretching her bones.
She'd carried eight children,
three had sunk in her belly, *náufragos*,
she'd called them, shipwrecked babies
drowned in her black waters.
Children are made in the night and
steal your days
for the rest of your life, amen. She said this

to each of her daughters in turn.
Once she had made a pact with man and nature
and kept it. Now like the sea
she is claiming back her territory.

Since then I have thought back through my mothers through dozens of poems, essays, short stories, and a novel. And not just my mothers through biology, but also my literary mothers who include a wealthy Victorian called Woolf; several African American matriarchs such as Mother Morrison and Sisters Walker and Dove; my southern muses, greatest among them Flannery O'Connor; the cousins from South and Central America, [p. 112] Allende and Esquivel; my closest contemporary Puerto Rican kin-through-art from my own Island and the U.S.; and the work of my contemporary Latina writers whose example inspires and encourages me. My mothers are all strong women, but they are not all *puertorriqueñas*.

Finally, I am not lost in America. I am not searching for an identity. I know who I am and what I am. And although community is nice for a writer to have — a group to discuss work in progress with, a cafe to socialize with others who share her interests — I do not believe those things are necessary to the production of a work. In my case, specifically, I don't feel a need to have others authenticate my work as "Puerto Rican" literature.

Although I often seek the counsel of my scholarly colleagues who are 15 experts in the field of Puerto Rican literature and culture — which I'm not, and I freely and gratefully accept their assistance and expertise — I do my best work in a room alone. I am not confused about my cultural identity. I know what I am because my *puertorricanness* was not awarded to me: it is part of me; it cannot be legislated out. It can be said and it can be written that one is or is not a Puerto Rican writer, but one's [p. 113] essence cannot be either given or taken away. Whether I write in Spanish or English, I am who I am: a writer who is a Puerto Rican woman, whether I live in New York City or on a farm in Georgia.

Because I am vigilant about keeping my work free from the constraints of external interference, the push for political and other agendas, I have an even greater need to get back to what Octavio Paz described as "that time I wrote without wondering why I was doing it."

In my books I follow memories, *cuentos*,° events, and characters that I see as my guides back to what Virginia Woolf calls "moments of being" in my life, both in Puerto Rico and in the United States. It is a process of discovery. My books are neither Puerto Rican emigrant history nor sociological case studies; at least, I didn't write them as such. I tell stories that recount the suffering and joy of the Puerto Rican emigrants of my experience, mainly women; I re-envision the scenes of my youth and transform them through my imagination, attempting to synthesize the collective yearnings of these souls into a collage that

---

cuentos: Stories.

means Puerto Rican to me, that gives shape to my individual vision. If these *cuentos* I create out of my memory and imbue with my perceptions add up to a universal message, then [p. 114] I consider myself fortunate to have accomplished much more than I allow myself to hope for when I sit down in front of that blank sheet of paper that calls to my restless spirit like a believer's candle. No longer the idealistic young poet hoping to find big answers to big questions, I am content now to be the solitary traveler, the *caminante*: my main hope — to find a pattern in the trees, the path less traveled by in the woods. I know to whom these woods belong: if I'm lucky I will find her *casa*° in the clearing, always just ahead of me — my little-old-lady muse, my *abuela*,° sitting in her rocking chair waiting to tell me another *cuento*; through her storytelling, she teaches me the way back home. [p. 115]

---

casa: House.   *abuela*: Grandmother.

Rafael Ocasio

Speaking in Puerto Rican: An Interview with Judith Ortiz Cofer°   [1992]

Rafael Ocasio: *Maybe you should start by talking about your poetry. You are a poet by trade and that was your first literary work.*

Judith Ortiz Cofer: Poetry is my obsession. I think that poetry has taught me the craft of writing. I have known for a long time that I needed to express myself creatively. For a while I wanted to be a sociologist and save the world. Eventually, I even looked into the visual arts but found out very rapidly that I had no talent in that area. It dawned on me that the one thing I had consistently been doing was writing and that I loved studying literature, particularly poetry.

RO: *When did you start publishing your poetry?*

JOC: Only after I finished graduate school did I really attempt to write poems that I wanted to show other people. I was frankly surprised when they were taken for publication, because one of the first poems that was published was called "Latin Women Pray." It's an ironic little poem about being a Puerto Rican and praying to an Anglo god with a Jewish heritage, and all you can hope is that He's bilingual. It was a political statement as well as a sarcastic poem. It was published in *The New Mexico Humanities Review* and an editorial member wrote a note and said, "Please send us more, we don't get this kind of stuff." . . .

This interview was conducted in November 1990 at Lanier Plaza Hotel, Atlanta, Georgia, by Rafael Ocasio. The written transcript was edited by Rita Ganey. Ocasio, Rafael. "Speaking in Puerto Rican: An Interview with Judith Ortiz Cofer." *The Bilingual Review,* 17.2 (May–Aug 1992): 143–46. Print.

RO: *How would you describe your poetry?*   5

JOC: The more I wrote poetry, the more I learned about it, the more I understood that I was passionately committed to the art form. Writing a poem is a discipline; most people think that you just sit down and you let the Muse strike you on the head and out comes a poem. My poems go through 15, 20, 25 drafts. In fact, I'm working on one now about going back to see my mother ten years after my father had died and finding out that she had a lover. It was a traumatic experience for me. I must have 30 drafts of that. It's a delicate subject, and I love [p. 143]° my mother so much that if she ever reads it, I want her to understand that it's done with affection. Poetry fine tunes my writing. When I go from working on my poetry to working on a novel, the demands of language are already established. I don't want to write 20 pages a day and find 18 of them are disposable. When I sit down to write a page of prose, it is as economical, as concentrated, and as strong as a poem.

RO: *Does poetry writing have a personal commitment for you?*

JOC: Yes. Because I've lived physically isolated from the Puerto Rican community, my poetry has kept me connected emotionally. Even though I live in rural Georgia, my husband is North American, and my daughter was born here, I feel connected to the island and to my heritage. Every time I sit down to write a poem about my grandmother, I have to call her back. In a sense it's like being a medium. You sit down at a table and call back the spirits of your ancestors. When the novel [*The Line of the Sun* (1989)] was published, my mother said, "Everybody is amazed that you write as if you've been here all your life." In a sense I have been connected through my imagination. It's like having a child who is away. You don't stop loving them. My poetry is my emotional and intellectual connection to my heritage. . . .

RO: *It is obvious that women, specifically your grandmother, are influences in your work.*

JOC: A lot of my stories have to do with the fact that my grandmother, who   10 is slightly suspicious of books, is a woman connected to her work, her children, her family, and has not had the opportunity or the time to be educated. She loves storytelling, though. If she can teach something by telling a story, she'll do it. My book of essays, *Silent Dancing*, is dedicated to that very strong narrative impulse. Most of the stories in my work date back to the times when I would sit around at my grandmother's house and listen to the women telling their stories.

RO: *How did you make the transition from poetry to prose writing?*

JOC: I don't feel that I've made a transition. I've added a genre. I've never stopped writing poetry. What the public mainly sees between books is my poems. The poem is an immediate source for telling a story. I found a few years ago that I got an immense amount of satisfaction from telling a story. I knew that there were certain characters I wanted to create and let them act. I chose my black sheep Angel Guzmán, who is a real person and who was a real black sheep of my family. In my childhood, I had heard only stories that my mother thought a small child should hear about Guzmán. I let my imagination run

---

(Page numbers in square brackets refer to the original publication.)

wild. The novel developed out of my strong sense that I could tell a story and that the natural form for it should be a novel. . . . [p. 144]

RO: *Let's talk more specifically about your novel. The Spanish tone which permeates your English prose resembles the* criollismo *[mixed languages] techniques as it presents universal values through original Latin American motifs. Would you comment on that particular style or do you feel that there is a special affinity with American and Spanish American, including Puerto Rican writers?*

JOC: I intended to make the language relate to the theme. I was writing about rural Puerto Ricans, leading their lives in connections to each other and the land. I felt that idiomatic American English would defeat that purpose, because Spanish is lyrical. These people were thinking and speaking in Spanish, but I was writing my novel in English. I wrote as if it were being translated at the moment of writing. It preserved the flavor of the Spanish, because Spanish is syntactically different from English. It is also more poetic in its expression. My poems that deal with Puerto Rico are syntactically different than my poems that deal with my life in the United States. The tone is a direct result of the different syntactical construction I used in order to make it seem credible and feasible that these people were actually Spanish speakers and thinkers, not Americans impersonating Puerto Ricans. . . .

RO: *What do you think will be the reaction of the Puerto Rican scholar and reader* 15 *to your novel? What will be the reaction of the American scholar and reader?* [p. 145]

JOC: Interestingly enough, I've gotten mainly the reaction of the American readers to my novel. . . . I was at a conference in Paris where different writers were being discussed. A publisher said, "We don't know where to put Judith Cofer." Judith Cofer is writing in standard English, and she lives in Georgia. Until recently, I was somewhere in limbo. I'm not a mainstream North American writer, but I publish in mainstream North American journals. I'm not an island writer. All I know is that I'm a writer, period, writing about the one thing that defines me as a human being—my biculturalism. [p. 146]

Marilyn Kallet

The Art of Not Forgetting: An Interview with Judith Ortiz Cofer°   [1994]

MK: *The concept of "not forgetting" plays a central part in your work and aesthetics. Why is "not forgetting" so important to you as a writer?*

JOC: It's a complex concept for me. Many people of my parents' generation felt that if we assimilated, if we learned to live within the culture, it would be easier for us. I can see that as an economic survival technique, but as an artist I

Kallet, Marilyn. "The Art of Not Forgetting: An Interview with Judith Ortiz Cofer." *Prairie Schooner* 68.4 (Winter 1994): 68–75. Print.

discovered that assimilation is exactly what destroys the artistic—to blend so well that you forget what makes you unique. When I started to write I really thought—like most English majors and graduate students—that I had to abstract all my ideas to be able to communicate the large concepts. I found out that what I really needed to communicate were the basics in our culture. Language and memory became important, because I realized that memory was the treasure in my backyard. My education had allowed me to become perceptive enough to be able to use memory plus imagination, to transform remembering into art. Not forgetting is a spiritual matter with me. It connects me to the reality of my life. As long as I understand that, I will continue to produce art. One falls into the error of forgetting basic concepts like language and its power to affect reality. The language one speaks at home shapes the original reality and then one learns other versions of that fact to survive in the world. As a poet I have to be able to tell the difference, to transmit it. In a poem like "The Latin Deli" I don't just put in Spanish words as decoration. They are used to transmit a special kind of reality, to communicate to my English-speaking reader, to say, "Yes, this is a different reality, but you can understand it by paying close attention." . . . [p. 68]°

MK: *When you were little, was Spanish spoken at home?*

JOC: Absolutely, especially since my mother was the one who was with us in the house all the time. She spoke nothing but Spanish. Our apartments were a microcosm of her *casa*. This is where she listened to her Spanish language records, where the Spanish language newspaper came in, and her books. She encouraged us to succeed in the outside world, but that was not her reality. . . . [p. 69]

MK: *Was your father bilingual?*

JOC: Fully. He spoke textbook English. He was a perfectionist and he insisted on the correct pronunciation. I remember clearly one time when he had come to pick me up at catechism. One of my friends, a Puerto Rican, said "tousand" instead of "thousand." He was too kind to correct her but later he said, "I want you to know that the word is 'thousand.'" He made me repeat it and I thought that he was just being pushy. I finally understood that he felt that he would be treated better if he spoke well and he transmitted that to us. [p. 69]

MK: *Language was a passport to—?*

JOC: The usual immigrant idea that if you speak intelligently people will treat you with respect. He was of that mind. Even though he was very authoritarian and the military shaped him, he understood that I needed books, and he encouraged me in that area and bought me books. In fact, he was the one who told my mother not to push me to cook if I didn't want to, that that was something I wasn't going to need. That was the most liberated decision he ever made in the sense that he thought my intelligence could take me farther than he had gone. He was the one who emphasized the importance of education. He insisted that my brother and I keep up with our studies no matter how unstable our lives

---

(Page citations in square brackets refer to the original interview.)

were. He facilitated my move into the literary life by encouraging me to read voraciously, to think of education as empowering.

MK: *Do you remember which books you were looking at, which ones influenced you at the beginning?*

JOC: In fact I do. I have an essay called "The Paterson Public Library" in   10
my book *The Latin Deli*. In it, I talk about how nothing prevented me from going to the library. I was allowed a certain amount of time to go on Saturday mornings. There was a girl who hated me because the teacher used to humiliate her by making me tutor her in spelling. She lived on the way to the library and she had promised to beat me up. I remember fearing this girl — she was twice as big as I was. I guess I wanted books more than to save my life because she did carry through with her threat. That hour or so that I was given to go and get books was my best time. The library was impressive to a little girl. I don't know what it would look like now and I have resisted going back because at that time I felt like I was in one of those paintings of philosophers and their disciples sitting on the steps of a great temple. I would approach this magnificent library which was incongruously placed in the worst neighborhood you can imagine where this Greek temple arose from chaos with its lions and its columns.

I had a pink card which meant for a long time I could only check out children's books. So I started reading the world's fairy tales and folk tales at one end of the children's room and worked my way to the other. I experienced a sense of discovery when I found out that the Cinderella story appears in Africa and China, and that heroines didn't have to have pink skin and gold hair, that sometimes they had braided kinky hair and sometimes they had Asian features. That reassured me in my reality that the world was populated by people as different-looking as I thought I was. . . . [p. 70]

MK: *In "Casa" language becomes a place; I can see you sitting there in the late afternoon.*

JOC: Wasn't it Milosz who said that "language is the only homeland"? I believe that. The women spoke in Spanish of course, and I have to translate that into English. Something *is* lost. What people say to one another under intimate circumstances can never [p. 72] fully survive translation. There's a lot of non-verbal communication going on, many shared intimacies. The only way I can regain the power of the original storytelling is not to be a slave to the factual story, but rather to present it as drama, with me as the witness or audience. I try to give back to the women's voices the original power that they had for me as a child by using the techniques of the poet and fiction writer. . . .

MK: *Which poets have influenced you most?*

JOC: I've been an avid reader of poetry for many years. While I was in   15
graduate school I read the "standard" poets. The first poet who gave me that "jolt," that shock of recognition, who made me feel that she was speaking directly to me was Denise Levertov. After I looked up her poetry I seriously began to think of writing poetry myself.

MK: *What was it about her work that impressed you?*

JOC: It was both the control and the flexibility. She was speaking with emotion about certain subjects that were close to her, but she kept a certain control. The lines were naturally flowing and yet they seemed to have a reason for being. Later I read some of her essays about the line. She was very conscious of what she was [p. 73] doing without being self-conscious. By studying Levertov's poetry I realized the art and craft involved in writing poetry, as well as the emotional release and self-discovery involved. . . . .

MK: *How do you decide which genre to pursue, or does the work itself make that decision for you?*

JOC: The work itself sometimes makes a double decision. Right now I'm working on a short story based on the character in "The Latin Deli" [a poem]. The direction is based on the strength of my obsession. If I write a poem and the subject continues to intrigue me, and I need to explore it in a more ample way, it might become an essay, a short story, or even a novel. I now have twenty pages of a story called "Corazon's Cafe." In this story, the woman from my poem has a husband who has just died and she is considering closing their grocery store. This woman intrigued me and I wanted to explore her character in more depth.

I recently wrote an essay called "The Story of My Body" for an anthology. . . .   20
It's about how walking around in this body has [p. 74] affected my life. About how not being tall, being a "shrimp," and unathletic has influenced my individual reality. When I started writing it I knew that it couldn't be a poem, it couldn't be anything but a very structured essay which I divided into skin color, size, and physical appearance and the relativity of these to my sense of self. To my mother I'm tall, because she's 4´11˝. To everyone else, I'm short.

MK: *Physical appearance does affect our reality, but it's not something we talk about.*

JOC: I resisted writing about it. . . . And then I started thinking about how having been the last chosen for sports at school inspired my best secret stories. . . . I fantasized about being Wonder Woman and scooping up all of the P.E. teachers and putting them on a barren asteroid where they would perish because they had no inner resources. I didn't realize how much I disliked them until I wrote that! I needed to say this in an essay. An essay is an attempt to explore ideas. A poem is an attempt to concentrate ideas into their essential core. [p. 75]

Lorraine M. López

Possibilities for Salsa Music in the Mainstream: An Interview with Judith Ortiz Cofer°   [1999]

LÓPEZ: *What inspired you to become a writer?*

COFER: I have always had a need for creative expression. Even as a child I was always acting in little plays that I made up. For a long time, all of my energies were put into school. I was the "Scholarship Kid." I married young and had

López, Lorraine M. "Possibilities for Salsa Music in the Mainstream: An Interview with Judith Ortiz Cofer." *Crab Orchard Review* (Fall 1999): 23–34. Print.

a child. After I accomplished my immediate goals of becoming a teacher and getting my graduate degree, I still felt a need that I could not identify at first. It was a vacuum that didn't get filled until I started to jot down notes and stories and made a few hesitant attempts at poetry.

When I began to write every day, I realized writing is something I need to do. But I didn't really start writing seriously until I had finished my education because I had so little time. I have an essay about this called "Five A.M." I had tried to do everything at once — get married, have a child, go to school. I literally didn't have [enough] hours in the day. So I started making the time by waking [p. 23]° up at five in the morning, which I still do whenever possible. Writing for two hours a day, minimum, has become an intrinsic part of my life. . . .

LÓPEZ: *William Faulkner said the inspiration for* The Sound and the Fury *came to him from a single image. He had spied a young child in soiled underclothes climbing into a window from the branch of a tree, and the idea for the novel was triggered immediately by this sight. What are the sources of your inspiration? Images? Words? Dreams?*

COFER: Poetry inspires me. I started out writing nothing but poetry. The first thing I do in the morning is turn to poetry. I either read it or write it. To me the music and the images [poetry evokes] is just like listening to a song. A lot of my essays in *Silent Dancing* are directly related to my poems. [p. 24]

In one essay, I write about my paternal grandmother, a woman who was oppressed, but who found ways of being rebellious. One of the things that I found very incongruous about this very shy and introverted Puerto Rican woman was that she always had a huge pack of cigarettes in her pocket. Her husband had never allowed her to smoke, even though *he* did. After he died, she smoked like a chimney, and she also displayed her vice. So out of that image of this shy little person with a huge pack of unfiltered cigarettes in her pocket grew an essay.

In another essay about my parents' marriage, I attribute [the inspiration] to their wedding picture. So images are very crucial in the genesis of poetry for me. But also sometimes, it's a musical phrase of some sort, something that I can't stop hearing, sometimes Spanish words hit me as in "El Olvido," that poem I have explained many times. I heard a conversation between my mother and a woman in which the phrase was used so dramatically. *Ai, el olvido!*° It explained everything! I could not be free of it until I wrote a sort of dramatic definition of what that meant.

Sometimes I have to wait until the idea becomes totally sublimated, becomes part of my subconscious, and then I can create characters that are made out of the stuff of that idea, but they are not mere symbols of that idea. I don't want to write a sermon; I want to write a novel.

LÓPEZ: *Which genre do you find most satisfying for the expression of your inspiration, your ideas?*

(Page citations in square brackets refer to the original interview.)   *Ai, el olvido!*: Oh, the forgetting!

COFER: I think poetry because it provides the satisfaction that I imagine a 10 sculptor has after taking fifteen years to make a huge statue. But in two or three days, one can make a beautiful vase, maybe. For me, it's not that the poem doesn't take long; sometimes I'll work on a poem for years. But it takes *shape* before your eyes. It *becomes*. It starts looking like what it will be. It's a creation you can add to, but it's already there. Whereas the novel is this great, plastic thing, a huge thing filling the room of your life, and you're trying to deal with it and mold it. And you have no idea whether (a) you'll be able to do it, or (b) what shape it will be when it's finished, or (c) whether you'll even have the energy to do it. With a poem, there's this beautiful time when you are shaping it and you say, yes, it looks like a poem, it sounds like a poem. It *is* a poem! I would [p. 25] never call it immediate gratification because I have poems I have been working on for years. In fact this morning, I printed out three poems. One had a date of 1995 on it! So I wouldn't exactly call it a quick process.

With a novel or even a short story, your labor may or may not turn into an identifiable story or novel. I have thrown out hundreds of pages after several years of work on something that refused to become a novel or story. I also think that poetry contains the whole spectrum of pleasure that language can offer. You can read a chapter in a beautifully written novel and say, "Ah, yes that was satisfying." But you read a poem and it fills you like good wine. I literally cannot stop myself from getting goose bumps if a poem touches me. It's hard to sustain goose bumps through fifty pages of prose. It might become a permanent condition! I don't think that I am necessarily better at poetry, but for me, it is the most satisfying form.

LÓPEZ: *When inspiration strikes you, how do you, as a multi-genre writer, know what form your idea will take?*

COFER: That's a hard one to answer, but I think it has to do with the concentration, the level of concentration. In my mind, I think of it in the way one knows if a substance is going to be juice or jelly. How do you know the consistency of it? It all depends on how much of the ingredients you choose to put into it.

When I need to write a poem, the image is so concentrated and the impulse is so strong that I want to immediately put it in its right container and shape it as such. For example, I have a very old poem in which I talk about my mother's hands, how she held my hand. The way she held my hand was like a Braille code telegraphing her fear and her anxiety. I suppose I could have written an essay about that, but it didn't feel like an essay. I didn't want that image of my mother's hands to have many tangents or to go off in many directions. I wanted it to be just about that image, to be concentrated and fully about that.

It's the difference between a close-up and panning. Do you want to show a 15 scene of a funeral with everyone hunched over and crying or do you focus the camera right on a tear falling down that child's face? To me, the essay or the short story is the camera moving further away and trying to take in a scene. If it's everything that led to that scene, then it's a novel. But if it's just that one close up, that one image that has to represent everything—then it's a poem. . . . [p. 26]

LÓPEZ: *Those who are familiar with your work are aware that family figures prominently in your writing. How has your family dealt with the idea that they may — or, in some cases, they may not — become subjects in your poetry and prose?*

COFER: I have tried to be very well aware of their sensibilities. I dealt with that very directly when I wrote *The Line of the Sun* and was actually afraid that my mother might be offended by some of the things [in that novel] because she is recognizably in it. But she saw that my imagination took over. Though I based a lot of the characters on real people, I also departed significantly from them.

The other book that was more direct in its approach to the use of family as the basis for the work was *Silent Dancing*. I took care, first of all, to write a foreword in which I discussed Virginia Woolf's theory that the past really belongs to the teller [who is] basically a witness and a participant and not liable for getting everyone else's version of the past right. I wanted to express that this is how *I* absorbed the events around me.

I did it in the form of creative nonfiction, which means I put at the core of each of the pieces real events in real time. I was accurate in my historical time, but I felt free to dramatize conversations that I remembered or recalled without claiming that they were word for word accurate. I also took care to change the names of the people and to [p. 29] make sure that their physical descriptions didn't match so closely that someone was backed into a corner. I was after a poetic truth. . . . [p. 30]

LÓPEZ: *How does teaching and creating literature — in its various permuta-* 20 *tions — inform your vision of what literature will be in this country in the next ten or twenty years? What changes do you foresee?*

COFER: I foresee an opening up of literature. For the longest time, we seem to have been in a fortress called the Western canon. It was a wonderful fortress and very solid, but it did not allow much change. It was somewhat like [saying] we live in a palace, we don't have electricity, still we live in a palace. It's time to rewire the structure, to allow for different ways of seeing and speaking. I cannot believe that anyone can still claim we are not enriched by having Toni Morrison or Louise Erdrich or Rudolfo Anaya or any voices like these added to the so-called canon. [p. 33]

What I think will happen is that a new generation of people, who are multiracial and multi-ethnic (they are already appearing), people who speak standard English, who have gone through the educational process, but come from a multitude of cultures, will be creating a literature that will represent the true diversity of this country, not just pockets. These young kids, like my daughter and your children are going to be working together and communicating easily with each other, but they will be very aware that they are different in some ways.

That's my idealized view of the new literature that encompasses an easier acceptance of the certitude of diversity in the United States, much like my daughter doesn't get up in the morning and think, "I'm half-white and half-Puerto Rican. What shall I wear today?" But many days I had to get up, feeling

I didn't want to go to school, dreading things [at school] that I didn't understand. As times change, I foresee an easier acceptance of difference and thus art and literature are going to represent the vision that, for example, salsa music is possible in the mainstream. [p. 34]

Bridget Kevane and Juanita Heredia

The Poetic Truth: An Interview with Judith Ortiz Cofer°

[2000]

BK: *You once said that you don't believe in the muse. Why?*

JOC: Although my writing gives me a spiritual life, I don't depend on anything extraordinary or supernatural or this thing called inspiration, which I believe is something other than what most people think it is. In my essay "5:00 A.M." in *The Latin Deli,* I said that for me the mysterious part is why I need to write. I need to write like some people need to run, like some people need to play a musical instrument, or like some people need to cook as a form of self-expression. Actually, I don't write for self-expression but for self-discovery. I started giving myself an assigned time, which was five to seven in the morning before my child got up and I had to prepare for my job and everything else. I found that I could will myself to be creative at that hour and that it was a process very similar to exercise. I don't like to exercise, but at a certain point in my day I say that I'm going to do an hour of exercise because I need to. If I don't, I'll regret it and my day will be less than it should be. So I found that it's a combination of the mystical and the practical. . . . [p. 110]°

BK: *But there must be some reward for all the effort in writing poetry?*

JOC: For me, it's become like deep analysis. When I start thinking of a poem somehow my synapses connect and lead me to a place where I don't normally wander into. I know a poem works if it surprises me, if I discover something. The same thing happens over and over, and I always feel a sense of release and almost intense joy for a moment when that happens. Because I know that even if the poem never gets published, even if no one else ever reads it, it has shown me something. The discoveries are not earthshaking. They're discoveries that most people make if they lead [p. 111] examined lives over a long period of time. If you can make them into universal discoveries, then they become art. . . .

BK: *Which writers have served as models for you?*

JOC: When I'm addressing a Latino audience and they ask me about models I pause because I know that they want me to say that my models were

5

Kevane, Bridget, and Juanita Heredia. "The Poetic Truth: An Interview with Judith Ortiz Cofer." *Latina Self-Portraits: Interviews with Contemporary Women Writers.* Albuquerque: New Mexico UP, 2000. 109–23. Print.   (Page citations in square brackets refer to the original interview.)

Puerto Rican writers. I can't say that. Because if you're talking about the models that formed me as an artist twenty years ago, well, there was no big multicultural drive in the United States, there were no Latino studies, nothing like it. In fact, when I was in graduate school, studying American and British literature was the only way that I could do what I wanted to do. Spanish literature from Spain did not represent my interests as closely as did American literature. My only model was Virginia Woolf, because she was the only woman who was allowed on the syllabus. But I didn't feel the shock of recognition until I happened to take a course in Southern literature where I encountered the work of Flannery O'Connor and Eudora Welty. I realized that these were women writing about ordinary lives that they had transformed through art. They weren't rich British women who could be counted among the world's Dead Englishman geniuses; these were women who were writing about family, land, religion. I would say Flannery O'Connor was the first one to give me that jolt, and years later, Alice Walker. Then followed Toni Morrison, because once you get into that era, then African-American and other people start publishing. [p. 112] But it wasn't until Gabriel García Márquez won the Nobel Prize and the so-called Latin American literary boom, when other Latin American writers were "discovered" by American publishers, that we then got Isabel Allende and other people in translation. It's been a long road. Now I do seek out and read the works of Puerto Rican women on the island.

. . . I have had the distinction, if one can call it that, of having been one of the original Puerto Rican writers writing in English, as opposed to being translated, or Latina writers in English. I had to make do, and it hasn't hurt me. I find that I can put into my work many things because I'm aware of the mainstream and have studied contemporary literature by all writers, not just limiting myself to Latino studies, because I think a writer needs to absorb everything. [p. 113]

BK: *Why do your works rely on oral histories? What's special about the oral quality of Puerto Rican literature for you?*

JOC: I think that many cultures have that oral quality. In fact, my husband is a Southerner and comes from a storytelling family. But they tell their stories differently. There are certain stories that define a family and certain keywords that call them up and everyone knows that if you say something about someone or something in front of his grandmother, that she [p. 115] will immediately tell that story. And even though she usually tells it in the same way, it's expected and everyone enjoys it. What my grandmother liked to do that made her, at least I thought, different and unique was that she didn't mind changing the story for her audience. So I would hear her tell one story for my aunts in a particular way and assure us that it was absolutely true and then tell it to us in a different way to make a different point. What I learned about art from her was that it wasn't so much the facts as the poetic truth that was being made. I thought that was a great lesson to learn. She made an art out of stories that could've been just simple gossip. . . . [p. 116]

BK: *Why did you settle on* Silent Dancing *as the title for your collection of* 10 *memoirs?*

JOC: One of my main obsessions and motifs is the island, the isolation of everyone being an island and how isolated you are when you don't know the language. I chose Silent Dancing mainly because it went well with the idea of the silent movie and I thought it was both poignant and slightly absurd to see people dancing without music. To me that had symbolic meaning for the life of the immigrant. We are trying to re-create island life in a hostile environment. That's a crucial essay for me because it reflected the sort of sad paradox of the Puerto Rican in the city. . . . [p. 117]

BK: *Do your readers demand a certain Puerto Ricanness from you?*

JOC: Yes, they really do. When I go places I'm supposed to know about the political status of Puerto Rico, the history, the geography. Of course, I try and keep up. But my main message in my books is that a lifetime is an ongoing process and that evolution doesn't have to always equal progress, but it's inevitable culturally. My daughter is living in a different world than I lived in, and she will be a different kind of woman. I think that's what happens with these trends, what the country adopts right now, where we are in a frenzy where we are trying to pigeonhole people. I don't think that's going to work. When kids talk to me about that I tell them to define themselves and what they feel themselves to be first and then to go back and see what they have adapted from each culture and how much of it they actually need.

BK: *What's your relationship to the island now? Do you return as a visitor to the past, or do you feel that you're returning home?*

JOC: Well, that is the question, isn't it? When people ask me what are you 15 and they mean where do you come from, I always say I'm Puerto Rican, which is obviously what I am. But I think that culture is a very complex concept. You could say that I am Puerto Rican by birth. I certainly enjoy and appreciate my heritage, and have used a lot of my culture for my art and incorporated it into my life. But then there are larger elements to living such as economics and politics and employment and sexual roles and that sort of thing. I'm culturally an American woman and a native Puerto Rican. My mother is a Puerto Rican who never became culturally an American woman. She's never happier than when she is on the island doing the things that she thinks are familiar and are her way of life, which is very different from me. I love going to the island, but it's no longer as familiar to me as Georgia. So, at the risk of sounding like I am betraying my ethnicity, when I go there I have to be more aware. It's like if you stop driving for years you become more aware of driving. It's not automatic anymore. When I go to Puerto Rico I act as when I go to Europe; I spend a lot of time observing and making sure that I know what's going [p. 122] on. Whereas here I'm on automatic pilot a lot of the time. For better or worse, I'm no longer the same kind of puertorriqueña that my mother is. I refuse to be politically correct and say that I'm a pure, unadulterated, native puertorriqueña. No. I've undergone an evolutionary process as has everyone who has ever left their homeland. [p. 123]

RESPONDING THROUGH WRITING

Here are some suggestions for writing on Judith Ortiz Cofer, but for a chapter like this one, you should not limit yourself to these topics. An important lesson in studying an author in depth is learning how to find good topics on your own.

PAPERS USING ONLY THE POETRY IN THE CHAPTER

Literary Analysis Papers

1. Write a paper discussing nostalgia as a theme in "The Latin Deli: An Ars Poetica" (p. 727).

2. Write a paper on remembrances, reversals, and religious imagery in "Cold as Heaven" (in Ch. 15, p. 646).

Comparison-Contrast Papers

3. Write a paper analyzing the use of comparisons and contrasts as both theme and technique in "The Changeling" (p. 725).

4. Write a paper comparing and contrasting the picture of home, "the island" (Puerto Rico), that is depicted in "The Birthplace" (p. 726) and "On the Island I Have Seen" (p. 726).

Cultural Studies Papers

5. Write a paper on the use of gender and ethnic stereotypes in "First Job: The Southern Sweets Sandwich Shop and Bakery" (p. 729).

6. Write a paper examining how the issue of identity for people born in Puerto Rico but living in the United States appears and is handled in poems by Ortiz Cofer included in this chapter.

PAPERS USING BOTH POETRY AND PROSE IN THE CHAPTER

Literary Analysis Papers

1. Write an analytic paper on figures of speech and theme in "The Birthplace" (p. 726) relating the poem to ideas and images in "Silent Dancing" (p. 731) and "And Are You a Latina Writer?" (p. 738).

2. Write a thematic paper on what Ortiz Cofer says in "And Are You a Latina Writer?" (p. 738) and "Speaking in Puerto Rican" (p. 742) about "thinking back through mothers" and the importance of mothers and grandmothers, and their stories, in her poems and stories.

Comparison-Contrast Papers

3. The subtitle of Ortiz Cofer's poem "The Latin Deli" is "An Ars Poetica." *Ars Poetica* is the title of a poem by the Roman poet Horace (65 BCE–8 BCE). The "Art of Poetry" is his theory of literature that spells out the qualities that should be evident in literary works and in writers of them. Write a paper relating "The Latin Deli" to what Ortiz Cofer says about writing in other works included in this chapter and explain in what sense this poem can be seen as her "art of poetry."

4. Ortiz Cofer says her work was strongly influenced by the storytelling of her grandmother and other Puerto Rican women. Write a paper in which you use what she says about storytelling in "Silent Dancing" (p. 731) and the interviews in this chapter as the basis for analyzing storytelling techniques in some of her poetry.

Cultural Studies Papers

5. Critics have pointed out that writers like Ortiz Cofer deal with the need to find both a racial and a gender identity; they are "outsiders" as Latinas and as women. Write a paper on the way this theme appears and is handled in Ortiz Cofer's personal writings and in her poetry.

6. Write a paper exploring the image and importance of family in Ortiz Cofer's personal prose and in the poems included in this book.

PAPERS INCLUDING OUTSIDE RESEARCH

Literary Analysis Papers

1. In "And Are You a Latina Writer?" (p. 738) Ortiz Cofer refers to Mexican writer Octavio Paz's Nobel Prize lecture in which he says aloneness is the condition of humankind and artists build bridges "to overcome the separation and reunite us with the world and our fellow human beings." Write a paper on ways literature achieves that goal for you, personally, using the work of Ortiz Cofer and another author to illustrate.

2. Critic Teresa Derrickson ("'Cold/Hot, English/Spanish': The Puerto Rican American Divide in Judith Ortiz Cofer's *Silent Dancing*," *MELUS* 28.2 [Summer 2003]) points out the difference between having a concrete land border, like that between the United States and Mexico, and an imaginary border, like that between the mainland United States and Puerto Rico. The latter becomes a movable border, surrounding the barrio in Paterson, New Jersey, or even the apartment in which the Ortiz family lives. People can go back and forth across that border—they live simultaneously in two cultures, rather than move from one and settle in the other. Find and read Dickerson's essay. Write a paper discussing such cultural simultaneity and how it appears in Ortiz Cofer's poems and stories.

Comparison-Contrast Papers

3. Write a research paper comparing and contrasting what Ortiz Cofer says about her *abuela,* or grandmother, in "And Are You a Latina Writer?" (p. 738) and "Speaking in Puerto Rican" (p. 742) and how she treats grandmothers in her poetry and stories — ones in this book, such as "Cold as Heaven" (p. 646), and ones you find in other books by her.

4. In her interview with Marilyn Kallet (p. 744) Ortiz Cofer says Denise Levertov was the poet who made her think seriously of writing poetry. Read carefully what she says about Levertov in the interview (paras. 15–17). Then read some poetry by Levertov (pp. 759 and 833) and write a paper comparing and contrasting their styles and techniques as poets.

Cultural Studies Papers

5. Learn more about the experiences of other writers with Puerto Rican origins or heritage — such as Julia de Burgos, Jesus Colon, Victor Hernández Cruz, and Sandra Maria Esteves, to name just a few — and write a paper discussing how Ortiz Cofer's response to her cultural background is similar to and different from theirs.

6. Watch the much-acclaimed early 1960s film *West Side Story* and research its background and effectiveness. Then compare that film's depiction of Puerto Rican–American culture with that depicted in works by Ortiz Cofer. Or do the same with a film of your choice. (Be sure to ask your instructor if your film choice is applicable.)

A Collection of Poems

CHAPTER **20**

Valuing Various Voices

A DOZEN VERY SHORT POEMS

For pedagogical purposes, the majority of poems selected for this book are not very long. There are, of course, many significant, long poems, from the book-length verses of Dante's *The Divine Comedy*, John Milton's *Paradise Lost*, and William Wordsworth's *The Prelude* to myriad others that are several pages in length and composed by equally accomplished writers. So what then is poetry's version of "short short" or "sudden fiction"? Of the one-act or "ten-minute" play of drama? Is it a poem that can be read in ten seconds?

Time, of course, is not the issue: Many short poems create an experience outside those parameters measured by a clock. Instead, the "short short poem" has to have an impact with very little, if any, buildup. It must "hit home" soon after the first line or the first few lines, creating a kind of whip crack of sudden realization, of an arresting moment, of blinding insight, or of a shift in attention or a change in perception. There is no time for the poet to lead up to the situation, to create an extended description of setting or context, to give a thorough background; there is no time to build to a conclusion, resolution, or surprise in a gradually unfolding manner. It's hit or miss. See how the following poems hit or miss you.

For additional information on these authors, see Biographical Sketches, pages 1371–1421.

Anonymous

Western Wind

[15th century]

Western wind, when will thou blow,
    The small rain down can rain?
Christ, if my love were in my arms
    And I in my bed again!

Margaret Atwood b. 1939

you fit into me

[1971]

you fit into me
like a hook into an eye

a fish hook
an open eye

Lucille Clifton 1936–2010

adam and eve

[1972]

the names
of the things
bloom in my mouth

my body opens
into brothers

5

Countee Cullen 1903–1946

For a Lady I Know

[1925]

She even thinks that up in heaven
    Her class lies late and snores,
While poor black cherubs rise at seven
    To do celestial chores.

Lance Henson   b. 1944

song in january   [1987]

a single ember in the fireplace
sends a trail of woodsmoke up the chimney

the house grown cold

the clear note of winter on everything

Randall Jarrell   1914–1965

The Death of the Ball Turret Gunner°   [1945]

From my mother's sleep I fell into the State,
And I hunched in its belly till my wet fur froze.
Six miles from earth, loosed from its dream of life,
I woke to black flak and the nightmare fighters.
When I died they washed me out of the turret with a hose.   5

Ball Turret Gunner: "A ball turret was a plexiglass sphere set into the belly of a B-17 or B-24, and inhabited by two .50 caliber machine-guns and one man, a short small man. When this gunner tracked with his machine guns a fighter attacking his bomber from below, he revolved with the turret; hunched upside-down in his little sphere, he looked like the foetus in the womb. The fighters that attacked him were armed with cannon-firing explosive shells. The hose was a steam hose" [Jarrell's note].

Denise Levertov   1923–1997

Leaving Forever   [1964]

He says the waves in the ship's wake
are like stones rolling away.
I don't see it that way.
But I see the mountain turning,
turning away its face as the ship   5
takes us away.

Marianne Moore   1887–1972

Poetry°   [1967]

I, too, dislike it.
　　Reading it, however, with a perfect contempt for it, one discovers in
　　it, after all, a place for the genuine.

Poetry: For an earlier version of this poem, see p. 843.

Dorothy Parker   1893–1967

Résumé   [1926]

Razors pain you;
Rivers are damp;
Acids stain you;
And drugs cause cramp.
Guns aren't lawful;   5
Nooses give;
Gas smells awful;
You might as well live.

Ezra Pound   1885–1972

In a Station of the Metro   [1916]

The apparition of these faces in the crowd;
Petals on a wet, black bough.

Mary Ruefle   b. 1952

Barbarians   [1987]

Here and there, between trees,
cows lie down in the forest
in the mid-afternoon
as though sleep were an idea
for which they were willing   5
to die.

Carl Sandburg 1878–1967

Fog [1916]

The fog comes
on little cat feet.

It sits looking
over harbor and city
on silent haunches   5
and then moves on.

A VARIETY OF POEMS FOR FURTHER READING

For additional information about the poets included here, see
"Biographical Sketches" pages 1371–1421.

> **APPROACHING THE AUTHOR**
>
> **Ai** described herself as "One-half Japanese, one-eighth Choctaw, one-fourth
> Black, and one-sixteenth Irish. This history of my family is itself a history of
> America." *Ai* means "love" in Japanese.
>   For more about her, see page 1371.

Ai 1947–2010

Why Can't I Leave You? [1973]

You stand behind the old black mare,
dressed as always in that red shirt,
stained from sweat, the crying of the armpits,
that will not stop for anything,
stroking her rump, while the barley goes unplanted.   5
I pick up my suitcase and set it down,
as I try to leave you again.
I smooth the hair back from your forehead.
I think with your laziness and the drought too,
you'll be needing my help more than ever.   10
You take my hands, I nod
and go to the house to unpack,
having found another reason to stay.

I undress, then put on my white lace slip
for you to take off, because you like that   15
and when you come in, you pull down the straps

and I unbutton your shirt.
I know we can't give each other any more
or any less than what we have.
There is safety in that, so much   20
that I can never get past the packing,
the begging you to please, if I can't make you happy,
come close between my thighs
and let me laugh for you from my second mouth.

Agha Shahid Ali 1949–2001

I Dream It Is Afternoon When I Return to Delhi   [1987]

At Purana Qila I am alone, waiting
for the bus to Daryaganj. I see it coming,
but my hands are empty.
"Jump on, jump on," someone shouts,
"I've saved this change for you   5
for years. Look!"
A hand opens, full of silver rupees.
"Jump on, jump on." The voice doesn't stop.
There's no one I know. A policeman,
handcuffs silver in his hands,   10
asks for my ticket.

I jump off the running bus,
sweat pouring from my hair.
I run past the Doll Museum, past
headlines on the Times of India   15
building, PRISONERS BLINDED IN A BIHAR
JAIL, HARIJAN VILLAGES BURNED BY LANDLORDS.
Panting, I stop in Daryaganj,
outside Golcha Cinema.

Sunil is there, lighting   20
a cigarette, smiling. I say,
"It must be ten years, you haven't changed,
it was your voice on the bus!"
He says, "The film is about to begin,
I've bought an extra ticket for you,"   25
and we rush inside:

Anarkali is being led away,
her earrings lying on the marble floor.
Any moment she'll be buried alive.
"But this is the end," I turn   30
toward Sunil. He is nowhere.

The usher taps my shoulder, says
my ticket is ten years old.

Once again my hands are empty.
I am waiting, alone, at Purana Qila.   35
Bus after empty bus is not stopping.
Suddenly, beggar women with children
are everywhere, offering
me money, weeping for me.

Anonymous

Sir Patrick Spens   [1765]

The king sits in Dumferling town,
    Drinking the blude-reid° wine;   *blood-red*
"O whar will I get guid sailor,
    To sail this ship of mine?"

Up and spak an eldern knicht,°   *elderly knight* 5
    Sat at the king's richt° knee;   *right*
"Sir Patrick Spens is the best sailor
    That sails upon the sea."

The king has written a braid° letter   *broad (clear)*
    And signed it wi' his hand,   10
And sent it to Sir Patrick Spens,
    Was walking on the sand.

The first line that Sir Patrick read,
    A loud lauch° lauched he;   *laugh*
The next line that Sir Patrick read,   15
    The tear blinded his ee.°   *eye*

"O wha° is this has done this deed,   *who*
    This ill deed done to me,
To send me out this time o' the year,
    To sail upon the sea?   20

"Mak haste, mak haste, my mirry men all,
    Our guid ship sails the morn."
"O say na° sae,° my master dear,   *not/so*
    For I fear a deadly storm.

"Late, late yestre'en I saw the new moon   25
    Wi' the auld moon in hir arm,
And I fear, I fear, my dear master,
    That we will come to harm."

O our Scots nobles were richt laith°   *loath*
   To weet° their cork-heeled shoon,°   *wet; shoes*   30
But lang or° a' the play were played   *before*
   Their hats they swam aboon.°   *above*

O lang, lang may their ladies sit,
   Wi' their fans into their hand,
Or ere they see Sir Patrick Spens   35
   Come sailing to the land.

O lang, lang may the ladies stand
   Wi' their gold kems° in their hair,   *combs*
Waiting for their ain° dear lords,   *own*
   For they'll see them na mair.°   *more*   40

Half o'er, half o'er to Aberdour
   It's fifty fadom° deep,   *fathoms*
And there lies guid Sir Patrick Spens
   Wi' the Scots lords at his feet.

A PAIRING OF POEMS

Margaret Atwood's "True Stories" leads us to wonder what truth actually is.
What is the truth in stories? Why is it important? Or in some cases, why
isn't it important? Compare what her poem says about the truth in stories
with Richard Garcia's truth in the stories he tells in "Why I Left the Church."
Think about the ways truth is told in the poems. What do you think the
writers are trying to get us to consider in terms of ideas about truth?

Margaret Atwood   b. 1939

True Stories   [1981]

i

Don't ask for the true story;
why do you need it?

It's not what I set out with
or what I carry.

What I'm sailing with,
a knife, blue fire,   5

luck, a few good words
that still work, and the tide.

ii

The true story was lost
on the way down to the beach, it's something   10

I never had, that black tangle
of branches in a shifting light,

my blurred footprints
filling with salt

water, this handful   15
of tiny bones, this owl's kill;

a moon, crumpled papers, a coin,
the glint of an old picnic,

the hollows made by lovers
in sand a hundred   20

years ago: no clue.

iii

The true story lies
among the other stories,

a mess of colours, like jumbled clothing
thrown off or away,   25

like hearts on marble, like syllables, like
butchers' discards.

The true story is vicious
and multiple and untrue

after all. Why do you   30
need it? Don't ever

ask for the true story.

Richard Garcia   b. 1941

Why I Left the Church   [1993]

Maybe it was
because the only time
I hit a baseball
it smashed the neon cross
on the church across   5
the street. Even

twenty-five years later
when I saw Father Harris
I would wonder
if he knew it was me.   10
Maybe it was the demon-stoked
rotisseries of purgatory
where we would roast
hundreds of years
for the smallest of sins.   15
Or was it the day
I wore my space helmet
to catechism? Clear plastic
with a red-and-white
inflatable rim.   20
Sister Mary Bernadette
pointed toward the door
and said, "Out! Come back
when you're ready."
I rose from my chair   25
and kept rising
toward the ceiling
while the children
screamed and Sister
kept crossing herself.   30
The last she saw of me
was my shoes disappearing
through cracked plaster.
I rose into the sky and beyond.
It is a good thing   35
I am wearing my helmet,
I thought as I floated
and turned in the blackness
and brightness of outer space,
my body cold on one side and hot   40
on the other. It would
have been very quiet
if my blood had not been
rumbling in my ears so loud.
I remember thinking,   45
Maybe I will come back
when I'm ready.
But I won't tell
the other children
what it was like.   50
I'll have to make something up.

W. H. Auden   1907–1973

Musée des Beaux Arts°   [1940]

About suffering they were never wrong,
The Old Masters: how well they understood
Its human position; how it takes place
While someone else is eating or opening a window or just
    walking dully along;
How, when the aged are reverently, passionately waiting   5
For the miraculous birth, there always must be
Children who did not specially want it to happen, skating
On a pond at the edge of the wood:
They never forgot
That even the dreadful martyrdom must run its course   10
Anyhow in a corner, some untidy spot
Where the dogs go on with their doggy life and the torturer's horse
Scratches its innocent behind on a tree.

Pieter Brueghel the Elder (c. 1525–1569), Landscape with the Fall of Icarus, *1558.*
Scala/Art Resource, NY.

Musée des Beaux Arts: The painting *Landscape with the Fall of Icarus* (above), on which the
poem is based, is in the Musées Royaux des Beaux-Arts in Brussels.

In Breughel's *Icarus*, for instance: how everything turns away
Quite leisurely from the disaster; the ploughman may   15
Have heard the splash, the forsaken cry,
But for him it was not an important failure; the sun shone
As it had to on the white legs disappearing into the green
Water; and the expensive delicate ship that must have seen
Something amazing, a boy falling out of the sky,   20
Had somewhere to get to and sailed calmly on.

APPROACHING THE AUTHOR

Jimmy Santiago Baca taught himself to read and write and fashioned himself a poet while in prison. It was a fellow inmate who encouraged him to submit his work to *Mother Jones*, a move that would prove pivotal to launching his literary career.
For more about him, see page 1373.

Jimmy Santiago Baca b. 1952

Family Ties   [1989]

Mountain barbecue.
They arrive, young cousins singly,
older aunts and uncles in twos and threes,
like trees. I play with a new generation
of children, my hands in streambed silt   5
of their lives, a scuba diver's hands, dusting
surface sand for buried treasure.
Freshly shaved and powdered faces
of uncles and aunts surround taco
and tamale tables. Mounted elk head on wall,   10
brass rearing horse cowboy clock
on fireplace mantle. Sons and daughters
converse round beer and whiskey table.
Tempers ignite on land grant issues.
Children scurry round my legs.   15
Old bow-legged men toss horseshoes on lawn,
other farmhands from Mexico sit on a bench,
broken lives repaired for this occasion.
I feel no love or family tie here. I rise
to go hiking, to find abandoned rock cabins   20
in the mountains. We come to a grass clearing,
my wife rolls her jeans up past ankles,
wades ice cold stream, and I barefooted,
carry a son in each arm and follow.
We cannot afford a place like this.   25

At the party again, I eat bean and chile
burrito, and after my third glass of rum,
we climb in the car and my wife drives
us home. My sons sleep in the back,
dream of the open clearing,   30
they are chasing each other with cattails
in the sunlit pasture, giggling,
as I stare out the window
at no trespassing signs white flashing past.

Jim Barnes   b. 1933

Return to La Plata, Missouri   [1982]

The warping bandstand reminds you of the hard rage
you felt in the heart of the town the day you said goodbye
to the park, silver jet, and cicadas dead in the sage.

The town is basic red, although it browns. A cry
of murder, rape, or wrong will always bend the night   5
hard into the broken grass. You listen close for sighs

of lovers on the ground. The darkness gathers light
and throws it down: something glows that you cannot name,
something fierce, abstract, given time and space you might

on a journey leave behind, a stone to carve your fame   10
on, or a simple word like *love*. The sun is down
or always going down in La Plata, the same

sun. Same too the child's cry that turns the mother's frown
brittle as chalk or the town's face against the moon.
Same too the moan of dog and diesel circling the town   15

in an air so heavy with cloud that there is little room
for breath or moon. Strange: in a town so country, so
foreign, you never hear a song nor see a loom

pattern dark threads into a history you would know
and would not know. You think you see one silver star.   20
But the town offers only itself, and you must go.

Elizabeth Bishop 1911–1979

In the Waiting Room   [1976]

In Worcester, Massachusetts,
I went with Aunt Consuelo
to keep her dentist's appointment
and sat and waited for her
in the dentist's waiting room.   5
It was winter. It got dark
early. The waiting room
was full of grown-up people,
arctics and overcoats,
lamps and magazines.   10
My aunt was inside
what seemed like a long time
and while I waited I read
the *National Geographic*
(I could read) and carefully   15
studied the photographs:
the inside of a volcano,
black, and full of ashes;
then it was spilling over
in rivulets of fire.   20
Osa and Martin Johnson°
dressed in riding breeches,
laced boots, and pith helmets.
A dead man slung on a pole
— "Long Pig,"° the caption said.   25
Babies with pointed heads
wound round and round with string;
black, naked women with necks
wound round and round with wire
like the necks of light bulbs.   30
Their breasts were horrifying.
I read it right straight through.
I was too shy to stop.
And then I looked at the cover:
the yellow margins, the date.   35
Suddenly, from inside,

---

21. **Osa and Martin Johnson:** Husband-and-wife explorers and naturalists. 25. **Long Pig:**
Polynesian cannibals' name for a human carcass.

came an *oh!* of pain
—Aunt Consuelo's voice—
not very loud or long.
I wasn't at all surprised;   40
even then I knew she was
a foolish, timid woman.
I might have been embarrassed,
but wasn't. What took me
completely by surprise   45
was that it was *me*:
my voice, in my mouth.
Without thinking at all
I was my foolish aunt,
I—we—were falling, falling,   50
our eyes glued to the cover
of the *National Geographic*,
February, 1918.

I said to myself: three days
and you'll be seven years old.   55
I was saying it to stop
the sensation of falling off
the round, turning world
into cold, blue-black space.
But I felt: you are an *I*,   60
you are an *Elizabeth*,
you are one of *them*.
Why should you be one, too?
I scarcely dared to look
to see what it was I was.   65
I gave a sidelong glance
—I couldn't look any higher—
at shadowy gray knees,
trousers and skirts and boots
and different pairs of hands   70
lying under the lamps.
I knew that nothing stranger
had ever happened, that nothing
stranger could ever happen.
Why should I be my aunt,   75
or me, or anyone?
What similarities—
boots, hands, the family voice
I felt in my throat, or even
the *National Geographic*   80

and those awful hanging breasts —
held us all together
or made us all just one?
How — I didn't know any
word for it — how "unlikely"...   85
How had I come to be here,
like them, and overhear
a cry of pain that could have
got loud and worse but hadn't?

The waiting room was bright   90
and too hot. It was sliding
beneath a big black wave,
another, and another.

Then I was back in it.
The War was on. Outside,   95
in Worcester, Massachusetts,
were night and slush and cold,
and it was still the fifth
of February, 1918.

William Blake   1757–1827

The Chimney Sweeper   [1789]

When my mother died I was very young,
And my father sold me while yet my tongue
Could scarcely cry "'weep! 'weep! 'weep! 'weep!"
So your chimneys I sweep, and in soot I sleep.

There's little Tom Dacre, who cried when his head   5
That curled like a lamb's back, was shaved; so I said,
"Hush, Tom! never mind it, for when your head's bare,
You know that the soot cannot spoil your white hair."

And so he was quiet, and that very night,
As Tom was asleeping, he had such a sight!   10
That thousands of sweepers, Dick, Joe, Ned, and Jack,
Were all of them locked up in coffins of black;

And by came an Angel who had a bright key,
And he opened the coffins and set them all free.
Then down a green plain, leaping, laughing, they run,   15
And wash in a river, and shine in the Sun.

Then naked and white, all their bags left behind,
They rise upon clouds, and sport in the wind;
And the Angel told Tom, if he'd be a good boy,
He'd have God for his father, and never want joy.   20

And so Tom awoke, and we rose in the dark,
And got with our bags and our brushes to work.
Though the morning was cold, Tom was happy and warm;
So if all do their duty, they need not fear harm.

Eavan Boland b. 1944

The Pomegranate   [1994]

The only legend I have ever loved is
the story of a daughter lost in hell.
And found and rescued there.
Love and blackmail are the gist of it.
Ceres° and Persephone the names.   5
And the best thing about the legend is
I can enter it anywhere. And have.
As a child in exile in
a city of fogs and strange consonants,
I read it first and at first I was   10
an exiled child in the crackling dusk of
the underworld, the stars blighted. Later
I walked out in a summer twilight
searching for my daughter at bed-time.
When she came running I was ready   15
to make any bargain to keep her.
I carried her back past whitebeams
and wasps and honey-scented buddleias.°
But I was Ceres then and I knew
winter was in store for every leaf   20
on every tree on that road.

---

5. Ceres: Roman name of Demeter, the goddess of crops and harvest. Her daughter Persephone was kidnapped by Pluto (or Hades) and taken to the underworld. Demeter, grieving and angry, refused to let seeds germinate or crops grow. To save the human race from extinction, Zeus finally ordered Pluto to release Persephone. Pluto told her she was free to leave but tricked her by offering a pomegranate seed; anyone who eats food in the underworld must return there. Zeus therefore arranged a compromise: Persephone would spend a third of each year in the land of the dead with Pluto (winter, when Demeter went into mourning); but she would be with her mother for the other two-thirds of each year (spring and summer). **18. buddleias:** Butterfly bushes.

Was inescapable for each one we passed.
And for me.
        It is winter
and the stars are hidden.   25
I climb the stairs and stand where I can see
my child asleep beside her teen magazines,
her can of Coke, her plate of uncut fruit.
The pomegranate! How did I forget it?
She could have come home and been safe   30
and ended the story and all
our heart-broken searching but she reached
out a hand and plucked a pomegranate.
She put out her hand and pulled down
the French sound for apple° and   *pomme* 35
the noise of stone° and the proof   *granite*
that even in the place of death,
at the heart of legend, in the midst
of rocks full of unshed tears
ready to be diamonds by the time   40
the story was told, a child can be
hungry. I could warn her. There is still a chance.
The rain is cold. The road is flint-coloured.
The suburb has cars and cable television.
The veiled stars are above ground.   45
It is another world. But what else
can a mother give her daughter but such
beautiful rifts in time?
If I defer the grief I will diminish the gift.
The legend will be hers as well as mine.   50
She will enter it. As I have.
She will wake up. She will hold
the papery flushed skin in her hand.
And to her lips. I will say nothing.

Anne Bradstreet c. 1612–1672

To My Dear and Loving Husband   [1678]

If ever two were one, then surely we.
If ever man were loved by wife, then thee;
If ever wife was happy in a man,
Compare with me, ye women, if you can.
I prize thy love more than whole mines of gold,   5

Or all the riches that the East doth hold.
My love is such that rivers cannot quench,
Nor ought but love from thee give recompense.
Thy love is such I can no way repay;
The heavens reward thee manifold, I pray.   10
Then while we live, in love let's so persever,
That when we live no more we may live ever.

Olga Broumas b. 1949

Cinderella   [1977]

... the joy that isn't shared
I heard, dies young.
    Anne Sexton, 1928-1974

Apart from my sisters, estranged
from my mother, I am a woman alone
in a house of men
who secretly
call themselves princes, alone   5
with me usually, under cover of dark. I am the one allowed in

to the royal chambers, whose small foot conveniently
fills the slipper of glass. The woman writer, the lady
umpire, the madam chairman, anyone's wife.
I know what I know.   10
And I once was glad

of the chance to use it, even alone
in a strange castle, doing overtime on my own, cracking
the royal code. The princes spoke
in their fathers' language, were eager to praise me   15
my nimble tongue. I am a woman in a state of siege, alone

as one piece of laundry, strung on a windy clothesline a
mile long. A woman co-opted by promises: the lure
of a job, the ruse of a choice, a woman forced
to bear witness, falsely   20
against my kind, as each
other sister was judged inadequate, bitchy, incompetent,
jealous, too thin, too fat. I know what I know.
What sweet bread I make

for myself in this prosperous house   25
is dirty, what good soup I boil turns

in my mouth to mud. Give
me my ashes. A cold stove, a cinder-block pillow, wet
canvas shoes in my sisters', my sisters' hut. Or I swear

I'll die young   30
like those favored before me, hand-picked each one
for her joyful heart.

Sterling A. Brown 1901–1989

Riverbank Blues   [1932]

A man git his feet set in a sticky mudbank,
A man git dis yellow water in his blood,
No need for hopin', no need for doin',
Muddy streams keep him fixed for good.

Little Muddy, Big Muddy, Moreau and Osage,   5
Little Mary's, Big Mary's, Cedar Creek,
Flood deir muddy water roundabout a man's roots,
Keep him soaked and stranded and git him weak.

Lazy sun shinin' on a little cabin,
Lazy moon glistenin' over river trees;   10
Ole river whisperin', lappin' 'gainst de long roots:
"Plenty of rest and peace in these...."

Big mules, black loam, apple and peach trees,
But seems lak de river washes us down
Past de rich farms, away from de fat lands,   15
Dumps us in some ornery riverbank town.

Went down to the river, sot me down an' listened,
Heard de water talkin' quiet, quiet lak an' slow:
"Ain' no need fo' hurry, take yo' time, take yo' time...."
Heard it sayin'—*"Baby, hyeahs de way life go...."*   20

Dat is what it tole me as I watched it slowly rollin',
But somp'n way inside me rared up an' say,
"Better be movin'...better be travelin'...
Riverbank'll git you ef you stay...."

Towns are sinkin' deeper, deeper in de riverbank,   25
Takin' on de ways of deir sulky Ole Man—
Takin' on his creepy ways, takin' on his evil ways,
"Bes' git way, a long way...whiles you can."

"Man got his sea too lak de Mississippi
Ain't got so long for a whole lot longer way,   30
Man better move some, better not git rooted
Muddy water fool you, ef you stay...."

Elizabeth Barrett Browning 1806–1861

How do I love thee?
Let me count the ways   [1850]

How do I love thee? Let me count the ways.
I love thee to the depth and breadth and height
My soul can reach, when feeling out of sight
For the ends of Being and ideal Grace.
I love thee to the level of every day's   5
Most quiet need, by sun and candlelight.
I love thee freely, as men strive for Right;
I love thee purely, as they turn from Praise.
I love thee with the passion put to use
In my old griefs, and with my childhood's faith.   10
I love thee with a love I seemed to lose
With my lost saints—I love thee with the breath,
Smiles, tears, of all my life!—and, if God choose,
I shall but love thee better after death.

Jo Carson b. 1946

I Cannot Remember All the Times...   [1989]

I cannot remember all the times he hit me.
I might could count black eyes,
how many times I said I ran into doors
or fell down or stepped into the path
of any flying object except his fist.   5
Once I got a black eye playing softball.
The rest were him. Seven, eight.
I can name what of me he broke:
my nose, my arm, and four ribs
in the course of six years' marriage.   10
The ribs were after I said divorce
and in spite of a peace bond.

I spent the night in the hospital.
He did not even spend a night in jail.
The sheriff I helped elect does not   15
apply the law to family business.
He always swore he never meant to do it.
I do believe he never planned.
It was always just the day,
the way I looked at him afraid.   20
Maybe the first time he did not mean to do it,
maybe the broken ribs were for good luck.

I want to post this in ladies rooms,
write it on the tags of women's underwear,
write it on coupons to go in Tampax packages   25
because my ex-husband will want to marry again
and there is no tattoo where he can't see it
to tell the next woman who might fall in love with him.
After six months, maybe a year,
he will start with a slap you can brush off.   30
Leave when he slaps you.
When he begins to call you cunt and whore
and threatens to kill you if you try to go
it will almost be like teasing but it is not.
Keep two sets of car keys for yourself.   35
Take your children with you when you go.
If he is throwing things, he is drinking.
If he is drunk enough he cannot catch you.
A punch in the breast hurts worse than a punch in the jaw.
A hit with an object does more damage than a hit with a fist   40
unless he is so drunk he picks up a broom instead of a poker.
If you pick up the poker, he will try to get it.
If he gets it, he will hit you with it.
He probably will not kill you because you will pass out
and then, he is all the sudden sorry and he stops.   45
When he says he will not hit you again
as he drives you to the hospital,
both of you in tears and you in pain,
you have stayed much too long already.
Tell the people at the hospital the truth   50
no matter how much you think you love him.
Do not say you fell down stairs
no matter how much he swears he loves you.
He does love you, he loves you hurt
and he will hit you again.   55

Tina Chang b. 1969

Naming the Light   [2004]

My beautiful brother opens the garage door
on a Saturday morning, taking out the tools
to rake the leaves around the gated house.

He hates this job but does it anyway,
the way he makes his breakfast before daylight.   5
He gets up as my father would, without question.

The idea of infinity haunts me. The dark days boundless.
My brother raking the leaves on an autumn day
equals the loneliness I feel, waking up

on my mattress, the light not light yet.   10
My brother that comes in from the cold now
is the same brother that came in from the snow

20 years ago, pounding his boots to wet the carpet,
pieces of frost clinging to his winter hat. Taking off
his gloves, he lets the house warm him. The idea   15

of the present is that we will last, or that the minutes
might outlive us, that the universe within each
veined leaf will surpass the present tense.

When evening comes, lights dim from each window.
A figure stands by a lamp just about to shut it.   20
In this moment, it seems as if this job is important,

that if the light fades it will be one less marker of the night.
I realign the pens on my desk as if realigning the stars.
My brother once put his name on a slip of paper.

In his boyhood hand, he wrote his name, *Vincent*,   25
in script, the slanted letters uncertain and fragile.
Today, I found his name in my pocket.

APPROACHING THE AUTHOR

As a young child, **Marilyn Chin** had an intestinal parasite that caused her to cry
persistently. To soothe her, her illiterate grandmother would carry her around
the Wanchai district of Hong Kong where they lived, reciting songs and poems
as she walked. Chin says these chants have had a tremendous influence on her
poetry.

For more about her, see page 1377.

Marilyn Chin b. 1955

How I Got That Name   [1994]
an essay on assimilation

I am Marilyn Mei Ling Chin.
Oh, how I love the resoluteness
of that first person singular
followed by that stalwart indicative
of "be," without the uncertain i-n-g   5
of "becoming." Of course,
the name had been changed
somewhere between Angel Island° and the sea,
when my father the paperson°
in the late 1950s   10
obsessed with a bombshell blonde
transliterated "Mei Ling" to "Marilyn."
And nobody dared question
his initial impulse — for we all know
lust drove men to greatness,   15
not goodness, not decency.
And there I was, a wayward pink baby,
named after some tragic white woman
swollen with gin and Nembutal.°
My mother couldn't pronounce the "r."   20
She dubbed me "Numba one female offshoot"
for brevity: henceforth, she will live and die
in sublime ignorance, flanked
by loving children and the "kitchen deity."
While my father dithers,   25
a tomcat in Hong Kong trash —
a gambler, a petty thug,
who bought a chain of chopsuey joints
in Piss River, Oregon,
with bootlegged Gucci cash.   30
Nobody dared question his integrity given
his nice, devout daughters
and his bright, industrious sons
as if filial piety were the standard
by which all earthly men were measured.   35

---

8. **Angel Island:** An island in San Francisco Bay, site of the Angel Island Immigration Station
that processed approximately one million Asian immigrants between 1910 and 1940.   9. **paperson:**
A "paper son" is a term used for young Chinese males entering the United States who claimed
to be sons of U. S. citizens but were, in fact, sons on paper only.   19. **Nembutal:** A short-
acting barbituate (Pentobarbital) prescribed as a sedative but also used as an intoxicant.

Oh, how trustworthy our daughters,
how thrifty our sons!
How we've managed to fool the experts
in education, statistics and demography—
We're not very creative but not adverse to rote-learning.   40
Indeed, they can *use* us.
But the "Model Minority" is a tease.
We know you are watching now,
so we refuse to give you any!
Oh, bamboo shoots, bamboo shoots!   45
The further west we go, we'll hit east;
the deeper down we dig, we'll find China.
History has turned its stomach
on a black polluted beach—
where life doesn't hinge   50
on that red, red wheelbarrow,°
but whether or not our new lover
in the final episode of "Santa Barbara"°
will lean over a scented candle
and call us a "bitch."   55
Oh God, where have we gone wrong?
We have no inner resources!

Then, one redolent spring morning
the Great Patriarch Chin
peered down from his kiosk in heaven   60
and saw that his descendants were ugly.
One had a squarish head and a nose without a bridge.
Another's profile—long and knobbed as a gourd.
A third, the sad, brutish one
may never, never marry.   65
And I, his least favorite—
"not quite boiled, not quite cooked,"
a plump pomfret simmering in my juices—
too listless to fight for my people's destiny.
"To kill without resistance is not slaughter"   70
says the proverb. So, I wait for imminent death.
The fact that this death is also metaphorical
is testament to my lethargy.

So here lies Marilyn Mei Ling Chin,
married once, twice to so-and-so, a Lee and a Wong,   75
granddaughter of Jack "the patriarch"

---

51. red wheelbarrow: See the poem by William Carlos Williams on page 578.   **53. "Santa Barbara":** American television soap opera, 1984-1993, that focused on the lives of the wealthy Capwell family of Santa Barbara, California.

and the brooding Suilin Fong,
daughter of the virtuous Yuet Kuen Wong
and G. G. Chin the infamous,
sister of a dozen, cousin of a million,   80
survived by everybody and forgotten by all.
She was neither black nor white,
neither cherished nor vanquished,
just another squatter in her own bamboo grove
minding her poetry—   85
when one day heaven was unmerciful,
and a chasm opened where she stood.
Like the jowls of a mighty white whale,°
or the jaws of a metaphysical Godzilla,°
it swallowed her whole.   90
She did not flinch nor writhe,
nor fret about the afterlife,
but stayed! Solid as wood, happily
a little gnawed, tattered, mesmerized
by all that was lavished upon her   95
and all that was taken away!

---

88. **mighty white whale:** The whale in Herman Melville's 1851 novel *Moby Dick*.
89. **Godzilla:** A monster which appeared first in Ishirō Honda's 1954 film *Godzilla* and became a pop culture icon in twenty-eight additional films.

Lucille Clifton 1936–2010

homage to my hips   [1980]

these hips are big hips
they need space to
move around in.
they don't fit into little
petty places. these hips   5
are free hips.
they don't like to be held back.
these hips have never been enslaved,
they go where they want to go
they do what they want to do.   10
these hips are mighty hips.
these hips are magic hips.
i have known them
to put a spell on a man and
spin him like a top!   15

Samuel Taylor Coleridge 1772–1834

Kubla Khan   [c. 1797–1798; 1813]
Or, A Vision in a Dream. A Fragment°

In Xanadu did Kubla Khan
A stately pleasure dome decree:°
Where Alph,° the sacred river, ran
Through caverns measureless to man
    Down to a sunless sea.   5
So twice five miles of fertile ground
With walls and towers were girdled round:
And there were gardens bright with sinuous rills,
Where blossomed many an incense-bearing tree;
And here were forests ancient as the hills,   10
Enfolding sunny spots of greenery.

But oh! that deep romantic chasm which slanted
Down the green hill athwart a cedarn cover!
A savage place! as holy and enchanted
As e'er beneath a waning moon was haunted   15
By woman wailing for her demon lover!
And from this chasm, with ceaseless turmoil seething,
As if this earth in fast thick pants were breathing,
A mighty fountain momently was forced:
Amid whose swift half-intermitted burst   20
Huge fragments vaulted like rebounding hail,
Or chaffy grain beneath the thresher's flail:
And 'mid these dancing rocks at once and ever
It flung up momently the sacred river.
Five miles meandering with a mazy motion   25
Through wood and dale the sacred river ran,
Then reached the caverns measureless to man,
And sank in tumult to a lifeless ocean:
And 'mid this tumult Kubla heard from far
Ancestral voices prophesying war!   30

Or, a Vision…A Fragment: Coleridge stated in a preface that this poem composed itself in his mind during "a profound sleep" (actually an opium-induced reverie); that he began writing it down immediately upon waking but was interrupted by a caller; and that when he returned to his room an hour later he could not complete it.   **1–2. In…decree:** "In Xanadu did Cublai Can build a stately Palace, encompassing sixteene miles of plaine ground with a wall" (Samuel Purchas, *Purchas his Pilgrimage* [1613]). The historical Kublai Khan (1215–1294) was the founder of the Yüan dynasty of China and overlord of the Mongol Empire.   **3. Alph:** Probably derived from the name of the River Alpheus in southern Greece, which according to mythology ran under the sea and emerged at Syracuse (Italy) in the fountain of Arethusa.

The shadow of the dome of pleasure
Floated midway on the waves;
Where was heard the mingled measure
From the fountain and the caves.
It was a miracle of rare device,   35
A sunny pleasure dome with caves of ice!

A damsel with a dulcimer
In a vision once I saw:
It was an Abyssinian maid,
And on her dulcimer she played,   40
Singing of Mount Abora.°
Could I revive within me
Her symphony and song,
To such a deep delight 'twould win me,
That with music loud and long,   45
I would build that dome in air,
That sunny dome! those caves of ice!
And all who heard should see them there,
And all should cry, Beware! Beware!
His flashing eyes, his floating hair!   50
Weave a circle round him thrice,
And close your eyes with holy dread,
For he on honey-dew hath fed,
And drunk the milk of Paradise.

39–41. Abyssinian...Abora: See *Paradise Lost* 4.280–82: "where Abassin Kings their issue
Guard, / Mount Amara, though this by some supposed / True Paradise under the Ethiop Line."

APPROACHING THE AUTHOR

When **Billy Collins** served as poet laureate of the
United States, he created a poetry channel for Delta
Airlines so people can listen to recited poetry while
they fly and he developed Poetry 180, a program for
high schools that encourages a poem be read each day
with the morning announcements. His strong belief in
presenting poetry in unexpected places stems from the
example set by his mother, who would often recite lines of poetry at random during his childhood.
For more about him, see page 1379.

Billy Collins b. 1941

I Chop Some Parsley While Listening to Art Blakey's° Version of "Three Blind Mice"   [2001]

And I start wondering how they came to be blind.
If it was congenital, they could be brothers and sisters,
and I think of the poor mother
brooding over her sightless young triplets.

Or was it a common accident, all three caught   5
in a searing explosion, a firework perhaps?
If not,
if each came to his or her blindness separately,

how did they ever manage to find one another?
Would it not be difficult for a blind mouse   10
to locate even one fellow mouse with vision
let alone two other blind ones?

And how, in their tiny darkness,
could they possibly have run after a farmer's wife
or anyone else's wife for that matter?   15
Not to mention why.

Just so she could cut off their tails
with a carving knife, is the cynic's answer,
but the thought of them without eyes
and now without tails to trail through the moist grass   20

or slip around the corner of a baseboard
has the cynic who always lounges within me
up off his couch and at the window
trying to hide the rising softness that he feels.

By now I am on to dicing an onion   25
which might account for the wet stinging
in my own eyes, though Freddie Hubbard's°
mournful trumpet on "Blue Moon,"

which happens to be the next cut,
cannot be said to be making matters any better.   30

Art Blakey: Arthur Blakey (1919–1990), American jazz drummer and band leader whose drumming style was one of the primary innovations in bebop. **27. Freddie Hubbard:** Frederick Dewayne Hubbard (1938–2008), an influential American jazz and bebop trumpeter.

Victor Hernández Cruz b. 1949

Problems with Hurricanes   [1991]

A campesino looked at the air
And told me:
With hurricanes it's not the wind
or the noise or the water.

I'll tell you he said: 5
it's the mangoes, avocados
Green plantains and bananas
flying into town like projectiles.

How would your family
feel if they had to tell   10
The generations that you
got killed by a flying
Banana.

Death by drowning has honor
If the wind picked you up   15
and slammed you
Against a mountain boulder
This would not carry shame
But
to suffer a mango smashing   20
Your skull
or a plantain hitting your
Temple at 70 miles per hour
is the ultimate disgrace.

The campesino takes off his hat—   25
As a sign of respect
towards the fury of the wind
And says:
Don't worry about the noise
Don't worry about the water   30

Don't worry about the wind—
If you are going out
beware of mangoes
And all such beautiful
sweet things.   35

Todd Davis   b. 1965

Accident   [2010]

They tell the son, who tells his friends
at school, that the father's death was
an accident, that the rifle went off
while he was cleaning it. I'm not sure
why he couldn't wait. We understand   5
the ones who decide to leave us in February,
even as late as March. Snows swell.
Sun disappears. Hunting season ends.
With two deer in the freezer any family
can survive. I know sometimes   10
it feels like you've come to the end
of something. Sometimes you just want
to sit down beneath a hemlock and never go
back. But this late in the year, when plum
trees have opened their blossoms?   15
Yesterday it was so warm we slept
with the windows open. Smell of forsythia
right there in the room. I swear
you could hear the last few open,
silk petals come undone, a soft sound   20
like a pad sliding through a gun's barrel,
white cloth soaked in bore cleaner,
removing the lead, the copper, the carbon
that fouls everything. My son knows
you don't die cleaning your rifle: 25
the chamber's always open.
I told him to nod his head anyway
when his friend tells the story,
to say *yes* as many times as it takes,
to never forget the smell of smoke   30
and concrete, the little bit of light
one bulb gives off in a basement
with no windows.

Toi Derricotte b. 1941

A Note on My Son's Face   [1989]

I

Tonight, I look, thunderstruck
at the gold head of my grandchild.
Almost asleep, he buries his feet
between my thighs;
his little straw eyes   5
close in the near dark.
I smell the warmth of his raw
slightly foul breath, the new death
waiting to rot inside him.
Our breaths equalize our heartbeats;   10
every muscle of the chest uncoils,
the arm bones loosen in the nest
of nerves. I think of the peace
of walking through the house,
pointing to the name of this, the name of that,   15
an educator of a new man.

Mother. Grandmother. Wise
Snake-woman who will show the way;
Spider-woman whose black tentacles
hold him precious. Or will tear off his head,   20
her teeth over the little husband,
the small fist clotted in trust at her breast.

This morning, looking at the face of his father,
I remembered how, an infant, his face was too dark,
nose too broad, mouth too wide.   25
I did not look in that mirror
and see the face that could save me
from my own darkness.
Did he, looking in my eye, see
what I turned from: 30
my own dark grandmother
bending over gladioli in the field,
her shaking black hand defenseless
at the shining cock of flower?

I wanted that face to die,   35
to be reborn in the face of a white child.

I wanted the soul to stay the same,
for I loved to death,

to damnation and God-death,
the soul that broke out of me.   40
I crowed: My Son! My Beautiful!
But when I peeked in the basket,
I saw the face of a black man.

Did I bend over his nose
and straighten it with my fingers   45
like a vine growing the wrong way?
Did he feel my hand in malice?

Generations we prayed and fucked
for this light child,
the shining god of the second coming;   50
we bow down in shame
and carry the children of the past
in our wallets, begging forgiveness.

II

A picture in a book,
a lynching
The bland faces of men who watch   55
a Christ go up in flames, smiling,
as if he were a hooked
fish, a felled antelope, some
wild thing tied to boards and burned.   60
His charring body
gives off light—a halo
burns out of him.
His face scorched featureless;
the hair matted to the scalp   65
like feathers.
One man stands with his hand on his hip,
another with his arm
slung over the shoulder of a friend,
as if this moment were large enough   70
to hold affection.

III

How can we wake
from a dream
we are born into,
that shines around us,   75
the terrible bright air?

Having awakened,
having seen our own bloody hands,
how can we ask forgiveness,
bring before our children the real   80
monster of their nightmares?

The worst is true.
Everything you did not want to know.

Emily Dickinson 1830–1886

I heard a Fly buzz   [c. 1862; 1890]

I heard a Fly buzz—when I died—
The Stillness in the Room
Was like the Stillness in the Air—
Between the Heaves of Storm—

The Eyes around—had wrung them dry—   5
And Breaths were gathering firm
For that last Onset—when the King
Be witnessed—in the Room—

I willed my Keepsakes—Signed away
What portion of me be   10
Assignable—and then it was
There interposed a Fly—

With Blue—uncertain stumbling Buzz—
Between the light—and me—
And then the Windows failed—and then   15
I could not see to see—

Emily Dickinson 1830–1886

Because I could not stop for Death   [c. 1863; 1890]

Because I could not stop for Death—
He kindly stopped for me—
The Carriage held but just Ourselves—
And Immortality.

We slowly drove—He knew no haste   5
And I had put away
My labor and my leisure too,
For His Civility—

We passed the School, where Children strove
At Recess — in the Ring —   10
We passed the Fields of Gazing Grain —
We passed the Setting Sun —

Or rather — He passed Us —
The Dews drew quivering and chill —
For only Gossamer, my Gown —   15
My Tippet° — only Tulle° —   *scarf/silk net*

We paused before a House that seemed
A Swelling of the Ground —
The Roof was scarcely visible —
The Cornice — in the Ground —   20

Since then — 'tis Centuries — and yet
Feels shorter than the Day
I first surmised the Horses' Heads
Were toward Eternity —

Chitra Banerjee Divakaruni b. 1956

Nargis' Toilette   [1991]

The uncovered face of a woman is as a firebrand, inflaming men's desires and
reducing to ashes the honor of her family.

Muslim saying

Powder to whiten skin
unsnagged as a just-ripe peach.
Kohl° to underline the eye's mute deeps.
Attar of rose touched to the dip
behind the earlobe,   5
the shadow between the breasts,
the silk creases
of the crimson *kameez*.°

In the women's courtyard°
it is always quiet,   10
the carved iron gates locked.
The palm shivers by the marble fountain.
The *bulbul*° sings to its crimson double
in the mirrored cage.

---

3. Kohl: Ancient eye cosmetic, used to darken the eyelids and eyelashes.   **8. *kameez:*** Unisex
dress worn in south and central Asia.   **9. women's courtyard:** A courtyard often connected
to a larger house where women can socialize out of the view of men.   **13. *bulbul:*** A songbird.

Satin *dupattas*° rustle.   15
The women put henna°
on Nargis' hands. They braid,
down her back,
the forest's long shadows,
their laughter like the silver anklets   20
they are tying to her feet.

Today the women will take Nargis
to visit the women of the Amin family.
They will drink chilled pomegranate juice,
nibble pistachio *barfis*° green as ice.   25
The grandmothers will chew
betel leaves° and discuss the heat.
Nargis will sit, eyes down,
tracing the peacock pattern
on the mosaic floor.   30
If Allah wills, a marriage
will be arranged
with the Amins' second son
whose face Nargis will see
for the first time   35
in the square wedding mirror
placed in the bride's lap.

It is time to go.
They bring her *burkha*,°
slip it over her head.   40
Someone adjusts the lace slits to her eyes.
The *burkha* spills silk-black to her feet
and spreads, spreads,
over the land, dark wave
breaking over the women, quenching   45
their light.

Now all is ready.
Like a black candle
Nargis walks to the gate.

---

15. *dupattas:* Long scarves. 16. *henna:* A reddish dye for both hair and skin.
25. *barfis:* An Indian sweet made from condensed milk and sugar, often flavored with fruit or nuts. 27. *betel leaves:* Leaves of a South or Southeast Asian vine valued as a mild stimulant and for their medicinal properties. 39. *burkha:* Loose garment covering the body and head, with a veil covering the face, worn by women in some Islamic traditions in public places.

John Donne 1572–1631

Break of Day   [1622]

'Tis true, 'tis day; what though it be?
O wilt thou therefore rise from me?
Why should we rise because 'tis light?
Did we lie down because 'twas night?
Love, which in spite of darkness brought us hither,   5
Should in despite of light keep us together.

   Light hath no tongue, but is all eye;
If it could speak as well as spy,
This were the worst that it could say,
That being well, I fain° would stay,   *gladly*   10
And that I loved my heart and honor so
That I would not from him, that had them, go.

Must business thee from hence remove?
O, that's the worst disease of love.
The poor, the foul, the false, love can   15
Admit, but not the busied man.
He which hath business, and makes love, doth do
Such wrong, as when a married man doth woo.

John Donne 1572–1631

Death, be not proud   [1633]

Death, be not proud, though some have callèd thee
Mighty and dreadful, for thou art not so;
For those whom thou think'st thou dost overthrow
Die not, poor Death, nor yet canst thou kill me.
From rest and sleep, which but thy pictures be,   5
Much pleasure; then from thee much more must flow,
And soonest our best men with thee do go,
Rest of their bones, and soul's delivery.
Thou art slave to fate, chance, kings, and desperate men,
And dost with poison, war, and sickness dwell,   10
And poppy° or charms can make us sleep as well   *opium*
And better than thy stroke; why swell'st° thou then? *(with pride)*
One short sleep past, we wake eternally
And death shall be no more; Death, thou shalt die.

Mark Doty   b. 1953

Tiara   [1991]

Peter died in a paper tiara
cut from a book of princess paper dolls;
he loved royalty, sashes

and jewels. *I don't know,*
he said, when he woke in the hospice,   5
I was watching the Bette Davis film festival

on Channel 57 and then—
At the wake, the tension broke
when someone guessed

the casket closed because   10
he was *in there in a big wig
and heels,* and someone said,

*You know he's always late,
he probably isn't here yet—
he's still fixing his makeup.*   15

And someone said he asked for it.
Asked for it—
when all he did was go down

into the salt tide
of wanting as much as he wanted,   20
giving himself over so drunk

or stoned it almost didn't matter who,
though they were beautiful,
stampeding into him in the simple,

ravishing music of their hurry.   25
I think heaven is perfect stasis
poised over the realms of desire,

where dreaming and waking men lie
on the grass while wet horses
roam among them, huge fragments   30

of the music we die into
in the body's paradise.
Sometimes we wake not knowing

how we came to lie here,
or who has crowned us with these temporary,   35
precious stones. And given

the world's perfectly turned shoulders,
the deep hollows blued by longing,
given the irreplaceable silk

of horses rippling in orchards,   40
fruit thundering and chiming down,
given the ordinary marvels of form

and gravity, what could he do,
what could any of us ever do
but ask for it?   45

Rita Dove b. 1952

Fifth Grade Autobiography   [1989]

I was four in this photograph fishing
with my grandparents at a lake in Michigan.
My brother squats in poison ivy.
His Davy Crockett cap
sits squared on his head so the raccoon tail
flounces down the back of his sailor suit.

My grandfather sits to the far right
in a folding chair,
and I know his left hand is on
the tobacco in his pants pocket   10
because I used to wrap it for him
every Christmas. Grandmother's hips
bulge from the brush, she's leaning
into the ice chest, sun through the trees
printing her dress with soft   15
luminous paws.

I am staring jealously at my brother;
the day before he rode his first horse, alone.
I was strapped in a basket
behind my grandfather.   20
He smelled of lemons. He's died—

but I remember his hands.

> **APPROACHING THE AUTHOR**
>
> **Rita Dove** played the cello in her youth and later wrote song cycles for works by a variety of composers, one of which was performed by the revered Boston Symphony Orchestra. When not writing, she studies classical voice and practices the viola da gamba, a seventeenth-century forerunner of the modern cello. For more about her, see page 1381.

Cornelius Eady b. 1954

My Mother, If She Had Won Free Dance Lessons [1986]

Would she have been a person
With a completely different outlook on life?
There are times when I visit

And find her settled on a chair
In our dilapidated house,   5
The neighborhood crazy lady
Doing what the neighborhood crazy lady is supposed to do,
Which is absolutely nothing

And I wonder as we talk our sympathetic talk,
Abandoned in easy dialogue,   10
I, the son of the crazy lady,
Who crosses easily into her point of view
As if yawning
Or taking off an overcoat.
Each time I visit   15
I walk back into our lives

And I wonder, like any child who wakes up one day to find themself
Abandoned in a world larger than their
     Bad dreams,
I wonder as I see my mother sitting there,   20
Landed to the right-hand window in the living room,
Pausing from time to time in the endless loop of our dialogue
To peek for rascals through the
Venetian blinds,

I wonder a small thought.   25
I walk back into our lives.
Given the opportunity,
How would she have danced?
Would it have been as easily

As we talk to each other now,   30
The crazy lady
And the crazy lady's son,
As if we were old friends from opposite coasts
Picking up the thread of a long conversation,

Or two ballroom dancers   35
Who only know
One step?

What would have changed
If the phone had rung like a suitor,
If the invitation had arrived in the mail   40
Like Jesus, extending a hand?

T. S. Eliot 1888–1965

The Love Song of J. Alfred Prufrock   [1917]

S'io credesse che mia risposta fosse
A persona che mai tornasse al mondo,
Questa fiamma staria senza piu scosse.
Ma perciocche giammai di questo fondo
Non torno vivo alcun, s'i'odo il vero,
Senza tema d'infamia ti rispondo.°

Let us go then, you and I,
When the evening is spread out against the sky
Like a patient etherized upon a table;
Let us go, through certain half-deserted streets,
The muttering retreats   5
Of restless nights in one-night cheap hotels
And sawdust restaurants with oyster-shells:
Streets that follow like a tedious argument
Of insidious intent
To lead you to an overwhelming question...   10
Oh, do not ask, "What is it?"
Let us go and make our visit.

    In the room the women come and go
Talking of Michelangelo.

    The yellow fog that rubs its back upon the window-panes,   15
The yellow smoke that rubs its muzzle on the window-panes
Licked its tongue into the corners of the evening,
Lingered upon the pools that stand in drains,
Let fall upon its back the soot that falls from chimneys,
Slipped by the terrace, made a sudden leap,   20
And seeing that it was a soft October night,
Curled once about the house, and fell asleep.

    And indeed there will be time
For the yellow smoke that slides along the street,
Rubbing its back upon the window-panes;   25
There will be time, there will be time

Epigraph: "If I thought that my answer were being made to someone who would ever return to earth, this flame would remain without further movement; but since no one has ever returned alive from this depth, if what I hear is true, I answer you without fear of infamy" (Dante, *Inferno* 27.61–66). Dante encounters Guido de Montefeltro in the eighth circle of hell, where souls are trapped within flames (tongues of fire) as punishment for giving evil counsel. Guido tells Dante details about his evil life only because he assumes that Dante is on his way to an even deeper circle in hell and will never return to earth and be able to repeat what he has heard.

To prepare a face to meet the faces that you meet;
There will be time to murder and create,
And time for all the works and days° of hands
That lift and drop a question on your plate;   30
Time for you and time for me,
And time yet for a hundred indecisions,
And for a hundred visions and revisions,
Before the taking of a toast and tea.

    In the room the women come and go   35
Talking of Michelangelo.

    And indeed there will be time
To wonder, "Do I dare?" and, "Do I dare?"
Time to turn back and descend the stair,
With a bald spot in the middle of my hair —   40
(They will say: "How his hair is growing thin!")
My morning coat, my collar mounting firmly to the chin,
My necktie rich and modest, but asserted by a simple pin —
(They will say: "But how his arms and legs are thin!")
Do I dare   45
Disturb the universe?
In a minute there is time
For decisions and revisions which a minute will reverse.

    For I have known them all already, known them all: —
Have known the evenings, mornings, afternoons,   50
I have measured out my life with coffee spoons;
I know the voices dying with a dying fall°
Beneath the music from a farther room.
    So how should I presume?

    And I have known the eyes already, known them all —   55
The eyes that fix you in a formulated phrase,
And when I am formulated, sprawling on a pin,
When I am pinned and wriggling on the wall,
Then how should I begin
To spit out all the butt-ends of my days and ways?   60
    And how should I presume?

    And I have known the arms already, known them all —
Arms that are braceleted and white and bare
(But in the lamplight, downed with light brown hair!)
Is it perfume from a dress   65

---

29. works and days: *Works and Days* is the title of a didactic poem about farming by the Greek poet Hesiod (eighth century B.C.E.) that includes instruction about doing each task at the proper time.   **52. a dying fall:** An allusion to Shakespeare's *Twelfth Night* (1.1.4): "That strain [of music] again! It had a dying fall" (a cadence that falls away).

That makes me so digress?
Arms that lie along a table, or wrap about a shawl.
    And should I then presume?
    And how should I begin?

          ————————

Shall I say, I have gone at dusk through narrow streets   70
And watched the smoke that rises from the pipes
Of lonely men in shirt-sleeves, leaning out of windows?...

    I should have been a pair of ragged claws
Scuttling across the floors of silent seas.

          ————————

And the afternoon, the evening, sleeps so peacefully!   75
Smoothed by long fingers,
Asleep...tired...or it malingers,
Stretched on the floor, here beside you and me.
Should I, after tea and cakes and ices,
Have the strength to force the moment to its crisis?   80
But though I have wept and fasted, wept and prayed,
Though I have seen my head (grown slightly bald) brought in upon a
    platter,°
I am no prophet — and here's no great matter;
I have seen the moment of my greatness flicker,
And I have seen the eternal Footman hold my coat, and snicker,   85
And in short, I was afraid.

    And would it have been worth it, after all,
After the cups, the marmalade, the tea,
Among the porcelain, among some talk of you and me,
Would it have been worth while,   90
To have bitten off the matter with a smile,
To have squeezed the universe into a ball
To roll it toward some overwhelming question,
To say: "I am Lazarus,° come from the dead,
Come back to tell you all, I shall tell you all" —   95
If one, settling a pillow by her head,
    Should say: "That is not what I meant at all.
    That is not it, at all."

    And would it have been worth it, after all,
Would it have been worth while,   100
After the sunsets and the dooryards and the sprinkled streets,

————————

82. head...platter: As a reward for dancing before King Herod, Salome, his stepdaughter, asked for the head of John the Baptist to be presented to her on a platter (Matthew 14:1–12; Mark 6:17–28).   **94. Lazarus:** Either the beggar Lazarus, who in Luke 16:19–31 did not return from the dead, or Jesus' friend Lazarus, who did (John 11:1–44).

After the novels, after the teacups, after the skirts that trail along
    the floor —
And this, and so much more? —
It is impossible to say just what I mean!
But as if a magic lantern threw the nerves in patterns on a screen: 105
Would it have been worth while
If one, settling a pillow or throwing off a shawl,
And turning toward the window, should say:
    "That is not it at all,
      That is not what I meant, at all."   110

No! I am not Prince Hamlet, nor was meant to be;
Am an attendant lord, one that will do
To swell a progress,° start a scene or two,
Advise the prince; no doubt, an easy tool,
Deferential, glad to be of use,   115
Politic, cautious, and meticulous;
Full of high sentence,° but a bit obtuse;   *sententiousness*
At times, indeed, almost ridiculous —
Almost, at times, the Fool.

    I grow old . . . I grow old . . .   120
I shall wear the bottoms of my trousers rolled.°   *turned up, with cuffs*

    Shall I part my hair behind? Do I dare to eat a peach?
I shall wear white flannel trousers, and walk upon the beach.
I have heard the mermaids singing, each to each.

    I do not think that they will sing to me.   125

    I have seen them riding seaward on the waves
Combing the white hair of the waves blown back
When the wind blows the water white and black.

    We have lingered in the chambers of the sea
By sea-girls wreathed with seaweed red and brown   130
Till human voices wake us, and we drown.

---

113. **progress:** Ceremonial journey made by a royal court.

Gray Emerson b. 1986

The Indexer in Love   [2010]

Answer to My Prayers, 8
  See also You
Board Games (That I Let You Win), 122–124

Dancing, 42–44
  On the Ends of Your Eyelashes, 27   5
Eyelashes, 18–19
  See also Dancing
Hair, 83–85
  That You Complimented, 86
  That You Wrote a Poem About, 87   10
  That You Wrung Your Fingers Through, 88
Index, *Index*
  See also You
Kisses
  Never Given, 23–29   15
  Stolen/Ransomed/Returned, 81–85

Love, 99–100
  Not at First Sight, 10
Peculiarities (of You)
  Biting at Your Cuticles, 50   20
  Silent Sneezes, 113
  Words Used Out of Context, 103–105
Things, List of
  I Want to Do to You, *Appendix A*
  I Want to Do with You, *Appendix B*   25
Waiting
  In Line with You, 131
  See also You
You
  Answer to My Prayers, 1
  Index You (Unable to), 1   30
  Waiting for You, 1

APPROACHING THE AUTHOR

In her late twenties, **Carolyn Forché** worked as a human rights activist in South America. While having dinner at a high-ranking El Salvadoran officer's house, the colonel asked her to go back to Washington, D.C., and tell President Carter, "We've had enough of this human rights policy."
  For more about her, see page 1383.

Carolyn Forché   b. 1950

The Colonel   [1981]

What you have heard is true. I was in his house. His wife carried a tray of coffee and sugar. His daughter filed her nails, his son went out for the night. There were daily papers, pet dogs, a pistol on the cushion beside him. The moon swung bare on its black cord over the house. On the television was a cop show. It was in

English. Broken bottles were embedded in the walls around the house to scoop the kneecaps from a man's legs or cut his hands to lace. On the windows there were gratings like those in liquor stores. We had dinner, rack of lamb, good wine, a gold bell was on the table for calling the maid. The maid brought green mangoes, salt, a type of bread. I was asked how I enjoyed the country. There was a brief commercial in Spanish. His wife took everything away. There was some talk then of how difficult it had become to govern. The parrot said hello on the terrace. The colonel told it to shut up, and pushed himself from the table. My friend said to me with his eyes: say nothing. The colonel returned with a sack used to bring groceries home. He spilled many human ears on the table. They were like dried peach halves. There is no other way to say this. He took one of them in his hands, shook it in our faces, dropped it into a water glass. It came alive there. I am tired of fooling around he said. As for the rights of anyone, tell your people they can go fuck themselves. He swept the ears to the floor with his arm and held the last of his wine in the air. Something for your poetry, no? he said. Some of the ears on the floor caught this scrap of his voice. Some of the ears on the floor were pressed to the ground.

Vievee Francis b. 1963

1864, A Pocket Full of Rye   [2006]

Confederate anticipating Colored Union troops

The trees are so full in this light —
green petticoats the balls will mow flat.

If I hide tonight, beneath a mound
of dirt I will still die, trampled

by boot, or impaled on the dark beak   5
of a rifle. I long for my field,

my plow, my good wife,
the farm and its smell.

It took two years to clear a small plot.
I took down the black gums   10

with swings I then thought mighty,
muled the stumps, fought the weed,

spread the mulch, succulent
as flowers. I miss my daughters —

hear that? a rumble — rage from the portholes —   15
and I would have it over soon and

done. I won't survive these musings.
Into the pitch   the caws,

the crows rising quick, as if suddenly freed
from some great pie, a mad and mocking flock.   20

Robert Frost 1874–1963

After Apple-Picking   [1914]

My long two-pointed ladder's sticking through a tree
Toward heaven still,
And there's a barrel that I didn't fill
Beside it, and there may be two or three
Apples I didn't pick upon some bough.   5
But I am done with apple-picking now.
Essence of winter sleep is on the night,
The scent of apples: I am drowsing off.
I cannot rub the strangeness from my sight
I got from looking through a pane of glass   10
I skimmed this morning from the drinking trough
And held against the world of hoary grass.
It melted, and I let it fall and break.
But I was well
Upon my way to sleep before it fell,   15
And I could tell
What form my dreaming was about to take.
Magnified apples appear and disappear,
Stem end and blossom end,
And every fleck of russet showing clear.   20
My instep arch not only keeps the ache,
It keeps the pressure of a ladder-round.
I feel the ladder sway as the boughs bend.
And I keep hearing from the cellar bin
The rumbling sound   25
Of load on load of apples coming in.
For I have had too much
Of apple-picking: I am overtired
Of the great harvest I myself desired.
There were ten thousand thousand fruit to touch,   30
Cherish in hand, lift down, and not let fall.
For all
That struck the earth,
No matter if not bruised or spiked with stubble,
Went surely to the cider-apple heap   35
As of no worth.
One can see what will trouble
This sleep of mine, whatever sleep it is.

Were he not gone,
The woodchuck could say whether it's like his   40
Long sleep, as I describe its coming on,
Or just some human sleep.

Robert Frost   1874–1963

Birches   [1916]

When I see birches bend to left and right
Across the lines of straighter darker trees,
I like to think some boy's been swinging them.
But swinging doesn't bend them down to stay
As ice storms do. Often you must have seen them   5
Loaded with ice a sunny winter morning
After a rain. They click upon themselves
As the breeze rises, and turn many-colored
As the stir cracks and crazes their enamel.
Soon the sun's warmth makes them shed crystal shells   10
Shattering and avalanching on the snow crust—
Such heaps of broken glass to sweep away
You'd think the inner dome of heaven had fallen.
They are dragged to the withered bracken by the load,
And they seem not to break; though once they are bowed   15
So low for long, they never right themselves:
You may see their trunks arching in the woods
Years afterwards, trailing their leaves on the ground
Like girls on hands and knees that throw their hair
Before them over their heads to dry in the sun.   20
But I was going to say when Truth broke in
With all her matter of fact about the ice storm,
I should prefer to have some boy bend them
As he went out and in to fetch the cows—
Some boy too far from town to learn baseball,   25
Whose only play was what he found himself,
Summer or winter, and could play alone.
One by one he subdued his father's trees
By riding them down over and over again
Until he took the stiffness out of them,   30
And not one but hung limp, not one was left
For him to conquer. He learned all there was
To learn about not launching out too soon
And so not carrying the tree away
Clear to the ground. He always kept his poise   35

To the top branches, climbing carefully
With the same pains you use to fill a cup
Up to the brim, and even above the brim.
Then he flung outward, feet first, with a swish,
Kicking his way down through the air to the ground.   40
So was I once myself a swinger of birches.
And so I dream of going back to be.
It's when I'm weary of considerations,
And life is too much like a pathless wood
Where your face burns and tickles with the cobwebs   45
Broken across it, and one eye is weeping
From a twig's having lashed across it open.
I'd like to get away from earth awhile
And then come back to it and begin over.
May no fate willfully misunderstand me   50
And half grant what I wish and snatch me away
Not to return. Earth's the right place for love:
I don't know where it's likely to go better.
I'd like to go by climbing a birch tree,
And climb black branches up a snow-white trunk   55
Toward heaven, till the tree could bear no more,
But dipped its top and set me down again.
That would be good both going and coming back.
One could do worse than be a swinger of birches.

A PAIRING OF POEMS

Humankind has forever contemplated whether order lies behind what
happens in this world. Robert Frost's "Design" seriously describes an
everyday event in nature and then raises a profound question: Has this
occurred by chance, or is there a pattern, a "design," behind it — and by
extension — behind everything? David Hernandez's "The Butterfly Effect"
has a light tone, yet it too leads us to consider a serious point, one that
could be seen as similar to Frost's. Consider the poems together and be
ready to describe how they approach this subject, and what the tone of
each reveals about its speaker's attitude.

Robert Frost   1874–1963

Design   [1936]

I found a dimpled spider, fat and white,
On a white heal-all, holding up a moth
Like a white piece of rigid satin cloth—

Assorted characters of death and blight
Mixed ready to begin the morning right,   5
Like the ingredients of a witches' broth —
A snow-drop spider, a flower like a froth,
And dead wings carried like a paper kite.

What had that flower to do with being white,
The wayside blue and innocent heal-all?   10
What brought the kindred spider to that height,
Then steered the white moth thither in the night?
What but design of darkness to appall? —
If design govern in a thing so small.

David Hernandez   b. 1971

The Butterfly Effect   [2003]

If a butterfly flapping its wings in Beijing
could cause a hurricane off the coast of Florida,
so could a deck of cards shuffled at a picnic.
So could the clapping hands of a father
watching his son rounding the bases,   5
the wind sculpting his baggy pants.
So could a woman reading a book of poems,
a tiny current from a turned page
slipping out the open window, nudging
a passing breeze: an insignificant event   10
that could snowball months later into a monsoon
at a coastal village halfway around the world.
Palm trees bowing on the shore.
Grass huts disintegrating like blown dandelions.

Hard to believe, but when I rewind my life,   15
starting from a point when my heart
was destroyed, I see the dominoes rising,
how that storm was just a gale weeks earlier,
a gust days before that. Finally I see
where it all began: I say hello to a woman   20
sitting alone at the bar, a tattoo butterfly
perched on her ankle, ready to wreak havoc.

Tess Gallagher b. 1943

The Hug   [1984]

A woman is reading a poem on the street
and another woman stops to listen. We stop too,
with our arms around each other. The poem
is being read and listened to out here
in the open. Behind us   5
no one is entering or leaving the houses.

Suddenly a hug comes over me and I'm
giving it to you, like a variable star shooting light
off to make itself comfortable, then
subsiding. I finish but keep on holding   10
you. A man walks up to us and we know he hasn't
come out of nowhere, but if he could, he
would have. He looks homeless because of how
he needs. "Can I have one of those?" he asks you,
and I feel you nod. I'm surprised,   15
surprised you don't tell him how
it is—that I'm yours, only
yours, etc., exclusive as a nose to
its face. Love—that's what we're talking about, love
that nabs you with "for me   20
only" and holds on.

So I walk over to him and put my
arms around him and try to
hug him like I mean it. He's got an overcoat on
so thick I can't feel   25
him past it. I'm starting the hug
and thinking, "How big a hug is this supposed to be?
How long shall I hold this hug?" Already
we could be eternal, his arms falling over my
shoulders, my hands not   30
meeting behind his back, he is so big!

I put my head into his chest and snuggle
in. I lean into him. I lean my blood and my wishes
into him. He stands for it. This is his
and he's starting to give it back so well I know he's   35
getting it. This hug. So truly, so tenderly
we stop having arms and I don't know if
my lover has walked away or what, or

if the woman is still reading the poem, or the houses—
what about them?—the houses.   40

Clearly, a little permission is a dangerous thing.
But when you hug someone you want it
to be a masterpiece of connection, the way the button
on his coat will leave the imprint
of a planet in my cheek   45
when I walk away. When I try to find some place
to go back to.

Allen Ginsberg 1926–1997

A Supermarket in California   [1956]

What thoughts I have of you tonight, Walt Whitman, for I walked
down the sidestreets under the trees with a headache self-conscious
looking at the full moon.
    In my hungry fatigue, and shopping for images, I went into the
neon fruit supermarket, dreaming of your enumerations!
    What peaches and what penumbras! Whole families shopping at
night! Aisles full of husbands! Wives in the avocados, babies in the
tomatoes!—and you, García Lorca,° what were you doing down by
the watermelons?

    I saw you, Walt Whitman, childless, lonely old grubber, poking
among the meats in the refrigerator and eyeing the grocery boys.
    I heard you asking questions of each: Who killed the pork chops?
What price bananas? Are you my Angel?   5
    I wandered in and out of the brilliant stacks of cans following
you, and followed in my imagination by the store detective.
    We strode down the open corridors together in our solitary fancy
tasting artichokes, possessing every frozen delicacy, and never passing
the cashier.

    Where are we going, Walt Whitman? The doors close in an hour.
Which way does your beard point tonight?
    (I touch your book and dream of our odyssey in the supermarket
and feel absurd.)
    Will we walk all night through solitary streets? The trees add
shade to shade, lights out in the houses, we'll both be lonely.   10
    Will we stroll dreaming of the lost America of love past blue
automobiles in driveways, home to our silent cottage?

---

3. **García Lorca:** (1899–1936), Spanish surrealist poet and playwright.

Ah, dear father, graybeard, lonely old courage-teacher, what
America did you have when Charon° quit poling his ferry and you
got out on a smoking bank and stood watching the boat disappear
on the black waters of Lethe?°

Berkeley, 1955

12. **Charon:** The boatman in Greek mythology who carried the dead across the river Styx to Hades; **Lethe:** River of Forgetfulness in Hades.

APPROACHING THE AUTHOR

Wary of rejection, especially rejection rooted in racial discrimination, **Nikki Giovanni** formed her own publishing company to publish her first collection of poems. To this day, she has never sought out nor used a literary agent.
   For more about her, see page 1385.

Nikki Giovanni b. 1943

Nikki-Rosa   [1968]

childhood remembrances are always a drag
if you're Black
you always remember things like living in Woodlawn°
with no inside toilet
and if you become famous or something   5
they never talk about how happy you were to have your mother
all to yourself and
how good the water felt when you got your bath from one of those
big tubs that folk in chicago barbecue in
and somehow when you talk about home   10
it never gets across how much you
understood their feelings
as the whole family attended meetings about Hollydale°
and even though you remember
your biographers never understand   15
your father's pain as he sells his stock
and another dream goes
and though you're poor it isn't poverty that
concerns you
and though they fought a lot   20
it isn't your father's drinking that makes any difference
but only that everybody is together and you
and your sister have happy birthdays and very good christmasses

---

3. **Woodlawn:** A suburb of Cincinnati.   13. **Hollydale:** An all-black housing development in which Giovanni's father invested money.

and I really hope no white person ever has cause to write about me
because they never understand Black love is Black wealth and they'll   25
probably talk about my hard childhood and never understand that
all the while I was quite happy

Aracelis Girmay b. 1977

Consider the Hands That Write This Letter   [2007]

after Marina Wilson

Consider the hands
that write this letter.

Left palm pressed flat against paper,
as we have done before, over my heart,

in peace or reverence to the sea,   5
some beautiful thing

I saw once, felt once: snow falling
like rice flung from the giants' wedding,

or strangest of strange birds. & consider, then,
the right hand, & how it is a fist,   10

within which a sharpened utensil,
similar to the way I've held a spade,

the horse's reins, loping, the very fists
I've seen from roads through Limay & Estelí.

For years, I have come to sit this way: 15
one hand open, one hand closed,

like a farmer who puts down seeds & gathers up;
food will come from that farming.

Or, yes, it is like the way I've danced
with my left hand opened around a shoulder,   20

my right hand closed inside
of another hand. & how I pray,

I pray for this to be my way: sweet
work alluded to in the body's position to its paper:

left hand, right hand   25
like an open eye, an eye closed:

one hand flat against the trapdoor,
the other hand knocking, knocking.

Diane Glancy b. 1941

Emigrant   [1990]

While my braids were still short
I played at the teepee.
My doll, Two Sticks, slept beside me.
We whispered under the night
watching stars in the smoke-hole.   5
In winter
I kept her on a cradleboard
wrapped with the tail of a small buffalo.
The next year
the stars were brighter.   10
I was nine.
Two Sticks still slept with me.
She said jarum e to wah,
the stars walk toward us
in the tunnel of the smoke hole.   15
It was the winter of our hunger moon.
I sucked the arm of Two Sticks.
Her spirit whispered more distantly.
Soon we would see Grandmother
and Father, my brothers   20
who were shot in battle.
Our tattered robes, the thin horses we followed.
The night shone
like the membrane under rabbit fur
we hunted once.   25
Its tail the soft puff of stars
that fills our mouths.

Ray González b. 1952

Praise the Tortilla, Praise Menudo,
Praise Chorizo   [1994]

I praise the tortilla in honor of El Panzón,
who hit me in school every day and made me see
how the bruises on my arms looked like
the brown clouds on my mother's tortillas.
I praise the tortilla because I know   5

they can fly into our hands like
eager flesh of the one we love,
those soft yearnings we delight in biting
as we tear the tortilla and wipe the plate clean.

I praise the menudo° as visionary food that it is,   10
the tripas y posole° tight flashes of color
we see as the red caldo° smears across our notebooks
like a vision we have not had in years,
our lives going down like the empty bowl
of menudo exploding in our stomachs   15
with the chili piquin° of our poetic dreams.

I praise the chorizo° and smear it
across my face and hands,
the dayglow brown of it painting me
with the desire to find out   20
what happened to la familia,
why the chorizo sizzled in the pan
and covered the house with a smell
of childhood we will never have again,
the chorizo burrito hot in our hands,   25
as we ran out to play and show the vatos°
it's time to cut the chorizo,
tell it like it is before la manteca° runs down
our chins and drips away.

---

10. **menudo:** Mexican soup made with hominy and tripe; said to have special powers.
11. **tripas y posole:** Tripe and hominy.   12. **caldo:** Soup.   16. **chili piquin:** Type of pepper, added to menudo or other soups.   17. **chorizo:** Mexican sausage.   26. **vatos:** Guys.   28. **la manteca:** Lard or grease.

Kimiko Hahn   b. 1955

Mother's Mother   [1999]

...There is no mother tongue.
          —Elaine Showalter

The mother draws the shade down halfway
so the sunlight does not blind the pages
and she reads the story, *mukashi mukashi aruhi,*°
which is the way every story begins

---

3. *mukashi mukashi aruhi:* Once upon a time.

whether about a boy riding a tortoise beneath the sea   5
or a girl born from a bamboo stalk.
Her daughter does not speak Japanese
though she can write her name in the *kana*°
that resembles tv antennae

キ ミ コ°

and she knows not everyone speaks the same language: 10
see you, ciao, adios, sayonara. She knows
her mother knows more than one way to say things
and Japanese, which is also how she *looks,*
is the language her mother was taught,
like the island of Japan,   15
almost as far from this little house on the island of Maui.

The chickens are so loud grandma.
Urusai ne.°
So dusty.
Kitanai°   20
So —

She wants to learn every word her grandma knows.
She wants to be like her grandma
who she sees her mother loves and does not want to leave.
She wants to stay with her grandma also   25
and knows from her mother's shoulders they will not see her again.

If there is no mother tongue for women
there is for immigrant children
who play on the black volcanic beaches,
on the sharp coral reefs, in the salty rain, the plantation houses,   30
the fields of burning cane, the birds-of-paradise.
Who see the shark fins in the sunlight and linger on the blanket.

There is a mother's tongue and it is conveyed
by this mother to her daughters
who will carry the words at least in song   35
because when mother dies there will be no one else
unless there is an aunt or cousin
to correct the tense or word choice
with such affection and cause.

---

8. **kana:** A general term for the syllabic Japanese scripts *hiragana* and *katakana*, which were adapted from the logographic characters of Chinese origin known in Japan as *Kanji* and which are easier to master. 9. キ ミ コ: Ki - mi - ko. 18. *Urusai ne:* Annoying, isn't it? 20. **Kitanai:** Dirty, filthy.

そうよね。°

The same cause found in domestic arts and survival.   40
When the mother dies the daughter
or the daughter-in-law, or even the son,
becomes that figure in part
and the words the older woman knew
are the words this person will parent   45
despite lineage and its repressive roots.
Its often awful branches.
The root words and radicals the daughter memorizes.

氷　シ°

So when I toss my hair from my eyes I feel
it's mother tossing her head and when I cough   50
it is her cough I hear.
And when I tell my child to say *mama*
it may be that I am speaking to myself
as much as I am speaking to the small mouth
a few inches from my face.   55

---

39. そうよね。: That's just the way it is, isn't it?   **48. 氷　シ:** It is endless (the process of learning Chinese characters).

Thomas Hardy 1840–1928

The Man He Killed   [1902]

　　"Had he and I but met
　　　By some old ancient inn,
We should have sat us down to wet
　　　Right many a nipperkin!°

　　"But ranged as infantry,   5
　　　And staring face to face,
I shot at him as he at me,
　　　And killed him in his place.

　　"I shot him dead because—
　　　Because he was my foe,   10
Just so: my foe of course he was;
　　　That's clear enough; although

---

4. nipperkin: A small cup, half–pint or less.

"He thought he'd 'list, perhaps,
   Off-hand like—just as I—
Was out of work—had sold his traps—   15
   No other reason why.

"Yes; quaint and curious war is!
   You shoot a fellow down
You'd treat if met where any bar is,
   Or help to half-a-crown."   20

Michael S. Harper b. 1938

Nightmare Begins Responsibility   [1975]

I place these numbed wrists to the pane
watching white uniforms whisk over
him in the tube-kept
prison
fear what they will do in experiment   5
watch my gloved stickshifting gasolined hands
breathe *boxcar-information-please* infirmary tubes
distrusting white-pink mending paperthin
silkened end hairs, distrusting tubes
shrunk in his *trunk-skincapped*   10
shaven head, in thighs
distrusting-white-hands-picking-baboon-light
on this son who will not make his second night
of this wardstrewn intensive airpocket
where his father's asthmatic   15
hymns of *night-train*, train done gone
his mother can only know that he has flown
up into essential calm unseen corridor
going boxscarred home, *mamaborn, sweetsonchild*
gonedowntown into *researchtestingwarehousebatteryacid*   20
mama-son-done-gone/me telling her 'nother
train tonight, no music, no breathstroked
heartbeat in my infinite distrust of them:

and of my distrusting self
white-doctor-who-breathed-for-him-all-night   25
say it for two sons gone,
say nightmare, say it loud
panebreaking heartmadness:
nightmare begins responsibility.

Terrance Hayes b. 1971

Talk   [2006]

like a nigger now, my white friend, M, said
after my M.L.K. and Ronald Reagan impersonations,
the two of us alone and shirtless in the locker room,

and if you're thinking my knuckles knocked
a few times against his jaw or my fingers knotted   5
at his throat, you're wrong because I pretended

I didn't hear him, and when he didn't ask it again,
we slipped into our middle school uniforms
since it was November, the beginning

of basketball season, and jogged out   10
onto the court to play together
in that vision all Americans wish for

their children, and the point is we slipped
into our uniform harmony, and spit out *Go Team!*,
our hands stacked on and beneath the hands   15

of our teammates and that was as close
as I have come to passing for one
of the members of The Dream, my white friend

thinking I was so far from that word
that he could say it to me, which I guess   20
he could since I didn't let him taste the salt

and iron in the blood, I didn't teach him
what it's like to squint through a black eye,
and if I had I wonder if he would have grown

up to be the kind of white man who believes   25
all blacks are thugs or if he would have learned
to bite his tongue or let his belly be filled

by shame, but more importantly, would I be
the kind of black man who believes silence
is worth more than talk or that it can be   30

a kind of grace, though I'm not sure
that's the kind of black man I've become,
and in any case, M, wherever you are,

I'd just like to say I heard it, but let it go
because I was afraid to lose our friendship   35
or afraid we'd lose the game—which we did anyway.

Samuel Hazo b. 1928

For Fawzi in Jerusalem   [1968]

Leaving a world too old to name
and too undying to forsake,
I flew the cold, expensive sea
toward Columbus' mistake
where life could never be the same   5

for me. In Jerash° on the sand
I saw the colonnades of Rome
bleach in the sun like skeletons.
Behind a convalescent home,
armed soldiers guarded no man's land   10

between Jordanians and Jews.
Opposing sentries frowned and spat.
Fawzi, you mocked in Arabic
this justice from Jehoshophat°
before you shined my Pittsburgh shoes   15

for nothing. Why you never kept
the coins I offered you is still
your secret and your victory.
Saying you saw marauders kill
your father while Beershebans° wept   20

for mercy in their holy war,
you told me how you stole to stay
alive. You must have thought I thought
your history would make me pay
a couple of piastres more   25

than any shine was worth—and I
was ready to—when you said, "No,
I never take. I never want
America to think I throw
myself on you. I never lie."   30

I watched your young but old man's stare
demand the sword to flash again

---

6. **Jerash:** The ancient city of Gerasa, twenty-two miles north of Amman in present-day Jordan. Called Jerash by the Romans who rebuilt it in 65 C.E., it is the best-preserved Palestinian city of Roman times.   14. **Jehoshophat:** Hebrew king of Judah (c. 873–849 B.C.E.), the first to make a treaty with the neighboring kingdom of Israel.   20. **Beershebans:** Inhabitants of Beersheba, a city in southern Israel. Given to the Arabs in the partition of Palestine (1948), it was retaken by Israel in the Arab-Israeli war of 1948.

in blood and flame from Jericho°
and leave the bones of these new men
of Judah bleaching in the air   35

like Roman stones upon the plain
of Jerash. Then you faced away.
Jerusalem, Jerusalem,
I asked myself if I could pray
for peace and not recall the pain   40

you spoke. But what could praying do?
Today I live your loss in no
man's land but mine, and every time
I talk of fates not just but so,
Fawzi, my friend, I think of you.   45

---

33. Jericho: Ancient city in biblical Palestine, in the Jordan valley north of the Dead Sea, captured from the Canaanites by Joshua and destroyed (Joshua 6:1–21).

George Herbert 1593–1633

The Pulley   [1633]

When God at first made man,
Having a glass of blessings standing by,
"Let us," said he, "pour on him all we can.
Let the world's riches, which dispersèd lie,
    Contract into a span."   5

So strength first made a way;
Then beauty flowed, then wisdom, honor, pleasure.
When almost all was out, God made a stay,
Perceiving that, alone of all his treasure,
    Rest in the bottom lay.   10

"For if I should," said he,
"Bestow this jewel also on my creature,
He would adore my gifts instead of me,
And rest in Nature, not the God of Nature;
    So both should losers be.   15

"Yet let him keep the rest,
But keep them with repining restlessness.
Let him be rich and weary, that at least,
If goodness lead him not, yet weariness
    May toss him to my breast."   20

Robert Herrick 1591–1674

To the Virgins, to Make Much of Time   [1648]

Gather ye rosebuds while ye may,
  Old time is still a-flying;
And this same flower that smiles today
  Tomorrow will be dying.

The glorious lamp of heaven, the sun,   5
  The higher he's a-getting,
The sooner will his race be run,
  And nearer he's to setting.

That age is best which is the first,
  When youth and blood are warmer;   10
But being spent, the worse, and worst
  Times still succeed the former.

Then be not coy, but use your time,
  And while ye may, go marry;
For having lost but once your prime,   15
  You may forever tarry.

APPROACHING THE AUTHOR

Before he published his first book of poetry in his mid-thirties, **Bob Hicok** was an automotive die designer who owned his own company. For more about him, see page 1390.

Bob Hicok b. 1960

In the loop   [2010]

I heard from people after the shootings. People
I knew well or barely or not at all. Largely
the same message: how horrible it was, how little
there was to say about how horrible it was.
People wrote, called, mostly e-mailed   5
to say, there's nothing to say. Eventually
I answered these messages: there's nothing
to say back except of course there's nothing
to say, thank you for your willingness to say it.
Because this was about nothing. A boy who felt   10
that he was nothing, who erased and entered
that erasure, and guns that are good for nothing,
and talk of guns that is good for nothing,

and spring that is good for flowers, and Jesus
for some, and scotch for others, and "and"   15
for me in this poem, "and" that is good
for sewing the minutes together, which otherwise
go about going away, bereft of us and us
of them, like a scarf left on a train
and nothing like a scarf left on a train,   20
like the train, empty of everything but a scarf,
and still it opens its doors at every stop,
because this is what a train does,
this is what a man does with his hand on a lever,
because otherwise why the lever, why the hand,   25
and then it was over, and then it had just begun.

Jane Hirshfield   b. 1953

To Drink   [1988]

I want to gather your darkness
in my hands, to cup it like water
and drink.
I want this in the same way
as I want to touch your cheek—   5
it is the same—
the way a moth will come
to the bedroom window in late September,
beating and beating its wings against cold glass;
the way a horse will lower   10
his long head to water, and drink,
and pause to lift his head and look,
and drink again,
taking everything in with the water,
everything.   15

Tony Hoagland   b. 1953

History of Desire   [1992]

When you're seventeen, and drunk
on the husky, late-night flavor
of your first girlfriend's voice
along the wires of the telephone

what else to do but steal
your father's El Dorado from the drive,
and cruise out to the park on Driscoll Hill?
Then climb the county water tower

and aerosol her name in spraycan orange
a hundred feet above the town?
Because only the letters of that word,
DORIS, next door to yours,

in yard-high, iridescent script,
are amplified enough to tell the world
who's playing lead guitar
in the rock band of your blood.

You don't consider for a moment
the shock in store for you in 10 A.D.,
a decade after Doris, when,
out for a drive on your visit home,

you take the Smallville Road, look up
and see RON LOVES DORIS
still scorched upon the reservoir.
This is how history catches up—

by holding still until you
bump into yourself.
What makes you blush, and shove
the pedal of the Mustang

almost through the floor
as if you wanted to spray gravel
across the features of the past,
or accelerate into oblivion?

Are you so out of love that you
can't move fast enough away?
But if desire is acceleration,
experience is circular as any

Indianapolis. We keep coming back
to what we are—each time older,
more freaked out, or less afraid.
And you are older now.

You should stop today.
In the name of Doris, stop.

Linda Hogan b. 1947

Crow Law   [1993]

The temple where crow worships
walks forward in tall, black grass.
Betrayal is crow's way of saying grace
to the wolf
so it can eat   5
what is left
when blood is on the ground,
until what remains of moose
is crow
walking out   10
the sacred temple of ribs
in a dance of leaving
the red tracks of scarce and private gods.
It is the oldest war
where moose becomes wolf and crow,   15
where the road ceases
to become the old forest
where crow is calling,
where we are still afraid.

APPROACHING THE AUTHOR

Garrett Kaoru Hongo began writing poetry to create awareness of the Japanese
internments in the United States during World War II, a subject he found overlooked in school curricula. He believes that he has a moral responsibility to tell
the repressed story of this earlier generation of Japanese Americans.
    For more about him, see page 1391.

Garrett Kaoru Hongo b. 1951

Yellow Light   [1982]

One arm hooked around the frayed strap
of a tar-black patent-leather purse,
the other cradling something for dinner:
fresh bunches of spinach from a J-Town *yaoya*,°
sides of a split Spanish mackerel from Alviso's,   5

---

4. **J-Town** *yaoya*: A vegetable shop or stand in Japan-Town.

maybe a loaf of Langendorf;° she steps
off the hissing bus at Olympic and Fig,
begins the three-block climb up the hill,
passing gangs of schoolboys playing war,
Japs against Japs, Chicanas chalking sidewalks 10
with the holy double-yoked crosses of hopscotch,
and the Korean grocer's wife out for a stroll
around this neighborhood of Hawaiian apartments
just starting to steam with cooking
and the anger of young couples coming home 15
from work, yelling at kids, flicking on
TV sets for the Wednesday Night Fights.

If it were May, hydrangeas and jacaranda
flowers in the streetside trees would be
blooming through the smog of late spring. 20
Wisteria in Masuda's front yard would be
shaking out the long tresses of its purple hair.
Maybe mosquitoes, moths, a few orange butterflies
settling on the lattice of monkey flowers
tangled in chain-link fences by the trash. 25

But this is October, and Los Angeles
seethes like a billboard under twilight.
From used-car lots and the movie houses uptown,
long silver sticks of light probe the sky.
From the Miracle Mile, whole freeways away, 30
a brilliant fluorescence breaks out
and makes war with the dim squares
of yellow kitchen light winking on
in all the side streets of the Barrio.

She climbs up the two flights of flagstone 35
stairs to 201-B, the spikes of her high heels
clicking like kitchen knives on a cutting board,
props the groceries against the door,
fishes through memo pads, a compact,
empty packs of chewing gum, and finds her keys. 40

The moon then, cruising from behind
a screen of eucalyptus across the street,
covers everything, everything in sight,
in a heavy light like yellow onions.

---

6. **a loaf of Langendorf:** Bread from a well-known California bakery.

A PAIRING OF POEMS

Here are two poems about athletes and fame. As you read and then study them, describe the differences in their styles and what they reveal regarding how the speakers feel about their subjects. Then consider the similarities in their ideas and what that implies in light of their having been written in very different cultures and almost ninety years apart. Also think about the poems in light of our time, when many athletes are treated as celebrities.

A. E. Housman   1859–1936

To an Athlete Dying Young   [1896]

The time you won your town the race
We chaired you through the market-place;
Man and boy stood cheering by,
And home we brought you shoulder-high.

To-day, the road all runners come,   5
Shoulder-high we bring you home,
And set you at your threshold down,
Townsman of a stiller town.

Smart lad, to slip betimes away
From fields where glory does not stay   10
And early though the laurel grows
It withers quicker than the rose.

Eyes the shady night has shut
Cannot see the record cut,°   *broken*
And silence sounds no worse than cheers   15
After earth has stopped the ears:

Now you will not swell the rout
Of lads that wore their honours out,
Runners whom renown outran
And the name died before the man.   20

So set, before its echoes fade,
The fleet foot on the sill of shade,
And hold to the low lintel up
The still-defended challenge-cup.

And round that early-laurelled head   25
Will flock to gaze the strengthless dead,
And find unwithered on its curls
The garland briefer than a girl's.

Quincy Troupe b. 1943

A Poem For "Magic"°   [1991; rev. 1996]

for Earvin "Magic" Johnson, Donnell Reid & Richard Franklin

take it to the hoop, "magic" johnson,
take the ball dazzling down the open lane
herk & jerk & raise your six-feet, nine-inch frame
into air sweating screams of your neon name
"magic" johnson, nicknamed "windex" way back   5
in high school
                    cause you wiped glass backboards
so clean, where you first juked & shook
wiled your way to glory
                    a new-style fusion of shake-&-bake   10
energy, using everything possible, you created your own
space to fly through — any moment now
we expect your wings to spread feathers for that spooky takeoff
of yours — then, shake & glide & ride up in space
till you hammer home a clothes-lining deuce off glass   15
now, come back down with a reverse hoodoo gem
off the spin & stick in sweet, popping nets clean
from twenty feet, right side
put the ball on the floor again, "magic"
slide the dribble behind your back, ease it deftly   20
between your bony stork legs, head bobbing everwhichaway
up & down, you see everything on the court
off the high yoyo patter
               stop & go dribble
you thread a needle-rope pass sweet home   25
to kareem cutting through the lane
                        his skyhook pops the cords
now, lead the fastbreak, hit worthy on the fly
now, blindside a pinpoint behind-the-back pass for two more
off the fake, looking the other way, you raise off-balance   30
into electric space
sweating chants of your name
turn, 180 degrees off the move, your legs scissoring space
like a swimmer's yoyoing motion in deep water

"Magic": Earvin "Magic" Johnson Jr. (b. 1959), star basketball player at Lansing (Michigan) Everett High School (1973–77) and Michigan State University (1977–79) and for the Los Angeles Lakers (1979–91 and 1996). He was honored in 1996 as one of the Fifty Greatest Players in National Basketball Association History.

stretching out now toward free flight   35
you double-pump through human trees
                    hang in place
slip the ball into your left hand
then deal it like a las vegas card dealer off squared glass
into nets, living up to your singular nickname   40
so "bad" you cartwheel the crowd toward frenzy
wearing now your electric smile, neon as your name

in victory, we suddenly sense your glorious uplift
your urgent need to be champion
& so we cheer with you, rejoice with you   45
                   for this quicksilver, quicksilver,
quicksilver moment of fame
so put the ball on the floor again, "magic"
juke & dazzle, shake & bake down the lane
take the sucker to the hoop, "magic" johnson,   50
recreate reverse hoodoo gems off the spin
deal alley-oop dunkathon magician passes
now, double-pump, scissor, vamp through space
hang in place
             & put it all up in the sucker's face, "magic" johnson,   55
& deal the roundball like the juju man that you am
like the sho-nuff shaman that you am, "magic,"
like the sho-nuff spaceman you am

Langston Hughes   1902–1967

The Negro Speaks of Rivers   [1926]

I've known rivers:
I've known rivers ancient as the world and older than the flow of
    human blood in human veins.

My soul has grown deep like the rivers.

I bathed in the Euphrates when dawns were young.
I built my hut near the Congo and it lulled me to sleep.   5
I looked upon the Nile and raised the pyramids above it.
I heard the singing of the Mississippi when Abe Lincoln went down
    to New Orleans, and I've seen its muddy bosom turn all golden
    in the sunset.

I've known rivers:
Ancient, dusky rivers.

My soul has grown deep like the rivers.   10

Honorée Fanonne Jeffers b. 1967

Unidentified Female Student, Former Slave
(Talladega College, circa 1885)   [2003]

You might have heard a story like this one well
but I'm telling this one to you now.
I was five when the soldiers came.

Master worked me twenty years longer.
How could I know? One day he left me alone   5
and an unwatched pot started to boil. By the time

he came back home I was cleaned of him and singing,
There's a man going round taking names.
Ready, set, and I was gone, walking. Could I see

beyond his yard? Did I have a thought to read or write   10
or count past God's creation? A barefooted
girl!—and you remember, you woman who will take

your pen to write my life. This is what the truth was like:
Master's clouds followed me to the steps of this school.
Dear reader, when you think on this years after I have died   15

and I am dust, think on a great and awful morning
when I learned my freedom. Think that the skin on my
back was scared when I dared step out into the world,

when my Master stood trembling and weeping
on his front porch and he cursed me beyond knowing.   20

Ben Jonson 1572–1637

On My First Son   [1616]

Farewell, thou child of my right hand,° and joy;
     My sin was too much hope of thee, loved boy:
Seven years thou'wert lent to me, and I thee pay,

---

1. child...hand: A literal translation of the Hebrew name "Benjamin." The boy, named for his
father, was born in 1596 and died on his birthday ("the just day") in 1603.

Exacted by thy fate, on the just day.
O could I lose all father now! for why   5
  Will man lament the state he should envy,
To have so soon 'scaped world's and flesh's rage,
  And, if no other misery, yet age?
Rest in soft peace, and asked, say, "Here doth lie
  Ben Jonson his best piece of poetry."   10
For whose sake henceforth all his° vows be such   *(the father's)*
  As what he loves may never like° too much.

---

12. like: Archaic meaning both "want" and "please."

> **APPROACHING THE AUTHOR**
>
> **A. Van Jordan** has said, "A brother who can write is far more threatening to the status quo...than a brother with a gun and his pants hanging off his butt."
> For more about him, see page 1394.

A. Van Jordan b. 1965

From   [2004]

from (⇨) *prep.* 1. Starting at (a particular place or time): As in, John was *from* Chicago, but he played guitar straight *from* the Delta; he wore a blue suit *from* Robert Hall's; his hair smelled like coconut; his breath, like mint and bourbon; his hands felt like they were *from* slave times when he touched me—hungry, stealthy, trembling. 2. Out of: He pulled a knot of bills *from* his pocket, paid the man and we went upstairs. 3. Not near to or in contact with: He smoked the weed, but, surprisingly, he kept it *from* me. He said it would make me too self-conscious, and he wanted those feelings as far away *from* us as possible; he said a good part of my beauty was that I wasn't conscious of my beauty. Isn't that funny? So we drank Bloody Mothers (Hennessey and tomato juice), which was hard to keep *from* him—he always did like to drink. 4. Out of the control or authority of: I was released *from* my mama's house, *from* dreams of hands holding me down, *from* the threat of hands not pulling me up, *from* the man that knew me, but of whom I did not know; released *from* the dimming of twilight, *from* the brightness of morning; *from* the love I thought had to look like love; *from* the love I thought had to taste like love, *from* the love I thought I had to love like love. 5. Out of the totality of: I came *from* a family full of women; I came *from* a family full of believers; I came *from* a pack of witches—I'm just waiting to conjure my powers; I came *from* a legacy of lovers—I'm just waiting to seduce my seducer; I came *from* a pride of proud women, and we take good care of our young. 6. As being other or another than: He couldn't tell me *from* his mother; he couldn't tell me *from* his sister; he couldn't tell me *from* the last woman he had before me, and why should he—we're all the same woman. 7. With (some person, place, or thing) as the instrument, maker, or source: Here's a note *from* my mother, and you can take it as advice *from* me: A weak lover is more dangerous than a strong enemy; if you're going to love someone, make sure you know where they're coming *from*. 8. Because of: Becoming an alcoholic, learning to walk away, being a good speller, being good in bed, falling in love—they all come *from* practice. 9. Outside or beyond the possibility of: In the room, he kept me *from* leaving by keeping me curious; he kept me *from* drowning by holding my breath in his mouth; yes, he kept me *from* leaving till the next day when he said *Leave*. Then, he couldn't keep me *from* coming back.

John Keats 1795–1821

Ode on a Grecian Urn

[1820]

1

Thou still unravished bride of quietness,
    Thou foster child of silence and slow time,
Sylvan historian, who canst thus express
    A flowery tale more sweetly than our rhyme:
What leaf-fringed legend haunts about thy shape   5
    Of deities or mortals, or of both,
        In Tempe or the dales of Arcady?°
    What men or gods are these? What maidens loath?
What mad pursuit? What struggle to escape?
        What pipes and timbrels? What wild ecstasy?   10

2

Heard melodies are sweet, but those unheard
    Are sweeter; therefore, ye soft pipes, play on;
Not to the sensual ear,° but, more endeared,
    Pipe to the spirit ditties of no tone:
Fair youth, beneath the trees, thou canst not leave   15
    Thy song, nor ever can those trees be bare;
        Bold lover, never, never canst thou kiss,
Though winning near the goal—yet, do not grieve;
    She cannot fade, though thou hast not thy bliss,
    Forever wilt thou love, and she be fair!   20

---

7. Tempe, Arcady: Tempe, a valley in Greece, and Arcadia ("Arcady"), a region of ancient Greece, represent ideal pastoral landscapes. **13. Not...ear:** Not to the ear of the senses, but to the imagination.

3

Ah, happy, happy boughs! that cannot shed
  Your leaves, nor ever bid the spring adieu;
And, happy melodist, unwearièd,
  Forever piping songs forever new;
More happy love! more happy, happy love!   25
  Forever warm and still to be enjoyed,
    Forever panting, and forever young;
All breathing human passion far above,
  That leaves a heart high-sorrowful and cloyed,
    A burning forehead, and a parching tongue.   30

4

Who are these coming to the sacrifice?
  To what green altar, O mysterious priest,
Lead'st thou that heifer lowing at the skies,
  And all her silken flanks with garlands dressed?
What little town by river or sea shore,   35
  Or mountain-built with peaceful citadel,
    Is emptied of this folk, this pious morn?
And, little town, thy streets forevermore
  Will silent be; and not a soul to tell
    Why thou art desolate, can e'er return.   40

5

O Attic° shape! Fair attitude! with brede°
  Of marble men and maidens overwrought,
With forest branches and the trodden weed;
  Thou, silent form, dost tease us out of thought
As doth eternity: Cold Pastoral!   45
  When old age shall this generation waste,
    Thou shalt remain, in midst of other woe
Than ours, a friend to man, to whom thou say'st,
  "Beauty is truth, truth beauty,"° — that is all
    Ye know on earth, and all ye need to know.   50

---

41. Attic: Greek, specifically Athenian; **brede:** Interwoven pattern. **49. "Beauty...beauty":** The quotation marks around this phrase were found in its earliest printing, an 1820 volume of poetry by Keats, but not in a printing later that year or in written transcripts. This discrepancy has led to considerable critical controversy concerning the last two lines. Critics disagree whether "Beauty is truth, truth beauty" is spoken by the urn (and thus perhaps expressing a limited perspective not to be taken at face value) or by the speaker in the poem, or whether the last two lines in their entirety are said by the urn (some recent editors enclose both lines in quotation marks to make this explicit) or by the speaker.

APPROACHING THE AUTHOR

Etheridge Knight, in order to support his drug addiction, snatched a woman's purse. He was sentenced to a 10- to 25-year prison term during which he redirected his bitterness by writing poetry that liberated his soul. For more about him, see page 1396.

Etheridge Knight 1931–1991

Hard Rock Returns to Prison from the Hospital for the Criminal Insane   [1968]

Hard Rock / was / "known not to take no shit
From nobody," and he had the scars to prove it:
Split purple lips, lumbed ears, welts above
His yellow eyes, and one long scar that cut
Across his temple and plowed through a thick   5
Canopy of kinky hair.

The WORD / was / that Hard Rock wasn't a mean nigger
Anymore, that the doctors had bored a hole in his head,
Cut out part of his brain, and shot electricity
Through the rest. When they brought Hard Rock back,   10
Handcuffed and chained, he was turned loose,
Like a freshly gelded stallion, to try his new status.
And we all waited and watched, like a herd of sheep,
To see if the WORD was true.

As we waited we wrapped ourselves in the cloak   15
Of his exploits: "Man, the last time, it took eight
Screws° to put him in the Hole."° "Yeah, remember when he
Smacked the captain with his dinner tray?" "He set
The record for time in the Hole — 67 straight days!"
"Ol Hard Rock! man, that's one crazy nigger."   20
And then the jewel of a myth that Hard Rock had once bit
A screw on the thumb and poisoned him with syphilitic spit.

The testing came, to see if Hard Rock was really tame.
A hillbilly called him a black son of a bitch
And didn't lose his teeth, a screw who knew Hard Rock   25
From before shook him down and barked in his face.
And Hard Rock did *nothing*. Just grinned and looked silly,
His eyes empty like knot holes in a fence.

---

17. Screws: Guards; **the Hole:** Solitary confinement.

And even after we discovered that it took Hard Rock
Exactly 3 minutes to tell you his first name,   30
We told ourselves that he had just wised up,
Was being cool; but we could not fool ourselves for long,
And we turned away, our eyes on the ground. Crushed.
He had been our Destroyer, the doer of things
We dreamed of doing but could not bring ourselves to do,   35
The fears of years, like a biting whip,
Had cut deep bloody grooves
Across our backs.

Li-Young Lee b. 1957

Visions and Interpretations   [1986]

Because this graveyard is a hill,
I must climb up to see my dead,
stopping once midway to rest
beside this tree.

It was here, between the anticipation   5
of exhaustion, and exhaustion,
between vale and peak,
my father came down to me

and we climbed arm in arm to the top.
He cradled the bouquet I'd brought,   10
and I, a good son, never mentioned his grave,
erect like a door behind him.

And it was here, one summer day, I sat down
to read an old book. When I looked up
from the noon-lit page, I saw a vision   15
of a world about to come, and a world about to go.

Truth is, I've not seen my father
since he died, and, no, the dead
do not walk arm in arm with me.

If I carry flowers to them, I do so without their help,   20
the blossoms not always bright, torch-like,
but often heavy as sodden newspaper.

Truth is, I came here with my son one day,
and we rested against this tree,
and I fell asleep, and dreamed   25

a dream which, upon my boy waking me, I told.
Neither of us understood.
Then we went up.

Even this is not accurate.
Let me begin again: 30

Between two griefs, a tree.
Between my hands, white chrysanthemums, yellow chrysanthemums.

The old book I finished reading
I've since read again and again.

And what was far grows near,   35
and what is near grows more dear,

and all of my visions and interpretations
depend on what I see,

and between my eyes is always
the rain, the migrant rain.   40

Denise Levertov 1923–1997

Talking to Grief   [1978]

Ah, grief, I should not treat you
like a homeless dog
who comes to the back door
for a crust, for a meatless bone.
I should trust you.   5

I should coax you
into the house and give you
your own corner,
a worn mat to lie on,
your own water dish.   10

You think I don't know you've been living
under my porch.
You long for your real place to be readied
before winter comes. You need
your name,   15
your collar and tag. You need
the right to warn off intruders,
to consider

my house your own
and me your person   20
and yourself
my own dog.

Philip Levine b. 1928

What Work Is   [1991]

We stand in the rain in a long line
waiting at Ford Highland Park. For work.
You know what work is—if you're
old enough to read this you know what
work is, although you may not do it.   5
Forget you. This is about waiting,
shifting from one foot to another.
Feeling the light rain falling like mist
into your hair, blurring your vision
until you think you see your own brother   10
ahead of you, maybe ten places.
You rub your glasses with your fingers,
and of course it's someone else's brother,
narrower across the shoulders than
yours but with the same sad slouch, the grin   15
that does not hide the stubbornness,
the sad refusal to give in to
rain, to the hours wasted waiting,
to the knowledge that somewhere ahead
a man is waiting who will say, "No,   20
we're not hiring today," for any
reason he wants. You love your brother,
now suddenly you can hardly stand
the love flooding you for your brother,
who's not beside you or behind or   25
ahead because he's home trying to
sleep off a miserable night shift
at Cadillac so he can get up
before noon to study his German.
Works eight hours a night so he can sing   30
Wagner, the opera you hate most,
the worst music ever invented.
How long has it been since you told him
you loved him, held his wide shoulders,
opened your eyes wide and said those words,   35

and maybe kissed his cheek? You've never
done something so simple, so obvious,
not because you're too young or too dumb,
not because you're jealous or even mean
or incapable of crying in   40
the presence of another man, no,
just because you don't know what work is.

Larry Levis 1946–1996

The Poem You Asked For   [1972]

My poem would eat nothing.
I tried giving it water
but it said no,

worrying me.
Day after day,   5
I held it up to the light,

turning it over,
but it only pressed its lips
more tightly together.

It grew sullen, like a toad   10
through with being teased.
I offered it all my money,

my clothes, my car with a full tank.
But the poem stared at the floor.
Finally I cupped it in   15

my hands, and carried it gently
out into the soft air, into the
evening traffic, wondering how

to end things between us.
For now it had begun breathing,   20
putting on more and

more hard rings of flesh.
And the poem demanded the food,
it drank up all the water,

beat me and took my money,   25
tore the faded clothes
off my back,

said Shit,
and walked slowly away,
slicing its hair down.   30

Said it was going
over to your place.

Audre Lorde   1934–1992

Hanging Fire   [1978]

I am fourteen
and my skin has betrayed me
the boy I cannot live without
still sucks his thumb
in secret
how come my knees are   5
always so ashy
what if I die
before morning
and momma's in the bedroom   10
with the door closed.

I have to learn how to dance
in time for the next party
my room is too small for me
suppose I die before graduation   15
they will sing sad melodies
but finally
tell the truth about me
There is nothing I want to do
and too much   20
that has to be done
and momma's in the bedroom
with the door closed.

Nobody even stops to think
about my side of it   25
I should have been on Math Team
my marks were better than his
why do I have to be

the one
wearing braces   30
I have nothing to wear tomorrow
will I live long enough
to grow up
and momma's in the bedroom
with the door closed.   35

Richard Lovelace 1618–1657

To Lucasta, Going to the Wars   [1649]

Tell me not, Sweet, I am unkind,
   That from the nunnery
Of thy chaste breast and quiet mind
   To war and arms I fly.

True, a new mistress now I chase,   5
   The first foe in the field;
And with a stronger faith embrace
   A sword, a horse, a shield.

Yet this inconstancy is such
   As you too shall adore;   10
I could not love thee, dear, so much,
   Loved I not honor more.

Robert Lowell 1917–1978

Skunk Hour   [1963]

for Elizabeth Bishop°

Nautilus Island's hermit
heiress still lives through winter in her Spartan cottage;
her sheep still graze above the sea.
Her son's a bishop. Her farmer
is first selectman in our village;   5
she's in her dotage.

Thirsting for
the hierarchic privacy
of Queen Victoria's century,

Elizabeth Bishop: American poet (1911–1979); see her poems on pages 699 and 770 and the
biographical sketch on page 1374.

she buys up all   10
the eyesores facing her shore,
and lets them fall.

The season's ill —
we've lost our summer millionaire,
who seemed to leap from an L. L. Bean   15
catalogue. His nine-knot yawl
was auctioned off to lobstermen.
A red fox stain covers Blue Hill.

And now our fairy
decorator brightens his shop for fall;   20
his fishnet's filled with orange cork,
orange, his cobbler's bench and awl;
there is no money in his work,
he'd rather marry.

One dark night,   25
my Tudor Ford climbed the hill's skull;
I watched for love-cars. Lights turned down,
they lay together, hull to hull,
where the graveyard shelves on the town....
My mind's not right.   30

A car radio bleats,
"Love, O careless Love...." I hear
my ill-spirit sob in each blood cell,
as if my hand were at its throat....
I myself am hell;   35
nobody's here —

only skunks, that search
in the moonlight for a bite to eat.
They march on their soles up Main Street:
white stripes, moonstruck eyes' red fire   40
under the chalk-dry and spar spire
of the Trinitarian Church.

I stand on top
of our back steps and breathe the rich air —
a mother skunk with her column of kittens swills the garbage pail.   45
She jabs her wedge-head in a cup
of sour cream, drops her ostrich tail,
and will not scare.

Heather McHugh b. 1948

What He Thought [1994]

We were supposed to do a job in Italy
and, full of our feeling for
ourselves (our sense of being
Poets from America) we went
from Rome to Fano, met   5
the mayor, mulled
a couple matters over (what's
cheap date, they asked us; what's
flat drink). Among Italian literati

we could recognize our counterparts: 10
the academic, the apologist,
the arrogant, the amorous,
the brazen and the glib — and there was one

administrator (the conservative), in suit
of regulation gray, who like a good tour guide   15
with measured pace and uninflected tone narrated
sights and histories the hired van hauled us past.
Of all, he was most politic and least poetic,
so it seemed. Our last few days in Rome
(when all but three of the New World Bards had flown)   20
I found a book of poems this
unprepossessing one had written: it was there
in the *pensione* room (a room he'd recommended)
where it must have been abandoned by
the German visitor (was there a bus of *them*?)   25
to whom he had inscribed and dated it a month before.
I couldn't read Italian, either, so I put the book
back into the wardrobe's dark. We last Americans

were due to leave tomorrow. For our parting evening then
our host chose something in a family restaurant, and there   30
we sat and chatted, sat and chewed,
till, sensible it was our last
big chance to be poetic, make
our mark, one of us asked

                     "What's poetry?   35
Is it the fruits and vegetables and
marketplace of Campo dei Fiori, or
the statue there?" Because I was

the glib one, I identified the answer
instantly, I didn't have to think — "The truth   40

is both, it's both," I blurted out. But that
was easy. That was easiest to say. What followed
taught me something about difficulty,
for our underestimated host spoke out,
all of a sudden, with a rising passion, and he said: 45

The statue represents Giordano Bruno,
brought to be burned in the public square
because of his offense against
authority, which is to say
the Church. His crime was his belief   50
the universe does not revolve around
the human being: God is no
fixed point or central government, but rather is
poured in waves through all things. All things
move. "If God is not the soul itself, He is   55
the soul of the soul of the world." Such was
his heresy. The day they brought him
forth to die, they feared he might
incite the crowd (the man was famous
for his eloquence). And so his captors   60
placed upon his face
an iron mask, in which

he could not speak. That's
how they burned him. That is how
he died: without a word, in front   65
of everyone.
                    And poetry—
                         (we'd all
put down our forks by now, to listen to
the man in gray; he went on   70
softly)—
                    poetry is what

he thought, but did not say.

Christopher Marlowe   1564–1593

The Passionate Shepherd to His Love   [1599]

Come live with me and be my love,
And we will all the pleasures prove
That valleys, groves, hills, and fields,
Woods, or steepy mountain yields.

And we will sit upon the rocks,   5
Seeing the shepherds feed their flocks,
By shallow rivers, to whose falls
Melodious birds sing madrigals.

And I will make thee beds of roses
And a thousand fragrant posies,   10
A cap of flowers, and a kirtle°   *skirt, outer petticoat*
Embroidered all with leaves of myrtle.

A gown made of the finest wool
Which from our pretty lambs we pull,
Fair lined slippers for the cold,   15
With buckles of the purest gold.

A belt of straw and ivy buds,
With coral clasps and amber studs,
And if these pleasures may thee move,
Come live with me, and be my love.   20

The shepherd swains shall dance and sing
For thy delight each May morning.
If these delights thy mind may move,
Then live with me and be my love.

Andrew Marvell 1621–1678

To His Coy° Mistress   [*c. 1650*; 1681]

    Had we but world enough, and time,
This coyness, lady, were no crime.
We would sit down, and think which way
To walk, and pass our long love's day.
Thou by the Indian Ganges' side   5
Shouldst rubies find; I by the tide
Of Humber would complain.° I would
Love you ten years before the Flood,
And you should, if you please, refuse
Till the conversion of the Jews.°   10
My vegetable° love should grow   *living and growing*

Coy: In the seventeenth century, *coy* could carry its older meaning, "shy," or its modern sense
of "coquettish." **5–7. Indian Ganges', Humber:** The Ganges River in India, with its distant,
romantic associations, contrasts with the Humber River, running through Hull in northeast
England, Marvell's hometown. **10. conversion…Jews:** An occurrence foretold, in some
traditions, as one of the concluding events of human history.

Vaster than empires, and more slow;
An hundred years should go to praise
Thine eyes, and on thy forehead gaze;
Two hundred to adore each breast,   15
But thirty thousand to the rest;
An age at least to every part,
And the last age should show your heart.
For, lady, you deserve this state,°   *dignity*
Nor would I love at lower rate.   20
   But at my back I always hear
Time's wingèd chariot hurrying near;
And yonder all before us lie
Deserts of vast eternity.
Thy beauty shall no more be found,   25
Nor, in thy marble vault, shall sound
My echoing song; then worms shall try
That long-preserved virginity,
And your quaint honor turn to dust,
And into ashes all my lust: 30
The grave's a fine and private place,
But none, I think, do there embrace.
   Now therefore, while the youthful hue
Sits on thy skin like morning dew,
And while thy willing soul transpires°   *breathes forth*   35
At every pore with instant fires,°   *urgent passion*
Now let us sport us while we may,
And now, like amorous birds of prey,
Rather at once our time devour
Than languish in his slow-chapped° power.   40
Let us roll all our strength and all
Our sweetness up into one ball,
And tear our pleasures with rough strife
Thorough° the iron gates of life;   *through*
Thus, though we cannot make our sun   45
Stand still,° yet we will make him run.

You can explore Andrew Marvell and "To His Coy Mistress" in depth, including images and cultural documents, with VirtuaLit Poetry at bedfordstmartins.com/rewritinglit.

40. slow-chapped: Slow-jawed, devouring slowly.   45–46. make our sun Stand still: An allusion to Joshua 10:12. In answer to Joshua's prayer, God made the sun stand still, to prolong the day and give the Israelites more time to defeat the Amorites.

APPROACHING THE AUTHOR

John Milton became totally blind in 1652, in his early forties. He composed his long, famous works *Paradise Lost* (1667), *Paradise Regained* (1671), and *Samson Agonistes* (1671) in his head and dictated them to his daughter and others who wrote them down.

For more about him, see page 1400.

John Milton 1608–1674

When I consider how my light is spent   [c. 1652; 1673]

When I consider how my light is spent°
    Ere half my days, in this dark world and wide,
    And that one talent which is death to hide
    Lodged with me useless, though my soul more bent
To serve therewith my Maker, and present   5
    My true account, lest he returning chide.
    "Doth God exact day-labor, light denied?"
    I fondly° ask; but patience to prevent   *foolishly*
That murmur, soon replies, "God doth not need
    Either man's work or his own gifts; who best   10
    Bear his mild yoke, they serve him best. His state
Is kingly. Thousands at his bidding speed
    And post o'er land and ocean without rest:
    They also serve who only stand and wait."

---

1. When . . . spent: Milton went blind in 1652. Lines 1–2 allude to Matthew 25:1–13; line 3, to Matthew 25:14–30; and line 11, to Matthew 11:30.

Marianne Moore 1887–1972

Poetry°   [1921]

I, too, dislike it: there are things that are important beyond all this fiddle.
    Reading it, however, with a perfect contempt for it, one discovers in
    it after all, a place for the genuine.
        Hands that can grasp, eyes
        that can dilate, hair that can rise
           if it must, these things are important not because a   5

high-sounding interpretation can be put upon them but because they are
    useful. When they become so derivative as to become unintelligible,
    the same thing may be said for all of us, that we

Poetry: For a later revision of this poem, see p. 760.

do not admire what   10
we cannot understand: the bat
    holding on upside down or in quest of something to

eat, elephants pushing, a wild horse taking a roll, a tireless wolf under
a tree, the immovable critic twitching his skin like a horse that
                                    feels a flea, the base-
ball fan, the statistician—   15
    nor is it valid
        to discriminate against "business documents and

school-books"; all these phenomena are important. One must make
                                    a distinction
however: when dragged into prominence by half poets, the result
                                    is not poetry,
    nor till the poets among us can be   20
        "literalists of
        the imagination"—above
            insolence and triviality and can present

for inspection, "imaginary gardens with real toads in them," shall
                                    we have
    it. In the meantime, if you demand on the one hand,   25
    the raw material of poetry in
        all its rawness and
        that which is on the other hand
            genuine, you are interested in poetry.

Thylias Moss b. 1954

Rush Hour   [1983]

He boards the train downtown,
same time I get on in Lee Heights.

Eastbound passes westbound.
Can't pick him out,

square-shouldered every one of them,   5
under 40 years old, over 40 thousand a year,

never glancing up from their papers
till they pass Quincy, Central Avenue's

gutted brownstones, record and head shops,
Joe D's Tavern where I rent the back room.   10

He's ashamed of what we have in common.
I just left his house. Spotless.

Marilyn Nelson   b. 1946

Minor Miracle   [1997]

Which reminds me of another knock-on-wood
memory. I was cycling with a male friend,
through a small midwestern town. We came to a 4-way
stop and stopped, chatting. As we started again,
a rusty old pick-up truck, ignoring the stop sign,   5
hurricaned past scant inches from our front wheels.
My partner called, "Hey, that was a 4-way stop!"
The truck driver, stringy blond hair a long fringe
under his brand-name beer cap, looked back and yelled,
            "You fucking niggers!"   10
And sped off.
My friend and I looked at each other and shook our heads.
We remounted our bikes and headed out of town.
We were pedaling through a clear blue afternoon
between two fields of almost-ripened wheat   15
bordered by cornflowers and Queen Anne's lace
when we heard an unmuffled motor, a honk-honking.
We stopped, closed ranks, made fists.
It was the same truck. It pulled over.
A tall, very much in shape young white guy slid out: 20
greasy jeans, homemade finger tattoos, probably
a Marine Corps boot-camp footlockerful
of martial arts techniques.

"What did you say back there!" he shouted.
My friend said, "I said it was a 4-way stop.   25
You went through it."
"And what did I say?" the white guy asked.
"You said: 'You fucking niggers.'"
The afternoon froze.

"Well," said the white guy,   30
shoving his hands into his pockets
and pushing dirt around with the pointed toe of his boot,
"I just want to say I'm sorry."
He climbed back into his truck
and drove away.   35

Lorine Niedecker 1903–1970

My Life by Water   [1985]

My life
   by water—
      Hear

spring's
   first frog
      or board   5

out on the cold
   ground
      giving

Muskrats   10
   gnawing
      doors

to wild green
   arts and letters
      Rabbits   15

raided
   my lettuce
      One boat

two—
   pointed toward
      my shore   20

thru birdstart
   wingdrip
      weed-drift

of the soft   25
   and serious—
      Water

Naomi Shihab Nye b. 1952

The Small Vases from Hebron°   [1998]

Tip their mouths open to the sky.
Turquoise, amber,

Hebron: An ancient city in the West Bank area of Israel; a sacred place for both Muslims and Jews and a focus of tension between Israelis and Palestinians since the 1967 Arab-Israeli war.

the deep green with fluted handle,
pitcher the size of two thumbs,
tiny lip and graceful waist.   5

Here we place the smallest flower
which could have lived invisibly
in loose soil beside the road,
sprig of succulent rosemary,
bowing mint.   10

They grow deeper in the center of the table.

Here we entrust the small life,
thread, fragment, breath.
And it bends. It waits all day.
As the bread cools and the children   15
open their gray copybooks
to shape the letter that looks like
a chimney rising out of a house.

And what do the headlines say?

Nothing of the smaller petal   20
perfectly arranged inside the larger petal
or the way tinted glass filters light.
Men and boys, praying when they died,
fall out of their skins.
The whole alphabet of living,   25
heads and tails of words,
sentences, the way they said,
"Ya'Allah!" when astonished,
or "ya'ani" for "I mean" —
a crushed glass under the feet   30
still shines.
But the child of Hebron sleeps
with the thud of her brothers falling
and the long sorrow of the color red.

APPROACHING THE AUTHOR

Naomi Shihab Nye has traveled widely and lived in multiple countries, but she says she finds much of her inspiration in the local, drawing her poetry from the day-to-day goings-on and street conversations of her neighbors in San Antonio.

For more about her, see page 1403.

APPROACHING THE AUTHOR

Sharon Olds developed a program at Goldwater Hospital (a hospital in New York City for the severely disabled) that enables residents to create poems.

For more about her, see page 1404.

Sharon Olds b. 1942

I Go Back to May 1937   [1987]

I see them standing at the formal gates of their colleges,
I see my father strolling out
under the ochre sandstone arch, the
red tiles glinting like bent
plates of blood behind his head, I   5
see my mother with a few light books at her hip
standing at the pillar made of tiny bricks with the
wrought-iron gate still open behind her, its
sword-tips black in the May air,
they are about to graduate, they are about to get married,   10
they are kids, they are dumb, all they know is they are
innocent, they would never hurt anybody.
I want to go up to them and say Stop,
don't do it—she's the wrong woman,
he's the wrong man, you are going to do things   15
you cannot imagine you would ever do,
you are going to do bad things to children,
you are going to suffer in ways you never heard of,
you are going to want to die. I want to go
up to them there in the late May sunlight and say it,   20
her hungry pretty blank face turning to me,
her pitiful beautiful untouched body,
his arrogant handsome blind face turning to me,
his pitiful beautiful untouched body,
but I don't do it. I want to live. I   25
take them up like the male and female
paper dolls and bang them together
at the hips like chips of flint as if to
strike sparks from them, I say
Do what you are going to do, and I will tell about it.   30

Simon J. Ortiz b. 1941

Speaking   [1977]

I take him outside
under the trees,
have him stand on the ground.
We listen to the crickets,

cicadas, million years old sound.   5
Ants come by us.
I tell them,
"This is he, my son.
This boy is looking at you.
I am speaking for him."   10

The crickets, cicadas,
the ants, the millions of years
are watching us,
hearing us.
My son murmurs infant words,   15
speaking, small laughter
bubbles from him.
Tree leaves tremble.
They listen to this boy
speaking for me.   20

Linda Pastan b. 1932

love poem   [1988]

I want to write you
a love poem as headlong
as our creek
after thaw
when we stand   5
on its dangerous
banks and watch it carry
with it every twig
every dry leaf and branch
in its path   10
every scruple
when we see it
so swollen
with runoff
that even as we watch   15
we must grab
each other
and step back
we must grab each
other or   20
get our shoes
soaked we must
grab each other

Robert Pinsky b. 1940

Shirt   [1990]

The back, the yoke, the yardage. Lapped seams,
The nearly invisible stitches along the collar
Turned in a sweatshop by Koreans or Malaysians

Gossiping over tea and noodles on their break
Or talking money or politics while one fitted   5
This armpiece with its overseam to the band

Of cuff I button at my wrist. The presser, the cutter,
The wringer, the mangle. The needle, the union,
The treadle, the bobbin. The code. The infamous blaze

At the Triangle Factory° in nineteen-eleven.   *(in New York City)*   10
One hundred and forty-six died in the flames
On the ninth floor, no hydrants, no fire escapes —

The witness in a building across the street
Who watched how a young man helped a girl to step
Up to the windowsill, then held her out   15

Away from the masonry wall and let her drop.
And then another. As if he were helping them up
To enter a streetcar, and not eternity.

A third before he dropped her put her arms
Around his neck and kissed him. Then he held   20
Her into space, and dropped her. Almost at once

He stepped to the sill himself, his jacket flared
And fluttered up from his shirt as he came down,
Air filling up the legs of his gray trousers —

Like Hart Crane's Bedlamite, "shrill shirt ballooning."   25
Wonderful how the pattern matches perfectly
Across the placket and over the twin bar-tacked

Corners of both pockets, like a strict rhyme
Or a major chord. Prints, plaids, checks,
Houndstooth, Tattersall, Madras. The clan tartans   30

Invented by mill-owners inspired by the hoax of Ossian,°
To control their savage Scottish workers, tamed

---

31. Ossian: Legendary Gaelic poet, hero of a cycle of traditional tales and poems that place him in the third century C.E. The hoax involved Scottish author James Macpherson (1736–1796), who published two epic poems that he said were translations of works written by Ossian but were in fact mostly composed by Macpherson himself.

By a fabricated heraldry: MacGregor,

Bailey, MacMartin. The kilt, devised for workers
To wear among the dusty clattering looms.   35
Weavers, carders, spinners. The loader,

The docker, the navvy. The planter, the picker, the sorter
Sweating at her machine in a litter of cotton
As slaves in calico headrags sweated in fields:

George Herbert,° your descendant is a Black   40
Lady in South Carolina, her name is Irma
And she inspected my shirt. Its color and fit

And feel and its clean smell have satisfied
Both her and me. We have culled its cost and quality
Down to the buttons of simulated bone,   45

The buttonholes, the sizing, the facing, the characters
Printed in black on neckband and tail. The shape,
The label, the labor, the color, the shade. The shirt.

---

40. **George Herbert:** (1593–1633), English metaphysical poet. See pp. 818 and 1390.

Sylvia Plath   1932–1963

Daddy   [1962]

You do not do, you do not do
Any more, black shoe
In which I have lived like a foot
For thirty years, poor and white,
Barely daring to breathe or Achoo.   5

Daddy, I have had to kill you.
You died before I had time—
Marble-heavy, a bag full of God,
Ghastly statue with one grey toe
Big as a Frisco seal   10

And a head in the freakish Atlantic
Where it pours bean green over blue
In the waters off beautiful Nauset.
I used to pray to recover you.
Ach, du.°   *Oh, you (German)*   15

In the German tongue, in the Polish town
Scraped flat by the roller
Of wars, wars, wars.
But the name of the town is common.
My Polack friend   20

Says there are a dozen or two.
So I never could tell where you
Put your foot, your root,
I never could talk to you.
The tongue stuck in my jaw.   25

It stuck in a barb wire snare.
Ich, ich, ich, ich,°   I (German)
I could hardly speak.
I thought every German was you.
And the language obscene   30

An engine, an engine
Chuffing me off like a Jew.
A Jew to Dachau, Auschwitz, Belsen.°
I began to talk like a Jew.
I think I may well be a Jew.   35

The snows of the Tyrol,° the clear beer of Vienna
Are not very pure or true.
With my gypsy ancestress and my weird luck
And my Taroc pack and my Taroc pack
I may be a bit of a Jew.   40

I have always been scared of *you*,
With your Luftwaffe,° your gobbledygoo.
And your neat moustache
And your Aryan eye, bright blue.
Panzer°-man, panzer-man, O You—   45

Not God but a swastika
So black no sky could squeak through.
Every woman adores a Fascist,
The boot in the face, the brute
Brute heart of a brute like you.   50

You stand at the blackboard, daddy,
In the picture I have of you,

---

33. Dachau, Auschwitz, Belsen: Nazi concentration camps.   **36. the Tyrol:** An alpine region in western Austria and northern Italy.   **42. Luftwaffe:** The Nazi air force in World War II.
45. Panzer: An armored unit in the German army in World War II.

A cleft in your chin instead of your foot
But no less a devil for that, no not
Any less the black man who   55

Bit my pretty red heart in two.
I was ten when they buried you.
At twenty I tried to die
And get back, back, back to you.
I thought even the bones would do.   60

But they pulled me out of the sack,
And they stuck me together with glue.
And then I knew what to do.
I made a model of you,
A man in black with a Meinkampf° look   65

And a love of the rack and the screw.
And I said I do, I do.
So daddy, I'm finally through.
The black telephone's off at the root,
The voices just can't worm through.   70

If I've killed one man, I've killed two—
The vampire who said he was you
And drank my blood for a year,
Seven years, if you want to know.
Daddy, you can lie back now.   75

There's a stake in your fat black heart
And the villagers never liked you.
They are dancing and stamping on you.
They always *knew* it was you.
Daddy, daddy, you bastard, I'm through.   80

---

65. Mein Kampf: *My Struggle,* the title of Adolf Hitler's autobiography.

Dudley Randall   1914–2000

Ballad of Birmingham   [1969]
On the Bombing of a Church in Birmingham, Alabama, 1963

"Mother dear, may I go downtown
Instead of out to play,
And march the streets of Birmingham
In a Freedom March today?"

"No, baby, no, you may not go,   5
For the dogs are fierce and wild,
And clubs and hoses, guns and jails
Aren't good for a little child."

"But, mother, I won't be alone.
Other children will go with me,   10
And march the streets of Birmingham
To make our country free."

"No, baby, no, you may not go,
For I fear those guns will fire.
But you may go to church instead   15
And sing in the children's choir."

She has combed and brushed her night-dark hair,
And bathed rose petal sweet,
And drawn white gloves on her small brown hands,
And white shoes on her feet.   20

The mother smiled to know her child
Was in the sacred place,
But that smile was the last smile
To come upon her face.

For when she heard the explosion,   25
Her eyes grew wet and wild.
She raced through the streets of Birmingham
Calling for her child.

She clawed through bits of glass and brick,
Then lifted out a shoe.   30
"Oh, here's the shoe my baby wore,
But, baby, where are you?"

Henry Reed 1914–1986

Naming of Parts   [1946]

Today we have naming of parts. Yesterday,
We had daily cleaning. And tomorrow morning,
We shall have what to do after firing. But today,
Today we have naming of parts. Japonica
Glistens like coral in all of the neighbouring gardens,   5
            And today we have naming of parts.

This is the lower sling swivel. And this
Is the upper sling swivel, whose use you will see,
When you are given your slings. And this is the piling swivel,
Which in your case you have not got. The branches   10
Hold in the gardens their silent, eloquent gestures,
        Which in our case we have not got.

This is the safety-catch, which is always released
With an easy flick of the thumb. And please do not let me
See anyone using his finger. You can do it quite easy   15
If you have any strength in your thumb. The blossoms
Are fragile and motionless, never letting anyone see
        Any of them using their finger.

And this you can see is the bolt. The purpose of this
Is to open the breech, as you see. We can slide it   20
Rapidly backwards and forwards: we call this
Easing the spring. And rapidly backwards and forwards
The early bees are assaulting and fumbling the flowers:
        They call it easing the Spring.

They call it easing the Spring: it is perfectly easy   25
If you have any strength in your thumb: like the bolt,
And the breech, and the cocking-piece, and the point of balance,
Which in our case we have not got; and the almond-blossom
Silent in all of the gardens and the bees going backwards and forwards,
        For today we have naming of parts.   30

Adrienne Rich   b. 1929

Rape   [1972]

There is a cop who is both prowler and father:
he comes from your block, grew up with your brothers,
had certain ideals.
You hardly know him in his boots and silver badge,
on horseback, one hand touching his gun.   5

You hardly know him but you have to get to know him:
he has access to machinery that could kill you.
He and his stallion clop like warlords among the trash,
his ideals stand in the air, a frozen cloud
from between his unsmiling lips.   10

And so, when the time comes, you have to turn to him,
the maniac's sperm still greasing your thighs,

your mind whirling like crazy. You have to confess
to him, you are guilty of the crime
of having been forced.   15

And you see his blue eyes, the blue eyes of all the family
whom you used to know, grow narrow and glisten,
his hand types out the details
and he wants them all
but the hysteria in your voice pleases him best.   20

You hardly know him but now he thinks he knows you:
he has taken down your worst moment
on a machine and filed it in a file.
He knows, or thinks he knows, how much you imagined;
he knows, or thinks he knows, what you secretly wanted.   25

He has access to machinery that could get you put away;
and if, in the sickening light of the precinct,
and if, in the sickening light of the precinct,
your details sound like a portrait of your confessor,
will you swallow, will you deny them, will you lie your way home? 30

Jack Ridl b. 1944

First Cut   [2009]

The night before,
eight of the players
slept. Each of the rest
lay wondering if his name
would not be on the list.   5
"Tomorrow we'll post
first cuts," Coach had said.
"If you're not on the list,
you're still on the team.
If your name is there..."   10
He shrugged. Twenty-two
would go to look, hoping
to find themselves among
the chosen. For years
their names were only   15
something they had
answered to. But now,
hurled back to the earth's
first days, they could feel

the finger of the caller   20
of names point. God said,
"Smith," and Smith
walked on among the
elect. On the wall, next
to Coach's office door,   25
the list. Some came
early, stood, stared,
and left. Some waited.
Coach had told them
not to say a word.   30
Some held out past lunch,
then gave in, went,
and saw. That night,
Coach called the chosen
together at center court.   35
"All right," he said, "you
made it this far. There
will be one more cut.
Twelve of you will make it.
We'll go one more week. Now,   40
wind sprints." The others
went to look for something
else to do, wished
they'd never tried, felt a fire
burning around their names.   45

Alberto Ríos b. 1952

Nani°   [1982]

Sitting at her table, she serves
the sopa de arroz° to me   *rice soup*
instinctively, and I watch her,
the absolute *mamá*, and eat words
I might have had to say more   5
out of embarrassment. To speak,
now-foreign words I used to speak,
too, dribble down her mouth as she serves
me albondigas.° No more   *meatballs*
than a third are easy to me.   10

Nani: Diminutive for "grandmother."

By the stove she does something with words
and looks at me only with her
back. I am full. I tell her
I taste the mint, and watch her speak
smiles at the stove. All my words   15
make her smile. Nani never serves
herself, she only watches me
with her skin, her hair. I ask for more.

I watch the *mamá* warming more
tortillas for me. I watch her   20
fingers in the flame for me.
Near her mouth, I see a wrinkle speak
of a man whose body serves
the ants like she serves me, then more words
from more wrinkles about children, words   25
about this and that, flowing more
easily from these other mouths. Each serves
as a tremendous string around her,
holding her together. They speak
nani was this and that to me   30
and I wonder just how much of me
will die with her, what were the words
I could have been, was. Her insides speak
through a hundred wrinkles, now, more
than she can bear, steel around her,   35
shouting, then, What is this thing she serves?

She asks me if I want more.
I own no words to stop her.
Even before I speak, she serves.

Luis J. Rodriguez b. 1954

Running to America   [1989]

For Alfonso and María Estela; immigrants.

They are night shadows
violating borders;
fingers curled through chain-link fences,
hiding from infra-red eyes,
dodging 30-30 bullets.   5
They leave familiar smells,
warmth and sounds

as ancient
as the trampled stones.

Running to America.   10

There is a woman
in her finest
border-crossing wear:
A purple blouse from
an older sister, a pair of worn   15
shoes from church bazaar.
A tattered coat
from a former lover.

There is a child
dressed in black.   20
Fear sparkling from
dark Indian eyes;
clinging to
a beheaded Barbie doll.

And the men,   25
some hardened, quiet.
Others young and loud.
You see something like this
in prisons.

Soon they will cross   30
on their bellies; kissing
black earth.

Running to America.

Strange voices
whisper behind garbage cans,   35
beneath freeway passes,
next to broken bottles.
The spatter of words,
textured and multi-colored,
invoke demons.   40

They must run to America.

Their skin,
color of earth,
is a brand
for all the great ranchers,   45
for the killing floors
on Soto Street,

and as slaughter
for the garment row.
Still they come.   50
A hungry people
have no country.

Their tears
are the grease
of the bobbing machines   55
that rip into cloth
that make clothes
that keep you warm.

They have endured
the sun's stranglehold,   60
el cortito,°
foundry heats
and dark caves
of mines
hungry for men.   65

Still they come,
wandering bravely
through the thickness
of this strange land's
maddening ambivalence.   70

Their cries are singed
with fires of hope.
Their babies are born
with a lion
in their hearts.   75
Who can confine them?
Who can tell them
which lines never to cross?

For the green rivers,
for their looted gold,   80
escaping the blood of a land
that threatens to drown them,

they have come,
running to America.

---

61. el cortito: "The short one"—the short-handled hoe, which forces field laborers to work in
a stooped position; prolonged use can result in degeneration of the spine. It was banned from
California fields in 1975.

Wendy Rose b. 1948

Loo-Wit°   [1985]

The way they do
this old woman
no longer cares
what others think
but spits her black tobacco   5
any which way
stretching full length
from her bumpy bed.
Finally up
she sprinkles ashes   10
on the snow,
cold buttes
promise nothing
but the walk
of winter.   15
Centuries of cedar
have bound her
to earth,
huckleberry ropes
lay prickly   20
on her neck.
Around her
machinery growls,
snarls and ploughs
great patches   25
of her skin.
She crouches
in the north,
her trembling
the source   30
of dawn.
Light appears
with the shudder
of her slopes,
the movement   35
of her arm.
Blackberries unravel,

Loo-Wit: *Loo-wit* is the name by which the Cowlitz People know Mt. St. Helens — "lady of fire." [Poet's note.]

stones dislodge;
it's not as if
they weren't warned.   40

She was sleeping
but she heard the boot scrape,
the creaking floor,
felt the pull of the blanket
from her thin shoulder.   45
With one free hand
she finds her weapons
and raises them high;
clearing the twigs from her throat
she sings, she sings,   50
shaking the sky
like a blanket about her
Loo-wit sings and sings and sings!

William Shakespeare 1564–1616

Shall I compare thee to a summer's day?   *[1590s; 1609]*

Shall I compare thee to a summer's day?
Thou art more lovely and more temperate:
Rough winds do shake the darling buds of May,
And summer's lease° hath all too short a date;°   *allotted time; duration*
Sometimes too hot the eye of heaven shines,   5
And often is his gold complexion dimmed;
And every fair° from fair° sometimes declines,   *beautiful thing; beauty*
By chance or nature's changing course untrimmed;°   *stripped of its beauty*
But thy eternal summer shall not fade,
Nor lose possession of that fair thou ow'st;°   *beauty you own*   10
Nor shall death brag thou wand'rest in his shade,
When in eternal lines° to time thou grow'st:°
   So long as men can breathe, or eyes can see,
   So long lives this,° and this gives life to thee.   *this sonnet*

---

12. lines: (Of poetry); **grow'st:** You are grafted to time.

A PAIRING OF POEMS

Here are two poems about statues created as memorials: one for an Egyptian pharaoh, erected by himself, and the other for a Native American chief, commissioned by Lakota chief Henry Standing Bear, who wrote, "My fellow chiefs and I would like the white man to know that the red man has great heroes, too." As you read and look closely at the two poems, consider what is similar and what is different about the reflections the two poets express about the monuments.

Percy Bysshe Shelley 1792–1822

Ozymandias°   [1818]

I met a traveler from an antique land
Who said: Two vast and trunkless legs of stone
Stand in the desert.... Near them, on the sand,
Half sunk, a shattered visage lies, whose frown,
And wrinkled lip, and sneer of cold command,   5
Tell that its sculptor well those passions read
Which yet survive, stamped on these lifeless things,
The hand that mocked them, and the heart that fed:
And on the pedestal these words appear:
"My name is Ozymandias, king of kings: 10
Look on my works, ye Mighty, and despair!"
Nothing beside remains. Round the decay
Of that colossal wreck, boundless and bare
The lone and level sands stretch far away.

Ozymandias: The Greek name for Ramses II of Egypt (thirteenth century B.C.E.), who erected the largest statue in Egypt as a memorial to himself.

Peter Blue Cloud b. 1935

Crazy Horse Monument   [1995]

Hailstones falling like sharp blue sky chips
howling winds the brown grass bends, while
buffalo paw and stamp and blow billowing steam,
and prairie wolves chorus the moon in moaning.

The spotted snake of a village on the move   5
a silent file of horses rounding hills,

in a robe of grey, the sky chief clutches thunder
and winter seeks to find the strongest men.

    Crazy Horse rides the circle of his people's sleep,
        from Little Big Horn to Wounded Knee,   10
    Black Hills, their shadows are his only robe
        dark breast feathers of a future storm.

Those of broken bodies piled in death,
of frozen blood upon the white of snow,
yours is now the sky chant of spirit making,   15
pacing the rhythm of Crazy Horse's mount.

And he would cry in anger of a single death,
and dare the guns of mounted soldiers blue,
for his was the blood and pulse of rivers,
and mountains and plains taken in sacred trust.   20

    Crazy Horse rides the circle of his people's sleep,
        from Little Big Horn to Wounded Knee,
    Black Hills, their shadows are his only robe
        dark breast feathers of a future storm.

And what would he think of the cold steel chisel,   25
and of dynamite blasting mountain's face,
what value the crumbled glories of Greece and Rome,
to a people made cold and hungry?

To capture in stone the essence of a man's spirit,
to portray the love and respect of children and elders,   30
fashion instead the point of a hunting arrow sharp,
and leave to the elements the wearing-down of time.

    Crazy Horse rides the circle of his people's sleep,
        from Little Big Horn to Wounded Knee,
    Black Hills, their shadows are his only robe   35
        dark breast feathers of a future storm.

Charles Simic b. 1938

Classic Ballroom Dances   [1980]

Grandmothers who wring the necks
Of chickens; old nuns
With names like Theresa, Marianne,
Who pull schoolboys by the ear;

The intricate steps of pickpockets   5
Working the crowd of the curious
At the scene of an accident; the slow shuffle
Of the evangelist with a sandwich-board;

The hesitation of the early morning customer
Peeking through the window-grille   10
Of a pawnshop; the weave of a little kid
Who is walking to school with eyes closed;

And the ancient lovers, cheek to cheek,
On the dancefloor of the Union Hall,
Where they also hold charity raffles   15
On rainy Monday nights of an eternal November.

Gary Soto b. 1952

Moving Away   [1977]

Remember that we are moving away   brother
From those years
In the same house with a white stepfather
What troubled him has been forgotten

But what troubled us has settled   5
Like dirt
In the nests of our knuckles
And cannot be washed away

All those times you woke shivering
In the night   10
From a coldness I
Could not understand
And cupped a crucifix beneath the covers

All those summers we hoed our yard
In the afternoon sun   15
The heat waving across our faces
And we waved back wasps
While the one we hated
Watched us from under a tree and said nothing

We will remember those moments   brother   20

And now that we are far
From one another
What I want to speak of
Is the quiet of a room just before daybreak
And you next to me   sleeping   25

APPROACHING THE AUTHOR

Although **Gary Soto** grew up in a household devoid of books and spent much of his childhood laboring in fields and factories, he took his first steps into the literary world by reading Hemingway, Steinbeck, Frost, and other major writers in his school library.

For more about him, see page 1412.

Edmund Spenser 1552–1599

One day I wrote her name upon the strand [1595]

One day I wrote her name upon the strand,
But came the waves and washèd it away:
Again I wrote it with a second hand,
But came the tide, and made my pains his prey.
"Vain man," said she, "that dost in vain assay,   5
A mortal thing so to immortalize,
For I myself shall like to this decay,
And eek° my name be wipèd out likewise."   *also*
"Not so," quod° I, "let baser things devise,   *quoth (said)*
To die in dust, but you shall live by fame: 10
My verse your virtues rare shall eternize,
And in the heavens write your glorious name.
Where whenas death shall all the world subdue,
Our love shall live, and later life renew."

Wallace Stevens 1897–1955

Anecdote of the Jar [1923]

I placed a jar in Tennessee,
And round it was, upon a hill.
It made the slovenly wilderness
Surround that hill.

The wilderness rose up to it,   5
And sprawled around, no longer wild.
The jar was round upon the ground
And tall and of a port in air.

It took dominion everywhere.
The jar was gray and bare.   10
It did not give of bird or bush,
Like nothing else in Tennessee.

Mark Strand　b. 1934

Eating Poetry　[1968]

Ink runs from the corners of my mouth.
There is no happiness like mine.
I have been eating poetry.

The librarian does not believe what she sees.
Her eyes are sad　　　　　　　　　　　　　　　　　　　5
and she walks with her hands in her dress.

The poems are gone.
The light is dim.
The dogs are on the basement stairs and coming up.

Their eyeballs roll,　　　　　　　　　　　　　　　　　　10
their blond legs burn like brush.
The poor librarian begins to stamp her feet and weep.

She does not understand.
When I get on my knees and lick her hand,
she screams.　　　　　　　　　　　　　　　　　　　　15

I am a new man.
I snarl at her and bark.
I romp with joy in the bookish dark.

Virgil Suárez　b. 1962

Tea Leaves, *Caracoles*, Coffee Beans　[2005]

My mother, who in those Havana days believed in divination,
found her tea leaves at *El Volcán*, the Chinese market/apothecary,

brought the leaves in a precious silk paper bundle, unwrapped
them as if unwrapping her own skin, and then boiled water

to make my dying grandmother's tea; while my mother read　　5
its leaves, I simply saw *leaves floating* in steaming water,

vapor kissed my skin, my nose became moist as a puppy's.
My mother did this because my grandmother, her mother-in-law,

believed in all things. Her appetite for knowledge was vast,
the one thing we all agreed she passed down to me, the skinny　　10

kid sent to search for *caracoles*, these snail shells
that littered the underbrush of the empty lot next door.

My mother threw them on top of the table, cleaned them of dirt,
kept them in a mason jar and every morning before breakfast,

read them on top of the table, their way of falling, some up,   15
some down, their ridges, swirls of creamy lines, their broken

edges.... Everything she read looked bad, for my grandmother,
for us, for staying in our country, this island of suspended

disbelief. My mother read coffee beans too, with their wrinkled,
fleshy green and red skin. Orange-skinned beans she kept aside.   20

Orange meant death, and my mother didn't want to accept it.
I learned mostly of death from the way a sparrow fell

when I hit it in the chest with my slingshot and a lead pellet
I made by melting my toy soldiers. The sparrow's eyes

always hid behind droopy eyelids, which is how my grandmother   25
died, by closing her eyes to the world; truth became this fading

light, a tunnel, as everybody says, but instead of heaven
she went into the ground, to that one place that still nourishes

the tea leaves, *caracoles*, and the coffee beans, which, if I didn't
know better, I'd claim shone; those red-glowing beans   30

in starlight were the eyes of the dead looking out through
the darkness as those of us who believed in such things walked

through life with a lightness of feet, spirit, a vapor-aura
that could be read or sung.

May Swenson 1913–1989

The Shape of Death   [1970]

What does love look like?	We know the shape of death.
Death is a cloud, immense	and awesome. At first a
lid is lifted from the	eye of light. There is a
clap of sound. A white	blossom belches from the
jaw of fright. A	pillared cloud churns from 5
white to gray, like a	monstrous brain that bursts

and burns—then turns
away, filling the whole
Thickly it wraps, between
moon, the earth's green
cocoon, its choking
of death. Death is a

like? Is it a particle,
beyond the microscope and
the length of hope? Is
that we shall never dare
color, and its alchemy?
can it be dug? Or
it be bought? Can it be
a shy beast to be caught?
a clap of sound. Love is
nests within each cell,
is a ray, a seed, a note,
our air and blood. It is
our very skin, a sheath

sickly black, spilling
sky with ashes of dread.
the clean seas and the
head. Trapped in its   10
breath, we know the shape
cloud. What does love look

a star, invisible entirely,
Palomar?° A dimension past
it a climate far and fair,   15
discover? What is its
Is it a jewel in the earth,
dredged from the sea? Can
sown and harvested? Is it
Death is a cloud—immense,   20
little and not loud. It
and it cannot be split. It
a word, a secret motion of
not alien—it is near—
to keep us pure of fear.   25

---

14. **Palomar:** The Palomar Observatory in north San Diego County, California, features the 200-inch Hale Telescope, which from 1948 until 1993 was the world's largest telescope.

Arthur Sze b. 1950

The Shapes of Leaves   [2009]

Ginkgo, cottonwood, pin oak, sweet gum, tulip tree:
our emotions resemble leaves and alive
to their shapes we are nourished.

Have you felt the expanse and contours of grief
along the edges of a big Norway maple?   5
Have you winced at the orange flare

searing the curves of a curling dogwood?
I have seen from the air logged islands,
each with a network of branching gravel roads,

and felt a moment of pure anger, aspen gold.   10
I have seen sandhill cranes moving in an open field,
a single white whooping crane in the flock.

And I have traveled along the contours
of leaves that have no name. Here
where the air is wet and the light is cool,   15

I feel what others are thinking and do not speak,
I know pleasure in the veins of a sugar maple,
I am living at the edge of a new leaf.

APPROACHING THE AUTHOR

At age six, **Mary TallMountain** was the first child to be adopted out of
her village by an Anglo-American couple. She began writing letters to
"the little [Indian] girl who lived inside me." She did not publish her
poetry until she was fifty-five.

For more about her, see page 1415.

Mary TallMountain 1918–1994

Matmiya   [1990]

For my grandmother

I see you sitting
Implanted by roots
Coiled deep from your thighs.
Roots, flesh red, centuries pale.
Hairsprings wound tight   5
Through fertile earthscapes
Where each layer feeds the next
Into depths immutable.

Though you must rise, must
Move large and slow   10
When it is time, O my
Gnarled mother-vine, ancient
As vanished ages,
Your spirit remains
Nourished,   15
Nourishing me.

I see your figure wrapped in skins
Curved into a mound of earth
Holding your rich dark roots.
Matmiya, I see you sitting.   20

Alfred, Lord Tennyson 1809–1892

Ulysses°   [1833]

It little profits that an idle king,
By this still hearth, among these barren crags,
Matched with an agèd wife, I mete and dole
Unequal laws unto a savage race,°
That hoard, and sleep, and feed, and know not me.   5

    I cannot rest from travel; I will drink
Life to the lees. All times I have enjoyed
Greatly, have suffered greatly, both with those
That loved me, and alone; on shore, and when
Through scudding drifts° the rainy Hyades°   10
Vexed the dim sea. I am become a name;
For always roaming with a hungry heart
Much have I seen and known—cities of men
And manners, climates, councils, governments,
Myself not least, but honored of them all—   15
And drunk delight of battle with my peers,
Far on the ringing plains of windy Troy.
I am a part of all that I have met;
Yet all experience is an arch wherethrough
Gleams that untraveled world whose margin fades   20
Forever and forever when I move.
How dull it is to pause, to make an end,
To rust unburnished, not to shine in use!
As though to breathe were life! Life piled on life
Were all too little, and of one to me   25
Little remains; but every hour is saved
From that eternal silence, something more,
A bringer of new things; and vile it were

Ulysses (the Roman form of Odysseus): The hero of Homer's epic *The Odyssey,* which tells the story of Odysseus's adventures on his voyage back to his home, the little island of Ithaca, after he and the other Greek heroes had defeated Troy. It took Odysseus ten years to reach Ithaca, the small, rocky island of which he was king, where his wife (Penelope) and son (Telemachus) had been waiting for him. Upon his return he defeated the suitors who had been trying to marry the faithful Penelope, and he resumed the kingship and his old ways of life. Here Homer's story ends, but in Canto 26 of the *Inferno* Dante extended the story: Odysseus eventually became restless and dissatisfied with his settled life and decided to return to the sea and sail west, into the unknown sea, and seek whatever adventures he might find there. Tennyson's poem amplifies the speech delivered in Dante's poem as Ulysses challenges his men to accompany him on this new voyage.   **3–4. mete...race:** Administer inadequate (unequal to what is needed) laws to a still somewhat lawless race.   **10. scudding drifts:** Wind-driven spray; **Hyades:** Five stars in the constellation Taurus whose rising, it was assumed, would be followed by rain.

For some three suns° to store and hoard myself,   *years*
And this gray spirit yearning in desire   30
To follow knowledge like a sinking star,
Beyond the utmost bound of human thought.

    This is my son, mine own Telemachus,
To whom I leave the scepter and the isle—
Well-loved of me, discerning to fulfill   35
This labor, by slow prudence to make mild
A rugged people, and through soft degrees
Subdue them to the useful and the good.
Most blameless is he, centered in the sphere
Of common duties, decent not to fail   40
In offices of tenderness, and pay
Meet adoration to my household gods,
When I am gone. He works his work, I mine.

    There lies the port; the vessel puffs her sail;
There gloom the dark, broad seas. My mariners,   45
Souls that have toiled, and wrought, and thought with me—
That ever with a frolic welcome took
The thunder and the sunshine, and opposed
Free hearts, free foreheads—you and I are old;
Old age hath yet his honor and his toil.   50
Death closes all; but something ere the end,
Some work of noble note, may yet be done,
Not unbecoming men that strove with Gods.
The lights begin to twinkle from the rocks;
The long day wanes; the slow moon climbs; the deep   55
Moans round with many voices. Come, my friends,
'Tis not too late to seek a newer world.
Push off, and sitting well in order smite
The sounding furrows; for my purpose holds
To sail beyond the sunset, and the baths°   60
Of all the western stars, until I die.
It may be that the gulfs will wash us down;
It may be we shall touch the Happy Isles,°
And see the great Achilles,° whom we knew.
Though much is taken, much abides; and though   65

---

60. **baths:** The outer river or ocean surrounding the flat earth, in Greek cosmology, into which
the stars descended upon setting.   64. **Happy Isles:** The Islands of the Blessed, or Elysian
Fields, in Greek myth, which lay in the western seas beyond the Strait of Gibraltar and were
the abode of heroes after death.   64. **Achilles:** The hero of the Greeks, and Odysseus's comrade, in Homer's *Iliad*.

We are not now that strength which in old days
Moved earth and heaven, that which we are, we are—
One equal temper of heroic hearts,
Made weak by time and fate, but strong in will
To strive, to seek, to find, and not to yield.   70

APPROACHING THE AUTHOR

Dylan Thomas suffered from bronchitis and asthma throughout his life and was considered too frail to fight in World War II. Fittingly, he instead served the United Kingdom by writing scripts for the government. For more about him, see page 1416.

Dylan Thomas   1914–1953

Do not go gentle into that good night   [1952]

Do not go gentle into that good night,
Old age should burn and rave at close of day;
Rage, rage against the dying of the light.

Though wise men at their end know dark is right,
Because their words had forked no lightning they   5
Do not go gentle into that good night.

Good men, the last wave by, crying how bright
Their frail deeds might have danced in a green bay,
Rage, rage against the dying of the light.

Wild men who caught and sang the sun in flight,   10
And learn, too late, they grieved it on its way,
Do not go gentle into that good night.

Grave men, near death, who see with blinding sight
Blind eyes could blaze like meteors and be gay,
Rage, rage against the dying of the light.   15

And you, my father, there on the sad height,
Curse, bless, me now with your fierce tears, I pray.
Do not go gentle into that good night.
Rage, rage against the dying of the light.

Jean Toomer   1894–1967

Face   [1923]

Hair—
silver-gray,
like streams of stars,
Brows—
recurved canoes   5
quivered by the ripples blown by pain,
Her eyes—
mist of tears
condensing on the flesh below
And her channeled muscles   10
are cluster grapes of sorrow
purple in the evening sun
nearly ripe for worms.

James Welch   1940–2003

Christmas Comes to Moccasin Flat   [1976]

Christmas comes like this: Wise men
unhurried, candles bought on credit (poor price
for calves), warriors face down in wine sleep.
Winds cheat to pull heat from smoke.

Friends sit in chinked cabins, stare out   5
plastic windows and wait for commodities.
Charlie Blackbird, twenty miles from church
and bar, stabs his fire with flint.

When drunks drain radiators for love
or need, chiefs eat snow and talk of change,   10
an urge to laugh pounding their ribs.
Elk play games in high country.

Medicine Woman, clay pipe and twist tobacco,
calls each blizzard by name and predicts
five o'clock by spitting at her television.   15
Children lean into her breath to beg a story:

Something about honor and passion,
warriors back with meat and song,
a peculiar evening star, quick vision of birth.
Blackbird feeds his fire. Outside, a quick 30 below.   20

APPROACHING THE AUTHOR

Patricia Jabbeh Wesley lived through the devastation of her homeland, the massacre of thousands during the decades-long war in Liberia. She has said, "I will never let their stories die as long as I can write."
    For more about her, see page 1417.

Patricia Jabbeh Wesley b. 1955

There's Nothing You Can Do   [2010]

About the plane and the storm, coming at you.
Nothing, to quell that old fear of crashing.
Nothing about the first class seating
that's no longer there; nothing, to stop the agent

sitting next to you from recording your breathing   5
and your sighing; a stewardess, passing out
tiny packets of peanuts with a smile.
There's nothing, when your sweet girl

turns sixteen, and you awaken to a new little lion
growling at you, the one you grew   10
by mixing spices and herbs for stews.
Nothing you can do about aging,

about your wrinkling hands or being black
or white in America or just plain
being a person in America.   15
Nothing you can do about wanting,
about wanting to fall in love all over again.

If you could take back the one you didn't marry,
maybe. How could you pull out
every string of gray on your balding head?   20
The absoluteness of aging as inevitable as breath.

There's nothing you can do about birth pains
that still keep you awake at night
even though the child is now a college teenager,
lost in his own crowd. There's just nothing   25

you can do about God, about the earth as it now is.
You can no longer reshape this world
into something flat and simple, something
removable, something a finger can feel, a thing

with buttons, like a shirt. Not until the palm nut   30
becomes walnut and a man turns up
having babies. There's nothing you can do
about your sweet neighbor on her evening walk,

her golden retriever, so golden, he leaves his poop
to fertilize your lawn and your shoes too.   35

Roberta Hill Whiteman   b. 1947

The White Land   [1984]

When Orion° straddled his apex of sky,
over the white land we lingered loving.
The River Eridanus° flickered, foretelling
tropical waves and birds arrayed
in feathers of sunset, but we didn't waste   5
that prickling dark.

Not a dog barked our arrival before dawn.
Only in sleep did I drift vagabond
and suffer the patterns that constantly state
time has no time. Fate is a warlord.   10
That morning I listened to your long breath
for decades.

That morning you said bears
fell over the white land. Leaving their lair
in thick polar fur, they roused our joy   15
by leaving no footprint. Fat ones fell headlong,
but most of them danced, then without quarrel,
balanced on branches.

I couldn't breathe in the roar of that plane,
flying me back to a wooded horizon.   20
Regular rhythms bridge my uneven sleep.
What if the wind in the white land keeps you?
The dishwater's luminous; a truck
grinds down the street.

---

1. Orion: Prominent constellation located on the celestial equator.   **3. River Eridanus:** Large
southern constellation stretching southwest from Orion, identified with a river because of its
long winding shape.

Walt Whitman 1819–1892

From Song of Myself   [*1855*; 1891–1892]°

1

I celebrate myself, and sing myself,
And what I assume you shall assume,
For every atom belonging to me as good belongs to you.

I loafe and invite my soul,
I lean and loafe at my ease observing a spear of summer grass.   5

My tongue, every atom of my blood, form'd from this soil, this air,
Born here of parents born here from parents the same, and their parents
    the same,
I, now thirty-seven years old in perfect health begin,
Hoping to cease not till death.

Creeds and schools in abeyance,   10
Retiring back a while sufficed at what they are, but never forgotten,
I harbor for good or bad, I permit to speak at every hazard,
Nature without check with original energy.

21

I am the poet of the Body and I am the poet of the Soul,
The pleasures of heaven are with me and the pains of hell are
    with me,
The first I graft and increase upon myself, the latter I translate into
    a new tongue.

I am the poet of the woman the same as the man,   425
And I say it is as great to be a woman as to be a man,
And I say there is nothing greater than the mother of men.

I chant the chant of dilation or pride,
We have had ducking and deprecating about enough,
I show that size is only development.   430

Have you outstript the rest? are you the President?
It is a trifle, they will more than arrive there every one, and still
    pass on.

Date: The poem was first published in 1855 as an untitled section of *Leaves of Grass*. It was a rough, rude, and vigorous example of antebellum American cultural politics and free verse experimentation. The version excerpted here, from the sixth edition (1891–1892), is much longer, more carefully crafted, and more conventionally punctuated.

I am he that walks with the tender and growing night,
I call to the earth and sea half-held by the night.

Press close bare-bosom'd night—press close magnetic nourishing night!   435
Night of south winds—night of the large few stars!
Still nodding night—mad naked summer night.

Smile O voluptuous cool-breath'd earth!
Earth of the slumbering and liquid trees!
Earth of departed sunset—earth of the mountains misty-topt!   440
Earth of the vitreous pour of the full moon just tinged with blue!
Earth of shine and dark mottling the tide of the river!
Earth of the limpid gray of clouds brighter and clearer for my sake!
Far-swooping elbow'd earth—rich apple-blossom'd earth!
Smile, for your lover comes.   445

Prodigal, you have given me love—therefore I to you give love!
O unspeakable passionate love.

24

Walt Whitman, a kosmos, of Manhattan the son,
Turbulent, fleshy, sensual, eating, drinking and breeding,
No sentimentalist, no stander above men and women or apart
    from them,
No more modest than immodest.   500

Unscrew the locks from the doors!
Unscrew the doors themselves from their jambs!

Whoever degrades another degrades me,
And whatever is done or said returns at last to me.

Through me the afflatus° surging and surging, through me the
    current and index.   505

I speak the pass-word primeval, I give the sign of democracy,
By God! I will accept nothing which all cannot have their counterpart
    of on the same terms.

Through me many long dumb voices,
Voices of the interminable generations of prisoners and slaves,
Voices of the diseas'd and despairing and of thieves and dwarfs,   510
Voices of cycles of preparation and accretion,
And of the threads that connect the stars, and of wombs and of
    the father-stuff,
And of the rights of them the others are down upon.

---

505. **afflatus:** Inspiration, from Latin meaning "to blow on."

47

I am the teacher of athletes,
He that by me spreads a wider breast than my own proves the
    width of my own,   1235
He most honors my style who learns under it to destroy the teacher.

. . . .

52

The spotted hawk swoops by and accuses me, he complains of my
    gab and my loitering.

I too am not a bit tamed, I too am untranslatable,
I sound my barbaric yawp over the roofs of the world.

The last scud of day holds back for me,
It flings my likeness after the rest and true as any on the shadow'd
    wilds,   1335
It coaxes me to the vapor and the dusk.

I depart as air, I shake my white locks at the runaway sun,
I effuse my flesh in eddies, and drift it in lacy jags.

I bequeath myself to the dirt to grow from the grass I love,
If you want me again look for me under your boot-soles.   1340

You will hardly know who I am or what I mean,
But I shall be good health to you nevertheless,
And filter and fibre your blood.

Failing to fetch me at first keep encouraged,
Missing me one place search another,   1345
I stop somewhere waiting for you.

Richard Wilbur b. 1921

Love Calls Us to the Things of This World   [1956]

    The eyes open to a cry of pulleys,
And spirited from sleep, the astounded soul
Hangs for a moment bodiless and simple
As false dawn.
            Outside the open window
The morning air is all awash with angels.   5

Some are in bed-sheets, some are in blouses,
Some are in smocks: but truly there they are.
Now they are rising together in calm swells
Of halcyon feeling, filling whatever they wear
With the deep joy of their impersonal breathing;   10

   Now they are flying in place, conveying
The terrible speed of their omnipresence, moving
And staying like white water; and now of a sudden
They swoon down into so rapt a quiet
That nobody seems to be there.
                                    The soul shrinks   15

   From all that it is about to remember,
From the punctual rape of every blessèd day,
And cries,
              "Oh, let there be nothing on earth but laundry,
Nothing but rosy hands in the rising steam
And clear dances done in the sight of heaven."   20

   Yet, as the sun acknowledges
With a warm look the world's hunks and colors,
The soul descends once more in bitter love
To accept the waking body, saying now
In a changed voice as the man yawns and rises,   25

   "Bring them down from their ruddy gallows;
Let there be clean linen for the backs of thieves;
Let lovers go fresh and sweet to be undone,
And the heaviest nuns walk in a pure floating
Of dark habits,
                  keeping their difficult balance."   30

APPROACHING THE AUTHOR

Nancy Willard's son was a slow eater growing up, so she cut up an old copy of William Blake's *Songs of Innocence* and *Songs of Experience* and fashioned them into placemats. She noted that rather than staring at his broccoli, her son now spent his dinner reading Blake and enjoying the illustrations.

For more about her, see page 1418.

Nancy Willard b. 1936

Questions My Son Asked Me, Answers I Never Gave Him

[1982]

1. Do gorillas have birthdays?
   Yes. Like the rainbow, they happen.
   Like the air, they are not observed.

2. Do butterflies make a noise?
   The wire in the butterfly's tongue   5
   hums gold.
   Some men hear butterflies
   even in winter.

3. Are they part of our family?
   They forgot us, who forgot how to fly.   10

4. Who tied my navel? Did God tie it?
   God made the thread: O man, live forever!
   Man made the knot: enough is enough.

5. If I drop my tooth in the telephone
   will it go through the wires and bite someone's ear?   15
   I have seen earlobes pierced by a tooth of steel.
   It loves what lasts.
   It does not love flesh.
   It leaves a ring of gold in the wound.

6. If I stand on my head   20
   will the sleep in my eye roll up into my head?
   Does the dream know its own father?
   Can bread go back to the field of its birth?

7. Can I eat a star?
   Yes, with the mouth of time   25
   that enjoys everything.

8. Could we Xerox the moon?
   This is the first commandment:
   I am the moon, thy moon.
   Thou shalt have no other moons before thee.   30

9. Who invented water?
   The hands of the air, that wanted to wash each other.

10. What happens at the end of numbers?
    I see three men running toward a field.
    At the edge of the tall grass, they turn into light.   35

11. Do the years ever run out?
    God said, I will break time's heart.
    Time ran down like an old phonograph.
    It lay flat as a carpet.
    At rest on its threads, I am learning to fly.   40

William Carlos Williams 1883–1963

Spring and All   [1923]

By the road to the contagious hospital°
under the surge of the blue
mottled clouds driven from the
northeast—a cold wind. Beyond, the
waste of broad, muddy fields   5
brown with dried weeds, standing and fallen

patches of standing water
the scattering of tall trees

All along the road the reddish
purplish, forked, upstanding, twiggy   10
stuff of bushes and small trees
with dead, brown leaves under them
leafless vines—

Lifeless in appearance, sluggish
dazed spring approaches—   15

They enter the new world naked,
cold, uncertain of all
save that they enter. All about them
the cold, familiar wind—

Now the grass, tomorrow   20
the stiff curl of wildcarrot leaf

One by one objects are defined—
It quickens: clarity, outline of leaf

But now the stark dignity of
entrance—Still, the profound change   25
has come upon them: rooted, they
grip down and begin to awaken

---

1. **contagious hospital:** A hospital for the treatment of contagious diseases.

William Wordsworth 1770–1850

The world is too much with us   [1807]

The world is too much with us; late and soon,
Getting and spending, we lay waste our powers;
Little we see in Nature that is ours;
We have given our hearts away, a sordid boon!°   *gift*
This Sea that bares her bosom to the moon,   5
The winds that will be howling at all hours,
And are up-gathered now like sleeping flowers,
For this, for everything, we are out of tune;
It moves us not. — Great God! I'd rather be
A Pagan suckled in a creed outworn;   10
So might I, standing on this pleasant lea,°   *open meadow*
Have glimpses that would make me less forlorn;
Have sight of Proteus° rising from the sea;
Or hear old Triton° blow his wreathèd° horn.

---

13. Proteus: In Greek mythology, a sea god who could change his own form or appearance at will.   **14. Triton:** A Greek sea god with the head and upper body of a man and the tail of a fish, usually pictured as playing on a conch-shell trumpet. **wreathèd:** Curved.

Cheryl Savageau b. 1950

Bones – A City Poem   [1992]

forget the great blue heron flying low
   over the marsh, its footprints
   still fresh in the sand

forget the taste of wild mushrooms
    and where to find them   5

forget lichen-covered pines
    and iceland moss

forget the one-legged duck
    and the eggs of the snapping turtle
    laid in the bank   10

forget the frog found in the belly of a bass

forget the cove testing its breath
    against the autumn morning

forget the down-filled nest
    and the snake swimming at midday   15

forget the bullhead lilies
    and the whiskers
    of the pout

forget walking on black ice
    beneath the sky hunter's bow   20

forget the living waters
    of Quinsigamond

forget how to find the Pole star and why

forget the eyes of the red fox
    the hornets that made their home   25
    in the skull of a cow

forget waking to hear the call of the loon

forget that raccoons are younger brothers
    to the bear

forget that you are walking   30
    on the bones of your grandmothers

William Butler Yeats 1865–1939

The Second Coming°   [1921]

Turning and turning in the widening gyre
The falcon cannot hear the falconer;
Things fall apart; the centre cannot hold;
Mere anarchy is loosed upon the world,
The blood-dimmed tide is loosed, and everywhere   5
The ceremony of innocence is drowned;
The best lack all conviction, while the worst
Are full of passionate intensity.

Surely some revelation is at hand;
Surely the Second Coming is at hand.   10
The Second Coming! Hardly are those words out
When a vast image out of *Spiritus Mundi*°
Troubles my sight: somewhere in sands of the desert
A shape with lion body and the head of a man,
A gaze blank and pitiless as the sun,   15
Is moving its slow thighs, while all about it
Reel shadows of the indignant desert birds.
The darkness drops again; but now I know
That twenty centuries of stony sleep
Were vexed to nightmare by a rocking cradle,   20
And what rough beast, its hour come round at last,
Slouches towards Bethlehem to be born?

The Second Coming: Alludes to Matthew 24:3–44, on the return of Christ at the end of
the present age. Yeats viewed history as a series of 2,000-year cycles (imaged as gyres, cone-
shaped motions). The birth of Christ in Bethlehem brought to an end the cycle that ran
from the Babylonians through the Greeks and Romans. The approach of the year 2000,
then, anticipated for Yeats the end of another era (the Christian age). Yeats wrote this
poem shortly after the Russian Revolution of 1917 (lines 4–8), which may have confirmed
his sense of imminent change and of a new beginning of an unpredictable nature (Yeats
expected the new era to be violent and despotic).   **12. Spiritus Mundi:** Latin, "the spirit of
the universe." Yeats believed in a Great Memory, a universal storehouse of symbolic images
from the past. Individuals, drawing on it for images, are put in touch with the soul of the
universe.

Al Young b. 1939

A Dance for Ma Rainey°   [1969]

I'm going to be just like you, Ma
Rainey this monday morning
clouds puffing up out of my head
like those balloons
that float above the faces of white people   5
in the funnypapers

I'm going to hover in the corners
of the world, Ma
& sing from the bottom of hell
up to the tops of high heaven   10
& send out scratchless waves of yellow
& brown & that basic black honey
misery

I'm going to cry so sweet
& so low   15
& so dangerous,
Ma,
that the message is going to reach you
back in 1922
where you shimmer   20
snaggle-toothed
perfumed &
powdered
in your bauble beads

hair pressed & tied back   25
throbbing with that sick pain
I know
& hide so well
that pain that blues
jives the world with   30
aching to be heard
that downness
that bottomlessness
first felt by some stolen delta nigger
swamped under with redblooded american agony;   35
reduced to the sheer shit
of existence
that bred

Ma Rainey: Gertrude "Ma" Rainey (1886–1939), American singer known as the "Mother of
the Blues."

& battered us all,
Ma,   40
the beautiful people
our beautiful brave black people
who no longer need to jazz
or sing to themselves in murderous vibrations
or play the veins of their strong tender arms   45
with needles
to prove we're still here

APPROACHING THE AUTHOR

Ray A. Young Bear claims that the act of writing provides a personal link
to the writings of his grandfathers. He often pores over the journals of
his grandfathers, many of which date back to the early 1800s. "I...
believe that 'word-collecting' is genetically encoded in my blood," he says.
   For more about him, see page 1420.

Ray A. Young Bear   b. 1950

Green Threatening Clouds   [1990]

"Paint these green threatening clouds
a rose color," said Elvia near my shoulder.
"I mean around the fluffy sides to at least
give credence to these ceramic-looking pitchers
and their red corrugated brims. And how will you   5
convey the phenomena of luminous mountain plants
when they're nocturnal?"
She had two good points as far
as biology and the dispersal of colors
was concerned, but I was debating where   10
to hang the pitchers whose poisonous
contents, if consumed, would make this
jungle a lovely place to close one's eyes
in permanence and see that far-ahead time
when gravity-wise hawks would splinter   15
my hip bone against a mountainside
repeatedly for marrow access,
a time in respect when young bull
elks would nudge their antlers against
my half-submerged and decayed antlers   20
in the tundra, a time when my arctic
shadow would claim pieces of ice
as descendants and incubate them,
arguing with any penguin over
their ownership...   25

Outside, a Midwestern cardinal hovered
under the roof of my parent's prayer lodge
and delicately maneuvered itself to the tip
of an icicle for a nonexistent drop of water.
In the snow-covered garden, a bluejay   30
disappeared into a brittle corn husk
and gave it momentary life, but none
was received from a dance made from
hunger. (Here we cannot migrate
to low altitude for tropical weather   35
and abundant food. Instead, like cultures
who wait for their savior, we wait for
a young man who has a neverending source
of food in his Magic Tablecloth.)
In our efforts to help the hungry birds,   40
we impale a slice of bread on a treelimb,
but it freezes and becomes a violent wind
sculpture. At thirteen below zero, a poorly
clothed child walks by with a lonely sled
in hand.   45

And then Elvia began talking about Saskatchewan.
"I dreamt of a large green eagle, and it was
speaking to me in French. I understood that
the eagle was an elder, who had flown *down*
in response to a song when a person is allowed   50
to leave its body."
"Does such a song exist?" I questioned.
"Of course," she replied. "Green. Such an
important color."

Paul Zimmer b. 1934

Zimmer's Head Thudding against the Blackboard [1969]

At the blackboard I had missed
Five number problems in a row,
And was about to foul a sixth,
When the old, exasperated nun
Began to pound my head against   5
My six mistakes. When I cried
She threw me back into my seat,
Where I hid my head and swore
That very day I'd be a poet,
And curse her yellow teeth with this.   10

PART 4

Approaching
DRAMA

21 Reading Drama   891

22 Character, Conflict, and
Dramatic Action   897

23 Setting and Structure   920

24 Writing about Drama   948

25 August Wilson's *Fences* –
A Casebook   959

26 A Collection of Plays   1045

Overleaf: David Henry Hwang visiting a Seattle theater production of M. Butterfly, which won a Tony Award for Best Play in 1988 and established him as a major contemporary American playwright. In an interview he describes the common thread that runs throughout his work: "One of the most important themes . . . is the fluidity of identity. You can think you're one person, but in a different social context you can be transformed into somebody you may not recognize, somebody completely different." (See p. 1393 for a biographical sketch.)

Reading Drama

CHAPTER 21

Participating in Serious Play

"The play's the thing," said Hamlet. Drama has captured minds, hearts, and imaginations since the times of the ancient Greeks. Then and now, people and actions "come to life." As we laugh, cry, fear, hope, and despair with the characters of a drama, our own hopes, dreams, and fears are touched and our own lives enriched and enlarged. That happens when we attend a production, but it can also occur when we read a play. Duplicating the complex, interactive experience that live theater creates may be impossible when reading a play; but you can approximate it by bringing the characters and actions to life in the theater of your mind.

WHAT IS DRAMA?

Drama is one of the oldest forms of verbal art. From earliest times, people have enjoyed pretending, or "acting something out." This "let's pretend" became more highly developed as people planned and organized their playacting for the benefit and entertainment of an audience, composing words to say and instructions on how to move.

Drama has deep connections to religion: Greek tragedy grew out of the worship of Dionysus, Passover reenacts the flight of the Israelites from Egypt, and the Catholic Mass is a dramatic representation of the sacrificial death of Christ. Drama enables an audience to participate, vicariously, in some of the deeply meaningful archetypal or mythic events in cultural history. Before the printing press made wide dissemination of texts possible, drama was a basic form of verbal art, and performance was a viable way to present one's work. Thus study of literature is not complete without including written plays.

DRAMA AS PERFORMANCE   The word *drama* derives from the Greek word meaning "to do, act, or perform." From the time of the Greeks, *drama* was used to describe literary works that could be acted out or performed.

WATCHING A PERFORMANCE   Watching "live action" on the stage differs from watching a performance on film, on DVD, on television, or on-line—it demands a different use of imagination and intellect. At a play, the viewer constantly makes decisions about who or what to pay particular attention to, whether to focus in on one character's expressions or "pan out" to take in the entire stage. Trying to notice everything important and not to miss key words, glances, or gestures, in addition to responding emotionally to characters and situations, can be exhausting as well as exhilarating. For recorded performances, you watch what the camera shows you; the decisions you would make if you were watching a dramatic stage production are made by the camera's eye instead.

RISKS IN PERFORMANCE   Live theater also has a kind of "suspense of production" that film lacks. An actor risks missing a line or tripping during an entrance. Mistakes lead to another "take" in filming or are cut out, but in live theater they're evident for all to see. Actors live with the anxiety of potential embarrassment and enjoy the challenge of either coming through flawlessly or recovering beautifully from a slip. But audience members feel some anxiety too. They don't want to see actors embarrassed or the effect of the performance damaged, so in the back of their minds is the hope everything will go well (and a twinge of fear that it won't). There is no such anxiety in watching a film—we know all the slips, at least those that were caught, have been edited away.

AUDIENCE INTERACTION   Also, the audience at a live theater, by responding emotionally and imaginatively to the action on stage, makes a contribution to performance. Actors in live theater are aware of and energized by an involved, appreciative audience. A mutual synergy develops between actors and audience that leads to a deeper experience for both.

READING A PLAY   There is no question about it: All that a performance involves cannot be duplicated in reading a play. But awareness of what happens in a real theater enhances one's reading of a play. Reading a play well does take a lot of imaginative participation. Does it require more than fiction or poetry? Such comparisons aren't helpful, in the end. An active reader pours herself or himself into whatever reading is at hand. Drama, like all literature, demands a lot of a reader, but the rewards are well worth it.

WHY READ DRAMA?

When we read a play, we assume that there is value in treating a play as a literary work. In reading a play, we concentrate on the words, not on the performance. Those words embody the pure play, the play as written rather than as cut and rearranged and interpreted for a particular performance; the words last and remain the same. Reading allows us to pause and reflect, to go back and look at earlier lines, to do the kind of close analysis of structure, characters, and style we've been doing for stories and poems.

One of the most exciting types of theaters is the theater of your mind and imagination. Here you can stage, direct, and perform whatever play you are reading. Reading the texts of plays has long been regarded as an enjoyable and valuable thing to do. But we need to recognize from the start that this kind of reading differs from reading stories and poems. Imagining a play requires particular reading skills and approaches.

ACTIVE READING: Drama

A **play** is a "dramatic work": That is, it doesn't *tell* a story and doesn't have a narrator the way narrative does. A play *acts out* a story, bringing the people and events to life, imaginatively, on a stage. The text of a play looks different from the way a story or a poem looks on the page.

- *Consider the cast*. The first thing you see in most cases is the cast of characters, the **dramatis personae** (the "persons of the drama"), a list of the people who appear in the drama. The same list is included in the program when you attend a theater performance, with the names of the actors who play the roles.

  A good starting point for reading (or watching) a play is to go through the list carefully, trying to remember the names of the characters and their relationships with each other. When reading a play with a large cast of characters, such as a play by Shakespeare, some people jot down names and diagram their relationships on a slip of paper for easy reference.

- *Pay attention to stage directions*. After listing the cast of characters, the printed play may offer "**stage directions**," a description of what the playwright visualizes for the scenery on the stage and perhaps the age and appearance of the characters and the way they are dressed, sometimes even a personality characteristic. These are intended, of course, as guidelines for the director, set designer, and costume designer in planning how to produce the work on the stage. When reading a play, it's fun to fill these roles yourself and imagine the actors, their stage movements, the set design, and the costumes.

You are likely to find more extensive stage directions in a modern play than in one by Sophocles or Shakespeare. A dramatist always writes to fit the facilities available at the time (the kind of theater, scenery, and stage machinery). The scenery Sophocles or Shakespeare could count on was less elaborate than what came later, so they often used imagery in the text to indicate the scene. For example, many Elizabethan plays were acted in open-air theaters during the afternoon, so to indicate darkness Shakespeare has a character say that it's dark and may have someone carry a lantern. The directions included in modern plays vary widely. Some playwrights go into extensive detail illustrating everything from the color of the walls to the type of table sitting in a corner of a room, to the lighting and atmosphere they think is appropriate. Others may offer the sparest generalizations: "a room, some furniture."

- *Use your imagination.* Your imagination functions differently for a play than for a story or poem. The texts of stories, because they are meant to be read, include descriptions to help along your imagination ("the man with stringy brown hair plodded up the dimly lighted staircase"). A play assumes you are seeing the character on the stage, so it doesn't provide the same description. In watching a play, the role of the imagination is to accept the pretense that the actor really is the character and that what you see on the stage really is a kitchen or a forest. One of the challenges in reading a play is picturing the scene and characters in your mind. Stage directions help you to visualize the characters and action in your imagination.

- *Read the lines.* After the stage directions come the lines of the play itself, the script the actors memorize as they prepare to perform the play on stage, together with further stage directions for particular actions (including entrances and exits). What you see on the page is the name of the character, followed by words indicating what the character says or does. In reading the text of a play, first look at the name of the speaker — notice who and what the character is; then go on to what the character says. As you keep reading, use your intellect and imagination to connect the speeches to each other. Watch for interactions between characters and for the ways the diction varies among characters. Just as when you read a story, you will come to experience the characters developing as they reply to what other characters say.

- *Imagine the action.* The characters will also expand and develop as you imagine the movements that would take place on stage: people arriving and leaving, meeting each other, moving at various paces and with particular styles of movement and gestures, reacting to each other, using props, and interacting with the set. Remember always that this is a drama: You are observing the characters on the stage of your imagination as they act out a scene of considerable importance in the life of at least one of them.

REREADING: Drama

To experience a play fully, you need to read it more than once. As with a story or poem, during the first reading you primarily concentrate on what's going on. Only on the second or third time through do you begin to appreciate fully what the work offers. Many of the suggestions for rereading fiction and poetry (pp. 110–11 and 568–69) apply to rereading drama as well. We comment here on how they apply particularly to rereading a play.

- *The second time you read a play, slow down*. The first time through you usually read quickly because you want to find out what happens to the characters as they deal with a dramatic situation. You probably don't pay close attention to the way characters are expressing themselves or to the subtleties embedded in their speeches. Like poets and story writers, dramatists write carefully—each phrase is thoughtfully shaped and every word counts. On second reading, linger on speeches to enjoy the style, to catch the nuances that reveal subtleties in character, and to notice details that foreshadow later events that you now realize are significant.

- *Pay attention to little things*. The second time through, you can be more alert for easily overlooked details, things most readers do not notice the first time, and to the subtlety of techniques the author uses. (The same thing is true of watching a play. Seeing it a second time—like watching a movie a second or third or tenth time—helps you to appreciate it more fully.) You notice new things during subsequent readings—especially little things, like a gesture or an item on a table in act 1 that turns out to be significant in act 3. What may appear at first reading to be merely a set or stage direction is recognized on rereading to be of wider significance and thus is experienced more meaningfully.

- *Be selective about parts to reread, if you have to*. Because of the length of a three- or five-act play, it may be difficult to find the time to reread the whole work. In some cases (if you need to write a long paper studying the play thoroughly, for example), you'll need to find the time for a complete rereading. In other cases, if you can't reread the entire play, at least reread scenes and passages that are crucial to revealing character traits or plot development.

- *Remember the reading strategies we gave you for fiction and poetry*. Pay attention to the title; look up things that aren't familiar; research people, times, and places that relate to the plot; notice the opening and closing lines; reflect on what the characters are like and what motivates them, on the organization of the plot, and on the significance of the actions and events.

- *Read some parts aloud.* Dramatic dialogue is meant to be heard. Reading sections of the play aloud, working to interpret the expression, rhythms, and tone effectively, will help you hear other parts more clearly and meaningfully in your mind's ear as you read silently. And it can be fun. Divide up the parts among a few of your friends and see what happens.

William Shakespeare

(see pages 680, 862, and 1149)

Character, Conflict, and Dramatic Action

CHAPTER 22

Thinking about Who Does What to Whom and Why

Almost everyone enjoys watching stories acted out. Even if you don't attend live theater all that often, you probably watch television or movies. Television producers certainly recognize this appeal and place enormous importance on garnering huge audiences. Advertisers know it and tap into those shows that have the highest ratings, all because we love to watch everything from soaps to sitcoms to serious drama. There's something compelling about watching a skilled actor entering a role and bringing a character to life, making us laugh at comic characters and empathize with tragic ones.

Reading scripts can never substitute for watching an excellent performance: The script was meant for performance, after all. But reading plays, as we say in Chapter 21, has its own rewards, and learning to do it well is worth some effort. Whether you're watching or reading a play, the essential core is the same: character, conflict, and dramatic action. Drama usually focuses on characters, the created persons who appear or are referred to in a play. Those characters come to life primarily through conflict. And the conflict is presented through dramatic action on a stage, whether in a theater or in the imagination. You have already worked with conflict and character earlier in this book (see pp. 117–18 and 121–25). This chapter deals with how development of characters and conflicts is achieved through dialogue and dramatic action, the distinctive methods used by drama.

897

ENTRY POINTS   Plays and their productions are not always two hours (or more) in length and constructed in three or five acts. **One-act plays** — sometimes only ten or fifteen minutes in length — are an important theatrical form and work with the same elements as longer plays (see p. 1045). The guidelines for reading a play laid out in Chapter 21, especially the section "Active Reading: Drama" (pp. 893–94), apply just as well to one-act plays as to three- or five-act plays. Practice applying the guidelines to the following very short play, *The New New*.

This script does not start with a list of characters: They are instead identified in the stage directions. If you attended a performance of the play, the program would most likely list the names of the five characters (and of the actor playing each role), in order of appearance: Jenny, Marcy, Bradley, Craig, and Naomi. Because the text gives no details about their ages or appearance, you will need to make decisions about these as you imagine the play, just as a director would in planning a performance.

The text says nothing about where or when the action takes place. It presumably could take place in any large city and at any time (the program at a performance might well state, after the list of characters, "Time: the present"). The stage directions (in italics) supply guidance about staging the action: It alternates between two offices on opposite sides of the stage. Your imagination can furnish the offices in any way you like, though a performance could get by with simply a table, a couple of chairs, and a telephone on each side.

It is a dramatic convention that, when a stage is divided this way, the audience will assume that characters on the one side cannot hear characters talking on the other side. You will need to use your imagination to move back and forth between the two offices. In a performance, such movement might be signaled by lighting the side of the stage in which characters are talking, while darkening the other side. However, for a simple performance without special lighting equipment, the characters' voices will draw the audience's attention from side to side without it.

As you read the play itself, pay attention to who is speaking and thus, in this case, which side of the stage is active at the moment. Also be sure to notice the stage directions. As an active reader, you'll need to know what is happening in the present, especially any conflicts that emerge. You will also need to piece together what has happened in the past, what has led up to the present situation, and to figure out what each character is like from what they say and do and what is said about them (including two important characters who do not appear on the stage). And you will want to reflect on the choices the characters are making and the values their words and actions reveal.

Kelly Stuart b. 1961

The New New   [2002]

*Jenny and Marcy in one "office" area—they are stapling brochures or doing some
other type of repetitive office work. Bradley and Craig in another office—they
are actually separated by a long corridor, but should be represented as being in
isolated areas of the stage.*

JENNY: I'm going to have an affair with him.

MARCY: But Jenny, you're failing his class.

JENNY: He says I can take an incomplete if I
   want, and he'll help me make it up
   over the summer.

BRADLEY: I need a new word for new.

CRAIG: Fresh.

BRADLEY: Too hip hop. This is more white.

CRAIG *(opening a thesaurus)*: Thesaurus
   check.

*(Naomi, a nervous, down-at-the-heels woman appears and stands, hoping to engage
Marcy and Jenny's attention.)*

MARCY: Isn't he what, like, uh, married?

JENNY: Yeah, but we have this INTENSE CONNECTION. It's like, ECONOMICS
   is not my forte. I find the whole subject abysmal. But he's got this precision
   of mind and I want that. I think that's what's missing in me, and I'm so,
   like, attracted to that.

NAOMI: I'm here to see Bradley Zuckerman?

(Jenny and Marcy look at her, deciding she's a nonentity.)

CRAIG *(reading)*: Fresh, modern. Modernistic. Neoteric.

BRADLEY: Neoteric?

(They shrug in unison. Craig continues.)

CRAIG: Novel. Newfangled. Newsprung. Revived. Reinvigorating.

BRADLEY: ". . . Reinvigorated the genre of prison memoir."

CRAIG: That's stale.

BRADLEY: It's become stale to say something is NEW. What's the new new? We
   need the new NEW.

MARCY: Did you ask me a question?

NAOMI: Bradley Zuckerman?

MARCY: Do you have an appointment?

NAOMI: When is he back?

MARCY: Do you have an appointment?

NAOMI: When is he back?

JENNY: Do you have an appointment?

NAOMI: I'll wait.

MARCY: We discourage that.

JENNY: He's not coming in. He's with marketing. So you would simply be wasting your time.

NAOMI: Where's marketing?

(Marcy turns back to Jenny, leaving Naomi standing awkwardly. They whisper to each other, occasionally looking Naomi's way. Naomi watches. They giggle.)

BRADLEY: A laser-sharp vision. The voice. The, something, vision and voice. His. New. The . . . What. There's no more words.

CRAIG: I liked Neoteric.

BRADLEY: Nobody will know what that means.

CRAIG: A powerful neoteric account, of the agony behind prison walls.

BRADLEY: I'm sorry, that sounds like gobbledygook. Um . . . deadpan, self-deprecating and, witty. But it's also new and it's important we say that.

CRAIG: It's a first novel.

BRADLEY: It's a memoir.

CRAIG: Actually, we can't call it a memoir. It's a kind of memoiristic novel.

BRADLEY: Why can't we call it a memoir?

CRAIG: Legal affairs said—

BRADLEY: OK it's a novel in the form of a memoir, based on real-life authentic experience.

(Naomi continues to stand looking at the women. They ignore her. Their conversation has become audible again:)

JENNY: There is like, so much electricity there. When he's looking at me, it's like I get zapped.

MARCY: Well I really want you to meet this guy.

JENNY: The writer?

MARCY: Yeah. Jimmy.

BRADLEY: The absurdity and the agony of life as a convict.

CRAIG: Agony isn't a word that sells.

BRADLEY: Agonizing, and yet entertaining.

CRAIG: That sounds so *People* magazine.

(They scan a thesaurus.)

JENNY: What does he write about?

MARCY: Um, prison. Jail. The Penal system.

JENNY: Oh.

MARCY: He had like, an MBA from Yale but I think he was like, convicted of manslaughter.

JENNY: Oh. A murderer.

MARCY: Manslaughter. I think. It was accidental. Self Defense. Some kind of fight, with this guy named monster. This six foot two, three hundred pound monster. An accidental death that he was convicted of—I guess, I guess, he pled guilty.

JENNY: Oh.

MARCY: To spare something, more like, the death penalty. I mean, I guess he cut a deal.

(Jenny notices Naomi staring at her.)

JENNY: Can we help you with something else?

NAOMI: Who are you talking about?

MARCY: I'm going to have to ask you to leave, OK?

NAOMI: I need to see Bradley Zuckerman.

MARCY: Leave a number and go or I'll have to call security.

NAOMI: I'd like to know who you're talking about.

JENNY: Did you not hear us? Do we HAVE to call security?

(Naomi abruptly leaves. The two women shake their heads in disgust.)

MARCY: These people will do anything to make you take a manuscript. Anyway he's—he's just really charismatic and charming and smart. I mean, it is so odd, when you meet him, you'll see, what an odd juxtaposition to think of this guy in prison. I mean, I'm really FOND of him. And his writing is really super evocative of the, you know, of the Kafkaesque° nature of life in prison. He's sexy too.

JENNY: So why don't you sleep with him?

MARCY: I'm trying to be monogamous now. And Bradley is like, editing his book. I can't do that. Sleep with the guy Bradley edits.

(Naomi makes a cross past the stage. Disappears.)

BRADLEY: I used to get these calls from prison, collect calls every Tuesday. I thought of these calls as my "Tuesdays with Jimmy."° He was just this witty, sardonic ethnographer of prison life. Of the ingenuity. And the angle, the engagement I found with the theme of this—civilized business executive locked up with all these illiterate thugs, and how he survived.

CRAIG: I love that he used like, sales techniques.

BRADLEY: Yes.

CRAIG: Stuff he learned from corporate sales seminars: Body language mirroring.

BRADLEY: I guess it all works.

(For a beat, they mirror each other's body language. Naomi enters and stares at them. They ignore her.)

Kafkaesque: A feeling of senseless, sometimes menacing disorientation, as conveyed in the works of Austrian author Franz Kafka (1883–1924). **"Tuesdays with Jimmy":** Alluding to Mitch Albom's best-selling book *Tuesdays with Morrie* (1997).

CRAIG: In a way it doesn't matter how we market this thing because film rights have already gone to Ben Stiller.°

BRADLEY: Really?

CRAIG: Mike Medavoy° loved it. The release will coincide with the movie.

BRADLEY: But that's . . . I mean, there's a literary value.

CRAIG: It's great. Ben Stiller.

BRADLEY: Ben Stiller. That's great.

NAOMI: Excuse me —

CRAIG: It's a comedy. That's how they see it. It's going to sell like a mother-fucker.

NAOMI: Is this marketing?

CRAIG: Yes.

NAOMI: I'm looking for Bradley Zuckerman.

CRAIG: Bradley —

BRADLEY: He doesn't work here. You have the wrong department.

NAOMI: I was told he's in marketing.

MARCY: I just think you'd have more in common with him than with your economics professor.

JENNY: Why? Because he's a criminal?

MARCY: But he's not really.

BRADLEY: No, uh, he works in creative development.

NAOMI: But they said in his office that he was in here.

BRADLEY: No. He's not here. Have you seen him Craig?

CRAIG: Haven't seen him.

BRADLEY: Would you like to leave a message for him?

CRAIG: I'm sorry. You really can't wait here. Would you like to leave him a message? (*He hands her a notepad. She stands looking at it. She begins to write, furiously.*)

MARCY: Being convicted of manslaughter had nothing to do with the arc of his life. It was just, this aberration.

JENNY: Who did he kill again?

MARCY: This drug dealer guy. You're going to like him. I told him about you, he's interested in meeting you.

JENNY: So he's like, — out?

MARCY: On Parole.

(*Naomi has finished writing.*)

NAOMI: Will you make sure Bradley Zuckerman gets this?

BRADLEY: Certainly.

(*Naomi gives them the pad of paper and exits. The men giggle.*)

BRADLEY: Oh my God that was close.

CRAIG: "No I'm not Bradley."

Ben Stiller: Benjamin Edward Stiller (b. 1965), American actor, film director, and producer.   **Mike Medavoy:** Morris Mike Medavoy (b. 1941), American film producer and film studio executive.

BRADLEY: "BRADLEY? NO. I HAVEN'T SEEN HIM." Anyway, Jesus. What does she want? (*Craig is reading the pad of paper. He hands it to Bradley.*) My brother's name was Jeremy. Not Monster. He was five foot three, one hundred thirty pounds. Not six foot two, three hundred fifty. My brother was tortured and strangled over the course of a two-hour, period. The shape of a turtle and a steer were imprinted on my brother's neck, from the cowboy belt your so-called "author" used. My brother's face was badly beaten, bones protruded from his bloody face. My brother was a medical assistant. He was a human being, not a monster. To see this man profit, it's killing me and I wonder if you ever gave that a thought?

CRAIG: I still think, um. The SPIRIT of the—I mean, he was true to the SPIRIT of, the book's not about the crime in any case and uh, legally, there's no . . .

BRADLEY: You knew this?

CRAIG: It's not really an issue.

BRADLEY: I mean, the thing of it is, I—I really like Jimmy.

CRAIG: Yeah, and who is she? Who is she really? Like what do you know?

BRADLEY: And the thing of it is, it's about Jimmy's writing. I think his writing redeems him.

CRAIG: Yeah. That's why we never, like bothered to check.

MARCY: You know it's already been optioned as a movie? For Ben Stiller.

JENNY: I love Ben Stiller.

MARCY: Then I think, really, you're going to love Jimmy.

BRADLEY: I'm fixing him up with my girlfriend's sister. I wouldn't do that if I didn't like him, if I thought he wasn't, a good person. Yeah. It's fine. It's.

CRAIG: I mean, —this . . . —like, she's the victim's sister. That's all. What do you expect?

JENNY: So, what are we going to do, like, go out to dinner together? Are we—

MARCY: Yeah.

JENNY: I'm up for that.

(*Bradley looks seriously confused. Lights fade.*)

END OF PLAY

APPROACHING THE READING

1. Describe the characters—Jenny, Marcy, Bradley, Craig, and Naomi. What are you given that helps you get to know them? Which characters (if any) are you drawn to? Which ones are you put off by? Why?

2. There are two characters important to the play that we don't see, Jeremy and Jimmy. Describe what they are like. What are the advantages of not having Jimmy appear on stage? What is revealing about Naomi being the only one who knows Jeremy's name?

3. Identify different kinds of conflicts that appear within the play and ones that exist behind what occurs on stage. Do any of these conflicts raise issues that are meaningful or important to you? If so, explain.

4. Even though there isn't much action in this play, particular movements are important. Pick out those that we should notice and explain their significance.

READING FOR CHARACTER

Just as with fiction, some of the first questions to ask about a play likely involve the characters. Who are they? What are they like? Why do they act, speak, and feel the way they do? In drama, characters are developed in some of the same ways described earlier for fiction: showing, saying, telling, entering a character's mind, and naming (pp. 121–22). Saying and telling in particular are central in drama because of the significance of dialogue.

SHOWING   What a character is like comes out in part from the character's actions. We get to know about a character from what she or he does, often in a more reliable way than from what the character says or what is said about her or him: Actions in this case do speak louder than words. For Marcy and Jenny to turn their backs on Naomi and giggle at her, for example, especially when combined with the way they talk to her, reveals a good deal about them.

SAYING   Conversation between two or more characters, or **dialogue**, is the fundamental method of writing used in drama. Much of what occurs in a play starts from and relies on characters talking to each other. From what the characters say to each other, the audience or reader pieces the story together, including details about relevant events in the past and foreshadowings of what may occur in the future. And dialogue provides the primary means for becoming familiar with the characters: What they say and to whom, and especially how they say it, reveal things about them and about others and help us understand the conflicts and motivations that give rise to the action.

Thus, in *The New New*, what Jenny and Marcy talk about (using sex to pass an economics course, meeting a charming ex-con) and what Bradley and Craig talk about (finding ways to market a "memoiristic novel" about surviving in prison without verifying facts about the writer) evince the shallowness of their characters. For all of them, life centers in words, not realities, in words that instead of clarifying and revealing, avoid, cover up, and distort.

TELLING   We also learn about characters through dialogue as one character tells what another is like. When one character (whether in drama or fiction) tells us about another, the description may be accurate and reliable or it may be inaccurate and misleading. In *The New New* we know what

Naomi's brother is like from the note she writes, and we accept what she says as true because the other characters can't dispute it. And we learn about Jimmy first from what Marcy and Bradley say about him ("he's just really charismatic and charming and smart" and "He was just this witty, sardonic ethnographer of prison life") and then from what Naomi tells about him: "My brother was tortured and strangled over the course of a two-hour period." What Marcy and Bradley say reveals more about them than about the person they are discussing. Not only do they not actually know what Jimmy is like but they also don't seem to care. "And the thing of it is," Bradley says, "it's about Jimmy's writing. I think his writing redeems him." In other words, how one successfully manipulates words is more important than what one does.

ENTERING Entering a character's thoughts is less frequent in drama than in fiction, but it does occur in some instances (not, however, in *The New New*). In a **soliloquy**, a speaker alone onstage, or off to the side of the stage away from other characters, reveals to the audience what is going through her or his mind. Shakespeare uses soliloquies frequently, especially in his tragedies. In *Othello*, for example, the antagonist Iago has several soliloquies in which he reveals his intentions and motivations to the audience (see especially pp. 1168, 1176, and 1179).

> Review the discussion "Categories of Characterization," on pages 123–24. Most of the terminology introduced for fiction there — **protagonist**, **antagonist**; **major**, **minor**; **round**, **flat** — can be applied to drama as well.

READING FOR DIALOGUE

DIALOGUE IS CENTRAL Although all of the above methods are important, dialogue remains most significant. When we watch a play, we need to listen closely to the words of the dialogue; reading a play requires the same attentiveness and a great deal of imaginative involvement as well. Tone (p. 235) and style (p. 237) contribute in a significant way to dialogue in drama.

Aspects of style that we discussed earlier in the book apply here as well, and appropriateness remains the key factor: Word choice and sentence structure (see pp. 237–39) need to fit the character using the words and expressing the sentences. A good playwright is able to create stylistic differences in the dialogue of various characters as an aspect of characterization. And determining the tone is important in individual speeches as well as in a play as a whole.

One of the pleasures in reading a play is imagining how the dialogue would sound on stage — what pace, sound, inflections, and tones of voice fit each character. Should the actor shout or whisper "Shut up!"? How does she or he express anger or grief or bewilderment, or all three at once? What words should be emphasized? If you have ever acted or known an actor, you've likely experienced how many ways there are to say something seemingly as simple as "Where have you been?" In reading a play, we get to be the actors, experimenting with each line to decide how to express it most effectively and get across its meaning most completely, including what it reveals about the speaker.

Creating convincing dialogue is a challenge for playwrights: The discussions, arguments, questions, outbursts, seductions, and compliments must seem natural and appropriate to the speakers and "realistic" for their time and setting. At the same time, they must be carefully crafted to make every speech, even every word, count toward all the different things the dialogue needs to accomplish (for example, advancing the plot, revealing character, engaging the audience, focusing the conflict). Because watching or reading a play requires such close attention to the words of the dialogue, some people find it helpful to read a plot summary first. Knowing the broad plot outline can help you to pick up the signals and subtleties the words are conveying.

READING FOR CONFLICT

In drama, characters are most often found in a situation involving **conflict**, a struggle or confrontation between opposing characters or a character and opposing forces. Conflict is important to drama first because it usually creates action on the stage — whether external and physical or internal and psychological — and thus creates the kind of excitement, suspense, and tension we associate with the word *drama*. Even outside the theater, we hear *drama* used that way, as, for example, in describing a news story about a dramatic standoff. Second, conflict is important because the nature of the conflict, the issues involved, and the way it is handled generally bring out aspects of character: The essence and the depths of a person come out as she or he confronts a challenging situation.

The kinds of conflict in drama range as widely as those in fiction, but the same three broad categories discussed in Chapter 5 (pp. 112–58) — physical conflict, social conflict, and internal or psychological conflict — are useful here as well.

No physical conflict occurs in *The New New*, though the plot grows out of the brutal killing of Naomi's brother that occurred several years before. Social conflict appears in the contempt with which Marcy and Jenny treat the "nonentity" Naomi, a "nervous, down-at-the-heels" woman from a lower social stratum than theirs, who clearly lacks their education and sophistication (this is shown partly in the style in which her note to Bradley is written, especially the odd comma after "two-hour," which is apparent to a reader though perhaps not to someone watching the play). Internal conflict emerges when Bradley is confronted with the fact that he never did give a thought to the victim of Jimmy's crime, never investigated the truth of what Jimmy told him. Taken in by Jimmy's charm and charisma and by the opportunity to publish a best-selling book, he is converting a callous murderer into a wealthy celebrity.

Chapter 5 points out that watching for conflicts is a good way to get to the crucial issues in a work of fiction. That is even more true for a play. Identifying areas of conflict as you watch or read a play, or as you watch a movie or television show, usually takes you directly to the heart of its action and significance.

READING FOR DRAMATIC ACTION

Some dramatic productions do not use action on a stage. In reader's theater, for example, actors typically perch on stools and read their parts to each other and the audience. In most theater productions, however, actors move about onstage "acting out" what is going on.

MOVEMENT ON STAGE   Dramatic action is almost always a fundamental aspect of drama, and conflict in drama often becomes a part of the play's dramatic action: Characters differ, argue, quarrel, challenge each other, and find solutions to their problems or difficulties. Therefore, another challenge for you as the reader of a play is using your imagination to visualize the action while reading the text. For the play to be complete, the dramatic action needs to be seen, on stage or in the mind's theater.

ACTIONS ON STAGE   In some cases, the script of the play supplies guidelines for what actions should accompany the words, either in stage directions or in the lines themselves. Thus, a stage direction in *The New New* indicates that Craig "hands [Naomi] a notepad. She stands looking at it. She begins to write, furiously." For the most part, however, the actors and directors are left to decide how the characters should move on stage (called "blocking" in theater parlance) and what gestures they should use. As a reader, you are both director and actor, so you get to use your intelligence to try to understand the characters fully enough so that you can picture their actions, gestures, and expressions on the stage of your mind.

TIMING   A key part of any action is timing: When the text is acted out on stage, the pace depends on variations in the intensity of different moments. Words almost always take more time to say aloud than to read silently. Certain lines need to be spoken more slowly or quickly than others. Action on the stage occurs during lines, between lines, or while no one is speaking. Actions can be large—a sword fight—or smaller, perhaps a

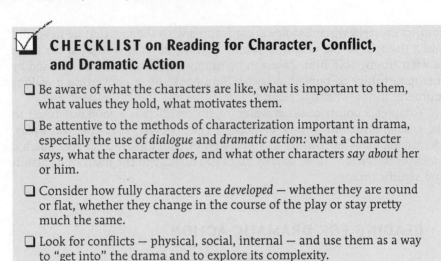

> ### ☑ CHECKLIST on Reading for Character, Conflict, and Dramatic Action
>
> ❑ Be aware of what the characters are like, what is important to them, what values they hold, what motivates them.
>
> ❑ Be attentive to the methods of characterization important in drama, especially the use of *dialogue* and *dramatic action:* what a character *says,* what the character *does,* and what other characters *say about* her or him.
>
> ❑ Consider how fully characters are *developed* — whether they are round or flat, whether they change in the course of the play or stay pretty much the same.
>
> ❑ Look for conflicts — physical, social, internal — and use them as a way to "get into" the drama and to explore its complexity.

character walking across the stage, looking out a window, or searching in a desk drawer. Both large and small actions can be significant. Sometimes characters come on stage, do something, and leave without saying any words at all. Sometimes pauses occur between sentences or between words in a speech, as one character looks angrily at another or ponders what another character has just said. In a play, as in life, pauses or silences often say as much as or even more than words do. For such reasons, a scene that takes five minutes to read might take ten minutes to act out.

> 🌐 You can further explore characters and conflict, including interactive exercises, with VirtuaLit Drama at bedfordstmartins.com/ rewritinglit.

Here too it is important for you the reader to imagine the pace at which things are taking place, especially where the script does not include specific indications.

FURTHER READING

ENTRY POINTS   In the following play, *dramatic action* certainly isn't dominant. A son stands at bat. His father throws him seven pitches, and the son hits the baseball three times. But between pitches they talk. By listening to the dialogue, we learn a great deal about the two characters and what their lives are like — the situations they face and the dreams they pursue or have pursued. Notice how their conversation reveals various conflicts, past and present, that contribute to the current situation. Even with minimal action, a lot is "going on." Note how the playwright focuses attention on important aspects of the conflict without detracting from the give-and-take of ordinary conversation.

Eduardo Machado   b. 1953

Crossing the Border   [2008]

CHARACTERS

MANUEL: Fifteen, thin, dark.
JACINTO: Early thirties, plump, less dark; father of Manuel.

SETTING

An alley in Playa Carmen, Mexico.

TIME

Late afternoon, the present.

You can hear Mexican rock music blaring from a car radio. The sound of motor bikes and bicycles. Manuel is holding a bat. His father, Jacinto, is pitching to him.

MANUEL: Papa. My teacher, she told me I write good essays. That I could win a contest. That she would help me after school. Isn't that great?

JACINTO: No.

MANUEL: No?

JACINTO: Hit the ball.

MANUEL: That's all you gotta say?

JACINTO: Hit it. You promise me you are going to hit it?

MANUEL: I'll try.

JACINTO: Not try. You are going to do it.

MANUEL: I'll try!

JACINTO: Trying is not enough.

MANUEL: That's all I can do.

JACINTO: Baseball is what you do best.

MANUEL: No. I can do physics and I know how to write in verse and I have read Lorca.

JACINTO: Lorca.

MANUEL: The great poet, killed by the fascists.

JACINTO: You know what fascists are?

MANUEL: Yes. The people who tried to take over the world.

JACINTO: The world?

MANUEL: They killed the gypsies and the Jews.

JACINTO: What?

MANUEL: And Garcia Lorca.°

Garcia Lorca: Federico García Lorca (1898–1936), Spanish poet, dramatist, and theater director. He was killed by fascist soldiers in the opening days of the Spanish civil war.

JACINTO: Why are you so smart, *mijo*°?   *my son*

MANUEL: 'Cause I read a lot.

JACINTO: You like reading.

MANUEL: I devour books.

JACINTO: You like science.

MANUEL: Yes.

JACINTO: And mathematics?

MANUEL: Numbers are an art form.

JACINTO: And poetry?

MANUEL: It fills my soul.

JACINTO: It does.

MANUEL: Yes!

JACINTO: Reading is not going to get you out of here.

MANUEL: I don't want to get out of here.

JACINTO: Yes, you do. Now get ready.

MANUEL: For what?

JACINTO: My pitch.

MANUEL: Baseball?

JACINTO: Yes.

MANUEL: Why?

JACINTO: Eyes on the ball.

MANUEL: Sure.

JACINTO: Yes?

MANUEL: Yes.

JACINTO: On the ball!

MANUEL: On the ball, Papa!

JACINTO: Here it comes. Might be a spit ball, keep your eye on my hand, the hand which is holding the ball, right?

MANUEL: Right!

JACINTO: Good son.

MANUEL: I'm ready!

(Jacinto pitches. Manuel misses.)

JACINTO: Goddam it! You missed the fucking ball!

MANUEL: I am sorry.

JACINTO: Sorry? You are sorry! You gotta concentrate.

MANUEL: I was.

JACINTO: Not good enough.

MANUEL: I am sorry.

JACINTO: Sorry ain't going to get you out of here.

MANUEL: I know. I am sorry.

JACINTO: Sorry will have you end up like me.

MANUEL: What's so bad.

JACINTO: What?

MANUEL: What's so bad with you?

JACINTO: My job.

MANUEL: What's wrong with your job?

JACINTO: Tour guide.

MANUEL: So?

JACINTO: A guide for tourists, French, German, Italians, but mostly gringos.

MANUEL: They come to the Mayan Riviera.

JACINTO: Mostly Texans.

MANUEL: Who can't afford to go anywhere but here.

JACINTO: That's right.

MANUEL: Sorry.

JACINTO: I make my living off a bunch of Texans.

MANUEL: You hate it?

JACINTO: What?

MANUEL: Your job?

JACINTO: It's what I have to do. What I have to do because I have one son, two daughters, another on the way. A wife that takes in sewing. And I live in Playa Carmen, Mexico, and there are thousands, millions. Just like me.

MANUEL: Just like you?

JACINTO: Fucked.

MANUEL: What do you mean?

JACINTO: 'Cause we were born in the wrong country, at the wrong time.

MANUEL: I see.

JACINTO: And I am trying to teach you something that will get you out of here, and you don't care.

MANUEL: I do!

JACINTO: You missed the ball!

MANUEL: Maybe I am no good at this.

JACINTO: Yes, you are.

MANUEL: Are you sure?

JACINTO: You got star potential, big leagues, U.S.A.

MANUEL: I don't see it, Papa.

JACINTO: I do.

MANUEL: I'm trying.

JACINTO: Believe it.

MANUEL: I take it very seriously. I try really hard to get better.

JACINTO: You are not trying hard enough!

MANUEL: What did I do wrong?

JACINTO: You missed the ball.

MANUEL: I know.

JACINTO: You did not concentrate hard enough.

MANUEL: Yes, I did.

JACINTO: Throw the ball back. Come on. Throw the ball to me.

MANUEL: Why?

JACINTO: 'Cause I told you to.

MANUEL: You have so many others right next to you.

JACINTO: But I want that one.

MANUEL: Why, Papa?

JACINTO: To punish you, son.

MANUEL: Punish me. I am punished enough.

JACINTO: No discipline, my son has no discipline.

MANUEL: I'm trying!

JACINTO: Not good enough.

MANUEL: It takes up all of my free time.

JACINTO: It has to!

MANUEL: We practice every day from when I get out of school at three till the sun goes down. That's enough punishment.

JACINTO: You think so?

MANUEL: Yes. I do, Papa.

JACINTO: You don't know what punishment is till you try to survive in this country . . . In this shit hole . . . in Mexico.

MANUEL: America is so much better?

JACINTO: So much more money.

MANUEL: For everybody?

JACINTO: Yes!

MANUEL: You sure?

JACINTO: If you are willing to work for it.

MANUEL: How do you know?

JACINTO: My brother.

MANUEL: Brother? You have a brother?

JACINTO: Yes. I had one.

MANUEL: Where is he?

JACINTO: Up north.

MANUEL: In California.

JACINTO: No. Tijuana.

MANUEL: Tijuana? He never came back here?

JACINTO: We don't speak. He ruined our chances. He got caught. He was supposed to go, then raise enough money so I could follow. But he got caught. Fucking idiot.

MANUEL: You should have gone first. You are smart.

JACINTO: You think so?

MANUEL: Yeah. You speak English.

JACINTO: Your mother. Didn't want me to land in jail. Like my brother. He went there to pick grapes. Went there to farm. To sweat. They need our sweat. But they hate us at the same time. Your mama needed to be here. A place where she knew she was wanted. Where she could starve, but with people that knew her.

MANUEL: Mama would not let you go?

JACINTO: After my brother was sent back . . .

MANUEL: Yes?

JACINTO: I was never able to raise enough to pay the coyotes.

MANUEL: How much money?

JACINTO: Couple of thousand.

MANUEL: Pesos.

JACINTO: Dollars.

MANUEL: Wow! High price.

JACINTO: It is.

MANUEL: I'm sorry. Here is the ball.

(*Manuel throws the ball at Jacinto, who catches it.*)

JACINTO: But you will get there.

MANUEL: To the U.S.A.?

JACINTO: Yes! Yes, you will! Right?

MANUEL: Maybe I don't want to get there.

JACINTO: Yes, you do.

MANUEL: They don't like us there.

JACINTO: They will . . .

MANUEL: They are building a huge wall.

JACINTO: I know. A wall to keep us out. They are sending an army to find us. The national guard. I read the paper. But we will change all that.

MANUEL: You think?

JACINTO: I know.

MANUEL: How?

JACINTO: For now, you hit this goddamn ball.

MANUEL: I will.

JACINTO: Good!

MANUEL: For you, Papa?

JACINTO: A home run?

MANUEL: I'll try.

JACINTO: But keep your eye on the ball!!

MANUEL: My eye is right on it, the ball, your hand, the pitch . . . Come on!

(*Jacinto pitches. Manuel hits it out of sight.*)

JACINTO: Out of the park! Yes! Good son! You are going to do it? Home run! Home run!

MANUEL: I don't know, Papa.

JACINTO: Yes! Yes, it is!

MANUEL: It only went down half a block.

JACINTO: A home run! That's what I said, that's what it is, Manuel.

MANUEL: Maybe in this alley, Papa. But not in America.

JACINTO: Don't think that. Don't say that!

MANUEL: We're cockroaches to them. They don't like us.

JACINTO: They like our tequila.

MANUEL: Yeah, tequila and guacamole. That's all.

JACINTO: They like the Dominicans . . .

MANUEL: Do they?

JACINTO: If they can hit.

MANUEL: Like David Ortiz°?

JACINTO: They like the Cubans . . .

MANUEL: No, they don't. They hate them.

JACINTO: Not if they can pitch.

MANUEL: Like "El Duque°"?

JACINTO: If you can pitch or hit, you get an instant green card.

MANUEL: Really?

JACINTO: Yes.

MANUEL: Are you sure?

JACINTO: Positive. Look at their teams, everybody has a Spanish name.

MANUEL: Maybe they were born there.

JACINTO: No, as soon as a Cuban baseball star defects to Canada, the next day they are a Yankee or a Dodger. They are welcomed and given millions. Millions.

MANUEL: That's true?

JACINTO: Yes, it is.

MANUEL: I see.

JACINTO: So hit the ball as if your life depended on it.

MANUEL: I want to be good, Papa.

JACINTO: I will teach you to be great.

MANUEL: Were you good at baseball, Papa?

JACINTO: Never played it till I started teaching you.

MANUEL: Did you like the game?

JACINTO: I'm doing this for you. When you started playing in the streets with your friends when you were eight, you out hit everybody. I knew it would be your way out. All we had to do was train and concentrate. I want you to have a future, son!

MANUEL: Thank you.

JACINTO: Poverty is a terrible thing, son. It takes away your pride.

MANUEL: So does ignorance.

JACINTO: When you become a baseball star, you can read any book you want. Now, your eye on the ball.

MANUEL: Yes.

JACINTO: Pick up the bat.

MANUEL: Yes, Papa.

(*Manuel picks up the bat.*)

JACINTO: Baseball Hall of Fame, that's what I want for my son.

MANUEL: Eye on the ball.

JACINTO: Good.

David Ortiz: David Américo Ortiz Arias (b. 1975 in the Dominican Republic), major league baseball player 1997–present.   **"El Duque":** Nickname of Orlando Hernández Pedroso (b. 1965 in Cuba), major league pitcher 1998–2007.

(Jacinto pitches. Manuel misses.)

MANUEL: Shit!

JACINTO: Good, you're angry. Come on!

MANUEL: Yeah!

JACINTO: You have to hit it.

MANUEL: Yeah!

JACINTO: Out of the park.

MANUEL: Yeah!

JACINTO: So they'll want you, like the Dominicans and the Cubans and the Venezuelans.

MANUEL: I'm going to do it.

JACINTO: So we can have some money. So your sisters can share in your dignity.

MANUEL: My sisters. Yes!

JACINTO: National League. American League!

MANUEL: Here I come.

JACINTO: Hot dogs, and peanuts and beers,

(Jacinto pitches. Manuel slams it out.)

JACINTO: Was that a foul ball?

MANUEL: No way. Hell no!

JACINTO: I don't know.

MANUEL: No way.

JACINTO: What?

MANUEL: It went so far down the street neither of us could see it. It had power. Home run.

JACINTO: Yes, it did.

MANUEL: Home run! Papa!

JACINTO: I like that.

MANUEL: What?

JACINTO: Are you beginning to see it?

MANUEL: Yes.

JACINTO: Your future. If you can hit that hard every time. Your future, son.

MANUEL: Will be full of endorsements?

JACINTO: For Nike, son.

MANUEL: Lots of girls?

JACINTO: With big tits, yeah.

(Jacinto pitches, a strike.)

MANUEL: Fuck, a strike.

JACINTO: A strike is OK, as long as you only get two.

(Jacinto pitches, a ball.)

MANUEL: Ball. Your fault.

JACINTO: My fault. It's going to click this time. Can you feel it?

MANUEL: I don't know.

JACINTO: Think of the names.° David Ortiz, Alex Rodriguez, Palimero, Juan Gonzalez, Sammy Sosa, Vinny Castillo, Ivan Rodriguez, Pedro Martinez, Roberto Clemente, Orlando "El Duque."

(Jacinto pitches. Manuel hits it hard.)

MANUEL: Wow! Yeah!
JACINTO: That's my son.
MANUEL: That was a home run. Two in a row.
JACINTO: Yes.
MANUEL: Wow!
JACINTO: Now you gotta do it every time.
MANUEL: Every time?
JACINTO: Yes. That's what it takes to get out of here.
MANUEL: Out of Mexico.
JACINTO: Yes. You'll do it?
MANUEL: Every time.

(Manuel grabs the bat.)

JACINTO: Good.
MANUEL: A home run!
JACINTO: Just think of the names. All the stars are Latinos, son, you'll be one of them! Ortiz, Rodriguez, Palimero, Gonzalez, Sosa, Castillo, Martinez, remember the names . . . Now pitching: Fernando Valenzuela, from Sonora, Mexico.
MANUEL: Wow.

(Jacinto gets ready to pitch. Black out.)

END OF PLAY

---

the names: All are current or former major league baseball players.

APPROACHING THE READING

1. Describe the characters and summarize their character traits. Are they round or flat, dynamic or static? Explain why you think so. Do you identify with one character more than the other? Why?

2. Explain how dialogue is used to fill in the background for what happens in the play.

3. List several conflicts in the play and label what kind of conflict each is.

4. What does the play "add up to"? (How would you describe its theme?)

5. Explain the significance of the play's title.

RESPONDING THROUGH **Writing**

WRITING ABOUT CHARACTER, CONFLICT, AND DRAMATIC ACTION

Journal Entries

1. Record two or more dialogues you have overheard or been involved in. Write a journal entry that discusses why the real-life dialogue seems artificial on the page and why the artful dialogue from a play seems real.

2. Write a journal entry in which you discuss what makes the dialogue of Jenny and Marcy distinct from that of Bradley and Craig in Kelly Stuart's *The New New* (p. 899).

> You can research the authors in this chapter with LitLinks, or take a quiz on the plays with LitQuiz, at bedfordstmartins.com/rewritinglit.

3. Watch a television sitcom or drama, paying attention to techniques used in developing characters. Write a journal entry explaining and evaluating them.

Literary Analysis Papers

4. Write a paper examining the use of style in Kelly Stuart's *The New New* (p. 899). You might focus on how the way characters express themselves is used to characterize them, individually and as a group.

5. Write an analysis of the two characters in Kelly Stuart's *The New New* (p. 899) whom we do not see, Jeremy and Jimmy. Touch on such aspects as what each is like, how we learn about them, why each is important to the play, and how the effect would be different if they did appear in the play.

6. Write a paper on Eduardo Machado's use of various types of conflict and their significance in *Crossing the Border* (p. 909).

Comparison-Contrast Papers

7. Write out the first page of Ernest Hemingway's dialogue-filled story "Hills Like White Elephants" (p. 196) the way it would look if it were a play instead of a short story, using Eduardo Machado's *Crossing the Border* (p. 909) as a model. Then compare and contrast the two versions and write a paper discussing how it would be different, or not much different, to read "Hills Like White Elephants" if it were written as a play rather than as a short story.

8. Write a paper comparing and contrasting the methods of characterization in Kelly Stuart's *The New New* (p. 899) and Mark Lambeck's *Intervention* (p. 1055).

TIPS for Writing about Character, Conflict, and Dramatic Action

- **Start with conflict.** Exploring and analyzing the conflicts in a play can lead to an effective paper topic, especially because conflict reveals many aspects of a play, such as themes, character, problems and their resolution or lack of resolution, ambiguities, and even setting. Watch for different kinds of conflict — physical, social, and internal/psychological. (The latter, when central to a play, can work especially well as a paper topic.)

- **Consider character.** If you decide to write a paper in which you discuss a single character or several characters, you should not only describe what that character or those characters are like but also explain how various character traits are revealed (pay attention especially to what the characters do, say, and tell about others) and how the characters change or grow or are confronted with a need to change.

- **Watch for juxtapositions.** Always look for juxtapositions — parallel or contrasting characters, scenes, actions, images, and similar elements — in any play that you decide to write about. Juxtaposition can be especially important in revealing character development and in the development of themes.

- **Focus on style or structure.** Some plays lend themselves to a useful analysis of style or dramatic strategies. A paper could examine how style is used for characterization by showing how such elements as diction, sentence structure and length, and choice of images and figures of speech are suited to the character and differ from those of other characters. A paper also could examine dramatic strategies: the way or ways the action is structured, in the play as a whole or in a key scene or two, perhaps the way it builds to a climax and is resolved, or the way an easily overlooked small action or incident is used as a pivotal point for the entire play.

- **Use specific details and illustrations.** It is very important when writing about drama to decide whether to deal with the whole play or to select a scene or two to examine thoroughly. In either case, you must support your points and explanations with specific details and illustrations from the text.

WRITING ABOUT CONNECTIONS

Making internal connections is standard dramatic technique, as the playwright establishes relationships (juxtapositions, comparisons, contrasts) between words, characters, dramatic actions, symbols, or ideas. For a reader, looking at two works and making external connections can also be a valuable way of understanding themes in a play, as these are brought out through character, conflict, and dramatic action. Here are some examples:

1. "Souls for Sale": The Cost of Devaluing Values in Kelly Stuart's *The New New* (p. 899) and Lorraine Hansberry's *A Raisin in the Sun* (p. 1300)
2. "I Gotta Be Me": Identity and Interrelationships in David Ives's *Sure Thing* (p. 1046) and Mark Lambeck's *Intervention* (p. 1055)
3. "A Sporting Chance": Athletics and the American Dream in Eduardo Machado's *Crossing the Border* (p. 909) and August Wilson's *Fences* (p. 963)

WRITING RESEARCH PAPERS

1. Dr. Rank in Henrik Ibsen's *A Doll House* (p. 1245) is dying from a sexually transmitted disease (STD) passed on from his father. Research nineteenth-century knowledge of and social attitudes toward STDs, and write a paper using what you find to discuss the importance of that motif in the play (and perhaps how it was regarded by readers then and how it might be regarded today).

2. In the past few years, there has been much controversy over a number of "memoirs" that included material that was not factual. This issue is the background for Kelly Stuart's *The New New* (p. 899). Research this controversy and its ethical implications and write a paper in which you take a stand on the issue, incorporating *The New New* in your discussion.

The color, the grace and levitation, the structural pattern in motion, the quick interplay of live beings, suspended like fitful lightning in a cloud, these things are the play, not words on paper, nor thoughts and ideas of an author.

Tennessee Williams

(*American Playwright, see p. 1083*)

CHAPTER **23 Setting and Structure**

Examining Where, When, and How It Happens

Think of the place shown each week in your favorite TV show. If it's an ongoing series, some or much of the action likely takes place in the same building, street, or room every week. You come to know those made-up places, those "sets" (the backdrops and properties constructed for staging a scene in a play or film), almost as well as the kitchen in your own house. For years one of the most popular shows on television, *Cheers*, took place almost completely in a Boston pub. The set of that imaginary neighborhood pub became so familiar that tourists visiting Boston expect to find and walk into the real Cheers.

Dramatic actions by characters occur in a location that is almost always significant and that is represented by a stage set. Reading as well as watching a play must include thoughtful consideration of sets and setting and of the way the dramatic action occurring in them is structured and connected in a meaningful way. Setting and structure in fiction are discussed earlier in this book. This chapter examines their significance for drama and the distinctive ways they are handled in a play.

READING FOR SETTING

The **setting** of a play—where, when, and in what circumstances the action occurs—is just as important in drama as it is in fiction. Significant aspects of setting include the *place* of the action (in broad terms such as region, country, or city and in narrow terms such as neighborhood, street, or building), the *time* at which the action occurs (the century, year, season, day, hour), and the *cultural context* of the action (social and historical circumstances that characterize the time and place). Each of these is discussed at length in Chapter 7. (Reviewing pages 200–03 will prepare you to consider the importance of setting in drama.)

THE SET ON STAGE   Sets are an important aspect of setting in plays, movies, and TV, an aspect not present in fiction and poetry because they lack the performance dimension of drama. The **set** is the physical setup on the stage, including the background (backdrop), structures, **properties** (or "props," all movable articles, such as furniture and objects handled by the actors), and lighting. Set is often the first thing you encounter when watching a play in a theater, but imagining how the play might be set is also an important part of staging the play in the theater of your mind.

PLAYWRIGHTS AND SETS   Plays written before the mid-1800s may indicate their setting but offer little guidance on how specific sets are to be designed. Modern playwrights, on the other hand, in addition to indicating the setting of a play, often give detailed instructions on how to construct the set and even how characters should look and be dressed. In *Trifles*, the play beginning on the next page, for example, such instructions offer guidance not only to set and costume designers but also to readers, who are given a host of detailed images to help them as they attempt to picture the set, characters, and action in their minds.

ENTRY POINTS   As you read the following one-act play, notice the way Susan Glaspell spells out how to construct the set and how characters should appear. Concentrate on visualizing the play in your mind as fully and sharply as you can. Also consider the importance of its rural, isolated setting — how it contributes to what has happened, and does happen, and to our reaction to it all. The play falls into the popular genre of the mystery story, as law officers attempt to solve a murder case. It also explores matters of human interest and of moral and legal importance. As you read, pay attention to the handling of dialogue and action, to the ways characters are revealed and developed, and to the conflicts presented.

Susan Glaspell 1882–1948

Trifles   [1916]

CHARACTERS

GEORGE HENDERSON (County Attorney)
HENRY PETERS (Sheriff)
LEWIS HALE, a neighboring farmer
MRS. PETERS
MRS. HALE

SCENE: *The kitchen in the now abandoned farmhouse of John Wright, a gloomy kitchen, and left without having been put in order—unwashed pans under the sink, a loaf of bread outside the bread-box, a dish-towel on the table—other signs of incompleted work. At the rear the outer door opens and the Sheriff comes in followed by the County Attorney and Hale. The Sheriff and Hale are men in middle life, the County Attorney is a young man; all are much bundled up and go at once to the stove. They are followed by the two women—the Sheriff's wife first; she is a slight wiry woman, a thin nervous face. Mrs. Hale is larger and would ordinarily be called more comfortable looking, but she is disturbed now and looks fearfully about as she enters. The women have come in slowly, and stand close together near the door.*

APPROACHING THE AUTHOR

Needing a break in 1922 from the theater group they founded in Provincetown,

Massachusetts, **Susan Glaspell** and her husband decided to act on a long-held dream of his and move to Greece. They settled in Delphi, on the slopes of Mt. Parnassus, where they adopted an archaic lifestyle, attempting to live as shepherds.

For more about her, see page 1386.

COUNTY ATTORNEY (*rubbing his hands*): This feels good. Come up to the fire, ladies.

MRS. PETERS (*after taking a step forward*): I'm not—cold.

SHERIFF (*unbuttoning his overcoat and stepping away from the stove as if to mark the beginning of official business*): Now, Mr. Hale, before we move things about, you explain to Mr. Henderson just what you saw when you came here yesterday morning.

COUNTY ATTORNEY: By the way, has anything been moved? Are things just as you left them yesterday?

SHERIFF (*looking about*): It's just the same. When it dropped below zero last night I thought I'd better send Frank out this morning to make a fire for us—no use getting pneumonia with a big case on, but I told him not to touch anything except the stove—and you know Frank.

COUNTY ATTORNEY: Somebody should have been left here yesterday.

SHERIFF: Oh—yesterday. When I had to send Frank to Morris Center for that man who went crazy—I want you to know I had my hands full yesterday. I knew you could get back from Omaha by today and as long as I went over everything here myself—

COUNTY ATTORNEY: Well, Mr. Hale, tell just what happened when you came here yesterday morning.

HALE: Harry and I had started to town with a load of potatoes. We came along the road from my place and as I got here I said, "I'm going to see if I can't get John Wright to go in with me on a party telephone." I spoke to Wright about it once before and he put me off, saying folks talked too much anyway, and all he asked was peace and quiet—I guess you know about how much he talked himself; but I thought maybe if I went to the house and talked about it before his wife, though I said to Harry that I didn't know as what his wife wanted made much difference to John —

COUNTY ATTORNEY: Let's talk about that later, Mr. Hale. I do want to talk about that, but tell now just what happened when you got to the house.

HALE: I didn't hear or see anything; I knocked at the door, and still it was all quiet inside. I knew they must be up, it was past eight o'clock. So I knocked again, and I thought I heard somebody say, "Come in." I wasn't sure, I'm not sure yet, but I opened the door—this door (*indicating the door by which the two women are still standing*) and there in that rocker— (*pointing to it*) sat Mrs. Wright.

(*They all look at the rocker.*)

COUNTY ATTORNEY: What—was she doing?

HALE: She was rockin' back and forth. She had her apron in her hand and was kind of—pleating it.

COUNTY ATTORNEY: And how did she—look?

HALE: Well, she looked queer.

COUNTY ATTORNEY: How do you mean—queer?

HALE: Well, as if she didn't know what she was going to do next. And kind of done up.

COUNTY ATTORNEY: How did she seem to feel about your coming?

HALE: Why, I don't think she minded—one way or other. She didn't pay much attention. I said, "How do, Mrs. Wright it's cold, ain't it?" And she said, "Is it?"—and went on kind of pleating at her apron. Well, I was surprised; she didn't ask me to come up to the stove, or to set down, but just sat there, not even looking at me, so I said, "I want to see John." And then she—laughed. I guess you would call it a laugh. I thought of Harry and the team outside, so I said a little sharp: "Can't I see John?" "No," she says, kind o' dull like. "Ain't he home?" says I. "Yes," says she, "he's home." "Then why can't I see him?" I asked her, out of patience. "'Cause he's dead," says she. *"Dead?"* says I. She just nodded her head, not getting a bit excited, but rockin' back and forth. "Why—where is he?" says I, not knowing what to say. She just pointed upstairs—like that (*himself pointing to the room above*). I got up, with the idea of going up there. I walked from there to here—then I says, "Why, what did he die of?" "He died of a rope round his neck," says she, and just went on pleatin' at her apron. Well, I went out and called Harry. I thought I might—need help. We went upstairs and there he was lyin' —

COUNTY ATTORNEY: I think I'd rather have you go into that upstairs, where you can point it all out. Just go on now with the rest of the story.

HALE: Well, my first thought was to get that rope off. It looked . . . (*stops, his face twitches*) . . . but Harry, he went up to him, and he said, "No, he's dead all right, and we'd better not touch anything." So we went back down stairs. She was still sitting that same way. "Has anybody been notified?" I asked. "No," says she unconcerned. "Who did this, Mrs. Wright?" said Harry. He said it business-like—and she stopped pleatin' of her apron. "I don't know," she says. "You don't *know*?" says Harry. "No," says she. "Weren't you sleepin' in the bed with him?" says Harry. "Yes," says she, "but I was on the inside." "Somebody slipped a rope round his neck and strangled him and you didn't wake up?" says Harry. "I didn't wake up," she said after him. We must 'a looked as if we didn't see how that could be, for after a minute she said, "I sleep sound." Harry was going to ask her more questions but I said maybe we ought to let her tell her story first to the coroner, or the sheriff, so Harry went fast as he could to Rivers' place, where there's a telephone.

COUNTY ATTORNEY: And what did Mrs. Wright do when she knew that you had gone for the coroner?

HALE: She moved from that chair to this one over here (*pointing to a small chair in the corner*) and just sat there with her hands held together and looking down. I got a feeling that I ought to make some conversation, so I said I had come in to see if John wanted to put in a telephone, and at that she started to laugh, and then she stopped and looked at me—scared. (*The County Attorney, who has had his notebook out, makes a note.*) I dunno, maybe it wasn't scared. I wouldn't like to say it was. Soon Harry got back, and then Dr. Lloyd came, and you, Mr. Peters, and so I guess that's all I know that you don't.

COUNTY ATTORNEY (*looking around*): I guess we'll go upstairs first—and then out to the barn and around there. (*to the Sheriff*) You're convinced that there was nothing important here—nothing that would point to any motive?

SHERIFF: Nothing here but kitchen things.

(*The County Attorney, after again looking around the kitchen, opens the door of a cupboard closet. He gets up on a chair and looks on a shelf. Pulls his hand away, sticky.*)

COUNTY ATTORNEY: Here's a nice mess.

(*The women draw nearer.*)

MRS. PETERS (*to the other woman*): Oh, her fruit; it did freeze. (*to the Lawyer*) She worried about that when it turned so cold. She said the fire'd go out and her jars would break.

SHERIFF: Well, can you beat the women! Held for murder and worryin' about her preserves.

COUNTY ATTORNEY: I guess before we're through she may have something more serious than preserves to worry about.

HALE: Well, women are used to worrying over trifles.

(*The two women move a little closer together.*)

COUNTY ATTORNEY (*with the gallantry of a young politician*): And yet, for all their worries, what would we do without the ladies? (*The women do not unbend. He goes to the sink, takes a dipperful of water from the pail and pouring it into a basin, washes his hands. Starts to wipe them on the roller-towel, turns it for a cleaner place.*) Dirty towels! (*kicks his foot against the pans under the sink*) Not much of a housekeeper, would you say, ladies?

MRS. HALE (*stiffly*): There's a great deal of work to be done on a farm.

COUNTY ATTORNEY: To be sure. And yet (*with a little bow to her*) I know there are some Dickson county farmhouses which do not have such roller towels.

(*He gives it a pull to expose its length again.*)

MRS. HALE: Those towels get dirty awful quick. Men's hands aren't always as clean as they might be.

COUNTY ATTORNEY: Ah, loyal to your sex, I see. But you and Mrs. Wright were neighbors. I suppose you were friends, too.

MRS. HALE (*shaking her head*): I've not seen much of her of late years. I've not been in this house—it's more than a year.

COUNTY ATTORNEY: And why was that? You didn't like her?

MRS. HALE: I liked her all well enough. Farmers' wives have their hands full, Mr. Henderson. And then —

COUNTY ATTORNEY: Yes—?

MRS. HALE (*looking about*): It never seemed a very cheerful place.

COUNTY ATTORNEY: No—it's not cheerful. I shouldn't say she had the homemaking instinct.

MRS. HALE: Well, I don't know as Wright had, either.

COUNTY ATTORNEY: You mean that they didn't get on very well?

MRS. HALE: No, I don't mean anything. But I don't think a place'd be any cheerfuller for John Wright's being in it.

COUNTY ATTORNEY: I'd like to talk more of that a little later. I want to get the lay of things upstairs now.

(*He goes to the left, where three steps lead to a stair door.*)

SHERIFF: I suppose anything Mrs. Peters does'll be all right. She was to take in some clothes for her, you know, and a few little things. We left in such a hurry yesterday.

COUNTY ATTORNEY: Yes, but I would like to see what you take, Mrs. Peters, and keep an eye out for anything that might be of use to us.

MRS. PETERS: Yes, Mr. Henderson.

(*The women listen to the men's steps on the stairs, then look about the kitchen.*)

MRS. HALE: I'd hate to have men coming into my kitchen, snooping around and criticizing.

(She arranges the pans under sink which the Lawyer had shoved out of place.)

MRS. PETERS: Of course it's no more than their duty.

MRS. HALE: Duty's all right, but I guess that deputy sheriff that came out to make the fire might have got a little of this on. *(gives the roller towel a pull)* Wish I'd thought of that sooner. Seems mean to talk about her for not having things slicked up when she had to come away in such a hurry.

MRS. PETERS *(who has gone to a small table in the left rear corner of the room, and lifted one end of a towel that covers a pan)*: She had bread set.

(Stands still.)

MRS. HALE *(eyes fixed on a loaf of bread beside the breadbox, which is on a low shelf at the other side of the room. Moves slowly toward it)*: She was going to put this in there. *(picks up loaf, then abruptly drops it. In manner of returning to familiar things)* It's a shame about her fruit. I wonder if it's all gone. *(gets up on the chair and looks)* I think there's some here that's all right, Mrs. Peters. Yes—here; *(holding it toward the window)* this is cherries, too. *(looking again)* I declare I believe that's the only one. *(Gets down, bottle in her hand. Goes to the sink and wipes it off on the outside.)* She'll feel awful bad after all her hard work in the hot weather. I remember the afternoon I put up my cherries last summer.

(She puts the bottle on the big kitchen table, center of the room. With a sigh, is about to sit down in the rocking-chair. Before she is seated realizes what chair it is; with a slow look at it, steps back. The chair which she has touched rocks back and forth.)

MRS. PETERS: Well, I must get those things from the front room closet. *(She goes to the door at the right, but after looking into the other room, steps back.)* You coming with me, Mrs. Hale? You could help me carry them.

(They go in the other room; reappear, Mrs. Peters carrying a dress and skirt, Mrs. Hale following with a pair of shoes.)

MRS. PETERS: My, it's cold in there.

(She puts the clothes on the big table, and hurries to the stove.)

MRS. HALE *(examining the skirt)*: Wright was close. I think maybe that's why she kept so much to herself. She didn't even belong to the Ladies Aid. I suppose she felt she couldn't do her part, and then you don't enjoy things when you feel shabby. She used to wear pretty clothes and be lively, when she was Minnie Foster, one of the town girls singing in the choir. But that—oh, that was thirty years ago. This all you was to take in?

MRS. PETERS: She said she wanted an apron. Funny thing to want, for there isn't much to get you dirty in jail, goodness knows. But I suppose just to make her feel more natural. She said they was in the top drawer in this cupboard. Yes, here. And then her little shawl that always hung behind the door. *(opens stair door and looks)* Yes, here it is.

(Quickly shuts door leading upstairs.)

MRS. HALE (*abruptly moving toward her*): Mrs. Peters?

MRS. PETERS: Yes, Mrs. Hale?

MRS. HALE: Do you think she did it?

MRS. PETERS (*in a frightened voice*): Oh, I don't know.

MRS. HALE: Well, I don't think she did. Asking for an apron and her little shawl. Worrying about her fruit.

MRS. PETERS (*starts to speak, glances up, where footsteps are heard in the room above. In a low voice*): Mr. Peters says it looks bad for her. Mr. Henderson is awful sarcastic in a speech and he'll make fun of her sayin' she didn't wake up.

MRS. HALE: Well, I guess John Wright didn't wake when they was slipping that rope under his neck.

MRS. PETERS: No, it's strange. It must have been done awful crafty and still. They say it was such a—funny way to kill a man, rigging it all up like that.

MRS. HALE: That's just what Mr. Hale said. There was a gun in the house. He says that's what he can't understand.

MRS. PETERS: Mr. Henderson said coming out that what was needed for the case was a motive; something to show anger, or—sudden feeling.

MRS. HALE (*who is standing by the table*): Well, I don't see any signs of anger around here. (*She puts her hand on the dish towel which lies on the table, stands looking down at table, one half of which is clean, the other half messy.*) It's wiped to here. (*Makes a move as if to finish work, then turns and looks at loaf of bread outside the breadbox. Drops towel. In that voice of coming back to familiar things.*) Wonder how they are finding things upstairs. I hope she had it a little more red-up° there. You know, it seems kind of *sneaking*. Locking her up in town and then coming out here and trying to get her own house to turn against her!

MRS. PETERS: But Mrs. Hale, the law is the law.

MRS. HALE: I s'pose 'tis. (*unbuttoning her coat*) Better loosen up your things, Mrs. Peters. You won't feel them when you go out.

(*Mrs. Peters takes off her fur tippet,° goes to hang it on hook at back of room, stands looking at the under part of the small corner table.*)

MRS. PETERS: She was piecing a quilt.

(*She brings the large sewing basket and they look at the bright pieces.*)

MRS. HALE: It's log cabin pattern. Pretty, isn't it? I wonder if she was goin' to quilt it or just knot it?

(*Footsteps have been heard coming down the stairs. The Sheriff enters followed by Hale and the County Attorney.*)

SHERIFF: They wonder if she was going to quilt it or just knot it!

(*The men laugh, the women look abashed.*)

---

red-up: Orderly; picked up.   **tippet:** A shoulder cape.

COUNTY ATTORNEY (*rubbing his hands over the stove*): Frank's fire didn't do much up there, did it? Well, let's go out to the barn and get that cleared up.

(*The men go outside.*)

MRS. HALE (*resentfully*): I don't know as there's anything so strange, our takin' up our time with little things while we're waiting for them to get the evidence. (*She sits down at the big table smoothing out a block with decision.*) I don't see as it's anything to laugh about.

MRS. PETERS (*apologetically*): Of course they've got awful important things on their minds.

(*Pulls up a chair and joins Mrs. Hale at the table.*)

MRS. HALE (*examining another block*): Mrs. Peters, look at this one. Here, this is the one she was working on, and look at the sewing! All the rest of it has been so nice and even. And look at this! It's all over the place! Why, it looks as if she didn't know what she was about!

(*After she has said this they look at each other, then start to glance back at the door. After an instant Mrs. Hale has pulled at a knot and ripped the sewing.*)

MRS. PETERS: Oh, what are you doing, Mrs. Hale?

MRS. HALE (*mildly*): Just pulling out a stitch or two that's not sewed very good. (*threading a needle*) Bad sewing always made me fidgety.

MRS. PETERS (*nervously*): I don't think we ought to touch things.

MRS. HALE: I'll just finish up this end. (*suddenly stopping and leaning forward*) Mrs. Peters?

MRS. PETERS: Yes, Mrs. Hale?

MRS. HALE: What do you suppose she was so nervous about?

MRS. PETERS: Oh—I don't know. I don't know as she was nervous. I sometimes sew awful queer when I'm just tired. (*Mrs. Hale starts to say something, looks at Mrs. Peters, then goes on sewing.*) Well I must get these things wrapped up. They may be through sooner than we think. (*putting apron and other things together*) I wonder where I can find a piece of paper, and string.

MRS. HALE: In that cupboard, maybe.

MRS. PETERS (*looking in cupboard*): Why, here's a bird-cage. (*holds it up*) Did she have a bird, Mrs. Hale?

MRS. HALE: Why, I don't know whether she did or not—I've not been here for so long. There was a man around last year selling canaries cheap, but I don't know as she took one; maybe she did. She used to sing real pretty herself.

MRS. PETERS (*glancing around*): Seems funny to think of a bird here. But she must have had one, or why would she have a cage? I wonder what happened to it.

MRS. HALE: I s'pose maybe the cat got it.

MRS. PETERS: No, she didn't have a cat. She's got that feeling some people have about cats—being afraid of them. My cat got in her room and she was real upset and asked me to take it out.

MRS. HALE: My sister Bessie was like that. Queer, ain't it?

MRS. PETERS (*examining the cage*): Why, look at this door. It's broke. One hinge is pulled apart.

MRS. HALE (*looking too*): Looks as if someone must have been rough with it.

MRS. PETERS: Why, yes.

(*She brings the cage forward and puts it on the table.*)

MRS. HALE: I wish if they're going to find any evidence they'd be about it. I don't like this place.

MRS. PETERS: But I'm awful glad you came with me, Mrs. Hale. It would be lonesome for me sitting here alone.

MRS. HALE: It would, wouldn't it? (*dropping her sewing*) But I tell you what I do wish, Mrs. Peters. I wish I had come over sometimes when *she* was here. I—(*looking around the room*)—wish I had.

MRS. PETERS: But of course you were awful busy, Mrs. Hale—your house and your children.

MRS. HALE: I could've come. I stayed away because it weren't cheerful—and that's why I ought to have come. I—I've never liked this place. Maybe because it's down in a hollow and you don't see the road. I dunno what it is, but it's a lonesome place and always was. I wish I had come over to see Minnie Foster sometimes. I can see now—(*shakes her head*)

MRS. PETERS: Well, you mustn't reproach yourself, Mrs. Hale. Somehow we just don't see how it is with other folks until—something comes up.

MRS. HALE: Not having children makes less work—but it makes a quiet house, and Wright out to work all day, and no company when he did come in. Did you know John Wright, Mrs. Peters?

MRS. PETERS: Not to know him; I've seen him in town. They say he was a good man.

MRS. HALE: Yes—good; he didn't drink, and kept his word as well as most, I guess, and paid his debts. But he was a hard man, Mrs. Peters. Just to pass the time of day with him—(*shivers*) Like a raw wind that gets to the bone. (*pauses, her eye falling on the cage*) I should think she would 'a wanted a bird. But what do you suppose went with it?

MRS. PETERS: I don't know, unless it got sick and died.

(*She reaches over and swings the broken door, swings it again, both women watch it.*)

MRS. HALE: You weren't raised round here, were you? (*Mrs. Peters shakes her head*) You didn't know—her?

MRS. PETERS: Not till they brought her yesterday.

MRS. HALE: She—come to think of it, she was kind of like a bird herself—real sweet and pretty, but kind of timid and—fluttery. How—she—did—change. (*silence; then as if struck by a happy thought and relieved to get back to everyday things*) Tell you what, Mrs. Peters, why don't you take the quilt in with you? It might take up her mind.

MRS. PETERS: Why, I think that's a real nice idea, Mrs. Hale. There couldn't possibly be any objection to it, could there? Now, just what would I take? I wonder if her patches are in here—and her things.

(*They look in the sewing basket.*)

MRS. HALE: Here's some red. I expect this has got sewing things in it. (*brings out a fancy box*) What a pretty box. Looks like something somebody would give you. Maybe her scissors are in here. (*Opens box. Suddenly puts her hand to her nose.*) Why — (*Mrs. Peters bends nearer, then turns her face away.*) There's something wrapped up in this piece of silk.

MRS. PETERS: Why, this isn't her scissors.

MRS. HALE (*lifting the silk*): Oh, Mrs. Peters — it's —

(*Mrs. Peters bends closer.*)

MRS. PETERS: It's the bird.

MRS. HALE (*jumping up*): But, Mrs. Peters — look at it! It's neck! Look at its neck! It's all — other side *to*.

MRS. PETERS: Somebody — wrung — its — neck.

(*Their eyes meet. A look of growing comprehension, of horror. Steps are heard outside. Mrs. Hale slips box under quilt pieces, and sinks into her chair. Enter Sheriff and County Attorney. Mrs. Peters rises.*)

COUNTY ATTORNEY (*as one turning from serious things to little pleasantries*): Well ladies, have you decided whether she was going to quilt it or knot it?

MRS. PETERS: We think she was going to — knot it.

COUNTY ATTORNEY: Well, that's interesting, I'm sure. (*seeing the birdcage*) Has the bird flown?

MRS. HALE (*putting more quilt pieces over the box*): We think the — cat got it.

COUNTY ATTORNEY (*preoccupied*): Is there a cat?

(*Mrs. Hale glances in quick covert way at Mrs. Peters.*)

MRS. PETERS: Well, not *now*. They're superstitious, you know. They leave.

COUNTY ATTORNEY (*to Sheriff Peters, continuing an interrupted conversation*): No sign at all of anyone having come from the outside. Their own rope. Now let's go up again and go over it piece by piece. (*They start upstairs.*) It would have to have been someone who knew just the —

(*Mrs. Peters sits down. The two women sit there not looking at one another, but as if peering into something and at the same time holding back. When they talk now it is in the manner of feeling their way over strange ground, as if afraid of what they are saying, but as if they can not help saying it.*)

MRS. HALE: She liked the bird. She was going to bury it in that pretty box.

MRS. PETERS (*in a whisper*): When I was a girl — my kitten — there was a boy took a hatchet, and before my eyes — and before I could get there — (*covers her face an instant*) If they hadn't held me back I would have — (*catches herself, looks upstairs where steps are heard, falters weakly*) — hurt him.

MRS. HALE (*with a slow look around her*): I wonder how it would seem never to have had any children around. (*pause*) No, Wright wouldn't like the bird — a thing that sang. She used to sing. He killed that, too.

MRS. PETERS (*moving uneasily*): We don't know who killed the bird.

MRS. HALE: I knew John Wright.

MRS. PETERS: It was an awful thing was done in this house that night, Mrs. Hale. Killing a man while he slept, slipping a rope around his neck that choked the life out of him.

MRS. HALE: His neck. Choked the life out of him.

(*Her hand goes out and rests on the birdcage.*)

MRS. PETERS (*with rising voice*): We don't know who killed him. We don't *know*.

MRS. HALE (*her own feeling not interrupted*): If there'd been years and years of nothing, then a bird to sing to you, it would be awful — still, after the bird was still.

MRS. PETERS (*something within her speaking*): I know what stillness is. When we homesteaded in Dakota, and my first baby died — after he was two years old, and me with no other then —

MRS. HALE (*moving*): How soon do you suppose they'll be through, looking for the evidence?

MRS. PETERS: I know what stillness is. (*pulling herself back*) The law has got to punish crime, Mrs. Hale.

MRS. HALE (*not as if answering that*): I wish you'd seen Minnie Foster when she wore a white dress with blue ribbons and stood up there in the choir and sang. (*a look around the room*) Oh, I *wish* I'd come over here once in a while! That was a crime! That was a crime! Who's going to punish that?

MRS. PETERS (*looking upstairs*): We mustn't — take on.

MRS. HALE: I might have known she needed help! I know how things can be — for women. I tell you, it's queer, Mrs. Peters. We live close together and we live far apart. We all go through the same things — it's all just a different kind of the same thing. (*brushes her eyes, noticing the bottle of fruit, reaches out for it*) If I was you, I wouldn't tell her her fruit was gone. Tell her it *ain't*. Tell her it's all right. Take this in to prove it to her. She — she may never know whether it was broke or not.

MRS. PETERS (*takes the bottle, looks about for something to wrap it in; takes petticoat from the clothes brought from the other room, very nervously begins winding this around the bottle. In a false voice*): My, it's a good thing the men couldn't hear us. Wouldn't they just laugh! Getting all stirred up over a little thing like a — dead canary. As if that could have anything to do with — with — wouldn't they *laugh*!

(*The men are heard coming down stairs.*)

MRS. HALE (*under her breath*): Maybe they would — maybe they wouldn't.

COUNTY ATTORNEY: No, Peters, it's all perfectly clear except a reason for doing it. But you know juries when it comes to women. If there was some definite thing. Something to show — something to make a story about — a thing that would connect up with this strange way of doing it —

(*The women's eyes meet for an instant. Enter Hale from outer door.*)

HALE: Well, I've got the team around. Pretty cold out there.

COUNTY ATTORNEY: I'm going to stay here a while by myself. (*to the Sheriff*) You can send Frank out for me, can't you? I want to go over everything. I'm not satisfied that we can't do better.

SHERIFF: Do you want to see what Mrs. Peters is going to take in?

(*The Lawyer goes to the table, picks up the apron, laughs.*)

COUNTY ATTORNEY: Oh, I guess they're not very dangerous things the ladies have picked out. (*Moves a few things about, disturbing the quilt pieces which cover the box. Steps back*) No, Mrs. Peters doesn't need supervising. For that matter, a sheriff's wife is married to the law. Ever think of it that way, Mrs. Peters?

MRS. PETERS: Not—just that way.

SHERIFF (*chuckling*): Married to the law. (*moves toward the other room*) I just want you to come in here a minute, George. We ought to take a look at these windows.

COUNTY ATTORNEY (*scoffingly*): Oh, windows!

SHERIFF: We'll be right out, Mr. Hale.

(*Hale goes outside. The Sheriff follows the County Attorney into the other room. Then Mrs. Hale rises, hands tight together, looking intensely at Mrs. Peters, whose eyes make a slow turn, finally meeting Mrs. Hale's. A moment Mrs. Hale holds her, then her own eyes point the way to where the box is concealed. Suddenly Mrs. Peters throws back quilt pieces and tries to put the box in the bag she is wearing. It is too big. She opens box, starts to take bird out, cannot touch it, goes to pieces, stands there helpless. Sound of a knob turning in the other room. Mrs. Hale snatches the box and puts it in the pocket of her big coat. Enter County Attorney and Sheriff.*)

COUNTY ATTORNEY (*facetiously*): Well, Henry, at least we found out that she was not going to quilt it. She was going to—what is it you call it, ladies?

MRS. HALE (*her hand against her pocket*): We call it—knot it, Mr. Henderson.

CURTAIN

APPROACHING THE READING

1. Summarize the action and explain the significance of details in the plot and setting (the mess in the kitchen, the jam and jam jars, the quilting and Mrs. Wright's way of working, the bird and birdcage, the choice of a rope as weapon, and so on).

2. Examine the way the story is presented as a mystery play. Do you notice situations or lines that are conventional in detective stories you've read or seen in movies or on television? Find uses of foreshadowing in the play and explain what makes them effective.

3. List several conflicts and several types of conflict in the play. Which conflicts focus your attention on issues that seem important in the play? List several such issues.

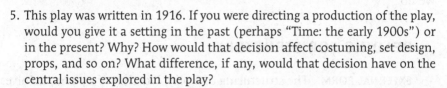

You can explore this author and play in depth, including images and cultural documents, with VirtuaLit Drama at bedfordstmartins.com/rewritinglit.

4. Reflect on the characters: Who are the major characters, what is important to them, what motivates them, how do they change (if they do), and why? How does your impression of them change? Who are the minor characters, and what are their roles and significance?

5. This play was written in 1916. If you were directing a production of the play, would you give it a setting in the past (perhaps "Time: the early 1900s") or in the present? Why? How would that decision affect costuming, set design, props, and so on? What difference, if any, would that decision have on the central issues explored in the play?

THE GENERAL SETTING   The stage directions locate the play in a farmhouse, apparently in western Iowa or eastern Nebraska, since Sheriff Peters mentions that the county attorney, George Henderson, has just returned from Omaha (p. 922). But the geographic region has little effect on this play. Glaspell was born and raised in Iowa and worked for a short time as a journalist in Des Moines. She moved to the Northeast more than a decade before she wrote *Trifles*, and its setting could just as easily be rural New England.

THE SPECIFIC SETTING   More significant for setting is that the farmhouse is isolated and depressing. As Mrs. Hale says, "I—I've never liked this place. Maybe because it's down in a hollow and you don't see the road. I dunno what it is, but it's a lonesome place and always was" (p. 929). Such isolation is important to the play: Mrs. Wright lacks contact with other people, sees neither neighbors nor friends. Her only source of companionship is a husband who rarely talks to or interacts with others.

THE OVERALL SET   In her headnote, Glaspell was more specific about set than setting. The set is the kitchen of the Wrights' home, and the detailed stage directions give a reader lots of help in imagining how the room appears (gloomy, probably sparsely furnished, in a state of considerable disorder, with a door to outside in the rear wall) and what the room contains (a breadbox, a sink with dirty pots under it, a stove, and a table). Glaspell also scatters stage directions throughout the text. We learn later, among other details, that the room contains a cupboard, a rocking chair, a small table in the left rear corner with a large sewing basket under it, a small chair in another corner, and a roller towel on the wall near the sink, and that there is at least one window, a door at the right into another room, and steps at the left leading to a door, behind which are the stairs to the second floor.

READING A SET   The way each stage designer envisions Glaspell's directions is individual and unique — just as the way you visualize it will be. Some stage designers will attempt to recreate authentic early twentieth-century details, while others will give it a more timeless feel and not try for historical "correctness." Reading a set, and reading a play, is like all other kinds of reading. There is no single set design, or a single interpretation of a text, that all readers must seek to attain. Instead, we should decide what is appropriate for the drama itself and relish the diversity and enrichment that results when others see things differently from the way we do.

READING FOR STRUCTURE

EXTERNAL FORM   The structuring of a play, like that of a poem, involves external form as well as internal form. The external form starts with such features as the list of characters, the stage directions, the division of the text into speeches headed by tags identifying the characters, and the stage directions guiding the actors on such things as action, tone, or expression.

DIVISION INTO ACTS   External form includes the division of longer plays into acts and scenes. An **act** is a major division of a drama, a significant section of the action. In performance, the end of an act is signaled by an intermission or by the lowering of the stage curtain. In reading, the text is usually marked as act 1, act 2, and so forth.

DIVISION INTO SCENES   Scenes are minor divisions in a drama — a single act may be divided into scenes, or a one-act play might consist of several scenes. Often a new scene jumps ahead to a different time or moves to a different location. Scene changes are signaled in different ways: The stage may empty while the curtain remains raised, or the lights may go out, or the scenery may be reconfigured. Sometimes locations are identified for the audience in the printed program. But it is left to the imagination of the reader or viewer to bridge such gaps by making the needed connections or by realizing what is only hinted at.

INTERNAL FORM   The internal structure of a play centers on **plot**, the structural pattern by which it is organized and developed. The plot in drama involves many of the same issues as plot in fiction. *Beginnings*: starting **in medias res**, for example, making use of **exposition** to explain things that occurred before the initial action of the play, and making use of **flashbacks** to clarify events prior to the beginning of the play. *Middles*: using conflicts, suspense, gaps, foreshadowings, and repetitions to increase plot "complications" and build to a climax. *Endings*: resolving (or in some cases not resolving) the mysteries, problems, or tensions that have developed in the beginning and middle. Terms and techniques dealing with structure are discussed thoroughly in Chapter 5. Reviewing pages 116–21 will prepare you for studying plot in drama.

THE FIVE-ACT PLAY Some theorists hold that the internal structure of a play involves a natural dramatic rhythm that develops in five divisions or steps, which they believe correspond with the traditional five-act structure of a play.

- *Introduction or exposition*: The introduction, or exposition, occurs early in the play, usually as one or more characters deliver speeches providing information required for following the action of the play: introducing characters, filling in prior action and the background from which the central conflict will develop, and establishing setting and tone.
- *Complication*: **Complication** is the rising action of the play; entanglements caused by the central conflict are set in motion.
- *Crisis or climax*: The **crisis** is the turning point in the action, the point at which the protagonist's situation turns for the better or worse. **Climax** is the point at which a significant emotional response is elicited. It does not always coincide with the moment of crisis.
- *Reversal*: Reversal is the falling action of a play, the depiction of the change in fortune experienced by the protagonist.
- *Catastrophe and resolution, or dénouement*: The term **catastrophe**, used mostly for tragedy, depicts the action, the unhappy ending, that results from crisis/climax and reversal. **Resolution**, or restoration of order, usually follows the catastrophe. **Dénouement** (French for "unknotting") is often used for the final unraveling of the plot complications in a comedy, though the unknotting at the end turns into a tying up of loose ends.

Compression and Contrast

COMPRESSION Dramatic works are shaped also by use of two key structural principles: compression and contrast. The first, *compression*, is necessary because although a work of fiction can extend to any length to tell its story, a playwright usually works under fairly strict time constraints. Audiences generally expect a play to last no more than three hours. There are plays that run four or five hours and some even for days, but those are the exceptions. Playwrights, therefore, are usually aware of time and use techniques that enable them to compress their material economically. Being aware of such techniques can help you understand how a play and a play's structure work and why some things have to be handled so as to fit the constraints of time.

To compress their material, playwrights tend to start close to the most exciting or significant scene (see "Beginnings," p. 934). *Trifles*, for example, opens the morning after Mr. Wright dies because the play is most concerned with the motivation for the murder and the way Mrs. Hale and Mrs. Peters come to regard that motivation. In reading or watching plays, you need to get used to arriving in the middle of a conversation and to use what is said to figure out what happened earlier. Often it is said that dramatic action occurs only in the present: What occurs on the stage is always "now." Even when a flashback is acted out, we see the past events occurring as we watch. Events that are not acted out are narrated through exposition, the way Mr. Hale fills in his experiences of the previous day. Playwrights also compress by using exposition to clarify information that the audience needs to know about earlier events and by using foreshadowing to alert us about things to watch for in what follows (see "Middles," p. 934). And they compress material by organizing events into moments, or scenes (p. 934).

SYMBOLS Playwrights can achieve compression through the use of **symbols**, images or actions or characters that are first and fundamentally themselves in the play but also embody an abstract idea. Symbols are discussed at length in Chapter 7. What is said on pages 203–206 about symbols in fiction applies equally to drama. The same types of symbols are used in drama, and the same formal devices convey to a reader or viewer that an image, action, or character may be symbolic: repetition, description, placement in noticeable positions (title, beginning, ending, climactic scene), or a sense of weightiness or significance beyond the literal function in the work. The birdcage in *Trifles*, for example, is a literal object in the story, but it also suggests qualities of the relationship between Mr. and Mrs. Wright. Mrs. Wright used to enjoy singing and her song, like the bird's, was stifled by Mr. Wright. She, like the bird, lived in a cage, trapped and broken figuratively in spirit, the way the bird's neck was broken literally. Symbols help achieve compression because the symbols — objects, character types, or actions — are seen on stage by the audience and require few words and little time to convey their meaning. The viewer, or the reader watching the play imaginatively, has the opportunity to recognize the symbol and to take part in discerning its appropriateness and meaning.

CONTRAST *Contrast* is important to playwrights both as a means of compression and as a way to establish relationships in a play. Dramatists regularly establish parallels or contrasts between two or more situations, characters, actions, or symbols to get us to notice things about each that we might miss without the pairing. Often parallel items reinforce a point or theme or serve as a means of repetition, a valuable technique for creating emphasis, while contrasts direct our attention to differences and distinctions more clearly and forcefully. In *Trifles*, the stillness in the house Mrs. Peters

> ☑ **CHECKLIST on Reading for Setting and Structure**
>
> ❑ Be attentive to setting, in terms of place, time, and historical, social, and cultural context, and to the effects of setting in a play.
>
> ❑ Be attentive to stage directions provided by the playwright, and use descriptions of set, props, costumes, stage movements, and character descriptions to sharpen your images as you visualize the plays.
>
> ❑ Be alert for symbols of different kinds (literary, conventional, traditional, and archetypal) and the various ways they can contribute to a play.
>
> ❑ Notice the structuring of plot in a play: its handling of beginning, middle, and ending; its use of gaps, flashbacks, suspense, foreshadowing, and repetition; and its use of compression and contrasts.
>
> ❑ Know the traditional five-part dramatic pattern (introduction, complication, climax, reversal, and resolution) and test to see if it applies to a particular play.

experienced after losing a child enabled her to empathize with the similar stillness Mrs. Wright must have felt after the death of the canary. The principal contrast of the play is between the women and the men, with their different approaches, outlooks, and attitudes. The term **foil** is used for a character who stands in contrast to another character and thus calls attention to distinctive features of the second character or to significant differences between the two. Naomi can be taken as a foil to Bradley in Kelly Stuart's play (p. 899).

You can further explore setting and structure, including using interactive exercises, with VirtuaLit Drama at bedfordstmartins.com/rewritinglit.

FURTHER READING

ENTRY POINTS   Setting is very important in the following play, as is the double set that depicts the two places where the action occurs. The setting for the action in the immediate present is a big, old, eerie house in Quebec, on a proverbial dark and stormy night. The events that set up the present situation took place some time ago in another old house, this one in Providence, Rhode Island. As you read, note when the action switches settings — from one side of the set to the other — as it did in *The New New*. You'll also need to piece together what happened in the past, making connections between certain things characters say and noticing subtle hints that lead to a surprising ending, one that will probably make you want to read the play again.

Don Nigro   b. 1949

Letters from Quebec to Providence in the Rain   [2008]

CHARACTERS

PETRUS: Late twenties.
VANESSA: Late twenties.
JONATHAN: Early twenties.
MARIANNE: Early twenties.

SETTING

An old house in Quebec, and another old house in Providence. Both are present onstage at once. Some furniture, which is part of both houses. Time and space interpenetrate. There's a desk and chair down right, a bed right, an old-fashioned clawfoot bathtub up center, a sofa left, and a chair and small round table down left.

TIME

The present, and the not too distant past.

Sound of whippoorwills in the darkness. Lights up on Petrus at the desk down right and, in dimmer light for the moment, Jonathan sitting in his chair down left and Marianne in the bathtub up center.

APPROACHING THE AUTHOR

Don Nigro says of his beginnings as a writer: "I started writing when I was a young child, and I started lying, and lying turned me into a writer." Aside from lying, he has said that an ability to empathize with people has helped him develop as a playwright.
  For more about him, see page 1403.

PETRUS (*taking some letters out of an old book*): This is very odd.

VANESSA (*coming into the light, in bathrobe, barefoot*): This is Quebec. Everything is odd here. Not very odd. Just a little bit odd. Just a bit off center, as if one were living in two places at the same time. Everything has two reflections here.

PETRUS: I've found some letters in this old book.

VANESSA: Whose book is it? Yours or mine?

PETRUS: I don't know whose book it is. Well, it's mine now. I bought it this morning, on impulse, from a girl selling books by the river. When I got home, I opened it up, and these letters fell out.

VANESSA: You didn't open the book before you bought it?

PETRUS: It was raining. I was rushing to get home.

VANESSA: You were rushing to get home, so you stopped to buy an old book?

PETRUS: I had a sudden impulse. She looked so lonely, there in the rain.

VANESSA: She was selling books in the rain?

PETRUS: It's Drago's *Occult Notebooks*. I've been looking for this book for many, many years. I thought I'd never find a copy.

VANESSA: Who is Drago?

PETRUS: N. J. Drago. A Romanian writer. Rather obscure and difficult, but brilliant. It's quite a rare book. I got it for practically nothing.

VANESSA: So you stole from the poor girl?

PETRUS: I didn't steal from her. I paid what she asked for it.

VANESSA: But you knew it was worth more. The creature is half mad, selling books in the rain, and you're drawn to her on impulse, no doubt because of her melancholy beauty, and then you cheat her out of a rare book.

PETRUS: You're missing the point here.

VANESSA: No I'm not. I have always very much appreciated the romance of found objects. At least, I seem to remember that I have. Everything is still a little blurry in my head. Found objects can seem to radiate a powerful numinosity. Now there's a word I didn't know I knew. Numinosity. Is that a word? A sense that objects or events or even certain persons or places possess tremendous significance, that one has stumbled upon them for some purpose unknown to one, that one is suddenly able to perceive the vague outline of a pattern in what would appear to be entirely random events. It appears I may be more intelligent than I'd realized. Or possibly just demented.

PETRUS: What's really interesting here is the letters.

VANESSA: You found some letters in an old book. One's likely to stumble upon anything in the pages of an old book. Flowers. Note cards. Fragments of human skin.

PETRUS: They're written to someone named Vanessa.

VANESSA: And that is interesting because—?

PETRUS: Because your name is Vanessa.

VANESSA: And?

PETRUS: Doesn't that seem an odd coincidence to you?

VANESSA: I have no doubt there are a number of persons in Quebec named Vanessa. This is still Quebec, isn't it? Sometimes I wake up from a dream and I seem to be in an entirely different place. I suppose it's the medication.

PETRUS: I'm sure there are other persons named Vanessa in Quebec. But they're not living in my house, are they?

VANESSA: Not that I know of. Who are the letters from?

PETRUS: They're from somebody named Jonathan. And they were mailed from Quebec to Providence.

VANESSA: So this is Providence?

PETRUS: No. This is Quebec.

VANESSA: If they were mailed to Providence, then how did they get back to Quebec?

PETRUS: Clearly, in this book.

(*Lights up on Jonathan, sitting at the table down left, speaking as a letter but not writing.*)

JONATHAN: Dearest Vanessa. I got the key to Rum House from a horrible old woman with a face like a salamander and moved in three days ago. The plaster is flaking off the walls, and there's something scuttling in the cupboards, but I feel surprisingly at home in Quebec, as if I'd lived here in a previous life.

VANESSA: I had a brother named Jonathan.

PETRUS: A brother? Did you?

JONATHAN: It rains here every evening, and in the morning there is fog, and always the song of the whippoorwills in the cherry trees by the river.

PETRUS: You've never mentioned having a brother.

JONATHAN: I've been exploring the overgrown garden, which is a miasma of tangled vines.

VANESSA: I don't any more. He's dead now.

JONATHAN: I have on more than one occasion had the overwhelming sensation that I am not alone in this house. Last night I could have sworn I heard a young girl talking to herself upstairs in the bath.

(Lights up on Marianne in the tub.)

MARIANNE: Once upon a time, she said, Vanessa and Jonathan lived in Quebec.

PETRUS: What did your brother die of?

MARIANNE: Then Vanessa went to college, to Brown University, in Providence, Rhode Island, to study creative writing, and there she met her roommate, Marianne.

JONATHAN: When I made my way up the creaking steps to the lavatory, I saw that I had apparently left the light on.

VANESSA: He fell down a staircase and broke his neck.

JONATHAN: I opened the creaking door. The water was running. The tub was about to overflow. But nobody was there.

MARIANNE: Marianne was an apothecary's daughter who loved telling herself stories in the bath.

PETRUS: Did your brother write you letters?

MARIANNE: Petrus, you wicked boy, will you close that door? You're letting in goblins.

VANESSA: Yes. As a matter of fact, I believe he did. When I lived in Providence. I went to school there. At Brown. I went to Brown.

MARIANNE: At Christmas break, Vanessa brought her roommate Marianne home to Quebec to meet her brother. Marianne was a very beautiful creative writing major, and when Jonathan met her, he fell hopelessly in love with her, as nearly everybody did.

JONATHAN: The bathroom smelled like the freshly shampooed hair of Marianne.

VANESSA: I might have gone to Princeton or to Harvard, but I was fascinated by Lovecraft.° The writer. H. P. Lovecraft. Dark creatures lurking in basements. Unspeakable impossibly ancient gelatinous beings from outer space. Lovecraft

---

Lovecraft: H. P. Lovecraft (1890–1937), American writer of horror, fantasy, and science fiction.

lived in Providence. He prowled the streets at night, looking for God knows what. He was terribly lonely. I used to walk the streets at night and think of him.

PETRUS: He mentions a girl named Marianne in these letters.

VANESSA: I knew a girl named Marianne. I brought her home for Christmas break, and my brother fell hopelessly in love with her. But she was used to it. Many people fell in love with her. She had a certain melancholy beauty. It was very annoying. The surest way to make someone not want you is to love them. Don't you find that?

MARIANNE: I used to walk by Lovecraft's house at night, in Providence. (*Sound of whippoorwills.*) He was haunted by the sound of whippoorwills.

JONATHAN: How is Marianne? I haven't seen her in so long. Does she ever speak of me? You never mention her any more in your letters.

MARIANNE: Petrus? Is that you out there on the staircase?

VANESSA: Idea for a story. A man stops at a girl's book stall by the river one morning in the rain, drawn there perhaps by the melancholy beauty of the girl. He opens one of the books and some old letters fall out. He's always been fond of the little mysterious things found in old books. He has always appreciated the romance of found objects. Query to self: What is the book? Lovecraft's *Color Out of Space?* The *Occult Notebooks* of N. J. Drago? How old are the letters? Do they smell like perfume? Sweet or citrus? His name is Petrus Van Hoek. He's an artist.

MARIANNE: After her return to Providence, Jonathan wrote Marianne hundreds of love letters, passionate, desperately tender, beautiful letters. But Marianne never wrote back.

VANESSA: Is there perhaps a photograph in among the letters? A photograph of a girl?

JONATHAN: Dearest Marianne. I am writing to tell you that I've fallen desperately and hopelessly in love with you. It would perhaps be more prudent to pretend this was not the case, but I feel so strongly that all deception in my relations to you are repugnant to me.

MARIANNE: I love a strange city where I do not speak the language. I prefer it that way.

PETRUS: There is a photograph in this letter. Of a very pretty girl.

VANESSA: Does she have a melancholy beauty?

PETRUS: She looks rather familiar.

VANESSA: Yes. That's good. A girl who looks oddly familiar. He's overcome by the eerie sensation that he's known her before, in another life, perhaps. On the back of the photograph it says "From Marianne, With Love."

PETRUS: It does say that, actually.

VANESSA: Of course it does. Does the man who buys the book fall in love with the girl in the photograph?

PETRUS: I don't know. Does he?

MARIANNE: Everybody falls in love with me.

JONATHAN: I wonder if somehow my letters to you have gone astray.

VANESSA: The man is convinced he knows the girl. But he can't quite remember. Perhaps he doesn't want to remember.

MARIANNE: Petrus, is that you?

VANESSA: Perhaps it involves the memory of something terrible that happened. Something he wants to forget. Is the girl in some danger? Is there something about the letter that terrifies him? Is there a lock of hair, perhaps?

PETRUS: Vanessa, look at the photograph. Do you know this girl?

VANESSA: (*Examining the photograph.*) I'm not certain. It's so difficult to tell what's real. You know I've just got out of that place. Between the drugs I took before I went there, and all the drugs they gave me, and the shock treatments, my memory is like scrambled eggs.

MARIANNE: Oh, Vanessa, I have met the most wonderful young man. His name is Petrus Van Hoek, and he is an artist who studies the anatomy of young women. He has been studying my anatomy in great detail, and he reports that it is magnificent. He says I have a marvelous, melancholy beauty. He is presently taking photographs of me in the bath.

VANESSA: I remember a basement full of embalming bottles. And the cries of the whippoorwills.

JONATHAN: Dearest Vanessa. I have seen her. I have seen her naked in her bath.

VANESSA: There are some things I don't exactly remember, but I seem to remember having once been able to remember. Unless of course I've made them up. But are they my stories, or Marianne's stories? And are they fiction, or are they reminiscence? Madness must be like this.

MARIANNE: Petrus? Would you like to come up and wash my back?

VANESSA: I remember that she had a lover.

PETRUS: Why wouldn't she have a lover? A beautiful girl like that.

VANESSA: Yes, but up until then, you see, it had been just us two. Just Marianne and me. Many were in love with me, and everybody was in love with her, but mostly we two laughed at them. We were very happy, in our little world in Providence. We didn't want to spoil it by letting men in. Men exist to defile beauty. But then she found this artist. Or he found her. Perhaps she was modeling to put herself through school. It's very expensive, you know. But this one, for some reason, she wanted. And I was jealous.

MARIANNE: I've just met a wonderful man. His name is Petrus Van Hoek.

VANESSA: So the roommate finds her in the tub. She is forever taking long baths.

MARIANNE: Is somebody out there?

VANESSA: And the roommate confronts her.

MARIANNE: Petrus? Is that you?

VANESSA: Why do you give yourself to such a person? she says. He doesn't care about you. Not like I do. Why would you want to spoil everything by allowing this person to violate you?

JONATHAN: I don't understand why she won't answer my letters. It's driving me insane.

VANESSA: He's just a man, she says. He doesn't know how to care about you. But I love you.

MARIANNE: And I love you too, dear.

VANESSA: Says Marianne.

MARIANNE: Would you hand me the towel? I have a date with Petrus.

JONATHAN: I can't stand it any more. I must go to Providence to see her, confront her, tell her how much I love her.

VANESSA: Idea for the ending: jealous girl strangles her beloved in the bathtub.

JONATHAN: I knock and knock at the door but nobody answers. The door is unlocked. I walk into the old house. Vanessa? I say. Marianne? There is no answer. I can hear water dripping upstairs. I walk up the creaking staircase. I open the door to the bathroom. I find her lying dead in the tub. Then suddenly there is only darkness.

VANESSA: The murderess is hiding behind the door. She strikes him violently on the head with the bulldog door stop, and only later realizes that it's her brother. He is never quite right in the head after. But then, he was a man, after all. He'd never been all that bright.

JONATHAN: Lying naked there in the water. So beautiful.

VANESSA: Then she begins receiving mysterious letters from Quebec. She knows her brother must be sending them. Sometimes there are three or four letters a day, all about Marianne. She can't take it any more. Finally she goes back to Quebec to convince him to stop writing her these letters. She confronts him on the staircase.

PETRUS: What does she do?

(*Sound of whippoorwills.*)

VANESSA: She can hear the sound of whippoorwills.

PETRUS: What did you do?

VANESSA: They find her wandering in the streets of Quebec in the rain. Only she insists that it's not Quebec. It's Providence, she says. You may think it's Quebec, but just look in the mirror. My image in the mirror does not speak this language.

PETRUS: Vanessa, what did you do?

VANESSA: She woke up in another place. A quiet place. And every day a man came to see her. He sat with her every day and read to her. Spoke with her. He read to her from a very odd book.

JONATHAN: I go all about the house, calling her name. But nobody is there. The library is full of old books and papers. I wonder if they're my books and papers. I open an old book on the desk. It's the *Occult Notebooks* of N. J. Drago. The name written on the inside front cover is Petrus Van Hoek.

MARIANNE: Petrus? Is that you?

JONATHAN: I open the book to a random page and read: On my antiquarian trip from Oswego and Ticonderoga to Quebec, I was often confused by the cries of whippoorwills.

VANESSA: You're Petrus. You're the one who loved her.

PETRUS: Yes.

VANESSA: But why did you come to see me every day? Why have you brought me here?

PETRUS: I think you know.

VANESSA: I didn't mean to hurt her.

PETRUS: It's time for your bath now.

VANESSA: Yes. My bath.

MARIANNE: A beautiful girl, drowned in her bath.

VANESSA: I must take my bath now.

MARIANNE: Petrus? Is that you? Is somebody on the stairs?

PETRUS: I'll be up soon.

(*The light fades on them and goes out. Sound of whippoorwills in the darkness.*)

END OF PLAY

APPROACHING THE READING

1. In this play, the flashbacks make it challenging to follow exactly what has happened and is happening and why. It will help if you outline the important events in chronological order. Be ready to explain what happened to whom and why and how the play's structure achieves the playwright's desired effects.

2. What characteristics usually associated with horror stories (starting with setting) do you find in the play?

3. It is important to pay especially close attention to Petrus and Vanessa, to the way their character traits are revealed through the whole play. Does your view of them change as the play progresses? By the conclusion what is each like? How does the way they are characterized fit the horror-story genre?

4. Don Nigro seems to have made up N. J. Drago, but H. P. Lovecraft was an actual person—a writer of horror stories—who lived in Providence for much of his life. Stephen King called him "the twentieth century's greatest practitioner of the classic horror tale." Check the Internet for information about him. Then think about how Nigro makes Lovecraft part of the story and what impact his presence has. Consider, too, what particular ways Lovecraft's works may have influenced the play.

RESPONDING THROUGH Writing

WRITING ABOUT SETTING AND STRUCTURE

Journal Entries

1. Write a journal entry listing ways the structuring of Susan Glaspell's *Trifles* (p. 922) both corresponds to and doesn't correspond to a popular TV detective drama.

2. In your journal, write a list of stage movements in Susan Glaspell's *Trifles* (p. 922), both those noted in the stage directions and those suggested by the text, and comment on their significance. Note especially what is indicated by the way characters are positioned in relation to one another.

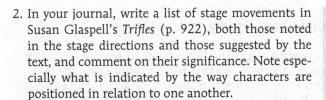

You can research the authors in this chapter with LitLinks, or take a quiz on the plays with LitQuiz, at bedfordstmartins.com/rewritinglit.

3. Write a journal entry listing various uses of irony in Susan Glaspell's *Trifles* (p. 922) and commenting on their importance to the effect and meaning of the play.

Literary Analysis Papers

4. Write a paper analyzing the means of characterization in Susan Glaspell's *Trifles* (p. 922) and the relation of characters to the play's theme. Include the two key characters who do not appear on the stage, Mr. and Mrs. Wright.

5. Write a paper analyzing the unity of structure and theme in Susan Glaspell's *Trifles* (p. 922) or Tennessee Williams's *This Property Is Condemned* (p. 1083).

6. Write a paper examining the dramatic structure of Don Nigro's *Letters from Quebec to Providence in the Rain* (p. 938) and its contribution to the effect of the play.

Comparison-Contrast Papers

7. Compare and contrast the birdcage in Susan Glaspell's *Trifles* (p. 922) and the doll house in Henrik Ibsen's *A Doll House* (p. 1245) as feminist metaphors.

8. Compare and contrast Susan Glaspell's *Trifles* (p. 922) to a contemporary TV detective program, focusing on generic conventions they have in common and ones they do not share.

WRITING ABOUT CONNECTIONS

Setting and structure invariably offer opportunities for you to work with connections within a play. When you attend to the setting, pay special attention to how any action connects to its location in a meaningful way and notice how the structure arranges the various parts of a play, interconnecting them in an orderly and illuminating fashion. Equally interesting is the examination of thematic connections between different plays that have implications regarding setting and structure. Here are a few examples:

1. "By a Higher Standard": The Conflict of Law and Justice in Susan Glaspell's *Trifles* (p. 922) and Sophocles' *Antigone* (p. 1103)

TIPS for Writing about Setting and Structure

- **Specific settings.** Even though the importance of setting in drama varies depending on the play, it often has a key role. For the location of the action to be described in specific detail usually indicates that it will be influential, affecting characterization, tone, assumptions about social and cultural attitudes, and themes. In such cases, it should at least be referred to, even in a paper on a different topic. It might also be suitable in itself as the main focus of a paper.

- **General settings.** When setting is general or unspecified (when the action could occur anywhere at any time), it could mean that it is less significant than a specific setting. However, there are plays, such as some by Samuel Beckett, in which the abstract setting and time hold important meaning. It will be helpful and valuable to mention and explain how an unspecified setting affects or does not affect the impact of the play.

- **Arrangement.** The way a play's action is organized structurally often contributes significantly to its impact. When this is the case, analyzing that arrangement can be an insightful topic for a paper. Pay attention especially to the opening, to the means by which background information is supplied, to the way the action builds to a climax, and to how things are brought to a conclusion.

- **Crucial scenes.** Because full-length plays are difficult to cover completely in a short paper, it may be necessary to focus on key scenes in a paper on structure. Often it works best to choose scenes that are the most dramatic, in which characters and ideas are involved in crucial conflicts. However, in some plays the crucial conflict may occur in a very subtle manner, so don't overlook what may appear at first to be a less important scene. Revealing the impact of a seemingly minor or insignificant scene can be an interesting and effective paper topic.

- **Contrast.** Analyzing contrast — the structural juxtaposition of scenes, images, and ideas, and the use of one character as a foil to another — can be one of the most interesting and effective ways to find a topic and focus a paper on drama.

2. "Living on a Smile and a Handshake": Selling Yourself in David Ives's *Sure Thing* (p. 1046) and Mark Lambeck's *Intervention* (p. 1055)
3. "Serving Time in Invisible Prisons": Social Entrapments in Tennessee Williams's *This Property Is Condemned* (p. 1083) and Eduardo Machado's *Crossing the Border* (p. 909)

WRITING RESEARCH PAPERS

1. Read the description of feminist criticism on pages 1458–60 and do additional research into feminist approaches to literature. Apply what you find in a paper analyzing Susan Glaspell's *Trifles* (p. 922) and/or Henrik Ibsen's *A Doll House* (p. 1245).

2. Do research on the appeal of detective stories (in books, on TV, in movies and plays), including Susan Glaspell's *Trifles* (p. 922), as a cultural phenomenon. What is it about our culture that makes such stories popular? Try to find out if that popularity extends to other cultures and include that in your consideration. Write a research paper on what you find.

Writing has been to me like a bath from which I have risen feeling cleaner, healthier, and freer.

Henrik Ibsen

(Norwegian Playwright, see p. 1245)

(Norwegian Playwright, see p. 1245)

CHAPTER **24** # Writing about Drama

Applying What You've Learned

Drama enters the ongoing conversation about literature most often through performances of plays. People attend a play and then talk about what they experienced, especially with others who saw the same production. Writing extends the conversation in the form of drama reviews in newspapers and periodicals and on the Web. This chapter, however, does not focus on writing (or talking) about drama on the stage—about the director's interpretation, how the actors played their roles, and the effect of the sets, lighting, other technical devices, and costumes. Instead it discusses how to write effectively about plays when you read them as literature (the same as our emphasis in Chapters 21–23). We concentrate not on the way a particular production handled the play but rather on the way a reader interacts with a text's presentation of action, characters, and setting.

The suggestions offered in "Writing Short Papers" in Chapter 2 (pp. 30–43) apply to writing about drama, as they do to any literary paper. And much that is covered in Chapters 9 and 18 on writing about fiction and poetry carries over to writing about drama as well. This chapter adds to those chapters by offering suggestions particularly applicable if you are asked to write about plays.

We gave one of our introduction to literature classes the assignment to write a paper on an aspect of theme or dramatic technique in one of the short plays in Chapters 22 or 23. This chapter will follow one of the students, Julian Hinson, as he wrote about Kelly Stuart's *The New New* (p. 899). If you haven't read the play or don't remember it well, reading or rereading it now will make this chapter easier to follow and apply to your own work.

Step 1. Prewriting: Finding a Topic

Looking for a topic on drama has a lot in common with looking for a topic on fiction. In both cases you usually have a story involving conflict and theme and characters whose personalities and/or actions are explored and developed. Focusing on one or more of these elements could lead you to a topic. Plays often deal with issues of general human interest, moral significance, or social or relational problems. Looking at the way the play handles these and explores the ideas connected to them could lead you to a paper topic. In a play, dialogue and dramatic action take the place of narrative. You might be able to find a topic by focusing on dramatic techniques—on how the playwright individualizes characters through differences in dialogue, for example, or how the playwright uses foreshadowing, symbolism, contrasting scenes, or juxtaposition of characters (foils) to affect an audience's response.

In the box, Julian explains how he arrived at his topic.

We have provided suggestions for paper topics at the ends of Chapters 22 and 23. If you're still looking for a topic, you might look at those again (pp. 917 and 944). Here are a dozen additional possibilities:

A student, Julian Hinson, on finding a topic: "When we were given the assignment, I decided almost at once to work on the play I liked best when we read it for class earlier, Kelly Stuart's *The New New*. I sat down right after class to reread the play. The first time I read it, a week or so ago, it was confusing, partly because of its odd title and partly because of the way it jumps back and forth between the two men and the two women. This time as I read it I drew lines in the text each time the focus shifted from the one group to the other, and that made it easier to follow. Then I read the play aloud with another student, dividing the roles between us. That helped clarify what the lines mean because we had to concentrate on their tone and expression. After doing this, I realized that what interested me most were the moral issues brought up by the play. I decided that would be my topic."

1. The presence and importance of *hubris* (pride) in Sophocles' *Antigone* (p. 1103)
2. The nonrealistic dramatization of death and the use of symbolism in Woody Allen's *Death Knocks* (p. 1066) and David Henry Hwang's *As the Crow Flies* (p. 1073)
3. Parent and child conflicts in August Wilson's *Fences* (p. 963) and Lorraine Hansberry's *A Raisin in the Sun* (p. 1300)
4. The use and effect of Emilia as a foil to Desdemona in William Shakespeare's *Othello* (p. 1149)
5. An explication of one of the following passages, relating it to the play as a whole: Antigone's speech on human and divine law in lines 499–525 of *Antigone* (p. 1103); Othello's monologue in *Othello*

5.2.1–22 (p. 1149); Helmer's "calm yourself and collect your thoughts speech" in *A Doll House* (p. 1245); or what Walter says in the dialogue with his mother in the last two pages of act 1 of *A Raisin in the Sun* (p. 1300)

6. Similarities and differences of men's attitudes toward women and women's attitudes toward themselves and other women as shown in Susan Gaspell's *Trifles* (p. 922) and Henrik Ibsen's *A Doll House* (p. 1245)

7. Characters and coping devices in Tennessee Williams's *This Property Is Condemned* (p. 1083) or Marco Ramirez's *I Am Not Batman* (p. 1090) or in both plays together

8. The role and effect of class distinctions in Kelly Stuart's *The New New* (p. 899), August Wilson's *Fences* (p. 963), and/or Henrik Ibsen's *A Doll House* (p. 1245)

9. The way monologue works as a play, focusing on Joyce Carol Oates's *When I Was a Little Girl and My Mother Didn't Want Me* (p. 1062). Discuss why it can be considered a play and what makes such a single-character drama effective.

10. The use of horror story conventions and their effect in Don Nigro's *Letters from Quebec to Providence in the Rain* (p. 938)

11. The role and importance of sports in Eduardo Machado's *Crossing the Border* (p. 909) and August Wilson's *Fences* (p. 963)

12. A film version of a play versus its written text, perhaps using *Othello*—the 1995 version starring Laurence Fishburne as Othello and Kenneth Branagh as Iago or the 1981 version by the BBC starring Anthony Hopkins and Bob Hoskins or a comparison of the two—or using *A Raisin in the Sun*—the 1961 version starring Sidney Poitier, Ruby Dee, and Claudia McNeil or the 2008 television version starring Sean Combs, Audra McDonald, and Phylicia Rashad or a comparison of the two. Does the movie stick closely to the text or does it take considerable liberties? Is the result effective and satisfying or a disappointment? What things can the play do that the film version cannot, and what is the film able to do that the play can not?

PLAYING DIRECTOR   A topic possibility unique to drama is a paper in which you assume the role of director. In this sort of paper, you would explain how you as director interpret the play, how you want your cast to present the characters, and why. You might describe how you would stage the play—what kind of set, props, costumes, lighting, sound, and music you would use and what kind of stage movement (called "blocking") and action you would want. The decisions you make and descriptions you give will clarify your reading and interpretation of the play. This kind of paper, like any of the others suggested in this chapter, needs a thesis that develops an idea about the play. It also must discuss and illustrate whatever points you use to develop and support that thesis.

Step 2. Prewriting: Narrowing the Topic

Just as with a short story or novel, you can't write about everything in a play. You need to narrow your focus to what is especially pertinent to or valuable for your topic. Benjamin De Mott's technique of focusing on "key passages" (see p. 40) works very well for plays. As you reread the play or crucial parts of it, watch for and mark key passages. Write notes on what seems most important or pertinent in them. As you go over the passages you've marked and the notes you've written, check if they connect with each other. That could point you toward a way of limiting or narrowing the topic from the whole story to related parts.

Notice how Julian went about narrowing and focusing his topic (box at right).

> A student, Julian Hinson, on narrowing his topic: "When I returned to the assignment the next evening, the open-endedness of the assignment led me to explore as many aspects of morality in the play as I could. After some false starts I jotted down a tentative title, 'The Degeneration of Morals in *The New New*,' and drafted a working thesis: 'The use and abuse of language in *The New New* reflects a breakdown in contemporary moral values.'"

Step 3. Prewriting: Deciding on an Approach

Chapter 2 discusses several major categories of approaches you can take in a paper about literature: literary analysis, comparison-contrast, social and cultural analysis, or a combination of these (see pp. 34–36). Sometimes, of course, the topic you select has an approach built in, as, for example, if you decide to write a paper on the use and effect of foreshadowing and symbolism in *A Doll House* (p. 1245). That would require an analytical approach — as Julian's topic did as well. For drama, analyses of dramatic structure (the way action is arranged to build in dramatic intensity) or of dramatic conflict as a way of compressing the tensions in a play can turn into solid topics.

If you want to examine how Shakespeare's conception of tragedy was similar to and/or different from that of the Greek tragedies, you would necessarily be comparing and contrasting. Examining the use of foils (such as the function of Mrs. Linde as a foil to Nora Helmer in *A Doll House*) can often result in a valuable comparison-contrast paper.

> A student, Julian Hinson, on deciding on an approach: "After reflecting a bit on the topic and preliminary thesis I had drafted, it seemed clear to me that I was undertaking a thematic analysis of the play. So I proceeded to take further analytical steps. I returned to the play and began searching for examples of major distortions of ethics and minor misdemeanors, hoping to show that in their essence both 'little white lies' and multimillion-dollar cover-ups differ very little from each other. In order to properly write an analysis involving a new *new*, I figured it would be wise to struggle through the same problem Bradley and Craig did. I looked up the word *new* in a dictionary (NOT a thesaurus!) and found the following definitions: 'something of recent origin' or 'recently brought into being.'"

If you would like to study how accurately Lorraine Hansberry's *A Raisin in the Sun* (p. 1300) reflects housing discrimination practices in the 1950s, you would be doing a research paper dealing with social and cultural analysis. You would also be doing social or cultural analysis if you decide to investigate whether *A Doll House* had a direct influence on changing attitudes toward women in the period following its appearance or if Ibsen's 1881 play *Ghosts*, which deals directly with the topic of congenital venereal disease and which created quite a controversy, had an effect on public awareness and attitudes toward sexuality.

Step 4. Prewriting: Framing a Thesis and Preparing an Outline

In previous chapters on writing, we said that an effective literary paper needs to have a thesis—a statement of the paper's central idea or claim that is to be discussed and supported. As you write the paper, you are seeking to convince readers that your position is sound or worthy of serious consideration. Review pages 36–38 on making sure you have an idea-based thesis. In writing about drama (just as with fiction), some students slip into plot summary. Your paper must go further. It must illuminate or clarify the drama in some way, presenting your ideas with convincing support. In this respect, Julian was fortunate that the preliminary thesis he wrote while narrowing his topic was idea-based and continued to be what he wanted to examine in the paper. As he said, "It doesn't always work out this way for me."

Next he concentrated on coming up with an outline to organize the ideas he was interested in:

The Values of Society as Seen in *The New New*
Introduction: implications of "new"
1. Connections between distortions of words and distortions in morals
2. Decline in media values during the lifetimes of generation Y
3. Music on MTV and BET are evidence of a decline in morals
4. Spin doctors make decline seem like improvement
5. Society allows success to transcend ethical concerns
6. The problem is apathy, that people no longer really care

Step 5. Writing: Developing and Supporting the Thesis

Methods of developing and supporting the ideas in a literature paper are discussed fully in Chapter 2. It might be good to go back and reread the sections "Illustrate and Explain," "Include Quotations," "Focus on Key Passages," and "Avoid Summary" (see pp. 40–42). Before starting a paper on drama, it might be helpful to review the section on using the literary present (p. 42). The way you develop and support your arguments is central to your paper's success: The most amazing ideas in the world are of little value if they are not supported convincingly.

Julian says he returned to his paper a day or two later and worked on development and support.

"I reread the play, looking for phrases I could use in developing my points. Here's what I came up with:

1. redeems; neoteric; witty sardonic ethnographer; Thesaurus check (searching for *synonyms*, not *meanings*)
2. Jenny's affair with a teacher; INTENSE CONNECTION
3. (I decided to drop this point [that music on MTV and BET are evidence of a decline in morals] because there isn't support for it in the play.)
4. we can't *call it* a memoir; Monster; marketing department
5. failing his class; his writing redeems him; witty sardonic ethnographer
6. the way they proceed despite what Naomi told them; never bother to check

I then began working on a rough draft, incorporating those phrases and using them to develop my ideas."

Step 6. Revising, Proofreading, and Formatting

In Chapter 2 we explained the importance of careful revision and editing (proofreading) and offered suggestions for how to do them well. Reviewing them before you proceed with this step might be helpful (pp. 43–45).

A student, Julian Hinson, on revising and proofreading: "When I reread my rough draft the next day, I felt the paper didn't 'flow' in logical sequence. So I reread the play and reread what I had written and decided my points would be better integrated if I rearranged paragraphs to follow the structure of Kelly Stuart's ideas as they develop in the beginning, middle, and end of her play. I also revised the title to something that would be catchier and convey the point of the paper more clearly. Here's the final outline:

Out with the Old, in with the New: The Spin on Contemporary Values in *The New New*
Introduction: implications of 'new'
1. In contemporary society, success transcends ethics
2. That's particularly evident in the entertainment industry
3. Distortions of words connect to decline in morals
4. Spin doctors make decline seem like improvement
5. The problem is apathy, that people no longer really care

Conclusion

What initially seemed a simple play turned out to be a fairly complex and nuanced consideration of modern attitudes toward social and personal ethics. That led me to do a lot of thinking in the shower long after I finished the paper."

TIPS for Quoting Drama

For general advice on fitting quotations into your paragraphs and sentences, review the sections on handling quotations (p. 41) and "A Closer Look at Punctuating and Formatting Quotations" (p. 53). Much of what is said on those pages applies to quoting from a play. But quoting from a play poses some special challenges. Here are some tips on how to handle drama quotations:

- **Quote economically.** Whenever possible, make the quotations you use short and pointed. Focus on key lines, phrases, or words instead of typing out extended passages. Often a careful lead-in phrase or introductory sentence or two can clarify the context and your point and thus reduce the need for a long quotation.

- **Quoting one speech, prose.** Handle prose passages from one speech in a play as you do quotations from any other prose. Merge quotations of four or fewer lines into your sentence; format longer passages as block quotations (see p. 53).

- **Quoting one speech, verse.** Handle passages from one speech in a play written in verse (many of Shakespeare's plays, for example) as you do quotations from poetry. Merge quotations of one to three lines into your sentence, using slashes to indicate line divisions; format passages of four lines or more as block quotations (see p. 53).

- **Quoting more than one speech.** Format passages quoting from more than one speech as block quotations. For each character, indent the first line a half inch; type the character's name in capitals, followed by a colon, and then the text of the speech; indent additional lines in the same speech another half inch (using hanging indents). For an example, see Julian's paper, page 955.

- **Citing passages from plays in verse.** For plays written in verse and divided into acts and scenes, identify passages by giving the act, scene, and line numbers in parentheses after the quotation. Use arabic numbers, separated by periods, even if the original uses roman numerals. This is especially helpful for older plays that have been reprinted many times. A page number isn't much help if you have a different edition from the one used in someone's paper. Thus, a citation of the famous "It is the cause, it is the cause" speech in the final act of *Othello* (p. 1231) would appear as (5.2.1–15). Include the title of the play if other plays are cited in the paper. Give the edition from which you are quoting on the Works Cited page.

- **Citing passages from plays in prose.** For plays written in prose, cite passages by page number in parentheses after the quotation. Give the edition from which you are quoting on the Works Cited page.

SAMPLE SHORT PAPER

Julian Hinson
Professor Schakel
English 105-04
1 December 2010

Out with the Old, in with the New:
The Spin on Contemporary Values in *The New New*

Authors often think of their titles last. The title, however, is the first thing that the reader sees and it has a significant impact as the reader considers it before, during, and after finishing the work. *The New New* may seem at first a confusing title, yet it is intriguing as well. *New*, when used as an adjective, describes something unfamiliar, previously unseen, and recently brought into being. Yet when used as a noun, *New* can be seen as a socially acceptable norm, as in the phrases "Ring in the new" or "What's new?" Kelly Stuart combines both forms of the word into a title and uses her short play *The New New* to show that new attitudes toward language reflect unfavorable changes in society's attitude toward morals.

Thesis sentence.

The play opens with lines that indicate "new" grounds for making decisions that have moral implications. Stuart opens her play with lines that once, at least, would have shocked readers:

Quotation introduced formally with colon.

JENNY: I'm going to have an affair with him.
MARCY: But Jenny, you're failing his class.
JENNY: He says I can take an incomplete if I want, and he'll
       help me make it up over the summer. (899)

Marcy's reply establishes that there is something fundamentally wrong with Jenny's statement, but her reply does not follow along ethical lines. It is, instead, based on Jenny's poor performance in the class. Marcy's response assumes that were Jenny acing the class, her actions

Builds argument with assertions and illustrations.

Hinson 2

Quotation blended into sentence.

would be acceptable, a reflection on the immunity of the successful in our society. Since Jimmy, the man convicted of manslaughter and the author of the new book, is an excellent writer — "his writing redeems him" (903) — neither Craig nor Bradley nor anyone else in their company ever bothered to check the validity of his story. In the play and often in modern society, morals take a backseat to pleasure. Bradley's diction as he describes talking to Jimmy shows how immune a successful, entertaining man can be:

Block quotation with speaker identified in the text.

> I used to get these calls from prison, collect calls every Tuesday. I thought of these calls as my "Tuesdays with Jimmy." He was just this witty, sardonic ethnographer of prison life. . . . [This] civilized business executive locked up with all these illiterate thugs. . . . (901)

If Bradley had not found it "engaging" to hear about a businessman spending time in jail with petty thieves, he might have paid more attention to the fact that Jimmy survived prison, and probably managed to get his conviction reduced to manslaughter, through his ability to use "sales techniques."

Transition and topic sentence.

The tendency to allow success to trump ethics is evident in much of the contemporary entertainment industry. One can, for example, attend a movie rated PG and find that the previews contain distinctly R images, yet each of those previews contains the disclaimer: "The following preview is suitable for all ages." Selling a new movie is more important than being sensitive to what ratings guidelines are supposed to achieve. An evening in front of the TV offers ample evidence of a significant decline in media values, despite claims to the contrary by corporate executives. Stuart reveals the current susceptibility to "spin doctors" through Bradley and Craig's manipulation of the story of Naomi's murdered brother, Jeremy. Bradley and Craig are in the marketing department: Their job is to use words to sell a product. As Craig puts it, "Agony isn't a word that sells" (900). By changing Jeremy's name to "Monster" and placing the emphasis on Jimmy's writing, they are able to promote this "memoiristic novel" as good literature.

Hinson 3

The New New shows how the meanings of words can be
severely distorted. Before the advent of this new "norm," an
"INTENSE CONNECTION" (899) did not warrant sleeping with one's
professor. In the same manner that the word "New" is replaced
by "neoteric," Bradley views "agonizing" in the same light as
"entertaining." Marcy's attachment to Jimmy grows to "fondness"
without her knowledge of the truth of why this seemingly
"juxtaposed" man is actually in prison. Throughout the play, Stuart
attempts to show the reader that both for characters in her play
and for much of society words as a whole have lost their significance. Craig consults a thesaurus, looking for synonyms, not a
dictionary, looking for meanings. Words carry no consequence and,
without consequence, there can be no accountability, much less
responsibility. This explains how something as small as a "thesaurus check" can acquit a killer of his crime. Had Bradley used the
word "bitter" instead of "witty [and] sardonic," the book would
have been viewed in a distinctly different light.

Transition and topic sentence.

The end of the play shows the result of neglecting what
words actually mean. Naomi's note provides a benchmark for how
far the wordsmiths Bradley and Craig have traveled in arriving at
their distorted tale:

Transition and topic sentence.

> My brother's name was Jeremy. Not Monster. He was five
> foot three, one hundred thirty pounds. Not six foot two,
> three hundred fifty. My brother was tortured and strangled
> over the course of a two-hour, period. The shape of a turtle
> and a steer were imprinted on my brother's neck, from the
> cowboy belt your so-called "author" used. My brother's face
> was badly beaten, bones protruded from his bloody face. My
> brother was a medical assistant. He was a human being, not
> a monster. (903)

Despite this evidence to the contrary of everything
Bradley and Craig have sought to prove about Jimmy, they continue to justify their choice of author and remove his crime from

the "real" story in their book. As Craig puts it, "I still think, um. The SPIRIT of the — I mean, he was true to the SPIRIT of, the book's not about the crime in any case . . ." (903).

Transition.

Society is often willing to overlook an egregious fault in something as long as it works toward a desired end. When confronted, people are willing to justify the perpetrator on the basis of another "good" trait that works in her or his favor: "Being convicted of manslaughter had nothing to do with the arc of his life. It was just, this aberration" (902). The story has traveled so far from its original truth that a movie has been optioned for Ben Stiller, a comedy actor, and Marcy assumes that a "love" of Ben Stiller provides a basis for Jenny to love Jimmy.

Topic sentence.

Stuart is not trying to depict the two men as evil or saying that they are selfish enough to deliberately seek profit from another man's death. Instead, she shows that the problem in society is apathy: People don't care about words being emptied of meaning or about the results of doing so. Despite Naomi's plea — "To see this man profit, it's killing me and I wonder if you ever gave that a thought?" (903) — the two men are content to ignore the truth of the story because they "really like Jimmy" (000). Bradley continues to play matchmaker, placing his "girlfriend's sister" at risk because he thinks Jimmy is a good man, and Craig attributes Naomi's emotions to mere blood relation: ". . . [S] he's the victim's sister. That's all. What do you expect?" (903).

Conclusion.

At the end of the play, one can assume that Stuart gets the words of her title from Bradley and Craig's dilemma, but in spirit, her choice of a title slowly reveals and labels a problem embedded in contemporary society, the acceptance of a new new and a wrong norm.

he plays ultimately are about love, honor, duty, betrayal—what I call the Big Themes.

August Wilson

August Wilson's *Fences* — A Casebook

CHAPTER 25

Wrestling with One Writer's Work

August Wilson was born Frederick August Kittel on April 27, 1945, the son of Daisy Wilson, an African American cleaning woman, and Frederick August Kittel, a German immigrant baker who lived with the family only intermittently. His early years were spent in the Hill district, a black neighborhood of Pittsburgh. When his mother married David Bedford, a black ex-convict and former high-school football star, the family moved to the largely white community of Hazlewood, Pennsylvania, and later back to the Hill. Wilson's brothers kept their father's name, but Wilson decided, in 1965, to adopt his mother's maiden name, thus signaling his loyalty to his African American heritage.

He dropped out of Gladstone High School in 1960, after a ninth-grade teacher, believing Wilson could not have written or done the research for a twenty-page paper on Napoleon Bonaparte, accused him of plagiarism. From that point, he educated himself by reading his way through the section of black authors in the local library, discovering such writers as James Baldwin, Richard Wright, Langston Hughes, and Ralph Ellison. Reading works by black authors convinced him to be a writer himself, and he prepared by reading voraciously in fiction, poetry, and drama. He wrote and published some poetry, but soon found himself drawn to the theater. In 1968, he cofounded a theater company in Pittsburgh, Black Horizons on the Hill, through which he hoped to raise consciousness and politicize the community, and began writing one-act plays.

August Wilson performing his solo show How I Learned What I Learned *at the U.S. Comedy Arts Festival in March 2004 in Aspen, Colorado.*

E. Pablo Kosmicki/AP/ Wide World Photos.

He moved to St. Paul, Minnesota, in 1978, taking with him a satirical play, *Black Bart and the Sacred Hills*, adapted from his poems. He found a job writing for the Science Museum of Minnesota and in 1980 became involved with the Minneapolis Playwrights Center. He regarded *Jitney*, written in 1979, as his first real play. He submitted it and three other early plays, unsuccessfully, to the Eugene O'Neill Theater Center's National Playwrights Conference in Waterford, Connecticut. Finally, in 1982, *Ma Rainey's Black Bottom* was accepted. At the O'Neill, Wilson impressed Lloyd Richards, director of the O'Neill Workshop and artistic director of the Yale Drama School. Richards taught Wilson stagecraft and helped him learn to revise

August Wilson in front of Ann's Restaurant in Boston, Massachusetts, November 1990.

Photo copyright © by Michael Romanos. www.MichaelRomanos .com.

his work and went on to direct Wilson's first six plays from workshops through Broadway productions.

Ma Rainey (premiered in 1984) was followed by *Fences* (1985) and *Joe Turner's Come and Gone* (1986). All three won the prestigious New York Drama Critics Circle Award (he eventually won a total of seven). In addition he won a Tony award, three American Theatre Critics awards, and two Pulitzer Prizes for Drama, first for *Fences* and later for *The Piano Lesson* (1989). These works became part of a cycle of ten plays Wilson undertook, chronicling the experience of African Americans in the United States, one play for each decade of the twentieth century:

1900s — *Gem of the Ocean* (2003)

1910s — *Joe Turner's Come and Gone* (1984)

1920s — *Ma Rainey's Black Bottom* (1982)

1930s — *The Piano Lesson* (1989)

1940s — *Seven Guitars* (1995)

1950s — *Fences* (1985)

James Earl Jones as Troy Maxson in the 1987 Broadway production of Fences.
Photofest, Inc.

1960s – *Two Trains Running* (1990)

1970s – *Jitney* (1982)

1980s – *King Hedley II* (2001)

1990s – *Radio Golf* (2005)

The series is designed to inform later generations about the hardships and indignities earlier generations experienced but did not talk about to their children. All of the plays are set in Pittsburgh except *Ma Rainey's Black Bottom*, which is set in Chicago.

The final play in the cycle, *Radio Golf*, premiered in March 2005 at the Yale Repertory Theatre. Two months later Wilson was diagnosed with inoperable liver cancer. He died on 2 October 2005. Soon after his death the Virginia Theatre in New York was renamed the August Wilson Theatre. This is the first Broadway theater to be named for an African American and is a tribute to his stature as one of the seminal figures in twentieth-century American drama.

There are three ways to use the material in this chapter for writing assignments. The first is to write a paper on *Fences* without reading the secondary materials (the reviews, interviews, and critical essays) in the chapter. You would treat the play as if it were included in the "Collection of Plays" and

Lynn Thigpen and James Earl Jones in the 1987 Broadway production of Fences.

Photofest, Inc.

your paper would not draw on outside sources. If you choose this option, remember that if you do read any secondary materials, even parts of them, you must acknowledge it by including them in a bibliography, even if you don't quote from or refer to them.

In a second way of using this chapter, your instructor might ask you to write a paper on *Fences* using secondary sources but only those included in the chapter. Such a paper provides you practice working with and incorporating ideas from secondary sources, selecting passages to quote and blending quotations into your writing, and constructing a Works Cited page. But it isn't a full research paper because you aren't responsible for finding material to use in the paper. The reason an instructor might select this way of working is that it doesn't require as much time to complete as a full-blown research project does. You and your instructor will be working with material you are both familiar with. For such a paper, you should review the guidelines for handling quotations on pages 53-54 and you should read "Appendix on Reading Critical Essays" (pp. 1432-44) and the sections on incorporating sources, avoiding plagiarism, documenting sources, and preparing a Works Cited page in Chapter 3 (pp. 74-84). The secondary sources include original publication information and page references, which you can use for your in-text citations and Works Cited page, as if you had access to the actual books and periodicals.

A third way to use this chapter is as a starting point for an actual research paper. That is, after reading *Fences* and the secondary materials in this chapter, you would begin searching — perhaps only in the library, or perhaps also using electronic sources, as your instructor prefers — to locate additional sources. You might read more interviews with Wilson and additional plays or essays written by him, and you surely will be expected to read and use additional biographical or critical works about his thoughts and works. For such a project, in addition to reviewing the guidelines for handling quotations on pages 53-54 and reading the "Appendix on Reading Critical Essays" (pp. 1432-44), you should read or review all of Chapter 3, "Writing a Literary Research Paper."

August Wilson° 1945-2005

Fences [1985]

> When the sins of our fathers visit us
> We do not have to play host.
> We can banish them with forgiveness
> As God, in His Largeness and Laws.
> — *August Wilson* [p. x]°

Wilson, August. *Fences: A Play.* New York: New American Library, 1986. Print.
(Page citations in square brackets refer to the original publication.)

CHARACTERS

TROY MAXSON   GABRIEL, Troy's brother
JIM BONO, Troy's friend   CORY, Troy and Rose's son
ROSE, Troy's wife   RAYNELL, Troy's daughter [p. xiii]
LYONS, Troy's oldest son by
    previous marriage

SETTING

The setting is the yard which fronts the only entrance to the Maxson household, an ancient two-story brick house set back off a small alley in a big-city neighborhood. The entrance to the house is gained by two or three steps leading to a wooden porch badly in need of paint.

A relatively recent addition to the house and running its full width, the porch lacks congruence. It is a sturdy porch with a flat roof. One or two chairs of dubious value sit at one end where the kitchen window opens onto the porch. An old-fashioned icebox stands silent guard at the opposite end.

The yard is a small dirt yard, partially fenced, except for the last scene, with a wooden sawhorse, a pile of lumber, and other fence-building equipment set off to the side. Opposite is a tree from which hangs a ball made of rags. A baseball bat leans against the tree. Two oil drums serve as garbage receptacles and sit near the house at right to complete the setting. [p. xv]

THE PLAY

Near the turn of the century, the destitute of Europe sprang on the city with tenacious claws and an honest and solid dream. The city devoured them. They swelled its belly until it burst into a thousand furnaces and sewing machines, a thousand butcher shops and bakers' ovens, a thousand churches and hospitals and funeral parlors and money-lenders. The city grew. It nourished itself and offered each man a partnership limited only by his talent, his guile, and his willingness and capacity for hard work. For the immigrants of Europe, a dream dared and won true.

The descendants of African slaves were offered no such welcome or participation. They came from places called the Carolinas and the Virginias, Georgia, Alabama, Mississippi, and Tennessee. They came strong, eager, searching. The city rejected them and they fled and settled along the riverbanks and under bridges in shallow, ramshackle houses made of sticks and tar-paper. They collected rags and wood. They sold the use of their muscles and their bodies. They cleaned houses and washed clothes, they shined shoes, and in quiet desperation and vengeful pride, they stole, and lived in pursuit of their own dream. That they could breathe free, finally, and stand to meet life with the force of dignity and whatever eloquence the heart could call upon.

By 1957, the hard-won victories of the European immigrants had solidified the industrial might of America. War had been confronted and won with new energies that used loyalty and patriotism as its fuel. Life was rich, full, and flourishing. The Milwaukee Braves won the World Series, and the hot winds of

change that would make the sixties a turbulent, racing, dangerous, and provocative decade had not yet begun to blow full. [p. xvii]

ACT ONE / Scene One

*It is 1957. Troy and Bono enter the yard, engaged in conversation. Troy is fifty-three
years old, a large man with thick, heavy hands; it is this largeness that he strives to
fill out and make an accommodation with. Together with his blackness, his largeness
informs his sensibilities and the choices he has made in his life.*

*Of the two men, Bono is obviously the follower. His commitment to their friend-
ship of thirty-odd years is rooted in his admiration of Troy's honesty, capacity for
hard work, and his strength, which Bono seeks to emulate.*

*It is Friday night, payday, and the one night of the week the two men engage in
a ritual of talk and drink. Troy is usually the most talkative and at times he can be
crude and almost vulgar, though he is capable of rising to profound heights of expression. The men carry lunch buckets and wear or carry burlap aprons and are dressed
in clothes suitable to their jobs as garbage collectors.*

BONO: Troy, you ought to stop that lying!
TROY: I ain't lying! The nigger had a watermelon this big.

(He indicates with his hands.)

> Talking about . . . "What watermelon, Mr. Rand?" I liked to fell out! "What
> watermelon, Mr. Rand?" . . . And it sitting there big as life.
BONO: What did Mr. Rand say? [p. 3]
TROY: Ain't said nothing. Figure if the nigger too dumb to know he carrying a
    watermelon, he wasn't gonna get much sense out of him. Trying to hide
    that great big old watermelon under his coat. Afraid to let the white man
    see him carry it home.
BONO: I'm like you . . . I ain't got no time for them kind of people.
TROY: Now what he look like getting mad cause he see the man from the union
    talking to Mr. Rand?
BONO: He come to me talking about . . . "Maxson gonna get us fired." I told
    him to get away from me with that. He walked away from me calling you a
    troublemaker. What Mr. Rand say?
TROY: Ain't said nothing. He told me to go down the Commissioner's office
    next Friday. They called me down there to see them.
BONO: Well, as long as you got your complaint filed, they can't fire you. That's
    what one of them white fellows tell me.
TROY: I ain't worried about them firing me. They gonna fire me cause I asked a
    question? That's all I did. I went to Mr. Rand and asked him, "Why? Why
    you got the white mens driving and the colored lifting?" Told him, "what's
    the matter, don't I count? You think only white fellows got sense enough
    to drive a truck. That ain't no paper job! Hell, anybody can drive a truck.
    How come you got all whites driving and the colored lifting?" He told me

"take it to the union." Well, hell, that's what I done! Now they wanna come up with this pack of lies.

BONO: I told Brownie if the man come and ask him any questions . . . just tell the truth! It ain't nothing but [p. 4] something they done trumped up on you cause you filed a complaint on them.

TROY: Brownie don't understand nothing. All I want them to do is change the job description. Give everybody a chance to drive the truck. Brownie can't see that. He ain't got that much sense.

BONO: How you figure he be making out with that gal be up at Taylors' all the time . . . that Alberta gal?

TROY: Same as you and me. Getting just as much as we is. Which is to say nothing.

BONO: It is, huh? I figure you doing a little better than me . . . and I ain't saying what I'm doing.

TROY: Aw, nigger, look here . . . I know you. If you had got anywhere near that gal, twenty minutes later you be looking to tell somebody. And the first one you gonna tell . . . that you gonna want to brag to . . . is gonna be me.

BONO: I ain't saying that. I see where you be eyeing her.

TROY: I eye all the women. I don't miss nothing. Don't never let nobody tell you Troy Maxson don't eye the women.

BONO: You been doing more than eyeing her. You done bought her a drink or two.

TROY: Hell yeah, I bought her a drink! What that mean? I bought you one, too. What that mean cause I buy her a drink? I'm just being polite.

BONO: It's alright to buy her one drink. That's what you call being polite. But when you wanna be buying two or three . . . that's what you call eyeing her. [p. 5]

TROY: Look here, as long as you known me . . . you ever known me to chase after women?

BONO: Hell yeah! Long as I done known you. You forgetting I knew you when.

TROY: Naw, I'm talking about since I been married to Rose?

BONO: Oh, not since you been married to Rose. Now, that's the truth, there. I can say that.

TROY: Alright then! Case closed.

BONO: I see you be walking up around Alberta's house. You supposed to be at Taylors' and you be walking up around there.

TROY: What you watching where I'm walking for? I ain't watching after you.

BONO: I seen you walking around there more than once.

TROY: Hell, you liable to see me walking anywhere! That don't mean nothing cause you see me walking around there.

BONO: Where she come from anyway? She just kinda showed up one day.

TROY: Tallahassee. You can look at her and tell she one of them Florida gals. They got some big healthy women down there. Grow them right up out the ground. Got a little bit of Indian in her. Most of them niggers down in Florida got some Indian in them.

BONO: I don't know about that Indian part. But she damn sure big and healthy. Woman wear some big stockings. [p. 6] Got them great big old legs and hips as wide as the Mississippi River.

TROY: Legs don't mean nothing. You don't do nothing but push them out of the way. But them hips cushion the ride!

BONO: Troy, you ain't got no sense.

TROY: It's the truth! Like you riding on Goodyears!

(*Rose enters from the house. She is ten years younger than Troy, her devotion to him stems from her recognition of the possibilities of her life without him: a succession of abusive men and their babies, a life of partying and running the streets, the Church, or aloneness with its attendant pain and frustration. She recognizes Troy's spirit as a fine and illuminating one and she either ignores or forgives his faults, only some of which she recognizes. Though she doesn't drink, her presence is an integral part of the Friday night rituals. She alternates between the porch and the kitchen, where supper preparations are under way.*)

ROSE: What you all out here getting into?

TROY: What you worried about what we getting into for? This is men talk, woman.

ROSE: What I care what you all talking about? Bono, you gonna stay for supper?

BONO: No, I thank you, Rose. But Lucille say she cooking up a pot of pigfeet.

TROY: Pigfeet! Hell, I'm going home with you! Might even stay the night if you got some pigfeet. You got something in there to top them pigfeet, Rose? [p. 7]

ROSE: I'm cooking up some chicken. I got some chicken and collard greens.

TROY: Well, go on back in the house and let me and Bono finish what we was talking about. This is men talk. I got some talk for you later. You know what kind of talk I mean. You go on and powder it up.

ROSE: Troy Maxson, don't you start that now!

TROY (*puts his arm around her*): Aw, woman . . . come here. Look here, Bono . . . when I met this woman . . . I got out that place, say, "Hitch up my pony, saddle up my mare . . . there's a woman out there for me somewhere. I looked here. Looked there. Saw Rose and latched on to her." I latched on to her and told her—I'm gonna tell you the truth—I told her, "Baby, I don't wanna marry, I just wanna be your man." Rose told me . . . tell him what you told me, Rose.

ROSE: I told him if he wasn't the marrying kind, then move out the way so the marrying kind could find me.

TROY: That's what she told me. "Nigger, you in my way. You blocking the view! Move out the way so I can find me a husband." I thought it over two or three days. Come back—

ROSE: Ain't no two or three days nothing. You was back the same night.

TROY: Come back, told her . . . "Okay, baby . . . but I'm gonna buy me a banty rooster and put him out there in the backyard . . . and when he see a stranger come, he'll flap his wings and crow . . ." Look here, Bono, I could watch the front door by myself . . . it was that back door I was worried about. [p. 8]

ROSE: Troy, you ought not talk like that. Troy ain't doing nothing but telling a lie.

TROY: Only thing is . . . when we first got married . . . forget the rooster . . . we ain't had no yard!

BONO: I hear you tell it. Me and Lucille was staying down there on Logan Street. Had two rooms with the outhouse in the back. I ain't mind the outhouse none. But when that goddamn wind blow through there in the winter . . . that's what I'm talking about! To this day I wonder why in the hell I ever stayed down there for six long years. But see, I didn't know I could do no better. I thought only white folks had inside toilets and things.

ROSE: There's a lot of people don't know they can do no better than they doing now. That's just something you got to learn. A lot of folks still shop at Bella's.

TROY: Ain't nothing wrong with shopping at Bella's. She got fresh food.

ROSE: I ain't said nothing about if she got fresh food. I'm talking about what she charge. She charge ten cents more than the A&P.°

TROY: The A&P ain't never done nothing for me. I spends my money where I'm treated right. I go down to Bella, say, "I need a loaf of bread, I'll pay you Friday." She give it to me. What sense that make when I got money to go and spend it somewhere else and ignore the person who done right by me? That ain't in the Bible.

ROSE: We ain't talking about what's in the Bible. What sense it make to shop there when she overcharge?

TROY: You shop where you want to. I'll do my shopping where the people been good to me. [p. 9]

ROSE: Well, I don't think it's right for her to overcharge. That's all I was saying.

BONO: Look here . . . I got to get on. Lucille going be raising all kind of hell.

TROY: Where you going, nigger? We ain't finished this pint. Come here, finish this pint.

BONO: Well, hell, I am . . . if you ever turn the bottle loose.

TROY (*hands him the bottle*): The only thing I say about the A&P is I'm glad Cory got that job down there. Help him take care of his school clothes and things. Gabe done moved out and things getting tight around here. He got that job. . . . He can start to look out for himself.

ROSE: Cory done went and got recruited by a college football team.

TROY: I told that boy about that football stuff. The white man ain't gonna let him get nowhere with that football. I told him when he first come to me with it. Now you come telling me he done went and got more tied up in it. He ought to go and get recruited in how to fix cars or something where he can make a living.

ROSE: He ain't talking about making no living playing football. It's just something the boys in school do. They gonna send a recruiter by to talk to you. He'll tell you he ain't talking about making no living playing football. It's a honor to be recruited.

A&P: Chain of grocery stores operated by the Great Atlantic and Pacific Tea Company.

TROY: It ain't gonna get him nowhere. Bono'll tell you that.

BONO: If he be like you in the sports . . . he's gonna be alright. Ain't but two men ever played baseball as good as [p. 10] you. That's Babe Ruth and Josh Gibson.° Them's the only two men ever hit more home runs than you.

TROY: What it ever get me? Ain't got a pot to piss in or a window to throw it out of.

ROSE: Times have changed since you was playing baseball, Troy. That was before the war. Times have changed a lot since then.

TROY: How in hell they done changed?

ROSE: They got lots of colored boys playing ball now. Baseball and football.

BONO: You right about that, Rose. Times have changed, Troy. You just come along too early.

TROY: There ought not never have been no time called too early! Now you take that fellow . . . what's that fellow they had playing right field for the Yankees back then? You know who I'm talking about, Bono. Used to play right field for the Yankees.

ROSE: Selkirk?°

TROY: Selkirk! That's it! Man batting .269, understand? .269. What kind of sense that make? I was hitting .432 with thirty-seven home runs! Man batting .269 and playing right field for the Yankees! I saw Josh Gibson's daughter yesterday. She walking around with raggedy shoes on her feet. Now I bet you Selkirk's daughter ain't walking around with raggedy shoes on her feet! I bet you that!

ROSE: They got a lot of colored baseball players now. Jackie Robinson° was the first. Folks had to wait for Jackie Robinson. [p. 11]

TROY: I done seen a hundred niggers play baseball better than Jackie Robinson. Hell, I know some teams Jackie Robinson couldn't even make! What you talking about Jackie Robinson. Jackie Robinson wasn't nobody. I'm talking about if you could play ball then they ought to have let you play. Don't care what color you were. Come telling me I come along too early. If you could play . . . then they ought to have let you play.

(Troy takes a long drink from the bottle.)

ROSE: You gonna drink yourself to death. You don't need to be drinking like that.

Babe Ruth and Josh Gibson: George Herman Ruth (1895–1948) was a pitcher and then an outfielder for the Boston Red Sox (1914–1919), New York Yankees (1920–1934), and Boston Braves (1935). His sixty home runs in the 1927 season set a major league record that stood until 1961. Joshua Gibson (1911–1947), the greatest power hitter in the Negro Leagues and often referred to as the black Babe Ruth, was credited with having hit eighty-four home runs in a single season. In 1972 he was elected to the Baseball Hall of Fame, the second Negro League player (after Satchel Paige) to be so honored.   **Selkirk:** George Selkirk (1934–1987), successor to Babe Ruth in right field for the Yankees. In nine seasons (1934–1942) he had a cumulative batting average of .290 with 108 home runs. In 1940 his average was .269 with 19 home runs.   **Jackie Robinson:** Jack Roosevelt Robinson (1919–1972), first and second baseman for the Brooklyn Dodgers from 1947 to 1956, was the first African American to play in the major leagues.

TROY: Death ain't nothing. I done seen him. Done wrassled with him. You can't tell me nothing about death. Death ain't nothing but a fastball on the outside corner. And you know what I'll do to that! Lookee here, Bono . . . am I lying? You get one of them fastballs, about waist high, over the outside corner of the plate where you can get the meat of the bat on it . . . and good god! You can kiss it goodbye. Now, am I lying?

BONO: Naw, you telling the truth there. I seen you do it.

TROY: If I'm lying . . . that 450 feet worth of lying!

(*Pause.*)

That's all death is to me. A fastball on the outside corner.

ROSE: I don't know why you want to get on talking about death.

TROY: Ain't nothing wrong with talking about death. That's part of life. Everybody gonna die. You gonna die, I'm gonna die. Bono's gonna die. Hell, we all gonna die.

ROSE: But you ain't got to talk about it. I don't like to talk about it. [p. 12]

TROY: You the one brought it up. Me and Bono was talking about baseball . . . you tell me I'm gonna drink myself to death. Ain't that right, Bono? You know I don't drink this but one night out of the week. That's Friday night. I'm gonna drink just enough to where I can handle it. Then I cuts it loose. I leave it alone. So don't you worry about me drinking myself to death. 'Cause I ain't worried about Death. I done seen him. I done wrestled with him.

Look here, Bono . . . I looked up one day and Death was marching straight at me. Like Soldiers on Parade! The Army of Death was marching straight at me. The middle of July, 1941. It got real cold just like it be winter. It seem like Death himself reached out and touched me on the shoulder. He touch me just like I touch you. I got cold as ice and Death standing there grinning at me.

ROSE: Troy, why don't you hush that talk.

TROY: I say . . . What you want, Mr. Death? You be wanting me? You done brought your army to be getting me? I looked him dead in the eye. I wasn't fearing nothing. I was ready to tangle. Just like I'm ready to tangle now. The Bible say be ever vigilant. That's why I don't get but so drunk. I got to keep watch.

ROSE: Troy was right down there in Mercy Hospital. You remember he had pneumonia? Laying there with a fever talking plumb out of his head.

TROY: Death standing there staring at me . . . carrying that sickle in his hand. Finally he say, "You want bound over for another year?" See, just like that . . . "You want bound over for another year?" I told him, "Bound over hell! Let's settle this now!"

It seem like he kinda fell back when I said that, and all the cold went out of me. I reached down and grabbed that sickle and threw it just as far as I could throw it . . . and me and him commenced to wrestling. [p. 13]

We wrestled for three days and three nights. I can't say where I found the strength from. Every time it seemed like he was gonna get the best of me, I'd reach way down deep inside myself and find the strength to do him one better.

ROSE: Every time Troy tell that story he find different ways to tell it. Different things to make up about it.

TROY: I ain't making up nothing. I'm telling you the facts of what happened. I wrestled with Death for three days and three nights and I'm standing here to tell you about it.

(*Pause.*)

Alright. At the end of the third night we done weakened each other to where we can't hardly move. Death stood up, throwed on his robe . . . had him a white robe with a hood on it. He threwed on that robe and went off to look for his sickle. Say, "I'll be back." Just like that. "I'll be back." I told him, say, "Yeah, but . . . you gonna have to find me!" I wasn't no fool. I wan't going looking for him. Death ain't nothing to play with. And I know he's gonna get me. I know I got to join his army . . . his camp followers. But as long as I keep my strength and see him coming . . . as long as I keep up my vigilance . . . he's gonna have to fight to get me. I ain't going easy.

BONO: Well, look here, since you got to keep up your vigilance . . . let me have the bottle.

TROY: Aw hell, I shouldn't have told you that part. I should have left out that part.

ROSE: Troy be talking that stuff and half the time don't even know what he be talking about.

TROY: Bono know me better than that. [p. 14]

BONO: That's right. I know you. I know you got some Uncle Remus in your blood. You got more stories than the devil got sinners.

TROY: Aw hell, I done seen him too! Done talked with the devil.

ROSE: Troy, don't nobody wanna be hearing all that stuff.

(*Lyons enters the yard from the street. Thirty-four years old, Troy's son by a previous marriage, he sports a neatly trimmed goatee, sport coat, white shirt, tieless and buttoned at the collar. Though he fancies himself a musician, he is more caught up in the rituals and "idea" of being a musician than in the actual practice of the music. He has come to borrow money from Troy, and while he knows he will be successful, he is uncertain as to what extent his lifestyle will be held up to scrutiny and ridicule.*)

LYONS: Hey, Pop.

TROY: What you come "Hey, Popping" me for?

LYONS: How you doing, Rose?

(*He kisses her.*)

Mr. Bono. How you doing?

BONO: Hey, Lyons . . . how you been?

TROY: He must have been doing alright. I ain't seen him around here last week.

ROSE: Troy, leave your boy alone. He come by to see you and you wanna start all that nonsense.

TROY: I ain't bothering Lyons.

(*Offers him the bottle.*)

Here . . . get you a drink. We got an understanding. I know why he come by to see me and he know I know. [p. 15]

LYONS: Come on, Pop . . . I just stopped by to say hi . . . see how you was doing.

TROY: You ain't stopped by yesterday.

ROSE: You gonna stay for supper, Lyons? I got some chicken cooking in the oven.

LYONS: No, Rose . . . thanks. I was just in the neighborhood and thought I'd stop by for a minute.

TROY: You was in the neighborhood alright, nigger. You telling the truth there. You was in the neighborhood cause it's my payday.

LYONS: Well, hell, since you mentioned it . . . let me have ten dollars.

TROY: I'll be damned! I'll die and go to hell and play blackjack with the devil before I give you ten dollars.

BONO: That's what I wanna know about . . . that devil you done seen.

LYONS: What . . . Pop done seen the devil? You too much, Pops.

TROY: Yeah, I done seen him. Talked to him too!

ROSE: You ain't seen no devil. I done told you that man ain't had nothing to do with the devil. Anything you can't understand, you want to call it the devil.

TROY: Look here, Bono . . . I went down to see Hertzberger about some furniture. Got three rooms for two-ninety-eight. That what it say on the radio. "Three rooms . . . two-ninety-eight." Even made up a little song about it. Go down there . . . man tell me I can't get no [p. 16] credit. I'm working every day and can't get no credit. What to do? I got an empty house with some raggedy furniture in it. Cory ain't got no bed. He's sleeping on a pile of rags on the floor. Working every day and can't get no credit. Come back here—Rose'll tell you—madder than hell. Sit down . . . try to figure what I'm gonna do. Come a knock on the door. Ain't been living here but three days. Who know I'm here? Open the door . . . devil standing there bigger than life. White fellow . . . got on good clothes and everything. Standing there with a clipboard in his hand. I ain't had to say nothing. First words come out of his mouth was . . . "I understand you need some furniture and can't get no credit." I liked to fell over. He say, "I'll give you all the credit you want, but you got to pay the interest on it." I told him, "Give me three rooms worth and charge whatever you want." Next day a truck pulled up here and two men unloaded them three rooms. Man what drove the truck give me a book. Say send ten dollars, first of every month to the address in the book and everything will be alright. Say if I miss a payment the devil was coming back and it'll be hell to pay. That was fifteen years ago. To this day . . . the first of the month I send my ten dollars, Rose'll tell you.

ROSE: Troy lying.

TROY: I ain't never seen that man since. Now you tell me who else that could have been but the devil? I ain't sold my soul or nothing like that, you understand.

Naw, I wouldn't have truck with the devil about nothing like that. I got my furniture and pays my ten dollars the first of the month just like clockwork.

BONO: How long you say you been paying this ten dollars a month?

TROY: Fifteen years! [p. 17]

BONO: Hell, ain't you finished paying for it yet? How much the man done charged you?

TROY: Aw hell, I done paid for it. I done paid for it ten times over! The fact is I'm scared to stop paying it.

ROSE: Troy lying. We got that furniture from Mr. Glickman. He ain't paying no ten dollars a month to nobody.

TROY: Aw hell, woman. Bono know I ain't that big a fool.

LYONS: I was just getting ready to say . . . I know where there's a bridge for sale.

TROY: Look here, I'll tell you this . . . it don't matter to me if he was the devil. It don't matter if the devil give credit. Somebody has got to give it.

ROSE: It ought to matter. You going around talking about having truck with the devil . . . God's the one you gonna have to answer to. He's the one gonna be at the Judgment.

LYONS: Yeah, well, look here, Pop . . . let me have that ten dollars. I'll give it back to you. Bonnie got a job working at the hospital.

TROY: What I tell you, Bono? The only time I see this nigger is when he wants something. That's the only time I see him.

LYONS: Come on, Pop, Mr. Bono don't want to hear all that. Let me have the ten dollars. I told you Bonnie working.

TROY: What that mean to me? "Bonnie working." I don't care if she working. Go ask her for the ten dollars if she working. Talking about "Bonnie working." Why ain't you working? [p. 18]

LYONS: Aw, Pop, you know I can't find no decent job. Where am I gonna get a job at? You know I can't get no job.

TROY: I told you I know some people down there. I can get you on the rubbish if you want to work. I told you that the last time you came by here asking me for something.

LYONS: Naw, Pop . . . thanks. That ain't for me. I don't wanna be carrying nobody's rubbish. I don't wanna be punching nobody's time clock.

TROY: What's the matter, you too good to carry people's rubbish? Where you think that ten dollars you talking about come from? I'm just supposed to haul people's rubbish and give my money to you cause you too lazy to work. You too lazy to work and wanna know why you ain't got what I got.

ROSE: What hospital Bonnie working at? Mercy?

LYONS: She's down at Passavant working in the laundry.

TROY: I ain't got nothing as it is. I give you that ten dollars and I got to eat beans the rest of the week. Naw . . . you ain't getting no ten dollars here.

LYONS: You ain't got to be eating no beans. I don't know why you wanna say that.

TROY: I ain't got no extra money. Gabe done moved over to Miss Pearl's paying her the rent and things done got tight around here. I can't afford to be giving you every payday.

LYONS: I ain't asked you to give me nothing. I asked you to loan me ten dollars. I know you got ten dollars. [p. 19]

TROY: Yeah, I got it. You know why I got it? Cause I don't throw my money away out there in the streets. You living the fast life . . . wanna be a musician . . . running around in them clubs and things . . . then, you learn to take care of yourself. You ain't gonna find me going and asking nobody for nothing. I done spent too many years without.

LYONS: You and me is two different people, Pop.

TROY: I done learned my mistake and learned to do what's right by it. You still trying to get something for nothing. Life don't owe you nothing. You owe it to yourself. Ask Bono. He'll tell you I'm right.

LYONS: You got your way of dealing with the world . . . I got mine. The only thing that matters to me is the music.

TROY: Yeah, I can see that! It don't matter how you gonna eat . . . where your next dollar is coming from. You telling the truth there.

LYONS: I know I got to eat. But I got to live too. I need something that gonna help me to get out of the bed in the morning. Make me feel like I belong in the world. I don't bother nobody. I just stay with the music cause that's the only way I can find to live in the world. Otherwise there ain't no telling what I might do. Now I don't come criticizing you and how you live. I just come by to ask you for ten dollars. I don't wanna hear all that about how I live.

TROY: Boy, your mamma did a hell of a job raising you.

LYONS: You can't change me, Pop. I'm thirty-four years old. If you wanted to change me, you should have been there when I was growing up. I come by to see you . . . ask for ten dollars and you want to talk about how I was raised. You don't know nothing about how I was raised. [p. 20]

ROSE: Let the boy have ten dollars, Troy.

TROY (*to Lyons*): What the hell you looking at me for? I ain't got no ten dollars. You know what I do with my money.

(*To Rose.*)

Give him ten dollars if you want him to have it.

ROSE: I will. Just as soon as you turn it loose.

TROY (*handing Rose the money*): There it is. Seventy-six dollars and forty-two cents. You see this, Bono? Now, I ain't gonna get but six of that back.

ROSE: You ought to stop telling that lie. Here, Lyons.

(*She hands him the money.*)

LYONS: Thanks, Rose. Look . . . I got to run . . . I'll see you later.

TROY: Wait a minute. You gonna say, "thanks, Rose" and ain't gonna look to see where she got that ten dollars from? See how they do me, Bono?

LYONS: I know she got it from you, Pop. Thanks. I'll give it back to you.

TROY: There he go telling another lie. Time I see that ten dollars . . . he'll be owing me thirty more.

LYONS: See you, Mr. Bono.
BONO: Take care, Lyons!
LYONS: Thanks, Pop. I'll see you again.

(*Lyons exits the yard.*) [p. 21]

TROY: I don't know why he don't go and get him a decent job and take care of
    that woman he got.
BONO: He'll be alright, Troy. The boy is still young.
TROY: The *boy* is thirty-four years old.
ROSE: Let's not get off into all that.
BONO: Look here . . . I got to be going. I got to be getting on. Lucille gonna be
    waiting.
TROY (*puts his arm around Rose*): See this woman, Bono? I love this woman. I love
    this woman so much it hurts. I love her so much . . . I done run out of ways of
    loving her. So I got to go back to basics. Don't you come by my house Monday
    morning talking about time to go to work . . . 'cause I'm still gonna be stroking!
ROSE: Troy! Stop it now!
BONO: I ain't paying him no mind, Rose. That ain't nothing but gin-talk. Go on,
    Troy. I'll see you Monday.
TROY: Don't you come by my house, nigger! I done told you what I'm gonna be
    doing.

(*The lights go down to black.*) [p. 22]

Scene Two

*The lights come up on Rose hanging up clothes. She hums and sings softly to herself.
It is the following morning.*

ROSE (*sings*): Jesus, be a fence all around me every day
    Jesus, I want you to protect me as I travel on my way.
    Jesus, be a fence all around me every day.

(*Troy enters from the house.*)

ROSE (*continued*): Jesus, I want you to protect me
    As I travel on my way.

(*To Troy.*)

    'Morning. You ready for breakfast? I can fix it soon as I finish hanging up
    these clothes.
TROY: I got the coffee on. That'll be alright. I'll just drink some of that this
    morning.
ROSE: That 651 hit yesterday. That's the second time this month. Miss Pearl hit
    for a dollar . . . seem like those that need the least always get lucky. Poor
    folks can't get nothing.
TROY: Them numbers don't know nobody. I don't know why you fool with
    them. You and Lyons both.

ROSE: It's something to do. [p. 23]

TROY: You ain't doing nothing but throwing your money away.

ROSE: Troy, you know I don't play foolishly. I just play a nickel here and a nickel there.

TROY: That's two nickels you done thrown away.

ROSE: Now I hit sometimes . . . that makes up for it. It always comes in handy when I do hit. I don't hear you complaining then.

TROY: I ain't complaining now. I just say it's foolish. Trying to guess out of six hundred ways which way the number gonna come. If I had all the money niggers, these Negroes, throw away on numbers for one week — just one week — I'd be a rich man.

ROSE: Well, you wishing and calling it foolish ain't gonna stop folks from playing numbers. That's one thing for sure. Besides . . . some good things come from playing numbers. Look where Pope done bought him that restaurant off of numbers.

TROY: I can't stand niggers like that. Man ain't had two dimes to rub together. He walking around with his shoes all run over bumming money for cigarettes. Alright. Got lucky there and hit the numbers . . .

ROSE: Troy, I know all about it.

TROY: Had good sense, I'll say that for him. He ain't throwed his money away. I seen niggers hit the numbers and go through two thousand dollars in four days. Man bought him that restaurant down there . . . fixed it up real nice . . . and then didn't want nobody to come in it! A Negro go in there and can't get no kind of service. I seen a white fellow come in there and order a bowl of stew. [p. 24] Pope picked all the meat out the pot for him. Man ain't had nothing but a bowl of meat! Negro come behind him and ain't got nothing but the potatoes and carrots. Talking about what numbers do for people, you picked a wrong example. Ain't done nothing but make a worser fool out of him than he was before.

ROSE: Troy, you ought to stop worrying about what happened at work yesterday.

TROY: I ain't worried. Just told me to be down there at the Commissioner's office on Friday. Everybody think they gonna fire me. I ain't worried about them firing me. You ain't got to worry about that.

(*Pause.*)

Where's Cory? Cory in the house? (*Calls.*) Cory?

ROSE: He gone out.

TROY: Out, huh? He gone out 'cause he know I want him to help me with this fence. I know how he is. That boy scared of work.

(*Gabriel enters. He comes halfway down the alley and, hearing Troy's voice, stops.*)

TROY (*continues*): He ain't done a lick of work in his life.

ROSE: He had to go to football practice. Coach wanted them to get in a little extra practice before the season start.

TROY: I got his practice . . . running out of here before he get his chores done.

ROSE: Troy, what is wrong with you this morning? Don't nothing set right with you. Go on back in there and go to bed . . . get up on the other side. [p. 25]

TROY: Why something got to be wrong with me? I ain't said nothing wrong with me.

ROSE: You got something to say about everything. First it's the numbers . . . then it's the way the man runs his restaurant . . . then you done got on Cory. What's it gonna be next? Take a look up there and see if the weather suits you . . . or is it gonna be how you gonna put up the fence with the clothes hanging in the yard.

TROY: You hit the nail on the head then.

ROSE: I know you like I know the back of my hand. Go on in there and get you some coffee . . . see if that straighten you up. 'Cause you ain't right this morning.

(*Troy starts into the house and sees Gabriel. Gabriel starts singing. Troy's brother, he is seven years younger than Troy. Injured in World War II, he has a metal plate in his head. He carries an old trumpet tied around his waist and believes with every fiber of his being that he is the Archangel Gabriel. He carries a chipped basket with an assortment of discarded fruits and vegetables he has picked up in the strip district and which he attempts to sell.*)

GABRIEL (*singing*): Yes, ma'am, I got plums
You ask me how I sell them
Oh ten cents apiece
Three for a quarter
Come and buy now
'Cause I'm here today
And tomorrow I'll be gone

(*Gabriel enters.*)

Hey, Rose! [p. 26]

ROSE: How you doing, Gabe?

GABRIEL: There's Troy . . . Hey, Troy!

TROY: Hey, Gabe.

(*Exit into kitchen.*)

ROSE (*to Gabriel*): What you got there?

GABRIEL: You know what I got, Rose. I got fruits and vegetables.

ROSE (*looking in basket*): Where's all these plums you talking about?

GABRIEL: I ain't got no plums today, Rose. I was just singing that. Have some tomorrow. Put me in a big order for plums. Have enough plums tomorrow for St. Peter and everybody.

(*Troy re-enters from kitchen, crosses to steps.*)
(*To Rose.*)

Troy's mad at me.

TROY: I ain't mad at you. What I got to be mad at you about? You ain't done nothing to me.

GABRIEL: I just moved over to Miss Pearl's to keep out from in your way. I ain't mean no harm by it.

TROY: Who said anything about that? I ain't said anything about that.

GABRIEL: You ain't mad at me, is you?

TROY: Naw . . . I ain't mad at you, Gabe. If I was mad at you I'd tell you about it. [p. 27]

GABRIEL: Got me two rooms. In the basement. Got my own door too. Wanna see my key?

(*He holds up a key.*)

That's my own key! Ain't nobody else got a key like that. That's my key! My two rooms!

TROY: Well, that's good, Gabe. You got your own key . . . that's good.

ROSE: You hungry, Gabe? I was just fixing to cook Troy his breakfast.

GABRIEL: I'll take some biscuits. You got some biscuits? Did you know when I was in heaven . . . every morning me and St. Peter would sit down by the gate and eat some big fat biscuits? Oh, yeah! We had us a good time. We'd sit there and eat us them biscuits and then St. Peter would go off to sleep and tell me to wake him up when it's time to open the gates for the judgment.

ROSE: Well, come on . . . I'll make up a batch of biscuits.

(*Rose exits into the house.*)

GABRIEL: Troy . . . St. Peter got your name in the book. I seen it. It say . . . Troy Maxson. I say . . . I know him! He got the same name like what I got. That's my brother!

TROY: How many times you gonna tell me that, Gabe?

GABRIEL: Ain't got my name in the book. Don't have to have my name. I done died and went to heaven. He got your name though. One morning St. Peter was looking at his book . . . marking it up for the judgment . . . and he let me see your name. Got it in there under M. Got Rose's name . . . I ain't seen it like I seen yours . . . but I know it's in there. He got a great big book. Got everybody's [p. 28] name what was ever been born. That's what he told me. But I seen your name. Seen it with my own eyes.

TROY: Go on in the house there. Rose going to fix you something to eat.

GABRIEL: Oh, I ain't hungry. I done had breakfast with Aunt Jemimah. She come by and cooked me up a whole mess of flapjacks. Remember how we used to eat them flapjacks?

TROY: Go on in the house and get you something to eat now.

GABRIEL: I got to sell my plums. I done sold some tomatoes. Got me two quarters. Wanna see?

(*He shows Troy his quarters.*)

I'm gonna save them and buy me a new horn so St. Peter can hear me when it's time to open the gates.

(*Gabriel stops suddenly. Listens.*)

Hear that? That's the hellhounds. I got to chase them out of here. Go on get out of here! Get out!

(*Gabriel exits singing.*)

Better get ready for the judgment
Better get ready for the judgment
My Lord is coming down

(*Rose enters from the house.*)

TROY: He gone off somewhere.

GABRIEL (*offstage*): Better get ready for the judgment
Better get ready for the judgment morning
Better get ready for the judgment
My God is coming down [p. 29]

ROSE: He ain't eating right. Miss Pearl say she can't get him to eat nothing.

TROY: What you want me to do about it, Rose? I done did everything I can for the man. I can't make him get well. Man got half his head blown away . . . what you expect?

ROSE: Seem like something ought to be done to help him.

TROY: Man don't bother nobody. He just mixed up from that metal plate he got in his head. Ain't no sense for him to go back into the hospital.

ROSE: Least he be eating right. They can help him take care of himself.

TROY: Don't nobody wanna be locked up, Rose. What you wanna lock him up for? Man go over there and fight the war . . . messin' around with them Japs, get half his head blown off . . . and they give him a lousy three thousand dollars. And I had to swoop down on that.

ROSE: Is you fixing to go into that again?

TROY: That's the only way I got a roof over my head . . . cause of that metal plate.

ROSE: Ain't no sense you blaming yourself for nothing. Gabe wasn't in no condition to manage that money. You done what was right by him. Can't nobody say you ain't done what was right by him. Look how long you took care of him . . . till he wanted to have his own place and moved over there with Miss Pearl.

TROY: That ain't what I'm saying, woman! I'm just stating the facts. If my brother didn't have that metal plate in his head . . . I wouldn't have a pot to piss in or a window to [p. 30] throw it out of. And I'm fifty-three years old. Now see if you can understand that!

(*Troy gets up from the porch and starts to exit the yard.*)

ROSE: Where you going off to? You been running out of here every Saturday for weeks. I thought you was gonna work on this fence?

TROY: I'm gonna walk down to Taylors'. Listen to the ball game. I'll be back in a bit. I'll work on it when I get back.

(*He exits the yard. The lights go to black.*) [p. 31]

Scene Three

The lights come up on the yard. It is four hours later. Rose is taking down the clothes from the line. Cory enters carrying his football equipment.

ROSE: Your daddy like to had a fit with you running out of here this morning without doing your chores.

CORY: I told you I had to go to practice.

ROSE: He say you were supposed to help him with this fence.

CORY: He been saying that the last four or five Saturdays, and then he don't never do nothing, but go down to Taylors'. Did you tell him about the recruiter?

ROSE: Yeah, I told him.

CORY: What he say?

ROSE: He ain't said nothing too much. You get in there and get started on your chores before he gets back. Go on and scrub down them steps before he gets back here hollering and carrying on.

CORY: I'm hungry. What you got to eat, Mama? [p. 33]

ROSE: Go on and get started on your chores. I got some meat loaf in there. Go on and make you a sandwich . . . and don't leave no mess in there.

(Cory exits into the house. Rose continues to take down the clothes. Troy enters the yard and sneaks up and grabs her from behind.)

Troy! Go on, now. You liked to scared me to death. What was the score of the game? Lucille had me on the phone and I couldn't keep up with it.

TROY: What I care about the game? Come here, woman. *(He tries to kiss her.)*

ROSE: I thought you went down Taylors' to listen to the game. Go on, Troy! You supposed to be putting up this fence.

TROY *(attempting to kiss her again)*: I'll put it up when I finish with what is at hand.

ROSE: Go on, Troy. I ain't studying you.

TROY *(chasing after her)*: I'm studying you . . . fixing to do my homework!

ROSE: Troy, you better leave me alone.

TROY: Where's Cory? That boy brought his butt home yet?

ROSE: He's in the house doing his chores.

TROY *(calling)*: Cory! Get your butt out here, boy!

(Rose exits into the house with the laundry. Troy goes over to the pile of wood, picks up a board, and starts sawing. Cory enters from the house.) [p. 34]

TROY: You just now coming in here from leaving this morning?

CORY: Yeah, I had to go to football practice.

TROY: Yeah, what?

CORY: Yessir.

TROY: I ain't but two seconds off you noway. The garbage sitting in there overflowing . . . you ain't done none of your chores . . . and you come in here talking about "Yeah."

CORY: I was just getting ready to do my chores now, Pop . . .

TROY: Your first chore is to help me with this fence on Saturday. Everything else come after that. Now get that saw and cut them boards.

(*Cory takes the saw and begins cutting the boards. Troy continues working. There is a long pause.*)

CORY: Hey, Pop . . . why don't you buy a TV?

TROY: What I want with a TV? What I want one of them for?

CORY: Everybody got one. Earl, Ba Bra . . . Jesse!

TROY: I ain't asked you who had one. I say what I want with one?

CORY: So you can watch it. They got lots of things on TV. Baseball games and everything. We could watch the World Series. [p. 35]

TROY: Yeah . . . and how much this TV cost?

CORY: I don't know. They got them on sale for around two hundred dollars.

TROY: Two hundred dollars, huh?

CORY: That ain't that much, Pop.

TROY: Naw, it's just two hundred dollars. See that roof you got over your head at night? Let me tell you something about that roof. It's been over ten years since that roof was last tarred. See now . . . the snow come this winter and sit up there on that roof like it is . . . and it's gonna seep inside. It's just gonna be a little bit . . . ain't gonna hardly notice it. Then the next thing you know, it's gonna be leaking all over the house. Then the wood rot from all that water and you gonna need a whole new roof. Now, how much you think it cost to get that roof tarred?

CORY: I don't know.

TROY: Two hundred and sixty-four dollars . . . cash money. While you thinking about a TV, I got to be thinking about the roof . . . and whatever else go wrong here. Now if you had two hundred dollars, what would you do . . . fix the roof or buy a TV?

CORY: I'd buy a TV. Then when the roof started to leak . . . when it needed fixing . . . I'd fix it.

TROY: Where you gonna get the money from? You done spent it for a TV. You gonna sit up and watch the water run all over your brand new TV.

CORY: Aw, Pop. You got money. I know you do.

TROY: Where I got it at, huh? [p. 36]

CORY: You got it in the bank.

TROY: You wanna see my bankbook? You wanna see that seventy-three dollars and twenty-two cents I got sitting up in there.

CORY: You ain't got to pay for it all at one time. You can put a down payment on it and carry it on home with you.

TROY: Not me. I ain't gonna owe nobody nothing if I can help it. Miss a payment and they come and snatch it right out your house. Then what you got? Now, soon as I get two hundred dollars clear, then I'll buy a TV. Right now, as soon as I get two hundred and sixty-four dollars, I'm gonna have this roof tarred.

CORY: Aw . . . Pop!

TROY: You go on and get you two hundred dollars and buy one if ya want it. I got better things to do with my money.

CORY: I can't get no two hundred dollars. I ain't never seen two hundred dollars.

TROY: I'll tell you what . . . you get you a hundred dollars and I'll put the other hundred with it.

CORY: Alright, I'm gonna show you.

TROY: You gonna show me how you can cut them boards right now.

(Cory begins to cut the boards. There is a long pause.)

CORY: The Pirates won today. That makes five in a row.

TROY: I ain't thinking about the Pirates. Got an all-white team. Got that boy . . . that Puerto Rican boy . . . Clemente.° [p. 37] Don't even half-play him. That boy could be something if they give him a chance. Play him one day and sit him on the bench the next.

CORY: He gets a lot of chances to play.

TROY: I'm talking about playing regular. Playing every day so you can get your timing. That's what I'm talking about.

CORY: They got some white guys on the team that don't play every day. You can't play everybody at the same time.

TROY: If they got a white fellow sitting on the bench . . . you can bet your last dollar he can't play! The colored guy got to be twice as good before he get on the team. That's why I don't want you to get all tied up in them sports. Man on the team and what it get him? They got colored on the team and don't use them. Same as not having them. All them teams the same.

CORY: The Braves got Hank Aaron and Wes Covington.° Hank Aaron hit two home runs today. That makes forty-three.

TROY: Hank Aaron ain't nobody. That's what you supposed to do. That's how you supposed to play the game. Ain't nothing to it. It's just a matter of timing . . . getting the right follow-through. Hell, I can hit forty-three home runs right now!

CORY: Not off no major-league pitching, you couldn't.

TROY: We had better pitching in the Negro leagues. I hit seven home runs off of Satchel Paige.° You can't get no better than that!

Clemente: Roberto Clemente (1934–1972), right fielder for the Pittsburgh Pirates from 1955 to 1971, was the first player of Latin American descent to be elected into the Baseball Hall of Fame. In 1956 he played in 147 games and had a .311 batting average; in 1957 he played in 111 games and his average dropped to .253. **Hank Aaron and Wes Covington:** Henry Louis Aaron (b. 1934), African American outfielder, hit 44 home runs for the Milwaukee Braves in 1957 and went on to break Babe Ruth's career home run record. John Wesley Covington (b. 1932), African American outfielder, hit 21 homers for the Milwaukee Braves in 1957. **Satchel Paige:** Leroy "Satchel" Paige (1906–1982), star pitcher in the Negro Leagues from 1926 to 1947, played in the major leagues for the Cleveland Indians (1948–1949), the St. Louis Browns (1951–1953), and the Kansas City Athletics (1965). He was the first African American elected to the Baseball Hall of Fame.

CORY: Sandy Koufax.° He's leading the league in strike-outs. [p. 38]

TROY: I ain't thinking of no Sandy Koufax.

CORY: You got Warren Spahn and Lew Burdette.° I bet you couldn't hit no home runs off of Warren Spahn.

TROY: I'm through with it now. You go on and cut them boards.

(*Pause.*)

Your mama tell me you done got recruited by a college football team? Is that right?

CORY: Yeah. Coach Zellman say the recruiter gonna be coming by to talk to you. Get you to sign the permission papers.

TROY: I thought you supposed to be working down there at the A&P. Ain't you suppose to be working down there after school?

CORY: Mr. Stawicki say he gonna hold my job for me until after the football season. Say starting next week I can work weekends.

TROY: I thought we had an understanding about this football stuff? You suppose to keep up with your chores and hold that job down at the A&P. Ain't been around here all day on a Saturday. Ain't none of your chores done . . . and now you telling me you done quit your job.

CORY: I'm gonna to be working weekends.

TROY: You damn right you are! And ain't no need for nobody coming around here to talk to me about signing nothing.

CORY: Hey, Pop . . . you can't do that. He's coming all the way from North Carolina. [p. 39]

TROY: I don't care where he coming from. The white man ain't gonna let you get nowhere with that football noway. You go on and get your book-learning so you can work yourself up in that A&P or learn how to fix cars or build houses or something, get you a trade. That way you have something can't nobody take away from you. You go on and learn how to put your hands to some good use. Besides hauling people's garbage.

CORY: I get good grades, Pop. That's why the recruiter wants to talk with you. You got to keep up your grades to get recruited. This way I'll be going to college. I'll get a chance . . .

TROY: First you gonna get your butt down there to the A&P and get your job back.

CORY: Mr. Stawicki done already hired somebody else 'cause I told him I was playing football.

Sandy Koufax: Sanford Koufax (b. 1935), pitcher for the Brooklyn and Los Angeles Dodgers from 1955 to 1966. He recorded 122 strikeouts in 1957. Jack Sanford ended up leading the league that year with 188 strikeouts for the Philadelphia Phillies. **Warren Spahn and Lew Burdette:** Warren Edward Spahn (1921–2003) is the winningest left-handed pitcher in major league history with 363 victories, all but seven of those wins coming with the Boston-Milwaukee Braves, 1942–1964. He had a 21-11 record in 1957 when he won the Cy Young Award and won the fourth game of the 1958 World Series. Selva Lewis Burdette (b. 1926), pitcher for six major league teams from 1950 to 1967, had a 17-9 record for Milwaukee in 1957, won three games in the 1957 World Series, and was named that series' Most Valuable Player.

TROY: You a bigger fool than I thought . . . to let somebody take away your job so you can play some football. Where you gonna get your money to take out your girlfriend and whatnot? What kind of foolishness is that to let somebody take away your job?

CORY: I'm still gonna be working weekends.

TROY: Naw . . . naw. You getting your butt out of here and finding you another job.

CORY: Come on, Pop! I got to practice. I can't work after school and play football too. The team needs me. That's what Coach Zellman say . . .

TROY: I don't care what nobody else say. I'm the boss . . . you understand? I'm the boss around here. I do the only saying what counts. [p. 40]

CORY: Come on, Pop!

TROY: I asked you . . . did you understand?

CORY: Yeah . . .

TROY: What?!

CORY: Yessir.

TROY: You go on down there to that A&P and see if you can get your job back. If you can't do both . . . then you quit the football team. You've got to take the crookeds with the straights.

CORY: Yessir.

(*Pause.*)

Can I ask you a question?

TROY: What the hell you wanna ask me? Mr. Stawicki the one you got the questions for.

CORY: How come you ain't never liked me?

TROY: Liked you? Who the hell say I got to like you? What law is there say I got to like you? Wanna stand up in my face and ask a damn fool-ass question like that. Talking about liking somebody. Come here, boy, when I talk to you.

(*Cory comes over to where Troy is working. He stands slouched over and Troy shoves him on his shoulder.*)

Straighten up, goddammit! I asked you a question . . . what law is there say I got to like you?

CORY: None.

TROY: Well, alright then! Don't you eat every day?

(*Pause.*)

Answer me when I talk to you! Don't you eat every day? [p. 41]

CORY: Yeah.

TROY: Nigger, as long as you in my house, you put that sir on the end of it when you talk to me!

CORY: Yes . . . sir.

TROY: You eat every day.

CORY: Yessir!

TROY: Got a roof over your head.

CORY: Yessir!

TROY: Got clothes on your back.

CORY: Yessir.

TROY: Why you think that is?

CORY: Cause of you.

TROY: Aw, hell I know it's 'cause of me . . . but why do you think that is?

CORY (*hesitant*): Cause you like me.

TROY: Like you? I go out of here every morning . . . bust my butt . . . putting up with them crackers every day . . . cause I like you? You about the biggest fool I ever saw.

(*Pause.*)

It's my job. It's my responsibility! You understand that? A man got to take care of his family. You live in my house . . . sleep you behind on my bedclothes . . . fill you belly up with my food . . . cause you my son. You my flesh and blood. Not 'cause I like you! Cause it's my duty to [p. 42] take care of you. I owe a responsibility to you! Let's get this straight right here . . . before it go along any further . . . I ain't got to like you. Mr. Rand don't give me my money come payday cause he likes me. He gives me cause he owe me. I done give you everything I had to give you. I gave you your life! Me and your mama worked that out between us. And liking your black ass wasn't part of the bargain. Don't you try and go through life worrying about if somebody like you or not. You best be making sure they doing right by you. You understand what I'm saying, boy?

CORY: Yessir.

TROY: Then get the hell out of my face, and get on down to that A&P.

(*Rose has been standing behind the screen door for much of the scene. She enters as Cory exits.*)

ROSE: Why don't you let the boy go ahead and play football, Troy? Ain't no harm in that. He's just trying to be like you with the sports.

TROY: I don't want him to be like me! I want him to move as far away from my life as he can get. You the only decent thing that ever happened to me. I wish him that. But I don't wish him a thing else from my life. I decided seventeen years ago that boy wasn't getting involved in no sports. Not after what they did to me in the sports.

ROSE: Troy, why don't you admit you was too old to play in the major leagues? For once . . . why don't you admit that?

TROY: What do you mean too old? Don't come telling me I was too old. I just wasn't the right color. Hell, I'm fifty-three years old and can do better than Selkirk's .269 right now! [p. 43]

ROSE: How's was you gonna play ball when you were over forty? Sometimes I can't get no sense out of you.

TROY: I got good sense, woman. I got sense enough not to let my boy get hurt over playing no sports. You been mothering that boy too much. Worried about if people like him.

ROSE: Everything that boy do . . . he do for you. He wants you to say "Good job, son." That's all.

TROY: Rose, I ain't got time for that. He's alive. He's healthy. He's got to make his own way. I made mine. Ain't nobody gonna hold his hand when he get out there in that world.

ROSE: Times have changed from when you was young, Troy. People change. The world's changing around you and you can't even see it.

TROY (*slow, methodical*): Woman . . . I do the best I can do. I come in here every Friday. I carry a sack of potatoes and a bucket of lard. You all line up at the door with your hands out. I give you the lint from my pockets. I give you my sweat and my blood. I ain't got no tears. I done spent them. We go upstairs in that room at night . . . and I fall down on you and try to blast a hole into forever. I get up Monday morning . . . find my lunch on the table. I go out. Make my way. Find my strength to carry me through to the next Friday.

(*Pause.*)

That's all I got, Rose. That's all I got to give. I can't give nothing else.

(*Troy exits into the house. The lights go down to black.*) [p. 44]

Scene Four

It is Friday. Two weeks later. Cory starts out of the house with his football equipment. The phone rings.

CORY (*calling*): I got it!

(*He answers the phone and stands in the screen door talking.*)

Hello? Hey, Jesse. Naw . . . I was just getting ready to leave now.

ROSE (*calling*): Cory!

CORY: I told you, man, them spikes is all tore up. You can use them if you want, but they ain't no good. Earl got some spikes.

ROSE (*calling*): Cory!

CORY (*calling to Rose*): Mam? I'm talking to Jesse.

(*Into phone.*)

When she say that? (*Pause.*) Aw, you lying, man. I'm gonna tell her you said that.

ROSE (*calling*): Cory, don't you go nowhere!

CORY: I got to go to the game, Ma!

(*Into the phone.*)

Yeah, hey, look, I'll talk to you later. Yeah, I'll meet you over Earl's house. Later. Bye, Ma. [p. 45]

(*Cory exits the house and starts out the yard.*)

ROSE: Cory, where you going off to? You got that stuff all pulled out and thrown all over your room.

CORY (*in the yard*): I was looking for my spikes. Jesse wanted to borrow my spikes.

ROSE: Get up there and get that cleaned up before your daddy get back in here.

CORY: I got to go to the game! I'll clean it up *when I get back.*

(*Cory exits.*)

ROSE: That's all he need to do is see that room all messed up.

(*Rose exits into the house. Troy and Bono enter the yard. Troy is dressed in clothes other than his work clothes.*)

BONO: He told him the same thing he told you. Take it to the union.

TROY: Brownie ain't got that much sense. Man wasn't thinking about nothing. He wait until I confront them on it . . . then he wanna come crying seniority.

(*Calls.*)

Hey, Rose!

BONO: I wish I could have seen Mr. Rand's face when he told you.

TROY: He couldn't get it out of his mouth! Liked to bit his tongue! When they called me down there to the Commissioner's office . . . he thought they was gonna fire me. Like everybody else. [p. 46]

BONO: I didn't think they was gonna fire you. I thought they was gonna put you on the warning paper.

TROY: Hey, Rose!

(*To Bono.*)

Yeah, Mr. Rand like to bit his tongue.

(*Troy breaks the seal on the bottle, takes a drink, and hands it to Bono.*)

BONO: I see you run right down to Taylors' and told that Alberta gal.

TROY (*calling*): Hey Rose! (*To Bono.*) I told everybody. Hey, Rose! I went down there to cash my check.

ROSE (*entering from the house*): Hush all that hollering, man! I know you out here. What they say down there at the Commissioner's office?

TROY: You supposed to come when I call you, woman. Bono'll tell you that.

(*To Bono.*)

Don't Lucille come when you call her?

ROSE: Man, hush your mouth. I ain't no dog . . . talk about "come when you call me."

TROY (*puts his arm around Rose*): You hear this, Bono? I had me an old dog used to get uppity like that. You say, "C'mere, Blue!" . . . and he just lay there and look at you. End up getting a stick and chasing him away trying to make him come.

ROSE: I ain't studying you and your dog. I remember you used to sing that old song.

TROY (*he sings*): Hear it ring! Hear it ring!

I had a dog his name was Blue. [p. 47]

ROSE: Don't nobody wanna hear you sing that old song.

TROY (*sings*): You know Blue was mighty true.

ROSE: Used to have Cory running around here singing that song.

BONO: Hell, I remember that song myself.

TROY (*sings*): You know Blue was a good old dog.

Blue treed a possum in a hollow log.

That was my daddy's song. My daddy made up that song.

ROSE: I don't care who made it up. Don't nobody wanna hear you sing it.

TROY (*makes a song like calling a dog*): Come here, woman.

ROSE: You come in here carrying on, I reckon they ain't fired you. What they say down there at the Commissioner's office?

TROY: Look here, Rose... Mr. Rand called me into his office today when I got back from talking to them people down there... it come from up top... he called me in and told me they was making me a driver.

ROSE: Troy, you kidding!

TROY: No I ain't. Ask Bono.

ROSE: Well, that's great, Troy. Now you don't have to hassle them people no more.

(*Lyons enters from the street.*) [p. 48]

TROY: Aw hell, I wasn't looking to see you today. I thought you was in jail. Got it all over the front page of the *Courier* about them raiding Sefus's place... where you be hanging out with all them thugs.

LYONS: Hey, Pop... that ain't got nothing to do with me. I don't go down there gambling. I go down there to sit in with the band. I ain't got nothing to do with the gambling part. They got some good music down there.

TROY: They got some rogues... is what they got.

LYONS: How you been, Mr. Bono? Hi, Rose.

BONO: I see where you playing down at the Crawford Grill tonight.

ROSE: How come you ain't brought Bonnie like I told you. You should have brought Bonnie with you, she ain't been over in a month of Sundays.

LYONS: I was just in the neighborhood... thought I'd stop by.

TROY: Here he come...

BONO: Your daddy got a promotion on the rubbish. He's gonna be the first colored driver. Ain't got to do nothing but sit up there and read the paper like them white fellows.

LYONS: Hey, Pop... if you knew how to read you'd be alright.

BONO: Naw... naw... you mean if the nigger knew how to *drive* he'd be all right. Been fighting with them people about driving and ain't even got a license. Mr. Rand know you ain't got no driver's license? [p. 49]

TROY: Driving ain't nothing. All you do is point the truck where you want it to go. Driving ain't nothing.

BONO: Do Mr. Rand know you ain't got no driver's license? That's what I'm talking about. I ain't asked if driving was easy. I asked if Mr. Rand know you ain't got no driver's license.

TROY: He ain't got to know. The man ain't got to know my business. Time he find out, I have two or three driver's licenses.

LYONS (*going into his pocket*): Say, look here, Pop . . .

TROY: I knew it was coming. Didn't I tell you, Bono? I know what kind of "Look here, Pop" that was. The nigger fixing to ask me for some money. It's Friday night. It's my payday. All them rogues down there on the avenue . . . the ones that ain't in jail . . . and Lyons is hopping in his shoes to get down there with them.

LYONS: See, Pop . . . if you give somebody else a chance to talk sometime, you'd see that I was fixing to pay you back your ten dollars like I told you. Here . . . I told you I'd pay you when Bonnie got paid.

TROY: Naw . . . you go ahead and keep that ten dollars. Put it in the bank. The next time you feel like you wanna come by here and ask me for something . . . you go on down there and get that.

LYONS: Here's your ten dollars, Pop. I told you I don't want you to give me nothing. I just wanted to borrow ten dollars.

TROY: Naw . . . you go on and keep that for the next time you want to ask me. [p. 50]

LYONS: Come on, Pop . . . here go your ten dollars.

ROSE: Why don't you go on and let the boy pay you back, Troy?

LYONS: Here you go, Rose. If you don't take it I'm gonna have to hear about it for the next six months. (*He hands her the money.*)

ROSE: You can hand yours over here too, Troy.

TROY: You see this, Bono. You see how they do me.

BONO: Yeah, Lucille do me the same way.

(*Gabriel is heard singing onstage. He enters.*)

GABRIEL: Better get ready for the Judgment! Better get ready for . . . Hey! . . . Hey! . . . There's Troy's boy!

LYONS: How you doing, Uncle Gabe?

GABRIEL: Lyons . . . The King of the Jungle! Rose . . . hey, Rose. Got a flower for you.

(*He takes a rose from his pocket.*)

     Picked it myself. That's the same rose like you is!

ROSE: That's right nice of you, Gabe.

LYONS: What you been doing, Uncle Gabe?

GABRIEL: Oh, I been chasing hellhounds and waiting on the time to tell St. Peter to open the gates.

LYONS: You been chasing hellhounds, huh? Well . . . you doing the right thing, Uncle Gabe. Somebody got to chase them. [p. 51]

GABRIEL: Oh, yeah . . . I know it. The devil's strong. The devil ain't no pushover. Hellhounds snipping at everybody's heels. But I got my trumpet waiting on the judgment time.

LYONS: Waiting on the Battle of Armageddon, huh?

GABRIEL: Ain't gonna be too much of a battle when God get to waving that Judgment sword. But the people's gonna have a hell of a time trying to get into heaven if them gates ain't open.

LYONS (*putting his arm around Gabriel*): You hear this, Pop. Uncle Gabe, you alright!

GABRIEL (*laughing with Lyons*): Lyons! King of the Jungle.

ROSE: You gonna stay for supper, Gabe? Want me to fix you a plate?

GABRIEL: I'll take a sandwich, Rose. Don't want no plate. Just wanna eat with my hands. I'll take a sandwich.

ROSE: How about you, Lyons? You staying? Got some short ribs cooking.

LYONS: Naw, I won't eat nothing till after we finished playing.

(*Pause.*)

You ought to come down and listen to me play, Pop.

TROY: I don't like that Chinese music. All that noise.

ROSE: Go on in the house and wash up, Gabe . . . I'll fix you a sandwich.

GABRIEL (*to Lyons, as he exits*): Troy's mad at me. [p. 52]

LYONS: What you mad at Uncle Gabe for, Pop.

ROSE: He thinks Troy's mad at him cause he moved over to Miss Pearl's.

TROY: I ain't mad at the man. He can live where he want to live at.

LYONS: What he move over there for? Miss Pearl don't like nobody.

ROSE: She don't mind him none. She treats him real nice. She just don't allow all that singing.

TROY: She don't mind that rent he be paying . . . that's what she don't mind.

ROSE: Troy, I ain't going through that with you no more. He's over there cause he want to have his own place. He can come and go as he please.

TROY: Hell, he could come and go as he please here. I wasn't stopping him. I ain't put no rules on him.

ROSE: It ain't the same thing, Troy. And you know it.

(*Gabriel comes to the door.*)

Now, that's the last I wanna hear about that. I don't wanna hear nothing else about Gabe and Miss Pearl. And next week . . .

GABRIEL: I'm ready for my sandwich, Rose.

ROSE: And next week . . . when that recruiter come from that school . . . I want you to sign that paper and go on and let Cory play football. Then that'll be the last I have to hear about that. [p. 53]

TROY (*to Rose as she exits into the house*): I ain't thinking about Cory nothing.

LYONS: What . . . Cory got recruited? What school he going to?

TROY: That boy walking around here smelling his piss . . . thinking he's grown. Thinking he's gonna do what he want, irrespective of what I say. Look here,

Bono . . . I left the Commissioner's office and went down to the A&P . . . that boy ain't working down there. He lying to me. Telling me he got his job back . . . telling me he working weekends . . . telling me he working after school . . . Mr. Stawicki tell me he ain't working down there at all!

LYONS: Cory just growing up. He's just busting at the seams trying to fill out your shoes.

TROY: I don't care what he's doing. When he get to the point where he wanna disobey me . . . then it's time for him to move on. Bono'll tell you that. I bet he ain't never disobeyed his daddy without paying the consequences.

BONO: I ain't never had a chance. My daddy came on through . . . but I ain't never knew him to see him . . . or what he had on his mind or where he went. Just moving on through. Searching out the New Land. That's what the old folks used to call it. See a fellow moving around from place to place . . . woman to woman . . . called it searching out the New Land. I can't say if he ever found it. I come along, didn't want no kids. Didn't know if I was gonna be in one place long enough to fix on them right as their daddy. I figured I was going searching too. As it turned out I been hooked up with Lucille near about as long as your daddy been with Rose. Going on sixteen years. [p. 54]

TROY: Sometimes I wish I hadn't known my daddy. He ain't cared nothing about no kids. A kid to him wasn't nothing. All he wanted was for you to learn how to walk so he could start you to working. When it come time for eating . . . he ate first. If there was anything left over, that's what you got. Man would sit down and eat two chickens and give you the wing.

LYONS: You ought to stop that, Pop. Everybody feed their kids. No matter how hard times is . . . everybody care about their kids. Make sure they have something to eat.

TROY: The only thing my daddy cared about was getting them bales of cotton in to Mr. Lubin. That's the only thing that mattered to him. Sometimes I used to wonder why he was living. Wonder why the devil hadn't come and got him. "Get them bales of cotton in to Mr. Lubin" and find out he owe him money . . .

LYONS: He should have just went on and left when he saw he couldn't get nowhere. That's what I would have done.

TROY: How he gonna leave with eleven kids? And where he gonna go? He ain't knew how to do nothing but farm. No, he was trapped and I think he knew it. But I'll say this for him . . . he felt a responsibility toward us. Maybe he ain't treated us the way I felt he should have . . . but without that responsibility he could have walked off and left us . . . made his own way.

BONO: A lot of them did. Back in those days what you talking about . . . they walk out their front door and just take on down one road or another and keep on walking.

LYONS: There you go! That's what I'm talking about.

BONO: Just keep on walking till you come to something else. Ain't you never heard of nobody having the walking [p. 55] blues? Well, that's what you call it when you just take off like that.

TROY: My daddy ain't had them walking blues! What you talking about? He stayed right there with his family. But he was just as evil as he could be. My mama couldn't stand him. Couldn't stand that evilness. She run off when I was about eight. She sneaked off one night after he had gone to sleep. Told me she was coming back for me. I ain't never seen her no more. All his women run off and left him. He wasn't good for nobody.

When my turn come to head out, I was fourteen and got to sniffing around Joe Canewell's daughter. Had us an old mule we called Greyboy. My daddy sent me out to do some plowing and I tied up Greyboy and went to fooling around with Joe Canewell's daughter. We done found us a nice little spot, got real cozy with each other. She about thirteen and we done figured we was grown anyway ... so we down there enjoying ourselves ... ain't thinking about nothing. We didn't know Greyboy had got loose and wandered back to the house and my daddy was looking for me. We down there by the creek enjoying ourselves when my daddy come up on us. Surprised us. He had them leather straps off the mule and commenced to whupping me like there was no tomorrow. I jumped up, mad and embarrassed. I was scared of my daddy. When he commenced to whupping on me ... quite naturally I run to get out of the way.

(*Pause.*)

Now I thought he was mad cause I ain't done my work. But I see where he was chasing me off so he could have the gal for himself. When I see what the matter of it was, I lost all fear of my daddy. Right there is where I become a man ... at fourteen years of age.

(*Pause.*)

Now it was my turn to run him off. I picked up them same reins that he had used on me. I picked up them reins and commenced to whupping on him. The gal jumped up [p. 56] and run off ... and when my daddy turned to face me, I could see why the devil had never come to get him ... cause he was the devil himself. I don't know what happened. When I woke up, I was laying right there by the creek, and Blue ... this old dog we had ... was licking my face. I thought I was blind. I couldn't see nothing. Both my eyes were swollen shut. I layed there and cried. I didn't know what I was gonna do. The only thing I knew was the time had come for me to leave my daddy's house. And right there the world suddenly got big. And it was a long time before I could cut it down to where I could handle it.

Part of that cutting down was when I got to the place where I could feel him kicking in my blood and knew that the only thing that separated us was the matter of a few years.

(*Gabriel enters from the house with a sandwich.*)

LYONS: What you got there, Uncle Gabe?

GABRIEL: Got me a ham sandwich. Rose gave me a ham sandwich.

TROY: I don't know what happened to him. I done lost touch with everybody except Gabriel. But I hope he's dead. I hope he found some peace.

LYONS: That's a heavy story, Pop. I didn't know you left home when you was fourteen.

TROY: And didn't know nothing. The only part of the world I knew was the forty-two acres of Mr. Lubin's land. That's all I knew about life.

LYONS: Fourteen's kinda young to be out on your own. (*Phone rings.*) I don't even think I was ready to be out on my own at fourteen. I don't know what I would have done. [p. 57]

TROY: I got up from the creek and walked on down to Mobile. I was through with farming. Figured I could do better in the city. So I walked the two hundred miles to Mobile.

LYONS: Wait a minute . . . you ain't walked no two hundred miles, Pop. Ain't nobody gonna walk no two hundred miles. You talking about some walking there.

BONO: That's the only way you got anywhere back in them days.

LYONS: Shhh. Damn if I wouldn't have hitched a ride with somebody!

TROY: Who you gonna hitch it with? They ain't had no cars and things like they got now. We talking about 1918.

ROSE (*entering*): What you all out here getting into?

TROY (*to Rose*): I'm telling Lyons how good he got it. He don't know nothing about this I'm talking.

ROSE: Lyons, that was Bonnie on the phone. She say you supposed to pick her up.

LYONS: Yeah, okay, Rose.

TROY: I walked on down to Mobile and hitched up with some of them fellows that was heading this way. Got up here and found out . . . not only couldn't you get a job . . . you couldn't find no place to live. I thought I was in freedom. Shhh. Colored folks living down there on the riverbanks in whatever kind of shelter they could find for themselves. Right down there under the Brady Street Bridge. Living in shacks made of sticks and tarpaper. Messed around there and went from bad to worse. Started stealing. First it was food. Then I figured, hell, if I steal [p. 58] money I can buy me some food. Buy me some shoes too! One thing led to another. Met your mama. I was young and anxious to be a man. Met your mama and had you. What I do that for? Now I got to worry about feeding you and her. Got to steal three times as much. Went out one day looking for somebody to rob . . . that's what I was, a robber. I'll tell you the truth. I'm ashamed of it today. But it's the truth. Went to rob this fellow . . . pulled out my knife . . . and he pulled out a gun. Shot me in the chest. I felt just like somebody had taken a hot branding iron and laid it on me. When he shot me I jumped at him with my knife. They told me I killed him and they put me in the penitentiary and locked me up for fifteen years. That's where I met Bono. That's where I learned how to play baseball. Got out that place and your mama had taken you and went on to make life without me. Fifteen years was a long time for her to wait. But that fifteen years cured me of that robbing stuff. Rose'll tell you.

She asked me when I met her if I had gotten all that foolishness out of my system. And I told her, "Baby, it's you and baseball all what count with me." You hear me, Bono? I meant it too. She say, "Which one comes first?" I told her, "Baby, ain't no doubt it's baseball . . . but you stick and get old with me and we'll both outlive this baseball." Am I right, Rose? And it's true.

ROSE: Man, hush your mouth. You ain't said no such thing. Talking about, "Baby, you know you'll always be number one with me." That's what you was talking.

TROY: You hear that, Bono. That's why I love her.

BONO: Rose'll keep you straight. You get off the track, she'll straighten you up.

ROSE: Lyons, you better get on up and get Bonnie. She waiting on you. [p. 59]

LYONS (*gets up to go*): Hey, Pop, why don't you come on down to the Grill and hear me play?

TROY: I ain't going down there. I'm too old to be sitting around in them clubs.

BONO: You got to be good to play down at the Grill.

LYONS: Come on, Pop . . .

TROY: I got to get up in the morning.

LYONS: You ain't got to stay long.

TROY: Naw, I'm gonna get my supper and go on to bed.

LYONS: Well, I got to go. I'll see you again.

TROY: Don't you come around my house on my payday.

ROSE: Pick up the phone and let somebody know you coming. And bring Bonnie with you. You know I'm always glad to see her.

LYONS: Yeah, I'll do that, Rose. You take care now. See you, Pop. See you, Mr. Bono. See you, Uncle Gabe.

GABRIEL: Lyons! King of the Jungle!

(*Lyons exits.*)

TROY: Is supper ready, woman? Me and you got some business to take care of. I'm gonna tear it up too.

ROSE: Troy, I done told you now! [p. 60]

TROY (*puts his arm around Bono*): Aw hell, woman . . . this is Bono. Bono like family. I done known this nigger since . . . how long I done know you?

BONO: It's been a long time.

TROY: I done known this nigger since Skippy was a pup. Me and him done been through some times.

BONO: You sure right about that.

TROY: Hell, I done know him longer than I known you. And we still standing shoulder to shoulder. Hey, look here, Bono . . . a man can't ask for no more than that.

(*Drinks to him.*)

I love you, nigger.

BONO: Hell, I love you too . . . but I got to get home see my woman. You got yours in hand. I got to go get mine.

(*Bono starts to exit as Cory enters the yard, dressed in his football uniform. He gives Troy a hard, uncompromising look.*)

CORY: What you do that for, Pop?

(*He throws his helmet down in the direction of Troy.*)

ROSE: What's the matter? Cory . . . what's the matter?

CORY: Papa done went up to the school and told Coach Zellman I can't play football no more. Wouldn't even let me play the game. Told him to tell the recruiter not to come.

ROSE: Troy . . .

TROY: What you Troying me for. Yeah, I did it. And the boy know why I did it. [p. 61]

CORY: Why you wanna do that to me? That was the one chance I had.

ROSE: Ain't nothing wrong with Cory playing football, Troy.

TROY: The boy lied to me. I told the nigger if he wanna play football . . . to keep up his chores and hold down that job at the A&P. That was the conditions. Stopped down there to see Mr. Stawicki . . .

CORY: I can't work after school during the football season, Pop! I tried to tell you that Mr. Stawicki's holding my job for me. You don't never want to listen to nobody. And then you wanna go and do this to me!

TROY: I ain't done nothing to you. You done it to yourself.

CORY: Just cause you didn't have a chance! You just scared I'm gonna be better than you, that's all.

TROY: Come here.

ROSE: Troy . . .

(*Cory reluctantly crosses over to Troy.*)

TROY: Alright! See. You done made a mistake.

CORY: I didn't even do nothing!

TROY: I'm gonna tell you what your mistake was. See . . . you swung at the ball and didn't hit it. That's strike one. See, you in the batter's box now. You swung and you missed. That's strike one. Don't you strike out!

(*Lights fade to black.*) [p. 62]

ACT TWO / Scene One

The following morning. Cory is at the tree hitting the ball with the bat. He tries to mimic Troy, but his swing is awkward, less sure. Rose enters from the house.

ROSE: Cory, I want you to help me with this cupboard.

CORY: I ain't quitting the team. I don't care what Poppa say.

ROSE: I'll talk to him when he gets back. He had to go see about your Uncle Gabe. The police done arrested him. Say he was disturbing the peace. He'll be back directly. Come on in here and help me clean out the top of this cupboard.

(Cory exits into the house. Rose sees Troy and Bono coming down the alley.)

Troy . . . what they say down there?

TROY: Ain't said nothing. I give them fifty dollars and they let him go. I'll talk to you about it. Where's Cory?

ROSE: He's in there helping me clean out these cupboards.

TROY: Tell him to get his butt out here.

(Troy and Bono go over to the pile of wood. Bono picks up the saw and begins sawing.) [p. 65]

TROY *(to Bono)*: All they want is the money. That makes six or seven times I done went down there and got him. See me coming they stick out their *hands*.

BONO: Yeah. I know what you mean. That's all they care about . . . that money. They don't care about what's right.

(Pause.)

Nigger, why you got to go and get some hard wood? You ain't doing nothing but building a little old fence. Get you some soft pine wood. That's all you need.

TROY: I know what I'm doing. This is outside wood. You put pine wood inside the house. Pine wood is inside wood. This here is outside wood. Now you tell me where the fence is gonna be?

BONO: You don't need this wood. You can put it up with pine wood and it'll stand as long as you gonna be here looking at it.

TROY: How you know how long I'm gonna be here, nigger? Hell, I might just live forever. Live longer than old man Horsely.

BONO: That's what Magee used to say.

TROY: Magee's a damn fool. Now you tell me who you ever heard of gonna pull their own teeth with a pair of rusty pliers.

BONO: The old folks . . . my granddaddy used to pull his teeth with pliers. They ain't had no dentists for the colored folks back then.

TROY: Get clean pliers! You understand? Clean pliers! Sterilize them! Besides we ain't living back then. All Magee had to do was walk over to Doc Goldblum's. [p. 66]

BONO: I see where you and that Tallahassee gal . . . that Alberta . . . I see where you all done got tight.

TROY: What you mean "got tight"?

BONO: I see where you be laughing and joking with her all the time.

TROY: I laughs and jokes with all of them, Bono. You know me.

BONO: That ain't the kind of laughing and joking I'm talking about.

(Cory enters from the house.)

CORY: How you doing, Mr. Bono?

TROY: Cory? Get that saw from Bono and cut some wood. He talking about the wood's too hard to cut. Stand back there, Jim, and let that young boy show you how it's done.

BONO: He's sure welcome to it.

(*Cory takes the saw and begins to cut the wood.*)

Whew-e-e! Look at that. Big old strong boy. Look like Joe Louis.° Hell, must be getting old the way I'm watching that boy whip through that wood.

CORY: I don't see why Mama want a fence around the yard noways.

TROY: Damn if I know either. What the hell she keeping out with it? She ain't got nothing nobody want.

BONO: Some people build fences to keep people out . . . and other people build fences to keep people in. Rose wants to hold on to you all. She loves you. [p. 67]

TROY: Hell, nigger, I don't need nobody to tell me my wife loves me. Cory . . . go on in the house and see if you can find that other saw.

CORY: Where's it at?

TROY: I said find it! Look for it till you find it!

(*Cory exits into the house.*)

What's that supposed to mean? Wanna keep us in?

BONO: Troy . . . I done known you seem like damn near my whole life. You and Rose both. I done know both of you all for a long time. I remember when you met Rose. When you was hitting them baseball out the park. A lot of them old gals was after you then. You had the pick of the litter. When you picked Rose, I was happy for you. That was the first time I knew you had any sense. I said . . . My man Troy knows what he's doing . . . I'm gonna follow this nigger . . . he might take me somewhere. I been following you too. I done learned a whole heap of things about life watching you. I done learned how to tell where the shit lies. How to tell it from the alfalfa. You done learned me a lot of things. You showed me how to not make the same mistakes . . . to take life as it comes along and keep putting one foot in front of the other.

(*Pause.*)

Rose a good woman, Troy.

TROY: Hell, nigger, I know she a good woman. I been married to her for eighteen years. What you got on your mind, Bono?

BONO: I just say she a good woman. Just like I say anything. I ain't got to have nothing on my mind.

TROY: You just gonna say she a good woman and leave it hanging out there like that? Why you telling me she a good woman? [p. 68]

BONO: She loves you, Troy. Rose loves you.

TROY: You saying I don't measure up. That's what you trying to say. I don't measure up cause I'm seeing this other gal. I know what you trying to say.

Joe Louis: Joseph Louis Barrow (1914–1981), African American boxer, was known as the "Brown Bomber" and held the world heavyweight title from 1937 to 1949, longer than any other man in history.

BONO: I know what Rose means to you, Troy. I'm just trying to say I don't want to see you mess up.

TROY: Yeah, I appreciate that, Bono. If you was messing around on Lucille I'd be telling you the same thing.

BONO: Well, that's all I got to say. I just say that because I love you both.

TROY: Hell, you know me... I wasn't out there looking for nothing. You can't find a better woman than Rose. I know that. But seems like this woman just stuck onto me where I can't shake her loose. I done wrestled with it, tried to throw her off me... but she just stuck on tighter. Now she's stuck on for good.

BONO: You's in control... that's what you tell me all the time. You responsible for what you do.

TROY: I ain't ducking the responsibility of it. As long as it sets right in my heart... then I'm okay. Cause that's all I listen to. It'll tell me right from wrong every time. And I ain't talking about doing Rose no bad turn. I love Rose. She done carried me a long ways and I love and respect her for that.

BONO: I know you do. That's why I don't want to see you hurt her. But what you gonna do when she find out? What you got then? If you try and juggle both of them... sooner or later you gonna drop one of them. That's common sense. [p. 69]

TROY: Yeah, I hear what you saying, Bono. I been trying to figure a way to work it out.

BONO: Work it out right, Troy. I don't want to be getting all up between you and Rose's business... but work it so it come out right.

TROY: Aw hell, I get all up between you and Lucille's business. When you gonna get that woman that refrigerator she been wanting? Don't tell me you ain't got no money now. I know who your banker is. Mellon don't need that money bad as Lucille want that refrigerator. I'll tell you that.

BONO: Tell you what I'll do... when you finish building this fence for Rose... I'll buy Lucille that refrigerator.

TROY: You done stuck your foot in your mouth now!

(Troy grabs up a board and begins to saw. Bono starts to walk out the yard.)

Hey, nigger... where you going?

BONO: I'm going home. I know you don't expect me to help you now. I'm protecting my money. I wanna see you put that fence up by yourself. That's what I want to see. You'll be here another six months without me.

TROY: Nigger, you ain't right.

BONO: When it comes to my money... I'm right as fireworks on the Fourth of July.

TROY: Alright, we gonna see now. You better get out your bankbook.

(Bono exits, and Troy continues to work. Rose enters from the house.) [p. 70]

ROSE: What they say down there? What's happening with Gabe?

TROY: I went down there and got him out. Cost me fifty dollars. Say he was disturbing the peace. Judge set up a hearing for him in three weeks. Say to show cause why he shouldn't be recommitted.

ROSE: What was he doing that cause them to arrest him?

TROY: Some kids was teasing him and he run them off home. Say he was howling and carrying on. Some folks seen him and called the police. That's all it was.

ROSE: Well, what's you say? What'd you tell the judge?

TROY: Told him I'd look after him. It didn't make no sense to recommit the man. He stuck out his big greasy palm and told me to give him fifty dollars and take him on home.

ROSE: Where's he at now? Where'd he go off to?

TROY: He's gone about his business. He don't need nobody to hold his hand.

ROSE: Well, I don't know. Seem like that would be the best place for him if they did put him into the hospital. I know what you're gonna say. But that's what I think would be best.

TROY: The man done had his life ruined fighting for what? And they wanna take and lock him up. Let him be free. He don't bother nobody.

ROSE: Well, everybody got their own way of looking at it I guess. Come on and get your lunch. I got a bowl of lima [p. 71] beans and some cornbread in the oven. Come and get something to eat. Ain't no sense you fretting over Gabe.

(*Rose turns to go into the house.*)

TROY: Rose . . . got something to tell you.

ROSE: Well, come on . . . wait till I get this food on the table.

TROY: Rose!

(*She stops and turns around.*)

I don't know how to say this.

(*Pause.*)

I can't explain it none. It just sort of grows on you till it gets out of hand. It starts out like a little bush . . . and the next thing you know it's a whole forest.

ROSE: Troy . . . what is you talking about?

TROY: I'm talking, woman, let me talk. I'm trying to find a way to tell you . . . I'm gonna be a daddy. I'm gonna be somebody's daddy.

ROSE: Troy . . . you're not telling me this? You're gonna be . . . what?

TROY: Rose . . . now . . . see . . .

ROSE: You telling me you gonna be somebody's daddy? You telling your *wife* this?

(*Gabriel enters from the street. He carries a rose in his hand.*)

GABRIEL: Hey, Troy! Hey, Rose!

ROSE: I have to wait eighteen years to hear something like this. [p. 72]

GABRIEL: Hey, Rose . . . I got a flower for you.

(*He hands it to her.*)

That's a rose. Same rose like you is.

ROSE: Thanks, Gabe.

GABRIEL: Troy, you ain't mad at me is you? Them bad mens come and put me away. You ain't mad at me is you?

TROY: Naw, Gabe, I ain't mad at you.

ROSE: Eighteen years and you wanna come with this.

GABRIEL (*takes a quarter out of his pocket*): See what I got? Got a brand new quarter.

TROY: Rose . . . it's just . . .

ROSE: Ain't nothing you can say, Troy. Ain't no way of explaining that.

GABRIEL: Fellow that give me this quarter had a whole mess of them. I'm gonna keep this quarter till it stop shining.

ROSE: Gabe, go on in the house there. I got some watermelon in the frigidaire. Go on and get you a piece.

GABRIEL: Say, Rose . . . you know I was chasing hellhounds and them bad mens come and get me and take me away. Troy helped me. He come down there and told them they better let me go before he beat them up. Yeah, he did!

ROSE: You go on and get you a piece of watermelon, Gabe. Them bad mens is gone now. [p. 73]

GABRIEL: Okay, Rose . . . gonna get me some watermelon. The kind with the stripes on it.

(*Gabriel exits into the house.*)

ROSE: Why, Troy? Why? After all these years to come dragging this in to me now. It don't make no sense at your age. I could have expected this ten or fifteen years ago, but not now.

TROY: Age ain't got nothing to do with it, Rose.

ROSE: I done tried to be everything a wife should be. Everything a wife could be. Been married eighteen years and I got to live to see the day you tell me you been seeing another woman and done fathered a child by her. And you know I ain't never wanted no half nothing in my family. My whole family is half. Everybody got different fathers and mothers . . . my two sisters and my brother. Can't hardly tell who's who. Can't never sit down and talk about Papa and Mama. It's your papa and your mama and my papa and my mama . . .

TROY: Rose . . . stop it now.

ROSE: I ain't never wanted that for none of my children. And now you wanna drag your behind in here and tell me something like this.

TROY: You ought to know. It's time for you to know.

ROSE: Well, I don't want to know, goddamn it!

TROY: I can't just make it go away. It's done now. I can't wish the circumstance of the thing away.

ROSE: And you don't want to either. Maybe you want to wish me and my boy away. Maybe that's what you want? Well, you can't wish us away. I've got eighteen years of my [p. 74] life invested in you. You ought to have stayed upstairs in my bed where you belong.

TROY: Rose . . . now listen to me . . . we can get a handle on this thing. We can talk this out . . . come to an understanding.

ROSE: All of a sudden it's "we." Where was "we" at when you was down there rolling around with some god-forsaken woman? "We" should have come to an understanding before you started making a damn fool of yourself. You're a day late and a dollar short when it comes to an understanding with me.

TROY: It's just . . . She gives me a different idea . . . a different understanding about myself. I can step out of this house and get away from the pressures and problems . . . be a different man. I ain't got to wonder how I'm gonna pay the bills or get the roof fixed. I can just be a part of myself that I ain't never been.

ROSE: What I want to know . . . is do you plan to continue seeing her. That's all you can say to me.

TROY: I can sit up in her house and laugh. Do you understand what I'm saying. I can laugh out loud . . . and it feels good. It reaches all the way down to the bottom of my shoes.

(*Pause.*)

Rose, I can't give that up.

ROSE: Maybe you ought to go on and stay down there with her . . . if she a better woman than me.

TROY: It ain't about nobody being a better woman or nothing. Rose, you ain't the blame. A man couldn't ask for no woman to be a better wife than you've been. I'm responsible [p. 75] for it. I done locked myself into a pattern trying to take care of you all that I forgot about myself.

ROSE: What the hell was I there for? That was my job, not somebody else's.

TROY: Rose, I done tried all my life to live decent . . . to live a clean . . . hard . . . useful life. I tried to be a good husband to you. In every way I knew how. Maybe I come into the world backwards, I don't know. But . . . you born with two strikes on you before you come to the plate. You got to guard it closely . . . always looking for the curve ball on the inside corner. You can't afford to let none get past you. You can't afford a call strike. If you going down . . . you going down swinging. Everything lined up against you. What you gonna do. I fooled them, Rose. I bunted. When I found you and Cory and a halfway decent job . . . I was safe. Couldn't nothing touch me. I wasn't gonna strike out no more. I wasn't going back to the penitentiary. I wasn't gonna lay in the streets with a bottle of wine. I was safe. I had me a family. A job. I wasn't gonna get that last strike. I was on first looking for one of them boys to knock me in. To get me home.

ROSE: You should have stayed in my bed, Troy.

TROY: Then when I saw that gal . . . she firmed up my backbone. And I got to thinking that if I tried . . . I just might be able to steal second. Do you understand after eighteen years I wanted to steal second.

ROSE: You should have held me tight. You should have grabbed me and held on.

TROY: I stood on first base for eighteen years and I thought . . . well, goddamn it . . . go on for it! [p. 76]

ROSE: We're not talking about baseball! We're talking about you going off to lay in bed with another woman . . . and then bring it home to me. That's what we're talking about. We ain't talking about no baseball.

TROY: Rose, you're not listening to me. I'm trying the best I can to explain it to you. It's not easy for me to admit that I been standing in the same place for eighteen years.

ROSE: I been standing with you! I been right here with you, Troy. I got a life too. I gave eighteen years of my life to stand in the same spot with you. Don't you think I ever wanted other things? Don't you think I had dreams and hopes? What about my life? What about me? Don't you think it ever crossed my mind to want to know other men? That I wanted to lay up somewhere and forget about my responsibilities? That I wanted someone to make me laugh so I could feel good? You not the only one who's got wants and needs. But I held on to you, Troy. I took all my feelings, my wants and needs, my dreams . . . and I buried them inside you. I planted a seed and watched and prayed over it. I planted myself inside you and waited to bloom. And it didn't take me no eighteen years to find out the soil was hard and rocky and it wasn't never gonna bloom.

But I held on to you, Troy. I held you tighter. You was my husband. I owed you everything I had. Every part of me I could find to give you. And upstairs in that room . . . with the darkness falling in on me . . . I gave everything I had to try and erase the doubt that you wasn't the finest man in the world. And wherever you was going . . . I wanted to be there with you. Cause you was my husband. Cause that's the only way I was gonna survive as your wife. You always talking about what you give . . . and what you don't have to give. But you take too. You take . . . and don't even know nobody's giving!

(Rose turns to exit into the house; Troy grabs her arm.) [p. 77]

TROY: You say I take and don't give!

ROSE: Troy! You're hurting me!

TROY: You say I take and don't give.

ROSE: Troy . . . you're hurting my arm! Let go!

TROY: I done give you everything I got. Don't you tell that lie on me.

ROSE: Troy!

TROY: Don't you tell that lie on me!

(Cory enters from the house.)

CORY: Mama!

ROSE: Troy. You're hurting me.

TROY: Don't you tell me about no taking and giving.

(Cory comes up behind Troy and grabs him. Troy, surprised, is thrown off balance just as Cory throws a glancing blow that catches him on the chest and knocks him down. Troy is stunned, as is Cory.)

ROSE: Troy. Troy. No!

(Troy gets to his feet and starts at Cory.)

Troy . . . no. Please! Troy!

(*Rose pulls on Troy to hold him back. Troy stops himself.*)

TROY (*to Cory*): Alright. That's strike two. You stay away from around me, boy. Don't you strike out. You living with a full count. Don't you strike out.

(*Troy exits out the yard as the lights go down.*) [p. 78]

Scene Two

It is six months later, early afternoon. Troy enters from the house and starts to exit the yard. Rose enters from the house.

ROSE: Troy, I want to talk to you.

TROY: All of a sudden, after all this time, you want to talk to me, huh? You ain't wanted to talk to me for months. You ain't wanted to talk to me last night. You ain't wanted no part of me then. What you wanna talk to me about now?

ROSE: Tomorrow's Friday.

TROY: I know what day tomorrow is. You think I don't know tomorrow's Friday? My whole life I ain't done nothing but look to see Friday coming and you got to tell me it's Friday.

ROSE: I want to know if you're coming home.

TROY: I always come home, Rose. You know that. There ain't never been a night I ain't come home.

ROSE: That ain't what I mean . . . and you know it. I want to know if you're coming straight home after work.

TROY: I figure I'd cash my check . . . hang out at Taylors' with the boys . . . maybe play a game of checkers . . . [p. 79]

ROSE: Troy, I can't live like this. I won't live like this. You livin' on borrowed time with me. It's been going on six months now you ain't been coming home.

TROY: I be here every night. Every night of the year. That's 365 days.

ROSE: I want you to come home tomorrow after work.

TROY: Rose . . . I don't mess up my pay. You know that now. I take my pay and I give it to you. I don't have no money but what you give me back. I just want to have a little time to myself . . . a little time to enjoy life.

ROSE: What about me? When's my time to enjoy life?

TROY: I don't know what to tell you, Rose. I'm doing the best I can.

ROSE: You ain't been home from work but time enough to change your clothes and run out . . . and you wanna call that the best you can do?

TROY: I'm going over to the hospital to see Alberta. She went into the hospital this afternoon. Look like she might have the baby early. I won't be gone long.

ROSE: Well, you ought to know. They went over to Miss Pearl's and got Gabe today. She said you told them to go ahead and lock him up.

TROY: I ain't said no such thing. Whoever told you that is telling a lie. Pearl ain't doing nothing but telling a big fat lie.

ROSE: She ain't had to tell me. I read it on the papers.

TROY: I ain't told them nothing of the kind. [p. 80]

ROSE: I saw it right there on the papers.

TROY: What it say, huh?

ROSE: It said you told them to take him.

TROY: Then they screwed that up, just the way they screw up everything. I ain't worried about what they got on the paper.

ROSE: Say the government send part of his check to the hospital and the other part to you.

TROY: I ain't got nothing to do with that if that's the way it works. I ain't made up the rules about how it work.

ROSE: You did Gabe just like you did Cory. You wouldn't sign the paper for Cory . . . but you signed for Gabe. You signed that paper.

(*The telephone is heard ringing inside the house.*)

TROY: I told you I ain't signed nothing, woman! The only thing I signed was the release form. Hell, I can't read, I don't know what they had on that paper! I ain't signed nothing about sending Gabe away.

ROSE: I said send him to the hospital . . . you said let him be free . . . now you done went down there and signed him to the hospital for half his money. You went back on yourself, Troy. You gonna have to answer for that.

TROY: See now . . . you been over there talking to Miss Pearl. She done got mad cause she ain't getting Gabe's rent money. That's all it is. She's liable to say anything.

ROSE: Troy, I seen where you signed the paper. [p. 81]

TROY: You ain't seen nothing I signed. What she doing got papers on my brother anyway? Miss Pearl telling a big fat lie. And I'm gonna tell her about it too! You ain't seen nothing I signed. Say . . . you ain't seen nothing I signed.

(*Rose exits into the house to answer the telephone. Presently she returns.*)

ROSE: Troy . . . that was the hospital. Alberta had the baby.

TROY: What she have? What is it?

ROSE: It's a girl.

TROY: I better get on down to the hospital to see her.

ROSE: Troy . . .

TROY: Rose . . . I got to go see her now. That's only right . . . what's the matter . . . the baby's all right, ain't it?

ROSE: Alberta died having the baby.

TROY: Died . . . you say she's dead? Alberta's dead?

ROSE: They said they done all they could. They couldn't do nothing for her.

TROY: The baby? How's the baby?

ROSE: They say it's healthy. I wonder who's gonna bury her.

TROY: She had family, Rose. She wasn't living in the world by herself.

ROSE: I know she wasn't living in the world by herself. [p. 82]

TROY: Next thing you gonna want to know if she had any insurance.

ROSE: Troy, you ain't got to talk like that.

TROY: That's the first thing that jumped out your mouth. "Who's gonna bury her?" Like I'm fixing to take on that task for myself.

ROSE: I am your wife. Don't push me away.

TROY: I ain't pushing nobody away. Just give me some space. That's all. Just give me some room to breathe.

(*Rose exits into the house. Troy walks about the yard.*)

TROY (*with a quiet rage that threatens to consume him*): Alright . . . Mr. Death. See now . . . I'm gonna tell you what I'm gonna do. I'm gonna take and build me a fence around this yard. See? I'm gonna build me a fence around what belongs to me. And then I want you to stay on the other side. See? You stay over there until you're ready for me. Then you come on. Bring your army. Bring your sickle. Bring your wrestling clothes. I ain't gonna fall down on my vigilance this time. You ain't gonna sneak up on me no more. When you ready for me . . . when the top of your list say Troy Maxson . . . that's when you come around here. You come up and knock on the front door. Ain't nobody else got nothing to do with this. This is between you and me. Man to man. You stay on the other side of that fence until you ready for me. Then you come up and knock on the front door. Anytime you want. I'll be ready for you.

(*The lights go down to black.*) [p. 83]

Scene Three

The lights come up on the porch. It is late evening three days later. Rose sits listening to the ball game waiting for Troy. The final out of the game is made and Rose switches off the radio. Troy enters the yard carrying an infant wrapped in blankets. He stands back from the house and calls.

(*Rose enters and stands on the porch. There is a long, awkward silence, the weight of which grows heavier with each passing second.*)

TROY: Rose . . . I'm standing here with my daughter in my arms. She ain't but a wee bittie little old thing. She don't know nothing about grownups' business. She innocent . . . and she ain't got no mama.

ROSE: What you telling me for, Troy?

(*She turns and exits into the house.*)

TROY: Well . . . I guess we'll just sit out here on the porch.

(*He sits down on the porch. There is an awkward indelicateness about the way he handles the baby. His largeness engulfs and seems to swallow it. He speaks loud enough for Rose to hear.*)

A man's got to do what's right for him. I ain't sorry for nothing I done. It felt right in my heart.

(*To the baby.*)

What you smiling at? Your daddy's a big man. Got these great big old hands. But sometimes he's scared. And right [p. 85] now your daddy's scared cause we sitting out here and ain't got no home. Oh, I been homeless before. I ain't had no little baby with me. But I been homeless. You just be out on the road by your lonesome and you see one of them trains coming and you just kinda go like this . . .

(*He sings as a lullaby.*)

Please, Mr. Engineer let a man ride the line
Please, Mr. Engineer let a man ride the line
I ain't got no ticket please let me ride the blinds

(*Rose enters from the house. Troy, hearing her steps behind him, stands and faces her.*)

She's my daughter, Rose. My own flesh and blood. I can't deny her no more than I can deny them boys.

(*Pause.*)

You and them boys is my family. You and them and this child is all I got in the world. So I guess what I'm saying is . . . I'd appreciate it if you'd help me take care of her.

ROSE: Okay, Troy . . . you're right. I'll take care of your baby for you . . . cause . . . like you say . . . she's innocent . . . and you can't visit the sins of the father upon the child. A motherless child has got a hard time.

(*She takes the baby from him.*)

From right now . . . this child got a mother. But you a womanless man.

(*Rose turns and exits into the house with the baby. Lights go down to black.*) [p. 86]

Scene Four

It is two months later. Lyons enters from the street. He knocks on the door and calls.

LYONS: Hey, Rose! (*Pause.*) Rose!

ROSE (*from inside the house*): Stop that yelling. You gonna wake up Raynell. I just got her to sleep.

LYONS: I just stopped by to pay Papa this twenty dollars I owe him. Where's Papa at?

ROSE: He should be here in a minute. I'm getting ready to go down to the church. Sit down and wait on him.

LYONS: I got to go pick up Bonnie over her mother's house.

ROSE: Well, sit it down there on the table. He'll get it.

LYONS (*enters the house and sets the money on the table*): Tell Papa I said thanks. I'll see you again.

ROSE: Alright, Lyons. We'll see you.

(*Lyons starts to exit as Cory enters.*)

CORY: Hey, Lyons. [p. 87]

LYONS: What's happening, Cory? Say man, I'm sorry I missed your graduation. You know I had a gig and couldn't get away. Otherwise, I would have been there, man. So what you doing?

CORY: I'm trying to find a job.

LYONS: Yeah I know how that go, man. It's rough out here. Jobs are scarce.

CORY: Yeah, I know.

LYONS: Look here, I got to run. Talk to Papa . . . he know some people. He'll be able to help get you a job. Talk to him . . . see what he say.

CORY: Yeah . . . alright, Lyons.

LYONS: You take care. I'll talk to you soon. We'll find some time to talk.

(*Lyons exits the yard. Cory wanders over to the tree, picks up the bat, and assumes a batting stance. He studies an imaginary pitcher and swings. Dissatisfied with the result, he tries again. Troy enters. They eye each other for a beat. Cory puts the bat down and exits the yard. Troy starts into the house as Rose exits with Raynell. She is carrying a cake.*)

TROY: I'm coming in and everybody's going out.

ROSE: I'm taking this cake down to the church for the bakesale. Lyons was by to see you. He stopped by to pay you your twenty dollars. It's laying in there on the table.

TROY (*going into his pocket*): Well . . . here go this money. [p. 88]

ROSE: Put it in there on the table, Troy. I'll get it.

TROY: What time you coming back?

ROSE: Ain't no use in you studying me. It don't matter what time I come back.

TROY: I just asked you a question, woman. What's the matter . . . can't I ask you a question?

ROSE: Troy, I don't want to go into it. Your dinner's in there on the stove. All you got to do is heat it up. And don't you be eating the rest of them cakes in there. I'm coming back for them. We having a bakesale at the church tomorrow.

(*Rose exits the yard. Troy sits down on the steps, takes a pint bottle from his pocket, opens it, and drinks. He begins to sing.*)

TROY: Hear it ring! Hear it ring!
    Had an old dog his name was Blue
    You know Blue was mighty true
    You know Blue was a good old dog
    Blue trees a possum in a hollow log
    You know from that he was a good old dog

(*Bono enters the yard.*)

BONO: Hey, Troy.

TROY: Hey, what's happening, Bono?

BONO: I just thought I'd stop by to see you.

TROY: What you stop by and see me for? You ain't stopped by in a month of Sundays. Hell, I must owe you money or something. [p. 89]

BONO: Since you got your promotion I can't keep up with you. Used to see you every day. Now I don't even know what route you working.

TROY: They keep switching me around. Got me out in Greentree now . . . hauling white folks' garbage.

BONO: Greentree, huh? You lucky, at least you ain't got to be lifting them barrels. Damn if they ain't getting heavier. I'm gonna put in my two years and call it quits.

TROY: I'm thinking about retiring myself.

BONO: You got it easy. You can *drive* for another five years.

TROY: It ain't the same, Bono. It ain't like working the back of the truck. Ain't got nobody to talk to . . . feel like you working by yourself. Naw, I'm thinking about retiring. How's Lucille?

BONO: She alright. Her arthritis get to acting up on her sometime. Saw Rose on my way in. She going down to the church, huh?

TROY: Yeah, she took up going down there. All them preachers looking for somebody to fatten their pockets.

(Pause.)

Got some gin here.

BONO: Naw, thanks. I just stopped by to say hello.

TROY: Hell, nigger . . . you can take a drink. I ain't never known you to say no to a drink. You ain't got to work tomorrow.

BONO: I just stopped by. I'm fixing to go over to Skinner's. We got us a domino game going over his house every Friday. [p. 90]

TROY: Nigger, you can't play no dominoes. I used to whup you four games out of five.

BONO: Well, that learned me. I'm getting better.

TROY: Yeah? Well, that's alright.

BONO: Look here . . . I got to be getting on. Stop by sometime, huh?

TROY: Yeah, I'll do that, Bono. Lucille told Rose you bought her a new refrigerator.

BONO: Yeah, Rose told Lucille you had finally built your fence . . . so I figured we'd call it even.

TROY: I knew you would.

BONO: Yeah . . . okay. I'll be talking to you.

TROY: Yeah, take care, Bono. Good to see you. I'm gonna stop over.

BONO: Yeah. Okay, Troy.

(Bono exits. Troy drinks from the bottle.)

TROY: Old Blue died and I dig his grave
　　Let him down with a golden chain
　　Every night when I hear old Blue bark

I know Blue treed a possum in Noah's Ark.
Hear it ring! Hear it ring!

(*Cory enters the yard. They eye each other for a beat. Troy is sitting in the middle of the steps. Cory walks over.*)

CORY: I got to get by. [p. 91]

TROY: Say what? What's you say?

CORY: You in my way. I got to get by.

TROY: You got to get by where? This is my house. Bought and paid for. In full. Took me fifteen years. And if you wanna go in my house and I'm sitting on the steps . . . you say excuse me. Like your mama taught you.

CORY: Come on, Pop . . . I got to get by.

(*Cory starts to maneuver his way past Troy. Troy grabs his leg and shoves him back.*)

TROY: You just gonna walk over top of me?

CORY: I live here too!

TROY (*advancing toward him*): You just gonna walk over top of me in my own house?

CORY: I ain't scared of you.

TROY: I ain't asked if you was scared of me. I asked you if you was fixing to walk over top of me in my own house? That's the question. You ain't gonna say excuse me? You just gonna walk over top of me?

CORY: If you wanna put it like that.

TROY: How else am I gonna put it?

CORY: I was walking by you to go into the house cause you sitting on the steps drunk, singing to yourself. You can put it like that.

TROY: Without saying excuse me???

(*Cory doesn't respond.*)

I asked you a question. Without saying excuse me??? [p. 92]

CORY: I ain't got to say excuse me to you. You don't count around here no more.

TROY: Oh, I see . . . I don't count around here no more. You ain't got to say excuse me to your daddy. All of a sudden you done got so grown that your daddy don't count around here no more . . . Around here in his own house and yard that he done paid for with the sweat of his brow. You done got so grown to where you gonna take over. You gonna take over my house. Is that right? You gonna wear my pants. You gonna go in there and stretch out on my bed. You ain't got to say excuse me cause I don't count around here no more. Is that right?

CORY: That's right. You always talking this dumb stuff. Now, why don't you just get out my way.

TROY: I guess you got someplace to sleep and something to put in your belly. You got that, huh? You got that? That's what you need. You got that, huh?

CORY: You don't know what I got. You ain't got to worry about what I got.

TROY: You right! You one hundred percent right! I done spent the last seventeen years worrying about what you got. Now it's your turn, see? I'll tell you what to do. You grown . . . we done established that. You a man. Now, let's see you act like one. Turn your behind around and walk out this yard. And when you get out there in the alley . . . you can forget about this house. See? Cause this is my house. You go on and be a man and get your own house. You can forget about this. Cause this is mine. You go on and get yours cause I'm through with doing for you.

CORY: You talking about what you did for me . . . what'd you ever give me? [p. 93]

TROY: Them feet and bones! That pumping heart, nigger! I give you more than anybody else is ever gonna give you.

CORY: You ain't never gave me nothing! You ain't never done nothing but hold me back. Afraid I was gonna be better than you. All you ever did was try and make me scared of you. I used to tremble every time you called my name. Every time I heard your footsteps in the house. Wondering all the time . . . what's Papa gonna say if I do this? . . . What's he gonna say if I do that? . . . What's Papa gonna say if I turn on the radio? And Mama, too . . . she tries . . . but she's scared of you.

TROY: You leave your mama out of this. She ain't got nothing to do with this.

CORY: I don't know how she stand you . . . after what you did to her.

TROY: I told you to leave your mama out of this!

(He advances toward Cory.)

CORY: What you gonna do . . . give me a whupping? You can't whup me no more. You're too old. You just an old man.

TROY *(shoves him on his shoulder)*: Nigger! That's what you are. You just another nigger on the street to me!

CORY: You crazy! You know that?

TROY: Go on now! You got the devil in you. Get on away from me!

CORY: You just a crazy old man . . . talking about I got the devil in me.

TROY: Yeah, I'm crazy! If you don't get on the other side of that yard . . . I'm gonna show you how crazy I am! Go on . . . get the hell out of my yard. [p. 94]

CORY: It ain't your yard. You took Uncle Gabe's money he got from the army to buy this house and then you put him out.

TROY *(advances on Cory)*: Get your black ass out of my yard!

(Troy's advance backs Cory up against the tree. Cory grabs up the bat.)

CORY: I ain't going nowhere! Come on . . . put me out! I ain't scared of you.

TROY: That's my bat!

CORY: Come on!

TROY: Put my bat down!

CORY: Come on, put me out.

(Cory swings at Troy, who backs across the yard.)

What's the matter? You so bad . . . put me out!

(Troy advances toward Cory.)

CORY *(backing up)*: Come on! Come on!

TROY: You're gonna have to use it! You wanna draw that bat back on me . . . you're gonna have to use it.

CORY: Come on! . . . Come on!

(*Cory swings the bat at Troy a second time. He misses. Troy continues to advance toward him.*)

TROY: You're gonna have to kill me! You wanna draw that bat back on me. You're gonna have to kill me. [p. 95]

(*Cory, backed up against the tree, can go no farther. Troy taunts him. He sticks out his head and offers him a target.*)

Come on! Come on!

(*Cory is unable to swing the bat. Troy grabs it.*)

TROY: Then I'll show you.

(*Cory and Troy struggle over the bat. The struggle is fierce and fully engaged. Troy ultimately is the stronger and takes the bat from Cory and stands over him ready to swing. He stops himself.*)

Go on and get away from around my house.

(*Cory, stung by his defeat, picks himself up, walks slowly out of the yard and up the alley.*)

CORY: Tell Mama I'll be back for my things.

TROY: They'll be on the other side of that fence.

(*Cory exits.*)

TROY: I can't taste nothing. Helluljah! I can't taste nothing no more. (*Troy assumes a batting posture and begins to taunt Death, the fastball on the outside corner.*) Come on! It's between you and me now! Come on! Anytime you want! Come on! I be ready for you . . . but I ain't gonna be easy.

(*The lights go down on the scene.*) [p. 96]

Scene Five

The time is 1965. The lights come up in the yard. It is the morning of Troy's funeral. A funeral plaque with a light hangs beside the door. There is a small garden plot off to the side. There is noise and activity in the house as Rose, Gabriel, and Bono have gathered. The door opens and Raynell, seven years old, enters dressed in a flannel nightgown. She crosses to the garden and pokes around with a stick. Rose calls from the house.

ROSE: Raynell!

RAYNELL: Mam?

ROSE: What you doing out there?

RAYNELL: Nothing.

(*Rose comes to the door.*)

ROSE: Girl, get in here and get dressed. What you doing?

RAYNELL: Seeing if my garden growed.

ROSE: I told you it ain't gonna grow overnight. You got to wait.

RAYNELL: It don't look like it never gonna grow. Dag! [p. 97]

ROSE: I told you a watched pot never boils. Get in here and get dressed.

RAYNELL: This ain't even no pot, Mama.

ROSE: You just have to give it a chance. It'll grow. Now you come on and do what I told you. We got to be getting ready. This ain't no morning to be playing around. You hear me?

RAYNELL: Yes, mam.

(*Rose exits into the house. Raynell continues to poke at her garden with a stick. Cory enters. He is dressed in a Marine corporal's uniform, and carries a duffel bag. His posture is that of a military man, and his speech has a clipped sternness.*)

CORY (*to Raynell*): Hi.

(*Pause.*)

I bet your name is Raynell.

RAYNELL: Uh huh.

CORY: Is your mama home?

(*Raynell runs up on the porch and calls through the screendoor.*)

RAYNELL: Mama . . . there's some man out here. Mama?

(*Rose comes to the door.*)

ROSE: Cory? Lord have mercy! Look here, you all!

(*Rose and Cory embrace in a tearful reunion as Bono and Lyons enter from the house dressed in funeral clothes.*)

BONO: Aw, looka here . . . [p. 98]

ROSE: Done got all grown up!

CORY: Don't cry, Mama. What you crying about?

ROSE: I'm just so glad you made it.

CORY: Hey Lyons. How you doing, Mr. Bono.

(*Lyons goes to embrace Cory.*)

LYONS: Look at you, man. Look at you. Don't he look good, Rose. Got them Corporal stripes.

ROSE: What took you so long.

CORY: You know how the Marines are, Mama. They got to get all their paper-work straight before they let you do anything.

ROSE: Well, I'm sure glad you made it. They let Lyons come. Your Uncle Gabe's still in the hospital. They don't know if they gonna let him out or not. I just talked to them a little while ago.

LYONS: A Corporal in the United States Marines.

BONO: Your daddy knew you had it in you. He used to tell me all the time.

LYONS: Don't he look good, Mr. Bono?

BONO: Yeah, he remind me of Troy when I first met him.

(*Pause.*)

> Say, Rose, Lucille's down at the church with the choir. I'm gonna go down and get the pallbearers lined up. I'll be back to get you all.

ROSE: Thanks, Jim. [p. 99]

CORY: See you, Mr. Bono.

LYONS (*with his arm around Raynell*): Cory . . . look at Raynell. Ain't she precious? She gonna break a whole lot of hearts.

ROSE: Raynell, come and say hello to your brother. This is your brother, Cory. You remember Cory.

RAYNELL: No, Mam.

CORY: She don't remember me, Mama.

ROSE: Well, we talk about you. She heard us talk about you. (*To Raynell.*) This is your brother, Cory. Come on and say hello.

RAYNELL: Hi.

CORY: Hi. So you're Raynell. Mama told me a lot about you.

ROSE: You all come on into the house and let me fix you some breakfast. Keep up your strength.

CORY: I ain't hungry, Mama.

LYONS: You can fix me something, Rose. I'll be in there in a minute.

ROSE: Cory, you sure you don't want nothing? I know they ain't feeding you right.

CORY: No, Mama . . . thanks. I don't feel like eating. I'll get something later.

ROSE: Raynell . . . get on upstairs and get that dress on like I told you. [p. 100]

(*Rose and Raynell exit into the house.*)

LYONS: So . . . I hear you thinking about getting married.

CORY: Yeah, I done found the right one, Lyons. It's about time.

LYONS: Me and Bonnie been split up about four years now. About the time Papa retired. I guess she just got tired of all them changes I was putting her through.

(*Pause.*)

> I always knew you was gonna make something out yourself. Your head was always in the right direction. So . . . you gonna stay in . . . make it a career . . . put in your twenty years?

CORY: I don't know. I got six already, I think that's enough.

LYONS: Stick with Uncle Sam and retire early. Ain't nothing out here. I guess Rose told you what happened with me. They got me down the workhouse. I thought I was being slick cashing other people's checks.

CORY: How much time you doing?

LYONS: They give me three years. I got that beat now. I ain't got but nine more months. It ain't so bad. You learn to deal with it like anything else. You got to take the crookeds with the straights. That's what Papa used to say. He used to say that when he struck out. I seen him strike out three times in a row . . . and the next time up he hit the ball over the grandstand. Right out there in Homestead Field. He wasn't satisfied hitting in the seats . . . he want to hit it over everything! After the game he had two hundred people standing around waiting to shake his hand. You got to take the crookeds with the straights. Yeah, Papa was something else. [p. 101]

CORY: You still playing?

LYONS: Cory . . . you know I'm gonna do that. There's some fellows down there we got us a band . . . we gonna try and stay together when we get out . . . but yeah, I'm still playing. It still helps me to get out of bed in the morning. As long as it do that I'm gonna be right there playing and trying to make some sense out of it.

ROSE (*calling*): Lyons, I got these eggs in the pan.

LYONS: Let me go on and get these eggs, man. Get ready to go bury Papa.

(*Pause.*)

How you doing? You doing alright?

(*Cory nods. Lyons touches him on the shoulder and they share a moment of silent grief. Lyons exits into the house. Cory wanders about the yard. Raynell enters.*)

RAYNELL: Hi.

CORY: Hi.

RAYNELL: Did you used to sleep in my room?

CORY: Yeah . . . that used to be my room.

RAYNELL: That's what Papa call it. "Cory's room." It got your football in the closet.

(*Rose comes to the door.*)

ROSE: Raynell, get in there and get them good shoes on.

RAYNELL: Mama, can't I wear these? Them other one hurt my feet. [p. 102]

ROSE: Well, they just gonna have to hurt your feet for a while. You ain't said they hurt your feet when you went down to the store and got them.

RAYNELL: They didn't hurt then. My feet done got bigger.

ROSE: Don't you give me no backtalk now. You get in there and get them shoes on.

(*Raynell exits into the house.*)

Ain't too much changed. He still got that piece of rag tied to that tree. He was out here swinging that bat. I was just ready to go back in the house. He swung that bat and then he just fell over. Seem like he swung it and stood there with this grin on his face . . . and then he just fell over. They carried him on down to the hospital, but I knew there wasn't no need . . . why don't you come on in the house?

CORY: Mama . . . I got something to tell you. I don't know how to tell you this . . . but I've got to tell you . . . I'm not going to Papa's funeral.

ROSE: Boy, hush your mouth. That's your daddy you talking about. I don't want hear that kind of talk this morning. I done raised you to come to this? You standing there all healthy and grown talking about you ain't going to your daddy's funeral?

CORY: Mama . . . listen . . .

ROSE: I don't want to hear it, Cory. You just get that thought out of your head.

CORY: I can't drag Papa with me everywhere I go. I've got to say no to him. One time in my life I've got to say no.

ROSE: Don't nobody have to listen to nothing like that. I know you and your daddy ain't seen eye to eye, but I ain't [p. 103] got to listen to that kind of talk this morning. Whatever was between you and your daddy . . . the time has come to put it aside. Just take it and set it over there on the shelf and forget about it. Disrespecting your daddy ain't gonna make you a man, Cory. You got to find a way to come to that on your own. Not going to your daddy's funeral ain't gonna make you a man.

CORY: The whole time I was growing up . . . living in his house . . . Papa was like a shadow that followed you everywhere. It weighed on you and sunk into your flesh. It would wrap around you and lay there until you couldn't tell which one was you anymore. That shadow digging in your flesh. Trying to crawl in. Trying to live through you. Everywhere I looked, Troy Maxson was staring back at me . . . hiding under the bed . . . in the closet. I'm just saying I've got to find a way to get rid of that shadow, Mama.

ROSE: You just like him. You got him in you good.

CORY: Don't tell me that, Mama.

ROSE: You Troy Maxson all over again.

CORY: I don't want to be Troy Maxson. I want to be me.

ROSE: You can't be nobody but who you are, Cory. That shadow wasn't nothing but you growing into yourself. You either got to grow into it or cut it down to fit you. But that's all you got to make life with. That's all you got to measure yourself against that world out there. Your daddy wanted you to be everything he wasn't . . . and at the same time he tried to make you into everything he was. I don't know if he was right or wrong . . . but I do know he meant to do more good than he meant to do harm. He wasn't always right. Sometimes when he touched he bruised. And sometimes when he took me in his arms he cut. [p. 104]

When I first met your daddy I thought . . . Here is a man I can lay down with and make a baby. That's the first thing I thought when I seen him. I was thirty years old and had done seen my share of men. But when he walked up to me and said, "I can dance a waltz that'll make you dizzy," I thought, Rose Lee, here is a man that you can open yourself up to and be filled to bursting. Here is a man that can fill all them empty spaces you been tipping around the edges of. One of them empty spaces was being somebody's mother.

I married your daddy and settled down to cooking his supper and keeping clean sheets on the bed. When your daddy walked through the house he was so big he filled it up. That was my first mistake. Not to make him leave some room for me. For my part in the matter. But at that time I wanted that. I wanted a house that I could sing in. And that's what your daddy gave me. I didn't know to keep up his strength I had to give up little pieces of mine. I did that. I took on his life as mine and mixed up the pieces so that you couldn't hardly tell which was which anymore. It was my choice. It was my life and I didn't have to live it like that. But that's what life offered me in the way of being a woman and I took it. I grabbed hold of it with both hands.

By the time Raynell came into the house, me and your daddy had done lost touch with one another. I didn't want to make my blessing off of nobody's misfortune . . . but I took on to Raynell like she was all them babies I had wanted and never had.

(The phone rings.)

Like I'd been blessed to relive a part of my life. And if the Lord see fit to keep up my strength . . . I'm gonna do her just like your daddy did you . . . I'm gonna give her the best of what's in me.

RAYNELL *(entering, still with her old shoes)*: Mama . . . Reverend Tollivier on the phone. [p. 105]

(Rose exits into the house.)

RAYNELL: Hi.

CORY: Hi.

RAYNELL: You in the Army or the Marines?

CORY: Marines.

RAYNELL: Papa said it was the Army. Did you know Blue?

CORY: Blue? Who's Blue?

RAYNELL: Papa's dog what he sing about all the time.

CORY *(singing)*: Hear it ring! Hear it ring!
I had a dog his name was Blue
You know Blue was mighty true
You know Blue was a good old dog
Blue treed a possum in a hollow log
You know from that he was a good old dog.
Hear it ring! Hear it ring!

(Raynell joins in singing.)

CORY AND RAYNELL: Blue treed a possum out on a limb
Blue looked at me and I looked at him
Grabbed that possum and put him in a sack
Blue stayed there till I came back
Old Blue's feets was big and round
Never allowed a possum to touch the ground.

Old Blue died and I dug his grave
I dug his grave with a silver spade
Let him down with a golden chain
And every night I call his name [p. 106]
Go on Blue, you good dog you
Go on Blue, you good dog you

RAYNELL: Blue laid down and died like a man
Blue laid down and died . . .

BOTH: Blue laid down and died like a man
Now he's treeing possums in the Promised Land
I'm gonna tell you this to let you know
Blue's gone where the good dogs go
When I hear old Blue bark
When I hear old Blue bark
Blue treed a possum in Noah's Ark
Blue treed a possum in Noah's Ark.

(Rose comes to the screen door.)

ROSE: Cory, we gonna be ready to go in a minute.

CORY *(to Raynell)*: You go on in the house and change them shoes like Mama
told you so we can go to Papa's funeral.

RAYNELL: Okay, I'll be back.

*(Raynell exits into the house. Cory gets up and crosses over to the tree. Rose stands
in the screen door watching him. Gabriel enters from the alley.)*

GABRIEL *(calling)*: Hey, Rose!

ROSE: Gabe?

GABRIEL: I'm here, Rose. Hey Rose, I'm here!

(Rose enters from the house.)

ROSE: Lord . . . Look here, Lyons! [p. 107]

LYONS: See, I told you, Rose . . . I told you they'd let him come.

CORY: How you doing, Uncle Gabe?

LYONS: How you doing, Uncle Gabe?

GABRIEL: Hey, Rose. It's time. It's time to tell St. Peter to open the gates. Troy,
you ready? You ready, Troy. I'm gonna tell St. Peter to open the gates. You
get ready now.

*(Gabriel, with great fanfare, braces himself to blow. The trumpet is without a
mouthpiece. He puts the end of it into his mouth and blows with great force, like a
man who has been waiting some twenty-odd years for this single moment. No sound
comes out of the trumpet. He braces himself and blows again with the same result.
A third time he blows. There is a weight of impossible description that falls away and
leaves him bare and exposed to a frightful realization. It is a trauma that a sane and
normal mind would be unable to withstand. He begins to dance. A slow, strange*

dance, eerie and life-giving. A dance of atavistic signature and ritual. Lyons attempts to embrace him. Gabriel pushes Lyons away. He begins to howl in what is an attempt at song, or perhaps a song turning back into itself in an attempt at speech. He finishes his dance and the gates of heaven stand open as wide as God's closet.)

That's the way that go!

(*BLACKOUT.*) [p. 108]

Lloyd Richards
Director's Introduction°   [1986]

Fences is the second major play of a poet turned playwright, August Wilson. One of the most compelling storytellers to begin writing for the theater in many years, he has taken the responsibility of telling the tale of the encounter of the released black slaves with a vigorous and ruthless growing America decade by decade. *Fences* encompasses the 1950s and a black family trying to put down roots in the slag-slippery hills of a middle American urban industrial city that one might correctly mistake for Pittsburgh, Pennsylvania.

To call August Wilson a storyteller is to align him at one and the same time with the ancient aristocrats of dramatic writing who stood before the tribes and made compelling oral history into legend, as well as with the modern playwrights who bring an audience to their feet at the end of an evening of their work because that audience knows that they have encountered themselves, their concerns, and their passions, and have been moved and enriched by the experience. In *Fences*, August Wilson tells the story of four generations of black Americans and of how they have passed on a legacy of morals, mores, attitudes, and patterns through stories with and without music.

He tells the story of Troy Maxson, born to a sharecropper father who was frustrated by the fact that every crop took him further into debt. The father knew himself as a failure and took it out on everyone at hand, including his young son, Troy, and his wives, all of whom "leave him." Troy learns violence from him, but he also learns the value of work and the fact that a man takes responsibility for his family no matter how difficult circumstances may be. He learns respect [p. vii]° for a home, the importance of owning land, and the value of an education because he doesn't have one.

An excellent baseball player, Troy learns that in the land of equal opportunity, chances for a black man are not always equal, and that the same country that deprived him asked sacrifice of his brother in World War II and got it. Half his brother's head was blown away, and he is now a disoriented and confused beautiful man. He learns that he must fight and win the little victories

Richards, Lloyd. Director's Introduction. *Fences: A Play*. By August Wilson. New York: New American Library, 1986. vii–viii. Print.
(Page citations in square brackets refer to the original publication.)

that—given his life—must assume the proportion of major triumphs. He learns that day to day and moment to moment he lives close to death and must wrestle with death to survive. He learns that to take a chance and grab a moment of beauty can crumble the delicate fabric of an intricate value system and leave one desolate and alone. Strength of body and strength of purpose are not enough. Chance and the color of one's skin, chance again, can tip the balance. "You've got to take the crooked with the straight."

Troy Maxson spins yarns, raps, tells stories to his family and friends in that wonderful environment of the pretelevision, pre-airconditioned era when the back porch and the backyard were the platform for some of the most exciting tales of that time. From this platform and through his behavior he passes on to his extended family principles for living, which members of his family accept or refute through the manner in which they choose to live their own lives.

How is this reformed criminal perceived? What should be learned from him? What accepted? What passed on? Is his life to be discarded or honored? That is the story of *Fences*, which we build to keep things and people out or in.

New Haven, Connecticut
March 6, 1986 [p. viii]

Clive Barnes

Fiery *Fences*: A Review°   [1987]

Once in a rare while, you come across a play—or a movie or a novel—that seems to break away from the confines of art into a dense, complex realization of reality. A veil has been torn aside, the artist has disappeared into a transparency. We look with our own eyes, feel with our own hearts.

That was my reaction to August Wilson's pulsing play *Fences*, which opened last night at the Forty-sixth Street Theater, with James Earl Jones in full magnificent cry heading a cast of actors as good as you could find anywhere.

I wasn't just moved. I was transfixed—by intimations of a life, impressions of a man, images of a society.

Wilson, who a couple of seasons back gave us the arresting but fascinatingly flawed *Ma Rainey's Black Bottom*, always insists in interviews that he is writing from the wellspring of black experience in America.

This is undoubtedly true. Had Wilson been white, his plays would have been different—they would have had a different fire in a different belly.

But calling Wilson a "black" playwright is irrelevant. What makes *Fences* so engrossing, so embracing, so simply powerful, is his startling ability to tell a story, reveal feeling, paint emotion.

In many respects, *Fences* falls into the classic pattern of the American realistic drama—a family play, with a tragically doomed American father locked in conflict with his son. Greek tragedy with a Yankee accent.

Barnes, Clive. "Fiery *Fences*: A Review." *New York Post* 27 March 1987: C23. Print.

The timing of the play — the late '50s — is carefully pinpointed in the history of black America as that turning point in the civil rights movement when a dream unfulfilled became a promise deferred.

The hero is Troy Maxson — and I suggest that he will be remembered as one of the great characters in American drama, and Jones always recalled as the first actor to play him.

Troy is as complex and as tormented as black America itself. He started life as a refugee from the South, and as a thief and, eventually, a killer.

Life in a penitentiary gave him the iron determination to reshape his life — as did, later, a feverish brush with death.

Prison also taught him baseball; when he came out, he became a temperamental star of the Negro Leagues. And now — in 1957 — he can look at the likes of Jackie Robinson and Hank Aaron, making it in the Major Leagues of big-time whiteball, with a mixture of anger, envy, and contempt.

A garbage collector, Troy has typically had to fight through his union to become the first black driver of a garbage truck. Equally typically, he hasn't even got a driver's license.

He sees himself as a man fenced in with responsibilities, but he has created some of those fences himself — some intended to keep people out, some to keep people in.

He is a family man — with a second wife, Rose, and their son Cory, as well as Gabriel, his brother, half-crazed by a war injury, and Lyons, Troy's older son by a previous marriage.

His life is secure — but limited. His son wants to go to college on a football scholarship, but Troy, wary of professional sports, refuses to let him try his luck.

Troy — although fully aware of his wife's qualities and warned by his best friend, Jim — falls in love with a younger woman, who becomes pregnant.

What is particularly pungent about Wilson's play is how the story and the characters are plugged into their particular historic relevance, ranging from the lessons of prison to the metaphors of baseball. It is this that makes the play resonate with all its subtle vibrations of truth and actuality.

This is in no sense a political play — but quite dispassionately it says: This is what it was like to be a black man of pride and ambition from the South, trying to live and work in the industrial North in the years just before and just after World War II.

The writing is perfectly geared to its people and its place. It jumps from the author's mind onto the stage, its language catching fire in the rarefied atmosphere of drama.

However fine the play is — and it is the strongest, most passionate American dramatic writing since Tennessee Williams — no praise can be too high for the staging by Lloyd Richards.

Helped by the cinematic accuracy of James D. Sandefur's setting, Richards has made the play into a microcosm in which we can see the tiny reflections of parts of ourselves, parts of America, and parts of history.

He gives every actor a sense of purpose and belonging — and makes the play their nightly story. Wonderful acting, but also marvelous direction.

James Earl Jones remakes himself in Troy's image. It is a performance of such astonishing credibility that it offers the audience a guilty sense of actually spying on the character, unobserved and unwanted.

But this is only one performance of note; in her way, Mary Alice, as Troy's wife, is just as powerful, her pain and reality just as painfully real. And then there is Courtney B. Vance as Troy's alienated son, another performance of bewildering truth and honesty.

Add to these Ray Aranha, Charles Brown, Frankie F. Faison, and Karima Miller, and you have an ensemble cast as good as you will ever find.

Fences gave me one of the richest experiences I have ever had in the theater.

Frank Rich

Family Ties in Wilson's *Fences*: A Review°　　　　[1987]

To hear his wife tell it, Troy Maxson, the middle-aged Pittsburgh sanitation worker at the center of *Fences*, is "so big" that he fills up his tenement house just by walking through it. Needless to say, that description could also apply to James Earl Jones, the actor who has found what may be the best role of his career in August Wilson's new play, at the Forty-sixth Street Theater. But the remarkable stature of the character — and of the performance — is not a matter of sheer size. If Mr. Jones's Troy is a mountainous man prone to tyrannical eruptions of rage, he is also a dignified, delicate figure capable of cradling a tiny baby, of pleading gravely to his wife for understanding, of standing still to stare death unflinchingly in the eye. A black man, a free man, a descendant of slaves, a menial laborer, a father, a husband, a lover — Mr. Jones's Troy embraces all the contradictions of being black and male and American in his time.

That time is 1957 — three decades after the period of Mr. Wilson's previous and extraordinary *Ma Rainey's Black Bottom*. For blacks like Troy in the industrial North of *Fences*, social and economic equality is more a legal principle than a reality: The Maxsons' slum neighborhood, a panorama of grimy brick and smokestack-blighted sky in James D. Sandefur's eloquent design, is a cauldron of busted promises, waiting to boil over. The conflagration is still a decade away — the streetlights burn like the first sparks of distant insurrection — so Mr. Wilson writes about the pain of an extended family lost in the wilderness of de facto segregation and barren hope.

It speaks of the power of the play — and of the cast assembled by the director, Lloyd Richards — that Mr. Jones's patriarch doesn't devour the rest of *Fences* so much as become the life force that at once nurtures and stunts the characters who share his blood. The strongest countervailing player is his wife, Rose, luminously acted by Mary Alice. Rose is a quiet woman who, as she says "planted

---

Rich, Frank. "Family Ties in Wilson's *Fences*: A Review." *New York Times* 27 March 1987: C3. Print.

herself" in the "hard and rocky" soil of her husband. But she never bloomed: Marriage brought frustration and betrayal in equal measure with affection.

Even so, Ms. Alice's performance emphasizes strength over self-pity, open anger over festering bitterness. The actress finds the spiritual quotient in the acceptance that accompanies Rose's love for a scarred, profoundly complicated man. It's rare to find a marriage of any sort presented on stage with such balance — let alone one in which the husband has fathered children by three different women. Mr. Wilson grants both partners the right to want to escape the responsibilities of their domestic drudgery while affirming their respective claims to forgiveness.

The other primary relationship of *Fences* is that of Troy to his son Cory (Courtney B. Vance) — a promising 17-year-old football player being courted by a college recruiter. Troy himself was once a baseball player in the Negro Leagues — early enough to hit homers off Satchel Paige, too early to benefit from Jackie Robinson's breakthrough — and his bitter, long-ago disappointment leads him to decree a different future for his son. But while Troy wants Cory to settle for a workhorse trade guaranteeing a weekly paycheck, the boy resists. The younger Maxson is somehow convinced that the dreams of his black generation need not end in the city's mean alleys with the carting of white men's garbage.

The struggle between father and son over conflicting visions of black identity, aspirations, and values is the play's narrative fulcrum, and a paradigm of violent divisions that would later tear apart a society. As written, the conflict is also a didactic one, reminiscent of old-fashioned plays, black and white, about disputes between first-generation American parents and their rebellious children.

In *Ma Rainey* — set at a blues recording session — Mr. Wilson's characters were firecrackers exploding in a bottle, pursuing jagged theatrical riffs reflective of their music and of their intimacy with the Afro-American experience that gave birth to that music. The relative tameness of *Fences* — with its laboriously worked-out titular metaphor, its slow-fused act 1 exposition — is as much an expression of its period as its predecessor was of the hotter '20s. Intentionally or not — and perhaps to the satisfaction of those who found the more esthetically daring *Ma Rainey* too "plotless" — Mr. Wilson invokes the clunkier dramaturgy of Odets, Miller, and Hansberry on this occasion.

Such formulaic theatrical tidiness, while exasperating at times, proves a minor price for the gripping second act (strengthened since the play's Yale debut in 1985) and for the scattered virtuoso passages throughout. Like *Ma Rainey* and the latest Wilson work seen at Yale (*Joe Turner's Come and Gone*, also promised for New York), *Fences* leaves no doubt that Mr. Wilson is a major writer, combining a poet's ear for vernacular with a robust sense of humor (political and sexual), a sure instinct for crackling dramatic incident, and a passionate commitment to a great subject.

Mr. Wilson continues to see history as fully as he sees his characters. In one scene, Troy and his oldest friend (played with brimming warmth by Ray Aranha) weave an autobiographical "talking blues" — a front-porch storytelling jaunt from the antebellum plantation through the preindustrial urban South, jail, and northward migration. *Fences* is pointedly bracketed by two disparate wars that swallowed up black manhood, and, as always with Mr. Wilson, is as keenly cognizant of its characters' bonds to Africa, however muted here, as their bondage to white America. One hears the cadences of a centuries-old heritage in Mr. Jones's efforts to shout down the devil. It is a frayed scrap of timeless blues singing, unpretty but unquenchable, that proves the overpowering cathartic link among the disparate branches of the Maxson family tree.

Under the exemplary guidance of Mr. Richards — whose staging falters only in the awkward scene transitions — the entire cast is impressive, including Frankie R. Faison in the problematic (but finally devastating) role of a brain-damaged, horn-playing uncle named Gabriel, and Charles Brown, as a Maxson son who falls into the sociological crack separating the play's two principal generations. As Cory, Courtney B. Vance is not only formidable in challenging Mr. Jones to a psychological (and sometimes physical) kill-or-be-killed battle for supremacy but also seems to grow into Troy's vocal timbre and visage by the final scene. Like most sons, Mr. Vance just can't elude "the shadow" of his father, no matter how hard he tries. Such is the long shadow Mr. Jones's father casts in *Fences* that theatergoers from all kinds of families may find him impossible to escape.

Bonnie Lyons

An Interview with August Wilson°   [1999]

Q: Elsewhere you've talked about writing as a way of effecting social change and said that all your plays are political, but that you try not to make them didactic or polemical. Can you talk a little about how plays can effect social change without being polemical or didactic?

A: I don't write primarily to effect social change. I believe writing can do that, but that's not why I write. I work as an artist. However, all art is political in the sense that it serves the politics of someone. Here in America whites have a particular view of blacks, and I think my plays offer them a different and new way to look at black Americans. For instance, in *Fences* they see a garbageman, a person they really don't look at, although they may see a garbageman every day. By looking at Troy's life, white people find out that the content of this black garbageman's life is very similar to their own, that he is affected by the same things — love, honor, beauty, betrayal, duty. Recognizing that these things are as much a part of his life as of theirs can [p. 2]° be revolutionary and can affect how they think about and deal with black people in their lives.

Lyons, Bonnie. "An Interview with August Wilson." *Contemporary Literature* 40.1 (Spring 1999): 1–21. Print.
(Page citations in square brackets refer to the original publication.)

Q: How would that same play, *Fences*, affect a black audience?

A: Blacks see the content of their lives being elevated into art. They don't always know that is possible, and it's important to know that.

Q: You've talked about how important black music was for your development. Was there any black literature that showed you that black lives can be the subject of great art?

A: *Invisible Man.* When I was fourteen I discovered the Negro section of the library. I read *Invisible Man*, Langston Hughes, and all the thirty or forty books in the section, including the sociology. I remember reading a book that talked about the "Negro's power of hard work" and how much that phrase affected me. At the time I used to cut the lawn for a blind man named Mr. Douglas, who was the father of the Olympic track star. After I read that, I didn't so much cut his lawn as plow it, to show the Negro power of hard work. Looking back, I see that I had never seen those words together: "Negro power." Later of course in the sixties that became "black power." Forty years ago we had few black writers compared to today. There have been forty years of education and many more college graduates. And it's important to remember that blacks don't have a long history of writing. We come from an oral tradition. At one point in America it was a crime to teach blacks to read and write. So it's only in the past 150 years that we've been writing in this country.

Q: Elsewhere you've said that the primary opposition in your plays is between blacks who deny their African roots and those who don't. Would you still describe your work that way?

A: Today I would say that the conflict in black America is between the middle class and the so-called underclass, and that conflict goes back to those who deny themselves and those who aren't willing to. America offers blacks a contract that says, "If you leave all that African stuff over there and adopt the values of the dominant culture, you can participate." For the most part, black Americans have [p. 3] rejected that sort of con job. Many blacks in the ghettos say, "If I got to give up who I am, if I can't be like me, then I don't want it." The ones who accept go on to become part of the growing black middle class and in some areas even acquire some power and participation in society, but when they finally arrive where they arrive, they are no longer the same people. They are clothed in different manners and ways of life, different thoughts and ideas. They've acculturated and adopted white values. . . . [p. 4]

Q: Elsewhere you've said you want your audience to see your characters as Africans, not just black folks in America. Can you talk about that?

A: I'm talking about black Americans having uniquely African ways of participating in the world, of doing things, different ways of socializing. I have no fascination with Africa itself. I've never been to Africa and have no desire to go. I've been invited several times and turned down the invitations because I don't like to travel. When my daughter went to college, she called me all excited that she was studying about Timbuktu. I told her, "You study your grandma and her grandmother before you go back to Timbuktu." People don't want to do that because soon you wind up with slavery, and that's a [p. 7] condition people want to run away from. It's much easier to go back to the glory days of Timbuktu, but to do that is falsely romantic. It doesn't get you anywhere. I remember when I first went with a friend to a Passover seder and heard them say, "When we were slaves in the land of Egypt." I met a kid in 1987 in New York who thought slavery ended in 1960. This is God's honest truth. He was seventeen years old and he thought slavery ended in 1960. That's our fault. Like the Jews, we need to celebrate our emancipation; it would give us a way of identifying and expressing a sense of unity.

Q: Do you see anything anomalous about your wanting blacks to see themselves as Africans but your not having any desire even to visit Africa?

A: I'm simply saying blacks should hold on to what they are. You don't have to go to Africa to be an African. I live and breathe that. Even in the sixties, with all the romantic involvement with Africa, I never wore a dashiki to participate in the black power movement. Africa is right here in the southern part of the United States, which is our ancestral homeland. I don't need to make that leap across the ocean. When the first African died on the continent of North America, that was the beginning of my history.

Q: Speaking of your history, I remember reading that you said the first word you typed was your own name. Do you have any interest in autobiography?

A: Not about me as an individual. I don't like to read biographies or autobiographies myself. And if your material is autobiographical, sooner or later you're going to run out of material. I take the entire black experience in America, from the first black in 1619 until now, and claim that as my material. That's my story, my life story, and that's a lot to write about. But in truth, whatever subject you take, you as a writer are going to come up with something that is based on who you are, so even in choosing the black experience I am writing it from my own perspective. . . . [p. 8]

Q: Do you think you define plot the same way Aristotle did?

A: For me plot grows out of characterization, so there are no plot points. The play doesn't flow from plot point to plot point. I guess it's easy to plot that way, since every TV drama moves along those lines. It becomes very mechanical. Some people call my plays plotless; that's simply because they haven't been able to recognize the plot in [p. 11] them. In my plays you don't say, "Here is a point here, hold on to this because we're going to need it." I think you need to hold on to everything. In my plays things happen gradually, and you come to see why things are in the play. For example, in *Seven Guitars* you hear four men talking, and you may think the play is not going anywhere. But it is. All that stuff, every single thing they talk about, connects and is important to your understanding of the drama.

Q: It may seem a strange connection, but are your plays more like Chekhov's° than most playwrights', both in their being ensemble plays and in their seeming plotlessness?

A: I think you're right. I didn't know Chekhov's work, so there is no question of influence, but when I saw *Uncle Vanya*, I thought, "He's cool. I like this play. Yes, it's just people sitting around talking, and the drama is made out of the talk, but there are things going on, a lot of stuff is happening." . . . [p. 12]

Chekhov: Anton Chekhov (1860–1904), Russian playwright and short-story writer.

Q: In the past you've mentioned the importance of listening to your characters and trusting them. Can you talk about that a bit?

A: You listen to them, but you never lose consciousness that they are your creations. When I first started writing plays I couldn't write good dialogue because I didn't respect how black people talked. I thought that in order to make art out of it I had to change it, make it into something different. Once I learned to value and respect my characters, I could really hear them. How you talk is how you think; the language describes the one who speaks it. When I have characters, I just let them start talking. The important thing is not to censor them, to trust them to just talk. What they are talking about may not seem to have anything to do with what you as a writer were writing about, but it does. Just let them talk and it will connect, because you as the artist will make it connect.... [p. 13] The more my characters talk, the more I find out about them. And the more I find out about them, the more material I have. So I encourage them, I tell them, "Tell me some more." I just write it down, and it starts to make connections.... [p. 14]

Q: In your cycle of plays, you'll have one play per decade of this century, but in your introductory note to *Seven Guitars* you say, "Despite my interest in history, I've always been more concerned with culture." Could you talk a little about history versus culture?

A: I'm more interested in the historical context than in actual history, so for example I changed the actual historical date of a Joe Louis boxing match because it suited my dramatic purposes. I always come back to the quote from James Baldwin about the black tradition, which he defined as "That field of manners and rituals of intercourse that will sustain a man once he's left his father's house." [p. 16] The primary focus of my work is looking at black culture as it changes and grows in evolving historical contexts ...

Q: In addition to plays, you've written poetry, and now you're also writing a novel. Can you talk about the differences between those forms, and whether material comes to you in one form or another?

A: For me, poetry is distilled language. Somewhere I read poetry defined as enlarging the sayable. I like that definition, and I think poetry is the highest form of literature. Writing a novel is like setting [p. 17] out on this vast, uncharted ocean. I never knew how anyone could do it. But now I see that like any kind of writing, you start with the first word and finish the first page. Then you've got a page and you go on to the next. I realized that writing a novel is like writing a play in that you don't have to know where you're going. You just go and you find out as you go along ...

Q: Playwrights have taken quite varying positions about the importance of production. Edward Albee° has taken an extreme position, saying, "A first-rate

---

Edward Albee: U.S. playwright, b. 1928. For the position expressed, see *Conversations with Edward Albee*, ed. Philip C. Kolin (Jackson: University Press of Mississippi, 1988), 137.

play exists completely on the page and is never improved by production; it is only proved by production." Do you agree?

A: I agree with that, because the play is there on the page; it provides a road map or a blueprint. I don't write for a production; I write for the page, just like a poem. A play, like a poem, exists on the page even if no one ever reads it aloud. But I don't want to underestimate what a good production with actors embodying the characters offers. But depending on the imagination of the reader, he may get more by reading the play than by seeing a weak production. . . . [p. 18]

Q: One playwright has said that drama is made up of sound and silence. Do you see drama that way?

A: No doubt drama is made up of sound and silence, but I see conflict at the center. What you do is set up a character who has certain beliefs and you establish a situation where those beliefs are challenged and that character is forced to examine those beliefs and perhaps change them. That's the kind of dramatic situation which engages an audience.

Q: Then is the conflict primarily internal rather than external, between characters?

A: Internal, right, where the character has to reexamine his whole body of beliefs. The play has to shake the very foundation of his whole system of beliefs and force him to make a choice. Then I think [p. 19] you as a playwright have accomplished something, because that process also forces the audience to go through the same inner struggle. When I teach my workshops I tell my students that if a guy announces, "I'm going to kill Joe," and there's a knock on the door, the audience is going to want to know if that's Joe and why this guy wants to kill him and whether we would also want to kill him if we were in the same situation. The audience is engaged in the questions. [p. 20]

Miles Marshall Lewis

Miles Marshall Lewis Talks with August Wilson° [2005]

Miles Marshall Lewis: Despite the similarities between *Fences* and *Death of a Salesman*, and the art of playwriting as a predominantly white discipline, you've cited your greatest literary influence as poet-playwright Amiri Baraka.° How would you say he influenced you?

August Wilson: I'm not sure what they say about *Fences* as it relates to *Death of a Salesman*. At the time I wrote *Fences*, I had not read *Death of a Salesman*, had not seen *Death of a Salesman*, did not know anything about *Death of a Salesman*.

Lewis, Miles Marshall. "Miles Marshall Lewis Talks with August Wilson." *The Believer Book of Writers Talking to Writers.* Ed. Vendela Vida. San Francisco: Believer Books, 2005. 409–27. Print. **Amiri Baraka:** U.S. poet, playwright, essayist, and music critic; born Everett LeRoy Jones in 1934, he changed his name to LeRoi Jones in 1952, to Imamu Ameer Baraka in 1967, and later to Amiri Baraka.

My greatest influence has been the blues. And that's a literary influence, because I think the blues is the best literature that we as [p. 410]° black Americans have. My interest in Baraka comes from the '60s and the Black Power movement. So it's more for Baraka's political ideas, which I loved and still am an exponent of. Through all those years I was a follower, if you will, of Baraka. He had an influence on my thinking.

MML: Were you exposed first to his poetry or his plays?

AW: The poetry in particular. The book called *Black Magic*, which is sort of a collection of several books. That's '69 – I wore that book out, the cover got taped up with Scotch tape, the pages falling out. That was my bible, I carried it wherever I went. So that in particular. I wasn't writing plays back then, so I wasn't influenced by his playwriting – although, to me, his best plays are collected in a book called *Four Black Revolutionary Plays*, with *Madheart*, *Great Goodness of Life*, *A Black Mass*, and *Experimental Death Unit 1*. They contributed a lot to my thinking just in terms of getting stuff on the page.

MML: How specifically was the blues an influence on your work?

AW: Blues is the bedrock of everything I do. All the characters in my plays, their ideas and their attitudes, the stance that they adopt in the world, are all ideas and attitudes that are expressed in the blues. If all this were to disappear off the face of the earth and some people two million unique years from now would dig out this civilization and come across some blues records, working as anthropologists, they would be able to piece together who these people were, what they thought about, what their ideas and attitudes toward pleasure and pain were, all of that. All the components of culture. Just like they do with the Egyptians, they piece together all that stuff. And all you need is the blues. So to me the blues is the book, it's the bible, it's everything. . . . [p. 411]

MML: Your characters also often riff off of each other like jazz musicians, particularly in *Seven Guitars*. Your work in general is like improvising on a theme: the life of southern blacks who migrated to the North in the twentieth century. How has jazz impacted your creative process?

AW: I think that's the core of black aesthetics: the ability to improvise. That is what has enabled our survival. . . . [p. 412]

AW: People say, "Well, you writin a play in 1911 and you weren't alive in 1911. Did you do any research?" I say, I don't do research. They say, "Well, how do you know?" Because the plays ultimately are about love, honor, duty, betrayal – what I call the Big Themes. So you could set it in the '80s and make use of various things, but you're telling a story that is using the Big Themes. . . . [p. 417]

MML: Essayist Sandra Shannon has criticized the women in your plays, saying, "His feminine portrayals tend to slip into comfort zones of what seem to be male-fantasized roles." Feminist critic bell hooks said of *Fences* that "patriarchy is not critiqued" and "sexist values are reinscribed." I was wondering if you've given thought to this in relation to approaching the final play in your

---

(Page citations in square brackets refer to the original publication.)

cycle, which takes place in the 1990s, a time when women are arguably their most liberated and independent.

AW: I can't approach them any different than I have, man, cause all my women are independent. People can say anything they want, that's valid, they're liable to say anything they want. I don't agree with that. You gotta write women like . . . they can't express ideas and attitudes that women of the feminist movement in the '60s made. Even though I'm aware of all that, you gotta be very careful if you're trying to create a character like that, that they don't come up with any greater understanding of themselves and their relationship to the world than women had at that time.

As a matter of fact, all my characters are at the edge of that, they pushing them boundaries, they have more understanding. I had to cut back and say, "These are feminist ideas." My mother was a feminist, though she wouldn't express it that way. She don't know nothing about no feminist women and whatnot but she didn't accept her place. She raised three daughters, and my sisters are the same way. So that's where I get my women from. I grew up in a household with four women. [p. 422]

Missy Dehn Kubitschek

August Wilson's Gender Lesson°   [1994]

Like much African American literature of the last two decades, August Wilson's cycle of plays takes its readers/viewers on an extended historical examination of gendered interactions in the black community. Although his earliest play, *Ma Rainey's Black Bottom* (1984), does not focus on gender to the same extent as his later works, it sets the premises under which they develop their statements: the presence of a powerful African American spirituality and the difficulty of preserving it in an economic system controlled by white racists. *Fences* (1985) forcefully demonstrates the spiritual alienation of men and women from one another, and of men from their children. The play shows men and women speaking different languages, reflecting different understandings of the spiritual cosmos. . . . [p. 183]°

Centered on the economic disruption of black men's and women's relationships, *Fences* shows men and women speaking the different languages imposed/derived from their unconscious acceptance of an implicitly Eurocentric view of separate male and female spheres. The development of a situation in which men and women are speaking different languages that no longer refer to the same spiritual realities can be approached through a juxtaposition of two models of gender relations. Nineteenth-century European models divide sex

Kubitschek, Missy Dehn. "August Wilson's Gender Lesson." *May All Your Fences Have Gates: Essays on the Drama of August Wilson.* Ed. Alan Nadel. Iowa City: Iowa UP, 1994. 183–99. Print. (Page citations in square brackets refer to the original publication.)

roles into separate spheres in a hierarchical schema. A second set of models derives from the experiences of women in traditional nonindustrial societies or in minority communities in the United States.

Delineated by Paula Gunn Allen's *The Sacred Hoop* and Trinh Minh-ha's *Woman, Native, Other*, and implied by other works such as Gloria Anzaldua's *Borderlands/La Frontera* and bell hooks's *Feminist Theory: From Margin to Center*, this second paradigm represents men and women as possessing somewhat differ-ent spiritual gifts and hence different social responsibilities, but sharing some areas of influence. Men's and women's spheres of activity are fundamentally con-nected, mutually contributive parts of community. . . . [p. 184]

Separate spheres were for black Americans unachievable in the nineteenth century and available only to a small middle class in the twentieth. Historically, the separate-spheres ideology has combined with white male economic control to erode African American families and communities by preventing black men from achieving the only culturally endorsed definition of manhood and by subordinating the activities of black women, sometimes making them competi-tive in formerly common arenas of endeavor. *Fences* explores the damage that results when European constructions of sex roles separate, hierarchically order, and then alienate men and women; at the same time, the play suggests a palimpsest of a more empowering traditional model.

Troy Maxson's definition of his manhood centers on his ability to support his family economically, though he intermittently glimpses the inadequacy of this conception. He describes, for example, his own father's economically pres-sured definition of his children as workers, and only workers, with considerable pain. He also recognizes his father's lack of joy, his selfishness, his demeaning treatment of his children, his abuse of his wife. Simultaneously [p. 185] Troy says, "He wasn't good for nobody" (992) but affirms that he strove to accom-plish the one thing necessary, securing the necessities for his family.

Under this superimposed definition of manhood, another, broader, defini-tion struggles to reemerge, the sense that economic relations ought not to be the whole of a father's relationship to his children. Troy cannot express such an idea directly. Though he suffered for lack of his father's love (and was further deprived when his mother left), he tries to force Cory to be satisfied with the same father/son relationship:

> It's my job. It's my responsibility! You understand that? A man got to take care of his family. You live in my house . . . sleep you behind on my bed-clothes . . . fill you belly up with my food . . . cause you my son. You my flesh and blood. Not 'cause I like you! Cause it's my duty to take care of you. I owe a responsibility to you! (985)

His intermittent recognition of his father's inadequacy does not lead to any other conception of fatherhood.

Trying not to fail Cory as he failed Lyons (imprisonment prevented him from supporting his first family), Troy virtually recreates the destructive relationship between his father and himself. Not only does he insist on Cory's working for salary, he identifies the family's resources—the house and its furnishings, food—as his own property, his son as a dependent rather than a contributor. Troy expresses disgust at Lyons's easy acceptance of such a relationship; only a boy accepts such a position, and only because he has no choice.

Troy's bitterness at whites' power to exclude him from prestigious and well-paid labor (major league baseball) makes the likenesses between himself and Cory into threats. Unable to recognize changes in social conditions, he sees Cory's talents as a temptation to irresponsibility. He insists on conditions that make it impossible for Cory to satisfy his work requirement and also to attend necessary athletic practices. Although he claims to be protecting Cory from inevitable disappointment, he is deforming another generation with Procrustean° gender definitions.

Following his only model, he plays his father's role with a slightly different script. Troy breaks from his father at fourteen, but the separation is temporary, geographic rather than temperamental or psychic; he understands his father later, when "I could feel him kicking in my blood and knew that the only thing that separated us was the matter of a few years" (992). Given the [p. 186] economic conditions and his understanding of his role, Troy can only recreate in another generation the economic exploitation and competition between father and son.

Fences demonstrates that, as the European/Victorian doctrine of separate spheres combines with very limited economic opportunities, relationships between black men and women deteriorate. The very list of characters for *Fences* testifies to patriarchal hegemony, with its implications of subordination for women—all but one of the characters are identified solely by their relationship to Troy, as "Troy's oldest son" or "Troy's wife"; significantly, Cory is identified as "Troy and Rose's son," an assertion of women's ongoing presence and importance for heritage.

Men's and women's languages in *Fences* reflect the separation of their spheres of activity. In their most intensely emotional scene (act 2, scene 1), Troy and Rose attempt to communicate with metaphors that diverge sharply. Troy repeatedly uses baseball metaphors that Rose implicitly rejects by returning always to the concrete level of action:

> ROSE: You should have held me tight. You should have grabbed me and held
> on.
> TROY: I stood on first base for eighteen years and I thought . . . well, god-
> damn it . . . go on for it!
> ROSE: We're not talking about baseball! We're talking about you going off
> to lay in bed with another woman. (1001)

Troy's account doesn't lose track of the concrete level, but his metaphorical expression is confined to—and confines—the experience to an arena that he has only limited access to and that excludes Rose entirely. Troy chooses baseball,

---

Procrustean: Creating uniformity or conformity forcefully, without allowing for variety or individuality.

the game whose racial segregation has prevented his enjoying the economic or status benefits of his athletic prowess, as his vehicle. But baseball is, of course, also sex-segregated. Troy hopes for "one of them boys to knock me in" because metaphorically and literally, it has become impossible for any woman to play on his team, to advance him in his competitive quest. Instead, Rose disappears entirely from the metaphor, and Alberta is objectified, a base to steal. Inevitably Rose refuses the metaphor that excludes her and includes women only as objects.

Whereas Troy's metaphor comes from the social (and therefore hierarchical) world, Rose's metaphor in this scene derives from the natural world. Her expression emphasizes her expectation that her experience will partake of the [p. 187] cycle of living things, and her frustration that it does not come to fulfillment: "I took all my feelings, my wants and needs, my dreams . . . and I buried them inside you. I planted a seed and watched and prayed over it. I planted myself inside you and waited to bloom. And it didn't take me no eighteen years to find out the soil was hard and rocky and it wasn't never gonna bloom" (1002). In his role as divine fool, Gabriel underlines Rose's connections to nature by giving her flowers and commenting that she shares their essence. Rose's imagery, moreover, leaves open the possibility of shared ground as Troy's does not, for Troy at least appears in Rose's imagery, even though he is represented as an environment of dubious hospitality. Rose's natural imagery suggests continuity, as Troy's game imagery suggests a discrete series, and although women's experience provides the source of this natural imagery, the experience is itself not socially limited to one gender.

Fences does not, of course, present black men as failed human beings and women as the preservers of undamaged original spiritualities (a conception that would result from the separate-spheres doctrine's idealization of women's purity). The division into separate spheres affects Rose as well as Troy. Her impassioned denunciation of his affair and its results reveals the conflict between European and African ideals of kinship: "And you know I ain't never wanted no half nothing in my family. My whole family is half. Everybody got different fathers and mothers . . . my two sisters and my brother. Can't hardly tell who's who. Can't never sit down and talk about Papa and Mama. It's your papa and your mama and my papa and my mama" (1000). On the one hand, Rose is angry about a kind of confused ancestral heritage, the lack of archetypal Mama and Papa, and their replacement by lowercase, less powerful specifics. On the other, her idea of a proper family reflects the European, nuclear ideal rather than the traditional African or African American conception of extended family.

The last scene shows the simultaneous influence of both paradigms. On the one hand, Raynell, like Rose, is associated with the natural world of the garden while Cory appears in military uniform, a clear suggestion of continued separation of sex roles. On the other hand, a shared spirituality persists. Troy's father's song, "Old Blue," for instance, survives because both Raynell and Cory have heard Troy's version. Singing it together, they ritually evoke the ancestors.

More important, both Rose and Gabriel reclaim spiritual powers by refusing European systems and returning to traditional understandings and roles. Rose, however equivocally, finally refuses the role offered to her by separate [p. 188] spheres — female victim of a superior male power — to embrace her own responsibility for constructing a shared space with Troy:

> When I first met your daddy I thought . . . Here is a man I can lay down with and make a baby. [. . .] I thought, Rose Lee, here is a man that you can open yourself up to and be filled to bursting. [. . .]
>
> When your daddy walked through the house he was so big he filled it up. That was my first mistake. Not to make him leave some room for me. For my part in the matter. But at that time I wanted that. I wanted a house that I could sing in. And that's what your daddy gave me. I didn't know to keep up his strength I had to give up little pieces of mine. I did that. [. . .] It was my choice. It was my life and I didn't have to live it like that. But that's what life offered me in the way of being a woman and I took it. (1015–16, first ellipsis Wilson's)

Troy controlled what should have been their shared space because Rose did not claim and exercise her power. Rose does not blame Troy, however, indicating that a different outcome would have been possible if she had understood the implications of ceding power. At the same time, she implies that her choice was not entirely determined by personality: "That's what life offered me in the way of being a woman."

Fences shows mutual autonomy with shared responsibilities as a more fulfilling paradigm than that of separate spheres. Rose tells Cory directly that reclaiming her power and independence made her happier. Although she had initially rejected traditional ideas of kinship, referring to Raynell as "your baby," Rose went on to agree to Troy's request to care for her with "this child got a mother. But you a womanless man" (1006). Thus, she no longer accepted Troy's presence throughout the shared house; instead, as the price of having shared responsibilities for Raynell, she insisted on redefining the whole relationship. The timing of Rose's communication of joint responsibility — Cory is engaged — makes an alternative available to her son that he did not witness in their home. Troy's mother had left by the time he rejected his father, and with no other model to emulate, Troy inevitably recreates his father's role and vision. Rose's presence — more important, her communication — opens other possibilities for Cory.

In a more direct and absolute critique of Western models, Gabriel replaces a failed Christianity with an empowering African spirituality. Convinced that it's time for him to perform the role that Christianity assigns to the Archangel Gabriel, Gabriel decides to end the world by blowing his trumpet. When the [p. 189] damaged instrument makes no noise, "a weight of impossible description [. . .] falls away" (1017). His consequent "frightful realization" makes him begin to dance, then to howl. This "atavistic signature and ritual" (1018) of dance and sound then opens the gate of heaven, and the last words of the play are Gabriel's triumphant "That's the way that go!" [p. 190]

Works Cited

Allen, Paula Gunn. *The Sacred Hoop: Recovering the Feminine in American Indian Traditions*. Boston: Beacon, 1986. Print.

Anzaldua, Gloria. *Borderlands/La Frontera*. San Francisco: Spinsters/Aunt Lute, 1987. Print.

hooks, bell. *Feminist Theory: From Margin to Center*. Boston: South End Press, 1984. Print.

Trinh, Minh-ha. *Woman, Native, Other*. Bloomington: Indiana UP, 1989. Print.

Wilson, August. *Fences*. New York: New American Library/Signet, 1986. Print.

——. *Ma Rainey's Black Bottom*. New York: New American Library, Plume, 1985. Print.

Harry J. Elam, Jr.

August Wilson°   [2005]

With two Pulitzer Prizes, two Tony awards, and numerous other accolades, August Wilson stands out as one of if not the most preeminent playwrights in the contemporary American theater. Wilson's self-imposed dramatic project is to review African American history in the twentieth century by writing a play for each decade. With each work, he recreates and reevaluates the choices that blacks have made in the past by refracting them through the lens of the present. Wilson focuses on the experiences and daily lives of ordinary black people within particular historical circumstances. Carefully situating each play at critical junctures in African American history, Wilson explores the pain and perseverance, the determination and dignity in these black lives. . . . [p. 318]°

Critical to each play in Wilson's historical cycle is the concept that one must go backwards in order to move forward. Repeatedly, Wilson creates black characters who are displaced and disconnected from their history and from their individual identity, and are in search of spiritual resurrection and cultural reconnection. For these characters, past events have a commanding influence on their present dreams and aspirations. Their personal stories are inextricably linked to the history of African American struggle and survival in this country. Wilson's dramatic cycle demonstrates the impact of the past on the present. Ethics and aesthetics conjoin as the personal dynamics of his characters' lives have profound political consequences. He terms his project "a four hundred-year-old autobiography, which is the black experience" (qtd. in Shannon 179–80). As an African American "autobiography," Wilson's work links African American collective memory with Wilson's own memories and with his activist

Elam, Harry J., Jr. "August Wilson." *A Companion to Twentieth-Century American Drama*. Ed. David Krasner. Malden, MA: Blackwell Publishing, 2005. 318–33. Print.
(Page citations in square brackets refer to the original publication.)

racial agenda. His family background and own life experiences are evident in this project. [p. 319]

Wilson . . . found his own true voice as a dramatist as the decade of the 1960s drew to a close. Affected by the urgencies around black cultural nationalism of the late 1960s, Wilson, along with his friend Rob Penny, cofounded Pittsburgh's Black Horizon's Theatre, a revolutionary-inclined African American theater. With his work at Black Horizon's, Wilson encountered one of the influences that continue to shape his dramas, the fiery playwright and poet Amiri Baraka (LeRoi Jones), the leading theater practitioner of the black revolutionary theater movement of the late 1960s and early 1970s. . . . Wilson maintains that Baraka's words and cultural politics inspired his own desire to use drama as a means to social ends.

In and around the same time, Wilson discovered three more influences: Jorge Luis Borges, Romare Bearden, and the blues. Argentinean short-story writer Borges became significant to Wilson because of his ability to blend the metaphysical and the mystical within his complex plot lines. With his skillful use of narration, Borges mixes the fantastical and the spiritual as his characters follow difficult and convoluted pathways. Within plays such as *Fences*, *Joe Turner's Come and Gone*, *The Piano Lesson*, and *Gem of the Ocean*, Wilson's incorporation of the supernatural and metaphysical has been influenced by the writing of Borges.

Wilson discovered the work of fellow Pittsburgh native Romare Bearden in 1977, when his friend Charles Purdy purchased a copy of his collage *The Prevalence of Ritual* (1964). Viewing this artwork had a profound effect on Wilson: "My response was visceral. I was looking at myself in ways I hadn't thought of before and have never ceased to think of since. In Bearden I found my artistic mentor and sought, and still aspire, to make my plays the equal of his canvases" (qtd. in Fishman 134). Bearden's collages *Millhands Lunch Bucket* (1978) and *The Piano Lesson* (1984) directly inspired Wilson's plays *Joe Turner* and *Piano Lesson*, respectively. Bearden's formula for [p. 320] collage, his use of found objects, and his blending of past and present are examples reflected in Wilson's pastiche style of playwriting and his interest in the impact of history upon present conditions. Within the artistry of both men, the metaphorical and ritualistic coexist with everyday experiences of African Americans. Unfortunately, the two men never met in Bearden's lifetime.

Despite the impact of Bearden, Borges, and Baraka on Wilson and his work, the most significant and most transformative of the four influences (referred to as the "4Bs" because all begin with the letter "B") is the blues. Twelve years prior to encountering Bearden in 1965, Wilson discovered the blues while listening to an old recording of Bessie Smith's "Nobody in Town Can Bake a Sweet Jellyroll Like Mine." This recording transformed his life and his cultural ideology. The blues become not only a guiding force in his writing, but also the foundation he discovers for African American expressive culture and for what Wilson believes is a distinctly African American way of "being" (*Three Plays* ix–x). According to Wilson, the cultural, social, political, and spiritual all interact within the blues. Forged in and from the economics of slavery as a method of mediating the pains and dehumanization of that experience, the blues are purposefully duplicitous, containing a matrix of meanings. The blues for Wilson continue to offer a methodology for negotiating the difficult spaces of African American existence and achieving African American survival.

Structurally, Wilson's "bluesology" acts as an aesthetic and cultural intervention disrupting the conventional frame of realism. Rather than plot or action, character and the lyrical music of the dialogue drive the plays. Wilson, a poet before he became a playwright, celebrates the poetic power contained in the speech of poor and uneducated peoples. Wilson allows his characters to voice their history in the verbal equivalent of musical solos. For instance, Troy Maxson—an illiterate garbage man and central figure in *Fences*—fashions his identity and self-awareness through bold expressive tales. Like the ancient city of Troy, he is an epic force, impregnable and larger than life. Troy's stories, which serve to describe the African American experiences as well as his individual life, expand the realistic canvas of the play, reaching beyond the conventional temporal and spatial limits to reveal the inner presence of history impacting on an individual.

Ralph Ellison calls the blues a unique combination of "the tragic and the comic," of poetry and ritual (256). Wilson's plays embody this blues formula on a multitude of occasions. In each of the plays, Wilson's characters engage in a series of vernacular games, the dozens, and signifyin'. All these cultural activities are extensions of the blues or variations on a blues theme. Wilson sets his works in sites that enable such communal engagement, verbal jousting, and oral transmission of culture. . . . [p. 321]

In Wilson's plays, music and song act as metaphors for African American identity, spirit, and soul. Through the invisible presence and symbolic activities of off-stage white characters, Wilson suggests that the dominant culture has continually sought to subjugate African American humanity and suppress the power and ability of African Americans to sing their song without looking over their shoulder.

Wilson's blues theology privileges the blues musician. He posits the blues musician as a potentially powerful site of black resistive agency. Too often, however, the [p. 323] musicians fail to realize the power they possess. As with any gift or power, the power of the blues musician exacts certain costs and expectations from the ones to whom it is given. Lyons in *Fences*, Jeremy in *Joe Turner's Come and Gone*, and Winning Boy in *The Piano Lesson*, for instance, all represent blues musicians who have misunderstood the spiritual force of the blues song and the cultural responsibility inherent in their ability to play the blues. As a result, they are exploited for their music and fall victim to those who wish to control their spirit and song. . . . Still, it is on and through these musicians that Wilson positions himself as blues musician improvising on a theme. Toledo's° declarations of the need for African Americans to recognize their connections to Africa represent an important element of Wilson's blues theology. Wilson believes that in order for African Americans to be able to sing their own song, to feel truly liberated in the American context, they must rediscover their "African-ness." Wilson puts it this way: "One of the things I'm trying to say in my writing is that

---

Toledo: Philosophical pianist in *Ma Rainey's Black Bottom*.

we can never begin to make a contribution to the society except as Africans" (qtd. in Savran 296). Toledo, accordingly, reprimands the band and himself for not being African and for being imitation white men. . . .

The ending of *Ma Rainey*, in which one of the band members murders another, is a complex and confounding blues moment. It stands in stark contrast to endings of Wilson's later dramas such as *Fences*, *Joe Turner*, and *Piano Lesson*, in which characters reach moments of spiritual fulfillment, acknowledge their relationships to the African American past, and perform actions of self-actualization, self-determination, and collective communion. . . . [p. 324]

Wilson claims that he started *Fences* (1986), his first Pulitzer Prize–winning play, with "the image of a man standing in his yard with a baby in his arms" (qtd. in DeVries 25). Beginning with this image, Wilson sought to subvert the dominant culture's representations of African American men as irresponsible, absentee fathers. Wilson creates Troy Maxson, a larger-than-life figure, who feels an overwhelming sense of duty and responsibility to his family. With an impenetrable resolve, he perceives familial values only from his perspective. Troy's self-involved concept of familial duty and responsibility prevents him from seeing the harm he causes, the pain his decisions inflict on other family members.

Through a series of retrospective stories performed by Troy, Wilson reveals Troy's victimization by and resentment of the forces of social and economic oppression. Wilson also uses these moments to disclose the influence that Troy's prior relationship with his father now exacts on his relationship with his own son Cory. Physically beaten by his father, Troy was forced to strike out on his own. During the course of the play, Cory must undergo a similar rite of passage. Repeating the family history, Cory physically confronts his father, is beaten by Troy, and is forced to leave his father's house. The repetition of behavior patterns by father and son underscores Wilson's conviction that history plays an important role in determining contemporary identity. Only by literally confronting the embodiment of the past, one's father or "forefathers," can one gain entrance into the future or ascendancy into adulthood.

In the play's second act, Troy's adultery provides the catalyst that propels his wife, Rose, to reassess her position, to gain a greater self-awareness, and to change. Rose blooms. Although Rose spiritually distances herself from Troy, she does not leave the marriage. Her final assessment of their marriage, delivered to her son Cory in the last scene, functions to reconcile father and son and emphasizes Rose's own resignation to "what life offered me in terms of being a woman" (1016). At the close of *Fences*, Cory is able to accept the continued "presence" of his father in his life. This acceptance comes after Cory has returned home from the Marines and announces to Rose his intent to boycott his father's funeral. Wilson juxtaposes Cory's return with the entrance of a new character, Troy's seven-year-old daughter from his affair, Raynell (Cory's half-sister). Wilson uses Raynell as a critical element in his redemptive strategy. Raynell visually represents the inextricable connection between past and present. Not only is she the manifestation of Troy's past infidelities but the signifier of his redemption. Her appearance enables both the audience and Cory to understand better the importance of inheritance, the perpetuation and veneration of history. In addition, here as in other Wilson works the child, Raynell, symbolizes the hope for [p. 325] the family's future. Significantly, her entrance into the action occurs not just on the day of Troy's funeral, but in the year 1965, in the midst of the civil rights era, a period of intense struggle and new opportunity for African Americans. [p. 326]

Works Cited

DeVries, Hilary. "A Song in Search of Itself." *American Theatre* 3.10 (January 1987): 22–25. Print.

Ellison, Ralph. "Blues People." *Shadow and Act*. New York: Random House, 1964. 247–58. Print.

Fishman, Joan. "Romare Bearden, August Wilson, and the Traditions of African Performance." *May All Your Fences Have Gates: Essays on the Drama of August Wilson*. Ed. Alan Nadel. Iowa City: U Iowa P, 1994. 133–49. Print.

Savran, David. *In Their Own Words: Contemporary American Playwrights*. New York: Theatre Communications Group, 1988. Print.

Shannon, Sandra G. "The Role of Memory in August Wilson's Four-Hundred-Year Autobiography." *Memory and Cultural Politics: New Approaches to American Ethnic Literature*. Ed. Amritjit Singh, Commas Skerrett, and Robert E. Hogan. Boston: Northeastern UP, 1996. 175–93. Print.

Wilson, August. *Fences*. New York: New American Library, 1986. Print.

———. *Joe Turner's Come and Gone*. New York: New American Library, 1988. Print.

———. *Ma Rainey's Black Bottom*. New York: New American Library, 1985. Print.

———. *The Piano Lesson*. New York: Plume, 1990. Print.

———. *Three Plays*. Pittsburgh: University of Pittsburgh Press, 1991. Print.

Susan Koprince

Baseball as History and Myth in August Wilson's *Fences*°   [2006]

The game of baseball has long been regarded as a metaphor for the American dream – an expression of hope, democratic values, and the drive for individual success. According to John Thorn, baseball has become "the great repository of national ideals, the symbol of all that [is] good in American life: fair play (sportsmanship); the rule of law (objective arbitration of disputes); equal opportunity (each side has its innings); the brotherhood of man (bleacher harmony); and more" (qtd. in Elias 3). Baseball's playing field itself has been viewed as archetypal – a walled garden, an American Eden marked by youth and timelessness. (There are no clocks in the game, and the runners move counterclockwise around the bases.) As former Yale University president and former

---

Koprince, Susan. "Baseball as History and Myth in August Wilson's *Fences*." *African American Review* 40.3 (2006): 349–58. Print.

baseball commissioner Bart Giamatti once wrote, baseball is "the last pure place where Americans can dream" (qtd. in Elias 9).

In his Pulitzer Prize–winning drama *Fences...*, however, August Wilson uses...the mythology of baseball to reveal the failed promise of the American dream. As Deeanne Westbrook observes in *Ground Rules: Baseball and Myth* (1996), baseball's playing field can be understood as an archetypal garden—an image of innocence and timeless space—an American Eden. In W. P. Kinsella's novel *Shoeless Joe* (1982), for example, the protagonist Ray Kinsella rediscovers Eden by building a baseball park in his Iowa cornfield, creating "a walled garden of eternal youth." Players from baseball's past enter this magical garden, "not middle-aged or elderly, as they were at their deaths, but young, as they were at their moments of peak performance. They occupy the mythic present" (Westbrook 102).

In *Fences* the closest that Troy comes to participating in the American dream—and hence inhabiting such a paradise—is during his life in the Negro Leagues. Wilson associates the American dream with Troy's younger days as a ball-player: with self-affirmation, limitless possibilities, and the chance for heroic success. The very act of hitting a home run—especially when the ball is hit over the fence—suggests extraordinary strength and the ability to transcend limits. Troy's son Lyons recalls seeing his father hit a home run over the grandstand: "Right out there in Homestead Field. He wasn't satisfied hitting in the seats... he want to hit it over everything! After the game he had two hundred people standing around waiting to shake his hand" (1014). Troy himself claims that he hit seven home runs off of Satchel Paige. "You can't get no better than that," he boasts (982).

For Troy, however, the American dream has turned into a prolonged nightmare. Instead of limitless opportunity, he has come to know racial discrimination and poverty. At age fifty-three, this former Negro League hero is a garbage collector who ekes out a meager existence, working arduously to support his family and living from hand to mouth. "I do the best I can do," he tells Rose. "I come in here every Friday. I carry a sack of potatoes and a bucket of lard. You all line up at the door with your hands out. I give you the lint from my pockets. I give you my sweat and my blood. I ain't got no tears. I done spent them" (986). Troy claims that he would not even have a roof over his head if it were not for the $3,000 that the government gave to his mentally disabled brother, Gabriel, following a serious head injury in World War II.

Wilson accentuates Troy's exclusion from the American Eden by converting baseball's mythical garden into an ironic version of paradise. In the stage directions to *Fences*, Wilson indicates that the legendary "field of dreams" has been reduced to the "small dirt yard" (964) in front of Troy's home—his current playing field. Incompletely fenced, the yard contains lumber and other fence-building materials, as well as two oil drums used as garbage containers. A baseball bat—"the most visible symbol of [Troy's] deferred dreams" (Shannon, *Fences* 46)—is propped up against a tree, from which there hangs "a ball made of rags" (964). As the setting reveals, Troy does not inhabit a walled garden of timeless youth. At fifty-three, he cannot reclaim his past glory as a power hitter; nor can he participate in the American dream. His playing field in 1957 has deteriorated into one of dirt, garbage, and rags. Indeed, only after Troy's death at the end of the play, when his fence is completed and when his daughter Raynell plants a small garden in front of the house, is there even a suggestion of a walled paradise.

According to Westbrook, baseball's archetypal playing field can also become a battleground—a scene of violent confrontation—much like the heroic fights at Valhalla, the "home of the slain" in Norse mythology. Each morning the warriors arm themselves for combat and battle one another fiercely in the great courtyard, returning to the banquet hall in the evening to feast and boast of their exploits. As Westbrook notes, "The ritualized aggression of both Valhalla and baseball field is rule governed . . . and endlessly repeatable" (109). The baseball players are modern-day warriors, the bat and ball are weapons, and the game itself a substitute for combat.

In *Fences* Wilson converts Troy's playing field into a battleground—an image reinforced by references to World War II (during which Gabriel got "half his head blown off" [979]), to the "Army of Death" (970), and to the Battle of Armageddon (when, according to Gabriel, "God get to waving that Judgment sword" [990]). Throughout the play Troy is pictured as a batter/warrior, fighting to earn a living and to stay alive in a world that repeatedly discriminates against him. As Shannon has noted, Troy sees life as a baseball contest; he sees himself as perpetually in the batter's box (*Dramatic Vision* 110). He tells Rose: "You got to guard [the plate] closely . . . always looking for the curve ball on the inside corner. You can't afford to let none get past you. You can't afford a call strike. If you going down . . . you going down swinging" (1001).

Troy's front yard is literally turned into a battleground during his confrontations with his younger son, Cory. Bitter about his own exclusion from major-league baseball, Troy is resistant when Cory wants to attend college on a football scholarship, telling his son that black athletes have to be twice as talented to make the team and that "the white man ain't gonna let you get nowhere with that football noway" (983). But Cory, who seems to believe in the promise of the American dream—particularly for black athletes in the 1950s—insists that Troy is selfishly holding him back from success: "You just scared I'm gonna be better than you, that's all" (995). The intergenerational conflict reaches a climax in act 2, when Troy and Cory engage in an ironic version of the all-American father-and-son game of catch (Birdwell 91). "Get your black ass out of my yard!" (1010), Troy warns Cory, after which the two combatants fight furiously over Troy's bat/weapon until Cory is expelled from his father's playing field.

Troy's efforts to prevent his son from playing football can be viewed as a form of what Harry J. Elam Jr. calls "racial madness"—a term that suggests that social and political forces can impact the black psyche and that decades of oppression can induce a collective psychosis.[1] In *Fences* this racial madness is illustrated most vividly in the character of Troy's mentally handicapped brother, Gabriel, but it is also revealed in Troy himself, who is so overwhelmed by bitterness that he destroys his son's dream of a college education—a dream that most fathers would happily support. Instead, Troy instructs Cory to stick with his job at the A & P or learn a trade like carpentry or auto mechanics: "That way you have something can't nobody take away from you" (983). There is a certain method, however, to Troy's madness; for why should he expect college football (another white power structure) to treat his son any better than major-league baseball treated him? Why should he believe, in 1957, that times have really changed for black men? Anxious for Cory to find economic security, and, more importantly, self-respect, Troy exclaims to Rose, "I don't want him to be like me! I want him to move as far away from my life as he can get" (985).

In Amiri Baraka's play *Dutchman* (1964), the African American protagonist Clay advocates a violent solution to the problem of racial madness, telling his white adversary, Lula, that "the only thing that would cure the neurosis would be your murder. Simple as that. . . . Crazy niggers turning their backs on sanity. When all it need is that simple act. Murder. Just Murder!" (qtd. in Elam 63). In *Fences* Troy's response to the racial madness that infects him is much less revolutionary than Clay's, but it is combative nonetheless. Troy chooses to challenge the white man, literally, by engaging in a form of social activism, that is, by taking a job complaint to his boss, Mr. Rand, and then to the commissioner's office. Moreover, he teaches his son how to fight. During their climactic struggle in act 2, Troy deliberately confronts Cory, taunting him, grabbing the bat from him, and insisting that he teach Cory how to swing. Determined to prepare his son for combat in a racist society, Troy uses the weapons and language of baseball as his teaching tools. "Don't you strike out," he tells Cory after an earlier altercation. "You living with a full count. Don't you strike out" (1003).

Troy's playing field is the scene not only of father-son conflict, but of marital strife as well. In act 2 Rose learns that Troy has been unfaithful to her and has fathered a child with his mistress, Alberta. When Troy tries to explain (and even justify) his infidelity by using baseball analogies, Rose is not impressed. "We're not talking about baseball!" she says. "We're talking about you going off to lay in bed with another woman . . . and then bring it home to me. That's what we're talking about. We ain't talking about no baseball" (1001). After the conflict between Rose and Troy escalates into a cold war—the two of them rarely speaking to one another—it is the wounded Rose, rather than Troy, who eventually dominates the battle, taking in his motherless daughter and telling Troy: "From right now . . . this child got a mother. But you a womanless man" (1006) . . .

Although Wilson's dramas are typically grounded in elements of African and African American cultures—including ritual, superstition, the blues, and jazz—*Fences* is unique in that it appropriates a traditionally white cultural form—baseball—in order to portray an African American experience in the twentieth century. By adopting this white cultural form, Wilson artfully expresses Troy Maxson's double consciousness—his complicated experience as a black man in a white-dominated world. At the same time, Wilson creates a "subversive narrative" that competes with the American Dream itself (Shannon, *Fences* 20). Thus, he demonstrates that the national pastime has been stained by racism, that the Edenic promise of America is illusory, and that the traditional mythology of baseball must ultimately make room for a new and revolutionary mythos: that of the defiant African American warrior.

Note

[1]Invoking the theories of psychiatrist-philosopher Frentz Fanon as well as the perspectives of Du Bois, Ellison, and others, Elam emphasizes that "racial madness" does not imply a pathology in blackness itself. Rather it is "a trope that became operative in clinical practice, literary creation, and cultural theory in the modern period as artists, critics, and practitioners identified social and cultural roots for black psychological impairment" (59). During his discussion of racial madness in *Fences*, Elam focuses on Troy's brain-damaged brother, Gabriel, whom he describes as a force for redemption.

Works Cited

Birdwell, Christine. "Death as a Fastball on the Outside Corner: *Fences'* Troy Maxson and the American Dream." *Aethlon: The Journal of Sport Literature* 8.1 (Fall 1990): 87–96. Print.

Elam, Harry J. Jr. *The Past as Present in the Drama of August Wilson*. Ann Arbor: U Michigan P, 2004. Print.

Elias, Robert. "A Fit for a Fractured Society." *Baseball and the American Dream: Race, Class, Gender, and the National Pastime*. Ed. Robert Elias. Armonk, N.Y.: M. E. Sharpe, 2001. 3–33. Print.

Kinsella, W. P. *Shoeless Joe*. 1982. New York: Ballantine, 1990. Print.

Shannon, Sandra G. *August Wilson's* Fences: *A Reference Guide*. Westport, Conn.: Greenwood, 2003. Print.

———. *The Dramatic Vision of August Wilson*. Washington, D.C.: Howard UP, 1995. Print.

Westbrook, Deeanne. *Ground Rules: Baseball and Myth*. Urbana: U Illinois P, 1996. Print.

Wilson, August. *Fences*. New York: New American Library, 1986. Print.

RESPONDING THROUGH Writing

Here are some suggestions for writing on August Wilson, but for a chapter like this one, you should not limit yourself to these topics. An important purpose behind the chapter is to help you learn how to find good topics on your own. You may make changes in the topics (with your instructor's permission) and make changes in how they are categorized (using a topic from the first six as a research topic, for example, instead of one using no outside sources.)

PAPERS USING NO OUTSIDE SOURCES

Literary Analysis Papers

1. Write a paper analyzing the use of baseball as a plot element and as a metaphor for life in *Fences*.

2. Write a paper exploring different kinds of fences, literal ones and figurative ones suggesting enclosures, in *Fences*.

Comparison-Contrast Papers

3. Write a paper comparing and contrasting the attitudes toward change evinced by Troy and by other characters in *Fences*.

4. Write a comparison-contrast paper showing how Bono serves as a foil for Troy or how Lyons serves as a foil for Cory in *Fences*.

Cultural Studies Papers

5. The church has traditionally been an important part of African American culture. Write a paper examining the use and effect of the language of and the practice of Christianity in *Fences*.

6. Write a paper on the attitudes toward and meaning of work in *Fences*.

PAPERS USING LIMITED OUTSIDE SOURCES

Literary Analysis Papers

1. In his interview with Bonnie Lyons, August Wilson says that inner conflict is at the center of drama (p. 1027). Using what he says there and what reviewers and critics included in this chapter say, write a paper discussing the inner conflicts that drive the action in *Fences*.

2. In his interview with Miles Marshall Lewis, August Wilson says his plays are about the "Big Themes" — "love, honor, duty, betrayal" (p. 1028). Drawing on that interview and other secondary writings in this chapter, write a paper discussing the extent to which those themes are present and influential in *Fences*.

Comparison-Contrast Papers

3. Frank Rich's reference to the "conflicting visions" of Troy and Cory (p. 1022) is echoed by other secondary works included in this chapter. Building on their comments, write a paper comparing and contrasting the visions of the two men and discussing the reasons for and effects of the tensions between them.

4. Lloyd Richards, the original director of *Fences*, writes that the play tells the story of four generations of black Americans (p. 1018). Write a paper examining differences and similarities in what happens to them, especially changes — or lack of change — in their relationships with white Americans. Use secondary materials in this chapter, as well as the play, for support.

Cultural Studies Papers

5. Write a paper examining the roles of and attitudes toward women in *Fences*, using the secondary materials in this chapter as well as the play itself for illustrations and supporting details.

6. Harry J. Elam, Jr. says that at the heart of Wilson's plays is "the concept that one must go backwards in order to move forward" (p. 1034). Write a paper in which you explore the applicability of that claim in *Fences*, using the secondary materials in this chapter as well as the play for support.

PAPERS INVOLVING FURTHER RESEARCH

Literary Analysis Papers

1. Wilson once said that listening to a recording of Bessie Smith's "Nobody in Town Can Bake a Jelly Roll Like Mine" awakened his interest in the blues. Write a research paper on the use and influence of the blues on his play *Fences* (consider the rhythms, outlook, and sensibility that characterize the blues).

2. Harry J. Elam, Jr. says that Wilson, who wrote poetry before turning to drama, "allows his characters to voice their history in the verbal equivalent of musical solos" (p. 1036). Write a paper analyzing the "poetic" or "musical" style Wilson gives to characters in *Fences*, especially in major speeches. Focus on the text of the play, but bring in the secondary materials in this chapter and other critical materials you find elsewhere for additional support.

Comparison-Contrast Papers

3. Susan Koprince (p. 1038) is one of several critics who write about the mythic implications of baseball as a metaphor for the American dream in *Fences*. Write a paper comparing and contrasting her insights with those of two or three other critics and explain which you find most helpful or convincing and why.

4. Do research on August Wilson's life, using the material in this chapter and going beyond it. Write a paper in which you compare and contrast what happens in Troy Maxson's life to events in or associated with Wilson's life or the lives of people he knew, focusing on how Wilson transforms biographical material to make the play "work."

Cultural Studies Papers

5. Write a research paper examining August Wilson's incorporation and adaptation of African American folklore traditions in *Fences*.

6. In August Wilson's master plan of writing ten plays, one embodying the spirit of each of the decades of the twentieth century, *Fences* was the play for the 1950s. Write a research paper on how *Fences* is representative of—or epitomizes—events and changes taking place in that decade.

A Collection of Plays

CHAPTER 26

Viewing from Various Vantage Points

FOUR TEN-MINUTE PLAYS

You can research the authors in this collection with LitLinks, or take a quiz on the plays with LitQuiz, at bedfordstmartins.com/rewritinglit.

Unlike the idiosyncratic nature of flash fiction and short-short poems, which defy easy categorization, the short play doesn't differ all that much from a play of standard length. Its primary distinction from longer plays is that it is more constrained by performance time and therefore more often than not is only one act long.

The dramatic elements of a short play do not differ from those of a longer play either. However, the climax, instead of happening after a developed buildup, is more like that of a conventional short story, in which a particular moment has a sudden, profound effect on a character. The dramatic intensity of such a moment is crafted into the structures of both short plays and plays with several acts. Again, the difference lies in the length of time leading to and following the climax. Think about it in terms of a crucial moment in a long-term relationship and one on a first date: Both can be dramatic. The difference is in the length of time the drama develops.

As you read the following ten-minute plays, bring to them all the resources you would bring to a play of two, three, four, or five acts.

David Ives   b. 1950

Sure Thing   [1988]

This play is for Jason Buzas

Betty, a woman in her late twenties, is reading at a café table. An empty chair is opposite her. Bill, same age, enters.

BILL: Excuse me. Is this chair taken?
BETTY: Excuse me?
BILL: Is this taken?
BETTY: Yes it is.
BILL: Oh. Sorry.
BETTY: Sure thing.

(*A bell rings softly.*)

BILL: Excuse me. Is this chair taken?
BETTY: Excuse me?
BILL: Is this taken?
BETTY: No, but I'm expecting somebody in a minute.
BILL: Oh. Thanks anyway.
BETTY: Sure thing.

(*A bell rings softly.*)

BILL: Excuse me. Is this chair taken?
BETTY: No, but I'm expecting somebody very shortly.
BILL: Would you mind if I sit here till he or she or it comes?
BETTY (*glances at her watch*): They do seem to be pretty late. . . .
BILL: You never know who you might be turning down.
BETTY: Sorry. Nice try, though.
BILL: Sure thing.

(*Bell.*)

Is this seat taken?
BETTY: No it's not.
BILL: Would you mind if I sit here?
BETTY: Yes I would.
BILL: Oh.

(*Bell.*)

Is this chair taken?

BETTY: No it's not.

BILL: Would you mind if I sit here?

BETTY: No. Go ahead.

BILL: Thanks. (*He sits. She continues reading.*) Everyplace else seems to be taken.

BETTY: Mm-hm.

BILL: Great place.

BETTY: Mm-hm.

BILL: What's the book?

BETTY: I just wanted to read in quiet, if you don't mind.

BILL: No. Sure thing.

(*Bell.*)

BILL: Everyplace else seems to be taken.

BETTY: Mm-hm.

BILL: Great place for reading.

BETTY: Yes, I like it.

BILL: What's the book?

BETTY: *The Sound and the Fury.*

BILL: Oh. Hemingway.

(*Bell.*)

What's the book?

BETTY: *The Sound and the Fury.*

BILL: Oh. Faulkner.

BETTY: Have you read it?

BILL: Not . . . actually. I've sure read *about* it, though. It's supposed to be great.

BETTY: It is great.

BILL: I hear it's great. (*Small pause.*) Waiter?

(*Bell.*)

What's the book?

BETTY: *The Sound and the Fury.*

BILL: Oh. Faulkner.

BETTY: Have you read it?

BILL: I'm a Mets fan, myself.

(*Bell.*)

BETTY: Have you read it?

BILL: Yeah, I read it in college.

BETTY: Where was college?

BILL: I went to Oral Roberts University.

(*Bell.*)

BETTY: Where was college?

BILL: I was lying. I never really went to college. I just like to party.

(*Bell.*)

BETTY: Where was college?

BILL: Harvard.

BETTY: Do you like Faulkner?

BILL: I love Faulkner. I spent a whole winter reading him once.

BETTY: I've just started.

BILL: I was so excited after ten pages that I went out and bought everything else he wrote. One of the greatest reading experiences of my life. I mean, all that incredible psychological understanding. Page after page of gorgeous prose. His profound grasp of the mystery of time and human existence. The smells of the earth . . . What do you think?

BETTY: I think it's pretty boring.

(*Bell.*)

BILL: What's the book?

BETTY: *The Sound and the Fury.*

BILL: Oh! Faulkner!

BETTY: Do you like Faulkner?

BILL: I love Faulkner.

BETTY: He's incredible.

BILL: I spent a whole winter reading him once.

BETTY: I was so excited after ten pages that I went out and bought everything else he wrote.

BILL: All that incredible psychological understanding.

BETTY: And the prose is so gorgeous.

BILL: And the way he's grasped the mystery of time —

BETTY: — and human existence. I can't believe I've waited this long to read him.

BILL: You never know. You might not have liked him before.

BETTY: That's true.

BILL: You might not have been ready for him. You have to hit these things at the right moment or it's no good.

BETTY: That's happened to me.

BILL: It's all in the timing. (*Small pause.*) My name's Bill, by the way.

BETTY: I'm Betty.

BILL: Hi.

BETTY: Hi. (*Small pause.*)

BILL: Yes I thought reading Faulkner was . . . a great experience.

BETTY: Yes. (*Small pause.*)

BILL: *The Sound and the Fury* . . . (*Another small pause.*)

BETTY: Well. Onwards and upwards. (*She goes back to her book.*)

BILL: Waiter — ?

(*Bell.*)

You have to hit these things at the right moment or it's no good.

BETTY: That's happened to me.

BILL: It's all in the timing. My name's Bill, by the way.

BETTY: I'm Betty.

BILL: Hi.

BETTY: Hi.

BILL: Do you come in here a lot?

BETTY: Actually I'm just in town for two days from Pakistan.

BILL: Oh. Pakistan.

(*Bell.*)

My name's Bill, by the way.

BETTY: I'm Betty.

BILL: Hi.

BETTY: Hi.

BILL: Do you come in here a lot?

BETTY: Every once in a while. Do you?

BILL: Not so much anymore. Not as much as I used to. Before my nervous break-down.

(*Bell.*)

Do you come in here a lot?

BETTY: Why are you asking?

BILL: Just interested.

BETTY: Are you really interested, or do you just want to pick me up?

BILL: No, I'm really interested.

BETTY: Why would you be interested in whether I come in here a lot?

BILL: I'm just . . . getting acquainted.

BETTY: Maybe you're only interested for the sake of making small talk long enough to ask me back to your place to listen to some music, or because you've just rented this great tape for your VCR, or because you've got some terrific unknown Django Reinhardt record, only all you really want to do is fuck—which you won't do very well—after which you'll go into the bathroom and pee very loudly, then pad into the kitchen and get yourself a beer from the refrigerator without asking me whether I'd like anything, and then you'll pro-ceed to lie back down beside me and confess that you've got a girlfriend named Stephanie who's away at medical school in Belgium for a year, and that you've been involved with her—*off and on*—in what you'll call a very "intricate" rela-tionship, for the past *seven YEARS*. None of which *interests* me, mister!

BILL: Okay.

(*Bell.*)

Do you come in here a lot?

BETTY: Every other day, I think.

BILL: I come in here quite a lot and I don't remember seeing you.

BETTY: I guess we must be on different schedules.

BILL: Missed connections.

BETTY: Yes. Different time zones.

BILL: Amazing how you can live right next door to somebody in this town and never even know it.

BETTY: I know.

BILL: City life.

BETTY: It's crazy.

BILL: We probably pass each other in the street every day. Right in front of this place, probably.

BETTY: Yep.

BILL (*looks around*): Well the waiters here sure seem to be in some different time zone. I can't seem to locate one anywhere. . . . Waiter! (*He looks back.*) So what do you— (*He sees that she's gone back to her book.*)

BETTY: I beg pardon?

BILL: Nothing. Sorry.

(*Bell.*)

BETTY: I guess we must be on different schedules.

BILL: Missed connections.

BETTY: Yes. Different time zones.

BILL: Amazing how you can live right next door to somebody in this town and never even know it.

BETTY: I know.

BILL: City life.

BETTY: It's crazy.

BILL: You weren't waiting for somebody when I came in, were you?

BETTY: Actually I was.

BILL: Oh. Boyfriend?

BETTY: Sort of.

BILL: What's a sort-of boyfriend?

BETTY: My husband.

BILL: Ah-ha.

(*Bell.*)

You weren't waiting for somebody when I came in, were you?

BETTY: Actually I was.

BILL: Oh. Boyfriend?

BETTY: Sort of.

BILL: What's a sort-of boyfriend?

BETTY: We were meeting here to break up.

BILL: Mm-hm . . .

(*Bell.*)

What's a sort-of boyfriend?

BETTY: My lover. Here she comes right now!

(*Bell.*)

BILL: You weren't waiting for somebody when I came in, were you?

BETTY: No, just reading.

BILL: Sort of a sad occupation for a Friday night, isn't it? Reading here, all by yourself?

BETTY: Do you think so?

BILL: Well sure. I mean, what's a good-looking woman like you doing out alone on a Friday night?

BETTY: Trying to keep away from lines like that.

BILL: No, listen —

(*Bell.*)

You weren't waiting for somebody when I came in, were you?

BETTY: No, just reading.

BILL: Sort of a sad occupation for a Friday night, isn't it? Reading here all by yourself?

BETTY: I guess it is, in a way.

BILL: What's a good-looking woman like you doing out alone on a Friday night anyway? No offense, but . . .

BETTY: I'm out alone on a Friday night for the first time in a very long time.

BILL: Oh.

BETTY: You see, I just recently ended a relationship.

BILL: Oh.

BETTY: Of rather long standing.

BILL: I'm sorry. (*Small pause.*) Well listen, since reading by yourself is such a sad occupation for a Friday night, would you like to go elsewhere?

BETTY: No . . .

BILL: Do something else?

BETTY: No thanks.

BILL: I was headed out to the movies in a while anyway.

BETTY: I don't think so.

BILL: Big chance to let Faulkner catch his breath. All those long sentences get him pretty tired.

BETTY: Thanks anyway.

BILL: Okay.

BETTY: I appreciate the invitation.

BILL: Sure thing.

(*Bell.*)

You weren't waiting for somebody when I came in, were you?

BETTY: No, just reading.

BILL: Sort of a sad occupation for a Friday night, isn't it? Reading here all by yourself?

BETTY: I guess I was trying to think of it as existentially romantic. You know — cappuccino, great literature, rainy night . . .

BILL: That only works in Paris. We *could* hop the late plane to Paris. Get on a Concorde. Find a café . . .

BETTY: I'm a little short on plane fare tonight.

BILL: Darn it, so am I.

BETTY: To tell you the truth, I was headed to the movies after I finished this section. Would you like to come along? Since you can't locate a waiter?

BILL: That's a very nice offer, but . . .

BETTY: Uh-huh. Girlfriend?

BILL: Two, actually. One of them's pregnant, and Stephanie —

(*Bell.*)

BETTY: Girlfriend?

BILL: No, I don't have a girlfriend. Not if you mean the castrating bitch I dumped last night.

(*Bell.*)

BETTY: Girlfriend?

BILL: Sort of. Sort of.

BETTY: What's a sort-of girlfriend?

BILL: My mother.

(*Bell.*)

I just ended a relationship, actually.

BETTY: Oh.

BILL: Of rather long standing.

BETTY: I'm sorry to hear it.

BILL: This is my first night out alone in a long time. I feel a little bit at sea, to tell you the truth.

BETTY: So you didn't stop to talk because you're a Moonie, or you have some weird political affiliation — ?

BILL: Nope. Straight-down-the-ticket Republican.

(*Bell.*)

Straight-down-the-ticket Democrat.

(*Bell.*)

Can I tell you something about politics?

(*Bell.*)

I like to think of myself as a citizen of the universe.

(*Bell.*)

I'm unaffiliated.

BETTY: That's a relief. So am I.

BILL: I vote my beliefs.

BETTY: Labels are not important.

BILL: Labels are not important, exactly. Take me, for example. I mean, what does it matter if I had a two-point at—

(*Bell.*)

three-point at—

(*Bell.*)

four-point at college? Or if I did come from Pittsburgh—

(*Bell.*)

Cleveland—

(*Bell.*)

Westchester County?

BETTY: Sure.

BILL: I believe that a man is what he is.

(*Bell.*)

A person is what he is.

(*Bell.*)

A person is . . . what they are.

BETTY: I think so too.

BILL: So what if I admire Trotsky?

(*Bell.*)

So what if I once had a total-body liposuction?

(*Bell.*)

So what if I don't have a penis?

(*Bell.*)

So what if I spent a year in the Peace Corps? I was acting on my convictions.

BETTY: Sure.

BILL: You just can't hang a sign on a person.

BETTY: Absolutely. I'll bet you're a Scorpio.

(*Many bells ring.*)

Listen, I was headed to the movies after I finished this section. Would you like to come along?

BILL: That sounds like fun. What's playing?

BETTY: A couple of the really early Woody Allen movies.

BILL: Oh.

BETTY: You don't like Woody Allen?

BILL: Sure. I like Woody Allen.

BETTY: But you're not crazy about Woody Allen.

BILL: Those early ones kind of get on my nerves.

BETTY: Uh-huh.

(*Bell.*)

BILL: Y'know I was headed to the—

BETTY (*simultaneously*): I was thinking about—

BILL: I'm sorry.

BETTY: No, go ahead.

BILL: I was going to say that I was headed to the movies in a little while, and . . .

BETTY: So was I.

BILL: The Woody Allen festival?

BETTY: Just up the street.

BILL: Do you like the early ones?

BETTY: I think anybody who doesn't ought to be run off the planet.

BILL: How many times have you seen *Bananas*?

BETTY: Eight times.

BILL: Twelve. So are you still interested (*Long pause.*)

BETTY: Do you like Entenmann's crumb cake . . . ?

BILL: Last night I went out at two in the morning to get one. Did you have an Etch-a-Sketch as a child?

BETTY: Yes! And do you like Brussels sprouts? (*Pause.*)

BILL: No, I think they're disgusting.

BETTY: They *are* disgusting!

BILL: Do you still believe in marriage in spite of current sentiments against it?

BETTY: Yes.

BILL: And children?

BETTY: Three of them.

BILL: Two girls and a boy.

BETTY: Harvard, Vassar, and Brown.

BILL: And will you love me?

BETTY: Yes.

BILL: And cherish me forever?

BETTY: Yes.

BILL: Do you still want to go to the movies?

BETTY: Sure thing.

BILL AND BETTY (*together*): *Waiter!*

BLACKOUT

Mark Lambeck

Intervention

[2008]

CHARACTERS

JULIA, early thirties, a pushy, female executive-type
MIKE, late thirties, Craig's best friend and Julia's husband
AMY, early thirties, Craig's loving wife
CRAIG, late thirties, an accountant who is unaffiliated, the object of the
   intervention

SETTING

Various street locations; no set
   required.

TIME

The present.

PROPS

JULIA, a shoulder bag and a cell phone
MIKE, a cell phone
AMY, a shoulder bag and a cell phone
CRAIG, an attaché case

APPROACHING THE AUTHOR

When Temple Beth Sholom in Stratford shut
down its bingo operation in the spring of
1998, **Mark Lambeck** organized the Temple
Players as a means not only to raise funds
but also to present plays with "identifiable
Jewish characters or themes" to a diverse
audience of Connecticut theatergoers, which
it continues to do.

For more about him, see page 1397.

*At rise, Mike walks on downstage left with a cell phone at his ear. He continues
walking in place once he reaches his mark.*

MIKE (*into phone*): Did you talk to Amy?

JULIA (*walks on downstage right with a cell phone, walking in place*): He's coming.

MIKE: How'd she do it?

JULIA: She told him it was our anniversary and he had to help us celebrate at La
   Scala.

MIKE: Anniversary? (*Looks at phone, quickly presses a few buttons—beeping
   sounds—till he gets to his calendar.*)

JULIA: I heard that!

MIKE (*finds calendar*): But our anniversary's in June. (*Pause.*) Right?

JULIA: Are you trying to piss me off?

MIKE: No . . . I.

JULIA: I heard the beeping. I know you were surfing through your calendar to
   check the date.

MIKE: No. I wouldn't forget. . . .

JULIA (*annoyed*): Can we just focus on Craig for a minute, please?

MIKE: Sure. I'm with ya.

JULIA: I'm walking down Chapel headed toward Elm. Where are you?

MIKE (*still walking in place*): I'm at Arbor heading toward Main. (*Pause.*) Look, are you sure we're doing the right thing?

JULIA: He's refused to join the rest of modern civilization. He's refused to adapt. He blew up at Amy when she even suggested it. She needs us there. We don't know how he's gonna react.

MIKE: What? Craig's not gonna get violent. I've known him since high school. Accountants don't throw punches.

JULIA: He got into a screaming match with Amy.

MIKE: We're all in this together. He knows we all love him. (*Pause.*) Plus, we can take him!

JULIA: I don't wanna take him. Craig's our friend. We're just looking out for his best interest. (*Intent.*) He has to understand that this intervention is for his own good. He can't go on refusing... Oh. Hold on, I have another call coming in. (*Presses buttons.*) Hello?

MIKE (*looks at phone, reads text message*): Where are you two? With the letters R, U, and the number two. Gotta love text messaging.

JULIA: What? I can't hear you. What? Oh, hi Ian. Sorry. Bad connection. You're in the lobby? He hasn't left his office yet? What? You're breaking up. Move outside so you can get a better signal. Wait. Hold on a minute.

(*Presses button.*)

MIKE: So what's the story?

JULIA: I have Ian on the other line. He's in the lobby at Craig's work.

MIKE: In the lobby? Man, is he crazy? He could be spotted.

JULIA: I know. I didn't even get to say anything yet. He keeps cutting out. Look, we're running out of time. He's still on the other line...

MIKE: I just got a text message from Chuck. He's at Point Zero wondering where we are. We were supposed to be the first ones there, and we haven't even gotten to our meeting point yet! Oh, hang on, honey, I'm getting another call. (*Pushes button.*) Hello?

JULIA (*pushes button*): Are you there, Ian? Yeah. Better. Look, you gotta stay out of sight. He's gonna know something's up.

AMY (*enters upstage on a cell phone*): Mike, where are you guys? I tried calling Julia but it went straight to her voice mail.

JULIA: Hold on a minute, Ian, I got a new voice mail. (*Pushes button.*)

MIKE: That's because she's on the other line with Ian. I have her on hold.

AMY: We're never gonna pull this. Craig's resisted for so long. I think he actually prides himself on being the last person in America who... Hold on. I have another call coming in. (*Presses button.*) Hello?

JULIA: He's what? Oh my God. Don't let him see you!

AMY: I know, Chuck. They're late. The plan is to intercept him on Main before he gets to La Scala. Just wait outside the restaurant—we'll see you. I have Mike on hold now. He's got Julia on the other line... Hello? Are you there? I'm losing you. Chuck? Hello?

JULIA: He what? Oh my God. How did that happen? Is he OK? No. Wait. I'm texting Mike right now. (*Presses buttons. Back into the phone.*)

AMY: Lost him. (*Presses button.*) Hello? Mike? Are you there?

MIKE: Yeah. I'm here.

AMY: Chuck called to find out where everybody is. But I lost him.

MIKE: I know. He just texted me, "Where R–U–2?"

JULIA: You know, they shouldn't be cleaning those floors till after six. They're lucky he didn't get hurt. He's not hurt, is he Ian?

AMY: I don't know why I let you guys talk me into this. Craig is adamant.

MIKE: Look Amy, it's under control. All the spotters are in place. Ian's at Craig's office. Chuck is at Point Zero. Julia's on her way, and I'm walking toward Main right now. Where are you?

AMY: I'm just turning onto Main.

MIKE: We'll meet you at the corner of Main and Hollister in (*Looks at watch.*) ten minutes.

JULIA: What? Say that again. I can't hear you.

AMY: I'm really having second thoughts. Craig's gonna think we're ganging up on him.

MIKE: We ARE ganging up on him! That's what you do in an intervention. Craig's my best friend. We only want to . . . Oh, hold on, Amy, I'm getting a text message. (*Puts her on hold. Reads.*) Craig fell in the lobby. Got up. Looks OK. Oh, man! (*Presses button.*) Amy? OK, now don't panic . . .

AMY: You know it's never comforting to the person you're talking to when you tell them "don't panic."

MIKE: Apparently Craig fell in the lobby but he's fine.

AMY: Oh my God. What happened?

MIKE: Wait, there's another text message.

JULIA: OK, I'll check. You just sent it through?

MIKE (*reads*): Uh, Amy, put me on hold and check your phone e-mail. Ian shot some video of Craig's fall on his cell and e-mailed it.

JULIA (*Presses buttons. Looks at phone.*): Got it. Great action shot. You sure he's OK. Looks like a nasty spill.

AMY: Wait. Something's coming in. (*Pulls phone away, then back into it.*) It's an e-mail from Chuck. What's going on? Is Craig OK?

MIKE: Hang on, Amy. (*Holds phone away to look at it.*) OK, Chuck's e-mail has a link to the video footage Ian sent. Apparently it shows Craig getting up and moving. Ya see? He's fine.

JULIA (*into phone*): Nice video work, Ian. Did you send this to Amy? You know how she worries.

MIKE: Amy? Are you there? Did you check out the video? Amy? Hello?

AMY (*looking at phone video*): I can't believe Craig wore that red tie today. I told him to go with the blue. He never listens to me.

JULIA: That video footage is hilarious. (*Giggles.*) The way his portfolio flew up in the air like that and his leg bent under.

MIKE: Amy?

AMY (*Presses buttons; listens*): Hello?

MIKE: Man, I thought I lost you.

AMY: I'm here. I was watching the video.

JULIA: Good work, Ian. Now get out of there before he sees you. We'll call you later and let you know how it goes. (*Presses buttons.*)

MIKE: Hang on, I got another call coming in. (*Presses button.*) Hello?

JULIA: Mike? Good you're still there. Look, I got a voice mail from Amy.

MIKE: I know. I have her on the other line right now.

JULIA: Great! Conference me in.

MIKE: Hang on. (*Presses buttons.*) Hello? Amy are you still there?

AMY: I'm still here.

MIKE: Julia? Can you hear me?

JULIA: Loud and clear.

AMY: Hi, Julia.

JULIA: Hi, Ames. Where ARE you?

AMY: I'm on Main heading toward Hollister.

MIKE: That was fast. Me too.

JULIA: Amy, I know you're worried but it's gonna be fine. Mike and Chuck and me will be there with you.

AMY: What about Ian?

JULIA: He was just a spotter. I sent him home. We don't want to overwhelm Craig. That Ian . . . so quick with the camera work, huh?

MIKE: Fastest thumbs on the East Coast.

AMY: Oh . . . you guys. I knew I can depend on you. I'm so grateful . . .

JULIA: What are friends for?

MIKE: Oh, man! I think I see him coming. (*Pointing to distance.*) Way down the street. Where are you now Amy?

AMY (*Coming up behind him on phone; taps Mike.*): Turn around.

MIKE (*yelps and literally jumps*): Ahhhhh . . . Jesus!

JULIA: What's going on?

MIKE: Amy's here. We can see Craig down the street. Where are you?

JULIA: I'm on Hollister. I'll be there in a minute.

MIKE (*to Amy*): Should we duck behind a bush or something?

AMY: Craig just came from work—he's still deep in thought.

MIKE: Right, he won't even see us until he's practically on top of us.

JULIA (*exits stage left*): OK, I see you guys on the street. Look left.

(*Mike and Amy both look left. They start waving.*)

AMY (*waving*): Hey, Julia!

MIKE: Here he comes.

CRAIG (*Enters limping—almost walks into Mike.*): Oh excuse . . . Mike? Amy? I thought you guys were gonna meet me at La Scala. (*Looks at watch.*) Am I late?

AMY (*takes his arm*): No, sweetie. (*Rubs his back.*) You're fine.

MIKE: Everything's gonna be fine.

CRAIG (*confused*): What?

JULIA (*Enters stage right coming up behind Craig.*): We're here for you, Craig. You know how much we all care about you.

CRAIG: Julia? What are you talking about?

MIKE: It's time you faced reality, Craig.

JULIA: You can't hold out any longer. You HAVE to give in.

AMY: Oh, sweetie. I love you! It's for your own good.

MIKE: We all love you, man!

JULIA (*opens purse, takes out a cell phone*): Here. Take it. It's yours.

CRAIG: What? NO!

MIKE: You're the last man in America without a cell phone.

JULIA: Did you really think you could hold out forever?

CRAIG: NO! I won't take it.

JULIA: Grab him!

(*Mike and Amy both grab Craig as he struggles to pull away.*)

JULIA (*putting cell in Craig's hand*): Your number is 918-2773.

CRAIG: NO! (*Gets loose; drops portfolio and puts his hands over his ears; yells.*)
    NO! (*Looks at Mike, then Amy.*) My God. How could you?

MIKE: We could because we're your friends, man.

AMY: I'm your wife. I love you.

JULIA: This is an intervention, Craig.

CRAIG: But an intervention is for someone who's addicted to something.
    YOU'RE the ones addicted to cell phones. Everyone's obsessed! (*Raising his
    voice.*) People walking down the street with earpieces looking like they're
    talking to themselves. Car crashes because drivers are on hands-free sys-
    tems. The other day I was in the men's room and the guy in the next stall
    was making a business deal on his cell while . . . multitasking!

AMY: Sweetie, it's time.

CRAIG: My God—even my own wife.

AMY: Please Craig. I worry about you when you go on those bike rides alone
    without your wallet, without ID. What if you were hit by a car?

MIKE: With a cell phone, you could call for help.

JULIA: You could program in an ICE.

CRAIG: An Ice?

MIKE: I-C-E. In case of emergency. They could speed-dial Amy.

AMY: It's for your own safety.

JULIA: What if you broke down on the road and couldn't call Triple-A?

CRAIG: No! It's a cult. You're the ones who need an intervention!

MIKE: What if you were running late and were supposed to meet Amy at her
    mother's, but you were stuck in traffic—while she worried.

AMY: Or if I needed you to pick up a pizza for dinner.

MIKE: Or I canceled our squash court because I twisted my ankle and you were
    already heading for the Y.

CRAIG: No. I can't do it!

JULIA: What if Amy sent you to pick up her favorite shampoo and there you
    were, in the personal-care aisle, looking over rows and rows . . .

MIKE: Shelves and shelves . . .

JULIA: Of hair products but you couldn't remember the one she wanted!

AMY: All you'd have to do is call.

CRAIG: But what about the monthly bill? Roaming charges. Minutes that should have rolled over but didn't. Contracts that lock you in for two years even if the service sucks. Erroneous charges they won't remove. (*Hyperventilating.*) Text messaging fees!!!

MIKE (*patting Craig*): Take a deep breath, buddy. We've all been there.

JULIA: It's part of being a member of a technologically advanced society.

MIKE: Yeah, you don't wanna be an outcast, man.

(*Cell rings. Amy, Julia, and Mike dive for their phones.*)

JULIA (*holding up her phone victoriously*): It's me. Hello? Not now, Ian. I'll call you when it's over. (*Hangs up.*)

AMY (*to Craig*): It's so humiliating when I can't reach you at a moment's notice. At work, my coworkers look at me with pity when I have to leave a message on the land line at your office.

JULIA: I hear they're reviewing legislation mandating everyone over the age of six carries a cell phone. For emergencies.

MIKE: So kids won't get nabbed by psychos.

JULIA: Our government can't be responsible if someone can't reach 911.

CRAIG (*starts breaking down*): Oh my God. I can't. I just . . .

JULIA: It's all about accessibility.

MIKE: Yeah, man, don't you want to be accessible?

(*A cell phone rings again. Julia, Amy, and Mike all dive into their purses/pockets to retrieve theirs again.*)

JULIA (*holding up phone*): It's me! (*Presses button.*) Hello? Chuck? Yes. It's done. No. He's actually holding it in his hand.

CRAIG (*looks at the phone in his hand*): My God, I'm holding it in my hand.

JULIA: We'll be there in a few minutes. What? You're breaking up.

AMY (*comforting Craig*): Oh, sweetie, you'll grow to love it. You'll grow to depend on it just like the rest of us.

JULIA: Ian posted the video of Craig's fall on YouTube? (*Looks at the others excitedly.*) It's already gotten over a thousand hits?

MIKE: Hey, man, you're a star.

CRAIG: Oh my God. Ian was there? How did he . . . ?

AMY: Call your mother. I'll show you how to program in her number.

JULIA: Chuck, I gotta go. I promised Ian I'd call him when it was over.

(*A cell phone rings again.*)

MIKE/AMY (*Together. Answering their phones.*): Hello?

(*Blackout.*)

END OF PLAY

Suzan-Lori Parks (b. 1964)

Father Comes Home from the Wars (Part 1)   [2006]
from *365 Days/365 Plays*

FATHER: Hi honey, Im home.

MOTHER: Yr home.

FATHER: Yes.

MOTHER: I wasnt expecting you. Ever.

FATHER: Should I go back out and come back in again?

MOTHER: Please.

(*He goes back out and comes back in again.*)

MOTHER: Once more.

FATHER: Yr kidding.

MOTHER: Please.

(*He goes back out and comes back in again.*)

MOTHER: Yr home.

FATHER: Yes.

MOTHER: Let me get a good look at you.

FATHER: I'll just turn around.

MOTHER: Please.

(*He turns around once. Counterclockwise.*)

MOTHER: They should of sent a letter. A letter saying you were coming home. Or at least a telephone call. That is the least they could do. Give a woman and her family and her friends and neighbors a chance to get ready. A chance to spruce things up. Put new ribbons in the hair of the dog. Get the oil changed. Have everything running. Smoothly. And bake a cake of course. Hang streamers. Tell the yard man to—tidy up his act. Oh God. Long story. Oh God. Long story. I woulda invited the neighbors over. Had everyone on the block jump out from their hiding places from behind the brand-new furniture with the plastic still on it and say—WHAT? Say: "Welcome Home" of course. And then after a few slices of cake and a few drinks theyd all get the nerve to say what theyre really thinking. For now itll stay unthought and unsaid. Well. You came home. All in one piece looks like. We're lucky. I guess. We're lucky, right? Hhhhh.

FATHER: They sent a letter saying I was coming or at least they telephoned. Maybe you didnt open the letter. I dont blame you. It could have been bad news. I see yr unopened envelopes piled up. I dont blame you. I dont blame you at all. They called several times. Maybe you were out. Maybe you were screwing the yard man. If you had known I was coming you woulda put new ribbons in the hair of the dog, got the oil changed, baked a cake and

APPROACHING THE AUTHOR

From November 2002 to November 2003, **Suzan-Lori Parks** wrote a short play each day, for the "365 Days/365 Plays" project. The plays were premiered in various cities across the United States during 2006–2007. According to the *New York Times*, "subject matter for the plays, most only a few pages long, ranges from deities to soldiers to what Ms. Parks saw out of her plane window." For more about her, see page 1406.

invited all the neighbors over so they could jump out of their various hiding places behind the brand-new furniture purchased with the blood of some people I used to know—and some blood of some people I used to kill. Oh God. Long story. Oh God. Long story. And theyd shout at me—WHAT? "Welcome Home" of course. And then after a few slices of cake and a few drinks theyd get the nerve to tell me what they really think: "Murderer, baby killer, racist, government pawn, ultimate patsy, stooge, fall guy, camp follower, dumbass, dope fiend, loser." Hhhhh.

MOTHER
FATHER

(*Rest.*)

MOTHER: I cant understand a word yr saying.
FATHER: I dont speak English anymore.
MOTHER: I dont blame you. SIT DOWN, I'LL FIX YOU SOMETHING.

(*He sits. She takes a heavy frying pan and holds it over his head. Almost murder. She lowers the pan.*)

MOTHER
FATHER

(*Rest.*)

(*He sits. Again she raises the frying pan and holds it over his head. Almost murder. She lowers the pan.*)

FATHER: Where are the children?
MOTHER: What children?

(*Sound of the wind and the rain.*)

Joyce Carol Oates (b. 1938)

When I Was a Little Girl and My Mother Didn't Want Me   [1997]

Lights up. An elderly woman speaks. Her voice alternates between urgency and bemusement; emotion and reflection.

My father was killed and I never knew why.
Then, I was given away. By my mother.
I was so little . . . six months.
There were too many of us, nine of us,
    my mother gave me away.
When I was old enough to know . . . I cried a lot.   5

My father was killed and I never knew
    why.
No one would tell me.
Now there's no one I can ask.
"Why? Why?"
It happened in a fight, in a tavern, he
    was only forty-four years old.
My father I never knew. Forty-four!
    Now, he could be my son.

I wasn't always an . . . old woman.
    Eighty-one.
I was a girl for so long.
I was a little girl for so long.
I was six months old when my father
    died.   15
And there were too many of us to feed, and my mother . . . gave me away.

APPROACHING THE AUTHOR

Joyce Carol Oates didn't read and write
until first grade, but before then she was
already "writing" books. She has said of
these books, "My earliest fictional
characters were zestfully if crudely drawn,
upright chickens and cats engaged in
various dramatic confrontations; the title
of my first full half-length novel, on tablet
paper, was *The Cat House.*"
    For more about her, see page 1404.

(*Woman hides her face very briefly in her hands; face composed.*)

There were nine children. I was the baby.
I was born late, I was the baby.
My mother gave me to her sister Lena who didn't have
    children. This was in 1918.
This was in the Black Rock section of Buffalo,
    the waterfront on the Niagara River.   20
Germans, Poles, Hungarians . . . immigrants.
We were Hungarians. We were called "Hunkies."
I don't know why people hated us . . .

(*Woman pauses; decides not to explore this.*)

Uncle John and Aunt Lena were my "parents."
We moved to a farm far away in the country.   25
And my real mother and my brothers and sisters
    moved to a farm a few miles away.

Uncle John and Aunt Lena were good to me.
I don't know if I loved them . . . I think I loved them.
I think . . . I think they loved me.
They wanted children but couldn't have them so it was
    right, I think, that my mother gave me to them . . .   30
it was a, a good thing, it was a . . . (*Pause.*)
necessary thing.
I would learn one day that it happened often.
In immigrant families in those days.
In poor immigrant families.   35

My father was killed and I never knew why.
They said he was a bad drinker, he got drunk
   and was always in fights.
The Hungarians were the worst, they
   said—the drinking, and the fighting.
They said he was so handsome, my father.
My mother Elizabeth was so pretty.   40
Curly hair like mine.
They said he had a temper "like the devil."
In the tavern there was a fight, and he died.
A man took up a poker and beat my father to death.
I never knew why, I never knew who it had been.   45
Yet this was how my life was decided.

There is the moment of conception—you don't know.
There is the moment of birth—you don't know.
There is the moment your life is decided—you don't know.
Yet you say, "This is my life."   50
You say, "This is me."

(Woman regards herself in wonder like a stroke victim regaining some of her awareness.)

When I was a little girl and my mother didn't want me
I hid away to cry.
I felt so bad and I felt so ashamed.
My mother didn't want me.   55
When I was old enough I would walk to the other farm.
There was a bridge over the Tonawanda Creek a few
   miles away.
They didn't really want to see me I guess.
My name was Carolina, but they didn't call me that.
I don't remember if there was a name they called me.   60
They weren't very nice to me I guess.
They didn't want me, I guess I was a reminder of . . .
   something.

Elizabeth, my mother, never learned English.
She spoke Hungarian all her life.
She never learned to read. She never learned to drive a car.   65
My Aunt Lena never learned to drive, so the sisters didn't
   see much of each other.
They lived only a few miles apart, and were the only
   sisters of their family in America, but they didn't
   see much of each other.
That was how women were in the old days.

————————

I loved my mother.
She was a short, plump woman.   70
Curly brown hair like mine.
People would say, "You look just like your momma!"
Then they would be surprised, I'd start to cry.
My mother was busy, she scolded me in Hungarian—
"Go away, go home where you belong. You have a home.   75
Your home is not here."

I loved my big brothers and sisters.
There was Leslie, he was the oldest.
He took over when my father died.
There was Mary, I didn't get to know real well.   80
They were born in Budapest.
There was Steve, who'd been kicked and trampled by a horse.
    His brain was injured, he would never leave home.
There was Elsie who was my "big sister."
There was Frank who was my "big brother."
There was Johnny . . . and Edith . . .   85
There was George, I wasn't too close with George.
There was Joseph, I wasn't too close with.

(Pause.)

They are all dead now.
I loved them, but . . .
I am the only one remaining.   90
Sometimes I think: The soul is just a burning match!
It burns awhile and then . . .
And then that's all.

It's a long time ago now, but I remember hiding
    away to cry.
When I was a little girl and my mother didn't want me.   95

Lights out.

> ## TWO PAIRINGS OF TEN-MINUTE PLAYS
>
> The following two plays deal with death. While they have similarities primarily because of the theme, they also have distinctive differences. As you read them, consider the ways that the plots differ. Notice how each playwright has chosen to use the situation and action and its ultimate effect. Why might the writers have used nonrealistic approaches for this most realistic of themes? What distinguishes each playwright's approach? Be alert for symbols in both plays and reflect on the effects achieved by using them.

Woody Allen b. 1935

Death Knocks   [1968]

The play takes place in the bedroom of Nat Ackerman's two-story house, somewhere in Kew Gardens.° The carpeting is wall-to-wall. There is a big double bed and a large vanity. The room is elaborately furnished and curtained, and on the walls there are several paintings and a not really attractive barometer. Soft theme music as the curtain rises. Nat Ackerman, a bald, paunchy fifty-seven-year-old dress manufacturer, is lying on the bed finishing off tomorrow's Daily News.° *He wears a bathrobe and slippers, and reads by a bed light clipped to the white headboard of the bed. The time is near midnight. Suddenly we hear a noise, and Nat sits up and looks at the window.*

> ### APPROACHING THE AUTHOR
>
> Although **Woody Allen** has received many distinctive recognitions for his writing, directing, and acting, including three Academy Awards and the Lifetime Achievement Award from the American Directors Guild, he perhaps most enjoys the times he plays clarinet at jazz venues throughout his beloved Manhattan.
>
> For more about him, see page 1371.

NAT: What the hell is that?

(*Climbing awkwardly through the window is a somber, caped figure. The intruder wears a black hood and skintight black clothes. The hood covers his head but not his face, which is middle-aged and stark white. He is something like Nat in appearance. He huffs audibly and then trips over the windowsill and falls into the room.*)

DEATH (*for it is no one else*): Jesus Christ. I nearly broke my neck.

Kew Gardens: An ethnically diverse middle-class neighborhood in the New York City borough of Queens.   **tomorrow's** *Daily News:* The New York *Daily News* was the first U.S. daily tabloid paper; at the time in which the play is set, the morning edition was still distributed around 10:00 the previous night.

NAT (*watching with bewilderment*): Who are you?

DEATH: Death.

NAT: Who?

DEATH: Death. Listen—can I sit down? I nearly broke my neck. I'm shaking like a leaf.

NAT: Who *are* you?

DEATH: *Death.* You got a glass of water?

NAT: Death? What do you mean, Death?

DEATH: What is wrong with you? You see the black costume and the whitened face?

NAT: Yeah.

DEATH: Is it Halloween?

NAT: No.

DEATH: Then I'm Death. Now can I get a glass of water—or a Fresca?

NAT: If this is some joke—

DEATH: What kind of joke? You're fifty-seven? Nat Ackerman? One eighteen Pacific Street? Unless I blew it—where's the call sheet? (*He fumbles through pocket, finally producing a card with an address on it. It seems to check.*)

NAT: What do you want with me?

DEATH: What do I want? What do you think I want?

NAT: You must be kidding. I'm in perfect health.

DEATH (*unimpressed*): Un-huh. (*Looking around.*) This is a nice place. You do it yourself?

NAT: We had a decorator, but we worked with her.

DEATH (*looking at picture on the wall*): I love those kids with the big eyes.

NAT: I don't want to go yet.

DEATH: *You* don't want to go? Please don't start in. As it is, I'm nauseous from the climb.

NAT: What climb?

DEATH: I climbed up the drainpipe. I was trying to make a dramatic entrance. I see the big windows and you're awake reading. I figure it's worth a shot. I'll climb up and enter with a little—you know . . . (*Snaps fingers.*) Meanwhile, I get my heel caught on some vines, the drainpipe breaks, and I'm hanging by a thread. Then my cape begins to tear. Look, let's just go. It's been a rough night.

NAT: You broke my drainpipe?

DEATH: Broke. It didn't break. It's a little bent. Didn't you hear anything? I slammed into the ground.

NAT: I was reading.

DEATH: You must have really been engrossed. (*Lifting newspaper Nat was reading.*) "NAB COEDS IN POT ORGY." Can I borrow this?

NAT: I'm not finished.

DEATH: Er—I don't know how to put this to you, pal. . . .

NAT: Why didn't you just ring downstairs?

DEATH: I'm telling you, I could have, but how does it look? This way I get a little drama going. Something. Did you read "Faust"?°

NAT: What?

DEATH: And what if you had company? You're sitting there with important people. I'm Death—I should ring the bell and traipse right in the front? Where's your thinking?

NAT: Listen, Mister, it's very late.

DEATH: Yeah. Well, you want to go?

NAT: Go where?

DEATH: Death. It. The Thing. The Happy Hunting Grounds. (*Looking at his own knee.*) Y'know, that's a pretty bad cut. My first job, I'm liable to get gangrene yet.

NAT: Now, wait a minute. I need time. I'm not ready to go.

DEATH: I'm sorry. I can't help you. I'd like to, but it's the moment.

NAT: How can it be the moment? I just merged with Modiste Originals.

DEATH: What's the difference, a couple bucks more or less.

NAT: Sure, what do you care? You guys probably have all your expenses paid.

DEATH: You want to come along now?

NAT: (*studying him*): I'm sorry, but I cannot believe you're Death.

DEATH: Why? What'd you expect—Rock Hudson?°

NAT: No it's not that.

DEATH: I'm sorry if I disappointed you.

NAT: Don't get upset. I don't know, I always thought you'd be . . . uh . . . taller.

DEATH: I'm five seven. It's average for my weight.

NAT: You look a little like me.

DEATH: Who should I look like? I'm your death.

NAT: Give me some time. Another day.

DEATH: I can't. What do you want me to say?

NAT: One more day. Twenty-four hours.

DEATH: What do you need it for? The radio said rain tomorrow.

NAT: Can't we work out something?

DEATH: Like what?

NAT: You play chess?

DEATH: No, I don't.

NAT: I once saw a picture of you playing chess.

DEATH: Couldn't be me, because I don't play chess. Gin rummy, maybe.

NAT: You play gin rummy?

DEATH: Do I play gun rummy? Is Paris a city?

NAT: You're good, huh?

DEATH: Very good.

NAT: I'll tell you what I'll do—

"**Faust**": German poetic drama in two parts (1806, 1832) by Johann Wolfgang von Goethe, exploring eternal questions of the meaning of life and the universe. **Rock Hudson:** Roy Harold Scherer Jr. (1925–1985) was an American actor, appearing in nearly seventy films, best known as leading man in romantic comedies with Doris Day.

DEATH: Don't make any deals with me.

NAT: I'll play you gin rummy. If you win, I'll go immediately. If I win, give me some more time. A little bit—one more day.

DEATH: Who's got time to play gin rummy?

NAT: Come on. If you're so good.

DEATH: Although I feel like a game . . .

NAT: Come on. Be a sport. We'll shoot for a half hour.

DEATH: I really shouldn't.

NAT: I got the cards right here. Don't make a production.

DEATH: All right, come on. We'll play a little. It'll relax me.

NAT (*getting cards, pad, and pencil*): You won't regret this.

DEATH: Don't give me a sales talk. Get the cards and give me a Fresca and put out something. For God's sake, a stranger drops in, you don't have potato chips or pretzels.

NAT: There's M&M's downstairs in a dish.

DEATH: M&M's. What if the President came? He'd get M&M's too?

NAT: You're not the President.

DEATH: Deal.

(*Nat deals, turns up a five.*)

NAT: You want to play a tenth of a cent a point to make it interesting?

DEATH: It's not interesting enough for you?

NAT: I play better when money's at stake.

DEATH: Whatever you say, Newt.

NAT: Nat, Nat Ackerman. You don't know my name?

DEATH: Newt, Nat—I got such a headache.

NAT: You want that five?

DEATH: No.

NAT: So pick.

DEATH (*surveying his hand as he picks*): Jesus, I got nothing here.

NAT: What's it like?

DEATH: What's what like?

(*Throughout the following, they pick and discard.*)

NAT: Death.

DEATH: What should it be like? You lay there.

NAT: Is there anything after?

DEATH: Aha, you're saving twos.

NAT: I'm asking. Is there anything after?

DEATH: (*absently*): You'll see.

NAT: Oh, then I will actually see something?

DEATH: Well, maybe I shouldn't have put it that way. Throw.

NAT: To get an answer from you is a big deal.

DEATH: I'm playing cards.

NAT: All right, play, play.

DEATH: Meanwhile, I'm giving you one card after another.

NAT: Don't look through the discards.

DEATH: I'm not looking. I'm straightening them up. What was the knock card?

NAT: Four. You ready to knock already?

DEATH: Who said I'm ready to knock? All I asked was what was the knock card?

NAT: And all I asked was is there anything for me to look forward to.

DEATH: Play.

NAT: Can't you tell me anything? Where do we go?

DEATH: We? To tell you the truth, *you* fall in a crumpled heap on the floor.

NAT: Oh, I can't wait for that! Is it going to hurt?

DEATH: Be over in a second.

NAT: Terrific. (*Sighs.*) I needed this. A man merges with Modiste Originals . . .

DEATH: How's four points?

NAT: You're knocking?

DEATH: Four points is good?

NAT: No, I got two.

DEATH: You're kidding.

NAT: No, you lose.

DEATH: Holy Christ, and I thought you were saving sixes.

NAT: No. Your deal. Twenty points and two boxes. Shoot. (*Death deals.*) I must fall on the floor, eh? I can't be standing over the sofa when it happens?

DEATH: No. Play.

NAT: Why not?

DEATH: Because you fall on the floor! Leave me alone. I'm trying to concentrate.

NAT: Why must it be on the floor? That's all I'm saying! Why can't the whole thing happen and I'll stand next to the sofa?

DEATH: I'll try my best. Now can we play?

NAT: That's all I'm saying. You remind me of Moe Lefkowitz. He's also stubborn.

DEATH: I remind him of Moe Lefkowitz. I'm one of the most terrifying figures you could possibly imagine, and him I remind of Moe Lefkowitz. What is he, a furrier?

NAT: You should be such a furrier. He's good for eighty thousand a year. Passementeries. He's got his own factory. Two points.

DEATH: What?

NAT: Two points. I'm knocking. What have you got?

DEATH: My hand is like a basketball score.

NAT: And it's spades.

DEATH: If you didn't talk so much.

(*They redeal and play on.*)

NAT: What'd you mean before when you said this was your first job?

DEATH: What does it sound like?

NAT: What are you telling me — that nobody ever went before?

DEATH: Sure they went. But I didn't take them.

NAT: So who did?

DEATH: Others

NAT: There's others?

DEATH: Sure. Each one has his own personal way of going.

NAT: I never knew that.

DEATH: Why should you know? Who are you?

NAT: What do you mean who am I? Why — I'm nothing?

DEATH: Not nothing. You're a dress manufacturer. Where do you come to knowledge of the eternal mysteries?

NAT: What are you talking about? I make a beautiful dollar. I sent two kids through college. One is in advertising, the other's married. I got my own home. I drive a Chrysler. My wife has whatever she wants. Maids, mink coat, vacations. Right now she's at the Eden Roc.° Fifty dollars a day because she wants to be near her sister. I'm supposed to join her next week, so what do you think I am — some guy off the street?

DEATH: All right. Don't be so touchy.

NAT: Who's touchy?

DEATH: How would you like it if I got insulted quickly?

NAT: Did I insult you?

DEATH: You didn't say you were disappointed in me?

NAT: What do you expect? You want me to throw you a block party?

DEATH: I'm not talking about that. I mean me personally. I'm too short, I'm this, I'm that.

NAT: I said you looked like me. It's like a reflection.

DEATH: All right, deal, deal.

(*They continue to play as music steals in and the lights dim until all is in total darkness. The lights slowly come up again, and now it is later and their game is over. Nat tallies.*)

NAT: Sixty-eight . . . one-fifty . . . Well, you lose.

DEATH (*dejectedly looking through the deck*): I knew I shouldn't have thrown that nine. Damn it.

NAT: So I'll see you tomorrow.

DEATH: What do you mean you'll see me tomorrow?

NAT: I won the extra day. Leave me alone.

DEATH: You were serious?

NAT: We made a deal.

DEATH: Yeah, but—

NAT: Don't "but" me. I won twenty-four hours. Come back tomorrow.

DEATH: I didn't know we were actually playing for time.

NAT: That's too bad for you. You should pay attention.

DEATH: Where am I going to go for twenty-four hours?

NAT: What's the difference? The main thing is I won an extra day.

Eden Roc: An upscale resort and spa which opened in Miami in 1956.

DEATH: What do you want me to do—walk the streets?

NAT: Check into a hotel and go to a movie. Take a *schvitz*.° Don't make a federal case.

DEATH: Add the score again.

NAT: Plus you owe me twenty-eight dollars.

DEATH: *What?*

NAT: That's right, Buster. Here it is—read it.

DEATH (*going through pockets*): I have a few singles—not twenty-eight dollars.

NAT: I'll take a check.

DEATH: From what account?

NAT: Look who I'm dealing with.

DEATH: Sue me. Where do I keep my checking account?

NAT: All right, gimme what you got and we'll call it square.

DEATH: Listen, I need that money.

NAT: Why should you need money?

DEATH: What are you talking about? You're going to the Beyond.

NAT: So?

DEATH: So—you know how far that is?

NAT: So?

DEATH: So where's gas? Where's tolls?

NAT: We're going by car!

DEATH: You'll find out. (*Agitatedly.*) Look—I'll be back tomorrow, and you'll give me a chance to win my money back. Otherwise I'm in definite trouble.

NAT: Anything you want. Double or nothing we'll play. I'm liable to win an extra week or a month. The way you play, maybe years.

DEATH: Meantime I'm stranded.

NAT: See you tomorrow.

DEATH (*being edged to the doorway*): Where's a good hotel? What am I talking about hotel, I got no money. I'll go sit in Bickford's.° (*He picks up the* News.)

NAT: Out. Out. That's my paper. (*He takes it back.*)

DEATH (*exiting*): I couldn't just take him and go. I had to get involved in rummy.

NAT (*calling after him*): And be careful going downstairs. On one of the steps the rug is loose.

(*And, on cue, we hear a terrific crash. Nat sighs, then crosses to the bedside table and makes a phone call.*)

NAT: Hello, Moe? Me. Listen, I don't know if somebody's playing a joke, or what, but Death was just here. We played a little gin . . . No, *Death*. In person. Or somebody who claims to be Death. But, Moe, he's such a *schlep*!°

Curtain

---

schvitz: Steam bath, sauna (Yiddish). **Bickford's:** A chain of low-cost all-night restaurants and cafeterias well known in New York City from the 1920s through the 1970s. **schlep:** An awkward or tedious person (Yiddish).

David Henry Hwang b. 1957

As the Crow Flies   [1986]

CHARACTERS

HANNAH, a black woman in her 60s
MRS. CHAN, a Chinese woman in her
  70s, sometimes called Popo
  (Grandma)
P. K., a Chinese man in his 70s, some-
  times called Gung Gung
  (Grandfather)
SANDRA, a black woman in her 40s

TIME AND PLACE

The living room of an upper middle-
class home. The present.

APPROACHING THE AUTHOR

When his grandmother's death appeared
imminent, ten-year-old **David Henry Hwang**
flew to the Philippines to visit her. The
interviews with her he recorded on cassette
tapes became the basis for a ninety-page
novel, which as an adult he transformed
into the successful Broadway stage drama
Golden Child.

For more about him, see page 1392.

*A living room in an upper middle-class home, owned by Mrs. Chan, a Chinese
woman in her seventies, and her husband, P. K. Up right, a door leads out to the
front driveway. Stage left is a door leading to the rest of the house. Mrs. Chan sits
in a large chair, center stage, looking downstage out into a garden. Around her,
Hannah, a black woman in her late sixties, cleans. She has been their cleaning woman
for over a decade.*

HANNAH: I guess I never told you this before, Mrs. Chan, but I think the time is
  right now. See, I'm really two different folks. You've been knowin' me as
  Hannah Carter, 'cuz when I'm over here cleanin', that's who I am. But at
  night, or when I'm outside and stuff, I turn into Sandra Smith. (*Beat*) Is
  that all clear?
CHAN: Um. Yeah.
HANNAH: You got all that?
CHAN: When you are here, you are Hannah Carter—
HANNAH: Right.
CHAN: And, then, you go outside, and you are . . . someone . . . someone . . .
HANNAH: Sandra Smith.
CHAN: Um. Okay.

Pause.

HANNAH: You don't have any questions 'bout that?
CHAN: Hannah Carter, Sandra Smith—I understand.
HANNAH: Well, you know how you can tell the two apart?
CHAN: No. Because I have not seen Sandra—Sandra . . .
HANNAH: Smith. Well, when I'm Sandra Smith, see, I look different. First of all,
  I'm a lot younger.

CHAN: Good.

HANNAH: And, you know, since I'm younger, well, guess I'm looser, too. What I mean by that, is, when I talk, well, I use different words. Young words. And, Mrs. Chan, since I'm younger, my hair color's a lot different too. And I don't clean floors. 'Cuz young people nowadays, they don't clean floors. They stay up around the clock, and make themselves into lazy good-for-nothings, and drink a lot, and dance themselves into a state. Young people — just don't know what's got into them. But whatever it is, the same thing's gotten into Sandra Smith. (*Pause*) You don't think this is all a little strange?

CHAN: No.

HANNAH: Well, that's the first time . . . I remember when I told Mrs. Washburn about Sandra Smith — she just fell right over.

CHAN: So what? So you have two different people.

HANNAH: That's right. Living inside me.

CHAN: So what? My uncle had six!

HANNAH: Six people?

CHAN: Maybe even seven. Who can keep count?

HANNAH: Seven? All in one guy?

CHAN: Way back in China — my second uncle — he had seven, maybe even eight, people — inside here. I don't . . . is hard to remember all their name.

HANNAH: I can believe that.

CHAN: Chan Yup Lee — he was, uh, I think, the businessman. He runs Uncle's import-export association. Good man. Very stingy. I like him. Then, I think there was another: ah, C. Y. Sing — he is the family man. Then, one man, Fat-Fingers Lew. Introduce this sport — what is the name? Ball goes through big hoop.

HANNAH: Basketball?

CHAN: Yes, yes — introduce that to our village. Then, there is Big Ear Tong — collects debt for C. Y.'s company. Never talks, only fight. Then, also, one who has been to America — Morty Fong. He all the time warns us about Communists. And, then, oh, maybe two or three others that I hardly ever meet.

HANNAH: This is all one guy?

CHAN: Mmmmm.

HANNAH: Isn't that somethin'?

CHAN: No.

HANNAH: Huh?

CHAN: Whatever you can tell me — man with six persons inside, man with three heads, man who sees a flying ghost, a sitting ghost, a ghost disguise to look like his dead wife — none of these are so unusual.

HANNAH: No?

CHAN: I have lived a long time.

HANNAH: Well, so have I, Mrs. Chan, so have I. And I'm still scared of Sandra Smith.

CHAN: Scare? Why scare? Happens all the time.

HANNAH: I don't want Sandra comin' round to any of my houses that I clean.

CHAN: Aaah—do not worry.

HANNAH: Whaddya mean? Sandra's got no respect for authority.

CHAN: Do not worry. She will not come into any house.

HANNAH: What makes you so sure?

CHAN: You have to know how ghosts think. You say, Sandra appears outdoors. Therefore, she is the outside ghost. She cannot come inside.

HANNAH: Yeah? They got rules like that? In ghost-land?

CHAN: Yes—there are rules everyplace! Have you ever been someplace where there were none?

HANNAH: Well, no, but—

CHAN: You see? Ghosts cannot kill a man if there is a goldfish in the room. They will think the fish is gold, and take it instead. They cannot enter a house if there is a raised step in the doorway. Ghosts do not look, so they trip over it instead.

HANNAH: These ghosts don't sound like they got a lot on the ball.

CHAN: Some ghosts, they are smart. But most ghosts, they are like most people. When alive, they were stupid. After death, they remain the same.

HANNAH: Well, I don't think Sandra's got much respect for those rules. That's probably why she showed up at Mrs. Washburn's.

CHAN: Inside the house?

HANNAH: 'Fraid so.

CHAN: Oh. Mrs. Washburn—does she have a goldfish?

HANNAH: No, no—I don't think so.

CHAN: There—you see?

HANNAH: Anyway, Mrs. Chan, I just thought I oughta tell you about her, on account of what happened to Mrs. Washburn. I been working for all you people ten, sometimes twenty years. All my clients—they're gettin' up there. We're all startin' to show our age. Can't compete with the young girls no more.

CHAN: I never try—even when I was one.

HANNAH: Well, the older I get, the more I see of Sandra, so I just thought I oughta be warnin' you.

CHAN: I am not afraid of Sandra Smith.

HANNAH: Well, good then. Good for you.

CHAN: She comes here, I will fight her. Not like these Americans. So stupid. Never think of these things. Never think of ghost. Never think of death. Never prepare for anything. Always think, life goes on and on, forever. And so, always, it ends.

HANNAH: Okay. Glad to hear it. Guess I'll go take the slime off the shower walls.

Hannah exits, into the house. Chan just stares downstage, from her chair. Silence. P. K. enters from the driveway, golf clubs slung over his shoulder.

P. K.: Hi, Popo!

CHAN: Hello.

P. K.: Do you have a beer?

CHAN: Look in 'frigerator.

P. K.: Just return from a good game of golf!

CHAN: Ah! What are you talking about?

P. K.: Eighteen holes, Popo!

CHAN: Ai! You cannot remember anything anymore!

P. K.: So? I remember that I go to golf!

CHAN: How can this be? You do not drive!

P. K.: What do you mean? I drive the Eldorado.

CHAN: You cannot drive the Eldorado.

P. K.: I do!

CHAN: Hanh! We sell it many years ago!

P. K.: What?

CHAN: Yes! Remember? We sell it! To John, your nephew.

P. K.: Huh? How much did he pay?

CHAN: Who cares?

P. K.: I want to know!

CHAN: I always tell you, John buys the car; you always ask me, how much does
  he pay?

P. K.: It is important! It is worth—lots of money!

CHAN: Ah, not so much money.

P. K.: No! Lots!

CHAN: Not after Humphrey breaks the back window by trying to lower top while
  driving.

P. K.: Yes! I tell Humphrey—cannot lower while driving. He says, "Of course!
  Can! This is a luxury car!" How come we sell the car?

CHAN: Ah! You cannot remember anything!

P. K.: No. Gung Gung cannot remember anything anymore.

CHAN: We sell, because you can no longer drive.

P. K.: I can! I can!

CHAN: You cannot pass the test.

P. K.: Can Humphrey pass the test?

CHAN: Of course! Of course, he passes it.

P. K.: How can? He is the one who lowers top while driving!

CHAN: Gung Gung! Because he is young, so he can pass the test!

P. K.: Young, but not so smart.

CHAN: Stupid.

P. K.: Sometimes, stupid.

CHAN: Stupid does not matter. Many stupid people drive.

Pause.

P. K.: So I did not go to golf?

CHAN: No! How can you go to golf? You cannot go anyplace.

P. K. (*Points to clubs*): Then, what are these?

CHAN: You just put them on your shoulder, then walk outside. Two hour later, you return.

P. K.: Where did I go?

CHAN: I don't know! You tell me!

P. K.: I cannot remember anything, anymore. I thought that I go to play eighteen hole golf. But there is no golf course. So perhaps I walk into those hills. Maybe I shoot a few balls in the hills. Maybe I sink a putt into a gopher hole.

Pause.

CHAN: Gung Gung.

P. K.: Yes, Popo?

CHAN: I saw a ghost today.

P. K.: Popo! A ghost?

CHAN: Yes—a warning ghost.

P. K.: Which is this?

CHAN: They warn that another ghost will soon come. Bigger. More dangerous. Fatter.

P. K.: Oh! Popo! Why do they send this warning ghost?

CHAN: Because, they are stupid! This is how, they become dead to begin with. Because when they were living, they were too stupid to listen to the warning ghost!

P. K.: Popo! Will you die? (*He starts to cry*) What will Gung Gung do without you?

CHAN: No.

P. K.: Without Popo, I will be completely all lost.

CHAN: No, Gung Gung.

P. K.: I will walk around all day, not know where I am going, not know where I come from, only saying, "Popo? Where is Popo? Where is—?"

CHAN: No! Will you listen to me? You ask the question, then you will not listen to the answer! Talk, talk, talk! If I die, leave you alone, I would be lucky!

P. K.: You mean, you will not die?

CHAN: No, I will not die.

P. K.: How can this be?

CHAN: They are stupid enough to send the warning ghost. This is how I know, they will not defeat me.

P. K.: But, when the ghost come, no one can resist.

CHAN: Who says this?

P. K.: Ummm . . .

CHAN: See? Maybe, Gung Gung, *you* cannot resist.

P. K.: No. I cannot resist.

CHAN: But you have no responsibilities. I have. I have responsibility. I cannot leave you alone, Gung Gung. And also, I must watch the grandchildren grow to adults.

P. K.: Yes—this would be good.

CHAN: So, you see, I cannot die.

P. K.: This makes me so happy.

CHAN: I will defeat the ghost.

P. K.: Yes! Popo! You can do it! Popo is very smart!

CHAN: Yeah, yeah, yeah, we all know this already.

P. K.: I am fortunate to marry such a smart wife.

CHAN: Not smart. Smart is not enough.

P. K.: More than smart.

CHAN: Fight. Fight is more important. I am willing to fight. I like to fight.

Pause.

P. K.: Why do I carry these golf clubs?

CHAN: I do not know! You ask so many times already!

P. K.: Oh—I suppose—I must go to golf.

Pause.

CHAN: Yes—you must go to golf.

P. K.: Okay. I will leave now. Take the Eldorado. Bye, Popo.

CHAN: Bye, Gung Gung.

P. K.: You will have a cold can of beer in the 'frigerator, for when I return?

CHAN: I will, Gung Gung. I will.

P. K. starts to exit out the upstage door.

Gung Gung!

P. K.: Yes, Popo?

CHAN: Have a good game, okay, Gung Gung?

P. K.: I will have a good game, okay, Popo. (*He exits*)

CHAN: I arrive in America one day, June 16, 1976. Many times, I have come here before, to visit children, but on this day, I arrive to stay. All my friends, all the Chinese in the Philippine, they tell me, "We thought you are stupid when you send all your children to America. We even feel sorry for you, that you will grow old all alone—no family around you." This is what they tell me.

The day I arrive in America, I do not feel sorry. I do not miss the Philippine, I do not look forward live in America. Just like, I do not miss China, when I leave it many years ago—go live in Philippine. Just like, I do not miss Manila, when Japanese take our home during wartime, and we are all have to move to Baguio, and live in haunted house. It is all same to me. Go, one home to the next, one city to another, nation to nation, across ocean big and small.

We are born traveling. We travel—all our lives. I am not looking for a home. I know there is none. The day I was marry, my mother put many gold bracelets on my arm, and so many necklaces that the back of my head grows sore. "These," she tells me. "These are for the times when you will have to run."

The upstage door opens. Hannah is standing there, dressed as Sandra Smith. Sandra wears a bright orange fright wig and a tight dress, sports huge sunglasses, and swings a small purse.

SANDRA: Well, hello there! Howdy, howdy, howdy!

CHAN: Hi.

SANDRA: Say, you seen Hannah? Hannah Carter? I understand she works here on Wednesdays.

CHAN: I think, she just leave.

SANDRA: Oh, well, that's a shame. I usually don't get to visit where she works. We were supposed to go for dinner at Chicken on Fire, but, looks like we're just not connecting. Damn! Always happens, whenever I try to meet her at one of these houses.

CHAN: So, would you like to go home, now?

SANDRA: Mmmm. Guess I could, but I wouldn't mind enjoying some of your hospitality.

CHAN: What is this, hospitality?

SANDRA: You know. What you show your guests.

CHAN: We do not have guests here! Only relatives, and, ah, servants.

SANDRA: Well, what do you do when someone comes over?

CHAN: They tell me what they want. Then, they leave.

SANDRA: No time to socialize?

CHAN: What is, socialize?

SANDRA: You know. You're not gonna offer me a tea, coffee, cake, Sanka?

CHAN: No.

SANDRA: I can't hardly believe this house.

CHAN: People—they are like cats. If you feed them, they will always return.

SANDRA: What ever happened to old-fashioned manners?

CHAN: My manners—they are very old. We act like this for centuries.

SANDRA: My name's Sandra. Sandra Smith.

CHAN: This is no surprise. Are you finish, now? Hannah is not here.

SANDRA: No—I can see that. (*Pause*) You know, I've known Hannah—well, ever since she was a little girl. She wasn't very pretty. No one in Louisville paid much attention to her. Yeah, she's had five husbands and all, okay, that's true, but my personal guess is that most of 'em married her because she was a hard-working woman who could bring home the bacon week after week. Certain men will hold their noses for a free lunch. Hannah thinks the same thing, though she hardly ever talks about it. How can she think anything else when all five of them left her as soon as they got a whiff of some girl with pipe cleaners for legs? Hard for her to think she's much more than some mule, placed on this earth to work her back. She spends most of her life wanderin' from one beautiful house to the next, knowing intimately every detail, but never layin' down her head in any of 'em. She's what they call a good woman. Men know it, rich folks know it. Everyplace is beautiful, 'cept the place where she lives. Home is a dark room, she knows it well, knows its limits. She knows she can't travel nowhere without returnin' to that room once the sun goes down. Home is fixed, it does not move, even as the rest of the world circles 'round and 'round, picking up speed.

CHAN: You are a ghost.

SANDRA: I have a good time, if that's what you mean.

CHAN: I was warned that you would come.

SANDRA: By Hannah? She's always tellin' people about me. Like I was some kinda celebrity or somethin'.

CHAN: I fight ghosts. I chase them.

SANDRA: Can't chase anything, unless you get it runnin' from ya first.

CHAN: In Baguio, we live in a haunted house.

SANDRA: In where?

CHAN: Baguio. In the Philippine.

SANDRA: I never been there.

CHAN: During the war, we live in a haunted house. I chase the ghost out, with pots and pan. So, I know I can defeat them.

SANDRA: Hannah — she lives in a haunted house right now.

CHAN: Yes — haunted with you.

SANDRA: I show her how to make her life a little easier. Someone's gotta do it, after all her sixty-some-odd years. How 'bout you? Anything I can help you with?

CHAN: Ha! I do not need a thing!

SANDRA: I'm not sure if I believe that, Mrs. . . . Mrs. . . . whatever. Hannah sees you sittin' here, day after day —

CHAN: I am old! Of course I sit!

SANDRA: — starin' out into that garden —

CHAN: So?

SANDRA: First off, it's mostly dirt.

CHAN: This way, easier to take care of.

SANDRA: But you stare like there's somethin' out there.

CHAN: Yes! The sun is out there!

SANDRA: Lookin' at the sun, Mrs. — ma'am? Gotta be careful you don't burn your eyeballs out.

CHAN: I only look outside because — sky, clouds, sun — they are all there — interesting to watch.

SANDRA: Real pretty, huh?

CHAN: Yes. Sometimes pretty.

SANDRA: Looks like home.

CHAN: What is this? All the time, you talk about home, home, home?

SANDRA: Just like you do.

CHAN: I never talk about home. Barely talk at all.

SANDRA: You think, you keep your lips buttoned, that means all your secrets are safe inside? If they're strong enough, things make themselves known, one way or another. Hannah knows, she's not stupid. She'd never tell anyone but me. But me, I'd tell anybody. (*Pause*) Want me to tell you?

CHAN: Tell me what?

SANDRA: What you're lookin' at out there?

Pause.

CHAN: I can defeat you. I defeat ghost before.

SANDRA: Honey, it's not a fight no more. I've been around fifteen years. I already know you. You know me. We see the same thing. Out there. (*Pause*) There's a crow sitting on a window sill. And two kids who chase it down a steep ravine. Their path grows darker and darker, but the crow continues, and the kids don't tire, even when the blisters start to show on their feet. Mud, sleet, rain, and snow, all try to make the kids give up the chase. The crow caws—mountains fall in its wake, but still the children continue. And then it becomes dark, so dark, and the crow throws disasters at their feet. Floods, droughts, wars. The children see nothing, now. They follow the crow only by the catastrophes it leaves in its path. Where there is famine, the crow must have been. Where there are earthquakes, it has rested. They run on faith now, passing through territories uncharted, following the sound of their suffering. And it is in this way that they pass through their lives. Hardly noticing that they've entered. Without stopping to note its passing. Just following a crow, with single dedication, forgetting how they started, or why they're chasing, or even what may happen if they catch it. Running without pause or pleasure, past the point of their beginning.

Over the next section, Mrs. Chan's dress slowly rises into the air. She wears a white slip beneath. She stands up from the chair, for the first time in the play, and walks over to Sandra.

I see it in the distance.

CHAN: It is waiting for me.

SANDRA: I cannot stop my running.

CHAN: I cannot rest, even for a second.

SANDRA: There's a field out in the distance.

CHAN: There's a wooden gate in that field.

SANDRA: There is a crow sitting on that gate.

CHAN: It caws.

SANDRA: It caws.

CHAN: And disaster comes.

SANDRA: Once again.

CHAN: Nothing new.

SANDRA: Nothing blue.

CHAN: Only the scent of home.

SANDRA: I don't know why I follow it.

CHAN: I don't care to know.

SANDRA: Not now.

CHAN: Not here.

SANDRA: Not ever. Perhaps someday.

CHAN: Maybe to remember.
SANDRA: Why I run.
CHAN: Why I chase.
SANDRA: Until I am so—
CHAN: So tired.
SANDRA: Another disaster.
CHAN: Another lonely child.
SANDRA: We follow the scent of home.

Sandra removes her wig, glasses, tight dress. She too wears a white slip. She is Hannah again. Mrs. Chan moves towards the door. Hannah ever so slowly lowers herself into Mrs. Chan's chair. Hannah sits in it, beams.

HANNAH: Ooooh. Nice home, Mrs. Chan.
CHAN: I see it.
HANNAH: So do I, so do I.
CHAN: I see all the way past those mountains.
HANNAH: Welcome home, Mrs. Chan.
CHAN: Welcome home, Hannah.

Mrs. Chan exits through the garden. Hannah looks around her like a kid with a new toy. Upstage, P. K. enters with golf clubs. He cannot see Hannah in the chair.

P. K.: Hi, Popo! (*Pause*) Where is my beer?

Hannah closes her eyes, a smile on her face.

You leave a beer in the 'frigerator? (*Pause*) Popo? Popo?

P. K. is walking towards the chair as lights fade to black.

END OF PLAY

Even though the following two plays were written more than sixty years apart and differ in many ways, they have striking similarities. Both are about young characters who have encountered extraordinary difficulties. But even more striking are the unusual ways in which they are forced to cope. As you read and reread the plays, pay attention to plot, setting, and characters. Note what the girl in the first play and the boy in the second have had to deal with. Then consider the defenses each has built up. Reflect on what you feel about them during and at the end of the plays. Think of their later lives. What kind of future do you surmise each might look forward to?

Tennessee Williams (1911–1983)

This Property Is Condemned   [1946]

CHARACTERS

WILLIE, a young girl
TOM, a boy

SCENE: *A railroad embankment on the outskirts of a small Mississippi town on one of those milky white winter mornings peculiar to that part of the country. The air is moist and chill. Behind the low embankment of the tracks is a large yellow frame house which has a look of tragic vacancy. Some of the upper*

APPROACHING THE AUTHOR

Tennessee Williams was born in Mississippi, but when he was seven his family moved to St. Louis so his father could work in a shoe factory. Because his family was poor and because he had an accent from the Deep South, children at school made fun of him and his sister, Rose.

For more about him, see page 1419.

windows are boarded, a portion of the roof has fallen away. The land is utterly flat. In the left background is a billboard that says "GIN WITH JAKE" and there are some telephone poles and a few bare winter trees. The sky is a great milky whiteness: crows occasionally make a sound of roughly torn cloth.

The girl Willie is advancing precariously along the railroad track, balancing herself with both arms outstretched, one clutching a banana, the other an extraordinarily dilapidated doll with a frowsy blond wig.

She is a remarkable apparition — thin as a beanpole and dressed in outrageous cast-off finery. She wears a long blue velvet party dress with a filthy cream lace collar and sparkling rhinestone beads. On her feet are battered silver kid slippers with large ornamental buckles. Her wrists and her fingers are resplendent with dimestore jewelry. She has applied rouge to her childish face in artless crimson daubs and her lips are made up in a preposterous Cupid's bow. She is about thirteen and there is something ineluctably childlike and innocent in her appearance despite the makeup. She laughs frequently and wildly and with a sort of precocious, tragic abandon.

The boy Tom, slightly older, watches her from below the embankment. He wears corduroy pants, blue shirt and a sweater and carries a kite of red tissue paper with a gaudily ribboned tail.

TOM: Hello. Who are you?

WILLIE: Don't talk to me till I fall off. (*She proceeds dizzily. Tom watches with mute fascination. Her gyrations grow wider and wider. She speaks breathlessly.*) Take my—crazy doll—will you?

TOM (*scrambling up the bank*): Yeh.

WILLIE: I don't wanta—break her when—I fall! I don't think I can—stay on much—longer—do you?

TOM: Naw.

WILLIE: I'm practically—off—right now! (*Tom offers to assist her.*) No, don't touch me. It's no fair helping. You've got to do it—all—by yourself! God, I'm wobbling! I don't know what's made me so nervous! You see that water-tank way back yonder?

TOM: Yeah?

WILLIE: That's where I—started—from! This is the furthest—I ever gone—without once—falling off. I mean it will be—if I can manage to stick on—to the next—telephone—pole! Oh! Here I go! (*She becomes completely unbalanced and rolls down the bank.*)

TOM (*standing above her now*): Hurtcha self?

WILLIE: Skinned my knee a little. Glad I didn't put my silk stockings on.

TOM (*coming down the bank*): Spit on it. That takes the sting away.

WILLIE: Okay.

TOM: That's animal's medicine, you know. They always lick their wounds.

WILLIE: I know. The principal damage was done to my bracelet, I guess. I knocked out one of the diamonds. Where did it go?

TOM: You never could find it in all them cinders.

WILLIE: I don't know. It had a lot of shine.

TOM: It wasn't a genuine diamond.

WILLIE: How do you know?

TOM: I just imagine it wasn't. Because if it was you wouldn't be walking along a railroad track with a banged-up doll and a piece of a rotten banana.

WILLIE: Oh, I wouldn't be so sure. I might be peculiar or something. You never can tell. What's your name?

TOM: Tom.

WILLIE: Mine's Willie. We've both got boy's names.

TOM: How did that happen?

WILLIE: I was expected to be a boy but I wasn't. They had one girl already. Alva. She was my sister. Why ain't you at school?

TOM: I thought it was going to be windy so I could fly my kite.

WILLIE: What made you think that?

TOM: Because the sky was so white.

WILLIE: Is that a sign?

TOM: Yeah.

WILLIE: I know. It looks like everything had been swept off with a broom. Don't it?

TOM: Yeah.

WILLIE: It's perfectly white. It's white as a clean piece of paper.

TOM: Uh-huh.

WILLIE: But there isn't a wind.

TOM: Naw.

WILLIE: It's up too high for us to feel it. It's way, way up in the attic sweeping the dust off the furniture up there!

TOM: Uh-huh. Why ain't you at school?

WILLIE: I quituated. Two years ago this winter.

TOM: What grade was you in?

WILLIE: Five A.

TOM: Miss Preston.

WILLIE: Yep. She used to think my hands was dirty until I explained that it was cinders from falling off the railroad tracks so much.

TOM: She's pretty strict.

WILLIE: Oh, no, she's just disappointed because she didn't get married. Probably never had an opportunity, poor thing. So she has to teach Five A for the rest of her natural life. They started teaching algebra an' I didn't give a goddam what X stood for so I quit.

TOM: You'll never get an education walking the railroad tracks.

WILLIE: You won't get one flying a red kite neither. Besides . . .

TOM: What?

WILLIE: What a girl needs to get along is social training. I learned all of that from my sister Alva. She had a wonderful popularity with the railroad men.

TOM: Train engineers?

WILLIE: Engineers, firemen, conductors. Even the freight sup'rintendent. We run a boarding-house for railroad men. She was I guess you might say The Main Attraction. Beautiful? Jesus, she looked like a movie star!

TOM: Your sister?

WILLIE: Yeah. One of 'em used to bring her regular after each run a great big heart-shaped red-silk box of assorted chocolates and nuts and hard candies. Marvelous?

TOM: Yeah. (*The cawing of crows sounds through the chilly air.*)

WILLIE: You know where Alva is now?

TOM: Memphis?

WILLIE: Naw.

TOM: New Awleuns?

WILLIE: Naw.

TOM: St. Louis?

WILLIE: You'll never guess.

TOM: Where is she then? (*Willie does not answer at once.*)

WILLIE (*very solemnly*): She's in the bone-orchard.

TOM: What?

WILLIE (*violently*): Bone-orchard, cemetery, graveyard! Don't you understand English?

TOM: Sure. That's pretty tough.

WILLIE: You don't know the half of it, buddy. We used to have some high old times in that big yellow house.

TOM: I bet you did.

WILLIE: Musical instruments going all of the time.

TOM: Instruments? What kind?

WILLIE: Piano, victrola, Hawaiian steel guitar. Everyone played on something. But now it's—awful quiet. You don't hear a sound from there, do you?

TOM: Naw. Is it empty?

WILLIE: Except for me. They got a big sign stuck up.

TOM: What does it say?

WILLIE (*loudly but with a slight catch*): "THIS PROPERTY IS CONDEMNED!"

TOM: You ain't still living there?

WILLIE: Uh-huh.

TOM: What happened? Where did everyone go?

WILLIE: Mama run off with a brakeman on the C. & E. I. After that everything went to pieces. (*A train whistles far off.*) You hear that whistle? That's the Cannonball Express. The fastest thing on wheels between St. Louis, New Awleuns an' Memphis. My old man got to drinking.

TOM: Where is he now?

WILLIE: Disappeared. I guess I ought to refer his case to the Bureau of Missing Persons. The same as he done with Mama when she disappeared. Then there was me and Alva. Till Alva's lungs got affected. Did you see Greta Garbo in *Camille*? It played at the Delta Brilliant one time las' spring. She had the same what Alva died of. Lung affection.

TOM: Yeah?

WILLIE: Only it was—very beautiful the way she had it. You know. Violins playing. And loads and loads of white flowers. All of her lovers come back in a beautiful scene!

TOM: Yeah?

WILLIE: But Alva's all disappeared.

TOM: Yeah?

WILLIE: Like rats from a sinking ship! That's how she used to describe it. Oh, it—wasn't like death in the movies.

TOM: Naw?

WILLIE: She says, "Where is Albert? Where's Clemence?" None of them was around. I used to lie to her, I says, "They send their regards. They're coming to see you tomorrow." "Where's Mr. Johnson?" she asked me. He was the freight sup'rintendent, the most important character we ever had in our rooming-house. "He's been transferred to Grenada," I told her. "But wishes to be remembered." She known I was lying.

TOM: Yeah?

WILLIE: "This here is the pay-off!" she says. "They all run out on me like rats from a sinking ship!" Except Sidney.

TOM: Who was Sidney?

WILLIE: The one that used to give her the great big enormous red-silk box of American Beauty choc'lates.

TOM: Oh.

WILLIE: He remained faithful to her.

TOM: That's good.

WILLIE: But she never did care for Sidney. She said his teeth was decayed so he didn't smell good.

TOM: Aw!

WILLIE: It wasn't like death in the movies. When somebody dies in the movies they play violins.

TOM: But they didn't for Alva.

WILLIE: Naw. Not even a goddam victrola. They said it didn't agree with the hospital regulations. Always singing around the house.

TOM: Who? Alva?

WILLIE: Throwing enormous parties. This was her favorite number. (*She closes her eyes and stretches out her arms in the simulated rapture of the professional blues singer. Her voice is extraordinarily high and pure with a precocious emotional timbre.*)

> You're the only star
> In my blue hea-ven
> And you're shining just
> For me!

This is her clothes I got on. Inherited from her. Everything Alva's is mine. Except her solid gold beads.

TOM: What happened to them?

WILLIE: Them? She never took 'em off.

TOM: Oh!

WILLIE: I've also inherited all of my sister's beaux. Albert and Clemence and even the freight sup'rintendent.

TOM: Yeah?

WILLIE: They all disappeared. Afraid that they might get stuck for expenses I guess. But now they turn up again, all of 'em, like a bunch of bad pennies. They take me out places at night. I've got to be popular now. To parties an' dances an' all of the railroad affairs. Lookit here!

TOM: What?

WILLIE: I can do bumps! (*She stands in front of him and shoves her stomach toward him in a series of spasmodic jerks.*)

TOM: Frank Waters said that . . .

WILLIE: What?

TOM: You know.

WILLIE: Know what?

TOM: You took him inside and danced for him with your clothes off.

WILLIE: Oh. Crazy Doll's hair needs washing. I'm scared to wash it though 'cause her head might come unglued where she had that compound fracture of the skull. I think that most of her brains spilled out. She's been acting silly ever since. Saying an' doing the most outrageous things.

TOM: Why don't you do that for me?

WILLIE: What? Put glue on your compound fracture?

TOM: Naw. What you did for Frank Waters.

WILLIE: Because I was lonesome then an' I'm not lonesome now. You can tell Frank Waters that. Tell him that I've inherited all of my sister's beaux. I go out steady with men in responsible jobs. The sky sure is white. Ain't it? White as a clean piece of paper. In Five A we used to draw pictures. Miss Preston would give us a piece of white foolscap an' tell us to draw what we pleased.

TOM: What did you draw?

WILLIE: I remember I drawn her a picture one time of my old man getting conked with a bottle. She thought it was good, Miss Preston, she said, "Look here. Here's a picture of Charlie Chaplin with his hat on the side of his head!" I said, "Aw, naw, that's not Charlie Chaplin, that's my father, an' that's not his hat, it's a bottle!"

TOM: What did she say?

WILLIE: Oh, well. You can't make a school-teacher laugh.

> You're the only star
> In my blue hea-VEN . . .

The principal used to say there must've been something wrong with my home atmosphere because of the fact that we took in railroad men an' some of 'em slept with my sister.

TOM: Did they?

WILLIE: She was The Main Attraction. The house is sure empty now.

TOM: You ain't still living there, are you?

WILLIE: Sure.

TOM: By yourself?

WILLIE: Uh-huh. I'm not supposed to be but I am. The property is condemned but there's nothing wrong with it. Some county investigator come snooping around yesterday. I recognized her by the shape of her hat. It wasn't exactly what I would call stylish-looking.

TOM: Naw?

WILLIE: It looked like something she took off the lid of the stove. Alva knew lots about style. She had ambitions to be a designer for big wholesale firms in Chicago. She used to submit her pictures. It never worked out.

> You're the only star
> In my blue hea-ven . . .

TOM: What did you do? About the investigators?

WILLIE: Laid low upstairs. Pretended like no one was home.

TOM: Well, how do you manage to keep on eating?

WILLIE: Oh, I don't know. You keep a sharp look-out you see things lying around. This banana, perfectly good, for instance. Thrown in a garbage pail in back of the Blue Bird Café. (*She finishes the banana and tosses away the peel.*)

TOM (*grinning*): Yeh. Miss Preston for instance.

WILLIE: Naw, not her. She gives you a white piece of paper, says "Draw what you please!" One time I drawn her a picture of— Oh, but I told you that, huh? Will you give Frank Waters a message?

TOM: What?

WILLIE: Tell him the freight sup'rintendent has bought me a pair of kid slippers. Patent. The same as the old ones of Alva's. I'm going to dances with them at Moon Lake Casino. All night I'll be dancing an' come home drunk in the morning! We'll have serenades with all kinds of musical instruments. Trumpets an' trombones. An' Hawaiian steel guitars. Yeh! Yeh! (*She rises excitedly.*) The sky will be white like this.

TOM (*impressed*): Will it?

WILLIE: Uh-huh. (*She smiles vaguely and turns slowly toward him.*) White—as a clean—piece of paper . . . (*then excitedly*) I'll draw—pictures on it!

TOM: Will you?

WILLIE: Sure!

TOM: Pictures of what?

WILLIE: Me dancing! With the freight sup'rintendent! In a pair of patent kid shoes! Yeh! Yeh! With French heels on them as high as telegraph poles! An' they'll play my favorite music!

TOM: Your favorite?

WILLIE: Yeh. The same as Alva's. (*breathlessly, passionately*)

> You're the only STAR—
> In my blue HEA-VEN . . .

I'll—

TOM: What?

WILLIE: I'll—wear a corsage!

TOM: What's that?

WILLIE: Flowers to pin on your dress at a formal affair! Rosebuds! Violets! And lilies-of-the-valley! When you come home it's withered but you stick 'em in a bowl of water to freshen 'em up.

TOM: Uh-huh.

WILLIE: That's what Alva done. (*She pauses, and in the silence the train whistles.*) The Cannonball Express . . .

TOM: You think a lot about Alva. Don't you?

WILLIE: Oh, not so much. Now an' then. It wasn't like death in the movies. Her beaux disappeared. An' they didn't have violins playing. I'm going back now.

TOM: Where to, Willie?

WILLIE: The water-tank.

TOM: Yeah?

WILLIE: An' start all over again. Maybe I'll break some kind of continuous record. Alva did once. At a dance marathon in Mobile. Across the state line. Alabama. You can tell Frank Waters everything that I told you. I don't have time for inexperienced people. I'm going out now with popular railroad men, men with good salaries, too. Don't you believe me?

TOM: No. I think you're drawing an awful lot on your imagination.

WILLIE: Well, if I wanted to I could prove it. But you wouldn't be worth convincing. (*She smooths out Crazy Doll's hair.*) I'm going to live for a long, long time like my sister. An' when my lungs get affected I'm going to die like she did — maybe not like in the movies, with violins playing — but with my pearl earrings on an' my solid gold beads from Memphis. . . .

TOM: Yes?

WILLIE (*examining Crazy Doll very critically*): An' then I guess —

TOM: What?

WILLIE (*gaily but with a slight catch*): Somebody else will inherit all of my beaux! The sky sure is white.

TOM: It sure is.

WILLIE: White as a clean piece of paper. I'm going back now.

TOM: So long.

WILLIE: Yeh. So long. (*She starts back along the railroad track, weaving grotesquely to keep her balance. She disappears. Tom wets his finger and holds it up to test the wind. Willie is heard singing from a distance.*)

> You're the only star
> In my blue heaven —

(*There is a brief pause. The stage begins to darken.*)

> An' you're shining just —
> For me!

CURTAIN

Marco Ramirez (b. 1983)

I Am Not Batman   [2007]

Sudden drumming, then quiet. Lights up on a BOY, *maybe 7, maybe 27, wearing a hooded sweatshirt. He looks out directly before him, breathing nervously. A* DRUMMER *sits behind a drum set placed in the middle of the stage, in some kind of silhouette. The* BOY *is excited, but never gets ahead of himself.*

BOY: It's the middle of the night and the sky is glowing like mad radioactive red. And if you squint you could maybe see the moon through a thick layer of cigarette smoke and airplane exhaust that covers the whole city, like a mosquito net that won't let the angels in.

(*LIGHT SNARE DRUMMING.*)

And if you look up high enough you could see me. Standing on the edge of a eighty-seven story building, —

(*Thick steam shoots out of some pipes behind him —*)

—And up there, a place for gargoyles and broken clock towers that have stayed still and dead for maybe like a hundred years — up there is *me*.

(*DRUMS.*)

And I'm freakin' *Batman*.

(*CYMBAL.*)

And I gots Bat-mobiles and Bat-a-rangs and freakin' Bat-caves like for real, and all it takes is a broom closet or a back room or a fire escape, and Danny's hand-me-down jeans are gone.

(*BOOM.*)

And my navy blue polo shirt? —

(*—BOOM —*)

—The-one-that-looks-kinda-good-on-me-but-has-that-hole-on-it-near-the-butt-from-when-it-got-snagged-on-the-chain-link-fence-behind-Arturo's-but-it-isn't-even-a-big-deal-'cause-I-tuck-that-part-in-and-it's-like-all-good? —

(*—BOOM —*)

—*that* blue polo shirt? —

(*—BOOM —*)

—It's gone too. And I get like, like transformation-al.

(*BOOM. SNARE.*)

And nobody pulls out a belt and whips Batman for talking back —

APPROACHING THE AUTHOR

When **Marco Ramirez** was in high school, he wrote a one-act play about his grandfathers playing dominoes and discussing their experiences as Cuban refugees. He said of the composition process, "To get my first draft written, it took three or four days of working from six in the afternoon to about three in the morning, with Mom coming by and hitting me in the head and saying, 'Go to bed already.' . . . I thought, 'When she reads it she'll understand.'" The play was such a hit at his high school that the Coconut Grove Playhouse in Miami invited the troupe to perform it at a professional theater.

For more about him, see page 1408.

(—*SNARE*—)

—Or for *not* talking back,—

(—*SNARE, CRASH*—)

And nobody calls Batman simple—

(—*SNARE*—)

—Or stupid—

(—*SNARE*—)

—Or skinny—

(—*CYMBAL*—)

—And *nobody* fires Batman's brother from the Eastern Taxi Company 'cause they was making cutbacks, neither, ' cause they got nothing but respect, and not like *afraid*-respect. Just like *respect*-respect. 'Cause nobody's afraid of you.

'Cause Batman doesn't mean nobody no harm.

(*BOOM.*)

Ever.

(*SNARE, SNARE.*)

'Cause all Batman really wants to do is save people and maybe pay Abuela's bills one day and die happy and maybe get like mad famous. For real.

. . . And kill the Joker.

(*DRUMS.*)

Tonight, like most nights, I'm all alone. And I'm watching. . . And I'm waiting. . .

Like a eagle. Or like a—no, yea, like a eagle.

(*The DRUMS start low but constant, almost tribal.*)

And my cape is flappin' in the wind ('cause it's freakin' long), and my pointy ears are on, and that mask that covers like half my face is on too, and I got like bulletproof stuff all in my chest so no one could hurt me and nobody—*nobody*—is gonna come between Batman,

(*CYMBAL.*)

and Justice.

(*The SLOW KICKS continue, now there are SHORT hits randomly placed on the drum set. They somehow resemble city noises.*)

From where I am I could hear everything.

(*The DRUMS build, then STOP.*)

Somewhere in the city there's a old lady picking Styrofoam leftovers up outta a trash can and she's putting a piece of sesame chicken someone spit out into her own mouth.

(*SNARE.*)

And somewhere there's a doctor with a whack haircut in a black lab coat trying to find a cure for the diseases that are gonna make us all extinct for real one day.

(*SNARE. SNARE.*)

And somewhere there's a man, a man in a janitor's uniform, stumbling home drunk and dizzy after spending half his paycheck on forty-ounce bottles of twist-off beer and the other half on a four hour visit to some lady's house on a street where the lights have all been shot out by people who'd rather do what they do, in *this* city, in the dark.

And half a block away from JanitorMan there's a group of good-for-nothings who don't know no better waiting to beat JanitorMan with rusted bicycle chains and imitation Louisville Sluggers, and if they don't find a cent on him—which they won't—they'll just pound at him till the muscles in their arms start burning, till there's no more teeth to crack out.

But they don't count on me.

(*The BOY becomes proud, stands up straight.*)

They don't count on no dark knight (with a stomach full of grocery store brand macaroni-and-cheese and cut up Vienna sausages),

'Cause they'd rather believe I don't exist,

(*CYMBAL. The DRUMS start to build slowly again. The steam comes out thicker and thicker.*)

And from eighty-seven stories up I could hear one of the good-for-nothings say "Gimmethecash" real fast (like that) just "Gimmethefuckingcash" and I see JanitorMan mumble something in drunk language and turn pale and from eighty-seven stories up I could hear his stomach trying to hurl its way out of his Dickies.

So I swoop down like mad fast and I'm like darkness. I'm like SWOOSH—

(—*A LIGHT DRUMROLL*—)

—And I throw a Bat-a-rang at the one naked lightbulb—

(—*Light CYMBAL*—)

And they're all like "whoa-motherfucker-who-just-turned-out-the-lights?"—

(*Silence. The BOY breathes, re-enacting their fear, the largest and lowest CYMBAL builds slowly throughout this.*)

"What's that over there?" —

— "What?" —

— "Gimme whatchou got old man" —

— "Did anybody hear that?!" —

— "Hear what? There ain't nothing" —

— "No, really" —

— "There ain't. No. Bat."

(*The CYMBAL reaches its height.*)

But then —

(—*A KICK on the drums as the BOY suddenly springs into action*—)

— One out of three good-for-nothings gets it to the head!

And number Two swings blindly into the dark cape before him but before his fist hits anything I grab a trash can lid and —

(—*A CRASH on a CYMBAL*—)

— right in the gut, and number One comes back with a jump-kick but I know judo-karate too so I'm like —

(—*CRASH, happy from the response, he adds this part.*)

— Twice —

(—*CRASH*—)

— but before I can do any more damage suddenly we all hear a CLIC — CLIC —

(—*The DRUMMER's TOMS finish, BOOM. The steam stops.*)

And suddenly everything gets quiet.

(*The steam clears.*)

And the one good-for-nothing left standing grips a handgun and aims straight up, like he's holding Jesus hostage, like he's threatening maybe to blow a hole in the moon.

And the good-for-nothing who got it to the head who tried to jump-kick me and the other good-for-nothing who got it in the gut is both scrambling back away from the dark figure before him.

And the drunk man the JanitorMan is huddled in a corner, praying to Saint Anthony 'cause that's the only one he could remember.

(*HIT. HIT.*)

And there's me,

(*CYMBAL. HIT HIT.*)

Eyes glowing white, cape blowing softly in the wind.

(*HIT. HIT.*)

Bulletproof chest heaving. My heart beating right through it in a Morse code for "fuck with me, just once, come on, just try."

(*HIT. HIT. HIT.*)

And the one good-for-nothing left standing, the one with the handgun, he laughs, he lowers his arm, and he points it at me and gives the moon a break, and he aims it right between my pointy ears, like goalposts and he's special teams.

(*The BOY stands, frozen, afraid.*)

And JanitorMan is still calling Saint Anthony but he ain't pickin' up,

(*Silence.*)

And for a second it seems like . . . *maybe I'm gonna lose.*

(*The BOY takes a breath. Sudden courage.*)

Naw.

(*—SNARE. The BOY mimes the fight.*)

SHOO—SHOO! FUACATA!—

(*—SNARE—*)

—"Don't kill me mannn!!"—

(*—CYMBAL—*)

—SNAP!—

(*—SNARE—*)

—Wrist CRACK—

(*—SNARE—*)

—Neck—

(*—SNARE—*)

—SLASH!—

(*—CYMBAL—*)

—Skin—meets—acid—

(*—SNARE—*)

—"AHH!!"—

(—*SNARE.*)

And he's on the floor. And I'm standing over him. And I got the gun in MY hands now. And I hate guns, I hate holding 'em cause I'm Batman, and—

ASTERICKS: Batman don't like guns 'cause his parents got iced by guns a long time ago—but for just a second, my eyes glow white, and I hold this thing, for I could speak to the good-for-nothing in a language he maybe understands,

(*He aims the gun up at the sky.*)

...CLIC—CLIC...

(*The BASS DRUM.*)

And the good-for-nothings become good-for-disappearing into whatever toxic-waste-chemical-sludge-shit-hole they crawled out of.

(*A pause.*)

And it's just me and JanitorMan.

And I pick him up.

And I wipe sweat and cheap perfume off his forehead.

And he begs me not to hurt him and I grab him tight by his JanitorMan shirt collar and I pull him to my face, and he's taller than me, but the cape helps, so he listens when I look him straight in the eyes and I say two words to him:

"Go home."

And he does, checking behind his shoulder every ten feet.

And I SWOOSH from building to building on his way there, 'cause I know where he lives. And I watch his hands tremble as he pulls out his keychain and opens the door to his building.

And I'm back in bed before he even walks in through the front door.

(*SNARE.*)

And I hear him turn on the faucet and pour himself a glass of warm tap water.

And he puts the glass back in the sink.

(*SNARE.*)

And I hear his footsteps,

(*BOOM. BOOM.*)

And they get slower as they get to my room.

(*BOOM.*)

And he creaks my door open like mad slow.

(*Silence.*)

And he takes a step in, which he never does.

(*BOOM.*)

And he's staring off into nowhere, his face the color of sidewalks in summer, and I act like I'm just waking up, and I say,

"What's up, Pop?"

And JanitorMan says nothing to me.

But I see, in the dark, I see his arms go limp and his head turns back, like towards me, and he lifts it for I could see his face,

For I could see his eyes,

And his cheeks is dripping but not with sweat.

And he just stands there, breathing, like he remembers my eyes glowing white.

Like he remembers my bulletproof chest.

Like he remembers he's my pop.

(*Silence.*)

And for a long time I don't say nothing.

(*SILENCE.*)

And he turns around, hand on the doorknob, and he ain't looking my way but I hear him mumble two words to me.

(*A pause.*)

"I'm sorry."

(*A pause, the BOY is suddenly strong again.*)

And I lean over and open my window just a crack.

. . . If you look up high enough you could see me.

(*A couple SLOW KICKS, and some more, quiet, echoing SHORT hits.*)

And from where I am?. . . I could hear everything.

(*A slow blackout.*)

END OF PLAY

FOUR CLASSIC PLAYS

The Impact of Genre and Theater

Chapters 22 and 23 focus on the elements of drama that need attention as you read a play—the handling of character, dialogue, dramatic action, setting, and structure. For drama, however, you also need some familiarity with the traditional dramatic genres and how they changed—for example, what *comedy* and *tragedy* meant at the time a playwright was writing. And you need to be aware of the kind of theaters in which plays were and are acted. Playwrights nearly always write with specific stage structures in mind, usually reflecting the theater designs and practices of their day. For the four plays that follow, from very different time periods, we provide introductions giving information regarding the assumptions about genre and the theater designs in use when the playwright was writing.

In looking at theaters we consider not just the shape and size of the buildings and stages, but also the conventions used on those stages. **Conventions**, in this case, are assumptions shared by playwrights and audiences about how an action on the stage can be accepted as believable, even real. Conventions rely on what nineteenth-century poet and critic Samuel Taylor Coleridge called a "willing suspension of disbelief"—that is, a willingness not to question the truth, accuracy, or probability of what occurs in a work so that one can enter and enjoy it as if it were real. For example, lighting could not be controlled on an outdoor Elizabethan stage; so, if in a drama from that time period an actor says it is so dark he can't even see his hand in front of his face, the playwright and audience accept it as true, even though they can see the actor clearly.

The Greek Theater

The first of the four plays, *Antigone*, was originally performed in Athens in a large, open-air stadium designed for the annual festival of Dionysus, the Greek god of fertility. At the center of the structure was the circular "orchestra," or "dancing place," where the chorus moved from side to side and chanted their lines. At its center was an altar used for religious ceremonies, of which the drama was a part. Circling two-thirds of the orchestra was the *theatron* or "seeing place": tiers of wooden or stone seats for the audience, which rose up a hillside and created a bowl large enough to hold 15,000 people. Comparing that to today, when a 1,500–2,000-seat capacity is considered a large theater, gives some indication of how important these ceremonies were in Athenian culture.

Closing off the circle was the *skene* (literally, the "hut"), a wooden building where actors changed masks or costumes. Three doors opened onto the *proskenion*, a long, narrow section that served as the main acting area.

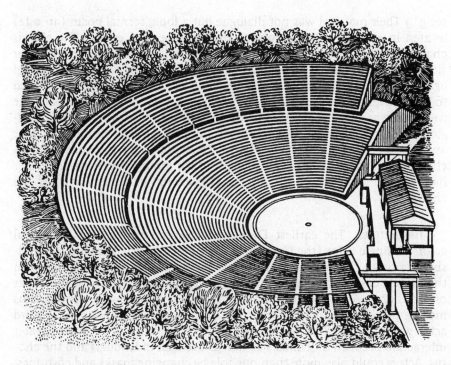

Classical Greek Theater. Based on scholarly sources, this drawing represents the features typical of a classical theater. (Macgowan & Melnitz, *The Living Stage: A History of the World Theater*, illustration of a classical Greek theatre by Gerda Becker, p. 148, © 1982. Reproduced by permission of Pearson Education, Inc.)

(The term ***proscenium***, for the apron or forestage of a modern theater, came from the Greek word.) The actors moved back and forth between the *proskenion* and the orchestra. The roof of the *skene* was also used as an acting area; it could, for example, suggest a cliff or the place of the gods.

ACTING STYLE   Performing in such a huge theater made it impossible to rely on subtle voice inflections, slight gestures, or facial expressions. Actors wore large masks to identify their characters, with megaphonic mouthpieces to project their voices; they used exaggerated gestures so even those seated at the top of the *theatron* could see them. In reading a Greek play, therefore, think of a stately style of acting, with the flowing movements of a formal dance company and the dignity of a traditional religious celebration. Visualizing it as a kind of ballet or pageant without music comes closer to its spirit than imagining it as a realistic drama.

THE CHORUS   The earliest Dionysian religious celebrations used only a **chorus** of ten to twelve men dressed in goat skins who chanted in unison, with no individual speakers. (*Tragedy* derives from the Greek word for "goat song".) Their material was not dialogue but a long, formal poem (an **ode**) written in sections called **strophe**, **antistrophe**, and **epode**. The chorus chanted the strophe on one side of the orchestra, moved across to the other side in a choreographed pattern to deliver the antistrophe, and then moved again for the epode, if the play included epodes. The choral lyric continued to be a convention of later Greek drama as well, and the chorus grew in size to as many as fifty people: When you read speeches by the chorus in *Antigone*, as on page 1107, imagine hearing numerous voices reciting together and moving about the orchestra in a stately rhythm—the entire chorus chanting and moving at times, or half of the group addressing the other half, or the members of the chorus conversing with the leader of the chorus.

THE ACTORS   The earliest Dionysian celebrations had no individual actors. A single actor (the Greek word is *hypocrites*) was added in the mid-sixth century B.C.E., reputedly by Thespis of Athens. The actor spoke between the choral odes, acting out parts in the story and conversing with the leader of the chorus. A second actor was added by the dramatist Aeschylus, thus making possible conflict between protagonist and antagonist, and a third actor was introduced by Sophocles, in the next century, allowing greater interaction between individuals as well as between individuals and the chorus. Actors could play more than one role by changing masks and costumes, which they would have done in performing *Antigone*.

THE ROLE OF THE CHORUS   Although the focus shifted increasingly to the actors, the chorus continued to be an important part of Greek drama. Actors entered and exited, but the chorus was present for most of the performance. In *Antigone*, they are onstage from the time they enter after line 116. The chorus—or the leader speaking for the rest—at times stands outside the action to provide background information, as in lines 117–79. They listen in on what characters say and comment on it or react to what is done (as, for example, in lines 377–424) or point out the moral (lines 1466–70). Sometimes the chorus interacts with characters (Antigone addresses them in lines 564–65) and gives characters advice or warnings (lines 1035–89). Sometimes the chorus does not "get" what is going on and requires more explanation from the characters—which enlightens the audience as well (lines 417–24). The chorus provides a continuous point of reference for the audience and serves as an intermediary, often addressing the audience directly.

ACTION OFFSTAGE   A convention of Greek drama is that little action occurs on the stage. What conflict does happen onstage is not a physical clash, but rather verbal and emotional sparring. Violence was never shown on the Greek stage; when it was part of the plot, it was reported to the audience. You will find that to be the case in *Antigone*.

GREEK TRAGEDY AS GENRE   As stated earlier, *tragedy* comes from the Greek word *tragōidía*, for "goat-song," and was likely connected to the sacrifice of goats as part of an annual festival honoring Dionysus. The festival included an ode, or *dithyramb*, chanted by a chorus, lamenting the death of Dionysus (see lines 1238–72 for an ode to Dionysus). Thespis is usually given credit for transforming the content of the *dithyramb* from a hymn honoring the god to tragic stories about famous heroes. A **tragedy** in literary usage is a play or work characterized by serious and significant actions that often lead to a disastrous result for the protagonist. Until the 1700s, tragedies were usually written in poetry and mostly in an elevated and dignified literary style. Their tone is correspondingly sober and weighty. Although the central character comes to a tragic end, Greek tragedies usually conclude with a restoration of order and an expectation of a brighter future for those who survive.

FAMILIAR PLOTS, DRAMATIC IRONY   Greek tragic plots were generally drawn from old, familiar myths, so the audience already knew the story when they attended a play. The audience's interest was in the way the story was handled. Perhaps the play would change the primary emphasis, present the theme from an alternative angle, or change the way the characters express themselves. Knowing that the plots would be familiar to the audience permitted playwrights to use **dramatic irony** liberally, for the viewers knew what lay ahead for the characters, though the characters themselves did not.

EFFECTS OF TRAGEDY   Aristotle, discussing literature in his *Poetics* (c. 330 B.C.E.), described tragedy as raising fear and pity in its audience and as having the effect of a **catharsis**, which has usually been translated as "purgation" or "purification." What he meant by this is widely disputed, but a common summation is as follows. The play first raises emotions: Members of the audience pity the hero and feel fear lest they encounter a fate similar to the hero's. But the artistic handling of the conclusion releases and quiets those emotions, as order is restored and the hero faces her or his destiny with fortitude, thus affirming the courage and dignity of humankind. In Aristotle's view, such raising and releasing of emotion has a healthy effect, psychologically and physically: The audience goes away feeling not dejected but relieved and strengthened.

TRAGIC HEROES   Because the central figures in myths are heroes and gods, the protagonists of Greek tragedies are persons of high rank or great importance. However, it is interesting that Aristotle, in his analysis of tragedy, said the hero should *not* be superhumanly good, for any calamity falling on such a person would be too hard to accept, nor should any character be thoroughly evil, for the downfall of such a person is deserved and therefore would not elicit pity. As you read Sophocles' *Antigone*, look for the traits Aristotle described, those that make Antigone and Creon good but not perfect. The important issue for Aristotle is the reason such a change from prosperity to adversity in fortune occurs. Think about that as you read and reflect on the play.

HAMARTIA The Greek tragic hero goes from prosperity to adversity as a result of a mistake, an error in judgment, a frailty. Aristotle's word for this is *hamartia*. It's important to keep in mind that *hamartia* is not the same as a character flaw. Some critics explain all tragedies in terms of a "**tragic flaw**" in the hero and cite Aristotle as their source; but the cause of a character's downfall is not always a defect or flaw. As you read or view the play and consider what leads to the tragic downfall, watching for an error or a misstep (*hamartia*) is preferable to looking for character defects. As you read *Antigone*, watch for missteps, or errors in judgment, that Antigone and Creon make, rather than for flaws in them.

PITY AND FEAR If Aristotle is right, you should feel a sense of pity for Antigone and Creon because of what happens as a result of their mistakes and a sense of fear that, if these basically good and decent characters could experience such a tragic series of events, it could happen to anyone. You should also experience a sense of relief ("purgation") — relief that Creon accepts the outcome with piety and humility and that order is restored in Thebes.

ENTRY POINTS Before you start reading *Antigone*, it's important to read the footnote to line 2, which summarizes the saga up to this point. *Antigone* is a sequel to Sophocles' equally famous play *Oedipus Rex*, or *Oedipus the King*, the sad story of the downfall of Oedipus as a result of mistakes, errors of judgment, that he makes. There is a similar plot in *Antigone*, involving Creon, Oedipus's successor as king of Thebes. But *Antigone* raises an additional theme that you will encounter first: the dilemma a character faces when the morally right thing to do has been made illegal by political authorities. That is the situation Antigone faces as the play begins, believing she is duty bound to bury her brother Polynices, although Creon, who considers Polynices a traitor, has forbidden it.

APPROACHING THE AUTHOR

In the years after **Sophocles** died, several legends cropped up as to the cause of death: The most famous is that he died while trying to recite a long line from *Antigone* without taking a breath. Another holds that he choked on grapes at a festival. Still another says he died of happiness after hearing of *Antigone*'s success at a theater competition.

For more about him, see page 1412.

Sophocles 496?–406 B.C.E.

Antigone   [c. 441 B.C.E.]

Translated by Robert Fagles

CHARACTERS

ANTIGONE, daughter of Oedipus
   and Jocasta
ISMENE, sister of Antigone
A CHORUS of old Theban citizens
   and their LEADER
CREON, king of Thebes, uncle of
   Antigone and Ismene

A SENTRY
HAEMON, son of Creon and
   Eurydice
TIRESIAS, a blind prophet
A MESSENGER
EURYDICE, wife of Creon
GUARDS, ATTENDANTS, AND A BOY

TIME AND SCENE

The royal house of Thebes. It is still night, and the invading armies of Argos
have just been driven from the city. Fighting on opposite sides, the sons of
Oedipus, Eteocles and Polynices, have killed each other in combat. Their uncle,
Creon, is now king of Thebes.

*Enter Antigone, slipping through the central doors of the palace. She motions to her
sister, Ismene, who follows her cautiously toward an altar at the center of the
stage.*

ANTIGONE: My own flesh and blood — dear sister, dear Ismene,
   how many griefs our father Oedipus handed down!°

---

2. Oedipus handed down: Oedipus, the father of Antigone and Ismene, was abandoned as an
infant when an oracle told his parents he would someday kill his father and marry his mother.
He was found by a shepherd and brought to Polybus, king of Corinth, who adopted him. Told
by a drunken man that Polybus was not his father, Oedipus went to an oracle to learn the truth
and was told that he would kill his father and marry his mother. Oedipus decided to leave
Corinth, in order to escape this fate. Forced off the road by a chariot, he killed the driver (Laius,
king of Thebes, his biological father), thus unknowingly fulfilling the first part of the oracle's
prophecy. He went on to Thebes, which was held in thrall by a sphinx who killed all those who
could not solve her riddle. Oedipus answered it correctly and became king by marrying the widowed queen, Jocasta. The couple had two sons, Polynices and Eteocles, and two daughters, Antigone and Ismene. *Oedipus the King*, the prequel to *Antigone*, tells how, when Thebes was
suffering from a plague, an oracle declared that the land was polluted by the presence of the
murderer of its king, who had to be expelled. In a series of painful revelations, Oedipus and Jocasta learn the truth about each other and their situation. In grief and horror, Jocasta kills
herself and Oedipus puts out his eyes and goes into exile, giving the kingdom to his sons, who
agree to rule in alternate years. After the first year, Eteocles refuses to step down and Polynices
attacks Thebes, with the support of the army from a nearby city, Argos. The brothers kill each
other in hand-to-hand combat in front of the gates of Thebes, and Creon, brother of Jocasta,
takes over as king. He orders that Eteocles be given full burial honors, but that Polynices must
go unburied and thus be dishonored. *Antigone* opens at this point.

Do you know one, I ask you, one grief
that Zeus will not perfect for the two of us
while we still live and breathe? There's nothing,   5
no pain — our lives are pain — no private shame,
no public disgrace, nothing I haven't seen
in your griefs and mine. And now this:
an emergency decree, they say, the Commander°
has just declared for all of Thebes.   10
What, haven't you heard? Don't you see?
The doom reserved for enemies
marches on the ones we love the most.

ISMENE: Not I, I haven't heard a word, Antigone.
Nothing of loved ones,   15
no joy or pain has come my way, not since
the two of us were robbed of our two brothers,
both gone in a day, a double blow —
not since the armies of Argos vanished,
just this very night. I know nothing more,   20
whether our luck's improved or ruin's still to come.

ANTIGONE: I thought so. That's why I brought you out here,
past the gates, so you could hear in private.

ISMENE: What's the matter? Trouble, clearly . . .
you sound so dark, so grim.   25

ANTIGONE: Why not? Our own brothers' burial!
Hasn't Creon graced one with all the rites,
disgraced the other? Eteocles, they say,
has been given full military honors,
rightly so — Creon's laid him in the earth   30
and he goes with glory down among the dead.
But the body of Polynices, who died miserably —
why, a city-wide proclamation, rumor has it,
forbids anyone to bury him, even mourn him.
He's to be left unwept, unburied, a lovely treasure   35
for birds that scan the field and feast to their heart's content.

Such, I hear, is the martial law our good Creon
lays down for you and me — yes, me, I tell you —
and he's coming here to alert the uninformed
in no uncertain terms,   40
and he won't treat the matter lightly. Whoever
disobeys in the least will die, his doom is sealed:
stoning to death inside the city walls!

_____

9. **the Commander:** Creon.

There you have it. You'll soon show what you are,
worth your breeding, Ismene, or a coward—   45
for all your royal blood.
ISMENE: My poor sister, if things have come to this,
who am I to make or mend them, tell me,
what good am I to you?
ANTIGONE: Decide.
Will you share the labor, share the work?   50
ISMENE: What work, what's the risk? What do you mean?
ANTIGONE:

(*Raising her hands.*)

Will you lift up his body with these bare hands
and lower it with me?
ISMENE: What? You'd bury him—
when a law forbids the city?
ANTIGONE: Yes!
He is my brother and—deny it as you will—   55
your brother too.
No one will ever convict me for a traitor.
ISMENE: So desperate, and Creon has expressly—
ANTIGONE: No,
he has no right to keep me from my own.
ISMENE: Oh my sister, think—   60
think how our own father died,° hated,
his reputation in ruins, driven on
by the crimes he brought to light himself
to gouge out his eyes with his own hands—
then mother . . . his mother and wife, both in one,   65
mutilating her life in the twisted noose—
and last, our two brothers dead in a single day,
both shedding their own blood, poor suffering boys,
battling out their common destiny hand-to-hand.

Now look at the two of us, left so alone . . .   70
think what a death we'll die, the worst of all
if we violate the laws and override
the fixed decree of the throne, its power—
we must be sensible. Remember we are women,
we're not born to contend with men. Then too,   75
we're underlings, ruled by much stronger hands,
so we must submit in this, and things still worse.

---

61. our own father died: *Oedipus the King* and *Oedipus at Colonus*, written later than *Antigone,*
give a different account of Oedipus's later life and death.

I, for one, I'll beg the dead to forgive me—
I'm forced, I have no choice—I must obey
the ones who stand in power. Why rush to extremes?   80
It's madness, madness.

ANTIGONE: I won't insist,
no, even if you should have a change of heart,
I'd never welcome you in the labor, not with me.
So, do as you like, whatever suits you best—
I will bury him myself.   85
And even if I die in the act, that death will be a glory.
I will lie with the one I love and loved by him—
an outrage sacred to the gods! I have longer
to please the dead than please the living here:
in the kingdom down below I'll lie forever.   90
Do as you like, dishonor the laws
the gods hold in honor.

ISMENE: I'd do them no dishonor . . .
but defy the city? I have no strength for that.

ANTIGONE: You have your excuses. I am on my way,
I will raise a mound for him, for my dear brother.   95

ISMENE: Oh Antigone, you're so rash—I'm so afraid for you!

ANTIGONE: Don't fear for me. Set your own life in order.

ISMENE: Then don't, at least, blurt this out to anyone.
Keep it a secret. I'll join you in that, I promise.

ANTIGONE: Dear god, shout it from the rooftops. I'll hate you   100
all the more for silence—tell the world!

ISMENE: So fiery—and it ought to chill your heart.

ANTIGONE: I know I please where I must please the most.

ISMENE: Yes, if you can, but you're in love with impossibility.

ANTIGONE: Very well then, once my strength gives out   105
I will be done at last.

ISMENE: You're wrong from the start,
you're off on a hopeless quest.

ANTIGONE: If you say so, you will make me hate you,
and the hatred of the dead, by all rights,
will haunt you night and day.   110
But leave me to my own absurdity, leave me
to suffer this—dreadful thing. I will suffer
nothing as great as death without glory.

(*Exit to the side.*)

ISMENE: Then go if you must, but rest assured,
wild, irrational as you are, my sister,   115
you are truly dear to the ones who love you.

(Withdrawing to the palace. Enter a Chorus, the old citizens of Thebes, chanting as the sun begins to rise.)

CHORUS: Glory! — great beam of sun, brightest of all
    that ever rose on the seven gates of Thebes,
        you burn through night at last!
            Great eye of the golden day,   120
    mounting the Dirce's° banks you throw him back —
    the enemy out of Argos, the white shield, the man of bronze —
    he's flying headlong now
           the bridle of fate stampeding him with pain!

    And he had driven against our borders,   125
    launched by the warring claims of Polynices —
    like an eagle screaming, winging havoc
    over the land, wings of armor
    shielded white as snow,
    a huge army massing,   130
    crested helmets bristling for assault.

He hovered above our roofs, his vast maw gaping
closing down around our seven gates,
    his spears thirsting for the kill
            but now he's gone, look,   135
before he could glut his jaws with Theban blood
or the god of fire put our crown of towers to the torch.
He grappled the Dragon° none can master — Thebes —
        the clang of our arms like thunder at his back!

    Zeus hates with a vengeance all bravado,   140
    the mighty boasts of men. He watched them
    coming on in a rising flood, the pride
    of their golden armor ringing shrill —
    and brandishing his lightning
    blasted the fighter° just at the goal,   145
    rushing to shout his triumph from our walls.

Down from the heights he crashed, pounding down on the earth!
And a moment ago, blazing torch in hand —
        mad for attack, ecstatic
he breathed his rage, the storm   150

---

121. the Dirce's: A river near Thebes.   **138. the Dragon:** Alluding to the legend that the Thebans grew from dragon's teeth sown by Cadmus.   **145. blasted the fighter:** Capaneus, ally of Polynices, boasted from the top of a siege ladder that not even Zeus could keep him from entering Thebes. Zeus punished this impiety by striking him at the top of the ladder with a thunderbolt.

of his fury hurling at our heads!
But now his high hopes have laid him low
and down the enemy ranks the iron god of war
        deals his rewards, his stunning blows—Ares°
        rapture of battle, our right arm in the crisis.   155

        Seven captains marshaled at seven gates
        seven against their equals, gave
        their brazen trophies up to Zeus,
        god of the breaking rout of battle,
        all but two: those blood brothers,   160
        one father, one mother—matched in rage,
        spears matched for the twin conquest—
        clashed and won the common prize of death.

But now for Victory! Glorious in the morning,
joy in her eyes to meet our joy   165
        she is winging down to Thebes,
our fleets of chariots wheeling in her wake—
        Now let us win oblivion from the wars,
thronging the temples of the gods
in singing, dancing choirs through the night!   170
        Lord Dionysus,° god of the dance
        that shakes the land of Thebes, now lead the way!

(*Enter Creon from the palace, attended by his guard.*)

        But look, the king of the realm is coming,
        Creon, the new man for the new day,
        whatever the gods are sending now . . .   175
        what new plan will he launch?
        Why this, this special session?
        Why this sudden call to the old men
        summoned at one command?

CREON: My countrymen,
the ship of state is safe. The gods who rocked her,   180
after a long, merciless pounding in the storm,
have righted her once more.
                 Out of the whole city
I have called you here alone. Well I know,
first, your undeviating respect
for the throne and royal power of King Laius.   185
Next, while Oedipus steered the land of Thebes,
and even after he died, your loyalty was unshakable,

---

154. **Ares:** God of savage warfare; a patron deity of Thebes.   **171. Dionysus:** God of fertility
and wine, at whose festival Greek tragedies originally were performed.

you still stood by their children. Now then,
since the two sons are dead—two blows of fate
in the same day, cut down by each other's hands,   190
both killers, both brothers stained with blood—
as I am next in kin to the dead,
I now possess the throne and all its powers.

Of course you cannot know a man completely,
his character, his principles, sense of judgment,   195
not till he's shown his colors, ruling the people,
making laws. Experience, there's the test.
As I see it, whoever assumes the task,
the awesome task of setting the city's course,
and refuses to adopt the soundest policies   200
but fearing someone, keeps his lips locked tight,
he's utterly worthless. So I rate him now,
I always have. And whoever places a friend
above the good of his own country, he is nothing:
I have no use for him. Zeus my witness,   205
Zeus who sees all things, always—
I could never stand by silent, watching destruction
march against our city, putting safety to rout,
nor could I ever make that man a friend of mine
who menaces our country. Remember this: 210
our country *is* our safety.
Only while she voyages true on course
can we establish friendships, truer than blood itself.
Such are my standards. They make our city great.

Closely akin to them I have proclaimed,   215
just now, the following decree to our people
concerning the two sons of Oedipus.
Eteocles, who died fighting for Thebes,
excelling all in arms: he shall be buried,
crowned with a hero's honors, the cups we pour°   220
to soak the earth and reach the famous dead.

But as for his blood brother, Polynices,
who returned from exile, home to his father-city
and the gods of his race, consumed with one desire—
to burn them roof to roots—who thirsted to drink   225
his kinsmen's blood and sell the rest to slavery:
that man—a proclamation has forbidden the city
to dignify him with burial, mourn him at all.

---

220. the cups we pour: Libations—a ritual pouring out of wine or another liquid.

No, he must be left unburied, his corpse   230
carrion for the birds and dogs to tear,
an obscenity for the citizens to behold!

These are my principles. Never at my hands
will the traitor be honored above the patriot.
But whoever proves his loyalty to the state —
I'll prize that man in death as well as life.   235

LEADER: If this is your pleasure, Creon, treating
  our city's enemy and our friend this way . . .
  The power is yours, I suppose, to enforce it
  with the laws, both for the dead and all of us,
  the living.

CREON: Follow my orders closely then,   240
  be on your guard.

LEADER: We're too old.
  Lay that burden on younger shoulders.

CREON: No, no,
  I don't mean the body—I've posted guards already.

LEADER: What commands for us then? What other service?

CREON: See that you never side with those who break my orders.   245

LEADER: Never. Only a fool could be in love with death.

CREON: Death is the price—you're right. But all too often
  the mere hope of money has ruined many men.

(*A Sentry enters from the side.*)

SENTRY: My lord,
  I can't say I'm winded from running, or set out
  with any spring in my legs either—no sir,   250
  I was lost in thought, and it made me stop, often,
  dead in my tracks, wheeling, turning back,
  and all the time a voice inside me muttering,
  "Idiot, why? You're going straight to your death."
  Then muttering, "Stopped again, poor fool?   255
  If somebody gets the news to Creon first,
  what's to save your neck?"
                          And so,
  mulling it over, on I trudged, dragging my feet,
  you can make a short road take forever . . .
  but at last, look, common sense won out,   260
  I'm here, and I'm all yours,
  and even though I come empty-handed
  I'll tell my story just the same, because
  I've come with a good grip on one hope,
  what will come will come, whatever fate—   265

CREON: Come to the point!

What's wrong—why so afraid?
SENTRY: First, myself, I've got to tell you,
    I didn't do it, didn't see who did—
    Be fair, don't take it out on me.   270
CREON: You're playing it safe, soldier,
    barricading yourself from any trouble.
    It's obvious, you've something strange to tell.
SENTRY: Dangerous too, and danger makes you delay
    for all you're worth.   275
CREON: Out with it—then dismiss!
SENTRY: All right, here it comes. The body—
    someone's just buried it, then run off . . .
    sprinkled some dry dust° on the flesh,
    given it proper rites.
CREON: What?   280
    What man alive would dare—
SENTRY: I've no idea, I swear it.
    There was no mark of a spade, no pickaxe there,
    no earth turned up, the ground packed hard and dry,
    unbroken, no tracks, no wheelruts, nothing,
    the workman left no trace. Just at sunup   285
    the first watch of the day points it out—
    it was a wonder! We were stunned . . .
    a terrific burden too, for all of us, listen:
    you can't see the corpse, not that it's buried,
    really, just a light cover of road-dust on it,   290
    as if someone meant to lay the dead to rest
    and keep from getting cursed.
    Not a sign in sight that dogs or wild beasts
    had worried the body, even torn the skin.

But what came next! Rough talk flew thick and fast,   295
    guard grilling guard—we'd have come to blows
    at last, nothing to stop it; each man for himself
    and each the culprit, no one caught red-handed,
    all of us pleading ignorance, dodging the charges,
    ready to take up red-hot iron in our fists,   300
    go through fire, swear oaths to the gods—
    "I didn't do it, I had no hand in it either,
    not in the plotting, not in the work itself!"

Finally, after all this wrangling came to nothing,
    one man spoke out and made us stare at the ground,   305

---

279. sprinkled some dry dust: As a symbolic burial, all that Antigone could do since Polynices'
body was being guarded closely.

hanging our heads in fear. No way to counter him,
no way to take his advice and come through
safe and sound. Here's what he said:
"Look, we've got to report the facts to Creon,
we can't keep this hidden." Well, that won out,   310
and the lot fell to me, condemned me,
unlucky as ever, I got the prize. So here I am,
against my will and yours too, well I know—
no one wants the man who brings bad news.

LEADER: My king,
ever since he began I've been debating in my mind,   315
could this possibly be the work of the gods?

CREON: Stop—
before you make me choke with anger—the gods!
You, you're senile, must you be insane?
You say—why it's intolerable—say the gods
could have the slightest concern for that corpse?   320
Tell me, was it for meritorious service
they proceeded to bury him, prized him so? The hero
who came to burn their temples ringed with pillars,
their golden treasures—scorch their hallowed earth
and fling their laws to the winds.   325
Exactly when did you last see the gods
celebrating traitors? Inconceivable!

No, from the first there were certain citizens
who could hardly stand the spirit of my regime,
grumbling against me in the dark, heads together,   330
tossing wildly, never keeping their necks beneath
the yoke, loyally submitting to their king.
These are the instigators, I'm convinced—
they've perverted my own guard, bribed them
to do their work.

                        Money! Nothing worse   335
in our lives, so current, rampant, so corrupting.
Money—you demolish cities, root men from their homes,
you train and twist good minds and set them on
to the most atrocious schemes. No limit,
you make them adept at every kind of outrage,   340
every godless crime—money!

                        Everyone—
the whole crew bribed to commit this crime,
they've made one thing sure at least:
sooner or later they will pay the price.

(*Wheeling on the Sentry.*)

                                                You —
   I swear to Zeus as I still believe in Zeus,   345
   if you don't find the man who buried that corpse,
   the very man, and produce him before my eyes,
   simple death won't be enough for you,
   not till we string you up alive
   and wring the immorality out of you.   350
   Then you can steal the rest of your days,
   better informed about where to make a killing.
   You'll have learned, at last, it doesn't pay
   to itch for rewards from every hand that beckons.
   Filthy profits wreck most men, you'll see —   355
   they'll never save your life.
SENTRY: Please,
   may I say a word or two, or just turn and go?
CREON: Can't you tell? Everything you say offends me.
SENTRY: Where does it hurt you, in the ears or in the heart?
CREON: And who are you to pinpoint my displeasure?   360
SENTRY: The culprit grates on your feelings,
   I just annoy your ears.
CREON: Still talking?
   You talk too much! A born nuisance —
SENTRY: Maybe so,
   but I never did this thing, so help me!
CREON: Yes you did —
   what's more, you squandered your life for silver!   365
SENTRY: Oh it's terrible when the one who does the judging
   judges things all wrong.
CREON: Well now,
   you just be clever about your judgments —
   if you fail to produce the criminals for me,
   you'll swear your dirty money brought you pain.   370

(Turning sharply, reentering the palace.)

SENTRY: I hope he's found. Best thing by far.
   But caught or not, that's in the lap of fortune;
   I'll never come back, you've seen the last of me.
   I'm saved, even now, and I never thought,
   I never hoped —   375
   dear gods, I owe you all my thanks!

(Rushing out.)

CHORUS: Numberless wonders
   terrible wonders walk the world but none the match for man —
   that great wonder crossing the heaving gray sea,

driven on by the blasts of winter
on through breakers crashing left and right, 380
   holds his steady course
and the oldest of the gods he wears away—
the Earth, the immortal, the inexhaustible—
as his plows go back and forth, year in, year out
   with the breed of stallions turning up the furrows. 385

And the blithe, lightheaded race of birds he snares,
the tribes of savage beasts, the life that swarms the depths—
   with one fling of his nets
woven and coiled tight, he takes them all,
   man the skilled, the brilliant! 390
He conquers all, taming with his techniques
the prey that roams the cliffs and wild lairs,
training the stallion, clamping the yoke across
   his shaggy neck, and the tireless mountain bull.

And speech and thought, quick as the wind 395
and the mood and mind for law that rules the city—
   all these he has taught himself
and shelter from the arrows of the frost
when there's rough lodging under the cold clear sky
and the shafts of lashing rain— 400
   ready, resourceful man!
      Never without resources
never an impasse as he marches on the future—
only Death, from Death alone he will find no rescue
but from desperate plagues he has plotted his escapes. 405

Man the master, ingenious past all measure
past all dreams, the skills within his grasp—
   he forges on, now to destruction
now again to greatness. When he weaves in
the laws of the land, and the justice of the gods 410
that binds his oaths together
   he and his city rise high—
      but the city casts out
that man who weds himself to inhumanity
thanks to reckless daring. Never share my hearth 415
never think my thoughts, whoever does such things.

(Enter Antigone from the side, accompanied by the Sentry.)

Here is a dark sign from the gods—
what to make of this? I know her,
how can I deny it? That young girl's Antigone!

Wretched, child of a wretched father,   420
Oedipus. Look, is it possible?
They bring you in like a prisoner —
why? did you break the king's laws?
Did they take you in some act of mad defiance?
SENTRY: She's the one, she did it single-handed —   425
we caught her burying the body. Where's Creon?

(*Enter Creon from the palace.*)

LEADER: Back again, just in time when you need him.
CREON: In time for what? What is it?
SENTRY: My king,
there's nothing you can swear you'll never do —
second thoughts make liars of us all.   430
I could have sworn I wouldn't hurry back
(what with your threats, the buffeting I just took),
but a stroke of luck beyond our wildest hopes,
what a joy, there's nothing like it. So,
back I've come, breaking my oath, who cares?   435
I'm bringing in our prisoner — this young girl —
we took her giving the dead the last rites.
But no casting lots this time; this is *my* luck,
my prize, no one else's.
                         Now, my lord,
here she is. Take her, question her,   440
cross-examine her to your heart's content.
But set me free, it's only right —
I'm rid of this dreadful business once for all.
CREON: Prisoner! Her? You took her — where, doing what?
SENTRY: Burying the man. That's the whole story.
CREON: What?   445
You mean what you say, you're telling me the truth?
SENTRY: She's the one. With my own eyes I saw her
bury the body, just what you've forbidden.
There. Is that plain and clear?
CREON: What did you see? Did you catch her in the act?   450
SENTRY: Here's what happened. We went back to our post,
those threats of yours breathing down our necks —
we brushed the corpse clean of the dust that covered it,
stripped it bare . . . it was slimy, going soft,
and we took to high ground, backs to the wind   455
so the stink of him couldn't hit us;
jostling, baiting each other to keep awake,
shouting back and forth — no napping on the job,
not this time. And so the hours dragged by

until the sun stood dead above our heads,   460
a huge white ball in the noon sky, beating,
blazing down, and then it happened—
suddenly, a whirlwind!
Twisting a great dust-storm up from the earth,
a black plague of the heavens, filling the plain,   465
ripping the leaves off every tree in sight,
choking the air and sky. We squinted hard
and took our whipping from the gods.

And after the storm passed—it seemed endless—
there, we saw the girl!   470
And she cried out a sharp, piercing cry,
like a bird come back to an empty nest,
peering into its bed, and all the babies gone . . .
Just so, when she sees the corpse bare
she bursts into a long, shattering wail   475
and calls down withering curses on the heads
of all who did the work. And she scoops up dry dust,
handfuls, quickly, and lifting a fine bronze urn,
lifting it high and pouring, she crowns the dead
with three full libations.
               Soon as we saw   480
we rushed her, closed on the kill like hunters,
and she, she didn't flinch. We interrogated her,
charging her with offenses past and present—
she stood up to it all, denied nothing. I tell you,
it made me ache and laugh in the same breath.   485
It's pure joy to escape the worst yourself,
it hurts a man to bring down his friends.
But all that, I'm afraid, means less to me
than my own skin. That's the way I'm made.

CREON:

(*Wheeling on Antigone.*)

                                  You,   490
with your eyes fixed on the ground—speak up.
Do you deny you did this, yes or no?

ANTIGONE: I did it. I don't deny a thing.

CREON:

(*To the Sentry.*)

You, get out, wherever you please—
you're clear of a very heavy charge.

(*He leaves; Creon turns back to Antigone.*)

You, tell me briefly, no long speeches —   495
were you aware a decree had forbidden this?
ANTIGONE: Well aware. How could I avoid it? It was public.
CREON: And still you had the gall to break this law?
ANTIGONE: Of course I did. It wasn't Zeus, not in the least,
who made this proclamation — not to me.   500
Nor did that Justice, dwelling with the gods
beneath the earth, ordain such laws for men.
Nor did I think your edict had such force
that you, a mere mortal, could override the gods,
the great unwritten, unshakeable traditions.   505
They are alive, not just today or yesterday:
they live forever, from the first of time,
and no one knows when they first saw the light.

These laws — I was not about to break them,
not out of fear of some man's wounded pride,   510
and face the retribution of the gods.
Die I must, I've known it all my life —
how could I keep from knowing? — even without
your death-sentence ringing in my ears.
And if I am to die before my time   515
I consider that a gain. Who on earth,
alive in the midst of so much grief as I,
could fail to find his death a rich reward?
So for me, at least, to meet this doom of yours
is precious little pain. But if I had allowed   520
my own mother's son to rot, an unburied corpse —
that would have been an agony! This is nothing.
And if my present actions strike you as foolish,
let's just say I've been accused of folly
by a fool.
LEADER: Like father like daughter,   525
passionate, wild . . .
she hasn't learned to bend before adversity.
CREON: No? Believe me, the stiffest stubborn wills
fall the hardest; the toughest iron,
tempered strong in the white-hot fire,   530
you'll see it crack and shatter first of all.
And I've known spirited horses you can break
with a light bit — proud, rebellious horses.
There's no room for pride, not in a slave,
not with the lord and master standing by.   535

This girl was an old hand at insolence
when she overrode the edicts we made public.

But once she'd done it—the insolence,
twice over—to glory in it, laughing,
mocking us to our face with what she'd done.   540
I'm not the man, not now: she is the man
if this victory goes to her and she goes free.

Never! Sister's child or closer in blood
than all my family clustered at my altar
worshiping Guardian Zeus—she'll never escape,   545
she and her blood sister, the most barbaric death.
Yes, I accuse her sister of an equal part
in scheming this, this burial.

(To his attendants.)

                              Bring her here!
I just saw her inside, hysterical, gone to pieces.
It never fails: the mind convicts itself   550
in advance, when scoundrels are up to no good,
plotting in the dark. Oh but I hate it more
when a traitor, caught red-handed,
tries to glorify his crimes.
ANTIGONE: Creon, what more do you want   555
than my arrest and execution?
CREON: Nothing. Then I have it all.
ANTIGONE: Then why delay? Your moralizing repels me,
every word you say—pray god it always will.
So naturally all I say repels you too.
                                   Enough.   560
Give me glory! What greater glory could I win
than to give my own brother decent burial?
These citizens here would all agree,

(To the Chorus.)

they would praise me too
if their lips weren't locked in fear.   565

(Pointing to Creon.)

Lucky tyrants—the perquisites of power!
Ruthless power to do and say whatever pleases *them*.
CREON: You alone, of all the people in Thebes,
see things that way.
ANTIGONE: They see it just that way
but defer to you and keep their tongues in leash.   570
CREON: And you, aren't you ashamed to differ so from them?
So disloyal!

ANTIGONE: Not ashamed for a moment,
    not to honor my brother, my own flesh and blood.
CREON: Wasn't Eteocles a brother too—cut down, facing him?
ANTIGONE: Brother, yes, by the same mother, the same father.   575
CREON: Then how can you render his enemy such honors,
    such impieties in his eyes?
ANTIGONE: He will never testify to that,
    Eteocles dead and buried.
CREON: He will—
    if you honor the traitor just as much as him.   580
ANTIGONE: But it was his brother, not some slave that died—
CREON: Ravaging our country!—
    but Eteocles died fighting in our behalf.
ANTIGONE: No matter—Death longs for the same rites for all.
CREON: Never the same for the patriot and the traitor.   585
ANTIGONE: Who, Creon, who on earth can say the ones below
    don't find this pure and uncorrupt?
CREON: Never. Once an enemy, never a friend,
    not even after death.
ANTIGONE: I was born to join in love, not hate—   590
    that is my nature.
CREON: Go down below and love,
    if love you must—love the dead! While I'm alive,
    no woman is going to lord it over me.

(Enter Ismene from the palace, under guard.)

CHORUS: Look,
    Ismene's coming, weeping a sister's tears,
    loving sister, under a cloud . . .   595
    her face is flushed, her cheeks streaming.
    Sorrow puts her lovely radiance in the dark.
CREON: You—
    in my own house, you viper, slinking undetected,
    sucking my life-blood! I never knew
    I was breeding twin disasters, the two of you   600
    rising up against my throne. Come, tell me,
    will you confess your part in the crime or not?
    Answer me. Swear to me.
ISMENE: I did it, yes—
    if only she consents—I share the guilt,
    the consequences too.
ANTIGONE: No,   605
    Justice will never suffer that—not you,
    you were unwilling. I never brought you in.
ISMENE: But now you face such dangers . . . I'm not ashamed

to sail through trouble with you,
make your troubles mine.

ANTIGONE: Who did the work?   610
Let the dead and the god of death bear witness!
I have no love for a friend who loves in words alone.

ISMENE: Oh no, my sister, don't reject me, please,
let me die beside you, consecrating
the dead together.

ANTIGONE: Never share my dying,   615
don't lay claim to what you never touched.
My death will be enough.

ISMENE: What do I care for life, cut off from you?

ANTIGONE: Ask Creon. Your concern is all for him.

ISMENE: Why abuse me so? It doesn't help you now.

ANTIGONE: You're right—   620
if I mock you, I get no pleasure from it,
only pain.

ISMENE: Tell me, dear one,
what can I do to help you, even now?

ANTIGONE: Save yourself. I don't grudge you your survival.

ISMENE: Oh no, no, denied my portion in your death?   625

ANTIGONE: You chose to live, I chose to die.

ISMENE: Not, at least,
without every kind of caution I could voice.

ANTIGONE: Your wisdom appealed to one world—mine, another.

ISMENE: But look, we're both guilty, both condemned to death.

ANTIGONE: Courage! Live your life. I gave myself to death,   630
long ago, so I might serve the dead.

CREON: They're both mad, I tell you, the two of them.
One's just shown it, the other's been that way
since she was born.

ISMENE: True, my king,
the sense we were born with cannot last forever . . .   635
commit cruelty on a person long enough
and the mind begins to go.

CREON: Yours did,
when you chose to commit your crimes with her.

ISMENE: How can I live alone, without her?

CREON: Her?
Don't even mention her—she no longer exists.   640

ISMENE: What? You'd kill your own son's bride?

CREON: Absolutely:
there are other fields for him to plow.

ISMENE: Perhaps,
but never as true, as close a bond as theirs.

CREON: A worthless woman for my son? It repels me.
ISMENE: Dearest Haemon, your father wrongs you so!   645
CREON: Enough, enough—you and your talk of marriage!
ISMENE: Creon—you're really going to rob your son of Antigone?
CREON: Death will do it for me—break their marriage off.
LEADER: So, it's settled then? Antigone must die?
CREON: Settled, yes—we both know that.   650

(*To the guards.*)

> Stop wasting time. Take them in.
> From now on they'll act like women.
> Tie them up, no more running loose;
> even the bravest will cut and run,
> once they see Death coming for their lives.   655

(*The guards escort Antigone and Ismene into the palace. Creon remains while the old citizens form their chorus.*)

CHORUS: Blest, they are the truly blest who all their lives
    have never tasted devastation. For others, once
    the gods have rocked a house to its foundations
        the ruin will never cease, cresting on and on
    from one generation on throughout the race—   660
    like a great mounting tide
    driven on by savage northern gales,
        surging over the dead black depths
    roiling up from the bottom dark heaves of sand
    and the headlands, taking the storm's onslaught full-force,   665
    roar, and the low moaning
                echoes on and on
                      and now
    as in ancient times I see the sorrows of the house,
    the living heirs of the old ancestral kings,
    piling on the sorrows of the dead
        and one generation cannot free the next—   670
    some god will bring them crashing down,
    the race finds no release.
    And now the light, the hope
        springing up from the late last root
    in the house of Oedipus, that hope's cut down in turn   675
    by the long, bloody knife swung by the gods of death
    by a senseless word
        by fury at the heart.
                    Zeus,
    yours is the power, Zeus, what man on earth
    can override it, who can hold it back?

Power that neither Sleep, the all-ensnaring   680
    no, nor the tireless months of heaven
can ever overmaster—young through all time,
mighty lord of power, you hold fast
    the dazzling crystal mansions of Olympus.
And throughout the future, late and soon   685
as through the past, your law prevails:
no towering form of greatness
        enters into the lives of mortals
            free and clear of ruin.
                          True,
our dreams, our high hopes voyaging far and wide   690
bring sheer delight to many, to many others
    delusion, blithe, mindless lusts
and the fraud steals on one slowly . . . unaware
till he trips and puts his foot into the fire.
    He was a wise old man who coined   695
the famous saying: "Sooner or later
foul is fair, fair is foul
to the man the gods will ruin"—
    He goes his way for a moment only
            free of blinding ruin.   700

(Enter Haemon from the palace.)

    Here's Haemon now, the last of all your sons.
    Does he come in tears for his bride,
    his doomed bride, Antigone—
    bitter at being cheated of their marriage?
CREON: We'll soon know, better than seers could tell us.   705

(Turning to Haemon.)

    Son, you've heard the final verdict on your bride?
    Are you coming now, raving against your father?
    Or do you love me, no matter what I do?
HAEMON: Father, I'm your *son* . . . you in your wisdom
    set my bearings for me—I obey you.   710
    No marriage could ever mean more to me than you,
    whatever good direction you may offer.
CREON: Fine, Haemon.
    That's how you ought to feel within your heart,
    subordinate to your father's will in every way.
    That's what a man prays for: to produce good sons—   715
    a household full of them, dutiful and attentive,
    so they can pay his enemy back with interest
    and match the respect their father shows his friend.

But the man who rears a brood of useless children,
what has he brought into the world, I ask you?   720
Nothing but trouble for himself, and mockery
from his enemies laughing in his face.
                                        Oh Haemon,
never lose your sense of judgment over a woman.
The warmth, the rush of pleasure, it all goes cold
in your arms, I warn you . . . a worthless woman   725
in your house, a misery in your bed.
What wound cuts deeper than a loved one
turned against you? Spit her out,
like a mortal enemy — let the girl go.
Let her find a husband down among the dead.   730

Imagine it: I caught her in naked rebellion,
the traitor, the only one in the whole city.
I'm not about to prove myself a liar,
not to my people, no, I'm going to kill her!
That's right — so let her cry for mercy, sing her hymns   735
to Zeus who defends all bonds of kindred blood.
Why, if I bring up my own kin to be rebels,
think what I'd suffer from the world at large.
Show me the man who rules his household well:
I'll show you someone fit to rule the state.   740
That good man, my son,
I have every confidence he and he alone
can give commands and take them too. Staunch
in the storm of spears he'll stand his ground,
a loyal, unflinching comrade at your side.   745

But whoever steps out of line, violates the laws
or presumes to hand out orders to his superiors,
he'll win no praise from me. But that man
the city places in authority, his orders
must be obeyed, large and small,   750
right and wrong.
                Anarchy —
show me a greater crime in all the earth!
She, she destroys cities, rips up houses,
breaks the ranks of spearmen into headlong rout.
But the ones who last it out, the great mass of them   755
owe their lives to discipline. Therefore
we must defend the men who live by law,
never let some woman triumph over us.
Better to fall from power, if fall we must,
at the hands of a man — never be rated   760

inferior to a woman, never.

LEADER: To us,
    unless old age has robbed us of our wits,
    you seem to say what you have to say with sense.

HAEMON: Father, only the gods endow a man with reason,
    the finest of all their gifts, a treasure.   765
    Far be it from me—I haven't the skill,
    and certainly no desire, to tell you when,
    if ever, you make a slip in speech . . . though
    someone else might have a good suggestion.

    Of course it's not for you,   770
    in the normal run of things, to watch
    whatever men say or do, or find to criticize.
    The man in the street, you know, dreads your glance,
    he'd never say anything displeasing to your face.
    But it's for me to catch the murmurs in the dark,   775
    the way the city mourns for this young girl.
    "No woman," they say, "ever deserved death less,
    and such a brutal death for such a glorious action.
    She, with her own dear brother lying in his blood—
    she couldn't bear to leave him dead, unburied,   780
    food for the wild dogs or wheeling vultures.
    Death? She deserves a glowing crown of gold!"
    So they say, and the rumor spreads in secret,
    darkly . . .
               I rejoice in your success, father—
    nothing more precious to me in the world.   785
    What medal of honor brighter to his children
    than a father's growing glory? Or a child's
    to his proud father? Now don't, please,
    be quite so single-minded, self-involved,
    or assume the world is wrong and you are right.   790
    Whoever thinks that he alone possesses intelligence,
    the gift of eloquence, he and no one else,
    and character too . . . such men, I tell you,
    spread them open—you will find them empty.
                    No,
    it's no disgrace for a man, even a wise man,   795
    to learn many things and not to be too rigid.
    You've seen trees by a raging winter torrent,
    how many sway with the flood and salvage every twig,
    but not the stubborn—they're ripped out, roots and all.
    Bend or break. The same when a man is sailing: 800
    haul your sheets too taut, never give an inch,

you'll capsize, go the rest of the voyage
keel up and the rowing-benches under.

Oh give way. Relax your anger—change!
I'm young, I know, but let me offer this: 805
it would be best by far, I admit,
if a man were born infallible, right by nature.
If not—and things don't often go that way,
it's best to learn from those with good advice.

LEADER: You'd do well, my lord, if he's speaking to the point,   810
to learn from him,

(*Turning to Haemon.*)

                and you, my boy, from him.
You both are talking sense.

CREON: So,
men our age, we're to be lectured, are we?—
schooled by a boy his age?

HAEMON: Only in what is right. But if I seem young,   815
look less to my years and more to what I do.

CREON: Do? Is admiring rebels an achievement?

HAEMON: I'd never suggest that you admire treason.

CREON: Oh?—
isn't that just the sickness that's attacked her?

HAEMON: The whole city of Thebes denies it, to a man.   820

CREON: And is Thebes about to tell me how to rule?

HAEMON: Now, you see? Who's talking like a child?

CREON: Am I to rule this land for others—or myself?

HAEMON: It's no city at all, owned by one man alone.

CREON: What? The city *is* the king's—that's the law!   825

HAEMON: What a splendid king you'd make of a desert island—
you and you alone.

CREON:

(*To the Chorus.*)

                This boy, I do believe,
is fighting on her side, the woman's side.

HAEMON: If you are a woman, yes;
my concern is all for you.   830

CREON: Why, you degenerate—bandying accusations,
threatening me with justice, your own father!

HAEMON: I see my father offending justice—wrong.

CREON: Wrong?
To protect my royal rights?

HAEMON: Protect your rights?

When you trample down the honors of the gods?   835
CREON: You, you soul of corruption, rotten through—
    woman's accomplice!
HAEMON: That may be,
    but you will never find me accomplice to a criminal.
CREON: That's what *she* is,
    and every word you say is a blatant appeal for her—   840
HAEMON: And you, and me, and the gods beneath the earth.
CREON: You will never marry her, not while she's alive.
HAEMON: Then she'll die . . . but her death will kill another.
CREON: What, brazen threats? You go too far!
HAEMON: What threat?
    Combating your empty, mindless judgments with a word?   845
CREON: You'll suffer for your sermons, you and your empty wisdom!
HAEMON: If you weren't my father, I'd say you were insane.
CREON: Don't flatter me with Father—you woman's slave!
HAEMON: You really expect to fling abuse at me
    and not receive the same?
CREON: Is that so!   850
    Now, by heaven, I promise you, you'll pay—
    taunting, insulting me! Bring her out,
    that hateful—she'll die now, here,
    in front of his eyes, beside her groom!
HAEMON: No, no, she will never die beside me—   855
    don't delude yourself. And you will never
    see me, never set eyes on my face again.
    Rage your heart out, rage with friends
    who can stand the sight of you.

(*Rushing out.*)

LEADER: Gone, my king, in a burst of anger.   860
    A temper young as his . . . hurt him once,
    he may do something violent.
CREON: Let him do—
    dream up something desperate, past all human limit!
    Good riddance. Rest assured,
    he'll never save those two young girls from death.   865
LEADER: Both of them, you really intend to kill them both?
CREON: No, not her, the one whose hands are clean —
    you're quite right.
LEADER: But Antigone—
    what sort of death do you have in mind for her?
CREON: I will take her down some wild, desolate path   870
    never trod by men, and wall her up alive
    in a rocky vault, and set out short rations,

just the measure piety demands
to keep the entire city free of defilement.
There let her pray to the one god she worships: 875
Death—who knows?—may just reprieve her from death.
Or she may learn at last, better late than never,
what a waste of breath it is to worship Death.

(*Exit to the palace.*)

CHORUS: Love, never conquered in battle
Love the plunderer laying waste the rich!   880
Love standing the night-watch
          guarding a girl's soft cheek,
you range the seas, the shepherds' steadings off in the wilds—
not even the deathless gods can flee your onset,
nothing human born for a day—   885
whoever feels your grip is driven mad.
                   Love!—
you wrench the minds of the righteous into outrage,
swerve them to their ruin—you have ignited this,
this kindred strife, father and son at war
          and Love alone the victor—   890
warm glance of the bride triumphant, burning with desire!
Throned in power, side-by-side with the mighty laws!
Irresistible Aphrodite,° never conquered—
Love, you mock us for your sport.

(*Antigone is brought from the palace under guard.*)

    But now, even I would rebel against the king,   895
    I would break all bounds when I see this—
    I fill with tears, I cannot hold them back,
    not any more . . . I see Antigone make her way
    to the bridal vault where all are laid to rest.
ANTIGONE: Look at me, men of my fatherland,   900
    setting out on the last road
looking into the last light of day
the last I'll ever see . . .
the god of death who puts us all to bed
takes me down to the banks of Acheron° alive—   905
    denied my part in the wedding-songs,
no wedding-song in the dusk has crowned my marriage—
I go to wed the lord of the dark waters.
CHORUS: Not crowned with glory, or with a dirge,

---

893. Aphrodite: Goddess of love. **905. Acheron:** A river in the underworld, the realm of the dead.

you leave for the deep pit of the dead.   910
No withering illness laid you low,
no strokes of the sword—a law to yourself,
alone, no mortal like you, ever, you go down
to the halls of Death alive and breathing.

ANTIGONE: But think of Niobe°—well I know her story—   915
think what a living death she died,
Tantalus' daughter, stranger queen from the east:
there on the mountain heights, growing stone
binding as ivy, slowly walled her round
and the rains will never cease, the legends say   920
the snows will never leave her . . .
            wasting away, under her brows the tears
showering down her breasting ridge and slopes—
a rocky death like hers puts me to sleep.

CHORUS: But she was a god, born of gods,   925
and we are only mortals born to die.
And yet, of course, it's a great thing
for a dying girl to hear, just to hear
she shares a destiny equal to the gods,
during life and later, once she's dead.

ANTIGONE: O you mock me!   930
Why, in the name of all my fathers' gods
why can't you wait till I am gone—
            must you abuse me to my face?
O my city, all your fine rich sons!
And you, you springs of the Dirce,   935
holy grove of Thebes where the chariots gather,
            you at least, you'll bear me witness, look,
unmourned by friends and forced by such crude laws
I go to my rockbound prison, strange new tomb—
            always a stranger, O dear god,   940
I have no home on earth and none below,
            not with the living, not with the breathless dead.

CHORUS: You went too far, the last limits of daring—
smashing against the high throne of Justice!
            Your life's in ruins, child—I wonder . . .   945
            do you pay for your father's terrible ordeal?

ANTIGONE: There—at last you've touched it, the worst pain
the worst anguish! Raking up the grief for father
            three times over, for all the doom

---

915. Niobe: A queen of Thebes who boasted that she had more children than Leto, mother of
Apollo and Artemis. To punish her, Apollo and Artemis killed her children, and she was turned
into a rock on Mount Sipylus, where she weeps constantly.

that's struck us down, the brilliant house of Laius.   950
O mother, your marriage-bed
the coiling horrors, the coupling there —
    you with your own son, my father — doomstruck mother!
Such, such were my parents, and I their wretched child.
I go to them now, cursed, unwed, to share their home —   955
    I am a stranger! O dear brother, doomed
in your marriage — your marriage° murders mine,
    your dying drags me down to death alive!

(*Enter Creon.*)

CHORUS: Reverence asks some reverence in return —
    but attacks on power never go unchecked,   960
        not by the man who holds the reins of power.
    Your own blind will, your passion has destroyed you.
ANTIGONE: No one to weep for me, my friends,
    no wedding-song — they take me away
    in all my pain . . . the road lies open, waiting.   965
    Never again, the law forbids me to see
    the sacred eye of day. I am agony!
    No tears for the destiny that's mine,
    no loved one mourns my death.
CREON: Can't you see?
If a man could wail his own dirge *before* he dies,   970
he'd never finish.

(*To the guards.*)

          Take her away, quickly!
Wall her up in the tomb, you have your orders.
Abandon her there, alone, and let her choose —
death or a buried life with a good roof for shelter.
As for myself, my hands are clean. This young girl —   975
dead or alive, she will be stripped of her rights,
her stranger's° rights, here in the world above.
ANTIGONE: O tomb, my bridal-bed — my house, my prison
cut in the hollow rock, my everlasting watch!
I'll soon be there, soon embrace my own,   980
the great growing family of our dead
Persephone° has received among her ghosts.

---

957. **your marriage:** Polynices had married a daughter of Adrastus, king of Argos, to forge their alliance to overcome Eteocles.   977. **stranger's:** Because of her disobedience, Creon treats Antigone as a traitor, no longer a citizen.   982. **Persephone:** Daughter of Demeter, abducted by Pluto, god of the underworld, to be his queen.

                                        I,
the last of them all, the most reviled by far,
go down before my destined time's run out.
But still I go, cherishing one good hope: 985
my arrival may be dear to father,
dear to you, my mother,
dear to you, my loving brother, Eteocles—
When you died I washed you with my hands,
I dressed you all, I poured the cups   990
across your tombs. But now, Polynices,
because I laid your body out as well,
this, this is my reward. Nevertheless
I honored you—the decent will admit it—
well and wisely too.   995
                            Never, I tell you,
if I had been the mother of children
or if my husband died, exposed and rotting—
I'd never have taken this ordeal upon myself,
never defied our people's will. What law,
you ask, do I satisfy with what I say?   1000
A husband dead, there might have been another.
A child by another too, if I had lost the first.
But mother and father both lost in the halls of Death,
no brother could ever spring to light again.
For this law alone I held you first in honor.   1005
For this, Creon, the king, judges me a criminal
guilty of dreadful outrage, my dear brother!
And now he leads me off, a captive in his hands,
with no part in the bridal-song, the bridal-bed,
denied all joy of marriage, raising children—   1010
deserted so by loved ones, struck by fate,
I descend alive to the caverns of the dead.

What law of the mighty gods have I transgressed?
Why look to the heavens any more, tormented as I am?
Whom to call, what comrades now? Just think,   1015
my reverence only brands me for irreverence!
Very well: if this is the pleasure of the gods,
once I suffer I will know that I was wrong.
But if these men are wrong, let them suffer
nothing worse than they mete out to me—   1020
these masters of injustice!
LEADER: Still the same rough winds, the wild passion
        raging through the girl.
CREON:

(*To the guards.*)

Take her away.

You're wasting time—you'll pay for it too.

ANTIGONE: Oh god, the voice of death. It's come, it's here.　　　　1025

CREON: True. Not a word of hope—your doom is sealed.

ANTIGONE: Land of Thebes, city of all my fathers—
　　　O you gods, the first gods of the race!
　　　They drag me away, now, no more delay.
　　　Look on me, you noble sons of Thebes—　　　　1030
　　　the last of a great line of kings,
　　　I alone, see what I suffer now
　　　at the hands of what breed of men—
　　　all for reverence, my reverence for the gods!

(*She leaves under guard; the Chorus gathers.*)

CHORUS: Danaë, Danaë°—　　　　1035
　　　even she endured a fate like yours,
　　　　in all her lovely strength she traded
　　　the light of day for the bolted brazen vault—
　　　buried within her tomb, her bridal-chamber,
　　　wed to the yoke and broken.　　　　1040
　　　　But she was of glorious birth
　　　　　　　my child, my child
　　　and treasured the seed of Zeus within her womb,
　　　the cloudburst streaming gold!
　　　　The power of fate is a wonder,　　　　1045
　　　dark, terrible wonder—
　　　neither wealth nor armies
　　　towered walls nor ships
　　　black hulls lashed by the salt
　　　can save us from that force.　　　　1050

The yoke tamed him too
　　　young Lycurgus° flaming in anger
king of Edonia, all for his mad taunts
Dionysus clamped him down, encased
　　　in the chain-mail of rock　　　　1055
　　　　and there his rage
　　　　　　　his terrible flowering rage burst—

1035. **Danaë:** Daughter of Acrisius, king of Argos, who imprisoned her in a bronze tower because of a prophecy that he would be killed by his daughter's son. Zeus entered the tower as a golden rain shower and she bore a son, Perseus, by whose hands Acrisius eventually was killed.　　**1052. Lycurgus:** Thracian king imprisoned and driven mad by Dionysus because he would not worship him.

sobbing, dying away . . . at last that madman
came to know his god —
> the power he mocked, the power   1060
> he taunted in all his frenzy
> trying to stamp out
> the women strong with the god —
> the torch, the raving sacred cries —
> enraging the Muses° who adore the flute.   1065

And far north where the Black Rocks
> cut the sea in half
and murderous straits
split the coast of Thrace
> a forbidding city stands   1070
where once, hard by the walls
the savage Ares thrilled to watch
a king's new queen,° a Fury rearing in rage
> against his two royal sons —
> her bloody hands, her dagger-shuttle   1075
stabbing out their eyes — cursed, blinding wounds —
their eyes blind sockets screaming for revenge!

They wailed in agony, cries echoing cries
> the princes doomed at birth . . .
and their mother doomed to chains,   1080
walled up in a tomb of stone —
> but she traced her own birth back
to a proud Athenian line and the high gods
and off in caverns half the world away,
born of the wild North Wind   1085
> she sprang on her father's gales,
> racing stallions up the leaping cliffs —
child of the heavens. But even on her the Fates
the gray everlasting Fates rode hard
my child, my child.

(*Enter Tiresias, the blind prophet, led by a boy.*)

TIRESIAS: Lords of Thebes,   1090
I and the boy have come together,

1065. **the Muses:** Nine sister goddesses who preside over the arts. 1073. **a king's new queen:** Phineas, a Thracian king, abandoned his first wife, Cleopatra, daughter of the Athenian princess Orithyia, and imprisoned her in a cave. The king's new wife, Eidothea, blinded Cleopatra's two sons in order to solidify her children's claim to succeed Phineas. Ares, who was born in Thrace, watched her savage deed with pleasure.

hand in hand. Two see with the eyes of one . . .
so the blind must go, with a guide to lead the way.
CREON: What is it, old Tiresias? What news now?
TIRESIAS: I will teach you. And you obey the seer.
CREON: I will,   1095
I've never wavered from your advice before.
TIRESIAS: And so you kept the city straight on course.
CREON: I owe you a great deal, I swear to that.
TIRESIAS: Then reflect, my son: you are poised,
once more, on the razor-edge of fate.   1100
CREON: What is it? I shudder to hear you.
TIRESIAS: You will learn
when you listen to the warnings of my craft.
As I sat on the ancient seat of augury,°
in the sanctuary where every bird I know
will hover at my hands—suddenly I heard it,   1105
a strange voice in the wingbeats, unintelligible,
barbaric, a mad scream! Talons flashing, ripping,
they were killing each other—that much I knew—
the murderous fury whirring in those wings
made that much clear!
                                    I was afraid,   1110
I turned quickly, tested the burnt-sacrifice,
ignited the altar at all points—but no fire,
the god in the fire never blazed.
Not from those offerings . . . over the embers
slid a heavy ooze from the long thighbones,   1115
smoking, sputtering out, and the bladder
puffed and burst—spraying gall into the air—
and the fat wrapping the bones slithered off
and left them glistening white. No fire!
The rites failed that might have blazed the future   1120
with a sign. So I learned from the boy here:
he is my guide, as I am guide to others.
                                            And it is you—
your high resolve that sets this plague on Thebes.
The public altars and sacred hearths are fouled,
one and all, by the birds and dogs with carrion   1125
torn from the corpse, the doomstruck son of Oedipus!
And so the gods are deaf to our prayers, they spurn
the offerings in our hands, the flame of holy flesh.
No birds cry out an omen clear and true—

1103. seat of augury: Where Tiresias sought omens among the birds.

they're gorged with the murdered victim's blood and fat.   1130
Take these things to heart, my son, I warn you.
All men make mistakes, it is only human.
But once the wrong is done, a man
can turn his back on folly, misfortune too,
if he tries to make amends, however low he's fallen,   1135
and stops his bullnecked ways. Stubbornness
brands you for stupidity—pride is a crime.
No, yield to the dead!
Never stab the fighter when he's down.
Where's the glory, killing the dead twice over?   1140

I mean you well. I give you sound advice.
It's best to learn from a good adviser
when he speaks for your own good:
it's pure gain.
CREON: Old man—all of you! So,
you shoot your arrows at my head like archers at the target—   1145
I even have *him* loosed on me, this fortune-teller.
Oh his ilk has tried to sell me short
and ship me off for years. Well,
drive your bargains, traffic—much as you like—
in the gold of India, silver-gold of Sardis.°   1150
You'll never bury that body in the grave,
not even if Zeus's eagles rip the corpse
and wing their rotten pickings off to the throne of god!
Never, not even in fear of such defilement
will I tolerate his burial, that traitor.   1155
Well I know, we can't defile the gods—
no mortal has the power.
                         No,
reverend old Tiresias, all men fall,
it's only human, but the wisest fall obscenely
when they glorify obscene advice with rhetoric—   1160
all for their own gain.
TIRESIAS: Oh god, is there a man alive
who knows, who actually believes . . .
CREON: What now?
What earth-shattering truth are you about to utter?
TIRESIAS: . . . just how much a sense of judgment, wisdom   1165
is the greatest gift we have?

1150. silver-gold of Sardis: Electrum, pale gold containing a considerable alloy of silver, found by some rivers in Asia Minor, especially the Pactolus, which ran through ancient Sardis.

CREON: Just as much, I'd say,
    as a twisted mind is the worst affliction going.
TIRESIAS: You are the one who's sick, Creon, sick to death.
CREON: I am in no mood to trade insults with a seer.
TIRESIAS: You have already, calling my prophecies a lie.
CREON: Why not?   1170
    You and the whole breed of seers are mad for money!
TIRESIAS: And the whole race of tyrants lusts for filthy gain.
CREON: This slander of yours—
    are you aware you're speaking to the king?
TIRESIAS: Well aware. Who helped you save the city?
CREON: You—   1175
    you have your skills, old seer, but you lust for injustice!
TIRESIAS: You will drive me to utter the dreadful secret in my heart.
CREON: Spit it out! Just don't speak it out for profit.
TIRESIAS: Profit? No, not a bit of profit, not for you.
CREON: Know full well, you'll never buy off my resolve.   1180
TIRESIAS: Then know this too, learn this by heart!
    The chariot of the sun will not race through
    so many circuits more, before you have surrendered
    one born of your own loins, your own flesh and blood,
    a corpse for corpses given in return, since you have thrust   1185
    to the world below a child sprung for the world above,
    ruthlessly lodged a living soul within the grave—
    then you've robbed the gods below the earth,
    keeping a dead body here in the bright air,
    unburied, unsung, unhallowed by the rites.   1190

    You, you have no business with the dead,
    nor do the gods above—this is violence
    you have forced upon the heavens.
    And so the avengers, the dark destroyers late
    but true to the mark, now lie in wait for you,   1195
    the Furies° sent by the gods and the god of death
    to strike you down with the pains that you perfected!

    There. Reflect on that, tell me I've been bribed.
    The day comes soon, no long test of time, not now,
    when the mourning cries for men and women break   1200
    throughout your halls. Great hatred rises against you—
    cities in tumult, all whose mutilated sons

1196. the Furies: Female spirits who avenge wrongdoing, especially crimes committed against close relations.

the dogs have graced with burial, or the wild beasts
or a wheeling crow that wings the ungodly stench of carrion
back to each city, each warrior's hearth and home.   1205

These arrows for your heart! Since you've raked me
I loose them like an archer in my anger,
arrows deadly true. You'll never escape
their burning, searing force.

(*Motioning to his escort.*)

Come, boy, take me home.   1210
So he can vent his rage on younger men,
and learn to keep a gentler tongue in his head
and better sense than what he carries now.

(*Exit to the side.*)

LEADER: The old man's gone, my king—
terrible prophecies. Well I know,   1215
since the hair on this old head went gray,
he's never lied to Thebes.
CREON: I know it myself—I'm shaken, torn.
It's a dreadful thing to yield . . . but resist now?
Lay my pride bare to the blows of ruin?   1220
That's dreadful too.
LEADER: But good advice,
Creon, take it now, you must.
CREON: What should I do? Tell me . . . I'll obey.
LEADER: Go! Free the girl from the rocky vault
and raise a mound for the body you exposed.   1225
CREON: That's your advice? You think I should give in?
LEADER: Yes, my king, quickly. Disasters sent by the gods
cut short our follies in a flash.
CREON: Oh it's hard.
giving up the heart's desire . . . but I will do it—
no more fighting a losing battle with necessity.   1230
LEADER: Do it now, go, don't leave it to others.
CREON: Now—I'm on my way! Come, each of you,
take up axes, make for the high ground,
over there, quickly! I and my better judgment
have come round to this—I shackled her,   1235
I'll set her free myself. I am afraid . . .
it's best to keep the established laws
to the very day we die.

(*Rushing out, followed by his entourage. The Chorus clusters around the altar.*)

CHORUS: God of a hundred names!°
                          Great Dionysus—
          Son and glory of Semele! Pride of Thebes—   1240
Child of Zeus whose thunder rocks the clouds—
Lord of the famous lands of evening—
King of the Mysteries!
                   King of Eleusis,° Demeter's plain
her breasting hills that welcome in the world—
Great Dionysus!
                    Bacchus,° living in Thebes   1245
the mother-city of all your frenzied women—
                          Bacchus
        living along the Ismenus'° rippling waters
standing over the field sown with the Dragon's teeth!

You—we have seen you through the flaring smoky fires,
         your torches blazing over the twin peaks   1250
where nymphs of the hallowed cave climb onward
                  fired with you, your sacred rage—
we have seen you at Castalia's running spring°
and down from the heights of Nysa° crowned with ivy
the greening shore rioting vines and grapes   1255
        down you come in your storm of wild women
            ecstatic, mystic cries—
                    Dionysus—
down to watch and ward the roads of Thebes!

First of all cities, Thebes you honor first
you and your mother, bride of the lightning—   1260
come, Dionysus! now your people lie
in the iron grip of plague,
come in your racing, healing stride
            down Parnassus'° slopes
or across the moaning straits.
                Lord of the dancing—   1265
dance, dance the constellations breathing fire!
Great master of the voices of the night!

1239–48. God of a hundred names . . . the Dragon's teeth: A litany of names for Dionysus. **1243. Eleusis:** Site near Athens for the worship of Demeter, goddess of grain and harvests, where young men were initiated into the rites of Dionysus. **1245. Bacchus:** Yet another of Dionysus's names. **1247. Ismenus:** River near which Cadmus sowed the dragon seeds that gave birth to the founders of Thebes. **1253. Castalia's running spring:** Spring on Mount Parnassus sacred to Apollo and the Muses. **1254. heights of Nysa:** Cliffs above Delphi where Dionysus spent the winter months. **1264. Parnassus:** Mountain in Greece sacred to the gods.

Child of Zeus, God's offspring, come, come forth!
Lord, king, dance with your nymphs, swirling, raving
arm-in-arm in frenzy through the night   1270
    they dance you, Iacchus° —
                                    Dance, Dionysus
    giver of all good things!

(*Enter a Messenger from the side.*)

MESSENGER: Neighbors,
    friends of the house of Cadmus° and the kings,
    there's not a thing in this life of ours
    I'd praise or blame as settled once for all.   1275
    Fortune lifts and Fortune fells the lucky
    and unlucky every day. No prophet on earth
    can tell a man his fate. Take Creon:
    there was a man to rouse your envy once,
    as I see it. He saved the realm from enemies;   1280
    taking power, he alone, the lord of the fatherland,
    he set us true on course — flourished like a tree
    with the noble line of sons he bred and reared . . .
    and now it's lost, all gone.
                                Believe me,
    when a man has squandered his true joys,   1285
    he's good as dead, I tell you, a living corpse.
    Pile up riches in your house, as much as you like —
    live like a king with a huge show of pomp,
    but if real delight is missing from the lot,
    I wouldn't give you a wisp of smoke for it,   1290
    not compared with joy.
LEADER: What now?
    What new grief do you bring the house of kings?
MESSENGER: Dead, dead — and the living are guilty of their death!
LEADER: Who's the murderer? Who is dead? Tell us.
MESSENGER: Haemon's gone, his blood spilled by the very hand — 1295
LEADER: His father's or his own?
MESSENGER: His own . . .
    raging mad with his father for the death —
LEADER: Oh great seer,
    you saw it all, you brought your word to birth!
MESSENGER: Those are the facts. Deal with them as you will.

(*As he turns to go, Eurydice enters from the palace.*)

1271. **Iacchus:** Dionysus (Bacchus).   1273. **Cadmus:** According to tradition, the founder of
Thebes.

LEADER: Look, Eurydice. Poor woman, Creon's wife,   1300
    so close at hand. By chance perhaps,
    unless she's heard the news about her son.

EURYDICE: My countrymen,
    all of you—I caught the sound of your words
    as I was leaving to do my part,
    to appeal to queen Athena° with my prayers.   1305
    I was just loosing the bolts, opening the doors,
    when a voice filled with sorrow, family sorrow,
    struck my ears, and I fell back, terrified,
    into the women's arms—everything went black.
    Tell me the news, again, whatever it is . . .   1310
    sorrow and I are hardly strangers;
    I can bear the worst.

MESSENGER: I—dear lady,
    I'll speak as an eye-witness. I was there.
    And I won't pass over one word of the truth.
    Why should I try to soothe you with a story,   1315
    only to prove a liar in a moment?
    Truth is always best.
               So,
    I escorted your lord, I guided him
    to the edge of the plain where the body lay,
    Polynices, torn by the dogs and still unmourned.   1320
    And saying a prayer to Hecate° of the Crossroads,
    Pluto° too, to hold their anger and be kind,
    we washed the dead in a bath of holy water
    and plucking some fresh branches, gathering . . .
    what was left of him, we burned them all together   1325
    and raised a high mound of native earth, and then
    we turned and made for that rocky vault of hers,
    the hollow, empty bed of the bride of Death.
    And far off, one of us heard a voice,
    a long wail rising, echoing   1330
    out of that unhallowed wedding-chamber;
    he ran to alert the master and Creon pressed on,
    closer—the strange, inscrutable cry came sharper,
    throbbing around him now, and he let loose
    a cry of his own, enough to wrench the heart,   1335
    "Oh god, am I the prophet now? going down
    the darkest road I've ever gone? My son—

1305. **Athena:** Goddess of wisdom.   1321–22. **Hecate, Pluto:** Gods of the underworld. Offerings to Hecate were left at crossroads.

it's *his* dear voice, he greets me! Go, men,
closer, quickly! Go through the gap,
the rocks are dragged back —   1340
right to the tomb's very mouth — and look,
see if it's Haemon's voice I think I hear,
or the gods have robbed me of my senses."

The king was shattered. We took his orders,
went and searched, and there in the deepest,   1345
dark recesses of the tomb we found her . . .
hanged by the neck in a fine linen noose,
strangled in her veils — and the boy,
his arms flung around her waist,
clinging to her, wailing for his bride,   1350
dead and down below, for his father's crimes
and the bed of his marriage blighted by misfortune.
When Creon saw him, he gave a deep sob,
he ran in, shouting, crying out to him,
"Oh my child — what have you done? what seized you,   1355
what insanity? what disaster drove you mad?
Come out, my son! I beg you on my knees!"
But the boy gave him a wild burning glance,
spat in his face, not a word in reply,
he drew his sword — his father rushed out,   1360
running as Haemon lunged and missed! —
and then, doomed, desperate with himself,
suddenly leaning his full weight on the blade,
he buried it in his body, halfway to the hilt.
And still in his senses, pouring his arms around her,   1365
he embraced the girl and breathing hard,
released a quick rush of blood,
bright red on her cheek glistening white.
And there he lies, body enfolding body . . .
he has won his bride at last, poor boy,   1370
not here but in the houses of the dead.

Creon shows the world that of all the ills
afflicting men the worst is lack of judgment.

(*Eurydice turns and reenters the palace.*)

LEADER: What do you make of that? The lady's gone,
without a word, good or bad.
MESSENGER: I'm alarmed too   1375
but here's my hope — faced with her son's death,
she finds it unbecoming to mourn in public.
Inside, under her roof, she'll set her women

to the task and wail the sorrow of the house.
She's too discreet. She won't do something rash. 1380
LEADER: I'm not so sure. To me, at least,
a long heavy silence promises danger,
just as much as a lot of empty outcries.
MESSENGER: We'll see if she's holding something back,
hiding some passion in her heart. 1385
I'm going in. You may be right—who knows?
Even too much silence has its dangers.

(*Exit to the palace. Enter Creon from the side, escorted by attendants carrying Haemon's body on a bier.*)

LEADER: The king himself! Coming toward us,
look, holding the boy's head in his hands.
Clear, damning proof, if it's right to say so— 1390
proof of his own madness, no one else's,
no, his own blind wrongs.
CREON: Ohhh,
so senseless, so insane . . . my crimes,
my stubborn, deadly—
Look at us, the killer, the killed, 1395
father and son, the same blood—the misery!
My plans, my mad fanatic heart,
my son, cut off so young!
Ai, dead, lost to the world,
not through your stupidity, no, my own.
LEADER: Too late, 1400
too late, you see what justice means.
CREON: Oh I've learned
through blood and tears! Then, it was then,
when the god came down and struck me—a great weight
shattering, driving me down that wild savage path,
ruining, trampling down my joy. Oh the agony, 1405
the heartbreaking agonies of our lives.

(*Enter the Messenger from the palace.*)

MESSENGER: Master,
what a hoard of grief you have, and you'll have more.
The grief that lies to hand you've brought yourself—

(*Pointing to Haemon's body.*)

the rest, in the house, you'll see it all too soon.
CREON: What now? What's worse than this?
MESSENGER: The queen is dead. 1410
The mother of this dead boy . . . mother to the end—

poor thing, her wounds are fresh.

CREON: No, no,
 harbor of Death, so choked, so hard to cleanse! —
 why me? why are you killing me?
 Herald of pain, more words, more grief?   1415
 I died once, you kill me again and again!
 What's the report, boy . . . some news for me?
 My wife dead? O dear god!
 Slaughter heaped on slaughter?

(The doors open; the body of Eurydice is brought out on her bier.)

MESSENGER: See for yourself:
 now they bring her body from the palace.

CREON: Oh no,   1420
 another, a second loss to break the heart.
 What next, what fate still waits for me?
 I just held my son in my arms and now,
 look, a new corpse rising before my eyes —
  wretched, helpless mother — O my son!   1425

MESSENGER: She stabbed herself at the altar,
 then her eyes went dark, after she'd raised
 a cry for the noble fate of Megareus,° the hero
 killed in the first assault, then for Haemon,
 then with her dying breath she called down   1430
 torments on your head — you killed her sons.

CREON: Oh the dread,
 I shudder with dread! Why not kill me too? —
 run me through with a good sharp sword?
 Oh god, the misery, anguish —
 I, I'm churning with it, going under.   1435

MESSENGER: Yes, and the dead, the woman lying there,
 piles the guilt of all their deaths on you.

CREON: How did she end her life, what bloody stroke?

MESSENGER: She drove home to the heart with her own hand,
 once she learned her son was dead . . . that agony.   1440

CREON: And the guilt is all mine —
  can never be fixed on another man,
  no escape for me. I killed you,
  I, god help me, I admit it all!

(To his attendants.)

———————————

1428. Megareus: Another son of Creon and Eurydice; he was killed in Polynices' attack on Thebes.

Take me away, quickly, out of sight.   1445
I don't even exist—I'm no one. Nothing.
LEADER: Good advice, if there's any good in suffering.
Quickest is best when troubles block the way.
CREON:

(*Kneeling in prayer.*)

Come, let it come!—that best of fates for me
that brings the final day, best fate of all.   1450
Oh quickly, now—
so I never have to see another sunrise.
LEADER: That will come when it comes;
we must deal with all that lies before us.
The future rests with the ones who tend the future.   1455
CREON: That prayer—I poured my heart into that prayer!
LEADER: No more prayers now. For mortal men
there is no escape from the doom we must endure.
CREON: Take me away, I beg you, out of sight.
A rash, indiscriminate fool!   1460
I murdered you, my son, against my will—
you too, my wife . . .
                            Wailing wreck of a man,
whom to look to? where to lean for support?

(*Desperately turning from Haemon to Eurydice on their biers.*)

Whatever I touch goes wrong—once more
a crushing fate's come down upon my head.   1465

(*The Messenger and attendants lead Creon into the palace.*)

CHORUS: Wisdom is by far the greatest part of joy,
and reverence toward the gods must be safeguarded.
The mighty words of the proud are paid in full
with mighty blows of fate, and at long last
those blows will teach us wisdom.   1470

(*The old citizens exit to the side.*)

Elizabethan Drama

England during the reigns of Elizabeth I (1558-1603) and James I
(1603-1625) witnessed an outpouring of splendidly written drama and an
increase in theatrical activity: It was one of the greatest periods for drama
in history. Dramatists such as Thomas Kyd, Christopher Marlowe, Ben
Jonson, Francis Beaumont, John Fletcher, John Webster, and, of course,

William Shakespeare wrote during this time, and theaters such as the Curtain, the Rose, the Globe, and the Fortune drew large audiences from across the social classes. To get a feel for the life of the theater during that time, watch the film *Shakespeare in Love* (1998), directed by John Madden and starring Gwyneth Paltrow and Joseph Fiennes. It offers a wonderfully lively, imaginative reenactment of the era's theater scene.

THE GLOBE In 1599, the Lord Chamberlain's Company, to which Shakespeare belonged—he was acting as well as writing plays for them— opened a new theater, the Globe. It was a typical theater of the time (see the sketch on page 1145): All were circular or octagonal structures with the center open to the sky. The audience was seated in several balconies on three sides, nearly surrounding the actors, who performed mostly on a "thrust stage" that extended out into the audience. The stage was covered to protect the actors from rain. These theaters could hold up to three thousand patrons, but the closeness of audience to stage, coupled with patrons standing in the "pit" around—and even leaning on—the edge of the stage, created an intimacy impossible in the large Greek theaters.

THE ACTING AREAS At the back of the thrust stage was a wall with two curtained doors used for entrances and exits and sometimes as places where characters hid and overheard what was said onstage. An upper gallery, normally used to seat wealthy patrons, was sometimes employed as an additional acting area. Most of the action, however, took place toward the front of the thrust stage, with audience members in the pit crowded around all three sides. This close proximity of the audience to the actors added to the effectiveness of Shakespeare's famous **soliloquies**. Imagine standing in the pit as a character comes to the front of the stage and expresses her or his most private thoughts and feelings, speaking directly to the audience (as is the case in Iago's famous soliloquies in *Othello*). Often the character is alone, but if other characters are onstage, the convention is that they do not hear or pay attention to the soliloquy.

POETIC DRAMA As you read *Othello*, you will find fairly long speeches, with most of the play written in blank verse (unrhymed iambic pentameter). Poetry was used because most serious literature at the time was written in verse: epics, ballads, and elegies as well as lyric poetry. Poetic drama is a convention of Elizabethan theater: It's certainly not realistic that a soldier on a battlefield would talk in iambic pentameter, but the audience accepted it by suspending their disbelief. And Shakespeare could count on members of the audience to be attentive listeners, on the whole able to follow speeches packed with meaning and to catch intricate wordplay. He was also fortunate to have excellent actors in his company, such as Richard Burbage and Will Kempe, who could deliver such speeches powerfully.

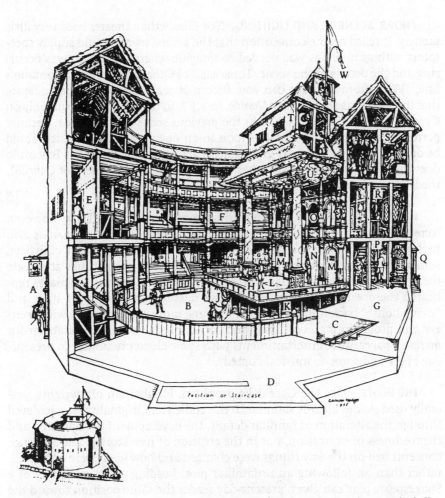

A   Main entrance
B   The yard
C   Entrances to lowest gallery
D   Position of entrances to staircase and
    upper galleries
E   Corridor serving the different sections of
    the middle gallery
F   Middle gallery ("Twopenny Rooms")
G   Position of "Gentlemen's Rooms" or
    "Lords' Rooms"
H   The stage
J   The hanging being put up round the
    stage
K   The "hell" under the stage

L   The stage trap leading down to the hell
M   Stage doors
N   Curtained "place behind the stage"
O   Gallery above the stage, used as required
    sometimes by musicians, sometimes by
    spectators, and often as part of the play
P   Backstage area (the tiring-house)
Q   Tiring-house door
R   Dressing-rooms
S   Wardrobe and storage
T   The hut housing the machine for lower-
    ing enthroned gods, etc., to the stage
U   The "heavens"
W   Hoisting the playhouse flag

A Conjectural Reconstruction of the Globe Theatre, 1599–1613. (Drawing by
C. Walter Hodges from his *Globe Restored*, published by Oxford University Press
© 1968 C. Walter Hodges. Reprinted with permission of Oxford University Press.)

PROPS, SCENERY, AND LIGHTING   The Elizabethan theater used very little scenery. It relied on the convention that the actors' words would supply spectators with as much as was needed to imagine where the action was occurring and the details of the scene. Thus, act 2 of *Othello* opens with Montano's line, "What from the cape can you discern at sea?" informing the audience that the scene has shifted from Venice, in act 1, to the seaside—presumably on Cyprus, where Othello was sent in the previous scene (1.3.220–26). Because performances were held midafternoon in an open-air structure, little could be done to indicate darkness in a scene. If actors call for a light (as Brabantio does in 1.1.140–44) or carry torches (as they do in act 1, scene 2 of *Othello*), the audience knows it is dark in that scene.

INDOOR PERFORMANCES   Performances in Shakespeare's day, however, were not limited to public theaters like the Globe. Acting companies also performed indoors, sometimes at court for the monarch and courtiers; sometimes in the banqueting halls of noble families; sometimes at private theaters such as the Blackfriars and the Whitefriars. These acting places replicated the open-air theaters as much as possible, with a thrust stage and "tiring house" backdrop with doors. Indoors, more could be done with scenery and props; in fact, costumes and scenery became quite spectacular for *masques*, pageantlike entertainments with some elements similar to present-day opera and some to musical comedy.

THE PLOTS   Like the Greeks before them, Elizabethan playwrights generally used stories already familiar to the audience: Originality was achieved through the alteration of familiar details, the development of character, and the freshness of expression, not in the creation of new stories. The audience concentrated on the way things were changed and how ideas were expressed, rather than on following an unfamiliar plot. Reading a plot summary of a Shakespeare play can give a present-day reader the same position toward the drama that Shakespeare's contemporaries were in. Unlike Greek plays, Elizabethan dramas showed a great deal of action on the stage, including violence: For example, murders and suicides, which occurred offstage and were only reported in Greek plays, are shown onstage in Elizabethan drama, as is the case in *Othello*.

EFFECTS OF EVIL   Tragedies from this era tend to deal with the results of evil in the world. Often they show how a misstep or an association with an antagonist harboring evil intentions results in a consequence that far exceeds what the protagonist seems to deserve. Or they show the destruction of an innocent victim caught in an evil web not of her or his own making, as seems true for *Othello*. As in Greek plays, the protagonists in Elizabethan dramas continue to be persons of high status and importance (whose actions affect many people) or, at least, from the upper ranks of society.

KINDS OF TRAGEDY

Elizabethan tragedy appears in several subtypes:

- One popular variety, influenced by drama of the Roman era, is *revenge tragedy,* in which an avenger who seeks to exact revenge for the death of a relative or comrade dies achieving that aim. The best-known tragedy of this type is Shakespeare's *Hamlet.*
- Another popular subtype, *tragedy of passion,* occurs when characters die as a result of excessively passionate reactions or relationships. Unrestrained passion that leads to an unbalanced life was believed to be a recipe for disaster; one was to use reason to restrain emotions and actions. Shakespeare's *Romeo and Juliet* (*c.* 1594–1596) illustrates this subtype: Love at first sight, a hasty marriage of young lovers, and other rash behavior are propelled by intense emotions, which lead the pair to their unfortunate and untimely deaths.
- A third subtype, *tragedy of fate,* depicts characters who cannot escape the doom that fortune has in store for them. *Romeo and Juliet* fits this category as well. From the opening lines, in which Romeo and Juliet are referred to as "star-crossed lovers," their doom seems inescapable. This fate is not the same as the divine inevitability of the Greeks, but rather it is an inexplicable, inescapable destiny, with chance, accident, and coincidence playing major roles.
- In still another subtype, *tragedy of character,* disastrous results stem from an individual's character traits—not necessarily weaknesses or flaws but often strengths and virtues that are carried too far or applied unwisely. Shakespeare's great tragedies—*Hamlet, Othello, King Lear, Macbeth*—are tragedies of character, with protagonists of great depth and complexity. To understand such characters well, it's important to read and reflect carefully.

A FEW NOTES ON COMEDY

Comedy, like tragedy, emerged from Greek religious ceremonies, particularly from Dionysian fertility rites. The word *comedy* derives from the Greek *kômos*, meaning "revel" or "merry-making." At its most basic, comedy is a narrative or drama with a happy ending. No matter what the characters go through, if the ending is happy, the play is a comedy. All's well that ends well.

THE PHYSICAL AND THE FOOLISH

In early Greek comedies, the revelry involved explicit sexuality. Although later comedies became less blatantly sexual, they retained the earthy,

physical qualities of their Dionysian origins. Comedy continues to emphasize the physical or sensuous nature of humans; their ridiculousness,
weaknesses, and foibles; their physical relationships; and their outrageous
behaviors and foolish misunderstandings.

CELEBRATION OF LIFE

The tone of comedy is lighter than that of tragedy and its style less elevated; it is usually written in prose. It uses humor to evoke smiles and
laughter from its readers and audience. Comedy generally has a realistic
strain, dealing with ordinary people in everyday activities, but the events
often include exaggeration and unrealistic circumstances, with characters
turning things upside down, breaking rules, reversing normal relationships, and falling into incongruous situations. Comedies celebrate life,
with all the disorder, misunderstandings, and confusion that often
accompany it. Comedies tend to begin in disorder and end with the restoration of order and often conclude with a dance, a marriage, or a celebration symbolizing harmony and happiness.

OLD COMEDY AND NEW COMEDY

Greek drama initiated two major strains of comedy that have remained
influential through the centuries. The earlier strain was **Old Comedy**, represented by the satiric works of Aristophanes (c. 450–385 B.C.E.), predecessor of later satiric comedy playwrights. Old Comedy was replaced by **New
Comedy**, originated by the Greek playwright Menander (c. 342–292 B.C.E.)
and developed further by the Roman dramatists Plautus (c. 254–184 B.C.E.)
and Terence (c. 190–159 B.C.E.). New Comedy concerns the obstacles faced
by young lovers and the unpredictable changes of fortune they encounter
and pokes fun at the foibles and attitudes of the lovers as well as those
around them. New Comedy developed later into the *comedy of manners*,
which laughs at people's behavior and attitudes, at their follies and vanities.

ELIZABETHAN COMEDY

In the Elizabethan era, two playwrights were successful in comedy: Ben
Jonson and William Shakespeare. Jonson was known for satiric comedy,
influenced by and adapting Old Comedy. Shakespeare was best known for
romantic comedy, in which he adapted New Comedy but also was influenced by Greek prose romances. Romantic comedy typically involves young
lovers who face obstacles to fulfilling their relationship (perhaps parental
opposition, a competing lover, their own differences, poverty, separation
because of war or travel, or coincidences that prevent them from being
together). After facing numerous complications and encountering several
near disasters, all of which make a favorable outcome seem impossible,
the lovers at last are united and their union accepted. Hollywood movies
and TV shows continue the romantic comedy tradition today.

ENTRY POINTS *Othello* opens in the midst of conflict: Iago and Roderigo are irate with Othello for having stolen a promotion from the former and the woman he loves from the latter. The conflict intensifies as they inform Brabantio that his daughter, Desdemona, has eloped with Othello, a black soldier. Conflicts continue, almost without reprieve, for the remainder of the drama. As you read, watch for the presence and effects of evil in the play. What mistakes does Othello make? Is he responsible for his fate, or is he a victim as much as Desdemona is? Do you think Othello deserves what happens to him, or does it exceed what he deserves? In what ways does *Othello* illustrate a tragedy of character? Does *Othello* also contain elements of the other three tragedy types discussed above? If so, explain the reasoning that led to your conclusion.

APPROACHING THE AUTHOR

Virtually no evidence of any kind, let alone writings, exist for **William Shakespeare** in the years between 1585 and 1592. Numerous theories abound about these "lost years," including one that contends he was caught poaching near Strafford and escaped to London to avoid persecution. More probable is that he worked as a schoolmaster during those years.

For more about him, see page 1411.

William Shakespeare 1564–1616

Othello the Moor of Venice   [1604]

THE NAMES OF THE ACTORS

OTHELLO, THE MOOR
BRABANTIO, [a Venetian senator,] father to Desdemona
CASSIO, an honorable lieutenant [to Othello]
IAGO, [Othello's ancient,] a villain
RODERIGO, a gulled gentleman
DUKE OF VENICE
SENATORS [of Venice]
MONTANO, governor of Cyprus

LODOVICO AND GRATIANO, [kinsmen to Brabantio,] two noble Venetians
SAILORS
CLOWNS
DESDEMONA, wife to Othello
EMILIA, wife to Iago
BIANCA, a courtesan
[MESSENGER, HERALD, OFFICERS, VENETIAN GENTLEMEN, MUSICIANS, ATTENDANTS

Note: *Othello* was first published in 1622, some six years after Shakespeare's death, in a slender book called a "quarto" (made up of printer's paper folded twice, creating four leaves—eight pages—approximately 9 ½ by 12 inches in size). The following year the play was printed a second time, in the 1623 collected edition of Shakespeare's plays called the First Folio (with paper folded once, creating pages twice as large as a quarto). The Folio text is around 160 lines longer, but the quarto text contains some things omitted from the Folio text. The play as printed here mainly follows the Folio text, but passages from the quarto text have been inserted and enclosed in square brackets.

SCENE
Venice and Cyprus]

ACT I / Scene I

A street in Venice.

Enter Roderigo and Iago.

RODERIGO: Tush, never tell me! I take it much unkindly
    That thou, Iago, who hast had my purse
    As if the strings were thine, shouldst know of this.°
IAGO: 'Sblood,° but you'll not hear me!
    If ever I did dream of such a matter,   5
    Abhor me.
RODERIGO: Thou told'st me thou didst hold him in thy hate.
IAGO: Despise me if I do not. Three great ones of the city,
    In personal suit to make me his lieutenant,
    Off-capped to him;° and, by the faith of man,   10
    I know my price; I am worth no worse a place.
    But he, as loving his own pride and purposes,
    Evades them with a bombast circumstance.°
    Horribly stuffed with epithets of war;
    [And, in conclusion,]   15
    Nonsuits° my mediators; for, "Certes," says he,
    "I have already chose my officer."
    And what was he?
    Forsooth, a great arithmetician,°
    One Michael Cassio, a Florentine   20
    (A fellow almost damned in a fair wife°)
    That never set a squadron in the field,
    Nor the division of a battle knows
    More than a spinster; unless the bookish theoric,
    Wherein the togèd consuls can propose°   25
    As masterly as he. Mere prattle without practice
    Is all his soldiership. But he, sir, had th' election;
    And I (of whom his eyes had seen the proof
    At Rhodes, at Cyprus, and on other grounds
    Christian and heathen) must be belee'd and calmed°   30
    By debitor and creditor; this counter-caster,°

ACT I, SCENE I. **3. this:** I.e., Desdemona's elopement. **4. 'Sblood:** By God's blood. **10. him:** I.e., Othello. **13. a bombast circumstance:** Pompous circumlocutions. **16. Nonsuits:** Rejects. **19. arithmetician:** Theoretician. **21. almost . . . wife:** (An obscure allusion; Cassio is unmarried, but see 4.1.125–26). **25. Wherein . . . propose:** In which the toga-wearing senators can debate. **30. belee'd and calmed:** Left in the lurch. **31. counter-caster:** Bookkeeper.

He, in good time, must his lieutenant be,
And I—God bless the mark!—his Moorship's ancient.°
RODERIGO: By heaven, I rather would have been his hangman.
IAGO: Why, there's no remedy; 'tis the curse of service.   35
Preferment goes by letter and affection,°
And not by old gradation, where each second
Stood heir to th' first. Now, sir, be judge yourself,
Whether I in any just term° am affined°
To love the Moor.
RODERIGO: I would not follow him then.   40
IAGO: O, sir, content you;
I follow him to serve my turn upon him.
We cannot all be masters, nor all masters
Cannot be truly followed. You shall mark
Many a duteous and knee-crooking knave   45
That, doting on his own obsequious bondage,
Wears out his time, much like his master's ass,
For naught but provender; and when he's old, cashiered.°
Whip me such honest knaves! Others there are
Who, trimmed° in forms and visages of duty,   50
Keep yet their hearts attending on themselves;
And, throwing but shows of service on their lords,
Do well thrive by them, and when they have lined their coats,°
Do themselves homage. These fellows have some soul;
And such a one do I profess myself. For, sir,   55
It is as sure as you are Roderigo,
Were I the Moor, I would not be Iago.
In following him, I follow but myself;
Heaven is my judge, not I for love and duty,
But seeming so, for my peculiar end;   60
For when my outward action doth demonstrate
The native act and figure of my heart°
In compliment extern,° 'tis not long after
But I will wear my heart upon my sleeve
For daws to peck at; I am not what I am.°   65
RODERIGO: What a full fortune does the thick-lips° owe°
If he can carry't thus!
IAGO: Call up her father,
Rouse him. Make after him, poison his delight,

---

33. ancient: Ensign. **36. affection:** Favoritism. **39. term:** Respect; **affined:**
Obliged. **48. cashiered:** Dismissed. **50. trimmed:** Dressed up. **53. lined their coats:** Filled
their purses. **62. The . . . heart:** What I really believe and intend. **63. compliment extern:**
Outward appearance. **65. What I am:** What I seem. **66. thick-lips:** An Elizabethan epi-
thet for blacks, including Moors; **owe:** Own.

Proclaim him in the streets. Incense her kinsmen,
And though he in a fertile climate dwell,   70
Plague him with flies; though that his joy be joy,
Yet throw such changes of vexation on't
As it may lose some color.

RODERIGO: Here is her father's house. I'll call aloud.

IAGO: Do, with like timorous° accent and dire yell   75
As when, by night and negligence, the fire
Is spied in populous cities.

RODERIGO: What, ho, Brabantio! Signior Brabantio, ho!

IAGO: Awake! What, ho, Brabantio! Thieves! thieves! thieves!
Look to your house, your daughter, and your bags!   80
Thieves! thieves!

Brabantio at a window.°

BRABANTIO (*above*): What is the reason of this terrible summons?
What is the matter there?

RODERIGO: Signior, is all your family within?

IAGO: Are your doors locked?

BRABANTIO: Why, wherefore ask you this?   85

IAGO: Zounds, sir, y' are robbed! For shame, put on your gown!
Your heart is burst; you have lost half your soul.
Even now, now, very now, an old black ram
Is tupping° your white ewe. Arise, arise!
Awake the snorting° citizens with the bell.   90
Or else the devil will make a grandsire of you.
Arise, I say!

BRABANTIO: What, have you lost your wits?

RODERIGO: Most reverend signior, do you know my voice?

BRABANTIO: Not I. What are you?   95

RODERIGO: My name is Roderigo.

BRABANTIO: The worser welcome!
I have charged thee not to haunt about my doors.
In honest plainness thou hast heard me say
My daughter is not for thee; and now, in madness,
Being full of supper and distemp'ring° draughts,   100
Upon malicious knavery dost thou come
To start° my quiet.

RODERIGO: Sir, sir, sir—

BRABANTIO: But thou must needs be sure
My spirit and my place have in them power   105

----

75. timorous: Terrifying.   *s.d.* **Brabantio at a window:** (added from quarto).   **89. tupping:**
Copulating with.   **90. snorting:** Snoring.   **100. distemp'ring:** Intoxicating.   **102. start:** Startle, disturb.

To make this bitter to thee.

RODERIGO: Patience, good sir.

BRABANTIO: What tell'st thou me of robbing? This is Venice;
    My house is not a grange.°

RODERIGO: Most grave Brabantio,
    In simple° and pure soul I come to you.

IAGO: Zounds, sir, you are one of those that will not serve God if the devil bid   110
    you. Because we come to do you service, and you think we are ruffians,
    you'll have your daughter covered with a Barbary horse; you'll have your
    nephews° neigh to you; you'll have coursers for cousins, and gennets for
    germans.°

BRABANTIO: What profane wretch art thou?   115

IAGO: I am one, sir, that comes to tell you your daughter and the Moor are now
    making the beast with two backs.

BRABANTIO: Thou art a villain.

IAGO: You are—a senator.

BRABANTIO: This thou shalt answer. I know thee, Roderigo.

RODERIGO: Sir, I will answer anything. But I beseech you,   120
    If 't be your pleasure and most wise consent,
    As partly I find it is, that your fair daughter,
    At this odd-even° and dull watch o' th' night,
    Transported, with° no worse nor better guard
    But with a knave of common hire, a gondolier,   125
    To the gross clasps of a lascivious Moor—
    If this be known to you, and your allowance,°
    We then have done you bold and saucy wrongs;
    But if you know not this, my manners tell me
    We have your wrong rebuke. Do not believe   130
    That, from° the sense of all civility,
    I thus would play and trifle with your reverence.
    Your daughter, if you have not given her leave,
    I say again, hath made a gross revolt,
    Tying her duty, beauty, wit, and fortunes   135
    In an extravagant and wheeling° stranger
    Of here and everywhere. Straight satisfy yourself.
    If she be in her chamber, or your house,
    Let loose on me the justice of the state
    For thus deluding you.

BRABANTIO: Strike on the tinder, ho!   140
    Give me a taper!° Call up all my people!

---

108. **grange:** Isolated farmhouse. 109. **simple:** Sincere. 113. **nephews:** I.e., grand-
sons. 114. **gennets for germans:** Spanish horses for near kinsmen. 123. **odd-even:** Between
night and morning. 124. **with:** By. 127. **allowance:** Approval. 131. **from:** Contrary
to. 136. **extravagant and wheeling:** Expatriate and roving. 141. **taper:** Candle.

This accident° is not unlike my dream.
Belief of it oppresses me already.
Light, I say! light!   *Exit [above].*

IAGO: Farewell, for I must leave you.
It seems not meet,° nor wholesome to my place,°   145
To be produced°—as, if I stay, I shall—
Against the Moor. For I do know the state,
However this may gall him with some check,°
Cannot with safety cast° him; for he's embarked
With such loud reason to the Cyprus wars,   150
Which even now stand in act,° that for their souls
Another of his fathom° they have none
To lead their business; in which regard,
Though I do hate him as I do hell-pains,
Yet, for necessity of present life,°   155
I must show out a flag and sign of love,
Which is indeed but sign. That you shall surely find him,
Lead to the Sagittary° the raisèd search;
And there will I be with him. So farewell.   *Exit.*

Enter [below] Brabantio in his nightgown,° and Servants with torches.

BRABANTIO: It is too true an evil. Gone she is;   160
And what's to come of my despisèd time
Is naught but bitterness. Now, Roderigo,
Where didst thou see her?—O unhappy girl!—
With the Moor, say'st thou?—Who would be a father?—
How didst thou know 'twas she!—O, she deceives me   165
Past thought!—What said she to you?—Get moe° tapers!
Raise all my kindred!—Are they married, think you?

RODERIGO: Truly I think they are.

BRABANTIO: O heaven! How got she out? O treason of the blood!
Fathers, from hence trust not your daughters' minds   170
By what you see them act. Is there not charms
By which the property° of youth and maidhood
May be abused? Have you not read, Roderigo,
Of some such thing?

RODERIGO: Yes, sir, I have indeed.

BRABANTIO: Call up my brother.—O, would you had had her!— 175
Some one way, some another.—Do you know
Where we may apprehend her and the Moor?

---

142. **accident:** Occurrence. 145. **meet:** Fitting. **place:** Position. 146. **produced:** Called as a witness. 148. **check:** Reprimand. 149. **cast:** Discharge. 151. **stand in act:** Are going on. 152. **fathom:** Capacity. 155. **life:** Livelihood. 158. **Sagittary:** An inn. *s.d.* **nightgown:** Dressing gown. 166. **moe:** More. 172. **property:** Nature.

RODERIGO: I think I can discover him, if you please
    To get good guard and go along with me.
BRABANTIO: I pray you lead on. At every house I'll call;   180
    I may command at most.—Get weapons, ho!
    And raise some special officers of night.—
    On, good Roderigo; I'll deserve° your pains.   *Exeunt.*

Scene II

Before the lodgings of Othello.

Enter Othello, Iago, and Attendants with torches.

IAGO: Though in the trade of war I have slain men,
    Yet do I hold it very stuff o' th' conscience
    To do no contrived° murther. I lack iniquity
    Sometimes to do me service. Nine or ten times
    I had thought t' have yerked° him here under the ribs.   5
OTHELLO: 'Tis better as it is.
IAGO: Nay, but he prated,
    And spoke such scurvy and provoking terms
    Against your honor
    That with the little godliness I have
    I did full hard forbear him.° But I pray you, sir,   10
    Are you fast° married? Be assured of this,
    That the magnifico° is much beloved,
    And hath in his effect° a voice potential°
    As double° as the Duke's. He will divorce you,
    Or put upon you what restraint and grievance   15
    The law, with all his might to enforce it on,
    Will give him cable.
OTHELLO: Let him do his spite.
    My services which I have done the signiory°
    Shall out-tongue his complaints. 'Tis yet to know°—
    Which, when I know that boasting is an honor,   20
    I shall promulgate—I fetch my life and being
    From men of royal siege;° and my demerits°
    May speak unbonneted to as proud a fortune
    As this that I have reached.° For know, Iago,
    But that I love the gentle Desdemona,   25

---

183. deserve: Show gratitude for. SCENE II. **3. contrived:** Premeditated **5. yerked:** Stabbed.
10. I . . . him: I restrained myself with difficulty from attacking him. **11. fast:** Securely. **12.**
magnifico: Grandee (Brabantio). **13. in his effect:** At his command. **Potential:** Powerful. **14. double:** Doubly influential. **18. signiory:** Venetian government. **19. yet to know:**
Still not generally known. **22. siege:** Rank; **demerits:** Deserts. **23–24. May speak . . . reached:**
Are equal, I modestly assert, to those of Desdemona's family.

I would not my unhousèd° free condition
Put into circumscription and confine
For the sea's worth. But look what lights come yond?
IAGO: Those are the raisèd father and his friends.
    You were best go in.
OTHELLO: Not I; I must be found.   30
    My parts, my title, and my perfect soul°
    Shall manifest me rightly. Is it they?
IAGO: By Janus, I think no.

Enter Cassio, with torches, Officers.

OTHELLO: The servants of the Duke, and my lieutenant.
    The goodness of the night upon you, friends!   35
    What is the news?
CASSIO: The Duke does greet you, general;
    And he requires your haste-post-haste appearance
    Even on the instant.
OTHELLO: What's the matter, think you?
CASSIO: Something from Cyprus, as I may divine.
    It is a business of some heat.° The galleys   40
    Have sent a dozen sequent° messengers
    This very night at one another's heels,
    And many of the consuls,° raised and met,
    Are at the Duke's already. You have been hotly called for;
    When, being not at your lodging to be found,   45
    The Senate hath sent about three several° quests
    To search you out.
OTHELLO: 'Tis well I am found by you.
    I will but spend a word here in the house,
    And go with you.   [*Exit*]
CASSIO: Ancient, what makes° he here?
IAGO: Faith, he to-night hath boarded a land carack.°   50
    If it prove lawful prize,° he's made for ever.
CASSIO: I do not understand.
IAGO: He's married.
CASSIO: To who?

[*Enter Othello.*]

IAGO: Marry,° to—Come, captain, will you go?

---

26. unhousèd: Unrestrained. **31. my . . . soul:** My natural gifts, my position, and my stainless conscience. **40. heat:** Urgency. **41. sequent:** Consecutive. **43. consuls:** Senators. **46. several:** Separate. **49. makes:** Does. **50. carack:** Treasure ship. **51. prize:** Booty. **53. Marry:** By Mary (a mild oath).

OTHELLO: Have with you.

CASSIO: Here comes another troop to seek for you.

Enter Brabantio, Roderigo, and others with lights and weapons.

IAGO: It is Brabantio. General, be advised.°   55
    He comes to bad intent.

OTHELLO: Holla! stand there!

RODERIGO: Signior, it is the Moor.

BRABANTIO: Down with him, thief!

[They draw on both sides.]

IAGO: You, Roderigo! Come, sir, I am for you.

OTHELLO: Keep up° your bright swords, for the dew will rust them.
    Good signior, you shall more command with years   60
    Than with your weapons.

BRABANTIO: O thou foul thief, where hast thou stowed my daughter?
    Damned as thou art, thou hast enchanted her!
    For I'll refer me to all things of sense,°
    If she in chains of magic were not bound,   65
    Whether a maid so tender, fair, and happy,
    So opposite to marriage that she shunned
    The wealthy curlèd darlings of our nation,
    Would ever have, t' incur a general mock,
    Run from her guardage° to the sooty bosom   70
    Of such a thing as thou—to fear, not to delight.
    Judge me the world if 'tis not gross in sense°
    That thou hast practiced on her with foul charms,
    Abused her delicate youth with drugs or minerals
    That weaken motion.° I'll have't disputed on;   75
    'Tis probable, and palpable to thinking.
    I therefore apprehend and do attach° thee
    For an abuser of the world, a practicer
    Of arts inhibited° and out of warrant.°
    Lay hold upon him. If he do resist,   80
    Subdue him at his peril.

OTHELLO: Hold your hands,
    Both you of my inclining and the rest.
    Were it my cue to fight, I should have known it
    Without a prompter. Where will you that I go
    To answer this your charge?

---

55. be advised: Be on your guard. **59. Keep up:** I.e., sheath. **64. I'll . . . sense:** I'll submit my case to everyone. **70. guardage:** Guardianship. **72. gross in sense:** Obvious. **75. weaken motion:** Impair perception. **77. attach:** Arrest. **79. arts inhibited:** Prohibited arts, black magic. **out of warrant:** Illegal.

BRABANTIO: To prison, till fit time   85
  Of law and course of direct session°
  Call thee to answer.
OTHELLO: What if I do obey?
  How may the Duke be therewith satisfied,
  Whose messengers are here about my side
  Upon some present business of the state   90
  To bring me to him?
OFFICER: 'Tis true, most worthy signior.
  The Duke's in council, and your noble self
  I am sure is sent for.
BRABANTIO: How? The Duke in council?
  In this time of the night? Bring him away.
  Mine's not an idle° cause. The Duke himself,   95
  Or any of my brothers of the state,
  Cannot but feel this wrong as 'twere their own;
  For if such actions may have passage free,°
  Bondslaves and pagans shall our statesmen be.   *Exeunt.*

Scene III

The Venetian Senate Chamber.

Enter Duke and Senators, set at a table, with lights and Attendants.

DUKE: There is no composition° in these news
  That gives them credit.
FIRST SENATOR: Indeed they are disproportioned.°
  My letters say a hundred and seven galleys.
DUKE: And mine a hundred forty.
SECOND SENATOR: And mine two hundred.
  But though they jump° not on a just° account—   5
  As in these cases where the aim° reports
  'Tis oft with difference—yet do they all confirm
  A Turkish fleet, and bearing up to Cyprus.
DUKE: Nay, it is possible enough to judgment.
  I do not so secure me° in the error   10
  But the main article° I do approve°
  In fearful sense.
SAILOR (*within*):   What, ho! what, ho! what, ho!
OFFICER: A messenger from the galleys.

---

86. **direct session:** Regular trial.   95. **idle:** Trifling.   98. **may . . . free:** Are allowed to go unrestrained.   SCENE III.   1. **composition:** Consistency.   2. **disproportioned:** Inconsistent.
5. **jump:** Agree; **just:** Exact.   6. **aim:** Conjecture.   10. **so secure me:** Take such comfort.
11. **article:** Substance; **approve:** Accept.

Enter Sailor.

DUKE: Now, what's the business?

SAILOR: The Turkish preparation makes for Rhodes.
  So was I bid report here to the state   15
  By Signior Angelo.

DUKE: How say you by° this change?

FIRST SENATOR: This cannot be
  By no assay° of reason. 'Tis a pageant
  To keep us in false gaze.° When we consider
  Th' importancy of Cyprus to the Turk,   20
  And let ourselves again but understand
  That, as it more concerns the Turk than Rhodes,
  So may he with more facile question bear° it,
  For that it stands not in such warlike brace,°
  But altogether lacks th' abilities   25
  That Rhodes is dressed in — if we make thought of this,
  We must not think the Turk is so unskillful
  To leave that latest which concerns him first,
  Neglecting an attempt of ease and gain
  To wake and wage° a danger profitless.   30

DUKE: Nay, in all confidence, he's not for Rhodes.

OFFICER: Here is more news.

Enter a Messenger.

MESSENGER: The Ottomites, reverend and gracious,
  Steering with due course toward the isle of Rhodes,
  Have there injointed them° with an after fleet.   35

FIRST SENATOR: Ay, so I thought. How many, as you guess?

MESSENGER: Of thirty sail; and now they do restem°
  Their backward course, bearing with frank appearance°
  Their purposes toward Cyprus. Signior Montano,
  Your trusty and most valiant servitor,   40
  With his free duty recommends you thus,
  And prays you to believe him.

DUKE: 'Tis certain then for Cyprus.
  Marcus Luccicos,° is not he in town?

FIRST SENATOR: He's now in Florence.   45

DUKE: Write from us to him, post, post-haste. Dispatch.

FIRST SENATOR: Here comes Brabantio and the valiant Moor.

---

17. **by:** About. 18. **assay:** Test. 19. **in false gaze:** Looking the wrong way. 23. **with . . . bear:** More easily capture. 24. **brace:** Posture of defense. 30. **wake and wage:** Rouse and risk. 35. **injointed them:** Joined themselves. 37. **restem:** Steer again. 38. **frank appearance:** Undisguised intent. 44. **Marcus Luccicos:** (Presumably a Venetian envoy).

Enter Brabantio, Othello, Cassio, Iago, Roderigo, and Officers.

DUKE: Valiant Othello, we must straight employ you
    Against the general enemy Ottoman.
    [*To Brabantio.*] I did not see you. Welcome, gentle signior.   50
    We lacked your counsel and your help to-night.
BRABANTIO: So did I yours. Good your grace, pardon me.
    Neither my place, nor aught I heard of business,
    Hath raised me from my bed; nor doth the general care
    Take hold on me; for my particular grief   55
    Is of so floodgate° and o'erbearing nature
    That it engluts° and swallows other sorrows,
    And it is still itself.
DUKE: Why, what's the matter?
BRABANTIO: My daughter! O, my daughter!
ALL: Dead?
BRABANTIO: Ay, to me.
    She is abused,° stol'n from me, and corrupted   60
    By spells and medicines bought of mountebanks;
    For nature so prepost'rously to err,
    Being not deficient,° blind, or lame of sense,
    Sans witchcraft could not.
DUKE: Whoe'er he be that in this foul proceeding   65
    Hath thus beguiled your daughter of herself,
    And you of her, the bloody book of law
    You shall yourself read in the bitter letter
    After your own sense; yea, though our proper° son
    Stood in your action.°
BRABANTIO: Humbly I thank your grace.   70
    Here is the man — this Moor, whom now, it seems,
    Your special mandate for the state affairs
    Hath hither brought.
ALL: We are very sorry for't.
DUKE [*to Othello*]: What, in your own part, can you say to this?
BRABANTIO: Nothing, but this is so.   75
OTHELLO: Most potent, grave, and reverend signiors,
    My very noble, and approved° good masters,
    That I have ta'en away this old man's daughter,
    It is most true; true I have married her.
    The very head and front of my offending   80
    Hath this extent, no more. Rude° am I in my speech,

---

56. **floodgate:** Torrential. 57. **engluts:** Engulfs. 60. **abused:** Deceived. 63. **deficient:** Feeble-minded. 69. **our proper:** My own. 70. **Stood in your action:** Were accused by you. 77. **approved:** Tested by experience. 81. **Rude:** Unpolished.

And little blessed with the soft phrase of peace;
For since these arms of mine had seven years' pith°
Till now some nine moons wasted,° they have used
Their dearest action in the tented field;   85
And little of this great world can I speak
More than pertains to feats of broil and battle;
And therefore little shall I grace my cause
In speaking for myself. Yet, by your gracious patience,
I will a round° unvarnished tale deliver   90
Of my whole course of love—what drugs, what charms,
What conjuration, and what mighty magic
(For such proceeding am I charged withal°)
I won his daughter.

BRABANTIO: A maiden never bold;
Of spirit so still and quiet that her motion   95
Blushed° at herself; and she—in spite of nature,
Of years,° of country, credit, everything—
To fall in love with what she feared to look on!
It is a judgment maimed and most imperfect
That will confess perfection so could err   100
Against all rules of nature, and must be driven
To find out practices° of cunning hell
Why this should be. I therefore vouch° again
That with some mixtures pow'rful o'er the blood,°
Or with some dram, conjured° to this effect,   105
He wrought upon her.

DUKE: To vouch this is no proof,
Without more certain and more overt test
Than these thin habits° and poor likelihoods
Of modern seeming° do prefer against him.

FIRST SENATOR: But, Othello, speak.   110
Did you by indirect and forcèd° courses
Subdue and poison this young maid's affections?
Or came it by request, and such fair question°
As soul to soul affordeth?

OTHELLO: I do beseech you,
Send for the lady to the Sagittary   115
And let her speak of me before her father.

---

83. **pith:** Strength (i.e., since I was seven years old).   84. **Till . . . wasted:** Until about nine months
ago.   90. **round:** Plain.   93. **withal:** With.   95–96. **her motion Blushed:** Her own emotions
caused her to blush.   97. **years:** (Difference in age).   102. **practices:** Plots.   103. **vouch:** Assert.   104. **blood:** Passions.   105. **dram, conjured:** Potion, prepared by magic.   108. **thin
habits:** Slight appearances.   109. **modern seeming:** Everyday supposition.   111. **forcèd:** Violent.   113. **question:** Conversation.

If you do find me foul in her report,
The trust, the office, I do hold of you
Not only take away, but let your sentence
Even fall upon my life.

DUKE: Fetch Desdemona hither. 120

OTHELLO: Ancient, conduct them; you best know the place.

Exit [Iago, with] two or three [Attendants].

And till she come, as truly as to heaven
I do confess the vices of my blood,
So justly to your grave ears I'll present
How I did thrive in this fair lady's love, 125
And she in mine.

DUKE: Say it, Othello.

OTHELLO: Her father loved me, oft invited me;
Still° questioned me the story of my life
From year to year—the battles, sieges, fortunes 130
That I have passed.
I ran it through, even from my boyish days
To th' very moment that he bade me tell it.
Wherein I spoke of most disastrous chances,
Of moving accidents by flood and field; 135
Of hairbreadth scapes i' th' imminent deadly breach;
Of being taken by the insolent foe
And sold to slavery; of my redemption thence
And portance° in my travels' history;
Wherein of antres° vast and deserts idle, 140
Rough quarries, rocks, and hills whose heads touch heaven,
It was my hint° to speak—such was the process;
And of the Cannibals that each other eat,
The Anthropophagi,° and men whose heads
Do grow beneath their shoulders. This to hear 145
Would Desdemona seriously incline;
But still the house affairs would draw her thence;
Which ever as she could with haste dispatch,
She'ld come again, and with a greedy ear
Devour up my discourse. Which I observing, 150
Took once a pliant° hour, and found good means
To draw from her a prayer of earnest heart
That I would all my pilgrimage dilate,°
Whereof by parcels° she had something heard,
But not intentively.° I did consent, 155

---

129. **Still:** Continually. 139. **portance:** Behavior. 140. **antres:** Caves. 142. **hint:** Occasion. 144. **Anthropophagi:** Man-eaters. 151. **pliant:** Suitable. 153. **dilate:** Recount in full. 154. **parcels:** Portions. 155. **intentively:** With full attention.

And often did beguile her of her tears
When I did speak of some distressful stroke
That my youth suffered. My story being done,
She gave me for my pains a world of sighs.
She swore, i' faith, 'twas strange, 'twas passing° strange;   160
'Twas pitiful, 'twas wondrous pitiful.
She wished she had not heard it; yet she wished
That heaven had made her such a man. She thanked me;
And bade me, if I had a friend that loved her,
I should but teach him how to tell my story,   165
And that would woo her. Upon this hint° I spake.
She loved me for the dangers I had passed,
And I loved her that she did pity them.
This only is the witchcraft I have used.
Here comes the lady. Let her witness it.   170

Enter Desdemona, Iago, Attendants.

DUKE: I think this tale would win my daughter too.
    Good Brabantio,
    Take up this mangled matter at the best.°
    Men do their broken weapons rather use
    Than their bare hands.
BRABANTIO: I pray you hear her speak.   175
    If she confess that she was half the wooer,
    Destruction on my head if my bad blame
    Light on the man! Come hither, gentle mistress.
    Do you perceive in all this noble company
    Where most you owe obedience?
DESDEMONA: My noble father,   180
    I do perceive here a divided duty.
    To you I am bound for life and education;°
    My life and education both do learn me
    How to respect you: you are the lord of duty;°
    I am hitherto your daughter. But here's my husband;   185
    And so much duty as my mother showed
    To you, preferring you before her father,
    So much I challenge° that I may profess
    Due to the Moor my lord.
BRABANTIO: God be with you! I have done.
    Please it your grace, on to the state affairs.   190
    I had rather to adopt a child than get° it.

---

160. **passing:** Exceedingly. 166. **hint:** Opportunity. 173. **Take . . . best:** Make the best
of this situation. 182. **education:** Upbringing. 184. **of duty:** To whom duty is due.
188. **challenge:** Claim the right. 191. **get:** Beget.

Come hither, Moor.
I here do give thee that with all my heart
Which, but thou hast already, with all my heart
I would keep from thee. For your sake,° jewel,   195
I am glad at soul I have no other child;
For thy escape° would teach me tyranny,
To hang clogs on them. I have done, my lord.
DUKE: Let me speak like yourself° and lay a sentence°
    Which, as a grise° or step, may help these lovers   200
    [Into your favor.]
    When remedies are past, the griefs are ended
    By seeing the worst, which late on hopes depended.
    To mourn a mischief that is past and gone
    Is the next way to draw new mischief on.   205
    What cannot be preserved when fortune takes,
    Patience her injury a mock'ry makes.
    The robbed that smiles steals something from the thief;
    He robs himself that spends a bootless grief.
BRABANTIO: So let the Turk of Cyprus us beguile: 210
    We lose it not so long as we can smile.
    He bears the sentence well that nothing bears
    But the free comfort which from thence he hears;
    But he bears both the sentence and the sorrow
    That to pay grief must of poor patience borrow.   215
    These sentences, to sugar, or to gall,
    Being strong on both sides, are equivocal.
    But words are words. I never yet did hear
    That the bruisèd heart was piercèd through the ear.
    Beseech you, now to the affairs of state.   220
DUKE: The Turk with a most mighty preparation makes for Cyprus. Othello, the
    fortitude° of the place is best known to you; and though we have there a
    substitute of most allowed° sufficiency, yet opinion,° a more sovereign
    mistress of effects, throws a more safer voice on you. You must therefore be
    content to slubber° the gloss of your new fortunes with this more stubborn 225
    and boist'rous expedition.
OTHELLO: The tyrant custom, most grave senators,
    Hath made the flinty and steel couch of war
    My thrice-driven bed of down. I do agnize
    A natural and prompt alacrity   230
    I find in hardness;° and do undertake

---

195. **For your sake:** Because of you. 197. **escape:** Escapade. 199. **like yourself:** As you
should; **sentence:** Maxim. 200. **grise:** Step. 222. **fortitude:** Fortification. 223. **allowed:** Acknowledged; **opinion:** Public opinion. 225. **slubber:** Sully. 229–31. **agnize . . .
hardness:** Recognize in myself a natural and easy response to hardship.

These present wars against the Ottomites.
Most humbly, therefore, bending to your state,
I crave fit disposition for my wife,
Due reference of place, and exhibition,°   235
With such accommodation and besort°
As levels° with her breeding.

DUKE: If you please,
Be't at her father's.

BRABANTIO: I will not have it so.

OTHELLO: Nor I.

DESDEMONA: Nor I. I would not there reside,   240
To put my father in impatient thoughts
By being in his eye. Most gracious Duke,
To my unfolding lend your prosperous° ear,
And let me find a charter in your voice,
T' assist my simpleness.°   245

DUKE: What would you, Desdemona?

DESDEMONA: That I did love the Moor to live with him,
My downright violence, and storm of fortunes,°
May trumpet to the world. My heart's subdued
Even to the very quality of my lord.   250
I saw Othello's visage in his mind,
And to his honors and his valiant parts
Did I my soul and fortunes consecrate.
So that, dear lords, if I be left behind,
A moth of peace, and he go to the war,   255
The rites for which I love him are bereft me,
And I a heavy interim shall support
By his dear° absence. Let me go with him.

OTHELLO: Let her have your voice.°
Vouch with me, heaven, I therefore beg it not   260
To please the palate of my appetite,
Not to comply with heat°—the young affects°
In me defunct—and proper satisfaction;
But to be free and bounteous to her mind;
And heaven defend your good souls that you think   265
I will your serious and great business scant
When she is with me. No, when light-winged toys
Of feathered Cupid seel° with wanton dullness

---

235. exhibition: Allowance of money. **236. besort:** Suitable company. **237. levels:** Corresponds. **243. prosperous:** Favorable. **245. simpleness:** Lack of skill. **248. My . . . fortunes:** My clear and complete breaking of social customs. **258. dear:** Grievous. **259. voice:** Consent. **262. heat:** Passions; **young affects:** Tendencies of youth. **268. seel:** Blind.

My speculative and officed instruments,°
That° my disports corrupt and taint my business,   270
Let housewives make a skillet of my helm,
And all indign° and base adversities
Make head against my estimation!°
DUKE: Be it as you shall privately determine,
Either for her stay or going. Th' affair cries haste,   275
And speed must answer it.
FIRST SENATOR: You must away to-night.
OTHELLO: With all my heart.
DUKE: At nine i' th' morning here we'll meet again.
Othello, leave some officer behind,
And he shall our commission bring to you,   280
With such things else of quality and respect
As doth import° you.
OTHELLO: So please your grace, my ancient;
A man he is of honesty and trust.
To his conveyance I assign my wife,
With what else needful your good grace shall think   285
To be sent after me.
DUKE: Let it be so.
Good night to every one.
        [*To Brabantio.*]   And, noble signior,
If virtue no delighted° beauty lack,
Your son-in-law is far more fair than black.
FIRST SENATOR: Adieu, brave Moor. Use Desdemona well.   290
BRABANTIO: Look to her, Moor, if thou hast eyes to see:
She has deceived her father, and may thee.
                            Exeunt [Duke, Senators, Officers, &c.].
OTHELLO: My life upon her faith! — Honest Iago,
My Desdemona must I leave to thee.
I prithee let thy wife attend on her,   295
And bring them after in the best advantage.°
Come, Desdemona. I have but an hour
Of love, of worldly matters and direction,
To spend with thee. We must obey the time.
                            Exit Moor and Desdemona.
RODERIGO: Iago, —   300
IAGO: What say'st thou, noble heart?
RODERIGO: What will I do, think'st thou?

---

269. My ... instruments: My perceptive and responsible faculties. **270. That:** So that.
272. indign: Unworthy. **273. estimation:** Reputation. **282. import:** Concern.
288. delighted: Delightful. **296. in the best advantage:** At the best opportunity.

IAGO: Why, go to bed and sleep.

RODERIGO: I will incontinently° drown myself.

IAGO: If thou dost, I shall never love thee after. Why, thou silly gentleman!   305

RODERIGO: It is silliness to live when to live is torment; and then have we a prescription to die when death is our physician.

IAGO: O villainous! I have looked upon the world for four times seven years; and since I could distinguish betwixt a benefit and an injury, I never found man that knew how to love himself. Ere I would say I would drown 310 myself for the love of a guinea hen,° I would change my humanity with a baboon.

RODERIGO: What should I do? I confess it is my shame to be so fond,° but it is not in my virtue° to amend it.

IAGO: Virtue? a fig! 'Tis in ourselves that we are thus or thus. Our bodies are 315 our gardens, to which our wills are gardeners; so that if we will plant nettles or sow lettuce, set hyssop and weed up thyme, supply it with one gender° of herbs or distract it with many—either to have it sterile with idleness or manured with industry—why, the power and corrigible authority° of this lies in our wills. If the balance of our lives had not one scale of reason to 320 poise° another of sensuality, the blood and baseness° of our natures would conduct us to most preposterous conclusions. But we have reason to cool our raging motions,° our carnal strings, our unbitted° lusts; whereof I take this that you call love to be a sect or scion.°

RODERIGO: It cannot be.   325

IAGO: It is merely a lust of the blood and a permission of the will. Come, be a man! Drown thyself? Drown cats and blind puppies! I have professed me thy friend, and I confess me knit to thy deserving with cables of per- durable toughness. I could never better stead thee than now. Put money in thy purse. Follow thou the wars; defeat thy favor° with an usurped 330 beard. I say, put money in thy purse. It cannot be that Desdemona should long continue her love to the Moor—put money in thy purse—nor he his to her. It was a violent commencement in her, and thou shalt see an answerable sequestration°—put but money in thy purse. These Moors are changeable in their wills—fill thy purse with money. The food that to 335 him now is as luscious as locusts shall be to him shortly as bitter as colo- quintida.° She must change for youth: when she is sated with his body, she will find the error of her choice. [She must have change, she must.] Therefore put money in thy purse. If thou wilt needs damn thyself, do it

---

304. incontinently: Forthwith. **311. guinea hen:** Prostitute (slang). **313. fond:** Foolish. **314. virtue:** Strength, ability. **317. gender:** Species. **319. corrigible authority:** Corrective power. **321. poise:** Counterbalance; **blood and baseness:** Animal instincts. **323. motions:** Appetites; **unbitted:** Uncontrolled. **324. sect or scion:** Offshoot, cutting. **330. defeat thy favor:** Disguise thy appearance. **334. sequestration:** Estrangement. **336–37. coloquin-tida:** A medicine.

a more delicate way than drowning. Make° all the money thou canst. If 340
sanctimony and a frail vow betwixt an erring° barbarian and a super-
subtle Venetian be not too hard for my wits and all the tribe of hell, thou
shalt enjoy her. Therefore make money. A pox of drowning thyself! 'Tis
clean out of the way. Seek thou rather to be hanged in compassing thy
joy than to be drowned and go without her.   345

RODERIGO: Wilt thou be fast to my hopes, if I depend on the issue?

IAGO: Thou art sure of me. Go, make money. I have told thee often, and I
retell thee again and again, I hate the Moor. My cause is hearted;° thine
hath no less reason. Let us be conjunctive° in our revenge against him.
If thou canst cuckold him, thou dost thyself a pleasure, me a sport. There 350
are many events in the womb of time, which will be delivered. Traverse,°
go, provide thy money! We will have more of this to-morrow. Adieu.

RODERIGO: Where shall we meet i' th' morning?

IAGO: At my lodging.

RODERIGO: I'll be with thee betimes.°   355

IAGO: Go to, farewell — Do you hear, Roderigo?

[RODERIGO: What say you?

IAGO: No more of drowning, do you hear?

RODERIGO: I am changed.

IAGO: Go to, farewell. Put money enough in your purse.]   360

RODERIGO: I'll sell all my land.   *Exit.*

IAGO: Thus do I ever make my fool my purse;
    For I mine own gained knowledge should profane
    If I would time expend with such a snipe°
    But for my sport and profit. I hate the Moor;   365
    And it is thought abroad° that 'twixt my sheets
    H'as done my office. I know not if't be true;
    But I, for mere suspicion in that kind,
    Will do as if for surety.° He holds me well;°
    The better shall my purpose work on him.   370
    Cassio's a proper man. Let me see now:
    To get his place, and to plume up° my will
    In double knavery — How, how? — Let's see: —
    After some time, to abuse° Othello's ears
    That he° is too familiar with his° wife.   375
    He hath a person and a smooth dispose°
    To be suspected — framed to make women false.
    The Moor is of a free° and open nature

---

340. **Make:** Raise. 341. **erring:** Wandering. 348. **hearted:** Fixed in my heart. 349. **con-
junctive:** United. 351. **Traverse:** Forward march. 355. **betimes:** Early. 364. **snipe:** Fool.
366. **thought abroad:** Rumored. 369. **do ... surety:** Act on it as if certain; **well:** In high regard. 372. **plume up:** Gratify. 374. **abuse:** Deceive. 375. **he:** (Cassio); **his:** (Othello's). 376.
dispose: Manner. 378. **free:** Frank.

That thinks men honest that but seem to be so;
And will as tenderly be led by th' nose   380
As asses are.
I have't! It is engend'red! Hell and night
Must bring this monstrous birth to the world's light.   *Exit.*

ACT II / Scene I

An open place in Cyprus, near the harbor.

Enter Montano and two Gentlemen.

MONTANO: What from the cape can you discern at sea?
FIRST GENTLEMAN: Nothing at all: it is a high-wrought flood.°
    I cannot 'twixt the heaven and the main
    Descry a sail.
MONTANO: Methinks the wind hath spoke aloud at land;   5
    A fuller blast ne'er shook our battlements.
    If it hath ruffianed° so upon the sea,
    What ribs of oak, when mountains° melt on them,
    Can hold the mortise?° What shall we hear of this?
SECOND GENTLEMAN: A segregation° of the Turkish fleet.   10
    For do but stand upon the foaming shore,
    The chidden billow seems to pelt the clouds;
    The wind-shaked surge, with high and monstrous mane,
    Seems to cast water on the burning Bear
    And quench the Guards° of th' ever-fixèd pole.°   15
    I never did like molestation° view
    On the enchafèd° flood.
MONTANO: If that° the Turkish fleet
    Be not ensheltered and embayed, they are drowned;
    It is impossible to bear it out.

Enter a third Gentleman.

THIRD GENTLEMAN: News, lads! Our wars are done.   20
    The desperate tempest hath so banged the Turks
    That their designment halts.° A noble ship of Venice
    Hath seen a grievous wrack° and sufferance°
    On most part of their fleet.
MONTANO: How? Is this true?
THIRD GENTLEMAN: The ship is here put in,   25

ACT II, SCENE I. **2. high-wrought flood:** Very agitated sea. **7. ruffianed:** Raged. **8. mountains:** I.e., of water. **9. hold the mortise:** Hold their joints together. **10. segregation:** Scattering. **15. Guards:** Stars near the North Star; **pole:** Polestar. **16. molestation:** Tumult. **17. enchafèd:** Angry; **If that:** If. **22. designment halts:** Plan is crippled. **23. wrack:** Shipwreck; **sufferance:** Disaster.

A Veronesa;° Michael Cassio,
Lieutenant to the warlike Moor Othello,
Is come on shore; the Moor himself at sea,
And is in full commission here for Cyprus.
MONTANO: I am glad on't. 'Tis a worthy governor.   30
THIRD GENTLEMAN: But this same Cassio, though he speak of comfort
Touching the Turkish loss, yet he looks sadly
And prays the Moor be safe, for they were parted
With foul and violent tempest.
MONTANO: Pray heaven he be;
For I have served him, and the man commands   35
Like a full° soldier. Let's to the seaside, ho!
As well to see the vessel that's come in
As to throw out our eyes for brave Othello,
Even till we make the main and th' aerial blue
An indistinct regard.°
THIRD GENTLEMAN: Come, let's do so;   40
For every minute is expectancy
Of more arrivance.

Enter Cassio.

CASSIO: Thanks, you the valiant of this warlike isle,
That so approve° the Moor! O, let the heavens
Give him defense against the elements,   45
For I have lost him on a dangerous sea!
MONTANO: Is he well shipped?
CASSIO: His bark is stoutly timbered, and his pilot
Of very expert and approved allowance;°
Therefore my hopes, not surfeited to death,°   50
Stand in bold cure.°
(*Within.*)   A sail, a sail, a sail!   *Enter a messenger.*
CASSIO: What noise?
MESSENGER: The town is empty; on the brow o' th' sea
Stand ranks of people, and they cry "A sail!"
CASSIO: My hopes do shape him for the governor.   55

A shot.

SECOND GENTLEMAN: They do discharge their shot of courtesy:
Our friends at least.
CASSIO: I pray you, sir, go forth
And give us truth who 'tis that is arrived.

---

26. Veronesa: Ship furnished by Verona.   **36. full:** Perfect.   **40. An indistinct regard:** Indistinguishable.   **44. approve:** Commend, admire.   **49. approved allowance:** Tested reputation.   **50. surfeited to death:** Overindulged.   **51. in bold cure:** A good chance of fulfillment.

SECOND GENTLEMAN: I shall.   *Exit.*

MONTANO: But, good lieutenant, is your general wived?   60

CASSIO: Most fortunately. He hath achieved a maid
    That paragons° description and wild fame;
    One that excels the quirks° of blazoning° pens,
    And in th' essential vesture of creation
    Does tire the ingener.°

Enter Second Gentleman.

                        How now? Who has put in?   65

SECOND GENTLEMAN: 'Tis one Iago, ancient to the general.

CASSIO: He's had most favorable and happy speed:
    Tempests themselves, high seas, and howling winds,
    The guttered° rocks and congregated sands,
    Traitors ensteeped° to clog the guiltless keel,   70
    As having sense of beauty, do omit
    Their mortal° natures, letting go safely by
    The divine Desdemona.

MONTANO: What is she?

CASSIO: She that I spake of, our great captain's captain,
    Left in the conduct of the bold Iago,   75
    Whose footing° here anticipates our thoughts
    A se'nnight's° speed. Great Jove, Othello guard,
    And swell his sail with thine own pow'rful breath,
    That he may bless this bay with his tall ship,
    Make love's quick pants in Desdemona's arms,   80
    Give renewed fire to our extincted spirits,
    [And bring all Cyprus comfort!]

Enter Desdemona, Iago, Roderigo, and Emilia [with Attendants].

                        O, behold!
    The riches of the ship is come on shore!
    You men of Cyprus, let her have your knees.°
    Hail to thee, lady! and the grace of heaven,   85
    Before, behind thee, and on every hand,
    Enwheel thee round!

DESDEMONA: I thank you, valiant Cassio.
    What tidings can you tell me of my lord?

CASSIO: He is not yet arrived; nor know I aught
    But that he's well and will be shortly here.   90

---

62. **paragons:** Surpasses. 63. **quirks:** Ingenuities; **blazoning:** Describing in heraldic language. 64–65. **And . . . ingener:** Merely to describe her as God made her exhausts her praiser.
69. **guttered:** Jagged. 70. **ensteeped:** Submerged. 72. **mortal:** Deadly. 76. **footing:**
Landing. 77. **se'nnight's:** Week's. 84. **knees:** I.e., kneeling.

DESDEMONA: O but I fear! How lost you company?

CASSIO: The great contention of the sea and skies
　　Parted our fellowship.
　　　　(*Within.*)　　　　　A sail, a sail! [*A shot.*]
　　　　　　　　　　　　　　　　　　　　But hark. A sail!

SECOND GENTLEMAN: They give their greeting to the citadel;
　　This likewise is a friend.

CASSIO:　　　　　　　　　　See for the news.　　　　　　　　　95

　　　　　　　　　　　　　　　　[*Exit Gentleman.*]

　　Good ancient, you are welcome.
　　　　[*To Emilia.*]　　　　　Welcome, mistress. —
　　Let it not gall your patience, good Iago,
　　That I extend my manners. 'Tis my breeding
　　That gives me this bold show of courtesy.
　　　　[*Kisses Emilia.°*]

IAGO: Sir, would she give you so much of her lips　　　　　100
　　As of her tongue she oft bestows on me,
　　You would have enough.

DESDEMONA:　　　　　　　　Alas, she has no speech!

IAGO: In faith, too much.
　　I find it still° when I have list° to sleep.
　　Marry, before your ladyship, I grant,　　　　　　　　105
　　She puts her tongue a little in her heart
　　And chides with thinking.

EMILIA: You have little cause to say so.

IAGO: Come on, come on! You are pictures out of doors,°
　　Bells° in your parlors, wildcats in your kitchens,　　　110
　　Saints° in your injuries, devils being offended,
　　Players in your housewifery,° and housewives° in your beds.

DESDEMONA: O, fie upon thee, slanderer!

IAGO: Nay, it is true, or else I am a Turk:°
　　You rise to play, and go to bed to work.　　　　　　　115

EMILIA: You shall not write my praise.

IAGO:　　　　　　　　　　No, let me not.

DESDEMONA: What wouldst thou write of me, if thou shouldst praise me?

IAGO: O gentle lady, do not put me to't,
　　For I am nothing if not critical.

DESDEMONA: Come on, assay.° — There's one gone to the harbor?　　120

IAGO: Ay, madam.

---

s.d. **Kisses Emilia:** (Kissing was a common Elizabethan form of social courtesy).　**104. still:** Always; **list:** Desire.　**109. pictures out of doors:** Well-behaved in public.　**110. Bells:** Noisy, jangling.　**111. Saints:** Martyrs.　**112. housewifery:** Housekeeping; **housewives:** Hussies.　**114. Turk:** Infidel, not to be believed.　**120. assay:** Try.

DESDEMONA: I am not merry; but I do beguile
  The thing I am by seeming otherwise. —
  Come, how wouldst thou praise me?
IAGO: I am about it; but indeed my invention   125
  Comes from my pate as birdlime° does from frieze° —
  It plucks out brains and all. But my Muse labors,
  And thus she is delivered:
  If she be fair and wise, fairness and wit —
  The one's for use, the other useth it.   130
DESDEMONA: Well praised! How if she be black° and witty?
IAGO: If she be black, and thereto have a wit,
  She'll find a white° that shall her blackness fit.
DESDEMONA: Worse and worse!
EMILIA: How if fair and foolish?   135
IAGO: She never yet was foolish that was fair,
  For even her folly° helped her to an heir.
DESDEMONA: These are old fond° paradoxes to make fools laugh i' th' alehouse.
  What miserable praise hast thou for her that's foul° and foolish?
IAGO: There's none so foul, and foolish thereunto,   140
  But does foul pranks which fair and wise ones do.
DESDEMONA: O heavy ignorance! Thou praisest the worst best. But what
  praise couldst thou bestow on a deserving woman indeed — one that in
  the authority of her merit did justly put on the vouch° of very malice
  itself?   145
IAGO: She that was ever fair, and never proud;
  Had tongue at will, and yet was never loud;
  Never lacked gold, and yet went never gay;°
  Fled from her wish, and yet said "Now I may";°
  She that, being ang'red, her revenge being nigh,   150
  Bade her wrong stay,° and her displeasure fly;
  She that in wisdom never was so frail
  To change the cod's head for the salmon's tail;°
  She that could think, and ne'er disclose her mind;
  See suitors following, and not look behind: 155
  She was a wight (if ever such wight° were) —
DESDEMONA: To do what?
IAGO: To suckle fools and chronicle small beer.°

---

126. birdlime: A sticky paste; **frieze:** Rough cloth. **131. black:** Brunette. **133. white:**
Wight (a person), and a fair person (pun). **137. folly:** Wantonness. **138. fond:** Foolish.
139. foul: Ugly. **144. put on the vouch:** Compel the approval. **148. gay:** Lavishly clothed.
149. Fled . . . may": Resisted temptation even when she had a choice. **151. Bade . . . stay:**
Decided to put up with her injury patiently. **153. To . . . tail:** I.e., to exchange the good for
the poor but expensive. **156. wight:** Person, human being. **158. chronicle small beer:**
Keep petty household accounts.

DESDEMONA: O most lame and impotent conclusion! Do not learn of him, Emilia, though he be thy husband. How say you, Cassio? Is he not a most 160 profane and liberal° counsellor?

CASSIO: He speaks home,° madam. You may relish him more in the soldier than in the scholar.

IAGO [*aside*]: He takes her by the palm. Ay, well said, whisper! With as little a web as this will I ensnare as great a fly as Cassio. Ay, smile upon her, do! I 165 will gyve thee in thine own courtship.° — You say true; 'tis so, indeed! — If such tricks as these strip you out of your lieutenantry, it had been better you had not kissed your three fingers so oft — which now again you are most apt to play the sir° in. Very good! well kissed! an excellent courtesy! 'Tis so, indeed. Yet again your fingers to your lips? Would they were clyster pipes° 170 for your sake! (*Trumpet within.*)

The Moor! I know his trumpet.

CASSIO: 'Tis truly so.

DESDEMONA: Let's meet him and receive him.

CASSIO: Lo, where he comes. 175

Enter Othello and Attendants.

OTHELLO: O my fair warrior!

DESDEMONA: My dear Othello!

OTHELLO: It gives me wonder great as my content
To see you here before me. O my soul's joy!
If after every tempest come such calms,
May the winds blow till they have wakened death! 180
And let the laboring bark climb hills of seas
Olympus-high, and duck again as low
As hell's from heaven! If it were now to die,
'Twere now to be most happy;° for I fear
My soul hath her content so absolute 185
That not another comfort like to this
Succeeds in unknown fate.

DESDEMONA: The heavens forbid
But that our loves and comforts should increase
Even as our days do grow.

OTHELLO: Amen to that, sweet powers!
I cannot speak enough of this content; 190
It stops me here; it is too much of joy.
And this, and this, the greatest discords be

They kiss.

---

161. **profane and liberal**: Worldly and licentious. 162. **home**: Bluntly. 166. **gyve ...
courtship**: Manacle you by means of your courtly manners. 169. **sir**: Courtly gentleman. 170. **clyster pipes**: Enema syringes. 184. **happy**: Fortunate.

That e'er our hearts shall make!
IAGO [*aside*]:   O, you are well tuned now!
But I'll set down° the pegs that make this music,
As honest as I am.
OTHELLO: Come, let us to the castle.   195
News, friends! Our wars are done; the Turks are drowned.
How does my old acquaintance of this isle? —
Honey, you shall be well desired° in Cyprus;
I have found great love amongst them. O my sweet,
I prattle out of fashion, and I dote   200
In mine own comforts. I prithee, good Iago,
Go to the bay and disembark my coffers.
Bring thou the master° to the citadel;
He is a good one, and his worthiness
Does challenge° much respect. — Come, Desdemona,   205
Once more well met at Cyprus.
                    Exit Othello [with all but Iago and Roderigo].
IAGO [*to an Attendant, who goes out*]: Do thou meet me presently at the har-
bor. [*To Roderigo.*] Come hither. If thou be'st valiant (as they say base
men being in love have then a nobility in their natures more than is
native to them), list me. The lieutenant to-night watches on the court of 210
guard.° First, I must tell thee this: Desdemona is directly in love with
him.
RODERIGO: With him? Why, 'tis not possible.
IAGO: Lay thy finger thus,° and let thy soul be instructed. Mark me with what
violence she first loved the Moor, but° for bragging and telling her fan- 215
tastical lies; and will she love him still for prating? Let not thy discreet
heart think it. Her eye must be fed; and what delight shall she have to
look on the devil? When the blood is made dull with the act of sport,°
there should be, again to inflame it and to give satiety a fresh appetite,
loveliness in favor,° sympathy° in years, manners, and beauties; all 220
which the Moor is defective in. Now for want of these required conveniences,° her delicate tenderness will find itself abused,° begin to heave the
gorge,° disrelish and abhor the Moor. Very nature° will instruct her in it
and compel her to some second choice. Now, sir, this granted — as it is a
most pregnant° and unforced position — who stands so eminent in the 225
degree of° this fortune as Cassio does? A knave very voluble; no further
conscionable° than in putting on the mere form of civil and humane°

---

194. **set down**: Loosen.   198. **well desired**: Warmly welcomed.   203. **master**: Ship captain.   205. **challenge**: Deserve.   210–11. **court of guard**: Headquarters.   214. **thus**: I.e., on
your lips.   215. **but**: Only.   218. **the act of sport**: Sex.   220. **favor**: Appearance; **sympathy**: Similarity.   221–22. **conveniences**: Compatibilities.   **abused**: Cheated.   222–23. **heave
the gorge**: Be nauseated.   223. **Very nature**: Her very instincts.   225. **pregnant**: Evident.
225–26. **in the degree of**: As next inline for.   227 **conscionable**: Conscientious; **humane**:
Polite.

seeming for the better compassing of his salt° and most hidden loose affection? Why, none! why, none! A slipper° and subtle knave; a finder-out of occasions; that has an eye can stamp° and counterfeit advantages,°   230 though true advantage never present itself; a devilish knave! Besides, the knave is handsome, young, and hath all those requisites in him that folly and green° minds look after. A pestilent complete knave! and the woman hath found him already.

RODERIGO: I cannot believe that in her; she's full of most blessed condition.°   235

IAGO: Blessed fig's-end! The wine she drinks is made of grapes. If she had been blessed, she would never have loved the Moor. Blessed pudding! Didst thou not see her paddle with the palm of his hand? Didst not mark that?

RODERIGO: Yes, that I did; but that was but courtesy.   240

IAGO: Lechery, by this hand! an index° and obscure° prologue to the history of lust and foul thoughts. They met so near with their lips that their breaths embraced together. Villainous thoughts, Roderigo! When these mutuali-ties° so marshal the way, hard at hand comes the master and main exercise, th' incorporate° conclusion. Pish! But, sir, be you ruled by me: I have   245 brought you from Venice. Watch you to-night; for the command, I'll lay't upon you.° Cassio knows you not. I'll not be far from you: do you find some occasion to anger Cassio, either by speaking too loud, or tainting° his discipline, or from what other course you please which the time shall more favorably minister.°   250

RODERIGO: Well.

IAGO: Sir, he's rash and very sudden in choler,° and haply with his truncheon may strike at you. Provoke him that he may; for even out of that will I cause these of Cyprus to mutiny; whose qualification° shall come into no true taste° again but by the displanting of Cassio. So shall you have a shorter   255 journey to your desires by the means I shall then have to prefer° them; and the impediment most profitably removed with-out the which there were no expectation of our prosperity.

RODERIGO: I will do this if you can bring it to any opportunity.

IAGO: I warrant thee. Meet me by and by at the citadel; I must fetch his neces-   260 saries ashore. Farewell.

RODERIGO: Adieu.   *Exit.*

IAGO: That Cassio loves her, I do well believe't;
That she loves him, 'tis apt° and of great credit.

---

228. **salt:** Lecherous. 229. **slipper:** Slippery. 230. **stamp:** Coin; **advantages:** Opportunities. 232–33. **folly and green:** Foolish and inexperienced. 235. **condition:** Character. 241. **index:** Table of contents; **obscure:** Hidden. 243–44. **mutualities:** Exchanges.
245. **incorporate:** Carnal. 246–47. **for . . . you:** I'll put you in charge. 248. **taint-
ing:** Discrediting. 250. **minister:** Provide. 252. **sudden in choler:** Violent in anger.
254. **qualification:** Appeasement. 254–55. **true taste:** Satisfactory state. 256. **prefer:** Advance. 264. **apt:** Probable.

The Moor, howbeit that I endure him not,   265
Is of a constant, loving, noble nature,
And I dare think he'll prove to Desdemona
A most dear husband. Now I do love her too;
Not out of absolute lust, though peradventure
I stand accountant° for as great a sin,   270
But partly led to diet° my revenge,
For that I do suspect the lusty Moor
Hath leaped into my seat; the thought whereof
Doth, like a poisonous mineral, gnaw my innards;
And nothing can or shall content my soul   275
Till I am evened with him, wife for wife;
Or failing so, yet that I put the Moor
At least into a jealousy so strong
That judgment cannot cure. Which thing to do,
If this poor trash of Venice, whom I trash°   280
For° his quick hunting, stand the putting on,°
I'll have our Michael Cassio on the hip,°
Abuse him to the Moor in the rank garb°
(For I fear Cassio with my nightcap too),
Make the Moor thank me, love me, and reward me   285
For making him egregiously an ass
And practicing upon° his peace and quiet
Even to madness. 'Tis here, but yet confused:
Knavery's plain face is never seen till used.   *Exit.*

Scene II

A street in Cyprus.

Enter Othello's Herald, with a proclamation.

HERALD: It is Othello's pleasure, our noble and valiant general, that, upon
    certain tidings now arrived, importing the mere perdition° of the Turkish
    fleet, every man put himself into triumph; some to dance, some to make
    bonfires, each man to what sport and revels his addiction leads him. For,
    besides these beneficial news, it is the celebration of his nuptial. So   5
    much was his pleasure should be proclaimed. All offices° are open, and
    there is full liberty of feasting from the present hour of five till the bell
    have told eleven. Heaven bless the isle of Cyprus and our noble general
    Othello!   *Exit.*

---

270. accountant: Accountable. **271. diet:** Feed. **280. I trash:** I weight down (in order to
keep under control). **281. For:** In order to develop; **stand the putting on:** Responds to my
inciting. **282. on the hip:** At my mercy. **283. rank garb:** Gross manner. **287. practicing upon:** Plotting against. SCENE II. **2. mere perdition:** Complete destruction. **6. offices:** Kitchens and storerooms.

Scene III

The Cyprian Castle.

Enter Othello, Desdemona, Cassio, and Attendants.

OTHELLO: Good Michael, look you to the guard to-night.
    Let's teach ourselves that honorable stop,
    Not to outsport discretion.°

CASSIO: Iago hath direction what to do;
    But not withstanding, with my personal eye   5
    Will I look to't.

OTHELLO: Iago is most honest.
    Michael, good night. To-morrow with your earliest
    Let me have speech with you.
        [*To Desdemona.*]   Come, my dear love.
    The purchase made, the fruits are to ensue;
    That profit 's yet to come 'tween me and you. —   10
    Good night.

                    Exit [Othello with Desdemona and Attendants].

Enter Iago.

CASSIO: Welcome, Iago. We must to the watch.

IAGO: Not this hour, lieutenant; 'tis not yet ten o' th' clock. Our general cast°
    us thus early for the love of his Desdemona; who let us not therefore
    blame. He hath not yet made wanton the night with her, and she is sport   15
    for Jove.

CASSIO: She's a most exquisite lady.

IAGO: And, I'll warrant her, full of game.

CASSIO: Indeed, she's a most fresh and delicate creature.

IAGO: What an eye she has! Methinks it sounds a parley to provocation.   20

CASSIO: An inviting eye; and yet methinks right modest.

IAGO: And when she speaks, is it not an alarum to love?

CASSIO: She is indeed perfection.

IAGO: Well, happiness to their sheets! Come, lieutenant, I have a stoup° of
    wine, and here without are a brace of Cyprus gallants that would fain have   25
    a measure to the health of black Othello.

CASSIO: Not to-night, good Iago. I have very poor and unhappy brains for drink-
    ing; I could well wish courtesy would invent some other custom of enter-
    tainment.

IAGO: O, they are our friends. But one cup! I'll drink for you.   30

CASSIO: I have drunk but one cup to-night, and that was craftily qualified° too;
    and behold what innovation° it makes here. I am unfortunate in the infir-
    mity and dare not task my weakness with any more.

SCENE III. **3. outsport discretion:** Let celebrating go too far. **13. cast:** Dismissed. **24.
stoup:** Two-quart tankard. **31. qualified:** Diluted. **32. innovation:** Disturbance.

IAGO: What, man! 'Tis a night of revels: the gallants desire it.
CASSIO: Where are they?   35
IAGO: Here at the door; I pray you call them in.
CASSIO: I'll do't, but it dislikes me.   *Exit.*
IAGO: If I can fasten but one cup upon him
    With that which he hath drunk to-night already,
    He'll be as full of quarrel and offense   40
    As my young mistress' dog. Now my sick fool Roderigo,
    Whom love hath turned almost the wrong side out,
    To Desdemona hath to-night caroused
    Potations pottle-deep;° and he's to watch.
    Three lads of Cyprus—noble swelling spirits,   45
    That hold their honors in a wary distance,°
    The very elements° of this warlike isle—
    Have I to-night flustered with flowing cups,
    And they watch too. Now, 'mongst this flock of drunkards
    Am I to put our Cassio in some action   50
    That may offend the isle.

Enter Cassio, Montano, and Gentlemen [; Servants following with wine].

                              But here they come.
    If consequence do but approve my dream,
    My boat sails freely, both with wind and stream.
CASSIO: 'Fore God, they have given me a rouse° already.
MONTANO: Good faith, a little one; not past a pint, as I am a soldier.   55
IAGO: Some wine, ho!
    [*Sings.*]   And let me the canakin° clink, clink;
                And let me the canakin clink
                   A soldier's a man;
                   A life's but a span,   60
                Why then, let a soldier drink.
    Some wine, boys!
CASSIO: 'Fore God, an excellent song!
IAGO: I learned it in England, where indeed they are most potent in potting.
    Your Dane, your German, and your swag-bellied Hollander—Drink,   65
    ho!—are nothing to your English.
CASSIO: Is your Englishman so expert in his drinking?
IAGO: Why, he drinks you with facility your Dane dead drunk; he sweats not to
    overthrow your Almain;° he gives your Hollander a vomit ere the next
    pottle can be filled.   70

---

44. **pottle-deep:** Bottoms up.   46. **That ... distance:** Are very sensitive about their honor.
47. **very elements:** True representatives.   54. **rouse:** Bumper.   57. **canakin:** Small drinking
cup.   69. **Almain:** German.

CASSIO: To the health of our general!

MONTANO: I am for it, lieutenant, and I'll do you justice.

IAGO: O sweet England!

[*Sings.*]   King Stephen was a worthy peer;
                     His breeches cost him but a crown;   75
                He held 'em sixpence all too dear,
                     With that he called the tailor lown.°
                He was a wight of high renown,
                     And thou art but of low degree.
                'Tis pride that pulls the country down;   80
                     Then take thine auld cloak about thee.

          Some wine, ho!

CASSIO: 'Fore God, this is a more exquisite song than the other.

IAGO: Will you hear't again?

CASSIO: No, for I hold him to be unworthy of his place that does those things.°   85
          Well, God's above all; and there be souls must be saved, and there be souls
          must not be saved.

IAGO: It's true, good lieutenant.

CASSIO: For mine own part—no offense to the general, nor any man of quality—I
          hope to be saved.   90

IAGO: And so do I too, lieutenant.

CASSIO: Ay, but, by your leave, not before me. The lieutenant is to be saved
          before the ancient. Let's have no more of this; let's to our affairs.—God
          forgive us our sins!—Gentlemen, let's look to our business. Do not think,
          gentlemen, I am drunk. This is my ancient; this is my right hand, and this   95
          is my left. I am not drunk now. I can stand well enough, and I speak well
          enough.

ALL: Excellent well!

CASSIO: Why, very well then. You must not think then that I am drunk.

                                                                    Exit.

MONTANO: To th' platform, masters. Come, let's set the watch.   100

IAGO: You see this fellow that is gone before.
          He's a soldier fit to stand by Caesar
          And give direction; and do but see his vice.
          'Tis to his virtue a just equinox,°
          The one as long as th' other. 'Tis pity of him.   105
          I fear the trust Othello puts him in,
          On some odd time of his infirmity,
          Will shake this island.

MONTANO: But is he often thus?

IAGO: 'Tis evermore his prologue to his sleep:

---

77. **lown:** Rascal. **85. does . . . things:** I.e., behaves in this fashion. **104. just equi-
nox:** Exact equivalent.

He'll watch the horologe a double set°   110
If drink rock not his cradle.
MONTANO: It were well
The general were put in mind of it.
Perhaps he sees it not, or his good nature
Prizes the virtue that appears in Cassio
And looks not on his evils. Is not this true?   115

Enter Roderigo.

IAGO [*aside to him*]: How now, Roderigo?
    I pray you, after the lieutenant, go!   *Exit Roderigo.*
MONTANO: And 'tis great pity that the noble Moor
    Should hazard such a place as his own second
    With one of an ingraft° infirmity.   120
    It were an honest action to say
    So to the Moor.
IAGO: Not I, for this fair island!
    I do love Cassio well and would do much
    To cure him of this evil.
          (*Within.*) Help! help!
                              But hark! What noise?   125

Enter Cassio, driving in Roderigo.

CASSIO: Zounds, you rogue! you rascal!
MONTANO: What's the matter, lieutenant?
CASSIO: A knave to teach me my duty?
    I'll beat the knave into a twiggen° bottle.
RODERIGO: Beat me?
CASSIO: Dost thou prate, rogue? [*Strikes him.*]
MONTANO: Nay, good lieutenant!
                                                    [*Stays him.*]
    I pray you, sir, hold your hand.
CASSIO: Let me go, sir,   130
    Or I'll knock you o'er the mazzard.°
MONTANO: Come, come, you're drunk!
CASSIO: Drunk?

They fight.

IAGO [*aside to Roderigo*]: Away, I say! Go out and cry a mutiny!
                                                    Exit Roderigo.
    Nay, good lieutenant. God's will, gentlemen!

---

110. **watch . . . set:** Stay awake twice around the clock (horologe). 120. **ingraft:** I.e., in-
grained. 128. **twiggen:** Wicker-covered. 131. **mazzard:** Head.

Help, ho! — lieutenant — sir — Montano — sir —   135
Help, masters! — Here's a goodly watch indeed!

A bell rung.

Who's that which rings the bell? Diablo,° ho!
The town will rise.° God's will, lieutenant, hold!
You'll be shamed for ever.

Enter Othello and Gentlemen with weapons.

OTHELLO: What is the matter here?
MONTANO: Zounds, I bleed still. I am hurt to th' death.   140
    He dies!
OTHELLO: Hold for your lives!
IAGO: Hold, hold! Lieutenant — sir — Montano — gentlemen!
    Have you forgot all sense of place and duty?
    Hold! The general speaks to you. Hold, for shame!   145
OTHELLO: Why, how now ho? From whence ariseth this?
    Are we turned Turks, and to ourselves do that
    Which heaven hath forbid the Ottomites?
    For Christian shame put by this barbarous brawl!
    He that stirs next to carve for° his own rage   150
    Holds his soul light;° he dies upon his motion.°
    Silence that dreadful bell! It frights the isle
    From her propriety.° What is the matter, masters?
    Honest Iago, that looks dead with grieving,
    Speak. Who began this? On thy love, I charge thee.   155
IAGO: I do not know. Friends all, but now, even now,
    In quarter,° and in terms like bride and groom
    Devesting them for bed; and then, but now —
    As if some planet had unwitted men —
    Swords out, and tilting one at other's breast   160
    In opposition bloody. I cannot speak
    Any beginning to this peevish odds,°
    And would in action glorious I had lost
    Those legs that brought me to a part of it!
OTHELLO: How comes it, Michael, you are thus forgot?°   165
CASSIO: I pray you pardon me; I cannot speak.
OTHELLO: Worthy Montano, you were wont to be civil;
    The gravity and stillness of your youth
    The world hath noted, and your name is great

---

137. Diablo: The devil.   **138. rise:** Grow riotous.   **150. carve for:** Indulge.   **151. Holds . . .
light:** Values his life lightly;   **upon his motion:** If he moves.   **153. propriety:** Proper self.
157. quarter: Friendliness.   **162. peevish odds:** Childish quarrel.   **165. are thus forgot:** Have
forgotten yourself this way.

In mouths of wisest censure.° What's the matter   170
That you unlace° your reputation thus
And spend your rich opinion° for the name
Of a night-brawler? Give me answer to it.
MONTANO: Worthy Othello, I am hurt to danger.
    Your officer, Iago, can inform you,   175
    While I spare speech, which something now offends° me,
    Of all that I do know; nor know I aught
    By me that's said or done amiss this night,
    Unless self-charity be sometimes a vice,
    And to defend ourselves it be a sin   180
    When violence assails us.
OTHELLO: Now, by heaven,
    My blood° begins my safer guides° to rule,
    And passion, having my best judgment collied,°
    Assays° to lead the way. If I once stir
    Or do but lift this arm, the best of you   185
    Shall sink in my rebuke. Give me to know
    How this foul rout began, who set it on;
    And he that is approved in° this offense,
    Though he had twinned with me, both at a birth,
    Shall lose me. What! in a town of war,   190
    Yet wild, the people's hearts brimful of fear,
    To manage° private and domestic quarrel?
    In night, and on the court and guard of safety?
    'Tis monstrous. Iago, who began't?
MONTANO: If partially affined, or leagued in office,°   195
    Thou dost deliver more or less than truth,
    Thou art no soldier.
IAGO: Touch me not so near.
    I had rather have this tongue cut from my mouth
    Than it should do offense to Michael Cassio;
    Yet I persuade myself, to speak the truth   200
    Shall nothing wrong him. This it is, general.
    Montano and myself being in speech,
    There comes a fellow crying out for help,
    And Cassio following him with determined sword
    To execute° upon him. Sir, this gentleman   205
    Steps in to Cassio and entreats his pause.°

---

170. **censure:** Judgment. 171. **unlace:** Undo. 172. **rich opinion:** High reputation. **176.**
offends: Pains. **182. blood:** Passion; **safer guides:** Reason. **183. collied:** Darkened. **184.**
Assays: Tries. **188. approved in:** Proved guilty of. **192. manage:** Carry on. **195. par-**
tially . . . office: Prejudiced by comradeship or official relations. **205. execute:** Work his
will. **206. his pause:** Him to stop.

Myself the crying fellow did pursue,
Lest by his clamor—as it so fell out—
The town might fall in fright. He, swift of foot,
Outran my purpose; and I returned the rather°   210
For that I heard the clink and fall of swords,
And Cassio high in oath;° which till to-night
I ne'er might say before. When I came back—
For this was brief—I found them close together
At blow and thrust, even as again they were   215
When you yourself did part them.
More of this matter cannot I report;
But men are men; the best sometimes forget.°
Though Cassio did some little wrong to him,
As men in rage strike those that wish them best,   220
Yet surely Cassio I believe received
From him that fled some strange indignity,
Which patience could not pass.°

OTHELLO: I know, Iago,
Thy honesty and love doth mince this matter,
Making it light to Cassio. Cassio, I love thee;   225
But never more be officer of mine.

Enter Desdemona, attended.

Look if my gentle love be not raised up!
I'll make thee an example.

DESDEMONA: What's the matter?

OTHELLO: All's well now, sweeting; come away to bed.
[*To Montano.*]
Sir, for your hurts, myself will be your surgeon.   230
Lead him off.

[*Montano is led off.*]

Iago, look with care about the town
And silence those whom this vile brawl distracted.°
Come, Desdemona; 'tis the soldiers' life
To have their balmy slumbers waked with strife.   235

                                 Exit [with all but Iago and Cassio].

IAGO: What, are you hurt, lieutenant?

CASSIO: Ay, past all surgery.

IAGO: Marry, God forbid!

---

210. rather: Sooner.   **212. high in oath:** Cursing.   **218. forget:** Forget themselves.   **223. pass:** Pass over, ignore.   **233. distracted:** Excited.

CASSIO: Reputation, reputation, reputation! O, I have lost my reputation! I have
lost the immortal part of myself, and what remains is bestial. My reputa- 240
tion, Iago, my reputation!

IAGO: As I am an honest man, I thought you had received some bodily wound.
There is more sense in that than in reputation. Reputation is an idle and
most false imposition; oft got without merit and lost without deserving. You
have lost no reputation at all unless you repute yourself such a loser. What, 245
man! there are ways to recover° the general again. You are but now cast in
his mood°—a punishment more in policy than in malice, even so as one
would beat his offenseless dog to affright an imperious lion. Sue to him
again, and he's yours.

CASSIO: I will rather sue to be despised than to deceive so good a commander 250
with so slight, so drunken, and so indiscreet an officer. Drunk! and speak
parrot!° and squabble! swagger! swear! and discourse fustian° with one's
own shadow! O thou invisible spirit of wine, if thou hast no name to be
known by, let us call thee devil!

IAGO: What was he that you followed with your sword? What had he done to 255
you?

CASSIO: I know not.

IAGO: Is't possible?

CASSIO: I remember a mass of things, but nothing distinctly; a quarrel, but nothing wherefore. O God, that men should put an enemy in their mouths to 260
steal away their brains! that we should with joy, pleasance, revel, and
applause° transform ourselves into beasts!

IAGO: Why, but you are now well enough. How came you thus recovered?

CASSIO: It hath pleased the devil drunkenness to give place to the devil wrath.
One unperfectness shows me another, to make me frankly despise my- 265
self.

IAGO: Come, you are too severe a moraler.° As the time, the place, and the condition of this country stands, I could heartily wish this had not so befall'n;
but since it is as it is, mend it for your own good.

CASSIO: I will ask him for my place again: he shall tell me I am a drunkard! Had 270
I as many mouths as Hydra,° such an answer would stop them all. To be
now a sensible man, by and by a fool, and presently a beast! O strange!
Every inordinate° cup is unblest, and the ingredient° is a devil.

IAGO: Come, come, good wine is a good familiar creature if it be well used.
Exclaim no more against it. And, good lieutenant, I think you think I love 275
you.

---

246. recover: Regain favor with. **246–47. in his mood:** Dismissed because of his anger.
252. parrot: Meaningless phrases; **fustian:** Bombastic nonsense. **262. applause:** Desire
to please. **267. moraler:** Moralizer. **271. Hydra:** Monster with many heads. **273. inor-
dinate:** Excessive; **ingredient:** Contents.

CASSIO: I have well approved it,° sir. I drunk!

IAGO: You or any man living may be drunk at some time, man. I'll tell you what
you shall do. Our general's wife is now the general. I may say so in this
respect, for that he hath devoted and given up himself to the contempla- 280
tion, mark, and denotement of her parts and graces. Confess yourself freely
to her; importune her help to put you in your place again. She is of so free,°
so kind, so apt, so blessed a disposition she holds it a vice in her goodness
not to do more than she is requested. This broken joint between you and
her husband entreat her to splinter;° and my fortunes against any lay° 285
worth naming, this crack of your love shall grow stronger than it was
before.

CASSIO: You advise me well.

IAGO: I protest, in the sincerity of love and honest kindness.

CASSIO: I think it freely; and betimes in the morning will I beseech the virtuous 290
Desdemona to undertake for me. I am desperate of my fortunes if they
check me here.°

IAGO: You are in the right. Good night, lieutenant; I must to the watch.

CASSIO: Good night, honest Iago.   *Exit Cassio.*

IAGO: And what's he then that says I play the villain,   295
When this advice is free I give and honest,
Probal° to thinking, and indeed the course
To win the Moor again? For 'tis most easy
Th' inclining Desdemona to subdue°
In any honest suit; she's framed as fruitful   300
As the free elements. And then for her
To win the Moor — were't to renounce his baptism,
All seals and symbols of redeemèd sin —
His soul is so enfettered to her love
That she may make, unmake, do what she list,   305
Even as her appetite shall play the god
With his weak function.° How am I then a villain
To counsel Cassio to this parallel° course,
Directly to his good? Divinity° of hell!
When devils will the blackest sins put on,°   310
They do suggest at first with heavenly shows,
As I do now. For whiles this honest fool
Plies Desdemona to repair his fortunes,
And she for him pleads strongly to the Moor,
I'll pour this pestilence into his ear,   315

---

277. **approved it:** Proved it by experience. 282. **free:** Bounteous. 285. **splinter:** Bind up
with splints; **lay:** Wager. 291–92. **I . . . here:** I despair of my future if my career is stopped
short here. 297. **Probal:** Probable. 299. **subdue:** Persuade. 307. **function:** Intelligence
(weakened by his fondness for her). 308. **parallel:** Corresponding. 309. **Divinity:** Theology. 310. **put on:** Incite.

That she repeals him° for her body's lust;
And by how much she strives to do him good,
She shall undo her credit with the Moor.
So will I turn her virtue into pitch,
And out of her own goodness make the net   320
That shall enmesh them all.

Enter Roderigo.

                     How, now, Roderigo?
RODERIGO: I do follow here in the chase, not like a hound that hunts, but one
    that fills up the cry.° My money is almost spent; I have been to-night
    exceedingly well cudgelled; and I think the issue will be—I shall have so
    much experience for my pains; and so, with no money at all, and a little 325
    more wit, return again to Venice.
IAGO: How poor are they that have not patience!
    What wound did ever heal but by degrees?
    Thou know'st we work by wit, and not by witchcraft;
    And wit depends on dilatory time.   330
    Does't not go well? Cassio hath beaten thee,
    And thou by that small hurt hast cashiered Cassio.°
    Though other things grow fair against the sun,
    Yet fruits that blossom first will first be ripe.°
    Content thyself awhile. By the mass, 'tis morning!   335
    Pleasure and action make the hours seem short.
    Retire thee; go where thou art billeted.
    Away, I say! Thou shalt know more hereafter.
    Nay, get thee gone!   *Exit Roderigo.*
               Two things are to be done:
    My wife must move for Cassio to her mistress;   340
    I'll set her on;
    Myself the while to draw the Moor apart
    And bring him jump° when he may Cassio find
    Soliciting his wife. Ay, that's the way!
    Dull no device by coldness and delay.   *Exit.* 345

ACT III / Scene I

Before the chamber of Othello and Desdemona.
Enter Cassio, with Musicians and the Clown.

CASSIO: Masters, play here, I will content° your pains:

---

316. **repeals him:** Seeks his recall. 323. **cry:** Pack. 332. **cashiered Cassio:** Maneuvered
Cassio's discharge. 333–34. **Though . . . ripe:** Although fruit ripens in the sun, yet the
first fruit to ripen will come from the earliest blossoms. 343. **jump:** At the exact moment.
ACT III, SCENE I. 1. **content:** Reward.

Something that's brief; and bid "Good morrow, general."

[*They play.*]

CLOWN: Why, masters, ha' your instruments been in Naples,° that they speak i'
     th' nose thus?

MUSICIAN: How, sir, how?   5

CLOWN: Are these, I pray you, called wind instruments?

MUSICIAN: Ay, marry, are they, sir.

CLOWN: O, thereby hangs a tail.

MUSICIAN: Whereby hangs a tale, sir?

CLOWN: Marry, sir, by many a wind instrument that I know. But, masters, here's   10
     money for you; and the general so likes your music that he desires you, for
     love's sake, to make no more noise with it.

MUSICIAN: Well, sir, we will not.

CLOWN: If you have any music that may not be heard, to't again: but, as they
     say, to hear music the general does not greatly care.   15

MUSICIAN: We have none such, sir.

CLOWN: Then put up your pipes in your bag, for I'll away. Go, vanish into air,
     away!   *Exit Musician [with his fellows].*

CASSIO: Dost thou hear, my honest friend?

CLOWN: No, I hear not your honest friend. I hear you.   20

CASSIO: Prithee keep up thy quillets.° There's a poor piece of gold for thee. If the
     gentlewoman that attends the general's wife be stirring, tell her there's one
     Cassio entreats her a little favor of speech. Wilt thou do this?

CLOWN: She is stirring sir. If she will stir hither, I shall seem to notify unto
     her.   25

CASSIO: [Do, good my friend.]   *Exit Clown.*

Enter Iago.

                              In happy time,° Iago.

IAGO: You have not been abed then?

CASSIO: Why, no; the day had broke
     Before we parted. I have made bold, Iago,
     To send in to your wife: my suit to her   30
     Is that she will to virtuous Desdemona
     Procure me some access.

IAGO: I'll send her to you presently;
     And I'll devise a mean to draw the Moor
     Out of the way, that your converse and business
     May be more free.   35

CASSIO: I humbly thank you for't.   *Exit [Iago].*

---

3. Naples: (Notorious for its association with venereal disease). **21. quillets:** Quips.
26. In happy time: Well met.

                           I never knew
A Florentine° more kind and honest.

Enter Emilia.

EMILIA: Good morrow, good lieutenant. I am sorry
    For your displeasure:° but all will sure be well.
    The general and his wife are talking of it,   40
    And she speaks for you stoutly. The Moor replied
    That he you hurt is of great fame in Cyprus
    And great affinity,° and that in wholesome wisdom
    He might not but refuse you; but he protests he loves you,
    And needs no other suitor but his likings   45
    [To take the safest occasion° by the front°]
    To bring you in again.
CASSIO: Yet I beseech you,
    If you think fit, or that it may be done,
    Give me advantage of some brief discourse
    With Desdemona alone.
EMILIA: Pray you come in.   50
    I will bestow you where you shall have time
    To speak your bosom° freely.
CASSIO: I am much bound to you.   *Exeunt.*

Scene II

The castle.

Enter Othello, Iago, and Gentlemen.

OTHELLO: These letters give, Iago, to the pilot
    And by him do my duties° to the Senate.
    That done, I will be walking on the works;°
    Repair there to me.
IAGO: Well, my good lord, I'll do't.
OTHELLO: This fortification, gentlemen, shall we see't?   5
GENTLEMEN: We'll wait upon your lordship.   *Exeunt.*

Scene III

The castle grounds.

Enter Desdemona, Cassio, and Emilia.

---

37. **Florentine:** I.e., even a Florentine (like Cassio; Iago was a Venetian).   39. **displeasure:** Fall
from favor.   43. **affinity:** Family connections.   46. **occasion:** Opportunity; **front:** Forelock.
52. **your bosom:** Your inmost thoughts.   SCENE II.   2. **do my duties:** Convey my respects.
3. **works:** Fortifications.

DESDEMONA: Be thou assured, good Cassio, I will do
    All my abilities in thy behalf.
EMILIA: Good madam, do. I warrant it grieves my husband
    As if the cause were his.
DESDEMONA: O, that's an honest fellow. Do not doubt, Cassio,   5
    But I will have my lord and you again
    As friendly as you were.
CASSIO: Bounteous madam,
    Whatever shall become of Michael Cassio,
    He's never anything but your true servant.
DESDEMONA: I know't; I thank you. You do love my lord;   10
    You have known him long; and be you well assured
    He shall in strangeness° stand no farther off
    Than in a politic distance.°
CASSIO: Ay, but, lady,
    That policy may either last so long,
    Or feed upon such nice and waterish diet,°   15
    Or breed itself so out of circumstance,
    That, I being absent, and my place supplied,
    My general will forget my love and service.
DESDEMONA: Do not doubt° that; before Emilia here
    I give thee warrant of thy place. Assure thee,   20
    If I do vow a friendship, I'll perform it
    To the last article. My lord shall never rest;
    I'll watch him tame° and talk him out of patience;
    His bed shall seem a school, his board a shrift;°
    I'll intermingle everything he does   25
    With Cassio's suit. Therefore be merry, Cassio,
    For thy solicitor shall rather die
    Than give thy cause away.

Enter Othello and Iago [at a distance].

EMILIA: Madam, here comes my lord.
CASSIO: Madam, I'll take my leave.   30
DESDEMONA: Why, stay, and hear me speak.
CASSIO: Madam, not now: I am very ill at ease,
    Unfit for mine own purposes.
DESDEMONA: Well, do your discretion.   *Exit Cassio.*
IAGO: Ha! I like not that.
OTHELLO: What dost thou say?   35
IAGO: Nothing, my lord; or if—I know not what.

SCENE III.   **12. strangeness:** Aloofness.   **13. Than . . . distance:** Than wise policy requires.
15. Or . . . diet: Or be continued for such slight reasons.   **19. doubt:** Fear.   **23. watch him
tame:** Keep him awake until he gives in.   **24. board a shrift:** Dining table confessional.

OTHELLO: Was not that Cassio parted from my wife?
IAGO: Cassio, my lord? No, sure, I cannot think it,
    That he would steal away so guilty-like,
    Seeing your coming.
OTHELLO: I do believe 'twas he.   40
DESDEMONA: How now, my lord?
    I have been talking with a suitor here,
    A man that languishes in your displeasure.
OTHELLO: What is't you mean?
DESDEMONA: Why, your lieutenant, Cassio. Good my lord,   45
    If I have any grace or power to move you,
    His present° reconciliation take;
    For if he be not one that truly loves you,
    That errs in ignorance, and not in cunning,°
    I have no judgment in an honest face,   50
    I prithee call him back.
OTHELLO: Went he hence now?
DESDEMONA: Yes, faith; so humbled
    That he hath left part of his grief with me
    To suffer with him. Good love, call him back.
OTHELLO: Not now, sweet Desdemon; some other time.   55
DESDEMONA: But shall't be shortly?
OTHELLO: The sooner, sweet, for you.
DESDEMONA: Shall't be to-night at supper?
OTHELLO: No, not to-night.
DESDEMONA: To-morrow dinner then?
OTHELLO: I shall not dine at home;
    I meet the captains at the citadel.
DESDEMONA: Why then, to-morrow night, or Tuesday morn,   60
    On Tuesday noon or night, or Wednesday morn.
    I prithee name the time, but let it not
    Exceed three days. I' faith, he's penitent;
    And yet his trespass, in our common reason
    (Save that, they say, the wars must make examples   65
    Out of their best), is not almost° a fault
    T' incur a private check.° When shall he come?
    Tell me, Othello. I wonder in my soul
    What you could ask me that I should deny
    Or stand so mamm'ring on.° What? Michael Cassio,   70
    That came a-wooing with you, and so many a time,
    When I have spoke of you dispraisingly,
    Hath ta'en your part—to have so much to do

---

47. present: Immediate. **49. in cunning:** Knowingly. **66. not almost:** Hardly. **67. a private check:** Even a private reprimand. **70. mamm'ring on:** Hesitating about.

To bring him in?° By'r Lady, I could do much—

OTHELLO: Prithee no more. Let him come when he will!   75
    I will deny thee nothing.

DESDEMONA: Why, this is not a boon;
    'Tis as I should entreat you wear your gloves,
    Or feed on nourishing dishes, or keep you warm,
    Or sue to you to do a peculiar profit
    To your own person. Nay, when I have a suit   80
    Wherein I mean to touch your love indeed,
    It shall be full of poise and difficult weight,
    And fearful° to be granted.

OTHELLO: I will deny thee nothing!
    Whereon I do beseech thee grant me this,
    To leave me but a little to myself.   85

DESDEMONA: Shall I deny you? No. Farewell, my lord.

OTHELLO: Farewell, my Desdemon: I'll come to thee straight.°

DESDEMONA: Emilia, come.—Be as your fancies teach you;°
    Whate'er you be, I am obedient.   *Exit [with Emilia].*

OTHELLO: Excellent wretch!° Perdition catch my soul   90
    But I do love thee! and when I love thee not,
    Chaos is come again.

IAGO: My noble lord—

OTHELLO: What dost thou say, Iago?

IAGO: Did Michael Cassio, when you wooed my lady,
    Know of your love?   95

OTHELLO: He did, from first to last. Why dost thou ask?

IAGO: But for a satisfaction of my thought;
    No further harm.

OTHELLO: Why of thy thought, Iago?

IAGO: I did not think he had been acquainted with her.

OTHELLO: O, yes, and went between us° very oft.   100

IAGO: Indeed?

OTHELLO: Indeed? Ay, indeed! Discern'st thou aught in that?
    Is he not honest?

IAGO: Honest, my lord?

OTHELLO: Honest. Ay, honest.

IAGO: My lord, for aught I know.

OTHELLO: What dost thou think?

IAGO: Think, my lord?

OTHELLO: "Think, my lord?"   105
    By heaven, he echoes me,

---

74. **To bring him in:** To restore him to favor. 83. **fearful:** Dangerous. 87. **straight:** Straight-way. 88. **Be . . . you:** Please yourself. 90. **wretch:** (A term of endearment). 100. **went . . . us:** (I.e., as messenger).

As if there were some monster in his thought
Too hideous to be shown. Thou dost mean something:
I heard thee say even now, thou lik'st not that,
When Cassio left my wife. What didst not like?   110
And when I told thee he was of my counsel
In my whole course of wooing, thou cried'st "Indeed?"
And didst contract and purse thy brow together,
As if thou then hadst shut up in thy brain
Some horrible conceit.° If thou dost love me,   115
Show me thy thought

IAGO: My lord, you know I love you.

OTHELLO: I think thou dost;
And, for° I know thou'rt full of love and honesty
And weigh'st thy words before thou giv'st them breath,
Therefore these stops° of thine fright me the more;   120
For such things in a false disloyal knave
Are tricks of custom;° but in a man that's just
They are close dilations, working from the heart
That passion cannot rule.°

IAGO: For Michael Cassio,
I dare be sworn I think that he is honest.   125

OTHELLO: I think so too.

IAGO: Men should be what they seem;
Or those that be not, would they might seem none!°

OTHELLO: Certain, men should be what they seem.

IAGO: Why then, I think Cassio's an honest man.

OTHELLO: Nay, yet there's more in this.   130
I prithee speak to me as to thy thinkings,
As thou dost ruminate, and give thy worst of thoughts
The worst of words.

IAGO: Good my lord, pardon me:
Though I am bound to every act of duty,
I am not bound to that all slaves are free to.°   135
Utter my thoughts? Why, say they are vile and false,
As where's that palace whereinto foul things
Sometimes intrude not? Who has a breast so pure
But some uncleanly apprehensions
Keep leets and law days,° and in Sessions sit   140
With meditations lawful?

---

115. conceit: Fancy. **118. for:** Because. **120. stops:** Pauses. **122. tricks of custom:** Customary, or usual, tricks. **123–24. close dilations . . . rule:** Secret emotions which well up and cannot be restrained. **127. seem none:** I.e., not pretend to be men when they are really monsters. **135. bound . . . free to:** Bound to tell that which even slaves are allowed to keep to themselves. **140. leets and law days:** Days when the courts sit.

OTHELLO: Thou dost conspire against thy friend, Iago,
    If thou but think'st him wronged, and mak'st his ear
    A stranger to thy thoughts.
IAGO: I do beseech you—
    Though I perchance am vicious° in my guess   145
    (As I confess it is my nature's plague
    To spy into abuses, and oft my jealousy°
    Shapes faults that are not), that your wisdom yet
    From one that so imperfectly conjects°
    Would take no notice, nor build yourself a trouble   150
    Out of his scattering° and unsure observance.
    It were not for your quiet nor your good,
    Nor for my manhood, honesty, and wisdom,
    To let you know my thoughts.
OTHELLO: What dost thou mean?
IAGO: Good name in man and woman, dear my lord,   155
    Is the immediate° jewel of their souls.
    Who steals my purse steals trash; 'tis something, nothing;
    'Twas mine, 'tis his, and has been slave to thousands;
    But he that filches from me my good name
    Robs me of that which not enriches him   160
    And makes me poor indeed.
OTHELLO: By heaven, I'll know thy thoughts!
IAGO: You cannot, if° my heart were in your hand;
    Nor shall not whilst 'tis in my custody.
OTHELLO: Ha!
IAGO: O, beware, my lord, of jealousy!   165
    It is the green-eyed monster, which doth mock°
    The meat it feeds on. That cuckold lives in bliss
    Who, certain of his fate, loves not his wronger;
    But O, what damnèd minutes tells he o'er
    Who dotes, yet doubts—suspects, yet strongly loves!   170
OTHELLO: O misery!
IAGO: Poor and content is rich, and rich enough;
    But riches fineless° is as poor as winter
    To him that ever fears he shall be poor.
    Good God, the souls of all my tribe defend   175
    From jealousy!
OTHELLO: Why, why is this?
    Think'st thou I'ld make a life of jealousy,
    To follow still the changes of the moon

---

145. **vicious:** Wrong. 147. **jealousy:** Suspicion. 149. **conjects:** Conjectures. 151. **scattering:** Random. 156. **immediate:** Nearest the heart. 163. **if:** Even if. 166. **mock:** Play with, like a cat with a mouse. 173. **fineless:** Unlimited.

With fresh suspicions? No! To be once in doubt
Is once to be resolved. Exchange me for a goat   180
When I shall turn the business of my soul
To such exsufflicate and blown° surmises,
Matching this inference. 'Tis not to make me jealous
To say my wife is fair, feeds well, loves company,
Is free of speech, sings, plays, and dances well;   185
Where virtue is, these are more virtuous.
Nor from mine own weak merits will I draw
The smallest fear or doubt of her revolt,°
For she had eyes, and chose me. No, Iago;
I'll see before I doubt; when I doubt, prove;   190
And on the proof there is no more but this—
Away at once with love or jealousy!
IAGO: I am glad of this; for now I shall have reason
To show the love and duty that I bear you
With franker spirit. Therefore, as I am bound,   195
Receive it from me. I speak not yet of proof.
Look to your wife; observe her well with Cassio;
Wear your eyes thus, not jealous nor secure:°
I would not have your free and noble nature,
Out of self-bounty,° be abused. Look to't.   200
I know our country disposition well:
In Venice they do let God see the pranks
They dare not show their husbands; their best conscience
Is not to leave't undone, but keep't unknown.
OTHELLO: Dost thou say so?   205
IAGO: She did deceive her father, marrying you;
And when she seemed to shake and fear your looks,
She loved them most.
OTHELLO: And so she did.
IAGO: Why, go to then!
She that, so young, could give out such a seeming
To seel° her father's eyes up close as oak°—   210
He thought 'twas witchcraft—but I am much to blame.
I humbly do beseech you of your pardon
For too much loving you.
OTHELLO: I am bound to thee for ever.
IAGO: I see this hath a little dashed your spirits.
OTHELLO: Not a jot, not a jot.

---

182. exsufflicate and blown: Spat out and flyblown. **188. revolt:** Unfaithfulness. **198 secure:** Overconfident. **200. self-bounty:** Natural goodness. **210. seel:** Close (a term from falconry); **close as oak:** Tight as oak grain.

IAGO: I' faith, I fear it has.   215
    I hope you will consider what is spoke
    Comes from my love. But I do see y' are moved.
    I am to pray you not to strain my speech
    To grosser issues° nor to larger reach
    Than to suspicion.   220
OTHELLO: I will not.
IAGO: Should you do so, my lord,
    My speech should fall into such vile success°
    As my thoughts aim not at. Cassio's my worthy friend—
    My lord, I see y' are moved.
OTHELLO: No, not much moved:
    I do not think but Desdemona's honest.°   225
IAGO: Long live she so! and long live you to think so!
OTHELLO: And yet, how nature erring from itself—
IAGO: Ay, there's the point! as (to be bold with you)
    Not to affect° many proposèd matches
    Of her own clime, complexion, and degree,°   230
    Whereto we see in all things nature tends—
    Foh! one may smell in such a will most rank,°
    Foul disproportion,° thoughts unnatural—
    But pardon me—I do not in position°
    Distinctly speak of her; though I may fear   235
    Her will, recoiling° to her better judgment,
    May fall to match° you with her country forms,
    And happily° repent.
OTHELLO: Farewell, farewell!
    If more thou dost perceive, let me know more.
    Set on thy wife to observe. Leave me, Iago.   240
IAGO: My lord, I take my leave.   *[Going.]*
OTHELLO: Why did I marry? This honest creature doubtless
    Sees and knows more, much more, than he unfolds.
IAGO *[returns]*: My lord, I would I might entreat your honor
    To scan this thing no further: leave it to time.   245
    Although 'tis fit that Cassio have his place,
    For sure he fills it up with great ability,
    Yet, if you please to hold off a while,
    You shall by that perceive him and his means.
    Note if your lady strain his entertainment°   250

---

219. To grosser issues: To mean something more monstrous. **222. vile success:** Evil outcome. **225. honest:** Chaste. **229. affect:** Prefer. **230. clime . . . degree:** Country, color,
and rank. **232. will most rank:** Desire most lustful. **233. disproportion:** Abnormality.
234. position: Definite assertion. **236. recoiling:** Reverting. **237. fall to match:** Happen
to compare. **238. happily:** Haply, perhaps. **250. strain his entertainment:** Urge his recall.

With any strong or vehement importunity;
Much will be seen in that. In the mean time
Let me be thought too busy° in my fears
(As worthy cause I have to fear I am)
And hold her free,° I do beseech your honor.   255
OTHELLO: Fear not my government.°
IAGO: I once more take my leave.   *Exit.*
OTHELLO: This fellow 's of exceeding honesty,
And knows all qualities,° with a learnèd spirit
Of° human dealings. If I do prove her haggard,°   260
Though that her jesses° were my dear heartstrings,
I'd whistle her off and let her down the wind
To prey at fortune.° Haply, for I am black
And have not those soft parts of conversation°
That chamberers° have, or for I am declined   265
Into the vale of years—yet that's not much—
She's gone. I am abused, and my relief
Must be to loathe her. O curse of marriage,
That we can call these delicate creatures ours,
And not their appetites! I had rather be a toad   270
And live upon the vapor of a dungeon
Than keep a corner in the thing I love
For others' uses. Yet 'tis the plague of great ones;°
Prerogatived° are they less than the base.
'Tis destiny unshunnable, like death.   275
Even then this forkèd plague° is fated to us
When we do quicken.° Look where she comes.

Enter Desdemona and Emilia.

If she be false, O, then heaven mocks itself!
I'll not believe't.
DESDEMONA: How now, my dear Othello?
Your dinner, and the generous° islanders   280
By you invited, do attend your presence.
OTHELLO: I am to blame.
DESDEMONA: Why do you speak so faintly?
Are you not well?

---

253. **busy:** Meddlesome.   255. **hold her free:** Consider her guiltless.   256. **government:** Self-control.   259. **qualities:** Natures.   259–60. **learnèd spirit Of:** Mind informed about.   260. **haggard:** A wild hawk.   261. **jesses:** Thongs for controlling a hawk.   262–63. **whistle . . . fortune:** Turn her out and let her take care of herself.   264. **soft . . . conversation:** Ingratiating manners.   265. **chamberers:** Courtiers.   273. **great ones:** Prominent men.   274. **Prerogatived:** Privileged.   276. **forkèd plague:** I.e., horns of a cuckold.   277. **do quicken:** Are born.   280. **generous:** Noble.

OTHELLO: I have a pain upon my forehead, here.

DESDEMONA: Faith, that's with watching;° 'twill away again.   285
    Let me but bind it hard, within this hour
    It will be well.

OTHELLO: Your napkin° is too little;

[*He pushes the handkerchief from him, and it falls unnoticed.*]

    Let it° alone. Come, I'll go in with you.

DESDEMONA: I am very sorry that you are not well.   *Exit* [*with Othello*].

EMILIA: I am glad I have found this napkin;   290
    This was her first remembrance from the Moor,
    My wayward husband hath a hundred times
    Wooed me to steal it; but she so loves the token
    (For he conjured her she should ever keep it)
    That she reserves it evermore about her   295
    To kiss and talk to. I'll have the work ta'en out°
    And give't Iago.
    What he will do with it heaven knows, not I;
    I nothing but to please his fantasy.°

Enter Iago.

IAGO: How now? What do you here alone?   300

EMILIA: Do not you chide; I have a thing for you.

IAGO: A thing for me? It is a common° thing° —

EMILIA: Ha?

IAGO: To have a foolish wife.

EMILIA: O, is that all? What will you give me now   305
    For that same handkerchief?

IAGO: What handkerchief?

EMILIA: What handkerchief!
    Why, that the Moor first gave to Desdemona;
    That which so often you did bid me steal.

IAGO: Hast stol'n it from her?   310

EMILIA: No, faith; she let it drop by negligence,
    And to th' advantage,° I, being here, took't up.
    Look, here it is.

IAGO: A good wench! Give it me.

EMILIA: What will you do with't, that you have been so earnest
    To have me filch it?

IAGO: Why, what is that to you?   315

[*Snatches it.*]

---

285. watching: Working late. **287. napkin:** Handkerchief. **288. it:** I.e., his forehead.
296. work ta'en out: Pattern copied. **299. fantasy:** Whim. **302. common:** Available to
everyone; **thing:** Slang term for vagina. **312. to th' advantage:** Opportunely.

EMILIA: If it be not for some purpose of import,°
    Give't me again. Poor lady, she'll run mad
    When she shall lack it.
IAGO: Be not acknown on't;° I have use for it.
    Go, leave me.   *Exit Emilia.* 320
    I will in Cassio's lodgings lose this napkin
    And let him find it. Trifles light as air
    Are to the jealous confirmations strong
    As proofs of holy writ. This may do something.
    The Moor already changes with my poison: 325
    Dangerous conceits° are in their nature poisons,
    Which at the first are scarce found to distaste,°
    But with a little act° upon the blood
    Burn like the mines of sulphur.

Enter Othello.

                     I did say so.
    Look where he comes! Not poppy nor mandragora,°   330
    Nor all the drowsy syrups of the world,
    Shall ever med'cine thee to that sweet sleep
    Which thou owedst yesterday.
OTHELLO: Ha! ha! false to me?
IAGO: Why, how now, general? No more of that!
OTHELLO: Avaunt! be gone! Thou hast set me on the rack.   335
    I swear 'tis better to be much abused
    Than but to know't a little.
IAGO: How now, my lord?
OTHELLO: What sense had I of her stol'n hours of lust?
    I saw't not, thought it not, it harmed not me;
    I slept the next night well, fed well, was free° and merry;   340
    I found not Cassio's kisses on her lips
    He that is robbed, not wanting° what is stol'n,
    Let him not know't, and he's not robbed at all.
IAGO: I am sorry to hear this.
OTHELLO: I had been happy if the general camp,   345
    Pioneers° and all, had tasted her sweet body,
    So° I had nothing known. O, now for ever
    Farewell the tranquil mind! farewell content!
    Farewell the plumèd troop, and the big° wars
    That make ambition virtue! O, farewell!   350

---

316. **import:** Importance. 319. **Be...on't:** Do not acknowledge it. 326. **conceits:** Ideas.
327. **distaste:** Be distasteful. 328. **act:** Action. 330. **mandragora:** A sleep-inducing drug
made from mandrake roots. 340. **free:** Carefree. 342. **wanting:** Missing. 346. **Pioneers:**
Sappers, laborers. 347. **So:** So long as. 349. **big:** Mighty.

Farewell the neighing steed and the shrill trump,
The spirit-stirring drum, th' ear-piercing fife,
The royal banner, and all quality,
Pride, pomp, and circumstance° of glorious war!
And O you mortal engines° whose rude throats   355
Th' immortal Jove's dread clamors counterfeit,°
Farewell! Othello's occupation's gone!

IAGO: Is't possible, my lord?

OTHELLO: Villain, be sure thou prove my love a whore!
Be sure of it; give me the ocular proof;   360
Or, by the worth of mine eternal soul,
Thou hadst been better have been born a dog
Than answer my waked wrath!

IAGO: Is't come to this?

OTHELLO: Make me to see't; or at the least so prove it
That the probation° bear no hinge nor loop   365
To hang a doubt on—or woe upon thy life!

IAGO: My noble lord—

OTHELLO: If thou dost slander her and torture me,
Never pray more; abandon all remorse;°
On horror's head horrors accumulate;   370
Do deeds to make heaven weep, all earth amazed;
For nothing canst thou to damnation add
Greater than that.

IAGO: O grace! O heaven forgive me!
Are you a man? Have you a soul or sense?—
God b' wi' you! take mine office. O wretched fool,°   375
That lov'st to make thine honesty a vice!°
O monstrous world! Take note, take note, O world,
To be direct and honest is not safe.
I thank you for this profit;° and from hence°
I'll love no friend, sith love breeds such offense.   380

OTHELLO: Nay, stay. Thou shouldst be honest.

IAGO: I should be wise; for honesty's a fool
And loses that it works for.

OTHELLO: By the world,
I think my wife be honest, and think she is not;
I think that thou art just, and think thou art not.   385
I'll have some proof. Her name, that was as fresh
As Dian's° visage, is now begrimed and black

---

354. **circumstance:** Pageantry. 355. **mortal engines:** Deadly artillery. 356. **counterfeit:** Imitate. 365. **probation:** Proof. 369. **remorse:** Penitence, hope of salvation. 375. **O wretched fool:** (Iago addressing himself). 376. **make...vice:** Take honesty too far. 379. **profit:** Profitable lesson; **hence:** Henceforth. 387. **Dian:** Diana, goddess of the moon and of chastity.

As mine own face. If there be cords, or knives,
Poison, or fire, or suffocating streams,
I'll not endure it. Would I were satisfied!°   390
IAGO: I see, sir, you are eaten up with passion:
I do repent me that I put it to you.
You would be satisfied?
OTHELLO: Would? Nay, I will.
IAGO: And may; but how? how satisfied, my lord?
Would you, the supervisor,° grossly gape on?   395
Behold her topped?
OTHELLO: Death and damnation! O!
IAGO: It were a tedious difficulty, I think,
To bring them to that prospect. Damn them then,
If ever mortal eyes do see them bolster°
More than their own! What then? How then?   400
What shall I say? Where's satisfaction?
It is impossible you should see this,
Were they as prime° as goats, as hot as monkeys,
As salt° as wolves in pride,° and fools as gross
As ignorance made drunk. But yet, I say,   405
If imputation and strong circumstances
Which lead directly to the door of truth
Will give you satisfaction, you may have't.
OTHELLO: Give me a living reason she's disloyal.
IAGO: I do not like the office.   410
But sith I am ent'red in this cause so far,
Pricked° to't by foolish honesty and love,
I will go on. I lay with Cassio lately,
And being troubled with a raging tooth,
I could not sleep.   415
There are a kind of men so loose of soul
That in their sleeps will mutter their affairs.
One of this kind is Cassio.
In sleep I heard him say, "Sweet Desdemona,
Let us be wary, let us hide our loves!"   420
And then, sir, would he grip and wring my hand,
Cry "O sweet creature!" and then kiss me hard,
As if he plucked up kisses by the roots
That grew upon my lips; then laid his leg
Over my thigh, and sighed, and kissed, and then   425
Cried "Cursèd fate that gave thee to the Moor!"

---

390. satisfied: Completely informed. **395. supervisor:** Spectator. **399. bolster:** Lie together. **403. prime:** Lustful. **404. salt:** Lecherous; **pride:** Heat. **412. Pricked:** Spurred.

OTHELLO: O monstrous! monstrous!

IAGO: Nay, this was but his dream.

OTHELLO: But this denoted a foregone conclusion;°
    'Tis a shrewd doubt,° though it be but a dream.

IAGO: And this may help to thicken other proofs   430
    That do demonstrate thinly.

OTHELLO: I'll tear her all to pieces!

IAGO: Nay, but be wise. Yet we see nothing done;
    She may be honest yet. Tell me but this—
    Have you not sometimes seen a handkerchief
    Spotted with strawberries in your wife's hand?   435

OTHELLO: I gave her such a one; 'twas my first gift.

IAGO: I know not that; but such a handkerchief—
    I am sure it was your wife's—did I to-day
    See Cassio wipe his beard with.

OTHELLO: If it be that—

IAGO: If it be that, or any that was hers,   440
    It speaks against her with the other proofs.

OTHELLO: O, that the slave had forty thousand lives!
    One is too poor, too weak for my revenge.
    Now do I see 'tis true. Look here, Iago:
    All my fond love thus do I blow to heaven.   445
    'Tis gone.
    Arise, black vengeance, from the hollow hell!
    Yield up, O love, thy crown and hearted throne
    To tyrannous hate! Swell, bosom, with thy fraught,°
    For 'tis of aspics'° tongues!

IAGO: Yet be content.   450

OTHELLO: O, blood, blood, blood!

IAGO: Patience, I say. Your mind perhaps may change.

OTHELLO: Never, Iago. Like to the Pontic sea,°
    Whose icy current and compulsive course
    Ne'er feels retiring ebb, but keeps due on   455
    To the Propontic and the Hellespont,
    Even so my bloody thoughts, with violent pace,
    Shall ne'er look back, ne'er ebb to humble love,
    Till that a capable° and wide revenge
    Swallow them up.
    (*He kneels.*)   Now, by yond marble heaven,   460
    In the due reverence of a sacred vow

---

428. **foregone conclusion:** Previous experience.   429. **a shrewd doubt:** Cursedly suspicious.
449. **fraught:** Burden.   450. **aspics:** Deadly poisonous snakes.   453. **Pontic sea:** Black Sea.
459. **capable:** All-embracing.

I here engage my words.
IAGO: Do not rise yet.
(*Iago kneels.*)
    Witness, you ever-burning lights above,
    You elements that clip° us round about,
    Witness that here Iago doth give up   465
    The execution° of his wit,° hands, heart
    To wronged Othello's service! Let him command,
    And to obey shall be in me remorse,°
    What bloody business ever.°

[*They rise.*]

OTHELLO: I greet thy love,
    Not with vain thanks but with acceptance bounteous,   470
    And will upon the instant put thee to't.
    Within these three days let me hear thee say
    That Cassio's not alive.
IAGO: My friend is dead; 'tis done at your request.
    But let her live.   475
OTHELLO: Damn her, lewd minx!° O, damn her! damn her!
    Come, go with me apart. I will withdraw
    To furnish me with some swift means of death
    For the fair devil. Now art thou my lieutenant.
IAGO: I am your own forever.   *Exeunt.* 480

Scene IV

The environs of the castle.

Enter Desdemona, Emilia, and Clown.

DESDEMONA: Do you know, sirrah, where Lieutenant Cassio lies?°
CLOWN: I dare not say he lies anywhere.
DESDEMONA: Why, man?
CLOWN: He's a soldier, and for me to say a soldier lies is stabbing.
DESDEMONA: Go to. Where lodges he?   5
CLOWN: To tell you where he lodges is to tell you where I lie.
DESDEMONA: Can anything be made of this?
CLOWN: I know not where he lodges; and for me to devise a lodging, and say he
    lies here or he lies there, were to lie in mine own throat.
DESDEMONA: Can you enquire him out, and be edified by report?   10
CLOWN: I will catechize the world for him; that is, make questions, and by
    them answer.

---

464. clip: Encompass.   466. execution: Activities; wit: Mind.   468. remorse: Pity.
469. ever: Soever.   476. minx: Wanton.   SCENE IV.   1. lies: Lives, lodges.

DESDEMONA: Seek him, bid him come hither. Tell him I have moved° my lord on
    his behalf and hope all will be well.
CLOWN: To do this is within the compass of man's wit, and therefore I'll attempt   15
    the doing of it.   *Exit.*
DESDEMONA: Where should I lose that handkerchief, Emilia?
EMILIA: I know not, madam.
DESDEMONA: Believe me, I had rather have lost my purse
    Full of crusadoes;° and but my noble Moor   20
    Is true of mind, and made of no such baseness
    As jealous creatures are, it were enough
    To put him to ill thinking.
EMILIA: Is he not jealous?
DESDEMONA: Who? he? I think the sun where he was born
    Drew all such humors° from him.

Enter Othello.

EMILIA: Look where he comes.   25
DESDEMONA: I will not leave him now till Cassio
    Be called to him—How is't with you, my lord?
OTHELLO: Well, my good lady. [*Aside.*] O, hardness to dissemble!—
    How do you, Desdemona?
DESDEMONA: Well, my good lord.
OTHELLO: Give me your hand. This hand is moist, my lady.   30
DESDEMONA: It yet hath felt no age nor known no sorrow.
OTHELLO: This argues fruitfulness and liberal heart.
    Hot, hot, and moist. This hand of yours requires
    A sequester° from liberty, fasting and prayer,
    Much castigation, exercise devout;   35
    For here's a young and sweating devil here
    That commonly rebels. 'Tis a good hand,
    A frank one.
DESDEMONA: You may, indeed, say so;
    For 'twas that hand that gave away my heart.   40
OTHELLO: A liberal hand! The hearts of old gave hands;
    But our new heraldry° is hands, not hearts.
DESDEMONA: I cannot speak of this. Come now, your promise!
OTHELLO: What promise, chuck?
DESDEMONA: I have sent to bid Cassio come speak with you.   45
OTHELLO: I have a salt and sorry rheum° offends me.
    Lend me thy handkerchief.
DESDEMONA: Here, my lord.

---

13. moved: Made proposals to. **20. crusadoes:** Portuguese gold coins. **25. humors:** Inclinations. **34. sequester:** Removal. **42. heraldry:** Heraldic symbolism. **46. salt . . . rheum:**
Distressing head cold.

OTHELLO: That which I gave you.

DESDEMONA: I have it not about me.

OTHELLO: Not?

DESDEMONA: No, faith, my lord.

OTHELLO: That's a fault.

That handkerchief   50
Did an Egyptian° to my mother give.
She was a charmer,° and could almost read
The thoughts of people. She told her, while she kept it,
'Twould make her amiable° and subdue my father
Entirely to her love; but if she lost it   55
Or made a gift of it, my father's eye
Should hold her loathèd, and his spirits should hunt
After new fancies. She, dying, gave it me,
And bid me, when my fate would have me wive,
To give it her. I did so; and take heed on't;   60
Make it a darling like your precious eye.
To lose't or give't away were such perdition°
As nothing else could match.

DESDEMONA: Is't possible?

OTHELLO: 'Tis true. There's magic in the web of it.
A sibyl that had numb'red in the world   65
The sun to course two hundred compasses,°
In her prophetic fury sewed the work;
The worms were hallowed that did breed the silk;
And it was dyed in mummy° which the skillful
Conserved of maidens' hearts.

DESDEMONA: I' faith? Is't true?   70

OTHELLO: Most veritable. Therefore look to't well.

DESDEMONA: Then would to God that I had never seen't!

OTHELLO: Ha! Wherefore?

DESDEMONA: Why do you speak so startingly and rash?

OTHELLO: Is't lost? Is't gone? Speak, is it out o' th' way?   75

DESDEMONA: Heaven bless us!

OTHELLO: Say you?

DESDEMONA: It is not lost. But what an if it were?

OTHELLO: How?

DESDEMONA: I say it is not lost.

OTHELLO: Fetch't, let me see't!   80

DESDEMONA: Why, so I can, sir; but I will not now.
This is a trick to put° me from my suit:

---

51. **Egyptian:** Gypsy.   52. **charmer:** Sorceress.   54. **amiable:** Lovable.   62. **perdition:** Disaster.   66. **compasses:** Annual rounds.   69. **mummy:** A drug made from mummies.   82. **put:** Divert.

Pray you let Cassio be received again.

OTHELLO: Fetch me the handkerchief! My mind misgives.

DESDEMONA: Come, come!   85
  You'll never meet a more sufficient man.

OTHELLO: The handkerchief!

[DESDEMONA: I pray talk me of Cassio.

OTHELLO: The handkerchief!]

DESDEMONA: A man that all his time°
  Hath founded his good fortunes on your love,
  Shared dangers with you —   90

OTHELLO: The handkerchief!

DESDEMONA: I' faith, you are to blame.

OTHELLO: Zounds!   *Exit Othello.*

EMILIA: Is not this man jealous?

DESDEMONA: I ne'er saw this before.   95
  Sure there's some wonder in this handkerchief;
  I am most unhappy in the loss of it.

EMILIA: 'Tis not a year or two shows us a man.
  They are all but° stomachs, and we all but food;
  They eat us hungerly, and when they are full,   100
  They belch us.

Enter Iago and Cassio.

      Look you — Cassio and my husband!

IAGO: There is no other way; 'tis she must do't.
  And lo the happiness!° Go and importune her.

DESDEMONA: How now, good Cassio? What's the news with you?

CASSIO: Madam, my former suit. I do beseech you   105
  That by your virtuous means I may again
  Exist, and be a member of his love
  Whom I with all the office° of my heart
  Entirely honor. I would not be delayed.
  If my offense be of such mortal° kind   110
  That neither service past, nor present sorrows,
  Nor purposed merit in futurity,
  Can ransom me into his love again,
  But to know so must be my benefit.
  So shall I clothe me in a forced content,   115
  And shut myself up in° some other course,
  To fortune's alms.

---

88. all . . . time: During his whole career.   99. but: Nothing but.   103. happiness: Good luck.   108. office: Loyal service.   110. mortal: Fatal.   116. shut myself up in: Confine myself to.

DESDEMONA: Alas, thrice-gentle Cassio!
  My advocation° is not now in tune.
  My lord is not my lord; nor should I know him,
  Were he in favor° as in humor altered.   120
  So help me every spirit sanctified
  As I have spoken for you all my best
  And stood within the blank° of his displeasure
  For my free speech! You must a while be patient.
  What I can do I will; and more I will   125
  Than for myself I dare. Let that suffice you.
IAGO: Is my lord angry?
EMILIA: He went hence but now,
  And certainly in strange unquietness.
IAGO: Can he be angry? I have seen the cannon
  When it hath blown his ranks into the air   130
  And, like the devil, from his very arm
  Puffed his own brother—and is he angry?
  Something of moment then. I will go meet him.
  There's matter in't indeed if he be angry.
DESDEMONA: I prithee do so.   *Exit [Iago]*.
                    Something sure of state,°   135
  Either from Venice or some unhatched practice°
  Made demonstrable here in Cyprus to him,
  Hath puddled° his clear spirit; and in such cases
  Men's natures wrangle with inferior things,
  Though great ones are their object. 'Tis even so;   140
  For let our finger ache, and it endues°
  Our other, healthful members even to a sense
  Of pain. Nay, we must think men are not gods,
  Nor of them look for such observancy°
  As fits the bridal. Beshrew me much, Emilia,   145
  I was, unhandsome warrior° as I am,
  Arraigning his unkindness with my soul;°
  But now I find I had suborned the witness,
  And he's indicted falsely.
EMILIA: Pray heaven it be state matters, as you think,   150
  And no conception nor no jealous toy°
  Concerning you.
DESDEMONA: Alas the day! I never gave him cause.

---

118. **advocation:** Advocacy. 120. **favor:** Appearance. 123. **blank:** Bull's-eye of the target. 135. **state:** Public affairs. 136. **unhatched practice:** Budding plot. 138. **puddled:** Muddied. 141. **endues:** Brings. 144. **observancy:** Attentiveness. 146. **unhandsome warrior:** Inadequate soldier. 147. **Arraigning . . . soul:** Indicting his unkindness before the bar of my soul. 151. **toy:** Fancy.

EMILIA: But jealous souls will not be answered so;
    They are not ever jealous for the cause,   155
    But jealous for° they're jealous. 'Tis a monster
    Begot upon itself,° born on itself.
DESDEMONA: Heaven keep that monster from Othello's mind!
EMILIA: Lady, amen.
DESDEMONA: I will go seek him. Cassio, walk here about: 160
    If I do find him fit, I'll move your suit
    And seek to effect it to my uttermost.
CASSIO: I humbly thank your ladyship.

                      Exeunt Desdemona and Emilia.

Enter Bianca.

BIANCA: Save° you, friend Cassio!
CASSIO: What make you from home?
    How is't with you, my most fair Bianca?   165
    I' faith, sweet love, I was coming to your house.
BIANCA: And I was going to your lodging, Cassio.
    What, keep a week away? seven days and nights?
    Eightscore eight hours? and lovers' absent hours,
    More tedious than the dial° eightscore times?   170
    O weary reck'ning!
CASSIO: Pardon me, Bianca:
    I have this while with leaden thoughts been pressed;
    But I shall in a more continuate° time
    Strike off this score° of absence. Sweet Bianca,

[*Gives her Desdemona's handkerchief.*]

    Take me this work out.°
BIANCA: O Cassio, whence came this?   175
    This is some token from a newer friend.
    To the felt absence now I feel a cause.
    Is't come to this? Well, well.
CASSIO: Go to, woman!
    Throw your vile guesses in the devil's teeth,
    From whence you have them. You are jealous now   180
    That this is from some mistress, some remembrance.
    No, by my faith, Bianca.
BIANCA: Why, whose is it?
CASSIO: I know not, sweet; I found it in my chamber.

---

156. **for:** Because. 157. **Begot . . . itself:** Self-engendered. 164. **Save:** God save. 170. **dial:** Complete revolution of the clock (or sundial). 173. **continuate:** Uninterrupted. 174. **Strike . . . score:** Settle this account. 175. **Take . . . out:** Copy this embroidery for me.

I like the work° well; ere it be demanded,
As like enough it will, I'd have it copied.   185
Take it and do't, and leave me for this time.
BIANCA: Leave you? Wherefore?
CASSIO: I do attend here on the general
  And think it no addition,° nor my wish,
  To have him see me womaned.
BIANCA: Why, I pray you?   190
CASSIO: Not that I love you not.
BIANCA: But that you do not love me!
  I pray you bring me on the way a little,
  And say if I shall see you soon at night.
CASSIO: 'Tis but a little way that I can bring you,
  For I attend here; but I'll see you soon.   195
BIANCA: 'Tis very good. I must be circumstanced.°   *Exeunt.*

ACT IV / Scene I

The environs of the castle.

Enter Othello and Iago.

IAGO: Will you think so?
OTHELLO: Think so, Iago?
IAGO: What,
  To kiss in private?
OTHELLO: An unauthorized kiss.
IAGO: Or to be naked with her friend in bed
  An hour or more, not meaning any harm?
OTHELLO: Naked in bed, Iago, and not mean harm?   5
  It is hypocrisy against the devil.°
  They that mean virtuously, and yet do so,
  The devil their virtue tempts, and they tempt heaven.
IAGO: So° they do nothing, 'tis a venial slip.
  But if I give my wife a handkerchief—   10
OTHELLO: What then?
IAGO: Why, then 'tis hers, my lord; and being hers,
  She may, I think, bestow't on any man.
OTHELLO: She is protectress of her honor too;
  May she give that?   15
IAGO: Her honor is an essence that's not seen;
  They have it very oft that have it not.

---

184. work: Needlework. 189. addition: (To my reputation). 196. circumstanced: Governed by circumstances. ACT IV, SCENE I. 6. hypocrisy . . . devil: I.e., feigned sin instead of feigned virtue. 9. So: So long as.

But for the handkerchief—

OTHELLO: By heaven, I would most gladly have forgot it!
Thou said'st—O, it comes o'er my memory   20
As doth the raven o'er the infected° house,
Boding to all!—he had my handkerchief.

IAGO: Ay, what of that?

OTHELLO: That's not so good now.

IAGO: What
If I had said I had seen him do you wrong?
Or heard him say—as knaves be such abroad   25
Who having, by their own importunate suit,
Or voluntary dotage of some mistress,
Convincèd or supplied° them, cannot choose
But they must blab—

OTHELLO: Hath he said anything?

IAGO: He hath, my lord; but be you well assured,   30
No more than he'll unswear.

OTHELLO: What hath he said?

IAGO: Faith, that he did—I know not what he did.

OTHELLO: What? what?

IAGO: Lie—

OTHELLO: With her?

IAGO: With her, on her; what you will.   35

OTHELLO: Lie with her? lie on her?—We say "lie on her" when they belie° her.—Lie
with her! Zounds, that's fulsome.°—Handkerchief—confessions—handkerchief!—To confess, and be hanged for his labor—first to be hanged, and
then to confess! I tremble at it. Nature would not invest herself in such
shadowing passion without some instruction.° It is not words that shakes 40
me thus.—Pish! Noses, ears, and lips? Is't possible?—Confess?—
Handkerchief?—O devil!

(Falls in a trance.)

IAGO: Work on,
My med'cine, work! Thus credulous fools are caught,
And many worthy and chaste dames even thus,   45
All guiltless, meet reproach.—What, ho! my lord!
My lord, I say! Othello!
Enter Cassio.   How now, Cassio?

CASSIO: What's the matter?

IAGO: My lord is fall'n into an epilepsy.

---

21. infected: Plague-stricken.   **28. Convincèd or supplied:** Overcome or gratified.   **36. belie:**
Slander.   **37. fulsome:** Foul.   **39–40. Nature . . . instruction:** My natural faculties would
not be so overcome by passion without reason.

This is his second fit; he had one yesterday.   50
CASSIO: Rub him about the temples.
IAGO: No, forbear.
   The lethargy° must have his quiet course.
   If not, he foams at mouth, and by and by
   Breaks out to savage madness. Look, he stirs.
   Do you withdraw yourself a little while.   55
   He will recover straight. When he is gone,
   I would on great occasion speak with you.   [*Exit Cassio.*]
   How is it, general? Have you not hurt your head?
OTHELLO: Dost thou mock me?
IAGO: I mock you? No, by heaven.
   Would you would bear your fortune like a man!   60
OTHELLO: A hornèd man's° a monster and a beast.
IAGO: There's many a beast then in a populous city,
   And many a civil° monster.
OTHELLO: Did he confess it?
IAGO: Good sir, be a man.
   Think every bearded fellow that's but yoked   65
   May draw with you. There's millions now alive
   That nightly lie in those unproper° beds
   Which they dare swear peculiar:° your case is better.
   O, 'tis the spite of hell, the fiend's arch-mock,
   To lip a wanton in a secure° couch,   70
   And to suppose her chaste! No, let me know;
   And knowing what I am, I know what she shall be.
OTHELLO: O, thou art wise! 'Tis certain.
IAGO: Stand you awhile apart;
   Confine yourself but in a patient list.°
   Whilst you were here, o'erwhelmèd with your grief—   75
   A passion most unsuiting such a man—
   Cassio came hither. I shifted him away
   And laid good 'scuse upon your ecstasy;°
   Bade him anon return, and here speak with me;
   The which he promised. Do but encave° yourself   80
   And mark the fleers, the gibes, and notable scorns
   That dwell in every region of his face;
   For I will make him tell the tale anew—
   Where, how, how oft, how long ago, and when

---

52. lethargy: Coma. **61. hornèd man:** Cuckold. **63. civil:** City-dwelling. **67. unproper:** Not exclusively their own. **68. peculiar:** Exclusively their own. **70. secure:** Free from fear of rivalry. **74. in a patient list:** Within the limits of self-control. **78. ecstasy:** Trance. **80. encave:** Conceal.

He hath, and is again to cope° your wife.   85
I say, but mark his gesture. Marry, patience!
Or I shall say y'are all in all in spleen,°
And nothing of a man.

OTHELLO: Dost thou hear, Iago?
I will be found most cunning in my patience;
But—dost thou hear?—most bloody.

IAGO: That's not amiss: 90
But yet keep time in all. Will you withdraw?

                                                  [*Othello retires.*]

Now will I question Cassio of Bianca,
A huswife° that by selling her desires
Buys herself bread and clothes. It is a creature
That dotes on Cassio, as 'tis the strumpet's plague   95
To beguile many and be beguiled by one.
He, when he hears of her, cannot refrain
From the excess of laughter. Here he comes.

Enter Cassio.

As he shall smile, Othello shall go mad;
And his unbookish° jealousy must conster°   100
Poor Cassio's smiles, gestures, and light behavior
Quite in the wrong. How do you now, lieutenant?

CASSIO: The worser that you give me the addition°
Whose want even kills me.

IAGO: Ply Desdemona well, and you are sure on't.   105
Now, if this suit lay in Bianca's power,
How quickly should you speed!

CASSIO: Alas, poor caitiff!°

OTHELLO: Look how he laughs already!

IAGO: I never knew a woman love man so.

CASSIO: Alas, poor rogue! I think, i' faith, she loves me.   110

OTHELLO: Now he denies it faintly, and laughs it out.

IAGO: Do you hear, Cassio?

OTHELLO: Now he importunes him
To tell it o'er. Go to! Well said, well said!

IAGO: She gives out that you shall marry her.
Do you intend it?   115

CASSIO: Ha, ha, ha!

OTHELLO: Do you triumph, Roman? Do you triumph?

---

85. **cope:** Meet.   87. **all in all in spleen:** Wholly overcome by your passion.   93. **hus-wife:** Hussy.   100. **unbookish:** Uninstructed; **conster:** Construe, interpret.   103. **addition:** Title.   107. **caitiff:** Wretch.

CASSIO: I marry her? What, a customer?° Prithee bear some charity to my wit;°
    do not think it so unwholesome.° Ha, ha, ha!
OTHELLO: So, so, so, so! They laugh that win!   120
IAGO: Faith, the cry goes that you shall marry her.
CASSIO: Prithee, say true.
IAGO: I am a very villain else.
OTHELLO: Have you scored me?° Well.
CASSIO: This is the monkey's own giving out. She is persuaded I will marry her 125
    out of her own love and flattery, not out of my promise.
OTHELLO: Iago beckons° me; now he begins the story.
CASSIO: She was here even now; she haunts me in every place. I was t' other day
    talking on the sea bank with certain Venetians, and thither comes the
    bauble,° and, by this hand, she falls me thus about my neck—   130
OTHELLO: Crying "O dear Cassio!" as it were. His gesture imports it.
CASSIO: So hangs, and lolls, and weeps upon me; so shakes and pulls me!
    Ha, ha, ha!
OTHELLO: Now he tells how she plucked him to my chamber. O, I see that nose
    of yours, but not that dog I shall throw it to.   135
CASSIO: Well, I must leave her company.

Enter Bianca.

IAGO: Before me!° Look where she comes.
CASSIO: 'Tis such another fitchew!° marry, a perfumed one. What do you mean
    by this haunting of me?
BIANCA: Let the devil and his dam haunt you! What did you mean by that same 140
    handkerchief you gave me even now? I was a fine fool to take it. I must take
    out the whole work? A likely piece of work that you should find it in your
    chamber and know not who left it there! This is some minx's token, and I
    must take out the work? There! Give it your hobby-horse.° Wheresoever
    you had it, I'll take out no work on't.   145
CASSIO: How now, my sweet Bianca? How now? how now?
OTHELLO: By heaven, that should be my handkerchief!
BIANCA: An° you'll come to supper to-night, you may; an you will not, come
    when you are next prepared for.   *Exit.*
IAGO: After her, after her!   150
CASSIO: Faith, I must; she'll rail in the street else.
IAGO: Will you sup there?
CASSIO: Yes, I intend so.
IAGO: Well, I may chance to see you; for I would very fain speak with you.

---

118. **customer:** Prostitute.   118. **bear . . . wit:** Be more generous in assessing my intelligence.   119. **unwholesome:** Impaired, defective.   124. **scored me:** Settled my account (?).
127. **beckons:** Signals.   130. **bauble:** Plaything.   137. **Before me:** By my soul.   138. **fitchew:**
Polecat (slang for whore).   144. **hobby-horse:** Harlot.   148. **An:** If.

CASSIO: Prithee come. Will you?   155
IAGO: Go to! say no more.   *Exit Cassio.*
OTHELLO [*comes forward*]: How shall I murder him, Iago?
IAGO: Did you perceive how he laughed at his vice?°
OTHELLO: O Iago!
IAGO: And did you see the handkerchief?   160
OTHELLO: Was that mine?
IAGO: Yours, by this hand! And to see how he prizes° the foolish woman your
   wife! She gave it him, and he hath giv'n it his whore.
OTHELLO: I would have him nine years a-killing—A fine woman! a fair woman!
   a sweet woman!   165
IAGO: Nay, you must forget that.
OTHELLO: Ay, let her rot, and perish, and be damned to-night; for she shall not
   live. No, my heart is turned to stone; I strike it, and it hurts my hand. O,
   the world hath not a sweeter creature! She might lie by an emperor's side
   and command him tasks.   170
IAGO: Nay, that's not your way.
OTHELLO: Hang her! I do but say what she is. So delicate with her needle! an
   admirable musician! O, she will sing the savageness out of a bear! Of so
   high and plenteous wit and invention°—
IAGO: She's the worse for all this.   175
OTHELLO: O, a thousand thousand times! And then, of so gentle a condition!°
IAGO: Ay, too gentle.°
OTHELLO: Nay, that's certain. But yet the pity of it, Iago! O Iago, the pity of it,
   Iago!
IAGO: If you are so fond over her iniquity, give her patent° to offend; for if it 180
   touch not you, it comes near nobody.
OTHELLO: I will chop her into messes!° Cuckold me!
IAGO: O, 'tis foul in her.
OTHELLO: With mine officer!
IAGO: That's fouler.   185
OTHELLO: Get me some poison, Iago, this night. I'll not expostulate with her,
   lest her body and beauty unprovide° my mind again. This night, Iago!
IAGO: Do it not with poison. Strangle her in her bed, even the bed she hath
   contaminated.
OTHELLO: Good, good! The justice of it pleases. Very good!   190
IAGO: And for Cassio, let me be his undertaker;° you shall hear more by mid-
   night.
OTHELLO: Excellent good!

A trumpet.

---

158. **vice:** I.e., vicious conduct. 162. **prizes:** Values. 174. **invention:** Imagination. 176.
condition: Disposition. 177. **gentle:** Generous. 180. **patent:** License. 182. **messes:** Small
pieces. 187. **unprovide:** Disarm. 191. **be his undertaker:** Undertake to deal with him.

What trumpet is that same?
IAGO: I warrant something from Venice.

Enter Lodovico, Desdemona, and Attendants.

          'Tis Lodovico.   195
 This comes from the Duke; and see, your wife is with him.
LODOVICO: God save you, worthy general!
OTHELLO: With all my heart, sir.
LODOVICO: The Duke and senators of Venice greet you.

[Gives him a letter.]

OTHELLO: I kiss the instrument of their pleasures.

[Opens the letter and reads.]

DESDEMONA: And what's the news, good cousin Lodovico? 200
IAGO: I am very glad to see you, signior.
 Welcome to Cyprus.
LODOVICO: I thank you. How does Lieutenant Cassio?
IAGO: Lives, sir.
DESDEMONA: Cousin, there's fall'n between him and my lord
 An unkind° breach; but you shall make all well. 205
OTHELLO: Are you sure of that?
DESDEMONA: My lord?
OTHELLO [*reads*]: "This fail you not to do, as you will—"
LODOVICO: He did not call; he's busy in the paper.
 Is there division 'twixt thy lord and Cassio? 210
DESDEMONA: A most unhappy one. I would do much
 T' atone° them, for the love I bear to Cassio.
OTHELLO: Fire and brimstone!
DESDEMONA: My lord?
OTHELLO: Are you wise?
DESDEMONA: What, is he angry?
LODOVICO: May be the letter moved him;
 For, as I think, they do command him home, 215
 Deputing Cassio in his government.
DESDEMONA: By my troth, I am glad on't.
OTHELLO: Indeed?
DESDEMONA: My lord?
OTHELLO: I am glad to see you mad.°
DESDEMONA: Why, sweet Othello—
OTHELLO: Devil!

[Strikes her.]

---

205. unkind: Unnatural. **212. atone:** Reconcile. **218. mad:** I.e., waggish.

DESDEMONA: I have not deserved this.   220
LODOVICO: My lord, this would not be believed in Venice,
    Though I should swear I saw't. 'Tis very much.
    Make her amends; she weeps.
OTHELLO: O devil, devil!
    If that the earth could teem° with woman's tears,
    Each drop she falls would prove a crocodile.°   225
    Out of my sight!
DESDEMONA: I will not stay to offend you.   [*Going.*]
LODOVICO: Truly, an obedient lady.
    I do beseech your lordship call her back.
OTHELLO: Mistress!
DESDEMONA: My lord?
OTHELLO: What would you with her, sir?   230
LODOVICO: Who? I, my lord?
OTHELLO: Ay! You did wish that I would make her turn.
    Sir, she can turn, and turn, and yet go on
    And turn again; and she can weep, sir, weep;
    And she's obedient; as you say, obedient,   235
    Very obedient. — Proceed you in your tears. —
    Concerning this, sir — O well-painted passion!° —
    I am commanded home. — Get you away;
    I'll send for you anon. — Sir, I obey the mandate
    And will return to Venice. — Hence, avaunt!   240
                         [*Exit Desdemona.*]
    Cassio shall have my place. And, sir, to-night
    I do entreat that we may sup together.
    You are welcome, sir, to Cyprus — Goats and monkeys!
                                          Exit.
LODOVICO: Is this the noble Moor whom our full Senate
    Call all in all sufficient? Is this the nature   245
    Whom passion could not shake? whose solid virtue
    The shot of accident nor dart of chance
    Could neither graze nor pierce?
IAGO: He is much changed.
LODOVICO: Are his wits safe? Is he not light of brain?
IAGO: He's that he is; I may not breathe my censure.   250
    What he might be — if what he might he is not —
    I would to heaven he were!
LODOVICO: What, strike his wife?
IAGO: Faith, that was not so well; yet would I knew

---

224. **teem:** Breed.   225. **crocodile:** (Crocodiles were supposed to shed hypocritical tears to lure men to destruction).   237. **passion:** Grief.

That stroke would prove the worst!
LODOVICO: Is it his use?°
Or did the letters work upon his blood°   255
And new-create this fault?
IAGO: Alas, alas!
It is not honesty in me to speak
What I have seen and known. You shall observe him,
And his own courses will denote° him so
That I may save my speech. Do but go after   260
And mark how he continues.
LODOVICO: I am sorry that I am deceived in him.   *Exeunt.*

Scene II

Within the castle.

Enter Othello and Emilia.

OTHELLO: You have seen nothing, then?
EMILIA: Nor ever heard, nor ever did suspect.
OTHELLO: Yes, you have seen Cassio and she together.
EMILIA: But then I saw no harm, and then I heard
    Each syllable that breath made up between them.   5
OTHELLO: What, did they never whisper?
EMILIA: Never, my lord.
OTHELLO: Nor send you out o' th' way?
EMILIA: Never.
OTHELLO: To fetch her fan, her gloves, her mask, nor nothing?
EMILIA: Never, my lord.   10
OTHELLO: That's strange.
EMILIA: I durst, my lord, to wager she is honest,
    Lay down my soul at stake.° If you think other,
    Remove your thought; it doth abuse your bosom.°
    If any wretch have put this in your head,   15
    Let heaven requite it with the serpent's curse!°
    For if she be not honest, chaste, and true,
    There's no man happy; the purest of their wives
    Is foul as slander.
OTHELLO: Bid her come hither. Go.   *Exit Emilia.*
    She says enough; yet she's a simple bawd   20
    That cannot say as much.° This is a subtle whore,
    A closet lock and key of villainous secrets;

---

254. use: Custom. 255. blood: Passions. 259. courses will denote: Actions will reveal.
SCENE II. 13. at stake: As the wager. 14. abuse . . . bosom: Deceive your heart. 16. serpent's curse: (cf. Genesis 3:14). 20–21. yet . . . much: Yet any procuress who couldn't
make up as believable a story as this would have to be pretty stupid.

And yet she'll kneel and pray; I have seen her do't.

Enter Desdemona and Emilia.

DESDEMONA: My lord, what is your will?

OTHELLO: Pray, chuck, come hither.

DESDEMONA: What is your pleasure?

OTHELLO: Let me see your eyes.   25
    Look in my face.

DESDEMONA: What horrible fancy's this?

OTHELLO [*to Emilia*]: Some of your function, mistress.
    Leave procreants° alone and shut the door;
    Cough or cry "hem" if anybody come.
    Your mystery, your mystery!° Nay, dispatch!   30

                                                            Exit Emilia.

DESDEMONA: Upon my knees, what doth your speech import?
    I understand a fury in your words,
    [But not the words.]

OTHELLO: Why, what art thou?

DESDEMONA: Your wife, my lord; your true
    And loyal wife.

OTHELLO: Come, swear it, damn thyself;   35
    Lest, being like one of heaven,° the devils themselves
    Should fear to seize thee. Therefore be double-damned—
    Swear thou art honest.°

DESDEMONA: Heaven doth truly know it.

OTHELLO: Heaven truly knows that thou art false as hell.

DESDEMONA: To whom, my lord? With whom? How am I false?   40

OTHELLO: Ah, Desdemona! away! away! away!

DESDEMONA: Alas the heavy day! Why do you weep?
    Am I the motive of these tears, my lord?
    If haply you my father do suspect
    An instrument° of this your calling back,   45
    Lay not your blame on me. If you have lost him,
    Why, I have lost him too.

OTHELLO: Had it pleased heaven
    To try me with affliction, had they rained
    All kinds of sores and shames on my bare head,
    Steeped me in poverty to the very lips,   50
    Given to captivity me and my utmost hopes,
    I should have found in some place of my soul
    A drop of patience. But, alas, to make me

---

28. **procreants:** Mating couples. 30. **mystery:** Trade, occupation. 36. **being . . . heaven:** Looking like an angel. 38. **honest:** Chaste. 45. **An instrument:** To be the cause.

A fixèd figure for the time of scorn°
To point his slow unmoving finger at!   55
Yet could I bear that too; well, very well.
But there where I have garnered up my heart,
Where either I must live or bear no life,
The fountain from the which my current runs
Or else dries up—to be discarded thence,   60
Or keep it as a cistern for foul toads
To knot and gender in—turn thy complexion there,°
Patience, thou young and rose-lipped cherubin!
Ay, there look grim as hell!

DESDEMONA: I hope my noble lord esteems me honest.   65

OTHELLO: O, ay; as summer flies are in the shambles,°
That quicken° even with blowing. O thou weed,
Who art so lovely fair, and smell'st so sweet,
That the sense aches at thee, would thou hadst ne'er been born!

DESDEMONA: Alas, what ignorant sin have I committed?   70

OTHELLO: Was this fair paper, this most goodly book,
Made to write "whore" upon? What committed?
Committed? O thou public commoner!°
I should make very forges of my cheeks
That would to cinders burn up modesty,   75
Did I but speak thy deeds. What committed?
Heaven stops the nose at it, and the moon winks;°
The bawdy wind, that kisses all it meets,
Is hushed within the hollow mine of earth
And will not hear it. What committed?   80
Impudent strumpet!

DESDEMONA: By heaven, you do me wrong!

OTHELLO: Are not you a strumpet?

DESDEMONA: No, as I am a Christian!
If to preserve this vessel for my lord
From any other foul unlawful touch
Be not to be a strumpet, I am none.   85

OTHELLO: What, not a whore?

DESDEMONA: No, as I shall be saved!

OTHELLO: Is't possible?

DESDEMONA: O, heaven forgive us!

OTHELLO: I cry you mercy° then.
I took you for that cunning whore of Venice

---

54. **time of scorn:** Scornful world.   62. **turn thy complexion there:** Change thy color at
that point.   66. **shambles:** Slaughterhouse.   67. **quicken:** Come to life.   73. **commoner:**
Harlot.   77. **winks:** Closes her eyes.   88. **cry you mercy:** Beg your pardon.

That married with Othello. — [*Calling.*] You, mistress,   90
That have the office opposite to Saint Peter
And keep the gate of hell!

Enter Emilia.

                       You, you, ay, you!
We have done our course; there's money for your pains:
I pray you turn the key, and keep our counsel.   *Exit.*
EMILIA: Alas, what does this gentleman conceive?   95
    How do you, madam? How do you, my good lady?
DESDEMONA: Faith, half asleep.°
EMILIA: Good madam, what's the matter with my lord?
DESDEMONA: With who?
EMILIA: Why, with my lord, madam.   100
DESDEMONA: Who is thy lord?
EMILIA: He that is yours, sweet lady.
DESDEMONA: I have none. Do not talk to me, Emilia.
    I cannot weep; nor answer have I none
    But what should go by water. Prithee to-night
    Lay on my bed my wedding sheets, remember;   105
    And call thy husband hither.
EMILIA: Here's a change indeed!   *Exit.*
DESDEMONA: 'Tis meet° I should be used so, very meet.
    How have I been behaved, that he might stick
    The small'st opinion° on my least misuse?°

Enter Iago and Emilia.

IAGO: What is your pleasure, madam? How is't with you?   110
DESDEMONA: I cannot tell. Those that do teach young babes
    Do it with gentle means and easy tasks:
    He might have chid me so; for, in good faith,
    I am a child to chiding.
IAGO: What is the matter, lady?
EMILIA: Alas, Iago, my lord hath so bewhored her,   115
    Thrown such despite and heavy terms upon her
    As true hearts cannot bear.
DESDEMONA: Am I that name, Iago?
IAGO: What name, fair lady?
DESDEMONA: Such as she said my lord did say I was.
EMILIA: He called her whore. A beggar in his drink   120
    Could not have laid such terms upon his callet.°

---

97. half asleep: I.e., stunned. **107. meet:** Fitting. **109. small'st opinion:** Least suspicion; **least misuse:** Slightest misconduct. **121. callet:** Whore.

IAGO: Why did he so?
DESDEMONA: I do not know; I am sure I am none such.
IAGO: Do not weep, do not weep. Alas the day!
EMILIA: Hath she forsook so many noble matches,   125
    Her father and her country, and her friends,
    To be called whore? Would it not make one weep?
DESDEMONA: It is my wretched fortune.
IAGO: Beshrew him for't!
    How comes this trick° upon him?
DESDEMONA: Nay, heaven doth know.
EMILIA: I will be hanged if some eternal villain,   130
    Some busy and insinuating° rogue,
    Some cogging, cozening° slave, to get some office,
    Have not devised this slander. I'll be hanged else.
IAGO: Fie, there is no such man! It is impossible.
DESDEMONA: If any such there be, heaven pardon him!   135
EMILIA: A halter° pardon him! and hell gnaw his bones!
    Why should he call her whore? Who keeps her company?
    What place? what time? what form? what likelihood?
    The Moor 's abused by some most villainous knave,
    Some base notorious knave, some scurvy fellow.   140
    O heaven, that such companions° thou 'dst unfold,°
    And put in every honest hand a whip
    To lash the rascals naked through the world
    Even from the east to th' west!
IAGO: Speak within door.°
EMILIA: O, fie upon them! Some such squire he was   145
    That turned your wit the seamy side without
    And made you to suspect me with the Moor.
IAGO: You are a fool. Go to.
DESDEMONA: Alas, Iago,
    What shall I do to win my lord again?
    Good friend, go to him; for, by this light of heaven,   150
    I know not how I lost him. Here I kneel:
    If e'er my will did trespass 'gainst his love
    Either in discourse° of thought or actual deed,
    Or that° mine eyes, mine ears, or any sense
    Delighted them in any other form,   155
    Or that I do not yet,° and ever did,
    And ever will (though he do shake me off

---

129. trick: Freakish behavior. **131. insinuating:** Ingratiating. **132. cogging, cozening:** Cheating, defrauding. **136. halter:** Hangman's noose. **141. companions:** Rogues; **unfold:** Expose. **144. within door:** With restraint. **153. discourse:** Course. **154. that:** If. **156. yet:** Still.

To beggarly divorcement) love him dearly,
Comfort forswear° me! Unkindness may do much;
And his unkindness may defeat° my life,   160
But never taint my love. I cannot say "whore."
It does abhor me now I speak the word;
To do the act that might the addition° earn
Not the world's mass of vanity° could make me.

IAGO: I pray you be content. 'Tis but his humor.   165
The business of the state does him offense,
[And he does chide with you.]

DESDEMONA: If 'twere no other—

IAGO: 'Tis but so, I warrant.

[Trumpets within.]

Hark how these instruments summon you to supper.
The messengers of Venice stay the meat: 170
Go in, and weep not. All things shall be well.

                                    Exeunt Desdemona and Emilia.

Enter Roderigo.

How now, Roderigo?

RODERIGO: I do not find that thou deal'st justly with me.

IAGO: What in the contrary?

RODERIGO: Every day thou daff'st me with some device,° Iago, and rather, as   175
it seems to me now, keep'st from me all conveniency° than suppliest
me with the least advantage° of hope. I will indeed no longer endure it;
nor am I yet persuaded to put up° in peace what already I have foolishly
suffered.

IAGO: Will you hear me, Roderigo?   180

RODERIGO: Faith, I have heard too much; for your words and performances
are no kin together.

IAGO: You charge me most unjustly.

RODERIGO: With naught but truth. I have wasted myself out of my means. The
jewels you have had from me to deliver to Desdemona would half have cor-   185
rupted a votarist.° You have told me she hath received them, and returned
me expectations and comforts of sudden respect° and acquaintance; but I
find none.

IAGO: Well, go to; very well.

RODERIGO: "Very well"! "go to"! I cannot go to, man; nor 'tis not very well. By   190
this hand, I say 'tis very scurvy, and begin to find myself fopped° in it.

---

159. **Comfort forswear:** May happiness forsake. 160. **defeat:** Destroy. 163. **addition:** Title.
164. **vanity:** Showy riches. 175. **thou...device:** You put me off with some trick. 176 **con-
veniency:** Favorable opportunities. 177. **advantage:** Increase. 178. **put up:** Tolerate. 186.
votarist: Nun. 187. **sudden respect:** Immediate notice. 191. **fopped:** Duped.

IAGO: Very well.

RODERIGO: I tell you 'tis not very well. I will make myself known to Desdemona.
If she will return me my jewels, I will give over my suit and repent my
unlawful solicitation; if not, assure yourself I will seek satisfaction of 195
you.

IAGO: You have said now.

RODERIGO: Ay, and said nothing but what I protest intendment° of doing.

IAGO: Why, now I see there's mettle in thee; and even from this instant do build
on thee a better opinion than ever before. Give me thy hand, Roderigo. 200
Thou has taken against me a most just exception; but yet I protest I have
dealt most directly° in thy affair.

RODERIGO: It hath not appeared.

IAGO: I grant indeed it hath not appeared, and your suspicion is not without
wit and judgment. But, Roderigo, if thou hast that in thee indeed which 205
I have greater reason to believe now than ever, I mean purpose, courage,
and valor, this night show it. If thou the next night following enjoy not
Desdemona, take me from this world with treachery and devise engines
for° my life.

RODERIGO: Well, what is it? Is it within reason and compass? 210

IAGO: Sir, there is especial commission come from Venice to depute Cassio in
Othello's place.

RODERIGO: Is that true? Why, then Othello and Desdemona return again to
Venice.

IAGO: O, no; he goes into Mauritania and takes away with him the fair 215
Desdemona, unless his abode be lingered here° by some accident; wherein
none can be so determinate° as the removing of Cassio.

RODERIGO: How do you mean removing of him?

IAGO: Why, by making him uncapable of Othello's place—knocking out his
brains. 220

RODERIGO: And that you would have me to do?

IAGO: Ay, if you dare do yourself a profit and a right. He sups to-night with a
harlotry, and thither will I go to him. He knows not yet of his honorable
fortune. If you will watch his going thence, which I will fashion to fall out°
between twelve and one, you may take him at your pleasure. I will be near 225
to second your attempt, and he shall fall between us. Come, stand not
amazed at it, but go along with me. I will show you such a necessity in his
death that you shall think yourself bound to put it on him. It is now high
supper time, and the night grows to waste. About it!

RODERIGO: I will hear further reason for this. 230

IAGO: And you shall be satisfied.   *Exeunt.*

---

198. **protest intendment**: Declare my intention.   202. **directly**: Straightforwardly.   208–9.
engines for: Plots against.   216. **abode . . . here**: Stay here be extended.   217. **determinate**:
Effective.   224. **fall out**: Occur.

Scene III

Within the castle.

Enter Othello, Lodovico, Desdemona, Emilia, and Attendants.

LODOVICO: I do beseech you, sir, trouble yourself no further.

OTHELLO: O, pardon me; 'twill do me good to walk.

LODOVICO: Madam, good night. I humbly thank your ladyship.

DESDEMONA: Your honor is most welcome.

OTHELLO: Will you walk, sir?

  O, Desdemona—   5

DESDEMONA: My lord?

OTHELLO: Get you to bed on th' instant; I will be returned forthwith.
  Dismiss your attendant there. Look't be done.

DESDEMONA: I will, my lord.

Exit [Othello, with Lodovico and Attendants].

EMILIA: How goes it now? He looks gentler than he did.   10

DESDEMONA: He says he will return incontinent.°
  He hath commanded me to go to bed,
  And bade me to dismiss you.

EMILIA: Dismiss me?

DESDEMONA: It was his bidding; therefore, good Emilia,
  Give me my nightly wearing, and adieu.   15
  We must not now displease him.

EMILIA: I would you had never seen him!

DESDEMONA: So would not I. My love doth so approve him
  That even his stubbornness,° his checks,° his frowns—
  Prithee unpin me—have grace and favor in them.   20

EMILIA: I have laid those sheets you bade me on the bed.

DESDEMONA: All's one.° Good faith, how foolish are our minds!
  If I do die before thee, prithee shroud me
  In one of those same sheets.

EMILIA: Come, come! You talk.°

DESDEMONA: My mother had a maid called Barbary.   25
  She was in love; and he she loved proved mad°
  And did forsake her. She had a song of "Willow";
  An old thing 'twas; but it expressed her fortune,
  And she died singing it. That song to-night
  Will not go from my mind; I have much to do   30
  But to go hang° my head all at one side
  And sing it like poor Barbary. Prithee dispatch.

SCENE III.   **11. incontinent:** At once.   **19. stubbornness:** Roughness; **checks:** Rebukes.
22. All's one: It doesn't matter.   **24. talk:** Prattle.   **26. mad:** Wild, faithless.   **30–31. I . . .
hang:** I can hardly keep from hanging.

EMILIA: Shall I go fetch your nightgown?°

DESDEMONA: No, unpin me here.

This Lodovico is a proper man.

EMILIA: A very handsome man.   35

DESDEMONA: He speaks well.

EMILIA: I know a lady in Venice would have walked barefoot to Palestine for
a touch of his nether lip.

DESDEMONA (*sings*): "The poor soul sat sighing by a sycamore tree
    Sing all a green willow;   40
  Her hand on her bosom, her head on her knee,
    Sing willow, willow, willow.
  The fresh streams ran by her and murmured her moans;
    Sing willow, willow, willow;
  Her salt tears fell from her, and soft'ned the stones" —   45
Lay by these.
    "Sing willow, willow, willow" —
Prithee hie thee;° he'll come anon.
    "Sing all a green willow must be my garland.
  Let nobody blame him; his scorn I approve" —   50
Nay, that's not next. Hark! who is't that knocks?

EMILIA: It's the wind.

DESDEMONA (*sings*): "I called my love false love; but what said he then?
    Sing willow, willow, willow:
  If I court more women, you'll couch with more men."   55
So get thee gone; good night. Mine eyes do itch.
Doth that bode weeping?

EMILIA: 'Tis neither here nor there.

DESDEMONA: I have heard it said so. O, these men, these men!
Dost thou in conscience think — tell me, Emilia —
That there be women do abuse their husbands   60
In such gross kind?

EMILIA: There be some such, no question.

DESDEMONA: Wouldst thou do such a deed for all the world?

EMILIA: Why, would not you?

DESDEMONA: No, by this heavenly light!

EMILIA: Nor I neither by this heavenly light.
I might do't as well i' th' dark.   65

DESDEMONA: Wouldst thou do such a deed for all the world?

EMILIA: The world's a huge thing; it is a great price for a small vice.

DESDEMONA: In troth, I think thou wouldst not.

EMILIA: In troth, I think I should; and undo't when I had done it. Marry, I would
not do such a thing for a joint-ring,° nor for measures of lawn, nor for   70

---

33. nightgown: Dressing gown. **48. hie thee:** Hurry. **70. joint-ring:** Ring made in separable halves.

gowns, petticoats, nor caps, nor any petty exhibition;° but, for all the whole
world—'Ud's pity! who would not make her husband a cuckold to make
him a monarch? I should venture purgatory for't.

DESDEMONA: Beshrew me if I would do such a wrong
For the whole world.   75

EMILIA: Why, the wrong is but a wrong i' th' world; and having the world for
your labor, 'tis a wrong in your own world, and you might quickly make
it right.

DESDEMONA: I do not think there is any such woman.

EMILIA: Yes, a dozen; and as many to th' vantage° as   80
would store° the world they played for.
But I do think it is their husbands' faults
If wives do fall. Say that they slack their duties
And pour our treasures into foreign laps;°
Or else break out in peevish° jealousies,   85
Throwing restraint upon us; or say they strike us,
Or scant our former having° in despite—
Why, we have galls;° and though we have some grace,
Yet have we some revenge. Let husbands know
Their wives have sense like them. They see, and smell,   90
And have their palates both for sweet and sour,
As husbands have. What is it that they do
When they change us for others? Is it sport?
I think it is. And doth affection breed it?
I think it doth. Is't frailty that thus errs?   95
It is so too. And have not we affections,
Desires for sport, and frailty, as men have?
Then let them use us well; else let them know,
The ills we do, their ills instruct us so.

DESDEMONA: Good night, good night. God me such usage° send,   100
Not to pick bad from bad, but by bad mend!°   *Exeunt.*

ACT V / Scene I

A street in Cyprus.

Enter Iago and Roderigo.

IAGO: Here, stand behind this bulk;° straight will he come.
Wear thy good rapier bare, and put it home.
Quick, quick! Fear nothing; I'll be at thy elbow.

---

71. **exhibition:** Gift.   80. **to th' vantage:** Besides.   82. **store:** Populate.   83–84. **slack . . .
laps:** Are unfaithful.   85. **peevish:** Senseless.   87. **having:** Allowance.   88. **galls:** Spirits to
resent.   100. **usage:** Habits.   101. **Not . . . mend:** As not to learn bad ways from others' bad-
ness, but to mend my ways by learning what evil is.   ACT V, SCENE I.   1. **bulk:** Projecting shop-
front.

It makes us, or it mars us—think on that,
And fix most firm thy resolution. 5
RODERIGO: Be near at hand; I may miscarry in't.
IAGO: Here, at thy hand. Be bold, and take thy stand.

[*Stands aside.*]

RODERIGO: I have no great devotion to the deed,
And yet he hath given me satisfying reasons.
'Tis but a man gone. Forth my sword! He dies! 10
IAGO: I have rubbed this young quat° almost to the sense,°
And he grows angry. Now whether he kill Cassio,
Or Cassio him, or each do kill the other,
Every way makes my gain. Live Roderigo,
He calls me to a restitution large 15
Of gold and jewels that I bobbed° from him
As gifts to Desdemona.
It must not be. If Cassio do remain,
He hath a daily beauty in his life
That makes me ugly; and besides, the Moor 20
May unfold me to him; there stand I in much peril.
No, he must die. Be't so! I hear him coming.

Enter Cassio.

RODERIGO: I know his gait. 'Tis he. Villain, thou diest!

[*Makes a pass at Cassio.*]

CASSIO: That thrust had been mine enemy indeed
But that my coat° is better than thou know'st. 25
I will make proof° of thine.

[*Draws, and wounds Roderigo.*]

RODERIGO: O, I am slain!

[*Iago darts from concealment behind Cassio, wounds him in the leg, and exits.*]

CASSIO: I am maimed for ever. Help, ho! Murder! murder!

[*Falls.*]
Enter Othello.

OTHELLO: The voice of Cassio. Iago keeps his word.
RODERIGO: O, villain that I am!
OTHELLO: It is even so.

---

11. quat: Pimple; sense: Quick. 16. bobbed: Swindled. 25. coat: Undershirt of mail.
26. proof: A test.

CASSIO: O, help, ho! light! a surgeon!   30
OTHELLO: 'Tis he. O brave Iago, honest and just,
   That hast such noble sense of thy friend's wrong!
   Thou teachest me. Minion,° your dear lies dead,
   And your unblest fate hies.° Strumpet, I come.
   Forth of my heart those charms, thine eyes, are blotted.   35
   Thy bed, lust-stained, shall with lust's blood be spotted.

                                                                          Exit Othello.

Enter Lodovico and Gratiano.

CASSIO: What, ho? No watch? No passage?° Murder! murder!
GRATIANO: 'Tis some mischance. The cry is very direful.
CASSIO: O, help!
LODOVICO: Hark!   40
RODERIGO: O wretched villain!
LODOVICO: Two or three groan. It is a heavy° night.
   These may be counterfeits. Let's think't unsafe
   To come in to the cry without more help.
RODERIGO: Nobody come? Then shall I bleed to death.   45
LODOVICO: Hark!

Enter Iago, with a light.

GRATIANO: Here's one comes in his shirt, with light and weapons.
IAGO: Who's there? Whose noise is this that cries on° murder?
LODOVICO: We do not know.
IAGO: Did not you hear a cry?
CASSIO: Here, here! For heaven's sake, help me!
IAGO: What's the matter?   50
GRATIANO: This is Othello's ancient, as I take it.
LODOVICO: The same indeed, a very valiant fellow.
IAGO: What are you here that cry so grievously?
CASSIO: Iago? O, I am spoiled, undone by villains!
   Give me some help.   55
IAGO: O me, lieutenant! What villains have done this?
CASSIO: I think that one of them is hereabout
   And cannot make° away.
IAGO: O treacherous villains!

[*To Lodovico and Gratiano.*]

   What are you there? Come in, and give some help.
RODERIGO: O, help me here!   60
CASSIO: That's one of them.

---

33. Minion: Mistress (Desdemona).   **34. hies:** Hurries on.   **37. passage:** Passersby.   **42.
heavy:** Cloudy, dark.   **48. cries on:** Raises the cry of.   **58. make:** Get.

IAGO: O murd'rous slave! O villain!

[*Stabs Roderigo.*]

RODERIGO: O damned Iago! O inhuman dog!
IAGO: Kill men i' th' dark? — Where be these bloody thieves? —
    How silent is this town! — Ho! murder! murder! —
    What may you be? Are you of good or evil?   65
LODOVICO: As you shall prove us, praise us.
IAGO: Signior Lodovico?
LODOVICO: He, sir.
IAGO: I cry you mercy.° Here's Cassio hurt by villains.
GRATIANO: Cassio?   70
IAGO: How is't, brother?
CASSIO: My leg is cut in two.
IAGO: Marry,° heaven forbid!
    Light, gentlemen. I'll bind it with my shirt.

Enter Bianca.

BIANCA: What is the matter, ho? Who is't that cried?
IAGO: Who is't that cried?   75
BIANCA: O my dear Cassio! my sweet Cassio!
    O Cassio, Cassio, Cassio!
IAGO: O notable strumpet! — Cassio, may you suspect
    Who they should be that have thus mangled you?
CASSIO: No.   80
GRATIANO: I am sorry to find you thus. I have been to seek you.
IAGO: Lend me a garter. So. O for a chair°
    To bear him easily hence!
BIANCA: Alas, he faints! O Cassio, Cassio, Cassio!
IAGO: Gentlemen all, I do suspect this trash   85
    To be a party in this injury. —
    Patience a while, good Cassio. — Come, come!
    Lend me a light. Know we this face or no?
    Alas, my friend and my dear countryman
    Roderigo? No — Yes, sure. — O heaven, Roderigo!   90
GRATIANO: What, of Venice?
IAGO: Even he, sir. Did you know him?
GRATIANO: Know him? Ay.
IAGO: Signior Gratiano? I cry your gentle° pardon.
    These bloody accidents° must excuse my manners
    That so neglected you.

---

69. I . . . mercy: I beg your pardon. **72. Marry:** (From "By Mary"). **82. chair:** Sedan chair (an enclosed seat carried on poles by two bearers). **93. gentle:** Noble. **94. accidents:** Sudden events.

GRATIANO: I am glad to see you.   95
IAGO: How do you, Cassio? — O, a chair, a chair!
GRATIANO: Roderigo?
IAGO: He, he, 'tis he!

[*A chair brought in.*]

O, that's well said;° the chair.
Some good man bear him carefully from hence.   100
I'll fetch the general's surgeon. [*To Bianca.*] For you, mistress,
Save you your labor. — He that lies slain here, Cassio,
Was my dear friend. What malice was between you?
CASSIO: None in the world; nor do I know the man.
IAGO [*To Bianca*]: What, look you pale? — O, bear him out o' th' air.   105

[*Cassio and Roderigo are borne off.*]

Stay you, good gentlemen. — Look you pale, mistress? —
Do you perceive the gastness° of her eye? —
Nay, if you stare, we shall hear more anon.
Behold her well; I pray you look upon her.
Do you see, gentlemen? Nay, guiltiness will speak.   110
Though tongues were out of use.

Enter Emilia.

EMILIA: 'Las, what's the matter? What's the matter, husband?
IAGO: Cassio hath here been set on in the dark
By Roderigo, and fellows that are scaped.
He's almost slain, and Roderigo dead.   115
EMILIA: Alas, good gentlemen! alas, good Cassio!
IAGO: This is the fruits of whoring. Prithee, Emilia,
Go know of° Cassio where he supped to-night.

[*To Bianca.*]

What, do you shake at that?
BIANCA: He supped at my house; but I therefore shake not.   120
IAGO: O, did he so? I charge you go with me.
EMILIA: Fie, fie upon thee, strumpet!
BIANCA: I am no strumpet, but of life as honest°
As you that thus abuse me.
EMILIA: As I? Foh! fie upon thee!
IAGO: Kind gentlemen, let's go see poor Cassio dressed°.   125

[*To Bianca.*]

---

99. well said: Well done. **107. gastness:** Terror. **118. know of:** Learn from. **123. honest:** Chaste. **125. Cassio dressed:** Cassio's wounds dressed.

Come, mistress, you must tell 's another tale.
Emilia, run you to the citadel
And tell my lord and lady what hath happed.

                                                 [Exit Emilia.]
Will you go on afore?   *Exeunt [all but Iago].*
                This is the night
That either makes me or fordoes° me quite.   *[Exit.]* 130

Scene II

A bedchamber in the castle.

Desdemona [asleep] in her bed. Enter Othello with a light.

OTHELLO: It is the cause, it is the cause,° my soul.
    Let me not name it to you, you chaste stars!
    It is the cause. Yet I'll not shed her blood,
    Nor scar that whiter skin of hers than snow,
    And smooth as monumental alabaster.°   5
    Yet she must die, else she'll betray more men.
    Put out the light, and then put out the light.
    If I quench thee, thou flaming minister,°
    I can again thy former light restore,
    Should I repent me;° but once put out thy light,   10
    Thou cunning'st pattern° of excelling nature,
    I know not where is that Promethean heat°
    That can thy light relume.° When I have plucked the rose,
    I cannot give it vital growth again;
    It needs must wither. I'll smell thee on the tree.   15

(*He kisses her.*)

    O balmy breath, that dost almost persuade
    Justice to break her sword! One more, one more!
    Be thus when thou art dead, and I will kill thee,
    And love thee after. One more, and that's the last!
    So sweet was ne'er so fatal. I must weep,   20
    But they are cruel tears. This sorrow's heavenly;
    It strikes where it doth love. She wakes.
DESDEMONA: Who's there? Othello?
OTHELLO: Ay, Desdemona.
DESDEMONA: Will you come to bed, my lord?

---

130. **fordoes:** Destroys. SCENE II. **1. cause:** Cause of justice. **5. monumental alabaster:** Alabaster stone used for tombs and monuments. **8. minister:** Servant. **10. repent me:** Change my mind. **11. cunning'st pattern:** Skillfully wrought example. **12. Promethean heat:** Divine fire. **13. relume:** Relight.

OTHELLO: Have you prayed to-night, Desdemon?

DESDEMONA: Ay, my lord.   25

OTHELLO: If you bethink yourself of any crime°
    Unreconciled as yet to heaven and grace,
    Solicit° for it straight.

DESDEMONA: Alack, my lord, what may you mean by that?

OTHELLO: Well, do it, and be brief; I will walk by.   30
    I would not kill thy unpreparèd spirit.
    No, heaven forfend!° I would not kill thy soul.

DESDEMONA: Talk you of killing?

OTHELLO: Ay, I do.

DESDEMONA: Then heaven
    Have mercy on me!

OTHELLO: Amen, with all my heart!

DESDEMONA: If you say so, I hope you will not kill me.   35

OTHELLO: Hum!

DESDEMONA: And yet I fear you; for you're fatal then
    When your eyes roll so. Why I should fear I know not,
    Since guiltiness I know not; but yet I feel I fear.

OTHELLO: Think on thy sins.

DESDEMONA: They are loves I bear to you.   40

OTHELLO: Ay, and for that thou diest.

DESDEMONA: That death 's unnatural that kills for loving.
    Alas, why gnaw you so your nether lip?
    Some bloody passion shakes your very frame.
    These are portents,° but yet I hope, I hope,   45
    They do not point on me.

OTHELLO: Peace and be still!

DESDEMONA: I will so. What's the matter?

OTHELLO: That handkerchief which I so loved and gave thee
    Thou gav'st to Cassio.

DESDEMONA: No, by my life and soul!
    Send for the man and ask him.

OTHELLO: Sweet soul, take heed,   50
    Take heed of perjury; thou art on thy deathbed.

DESDEMONA: Ay, but not yet to die.

OTHELLO: Yes, presently.°
    Therefore confess thee freely of thy sin;
    For to deny each article with oath
    Cannot remove nor choke the strong conception°   55
    That I do groan withal. Thou art to die.

---

26. **crime:** Sin. 28. **Solicit:** Pray. 32. **forfend:** Forbid. 45. **portents:** Signs of impending violence. 52. **presently:** At once. 55. **conception:** Belief.

DESDEMONA: Then Lord have mercy on me!

OTHELLO: I say amen.

DESDEMONA: And have you mercy too! I never did
 Offend° you in my life; never loved Cassio
 But with such general warranty of heaven   60
 As I might love. I never gave him token.

OTHELLO: By heaven, I saw my handkerchief in's hand!
 O perjured woman! thou dost stone my heart,°
 And mak'st me call what I intend to do
 A murder, which I thought a sacrifice.   65
 I saw the handkerchief.

DESDEMONA: He found it then.
 I never gave it him. Send for him hither.
 Let him confess a truth.

OTHELLO: He hath confessed.

DESDEMONA: What, my lord?

OTHELLO: That he hath used thee.

DESDEMONA: How? Unlawfully?

OTHELLO: Ay.   70

DESDEMONA: He will not say so.

OTHELLO: No, his mouth is stopped.
 Honest Iago hath ta'en order° for't.

DESDEMONA: O, my fear interprets. What, is he dead?

OTHELLO: Had all his hairs been lives, my great revenge
 Had stomach for them all.   75

DESDEMONA: Alas, he is betrayed, and I undone!   *[She weeps.]*

OTHELLO: Out, strumpet! Weep'st thou for him to my face?

DESDEMONA: O, banish me, my lord, but kill me not!

OTHELLO: Down, strumpet!

DESDEMONA: Kill me to-morrow; let me live to-night!   80

OTHELLO: Nay, if you strive—

DESDEMONA: But half an hour!

OTHELLO: Being done, there is no pause.

DESDEMONA: But while I say one prayer!

OTHELLO: It is too late.

(Smothers her.)

[DESDEMONA: O Lord, Lord, Lord!]

Emilia at the door.

EMILIA *(calls within)*: My lord, my lord! What, ho! my lord, my lord! 85

OTHELLO: What noise is this? Not dead? not yet quite dead?

---

59. Offend: Wrong. **63. stone my heart:** Turn my heart to stone. **72. ta'en order:** Taken measures.

I that am cruel am yet merciful;
I would not have thee linger in thy pain.
So, so.
EMILIA (*within*): What, ho! my lord, my lord!
OTHELLO: Who's there?   90
EMILIA (*within*): O, good my lord, I would speak a word with you!
OTHELLO: Yes, 'tis Emilia. — By and by.° — She's dead. —
    'Tis like° she comes to speak of Cassio's death.
    The noise was here. Ha! no more moving?
    Still as the grave. — Shall she come in? Were't good! —   95
    I think she stirs again. No. — What's best to do?
    If she come in, she'll sure speak to my wife.
    My wife! my wife! what wife? I have no wife.
    O, insupportable! O heavy hour!
    Methinks it should be now a huge eclipse   100
    Of sun and moon, and that th' affrighted globe
    Should yawn° at alteration.
EMILIA (*within*):   I do beseech you
    That I may speak with you, O good my lord!
OTHELLO: I had forgot thee. O, come in, Emilia.
    Soft, by and by. — Let me the curtains draw. —   105

[*Closes the bed-curtains.*]

    Where art thou?

[*Opens the door.*]
Enter Emilia.

                        What's the matter with thee now?
EMILIA: O my good lord, yonder's foul murder done!
OTHELLO: What? Now?
EMILIA: But now, my lord.
OTHELLO: It is the very error° of the moon.   110
    She comes more nearer earth than she was wont
    And makes men mad.
EMILIA: Cassio, my lord, hath killed a young Venetian
    Called Roderigo.
OTHELLO: Roderigo killed?
    And Cassio killed?
EMILIA: No, Cassio is not killed.   115
OTHELLO: Not Cassio killed? Then murder's out of tune,
    And sweet revenge grows harsh.

---

92. By and by: Just a moment (addressed to Emilia).   **93. like:** Likely.   **102. yawn:** Open,
as in an earthquake.   **110. error:** Straying off course.

DESDEMONA: O, falsely, falsely murdered?
EMILIA: O, Lord! what cry is that?
OTHELLO: That? What?
EMILIA: Out and alas! that was my lady's voice.   120
   Help! help, ho! help! O lady, speak again!
   Sweet Desdemona! O sweet mistress, speak!
DESDEMONA: A guiltless death I die.
EMILIA: O, who hath done this deed?
DESDEMONA: Nobody—I myself. Farewell.   125
   Commend° me to my kind lord. O, farewell!

(*She dies.*)

OTHELLO: Why, how should she be murd'red?
EMILIA: Alas, who knows?
OTHELLO: You heard her say herself, it was not I.
EMILIA: She said so. I must needs report the truth.
OTHELLO: She's like a liar gone to burning hell!   130
   'Twas I that killed her.
EMILIA: O, the more angel she,
   And you the blacker devil!
OTHELLO: She turned to folly, and she was a whore.
EMILIA: Thou dost belie° her, and thou art a devil.
OTHELLO: She was false as water.°
EMILIA: Thou art rash as fire to say   135
   That she was false. O, she was heavenly true!
OTHELLO: Cassio did top her. Ask thy husband else.°
   O, I were damned beneath all depth in hell
   But that I did proceed upon just grounds
   To this extremity. Thy husband knew it all.   140
EMILIA: My husband?
OTHELLO: Thy husband.
EMILIA: That she was false to wedlock?
OTHELLO: Ay, with Cassio. Nay, had she been true,
   If heaven would make me such another world
   Of one entire and perfect chrysolite,°   145
   I'd not have sold her for it.
EMILIA: My husband?
OTHELLO: Ay 'twas he that told me first.
   An honest man he is, and hates the slime
   That sticks on filthy deeds.
EMILIA: My husband?   150

---

126. Commend: Remember. **134. belie:** Slander. **135. water:** (Which is yielding).
137. else: If you don't believe me. **146. chrysolite:** (Precious topaz).

OTHELLO: What needs this iterance,° woman? I say thy husband.

EMILIA: O mistress, villainy hath made mocks with° love!
My husband say that she was false?

OTHELLO: He, woman.
I say, thy husband. Dost understand the word?
My friend, thy husband; honest, honest Iago.   155

EMILIA: If he say so, may his pernicious soul
Rot half a grain a day! he lies to th' heart.
She was too fond of her most filthy bargain.

OTHELLO: Ha!   [*He draws.*]

EMILIA: Do thy worst.   160
This deed of thine is no more worthy heaven
Than thou wast worthy her.

OTHELLO: Peace, you were best.°

EMILIA: Thou hast not half the power to do me harm
As I have to be hurt.° O gull! O dolt!
As ignorant as dirt! thou hast done a deed—   165
I care not for thy sword; I'll make thee known,
Though I lost twenty lives. Help! help! Ho! help!
The Moor hath killed my mistress! Murder! murder!

Enter Montano, Gratiano, Iago, and others.

MONTANO: What is the matter? How now, general?

EMILIA: O, are you come, Iago? You have done well,   170
That men must lay their murders on your neck.°

GRATIANO: What is the matter?

EMILIA: Disprove this villain, if thou be'st a man.
He says thou told'st him that his wife was false.
I know thou didst not; thou'rt not such a villain.   175
Speak, for my heart is full.

IAGO: I told him what I thought, and told no more
Than what he found himself was apt and true.

EMILIA: But did you ever tell him she was false?

IAGO: I did.   180

EMILIA: You told a lie, an odious damnèd lie!
Upon my soul, a lie! a wicked lie!
She false with Cassio? Did you say with Cassio?

IAGO: With Cassio, mistress. Go to, charm° your tongue.

EMILIA: I will not charm my tongue; I am bound to speak: 185
My mistress here lies murdered in her bed—

ALL: O heavens forfend!

---

151. **iterance:** Repetition.   152. **mocks with:** A mockery of.   162. **Peace . . . best:** You had better keep quiet.   164. **to be hurt:** To endure hurt.   171. **on your neck:** To your charge.
184. **charm:** Cast a spell on, silence.

EMILIA: And your reports have set the murder on.

OTHELLO: Nay, stare not, masters. It is true indeed.

GRATIANO: 'Tis a strange truth.   190

MONTANO: O monstrous act!

EMILIA: Villainy, villainy, villainy!
  I think upon't—I think I smell't!—O villainy!
  I thought so then.—I'll kill myself for grief.—
  O villainy, villainy!

IAGO: What, are you mad? I charge you get you home.   195

EMILIA: Good gentlemen, let me have leave to speak.
  'Tis proper I obey him, but not now.
  Perchance, Iago, I will ne'er go home.

OTHELLO: O! O! O!   (*Falls on the bed.*)

EMILIA: Nay, lay thee down and roar!
  For thou hast killed the sweetest innocent   200
  That e'er did lift up eye.°

OTHELLO: O, she was foul!

[*Rises.*]

  I scarce did know you, uncle. There lies your niece,
  Whose breath, indeed, these hands have newly stopped.
  I know this act shows° horrible and grim.

GRATIANO: Poor Desdemon! I am glad thy father's dead.   205
  Thy match was mortal to him, and pure grief
  Shore his old thread in twain. Did he live now,
  This sight would make him do a desperate turn;°
  Yea, curse his better angel from his side,
  And fall to reprobation.°   210

OTHELLO: 'Tis pitiful; but yet Iago knows
  That she with Cassio hath the act of shame
  A thousand times committed. Cassio confessed it;
  And she did gratify° his amorous works
  With that recognizance° and pledge of love   215
  Which I first gave her. I saw it in his hand.
  It was a handkerchief, an antique token
  My father gave my mother.

EMILIA: O God! O heavenly God!

IAGO: Zounds, hold your peace!

EMILIA: 'Twill out, 'twill out! I peace?   220
  No, I will speak as liberal as the north,°
  Let heaven and men and devils, let them all,

---

201. **lift up eye:** Lift her eyes to heaven. 204. **shows:** Appears. 208. **turn:** Act. 210. **reprobation:** Rejection by God, damnation. 214. **gratify:** Reward. 215. **recognizance:** Token. 221. **liberal as the north:** Unchecked as the north wind blows.

All, all, cry shame against me, yet I'll speak.
IAGO: Be wise, and get you home.
EMILIA: I will not.

[*Iago draws and threatens Emilia.*]

GRATIANO: Fie!
    Your sword upon a woman?   225
EMILIA: O thou dull Moor, that handkerchief thou speak'st of
    I found by fortune, and did give my husband;
    For often with a solemn earnestness—
    More than indeed belonged to such a trifle—
    He begged of me to steal't.
IAGO: Villainous whore!   230
EMILIA: She give it Cassio? No, alas, I found it,
    And I did give't my husband.
IAGO: Filth, thou liest!
EMILIA: By heaven, I do not, I do not, gentlemen.
    O murd'rous coxcomb!° what should such a fool
    Do with so good a wife?
OTHELLO: Are there no stones° in heaven   235
    But what serves for the thunder? Precious° villain!

The Moor runs at Iago [but is disarmed by Montano].

Iago kills his wife.

GRATIANO: The woman falls. Sure he hath killed his wife.
EMILIA: Ay, ay. O, lay me by my mistress' side.   *Exit Iago.*
GRATIANO: He's gone, but his wife's killed.
MONTANO: 'Tis a notorious° villain. Take you this weapon,   240
    Which I have here recovered from the Moor.
    Come, guard the door without. Let him not pass,
    But kill him rather. I'll after that same villain,
    For 'tis a damnèd slave.

Exit [Montano, with all but Othello and Emilia].

OTHELLO: I am not valiant neither;
    But every puny whipster° gets my sword.   245
    But why should honor outlive honesty?
    Let it go all.
EMILIA: What did thy song bode, lady?
    Hark, canst thou hear me? I will play the swan,
    And die in music. [*Sings.*] "Willow, willow, willow."

---

234. coxcomb: Fool. **235. stones:** Bolts like those used for thunderbolts. **236. Precious:** Absolute. **240. notorious:** Reprehensible. **245. puny whipster:** Whippersnapper.

Moor, she was chaste. She loved thee, cruel Moor: 250
So come my soul to bliss as I speak true.
So speaking as I think, alas, I die.

(*She dies.*)

OTHELLO: I have another weapon in this chamber;
It is a sword of Spain, the ice brook's° temper.
O, here it is.—Uncle, I must come forth.   255
GRATIANO (*within*): If thou attempt it, it will cost thee dear.
Thou hast no weapon, and perforce must suffer.
OTHELLO: Look in upon me then and speak with me,
Or, naked° as I am, I will assault thee.

[*Enter Gratiano.*]

GRATIANO: What is the matter?
OTHELLO: Behold, I have a weapon;   260
A better never did itself sustain
Upon a soldier's thigh. I have seen the day
That with this little arm and this good sword
I have made my way through more impediments
Than twenty times your stop.° But O vain boast!   265
Who can control his fate? 'Tis not so now.
Be not afraid, though you do see me weaponed.
Here is my journey's end, here is my butt,°
And very seamark° of my utmost sail:
Do you go back dismayed? 'Tis a lost° fear.   270
Man but a rush° against Othello's breast,
And he retires. Where should Othello go?
Now, how dost thou look now? O ill-starred wench!
Pale as thy smock! When we shall meet at compt,°
This look of thine will hurl my soul from heaven,   275
And fiends will snatch at it. Cold, cold, my girl?
Even like thy chastity.
O cursèd, cursèd slave! Whip me, ye devils,
From the possession of this heavenly sight!
Blow me about in winds! roast me in sulphur!   280
Wash me in steep-down gulfs of liquid fire!
Oh Desdemon! dead Desdemon! dead! Oh! Oh!

Enter Lodovico, Montano, Iago [as prisoner], and Officers; Cassio in a chair.

---

254. **ice brook:** I.e., a Spanish blade, tempered in cold running water. **259. naked:** Disarmed. **265. stop:** Power to stop. **268. butt:** Limit. **269. seamark:** Beacon, destination. **270. lost:** Groundless. **271. Man but a rush:** Wield only a reed. **274. compt:** Final accounting, Last Judgment.

LODOVICO: Where is this rash and most unfortunate man?

OTHELLO: That's he that was Othello. Here I am.

LODOVICO: Where is that viper? Bring the villain forth.   285

OTHELLO: I look down towards his feet° — but that's a fable.

    If that thou be'st a devil, I cannot kill thee.

[*Wounds Iago.*]

LODOVICO: Wrench his sword from him.

[*Othello is disarmed.*]

IAGO: I bleed, sir, but not killed.

OTHELLO: I am not sorry neither. I'ld have thee live;

    For in my sense, 'tis happiness to die.   290

LODOVICO: O thou Othello that wert once so good,

    Fall'n in the practice° of a damnèd slave,

    What shall be said to thee?

OTHELLO: Why, anything;

    An honorable murderer, if you will;

    For naught did I in hate, but all in honor.   295

LODOVICO: This wretch hath part confessed his villainy.

    Did you and he consent in° Cassio's death?

OTHELLO: Ay.

CASSIO: Dear general, I never gave you cause.

OTHELLO: I do believe it, and I ask your pardon.   300

    Will you, I pray, demand that demi-devil

    Why he hath thus ensnared my soul and body?

IAGO: Demand me nothing. What you know, you know.

    From this time forth I never will speak word.

LODOVICO: What, not to pray?

GRATIANO: Torments° will ope your lips.   305

OTHELLO: Well, thou dost best.

LODOVICO: Sir, you shall understand what hath befall'n,

    Which, as I think, you know not. Here is a letter

    Found in the pocket of the slain Roderigo;

    And here another. The one of them imports   310

    The death of Cassio to be undertook

    By Roderigo.

OTHELLO: O villain!

CASSIO: Most heathenish and most gross!

LODOVICO: Now here's another discontented° paper

    Found in the pocket too; and this, it seems,   315

---

286. I . . . feet: I.e., to see if they are cloven, like the Devil's. **292. practice:** Plot. **297. consent in:** Agree upon. **305. Torments:** Torture. **314. discontented:** Full of discontent.

Roderigo meant t' have sent this damnèd villain;
But that, belike, Iago in the nick°
Came in and satisfied him.

OTHELLO:　　　　　　　　　　　O thou pernicious caitiff! —
How came you, Cassio, by that handkerchief
That was my wife's?

CASSIO:　　　　　　　　　I found it in my chamber;　　　　　　　320
And he himself confessed but even now
That there he dropped it for a special purpose
Which wrought to his desire.

OTHELLO:　　　　　　　　　　O fool! fool! fool!

CASSIO: There is besides in Roderigo's letter,
How he upbraids Iago that he made him　　　　　　　　　325
Brave° me upon the watch; whereon it came°
That I was cast;° and even but now he spake,
After long seeming dead — Iago hurt him,
Iago set him on.

LODOVICO [*To Othello*]: You must forsake this room and go with us.　　330
Your power and your command is taken off,°
And Cassio rules in Cyprus. For this slave,
If there be any cunning cruelty
That can torment him much and hold him long,°
It shall be his. You shall close prisoner rest°　　　　　　　335
Till that the nature of your fault be known
To the Venetian state. Come, bring away.

OTHELLO: Soft you!° a word or two before you go.
I have done the state some service, and they know 't.
No more of that. I pray you, in your letters,　　　　　　　340
When you shall these unlucky° deeds relate,
Speak of me as I am. Nothing extenuate,
Nor set down aught in malice. Then must you speak
Of one that loved not wisely, but too well;
Of one not easily jealous, but, being wrought,°　　　　　　　345
Perplexed° in the extreme; of one whose hand,
Like the base Judean,° threw a pearl away
Richer than all his tribe; of one whose subdued° eyes,
Albeit unusèd to the melting mood,
Drop tears as fast as the Arabian trees　　　　　　　350
Their med'cinable gum. Set you down this.

---

317. nick: Nick of time.　**326. Brave:** Defy; **Whereon it came:** whereof it came about.
327. cast: Dismissed.　**331. off:** Away.　**334. hold him long:** Keep him alive a long time.
335. rest: Remain.　**338. Soft you:** Wait a moment.　**341. unlucky:** Unfortunate.　**345.**
wrought: Worked into a frenzy.　**346. Perplexed:** Distraught.　**347. Judean:** Judas Iscariot
(?) (quarto reads "Indian").　**348. subdued:** I.e., conquered by grief.

And say besides that in Aleppo once,
Where a malignant and a turbaned Turk
Beat a Venetian and traduced the state,
I took by th' throat the circumcisèd dog   355
And smote him—thus.

(He stabs himself.)

LODOVICO: O bloody period!°
GRATIANO: All that's spoke is marred.
OTHELLO: I kissed thee ere I killed thee. No way but this,
        Killing myself, to die upon a kiss.

(He [falls upon the bed and] dies.)

CASSIO: This did I fear, but thought he had no weapon;   360
        For he was great of heart.
LODOVICO [*to Iago*]:   O Spartan dog,
        More fell° than anguish, hunger, or the sea!
        Look on the tragic loading of this bed.
        This is thy work. The object poisons sight;
        Let it be hid.° Gratiano, keep° the house,   365
        And seize upon° the fortunes of the Moor,
        For they succeed on you. [*To Cassio*] To you, lord governor,
        Remains the censure° of this hellish villain,
        The time, the place, the torture. O, enforce it!
        Myself will straight aboard, and to the state   370
        This heavy act with heavy heart relate.

                                                                        Exeunt.

---

357. **period:** Ending.   362. **fell:** Cruel.   365. **Let it be hid:** I.e., draw the bed curtains;
keep: Guard.   366. **seize upon:** Take legal possession of.   368. **censure:** Judicial sentence.

You can research William Shakespeare in depth, including images and
cultural documents, with VirtuaLit Drama at bedfordstmartins.com/rewritinglit.

Post-Elizabethan Theaters

Theaters in England were closed for almost twenty years (1641–1660)
when the monarchy was replaced by a Puritan-led republic. When the monarchy was restored in 1660, theaters were allowed to reopen. Outdoor theaters were replaced with indoor ones, a trend influenced by theaters in
France, where many members of the English aristocracy had lived in exile
during Puritan rule. Like the Elizabethan indoor theaters (see p. 1146), the
new theaters had boxes on three sides (the expensive seats), a gallery above

(the cheap seats), and a seating area in front of the stage (the "pit," the fashionable place to be). A major innovation was the addition of a proscenium arch, with a curtain that opened at the beginning of the play. The acting was done in front of the arch, on the forestage. Behind the arch were a series of painted flats that could slide together and provide scenic backdrops for the action (as, for example, an indoor flat, a city street flat, a forest flat). Another major change was that, for the first time in England, women were allowed to act on stage. No longer were women's roles played by boys dressed as women.

MODERN THEATERS Growing increasingly larger in size, such theaters were the model in England from the late 1600s until the mid-1800s, when the "modern stage" developed. The modern era saw the action of a play moved behind the proscenium arch and the forestage pretty much eliminated. Thus, what had been called the rear stage (now referred to just as the "stage") became the main acting area.

BOX SET The result of the evolution of the stage area was the emergence of the "box set." Playwrights began writing for a stage that they thought of as a box behind the arch. They visualized the box as an actual room and instructed stage designers to build it with real windows and doors that could open and close and realistic carpets and furniture. Instead of the action taking place in front of artificial, painted flats, it took place within what looked like a room in an actual house. Three walls of the room were visible to the audience; the fourth wall, of course, was not. The major convention of the modern theater is the "invisible fourth wall" through which the audience can see into the room, though the actors behave as if the wall were present and couldn't be crossed.

THE QUEST FOR REALISM The modern stage was what Henrik Ibsen had in mind as he wrote *A Doll House*. His stage directions (p. 1246) are detailed and specific. The room described may seem old-fashioned and quaint to us, but for Ibsen's contemporaries it would have been typical of the upper-class society portrayed in the play. Ibsen wanted it to seem genuine, as he aimed for a realistic, totally believable story—in setting, plot, characters, and subject matter.

LIGHTING Creating a realistic effect was aided by improvements in lighting: Candles were replaced with gas lamps, which later were replaced with electric lights. The bare Elizabethan stage and the painted flats of its successor required a great deal of imaginative involvement by the audience. Realistic drama lessened how much the audience needed to imagine. Ideally audience members would forget they were watching a play and instead feel like they were observing real life.

UNITY OF PLACE One effect of the box set is a restriction on setting. Shakespeare's bare stage allowed him to change locations easily, just by having characters say the right words. Because the box set filled the stage and was difficult to move, *A Doll House* takes place entirely in the Helmers' living room. Nora is onstage much of the time. Mrs. Linde, Dr. Rank, and Krogstad visit her in that room; her scenes with her husband are there as well. A key event—Nora dancing her tarantella—occurs in the Stenborgs' apartment directly above the room shown onstage, so the audience doesn't see it; it is reported by Torvald. In the twentieth century, large theaters developed revolving platforms onstage that, by rotating between scenes, presented two or three realistic box-set stages. But nineteenth-century theaters were far from such technology, so playwrights had to accept unity of place, writing to fit the entire play into one location.

LATE EIGHTEENTH- AND NINETEENTH-CENTURY PLAYS Drama was at a low ebb from the mid-eighteenth century through the mid-nineteenth century. In general audiences did not like tragedy; some of Shakespeare's tragedies were even revised to give them happy endings. The preference among theatergoers was sentimental plays and melodramas, so that's what playwrights needed to write. There was also a reaction against plots that focused on only the upper classes. One result was the rise of the domestic tragedy, whose protagonists were ordinary members of the middle or lower classes. What audiences did love were spectacular productions, with lavish costumes and scenery and special effects, even if the texts needed to be cut back severely to accommodate such extravaganzas. Henrik Ibsen's *A Doll House* was part of a reaction against such sentimentalism and spectacle. Influenced by the realistic, or naturalistic, movement in fiction, Ibsen and several contemporary playwrights portrayed ordinary people and everyday life in as real and believable a way as they could. Their plays challenged audiences to respond to more important social issues and deeper psychological concerns than had the drama of the previous century.

THE PROBLEM PLAY Out of the realism movement a particular dramatic subtype arose: the **problem play**, a serious work that dramatizes and psychologically explores a real-life—usually contemporary—social, political, or ethical problem faced by ordinary people, all in an effort to confront the audience with relevant moral dilemmas. Although in a broad sense the term covers all drama dealing with problems of human life, it is used more narrowly for the "drama of ideas" that emerged in the late 1800s in the work of, for example, Ibsen, Irish playwright George Bernard Shaw (1856–1950), and English playwright John Galsworthy (1867–1933). Ibsen became famous (or, at the time, notorious) for a series of plays in which he dealt with marriage (*A Doll House*, 1879), syphilis and social and religious values (*Ghosts*, 1881), and communities faced with unpleasant truths exposed by outsiders (*An Enemy of the People*, 1882). In his later plays he moved on to psychological examinations of characters entangled in self-destructive relationships. The best-known of these is *Hedda Gabler* (1890).

ENTRY POINTS   *A Doll House* opens in the Christmas season, with the characters expecting a happy, carefree, family-centered celebration. They end up, however, facing a crisis created by thwarted expectations: Torvald Helmer and his wife, Nora, discover idealism is an unstable marriage foundation. Pay attention especially to the way characters (major ones and minor ones) are developed and to the dilemmas the characters (especially Nora) face. Think about what makes the conflicts realistic. Notice how complex the causes of the conflicts are, how you can't simply say "She/he is good/bad." Consider all the things that influence the characters and their reactions.

The ending was very controversial when the play was first produced. Consider whether what Nora does is the best thing to do. (And if so, best for whom?) Think about whether the play should be regarded as affirming women's rights or affirming human rights, or both. Consider also what performing the play with its original staging, in a box set, would have added to its impact.

Henrik Ibsen   1828–1906

A Doll House°   [1879]

Translated by Rolf Fjelde

THE CHARACTERS

TORVALD HELMER, a lawyer
NORA, his wife
DR. RANK
MRS. LINDE
NILS KROGSTAD, a bank clerk
THE HELMERS' THREE SMALL CHILDREN
ANNE-MARIE, their nurse
HELENE, a maid
A DELIVERY BOY

APPROACHING THE AUTHOR

Henrik Ibsen was born into a highly affluent family, but shortly after his birth his father's business collapsed, leaving the family in poverty. Financial difficulty is a theme throughout his plays, as it was throughout his life.

For more about him, see page 1393.

The action takes place in Helmer's residence.

A Doll House: Fjelde explains, in the foreword to his translation, that he translates the title as "A Doll House" instead of "A Doll's House" to avoid the suggestion that it is the house of the doll, Nora. Rather, he believes, Ibsen meant that both Torvald and Nora are living in an unreal, "let's pretend" situation.

ACT 1

(*A comfortable room, tastefully but not expensively furnished. A door to the right in the back wall leads to the entryway; another to the left leads to Helmer's study. Between these doors, a piano. Midway in the left-hand wall a door, and further back a window. Near the window a round table with an armchair and a small sofa. In the right-hand wall, toward the rear, a door, and nearer the foreground a porcelain stove with two armchairs and a rocking chair beside it. Between the stove and the side door, a small table. Engravings on the walls. An étagère° with china figures and other small art objects; a small bookcase with richly bound books; the floor carpeted; a fire burning in the stove. It is a winter day.*)

(*A bell rings in the entryway; shortly after we hear the door being unlocked. Nora comes into the room, humming happily to herself; she is wearing street clothes and carries an armload of packages, which she puts down on the table to the right. She has left the hall door open, and through it a Delivery Boy is seen holding a Christmas tree and a basket, which he gives to the Maid who let them in.*)

NORA: Hide the tree well, Helene. The children mustn't get a glimpse of it till this evening, after it's trimmed. (*To the Delivery Boy, taking out her purse.*) How much?

DELIVERY BOY: Fifty, ma'am.

NORA: There's a crown. No, keep the change. (*The Boy thanks her and leaves. Nora shuts the door. She laughs softly to herself while taking off her street things. Drawing a bag of macaroons from her pocket, she eats a couple, then steals over and listens at her husband's study door.*) Yes, he's home. (*Hums again as she moves to the table right.*)

HELMER (*from the study*): Is that my little lark twittering out there?

NORA (*busy opening some packages*): Yes, it is.

HELMER: Is that my squirrel rummaging around?

NORA: Yes!

HELMER: When did my squirrel get in?

NORA: Just now. (*Putting the macaroon bag in her pocket and wiping her mouth.*) Do come in, Torvald, and see what I've bought.

HELMER: Can't be disturbed. (*After a moment he opens the door and peers in, pen in hand.*) Bought, you say? All that there? Has the little spendthrift been out throwing money around again?

NORA: Oh, but Torvald, this year we really should let ourselves go a bit. It's the first Christmas we haven't had to economize.

HELMER: But you know we can't go squandering.

NORA: Oh yes, Torvald, we can squander a little now. Can't we? Just a tiny, wee bit. Now that you've got a big salary and are going to make piles and piles of money.

HELMER: Yes—starting New Year's. But then it's a full three months till the raise comes through.

NORA: Pooh! We can borrow that long.

---

s.d. étagère: A cabinet with a number of shelves.

HELMER: Nora! (*Goes over and playfully takes her by the ear.*) Are your scatter-brains off again? What if today I borrowed a thousand crowns, and you squandered them over Christmas week, and then on New Year's Eve a roof tile fell on my head, and I lay there —

NORA (*putting her hand on his mouth*): Oh! Don't say such things!

HELMER: Yes, but what if it happened — then what?

NORA: If anything so awful happened, then it just wouldn't matter if I had debts or not.

HELMER: Well, but the people I'd borrowed from?

NORA: Them? Who cares about them! They're strangers.

HELMER: Nora, Nora, how like a woman! No, but seriously, Nora, you know what I think about that. No debts! Never borrow! Something of freedom's lost — and something of beauty, too — from a home that's founded on borrowing and debt. We've made a brave stand up to now, the two of us; and we'll go right on like that the little while we have to.

NORA (*going toward the stove*): Yes, whatever you say, Torvald.

HELMER (*following her*): Now, now, the little lark's wings mustn't droop. Come on, don't be a sulky squirrel. (*Taking out his wallet.*) Nora, guess what I have here.

NORA (*turning quickly*): Money!

HELMER: There, see. (*Hands her some notes.*) Good grief, I know how costs go up in a house at Christmastime.

NORA: Ten — twenty — thirty — forty. Oh, thank you, Torvald; I can manage no end on this.

HELMER: You really will have to.

NORA: Oh yes, I promise I will! But come here so I can show you everything I bought. And so cheap! Look, new clothes for Ivar here — and a sword. Here a horse and a trumpet for Bob. And a doll and a doll's bed here for Emmy; they're nothing much, but she'll tear them to bits in no time anyway. And here I have dress material and handkerchiefs for the maids. Old Anne-Marie really deserves something more.

HELMER: And what's in that package there?

NORA (*with a cry*): Torvald, no! You can't see that till tonight!

HELMER: I see. But tell me now, you little prodigal, what have you thought of for yourself?

NORA: For myself? Oh, I don't want anything at all.

HELMER: Of course you do. Tell me just what — within reason — you'd most like to have.

NORA: I honestly don't know. Oh, listen, Torvald —

HELMER: Well?

NORA (*fumbling at his coat buttons, without looking at him*): If you want to give me something, then maybe you could — you could —

HELMER: Come on, out with it.

NORA (*hurriedly*): You could give me money, Torvald. No more than you think you can spare; then one of these days I'll buy something with it.

HELMER: But Nora —

NORA: Oh, please, Torvald darling, do that! I beg you, please. Then I could hang the bills in pretty gilt paper on the Christmas tree. Wouldn't that be fun?

HELMER: What are those little birds called that always fly through their fortunes?

NORA: Oh yes, spendthrifts; I know all that. But let's do as I say, Torvald; then I'll have time to decide what I really need most. That's very sensible, isn't it?

HELMER (*smiling*): Yes, very—that is, if you actually hung onto the money I give you, and you actually used it to buy yourself something. But it goes for the house and for all sorts of foolish things, and then I only have to lay out some more.

NORA: Oh, but Torvald—

HELMER: Don't deny it, my dear little Nora. (*Putting his arm around her waist.*) Spendthrifts are sweet, but they use up a frightful amount of money. It's incredible what it costs a man to feed such birds.

NORA: Oh, how can you say that! Really, I save everything I can.

HELMER (*laughing*): Yes, that's the truth. Everything you can. But that's nothing at all.

NORA (*humming, with a smile of quiet satisfaction*): Hm, if you only knew what expenses we larks and squirrels have, Torvald.

HELMER: You're an odd little one. Exactly the way your father was. You're never at a loss for scaring up money; but the moment you have it, it runs right out through your fingers; you never know what you've done with it. Well, one takes you as you are. It's deep in your blood. Yes, these things are hereditary, Nora.

NORA: Ah, I could wish I'd inherited many of Papa's qualities.

HELMER: And I couldn't wish you anything but just what you are, my sweet little lark. But wait; it seems to me you have a very—what should I call it?—a very suspicious look today—

NORA: I do?

HELMER: You certainly do. Look me straight in the eye.

NORA (*looking at him*): Well?

HELMER (*shaking an admonitory finger*): Surely my sweet tooth hasn't been running riot in town today, has she?

NORA: No. Why do you imagine that?

HELMER: My sweet tooth really didn't make a little detour through the confectioner's?

NORA: No, I assure you, Torvald—

HELMER: Hasn't nibbled some pastry?

NORA: No, not at all.

HELMER: Not even munched a macaroon or two?

NORA: No, Torvald, I assure you, really—

HELMER: There, there now. Of course I'm only joking.

NORA (*going to the table, right*): You know I could never think of going against you.

HELMER: No, I understand that; and you *have* given me your word. (*Going over to her.*) Well, you keep your little Christmas secrets to yourself, Nora darling. I expect they'll come to light this evening, when the tree is lit.

NORA: Did you remember to ask Dr. Rank?

HELMER: No. But there's no need for that, it's assumed he'll be dining with us. All the same, I'll ask him when he stops by here this morning. I've ordered some fine wine. Nora, you can't imagine how I'm looking forward to this evening.

NORA: So am I. And what fun for the children, Torvald!

HELMER: Ah, it's so gratifying to know that one's gotten a safe, secure job, and with a comfortable salary. It's a great satisfaction, isn't it?

NORA: Oh, it's wonderful!

HELMER: Remember last Christmas? Three whole weeks before, you shut yourself in every evening till long after midnight, making flowers for the Christmas tree, and all the other decorations to surprise us. Ugh, that was the dullest time I've ever lived through.

NORA: It wasn't at all dull for me.

HELMER (*smiling*): But the outcome *was* pretty sorry, Nora.

NORA: Oh, don't tease me with that again. How could I help it that the cat came in and tore everything to shreds.

HELMER: No, poor thing, you certainly couldn't. You wanted so much to please us all, and that's what counts. But it's just as well that the hard times are past.

NORA: Yes, it's really wonderful.

HELMER: Now I don't have to sit here alone, boring myself, and you don't have to tire your precious eyes and your fair little delicate hands—

NORA (*clapping her hands*): No, is it really true, Torvald, I don't have to? Oh, how wonderfully lovely to hear! (*Taking his arm.*) Now I'll tell you just how I've thought we should plan things. Right after Christmas—(*The doorbell rings.*) Oh, the bell. (*Straightening the room up a bit.*) Somebody would have to come. What a bore!

HELMER: I'm not at home to visitors, don't forget.

MAID (*from the hall doorway*): Ma'am, a lady to see you—

NORA: All right, let her come in.

MAID (*to Helmer*): And the doctor's just come too.

HELMER: Did he go right to my study?

MAID: Yes, he did.

(*Helmer goes into his room. The Maid shows in Mrs. Linde, dressed in traveling clothes, and shuts the door after her.*)

MRS. LINDE (*in a dispirited and somewhat hesitant voice*): Hello, Nora.

NORA (*uncertain*): Hello—

MRS. LINDE: You don't recognize me.

NORA: No, I don't know—but wait, I think—(*Exclaiming.*) What! Kristine! Is it really you?

MRS. LINDE: Yes, it's me.

NORA: Kristine! To think I didn't recognize you. But then, how could I? (*More quietly.*) How you've changed, Kristine!

MRS. LINDE: Yes, no doubt I have. In nine—ten long years.

NORA: Is it so long since we met! Yes, it's all of that. Oh, these last eight years have been a happy time, believe me. And so now you've come in to town, too. Made the long trip in the winter. That took courage.

MRS. LINDE: I just got here by ship this morning.

NORA: To enjoy yourself over Christmas, of course. Oh, how lovely! Yes, enjoy ourselves, we'll do that. But take your coat off. You're not still cold? (*Helping her.*) There now, let's get cozy here by the stove. No, the easy chair there! I'll take the rocker here. (*Seizing her hands.*) Yes, now you have your old look again; it was only in that first moment. You're a bit more pale, Kristine—and maybe a bit thinner.

MRS. LINDE: And much, much older, Nora.

NORA: Yes, perhaps a bit older; a tiny, tiny bit; not much at all. (*Stopping short; suddenly serious.*) Oh, but thoughtless me, to sit here, chattering away. Sweet, good Kristine, can you forgive me?

MRS. LINDE: What do you mean, Nora?

NORA (*softly*): Poor Kristine, you've become a widow.

MRS. LINDE: Yes, three years ago.

NORA: Oh, I knew it, of course; I read it in the papers. Oh, Kristine, you must believe me; I often thought of writing you then, but I kept postponing it, and something always interfered.

MRS. LINDE: Nora dear, I understand completely.

NORA: No, it was awful of me, Kristine. You poor thing, how much you must have gone through. And he left you nothing?

MRS. LINDE: No.

NORA: And no children?

MRS. LINDE: No.

NORA: Nothing at all, then?

MRS. LINDE: Not even a sense of loss to feed on.

NORA (*looking incredulously at her*): But Kristine, how could that be?

MRS. LINDE (*smiling wearily and smoothing her hair*): Oh, sometimes it happens, Nora.

NORA: So completely alone. How terribly hard that must be for you. I have three lovely children. You can't see them now; they're out with the maid. But now you must tell me everything—

MRS. LINDE: No, no, no, tell me about yourself.

NORA: No, you begin. Today I don't want to be selfish. I want to think only of you today. But there is something I must tell you. Did you hear of the wonderful luck we had recently?

MRS. LINDE: No, what's that?

NORA: My husband's been made manager in the bank, just think!

MRS. LINDE: Your husband? How marvelous!

NORA: Isn't it? Being a lawyer is such an uncertain living, you know, especially if one won't touch any cases that aren't clean and decent. And of course Torvald would never do that, and I'm with him completely there. Oh, we're simply delighted, believe me! He'll join the bank right after New Year's and start getting a huge salary and lots of commissions. From now on we can live quite differently—just as we want. Oh, Kristine, I feel so light and happy! Won't it be lovely to have stacks of money and not a care in the world?

MRS. LINDE: Well, anyway, it would be lovely to have enough for necessities.

NORA: No, not just for necessities, but stacks and stacks of money!

MRS. LINDE (*smiling*): Nora, Nora, aren't you sensible yet? Back in school you were such a free spender.

NORA (*with a quiet laugh*): Yes, that's what Torvald still says. (*Shaking her finger.*) But "Nora, Nora" isn't as silly as you all think. Really, we've been in no position for me to go squandering. We've had to work, both of us.

MRS. LINDE: You too?

NORA: Yes, at odd jobs—needlework, crocheting, embroidery, and such—(*casually*) and other things too. You remember that Torvald left the department when we were married? There was no chance of promotion in his office, and of course he needed to earn more money. But that first year he drove himself terribly. He took on all kinds of extra work that kept him going morning and night. It wore him down, and then he fell deathly ill. The doctors said it was essential for him to travel south.

MRS. LINDE: Yes, didn't you spend a whole year in Italy?

NORA: That's right. It wasn't easy to get away, you know. Ivar had just been born. But of course we had to go. Oh, that was a beautiful trip, and it saved Torvald's life. But it cost a frightful sum, Kristine.

MRS. LINDE: I can well imagine.

NORA: Four thousand, eight hundred crowns it cost. That's really a lot of money.

MRS. LINDE: But it's lucky you had it when you needed it.

NORA: Well, as it was, we got it from Papa.

MRS. LINDE: I see. It was just about the time your father died.

NORA: Yes, just about then. And, you know, I couldn't make that trip out to nurse him. I had to stay here, expecting Ivar any moment, and with my poor sick Torvald to care for. Dearest Papa, I never saw him again, Kristine. Oh, that was the worst time I've known in all my marriage.

MRS. LINDE: I know how you loved him. And then you went off to Italy?

NORA: Yes. We had the means now, and the doctors urged us. So we left a month after.

MRS. LINDE: And your husband came back completely cured?

NORA: Sound as a drum!

MRS. LINDE: But—the doctor?

NORA: Who?

MRS. LINDE: I thought the maid said he was a doctor, the man who came in with me.

NORA: Yes, that was Dr. Rank—but he's not making a sick call. He's our closest friend, and he stops by at least once a day. No, Torvald hasn't had a sick moment since, and the children are fit and strong, and I am, too. (*Jumping up and clapping her hands.*) Oh, dear God, Kristine, what a lovely thing to live and be happy! But how disgusting of me—I'm talking of nothing but my own affairs. (*Sits on a stool close by Kristine, arms resting across her knees.*) Oh, don't be angry with me! Tell me, is it really true that you weren't in love with your husband? Why did you marry him, then?

MRS. LINDE: My mother was still alive, but bedridden and helpless—and I had my two younger brothers to look after. In all conscience, I didn't think I could turn him down.

NORA: No, you were right there. But was he rich at the time?

MRS. LINDE: He was very well off, I'd say. But the business was shaky, Nora. When he died, it all fell apart, and nothing was left.

NORA: And then—?

MRS. LINDE: Yes, so I had to scrape up a living with a little shop and a little teaching and whatever else I could find. The last three years have been like one endless workday without a rest for me. Now, it's over, Nora. My poor mother doesn't need me, for she's passed on. Nor the boys, either; they're working now and can take care of themselves.

NORA: How free you must feel—

MRS. LINDE: No—only unspeakably empty. Nothing to live for now. (*Standing up anxiously.*) That's why I couldn't take it any longer out in that desolate hole. Maybe here it'll be easier to find something to do and keep my mind occupied. If I could only be lucky enough to get a steady job, some office work—

NORA: Oh, but Kristine, that's so dreadfully tiring, and you already look so tired. It would be much better for you if you could go off to a bathing resort.

MRS. LINDE (*going toward the window*): I have no father to give me travel money, Nora.

NORA (*rising*): Oh, don't be angry with me.

MRS. LINDE (*going to her*): Nora dear, don't you be angry with me. The worst of my kind of situation is all the bitterness that's stored away. No one to work for, and yet you're always having to snap up your opportunities. You have to live; and so you grow selfish. When you told me the happy change in your lot, do you know I was delighted less for your sakes than for mine?

NORA: How so? Oh, I see. You think maybe Torvald could do something for you.

MRS. LINDE: Yes, that's what I thought.

NORA: And he will, Kristine! Just leave it to me; I'll bring it up so delicately—find something attractive to humor him with. Oh, I'm so eager to help you.

MRS. LINDE: How very kind of you, Nora, to be so concerned over me—doubly kind, considering you really know so little of life's burdens yourself.

NORA: I—? I know so little—?

MRS. LINDE (*smiling*): Well, my heavens—a little needlework and such—Nora, you're just a child.

NORA (*tossing her head and pacing the floor*): You don't have to act so superior.

MRS. LINDE: Oh?

NORA: You're just like the others. You all think I'm incapable of anything serious—

MRS. LINDE: Come now—

NORA: That I've never had to face the raw world.

MRS. LINDE: Nora dear, you've just been telling me all your troubles.

NORA: Hm! Trivial! (*Quietly.*) I haven't told you the big thing.

MRS. LINDE: Big thing? What do you mean?

NORA: You look down on me so, Kristine, but you shouldn't. You're proud that you worked so long and hard for your mother.

MRS. LINDE: I don't look down on a soul. But it is true: I'm proud—and happy, too—to think it was given to me to make my mother's last days almost free of care.

NORA: And you're also proud thinking of what you've done for your brothers.

MRS. LINDE: I feel I've a right to be.

NORA: I agree. But listen to this, Kristine—I've also got something to be proud and happy for.

MRS. LINDE: I don't doubt it. But whatever do you mean?

NORA: Not so loud. What if Torvald heard! He mustn't, not for anything in the world. Nobody must know, Kristine. No one but you.

MRS. LINDE: But what is it, then?

NORA: Come here. (*Drawing her down beside her on the sofa.*) It's true—I've also got something to be proud and happy for. I'm the one who saved Torvald's life.

MRS. LINDE: Saved—? Saved how?

NORA: I told you about the trip to Italy. Torvald never would have lived if he hadn't gone south—

MRS. LINDE: Of course; your father gave you the means—

NORA (*smiling*): That's what Torvald and all the rest think, but—

MRS. LINDE: But—?

NORA: Papa didn't give us a pin. I was the one who raised the money.

MRS. LINDE: You? That whole amount?

NORA: Four thousand, eight hundred crowns. What do you say to that?

MRS. LINDE: But Nora, how was it possible? Did you win the lottery?

NORA (*disdainfully*): The lottery? Pooh! No art to that.

MRS. LINDE: But where did you get it from then?

NORA (*humming, with a mysterious smile*): Hmm, tra-la-la-la.

MRS. LINDE: Because you couldn't have borrowed it.

NORA: No? Why not?

MRS. LINDE: A wife can't borrow without her husband's consent.

NORA (*tossing her head*): Oh, but a wife with a little business sense, a wife who knows how to manage—

MRS. LINDE: Nora, I simply don't understand—

NORA: You don't have to. Whoever said I *borrowed* the money? I could have gotten it other ways. (*Throwing herself back on the sofa.*) I could have gotten it from some admirer or other. After all, a girl with my ravishing appeal—

MRS. LINDE: You lunatic.

NORA: I'll bet you're eaten up with curiosity, Kristine.

MRS. LINDE: Now listen here, Nora—you haven't done something indiscreet?

NORA (*sitting up again*): Is it indiscreet to save your husband's life?

MRS. LINDE: I think it's indiscreet that without his knowledge you—

NORA: But that's the point: He mustn't know! My Lord, can't you understand? He mustn't ever know the close call he had. It was to *me* the doctors came to say his life was in danger—that nothing could save him but a stay in the south. Didn't I try strategy then! I began talking about how lovely it would be for me to travel abroad like other young wives; I begged and I cried; I told him please to remember my condition, to be kind and indulge me; and then I dropped a hint that he could easily take out a loan. But at that, Kristine, he nearly exploded. He said I was frivolous, and it was his duty as man of the house not to indulge me in whims and fancies—as I think he called them. Aha, I thought, now you'll just have to be saved—and that's when I saw my chance.

MRS. LINDE: And your father never told Torvald the money wasn't from him?

NORA: No, never. Papa died right about then. I'd considered bringing him into my secret and begging him never to tell. But he was too sick at the time—and then, sadly, it didn't matter.

MRS. LINDE: And you've never confided in your husband since?

NORA: For heaven's sake, no! Are you serious? He's so strict on that subject. Besides—Torvald, with all his masculine pride—how painfully humiliating for him if he ever found out he was in debt to me. That would just ruin our relationship. Our beautiful, happy home would never be the same.

MRS. LINDE: Won't you ever tell him?

NORA (*thoughtfully, half smiling*): Yes—maybe sometime years from now, when I'm no longer so attractive. Don't laugh! I only mean when Torvald loves me less than now, when he stops enjoying my dancing and dressing up and reciting for him. Then it might be wise to have something in reserve—(*Breaking off.*) How ridiculous! That'll never happen—Well, Kristine, what do you think of my big secret? I'm capable of something too, hm? You can imagine, of course, how this thing hangs over me. It really hasn't been easy meeting the payments on time. In the business world there's what they call quarterly interest and what they call amortization, and these are always so terribly hard to manage. I've had to skimp a little here and there, wherever I could, you know. I could hardly spare anything from my house allowance, because Torvald has to live well. I couldn't let the children go poorly dressed; whatever I got for them, I felt I had to use up completely—the darlings!

MRS. LINDE: Poor Nora, so it had to come out of your own budget, then?

NORA: Yes, of course. But I was the one most responsible, too. Every time Torvald gave me money for new clothes and such, I never used more than half; always bought the simplest, cheapest outfits. It was a godsend that everything looks so well on me that Torvald never noticed. But it did weigh me down at times, Kristine. It *is* such a joy to wear fine things. You understand.

MRS. LINDE: Oh, of course.

NORA: And then I found other ways of making money. Last winter I was lucky enough to get a lot of copying to do. I locked myself in and sat writing every evening till late in the night. Ah, I was tired so often, dead tired. But still it was wonderful fun, sitting and working like that, earning money. It was almost like being a man.

MRS. LINDE: But how much have you paid off this way so far?

NORA: That's hard to say, exactly. These accounts, you know, aren't easy to figure. I only know that I've paid out all I could scrape together. Time and again I haven't known where to turn. (*Smiling.*) Then I'd sit here dreaming of a rich old gentleman who had fallen in love with me—

MRS. LINDE: What! Who is he?

NORA: Oh, really! And that he'd died, and when his will was opened, there in big letters it said, "All my fortune shall be paid over in cash, immediately, to that enchanting Mrs. Nora Helmer."

MRS. LINDE: But Nora dear—who *was* this gentleman?

NORA: Good grief, can't you understand? The old man never existed; that was only something I'd dream up time and again whenever I was at my wits' end for money. But it makes no difference now; the old fossil can go where he pleases for all I care; I don't need him or his will—because now I'm free. (*Jumping up.*) Oh, how lovely to think of that, Kristine! Carefree! To know you're carefree, utterly carefree; to be able to romp and play with the children, and to keep up a beautiful, charming home—everything just the way Torvald likes it! And think, spring is coming, with big blue skies. Maybe we can travel a little then. Maybe I'll see the ocean again. Oh yes, it *is* so marvelous to live and be happy!

(*The front doorbell rings.*)

MRS. LINDE (*rising*): There's the bell. It's probably best that I go.

NORA: No, stay. No one's expected. It must be for Torvald.

MAID (*from the hall doorway*): Excuse me, ma'am—there's a gentleman here to see Mr. Helmer, but I didn't know—since the doctor's with him—

NORA: Who is the gentleman?

KROGSTAD (*from the doorway*): It's me, Mrs. Helmer.

(*Mrs. Linde starts and turns away toward the window.*)

NORA (*stepping toward him, tense, her voice a whisper*): You? What is it? Why do you want to speak to my husband?

KROGSTAD: Bank business—after a fashion. I have a small job in the investment bank, and I hear now your husband is going to be our chief—

NORA: In other words, it's—

KROGSTAD: Just dry business, Mrs. Helmer. Nothing but that.

NORA: Yes, then please be good enough to step into the study. (*She nods indifferently as she sees him out by the hall door, then returns and begins stirring up the stove.*)

MRS. LINDE: Nora—who was that man?

NORA: That was a Mr. Krogstad—a lawyer.

MRS. LINDE: Then it really was him.

NORA: Do you know that person?

MRS. LINDE: I did once—many years ago. For a time he was a law clerk in our town.

NORA: Yes, he's been that.

MRS. LINDE: How he's changed.

NORA: I understand he had a very unhappy marriage.

MRS. LINDE: He's a widower now.

NORA: With a number of children. There now, it's burning. (*She closes the stove door and moves the rocker a bit to one side.*)

MRS. LINDE: They say he has a hand in all kinds of business.

NORA: Oh? That may be true; I wouldn't know. But let's not think about business. It's so dull.

(*Dr. Rank enters from Helmer's study.*)

RANK (*still in the doorway*): No, no, really—I don't want to intrude, I'd just as soon talk a little while with your wife. (*Shuts the door, then notices Mrs. Linde.*) Oh, beg pardon. I'm intruding here too.

NORA: No, not at all. (*Introducing him.*) Dr. Rank, Mrs. Linde.

RANK: Well now, that's a name much heard in this house. I believe I passed the lady on the stairs as I came.

MRS. LINDE: Yes, I take the stairs very slowly. They're rather hard on me.

RANK: Uh-hm, some touch of internal weakness?

MRS. LINDE: More overexertion, I'd say.

RANK: Nothing else? Then you're probably here in town to rest up in a round of parties?

MRS. LINDE: I'm here to look for work.

RANK: Is that the best cure for overexertion?

MRS. LINDE: One has to live, Doctor.

RANK: Yes, there's a common prejudice to that effect.

NORA: Oh, come on, Dr. Rank—you really do want to live yourself.

RANK: Yes, I really do. Wretched as I am, I'll gladly prolong my torment indefinitely. All my patients feel like that. And it's quite the same, too, with the morally sick. Right at this moment there's one of those moral invalids in there with Helmer—

MRS. LINDE (*softly*): Ah!

NORA: Who do you mean?

RANK: Oh, it's a lawyer, Krogstad, a type you wouldn't know. His character is rotten to the root—but even he began chattering all-importantly about how he had to *live.*

NORA: Oh? What did he want to talk to Torvald about?

RANK: I really don't know. I only heard something about the bank.

NORA: I didn't know that Krog—that this man Krogstad had anything to do with the bank.

RANK: Yes, he's gotten some kind of berth down there. (*To Mrs. Linde.*) I don't know if you also have, in your neck of the woods, a type of person who scuttles about breathlessly, sniffing out hints of moral corruption, and then maneuvers his victim into some sort of key position where he can keep an eye on him. It's the healthy these days that are out in the cold.

MRS. LINDE: All the same, it's the sick who most need to be taken in.

RANK (*with a shrug*): Yes, there we have it. That's the concept that's turning society into a sanatorium.

(*Nora, lost in her thoughts, breaks out into quiet laughter and claps her hands.*)

RANK: Why do you laugh at that? Do you have any real idea of what society is?

NORA: What do I care about dreary old society? I was laughing at something quite different—something terribly funny. Tell me, Doctor—is everyone who works in the bank dependent now on Torvald?

RANK: Is that what you find so terribly funny?

NORA (*smiling and humming*): Never mind, never mind! (*Pacing the floor.*) Yes, that's really immensely amusing: that we—that Torvald has so much power now over all those people. (*Taking the bag out of her pocket.*) Dr. Rank, a little macaroon on that?

RANK: See here, macaroons! I thought they were contraband here.

NORA: Yes, but these are some that Kristine gave me.

MRS. LINDE: What? I—?

NORA: Now, now, don't be afraid. You couldn't possibly know that Torvald had forbidden them. You see, he's worried they'll ruin my teeth. But hmp! Just this once! Isn't that so, Dr. Rank? Help yourself! (*Puts a macaroon in his mouth.*) And you too, Kristine. And I'll also have one, only a little one—or two, at the most. (*Walking about again.*) Now I'm really tremendously happy. Now's there's just one last thing in the world that I have an enormous desire to do.

RANK: Well! And what's that?

NORA: It's something I have such a consuming desire to say so Torvald could hear.

RANK: And why can't you say it?

NORA: I don't dare. It's quite shocking.

MRS. LINDE: Shocking?

RANK: Well, then it isn't advisable. But in front of us you certainly can. What do you have such a desire to say so Torvald could hear?

NORA: I have such a huge desire to say—to hell and be damned!

RANK: Are you crazy?

MRS. LINDE: My goodness, Nora!

RANK: Go on, say it. Here he is.

NORA (*hiding the macaroon bag*): Shh, shh, shh!

(*Helmer comes in from his study, hat in hand, overcoat over his arm.*)

NORA (*going toward him*): Well, Torvald dear, are you through with him?

HELMER: Yes, he just left.

NORA: Let me introduce you—this is Kristine, who's arrived here in town.

HELMER: Kristine—? I'm sorry, but I don't know—

NORA: Mrs. Linde, Torvald dear. Mrs. Kristine Linde.

HELMER: Of course. A childhood friend of my wife's, no doubt?

MRS. LINDE: Yes, we knew each other in those days.

NORA: And just think, she made the long trip down here in order to talk with you.

HELMER: What's this?

MRS. LINDE: Well, not exactly—

NORA: You see, Kristine is remarkably clever in office work, and so she's terribly eager to come under a capable man's supervision and add more to what she already knows—

HELMER: Very wise, Mrs. Linde.

NORA: And then when she heard that you'd become a bank manager—the story was wired out to the papers—then she came in as fast as she could and—Really, Torvald, for my sake you can do a little something for Kristine, can't you?

HELMER: Yes, it's not at all impossible. Mrs. Linde, I suppose you're a widow?

MRS. LINDE: Yes.

HELMER: Any experience in office work?

MRS. LINDE: Yes, a good deal.

HELMER: Well, it's quite likely that I can make an opening for you—

NORA (*clapping her hands*): You see, you see!

HELMER: You've come at a lucky moment, Mrs. Linde.

MRS. LINDE: Oh, how can I thank you?

HELMER: Not necessary. (*Putting his overcoat on.*) But today you'll have to excuse me—

RANK: Wait, I'll go with you. (*He fetches his coat from the hall and warms it at the stove.*)

NORA: Don't stay out long, dear.

HELMER: An hour; no more.

NORA: Are you going too, Kristine?

MRS. LINDE (*putting on her winter garments*): Yes, I have to see about a room now.

HELMER: Then perhaps we can all walk together.

NORA (*helping her*): What a shame we're so cramped here, but it's quite impossible for us to—

MRS. LINDE: Oh, don't even think of it! Good-bye, Nora dear, and thanks for everything.

NORA: Good-bye for now. Of course you'll be back this evening. And you too, Dr. Rank. What? If you're well enough? Oh, you've got to be! Wrap up tight now.

(*In a ripple of small talk the company moves out into the hall; children's voices are heard outside on the steps.*)

NORA: There they are! There they are! (*She runs to open the door. The children come in with their nurse, Anne-Marie.*) Come in, come in! (*Bends down and kisses them.*) Oh, you darlings—! Look at them, Kristine. Aren't they lovely!

RANK: No loitering in the draft here.

HELMER: Come, Mrs. Linde—this place is unbearable now for anyone but mothers.

(*Dr. Rank, Helmer, and Mrs. Linde go down the stairs. Anne-Marie goes into the living room with the children. Nora follows, after closing the hall door.*)

NORA: How fresh and strong you look. Oh, such red cheeks you have! Like apples and roses. (*The children interrupt her throughout the following.*) And it was so much fun? That's wonderful. Really? You pulled both Emmy and Bob on the sled? Imagine, all together! Yes, you're a clever boy, Ivar. Oh, let me hold her a bit, Anne-Marie. My sweet little doll baby! (*Takes the smallest from the nurse and dances with her.*) Yes, yes, Mama will dance with Bob as well. What? Did you throw snowballs? Oh, if I'd only been there! No, don't bother, Anne-Marie—I'll undress them myself. Oh yes, let me. It's such fun. Go in and rest; you look half frozen. There's hot coffee waiting for you on the stove. (*The nurse goes into the room to the left. Nora takes the children's winter things off, throwing them about, while the children talk to her all at once.*) Is that so? A big dog chased you? But it didn't bite? No, dogs never bite little, lovely doll babies. Don't peek in the packages, Ivar! What is it? Yes, wouldn't you like to know. No, no, it's an ugly something. Well? Shall we play? What shall we play? Hide-and-seek? Yes, let's play hide-and-seek. Bob must hide first. I must? Yes, let me hide first. (*Laughing and shouting, she and the children play in and out of the living room and the adjoining room to the right. At last Nora hides under the table. The children come storming in, search, but cannot find her, then hear her muffled laughter, dash over to the table, lift the cloth up and find her. Wild shouting. She creeps forward as if to scare them. More shouts. Meanwhile, a knock at the hall door; no one has noticed it. Now the door half opens, and Krogstad appears. He waits a moment; the game goes on.*)

KROGSTAD: Beg pardon, Mrs. Helmer—

NORA (*with a strangled cry, turning and scrambling to her knees*): Oh! What do you want?

KROGSTAD: Excuse me. The outer door was ajar; it must be someone forgot to shut it—

NORA (*rising*): My husband isn't home, Mr. Krogstad.

KROGSTAD: I know that.

NORA: Yes—then what do you want here?

KROGSTAD: A word with you.

NORA: With—? (*To the children, quietly.*) Go in to Anne-Marie. What? No, the strange man won't hurt Mama. When he's gone, we'll play some more. (*She leads the children into the room to the left and shuts the door after them. Then, tense and nervous:*) You want to speak to me?

KROGSTAD: Yes, I want to.

NORA: Today? But it's not yet the first of the month—

KROGSTAD: No, it's Christmas Eve. It's going to be up to you how merry a Christmas you have.

NORA: What is it you want? Today I absolutely can't—

KROGSTAD: We won't talk about that till later. This is something else. You do have a moment to spare, I suppose?

NORA: Oh yes, of course — I do, except —

KROGSTAD: Good. I was sitting over at Olsen's Restaurant when I saw your husband go down the street —

NORA: Yes?

KROGSTAD: With a lady.

NORA: Yes. So?

KROGSTAD: If you'll pardon my asking: Wasn't that lady a Mrs. Linde?

NORA: Yes.

KROGSTAD: Just now come into town?

NORA: Yes, today.

KROGSTAD: She's a good friend of yours?

NORA: Yes, she is. But I don't see —

KROGSTAD: I also knew her once.

NORA: I'm aware of that.

KROGSTAD: Oh? You know all about it. I thought so. Well, then let me ask you short and sweet: Is Mrs. Linde getting a job in the bank?

NORA: What makes you think you can cross-examine me, Mr. Krogstad — you, one of my husband's employees? But since you ask, you might as well know — yes, Mrs. Linde's going to be taken on at the bank. And I'm the one who spoke for her, Mr. Krogstad. Now you know.

KROGSTAD: So I guessed right.

NORA (*pacing up and down*): Oh, one does have a tiny bit of influence, I should hope. Just because I am a woman, don't think it means that — When one has a subordinate position, Mr. Krogstad, one really ought to be careful about pushing somebody who — hm —

KROGSTAD: Who has influence?

NORA: That's right.

KROGSTAD (*in a different tone*): Mrs. Helmer, would you be good enough to use your influence on my behalf?

NORA: What? What do you mean?

KROGSTAD: Would you please make sure that I keep my subordinate position in the bank?

NORA: What does that mean? Who's thinking of taking away your position?

KROGSTAD: Oh, don't play the innocent with me. I'm quite aware that your friend would hardly relish the chance of running into me again; and I'm also aware now whom I can thank for being turned out.

NORA: But I promise you —

KROGSTAD: Yes, yes, yes, to the point: There's still time, and I'm advising you to use your influence to prevent it.

NORA: But Mr. Krogstad, I have absolutely no influence.

KROGSTAD: You haven't? I thought you were just saying —

NORA: You shouldn't take me so literally. I! How can you believe that I have any such influence over my husband?

KROGSTAD: Oh, I've known your husband from our student days. I don't think the great bank manager's more steadfast than any other married man.

NORA: You speak insolently about my husband, and I'll show you the door.

KROGSTAD: The lady has spirit.

NORA: I'm not afraid of you any longer. After New Year's, I'll soon be done with the whole business.

KROGSTAD (*restraining himself*): Now listen to me, Mrs. Helmer. If necessary, I'll fight for my little job in the bank as if it were life itself.

NORA: Yes, so it seems.

KROGSTAD: It's not just a matter of income; that's the least of it. It's something else — All right, out with it! Look, this is the thing. You know, just like all the others, of course, that once, a good many years ago, I did something rather rash.

NORA: I've heard rumors to that effect.

KROGSTAD: The case never got into court; but all the same, every door was closed in my face from then on. So I took up those various activities you know about. I had to grab hold somewhere; and I dare say I haven't been among the worst. But now I want to drop all that. My boys are growing up. For their sakes, I'll have to win back as much respect as possible here in town. That job in the bank was like the first rung in my ladder. And now your husband wants to kick me right back down in the mud again.

NORA: But for heaven's sake, Mr. Krogstad, it's simply not in my power to help you.

KROGSTAD: That's because you haven't the will to — but I have the means to make you.

NORA: You certainly won't tell my husband that I owe you money?

KROGSTAD: Hm — what if I told him that?

NORA: That would be shameful of you. (*Nearly in tears.*) This secret — my joy and my pride — that he should learn it in such a crude and disgusting way — learn it from you. You'd expose me to the most horrible unpleasantness —

KROGSTAD: Only unpleasantness?

NORA (*vehemently*): But go on and try. It'll turn out the worse for you, because then my husband will really see what a crook you are, and then you'll never be able to hold your job.

KROGSTAD: I asked if it was just domestic unpleasantness you were afraid of?

NORA: If my husband finds out, then of course he'll pay what I owe at once, and then we'd be through with you for good.

KROGSTAD (*a step closer*): Listen, Mrs. Helmer — you've either got a very bad memory, or else no head at all for business. I'd better put you a little more in touch with the facts.

NORA: What do you mean?

KROGSTAD: When your husband was sick, you came to me for a loan of four thousand, eight hundred crowns.

NORA: Where else could I go?

KROGSTAD: I promised to get you that sum —

NORA: And you got it.

KROGSTAD: I promised to get you that sum, on certain conditions. You were so involved in your husband's illness, and so eager to finance your trip, that I guess you didn't think out all the details. It might just be a good idea to remind you. I promised you the money on the strength of a note I drew up.

NORA: Yes, and that I signed.

KROGSTAD: Right. But at the bottom I added some lines for your father to guarantee the loan. He was supposed to sign down there.

NORA: Supposed to? He did sign.

KROGSTAD: I left the date blank. In other words, your father would have dated his signature himself. Do you remember that?

NORA: Yes, I think—

KROGSTAD: Then I gave you the note for you to mail to your father. Isn't that so?

NORA: Yes.

KROGSTAD: And naturally you sent it at once—because only some five, six days later you brought me the note, properly signed. And with that, the money was yours.

NORA: Well, then; I've made my payments regularly, haven't I?

KROGSTAD: More or less. But—getting back to the point—those were hard times for you then, Mrs. Helmer.

NORA: Yes, they were.

KROGSTAD: Your father was very ill, I believe.

NORA: He was near the end.

KROGSTAD: He died soon after?

NORA: Yes.

KROGSTAD: Tell me, Mrs. Helmer, do you happen to recall the date of your father's death? The day of the month, I mean.

NORA: Papa died the twenty-ninth of September.

KROGSTAD: That's quite correct; I've already looked into that. And now we come to a curious thing— (*taking out a paper*) which I simply cannot comprehend.

NORA: Curious thing? I don't know—

KROGSTAD: This is the curious thing: that your father co-signed the note for your loan three days after his death.

NORA: How—? I don't understand.

KROGSTAD: Your father died the twenty-ninth of September. But look. Here your father dated his signature October second. Isn't that curious, Mrs. Helmer? (*Nora is silent.*) Can you explain it to me? (*Nora remains silent.*) It's also remarkable that the words "October second" and the year aren't written in your father's hand, but rather in one that I think I know. Well, it's easy to understand. Your father forgot perhaps to date his signature, and then someone or other added it, a bit sloppily, before anyone knew of his death. There's nothing wrong in that. It all comes down to the signature. And there's no question about *that*, Mrs. Helmer. It really *was* your father who signed his own name here, wasn't it?

NORA (*after a short silence, throwing her head back and looking squarely at him*): No, it wasn't. I signed Papa's name.

KROGSTAD: Wait, now—are you fully aware that this is a dangerous confession?

NORA: Why? You'll soon get your money.

KROGSTAD: Let me ask you a question—why didn't you send the paper to your father?

NORA: That was impossible. Papa was so sick. If I'd asked him for his signature, I also would have had to tell him what the money was for. But I couldn't tell him, sick as he was, that my husband's life was in danger. That was just impossible.

KROGSTAD: Then it would have been better if you'd given up the trip abroad.

NORA: I couldn't possibly. The trip was to save my husband's life. I couldn't give that up.

KROGSTAD: But didn't you ever consider that this was a fraud against me?

NORA: I couldn't let myself be bothered by that. You weren't any concern of mine. I couldn't stand you, with all those cold complications you made, even though you knew how badly off my husband was.

KROGSTAD: Mrs. Helmer, obviously you haven't the vaguest idea of what you've involved yourself in. But I can tell you this: It was nothing more and nothing worse that I once did—and it wrecked my whole reputation.

NORA: You? Do you expect me to believe that you ever acted bravely to save your wife's life?

KROGSTAD: Laws don't inquire into motives.

NORA: Then they must be very poor laws.

KROGSTAD: Poor or not—if I introduce this paper in court, you'll be judged according to law.

NORA: This I refuse to believe. A daughter hasn't a right to protect her dying father from anxiety and care? A wife hasn't a right to save her husband's life? I don't know much about laws, but I'm sure that somewhere in the books these things are allowed. And you don't know anything about it—you who practice the law? You must be an awful lawyer, Mr. Krogstad.

KROGSTAD: Could be. But business—the kind of business we two are mixed up in—don't you think I know about that? All right. Do what you want now. But I'm telling you this: If I get shoved down a second time, you're going to keep me company. (*He bows and goes out through the hall.*)

NORA (*pensive for a moment, then tossing her head*): Oh, really! Trying to frighten me! I'm not so silly as all that. (*Begins gathering up the children's clothes, but soon stops.*) But—? No, but that's impossible! I did it out of love.

THE CHILDREN (*in the doorway, left*): Mama, that strange man's gone out the door.

NORA: Yes, yes, I know it. But don't tell anyone about the strange man. Do you hear? Not even Papa!

THE CHILDREN: No, Mama. But now will you play again?

NORA: No, not now.

THE CHILDREN: Oh, but Mama, you promised.

NORA: Yes, but I can't now. Go inside; I have too much to do. Go in, go in, my sweet darlings. (*She herds them gently back in the room and shuts the door after them. Settling on the sofa, she takes up a piece of embroidery and makes some stitches, but soon stops abruptly.*) No! (*Throws the work aside, rises, goes to the hall door and calls out.*) Helene! Let me have the tree in here. (*Goes to the table, left, opens the table drawer, and stops again.*) No, but that's utterly impossible!

MAID (*with the Christmas tree*): Where should I put it, ma'am?

NORA: There. The middle of the floor.

MAID: Should I bring anything else?

NORA: No, thanks. I have what I need.

(*The Maid, who has set the tree down, goes out.*)

NORA (*absorbed in trimming the tree*): Candles here — and flowers here. That terrible creature! Talk, talk, talk! There's nothing to it at all. The tree's going to be lovely. I'll do anything to please you Torvald. I'll sing for you, dance for you —

(*Helmer comes in from the hall, with a sheaf of papers under his arm.*)

NORA: Oh! You're back so soon?

HELMER: Yes. Has anyone been here?

NORA: Here? No.

HELMER: That's odd. I saw Krogstad leaving the front door.

NORA: So? Oh yes, that's true. Krogstad was here a moment.

HELMER: Nora, I can see by your face that he's been here, begging you to put in a good word for him.

NORA: Yes.

HELMER: And it was supposed to seem like your own idea? You were to hide it from me that he'd been here. He asked you that, too, didn't he?

NORA: Yes, Torvald, but—

HELMER: Nora, Nora, and you could fall for that? Talk with that sort of person and promise him anything? And then in the bargain, tell me an untruth.

NORA: An untruth—?

HELMER: Didn't you say that no one had been here? (*Wagging his finger.*) My little songbird must never do that again. A songbird needs a clean beak to warble with. No false notes. (*Putting his arm about her waist.*) That's the way it should be, isn't it? Yes, I'm sure of it. (*Releasing her.*) And so, enough of that. (*Sitting by the stove.*) Ah, how snug and cozy it is here. (*Leafing among his papers.*)

NORA (*busy with the tree, after a short pause*): Torvald!

HELMER: Yes.

NORA: I'm so much looking forward to the Stenborgs' costume party, day after tomorrow.

HELMER: And I can't wait to see what you'll surprise me with.

NORA: Oh, that stupid business!

HELMER: What?

NORA: I can't find anything that's right. Everything seems so ridiculous, so inane.

HELMER: So my little Nora's come to *that* recognition?

NORA (*going behind his chair, her arms resting on its back*): Are you very busy, Torvald?

HELMER: Oh—

NORA: What papers are those?

HELMER: Bank matters.

NORA: Already?

HELMER: I've gotten full authority from the retiring management to make all necessary changes in personnel and procedure. I'll need Christmas week for that. I want to have everything in order by New Year's.

NORA: So that was the reason this poor Krogstad—

HELMER: Hm.

NORA (*still leaning on the chair and slowly stroking the nape of his neck*): If you weren't so very busy, I would have asked you an enormous favor, Torvald.

HELMER: Let's hear. What is it?

NORA: You know, there isn't anyone who has your good taste—and I want so much to look well at the costume party. Torvald, couldn't you take over and decide what I should be and plan my costume?

HELMER: Ah, is my stubborn little creature calling for a lifeguard?

NORA: Yes, Torvald, I can't get anywhere without your help.

HELMER: All right—I'll think it over. We'll hit on something.

NORA: Oh, how sweet of you. (*Goes to the tree again. Pause.*) Aren't the red flowers pretty—? But tell me, was it really such a crime that this Krogstad committed?

HELMER: Forgery. Do you have any idea what that means?

NORA: Couldn't he have done it out of need?

HELMER: Yes, or thoughtlessness, like so many others. I'm not so heartless that I'd condemn a man categorically for just one mistake.

NORA: No, of course not, Torvald!

HELMER: Plenty of men have redeemed themselves by openly confessing their crimes and taking their punishment.

NORA: Punishment—?

HELMER: But now Krogstad didn't go that way. He got himself out by sharp practices, and that's the real cause of his moral breakdown.

NORA: Do you really think that would—?

HELMER: Just imagine how a man with that sort of guilt in him has to lie and cheat and deceive on all sides, has to wear a mask even with the nearest and dearest he has, even with his own wife and children. And with the children, Nora—that's where it's most horrible.

NORA: Why?

HELMER: Because that kind of atmosphere of lies infects the whole life of a home. Every breath the children take in is filled with the germs of something degenerate.

NORA (*coming closer behind him*): Are you sure of that?

HELMER: Oh, I've seen it often enough as a lawyer. Almost everyone who goes bad early in life has a mother who's a chronic liar.

NORA: Why just—the mother?

HELMER: It's usually the mother's influence that's dominant, but the father's works in the same way, of course. Every lawyer is quite familiar with it. And still this Krogstad's been going home year in, year out, poisoning his own children with lies and pretense; that's why I call him morally lost. (*Reaching his hands out toward her.*) So my sweet little Nora must promise me never to plead his cause. Your hand on it. Come, come, what's this? Give me your hand. There, now. All settled. I can tell you it'd be impossible for me to work alongside of him. I literally feel physically revolted when I'm anywhere near such a person.

NORA (*withdraws her hand and goes to the other side of the Christmas tree*): How hot it is here! And I've got so much to do.

HELMER (*getting up and gathering his papers*): Yes, and I have to think about getting some of these read through before dinner. I'll think about your costume, too. And something to hang on the tree in gilt paper, I may even see about that. (*Putting his hand on her head.*) Oh you, my darling little songbird. (*He goes into his study and closes the door after him.*)

NORA (*softly, after a silence*): Oh, really! It isn't so. It's impossible. It must be impossible.

ANNE-MARIE (*in the doorway left*): The children are begging so hard to come in to Mama.

NORA: No, no, no, don't let them in to me! You stay with them, Anne-Marie.

ANNE-MARIE: Of course, ma'am. (*Closes the door.*)

NORA (*pale with terror*): Hurt my children—! Poison my home? (*A moment's pause; then she tosses her head.*) That's not true. Never. Never in all the world.

ACT 2

(*Same room. Beside the piano the Christmas tree now stands stripped of ornament, burned-down candle stubs on its ragged branches. Nora's street clothes lie on the sofa. Nora, alone in the room, moves restlessly about; at last she stops at the sofa and picks up her coat.*)

NORA (*dropping the coat again*): Someone's coming! (*Goes toward the door, listens.*) No—there's no one. Of course—nobody's coming today, Christmas Day—or tomorrow, either. But maybe—(*Opens the door and looks out.*) No, nothing in the mailbox. Quite empty. (*Coming forward.*) What nonsense! He won't do anything serious. Nothing terrible could happen. It's impossible. Why, I have three small children.

(*Anne-Marie, with a large carton, comes in from the room to the left.*)

ANNE-MARIE: Well, at last I found the box with the masquerade clothes.

NORA: Thanks. Put it on the table.

ANNE-MARIE (*does so*): But they're all pretty much of a mess.

NORA: Ahh! I'd love to rip them in a million pieces!

ANNE-MARIE: Oh, mercy, they can be fixed right up. Just a little patience.

NORA: Yes, I'll go get Mrs. Linde to help me.

ANNE-MARIE: Out again now? In this nasty weather? Miss Nora will catch cold — get sick.

NORA: Oh, worse things could happen — How are the children?

ANNE-MARIE: The poor mites are playing with their Christmas presents, but—

NORA: Do they ask for me much?

ANNE-MARIE: They're so used to having Mama around, you know.

NORA: Yes, but Anne-Marie, I *can't* be together with them as much as I was.

ANNE-MARIE: Well, small children get used to anything.

NORA: You think so? Do you think they'd forget their mother if she was gone for good?

ANNE-MARIE: Oh, mercy — gone for good!

NORA: Wait, tell me. Anne-Marie — I've wondered so often — how could you ever have the heart to give your child over to strangers?

ANNE-MARIE: But I had to, you know, to become little Nora's nurse.

NORA: Yes, but how could you *do* it?

ANNE-MARIE: When I could get such a good place? A girl who's poor and who's gotten in trouble is glad enough for that. Because that slippery fish, he didn't do a thing for me, you know.

NORA: But your daughter's surely forgotten you.

ANNE-MARIE: Oh, she certainly has not. She's written to me, both when she was confirmed and when she was married.

NORA (*clasping her about the neck*): You old Anne-Marie, you were a good mother for me when I was little.

ANNE-MARIE: Poor little Nora, with no other mother but me.

NORA: And if the babies didn't have one, then I know that you'd — What silly talk! (*Opening the carton.*) Go in to them. Now I'll have to — Tomorrow you can see how lovely I'll look.

ANNE-MARIE: Oh, there won't be anyone at the party as lovely as Miss Nora. (*She goes off into the room, left.*)

NORA (*begins unpacking the box, but soon throws it aside*): Oh, if I dared to go out. If only nobody would come. If only nothing would happen here while I'm out. What craziness — nobody's coming. Just don't think. This muff — needs a brushing. Beautiful gloves, beautiful gloves. Let it go. Let it go! One, two, three, four, five, six — (*With a cry.*) Oh, there they are! (*Poises to move toward the door, but remains irresolutely standing. Mrs. Linde enters from the hall, where she has removed her street clothes.*)

NORA: Oh, it's you, Kristine. There's no one else out there? How good that you've come.

MRS. LINDE: I hear you were up asking for me.

NORA: Yes, I just stopped by. There's something you really can help me with. Let's get settled on the sofa. Look, there's going to be a costume party tomorrow evening at the Stenborgs' right above us, and now Torvald wants me to go as a Neapolitan peasant girl and dance the tarantella° that I learned in Capri.

MRS. LINDE: Really, are you giving a whole performance?

NORA: Torvald says yes, I should. See, here's the dress. Torvald had it made for me down there; but now it's all so tattered that I just don't know—

MRS. LINDE: Oh, we'll fix that up in no time. It's nothing more than the trimmings—they're a bit loose here and there. Needle and thread? Good, now we have what we need.

NORA: Oh, how sweet of you!

MRS. LINDE (*sewing*): So you'll be in disguise tomorrow, Nora. You know what? I'll stop by then for a moment and have a look at you all dressed up. But listen, I've absolutely forgotten to thank you for that pleasant evening yesterday.

NORA (*getting up and walking about*): I don't think it was as pleasant as usual yesterday. You should have come to town a bit sooner, Kristine—Yes, Torvald really knows how to give a home elegance and charm.

MRS. LINDE: And you do, too, if you ask me. You're not your father's daughter for nothing. But tell me, is Dr. Rank always so down in the mouth as yesterday?

NORA: No, that was quite an exception. But he goes around critically ill all the time—tuberculosis of the spine, poor man. You know, his father was a disgusting thing who kept mistresses and so on—and that's why the son's been sickly from birth.

MRS. LINDE (*lets her sewing fall to her lap*): But my dearest Nora, how do you know about such things?

NORA (*walking more jauntily*): Hmp! When you've had three children, then you've had a few visits from—from women who know something of medicine, and they tell you this and that.

MRS. LINDE (*resumes sewing; a short pause*): Does Dr. Rank come here every day?

NORA: Every blessed day. He's Torvald's best friend from childhood, and *my* good friend, too. Dr. Rank almost belongs to this house.

MRS. LINDE: But tell me—is he quite sincere? I mean, doesn't he rather enjoy flattering people?

NORA: Just the opposite. Why do you think that?

MRS. LINDE: When you introduced us yesterday, he was proclaiming that he'd often heard my name in this house; but later I noticed that your husband hadn't the slightest idea who I really was. So how could Dr. Rank—?

NORA: But it's all true, Kristine. You see, Torvald loves me beyond words, and, as he puts it, he'd like to keep me all to himself. For a long time he'd almost be jealous if I even mentioned any of my old friends back home. So of course I dropped that. But with Dr. Rank I talk a lot about such things because he likes hearing about them.

MRS. LINDE: Now listen, Nora; in many ways you're still like a child. I'm a good deal older than you, with a little more experience. I'll tell you something: You ought to put an end to all this with Dr. Rank.

---

tarantella: A rapid whirling dance long popular in southern Italy.

NORA: What should I put an end to?

MRS. LINDE: Both parts of it, I think. Yesterday you said something about a rich admirer who'd provide you with money—

NORA: Yes, one who doesn't exist—worse luck. So?

MRS. LINDE: Is Dr. Rank well off?

NORA: Yes, he is.

MRS. LINDE: With no dependents?

NORA: No, no one. But—

MRS. LINDE: And he's over here every day?

NORA: Yes, I told you that.

MRS. LINDE: How can a man of such refinement be so grasping?

NORA: I don't follow you at all.

MRS. LINDE: Now don't try to hide it, Nora. You think I can't guess who loaned you the forty-eight hundred crowns?

NORA: Are you out of your mind? How could you think such a thing! A friend of ours, who comes here every single day. What an intolerable situation that would have been!

MRS. LINDE: Then it really wasn't him.

NORA: No, absolutely not. It never even crossed my mind for a moment—And he had nothing to lend in those days; his inheritance came later.

MRS. LINDE: Well, I think that was a stroke of luck for you, Nora dear.

NORA: No, it never would have occurred to me to ask Dr. Rank—Still, I'm quite sure that if I had asked him—

MRS. LINDE: Which you won't, of course.

NORA: No, of course not. I can't see that I'd ever need to. But I'm quite positive that if I talked to Dr. Rank—

MRS. LINDE: Behind your husband's back?

NORA: I've got to clear up this other thing; *that's* also behind his back. I've *got* to clear it all up.

MRS. LINDE: Yes, I was saying that yesterday, but—

NORA (*pacing up and down*): A man handles these problems so much better than a woman—

MRS. LINDE: One's husband does, yes.

NORA: Nonsense. (*Stopping.*) When you pay everything you owe, then you get your note back, right?

MRS. LINDE: Yes, naturally.

NORA: And can rip it into a million pieces and burn it up—that filthy scrap of paper!

MRS. LINDE (*looking hard at her, laying her sewing aside, and rising slowly*): Nora, you're hiding something from me.

NORA: You can see it in my face?

MRS. LINDE: Something's happened to you since yesterday morning. Nora, what is it?

NORA (*hurrying toward her*): Kristine! (*Listening.*) Shh! Torvald's home. Look, go in with the children a while. Torvald can't bear all this snipping and stitching. Let Anne-Marie help you.

MRS. LINDE (*gathering up some of the things*): All right, but I'm not leaving here until we've talked this out. (*She disappears into the room, left, as Torvald enters from the hall.*)

NORA: Oh, how I've been waiting for you, Torvald dear.

HELMER: Was that the dressmaker?

NORA: No, that was Kristine. She's helping me fix up my costume. You know, it's going to be quite attractive.

HELMER: Yes, wasn't that a bright idea I had?

NORA: Brilliant! But then wasn't I good as well to give in to you?

HELMER: Good—because you give in to your husband's judgment? All right, you little goose, I know you didn't mean it like that. But I won't disturb you. You'll want to have a fitting, I suppose.

NORA: And you'll be working?

HELMER: Yes. (*Indicating a bundle of papers.*) See. I've been down to the bank. (*Starts toward his study.*)

NORA: Torvald.

HELMER (*stops*): Yes.

NORA: If your little squirrel begged you, with all her heart and soul, for something—?

HELMER: What's that?

NORA: Then would you do it?

HELMER: First, naturally, I'd have to know what it was.

NORA: Your squirrel would scamper about and do tricks, if you'd only be sweet and give in.

HELMER: Out with it.

NORA: Your lark would be singing high and low in every room—

HELMER: Come on, she does that anyway.

NORA: I'd be a wood nymph and dance for you in the moonlight.

HELMER: Nora—don't tell me it's that same business from this morning?

NORA (*coming closer*): Yes, Torvald, I beg you, please!

HELMER: And you actually have the nerve to drag that up again?

NORA: Yes, yes, you've got to give in to me; you *have* to let Krogstad keep his job in the bank.

HELMER: My dear Nora, I've slated his job for Mrs. Linde.

NORA: That's awfully kind of you. But you could just fire another clerk instead of Krogstad.

HELMER: This is the most incredible stubbornness! Because you go and give an impulsive promise to speak up for him, I'm expected to—

NORA: That's not the reason, Torvald. It's for your own sake. That man does writing for the worst papers; you said it yourself. He could do you any amount of harm. I'm scared to death of him—

HELMER: Ah, I understand. It's the old memories haunting you.

NORA: What do you mean by that?

HELMER: Of course, you're thinking about your father.

NORA: Yes, all right. Just remember how those nasty gossips wrote in the papers about Papa and slandered him so cruelly. I think they'd have had him

dismissed if the department hadn't sent you up to investigate, and if you
hadn't been so kind and open-minded toward him.

HELMER: My dear Nora, there's a notable difference between your father and me.
Your father's official career was hardly above reproach. But mine is; and I
hope it'll stay that way as long as I hold my position.

NORA: Oh, who can ever tell what vicious minds can invent? We could be so
snug and happy now in our quiet, carefree home—you and I and the children, Torvald! That's why I'm pleading with you so—

HELMER: And just by pleading for him you make it impossible for me to keep him
on. It's already known at the bank that I'm firing Krogstad. What if it's
rumored around now that the new bank manager was vetoed by his wife—

NORA: Yes, what then—?

HELMER: Oh yes—as long as our little bundle of stubbornness gets her way—!
I should go and make myself ridiculous in front of the whole office—give
people the idea I can be swayed by all kinds of outside pressure. Oh, you
can bet I'd feel the effects of that soon enough! Besides—there's something
that rules Krogstad right out at the bank as long as I'm the manager.

NORA: What's that?

HELMER: His moral failings I could maybe overlook if I had to—

NORA: Yes, Torvald, why not?

HELMER: And I hear he's quite efficient on the job. But he was a crony of mine
back in my teens—one of those rash friendships that crop up again and
again to embarrass you later in life. Well, I might as well say it straight
out: We're on a first-name basis. And that tactless fool makes no effort at
all to hide it in front of others. Quite the contrary—he thinks that entitles
him to take a familiar air around me, and so every other second he comes
booming out with his, "Yes, Torvald!" and "Sure thing, Torvald!" I tell you,
it's been excruciating for me. He's out to make my place in the bank
unbearable.

NORA: Torvald, you can't be serious about all this.

HELMER: Oh no? Why not?

NORA: Because these are such petty considerations.

HELMER: What are you saying? Petty? You think I'm petty!

NORA: No, just the opposite, Torvald dear. That's exactly why—

HELMER: Never mind. You call my motives petty; then I might as well be just
that. Petty! All right! We'll put a stop to this for good. (*Goes to the hall door
and calls.*) Helene!

NORA: What do you want?

HELMER (*searching among his papers*): A decision. (*The Maid comes in.*) Look here;
take this letter; go out with it at once. Get hold of a messenger and have
him deliver it. Quick now. It's already addressed. Wait, here's some money.

MAID: Yes, sir. (*She leaves with the letter.*)

HELMER (*straightening his papers*): There, now, little Miss Willful.

NORA (*breathlessly*): Torvald, what was that letter?

HELMER: Krogstad's notice.

NORA: Call it back, Torvald! There's still time. Oh, Torvald, call it back! Do it for my sake—for your sake, for the children's sake! Do you hear, Torvald; do it! You don't know how this can harm us.

HELMER: Too late.

NORA: Yes, too late.

HELMER: Nora, dear, I can forgive you this panic, even though basically you're insulting me. Yes, you are! Or isn't it an insult to think that *I* should be afraid of a courtroom hack's revenge? But I forgive you anyway, because this shows so beautifully how much you love me. (*Takes her in his arms.*) This is the way it should be, my darling Nora. Whatever comes, you'll see: When it really counts, I have strength and courage enough as a man to take on the whole weight myself.

NORA (*terrified*): What do you mean by that?

HELMER: The whole weight, I said.

NORA (*resolutely*): No, never in all the world.

HELMER: Good. So we'll share it, Nora, as man and wife. That's as it should be. (*Fondling her.*) Are you happy now? There, there, there—not these frightened dove's eyes. It's nothing at all but empty fantasies—Now you should run through your tarantella and practice your tambourine. I'll go to the inner office, and shut both doors, so I won't hear a thing; you can make all the noise you like. (*Turning in the doorway.*) And when Rank comes, just tell him where he can find me. (*He nods to her and goes with his papers into the study, closing the door.*)

NORA (*standing as though rooted, dazed with fright, in a whisper*): He really could do it. He will do it. He'll do it in spite of everything. No, not that, never, never! Anything but that! Escape! A way out—(*The doorbell rings.*) Dr. Rank! Anything but that! *Anything*, whatever it is! (*Her hands pass over her face, smoothing it; she pulls herself together, goes over and opens the hall door. Dr. Rank stands outside, hanging his fur coat up. During the following scene, it begins getting dark.*)

NORA: Hello, Dr. Rank. I recognized your ring. But you mustn't go in to Torvald yet; I believe he's working.

RANK: And you?

NORA: For you, I always have an hour to spare—you know that. (*He has entered, and she shuts the door after him.*)

RANK: Many thanks. I'll make use of these hours while I can.

NORA: What do you mean by that? While you can?

RANK: Does that disturb you?

NORA: Well, it's such an odd phrase. Is anything going to happen?

RANK: What's going to happen is what I've been expecting so long—but I honestly didn't think it would come so soon.

NORA (*gripping his arm*): What is it you've found out? Dr. Rank, you have to tell me!

RANK (*sitting by the stove*): It's all over with me. There's nothing to be done about it.

NORA (*breathing easier*): Is it you—then—?

RANK: Who else? There's no point in lying to one's self. I'm the most miserable of all my patients, Mrs. Helmer. These past few days I've been auditing my internal accounts. Bankrupt! Within a month I'll probably be laid out and rotting in the churchyard.

NORA: Oh, what a horrible thing to say.

RANK: The thing itself is horrible. But the worst of it is all the other horror before it's over. There's only one final examination left; when I'm finished with that, I'll know about when my disintegration will begin. There's something I want to say. Helmer with his sensitivity has such a sharp distaste for anything ugly. I don't want him near my sickroom.

NORA: Oh, but Dr. Rank—

RANK: I won't have him in there. Under no condition. I'll lock my door to him—As soon as I'm completely sure of the worst, I'll send you my calling card marked with a black cross, and you'll know then the wreck has started to come apart.

NORA: No, today you're completely unreasonable. And I wanted you so much to be in a really good humor.

RANK: With death up my sleeve? And then to suffer this way for somebody else's sins. Is there any justice in that? And in every single family, in some way or another, this inevitable retribution of nature goes on—

NORA (*her hands pressed over her ears*): Oh, stuff! Cheer up! Please—be gay!

RANK: Yes, I'd just as soon laugh at it all. My poor, innocent spine, serving time for my father's gay army days.

NORA (*by the table, left*): He was so infatuated with asparagus tips and pâté de foie gras,° wasn't that it?

RANK: Yes—and with truffles.

NORA: Truffles, yes. And then with oysters, I suppose?

RANK: Yes, tons of oysters, naturally.

NORA: And then the port and champagne to go with it. It's so sad that all these delectable things have to strike at our bones.

RANK: Especially when they strike at the unhappy bones that never shared in the fun.

NORA: Ah, that's the saddest of all.

RANK (*looks searchingly at her*): Hm.

NORA (*after a moment*): Why did you smile?

RANK: No, it was you who laughed.

NORA: No, it was you who smiled, Dr. Rank!

RANK (*getting up*): You're even a bigger tease than I'd thought.

NORA: I'm full of wild ideas today.

RANK: That's obvious.

NORA (*putting both hands on his shoulders*): Dear, dear Dr. Rank, you'll never die for Torvald and me.

RANK: Oh, that loss you'll easily get over. Those who go away are soon forgotten.

NORA (*looks fearfully at him*): You believe that?

---

pâté de foie gras: Pâté of goose liver.

RANK: One makes new connections, and then—

NORA: Who makes new connections?

RANK: Both you and Torvald will when I'm gone. I'd say you're well under way already. What was that Mrs. Linde doing here last evening?

NORA: Oh, come—you can't be jealous of poor Kristine?

RANK: Oh yes, I am. She'll be my successor here in the house. When I'm down under, that woman will probably—

NORA: Shh! Not so loud. She's right in there.

RANK: Today as well. So you see.

NORA: Only to sew on my dress. Good gracious, how unreasonable you are. (*Sitting on the sofa.*) Be nice now, Dr. Rank. Tomorrow you'll see how beautifully I'll dance; and you can imagine then that I'm dancing only for you—yes, and of course for Torvald, too—that's understood. (*Takes various items out of the carton.*) Dr. Rank, sit over here and I'll show you something.

RANK (*sitting*): What's that?

NORA: Look here. Look.

RANK: Silk stockings.

NORA: Flesh-colored. Aren't they lovely? Now it's so dark here, but tomorrow—No, no, no, just look at the feet. Oh well, you might as well look at the rest.

RANK: Hm—

NORA: Why do you look so critical? Don't you believe they'll fit?

RANK: I've never had any chance to form an opinion on that.

NORA (*glancing at him a moment*): Shame on you. (*Hits him lightly on the ear with the stockings.*) That's for you. (*Puts them away again.*)

RANK: And what other splendors am I going to see now?

NORA: Not the least bit more, because you've been naughty. (*She hunts a little and rummages among her things.*)

RANK (*after a short silence*): When I sit here together with you like this, completely easy and open, then I don't know—I simply can't imagine—whatever would have become of me if I'd never come into this house.

NORA (*smiling*): Yes, I really think you feel completely at ease with us.

RANK (*more quietly, staring straight ahead*): And then to have to go away from it all—

NORA: Nonsense, you're not going away.

RANK (*his voice unchanged*): —and not even be able to leave some poor show of gratitude behind, scarcely a fleeting regret—no more than a vacant place that anyone can fill.

NORA: And if I asked you now for—No—

RANK: For what?

NORA: For a great proof of your friendship—

RANK: Yes, yes?

NORA: No, I mean—for an exceptionally big favor—

RANK: Would you really, for once, make me so happy?

NORA: Oh, you haven't the vaguest idea what it is.

RANK: All right, then tell me.

NORA: No, but I can't, Dr. Rank—it's all out of reason. It's advice and help, too—and a favor—

RANK: So much the better. I can't fathom what you're hinting at. Just speak out. Don't you trust me?

NORA: Of course. More than anyone else. You're my best and truest friend, I'm sure. That's why I want to talk to you. All right, then, Dr. Rank: There's something you can help me prevent. You know how deeply, how inexpressibly dearly Torvald loves me; he'd never hesitate a second to give up his life for me.

RANK (*leaning close to her*): Nora—do you think he's the only one—

NORA (*with a slight start*): Who—?

RANK: Who'd gladly give up his life for you.

NORA (*heavily*): I see.

RANK: I swore to myself you should know this before I'm gone. I'll never find a better chance. Yes, Nora, now you know. And also you know now that you can trust me beyond anyone else.

NORA (*rising, natural and calm*): Let me by.

RANK (*making room for her, but still sitting*): Nora—

NORA (*in the hall doorway*): Helene, bring the lamp in. (*Goes over to the stove.*) Ah, dear Dr. Rank, that was really mean of you.

RANK (*getting up*): That I've loved you just as deeply as somebody else? Was *that* mean?

NORA: No, but that you came out and told me. That was quite unnecessary—

RANK: What do you mean? Have you known—?

(*The Maid comes in with the lamp, sets it on the table, and goes out again.*)

RANK: Nora—Mrs. Helmer—I'm asking you: Have you known about it?

NORA: Oh, how can I tell what I know or don't know? Really, I don't know what to say—Why did you have to be so clumsy, Dr. Rank! Everything was so good.

RANK: Well, in any case, you now have the knowledge that my body and soul are at your command. So won't you speak out?

NORA (*looking at him*): After that?

RANK: Please, just let me know what it is.

NORA: You can't know anything now.

RANK: I have to. You mustn't punish me like this. Give me the chance to do whatever is humanly possible for you.

NORA: Now there's nothing you can do for me. Besides, actually, I don't need any help. You'll see—it's only my fantasies. That's what it is. Of course! (*Sits in the rocker, looks at him, and smiles.*) What a nice one you are, Dr. Rank. Aren't you a little bit ashamed, now that the lamp is here?

RANK: No, not exactly. But perhaps I'd better go—for good?

NORA: No, you certainly can't do that. You must come here just as you always have. You know Torvald can't do without you.

RANK: Yes, but *you*?

NORA: You know how much I enjoy it when you're here.

RANK: That's precisely what threw me off. You're a mystery to me. So many times I've felt you'd almost rather be with me than with Helmer.

NORA: Yes—you see, there are some people that one loves most and other people that one would almost prefer being with.

RANK: Yes, there's something to that.

NORA: When I was back home, of course I loved Papa most. But I always thought it was so much fun when I could sneak down to the maids' quarters, because they never tried to improve me, and it was always so amusing, the way they talked to each other.

RANK: Aha, so it's their place that I've filled.

NORA (*jumping up and going to him*): Oh, dear, sweet Dr. Rank, that's not what I meant at all. But you can understand that with Torvald it's just the same as with Papa—

(*The Maid enters from the hall.*)

MAID: Ma'am—please! (*She whispers to Nora and hands her a calling card.*)

NORA (*glancing at the card*): Ah! (*Slips it into her pocket.*)

RANK: Anything wrong?

NORA: No, no, not at all. It's only some—it's my new dress—

RANK: Really? But—there's your dress.

NORA: Oh, that. But this is another one—I ordered it—Torvald mustn't know—

RANK: Ah, now we have the big secret.

NORA: That's right. Just go in with him—he's back in the inner study. Keep him there as long as—

RANK: Don't worry. He won't get away. (*Goes into the study.*)

NORA (*to the Maid*): And he's standing waiting in the kitchen?

MAID: Yes, he came up by the back stairs.

NORA: But didn't you tell him somebody was here?

MAID: Yes, but that didn't do any good.

NORA: He won't leave?

MAID: No, he won't go till he's talked with you, ma'am.

NORA: Let him come in, then—but quietly. Helene, don't breathe a word about this. It's a surprise for my husband.

MAID: Yes, yes, I understand—(*Goes out.*)

NORA: This horror—it's going to happen. No, no, no, it can't happen, it mustn't. (*She goes and bolts Helmer's door. The Maid opens the hall door for Krogstad and shuts it behind him. He is dressed for travel in a fur coat, boots, and a fur cap.*)

NORA (*going toward him*): Talk softly. My husband's home.

KROGSTAD: Well, good for him.

NORA: What do you want?

KROGSTAD: Some information.

NORA: Hurry up, then. What is it?

KROGSTAD: You know, of course, that I got my notice.

NORA: I couldn't prevent it, Mr. Krogstad. I fought for you to the bitter end, but nothing worked.

KROGSTAD: Does your husband's love for you run so thin? He knows everything I can expose you to, and all the same he dares to —

NORA: How can you imagine he knows anything about this?

KROGSTAD: Ah, no — I can't imagine it either, now. It's not at all like my fine Torvald Helmer to have so much guts —

NORA: Mr. Krogstad, I demand respect for my husband!

KROGSTAD: Why, of course — all due respect. But since the lady's keeping it so carefully hidden, may I presume to ask if you're also a bit better informed than yesterday about what you've actually done?

NORA: More than you ever could teach me.

KROGSTAD: Yes, I *am* such an awful lawyer.

NORA: What is it you want from me?

KROGSTAD: Just a glimpse of how you are, Mrs. Helmer. I've been thinking about you all day long. A cashier, a night-court scribbler, a — well, a type like me also has a little of what they call a heart, you know.

NORA: Then show it. Think of my children.

KROGSTAD: Did you or your husband ever think of mine? But never mind. I simply wanted to tell you that you don't need to take this thing too seriously. For the present, I'm not proceeding with any action.

NORA: Oh no, really! Well — I knew that.

KROGSTAD: Everything can be settled in a friendly spirit. It doesn't have to get around town at all; it can stay just among us three.

NORA: My husband must never know anything of this.

KROGSTAD: How can you manage that? Perhaps you can pay me the balance?

NORA: No, not right now.

KROGSTAD: Or you know some way of raising the money in a day or two?

NORA: No way that I'm willing to use.

KROGSTAD: Well, it wouldn't have done you any good, anyway. If you stood in front of me with a fistful of bills, you still couldn't buy your signature back.

NORA: Then tell me what you're going to do with it.

KROGSTAD: I'll just hold onto it — keep it on file. There's no outsider who'll even get wind of it. So if you've been thinking of taking some desperate step —

NORA: I have.

KROGSTAD: Been thinking of running away from home —

NORA: I have!

KROGSTAD: Or even of something worse —

NORA: How could you guess that?

KROGSTAD: You can drop those thoughts.

NORA: How could you guess I was thinking of *that?*

KROGSTAD: Most of us think about *that* at first. I thought about it too, but I discovered I hadn't the courage —

NORA (*lifelessly*): I don't either.

KROGSTAD (*relieved*): That's true, you haven't the courage? You too?

NORA: I don't have it — I don't have it.

KROGSTAD: It would be terribly stupid, anyway. After that first storm at home blows out, why, then — I have here in my pocket a letter for your husband —

NORA: Telling everything?

KROGSTAD: As charitably as possible.

NORA (*quickly*): He mustn't ever get that letter. Tear it up. I'll find some way to get money.

KROGSTAD: Beg pardon, Mrs. Helmer, but I think I just told you —

NORA: Oh, I don't mean the money I owe you. Let me know how much you want from my husband, and I'll manage it.

KROGSTAD: I don't want any money from your husband.

NORA: What do you want, then?

KROGSTAD: I'll tell you what. I want to recoup, Mrs. Helmer; I want to get on in the world — and there's where your husband can help me. For a year and a half I've kept myself clean of anything disreputable — all that time struggling with the worst conditions; but I was satisfied, working my way up step by step. Now I've been written right off, and I'm just not in the mood to come crawling back. I tell you, I want to move on. I want to get back in the bank — in a better position. Your husband can set up a job for me —

NORA: He'll never do that!

KROGSTAD: He'll do it. I know him. He won't dare breathe a word of protest. And once I'm in there together with him, you just wait and see! Inside of a year, I'll be the manager's right-hand man. It'll be Nils Krogstad, not Torvald Helmer, who runs the bank.

NORA: You'll never see the day!

KROGSTAD: Maybe you think you can —

NORA: I have the courage now — for *that*.

KROGSTAD: Oh, you don't scare me. A smart, spoiled lady like you —

NORA: You'll see; you'll see!

KROGSTAD: Under the ice, maybe? Down in the freezing, coal-black water? There, till you float up in the spring, ugly, unrecognizable, with your hair falling out —

NORA: You don't frighten me.

KROGSTAD: Nor do you frighten me. One doesn't do these things, Mrs. Helmer. Besides what good would it be? I'd still have him safe in my pocket.

NORA: Afterwards? When I'm no longer — ?

KROGSTAD: Are you forgetting that *I'll* be in control then over your final reputation? (*Nora stands speechless, staring at him.*) Good; now I've warned you. Don't do anything stupid. When Helmer's read my letter, I'll be waiting for his reply. And bear in mind that it's your husband himself who's forced me back to my old ways. I'll never forgive him for that. Good-bye, Mrs. Helmer. (*He goes out through the hall.*)

NORA (*goes to the hall door, opens it a crack, and listens*): He's gone. Didn't leave the letter. Oh no, no, that's impossible too! (*Opening the door more and more.*) What's that? He's standing outside — not going downstairs. He's thinking it over? Maybe he'll—? (*A letter falls in the mailbox; then Krogstad's footsteps are heard, dying away down a flight of stairs. Nora gives a muffled cry and runs over toward the sofa table. A short pause.*) In the mailbox. (*Slips warily over to the hall door.*) It's lying there. Torvald, Torvald—now we're lost!

MRS. LINDE (*entering with the costume from the room, left*): There now, I can't see anything else to mend. Perhaps you'd like to try—

NORA (*in a hoarse whisper*): Kristine, come here.

MRS. LINDE (*tossing the dress on the sofa*): What's wrong? You look upset.

NORA: Come here. See that letter? There! Look—through the glass in the mailbox.

MRS. LINDE: Yes, yes, I see it.

NORA: That letter's from Krogstad—

MRS. LINDE: Nora—it's Krogstad who loaned you the money!

NORA: Yes, and now Torvald will find out everything.

MRS. LINDE: Believe me, Nora, it's best for both of you.

NORA: There's more you don't know. I forged a name.

MRS. LINDE: But for heaven's sake—?

NORA: I only want to tell you that, Kristine, so that you can be my witness.

MRS. LINDE: Witness? Why should I—?

NORA: If I should go out of my mind—it could easily happen—

MRS. LINDE: Nora!

NORA: Or anything else occurred—so I couldn't be present here—

MRS. LINDE: Nora, Nora, you aren't yourself at all!

NORA: And someone should try to take on the whole weight, all of the guilt, you follow me—

MRS. LINDE: Yes, of course, but why do you think—?

NORA: Then you're the witness that it isn't true, Kristine. I'm very much myself; my mind right now is perfectly clear; and I'm telling you: Nobody else has known about this; I alone did everything. Remember that.

MRS. LINDE: I will. But I don't understand all this.

NORA: Oh, how could you ever understand it? It's the miracle now that's going to take place.

MRS. LINDE: The miracle?

NORA: Yes, the miracle. But it's so awful, Kristine. It mustn't take place, not for anything in the world.

MRS. LINDE: I'm going right over and talk with Krogstad.

NORA: Don't go near him; he'll do you some terrible harm!

MRS. LINDE: There was a time once when he'd gladly have done anything for me.

NORA: He?

MRS. LINDE: Where does he live?

NORA: Oh, how do I know? Yes. (*Searches in her pocket.*) Here's his card. But the letter, the letter—!

HELMER (*from the study, knocking on the door*): Nora!

NORA (*with a cry of fear*): Oh! What is it? What do you want?

HELMER: Now, now, don't be so frightened. We're not coming in. You locked the door—are you trying on the dress?

NORA: Yes, I'm trying it. I'll look just beautiful, Torvald.

MRS. LINDE (*who has read the card*): He's living right around the corner.

NORA: Yes, but what's the use? We're lost. The letter's in the box.

MRS. LINDE: And your husband has the key?

NORA: Yes, always.

MRS. LINDE: Krogstad can ask for his letter back unread; he can find some excuse—

NORA: But it's just this time that Torvald usually—

MRS. LINDE: Stall him. Keep him in there. I'll be back as quick as I can. (*She hurries out through the hall entrance.*)

NORA (*goes to Helmer's door, opens it, and peers in*): Torvald!

HELMER (*from the inner study*): Well—does one dare set foot in one's own living room at last? Come on, Rank, now we'll get a look— (*In the doorway.*) But what's this?

NORA: What, Torvald dear?

HELMER: Rank had me expecting some grand masquerade.

RANK (*in the doorway*): That was my impression, but I must have been wrong.

NORA: No one can admire me in my splendor—not till tomorrow.

HELMER: But Nora dear, you look so exhausted. Have you practiced too hard?

NORA: No, I haven't practiced at all yet.

HELMER: You know, it's necessary—

NORA: Oh, it's absolutely necessary, Torvald. But I can't get anywhere without your help. I've forgotten the whole thing completely.

HELMER: Ah, we'll soon take care of that.

NORA: Yes, take care of me, Torvald, please! Promise me that? Oh, I'm so nervous. That big party—You must give up everything this evening for me. No business—don't even touch your pen. Yes? Dear Torvald, promise?

HELMER: It's a promise. Tonight I'm totally at your service—you little helpless thing. Hm—but first there's one thing I want to—(*Goes toward the hall door.*)

NORA: What are you looking for?

HELMER: Just to see if there's any mail.

NORA: No, no, don't do that, Torvald!

HELMER: Now what?

NORA: Torvald, please. There isn't any.

HELMER: Let me look, though. (*Starts out. Nora, at the piano, strikes the first notes of the tarantella. Helmer, at the door, stops.*) Aha!

NORA: I can't dance tomorrow if I don't practice with you.

HELMER (*going over to her*): Nora dear, are you really so frightened?

NORA: Yes, so terribly frightened. Let me practice right now; there's still time before dinner. Oh, sit down and play for me, Torvald. Direct me. Teach me, the way you always have.

HELMER: Gladly, if it's what you want. (*Sits at the piano.*)

NORA (*snatches the tambourine up from the box, then a long, varicolored shawl, which she throws around herself, whereupon she springs forward and cries out*): Play for me now! Now I'll dance!

(*Helmer plays and Nora dances. Rank stands behind Helmer at the piano and looks on.*)

HELMER (*as he plays*): Slower. Slow down.

NORA: Can't change it.

HELMER: Not so violent, Nora!

NORA: Has to be just like this.

HELMER (*stopping*): No, no, that won't do at all.

NORA (*laughing and swinging her tambourine*): Isn't that what I told you?

RANK: Let me play for her.

HELMER (*getting up*): Yes, go on. I can teach her more easily then.

(*Rank sits at the piano and plays, Nora dances more and more wildly. Helmer has stationed himself by the stove and repeatedly gives her directions; she seems not to hear them; her hair loosens and falls over her shoulders; she does not notice, but goes on dancing. Mrs. Linde enters.*)

MRS. LINDE (*standing dumbfounded at the door*): Ah—!

NORA (*still dancing*): See what fun, Kristine!

HELMER: But Nora darling, you dance as if your life were at stake.

NORA: And it is.

HELMER: Rank, stop! This is pure madness. Stop it, I say!

(*Rank breaks off playing, and Nora halts abruptly.*)

HELMER (*going over to her*): I never would have believed it. You've forgotten everything I taught you.

NORA (*throwing away the tambourine*): You see for yourself.

HELMER: Well, there's certainly room for instruction here.

NORA: Yes, you see how important it is. You've got to teach me to the very last minute. Promise me that, Torvald?

HELMER: You can bet on it.

NORA: You mustn't, either today or tomorrow, think about anything else but me; you mustn't open any letters—or the mailbox—

HELMER: Ah, it's still the fear of that man—

NORA: Oh yes, yes, that too.

HELMER: Nora, it's written all over you—there's already a letter from him out there.

NORA: I don't know. I guess so. But you mustn't read such things now; there mustn't be anything ugly between us before it's all over.

RANK (*quietly to Helmer*): You shouldn't deny her.

HELMER (*putting his arm around her*): The child can have her way. But tomorrow night, after you've danced—

NORA: Then you'll be free.

MAID (*in the doorway, right*): Ma'am, dinner is served.

NORA: We'll be wanting champagne, Helene.

MAID: Very good, ma'am. (*Goes out.*)

HELMER: So—a regular banquet, hm?

NORA: Yes, a banquet—champagne till daybreak! (*Calling out.*) And some macaroons, Helene. Heaps of them—just this once.

HELMER (*taking her hands*): Now, now, now—no hysterics. Be my own little lark again.

NORA: Oh, I will soon enough. But go on in—and you, Dr. Rank. Kristine, help me put up my hair.

RANK (*whispering, as they go*): There's nothing wrong—really wrong, is there?

HELMER: Oh, of course not. It's nothing more than this childish anxiety I was telling you about. (*They go out, right.*)

NORA: Well?

MRS. LINDE: Left town.

NORA: I could see by your face.

MRS. LINDE: He'll be home tomorrow evening. I wrote him a note.

NORA: You shouldn't have. Don't try to stop anything now. After all, it's a wonderful joy, this waiting here for the miracle.

MRS. LINDE: What is it you're waiting for?

NORA: Oh, you can't understand that. Go in to them; I'll be along in a moment.

(*Mrs. Linde goes into the dining room. Nora stands a short while as if composing herself; then she looks at her watch.*)

NORA: Five. Seven hours to midnight. Twenty-four hours to the midnight after, and then the tarantella's done. Seven and twenty-four? Thirty-one hours to live.

HELMER (*in the doorway, right*): What's become of the little lark?

NORA (*going toward him with open arms*): Here's your lark!

ACT 3

(*Same scene. The table, with chairs around it, has been moved to the center of the room. A lamp on the table is lit. The hall door stands open. Dance music drifts down from the floor above. Mrs. Linde sits at the table, absently paging through a book, trying to read, but apparently unable to focus her thoughts. Once or twice she pauses, tensely listening for a sound at the outer entrance.*)

MRS. LINDE (*glancing at her watch*): Not yet—and there's hardly any time left. If only he's not—(*Listening again.*) Ah, there it is. (*She goes out in the hall and cautiously opens the outer door. Quiet footsteps are heard on the stairs. She whispers.*) Come in. Nobody's here.

KROGSTAD (*in the doorway*): I found a note from you at home. What's back of all this?

MRS. LINDE: I just *had* to talk to you.

KROGSTAD: Oh? And it just *had* to be here in this house?

MRS. LINDE: At my place it was impossible; my room hasn't a private entrance. Come in, we're all alone. The maid's asleep, and the Helmers are at the dance upstairs.

KROGSTAD (*entering the room*): Well, well, the Helmers are dancing tonight? Really?

MRS. LINDE: Yes, why not?

KROGSTAD: How true—why not?

MRS. LINDE: All right, Krogstad, let's talk.

KROGSTAD: Do we two have anything more to talk about?

MRS. LINDE: We have a great deal to talk about.

KROGSTAD: I wouldn't have thought so.

MRS. LINDE: No, because you've never understood me, really.

KROGSTAD: Was there anything more to understand — except what's all too common in life? A calculating woman throws over a man the moment a better catch comes by.

MRS. LINDE: You think I'm so thoroughly calculating? You think I broke it off lightly?

KROGSTAD: Didn't you?

MRS. LINDE: Nils — is that what you really thought?

KROGSTAD: If you cared, then why did you write me the way you did?

MRS. LINDE: What else could I do? If I had to break off with you, then it was my job as well to root out everything you felt for me.

KROGSTAD (*wringing his hands*): So that was it. And this — all this, simply for money!

MRS. LINDE: Don't forget I had a helpless mother and two small brothers. We couldn't wait for you, Nils; you had such a long road ahead of you then.

KROGSTAD: That may be; but you still hadn't the right to abandon me for somebody else's sake.

MRS. LINDE: Yes — I don't know. So many, many times I've asked myself if I did have that right.

KROGSTAD (*more softly*): When I lost you, it was as if all the solid ground dissolved from under my feet. Look at me; I'm a half-drowned man now, hanging onto a wreck.

MRS. LINDE: Help may be near.

KROGSTAD: It was near — but then you came and blocked it off.

MRS. LINDE: Without my knowing it, Nils. Today for the first time I learned that it's you I'm replacing at the bank.

KROGSTAD: All right — I believe you. But now that you know, will you step aside?

MRS. LINDE: No, because that wouldn't benefit you in the slightest.

KROGSTAD: Not "benefit" me, hm! I'd step aside anyway.

MRS. LINDE: I've learned to be realistic. Life and hard, bitter necessity have taught me that.

KROGSTAD: And life's taught me never to trust fine phrases.

MRS. LINDE: Then life's taught you a very sound thing. But you do have to trust in actions, don't you?

KROGSTAD: What does that mean?

MRS. LINDE: You said you were hanging on like a half-drowned man to a wreck.

KROGSTAD: I've good reason to say that.

MRS. LINDE: I'm also like a half-drowned woman on a wreck. No one to suffer with; no one to care for.

KROGSTAD: You made your choice.

MRS. LINDE: There wasn't any choice then.

KROGSTAD: So — what of it?

MRS. LINDE: Nils, if only we two shipwrecked people could reach across to each other.

KROGSTAD: What are you saying?

MRS. LINDE: Two on one wreck are at least better off than each on his own.

KROGSTAD: Kristine!

MRS. LINDE: Why do you think I came into town?

KROGSTAD: Did you really have some thought of me?

MRS. LINDE: I have to work to go on living. All my born days, as long as I can remember, I've worked, and it's been my best and my only joy. But now I'm completely alone in the world; it frightens me to be so empty and lost. To work for yourself—there's no joy in that. Nils, give me something—someone to work for.

KROGSTAD: I don't believe all this. It's just some hysterical feminine urge to go out and make a noble sacrifice.

MRS. LINDE: Have you ever found me to be hysterical?

KROGSTAD: Can you honestly mean this? Tell me—do you know everything about my past?

MRS. LINDE: Yes.

KROGSTAD: And you know what they think I'm worth around here.

MRS. LINDE: From what you were saying before, it would seem that with me you could have been another person.

KROGSTAD: I'm positive of that.

MRS. LINDE: Couldn't it happen still?

KROGSTAD: Kristine—you're saying this in all seriousness? Yes, you are! I can see it in you. And do you really have the courage, then—?

MRS. LINDE: I need to have someone to care for, and your children need a mother. We both need each other. Nils, I have faith that you're good at heart—I'll risk everything together with you.

KROGSTAD (*gripping her hands*): Kristine, thank you, thank you—Now I know I can win back a place in their eyes. Yes—but I forgot—

MRS. LINDE (*listening*): Shh! The tarantella. Go now! Go on!

KROGSTAD: Why? What is it?

MRS. LINDE: Hear the dance up there? When that's over, they'll be coming down.

KROGSTAD: Oh, then I'll go. But—it's all pointless. Of course, you don't know the move I made against the Helmers.

MRS. LINDE: Yes, Nils, I know.

KROGSTAD: And all the same, you have the courage to—?

MRS. LINDE: I know how far despair can drive a man like you.

KROGSTAD: Oh, if I only could take it all back.

MRS. LINDE: You easily could—your letter's still lying in the mailbox.

KROGSTAD: Are you sure of that?

MRS. LINDE: Positive. But—

KROGSTAD (*looks at her searchingly*): Is that the meaning of it, then? You'll save your friend at any price. Tell me straight out. Is that it?

MRS. LINDE: Nils—anyone who's sold herself for somebody else once isn't going to do it again.

KROGSTAD: I'll demand my letter back.

MRS. LINDE: No, no.

KROGSTAD: Yes, of course. I'll stay here till Helmer comes down; I'll tell him to give me my letter again—that it only involves my dismissal—that he shouldn't read it—

MRS. LINDE: No, Nils, don't call the letter back.

KROGSTAD: But wasn't that exactly why you wrote me to come here?

MRS. LINDE: Yes, in that first panic. But it's been a whole day and night since then, and in that time I've seen such incredible things in this house. Helmer's got to learn everything; this dreadful secret has to be aired; those two have to come to a full understanding; all these lies and evasions can't go on.

KROGSTAD: Well, then, if you want to chance it. But at least there's one thing I can do, and do right away—

MRS. LINDE (*listening*): Go now, go, quick! The dance is over. We're not safe another second.

KROGSTAD: I'll wait for you downstairs.

MRS. LINDE: Yes, please do; take me home.

KROGSTAD: I can't believe it; I've never been so happy. (*He leaves by way of the outer door; the door between the room and the hall stays open.*)

MRS. LINDE (*straightening up a bit and getting together her street clothes*): How different now! How different! Someone to work for, to live for—a home to build. Well, it is worth the try! Oh, if they'd only come! (*Listening.*) Ah, there they are. Bundle up. (*She picks up her hat and coat. Nora's and Helmer's voices can be heard outside; a key turns in the lock, and Helmer brings Nora into the hall almost by force. She is wearing the Italian costume with a large black shawl about her; he has on evening dress, with a black domino open over it.*)

NORA (*struggling in the doorway*): No, no, no, not inside! I'm going up again. I don't want to leave so soon.

HELMER: But Nora dear—

NORA: Oh, I beg you, please, Torvald. From the bottom of my heart, *please*—only an hour more!

HELMER: Not a single minute, Nora darling. You know our agreement. Come on, in we go; you'll catch cold out here. (*In spite of her resistance, he gently draws her into the room.*)

MRS. LINDE: Good evening.

NORA: Kristine!

HELMER: Why, Mrs. Linde—are you here so late?

MRS. LINDE: Yes, I'm sorry, but I did want to see Nora in costume.

NORA: Have you been sitting here, waiting for me?

MRS. LINDE: Yes. I didn't come early enough; you were all upstairs; and then I thought I really couldn't leave without seeing you.

HELMER (*removing Nora's shawl*): Yes, take a good look. She's worth looking at, I can tell you that, Mrs. Linde. Isn't she lovely?

MRS. LINDE: Yes, I should say—

HELMER: A dream of loveliness, isn't she? That's what everyone thought at the party, too. But she's horribly stubborn—this sweet little thing. What's to be done with her? Can you imagine, I almost had to use force to pry her away.

NORA: Oh, Torvald, you're going to regret you didn't indulge me, even for just a half hour more.

HELMER: There, you see. She danced her tarantella and got a tumultuous hand—which was well earned, although the performance may have been a bit too naturalistic—I mean it rather overstepped the proprieties of art. But never mind—what's important is, she made a success, an overwhelming success. You think I could let her stay on after that and spoil the effect? Oh no; I took my lovely little Capri girl—my capricious little Capri girl, I should say—took her under my arm; one quick tour of the ballroom, a curtsy to every side, and then—as they say in novels—the beautiful vision disappeared. An exit should always be effective, Mrs. Linde, but that's what I can't get Nora to grasp. Phew, it's hot in here. (*Flings the domino on a chair and opens the door to his room.*) Why's it dark in here? Oh yes, of course. Excuse me. (*He goes in and lights a couple of candles.*)

NORA (*in a sharp, breathless whisper*): So?

MRS. LINDE (*quietly*): I talked with him.

NORA: And—?

MRS. LINDE: Nora—you must tell your husband everything.

NORA (*dully*): I knew it.

MRS. LINDE: You've got nothing to fear from Krogstad, but you have to speak out.

NORA: I won't tell.

MRS. LINDE: Then the letter will.

NORA: Thanks, Kristine. I know now what's to be done. Shh!

HELMER (*reentering*): Well, then, Mrs. Linde—have you admired her?

MRS. LINDE: Yes, and now I'll say good night.

HELMER: Oh, come, so soon? Is this yours, this knitting?

MRS. LINDE: Yes, thanks. I nearly forgot it.

HELMER: Do you knit, then?

MRS. LINDE: Oh yes.

HELMER: You know what? You should embroider instead.

MRS. LINDE: Really? Why?

HELMER: Yes, because it's a lot prettier. See here, one holds the embroidery so, in the left hand, and then one guides the needle with the right—so—in an easy, sweeping curve—right?

MRS. LINDE: Yes, I guess that's—

HELMER: But, on the other hand, knitting—it can never be anything but ugly. Look, see here, the arms tucked in, the knitting needles going up and down—there's something Chinese about it. Ah, that was really a glorious champagne they served.

MRS. LINDE: Yes, good night, Nora, and don't be stubborn anymore.

HELMER: Well put, Mrs. Linde!

MRS. LINDE: Good night, Mr. Helmer.

HELMER (*accompanying her to the door*): Good night, good night. I hope you get home all right. I'd be very happy to—but you don't have far to go. Good night, good night. (*She leaves. He shuts the door after her and returns.*) There, now, at last we got her out the door. She's a deadly bore, that creature.

NORA: Aren't you pretty tired, Torvald?

HELMER: No, not a bit.

NORA: You're not sleepy?

HELMER: Not at all. On the contrary, I'm feeling quite exhilarated. But you? Yes, you really look tired and sleepy.

NORA: Yes, I'm very tired. Soon now I'll sleep.

HELMER: See! You see! I was right all along that we shouldn't stay longer.

NORA: Whatever you do is always right.

HELMER (*kissing her brow*): Now my little lark talks sense. Say, did you notice what a time Rank was having tonight?

NORA: Oh, was he? I didn't get to speak with him.

HELMER: I scarcely did either, but it's a long time since I've seen him in such high spirits. (*Gazes at her a moment, then comes nearer her.*) Hm—it's marvelous, though, to be back home again—to be completely alone with you. Oh, you bewitchingly lovely young woman!

NORA: Torvald, don't look at me like that!

HELMER: Can't I look at my richest treasure? At all that beauty that's mine, mine alone—completely and utterly.

NORA (*moving around to the other side of the table*): You mustn't talk to me that way tonight.

HELMER (*following her*): The tarantella is still in your blood. I can see—and it makes you even more enticing. Listen. The guests are beginning to go. (*Dropping his voice.*) Nora—it'll soon be quiet through this whole house.

NORA: Yes, I hope so.

HELMER: You do, don't you, my love? Do you realize—when I'm out at a party like this with you—do you know why I talk to you so little, and keep such a distance away; just send you a stolen look now and then—you know why I do it? It's because I'm imagining then that you're my secret darling, my secret young bride-to-be, and that no one suspects there's anything between us.

NORA: Yes, yes; oh, yes, I know you're always thinking of me.

HELMER: And then when we leave and I place the shawl over those fine young rounded shoulders—over that wonderful curving neck—then I pretend that you're my young bride, that we're just coming from the wedding, that for the first time I'm bringing you into my house—that for the first time I'm alone with you—completely alone with you, your trembling young beauty!

All this evening I've longed for nothing but you. When I saw you turn and sway in the tarantella—my blood was pounding till I couldn't stand it—that's why I brought you down here so early—

NORA: Go away, Torvald! Leave me alone. I don't want all this.

HELMER: What do you mean? Nora, you're teasing me. You will, won't you? Aren't I your husband—?

(A knock at the outside door.)

NORA *(startled)*: What's that?

HELMER *(going toward the hall)*: Who is it?

RANK *(outside)*: It's me. May I come in a moment?

HELMER *(with quiet irritation)*: Oh, what does he want now? *(Aloud.)* Hold on. *(Goes and opens the door.)* Oh, how nice that you didn't just pass us by!

RANK: I thought I heard your voice, and then I wanted so badly to have a look in. *(Lightly glancing about.)* Ah, me, these old familiar haunts. You have it snug and cozy in here, you two.

HELMER: You seemed to be having it pretty cozy upstairs, too.

RANK: Absolutely. Why shouldn't I? Why not take in everything in life? As much as you can, anyway, and as long as you can. The wine was superb—

HELMER: The champagne especially.

RANK: You noticed that too? It's amazing how much I could guzzle down.

NORA: Torvald also drank a lot of champagne this evening.

RANK: Oh?

NORA: Yes, and that always makes him so entertaining.

RANK: Well, why shouldn't one have a pleasant evening after a well-spent day?

HELMER: Well spent? I'm afraid I can't claim that.

RANK *(slapping him on the back)*: But I can, you see!

NORA: Dr. Rank, you must have done some scientific research today.

RANK: Quite so.

HELMER: Come now—little Nora talking about scientific research!

NORA: And can I congratulate you on the results?

RANK: Indeed you may.

NORA: Then they were good?

RANK: The best possible for both doctor and patient—certainty.

NORA *(quickly and searchingly)*: Certainty?

RANK: Complete certainty. So don't I owe myself a gay evening afterwards?

NORA: Yes, you're right, Dr. Rank.

HELMER: I'm with you—just so long as you don't have to suffer for it in the morning.

RANK: Well, one never gets something for nothing in life.

NORA: Dr. Rank—are you very fond of masquerade parties?

RANK: Yes, if there's a good array of odd disguises—

NORA: Tell me, what should we two go as at the next masquerade?

HELMER: You little featherhead—already thinking of the next!

RANK: We two? I'll tell you what: You must go as Charmed Life—

HELMER: Yes, but find a costume for that!

RANK: Your wife can appear just as she looks every day.

HELMER: That was nicely put. But don't you know what you're going to be?

RANK: Yes, Helmer, I've made up my mind.

HELMER: Well?

RANK: At the next masquerade I'm going to be invisible.

HELMER: That's a funny idea.

RANK: They say there's a hat—black, huge—have you never heard of the hat that makes you invisible? You put it on, and then no one on earth can see you.

HELMER (*suppressing a smile*): Ah, of course.

RANK: But I'm quite forgetting what I came for. Helmer, give me a cigar, one of the dark Havanas.

HELMER: With the greatest pleasure. (*Holds out his case.*)

RANK: Thanks. (*Takes one and cuts off the tip.*)

NORA (*striking a match*): Let me give you a light.

RANK: Thank you. (*She holds the match for him; he lights the cigar.*) And now good-bye.

HELMER: Good-bye, good-bye, old friend.

NORA: Sleep well, Doctor.

RANK: Thanks for that wish.

NORA: Wish me the same.

RANK: You? All right, if you like—Sleep well. And thanks for the light. (*He nods to them both and leaves.*)

HELMER (*his voice subdued*): He's been drinking heavily.

NORA (*absently*): Could be. (*Helmer takes his keys from his pocket and goes out in the hall.*) Torvald—what are you after?

HELMER: Got to empty the mailbox; it's nearly full. There won't be room for the morning papers.

NORA: Are you working tonight?

HELMER: You know I'm not. Why—what's this? Someone's been at the lock.

NORA: At the lock—?

HELMER: Yes, I'm positive. What do you suppose—? I can't imagine one of the maids—? Here's a broken hairpin. Nora, it's yours—

NORA (*quickly*): Then it must be the children—

HELMER: You'd better break them of that. Hm, hm—well, opened it after all. (*Takes the contents out and calls into the kitchen.*) Helene! Helene, would you put out the lamp in the hall. (*He returns to the room, shutting the hall door, then displays the handful of mail.*) Look how it's piled up. (*Sorting through them.*) Now what's this?

NORA (*at the window*): The letter! Oh, Torvald, no!

HELMER: Two calling cards—from Rank.

NORA: From Dr. Rank?

HELMER (*examining them*): "Dr. Rank, Consulting Physician." They were on top. He must have dropped them in as he left.

NORA: Is there anything on them?

HELMER: There's a black cross over the name. See? That's a gruesome notion. He could almost be announcing his own death.

NORA: That's just what he's doing.

HELMER: What! You've heard something? Something he's told you?

NORA: Yes. That when those cards came, he'd be taking his leave of us. He'll shut himself in now and die.

HELMER: Ah, my poor friend! Of course I knew he wouldn't be here much longer. But so soon — And then to hide himself away like a wounded animal.

NORA: If it has to happen, then it's best it happens in silence — don't you think so, Torvald?

HELMER (*pacing up and down*): He's grown right into our lives. I simply can't imagine him gone. He with his suffering and loneliness — like a dark cloud setting off our sunlit happiness. Well, maybe it's best this way. For him, at least. (*Standing still.*) And maybe for us too, Nora. Now we're thrown back on each other, completely. (*Embracing her.*) Oh you, my darling wife, how can I hold you close enough? You know what, Nora — time and again I've wished you were in some terrible danger, just so I could stake my life and soul and everything, for your sake.

NORA (*tearing herself away, her voice firm and decisive*): Now you must read your mail, Torvald.

HELMER: No, no, not tonight. I want to stay with you, dearest.

NORA: With a dying friend on your mind?

HELMER: You're right. We've both had a shock. There's ugliness between us — these thoughts of death and corruption. We'll have to get free of them first. Until then — we'll stay apart.

NORA (*clinging about his neck*): Torvald — good night! Good night!

HELMER (*kissing her on the cheek*): Good night, little songbird. Sleep well, Nora. I'll be reading my mail now. (*He takes the letters into his room and shuts the door after him.*)

NORA (*with bewildered glances, groping about, seizing Helmer's domino, throwing it around her, and speaking in short, hoarse, broken whispers*): Never see him again. Never, never. (*Putting her shawl over her head.*) Never see the children either — them, too. Never, never. Oh, the freezing black water! The depths — down — Oh, I wish it were over — He has it now; he's reading it — now. Oh no, no, not yet. Torvald, good-bye, you and the children — (*She starts for the hall; as she does, Helmer throws open his door and stands with an open letter in his hand.*)

HELMER: Nora!

NORA (*screams*): Oh — !

HELMER: What is this? You know what's in this letter?

NORA: Yes, I know. Let me go! Let me out!

HELMER (*holding her back*): Where are you going?

NORA (*struggling to break loose*): You can't save me, Torvald!

HELMER (*slumping back*): True! Then it's true what he writes? How horrible! No, no, it's impossible — it can't be true.

NORA: It *is* true. I've loved you more than all this world.

HELMER: Ah, none of your slippery tricks.

NORA (*taking one step toward him*): Torvald—!

HELMER: What *is* this you've blundered into!

NORA: Just let me loose. You're not going to suffer for my sake. You're not going to take on my guilt.

HELMER: No more playacting. (*Locks the hall door.*) You stay right here and give me a reckoning. You understand what you've done? Answer! You understand?

NORA (*looking squarely at him, her face hardening*): Yes. I'm beginning to understand everything now.

HELMER (*striding about*): Oh, what an awful awakening! In all these eight years—she who was my pride and joy—a hypocrite, a liar—worse, worse—a criminal! How infinitely disgusting it all is! The shame! (*Nora says nothing and goes on looking straight at him. He stops in front of her.*) I should have suspected something of the kind. I should have known. All your father's flimsy values—Be still! All your father's flimsy values have come out in you. No religion, no morals, no sense of duty—Oh, how I'm punished for letting him off! I did it for your sake, and you repay me like this.

NORA: Yes, like this.

HELMER: Now you've wrecked all my happiness—ruined my whole future. Oh, it's awful to think of. I'm in a cheap little grafter's hands; he can do anything he wants with me, ask for anything, play with me like a puppet—and I can't breathe a word. I'll be swept down miserably into the depths on account of a featherbrained woman.

NORA: When I'm gone from this world, you'll be free.

HELMER: Oh, quit posing. Your father had a mess of those speeches too. What good would that ever do me if you were gone from this world, as you say? Not the slightest. He can still make the whole thing known; and if he does, I could be falsely suspected as your accomplice. They might even think that I was behind it—that I put you up to it. And all that I can thank you for—you that I've coddled the whole of our marriage. Can you see now what you've done to me?

NORA (*icily calm*): Yes.

HELMER: It's so incredible, I just can't grasp it. But we'll have to patch up whatever we can. Take off the shawl. I said, take it off! I've got to appease him somehow or other. The thing has to be hushed up at any cost. And as for you and me, it's got to seem like everything between us is just as it was—to the outside world, that is. You'll go right on living in this house, of course. But you can't be allowed to bring up the children; I don't dare trust you with them—Oh, to have to say this to someone I've loved so much! Well, that's done with. From now on happiness doesn't matter; all that matters is saving the bits and pieces, the appearance—(*The doorbell rings. Helmer starts.*) What's that? And so late. Maybe the worst—? You think he'd—? Hide, Nora! Say you're sick. (*Nora remains standing motionless. Helmer goes and opens the door.*)

MAID (*half dressed, in the hall*): A letter for Mrs. Helmer.

HELMER: I'll take it. (*Snatches the letter and shuts the door.*) Yes, it's from him. You don't get it; I'm reading it myself.

NORA: Then read it.

HELMER (*by the lamp*): I hardly dare. We may be ruined, you and I. But — I've got to know. (*Rips open the letter, skims through a few lines, glances at an enclosure, then cries out joyfully.*) Nora! (*Nora looks inquiringly at him.*) Nora! Wait — better check it again — Yes, yes, it's true. I'm saved. Nora, I'm saved!

NORA: And I?

HELMER: You too, of course. We're both saved, both of us. Look. He's sent back your note. He says he's sorry and ashamed — that a happy development in his life — oh, who cares what he says! Nora, we're saved! No one can hurt you. Oh, Nora, Nora — but first, this ugliness all has to go. Let me see — (*Takes a look at the note.*) No, I don't want to see it; I want the whole thing to fade like a dream. (*Tears the note and both letters to pieces, throws them into the stove and watches them burn.*) There — now there's nothing left — He wrote that since Christmas Eve you — Oh, they must have been three terrible days for you, Nora.

NORA: I fought a hard fight.

HELMER: And suffered pain and saw no escape but — No, we're not going to dwell on anything unpleasant. We'll just be grateful and keep on repeating: It's over now, it's over! You hear me, Nora? You don't seem to realize — it's over. What's it mean — that frozen look? Oh, poor little Nora, I understand. You can't believe I've forgiven you. But I have, Nora; I swear I have. I know that what you did, you did out of love for me.

NORA: That's true.

HELMER: You loved me the way a wife ought to love her husband. It's simply the means that you couldn't judge. But you think I love you any the less for not knowing how to handle your affairs? No, no — just lean on me; I'll guide you and teach you. I wouldn't be a man if this feminine helplessness didn't make you twice as attractive to me. You mustn't mind those sharp words I said — that was all in the first confusion of thinking my world had collapsed. I've forgiven you, Nora; I swear I've forgiven you.

NORA: My thanks for your forgiveness. (*She goes out through the door, right.*)

HELMER: No, wait — (*Peers in.*) What are you doing in there?

NORA (*inside*): Getting out of my costume.

HELMER (*by the open door*): Yes, do that. Try to calm yourself and collect your thoughts again, my frightened little songbird. You can rest easy now; I've got wide wings to shelter you with. (*Walking about close by the door.*) How snug and nice our home is, Nora. You're safe here; I'll keep you like a hunted dove I've rescued out of a hawk's claws. I'll bring peace to your poor, shuddering heart. Gradually it'll happen, Nora; you'll see. Tomorrow all this will look different to you; then everything will be as it was. I won't have to go on repeating I forgive you; you'll feel it for yourself. How can you imagine I'd ever conceivably want to disown you — or even blame you in any way? Ah, you don't know a man's heart, Nora. For a man there's something indescribably sweet and satisfying in knowing he's forgiven his wife—and forgiven her out of a full and open heart. It's as if she belongs to him in two ways now: In a sense he's given her fresh into the world again, and she's become his wife and his child as well. From now on that's what you'll be to me—you little, bewildered, helpless thing. Don't be afraid of anything, Nora; just open your heart to me, and I'll be conscience and will to you both— (*Nora enters in her regular clothes.*) What's this? Not in bed? You've changed your dress?

NORA: Yes, Torvald, I've changed my dress.

HELMER: But why now, so late?

NORA: Tonight I'm not sleeping.

HELMER: But Nora dear—

NORA (*looking at her watch*): It's still not so very late. Sit down, Torvald; we have a lot to talk over. (*She sits at one side of the table.*)

HELMER: Nora—what is this? That hard expression—

NORA: Sit down. This'll take some time. I have a lot to say.

HELMER (*sitting at the table directly opposite her*): You worry me, Nora. And I don't understand you.

NORA: No, that's exactly it. You don't understand me. And I've never understood you either—until tonight. No, don't interrupt. You can just listen to what I say. We're closing out accounts, Torvald.

HELMER: How do you mean that?

NORA (*after a short pause*): Doesn't anything strike you about our sitting here like this?

HELMER: What's that?

NORA: We've been married now eight years. Doesn't it occur to you that this is the first time we two, you and I, man and wife, have ever talked seriously together?

HELMER: What do you mean—seriously?

NORA: In eight whole years—longer even—right from our first acquaintance, we've never exchanged a serious word on any serious thing.

HELMER: You mean I should constantly go and involve you in problems you couldn't possibly help me with?

NORA: I'm not talking of problems. I'm saying that we've never sat down seriously together and tried to get to the bottom of anything.

HELMER: But dearest, what good would that ever do you?

NORA: That's the point right there: You've never understood me. I've been wronged greatly, Torvald—first by Papa, and then by you.

HELMER: What! By us—the two people who've loved you more than anyone else?

NORA (*shaking her head*): You never loved me. You've thought it fun to be in love with me, that's all.

HELMER: Nora, what a thing to say!

NORA: Yes, it's true now, Torvald. When I lived at home with Papa, he told me all his opinions, so I had the same ones too; or if they were different I hid them, since he wouldn't have cared for that. He used to call me his doll-child, and he played with me the way I played with my dolls. Then I came into your house—

HELMER: How can you speak of our marriage like that?

NORA (*unperturbed*): I mean, then I went from Papa's hands into yours. You arranged everything to your own taste, and so I got the same taste as you—or I pretended to; I can't remember. I guess a little of both, first one, then the other. Now when I look back, it seems as if I'd lived here like a beggar—just from hand to mouth. I've lived by doing tricks for you, Torvald. But that's the way you wanted it. It's a great sin what you and Papa did to me. You're to blame that nothing's become of me.

HELMER: Nora, how unfair and ungrateful you are! Haven't you been happy here?

NORA: No, never. I thought so—but I never have.

HELMER: Not—not happy!

NORA: No, only lighthearted. And you've always been so kind to me. But our home's been nothing but a playpen. I've been your doll-wife here, just as at home I was Papa's doll-child. And in turn the children have been my dolls. I thought it was fun when you played with me, just as they thought it fun when I played with them. That's been our marriage, Torvald.

HELMER: There's some truth in what you're saying—under all the raving exaggeration. But it'll all be different after this. Playtime's over; now for the schooling.

NORA: Whose schooling—mine or the children's?

HELMER: Both yours and the children's, dearest.

NORA: Oh, Torvald, you're not the man to teach me to be a good wife to you.

HELMER: And you can say that?

NORA: And I—how am I equipped to bring up children?

HELMER: Nora!

NORA: Didn't you say a moment ago that that was no job to trust me with?

HELMER: In a flare of temper! Why fasten on that?

NORA: Yes, but you were so very right. I'm not up to the job. There's another job I have to do first. I have to try to educate myself. You can't help me with that. I've got to do it alone. And that's why I'm leaving you now.

HELMER (*jumping up*): What's that?

NORA: I have to stand completely alone, if I'm ever going to discover myself and the world out there. So I can't go on living with you.

HELMER: Nora, Nora!

NORA: I want to leave right away. Kristine should put me up for the night—

HELMER: You're insane! You've no right! I forbid you!

NORA: From here on, there's no use forbidding me anything. I'll take with me whatever is mine. I don't want a thing from you, either now or later.

HELMER: What kind of madness is this!

NORA: Tomorrow I'm going home—I mean, home where I came from. It'll be easier up there to find something to do.

HELMER: Oh, you blind, incompetent child!

NORA: I must learn to be competent, Torvald.

HELMER: Abandon your home, your husband, your children! And you're not even thinking what people will say.

NORA: I can't be concerned about that. I only know how essential this is.

HELMER: Oh, it's outrageous. So you'll run out like this on your most sacred vows.

NORA: What do you think are my most sacred vows?

HELMER: And I have to tell you that! Aren't they your duties to your husband and children?

NORA: I have other duties equally sacred.

HELMER: That isn't true. What duties are they?

NORA: Duties to myself.

HELMER: Before all else, you're a wife and a mother.

NORA: I don't believe in that anymore. I believe that before all else, I'm a human being, no less than you—or anyway, I ought to try to become one. I know the majority thinks you're right, Torvald, and plenty of books agree with you, too. But I can't go on believing what the majority says, or what's written in books. I have to think over these things myself and try to understand them.

HELMER: Why can't you understand your place in your own home? On a point like that, isn't there one everlasting guide you can turn to? Where's your religion?

NORA: Oh, Torvald, I'm really not sure what religion is.

HELMER: What—?

NORA: I only know what the minister said when I was confirmed. He told me religion was this thing and that. When I get clear and away by myself, I'll go into that problem too. I'll see if what the minister said was right, or, in any case, if it's right for me.

HELMER: A young woman your age shouldn't talk like that. If religion can't move you, I can try to rouse your conscience. You do have some moral feeling? Or, tell me—has that gone too?

NORA: It's not easy to answer that, Torvald. I simply don't know. I'm all confused about these things. I just know I see them so differently from you. I find out for one thing, that the law's not at all what I'd thought—but I can't get it through my head that the law is fair. A woman hasn't a right to protect her dying father or save her husband's life! I can't believe that.

HELMER: You talk like a child. You don't know anything of the world you live in.

NORA: No, I don't. But now I'll begin to learn for myself. I'll try to discover who's right, the world or I.

HELMER: Nora, you're sick; you've got a fever. I almost think you're out of your head.

NORA: I've never felt more clearheaded and sure in my life.

HELMER: And—clearheaded and sure—you're leaving your husband and children?

NORA: Yes.

HELMER: Then there's only one possible reason.

NORA: What?

HELMER: You no longer love me.

NORA: No. That's exactly it.

HELMER: Nora! You can't be serious!

NORA: Oh, this is so hard, Torvald—you've been so kind to me always. But I can't help it. I don't love you anymore.

HELMER (*struggling for composure*): Are you also clearheaded and sure about that?

NORA: Yes, completely. That's why I can't go on staying here.

HELMER: Can you tell me what I did to lose your love?

NORA: Yes, I can tell you. It was this evening when the miraculous thing didn't come—then I knew you weren't the man I'd imagined.

HELMER: Be more explicit; I don't follow you.

NORA: I've waited now so patiently eight long years—for, my Lord, I know miracles don't come every day. Then this crisis broke over me, and such a certainty filled me: *Now* the miraculous event would occur. While Krogstad's letter was lying out there, I never for an instant dreamed that you could give in to his terms. I was so utterly sure you'd say to him: Go on, tell your tale to the whole wide world. And when he'd done that—

HELMER: Yes, what then? When I'd delivered my own wife into shame and disgrace—!

NORA: When he'd done that, I was so utterly sure that you'd step forward, take the blame on yourself and say: I am the guilty one.

HELMER: Nora—!

NORA: You're thinking I'd never accept such a sacrifice from you? No, of course not. But what good would my protests be against you? That was the miracle I was waiting for, in terror and hope. And to stave that off, I would have taken my life.

HELMER: I'd gladly work for you day and night, Nora—and take on pain and deprivation. But there's no one who gives up honor for love.

NORA: Millions of women have done just that.

HELMER: Oh, you think and talk like a silly child.

NORA: Perhaps. But you neither think nor talk like the man I could join myself to. When your big fright was over—and it wasn't from any threat against me, only for what might damage you—when all the danger was past, for you it was just as if nothing had happened. I was exactly the same, your little lark, your doll, that you'd have to handle with double care now that I'd turned out so brittle and frail. (*Gets up.*) Torvald—in that instant it dawned on me that for eight years I've been living here with a stranger, and that I'd even conceived three children—oh, I can't stand the thought of it! I could tear myself to bits.

HELMER (*heavily*): I see. There's a gulf that's opened between us—that's clear. Oh, but Nora, can't we bridge it somehow?

NORA: The way I am now, I'm no wife for you.

HELMER: I have the strength to make myself over.

NORA: Maybe—if your doll gets taken away.

HELMER: But to part! To part from you! No, Nora, no—I can't imagine it.

NORA (*going out, right*): All the more reason why it has to be. (*She reenters with her coat and a small overnight bag, which she puts on a chair by the table.*)

HELMER: Nora, Nora, not now! Wait till tomorrow.

NORA: I can't spend the night in a strange man's room.

HELMER: But couldn't we live here like brother and sister—

NORA: You know very well how long that would last. (*Throws her shawl about her.*) Good-bye, Torvald. I won't look in on the children. I know they're in better hands than mine. The way I am now, I'm no use to them.

HELMER: But someday, Nora—someday—?

NORA: How can I tell? I haven't the least idea what'll become of me.

HELMER: But you're my wife, now and wherever you go.

NORA: Listen, Torvald—I've heard that when a wife deserts her husband's house just as I'm doing, then the law frees him from all responsibility. In any case, I'm freeing you from being responsible. Don't feel yourself bound, any more than I will. There has to be absolute freedom for us both. Here, take your ring back. Give me mine.

HELMER: That too?

NORA: That too.

HELMER: There it is.

NORA: Good. Well, now it's all over. I'm putting the keys here. The maids know all about keeping up the house—better than I do. Tomorrow, after I've left town, Kristine will stop by to pack up everything that's mine from home. I'd like those things shipped up to me.

HELMER: Over! All over! Nora, won't you ever think about me?

NORA: I'm sure I'll think of you often, and about the children and the house here.

HELMER: May I write you?

NORA: No—never. You're not to do that.

HELMER: Oh, but let me send you—

NORA: Nothing. Nothing.

HELMER: Or help you if you need it.

NORA: No. I accept nothing from strangers.

HELMER: Nora—can I never be more than a stranger to you?

NORA (*picking up the overnight bag*): Ah, Torvald—it would take the greatest miracle of all—

HELMER: Tell me the greatest miracle!

NORA: You and I both would have to transform ourselves to the point that—Oh, Torvald, I've stopped believing in miracles.

HELMER: But I'll believe. Tell me! Transform ourselves to the point that—?

NORA: That our living together could be a true marriage. (*She goes out down the hall.*)

HELMER (*sinks down on a chair by the door, face buried in his hands*): Nora! Nora! (*Looking about and rising.*) Empty. She's gone. (*A sudden hope leaps in him.*) The greatest miracle—?

(*From below, the sound of a door slamming shut.*)

Twentieth-Century Theaters

Most theaters of the early and mid-twentieth century continued to have a proscenium arch. But dramatists and the theater as a whole have moved away from the realism of the late 1800s and early 1900s. In late modern and contemporary theater—both in the plays written now and productions of earlier plays—it is assumed that the audience knows the set is an artistic construction that requires imaginative participation. Playwrights as they write and producers as they plan productions no longer confine themselves to a realistic room in a box set, with all action occurring within that one space. They break through the "glass wall" and allow action to take place on the forestage as well as behind the arch. Thus the actors and audience are no longer always separated by the proscenium arch, as they are in Ibsen's theater. The action reaches out toward or into the audience. In some plays, characters even address the audience.

NONREALISTIC SET Lorraine Hansberry seems to have written *A Raisin in the Sun* with a conventional, realistic set behind the arch in mind. Her stage directions (p. 1301) sound a lot like those for *A Doll House* (p. 1246). But that kind of staging was already being replaced by a different approach. In 1949, for example, ten years before the premiere of *A Raisin in the Sun*, Arthur Miller conceived of the set for *Death of a Salesman* in a postmodern, nonrealistic way. While the proscenium stage and curtain are still there, what the audience sees on stage is not one room from the inside but several rooms from the outside. The outer and inner walls of the house are invisible (perhaps with only the bottom couple of feet of the walls, outlining the rooms), which allows spectators to see into several rooms. As Miller conceived it, "The kitchen at center seems actual enough, for there is a kitchen table with three chairs, and a refrigerator. But no other fixtures are seen. . . . To the right of the kitchen, on a level raised two feet, is a bedroom furnished only with a brass bedstead and a straight chair. . . . Behind the kitchen, on a level raised six and a half feet, is the boys' bedroom, at present barely visible. Two beds are dimly seen." *A Raisin in the Sun* also could be staged in such a nonrealistic way, with Walter and Ruth's bedroom visible as well as the living room. The point is that contemporary drama does not require realistic sets, the way modern drama did.

CONTEMPORARY THEATERS Theater in the mid- to late 1900s moved still further away from realism in text and stagecraft. Many contemporary theaters reach out to the audience not just through the imagination but also physically, by thrusting the stage out into the audience (returning to the Elizabethan methods) or by placing the stage in the center of the theater, with the audience surrounding it on all sides. Designers today take full advantage of a theater. Scenes might take place on the catwalks, in the audience, or in the aisles. Actors sometimes enter and exit through the audience, using the same aisles. Some plays even have a character initially seated in the audience who later rises and joins the action. Sets are changed between scenes while the audience watches, with the actors often moving furniture and props themselves.

SETS, PROPS, AND LIGHTING   A thrust stage or theater-in-the-round cannot, of course, have rooms with real walls. Sets and props usually are simple and minimal or impressionistic and symbolic rather than realistically detailed. Playwrights and stage designers often think in terms of platforms connected by ramps and stairways to allow multiple locations. Modern equipment produces lighting effects undreamed of even a few decades ago. All of this means that playwrights today are free to imagine a far greater variety of spaces.

NONCONVENTIONAL PRESENTATIONS OF DRAMA   Not all contemporary drama is produced in conventional theaters. Experimental or avant-garde drama uses the stage differently, often challenging the audience's ideas of theater itself. Ten-minute plays also, in many cases, make do with minimal settings and props. Some playwrights move outside of traditional theaters, writing plays to be performed in bare halls or even on the streets, sometimes with workers and ordinary people, instead of trained actors, playing the roles. Others utilize a single actor on an empty stage to deliver a monologue—as in, for example, Joyce Carol Oates's *When I Was a Little Girl and My Mother Didn't Want Me* (p. 1062). Today's productions of drama from earlier times often use such nonconventional staging methods. Imagine how watching *A Raisin in the Sun* (or *A Doll House* or *Othello*) would be different if set in one of these experimental ways.

SERIOUS DRAMA   The word *drama*, in addition to meaning a literary work intended for performance or the whole body of such works, also means any particularly striking or interesting event or series of events that involve conflict and tension. In literature or theater today, **drama** is often used to describe a play that is not a comedy and does not have a tragic ending but deals with serious events involving conflict and tension. *A Raisin in the Sun* is such a play, as is August Wilson's *Fences* (p. 963). So, too, are many of the works by late twentieth-century and early twenty-first-century playwrights. You may have noticed film genres such as *comedy*, *action*, and *drama*—not *tragedy*.

ENTRY POINTS   *A Raisin in the Sun* opens at daybreak on the Friday of a crucial weekend in the life of a family living on the South Side of Chicago. Tensions within the family quickly become apparent. It's important to notice that these tensions reveal character traits of family members and bring out their hopes, dreams, disappointments, and burdens. As you read the play and think back on it, consider what about it is mainly of 1950s historical interest and what about it holds continuing relevance. Consider also how the play is about a social problem—discrimination and its effects on people—as well as the universal problems of identity and self-worth and how those issues are woven together. Reflect on the title and the epigraph, Langston Hughes's poem "Harlem": Reread the discussion of the poem on pages 630–31 and ask yourself in what ways the play is exploring themes similar to those in the poem.

Lorraine Hansberry (1930–1965)

A Raisin in the Sun   [1959]

HARLEM (A Dream Deferred)

What happens to a dream deferred?

Does it dry up
like a raisin in the sun?
Or fester like a sore—
And then run?
Does it stink like rotten meat?
Or crust and sugar over—
like a syrupy sweet?

Maybe it just sags
like a heavy load.

Or does it explode?

—*Langston Hughes*

CHARACTERS

RUTH YOUNGER
TRAVIS YOUNGER
WALTER LEE YOUNGER (*Brother*)
BENEATHA YOUNGER
LENA YOUNGER (*Mama*)

JOSEPH ASAGAI
GEORGE MURCHISON
KARL LINDNER
BOBO
MOVING MEN

ACT 1

Scene 1: *Friday morning.*
Scene 2: *The following morning.*

ACT 2

Scene 1: *Later, the same day.*
Scene 2: *Friday night, a few weeks later.*
Scene 3: *Moving day, one week later.*

ACT 3

An hour later.

SCENE

The action of the play is set in Chicago's Southside, sometime between World War II and the present.

ACT I / Scene One

The YOUNGER *living room would be a comfortable and well-ordered room if it were not for a number of indestructible contradictions to this state of being. Its furnishings are typical and undistinguished and their primary feature now is that they have clearly had to accommodate the living of too many people for too many years—and they are tired. Still, we can see that at some time, a time probably no longer remembered by the family (except perhaps for* MAMA*), the furnishings of this room were actually selected with care and love and even hope—and brought to this apartment and arranged with taste and pride.*

That was a long time ago. Now the once loved pattern of the couch upholstery has to fight to show itself from under acres of crocheted doilies and couch covers which have themselves finally come to be more important than the upholstery. And here a table or a chair has been moved to disguise the worn places in the carpet; but the carpet has fought back by showing its weariness, with depressing uniformity, elsewhere on its surface.

Weariness has, in fact, won in this room. Everything has been polished, washed, sat on, used, scrubbed too often. All pretenses but living itself have long since vanished from the very atmosphere of this room.

Moreover, a section of this room, for it is not really a room unto itself, though the landlord's lease would make it seem so, slopes backward to provide a small kitchen area, where the family prepares the meals that are eaten in the living room proper, which must also serve as dining room. The single window that has been provided for these "two" rooms is located in this kitchen area. The sole natural light the family may enjoy in the course of a day is only that which fights its way through this little window.

At left, a door leads to a bedroom which is shared by MAMA *and her daughter,* BENEATHA. *At right, opposite, is a second room (which in the beginning of the life of this apartment was probably a breakfast room) which serves as a bedroom for* WALTER *and his wife,* RUTH.

Time: Sometime between World War II and the present.

Place: Chicago's Southside.

At Rise: It is morning dark in the living room, TRAVIS *is asleep on the make-down bed at center. An alarm clock sounds from within the bedroom at right, and presently* RUTH *enters from that room and closes the door behind her. She crosses sleepily toward the window. As she passes her sleeping son she reaches down and shakes him a little. At the window she raises the shade and a dusky Southside morning light comes in feebly. She fills a pot with water and puts it on to boil. She calls to the boy, between yawns, in a slightly muffled voice.*

RUTH *is about thirty. We can see that she was a pretty girl, even exceptionally so, but now it is apparent that life has been little that she expected, and disappointment has already begun to hang in her face. In a few years, before thirty-five even, she will be known among her people as a "settled woman."*

She crosses to her son and gives him a good, final, rousing shake.

RUTH: Come on now, boy, it's seven thirty! (*Her son sits up at last, in a stupor of sleepiness*) I say hurry up, Travis! You ain't the only person in the world got to use a bathroom ! (*The child, a sturdy, handsome little boy of ten or eleven, drags himself out of the bed and almost blindly takes his towels and "today's clothes" from drawers and a closet and goes out to the bathroom, which is in an outside hall and which is shared by another family or families on the same floor.* RUTH *crosses to the bedroom door at right and opens it and calls in to her husband*) Walter Lee! . . . It's after seven thirty! Lemme see you do some waking up in there now! (*She waits*) You better get up from there, man! It's after seven thirty I tell you. (*She waits again*) All right, you just go ahead and lay there and next thing you know Travis be finished and Mr. Johnson'll be in there and you'll be fussing and cussing round here like a madman! And be late too! (*She waits, at the end of patience*) Walter Lee — it's time for you to GET UP!

(*She waits another second and then starts to go into the bedroom, but is apparently satisfied that her husband has begun to get up. She stops, pulls the door to, and returns to the kitchen area. She wipes her face with a moist cloth and runs her fingers through her sleep-disheveled hair in a vain effort and ties an apron around her housecoat. The bedroom door at right opens and her husband stands in the doorway in his pajamas, which are rumpled and mismated. He is a lean, intense young man in his middle thirties, inclined to quick nervous movements and erratic speech habits — and always in his voice there is a quality of indictment*)

WALTER: Is he out yet?

RUTH: What you mean *out*? He ain't hardly got in there good yet.

WALTER: (*Wandering in, still more oriented to sleep than to a new day*) Well, what was you doing all that yelling for if I can't even get in there yet? (*Stopping and thinking*) Check coming today?

RUTH: They *said* Saturday and this is just Friday and I hopes to God you ain't going to get up here first thing this morning and start talking to me 'bout no money — 'cause I 'bout don't want to hear it.

WALTER: Something the matter with you this morning?

RUTH: No — I'm just sleepy as the devil. What kind of eggs you want?

WALTER: Not scrambled. (RUTH *starts to scramble eggs*) Paper come? (RUTH *points impatiently to the rolled up Tribune on the table, and he gets it and spreads it out and vaguely reads the front page*) Set off another bomb yesterday.

RUTH: (*Maximum indifference*) Did they?

WALTER: (*Looking up*) What's the matter with you?

RUTH: Ain't nothing the matter with me. And don't keep asking me that this morning.

WALTER: Ain't nobody bothering you. (*Reading the news of the day absently again*) Say Colonel McCormick is sick.

RUTH: (*Affecting tea-party interest*) Is he now? Poor thing.

WALTER: (*Sighing and looking at his watch*) Oh, me. (*He waits*) Now what is that boy doing in that bathroom all this time? He just going to have to start getting up earlier. I can't be being late to work on account of him fooling around in there.

RUTH: (*Turning on him*) Oh, no he ain't going to be getting up no earlier no such thing! It ain't his fault that he can't get to bed no earlier nights 'cause he got a bunch of crazy good-for-nothing clowns sitting up running their mouths in what is supposed to be his bedroom after ten o'clock at night . . .

WALTER: That's what you mad about, ain't it? The things I want to talk about with my friends just couldn't be important in your mind, could they?

(*He rises and finds a cigarette in her handbag on the table and crosses to the little window and looks out, smoking and deeply enjoying this first one*)

RUTH: (*Almost matter of factly, a complaint too automatic to deserve emphasis*) Why you always got to smoke before you eat in the morning?

WALTER: (*At the window*) Just look at 'em down there . . . Running and racing to work . . . (*He turns and faces his wife and watches her a moment at the stove, and then, suddenly*) You look young this morning, baby.

RUTH: (*Indifferently*) Yeah?

WALTER: Just for a second—stirring them eggs. Just for a second it was—you looked real young again. (*He reaches for her; she crosses away. Then, drily*) It's gone now—you look like yourself again!

RUTH: Man, if you don't shut up and leave me alone.

WALTER: (*Looking out to the street again*) First thing a man ought to learn in life is not to make love to no colored woman first thing in the morning. You all some eeeevil people at eight o'clock in the morning.

(TRAVIS *appears in the hall doorway, almost fully dressed and quite wide awake now, his towels and pajamas across his shoulders. He opens the door and signals for his father to make the bathroom in a hurry*)

TRAVIS: (*Watching the bathroom*) Daddy, come on!

(WALTER *gets his bathroom utensils and flies out to the bathroom*)

RUTH: Sit down and have your breakfast, Travis.

TRAVIS: Mama, this is Friday. (*Gleefully*) Check coming tomorrow, huh?

RUTH: You get your mind off money and eat your breakfast.

TRAVIS: (*Eating*) This is the morning we supposed to bring the fifty cents to school.

RUTH: Well, I ain't got no fifty cents this morning.

TRAVIS: Teacher say we have to.

RUTH: I don't care what teacher say. I ain't got it. Eat your breakfast, Travis.

TRAVIS: I *am* eating.

RUTH: Hush up now and just eat!

(*The boy gives her an exasperated look for her lack of understanding, and eats grudgingly*)

TRAVIS: You think Grandmama would have it?

RUTH: No! And I want you to stop asking your grandmother for money, you hear me?

TRAVIS: (*Outraged*) Gaaaleee! I don't ask her, she just gimme it sometimes!

RUTH: Travis Willard Younger—I got too much on me this morning to be—

TRAVIS: Maybe Daddy—

RUTH: *Travis!*

(*The boy hushes abruptly. They are both quiet and tense for several seconds*)

TRAVIS: (*Presently*) Could I maybe go carry some groceries in front of the super-market for a little while after school then?

RUTH: Just hush, I said. (*Travis jabs his spoon into his cereal bowl viciously, and rests his head in anger upon his fists*) If you through eating, you can get over there and make up your bed.

(*The boy obeys stiffly and crosses the room, almost mechanically, to the bed and more or less folds the bedding into a heap, then angrily gets his books and cap*)

TRAVIS: (*Sulking and standing apart from her unnaturally*) I'm gone.

RUTH: (*Looking up from the stove to inspect him automatically*) Come here. (*He crosses to her and she studies his head*) If you don't take this comb and fix this here head, you better! (TRAVIS *puts down his books with a great sigh of oppression, and crosses to the mirror. His mother mutters under her breath about his "slubbornness"*) 'Bout to march out of here with that head looking just like chickens slept in it! I just don't know where you get your slubborn ways . . . And get your jacket, too. Looks chilly out this morning.

TRAVIS: (*With conspicuously brushed hair and jacket*) I'm gone.

RUTH: Get carfare and milk money—(*Waving one finger*)—and not a single penny for no caps,° you hear me?

TRAVIS: (*With sullen politeness*) Yes'm.

(*He turns in outrage to leave. His mother watches after him as in his frustration he approaches the door almost comically. When she speaks to him, her voice has become a very gentle tease*)

RUTH: (*Mocking; as she thinks he would say it*) Oh, Mama makes me so mad sometimes, I don't know what to do! (*She waits and continues to his back as he stands stock-still in front of the door*) I wouldn't kiss that woman good-bye for nothing in this world this morning! (*The boy finally turns around and rolls his eyes at her, knowing the mood has changed and he is vindicated; he does not, however, move toward her yet*) Not for nothing in this world! (*She finally laughs aloud at him and holds out her arms to him and we see that it is*

---

caps: For his cap gun, a very popular toy in the 1950s and 1960s.

a way between them, very old and practiced. He crosses to her and allows her to embrace him warmly but keeps his face fixed with masculine rigidity. She holds him back from her presently and looks at him and runs her fingers over the features of his face. With utter gentleness) Now—whose little old angry man are you?

TRAVIS: *(The masculinity and gruffness start to fade at last)* Aw gaalee—Mama . . .

RUTH: *(Mimicking)* Aw gaaaaalleeeee, Mama! *(She pushes him, with rough playfulness and finality, toward the door)* Get on out of here or you going to be late.

TRAVIS: *(In the face of love, new aggressiveness)* Mama, could I *please* go carry groceries?

RUTH: Honey, it's starting to get so cold evenings.

WALTER: *(Coming in from the bathroom and drawing a make-believe gun from a make-believe holster and shooting at his son)* What is it he wants to do?

RUTH: Go carry groceries after school at the supermarket.

WALTER: Well, let him go . . .

TRAVIS: *(Quickly, to the ally)* I have to—she won't gimme the fifty cents . . .

WALTER: *(To his wife only)* Why not?

RUTH: *(Simply, and with flavor)* 'Cause we don't have it.

WALTER: *(To RUTH only)* What you tell the boy things like that for? *(Reaching down into his pants with a rather important gesture)* Here, son—

(He hands the boy the coin, but his eyes are directed to his wife's, TRAVIS *takes the money happily)*

TRAVIS: Thanks, Daddy.

(He starts out. RUTH *watches both of them with murder in her eyes.* WALTER *stands and stares back at her with defiance, and suddenly reaches into his pocket again on an afterthought)*

WALTER: *(Without even looking at his son, still staring hard at his wife)* In fact, here's another fifty cents . . . Buy yourself some fruit today—or take a taxicab to school or something!

TRAVIS: Whoopee—

(He leaps up and clasps his father around the middle with his legs, and they face each other in mutual appreciation; slowly WALTER LEE *peeks around the boy to catch the violent rays from his wife's eyes and draws his head back as if shot)*

WALTER: You better get down now—and get to school, man.

TRAVIS: *(At the door)* O.K. Good-bye. *(He exits)*

WALTER: *(After him, pointing with pride)* That's *my* boy.

(She looks at him in disgust and turns back to her work) You know what I was thinking 'bout in the bathroom this morning?

RUTH: No.

WALTER: How come you always try to be so pleasant!

RUTH: What is there to be pleasant 'bout!

WALTER: You want to know what I was thinking 'bout in the bathroom or not!

RUTH: I know what you thinking 'bout.

WALTER: (*Ignoring her*) 'Bout what me and Willy Harris was talking about last night.

RUTH: (*Immediately—a refrain*) Willy Harris is a good-for-nothing loudmouth.

WALTER: Anybody who talks to me has got to be a good-for-nothing loudmouth, ain't he? And what you know about who is just a good-for-nothing loud-mouth? Charlie Atkins was just a "good-for-nothing loudmouth" too, wasn't he! When he wanted me to go in the dry-cleaning business with him. And now—he's grossing a hundred thousand a year. A hundred thousand dollars a year! You still call *him* a loudmouth!

RUTH: (*Bitterly*) Oh, Walter Lee . . .

(*She folds her head on her arms over the table*)

WALTER: (*Rising and coming to her and standing over her*) You tired, ain't you? Tired of everything. Me, the boy, the way we live—this beat-up hole—every-thing. Ain't you? (*She doesn't look up, doesn't answer*) So tired—moaning and groaning all the time, but you wouldn't do nothing to help, would you? You couldn't be on my side that long for nothing, could you?

RUTH: Walter, please leave me alone.

WALTER: A man needs for a woman to back him up . . .

RUTH: Walter—

WALTER: Mama would listen to you. You know she listen to you more than she do me and Bennie. She think more of you. All you have to do is just sit down with her when you drinking your coffee one morning and talking 'bout things like you do and—(*He sits down beside her and demonstrates graphically what he thinks her methods and tone should be*)—you just sip your coffee, see, and say easy like that you been thinking 'bout that deal Walter Lee is so interested in, 'bout the store and all, and sip some more coffee, like what you saying ain't really that important to you—And the next thing you know, she be listening good and asking you questions and when I come home—I can tell her the details. This ain't no fly-by-night proposition, baby. I mean we figured it out, me and Willy and Bobo.

RUTH: (*With a frown*) Bobo?

WALTER: Yeah. You see, this little liquor store we got in mind cost seventy-five thousand and we figured the initial investment on the place be 'bout thirty thousand, see. That be ten thousand each. Course, there's a couple of hun-dred you got to pay so's you don't spend your life just waiting for them clowns to let your license get approved—

RUTH: You mean graft?

WALTER: (*Frowning impatiently*) Don't call it that. See there, that just goes to show you what women understand about the world. Baby, don't *nothing* happen for you in this world 'less you pay *somebody* off!

RUTH: Walter, leave me alone! (*She raises her head and stares at him vigorously—then says, more quietly*) Eat your eggs, they gonna be cold.

WALTER: (*Straightening up from her and looking off*) That's it. There you are. Man say to his woman: I got me a dream. His woman say: Eat your eggs. (*Sadly, but gaining in power*) Man say: I got to take hold of this here world, baby! And a woman will say: Eat your eggs and go to work. (*Passionately now*) Man say: I got to change my life, I'm choking to death, baby! And his woman say — (*In utter anguish as he brings his fists, down on his thighs*) — Your eggs is getting cold!

RUTH: (*Softly*) Walter, that ain't none of our money.

WALTER: (*Not listening at all or even looking at her*) This morning, I was lookin' in the mirror and thinking about it . . . I'm thirty-five years old; I been married eleven years and I got a boy who sleeps in the living room — (*Very, very quietly*) — and all I got to give him is stories about how rich white people live . . .

RUTH: Eat your eggs, Walter.

WALTER: (*Slams the table and jumps up*) — DAMN MY EGGS — DAMN ALL THE EGGS THAT EVER WAS!

RUTH: Then go to work.

WALTER: (*Looking up at her*) See — I'm trying to talk to you 'bout myself — (*Shaking his head with the repetition*) — and all you can say is eat them eggs and go to work.

RUTH: (*Wearily*) Honey, you never say nothing new. I listen to you every day, every night and every morning, and you never say nothing new. (*Shrugging*) So you would rather *be* Mr. Arnold than be his chauffeur. So — I would *rather* be living in Buckingham Palace.°

WALTER: That is just what is wrong with the colored woman in this world . . . Don't understand about building their men up and making 'em feel like they somebody. Like they can do something.

RUTH: (*Drily, but to hurt*) There *are* colored men who do things.

WALTER: No thanks to the colored woman.

RUTH: Well, being a colored woman, I guess I can't help myself none.

(*She rises and gets the ironing board and sets it up and attacks a huge pile of rough-dried clothes, sprinkling them in preparation for the ironing and then rolling them into tight fat balls*)

WALTER: (*Mumbling*) We one group of men tied to a race of women with small minds!

(*His sister BENEATHA enters. She is about twenty, as slim and intense as her brother. She is not as pretty as her sister-in-law, but her lean, almost intellectual face has a handsomeness of its own. She wears a bright-red flannel nightie, and her thick hair stands wildly about her head. Her speech is a mixture of many things; it is different from the rest of the family's insofar as education has permeated her sense of English — and perhaps the Midwest rather than the South has finally — at last — won out in her inflection; but not altogether, because over all of it is a soft slurring and transformed use of vowels which is the decided influence of the Southside. She passes*

Buckingham Palace: The London residence of the British royal family.

through the room without looking at either RUTH *or* WALTER *and goes to the outside door and looks, a little blindly, out to the bathroom. She sees that it has been lost to the Johnsons. She closes the door with a sleepy vengeance and crosses to the table and sits down a little defeated)*

BENEATHA: I am going to start timing those people.

WALTER: You should get up earlier.

BENEATHA: *(Her face in her hands. She is still fighting the urge to go back to bed)* Really—would you suggest dawn? Where's the paper?

WALTER: *(Pushing the paper across the table to her as he studies her almost clinically, as though he has never seen her before)* You a horrible-looking chick at this hour.

BENEATHA: *(Drily)* Good morning, everybody.

WALTER: *(Senselessly)* How is school coming?

BENEATHA: *(In the same spirit)* Lovely. Lovely. And you know, biology is the greatest. *(Looking up at him)* I dissected something that looked just like you yesterday.

WALTER: I just wondered if you've made up your mind and everything.

BENEATHA: *(Gaining in sharpness and impatience)* And what did I answer yesterday morning—and the day before that?

RUTH: *(From the ironing board, like someone disinterested and old)* Don't be so nasty, Bennie.

BENEATHA: *(Still to her brother)* And the day before that and the day before that!

WALTER: *(Defensively)* I'm interested in you. Something wrong with that? Ain't many girls who decide—

WALTER *and* BENEATHA: *(In unison)*—"to be a doctor." *(Silence)*

WALTER: Have we figured out yet just exactly how much medical school is going to cost?

RUTH: Walter Lee, why don't you leave that girl alone and get out of here to work?

BENEATHA: *(Exits to the bathroom and bangs on the door)* Come on out of there, please!

(She comes back into the room)

WALTER: *(Looking at his sister intently)* You know the check is coming tomorrow.

BENEATHA: *(Turning on him with a sharpness all her own)* That money belongs to Mama, Walter, and it's for her to decide how she wants to use it. I don't care if she wants to buy a house or a rocket ship or just nail it up somewhere and look at it. It's hers. Not ours—*hers.*

WALTER: *(Bitterly)* Now ain't that fine! You just got your mother's interest at heart, ain't you, girl? You such a nice girl—but if Mama got that money she can always take a few thousand and help you through school too—can't she?

BENEATHA: I have never asked anyone around here to do anything for me!

WALTER: No! And the line between asking and just accepting when the time comes is big and wide—ain't it!

BENEATHA: *(With fury)* What do you want from me, Brother—that I quit school or just drop dead, which!

WALTER: I don't want nothing but for you to stop acting holy 'round here. Me and Ruth done made some sacrifices for you—why can't you do something for the family?

RUTH: Walter, don't be dragging me in it.

WALTER: You are in it—Don't you get up and go work in somebody's kitchen for the last three years to help put clothes on her back?

RUTH: Oh, Walter—that's not fair . . .

WALTER: It ain't that nobody expects you to get on your knees and say thank you, Brother; thank you, Ruth; thank you, Mama—and thank you, Travis, for wearing the same pair of shoes for two semesters—

BENEATHA: (*Dropping to her knees*) Well—I *do*—all right?—thank everybody! And forgive me for ever wanting to be anything at all! (*Pursuing him on her knees across the floor*) FORGIVE ME, FORGIVE ME, FORGIVE ME!

RUTH: Please stop it! Your mama'll hear you.

WALTER: Who the hell told you you had to be a doctor? If you so crazy 'bout messing 'round with sick people—then go be a nurse like other women—or just get married and be quiet . . .

BENEATHA: Well—you finally got it said . . . It took you three years but you finally got it said. Walter, give up; leave me alone—it's Mama's money.

WALTER: *He was my father, too!*

BENEATHA: So what? He was mine, too—and Travis's grandfather—but the insurance money belongs to Mama. Picking on me is not going to make her give it to you to invest in any liquor stores—(*Underbreath, dropping into a chair*)—and I for one say, God bless Mama for that!

WALTER: (*To* RUTH) See—did you hear? Did you hear!

RUTH: Honey, please go to work.

WALTER: Nobody in this house is ever going to understand me.

BENEATHA: Because you're a nut.

WALTER: Who's a nut?

BENEATHA: You—you are a nut. Thee is mad, boy.

WALTER: (*Looking at his wife and his sister from the door, very sadly*) The world's most backward race of people, and that's a fact.

BENEATHA: (*Turning slowly in her chair*) And then there are all those prophets who would lead us out of the wilderness—(WALTER *slams out of the house*)— into the swamps!

RUTH: Bennie, why you always gotta be pickin' on your brother? Can't you be a little sweeter sometimes? (*Door opens.* WALTER *walks in. He fumbles with his cap, starts to speak, clears throat, looks everywhere but at* RUTH. *Finally:*)

WALTER: (*To* RUTH) I need some money for carfare.

RUTH: (*Looks at him, then warms; teasing, but tenderly*) Fifty cents? (*She goes to her bag and gets money*) Here—take a taxi!

(WALTER *exits,* MAMA *enters. She is a woman in her early sixties, full-bodied and strong. She is one of those women of a certain grace and beauty who wear it so unobtrusively that it takes a while to notice. Her dark-brown face is surrounded by the total whiteness of her hair, and, being a woman who has adjusted to many things in life and overcome many more, her face is full of strength. She has, we can see, wit and faith of a kind that keep her eyes lit and full of interest and expectancy. She is, in a word, a beautiful woman. Her bearing is perhaps most like the noble bearing of the women of the Hereros of Southwest Africa—rather as if she imagines that as she walks she still bears a basket or a vessel upon her head. Her speech, on the other hand, is as careless as her carriage is precise—she is inclined to slur everything—but her voice is perhaps not so much quiet as simply soft)*

MAMA: Who that 'round here slamming doors at this hour?

(She crosses through the room, goes to the window, opens it, and brings in a feeble little plant growing doggedly in a small pot on the windowsill. She feels the dirt and puts it back out)

RUTH: That was Walter Lee. He and Bennie was at it again.

MAMA: My children and they tempers. Lord, if this little old plant don't get more sun than it's been getting it ain't never going to see spring again. *(She turns from the window)* What's the matter with you this morning, Ruth? You looks right peaked. You aiming to iron all them things? Leave some for me. I'll get to 'em this afternoon. Bennie honey, it's too drafty for you to be sitting 'round half dressed. Where's your robe?

BENEATHA: In the cleaners.

MAMA: Well, go get mine and put it on.

BENEATHA: I'm not cold, Mama, honest.

MAMA: I know—but you so thin . . .

BENEATHA: *(Irritably)* Mama, I'm not cold.

MAMA: *(Seeing the make-down bed as* TRAVIS *has left it)* Lord have mercy, look at that poor bed. Bless his heart—he tries, don't he?

(She moves to the bed TRAVIS *has sloppily made up)*

RUTH: No—he don't half try at all 'cause he knows you going to come along behind him and fix everything. That's just how come he don't know how to do nothing right now—you done spoiled that boy so.

MAMA: *(Folding bedding)* Well—he's a little boy. Ain't supposed to know 'bout housekeeping. My baby, that's what he is. What you fix for his breakfast this morning?

RUTH: *(Angrily)* I feed my son, Lena!

MAMA: I ain't meddling—*(Underbreath; busy-bodyish)* I just noticed all last week he had cold cereal, and when it starts getting this chilly in the fall a child ought to have some hot grits or something when he goes out in the cold—

RUTH: *(Furious)* I gave him hot oats—is that all right!

MAMA: I ain't meddling. *(Pause)* Put a lot of nice butter on it? *(RUTH shoots her an angry look and does not reply)* He likes lots of butter.

RUTH: *(Exasperated)* Lena—

MAMA: (*To* BENEATHA. MAMA *is inclined to wander conversationally sometimes*)
   What was you and your brother fussing 'bout this morning?
BENEATHA: It's not important, Mama.

(*She gets up and goes to look out at the bathroom, which is apparently free, and she picks up her towels and rushes out*)

MAMA: What was they fighting about?
RUTH: Now you know as well as I do.
MAMA: (*Shaking her head*) Brother still worrying hisself sick about that money?
RUTH: You know he is.
MAMA: You had breakfast?
RUTH: Some coffee.
MAMA: Girl, you better start eating and looking after yourself better. You almost
   thin as Travis.
RUTH: Lena—
MAMA: Un-hunh?
RUTH: What are you going to do with it?
MAMA: Now don't you start, child. It's too early in the morning to be talking
   about money. It ain't Christian.
RUTH: It's just that he got his heart set on that store—
MAMA: You mean that liquor store that Willy Harris want him to invest in?
RUTH: Yes—
MAMA: We ain't no business people, Ruth. We just plain working folks.
RUTH: Ain't nobody business people till they go into business. Walter Lee say colored
   people ain't never going to start getting ahead till they start gambling on some
   different kinds of things in the world—investments and things.
MAMA: What done got into you, girl? Walter Lee done finally sold you on investing.
RUTH: No. Mama, something is happening between Walter and me. I don't
   know what it is—but he needs something—something I can't give him
   anymore. He needs this chance, Lena.
MAMA: (*Frowning deeply*) But liquor, honey—
RUTH: Well—like Walter say—I spec people going to always be drinking them-
   selves some liquor.
MAMA: Well—whether they drinks it or not ain't none of my business. But
   whether I go into business selling it to 'em *is,* and I don't want that on my
   ledger this late in life. (*Stopping suddenly and studying her daughter-in-law*)
   Ruth Younger, what's the matter with you today? You look like you could
   fall over right there.
RUTH: I'm tired.
MAMA: Then you better stay home from work today.
RUTH: I can't stay home. She'd be calling up the agency and screaming at them,
   "My girl didn't come in today—send me somebody! My girl didn't come
   in!" Oh, she just have a fit . . .
MAMA: Well, let her have it. I'll just call her up and say you got the flu—
RUTH: (*Laughing*) Why the flu?

MAMA: 'Cause it sounds respectable to 'em. Something white people get, too. They know 'bout the flu. Otherwise they think you been cut up or something when you tell 'em you sick.

RUTH: I got to go in. We need the money.

MAMA: Somebody would of thought my children done all but starved to death the way they talk about money here late. Child, we got a great big old check coming tomorrow.

RUTH: (*Sincerely, but also self-righteously*) Now that's your money. It ain't got nothing to do with me. We all feel like that—Walter and Bennie and me—even Travis.

MAMA: (*Thoughtfully, and suddenly very far away*) Ten thousand dollars—

RUTH: Sure is wonderful.

MAMA: Ten thousand dollars.

RUTH: You know what you should do, Miss Lena? You should take yourself a trip somewhere. To Europe or South America or someplace—

MAMA: (*Throwing up her hands at the thought*) Oh, child!

RUTH: I'm serious. Just pack up and leave! Go on away and enjoy yourself some. Forget about the family and have yourself a ball for once in your life—

MAMA: (*Drily*) You sound like I'm just about ready to die. Who'd go with me? What I look like wandering 'round Europe by myself?

RUTH: Shoot—these here rich white women do it all the time. They don't think nothing of packing up they suitcases and piling on one of them big steamships and—swoosh!—they gone, child.

MAMA: Something always told me I wasn't no rich white woman.

RUTH: Well—what are you going to do with it then?

MAMA: I ain't rightly decided. (*Thinking. She speaks now with emphasis*) Some of it got to be put away for Beneatha and her schoolin'—and ain't nothing going to touch that part of it. Nothing. (*She waits several seconds, trying to make up her mind about something, and looks at* RUTH *a little tentatively before going on*) Been thinking that we maybe could meet the notes on a little old two-story somewhere, with a yard where Travis could play in the summertime, if we use part of the insurance for a down payment and everybody kind of pitch in. I could maybe take on a little day work again, few days a week—

RUTH: (*Studying her mother-in-law furtively and concentrating on her ironing, anxious to encourage without seeming to*) Well, Lord knows, we've put enough rent into this here rat trap to pay for four houses by now . . .

MAMA: (*Looking up at the words "rat trap" and then looking around and leaning back and sighing—in a suddenly reflective mood—*) "Rat trap"—yes, that's all it is. (*Smiling*) I remember just as well the day me and Big Walter moved in here. Hadn't been married but two weeks and wasn't planning on living here no more than a year. (*She shakes her head at the dissolved dream*) We was going to set away, little by little, don't you know, and buy a little place out in Morgan Park. We had even picked out the house. (*Chuckling a little*) Looks right dumpy today. But Lord, child, you should know all the dreams I had 'bout buying that house and fixing it up and making me a little garden in the back—(*She waits and stops smiling*) And didn't none of it happen.

(*Dropping her hands in a futile gesture*)

RUTH: (*Keeps her head down, ironing*) Yes, life can be a barrel of disappointments, sometimes.

MAMA: Honey, Big Walter would come in here some nights back then and slump down on that couch there and just look at the rug, and look at me and look at the rug and then back at me—and I'd know he was down then . . . really down. (*After a second very long and thoughtful pause; she is seeing back to times that only she can see*) And then, Lord, when I lost that baby—little Claude—I almost thought I was going to lose Big Walter too. Oh, that man grieved hisself! He was one man to love his children.

RUTH: Ain't nothing' can tear at you like losin' your baby.

MAMA: I guess that's how come that man finally worked hisself to death like he done. Like he was fighting his own war with this here world that took his baby from him.

RUTH: He sure was a fine man, all right. I always liked Mr. Younger.

MAMA: Crazy 'bout his children! God knows there was plenty wrong with Walter Younger—hard-headed, mean, kind of wild with women—plenty wrong with him. But he sure loved his children. Always wanted them to have something—be something. That's where Brother gets all these notions, I reckon. Big Walter used to say, he'd get right wet in the eyes sometimes, lean his head back with the water standing in his eyes and say, "Seem like God didn't see fit to give the black man nothing but dreams—but He did give us children to make them dreams seem worth while." (*She smiles*) He could talk like that, don't you know.

RUTH: Yes, he sure could. He was a good man, Mr. Younger.

MAMA: Yes, a fine man—just couldn't never catch up with his dreams, that's all.

(BENEATHA *comes in, brushing her hair and looking up to the ceiling, where the sound of a vacuum cleaner has started up*)

BENEATHA: What could be so dirty on that woman's rugs that she has to vacuum them every single day?

RUTH: I wish certain young women 'round here who I could name would take inspiration about certain rugs in a certain apartment I could also mention.

BENEATHA: (*Shrugging*) How much cleaning can a house need, for Christ's sakes.

MAMA: (*Not liking the Lord's name used thus*) Bennie!

RUTH: Just listen to her—just listen!

BENEATHA: Oh, God—

MAMA: If you use the Lord's name just one more time—

BENEATHA: (*A bit of a whine*) Oh, Mama—

RUTH: Fresh—just fresh as salt, this girl!

BENEATHA: (*Drily*) Well—if the salt loses its savor—

MAMA: Now that will do. I just ain't going to have you 'round here reciting the scriptures in vain—you hear me?

BENEATHA: How did I manage to get on everybody's wrong side by just walking into a room?

RUTH: If you weren't so fresh—

BENEATHA: Ruth, I'm twenty years old.

MAMA: What time you be home from school today?

BENEATHA: Kind of late. (*With enthusiasm*) Madeline is going to start my guitar lessons today.

(MAMA *and* RUTH *look up with the same expression*)

MAMA: Your *what* kind of lessons?

BENEATHA: Guitar.

RUTH: Oh, Father!

MAMA: How come you done taken it in your mind to learn to play the guitar?

BENEATHA: I just want to, that's all.

MAMA: (*Smiling*) Lord, child, don't you know what to do with yourself? How long it going to be before you get tired of this now—like you got tired of that little playacting group you joined last year? (*Looking at* RUTH) And what was it the year before that?

RUTH: The horseback-riding club for which she bought that fifty-five-dollar riding habit that's been hanging in the closet ever since!

MAMA: (*To* BENEATHA) Why you got to flit so from one thing to another baby?

BENEATHA: (*Sharply*) I just want to learn to play the guitar. Is there anything wrong with that?

MAMA: Ain't nobody trying to stop you. I just wonders sometimes why you has to flit so from one thing to another all the time. You ain't never done nothing with all that camera equipment you brought home—

BENEATHA: I don't flit! I—I experiment with different forms of expression—

RUTH: Like riding a horse?

BENEATHA: — People have to express themselves one way or another.

MAMA: What is it you want to express?

BENEATHA: (*Angrily*) Me! (MAMA *and* RUTH *look at each other and burst into raucous laughter*) Don't worry—I don't expect you to understand.

MAMA: (*To change the subject*) Who you going out with tomorrow night?

BENEATHA: (*With displeasure*) George Murchison again.

MAMA: (*Pleased*) Oh—you getting a little sweet on him?

RUTH: You ask me, this child ain't sweet on nobody but herself— (*Underbreath*) Express herself!

(*They laugh*)

BENEATHA: Oh—I like George all right, Mama. I mean I like him enough to go out with him and stuff, but—

RUTH: (*For devilment*) What does *and stuff* mean?

BENEATHA: Mind your own business.

MAMA: Stop picking at her now, Ruth. (*She chuckles — then a suspicious sudden look at her daughter as she turns in her chair for emphasis*) What DOES it mean?

BENEATHA: (*Wearily*) Oh, I just mean I couldn't ever really be serious about George. He's — he's so shallow.

RUTH: Shallow — what do you mean he's shallow? He's *rich!*

MAMA: Hush, Ruth.

BENEATHA: I know he's rich. He knows he's rich, too.

RUTH: Well — what other qualities a man got to have to satisfy you, little girl?

BENEATHA: You wouldn't even begin to understand. Anybody who married Walter could not possibly understand.

MAMA: (*Outraged*) What kind of way is that to talk about your brother?

BENEATHA: Brother is a flip — let's face it.

MAMA: (*To* RUTH, *helplessly*) What's a flip?

RUTH: (*Glad to add kindling*) She's saying he's crazy.

BENEATHA: Not crazy. Brother isn't really crazy yet — he — he's an elaborate neurotic.

MAMA: Hush your mouth!

BENEATHA: As for George. Well. George looks good — he's got a beautiful car and he takes me to nice places and, as my sister-in-law says, he is probably the richest boy I will ever get to know and I even like him sometimes — but if the Youngers are sitting around waiting to see if their little Bennie is going to tie up the family with the Murchisons, they are wasting their time.

RUTH: You mean you wouldn't marry George Murchison if he asked you someday? That pretty, rich thing? Honey, I knew you was odd —

BENEATHA: No I would not marry him if all I felt for him was what I feel now. Besides, George's family wouldn't really like it.

MAMA: Why not?

BENEATHA: Oh, Mama — The Murchisons are honest-to-God-real-*live*-rich colored people, and the only people in the world who are more snobbish than rich white people are rich colored people. I thought everybody knew that. I've met Mrs. Murchison. She's a scene!

MAMA: You must not dislike people 'cause they well off, honey.

BENEATHA: Why not? It makes just as rnuch sense as disliking people 'cause they are poor, and lots of people do that.

RUTH: (*A wisdom-of-the-ages manner. To* MAMA) Well, she'll get over some of this —

BENEATHA: Get over it? What are you talking about, Ruth? Listen, I'm going to be a doctor. I'm not worried about who I'm going to marry yet — if I ever get married.

MAMA *and* RUTH: *If!*

MAMA: Now, Bennie —

BENEATHA: Oh, I probably will . . . but first I'm going to be a doctor, and George, for one, still thinks that's pretty funny. I couldn't be bothered with that. I am going to be a doctor and everybody around here better understand that!

MAMA: (*Kindly*) 'Course you going to be a doctor, honey, God willing.

BENEATHA: (*Drily*) God hasn't got a thing to do with it.

MAMA: Beneatha—that just wasn't necessary.

BENEATHA: Well—neither is God. I get sick of hearing about God.

MAMA: Beneatha!

BENEATHA: I mean it! I'm just tired of hearing about God all the time. What has He got to do with anything? Does he pay tuition?

MAMA: You 'bout to get your fresh little jaw slapped!

RUTH: That's just what she needs, all right!

BENEATHA: Why? Why can't I say what I want to around here, like everybody else?

MAMA: It don't sound nice for a young girl to say things like that—you wasn't brought up that way. Me and your father went to trouble to get you and Brother to church every Sunday.

BENEATHA: Mama, you don't understand. It's all a matter of ideas, and God is just one idea I don't accept. It's not important. I am not going out and be immoral or commit crimes because I don't believe in God. I don't even think about it. It's just that I get tired of Him getting credit for all the things the human race achieves through its own stubborn effort. There simply is no blasted God—there is only man and it is *he* who makes miracles!

(MAMA *absorbs this speech, studies her daughter and rises slowly and crosses to* BENEATHA *and slaps her powerfully across the face. After, there is only silence and the daughter drops her eyes from her mother's face, and* MAMA *is very tall before her*)

MAMA: Now—you say after me, in my mother's house there is still God. (*There is a long pause and* BENEATHA *stares at the floor wordlessly,* MAMA *repeats the phrase with precision and cool emotion*) In my mother's house there is still God.

BENEATHA: In my mother's house there is still God.

(*A long pause*)

MAMA: (*Walking away from* BENEATHA, *too disturbed for triumphant posture. Stopping and turning back to her daughter*) There are some ideas we ain't going to have in this house. Not long as I am at the head of this family.

BENEATHA: Yes, ma'am.

(MAMA *walks out of the room*)

RUTU: (*Almost gently, with profound understanding*) You think you a woman, Bennie—but you still a little girl. What you did was childish—so you got treated like a child.

BENEATHA: I see. (*Quietly*) I also see that everybody thinks it's all right for Mama to be a tyrant. But all the tyranny in the world will never put a God in the heavens!

(*She picks up her books and goes out. Pause*)

RUTH: (*Goes to* MAMA's *door*) She said she was sorry.

MAMA: (*Coming out, going to her plant*) They frightens me, Ruth. My children.

RUTH: You got good children, Lena. They just a little off sometimes—but they're good.

MAMA: No—there's something come down between me and them that don't let us understand each other and I don't know what it is. One done almost lost his mind thinking 'bout money all the time and the other done commence to talk about things I can't seem to understand in no form or fashion. What is it that's changing, Ruth.

RUTH: (*Soothingly, older than her years*) Now . . . you taking it all too seriously. You just got strong-willed children and it takes a strong woman like you to keep 'em in hand.

MAMA: (*Looking at her plant and sprinkling a little water on it*) They spirited all right, my children. Got to admit they got spirit—Bennie and Walter. Like this little old plant that ain't never had enough sunshine or nothing—and look at it . . .

(*She has her back to* RUTH, *who has had to stop ironing and lean against something and put the back of her hand to her forehead*)

RUTH: (*Trying to keep* MAMA *from noticing*) You . . . sure . . . loves that little old thing, don't you? . . .

MAMA: Well, I always wanted me a garden like I used to see sometimes at the back of the houses down home. This plant is close as I ever got to having one. (*She looks out of the window as she replaces the plant*) Lord, ain't nothing as dreary as the view from this window on a dreary day, is there? Why ain't you singing this morning, Ruth? Sing that "No Ways Tired." That song always lifts me up so—(*She turns at last to see that* RUTH *has slipped quietly to the floor, in a state of semiconsciousness*) Ruth! Ruth honey—what's the matter with you . . . Ruth!

Curtain

Scene Two

It is the following morning; a Saturday morning, and house cleaning is in progress at the YOUNGERS'. *Furniture has been shoved hither and yon and* MAMA *is giving the kitchen-area walls a washing down,* BENEATHA, *in dungarees, with a handkerchief tied around her face, is spraying insecticide into the cracks in the walls. As they work, the radio is on and a Southside disk-jockey program is inappropriately filling the house with a rather exotic saxophone blues.* TRAVIS, *the sole idle one, is leaning on his arms, looking out of the window.*

TRAVIS: Grandmama, that stuff Bennie is using smells awful. Can I go downstairs, please?

MAMA: Did you get all them chores done already? I ain't seen you doing much.

TRAVIS: Yes'm—finished early. Where did Mama go this morning?

MAMA: (*Looking at* BENEATHA) She had to go on a little errand.

(*The phone rings.* BENEATHA *runs to answer it and reaches it before* WALTER, *who has entered from bedroom*)

TRAVIS: Where?

MAMA: To tend to her business.

BENEATHA: Haylo ... (*Disappointed*) Yes, he is. (*She tosses the phone to* WALTER, *who barely catches it*) It's Willie Harris again.

WALTER: (*As privately as possible under* MAMA's *gaze*) Hello, Willie. Did you get the papers from the lawyer? ... No, not yet. I told you the mailman doesn't get here till ten-thirty ... No, I'll come there ... Yeah! Right away. (*He hangs up and goes for his coat*)

BENEATHA: Brother, where did Ruth go?

WALTER: (*As he exits*) How should I know!

TRAVIS: Aw come on, Grandma. Can I go outside?

MAMA: Oh, I guess so. You stay right in front of the house, though, and keep a good lookout for the postman.

TRAVIS: Yes'm. (*He darts into bedroom for stickball and bat, reenters, and sees* BENEATHA *on her knees spraying under sofa with behind upraised. He edges closer to the target, takes aim, and lets her have it. She screams*) Leave them poor little cockroaches alone, they ain't bothering you none! (*He runs as she swings the spray gun at him viciously and playfully*) Grandma! Grandma!

MAMA: Look out there, girl, before you be spilling some of that stuff on that child!

TRAVIS: (*Safely behind the bastion of* MAMA) That's right—look out, now! (*He exits*)

BENEATHA: (*Drily*) I can't imagine that it would hurt him—it has never hurt the roaches.

MAMA: Well, little boys' hides ain't as tough as Southside roaches. You better get over there behind the bureau. I seen one marching out of there like Napoleon yesterday.

BENEATHA: There's really only one way to get rid of them, Mama—

MAMA: How?

BENEATHA: Set fire to this building! Mama, where did Ruth go?

MAMA: (*Looking at her with meaning*) To the doctor, I think.

BENEATHA: The doctor? What's the matter? (*They exchange glances*) You don't think—

MAMA: (*With her sense of drama*) Now I ain't saying what I think. But I ain't never been wrong 'bout a woman neither.

(*The phone rings*)

BENEATHA: (*At the phone*) Hay-lo ... (*Pause, and a moment of recognition*) Well— when did you get back! ... And how was it? ... Of course I've missed you—in my way ... This morning? No ... house cleaning and all that and Mama hates it if I let people come over when the house is like this ... You have? Well, that's different ... What is it—Oh, what the hell, come on over ... Right, see you then. *Arrivederci*.

(*She hangs up*)

MAMA: (*Who has listened vigorously, as is her habit*) Who is that you inviting over here with this house looking like this? You ain't got the pride you was born with!

BENEATHA: Asagai doesn't care how houses look, Mama—he's an intellectual.

MAMA: *Who?*

BENEATHA: Asagai—Joseph Asagai. He's an African boy I met on campus. He's been studying in Canada all summer.

MAMA: What's his name?

BENEATHA: Asagai, Joseph. Ah-sah-guy . . . He's from Nigeria.

MAMA: Oh, that's the little country that was founded by slaves way back . . .

BENEATHA: No, Mama—that's Liberia.

MAMA: I don't think I never met no African before.

BENEATHA: Well, do me a favor and don't ask him a whole lot of ignorant questions about Africans. I mean, do they wear clothes and all that—

MAMA: Well, now, I guess if you think we so ignorant 'round here maybe you shouldn't bring your friends here—

BENEATHA: It's just that people ask such crazy things. All anyone seems to know about when it comes to Africa is Tarzan—

MAMA: (*Indignantly*) Why should I know anything about Africa?

BENEATHA: Why do you give money at church for the missionary work?

MAMA: Well, that's to help save people.

BENEATHA: You mean save them from *heathenism*—

MAMA: (*Innocently*) Yes.

BENEATHA: I'm afraid they need more salvation from the British and the French.

(RUTH *comes in forlornly and pulls off her coat with dejection. They both turn to look at her*)

RUTH: (*Dispiritedly*) Well, I guess from all the happy faces—everybody knows.

BENEATHA: You pregnant?

MAMA: Lord have mercy, I sure hope it's a little old girl. Travis ought to have a sister.

(BENEATHA *and* RUTH *give her a hopeless look for this grandmotherly enthusiasm*)

BENEATHA: How far along are you?

RUTH: Two months.

BENEATHA: Did you mean to? I mean did you plan it or was it an accident?

MAMA: What do you know about planning or not planning?

BENEATHA: Oh, Mama.

RUTH: (*Wearily*) She's twenty years old, Lena.

BENEATHA: Did you plan it, Ruth?

RUTH: Mind your own business.

BENEATHA: It is my business—where is he going to live, on the *roof*? (*There is silence following the remark as the three women react to the sense of it*) Gee—I didn't mean that, Ruth, honest. Gee, I don't feel like that at all. I—I think it is wonderful.

RUTH: (*Dully*) Wonderful.

BENEATHA: Yes—really. (*There is a sudden commotion from the street and she goes to the window to look out*) What on earth is going on out there? These kids. (*There are, as she throws open the window, the shouts of children rising up from the street. She sticks her head out to see better and calls out)* TRAVIS! TRAVIS . . . WHAT ARE YOU DOING DOWN THERE? *(She sees)* Oh Lord, they're chasing a rat!

(RUTH covers her face with hands and turns away)

MAMA: *(Angrily)* Tell that youngun to get himself up here, at once!

BENEATHA: TRAVIS . . . YOU COME UPSTAIRS . . . AT ONCE!

RUTH: *(Her face twisted)* Chasing a rat. . . . .

MAMA: *(Looking at RUTH, worried)* Doctor say everything going to be all right?

RUTH *(Far away)* Yes—she says everything is going to be fine . . .

MAMA: *(Immediately suspicious)* "She"—What doctor you went to?

(RUTH just looks at MAMA meaningfully and MAMA opens her mouth to speak as TRAVIS bursts in)

TRAVIS: *(Excited and full of narrative, coming directly to his mother)* Mama, you should of seen the rat . . . Big as a cat, honest! *(He shows an exaggerated size with his hands)* Gaaleee, that rat was really cuttin' and Bubber caught him with his heel and the janitor, Mr. Barnett, got him with a stick—and then they got him in a corner and—BAM! BAM! BAM!—and he was still jumping around and bleeding like everything too—there's rat blood all over the street—

(RUTH reaches out suddenly and grabs her son without even looking at him and clamps her hand over his mouth and holds him to her. MAMA crosses to them rapidly and takes the boy from her)

MAMA: You hush up now . . . talking all that terrible stuff. . . . *(TRAVIS is staring at his mother with a stunned expression, BENEATHA comes quickly and takes him away from his grandmother and ushers him to the door)*

BENEATHA: You go back outside and play . . . but not with any rats. *(She pushes him gently out the door with the boy straining to see what is wrong with his mother)*

MAMA: *(Worriedly hovering over RUTH)* Ruth honey—what's the matter with you—you sick?

(RUTH has her fists clenched on her thighs and is fighting hard to suppress a scream that seems to be rising in her)

BENEATHA: What's the matter with her, Mama?

MAMA: *(Working her fingers in RUTH's shoulders to relax her)* She be all right. Women gets right depressed sometimes when they get her way. *(Speaking softly, expertly, rapidly)* Now you just relax. That's right . . . just lean back, don't think 'bout nothing at all . . . nothing at all—

RUTH: I'm all right . . .

(The glassy-eyed look melts and then she collapses into a fit of heavy sobbing. The bell rings)

BENEATHA: Oh, my God—that must be Asagai.

MAMA: (*To* RUTH) Come on now, honey. You need to lie down and rest awhile ... then have some nice hot food.

(*They exit,* RUTH'*s weight on her mother-in-law.* BENEATHA, *herself profoundly disturbed, opens the door to admit a rather dramatic-looking young man with a large package*)

ASAGAI: Hello, Alaiyo —

BENEATHA: (*Holding the door open and regarding him with pleasure*) Hello ... (*Long pause*) Well — come in. And please excuse everything. My mother was very upset about my letting anyone come here with the place like this.

ASAGAI: (*Coming into the room*) You look disturbed too ... Is something wrong?

BENEATHA: (*Still at the door, absently*) Yes ... we've all got acute ghetto-itis. (*She smiles and comes toward him, finding a cigarette and sitting*) So — sit down! No! Wait! (*She whips the spray gun off sofa where she had left it and puts the cushions back. At last perches on arm of sofa. He sits*) So, how was Canada?

ASAGAI: (*A sophisticate*) Canadian.

BENEATHA: (*Looking at him*) Asagai, I'm very glad you are back.

ASAGAI: (*Looking back at her in turn*) Are you really?

BENEATHA: Yes — very.

ASAGAI: Why? — you were quite glad when I went away. What happened?

BENEATHA: You went away.

ASAGAI: Ahhhhhhhh.

BENEATHA: Before — you wanted to be so serious before there was time.

ASAGAI: How much time must there be before one knows what one feels?

BENEATHA: (*Stalling this particular conversation. Her hands pressed together, in a deliberately childish gesture*) What did you bring me?

ASAGAI: (*Handing her the package*) Open it and see.

BENEATHA: (*Eagerly opening the package and drawing out some records and the colorful robes of a Nigerian woman*) Oh, Asagai! ... You got them for me! ... How beautiful ... and the records too! (*She lifts out the robes and runs to the mirror with them and holds the drapery up in front of herself*)

ASAGAI: (*Coming to her at the mirror*) I shall have to teach you how to drape it properly. (*He flings the material about her for the moment and stands back to look at her*) Ah — Oh-pay-gay-day, oh-gbah-mu-shay. (*A Yoruba° exclamation for admiration*) You wear it well ... very well ... mutilated hair and all.

BENEATHA: (*Turning suddenly*) My hair — what's wrong with my hair?

ASAGAI: (*Shrugging*) Were you born with it like that?

BENEATHA: (*Reaching up to touch it*) No ... of course not.

(*She looks back to the mirror, disturbed*)

ASAGAI: (*Smiling*) How then?

BENEATHA: You know perfectly well how ... as crinkly as yours ... that's how.

ASAGAI: And it is ugly to you that way?

Yoruba: One of the largest ethnic groups in West Africa, known for its political and military strength and rich culture from A.D. 1100 to 1700.

BENEATHA: (*Quickly*) Oh, no — not ugly . . . (*More slowly, apologetically*) But it's so hard to manage when it's, well — raw.

ASAGAI: And so to accommodate that — you mutilate it every week?

BENEATHA: It's not mutilation!

ASAGAI: (*Laughing aloud at her seriousness*) Oh . . . please! I am only teasing you because you are so very serious about these things. (*He stands back from her and folds his arms across his chest as he watches her pulling at her hair and frowning in the mirror*) Do you remember the first time you met me at school? . . . (*He laughs*) You came up to me and you said — and I thought you were the most serious little thing I had ever seen — you said: (*He imitates her*) "Mr. Asagai — I want very much to talk with you. About Africa. You see, Mr. Asagai, I am looking for my *identity!*"

(*He laughs*)

BENEATHA: (*Turning to him, not laughing*) Yes —

(*Her face is quizzical, profoundly disturbed*)

ASAGAI: (*Still teasing and reaching out and taking her face in his hands and turning her profile to him*) Well . . . it is true that this is not so much a profile of a Hollywood queen as perhaps a queen of the Nile — (*A mock dismissal of the importance of the question*) But what does it matter? Assimilationism is so popular in your country.

BENEATHA: (*Wheeling, passionately, sharply*) I am not an assimilationist!

ASAGAI: (*The protest hangs in the room for a moment and* ASAGAI *studies her, his laughter fading*) Such a serious one. (*There is a pause*) So — you like the robes? You must take excellent care of them — they are from my sister's personal wardrobe.

BENEATHA: (*With incredulity*) You — you sent all the way home — for me?

ASAGAI: (*With charm*) For you — I would do much more . . . Well, that is what I came for. I must go.

BENEATHA: Will you call me Monday?

ASAGAI: Yes . . . We have a great deal to talk about. I mean about identity and time and all that.

BENEATHA: Time?

ASAGAI: Yes. About how much time one needs to know what one feels.

BENEATHA: You see! You never understood that there is more than one kind of feeling which can exist between a man and a woman — or, at least, there should be.

ASAGAI: (*Shaking his head negatively but gently*) No. Between a man and a woman there need be only one kind of feeling. I have that for you . . . Now even . . . right this moment . . .

BENEATHA: I know — and by itself — it won't do. I can find that anywhere.

ASAGAI: For a woman it should be enough.

BENEATHA: I know — because that's what it says in all the novels that men write. But it isn't. Go ahead and laugh — but I'm not interested in being someone's

little episode in America or—(*With feminine vengeance*)—one of them!
(ASAGAI *has burst into laughter again*) That's funny as hell, huh!

ASAGAI: It's just that every American girl I have known has said that to me.
White—black—in this you are all the same. And the same speech, too!

BENEATHA: (*Angrily*) Yuk, yuk, yuk!

ASAGAI: It's how you can be sure that the world's most liberated women are not
liberated at all. You all talk about it too much!

(MAMA *enters and is immediately all social charm because of the presence of a guest*)

BENEATHA: Oh—Mama—this is Mr. Asagai.

MAMA: How do you do?

ASAGAI: (*Total politeness to an elder*) How do you do, Mrs. Younger. Please forgive
me for coming at such an outrageous hour on a Saturday.

MAMA: Well, you are quite welcome. I just hope you understand that our house
don't always look like this. (*Chatterish*). You must come again. I would love
to hear all about—(*Not sure of the name*)—your country. I think it's so sad
the way our American Negroes don't know nothing about Africa 'cept
Tarzan and all that. And all that money they pour into these churches when
they ought to be helping you people over there drive out them French and
Englishmen done taken away your land.

(*The mother flashes a slightly superior look at her daughter upon completion of the
recitation*)

ASAGAI: (*Taken aback by this sudden and acutely unrelated expression of sympathy*)
Yes . . . yes . . .

MAMA: (*Smiling at him suddenly and relaxing and looking him over*) How many
miles is it from here to where you come from?

ASAGAI: Many thousands.

MAMA: (*Looking at him as she would* WALTER) I bet you don't half look after
yourself, being away from your mama either. I spec you better come 'round
here from time to time to get yourself some decent home-cooked meals . . .

ASAGAI: (*Moved*) Thank you. Thank you very much. (*They are all quiet, then—*)
Well . . . I must go. I will call you Monday, Alaiyo.

MAMA: What's that he call you?

ASAGAI: Oh—"Alaiyo." I hope you don't mind. It is what you would call a nickname, I think. It is a Yoruba word. I am a Yoruba.

MAMA: (*Looking at* BENEATHA) I—I thought he was from—(*Uncertain*)

ASAGAI: (*Understanding*) Nigeria is my country. Yoruba is my tribal origin—

BENEATHA: You didn't tell us what Alaiyo means . . . for all I know, you might be
calling me Little Idiot or something . . .

ASAGAI: Well . . . let me see . . . I do not know how just to explain it . . . The sense
of a thing can be so different when it changes languages.

BENEATHA: You're evading.

ASAGAI: No—really it is difficult . . . (*Thinking*) It means . . . it means One for
Whom Bread—Food—Is Not Enough. (*He looks at her*) Is that all right?

BENEATHA: (*Understanding, softly*) Thank you.

MAMA: (*Looking from one to the other and not understanding any of it*) Well . . . that's nice . . . You must come see us again — Mr. —

ASAGAI: Ah-sah-guy . . .

MAMA: Yes . . . Do come again.

ASAGAI: Good-bye.

(*He exits*)

MAMA: (*After him*) Lord, that's a pretty thing just went out here! (*Insinuatingly, to her daughter*) Yes, I guess I see why we done commence to get so interested in Africa 'round here. Missionaries my aunt Jenny!

(*She exits*)

BENEATHA: Oh, Mama! . . .

(*She picks up the Nigerian dress and holds it up to her in front of the mirror again. She sets the headdress on haphazardly and then notices her hair again and clutches at it and then replaces the headdress and frowns at herself. Then she starts to wriggle in front of the mirror as she thinks a Nigerian woman might.* TRAVIS *enters and stands regarding her*)

TRAVIS: What's the matter, girl, you cracking up?

BENEATHA: Shut up.

(*She pulls the headdress off and looks at herself in the mirror and clutches at her hair again and squinches her eyes as if trying to imagine something. Then, suddenly, she gets her raincoat and kerchief and hurriedly prepares for going out*)

MAMA: (*Coming back into the room*) She's resting now. Travis, baby, run next door and ask Miss Johnson to please let me have a little kitchen cleanser. This here can is empty as Jacob's kettle.

TRAVIS: I just came in.

MAMA: Do as you told. (*He exits and she looks at her daughter*) Where you going?

BENEATHA: (*Halting at the door*) To become a queen of the Nile!

(*She exits in a breathless blaze of glory.* RUTH *appears in the bedroom doorway*)

MAMA: Who told you to get up?

RUTH: Ain't nothing wrong with me to be lying in no bed for. Where did Bennie go?

MAMA: (*Drumming her fingers*) Far as I could make out — to Egypt. (RUTH *just looks at her*) What time is it getting to?

RUTH: Ten twenty. And the mailman going to ring that bell this morning just like he done every morning for the last umpteen years.

(TRAVIS *comes in with the cleanser can*)

TRAVIS: She say to tell you that she don't have much.

MAMA: (*Angrily*) Lord, some people I could name sure is tight-fisted! (*Directing her grandson*) Mark two cans of cleanser down on the list there. If she that hard up for kitchen cleanser, I sure don't want to forget to get her none!

RUTH: Lena—maybe the woman is just short on cleanser—

MAMA: (*Not listening*)—Much baking powder as she done borrowed from me all these years, she could of done gone into the baking business!

(*The bell sounds suddenly and sharply and all three are stunned—serious and silent—mid-speech. In spite of all the other conversation and distractions of the morning, this is what they have been waiting for, even* TRAVIS *who looks helplessly from his mother to his grandmother.* RUTH *is the first to come to life again*)

RUTH: (*To* TRAVIS) Get down them steps, boy!

(TRAVIS *snaps to life and flies out to get the mail*)

MAMA: (*Her eyes wide, her hand to her breast*) You mean it done really come?

RUTH: (*Excited*) Oh, Miss Lena!

MAMA: (*Collecting herself*) Well . . . I don't know what we all so excited about 'round here for. We known it was coming for months.

RUTH: That's a whole lot different from having it come and being able to hold it in your hands . . . a piece of paper worth ten thousand dollars . . . (TRAVIS *bursts back into the room. He holds the envelope high above his head, like a little dancer, his face is radiant and he is breathless. He moves to his grandmother with sudden slow ceremony and puts the envelope into her hands. She accepts it, and then merely holds it and looks at it*) Come on! Open it . . . Lord have mercy, I wish Walter Lee was here!

TRAVIS: Open it, Grandmama!

MAMA: (*Staring at it*) Now you all be quiet. It's just a check.

RUTH: Open it . . .

MAMA: (*Still staring at it*) Now don't act silly . . . We ain't never been no people to act silly 'bout no money—

RUTH: (*Swiftly*) We ain't never had none before—OPEN IT!

(MAMA *finally makes a good strong tear and pulls out the thin blue slice of paper and inspects it closely. The boy and his mother study it raptly over* MAMA's *shoulders*)

MAMA: Travis! (*She is counting off with doubt*) Is that the right number of zeros?

TRAVIS: Yes'm . . . ten thousand dollars. Gaalee, Grandmama, you rich.

MAMA: (*She holds the check away from her, still looking at it. Slowly her face sobers into a mask of unhappiness*) Ten thousand dollars. (*She hands it to* RUTH) Put it away somewhere, Ruth. (*She does not look at* RUTH; *her eyes seem to be seeing something somewhere very far off*) Ten thousand dollars they give you. Ten thousand dollars.

TRAVIS: (*To his mother, sincerely*) What's the matter with Grandmama—don't she want to be rich?

RUTH: (*Distractedly*) You go on out and play now, baby. (TRAVIS *exits.* MAMA *starts wiping dishes absently, humming intently to herself.* RUTH *turns to her, with kind exasperation*) You've gone and got yourself upset.

MAMA: (*Not looking at her*) I spec if it wasn't for you all . . . I would just put that money away or give it to the church or something.

RUTH: Now what kind of talk is that. Mr. Younger would just be plain mad if he could hear you talking foolish like that.

MAMA: (*Stopping and staring off*) Yes . . . he sure would. (*Sighing*) We got enough to do with that money, all right. (*She halts then, and turns and looks at her daughter-in-law hard;* RUTH *avoids her eyes and* MAMA *wipes her hands with finality and starts to speak firmly to* RUTH) Where did you go today, girl?

RUTH: To the doctor.

MAMA: (*Impatiently*) Now, Ruth . . . you know better than that. Old Doctor Jones is strange enough in his way but there ain't nothing 'bout him make somebody slip and call him "she" — like you done this morning.

RUTH: Well, that's what happened — my tongue slipped.

MAMA: You went to see that woman, didn't you?

RUTH: (*Defensively, giving herself away*) What woman you talking about?

MAMA: (*Angrily*) That woman who —

(WALTER *enters in great excitement*)

WALTER: Did it come?

MAMA: (*Quietly*) Can't you give people a Christian greeting before you start asking about money?

WALTER: (*To* RUTH) Did it come? (RUTH *unfolds the check and lays it quietly before him, watching him intently with thoughts of her own.* WALTER *sits down and grasps it close and counts off the zeros*) Ten thousand dollars — (*He turns suddenly, frantically to his mother and draws some papers out of his breast pocket*) Mama — look. Old Willy Harris put everything on paper —

MAMA: Son — I think you ought to talk to your wife . . . I'll go on out and leave you alone if you want —

WALTER: I can talk to her later — Mama, look —

MAMA: Son —

WALTER: WILL SOMEBODY PLEASE LISTEN TO ME TODAY!

MAMA: (*Quietly*) I don't 'low no yellin' in this house, Walter Lee, and you know it — (WALTER *stares at them in frustration and starts to speak several times*) And there ain't going to be no investing in no liquor stores.

WALTER: But, Mama, you ain't even looked at it.

MAMA: I don't aim to have to speak on that again.

(*A long pause*)

WALTER: You ain't looked at it and you don't aim to have to speak on that again? You ain't even looked at it and *you* have decided — (*Crumpling his papers*) Well, *you* tell that to my boy tonight when you put him to sleep on the living-room couch . . . (*Turning to* MAMA *and speaking directly to her*)

Yeah—and tell it to my wife, Mama, tomorrow when she has to go out of here to look after somebody else's kids. And tell it to *me*, Mama, every time we need a new pair of curtains and I have to watch *you* go out and work in somebody's kitchen. Yeah, you tell me then!

(WALTER *starts out*)

RUTH: Where you going?

WALTER: I'm going out!

RUTH: Where?

WALTER: Just out of this house somewhere —

RUTH: (*Getting her coat*) I'll come too.

WALTER: I don't want you to come!

RUTH: I got something to talk to you about, Walter.

WALTER: That's too bad.

MAMA: (*Still quietly*) Walter Lee — (*She waits and he finally turns and looks at her*) Sit down.

WALTER: I'm a grown man, Mama.

MAMA: Ain't nobody said you wasn't grown. But you still in my house and my presence. And as long as you are—you'll talk to your wife civil. Now sit down.

RUTH: (*Suddenly*) Oh, let him go on out and drink himself to death! He makes me sick to my stomach! (*She flings her coat against him and exits to bedroom*)

WALTER: (*Violently flinging the coat after her*) And you turn mine too, baby! (*The door slams behind her*) That was my biggest mistake —

MAMA: (*Still quietly*) Walter, what is the matter with you?

WALTER: Matter with me? Ain't nothing the matter with *me*!

MAMA: Yes there is. Something eating you up like a crazy man. Something more than me not giving you this money. The past few years I been watching it happen to you. You get all nervous acting and kind of wild in the eyes — (WALTER *jumps up impatiently at her words*) I said sit there now, I'm talking to you!

WALTER: Mama—I don't need no nagging at me today.

MAMA: Seem like you getting to a place where you always tied up in some kind of knot about something. But if anybody ask you 'bout it you just yell at 'em and bust out the house and go out and drink somewheres. Walter Lee, people can't live with that. Ruth's a good, patient girl in her way—but you getting to be too much. Boy, don't make the mistake of driving that girl away from you.

WALTER: Why—what she do for me?

MAMA: She loves you.

WALTER: Mama—I'm going out. I want to go off somewhere and be by myself for a while.

MAMA: I'm sorry 'bout your liquor store, son. It just wasn't the thing for us to do. That's what I want to tell you about—

WALTER: I got to go out, Mama—

(*He rises*)

MAMA: It's dangerous, son.

WALTER: What's dangerous?

MAMA: When a man goes outside his home to look for peace.

WALTER: (*Beseechingly*) Then why can't there never be no peace in this house then?

MAMA: You done found it in some other house?

WALTER: No—there ain't no woman! Why do women always think there's a woman somewhere when a man gets restless. (*Picks up the check*) Do you know what this money means to me? Do you know what this money can do for us? (*Puts it back*) Mama—Mama—I want so many things . . .

MAMA: Yes, son—

WALTER: I want so many things that they are driving me kind of crazy . . . Mama—look at me.

MAMA: I'm looking at you. You a good-looking boy. You got a job, a nice wife, a fine boy and—

WALTER: A job. (*Looks at her*) Mama, a job? I open and close car doors all day long. I drive a man around in his limousine and I say, "Yes, sir; no, sir; very good, sir; shall I take the Drive, sir?" Mama, that ain't no kind of job . . . that ain't nothing at all. (*Very quietly*) Mama, I don't know if I can make you understand.

MAMA: Understand what, baby?

WALTER: (*Quietly*) Sometimes it's like I can see the future stretched out in front of me—just plain as day. The future, Mama. Hanging over there at the edge of my days. Just waiting for me—a big, looming blank space—full of *nothing*. Just waiting for *me*. But it don't have to be. (*Pause. Kneeling beside her chair*) Mama—sometimes when I'm downtown and I pass them cool, quiet-looking restaurants where them white boys are sitting back and talking 'bout things . . . sitting there turning deals worth millions of dollars . . . sometimes I see guys don't look much older than me—

MAMA: Son—how come you talk so much 'bout money?

WALTER: (*With immense passion*) Because it is life, Mama!

MAMA: (*Quietly*) Oh—(*Very quietly*) So now it's life. Money is life. Once upon a time freedom used to be life—now it's money. I guess the world really do change . . .

WALTER: No—it was always money, Mama. We just didn't know about it.

MAMA: No . . . something has changed. (*She looks at him*) You something new, boy. In my time we was worried about not being lynched and getting to the North if we could and how to stay alive and still have a pinch of dignity too . . . Now here come you and Beneatha—talking 'bout things we ain't never even thought about hardly, me and your daddy. You ain't satisfied or proud of nothing we done. I mean that you had a home; that we kept you out of trouble till you was grown; that you don't have to ride to work on the back of nobody's streetcar—You my children—but how different we done become.

WALTER: (*A long beat. He pats her hand and gets up*) You just don't understand, Mama, you just don't understand.

MAMA: Son—do you know your wife is expecting another baby? (WALTER *stands, stunned, and absorbs what his mother has said*) That's what she wanted to talk to you about. (WALTER *sinks down into a chair*) This ain't for me to be telling—but you ought to know. (*She waits*) I think Ruth is thinking 'bout getting rid of that child.

WALTER: (*Slowly understanding*) No—no—Ruth wouldn't do that.

MAMA: When the world gets ugly enough—a woman will do anything for her family. *The part that's already living.*

WALTER: You don't know Ruth, Mama, if you think she would do that.

(RUTH *opens the bedroom door and stands there a little limp*)

RUTH: (*Beaten*) Yes I would too, Walter. (*Pause*) I gave her a five-dollar down payment.

(*There is total silence as the man stares at his wife and the mother stares at her son*)

MAMA: (*Presently*) Well—(*Tightly*) Well—son, I'm waiting to hear you say something . . . (*She waits*) I'm waiting to hear how you be your father's son. Be the man he was . . . (*Pause. The silence shouts*) Your wife say she going to destroy your child. And I'm waiting to hear you talk like him and say we a people who give children life, not who destroys them—(*She rises*) I'm waiting to see you stand up and look like your daddy and say we done give up one baby to poverty and that we ain't going to give up nary another one . . . I'm waiting.

WALTER: Ruth—(*He can say nothing*)

MAMA: If you a son of mine, tell her! (WALTER *picks up his keys and his coat and walks out. She continues, bitterly*) You . . . you are a disgrace to your father's memory. Somebody get me my hat!

Curtain

ACT II / Scene One

Time: Later the same day.

At rise: RUTH *is ironing again. She has the radio going. Presently* BENEATHA's *bedroom door opens and* RUTH's *mouth falls and she puts down the iron in fascination.*

RUTH: What have we got on tonight!

BENEATHA: (*Emerging grandly from the doorway so that we can see her thoroughly robed in the costume Asagai brought*) You are looking at what a well-dressed Nigerian woman wears—(*She parades for* RUTH, *her hair completely hidden by the headdress; she is coquettishly fanning herself with an ornate oriental fan, mistakenly more like Butterfly° than any Nigerian that ever was*) Isn't it beautiful?

Butterfly: Title character in Puccini's 1904 opera *Madame Butterfly,* set in Japan. She is a geisha entertainer who marries an American sailor.

(*She promenades to the radio and, with an arrogant flourish, turns off the good loud blues that is playing*) Enough of this assimilationist junk!(RUTH *follows her with her eyes as she goes to the phonograph and puts on a record and turns and waits ceremoniously for the music to come up. Then, with a shout*—) OCOMOGOSIAY!

(RUTH *jumps. The music comes up, a lovely Nigerian melody.* BENEATHA *listens, enraptured, her eyes far away*—"*back to the past.*" *She begins to dance.* RUTH *is dumbfounded*)

RUTH: What kind of dance is that?
BENEATHA: A folk dance.
RUTH: (*Pearl Bailey*)° What kind of folks do that, honey?
BENEATHA: It's from Nigeria. It's a dance of welcome.
RUTH: Who you welcoming?
BENEATHA: The men back to the village.
RUTH: Where they been?
BENEATHA: How should I know—out hunting or something. Anyway, they are coming back now . . .
RUTH: Well, that's good.
BENEATHA: (*With the record*)
Alundi, alundi
Alundi alunya
Jop pu a jeepua
Ang gu sooooooooooo

Ai yai yae . . .
Ayehaye—alundi . . .

(WALTER *comes in during this performance; he has obviously been drinking. He leans against the door heavily and watches his sister, at first with distaste. Then his eyes look off*—"*back to the past*"—*as he lifts both his fists to the roof, screaming*)

WALTER: YEAH . . . AND ETHIOPIA STRETCH FORTH HER HANDS AGAIN! . . .
RUTH: (*Drily, looking at him*) Yes—and Africa sure is claiming her own tonight. (*She gives them both up and starts ironing again*)
WALTER: (*All in a drunken, dramatic shout*) Shut up! . . . I'm digging them drums . . . them drums move me! . . . (*He makes his weaving way to his wife's face and leans in close to her*) In my heart of hearts—(*He thumps his chest*)—I am much warrior!
RUTH: (*Without even looking up*) In your heart of hearts you are much drunkard.
WALTER: (*Coming away from her and starting to wander around the room, shouting*) Me and Jomo° . . . (*Intently, in his sister's face. She has stopped dancing*

Pearl Bailey: Popular African American actress and singer (1918–1990), known for sly jokes as a part of her routine. **Jomo:** Jomo Kenyatta (1893?–1978) African anticolonialist activist and later first president of independent Kenya (1964–78).

to watch him in this unknown mood) That's my man, Kenyatta. *(Shouting and thumping his chest)* FLAMING SPEAR! HOT DAMN! *(He is suddenly in possession of an imaginary spear and actively spearing enemies all over the room)* OCOMOGOSIAY...

BENEATHA: *(To encourage* WALTER, *thoroughly caught up with this side of him)* OCOMOGOSIAY, FLAMING SPEAR!

WALTER: THE LION IS WAKING ... OWIMOWEH! *(He pulls his shirt open and leaps up on the table and gestures with his spear)*

BENEATHA: OWIMOWEH!

WALTER: *(On the table, very far gone, his eyes pure glass sheets. He sees what we cannot, that he is a leader of his people, a great chief, a descendant of Chaka,° and that the hour to march has come)* Listen, my black brothers —

BENEATHA: OCOMOGOSIAY!

WALTER: Do you hear the waters rushing against the shores of the coastlands —

BENEATHA: OCOMOGOSIAY!

WALTER: Do you hear the screeching of the cocks in yonder hills beyond where the chiefs meet in council for the coming of the mighty war —

BENEATHA: OCOMOGOSIAY!

(And now the lighting shifts subtly to suggest the world of WALTER's *imagination, and the mood shifts from pure comedy. It is the inner* WALTER *speaking: the Southside chauffeur has assumed an unexpected majesty)*

WALTER: Do you hear the beating of the wings of the birds flying low over the mountains and the low places of our land —

BENEATHA: OCOMOGOSIAY!

WALTER: Do you hear the singing of the women, singing the war songs of our fathers to the babies in the great houses? Singing the sweet war songs! *(The doorbell rings)* OH, DO YOU HEAR, MY BLACK BROTHERS!

BENEATHA: *(Completely gone)* We hear you, Flaming Spear —

*(*RUTH *shuts off the phonograph and opens the door.* GEORGE MURCHISON *enters)*

WALTER: Telling us to prepare for the GREATNESS OF THE TIME! *(Lights back to normal. He turns and sees* GEORGE) Black Brother!

(He extends his hand for the fraternal clasp)

GEORGE: Black Brother, hell!

RUTH: *(Having had enough, and embarrassed for the family)* Beneatha, you got company — what's the matter with you? Walter Lee Younger, get down off that table and stop acting like a fool ...

*(*WALTER *comes down off the table suddenly and makes a quick exit to the bathroom)*

Chaka: Shaka kaSenzangakhona (c. 1787–1828), also known as Shaka Zulu and sometimes spelled Chaka, was the most influential leader of the African Zulu Kingdom.

RUTH: He's had a little to drink ... I don't know what her excuse is.

GEORGE: (*To* BENEATHA) Look honey, we're going *to* the theatre — we're not going to be *in* it ... so go change, huh?

(BENEATHA *looks at him and slowly, ceremoniously, lifts her hands and pulls off the headdress. Her hair is close-cropped and unstraightened.* GEORGE *freezes mid-sentence and* RUTH's *eyes all but fall out of her head*)

GEORGE: What in the name of —

RUTH: (*Touching* BENEATHA's *hair*) Girl, you done lost your natural mind!? Look at your head!

GEORGE: What have you done to your head — I mean your hair!

BENEATHA: Nothing — except cut it off.

RUTH: Now that's the truth — it's what ain't been done to it! You expect this boy to go out with you with your head all nappy like that?

BENEATHA: (*Looking at* GEORGE) That's up to George. If he's ashamed of his heritage —

GEORGE: Oh, don't be so proud of yourself, Bennie — just because you look eccentric.

BENEATHA: How can something that's natural be eccentric?

GEORGE: That's what being eccentric means — being natural. Get dressed.

BENEATHA: I don't like that, George.

RUTH: Why must you and your brother make an argument out of everything people say?

BENEATHA: Because I hate assimilationist Negroes!

RUTH: Will somebody please tell me what assimila-who-ever means!

GEORGE: Oh, it's just a college girl's way of calling people Uncle Toms — but that isn't what it means at all.

RUTH: Well, what does it mean?

BENEATHA: (*Cutting* GEORGE *off and staring at him as she replies to* RUTH) It means someone who is willing to give up his own culture and submerge himself completely in the dominant, and in this case *oppressive* culture!

GEORGE: Oh, dear, dear, dear! Here we go! A lecture on the African past! On our Great West African Heritage! In one second we will hear all about the great Ashanti empires;° the great Songhay civilizations;° and the great sculpture of Bénin° — and then some poetry in the Bantu° — and the whole monologue will end with the word *heritage!* (*Nastily*) Let's face it, baby, your heritage is nothing but a bunch of raggedy-assed spirituals and some grass huts!

Ashanti empires: A precolonial West African empire in the eighteenth and nineteenth centuries in what is now Ghana. **Songhay civilizations:** (or Songhai) One of the largest and greatest West African empires, which lasted from the early fifteenth to the late sixteenth century. **sculpture of Bénin:** A collection of more than one thousand brass plaques, dating from the fifteenth and sixteenth centuries, in the Kingdom of Dahomey, renamed Bénin in 1975. **Bantu:** The predominant language spoken in central, eastern, and southern Africa.

BENEATHA: GRASS HUTS! (RUTH *crosses to her and forcibly pushes her toward the bedroom*) See there . . . you are standing there in your splendid ignorance talking about people who were the first to smelt iron on the face of the earth! (RUTH *is pushing her through the door*) The Ashanti were performing surgical operations when the English — (RUTH *pulls the door to, with* BENEATHA *on the other side, and smiles graciously at* GEORGE. BENEATHA *opens the door and shouts the end of the sentence defiantly at* GEORGE) — were still tattooing themselves with blue dragons! (*She goes back inside*)

RUTH: Have a seat, George (*They both sit.* RUTH *folds her hands rather primly on her lap, determined to demonstrate the civilization of the family*) Warm, ain't it? I mean for September. (*Pause*) Just like they always say about Chicago weather: If it's too hot or cold for you, just wait a minute and it'll change. (*She smiles happily at this cliché of clichés*) Everybody say it's got to do with them bombs and things they keep setting off. (*Pause*) Would you like a nice cold beer?

GEORGE: No, thank you. I don't care for beer. (*He looks at his watch*) I hope she hurries up.

RUTH: What time is the show?

GEORGE: It's an eight-thirty curtain. That's just Chicago, though. In New York standard curtain time is eight forty.

(*He is rather proud of this knowledge*)

RUTH: (*Properly appreciating it*) You get to New York a lot?

GEORGE: (*Offhand*) Few times a year.

RUTH: Oh — that's nice. I've never been to New York.

(WALTER *enters. We feel he has relieved himself, but the edge of unreality is still with him*)

WALTER: New York ain't got nothing Chicago ain't. Just a bunch of hustling people all squeezed up together — being "Eastern."

(*He turns his face into a screw of displeasure*)

GEORGE: Oh — you've been?

WALTER: Plenty of times.

RUTH: (*Shocked at the lie*) Walter Lee Younger!

WALTER: (*Staring her down*) Plenty! (*Pause*) What we got to drink in this house? Why don't you offer this man some refreshment. (*To* GEORGE) They don't know how to entertain people in this house, man.

GEORGE: Thank you — I don't really care for anything.

WALTER: (*Feeling his head; sobriety coming*) Where's Mama?

RUTH: She ain't come back yet.

WALTER: (*Looking* MURCHISON *over from head to toe, scrutinizing his carefully casual tweed sports jacket over cashmere V-neck sweater over soft eyelet shirt and tie, and soft slacks, finished off with white buckskin shoes*) Why all you college boys wear them faggoty-looking white shoes?

RUTH: Walter Lee!

(GEORGE MURCHISON *ignores the remark*)

WALTER: (*To* RUTH) Well, they look crazy as hell—white shoes, cold as it is.

RUTH: (*Crushed*) You have to excuse him—

WALTER: No he don't! Excuse me for what? What you always excusing me for! I'll excuse myself when I needs to be excused! (*A pause*) They look as funny as them black knee socks Beneatha wears out of here all the time.

RUTH: It's the college *style*, Walter.

WALTER: Style, hell. She looks like she got burnt legs or something!

RUTH: Oh, Walter—

WALTER: (*An irritable mimic*) Oh, Walter! Oh, Walter! (*To* MURCHISON) How's your old man making out? I understand you all going to buy that big hotel on the Drive?° (*He finds a beer in the refrigerator, wanders over to* MURCHISON, *sipping and wiping his lips with the back of his hand, and straddling a chair backwards to talk to the other man*) Shrewd move. Your old man is all right, man. (*Tapping his head and half winking for emphasis*) I mean he knows how to operate. I mean he thinks *big*, you know what I mean, I mean for a *home*, you know? But I think he's kind of running out of ideas now. I'd like to talk to him. Listen, man, I got some plans that could turn this city upside down. I mean think like he does. *Big*. Invest big, gamble big, hell, lose *big* if you have to, you know what I mean. It's hard to find a man on this whole Southside who understands my kind of thinking—you dig? (*He scrutinizes* MURCHISON *again, drinks his beer, squints his eyes and leans in close, confidential, man to man*) Me and you ought to sit down and talk sometimes, man. Man, I got me some ideas . . .

GEORGE: (*With boredom*) Yeah—sometimes we'll have to do that, Walter.

WALTER: (*Understanding the indifference, and offended*) Yeah—well, when you get the time, man. I know you a busy little boy.

RUTH: Walter, please—

WALTER: (*Bitterly, hurt*) I know ain't nothing in this world as busy as you colored college boys with your fraternity pins and white shoes . . .

RUTH: (*Covering her face with humiliation*) Oh, Walter Lee—

WALTER: I see you all all the time—with the books tucked under your arms—going to your (*British A—a mimic*) "clahsses." And for what! What the hell you learning over there? Filling up your heads—(*Counting off on his fingers*)—with the sociology and the psychology—but they teaching you how to be a man? How to take over and run the world? They teaching you how to run a rubber plantation or a steel mill? Naw—just to talk proper and read books and wear them faggoty-looking white shoes . . .

GEORGE: (*Looking at him with distaste, a little above it all*) You're all wacked up with bitterness, man.

The Drive: Lake Shore Drive, a waterfront expressway in Chicago lined with upscale residences and hotels.

WALTER: (*Intently, almost quietly, between the teeth, glaring at the boy*) And you — ain't you bitter, man? Ain't you just about had it yet? Don't you see no stars gleaming that you can't reach out and grab? You happy? — You contented son-of-a-bitch — you happy? You got it made? Bitter? Man, I'm a volcano. Bitter? Here I am a giant — surrounded by ants! Ants who can't even understand what it is the giant is talking about.

RUTH: (*Passionately and suddenly*) Oh, Walter — ain't you with nobody!

WALTER: (*Violently*) No! 'Cause ain't nobody with me! Not even my own mother!

RUTH: Walter, that's a terrible thing to say!

(BENEATHA *enters, dressed for the evening in a cocktail dress and earrings, hair natural*)

GEORGE: Well — hey — (*Crosses to* BENEATHA; *thoughtful, with emphasis, since this is a reversal*) You look great!

WALTER: (*Seeing his sister's hair for the first time*) What's the matter with your head?

BENEATHA: (*Tired of the jokes now*) I cut it off, Brother.

WALTER: (*Coming close to inspect it and walking around her*) Well, I'll be damned. So that's what they mean by the African bush . . .

BENEATHA: Ha ha. Let's go, George.

GEORGE: (*Looking at her*) You know something? I like it. It's sharp. I mean it really is. (*Helps her into her wrap*)

RUTH: Yes — I think so, too. (*She goes to the mirror and starts to clutch at her hair*)

WALTER: Oh no! You leave yours alone, baby. You might turn out to have a pin-shaped head or something!

BENEATHA: See you all later.

RUTH: Have a nice time.

GEORGE: Thanks. Good night. (*Half out the door, he reopens it. To* WALTER) Good night, Prometheus!°

(BENEATHA *and* GEORGE *exit*)

WALTER: (*To* RUTH) Who is Prometheus?

RUTH: I don't know. Don't worry about it.

WALTER: (*In fury, pointing after* GEORGE) See there — they get to a point where they can't insult you man to man — they got to go talk about something ain't nobody never heard of!

RUTH: How do you know it was an insult? (*To humor him*) Maybe Prometheus is a nice fellow.

WALTER: Prometheus! I bet there ain't even no such thing! I bet that simple-minded clown —

RUTH: Walter —

(*She stops what she is doing and looks at him*)

Prometheus: Greek god and one of the Titans, known for his crafty counsel (his name means "forethought"). The protector and benefactor of mankind, he bestowed on humans a number of gifts, including fire.

WALTER: (*Yelling*) Don't start!

RUTH: Start what?

WALTER: Your nagging! Where was I? Who was I with? How much money did I spend?

RUTH: (*Plaintively*) Walter Lee — why don't we just try to talk about it . . .

WALTER: (*Not listening*) I been out talking with people who understand me. People who care about the things I got on my mind.

RUTH: (*Wearily*) I guess that means people like Willy Harris.

WALTER: Yes, people like Willy Harris.

RUTH: (*With a sudden flash of impatience*) Why don't you all just hurry up and go into the banking business and stop talking about it!

WALTER: Why? You want to know why? 'Cause we all tied up in a race of people that don't know how to do nothing but moan, pray and have babies!

(*The line is too bitter even for him and he looks at her and sits down*)

RUTH: Oh, Walter . . . (*Softly*) Honey, why can't you stop fighting me?

WALTER: (*Without thinking*) Who's fighting you? Who even cares about you?

(*This line begins the retardation of his mood*)

RUTH: Well — (*She waits a long time, and then with resignation starts to put away her things*) I guess I might as well go on to bed . . . (*More or less to herself*) I don't know where we lost it . . . but we have . . . (*Then, to him*) I — I'm sorry about this new baby, Walter. I guess maybe I better go on and do what I started . . . I guess I just didn't realize how bad things was with us . . . I guess I just didn't really realize — (*She starts out to the bedroom and stops*) You want some hot milk?

WALTER: Hot milk?

RUTH: Yes — hot milk.

WALTER: Why hot milk?

RUTH: 'Cause after all that liquor you come home with you ought to have something hot in your stomach.

WALTER: I don't want no milk.

RUTH: You want some coffee then?

WALTER: No, I don't want no coffee. I don't want nothing hot to drink. (*Almost plaintively*) Why you always trying to give me something to eat?

RUTH: (*Standing and looking at him helplessly*) What else can I give you, Walter Lee Younger?

(*She stands and looks at him and presently turns to go out again. He lifts his head and watches her going away from him in a new mood which began to emerge when he asked her "Who cares about you?"*)

WALTER: It's been rough, ain't it, baby? (*She hears and stops but does not turn around and he continues to her back*) I guess between two people there ain't never as much understood as folks generally thinks there is. I mean like between me and you — (*She turns to face him*) How we gets to the place where we scared to talk softness to each other. (*He waits, thinking hard himself*) Why you think it got to be like that? (*He is thoughtful, almost as a child would be*) Ruth, what is it gets into people ought to be close?

RUTH: I don't know, honey. I think about it a lot.

WALTER: On account of you and me, you mean? The way things are with us. The way something done come down between us.

RUTH: There ain't so much between us, Walter . . . Not when you come to me and try to talk to me. Try to be with me . . . a little even.

WALTER: (*Total honesty*) Sometimes . . . sometimes . . . I don't even know how to try.

RUTH: Walter —

WALTER: Yes?

RUTH: (*Coming to him, gently and with misgiving, but coming to him*) Honey . . . life don't have to be like this. I mean sometimes people can do things so that things are better . . . You remember how we used to talk when Travis was born . . . about the way we were going to live . . . the kind of house . . . (*She is stroking his head*) Well, it's all starting to slip away from us . . .

(*He turns her to him and they look at each other and kiss, tenderly and hungrily. The door opens and* MAMA *enters —* WALTER *breaks away and jumps up. A beat*)

WALTER: Mama, where have you been?

MAMA: My — them steps is longer than they used to be. Whew! (*She sits down and ignores him*) How you feeling this evening, Ruth?

(RUTH *shrugs, disturbed at having been interrupted and watching her husband knowingly*)

WALTER: Mama, where have you been all day?

MAMA: (*Still ignoring him and leaning on the table and changing to more comfortable shoes*) Where's Travis?

RUTH: I let him go out earlier and he ain't come back yet. Boy, is he going to get it!

WALTER: Mama!

MAMA: (*As if she has heard him for the first time*) Yes, son?

WALTER: Where did you go this afternoon?

MAMA: I went downtown to tend to some business that I had to tend to.

WALTER: What kind of business?

MAMA: You know better than to question me like a child, Brother.

WALTER: (*Rising and bending over the table*) Where were you, Mama? (*Bringing his fists down and shouting*) Mama, you didn't go do something with that insurance money, something crazy?

(*The front door opens slowly, interrupting him, and* TRAVIS *peeks his head in, less than hopefully*)

TRAVIS: (*To his mother*) Mama, I —

RUTH: "Mama I" nothing! You're going to get it, boy! Get on in that bedroom and get yourself ready!

TRAVIS: But I —

MAMA: Why don't you all never let the child explain hisself.

RUTH: Keep out of it now, Lena.

(MAMA *clamps her lips together, and* RUTH *advances toward her son menacingly*)

RUTH: A thousand times I have told you not to go off like that—

MAMA: (*Holding out her arms to her grandson*) Well—at least let me tell him something. I want him to be the first one to hear . . . Come here, Travis. (*The boy obeys, gladly*) Travis—(*She takes him by the shoulder and looks into his face*)—you know that money we got in the mail this morning?

TRAVIS: Yes'm—

MAMA: Well—what you think your grandmama gone and done with that money?

TRAVIS: I don't know, Grandmama.

MAMA: (*Putting her finger on his nose for emphasis*) She went out and she bought you a house! (*The explosion comes from* WALTER *at the end of the revelation and he jumps up and turns away from all of them in a fury.* MAMA *continues, to* TRAVIS) You glad about the house? It's going to be yours when you get to be a man.

TRAVIS: Yeah—I always wanted to live in a house.

MAMA: All right, gimme some sugar then—(TRAVIS *puts his arms around her neck as she watches her son over the boy's shoulder. Then, to* TRAVIS, *after the embrace*) Now when you say your prayers tonight, you thank God and your grandfather—'cause it was him who give you the house—in his way.

RUTH: (*Taking the boy from* MAMA *and pushing him toward the bedroom*) Now you get out of here and get ready for your beating.

TRAVIS: Aw, Mama —

RUTH: Get on in there—(*Closing the door behind him and turning radiantly to her mother-in-law*) So you went and did it!

MAMA: (*Quietly, looking at her son with pain*) Yes, I did.

RUTH: (*Raising both arms classically*) PRAISE GOD! (*Looks at* WALTER *a moment, who says nothing. She crosses rapidly to her husband*) Please, honey—let me be glad . . . you be glad too. (*She has laid her hands on his shoulders, but he shakes himself free of her roughly, without turning to face her*) Oh Walter . . . a home . . . a home. (*She comes back to* MAMA) Well—where is it? How big is it? How much it going to cost?

MAMA: Well—

RUTH: When we moving?

MAMA: (*Smiling at her*) First of the month.

RUTH: (*Throwing back her head with jubilance*) Praise God!

MAMA: (*Tentatively, still looking at her son's back turned against her and* RUTH) It's—it's a nice house too . . . (*She cannot help speaking directly to him. An imploring quality in her voice, her manner, makes her almost like a girl now*) Three bedrooms—nice big one for you and Ruth . . . Me and Beneatha still have to share our room, but Travis have one of his own—and (*With diffi-culty*) I figure if the—new baby—is a boy, we could get one of them double-decker outfits . . . And there's a yard with a little patch of dirt where I could maybe get to grow me a few flowers . . . And a nice big basement . . .

RUTH: Walter honey, be glad—

MAMA: (*Still to his back, fingering things on the table*) 'Course I don't want to make it sound fancier than it is . . . It's just a plain little old house—but it's made good and solid—and it will be *ours*. Walter Lee—it makes a difference in a man when he can walk on floors that belong to *him* . . .

RUTH: Where is it?

MAMA: (*Frightened at this telling*) Well—well—it's out there in Clybourne Park—

(RUTH's *radiance fades abruptly, and* WALTER *finally turns slowly to face his mother with incredulity and hostility*)

RUTH: Where?

MAMA: (*Matter-of-factly*) Four o six Clybourne Street, Clybourne Park.

RUTH: Clybourne Park? Mama, there ain't no colored people living in Clybourne Park.

MAMA: (*Almost idiotically*) Well, I guess there's going to be some now.

WALTER: (*Bitterly*) So that's the peace and comfort you went out and bought for us today!

MAMA: (*Raising her eyes to meet his finally*) Son—I just tried to find the nicest place for the least amount of money for my family.

RUTH: (*Trying to recover from the shock*) Well—well—'course I ain't one never been 'fraid of no crackers,° mind you—but—well, wasn't there no other houses nowhere?

MAMA: Them houses they put up for colored in them areas way out all seem to cost twice as much as other houses. I did the best I could.

RUTH: (*Struck senseless with the news, in its various degrees of goodness and trouble, she sits a moment, her fists propping her chin in thought, and then she starts to rise, bringing her fists down with vigor, the radiance spreading from cheek to cheek again*) Well—well!—All I can say is—if this is my time in life—MY TIME—to say good-bye—(*And she builds with momentum as she starts to circle the room with an exuberant, almost tearfully happy release*)—to these god-damned cracking walls!—(*She pounds the walls*)—and these marching roaches!—(*She wipes at an imaginary army of marching roaches*)—and this cramped little closet which ain't now or never was no kitchen! . . . then I say it loud and good, HALLELUJAH! AND GOOD-BYE MISERY . . . I DON'T NEVER WANT TO SEE YOUR UGLY FACE AGAIN! (*She laughs joyously, hav-ing practically destroyed the apartment, and flings her arms up and lets them come down happily, slowly, reflectively, over her abdomen, aware for the first time perhaps that the life therein pulses with happiness and not despair*) Lena?

---

crackers: A disparaging term for lower-class white Southerners.

MAMA: (*Moved, watching her happiness*) Yes, honey?

RUTH: (*Looking off*) Is there—is there a whole lot of sunlight?

MAMA: (*Understanding*) Yes, child, there's a whole lot of sunlight.

(*Long pause*)

RUTH: (*Collecting herself and going to the door of the room* TRAVIS *is in*) Well—I guess I better see 'bout Travis. (*To* MAMA) Lord, I sure don't feel like whipping nobody today!

(*She exits*)

MAMA: (*The mother and son are left alone now and the mother waits a long time, considering deeply, before she speaks*) Son—you—you understand what I done, don't you? (WALTER *is silent and sullen*) I—I just seen my family falling apart today . . . just falling to pieces in front of my eyes . . . We couldn't of gone on like we was today. We was going backwards 'stead of forwards—talking 'bout killing babies and wishing each other was dead . . . When it gets like that in life—you just got to do something different, push on out and do something bigger . . . (*She waits*) I wish you say something, son . . . I wish you'd say how deep inside you you think I done the right thing—

WALTER: (*Crossing slowly to his bedroom door and finally turning there and speaking measuredly*) What you need me to say you done right for? *You* the head of this family. You run our lives like you want to. It was your money and you did what you wanted with it. So what you need for me to say it was all right for? (*Bitterly, to hurt her as deeply as he knows is possible*) So you butchered up a dream of mine—you—who always talking 'bout your children dreams . . .

MAMA: Walter Lee—

(*He just closes the door behind him.* MAMA *sits alone, thinking heavily*)

Curtain

Scene Two

Time: Friday night. A few weeks later.

   At rise: Packing crates mark the intention of the family to move. BENEATHA *and* GEORGE *come in, presumably from an evening out again.*

GEORGE: O.K. . . . O.K., whatever you say . . . (*They both sit on the couch. He tries to kiss her. She moves away*) Look, we've had a nice evening; let's not spoil it, huh? . . .

(*He again turns her head and tries to nuzzle in and she turns away from him, not with distaste but with momentary lack of interest; in a mood to pursue what they were talking about*)

BENEATHA: I'm *trying* to talk to you.

GEORGE: We always talk.

BENEATHA: Yes—and I love to talk.

GEORGE: (*Exasperated; rising*) I know it and I don't mind it sometimes . . . I want you to cut it out, see — The moody stuff, I mean. I don't like it. You're a nice-looking girl . . . all over. That's all you need, honey, forget the atmosphere. Guys aren't going to go for the atmosphere — they're going to go for what they see. Be glad for that. Drop the Garbo° routine. It doesn't go with you. As for myself, I want a nice — (*Groping*) — simple (*Thoughtfully*) — sophisticated girl . . . not a poet — O.K.?

(*He starts to kiss her, she rebuffs him again and he jumps up*)

BENEATHA: Why are you angry, George?

GEORGE: Because this is stupid! I don't go out with you to discuss the nature of "quiet desperation" or to hear all about your thoughts — because the world will go on thinking what it thinks regardless —

BENEATHA: Then why read books? Why go to school?

GEORGE: (*With artificial patience, counting on his fingers*) It's simple. You read books — to learn facts — to get grades — to pass the course — to get a degree. That's all — it has nothing to do with thoughts.

(*A long pause*)

BENEATHA: I see. (*He starts to sit*) Good night, George.

(GEORGE *looks at her a little oddly, and starts to exit. He meets* MAMA *coming in*)

GEORGE: Oh — hello, Mrs. Younger.

MAMA: Hello, George, how you feeling?

GEORGE: Fine — fine, how are you?

MAMA: Oh, a little tired. You know them steps can get you after a day's work. You all have a nice time tonight?

GEORGE: Yes — a fine time. A fine time.

MAMA: Well, good night.

GEORGE: Good night. (*He exits.* MAMA *closes the door behind her*) Hello, honey. What you sitting like that for?

BENEATHA: I'm just sitting.

MAMA: Didn't you have a nice time?

BENEATHA: No.

MAMA: No? What's the matter?

BENEATHA: Mama, George is a fool — honest. (*She rises*)

MAMA: (*Hustling around unloading the packages she has entered with. She stops*) Is he, baby?

BENEATHA: Yes.

(BENEATHA *makes up* TRAVIS's *bed as she talks*)

MAMA: You sure?

Garbo: Greta Garbo (1905–1990), Swedish-born actress known for her air of remote sophistication.

BENEATHA: Yes.

MAMA: Well—I guess you better not waste your time with no fools.

(BENEATHA *looks up at her mother, watching her put groceries in the refrigerator. Finally she gathers up her things and starts into the bedroom. At the door she stops and looks back at her mother*)

BENEATHA: Mama—

MAMA: Yes, baby—

BENEATHA: Thank you.

MAMA: For what?

BENEATHA: For understanding me this time.

(*She exits quickly and the mother stands, smiling a little, looking at the place where* BENEATHA *just stood.* RUTH *enters*)

RUTH: Now don't you fool with any of this stuff, Lena—

MAMA: Oh, I just thought I'd sort a few things out. Is Brother here?

RUTH: Yes.

MAMA: (*With concern*) Is he—

RUTH: (*Reading her eyes*) Yes.

(MAMA *is silent and someone knocks on the door.* MAMA *and* RUTH *exchange weary and knowing glances and* RUTH *opens it to admit the neighbor,* MRS. JOHNSON,° *who is a rather squeaky wide-eyed lady of no particular age, with a newspaper under her arm*)

MAMA: (*Changing her expression to acute delight and a ringing cheerful greeting*) Oh—hello there, Johnson.

JOHNSON: (*This is a woman who decided long ago to be enthusiastic about EVERYTHING in life and she is inclined to wave her wrist vigorously at the height of her exclamatory comments*) Hello there, yourself! H'you this evening, Ruth?

RUTH: (*Not much of a deceptive type*) Fine, Mis' Johnson, h'you?

JOHNSON: Fine. (*Reaching out quickly, playfully, and patting* RUTH's *stomach*) Ain't you starting to poke out none yet! (*She mugs with delight at the overfamiliar remark and her eyes dart around looking at the crates and packing preparation;* MAMA's *face is a cold sheet of endurance*) Oh, ain't we getting ready 'round here, though! Yessir! Lookathere! I'm telling you the Youngers is really getting ready to "move on up a little higher!"—Bless God!

MAMA: (*A little drily, doubting the total sincerity of the Blesser*) Bless God.

JOHNSON: He's good, ain't He?

MAMA: (*The same*) Oh yes, He's good.

JOHNSON: I mean sometimes He works in mysterious ways. . . but He works, don't He!

Mrs. Johnson: This character and the scene of her visit were cut from the original production and early editions of the play.

MAMA: (*The same*) Yes, he does.

JOHNSON: I'm just soooooo happy for y'all. And this here child — (*About* RUTH) looks like she could just pop open with happiness, don't she. Where's all the rest of the family?

MAMA: Bennie's gone to bed —

JOHNSON: Ain't no . . . (*The implication is pregnancy*) sickness done hit you — I hope . . . ?

MAMA: No — she just tired. She was out this evening.

JOHNSON: (*All is a coo, an emphatic coo*) Aw — ain't that lovely. She still going out with the little Murchison boy?

MAMA: (*Drily*) Ummmm huh.

JOHNSON: That's lovely. You sure got lovely children, Younger. Me and Isaiah talks all the time 'bout what fine children you was blessed with. We sure do.

MAMA: Ruth, give Mis' Johnson a piece of sweet potato pie and some milk.

JOHNSON: Oh honey, I can't stay hardly a minute — I just dropped in to see if there was anything I could do. (*Accepting the food easily*) I guess y'all seen the news what's all over the colored paper this week . . .

MAMA: No — didn't get mine yet this week.

JOHNSON: (*Lifting her head and blinking with the spirit of catastrophe*) You mean you ain't read 'bout them colored people that was bombed out their place out there?

(RUTH *straightens with concern and takes the paper and reads it.* JOHNSON *notices her and feeds commentary*)

JOHNSON: Ain't it something how bad these here white folks is getting here in Chicago! Lord, getting so you think you right down in Mississippi! (*With a tremendous and rather insincere sense of melodrama*) 'Course I thinks it's wonderful how our folks keeps on pushing out. You hear some of these Negroes 'round here talking 'bout how they don't go where they ain't wanted and all that — but not me, honey! (*This is a lie*) Wilhemenia Othella Johnson goes anywhere, any time she feels like it! (*With head movement for emphasis*) Yes I do! Why if we left it up to these here crackers, the poor niggers wouldn't have nothing — (*She clasps her hand over her mouth*) Oh, I always forgets you don't 'low that word in your house.

MAMA: (*Quietly, looking at her*) No — I don't 'low it.

JOHNSON: (*Vigorously again*) Me neither! I was just telling Isaiah yesterday when he come using it in front of me — I said, "Isaiah, it's just like Mis' Younger says all the time —"

MAMA: Don't you want some more pie?

JOHNSON: No — no thank you; this was lovely. I got to get on over home and have my midnight coffee. I hear some people say it don't let them sleep but I finds I can't close my eyes right lessen I done had that laaaast cup of coffee . . . (*She waits. A beat. Undaunted*) My Goodnight coffee, I calls it!

MAMA: (*With much eye-rolling and communication between herself and* RUTH) Ruth, why don't you give Mis' Johnson some coffee.

(RUTH *gives* MAMA *an unpleasant look for her kindness*)

JOHNSON: (*Accepting the coffee*) Where's Brother tonight?
MAMA: He's lying down.
JOHNSON: Mmmmmm, he sure gets his beauty rest, don't he? Good-looking man. Sure is a good-looking man! (*Reaching out to pat* RUTH'S *stomach again*) I guess that's how come we keep on having babies around here. (*She winks at* MAMA) One thing 'bout Brother, he always know how to have a *good* time. And soooooo ambitious! I bet it was his idea y'all moving out to Clybourne Park. Lord—I bet this time next month y'all's names will have been in the papers plenty—(*Holding up her hands to mark off each word of the headline she can see in front of her*) "NEGROES INVADE CLYBOURNE PARK—BOMBED!"
MAMA: (*She and* RUTH *look at the woman in amazement*) We ain't exactly moving out there to get bombed.
JOHNSON: Oh, honey—you know I'm praying to God every day that don't nothing like that happen! But you have to think of life like it is—and these here Chicago peckerwoods is some baaaad peckerwoods.
MAMA: (*Wearily*) We done thought about all that Mis' Johnson.

(BENEATHA *comes out of the bedroom in her robe and passes through to the bathroom.* MRS. JOHNSON *turns*)

JOHNSON: Hello there, Bennie!
BENEATHA: (*Crisply*) Hello, Mrs. Johnson.
JOHNSON: How is school?
BENEATHA: (*Crisply*) Fine, thank you. (*She goes out.*)
JOHNSON: (*Insulted*) Getting so she don't have much to say to nobody.
MAMA: The child was on her way to the bathroom.
JOHNSON: I know—but sometimes she act like ain't got time to pass the time of day with nobody ain't been to college. Oh—I ain't criticizing her none. It's just—you know how some of our young people gets when they get a little education. (MAMA *and* RUTH *say nothing, just look at her*) Yes—well. Well, I guess I better get on home. (*Unmoving*) 'Course I can understand how she must be proud and everything—being the only one in the family to make something of herself. I know just being a chauffeur ain't never satisfied Brother none. He shouldn't feel like that, though. Ain't nothing wrong with being a chauffeur.
MAMA: There's plenty wrong with it.
JOHNSON: What?
MAMA: Plenty. My husband always said being any kind of a servant wasn't a fit thing for a man to have to be. He always said a man's hands was made to make things, or to turn the earth with—not to drive nobody's car for 'em—or—(*She looks at her own hands*) carry they slop jars. And my boy is just like him—he wasn't meant to wait on nobody.

JOHNSON: (*Rising, somewhat offended*) Mmmmmmmmmm. The Youngers is too
much for me! (*She looks around*) You sure one proud-acting bunch of colored folks. Well—I always thinks like Booker T. Washington° said that
time—"Education has spoiled many a good plow hand"—

MAMA: Is that what old Booker T. said?

JOHNSON: He sure did.

MAMA: Well, it sounds just like him. The fool.

JOHNSON: (*Indignantly*) Well—he was one of our great men.

MAMA: Who said so?

JOHNSON: (*Nonplussed*) You know, me and you ain't never agreed about some
things, Lena Younger. I guess I better be going—

RUTH: (*Quickly*) Good night.

JOHNSON: Good night. Oh—(*Thrusting it at her*) You can keep the paper! (*With
a trill*) 'Night.

MAMA: Good night, Mis' Johnson.

(MRS. JOHNSON *exits*)

RUTH: If ignorance was gold . . .

MAMA: Shush. Don't talk about folks behind their backs.

RUTH: You do.

MAMA: I'm old and corrupted. (BENEATHA *enters*) You was rude to Mis' Johnson,
Beneatha, and I don't like it at all.

BENEATHA: (*At her door*) Mama, if there are two things we, as a people, have got
to overcome, one is the Ku Klux Klan—and the other is Mrs. Johnson. (*She
exits*)

MAMA: Smart aleck.

(*The phone rings*)

RUTH: I'll get it.

MAMA: Lord, ain't this a popular place tonight.

RUTH: (*At the phone*) Hello—Just a minute. (*Goes to door*) Walter, it's Mrs.
Arnold. (*Waits. Goes back to the phone. Tense*) Hello. Yes, this is his wife
speaking . . . He's lying down now. Yes . . . well, he'll be in tomorrow. He's
been very sick. Yes—I know we should have called, but we were so sure he'd
be able to come in today. Yes—yes, I'm very sorry. Yes . . . Thank you very
much. (*She hangs up.* WALTER *is standing in the doorway of the bedroom behind
her*) That was Mrs. Arnold.

WALTER: (*Indifferently*) Was it?

RUTH: She said if you don't come in tomorrow that they are getting a new
man . . .

WALTER: Ain't that sad—ain't that crying sad.

Booker T. Washington: Booker Taliaferro Washington (1856–1915) was an influential
African American educator and political leader, but controversial because of his willingness to
cooperate with supportive whites instead of actively confronting segregation policies.

RUTH: She said Mr. Arnold has had to take a cab for three days . . . Walter, you ain't been to work for three days! (*This is a revelation to her*) Where you been, Walter Lee Younger? (WALTER *looks at her and starts to laugh*) You're going to lose your job.

WALTER: That's right . . . (*He turns on the radio*)

RUTH: Oh, Walter, and with your mother working like a dog every day—

(*A steamy, deep blues pours into the room*)

WALTER: That's sad too—Everything is sad.

MAMA: What you been doing for these three days, son?

WALTER: Mama—you don't know all the things a man what got leisure can find to do in this city . . . What's this—Friday night? Well—Wednesday I borrowed Willy Harris's car and I went for a drive . . . just me and myself and I drove and drove . . . Way out . . . way past South Chicago, and I parked the car and I sat and looked at the steel mills all day long. I just sat in the car and looked at them big black chimneys for hours. Then I drove back and I went to the Green Hat. (*Pause*) And Thursday—Thursday I borrowed the car again and I got in it and I pointed it the other way and I drove the other way—for hours—way, way up to Wisconsin, and I looked at the farms. I just drove and looked at the farms. Then I drove back and I went to the Green Hat. (*Pause*) And today—today I didn't get the car. Today I just walked. All over the Southside. And I looked at the Negroes and they looked at me and finally I just sat down on the curb at Thirty-ninth and South Parkway and I just sat there and watched the Negroes go by. And then I went to the Green Hat. You all sad? You all depressed? And you know where I am going right now—

(RUTH *goes out quietly*)

MAMA: Oh, Big Walter, is this the harvest of our days?

WALTER: You know what I like about the Green Hat? I like this little cat they got there who blows a sax . . . He blows. He talks to me. He ain't but 'bout five feet tall and he's got a conked head and his eyes is always closed and he's all music—

MAMA: (*Rising and getting some papers out of her handbag*) Walter—

WALTER: And there's this other guy who plays the piano . . . and they got a sound. I mean they can work on some music . . . They got the best little combo in the world in the Green Hat . . . You can just sit there and drink and listen to them three men play and you realize that don't nothing matter worth a damn, but just being there—

MAMA: I've helped do it to you, haven't I, son? Walter I been wrong.

WALTER: Naw—you ain't never been wrong about nothing, Mama.

MAMA: Listen to me, now. I say I been wrong, son. That I been doing to you what the rest of the world been doing to you. (*She turns off the radio*) Walter—(*She stops and he looks up slowly at her and she meets his eyes pleadingly*) What you ain't never understood is that I ain't got nothing, don't own nothing, ain't never really wanted nothing that wasn't for you. There ain't nothing as precious to me . . . There ain't nothing worth holding on to, money, dreams, nothing else—if it means—if it means it's going to destroy my boy. (*She takes an envelope out of her handbag and puts it in front of him and he watches her without speaking or moving*) I paid the man thirty-five hundred dollars down on the house. That leaves sixty-five hundred dollars. Monday morning I want you to take this money and take three thousand dollars and put it in a savings account for Beneatha's medical schooling. The rest you put in a checking account—with your name on it. And from now on any penny that come out of it or that go in it is for you to look after. For you to decide. (*She drops her hands a little helplessly*) It ain't much, but it's all I got in the world and I'm putting it in your hands. I'm telling you to be the head of this family from now on like you supposed to be.

WALTER: (*Stares at the money*) You trust me like that, Mama?

MAMA: I ain't never stop trusting you. Like I ain't never stop loving you.

(*She goes out, and* WALTER *sits looking at the money on the table. Finally, in a decisive gesture, he gets up, and, in mingled joy and desperation, picks up the money. At the same moment,* TRAVIS *enters for bed*)

TRAVIS: What's the matter, Daddy? You drunk?

WALTER: (*Sweetly, more sweetly than we have ever known him*) No, Daddy ain't drunk. Daddy ain't going to never be drunk again. . . .

TRAVIS: Well, good night, Daddy.

(*The* FATHER *has come from behind the couch and leans over, embracing his son*)

WALTER: Son, I feel like talking to you tonight.

TRAVIS: About what?

WALTER: Oh, about a lot of things. About you and what kind of man you going to be when you grow up. . . . Son—son, what do you want to be when you grow up?

TRAVIS: A bus driver.

WALTER: (*Laughing a little*) A what? Man, that ain't nothing to want to be!

TRAVIS: Why not?

WALTER: 'Cause, man;—it ain't big enough—you know what I mean.

TRAVIS: I don't know then. I can't make up my mind. Sometimes Mama asks me that too. And sometimes when I tell her I just want to be like you—she says she don't want me to be like that and sometimes she says she does. . . .

WALTER: (*Gathering him up in his arms*) You know what, Travis? In seven years you going to be seventeen years old. And things is going to be very different with us in seven years, Travis. . . . One day when you are seventeen I'll come home—home from my office downtown somewhere—

TRAVIS: You don't work in no office, Daddy.

WALTER: No—but after tonight. After what your daddy gonna do tonight, there's going to be offices—a whole lot of offices. . . .

TRAVIS: What you gonna do tonight, Daddy?

WALTER: You wouldn't understand yet, son, but your daddy's gonna make a transaction . . . a business transaction that's going to change our lives. . . . That's
how come one day when you 'bout seventeen years old I'll come home and
I'll be pretty tired, you know what I mean, after a day of conferences and
secretaries getting things wrong the way they do . . . 'cause an executive's life
is hell, man—(*The more he talks the farther away he gets*) And I'll pull the car
up on the driveway . . . just a plain black Chrysler, I think, with white
walls—no—black tires. More elegant. Rich people don't have to be
flashy . . . though I'll have to get something a little sportier for Ruth—maybe
a Cadillac convertible to do her shopping in. . . . And I'll come up the steps to
the house and the gardener will be clipping away at the hedges and he'll say,
"Good evening, Mr. Younger." And I'll say, "Hello, Jefferson, how are you
this evening?" And I'll go inside and Ruth will come downstairs and meet me
at the door and we'll kiss each other and she'll take my arm and we'll go up
to your room to see you sitting on the floor with the catalogues of all the
great schools in America around you . . . All the great schools in the world!
And—and I'll say, all right son—it's your seventeenth birthday, what is it
you've decided? . . . Just tell me where you want to go to school and you'll *go*.
Just tell me, what it is you want to be—and you'll *be* it. . . . Whatever you
want to be—Yessir! (*He holds his arms open for* TRAVIS) You just name it,
son . . . (TRAVIS *leaps into them*) and I hand you the world!

(WALTER's *voice has risen in pitch and hysterical promise and on the last line he lifts*
TRAVIS *high*)

Blackout

Scene Three

Time: Saturday, moving day, one week later.
    Before the curtain rises, RUTH's *voice, a strident, dramatic church alto, cuts
through the silence.*
    *It is, in the darkness, a triumphant surge, a penetrating statement of expecta-
tion:* "Oh, Lord, I don't feel no ways tired! Children, oh, glory hallelujah!"
    As the curtain rises we see that RUTH *is alone in the living room, finishing up the
family's packing. It is moving day. She is nailing crates and tying cartons,* BENEATHA
enters, carrying a guitar case, and watches her exuberant sister-in-law.

RUTH: Hey!
BENEATHA: (*Putting away the case*) Hi.
RUTH: (*Pointing at a package*) Honey—look in that package there and see what I
    found on sale this morning at the South Center. (RUTH *gets up and moves to
    the package and draws out some curtains*) Lookahere—hand-turned hems!
BENEATHA: How do you know the window size out there?
RUTH: (*Who hadn't thought of that*) Oh—Well, they bound to fit something in
    the whole house. Anyhow, they was too good a bargain to pass up. (RUTH

slaps her head, suddenly remembering something) Oh, Bennie—I meant to put
a special note on that carton over there. That's your mama's good china
and she wants 'em to be very careful with it.

BENEATHA: I'll do it.

(BENEATHA *finds a piece of paper and starts to draw large letters on it*)

RUTH: You know what I'm going to do soon as I get in that new house?

BENEATHA: What?

RUTH: Honey—I'm going to run me a tub of water up to here . . . (*with her fingers practically up to her nostrils*) And I'm going to get in it—and I am going
to sit . . . and sit . . . and sit in that hot water and the first person who
knocks to tell me to hurry up and come out —

BENEATHA: Gets shot at sunrise.

RUTH: (*Laughing happily*) You said it, sister! (*Noticing how large* BENEATHA *is
absent-mindedly making the note*) Honey, they ain't going to read that from
no airplane.

BENEATHA: (*Laughing herself*) I guess I always think things have more emphasis
if they are big, somehow.

RUTH: (*Looking up at her and smiling*) You and your brother seem to have that
as a philosophy of life. Lord, that man—done changed so 'round here. You
know—you know what we did last night? Me and Walter Lee?

BENEATHA: What?

RUTH: (*Smiling to herself*) We went to the movies. (*Looking at* BENEATHA *to see if
she understands*) We went to the movies. You know the last time me and
Walter went to the movies together?

BENEATHA: No.

RUTH: Me neither. That's how long it been. (*Smiling again*) But we went last
night. The picture wasn't much good, but that didn't seem to matter. We
went—and we held hands.

BENEATHA: Oh, Lord!

RUTH: We held hands—and you know what?

BENEATHA: What?

RUTH: When we come out of the show it was late and dark and all the stores
and things was closed up . . . and it was kind of chilly and there wasn't
many people on the streets . . . and we was still holding hands, me and
Walter.

BENEATHA: You're killing me.

(WALTER *enters with a large package. His happiness is deep in him; he cannot keep
still with his newfound exuberance. He is singing and wiggling and snapping his
fingers. He puts his package in a corner and puts a phonograph record, which he has
brought in with him, on the record player. As the music, soulful and sensuous, comes
up he dances over to* RUTH *and tries to get her to dance with him. She gives in at last
to his raunchiness and in a fit of giggling allows herself to be drawn into his mood.
They dip and she melts into his arms in a classic, body-melding "slow drag"*)

BENEATHA: (*Regarding them a long time as they dance, then drawing in her breath for a deeply exaggerated comment which she does not particularly mean*) Talk about—olddddddddddd-fashionedddddddd—Negroes!

WALTER: (*Stopping momentarily*) What kind of Negroes? (*He says this in fun. He is not angry with her today, nor with anyone. He starts to dance with his wife again*)

BENEATHA: Old-fashioned.

WALTER: (*As he dances with* RUTH) You know, when these New Negroes have their convention—(*Pointing at his sister*)—that is going to be the chairman of the Committee on Unending Agitation. (*He goes on dancing, then stops*) Race, race, race! . . . Girl, I do believe you are the first person in the history of the entire human race to successfully brainwash yourself. (BENEATHA *breaks up and he goes on dancing. He stops again, enjoying his tease*) Damn, even the N double A C P takes a holiday sometimes! (BENEATHA *and* RUTH *laugh. He dances with* RUTH *some more and starts to laugh and stops and pantomimes someone over an operating table*) I can just see that chick someday looking down at some poor cat on an operating table and before she starts to slice him, she says . . . (*Pulling his sleeves back maliciously*) "By the way, what are your views on civil rights down there? . . ."

(*He laughs at her again and starts to dance happily. The bell sounds*)

BENEATHA: Sticks and stones may break my bones but . . . words will never hurt me!

(BENEATHA *goes to the door and opens it as* WALTER *and* RUTH *go on with the clowning.* BENEATHA *is somewhat surprised to see a quiet-looking middle-aged white man in a business suit holding his hat and a briefcase in his hand and consulting a small piece of paper*)

MAN: Uh—how do you do, miss. I am looking for a Mrs.—(*He looks at the slip of paper*) Mrs. Lena Younger? (*He stops short, struck dumb at the sight of the oblivious* WALTER *and* RUTH)

BENEATHA: (*Smoothing her hair with slight embarrassment*) Oh—yes, that's my mother. Excuse me (*She closes the door and turns to quiet the other two*) Ruth! Brother! (*Enunciating precisely but soundlessly: "There's a white man at the door!" They stop dancing,* RUTH *cuts off the phonograph,* BENEATHA *opens the door. The man casts a curious quick glance at all of them*) Uh—come in please.

MAN: (*Coming in*) Thank you.

BENEATHA: My mother isn't here just now. Is it business?

MAN: Yes. . . well, of a sort.

WALTER: (*Freely, the Man of the House*) Have a seat. I'm Mrs. Younger's son. I look after most of her business matters.

(RUTH *and* BENEATHA *exchange amused glances*)

MAN: (*Regarding* WALTER, *and sitting*) Well—My name is Karl Lindner . . .

WALTER: (*Stretching out his hand*) Walter Younger. This is my wife—(RUTH *nods politely*)—and my sister.

LINDNER: How do you do.

WALTER: (*Amiably, as he sits himself easily on a chair, leaning forward on his knees with interest and looking expectantly into the newcomer's face*) What can we do for you, Mr. Lindner!

LINDNER: (*Some minor shuffling of the hat and briefcase on his knees*) Well—I am a representative of the Clybourne Park Improvement Association—

WALTER: (*Pointing*) Why don't you sit your things on the floor?

LINDNER: Oh—yes. Thank you. (*He slides the briefcase and hat under the chair*) And as I was saying—I am from the Clybourne Park Improvement Association and we have had it brought to our attention at the last meeting that you people—or at least your mother—has bought a piece of residential property at—(*He digs for the slip of paper again*)—four o six Clybourne Street . . .

WALTER: That's right. Care for something to drink? Ruth, get Mr. Lindner a beer.

LINDNER: (*Upset for some reason*) Oh—no, really. I mean thank you very much, but no thank you.

RUTH: (*Innocently*) Some coffee?

LINDNER: Thank you, nothing at all.

(BENEATHA *is watching the man carefully*)

LINDNER: Well, I don't know how much you folks know about our organization. (*He is a gentle man; thoughtful and somewhat labored in his manner*) It is one of these community organizations set up to look after—oh, you know, things like block upkeep and special projects and we also have what we call our New Neighbors Orientation Committee . . .

BENEATHA: (*Drily*) Yes—and what do they do?

LINDNER: (*Turning a little to her and then returning the main force to* WALTER) Well—it's what you might call a sort of welcoming committee, I guess. I mean they, we—I'm the chairman of the committee—go around and see the new people who move into the neighborhood and sort of give them the lowdown on the way we do things out in Clybourne Park.

BENEATHA: (*With appreciation of the two meanings, which escape* RUTH *and* WALTER) Un-huh.

LINDNER: And we also have the category of what the association calls—(*He looks elsewhere*)—uh—special community problems . . .

BENEATHA: Yes—and what are some of those?

WALTER: Girl, let the man talk.

LINDNER: (*With understated relief*) Thank you. I would sort of like to explain this thing in my own way. I mean I want to explain to you in a certain way.

WALTER: Go ahead.

LINDNER: Yes. Well. I'm going to try to get right to the point. I'm sure we'll all appreciate that in the long run.

BENEATHA: Yes.

WALTER: Be still now!

LINDNER: Well—

RUTH: (*Still innocently*) Would you like another chair—you don't look comfortable.

LINDNER: (*More frustrated than annoyed*) No, thank you very much. Please. Well — to get right to the point I — (*A great breath, and he is off at last*) I am sure you people must be aware of some of the incidents which have happened in various parts of the city when colored people have moved into certain areas — (BENEATHA *exhales heavily and starts tossing a piece of fruit up and down in the air*) Well — because we have what I think is going to be a unique type of organization in American community life — not only do we deplore that kind of thing — but we are trying to do something about it. (BENEATHA *stops tossing and turns with a new and quizzical interest to the man*) We feel — (*gaining confidence in his mission because of the interest in the faces of the people he is talking to*) — we feel that most of the trouble in this world, when you come right down to it — (*He hits his knee for emphasis*) — most of the trouble exists because people just don't sit down and talk to each other.

RUTH: (*Nodding as she might in church, pleased with the remark*) You can say that again, mister.

LINDNER: (*More encouraged by such affirmation*) That we don't try hard enough in this world to understand the other fellow's problem. The other guy's point of view.

RUTH: Now that's right.

(BENEATHA *and* WALTER *merely watch and listen with genuine interest*)

LINDNER: Yes — that's the way we feel out in Clybourne Park. And that's why I was elected to come here this afternoon and talk to you people. Friendly like, you know, the way people should talk to each other and see if we couldn't find some way to work this thing out. As I say, the whole business is a matter of *caring* about the other fellow. Anybody can see that you are a nice family of folks, hard working and honest I'm sure, (BENEATHA *frowns slightly, quizzically, her head tilted regarding him*) Today everybody knows what it means to be on the outside of *something*. And of course, there is always somebody who is out to take advantage of people who don't always understand.

WALTER: What do you mean?

LINDNER: Well — you see our community is made up of people who've worked hard as the dickens for years to build up that little community. They're not rich and fancy people; just hard-working, honest people who don't really have much but those little homes and a dream of the kind of community they want to raise their children in. Now, I don't say we are perfect and there is a lot wrong in some of the things they want. But you've got to admit that a man, right or wrong, has the right to want to have the neighborhood he lives in a certain kind of way. And at the moment the overwhelming majority of our people out there feel that people get along better, take more of a common interest in the life of the community, when they share a common background. I want you to believe me when I tell you that race prejudice simply doesn't enter into it. It is a matter of the people of Clybourne Park believing, rightly or wrongly, as I say, that for the happiness of all concerned that our Negro families are happier when they live in their *own* communities.

BENEATHA: (*With a grand and bitter gesture*) This, friends, is the Welcoming Committee!

WALTER: (*Dumbfounded, looking at* LINDNER) Is this what you came marching all the way over here to tell us?

LINDNER: Well, now we've been having a fine conversation. I hope you'll hear me all the way through.

WALTER: (*Tightly*) Go ahead, man.

LINDNER: You see—in the face of all the things I have said, we are prepared to make your family a very generous offer. . .

BENEATHA: Thirty pieces and not a coin less!

WALTER: Yeah?

LINDNER: (*Putting on his glasses and drawing a form out of the briefcase*) Our association is prepared, through the collective effort of our people, to buy the house from you at a financial gain to your family.

RUTH: Lord have mercy, ain't this the living gall!

WALTER: All right, you through?

LINDNER: Well, I want to give you the exact terms of the financial arrangement—

WALTER: We don't want to hear no exact terms of no arrangements. I want to know if you got any more to tell us 'bout getting together?

LINDNER: (*Taking off his glasses*) Well—I don't suppose that you feel . . .

WALTER: Never mind how I feel—you got any more to say 'bout how people ought to sit down and talk to each other? . . . Get out of my house, man.

(*He turns his back and walks to the door*)

LINDNER: (*Looking around at the hostile faces and reaching and assembling his hat and briefcase*) Well—I don't understand why you people are reacting this way. What do you think you are going to gain by moving into a neighborhood where you just aren't wanted and where some elements—well—people can get awful worked up when they feel that their whole way of life and everything they've ever worked for is threatened.

WALTER: Get out.

LINDNER: (*At the door, holding a small card*) Well—I'm sorry it went like this.

WALTER: Get out.

LINDNER: (*Almost sadly regarding* WALTER) You just can't force people to change their hearts, son.

(*He turns and puts his card on a table and exits.* WALTER *pushes the door to with stinging hatred, and stands looking at it.* RUTH *just sits and* BENEATHA *just stands. They say nothing.* MAMA *and* TRAVIS *enter*)

MAMA: Well—this all the packing got done since I left out of here this morning. I testify before God that my children got all the energy of the *dead!* What time the moving men due?

BENEATHA: Four o'clock. You had a caller, Mama.

(*She is smiling, teasingly*)

MAMA: Sure enough—who?
BENEATHA: (*Her arms folded saucily*) The Welcoming Committee.

(WALTER *and* RUTH *giggle*)

MAMA: (*Innocently*) Who?
BENEATHA: The Welcoming Committee. They said they're sure going to be glad
    to see you when you get there.
WALTER: (*Devilishly*) Yeah, they said they can't hardly wait to see your face.

(*Laughter*)

MAMA: (*Sensing their facetiousness*) What's the matter with you all?
WALTER: Ain't nothing the matter with us. We just telling you 'bout the gentle-
    man who came to see you this afternoon. From the Clybourne Park
    Improvement Association.
MAMA: What he want?
RUTH: (*In the same mood as* BENEATHA *and* WALTER) To welcome you, honey.
WALTER: He said they can't hardly wait. He said the one thing they don't have,
    that they just *dying* to have out there is a fine family of fine colored people!
    (*To* RUTH *and* BENEATHA) Ain't that right!
RUTH: (*Mockingly*) Yeah! He left his card —
BENEATHA: (*Handing card to* MAMA) In case.

(MAMA *reads and throws it on the floor—understanding and looking off as she draws
her chair up to the table on which she has put her plant and some sticks and some cord*)

MAMA: Father, give us strength. (*Knowingly—and without fun*) Did he threaten
    us?
BENEATHA: Oh—Mama—they don't do it like that any more. He talked Brother-
    hood. He said everybody ought to learn how to sit down and hate each other
    with good Christian fellowship.

(*She and* WALTER *shake hands to ridicule the remark*)

MAMA: (*Sadly*) Lord, protect us . . .
RUTH: You should hear the money those folks raised to buy the house from us.
    All we paid and then some.
BENEATHA: What they think we going to do—eat 'em?
RUTH: No, honey, marry 'em.
MAMA: (*Shaking her head*) Lord, Lord, Lord . . .
RUTH: Well—that's the way the crackers crumble. (*A beat*) Joke.
BENEATHA: (*Laughingly noticing what her mother is doing*) Mama, what are you
    doing?
MAMA: Fixing my plant so it won't get hurt none on the way . . .
BENEATHA: Mama, you going to take *that* to the new house?
MAMA: Un-huh—
BENEATHA: That raggedy-looking old thing?

MAMA: (*Stopping and looking at her*) It expresses ME!

RUTH: (*With delight, to* BENEATHA) So there, Miss Thing!

(WALTER *comes to* MAMA *suddenly and bends down behind her and squeezes her in his arms with all his strength. She is overwhelmed by the suddenness of it and, though delighted, her manner is like that of* RUTH *and* TRAVIS)

MAMA: Look out now, boy! You make me mess up my thing here!

WALTER: (*His face lit, he slips down on his knees beside her, his arms still about her*) Mama . . . you know what it means to climb up in the chariot?

MAMA: (*Gruffly, very happy*) Get on away from me now . . .

RUTH: (*Near the gift-wrapped package, trying to catch* WALTER'S *eye*) Psst —

WALTER: What the old song say, Mama . . .

RUTH: Walter — Now?

(*She is pointing at the package*)

WALTER: (*Speaking the lines, sweetly, playfully, in his mother's face*)

I got wings . . . you got wings . . .
All God's children got wings . . .

MAMA: Boy — get out of my face and do some work . . .

WALTER:

When I get to heaven gonna put on my wings,
Gonna fly all over God's heaven . . .

BENEATHA: (*Teasingly, from across the room*) Everybody talking 'bout heaven ain't going there!

WALTER: (*To* RUTH, *who is carrying the box across to them*) I don't know, you think we ought to give her that . . . Seems to me she ain't been very appreciative around here.

MAMA: (*Eyeing the box, which is obviously a gift*) What is that?

WALTER: (*Taking it from* RUTH *and putting it on the table in front of* MAMA) Well — what you all think? Should we give it to her?

RUTH: Oh — she was pretty good today.

MAMA: I'll good you —

(*She turns her eyes to the box again*)

BENEATHA: Open it, Mama.

(*She stands up, looks at it, turns and looks at all of them, and then presses her hands together and does not open the package*)

WALTER: (*Sweetly*) Open it, Mama. It's for you. (MAMA *looks in his eyes. It is the first present in her life without its being Christmas. Slowly she opens her package and lifts out, one by one, a brand-new sparkling set of gardening tools.* WALTER *continues, prodding*) Ruth made up the note — read it . . .

MAMA: (*Picking up the card and adjusting her glasses*) "To our own Mrs. Miniver° — Love from Brother, Ruth and Beneatha." Ain't that lovely . . .

TRAVIS: (*Tugging at his father's sleeve*) Daddy, can I give her mine now?

WALTER: All right, son. (TRAVIS *flies to get his gift*)

MAMA: Now I don't have to use my knives and forks no more . . .

WALTER: Travis didn't want to go in with the rest of us, Mama. He got his own. (*Somewhat amused*) We don't know what it is . . .

TRAVIS: (*Racing back in the room with a large hatbox and putting it in front of his grandmother*) Here!

MAMA: Lord have mercy, baby. You done gone and bought your grandmother a hat?

TRAVIS: (*very proud*) Open it!

(*She does and lifts out an elaborate, but very elaborate, wide gardening hat, and all the adults break up at the sight of it*)

RUTH: Travis, honey, what is that?

TRAVIS: (*Who thinks it is beautiful and appropriate*) It's a gardening hat! Like the ladies always have on in the magazines when they work in their gardens.

BENEATHA: (*Giggling fiercely*) Travis — we were trying to make Mama Mrs. Miniver — not Scarlett O'Hara!°

MAMA: (*Indignantly*) What's the matter with you all! This here is a beautiful hat! (*Absurdly*) I always wanted me one just like it!

(*She pops it on her head to prove it to her grandson, and the hat is ludicrous and considerably oversized*)

RUTH: Hot dog! Go, Mama!

WALTER: (*Doubled over with laughter*) I'm sorry, Mama — but you look like you ready to go out and chop you some cotton sure enough!

(*They all laugh except* MAMA, *out of deference to* TRAVIS's *feelings*)

MAMA: (*Gathering the boy up to her*) Bless your heart — this is the prettiest hat I ever owned — (WALTER, RUTH *and* BENEATHA *chime in — noisily, festively and insincerely congratulating* TRAVIS *on his gift*) What are we all standing around here for? We ain't finished packin' yet. Bennie, you ain't packed one book.

(*The bell rings*)

BENEATHA: That couldn't be the movers . . . it's not hardly two good yet —

(BENEATHA *goes into her room,* MAMA *starts for door*)

WALTER: (*Turning, stiffening*) Wait — wait — I'll get it.

(*He stands and looks at the door*)

Mrs. Miniver: Character in the 1942 film *Mrs. Miniver,* a suburban British housewife who loves gardening.   **Scarlett O'Hara:** The strong, pragmatic, survivalist heroine in Margaret Mitchell's 1936 novel *Gone with the Wind.*

MAMA: You expecting company, son?
WALTER: (*Just looking at the door*) Yeah—yeah . . .

(MAMA *looks at* RUTH, *and they exchange innocent and unfrightened glances*)

MAMA: (*Not understanding*) Well, let them in, son.
BENEATHA: (*From her room*) We need some more string.
MAMA: Travis—you run to the hardware and get me some string cord.

(MAMA *goes out and* WALTER *turns and looks at* RUTH, TRAVIS *goes to a dish for money*)

RUTH: Why don't you answer the door, man?
WALTER: (*Suddenly bounding across the floor to embrace her*) 'Cause sometimes it
    hard to let the future begin! (*Stooping down in her face*)

    I got wings! You got wings!
    All God's children got wings!

(*He crosses to the door and throws it open. Standing there is a very slight little man
in a not too prosperous business suit and with haunted frightened eyes and a hat
pulled down tightly, brim up, around his forehead.* TRAVIS *passes between the men
and exits.* WALTER *leans deep in the man's face, still in his jubilance*)

    When I get to heaven gonna put on my wings,
    Gonna fly all over God's heaven . . .

(*The little man just stares at him*)

    Heaven—

    (*Suddenly he stops and looks past the little man into the empty hallway*)
    Where's Willy, man?

BOBO: He ain't with me.
WALTER: (*Not disturbed*) Oh—come on in. You know my wife.
BOBO: (*Dumbly, taking off his hat*) Yes—h'you, Miss Ruth.
RUTH: (*Quietly, a mood apart from her husband already, seeing* BOBO) Hello, Bobo.
WALTER: You right on time today . . . Right on time. That's the way! (*He slaps
    BOBO on his back*) Sit down . . . lemme hear.

(RUTH *stands stiffly and quietly in back of them, as though somehow she senses
death, her eyes fixed on her husband*)

BOBO: (*His frightened eyes on the floor, his hat in his hands*) Could I please get a
    drink of water, before I tell you about it, Walter Lee?

(WALTER *does not take his eyes off the man.* RUTH *goes blindly to the tap and gets a
glass of water and brings it to* BOBO)

WALTER: There ain't nothing wrong, is there?

BOBO: Lemme tell you—

WALTER: Man—didn't nothing go wrong?

BOBO: Lemme tell you—Walter Lee. (*Looking at* RUTH *and talking to her more than to* WALTER) You know how it was. I got to tell you how it was. I mean first I got to tell you how it was all the way . . . I mean about the money I put in, Walter Lee . . .

WALTER: (*With taut agitation now*) What about the money you put in?

BOBO: Well—it wasn't much as we told you—me and Willy—(*He stops*) I'm sorry, Walter. I got a bad feeling about it. I got a real bad feeling about it . . .

WALTER: Man, what you telling me about all this for? . . . Tell me what happened in Springfield . . .

BOBO: Springfield.

RUTH: (*Like a dead woman*) What was supposed to happen in Springfield?

BOBO: (*To her*) This deal that me and Walter went into with Willy—Me and Willy was going to go down to Springfield and spread some money 'round so's we wouldn't have to wait so long for the liquor license . . . That's what we were going to do. Everybody said that was the way you had to do, you understand, Miss Ruth?

WALTER: Man—what happened down there?

BOBO: (*A pitiful man, near tears*) I'm trying to tell you, Walter.

WALTER: (*Screaming at him suddenly*) THEN TELL ME, GODDAMMIT . . . WHAT'S THE MATTER WITH YOU?

BOBO: Man . . . I didn't go to no Springfield, yesterday.

WALTER: (*Halted, life hanging in the moment*) Why not?

BOBO: (*The long way, the hard way to tell*) 'Cause I didn't have no reasons to . . .

WALTER: Man, what are you talking about!

BOBO: I'm talking about the fact that when I got to the train station yesterday morning—eight o'clock like we planned . . . Man—Willy *didn't never show up.*

WALTER: Why . . . where was he . . . where is he?

BOBO: That's what I'm trying to tell you . . . I don't know . . . I waited six hours . . . I called his house . . . and I waited . . . six hours . . . I waited in that train station six hours . . . (*Breaking into tears*) That was all the extra money I had in the world . . . (*Looking up at* WALTER *with the tears running down his face*) Man, *Willy is gone.*

WALTER: Gone, what you mean Willy is gone? Gone where? You mean he went by himself. You mean he went off to Springfield by himself—to take care of getting the license—(*Turns and looks anxiously at* RUTH) You mean maybe he didn't want too many people in on the business down there? (*Looks to* RUTH *again, as before*) You know Willy got his own ways. (*Looks back to* BOBO) Maybe you was late yesterday and he just went on down there without you. Maybe—maybe—he's been callin' you at home tryin' to tell you what happened or something. Maybe—maybe—he just got sick. He's somewhere—he's got to be somewhere. We just got to find him—me and you got to find him. (*Grabs* BOBO *senselessly by the collar and starts to shake him*) We got to!

BOBO: (*In sudden angry, frightened agony*) What's the matter with you, Walter!
    When a cat take off with your money he don't leave you no road maps!
WALTER: (*Turning madly, as though he is looking for* WILLY *in the very room*)
    Willy! . . . Willy . . . don't do it . . . Please don't do it . . . Man, not with that
    money . . . Man, please, not with that money . . . Oh, God . . . Don't let it
    be true . . . (*He is wandering around, crying out for* WILLY *and looking for him
    or perhaps for help from God*) Man . . . I trusted you . . . Man, I put my life
    in your hands . . . (*He starts to crumple down on the floor as* RUTH *just covers
    her face in horror.* MAMA *opens the door and comes into the room, with* BENEATHA
    behind her) Man . . . (*He starts to pound the floor with his fists, sobbing
    wildly*) THAT MONEY IS MADE OUT OF MY FATHER'S FLESH—
BOBO: (*Standing over him helplessly*) I'm sorry, Walter . . . (*Only* WALTER'S *sobs
    reply,* BOBO *puts on his hat*) I had my life staked on this deal, too . . .

(*He exits*)

MAMA: (*To* WALTER) Son—(*She goes to him, bends down to him, talks to his bent
    head*) Son . . . Is it gone? Son, I gave you sixty-five hundred dollars. Is it
    gone? All of it? Beneatha's money too?
WALTER: (*Lifting his head slowly*) Mama . . . I never . . . went to the bank at all . . .
MAMA: (*Not wanting to believe him*) You mean . . . your sister's school
    money . . . you used that too . . . Walter? . . .
WALTER: Yessss! All of it . . . It's all gone . . .

(*There is total silence.* RUTH *stands with her face covered with her hands;* BENEATHA *leans
forlornly against a wall, fingering a piece of red ribbon from the mother's gift.* MAMA
*stops and looks at her son without recognition and then, quite without thinking about
it, starts to beat him senselessly in the face.* BENEATHA *goes to them and stops it*)

BENEATHA: Mama!

(MAMA *stops and looks at both of her children and rises slowly and wanders vaguely,
aimlessly away from them*)

MAMA: I seen . . . him . . . night after night . . . come in . . . and look at that
    rug . . . and then look at me . . . the red showing in his eyes . . . the veins
    moving in his head . . . I seen him grow thin and old before he was
    forty . . . working and working and working like somebody's old
    horse . . . killing himself . . . and you—you give it all away in a day—(*She
    raises her arms to strike him again*)
BENEATHA: Mama—
MAMA: Oh, God . . . (*She looks up to Him*) Look down here—and show me the
    strength.
BENEATHA: Mama—
MAMA: (*Folding over*) Strength . . .
BENEATHA: (*Plaintively*) Mama . . .
MAMA: Strength!

Curtain

ACT III

An hour later.

   At curtain, there is a sullen light of gloom in the living room, gray light not unlike that which began the first scene of Act One. At left we can see WALTER *within his room, alone with himself. He is stretched out on the bed, his shirt out and open, his arms under his head. He does not smoke, he does not cry out, he merely lies there, looking up at the ceiling, much as if he were alone in the world.*

   In the living room BENEATHA *sits at the table, still surrounded by the now almost ominous packing crates. She sits looking off. We feel that this is a mood struck perhaps an hour before, and it lingers now, full of the empty sound of profound disappointment. We see on a line from her brother's bedroom the sameness of their attitudes. Presently the bell rings and* BENEATHA *rises without ambition or interest in answering. It is* ASAGAI, *smiling broadly, striding into the room with energy and happy expectation and conversation.*

ASAGAI: I came over . . . I had some free time. I thought I might help with the packing. Ah, I like the look of packing crates! A household in preparation for a journey! It depresses some people . . . but for me . . . it is another feeling. Something full of the flow of life, do you understand? Movement, progress . . . It makes me think of Africa.

BENEATHA: Africa!

ASAGAI: What kind of a mood is this? Have I told you how deeply you move me?

BENEATHA: He gave away the money, Asagai . . .

ASAGAI: Who gave away what money?

BENEATHA: The insurance money. My brother gave it away.

ASAGAI: Gave it away?

BENEATHA: He made an investment! With a man even Travis wouldn't have trusted with his most worn-out marbles.

ASAGAI: And it's gone?

BENEATHA: Gone!

ASAGAI: I'm very sorry . . . And you, now?

BENEATHA: Me? . . . Me? . . . Me, I'm nothing . . . Me. When I was very small . . . we used to take our sleds out in the wintertime and the only hills we had were the ice-covered stone steps of some houses down the street. And we used to fill them in with snow and make them smooth and slide down them all day . . . and it was very dangerous, you know . . . far too steep . . . and sure enough one day a kid named Rufus came down too fast and hit the sidewalk and we saw his face just split open right there in front of us . . . And I remember standing there looking at his bloody open face thinking that was the end of Rufus. But the ambulance came and they took him to the hospital and they fixed the broken bones and they sewed it all up . . . and the next time I saw Rufus he just had a little line down the middle of his face . . . I never got over that . . .

ASAGAI: What?

BENEATHA: That that was what one person could do for another, fix him up — sew up the problem, make him all right again. That was the most marvelous thing in the world . . . I wanted to do that. I always thought it was the one concrete thing in the world that a human being could do. Fix up the sick, you know—and make them whole again. This was truly being God . . .

ASAGAI: You wanted to be God?

BENEATHA: No—I wanted to cure. It used to be so important to me. I wanted to cure. It used to matter. I used to care. I mean about people and how their bodies hurt . . .

ASAGAI: And you've stopped caring?

BENEATHA: Yes—I think so.

ASAGAI: Why?

BENEATHA: (*Bitterly*) Because it doesn't seem deep enough, close enough to what ails mankind! It was a child's way of seeing things—or an idealist's.

ASAGAI: Children see things very well sometimes—and idealists even better.

BENEATHA: I know that's what you think. Because you are still where I left off. You with all your talk and dreams about Africa! You still think you can patch up the world. Cure the Great Sore of Colonialism— (*Loftily, mocking it*) with the Penicillin of Independence—!

ASAGAI: Yes!

BENEATHA: Independence *and then what?* What about all the crooks and thieves and just plain idiots who will come into power and steal and plunder the same as before—only now they will be black and do it in the name of the new Independence—WHAT ABOUT THEM?!

ASAGAI: That will be the problem for another time. First we must get there.

BENEATHA: And where does it end?

ASAGAI: End? Who even spoke of an end? To life? To living?

BENEATHA: An end to misery! To stupidity! Don't you see there isn't any real progress, Asagai, there is only one large circle that we march in, around and around, each of us with our own little picture in front of us—our own little mirage that we think is the future.

ASAGAI: That is the mistake.

BENEATHA: What?

ASAGAI: What you just said about the circle. It isn't a circle—it is simply a long line—as in geometry, you know, one that reaches into infinity. And because we cannot see the end—we also cannot see how it changes. And it is very odd but those who see the changes—who dream, who will not give up—are called idealists . . . and those who see only the circle we call *them* the "realists"!

BENEATHA: Asagai, while I was sleeping in that bed in there, people went out and took the future right out of my hands! And nobody asked me, nobody consulted me—they just went out and changed my life!

ASAGAI: Was it your money?

BENEATHA: What?

ASAGAI: Was it your money he gave away?

BENEATHA: It belonged to all of us.

ASAGAI: But did you earn it? Would you have had it at all if your father had not died?

BENEATHA: No.

ASAGAI: Then isn't there something wrong in a house—in a world—where all dreams, good or bad, must depend on the death of a man? I never thought to see *you* like this, Alaiyo. You! Your brother made a mistake and you are grateful to him so that now you can give up the ailing human race on account of it! You talk about what good is struggle, what good is anything! Where are we all going and why are we bothering!

BENEATHA: AND YOU CANNOT ANSWER IT!

ASAGAI: (*Shouting over her*) I LIVE THE ANSWER! (*Pause*) In my village at home it is the exceptional man who can even read a newspaper . . . or who ever sees a book at all. I will go home and much of what I will have to say will seem strange to the people of my village. But I will teach and work and things will happen, slowly and swiftly. At times it will seem that nothing changes at all . . . and then again the sudden dramatic events which make history leap into the future. And then quiet again. Retrogression even. Guns, murder, revolution. And I even will have moments when I wonder if the quiet was not better than all that death and hatred. But I will look about my village at the illiteracy and disease and ignorance and I will not wonder long. And perhaps . . . perhaps I will be a great man . . . I mean perhaps I will hold on to the substance of truth and find my way always with the right course . . . and perhaps for it I will be butchered in my bed some night by the servants of empire . . .

BENEATHA: *The martyr!*

ASAGAI: (*He smiles*) . . . or perhaps I shall live to be a very old man, respected and esteemed in my new nation . . . And perhaps I shall hold office and this is what I'm trying to tell you, Alaiyo: Perhaps the things I believe now for my country will be wrong and outmoded, and I will not understand and do terrible things to have things my way or merely to keep my power. Don't you see that there will be young men and women—not British soldiers then, but my own black countrymen—to step out of the shadows some evening and slit my then useless throat? Don't you see they have always been there . . . that they always will be. And that such a thing as my own death will be an advance? They who might kill me even . . . actually replenish all that I was.

BENEATHA: Oh, Asagai, I know all that.

ASAGAI: Good! Then stop moaning and groaning and tell me what you plan to do.

BENEATHA: Do?

ASAGAI: I have a bit of a suggestion.

BENEATHA: What?

ASAGAI: (*Rather quietly for him*) That when it is all over—that you come home with me —

BENEATHA: (*Staring at him and crossing away with exasperation*) Oh—Asagai—at this moment you decide to be romantic!

ASAGAI: (*Quickly understanding the misunderstanding*) My dear, young creature of the New World—I do not mean across the city—I mean across the ocean: home—to Africa.

BENEATHA: (*Slowly understanding and turning to him with murmured amazement*)
To Africa?

ASAGAI: Yes! ... (*Smiling and lifting his arms playfully*) Three hundred years later
the African Prince rose up out of the seas and swept the maiden back across
the middle passage over which her ancestors had come —

BENEATHA: (*Unable to play*) To — to Nigeria?

ASAGAI: Nigeria. Home. (*Coming to her with genuine romantic flippancy*) I will
show you our mountains and our stars; and give you cool drinks from
gourds and teach you the old songs and the ways of our people — and, in
time, we will pretend that — (*Very softly*) — you have only been away for a
day. Say that you'll come (*He swings her around and takes her full in his arms
in a kiss which proceeds to passion*)

BENEATHA: (*Pulling away suddenly*) You're getting me all mixed up —

ASAGAI: Why?

BENEATHA: Too many things — too many things have happened today. I must sit
down and think. I don't know what I feel about anything right this minute.

(*She promptly sits down and props her chin on her fist*)

ASAGAI: (*Charmed*) All right, I shall leave you. No — don't get up. (*Touching her,
gently, sweetly*) Just sit awhile and think .. Never be afraid to sit awhile and
think. (*He goes to door and looks at her*) How often I have looked at you and
said, "Ah — so this is what the New World hath finally wrought ..."

(*He exits.* BENEATHA *sits on alone. Presently* WALTER *enters from his room and starts
to rummage through things, feverishly looking for something. She looks up and turns
in her seat*)

BENEATHA: (*Hissingly*) Yes — just look at what the New World hath wrought! ...
Just look! (*She gestures with bitter disgust*) There he is! *Monsieur le petit bourgeois noir*° — himself! There he is — Symbol of a Rising Class! Entrepreneur!
Titan of the system! (WALTER *ignores her completely and continues frantically
and destructively looking for something and hurling things to floor and tearing
things out of their place in his search.* BENEATHA *ignores the eccentricity of his
actions and goes on with the monologue of insult*) Did you dream of yachts on
Lake Michigan, Brother? Did you see yourself on that Great Day sitting
down at the Conference Table, surrounded by all the mighty bald-headed
men in America? All halted, waiting, breathless, waiting for your pronouncements on industry? Waiting for you — Chairman of the Board! (WALTER *finds
what he is looking for — a small piece of white paper — and pushes it in his pocket
and puts on his coat and rushes out without ever having looked at her. She shouts
after him*) I look at you and I see the final triumph of stupidity in the world!

(*The door slams and she returns to just sitting again.* RUTH *comes quickly out of*
MAMA'S *room*)

Monsieur . . . noir: Mr. black middle class (French).

RUTH: Who was that?

BENEATHA: Your husband.

RUTH: Where did he go?

BENEATHA: Who knows—maybe he has an appointment at U.S. Steel.

RUTH: (*Anxiously, with frightened eyes*) You didn't say nothing bad to him, did you?

BENEATHA: Bad? Say anything bad to him? No—I told him he was a sweet boy and full of dreams and everything is strictly peachy keen, as the ofay° kids say!

(MAMA *enters from her bedroom. She is lost, vague, trying to catch hold, to make some sense of her former command of the world, but it still eludes her. A sense of waste overwhelms her gait; a measure of apology rides on her shoulders. She goes to her plant, which has remained on the table, looks at it, picks it up and takes it to the windowsill and sits it outside, and she stands and looks at it a long moment. Then she closes the window, straightens her body with effort and turns around to her children*)

MAMA: Well—ain't it a mess in here, though? (*A false cheerfulness, a beginning of something*) I guess we all better stop moping around and get some work done. All this unpacking and everything we got to do. (RUTH *raises her head slowly in response to the sense of the line; and* BENEATHA *in similar manner turns very slowly to look at her mother*) One of you all better call the moving people and tell 'em not to come.

RUTH: Tell 'em not to come?

MAMA: Of course, baby. Ain't no need in 'em coming all the way here and having to go back. They charges for that too. (*She sits down, fingers to her brow, thinking*) Lord, ever since I was a little girl, I always remembers people saying, "Lena—Lena Eggleston, you aims too high all the time. You needs to slow down and see life a little more like it is. Just slow down some." That's what they always used to say down home—"Lord, that Lena Eggleston is a high-minded thing. She'll get her due one day!"

RUTH: No, Lena . . .

MAMA: Me and Big Walter just didn't never learn right.

RUTH: Lena, no! We gotta go. Bennie—tell her . . . (*She rises and crosses to* BENEATHA *with her arms outstretched.* BENEATHA *doesn't respond*) Tell her we can still move . . . the notes ain't but a hundred and twenty-five a month. We got four grown people in this house—we can work . . .

MAMA: (*To herself*) Just aimed too high all the time—

RUTH: (*Turning and going to* MAMA *fast—the words pouring out with urgency and desperation*) Lena—I'll work . . . I'll work twenty hours a day in all the kitchens in Chicago . . . I'll strap my baby on my back if I have to and scrub all the floors in America and wash all the sheets in America if I have to—but we got to MOVE! We got to get OUT OF HERE!!

(MAMA *reaches out absently and pats* RUTH's *hand*)

MAMA: No—I sees things differently now. Been thinking 'bout some of the things we could do to fix this place up some. I seen a secondhand bureau

---

ofay: White (slang).

over on Maxwell Street just the other day that could fit right there. (*She points to where the new furniture might go.* RUTH *wanders away from her*) Would need some new handles on it and then a little varnish and it look like something brand-new. And—we can put up them new curtains in the kitchen . . . Why this place be looking fine. Cheer us all up so that we forget trouble ever come . . . (To RUTH) And you could get some nice screens to put up in your room 'round the baby's bassinet . . . (*She looks at both of them, pleadingly*) Sometimes you just got to know when to give up some things . . . and hold on to what you got. . . .

(WALTER *enters from the outside, looking spent and leaning against the door, his coat hanging from him*)

MAMA: Where you been, son?

WALTER: (*Breathing hard*) Made a call.

MAMA: To who, son?

WALTER: To The Man. (*He heads for his room*)

MAMA: What man, baby?

WALTER: (*Stops in the door*) The Man, Mama. Don't you know who The Man is?

RUTH: Walter Lee?

WALTER: *The Man*. Like the guys in the streets say—The Man. Captain Boss— Mistuh Charley . . . Old Cap' n Please Mr. Bossman . . .

BENEATHA: (*Suddenly*) Lindner!

WALTER: That's right! That's good. I told him to come right over.

BENEATHA: (*Fiercely, understanding*) For what? What do you want to see him for!

WALTER: (*Looking at his sister*) We going to do business with him.

MAMA: What you talking 'bout, son?

WALTER: Talking 'bout life, Mama. You all always telling me to see life like it is. Well—I laid in there on my back today . . . and I figured it out. Life just like it is. Who gets and who don't get. (*He sits down with his coat on and laughs*) Mama, you know it's all divided up. Life is. Sure enough. Between the takers and the "tooken." (*He laughs*) I've figured it out finally. (*He looks around at them*) Yeah. Some of us always getting "tooken." (*He laughs*) People like Willy Harris, they don't never get "tooken." And you know why the rest of us do? 'Cause we all mixed up. Mixed up bad. We get to looking 'round for the right and the wrong; and we worry about it and cry about it and stay up nights trying to figure out 'bout the wrong and the right of things all the time . . . And all the time, man, them takers is out there operating, just taking and taking. Willy Harris? Shoot—Willy Harris don't even count. He don't even count in the big scheme of things. But I'll say one thing for old Willy Harris . . . he's taught me something. He's taught me to keep my eye on what counts in this world. Yeah—(*Shouting out a little*) Thanks, Willy!

RUTH: What did you call that man for, Walter Lee?

WALTER: Called him to tell him to come on over to the show. Gonna put on a show for the man. Just what he wants to see. You see, Mama, the man came here today and he told us that them people out there where you want us to move—well they so upset they willing to pay us *not* to move! (*He laughs again*) And—and oh, Mama you would of been proud of the way me and Ruth and Bennie acted. We told him to get out . . . Lord have mercy! We told the man to get out! Oh, we was some proud folks this afternoon, yeah. (*He lights a cigarette*) We were still full of that old-time stuff . . .

RUTH: (*Coming toward him slowly*) You talking 'bout taking them people's money to keep us from moving in that house?

WALTER: I ain't just talking 'bout it, baby—I'm telling you that's what's going to happen!

BENEATHA: Oh, God! Where is the bottom! Where is the real honest-to-God bottom so he can't go any farther!

WALTER: See—that's the old stuff. You and that boy that was here today you all want everybody to carry a flag and a spear and sing some marching songs, huh? You wanna spend your life looking into things and trying to find the right and the wrong part, huh? Yeah. You know what's going to happen to that boy someday—he'll find himself sitting in a dungeon, locked in forever—and the takers will have the key! Forget it, baby! There ain't no causes—there ain't nothing but taking in this world, and he who takes most is smartest—and it don't make a damn bit of difference *how*.

MAMA: You making something inside me cry, son. Some awful pain inside me.

WALTER: Don't cry, Mama. Understand. That white man is going to walk in that door able to write checks for more money than we ever had. It's important to him and I'm going to help him . . . I'm going to put on the show, Mama.

MAMA: Son—I come from five generations of people who was slaves and share-croppers—but ain't nobody in my family never let nobody pay 'em no money that was a way of telling us we wasn't fit to walk the earth. We ain't never been that poor. (*Raising her eyes and looking at him*) We ain't never been that—dead inside.

BENEATHA: Well—we are dead now. All the talk about dreams and sunlight that goes on in this house. It's all dead now.

WALTER: What's the matter with you all! I didn't make this world! It was give to me this way! Hell, yes, I want me some yachts someday! Yes, I want to hang some real pearls 'round my wife's neck. Ain't she supposed to wear no pearls? Somebody tell me—tell me, who decides which women is suppose to wear pearls in this world. I tell you I am a *man*—and I think my wife should wear some pearls in this world!

(*This last line hangs a good while and* WALTER *begins to move about the room. The word "Man" has penetrated his consciousness; he mumbles it to himself repeatedly between strange agitated pauses as he moves about*)

MAMA: Baby, how you going to feel on the inside?

WALTER: Fine! . . . Going to feel fine . . . a man . . .

MAMA: You won't have nothing left then, Walter Lee.

WALTER: (*Coming to her*) I'm going to feel fine, Mama. I'm going to look that son-of-a-bitch in the eyes and say—(*He falters*)—and say, "All right, Mr.

Lindner—(*He falters even more*)—that's *your* neighborhood out there! You got the right to keep it like you want! You got the right to have it like you want! Just write the check and—the house is yours." And—and I am going to say—(*His voice almost breaks*) "And you—you people just put the money in my hand and you won't have to live next to this bunch of stinking niggers! . . ." (*He straightens up and moves away from his mother, walking around the room*) And maybe—maybe I'll just get down on my black knees . . . (*He does so;* RUTH *and* BENNIE *and* MAMA *watch him in frozen horror*) "Captain, Mistuh, Bossman—(*Groveling and grinning and wringing his hands in profoundly anguished imitation of the slow-witted movie stereotype*) A-hee-hee-hee! Oh, yassuh boss! Yasssssuh! Great white—(*Voice breaking, he forces himself to go on*)—Father, just gi' ussen de money, fo' God's sake, and we's—we's ain't gwine come out deh and dirty up yo' white folks neighborhood . . . (*He breaks down completely*) And I'll feel fine! Fine! FINE! (*He gets up and goes into the bedroom*)

BENEATHA: That is not a man. That is nothing but a toothless rat.

MAMA: Yes—death done come in this here house. (*She is nodding, slowly, reflectively*) Done come walking in my house on the lips of my children. You what supposed to be my beginning again. You—what supposed to be my harvest. (*To* BENEATHA) You—you mourning your brother?

BENEATHA: He's no brother of mine.

MAMA: What you say?

BENEATHA: I said that that individual in that room is no brother of mine.

MAMA: That's what I thought you said. You feeling like you better than he is today? (BENEATHA *does not answer*) Yes? What you tell him a minute ago? That he wasn't a man? Yes? You give him up for me? You done wrote his epitaph too—like the rest of the world? Well, who give you the privilege?

BENEATHA: Be on my side for once! You saw what he just did, Mama! You saw him—down on his knees. Wasn't it you who taught me to despise any man who would do that? Do what he's going to do?

MAMA: Yes—I taught you that. Me and your daddy. But I thought I taught you something else too . . . I thought I taught you to love him.

BENEATHA: Love him? There is nothing left to love.

MAMA: There is *always* something left to love. And if you ain't learned that, you ain't learned nothing. (*Looking at her*) Have you cried for that boy today? I don't mean for yourself and for the family 'cause we lost the money. I mean for him: what he been through and what it done to him. Child, when do you think is the time to love somebody the most? When they done good and made things easy for everybody? Well then, you ain't through learning—because that ain't the time at all. It's when he's at his lowest and can't believe in hisself 'cause the world done whipped him so! When you starts measuring somebody, measure him right, child, measure him right. Make sure you done taken into account what hills and valleys he come through before he got to wherever he is.

(TRAVIS *bursts into the room at the end of the speech, leaving the door open*)

TRAVIS: Grandmama—the moving men are downstairs! The truck just pulled up.
MAMA: (*Turning and looking at him*) Are they, baby? They downstairs?

(*She sighs and sits.* LINDNER *appears in the doorway. He peers in and knocks lightly, to gain attention, and comes in. All turn to look at him*)

LINDNER: (*Hat and briefcase in hand*) Uh—hello . . .

(RUTH *crosses mechanically to the bedroom door and opens it and lets it swing open freely and slowly as the lights come up on* WALTER *within, still in his coat, sitting at the far corner of the room. He looks up and out through the room to* LINDNER)

RUTH: He's here.

(*A long minute passes and* WALTER *slowly gets up*)

LINDNER: (*Coming to the table with efficiency, putting his briefcase on the table and starting to unfold papers and unscrew fountain pens*) Well, I certainly was glad to hear from you people. (WALTER *has begun the trek out of the room, slowly and awkwardly, rather like a small boy, passing the back of his sleeve across his mouth from time to time*) Life can really be so much simpler than people let it be most of the time. Well—with whom do I negotiate? You, Mrs. Younger, or your son here? (MAMA *sits with her hands folded on her lap and her eyes closed as* WALTER *advances.* TRAVIS *goes closer to* LINDNER *and looks at the papers curiously*) Just some official papers, sonny.
RUTH: Travis, you go downstairs—
MAMA: (*Opening her eyes and looking into* WALTER'S) No. Travis, you stay right here. And you make him understand what you doing, Walter Lee. You teach him good. Like Willy Harris taught you. You show where our five generations done come to. (WALTER *looks from her to the boy, who grins at him innocently*) Go ahead, son—(*She folds her hands and closes her eyes*) Go ahead.
WALTER: (*At last crosses to* LINDNER, *who is reviewing the contract*) Well, Mr. Lindner. (BENEATHA *turns away*) We called you—(*There is a profound, simple groping quality in his speech*)—because, well, me and my family (*He looks around and shifts from one foot to the other*) Well—we are very plain people . . .
LINDNER: Yes—
WALTER: I mean—I have worked as a chauffeur most of my life—and my wife here, she does domestic work in people's kitchens. So does my mother. I mean—we are plain people . . .
LINDNER: Yes, Mr. Younger—
WALTER: (*Really like a small boy, looking down at his shoes and then up at the man*) And—uh—well, my father, well, he was a laborer most of his life. . . .
LINDNER: (*Absolutely confused*) Uh, yes—yes, I understand. (*He turns back to the contract*)
WALTER: (*A beat; staring at him*) And my father—(*With sudden intensity*) My father almost *beat a man to death* once because this man called him a bad name or something, you know what I mean?

LINDNER: (*Looking up, frozen*) No, no, I'm afraid I don't—

WALTER: (*A beat. The tension hangs; then* WALTER *steps back from it*) Yeah. Well—what I mean is that we come from people who had a lot of *pride*. I mean—we are very proud people. And that's my sister over there and she's going to be a doctor—and we are very proud—

LINDNER: Well—I am sure that is very nice, but—

WALTER: What I am telling you is that we called you over here to tell you that we are very proud and that this—(*Signaling to* TRAVIS) Travis, come here. (TRAVIS *crosses and* WALTER *draws him before him facing the man*) This is my son, and he makes the sixth generation our family in this country. And we have all thought about your offer—

LINDNER: Well, good . . . good—

WALTER: And we have decided to move into our house because my father—my father—he earned it for us brick by brick. (MAMA *has her eyes closed and is rocking back and forth as though she were in church, with her head nodding the Amen yes*) We don't want to make no trouble for nobody or fight no causes, and we will try to be good neighbors. And that's *all* we got to say about that. (*He looks the man absolutely in the eyes*) We don't want your money. (*He turns and walks away*)

LINDNER: (*Looking around at all of them*) I take it then—that you have decided to occupy . . .

BENEATHA: That's what the man said.

LINDNER: (*To* MAMA *in her reverie*) Then I would like to appeal to you, Mrs. Younger. You are older and wiser and understand things better I am sure . . .

MAMA: I am afraid you don't understand. My son said we was going to move and there ain't nothing left for me to say. (*Briskly*) You know how these young folks is nowadays, mister. Can't do a thing with 'em! (*As he opens his mouth, she rises*) Good-bye.

LINDNER: (*Folding up his materials*) Well—if you are that final about it . . . there is nothing left for me to say. (*He finishes, almost ignored by the family, who are concentrating on* WALTER LEE. *At the door* LINDNER *halts and looks around*) I sure hope you people know what you're getting into.

(*He shakes his head and exits*)

RUTH: (*Looking around and coming to life*) Well, for God's sake—if the moving men are here—LET'S GET THE HELL OUT OF HERE!

MAMA: (*Into action*) Ain't it the truth! Look at all this here mess. Ruth, put Travis's good jacket on him . . . Walter Lee, fix your tie and tuck your shirt in, you look like somebody's hoodlum! Lord have mercy, where is my plant? (*She flies to get it amid the general bustling of the family, who are deliberately trying to ignore the nobility of the past moment*) You all start on down . . . Travis child, don't go empty-handed . . . Ruth, where did I put that box with my skillets in it? I want to be in charge of it myself . . . I'm going to make us the biggest dinner we ever ate tonight . . . Beneatha, what's the matter with them stockings? Pull them things up, girl . . .

(*The family starts to file out as two moving men appear and begin to carry out the heavier pieces of furniture, bumping into the family as they move about*)

BENEATHA: Mama, Asagai asked me to marry him today and go to Africa —

MAMA: (*In the middle of her getting-ready activity*) He did? You ain't old enough to marry nobody — (*Seeing the moving men lifting one of her chairs precariously*) Darling, that ain't no bale of cotton, please handle it so we can sit in it again! I had that chair twenty-five years . . .

(*The movers sigh with exasperation and go on with their work*)

BENEATHA: (*Girlishly and unreasonably trying to pursue the conversation*) To go to Africa, Mama — be a doctor in Africa . . .

MAMA: (*Distracted*) Yes, baby —

WALTER: *Africa!* What he want you to go to Africa for?

BENEATHA: To practice there . . .

WALTER: Girl, if you don't get all them silly ideas out your head! You better marry yourself a man with some loot . . .

BENEATHA: (*Angrily, precisely as in the first scene of the play*) What have you got to do with who I marry!

WALTER: Plenty. Now I think George Murchison —

BENEATHA: *George Murchison!* I wouldn't marry him if he was Adam and I was Eve!

(WALTER *and* BENEATHA *go out yelling at each other vigorously and the anger is loud and real till their voices diminish.* RUTH *stands at the door and turns to* MAMA *and smiles knowingly*)

MAMA: (*Fixing her hat at last*) Yeah — they something all right, my children . . .

RUTH: Yeah — they're something. Let's go, Lena.

MAMA: (*Stalling, starting to look around at the house*) Yes — I'm coming. Ruth —

RUTH: Yes?

MAMA: (*Quietly, woman to woman*) He finally come into his manhood today, didn't he? Kind of like a rainbow after the rain . . .

RUTH: (*Biting her lip lest her own pride explode in front of* MAMA) Yes, Lena.

(WALTER's *voice calls for them raucously*)

WALTER: (*Off stage*) Y'all come on! These people charges by the hour, you know!

MAMA: (*Waving* RUTH *out vaguely*) All right, honey — go on down. I be down directly.

(RUTH *hesitates, then exits.* MAMA *stands, at last alone in the living room, her plant on the table before her as the lights start to come down. She looks around at all the walls and ceilings and suddenly, despite herself, while the children call below, a great heaving thing rises in her and she puts her fist to her mouth to stifle it, takes a final desperate look, pulls her coat about her, pats her hat and goes out. The lights dim down. The door opens and she comes back in, grabs her plant, and goes out for the last time*)

Curtain

Biographical Sketches

This section offers brief biographical sketches of the 235 known authors of the works included in this book. For fuller biographical information, the most convenient print sources are the *Dictionary of Literary Biography* (Detroit: Gale, 1978–), currently at 360 volumes, and *Contemporary Authors*, also published by Gale (original series, 248 volumes; new revised series, currently 312 volumes). Both are available online in many libraries.

Biographical information for many authors is also found on the Internet. The Academy of American Poets Web site is valuable and convenient for information about poets; we are indebted to it for many of our entries. *Voices from the Gaps: Women Writers of Color* also is very helpful. Sites for many individual authors are available as well, as are personal home pages for some contemporary poets and sites maintained by scholars or fans of writers old and new. To emphasize how writers work with each other and are influenced by other writers, when the names of authors represented in this anthology appear within a biographical entry, they are in small capital letters, as a reminder that those biographical notes will shed further light on the author at hand.

The Web site, bedfordstmartins.com/rewritinglit, provides access to LitLinks, which offers brief biographies of all of the writers in this book, with links to important related sites. After each biographical entry, we've included cross-references to this resource. It's a good place to start when researching individual authors.

AI (1947–2010), who described herself as "one-half Japanese, one-eighth Choctaw, one-fourth black, and one-sixteenth Irish," was born Florence Anthony in Albany, Texas, and grew up in Tucson, Arizona. She legally changed her name to *Ai*, which means "love" in Japanese. She received a B.A. in Japanese from the University of Arizona and an M.F.A. from the University of California at Irvine. She is the author of nine volumes of poetry, among them *Vice* (1999), which won the National Book Award for Poetry. Her last book was *No Surrender* (2010). She taught at Wayne State University, George Mason University, the University of Kentucky, and Oklahoma State University.

WEB: Further research this author with LitLinks at bedfordstmartins.com/rewritinglit.

WOODY ALLEN (b. 1935) was born and grew up in Brooklyn, New York. He attended New York University and City College of New York, but did not graduate. He began his writing career by writing jokes for New York newspapers and television talk shows. After becoming a popular stand-up comic in the 1960s, he turned to plays and movies. His first significant success was *What's New Pussycat* (1965), in which he played a small role. He began directing films he wrote, as well as acting in them. He won a best picture Oscar for *Annie Hall* (1977), and since then he has been considered a major figure in the American film industry. From 1978 to 2009 he directed at least one movie a year, except for 1981, including serious films such as *Crimes and Misdemeanors* (1989) and *Husbands and Wives* (1992), and lighthearted comedies such as *Zelig* (1983) and *Bullets over Broadway* (1994). His recent films include *Small Time Crooks* (2000), *Anything Else* (2002), *Match Point* (2005), and *Vicky Cristina Barcelona* (2008). He is an accomplished jazz clarinetist, a hobby featured in his 1998 documentary *Wild Man Blues*.

SHERMAN ALEXIE (b. 1966) — See page 278.

AGHA SHAHID ALI (1949–2001) was born in New Delhi and grew up Muslim in Kashmir. He was educated at the University of Kashmir, Srinagar, and at the University of Delhi. He earned a Ph.D. from Pennsylvania State University in 1984 and an M.F.A. from the University of Arizona in 1985. He was a poet (author of eight books of poetry), critic (author of *T. S. Eliot as Editor* [1986]), translator (*The Rebel's Silhouette: Selected Poems* by Faiz Ahmed Faiz, 1992), and editor (*Ravishing Disunities: Real Ghazals in English*, 2000). He held teaching positions at the University of Delhi and at several colleges and universities in the United States. "I Dream It Is Afternoon When I Return to Delhi" (p. 762) shows Ali's use of Western formal cultural principles in work that focuses on his own cultural background.

WEB: Further research this author with LitLinks at bedfordstmartins.com/rewritinglit.

ISABEL ALLENDE (b. 1942) was born in Lima, Peru. After the divorce of her mother and father (a Chilean diplomat), she lived with her maternal grandparents in Santiago, Chile, then in Bolivia, the Middle East, and Europe with her mother and stepfather, also a diplomat. She worked for the United Nations Food and Agricultural Organization in Santiago and then embarked on a promising career as a journalist for *Paula* magazine and on television and in movie newsreels. That career ended with the overthrow and assassination in 1973 of her uncle, Salvador Allende, president of Chile, when she, her husband, and her children had to flee to Venezuela for safety.

While in exile, she began to write her first novel, *The House of the Spirits* (1982), which traces personal and political conflicts in several generations of an imaginary family in a Latin American country and is based on memories of her own family and the political upheaval in Chile. She has since published many books, including novels, memoirs, and a collection of short stories — the most recent is a novel, *The Island Beneath the Sea* (2010). Her work is known for focusing on the experience (especially the struggles) of women and for its use of the "magic realism" often found in Latin American literature.

WEB: Further research this author with LitLinks at bedfordstmartins.com/rewritinglit.

JULIA ALVAREZ (b. 1950) was born in New York City, lived in the Dominican Republic until she was ten, and returned to New York when her father had to flee because he was involved in a plot to overthrow the dictator, Rafael Trujillo. Thus she needed to adjust to a new culture and a new language. Since childhood she says she loved stories — hearing them and telling them — so it was natural for her to decide she wanted to be a writer. She graduated from Middlebury College in Vermont and earned an M.A. in creative writing from Syracuse University. Since 1998 she has been writer-in-residence at Middlebury. Alvarez has published seven novels, many short stories, numerous books for children and young readers, three volumes of poetry, two nonfiction books, and a book of essays about herself and her writing life, *Something to Declare* (1998).

WEB: Further research this author with LitLinks at bedfordstmartins.com/rewritinglit.

MARGARET ATWOOD (b. 1939) was born in Ottawa and grew up in northern Ontario, in Quebec, and in Toronto. She began writing while attending high school in Toronto. She received her undergraduate degree from Victoria College at the University of Toronto and her master's degree from Radcliffe College. She won the E. J. Pratt Medal for her privately printed book of poems, *Double Persephone* (1961), and has published sixteen more collections of poetry. She is perhaps best known for her thirteen novels, which include *The*

Handmaid's Tale (1983), *The Robber Bride* (1994), and *The Blind Assassin* (2000—winner of the Booker Prize). She has also published seven collections of short stories, seven children's books, and nine books of nonfiction and edited several anthologies. Her work has been translated into more than thirty languages, including Farsi, Japanese, Turkish, Finnish, Korean, Icelandic, and Estonian.

WEB: Further research this author with LitLinks at bedfordstmartins.com/rewritinglit.

W.[YSTAN] H.[UGH] AUDEN (1907–1973) was born in York, England. He went to private school and then to Oxford University, where he began to write poetry. He supported himself by teaching and publishing and wrote books based on his travels to Iceland, Spain, and China. He also wrote (with Chester Kallman) several librettos, including one for Igor Stravinsky's *The Rake's Progress* (1951). He lived in the United States from 1939 until his death and became a U.S. citizen in 1946. His work combines lively intelligence, quick wit, and immense craftsmanship, and often focuses on social concerns.

WEB: Further research this author with LitLinks at bedfordstmartins.com/rewritinglit.

JIMMY SANTIAGO BACA (b. 1952) was born in Sante Fe, New Mexico, of Chicano and Apache heritage. Abandoned by his parents at the age of two, he lived with one of his grandparents for several years before being placed in an orphanage. He lived on the streets as a youth and was imprisoned for six years for drug possession. In prison, he taught himself to read and write, and began to compose poetry. A fellow inmate convinced him to submit some of his poems for publication. He has since published a dozen books of poetry, a memoir, a collection of stories and essays, a play, and a screenplay, with a novel forthcoming. He lives outside Albuquerque in a one-hundred-year-old adobe house.

WEB: Further research this author with LitLinks at bedfordstmartins.com/rewritinglit.

JAMES BALDWIN (1924–1987) was born in Harlem to an unmarried domestic worker. When Baldwin was three, his mother married a factory worker and storefront preacher who was a hard, cruel man. At age fourteen, Baldwin began preaching at the small Fireside Pentecostal Church in Harlem, and the cadences of black preaching continued to influence his writing style later in his life. His first story appeared in a church newspaper when he was about twelve. He left home at seventeen and lived in Greenwich Village, where he met Richard Wright, who encouraged him to continue his writing and helped him win a Eugene Saxton Fellowship. Strained relations with his stepfather, problems over sexual identity, the suicide of a friend, and racial oppression in the United States led Baldwin to move to France when he was nineteen, though he returned to the United States frequently to lecture and teach, and from 1957 on spent half of each year in New York City. His first novel, the partially autobiographical *Go Tell It on the Mountain*, was published in 1953. His second novel, *Giovanni's Room* (1956), dealt with a white American expatriate who must come to terms with his homosexuality, and *Another Country* (1962) explored racial and gay sexual tensions among New York intellectuals. He published several more novels, plays, and essay collections, including *Nobody Knows My Name* (1961) and *The Fire Next Time* (1963).

WEB: Further research this author with LitLinks at bedfordstmartins.com/rewritinglit.

TONI CADE BAMBARA (1939–1995) was born in New York City and grew up in Harlem and Bedford-Stuyvesant. She began writing stories when she was a child and continued writing and taking writing courses in high school and at Queens College, where she majored in Theater Arts and English. Bambara completed her master's degree in American literature while serving as program director at Colony Settlement House in Brooklyn; she then began teaching at City College of New York. She first became known for editing a groundbreaking collection of African American women's writing, *The Black Woman: An Anthology* (1970). She went on to publish four collections of stories, two novels, many screenplays, and a book for children. In addition to being an important figure among the group of African American writers who emerged in the 1960s, Bambara was an activist in the civil rights and women's movements.

WEB: Further research this author with LitLinks at bedfordstmartins.com/rewritinglit.

JIM BARNES (b. 1933), born in Oklahoma of Choctaw and Welsh heritage, worked for ten years as a lumberjack. He studied at Southeastern Oklahoma State University and received his M.A. and Ph.D. from the University of Arkansas. He has published many books of poetry, most recently *Visiting Picasso* (2007); several books of translations and criticism; and over 500 poems in more than 100 journals, including *Chicago Review, American Scholar, Prairie Schooner,* and *Georgia Review.* He is the founding editor of the Chariton Review Press and editor of *Chariton Review.* He taught at Truman State University from 1970 to 2003, then at Brigham Young University, and presently lives in Santa Fe.

WEB: Further research this author with LitLinks at bedfordstmartins.com/rewritinglit.

LYNDA BARRY (b. 1956) is a critically acclaimed American cartoonist, perhaps best known for her weekly comic *Ernie Pook's Comeek.* She has published many collections of graphic stories — including *The Freddie Stories* (1999), *The Greatest of Marlys* (2000), and *One Hundred Demons!* (2002) — and three graphic novels, *The Good Times Are Killing Me: A Novel* (1988), which was made into a musical play; *Cruddy: An Illustrated Novel* (2000); and *What It Is,* which won the 2009 Eisner Award for Best Reality-Based Work. She was born in Wisconsin and grew up in Seattle. She now lives near Footville, Wisconsin.

ANN BEATTIE (b. 1947) was born in Washington, D.C., and grew up in Chevy Chase, Maryland. She holds an undergraduate degree from American University and a master's degree from the University of Connecticut. In 1976, she published her first collection of short stories, *Distortions,* and her first novel, *Chilly Scenes of Winter,* which was later made into a film. She went on to publish eight more collections of stories — most recently *Follies: New Stories* (2005) and *The New Yorker Stories* (2010) — and seven more novels, including the recent *Walks with Men* (2010). She has taught at Harvard College, the University of Connecticut, and the University of Virginia, where she holds the Edgar Allan Poe Chair in the Department of English and Creative Writing. In 2005, she and her husband, the painter Lincoln Perry, collaborated on a published retrospective of Perry's paintings. She has received an award for excellence from the American Academy and Institute of Arts and Letters and a PEN/Bernard Malamud Award for excellence in the short story.

WENDELL BERRY (b. 1934) was born in Henry County, Kentucky, the first of four children of Virginia and John Berry, a lawyer and tobacco farmer. He attended Millersburg Military Institute, earned his B.A. and M.A. from the University of Kentucky, and was a Wallace Stegner Fellow at Stanford University. A prolific author of poetry, essays, short stories, and novels, he is also recognized for his academic, cultural, environmental, and economic criticism. His ancestors have farmed in Henry County for five generations, and since 1965 he has farmed a 125-acre homestead, Lane's Landing. His literary works focus on the life that he deeply values, one that includes sustainable agriculture, community, a connection to place, local economics, good work, and the interconnectedness of all life. He is a fellow at Britain's Temenos Academy, which is devoted to studying all faiths and spiritual paths.

ELIZABETH BISHOP (1911–1979), born in Worcester, Massachusetts, was raised in Nova Scotia by her grandparents after her father died and her mother was committed to an asylum. She attended Vassar College, intending to study medicine, but was encouraged by MARIANNE MOORE to be a poet. From 1935 to 1937 she traveled in France, Spain, northern Africa, Ireland, and Italy and then settled in Key West, Florida, for four years, after which she lived in Rio de Janeiro for almost twenty years. She wrote slowly and carefully and produced a small body of poetry (totaling only around one hundred poems), technically sophisticated, formally varied, witty and thoughtful, revealing in precise, true-to-life images her impressions of the physical world. She served as Consultant in Poetry at the Library of Congress from 1949 to 1950.

WEB: Further research this author with LitLinks at bedfordstmartins.com/rewritinglit.

The first appointment of a Consultant in Poetry at the Library of Congress was made in 1937. The title was changed to Poet Laureate Consultant in Poetry in 1986. Appointments are made for one year, beginning in September, and sometimes have been renewed for a second year.

WILLIAM BLAKE (1757–1827) was born and lived in London. His only formal schooling was in art—he studied for a year at the Royal Academy and was apprenticed to an engraver. He worked as a professional engraver, doing commissions and illustrations, assisted by his wife, Catherine Boucher. Blake started writing poetry at the age of eleven and later engraved and hand-printed his own poems, in very small batches, with his own hand-colored illustrations. His early work showed a strong social conscience, and his later work turned increasingly mythic and prophetic.

WEB: Further research this author with LitLinks at bedfordstmartins.com/rewritinglit.

PETER BLUE CLOUD (b. 1935), born in Quebec, is a Turtle Mohawk and former ironworker. In addition to editing such publications as the *Alcatraz Newsletter*, *Akwesasne Notes*, and *Coyote's Journal*, he has published several volumes of poetry, including *White Corn Sister* (1979) and *Clans of Many Nations: Selected Poems, 1969–1994* (1995). His visionary poems often draw on native storytelling traditions, native dance structures, and native chant and drumming. One can experience in his poems the influence of these as well as the impact of industrial values on native ways of life.

EAVAN BOLAND (b. 1944) was born in Dublin and was educated there and in London and New York. She has taught at Trinity College and University College, Bowdoin College, and the University of Iowa. She is currently the Bella Mabury and Eloise Mabury Knapp Professor in Humanities and the Melvin and Bill Lane Professor for the Director of the Creative Writing Program at Stanford University. An influential figure in Irish poetry, Boland has published a dozen volumes of poetry, including *The Journey and Other Poems* (1987), *Night Feed* (1994), *The Lost Land* (1998), *Code* (2001), *New Collected Poems* (2005), and *Domestic Violence* (2007), and has edited several other books including *Three Irish Poets: An Anthology* (2003) and *Irish Writers on Writing* (2007). Her poems and essays have appeared in magazines such as the *New Yorker*, *Atlantic*, *Kenyon Review*, and *American Poetry Review*. A collection of essays, *A Journey with Two Maps: Becoming a Woman Poet*, was published in 2011. She is a regular reviewer for the *Irish Times*.

WEB: Further research this author with LitLinks at bedfordstmartins.com/rewritinglit.

ANNE BRADSTREET (c. 1612–1672), born in Northampton, England, was educated by tutors, reading chiefly in religious writings and the Bible. In 1628, she married Simon Bradstreet, a brilliant young Puritan educated at Cambridge. They were among the earliest settlers of the Massachusetts Bay Colony, in 1630, and her father and husband were leading figures in its governance. She wrote regularly in both prose and verse throughout her busy and difficult years in Massachusetts.

WEB: Further research this author with LitLinks at bedfordstmartins.com/rewritinglit.

GWENDOLYN BROOKS (1917–2000), born in Topeka, Kansas, was raised in Chicago and wrote her first poems at age seven. She began studying poetry at the Southside Community Art Center. Her second collection of poems, *Annie Allen* (1949), earned the first Pulitzer Prize given to an African American poet. She served as Consultant in Poetry at the Library of Congress from 1985 to 1986 and worked in community programs and poetry workshops in Chicago to encourage young African American writers.

WEB: Further research this author with LitLinks at bedfordstmartins.com/rewritinglit.

OLGA BROUMAS (b. 1949) was born in Hermoupolis, Greece, and immigrated to the United States in 1967. She studied at the University of Pennsylvania and the University of Oregon and has taught at the University of

Oregon, the University of Idaho, and Boston University. She currently is Poet-in-Residence and Director of Creative Writing at Brandeis University. Her first collection of poems, *Beginning with O* (1977), was selected by Stanley Kunitz for the Yale Younger Poets Series, making her the first nonnative speaker of English to receive the award. She spends her summers in Provincetown, Massachusetts, where she founded and teaches at the Freehand Women Writers and Photographers Community.

STERLING A. BROWN (1901–1989) was born in Washington, D.C., and educated at Dunbar High School, Williams College, and Harvard University. He taught for more than fifty years at Howard University. Like many other black poets of the period, he expressed his concerns about race in America. His first book of poems, *Southern Road* (1932), was well received by critics, and Brown became part of the artistic tradition of the Harlem Renaissance. Brown was deeply interested in African American music and dialect. He became one of the great innovators in developing poetry related to jazz. His work is known for its frank, unsentimental portraits of black people and their experiences and its successful incorporation of African American folklore and contemporary idiom.

WEB: Further research this author with LitLinks at bedfordstmartins.com/rewritinglit.

ELIZABETH BARRETT BROWNING (1806–1861) was born in Durham, England, and studied with her brother's tutor. Her first book of poetry was published when she was thirteen, and she soon became the most famous female poet to that point in English history. A riding accident at the age of sixteen left her a semi-invalid in the house of her possessive father, who had forbidden any of his eleven children to marry. She and ROBERT BROWNING were forced to elope (she was thirty-nine at the time); they lived in Florence, Italy, where she died fifteen years later. Her best-known book of poems was *Sonnets from the Portuguese*, a sequence of forty-four sonnets recording the growth of her love for Robert.

WEB: Further research this author with LitLinks at bedfordstmartins.com/rewritinglit.

ROBERT BROWNING (1812–1889) was the son of a bank clerk in Camberwell, then a suburb of London. As an aspiring poet in 1844, he admired ELIZABETH BARRETT's poetry and began a correspondence with her that led to one of the world's most famous romances. Their courtship lasted until 1846 when they were secretly wed and ran off to Italy, where they lived until Elizabeth's death in 1861. The years in Florence were among the happiest for both of them. To her he dedicated *Men and Women*, which contains his best poetry. Although she was the more popular poet during her lifetime, his reputation grew upon his return to London after her death, assisted somewhat by public sympathy for him. The late 1860s were the peak of his career: He and ALFRED, LORD TENNYSON were mentioned together as the foremost poets of the age. His fame and influence continued to grow through the remainder of his life until his death in 1889.

WEB: Further research this author with LitLinks at bedfordstmartins.com/rewritinglit.

DENNIS BRUTUS (1924–2009) was born in Zimbabwe of South African parents. He attended the University of Witwaterstand and taught for fourteen years in South African high schools but was banned from teaching (and his university law studies) because of his leadership in the campaign to exclude South Africa from the Olympic Games as long as the country practiced apartheid in sports. He was arrested and sentenced to eighteen months of hard labor. His *Letters to Martha* (1968) are poems about his experiences as a prisoner on Robben Island. After leaving South Africa in 1966 with a Rhodesian passport, Brutus made his home in England, then moved to the United States, where he taught at the University of Denver, Northwestern University, and the University of Pittsburgh and published twelve books of poetry. In 1983, after engaging in a protracted legal struggle and appearing on ABC's *Nightline* with Ted Koppel, he won the right to stay in the United States as a political refugee. He returned to South Africa in 2007 and died at his home in Cape Town.

CHARLES BUKOWSKI (1920–1994), born in Andernach, Germany, came to the United

States at age three and grew up in poverty in Los Angeles, drifted extensively, and for much of his life made his home in San Pedro, working for many years in the U.S. Postal Service. He was familiar with the people of the streets, skid row residents, hustlers, and a transient lifestyle. He began writing in childhood and published his first story at age twenty-four and his first poetry when he was thirty-five. He published many books of poetry, in addition to novels and short stories reminiscent of ERNEST HEMINGWAY. He is very popular in Europe. His style, which exhibits a strong sense of immediacy and a refusal to embrace standard formal structures, was influenced by the Beat movement.

WEB: Further research this author with LitLinks at bedfordstmartins.com/rewritinglit.

JO CARSON (b. 1946) was born in Johnson City, Tennessee, and earned a degree in theater and speech from East Tennessee State University. Her best-known play is *Daytrips* (1991); her poetry is collected in *Stories I Ain't Told Nobody Yet* (1989); her story collection, *The Last of the "Waltz across Texas" and Other Stories*, was published in 1993. Most recently she has published two collections of performance stories, *Teller Tales: Histories* (2007) and *Liars, Thieves and Other Sinners on the Bench* (2009). She has published three books for children: *Pulling My Leg* (1990), *You Hold Me and I'll Hold You* (1992), and *The Great Shaking* (1994), an eyewitness account of the New Madrid earthquakes of 1811 and 1812, as told by a fictional bear.

RAYMOND CARVER (1938–1988) was born and grew up in Oregon. He decided he wanted to become a writer because he liked stories about hunting and fishing. He began to learn the craft of fiction in a creative writing course taught by novelist John Gardner at Chico State College in California. He earned his B.A. from Humboldt State College in California and attended the University of Iowa Writers' Workshop. Because Carver had married young and had a wife and children and little money, earning a living had to take precedence over writing and so his writing career progressed slowly. He kept at it, however, and eventually published a dozen collections of stories and books of poetry before his death from lung cancer at age fifty. He revised many of the stories in his first book, *Will You Please Be Quiet, Please?* (1976), as he moved into his much acclaimed and imitated hard-edged and minimalist style evident in the collection *What We Talk about When We Talk about Love* (1981).

WEB: Further research this author with LitLinks at bedfordstmartins.com/rewritinglit.

LORNA DEE CERVANTES (b. 1954) was born in San Francisco and grew up in San Jose. There she studied at San Jose City College and San Jose State University. She is the author of two volumes of poetry, *Emplumada* (1981), which won an American Book Award, and *From the Cables of Genocide: Poems on Love and Hunger* (Arte Público Press, 1991). She was also coeditor of *Red Dirt*, a cross-cultural poetry journal, and her work has been included in many anthologies. Cervantes, who considers herself "a Chicana writer, a feminist writer, a political writer," lives in Colorado and was a professor at the University of Colorado at Boulder.

WEB: Further research this author with LitLinks at bedfordstmartins.com/rewritinglit.

TINA CHANG (b. 1969) received her B.A. from the State University of New York–Binghamton and her M.F.A. from Columbia University. She is the author of *Half-Lit Houses* (2004), a finalist for the 2005 Asian American Literary Award, and coeditor of *Language for a New Century: Contemporary Poetry from the Middle East, Asia, and Beyond* (2008). Her poems have appeared in many literary journals and have been anthologized in such volumes as *Identity Lessons, Asian American Literature,* and *Asian-American Poetry: The Next Generation.* She has been awarded numerous residencies and fellowships. She teaches poetry at Sarah Lawrence College and Hunter College.

MARILYN CHIN (b. 1955) is a first-generation Chinese American, born in Hong Kong and raised in Portland, Oregon. She is the author of three volumes of poetry—*Dwarf Bamboo* (1987), *The Phoenix Gone, The Terrace Empty* (1994), and *Rhapsody in Plain Yellow* (2002)— and a novel, *Revenge of the Mooncake Vixen* (2009). She also is a coeditor of *Dissident Song: A Contemporary Asian American Anthology* (1991) and has translated poems by the modern Chinese poet Ai Qing and cotranslated poems by the Japanese poet Gozo Yoshimasu. She has received numerous awards for her poetry, including a Stegner Fellowship, the PEN/Josephine Miles Award, and four Pushcart Prizes. She is codirector of the M.F.A. program at San Diego State University.

WEB: Further research this author with LitLinks at bedfordstmartins.com/rewritinglit.

KATE CHOPIN (1851–1904) was born Katherine O'Flaherty in St. Louis. Her father, an Irish immigrant and a very successful businessman, died when she was four. Her mother was of a prominent French Creole family. Chopin received an excellent education at the Academy of the Sacred Heart and from her mother and grandmother, and on graduation was known as a brilliant storyteller, a youthful cynic, and an accomplished pianist. At age nineteen she married Oscar Chopin and had six children. They lived in the Creole community of Natchitoches Parish, Louisiana, until his death in 1882, when she moved back to St. Louis. After her mother died a year later, friends encouraged her to write as a way to deal with her grief and anger, and in doing so she turned to Creole country for her subjects and themes. She became both a nationally acclaimed and popular author. Her masterpiece, *The Awakening* (1899), a lyrical study of a young woman whose deep personal discontents lead to adultery and suicide, was praised for its craft but criticized for its content and created a scandal. Chopin, always sensitive to her critics and declining in health, wrote little after it.

WEB: Further research this author with LitLinks at bedfordstmartins.com/rewritinglit.

SANDRA CISNEROS (b. 1954) was born in Chicago to a Mexican father and Chicana mother. She grew up in ghetto neighborhoods of Chicago, moving frequently and thus never feeling settled. She spoke English at school and Spanish at home and on many trips to Mexico to visit her grandmother. She wrote poetry in high school and was editor of the school literary magazine and went on to earn a B.A. from Loyola University and an M.F.A. from the University of Iowa Writers' Workshop. She discovered her literary voice in a graduate seminar, when she experimented with writing about growing up as a poor Latina in Chicago. She has published two novels, three books of poetry, two books of stories, and a bilingual children's book. She was awarded a MacArthur Foundation Fellowship in 1995. Cisneros has taught at various colleges and universities, including the University of California, University of Michigan, and the University of New Mexico. She now lives in San Antonio, Texas.

WEB: Further research this author with LitLinks at bedfordstmartins.com/rewritinglit.

LUCILLE CLIFTON (1936–2010) was born in Depew, New York, and studied at Howard University. She published many books of poetry, including *Blessing the Boats: New and Selected Poems 1988-2000* (2000), which won the National Book Award. Her last book was *Voices* (2008). She also published a memoir and more than twenty books for children. She taught at several colleges and worked in the Office of Education in Washington, D.C. She served as poet laureate for the State of Maryland. Her poems typically reflect her ethnic pride, womanist principles, and race and gender consciousness.

WEB: Further research this author with LitLinks at bedfordstmartins.com/rewritinglit.

JUDITH ORTIZ COFER (b. 1952) — See page 720.

SAMUEL TAYLOR COLERIDGE (1772–1834) was born in Devonshire and sent to school in London after his father's death. He went to Jesus College, Cambridge, in 1791 and dropped out twice without a degree. In 1798 Coleridge and WILLIAM WORDSWORTH published *Lyrical Ballads*, which initiated the Romantic movement in English poetry and established both of their reputations. After 1802, Coleridge became addicted to opium, used as a treatment for physical discomfort and seizures. He and his wife were separated, his friendship with Wordsworth broke up, and his poetic output stopped. From 1816 to his death he lived under constant medical supervision but still managed to publish a journal and write several plays, pieces of criticism, and philosophical and religious treatises.

WEB: Further research this author with LitLinks at bedfordstmartins.com/rewritinglit.

BILLY COLLINS (b. 1941), born and raised in New York City, is the author of several collections of poems. Perhaps no poet since ROBERT FROST has managed to combine high critical acclaim with such broad popular appeal. The typical Collins poem opens on a clear and hospitable note but soon takes an unexpected turn; poems that begin in irony may end in a moment of lyric surprise. Collins sees his poetry as "a form of travel writing" and considers humor "a door into the serious." Collins is the author of numerous books of poetry, most recently, *She Was Just Seventeen* (2006) and *Ballistics* (2008). In 2009 he edited, with illustrator David Sibley, *Bright Wings: An Illustrated Anthology of Poems about Birds*. He served as Poet Laureate Consultant in Poetry at the Library of Congress from 2001 to 2003 and as New York State Poet Laureate from 2004 to 2006. He has taught at Columbia University, Sarah Lawrence College, and Lehman College, City University of New York.

WEB: Further research this author with LitLinks at bedfordstmartins.com/rewritinglit.

VICTOR HERNÁNDEZ CRUZ (b. 1949) was born in Aguas Buenas, Puerto Rico, and moved to New York City with his family at the age of five. His first book of poetry, *Papa Got His Gun, and Other Poems* (1966), was published when he was seventeen. Since then he has published numerous other collections, most recently *The Mountain in the Sea* (2006). In 1971 Cruz visited Puerto Rico and reconnected with his ancestral heritage; eighteen years later, he returned to Puerto Rico to live. He now divides his time between Puerto Rico and New York. Much of his work explores the relation between the English language and his native Spanish, playing with grammatical and syntactical conventions within both languages to create his own bilingual idiom.

WEB: Further research this author with LitLinks at bedfordstmartins.com/rewritinglit.

COUNTEE CULLEN (1903–1946) was born in either Louisville, Kentucky; Baltimore, Maryland; or (as he himself claimed) New York City. He was adopted by the Reverend Frederick A. Cullen and his wife and grew up, as he put it, "in the conservative atmosphere of a Methodist parsonage." He studied at New York University and Harvard University. A forerunner of the Harlem Renaissance movement, he was in the 1920s the most popular black literary figure in America. From the 1930s until his death, he wrote less and worked as a junior high French teacher. For many years after his death, his reputation was eclipsed by that of other Harlem Renaissance writers, particularly LANGSTON HUGHES and ZORA NEALE HURSTON; recently, however, there has been a resurgence of interest in his life and work.

WEB: Further research this author with LitLinks at bedfordstmartins.com/rewritinglit.

E. E. CUMMINGS (1894–1962) was born in Cambridge, Massachusetts, where his father was a Unitarian minister and a sociology lecturer at Harvard University. He graduated from Harvard and then served as an ambulance driver during World War I. *The Enormous Room* (1922) is an account of his confinement in a French prison camp during the war. After the war, he lived in rural Connecticut and Greenwich Village, with frequent visits to Paris. In his work, Cummings experimented radically with form, punctuation, spelling, and syntax, abandoning traditional techniques and structures to create a new, highly idiosyncratic means of poetic expression. At the time of his death, he was the second most widely read poet in the United States, after ROBERT FROST.

WEB: Further research this author with LitLinks at bedfordstmartins.com/rewritinglit.

LYDIA DAVIS (b. 1947) was born to a fiction writer and a book critic. In first grade, she learned to read English. In second grade, which she spent in Austria, she learned to read German. She has published many books of short stories, including *The Collected Stories of Lydia Davis* (2009). Her stories are known for their humor and brevity, many only one or two sentences long. She is also a translator of the works of Proust, Foucault, and other French writers, including a new version of *Madame Bovary* (2010). In 2003, she received a MacArthur Fellowship. She was nominated for the National Book Award in 2007 and was a PEN/Hemingway finalist for her collection *Break It Down* (1986).

TODD DAVIS (b. 1965) was born in Elkhart County, Indiana. He grew up there and in the Berkshires in Massachusetts, where his family had a farm. Spending time in both regions underscored the importance of place in his poetry. Davis's parents—particularly his father, a lover of words and poetry—helped fuel his love for poetry. He received his B.A. from Grace College in Indiana, where he began to write poetry in his junior year. He continued his studies at Northern Illinois University, where he received his M.A. and Ph.D. in English, studying with the Zen Buddhist poet Lucien Stryk. He taught at Goshen College from 1996 to 2002, and now teaches creative writing, environmental studies, and American literature at Penn State University's Altoona College. He has published three books of poems, *Ripe* (2002), *Some Heaven* (2007), and *The Least of These* (2010). He has won the Gwendolyn Brooks Poetry Prize and his poems have been nominated for the Pushcart Prize. In addition to his creative work, he is the author or editor of six scholarly books.

TOI DERRICOTTE (b. 1941) was born and raised in Detroit, where she earned a B.A. in special education from Wayne State University. She is the author of several collections of poetry as well as a memoir, *The Black Notebooks* (1997). With poet CORNELIUS EADY, she cofounded Cave Canem, which offers workshops and retreats for African American poets. Among many honors she has received is the Distinguished Pioneering of the Arts Award from the United Black Artists. Derricotte teaches creative writing at the University of Pittsburgh.

WEB: Further research this author with LitLinks at bedfordstmartins.com/rewritinglit.

EMILY DICKINSON (1830–1886) was born in Amherst, Massachusetts, and lived there her entire life, rarely leaving. She briefly attended a women's seminary but became homesick and left before a year was out. Dickinson never married and became reclusive later in life, forgoing even the village routines and revelries she enjoyed. She published very few

of the more than seventeen hundred poems she wrote; most were written for herself or for inclusion in her many letters. Not until 1955 was there a complete edition of her poems that attempted to present them as originally written.

WEB: Further research this author with LitLinks at bedfordstmartins.com/rewritinglit.

CHITRA BANERJEE DIVAKARUNI (b. 1956) was born in Calcutta, India. She received her B.A. from the University of Calcutta and that same year went to the United States to attend Wright State University where she earned a master's degree. She later received a Ph.D. from the University of California, Berkeley. She put herself through graduate school by taking on such jobs as store clerk, baby sitter, bread slicer, dining-hall attendant, and lab assistant. She has taught at Foothill College, Diablo Valley College, and the University of Houston. She is a cofounder and the former president of a help line for South Asian women dealing with domestic abuse. She has also served on the board of Pratham, an organization that works to bring literacy to disadvantaged Indian children. She began her writing career as a poet and has published several collections of poems—beginning with her first book, *The Reason for Nasturtiums* (1990)—and has won numerous awards for that genre. Her first collection of stories, *Arranged Marriage* (1995), won an American Book Award. In addition to poetry and short stories, she has written novels, essays, children's fiction and young adult fiction and has served as a reviewer and a columnist. She has written novels in multiple genres including realistic fiction, historical fiction, magical realism, and fantasy. Her work has been translated into eighteen languages.

JOHN DONNE (1572–1631) was born in London to a prosperous Catholic family (he was related to Sir Thomas More and the playwright John Heywood). Donne studied at Oxford University for several years but did not take a degree. He fought with Sir Walter Raleigh in two naval strikes against Spain. In 1601, Donne's promising political career was permanently derailed by his precipitous marriage to Anne More without her father's consent. He was briefly imprisoned, lost a very promising position with Sir Thomas Egerton, and spent years seeking further political employment before finally being convinced by King James in 1615 to take holy orders as priest of the Church of England. His life was described by Isaac Walton later in the century as being divided into two parts. In Phase I he was "Jack Donne" of Lincoln's Inn: When young, Donne employed a sophisticated urban wit in his earlier love poetry, like that of "A Valediction: Forbidding Mourning." In Phase II he was John Donne, dean of St. Paul's: After Donne took his vows in 1615, his poetry became markedly less amorous and more religious in tone. His *Holy Sonnets* are as dense and complex as his earlier work, with his talent now directed toward exploration of his relationship with God.

WEB: Further research this author with LitLinks at bedfordstmartins.com/rewritinglit.

MARK DOTY (b. 1953) is the author of twelve collections of poetry and three memoirs—*Heaven's Coast* (1996), about the loss of his partner, Wally Roberts; *Firebird* (1999), a gay coming-of-age story and a chronicle of a gradual process of finding in art a place of personal belonging; and *Dog Years* (2007), about the relationships between humans and the dogs they love. He has taught at Brandeis University, Sarah Lawrence College, Vermont College, and the University of Iowa Writers' Workshop. He now lives in New York City and Fire Island, New York, and teaches at Rutgers University.

WEB: Further research this author with LitLinks at bedfordstmartins.com/rewritinglit.

RITA DOVE (b. 1952) was born in Akron, Ohio. Her father was the first research chemist to break the race barrier in the tire industry. She graduated from Miami University in Oxford, Ohio, with a degree in English; after a year at Tübingen University in Germany on a Fulbright fellowship, she joined the University of Iowa Writers' Workshop, where she earned her M.F.A. in 1977. She has taught at Tuskegee Institute and Arizona State University and now is on the faculty of the University of Virginia. She was appointed Poet Laureate Consultant in Poetry at the Library of Congress in 1993, making her the youngest person to receive the highest official

honor in American letters. She is the author of numerous collections of poetry, including *Thomas and Beulah* (1986), a book-length sequence loosely based on the lives of her grandparents, which was awarded the Pulitzer Prize in 1987.

WEB: Further research this author with LitLinks at bedfordstmartins.com/rewritinglit.

PAUL LAURENCE DUNBAR (1872–1906) was the first African American to gain national eminence as a poet. Born and raised in Dayton, Ohio, he was the son of ex-slaves. He was an outstanding student: The only African American in his class, he was both class president and class poet. Although he lived to be only thirty-three years old, Dunbar was prolific, writing short stories, novels, librettos, plays, songs, and essays as well as the poetry for which he became well known. He was popular with both black and white readers of his day. His style encompasses two distinct voices—the standard English of the classical poet and the evocative dialect of the turn-of-the-century black community in America.

WEB: Further research this author with LitLinks at bedfordstmartins.com/rewritinglit.

CORNELIUS EADY (b. 1954) was born and raised in Rochester, New York, and attended Monroe Community College and Empire State College. He began writing as a teenager. His poems are his biography, their subjects ranging from blues musicians to the witnessing of his father's death. He has published eight volumes of poetry. With poet TOI DERRICOTTE, he cofounded Cave Canem, which offers workshops and retreats for African American poets, and with composer Diedre Murray he has collaborated on two highly acclaimed music dramas. Formerly the director of the Poetry Center at the State University of New York, Stony Brook, and Distinguished Writer-in-Residence at the City College of New York, he currently holds the Miller Family Endowed Chair in Literature and Writing at the University of Missouri.

WEB: Further research this author with LitLinks at bedfordstmartins.com/rewritinglit.

DAVE EGGERS (b. 1970) was born in Boston. His father was an attorney and his mother was a schoolteacher. The family moved to

Lake Forest, just north of Chicago, when he was still a child. He attended the University of Illinois hoping to major in journalism, but when his parents both died in 1991, he left school to care for his eight-year-old brother. He began writing as a *Salon.com* editor. His first book, *A Heartbreaking Work of Staggering Genius* (2000), about his parents' death from cancer and his struggles raising his brother, was a finalist for the Pulitzer Prize. He has since written many other works, including the screenplay for *Where the Wild Things Are* (2009). He is the founder of McSweeney's, an independent publishing house, and in 2002 he and educator Ninive Clements Calegari founded 826 Valencia, a non-profit writing and tutoring center for those ages six to eighteen. It has seven chapters in cities across the country. In 2007 the Heinz Family Foundation awarded him a $250,000 Heinz Award for "extraordinary achievement." He asked that the award money be given to 826 Valencia. The author of many books of fiction and non-fiction, he was presented the Courage in Media Award by the Council on American-Islamic Relations, was named by the *Utne Reader* as one of "Fifty Visionaries Who Are Changing the World," and in 2005 was awarded an honorary Doctor of Letters from Brown University.

T.[HOMAS] S.[TEARNS] ELIOT (1888–1965) was born and raised in St. Louis. He went to prep school in Massachusetts and then to Harvard University, where he earned an M.A. in philosophy in 1910 and started his doctoral dissertation. He studied at the Sorbonne, Paris, and then at Marburg, Germany, in 1914. The war forced him to Oxford, where he got married and abandoned philosophy for poetry. After teaching and working in a bank, he became an editor at Faber and Faber and editor of the journal *Criterion* and was the dominant force in English poetry for several decades. He became a British citizen and a member of the Church of England in 1927. He won the Nobel Prize for Literature in 1948. He also wrote plays, essays, and a series of poems on cats that became the basis of a musical by Andrew Lloyd Weber.

WEB: Further research this author with LitLinks at bedfordstmartins.com/rewritinglit.

RALPH ELLISON (1914–1994) was born in Oklahoma City, where his mother worked as a servant after the death of her husband when Ellison was three. She brought home discarded books and phonograph records from houses where she worked, and from them Ellison developed an interest in literature and music. He studied music at Tuskegee Institute in Alabama and then went to New York, where he met LANGSTON HUGHES and Richard Wright, who encouraged him in his writing. Ellison's literary reputation rests on one novel, *Invisible Man* (1952), which received the National Book Award for fiction and was listed in a Book Week poll in 1965 as the most distinguished American novel of the preceding twenty years. It deals with a young black man moving from the South to the North and learning about how racial prejudice leads to discrimination on the one hand and to being unnoticed and inconsequential on the other. "Battle Royal" (p. 402) is the first chapter of that novel. Ellison also published a scattering of short stories (collected posthumously in *Flying Home and Other Stories* [1996]) and two books of essays. A second novel was incomplete when he died (excerpts from the manuscript were published as *Juneteenth* in 1999).

WEB: Further research this author with LitLinks at bedfordstmartins.com/rewritinglit.

GRAY EMERSON (b. 1986), was born in Holland, Michigan. An English and philosophy graduate of Hope College, he has an interest in classic film and film history, graphic fiction and comics, and music. Four of his poems were included in *Time You Let Me In: 25 Poets Under 25*, edited by NAOMI SHIHAB NYE (Greenwillow Press, 2010). Gray plans on a career in library work and is currently working on a collection of poetry and writing a novel.

ANITA ENDREZZE (b. 1952), of Yaqui and European ancestry, was born in Long Beach, California, and earned her M.A. from Eastern Washington University. She is a poet, writer, and painter (in watercolor and acrylics) who also works in fiber and creates handmade books. She is a member of Atlatl, a Native American arts service organization. In addition to four volumes of poetry, she has published a children's novel, short stories, and nonfiction. She lives in Everett, Washington, where she is a storyteller, teacher, and writer.

WEB: Further research this author with LitLinks at bedfordstmartins.com/rewritinglit.

LOUISE ERDRICH (b. 1954) was born in Minnesota to a French-Ojibwe mother and a German-born father. She grew up near the Turtle Mountain Reservation in North Dakota and is a member of the Turtle Mountain Band of Chippewa. Her grandfather was tribal chief of the reservation. She was among the first women admitted to Dartmouth College, where she began writing; she also studied at Johns Hopkins University. She has published thirteen novels, six children's books, three collections of poetry, and three books of nonfiction. In 2009, her novel *The Plague of Doves* was named a finalist for the Pulitzer Prize in fiction. She lives in Minneapolis and is the owner of Birchbark Books, a small independent bookstore.

WEB: Further research this author with LitLinks at bedfordstmartins.com/rewritinglit.

MARTÍN ESPADA (b. 1957) was born in Brooklyn and has an eclectic résumé: radio journalist in Nicaragua, welfare rights paralegal, advocate for mental patients, night desk clerk in a transient hotel, attendant in a primate nursery, groundskeeper at a minor league ballpark, bindery worker in a printing plant, bouncer in a bar, and practicing lawyer in Chelsea, Massachusetts. Author of nine books of poetry, his latest collection is *The Trouble Ball* (2011). His earlier book, *Alabanza: New and Selected Poems, 1982-2002* (2003), received the Paterson Award for Sustained Literary Achievement and was named an American Library Association Notable Book of the Year. He is an essayist, editor, and translator as well as a poet. He lives in Amherst, Massachusetts, where he is professor of English at the University of Massachusetts–Amherst.

WEB: Further research this author with LitLinks at bedfordstmartins.com/rewritinglit.

WILLIAM FAULKNER (1897–1962) was born into an old southern family in New Albany, Mississippi. When he was five, his family moved to Oxford, a small city in northern Mississippi that was his home for most of the rest of his life. He attended the University of Mississippi for three semesters, having been admitted as a war veteran although he had not finished high school, and published poems and short stories in the campus newspaper. He continued writing while working at odd jobs for several years in New York and New Orleans and published his first novel, *Soldier's Pay*, in 1926. Success as a novelist came when he began writing about the northern Mississippi area he knew best, creating the mythical Yoknapatawpha County. His discovery that this "little postage stamp of native soil was worth writing about" enabled him to write a series of acclaimed experimental novels, including *The Sound and the Fury* (1920), *As I Lay Dying* (1930), *Light in August* (1932), and *Absalom, Absalom!* (1936), in which he traces the disintegration of the South through several generations. Until the publication of the anthology *The Portable Faulkner* brought him wide recognition in 1946, he supported himself by publishing short stories (nearly a hundred) in magazines and by writing screenplays in Hollywood. In 1949 he received the Nobel Prize for Literature and delivered one of the most influential acceptance speeches ever given at a Nobel ceremony (available online at nobelprize.org/nobel_prizes/literature/laureates/1949/faulkner-speech.html).

WEB: Further research this author with LitLinks at bedfordstmartins.com/rewritinglit.

CAROLYN FORCHÉ (b. 1950) was born in Detroit, attended Michigan State University, and earned an M.F.A. from Bowling Green State University. She achieved immediate success as a writer, winning a Yale Younger Poets Prize in 1976. Her work underwent a remarkable shift following a year spent on a Guggenheim Fellowship in El Salvador, where she worked with human-rights activist Archbishop Oscar Humberto Romero and with Amnesty International. The shock of witnessing countless atrocities in Central America led her to begin writing what she calls "poetry of witness." The volume *The Country between Us* (1981) stirred immediate controversy because of its overtly political topics and themes. "The Colonel" (p. 801), a prose poem in which the speaker conveys a horrific story with chilling flatness, is probably the most disturbing and memorable poem in the book. She is the author of four books of poetry, and the editor of *Against Forgetting: Twentieth-Century Poetry of Witness* (1993). She has also translated several books of poetry. She is director of the Lannan Center for Poetry and Poetics and holds the Lannan Chair in Poetry at Georgetown University in Washington, D.C.

WEB: Further research this author with LitLinks at bedfordstmartins.com/rewritinglit.

VIEVEE FRANCIS (b. 1963) worked for more than twenty years to develop her voice in poetry. She has had work published in many venues, including the *2003 Grolier Prize Annual, Callaloo, Margie,* and *Crab Orchard Review.* She spent several years doing exhaustive research for her first collection, *Blue-Tail Fly* (2006), a series of persona poems that treat the period of American history between the beginning of the Mexican-American War and the end of the Civil War. Francis gives voice to outsiders, from soldiers and common folk to influential politicians. Francis, who grew up in Detroit and has lived there all her life, teaches independent workshops for young adult writers there.

ROBERT FROST (1874–1963) was born in San Francisco and lived there until he was eleven. When his father died, the family moved to Massachusetts, where Robert did well in school, especially in the classics, but he dropped out of both Dartmouth College and Harvard University. He went unrecognized as a poet until 1913, when he was first published in England, where he had moved with his wife and four children. Upon returning to the United States, he quickly achieved success with more publications and became the most celebrated poet in mid-twentieth-century America. He held a teaching position at Amherst College and received many honorary degrees as well as an invitation to recite a poem at John F. Kennedy's inauguration. Although his work is principally associated with the life and landscape of New England, and though he is a poet of traditional verse forms and metrics, he is also a quintessentially modern poet in his adherence to language as it is actually spoken, in the psychological complexity of his portraits, and in the degree to which his work is infused with layers of ambiguity and irony.

WEB: Further research this author with LitLinks at bedfordstmartins.com/rewritinglit.

TESS GALLAGHER (b. 1943) was born in Port Angeles, Washington. She attended the University of Washington, where she studied under THEODORE ROETHKE, and received an M.F.A. from the University of Iowa. She is a poet, an essayist, a novelist, a screenwriter, a short story writer, and a playwright. Her second (and best-known) collection of poems, *Instructions to the Double*, won the 1976 Elliston Book Award for "best book of poetry published by a small press." Other collections include *Moon Crossing Bridge* (1992), *Owl-Spirit Dwelling* (1994), *My Black Horse: New and Selected Poems* (1995), and *Dear Ghosts* (2006). She married the author RAYMOND CARVER and her collection *Willingly* (1984) is written to and about him. After Carver's death in 1988, she became his literary executor. She has taught at many colleges and universities throughout the United States. She sings traditional Irish dirge, has traveled and lived in both Northern Ireland and the Irish Republic, and has become friends with and been influenced by many Northern Irish poets.

RICHARD GARCIA (b. 1941) was born in San Francisco, a first-generation American (his mother was from Mexico, his father from Puerto Rico). While still in high school, he had a poem published by City Lights in a Beat anthology. After publishing his first collection in 1972, however, he did not write poetry again for twelve years, until an unsolicited letter of encouragement from Octavio Paz inspired him to resume. Since then, his work has appeared widely in literary magazines as well as three later books, *The Flying Garcias* (1991), *Rancho Notorious* (2001), and *The Persistence of Objects* (2006). He is also the author of a bilingual children's book, *My Aunt Otilia's Spirits* (1987). For twelve years he was the poet-in-residence at Children's Hospital Los Angeles, where he conducted poetry and art workshops for hospitalized children. He teaches creative writing in the Antioch University Los Angeles M.F.A. program and at the College of Charleston.

WEB: Further research this author with LitLinks at bedfordstmartins.com/rewritinglit.

GABRIEL GARCÍA MÁRQUEZ (b. 1928) was born in the small town of Aracataca, situated in a tropical region of northern Colombia between the mountains and the Caribbean Sea, and he grew up there with his maternal grandparents. He studied law and then journalism at the National University of Colombia in Bogota and at the University of Cartagena. In 1954, he was sent to Rome on an assignment for his newspaper. Since then he has mostly lived abroad, in Paris, New York, Barcelona, and Mexico. He published his first book of short stories in 1955. His most famous work, the novel *One Hundred Years of Solitude*, was published in 1967. His fiction is characterized by magic realism, which, as he put it, "expands the categories of the real so as to encompass myth, magic and other extraordinary phenomena in Nature or experience" excluded by European realistic fiction. Besides his large output of fiction, he has written screenplays, a memoir, and has continued to work as a journalist. In 1982, he received the Nobel Prize for Literature. His most recent works are *Living to Tell the Tale* [2002], the first volume of a projected three-part memoir, and *Memories of My Melancholy Whores* (2004).

WEB: Further research this author with LitLinks at bedfordstmartins.com/rewritinglit.

DAGOBERTO GILB (b. 1950) was born and grew up in Los Angeles, raised by a Chicana mother who divorced his German father soon after Dagoberto was born. He attended the University of California, Santa Barbara, where he majored in philosophy and religion, after which he moved to El Paso and spent sixteen years making a living as a construction worker, twelve of them as a journeyman, high-rise carpenter. During this time, he began writing stories, several of which were published in a variety of journals. His collection of stories *The Magic of Blood* (1993) won the 1994 PEN/Hemingway Award, and his novel *The Last Known Residence of Mickey Acuña* (1994) was named a Notable Book of the Year by the *New York Times Book Review*. His most recent books are a collection of essays, *Gritos* (2003), and a novel, *The Flowers* (2008). He is writer-in-residence and executive director of Centro Victoria: Center for Mexican American Literature and Culture, at the University of Houston–Victoria.

ALLEN GINSBERG (1926–1997) was born in Newark, New Jersey, and graduated from Columbia University, after several suspensions, in 1948. Several years later, Ginsberg left for San Francisco to join other poets of the Beat movement. His poem "Howl," the most famous poem of the movement, was published in 1956 by Lawrence Ferlinghetti's City Lights Books; the publicity of the ensuing censorship trial brought the Beats to national attention. Ginsberg was cofounder with Anne Waldman of the Jack Kerouac School of Disembodied Poetics at the Naropa Institute in Boulder, Colorado. In his later years, he became a distinguished professor at Brooklyn College.

NIKKI GIOVANNI (b. 1943) was born in Knoxville, Tennessee, and returned there after spending her childhood years in Cincinnati. After receiving her B.A. from Fisk University, she organized the Black Arts Festival in Cincinnati and then entered graduate school at the University of Pennsylvania. She has received wide popular acclaim as a writer—having published around thirty collections of poetry for adults and children—and as a lecturer on literature and racial and social causes. She is currently professor of English and Gloria D. Smith Professor of Black Studies at Virginia Tech.

WEB: Further research this author with LitLinks at bedfordstmartins.com/rewritinglit.

ARACELIS GIRMAY (b. 1977), inheritor of Eritrean, Puerto Rican, and African American traditions, was born in Santa Ana, California, and grew up in southern California. Her future as a writer was given a boost when, at age seven, she received a red typewriter. She earned her B.A. from Connecticut College and her M.F.A. in poetry from New York University. A writer of poetry, essays, and fiction, her works have appeared in numerous journals and magazines. She received the Great Lakes Colleges Association's New Writers Award for her first poetry collection, *Teeth* (2007). Her second collection, *Kingdom Animalia* (2011), was awarded the Isabella Gardner Poetry Award. She teaches writing workshops in New York and California and has served as writer-in-residence at Hampshire College, where she is now on the faculty. In addition to her poetry collections, she has published a collage-based picture book, *Changing, Changing: Story and Collages* (2005).

DIANE GLANCY (b. 1941) was born in Kansas City, Missouri, to a Cherokee father and an English-German mother. She graduated from the University of Missouri in 1964, then married Duane Glancy and moved to Tulsa, Oklahoma. She completed her M.A. at Central State University in Edmond, Oklahoma, in 1983 and her M.F.A. at the University of Iowa Writers' Workshop in 1988. She taught in the English department at Macalaster College in Minneapolis from 1971 until 2009. Glancy, who writes in many genres, is the author of many plays and at least twenty books of fiction and other prose and twenty collections of poetry. Much of her work is based on Native American life, specifically how traditional values and lifestyles interact and are juxtaposed with those of modern America, often with harsh, even demeaning, results for her fiercely honorable characters.

SUSAN GLASPELL (1882–1948) was born and raised in Davenport, Iowa. She worked as a journalist before enrolling at Drake University in Des Moines; after graduating in 1899, she worked for two years as a reporter for the Des Moines *Daily News* and then returned to Davenport to write. Her short stories began to be accepted by magazines such as *Harper's* and the *American*. Her first novel, *The Glory of the Conquered*, was published in 1909. She married George Cram Cook, a novelist and utopian socialist, in 1916; they moved to New York and, at Cook's urging, she began to write plays. They founded the Provincetown Players in Provincetown, Massachusetts, in the summer of 1916 and moved the theater to New York that fall, where it served as a venue for producing innovative plays by American playwrights. Glaspell wrote *Trifles* (p. 922) for the Players' first season. Glaspell and Cook lived in Greece from 1922 until Cook's death in 1924, after which she settled in Provincetown for the rest of her life and continued writing. She published over fifty short stories, nine novels, eleven plays, and one biography. She was awarded a Pulitzer Prize for Drama for *Alison's House* (1931), based on the life of poet EMILY DICKINSON.

WEB: Further research this author with LitLinks at bedfordstmartins.com/rewritinglit.

RAY GONZÁLEZ (b. 1952) received his M.F.A. in creative writing from Southwest Texas State University. He has published ten books of poetry, including *The Heat of Arrivals* (which won the 1997 Josephine Miles Book Award) and *The Hawk Temple at Tierra Grande*, winner of a 2003 Minnesota Book Award in Poetry. He is the author of three books of nonfiction — *Memory Fever* (1999), *The Underground Heart* (2002), which received the 2003 Carr P. Collins/Texas Institute of Letters Award for Best Book of Nonfiction, and *Renaming the Earth* (2008) — and two collections of short stories — *The Ghost of John Wayne* (2001) and *Circling the Tortilla Dragon* (2002) — and is the editor of twelve anthologies. He has served as poetry editor for the *Bloomsbury Review* since 1980. He teaches creative writing at the University of Minnesota.

WEB: Further research this author with LitLinks at bedfordstmartins.com/rewritinglit.

ANGELINA WELD GRIMKÉ (1880–1958) was born in Boston to a mixed racial background: Her mother was from a prominent white family; her father was the son of a white man and a black slave. Grimké's father was able to earn a law degree from Harvard University (and become executive director of the NAACP) through the support of two white aunts in South Carolina who acknowledged their ties to their brother's mixed-race children. Her parents named her after her great aunt Angelina Grimké Weld, a famous white abolitionist and women's rights advocate. When Grimké was three years old, her mother left her father, taking her daughter with her. After four years she returned Angelina to her father and the child never saw her mother again. Grimké attended one of the finest schools in Massachusetts, the Carleton Academy in Ashburnham, graduated from the Boston Normal School with a degree in physical education, taught until 1907, and then moved to Washington, D.C., and taught English until she retired in 1926. While in Washington, she wrote poetry, fiction, reviews, and biographical sketches. Her best-known work, the only one published as a book, was the play *Rachel* (1916).

HA JIN (b. 1956) was born in Liaoning, China. At thirteen, he joined the People's Liberation Army during the Cultural Revolution. At sixteen, he began to educate himself in Chinese literature, and at nineteen he left the army and began teaching himself English while working the night shift as a railroad telegrapher. He then entered Heilongjiang University, earning a bachelor's degree in English studies. He received a master's degree in Anglo-American literature at Shandong University. He came to the United States to study at Brandeis University, and while he was there, the Tiananmen Square massacre occurred. The government's forcible repression of dissent led him to stay in the United States, complete his Ph.D., and write about China in English, "to preserve the integrity of his work." He went on to teach, first at Emory University and currently at Boston University. His first novel, *Waiting*, won the 1999 National Book Award for Fiction. He has published three volumes of poetry, five novels, four collections of short stories, and a book of essays. His work has resulted in increased attention to Chinese culture and history.

KIMIKO HAHN (b. 1955) was born in Mt. Kisco, New York, to two artists, a Japanese American mother from Hawaii and a German American father from Wisconsin. Hahn majored in English and East Asian studies at the University of Iowa and received an M.A. in Japanese literature from Columbia University. She is the author of seven collections of poetry, including *The Unbearable Heart* (1996), which received an American Book Award, and *The Narrow Road to the Interior* (2006). In 1995 she wrote ten portraits of women for a two-hour HBO special entitled *Ain't Nuthin' but a She-Thing*. She has taught at Parsons School of Design, the Poetry Project at St. Mark's Church, and

Yale University. She lives in New York and is a Distinguished Professor in the English Department at Queens College/CUNY.

WEB: Further research this author with LitLinks at bedfordstmartins.com/rewritinglit.

LORRAINE HANSBERRY (1930–1965) was born in Chicago, the daughter of parents who were intellectuals and activists. Her father's success in an antisegregation case brought before the Illinois Supreme Court was the inspiration for the events in *A Raisin in the Sun*. When she was eight, her parents bought a house in a white neighborhood and were subjected to racist attacks. The legal struggle over their move led to a landmark Supreme Court case, *Hansberry v. Lee*. The family home is now a designated landmark in Chicago. Her parents sent her to public schools rather than to private ones as a protest against segregation. She studied art at the University of Wisconsin and in Mexico. In 1950 she dropped out of college, moved to New York, and took classes in writing at The New School. She worked on the staff of the black newspaper *Freedom* under the direction of Paul Robeson, with W. E. B. DuBois whose office was in the same building, and as a waitress and cashier, while writing in any spare time she could find. During this period she completed *A Raisin in the Sun* (1959), the first play written by an African American woman to be produced on Broadway. At twenty-nine she became the youngest American playwright to receive the New York Drama Critics Circle Award for Best Play. Her premature death from pancreatic cancer cut short her promising career.

THOMAS HARDY (1840–1928) was born in a cottage in Higher Bockhampton, Dorset, near the regional market town of Dorchester in southwestern England. Apprenticed at age sixteen to an architect, he spent most of the next twenty years restoring old churches. He had always had an interest in literature and started writing novels in his thirties, publishing over a dozen. In 1896 Hardy gave up prose and turned to poetry, writing until his death at age eighty-eight. He had a consistently bleak, even pessimistic, outlook on life. Many of his works stress the dark effects of "hap" (happenstance, coincidence) in the world and include strong strains of irony.

JOY HARJO (b. 1951) was born in Tulsa, Oklahoma. Her mother was of Cherokee-French descent and her father was Creek. She moved to the Southwest and began writing poetry in her early twenties. She then earned her B.A. at the University of New Mexico and her M.F.A. from the University of Iowa Writers' Workshop. Harjo has published seven books of poetry, including *In Mad Love and War* (1990), which received an American Book Award and the Delmore Schwartz Memorial Award; *A Map to the Next World: Poems* (2000); and *How We Became Human: New and Selected Poems* (2002). She also performs her poetry and plays saxophone with her band, Poetic Justice. Of "She Had Some Horses" (p. 691) Harjo has said, "This is the poem I'm asked most about and the one I have the least to say about. I don't know where it came from."

WEB: Further research this author with LitLinks at bedfordstmartins.com/rewritinglit.

MICHAEL S. HARPER (b. 1938) was born in Brooklyn and grew up surrounded by jazz. When his family moved to Los Angeles, he worked at all kinds of jobs, from postal work to professional football. He studied at the City College of Los Angeles, California State University, Los Angeles, and the University of Iowa Writers' Workshop. He has written more than ten books of poetry, most recently *Selected Poems* (2002), and edited or coedited several collections of African American poetry. He is University Professor and professor of English at Brown University, where he has taught since 1970. He lives in Barrington, Rhode Island.

NATHANIEL HAWTHORNE (1804–1864) was born in Salem, Massachusetts, into a family that had been prominent in the area since colonial times. His father died when Nathaniel was four. Later, relatives recognized his literary talent and financed his education at Bowdoin College. After graduation, he lived at home writing short "tales" and a novel *Fanshawe*, which he self-published in 1828 and later dismissed as immature. He wrote prolifi-

cally in the 1830s, producing a number of successful short stories including "Young Goodman Brown" (p. 337). He published two collections of stories that were well received — *Twice-Told Tales* (1837; expanded edition 1842) and *Mosses from an Old Manse* (1846) — but had difficulty supporting himself by his writings. In 1845, he was appointed surveyor of the Boston Custom House by President James Polk but was dismissed from this post when Zachary Taylor became president. He then worked intensely on his most famous novel, *The Scarlet Letter*, published in 1850. In addition to five novels and romances, Hawthorne published nearly 120 stories and sketches and several books for children, and left behind numerous notebooks with sketches from his travels and ideas for additional stories and novels. He was one of the first American writers to explore the hidden motivations of his characters and often used allegorical approaches to explore the complexities of moral choices and his characters' struggles with sin and guilt.

WEB: Further research this author with LitLinks at bedfordstmartins.com/rewritinglit.

ROBERT HAYDEN (1913–1980) was raised in a poor neighborhood in Detroit and had an emotionally tumultuous childhood. Because of impaired vision, he was unable to participate in sports and spent his time reading instead. He graduated from high school in 1932 and attended Detroit City College (later Wayne State University). His first book of poems, *Heart-Shape in the Dust*, was published in 1940. After working for newspapers and on other projects, he studied under W. H. AUDEN in the graduate creative writing program at the University of Michigan. He taught at Fisk University and at the University of Michigan. His poetry gained international recognition in the 1960s, and he was awarded the grand prize for poetry at the First World Festival of Negro Arts in Dakar, Senegal, in 1966 for his book *Ballad of Remembrance*. In 1976, he became the first African American to be appointed as Consultant in Poetry at the Library of Congress.

WEB: Further research this author with LitLinks at bedfordstmartins.com/rewritinglit.

TERRANCE HAYES (b. 1971) was born in Columbia, South Carolina. In addition to being a writer, he is an accomplished artist and athlete. After receiving a B.A. from Coker College, where he was named an Academic All-American for his athletic and academic accomplishments, he earned an M.F.A. from the University of Pittsburgh. His first book of poetry, *Muscular Music* (1999), won both the Whiting Writers Award and the Kate Tufts Discovery Award. His next collection, *Hip Logic* (2002), won the National Poetry Series Award. His most recent book, *Lighthead*, won the National Book Award for Poetry in 2010. After teaching at Xavier University, he returned to Pittsburgh, where he is professor of creative writing at Carnegie Mellon University.

SAMUEL HAZO (b. 1928), of Lebanese and Syrian heritage, is a highly influential Arab American writer of verse, educator, and advocate on behalf of poetry. He is the author of numerous collections of poetry, fiction, and essays. He is founder, director, and president of the International Poetry Forum in Pittsburgh and the McAnulty Distinguished Professor of English Emeritus at Duquesne University. He is the recipient of the 1986 Hazlett Memorial Award for Excellence in the Arts. In 1993 he was chosen to be the first state poet of the Commonwealth of Pennsylvania, a position he still holds.

WEB: Further research this author with LitLinks at bedfordstmartins.com/rewritinglit.

SEAMUS HEANEY (b. 1939) grew up on a small farm near Castledawson, County Derry, Northern Ireland. He was educated at St. Columb's College, a Catholic boarding school situated in the city of Derry, forty miles from home, and then at Queen's University, Belfast. As a young English teacher in Belfast in the early 1960s, he joined a poetry workshop and began writing verse. Subsequently he became a major force in contemporary Irish literature. The author of many volumes of poetry, translations, and essays as well as two plays, he is well known for his best-selling verse translation of *Beowulf* (2000). He held the chair of professor of poetry at Oxford University from 1989 to 1994. He was awarded the Nobel Prize for Literature in 1995.

WEB: Further research this author with LitLinks at bedfordstmartins.com/rewritinglit.

ERNEST HEMINGWAY (1899–1961) was born in Oak Park, a conservative, upper-middle-class suburb of Chicago, but spent his summers at Walloon Lake in northern Michigan, where he learned to love the outdoors and fishing and hunting. He decided to become a journalist instead of going to college and worked as a reporter for the *Kansas City Star*, where he was taught to write with short sentences, short paragraphs, active verbs, compression, clarity, and immediacy, qualities apparent in his fiction writing. He tried to enlist for service in World War I but was turned down because of poor eyesight. Instead, he volunteered as a Red Cross ambulance driver. Shortly after arriving in Italy, he was seriously wounded, with over two hundred pieces of shrapnel in his legs. After the war he lived in Paris, worked as a newspaper correspondent for the *Toronto Daily Star*, and mingled with prominent writers and artists. Between 1925 and 1929 he published four major works of fiction, including two novels—*The Sun Also Rises* (1926) and *A Farewell to Arms* (1929)—and went from being unknown to being one of the most important writers of his generation. He moved first to Key West, Florida, where he grew to love big-game fishing, and later to Havana, Cuba. He continued writing, continued his interests in fishing and big-game hunting, and served as a war correspondent during the Spanish civil war and the Chinese-Japanese war, thus fostering further the macho persona he built throughout his life. His last major novels were *For Whom the Bell Tolls* (1940) and *The Old Man and the Sea* (1953), which was awarded the Pulitzer Prize for Fiction. He was awarded the Nobel Prize for Literature in 1954. Seven years later, in poor health and afflicted with severe depression, he committed suicide, as his father had some three decades earlier.

WEB: Further research this author with LitLinks at bedfordstmartins.com/rewritinglit.

LANCE HENSON (b. 1944), born in Washington, D.C., is Cheyenne, Oglala Sioux, and French. He was raised on a farm near Calumet, Oklahoma, by his great aunt and uncle,

Bertha and Bob Cook, in the Southern Cheyenne culture. He served in the United States Marine Corps after high school, during the Vietnam War, then attended Oklahoma College of Liberal Arts (now University of Science and Arts of Oklahoma) in Chickasha. He holds an M.F.A. in creative writing from the University of Tulsa. He has published twenty-eight books of poetry, half in the United States and half abroad. His work is known for its powerful imagery, brevity, and universal appeal. It incorporates Cheyenne philosophy and traditions as well as social and political commentary on the modern world. His poetry has been translated into twenty-five languages and he has read and lectured in nine countries.

GEORGE HERBERT (1593–1633) was the fifth son in an ancient and wealthy Welsh family. He studied at Cambridge University, graduating with honors, and was elected public orator of the university. He served in Parliament for two years but fell out of political favor and became rector of Bemerton near Salisbury. Herbert was a model Anglican priest and an inspiring preacher. All of his poetry, religious in nature, was published posthumously in 1633. "The Pulley" (p. 818) is a fine example of metaphysical poetry (see the Glossary of Literary Terms, p. 1478).

WEB: Further research this author with LitLinks at bedfordstmartins.com/rewritinglit.

DAVID HERNANDEZ (b. 1971) was born in Burbank, California. His first passion was drawing. His love of art continued through college at California State University, Long Beach, and it was there that his infatuation with poetry began and that he earned a B.A. in creative writing. He has published two poetry chapbooks and three full-length collections of poems: *A House Waiting for Music* (2003); *Always Danger* (2006), winner of the Crab Orchard Series in Poetry; and *Hoodwinked* (2011), winner of the Kathryn A. Morton Prize. He is also the author of two young adult novels, *Suckerpunch* (2007) and *No More Us for You* (2009). His drawings have appeared in literary magazines, including *Other Voices*, *Gargoyle*, and *Indiana Review*. He is married to writer Lisa Glatt. Their collection of collaborative poems, *A Merciful Bed*, was published in 2001. He teaches at the University of California–Irvine and in the

M.F.A. program at Antioch University–Los Angeles.

WEB: Further research this author with LitLinks at bedfordstmartins.com/rewritinglit.

ROBERT HERRICK (1591–1674), the son of a well-to-do London goldsmith, was apprenticed to his uncle (also a goldsmith), studied at Cambridge University, and then lived for nine years in London, where he hobnobbed with a group of poets that included BEN JONSON. Under familial pressure to do something more worthwhile, Herrick became an Anglican priest. He was given the parish of Dean Prior, Devonshire — a rural place that he at first hated — and there he quietly wrote poems about imagined mistresses and pagan rites as well as deft but devout religious poems. When he returned to London in 1648, having been ejected from his pulpit by the Puritan revolution, he published his poetry in a volume with two titles, *Hesperides* for the secular poems, *Noble Numbers* for those with sacred subjects. Probably his most famous poem is "To the Virgins, to Make Much of Time" (p. 819), a short lyric on the traditional *carpe diem* theme (see the Glossary of Literary Terms, p. 1471).

WEB: Further research this author with LitLinks at bedfordstmartins.com/rewritinglit.

BOB HICOK (b. 1960), in addition to writing poetry, spent years as an automotive die designer and computer system administrator in Ann Arbor, Michigan. His first collection of poetry, *The Legend of Light* (1995), won the Felix Pollack Prize for Poetry and was named an American Library Association Booklist Notable Book of the Year. He has published five more books: *Plus Shipping* (1998); *Animal Soul* (2001), a finalist for the National Book Critics Circle Award; *Insomnia Diary* (2004); *This Clumsy Living* (2007); and *Words for Empty and Words for Full* (2010). He teaches in the M.F.A. program at Virginia Tech University.

JANE HIRSHFIELD (b. 1953) is author of numerous award-winning books of poetry, editor and cotranslator of two anthologies of poetry by women, and author of a collection of essays, *Nine Gates: Entering the Mind of Poetry* (1997). A graduate of Princeton, she studied

Soto Zen from 1974 to 1982, including three years of monastic practice, the influence of which is apparent in her work. "For me, poetry, like Zen practice, is a path toward deeper and more life. There are ways to wake up into the actual texture of one's own existence, to widen it, to deepen and broaden it, and poetry is one of the things that does that." She has taught at the University of California, Berkeley, the University of San Francisco, and the University of Cincinnati, and at many writers' conferences.

TONY HOAGLAND (b. 1953) was born in Fort Bragg, North Carolina, the son of an army doctor. He grew up on military bases throughout the South. He was educated at Williams College, the University of Iowa, and the University of Arizona. He currently teaches at the University of Houston and Warren Wilson College. His collection *What Narcissism Means to Me* (2003) was a finalist for the National Book Critics Circle Award. His most recent book is *Unincorporated Persons in the Late Honda Dynasty* (2010). In 2002, he received the Academy Award in Literature from the American Academy of Arts and Letters, and in 2005 he was the recipient of the Poetry Foundation's Mark Twain Award in recognition of his contribution to humor in American poetry.

LINDA HOGAN (b. 1947), a poet, novelist, essayist, playwright, and activist widely considered to be one of the most influential and provocative Native American figures in the contemporary American literary landscape, was born in Denver. Because her father, who was from the Chickasaw Nation, was in the army and was transferred frequently during Hogan's childhood, she lived in various locations while she was growing up, but she considers Oklahoma to be her true home. In her late twenties, while working with children with orthopedic disabilities, she began writing during her lunch hours, though she had no previous experience as a writer and little experience reading literature. She pursued her writing by commuting to the University of Colorado, Colorado Springs, for her undergraduate degree and earning an M.A. in English and creative writing at the University of Colorado, Boulder, in 1978. She has written and edited many books—poetry, novels, and nonfiction—and received numerous awards for her work. She is a professor emeritus in the University of Colorado English department, and the writer in residence for the Chickasaw Nation.

WEB: Further research this author with LitLinks at bedfordstmartins.com/rewritinglit.

GARRETT KAORU HONGO (b. 1951) was born in Volcano, Hawaii, grew up on Oahu and in Los Angeles, and did graduate work in Japanese language and literature at the University of Michigan. Hongo has published two books of poetry, including *The River of Heaven* (1988), which was the Lamont Poetry Selection of the Academy of American Poets and a finalist for the Pulitzer Prize. He has also written *Volcano: A Memoir of Hawai'i* (1995) and edited collections of Asian American verse. He teaches at the University of Oregon, Eugene, where he directed the creative writing program from 1989 to 1993. His work often uses rich textures and sensuous details to comment on conditions endured by Japanese Americans during World War II and thereafter.

WEB: Further research this author with LitLinks at bedfordstmartins.com/rewritinglit.

GERARD MANLEY HOPKINS (1844–1889) was born in London, the eldest of eight children. His father was a ship insurer who also wrote a book of poetry. Hopkins studied at Balliol College, Oxford, and, after converting to Catholicism, taught in a school in Birmingham. In 1868, he became a Jesuit and burned all of his early poetry, considering it "secular" and worthless. He then worked as a priest and teacher in working-class London, Glasgow, and Merseyside, and later as professor of classics at University College, Dublin. Hopkins went on to write many poems on spiritual themes, but he published little during his lifetime; his poems were not known until they were published by his friend Robert Bridges in 1918. They convey a spiritual sensuality, celebrating the wonder of nature both in their language and their rhythms.

WEB: Further research this author with LitLinks at bedfordstmartins.com/rewritinglit.

A. E. HOUSMAN (1859–1936) was born in Fockbury, Worcestershire. A promising student at Oxford University, he failed his final exams because of emotional turmoil caused by his suppressed homosexual love for a fellow student and spent the next ten years feverishly studying and writing scholarly articles while working as a clerk at the patent office. Housman was rewarded with the chair of Latin at University College, London, and later at Cambridge. His poetry, like his scholarship, was meticulous, impersonal in tone, and limited in output: two slender volumes — *A Shropshire Lad* (1896) and *Last Poems* (1922) — during his lifetime, and a small book of *More Poems* (1936) after his death. His poems often take up the theme of doomed youths acting out their brief lives in the context of the human histories implicit in agricultural communities and activities, especially the English countryside and traditions he loved.

WEB: Further research this author with LitLinks at bedfordstmartins.com/rewritinglit.

LANGSTON HUGHES (1902–1967) was born in Joplin, Missouri, and grew up in Lincoln, Illinois, and Cleveland, Ohio. During his high-school years, he began writing poetry. He attended Columbia University for a year, then held odd jobs as an assistant cook, a launderer, and a busboy, and traveled to Africa and Europe working as a seaman. In 1924, he moved to Harlem. Hughes's first book of poetry, *The Weary Blues*, was published in 1926. He finished his college education at Lincoln University in Pennsylvania three years later. He wrote novels, short stories, plays, songs, children's books, essays, and memoirs as well as poetry and is also known for his engagement with the world of jazz and the influence it had on his writing. His life and work were enormously important in shaping the artistic contributions of the Harlem Renaissance of the 1920s.

ZORA NEALE HURSTON (1891–1960) was born to a family of sharecroppers in Notasula, Alabama, but grew up in Eatonville, Florida, a town founded by African Americans. After her mother's death in 1904, Hurston lived with various relatives. She never finished grade school. At sixteen she joined a traveling theater group and later did domestic work for a white household. The woman for whom she

worked arranged for her to attend high school at Morgan Academy (now known as Morgan State University) in Baltimore. In her twenties, she attended Howard University, where she published her first stories in student publications and later in newspapers and magazines. In 1925, she moved to New York City and became active in the Harlem Renaissance. She collaborated with LANGSTON HUGHES in a folk comedy, *Mule Bone* (1931). Her first book, *The Eatonville Anthology* (1927), gained her national attention. At Barnard College she took courses in anthropology and studied traditional folklore in Alabama and native culture in the Caribbean. During the 1930s and early 1940s, she completed graduate work at Columbia University and published four novels and an autobiography. Hurston published more books than any other African American woman writer of her time — novels, collections of stories, nonfiction, an autobiography — but she earned very little from her writing and spent her final years in near poverty. In the mid-1970s her work was rediscovered, and she is now recognized as an important American author.

WEB: Further research this author with LitLinks at bedfordstmartins.com/rewritinglit.

DAVID HENRY HWANG (b. 1957) was born in Los Angeles to parents who immigrated to the United States from China; his father was a banker, his mother a professor of music. Hwang attended Stanford University intending to study law, but he became interested in drama and changed his major to English. A year before he graduated in 1979, he wrote his first play, *FOB* [Fresh Off the Boat], which won the 1981 Obie Award as the best new play of the season for Joseph Papp's off-Broadway production in New York. Hwang attended the Yale School of Drama from 1980 to 1981. *The Dance and the Railroad* and *Family Devotions* were produced off-Broadway in 1981. Both, like *FOB*, deal with the problems of immigrants, the tension between trying to assimilate and trying to avoid assimilation in a new culture. Other plays followed in the 1980s, but his big breakthrough came with the 1988 Broadway hit, *M. Butterfly*, which won the Outer Critics Circle Award for best Broadway play, the Drama Desk Award for best new play, the John Gassner Award for best American play, and the Tony Award for best play of the year and established him as one of the leading young American playwrights.

WEB: Further research this author with LitLinks at bedfordstmartins.com/rewritinglit.

HENRIK IBSEN (1828–1906) was born in Skien, a tiny coastal town in southeast Norway. Although his father was successful and wealthy at the time of Ibsen's birth, his business failed soon after, and Ibsen grew up in poverty, familiar with the economic hardships he later depicted often in his plays. He worked for six years as apprentice to a druggist in the seaport town of Grimstad to help support his family, and he intended to study medicine but failed the university entrance examinations. By his early twenties, he was deeply involved in a small local theater in Bergen. In 1857, he was appointed artistic director for the new National Theatre and held that post until it went bankrupt in 1862. He received a travel grant from the government and moved with his wife and son to Rome, living for the next twenty-seven years in various European cities. In 1875, he began to experiment with realistic plays exploring social issues related to middle-class life. He is best known for a series of "problem plays" that shocked but also fascinated audiences, among them *A Doll House* (1879; see p. 1245) and *Hedda Gabler* (1890). In 1891, he returned to Norway for the rest of his life and continued to write until suffering a stroke in 1900. He received worldwide recognition on his seventieth birthday as the greatest dramatist of the nineteenth century.

WEB: Further research this author with LitLinks at bedfordstmartins.com/rewritinglit.

DAVID IVES (b. 1950) was born in Chicago and attended Northwestern University. After graduating, he moved to New York and worked as an editor for *Foreign Affairs*, in addition to writing plays and short stories. He enrolled in the Yale Drama School in 1981 and earned his M.F.A. degree. Many of his plays, often described as "wacky one-act comedies," have been staged at the Manhattan Punch Line's Festival of One-Act Comedies. His full-length comedy *Don Juan in Chicago* (1994) received the Outer Critics Circle's John Gassner Playwriting Award. He was named winner of the 1994 George and Elisabeth Martin Playwriting Award from Young Playwrights Inc. He has published many plays and collections of short plays as well as three books for children or young adults: *Monsieur Eck* (2001), *Scribe* (2005), and *Voss* (2008).

RANDALL JARRELL (1914–1965) was born in Nashville, Tennessee, and earned his B.A. and M.A. at Vanderbilt University. From 1937 to 1939 he taught at Kenyon College, where he met John Crowe Ransom and ROBERT LOWELL, and then at the University of Texas. He served in the air force during World War II. Jarrell's reputation as a poet was established in 1945 with the publication of his second book, *Little Friend, Little Friend*, which documents the intense fears and moral struggles of young soldiers. Other volumes followed, all characterized by great technical skill, empathy for others, and deep sensitivity. Following the war, Jarrell began teaching at the University of North Carolina, Greensboro, and remained there, except for occasional absences to teach elsewhere, until his death. Besides poetry, he wrote a satirical novel, several children's books, numerous poetry reviews—collected in *Poetry and the Age* (1953)—and a translation of Goethe's *Faust*.

HONORÉE FANONNE JEFFERS (b. 1967) has published fiction in addition to three books of poetry, *The Gospel of Barbecue* (2000), which won the 1999 Stan and Tom Wick Prize for Poetry and was the finalist for the 2001 Paterson Poetry Prize, *Outlandish Blues* (2003), and *Red Clay Suite* (2007). She won the 2002 Julia Peterkin Award for Poetry and awards from the Barbara Deming Memorial Fund and the Rona Jaffe Foundation. Her poetry has been published in the anthologies *At Our Core: Women Writing about Power*, *Dark Eros*, and *Identity Lessons* and in many journals, including *Callaloo*, *Kenyon Review*, and *Prairie Schooner*. She teaches at the University of Oklahoma.

HA JIN (b. 1956) was born in Liaoning, China. At thirteen, he joined the People's Liberation Army during the Cultural Revolution. At sixteen, he began to educate himself in Chinese literature, and at nineteen he left the army and began teaching himself English. He earned a bachelor's degree in English studies and a master's degree in Anglo-American literature. He came to the United States to study at Brandeis University, and while he was there, the Tiananmen Square massacre occurred. The government's repression of dissent led him to stay in the United States, complete his Ph.D., and write about China in English, "to preserve the integrity of his work." He has published three volumes of poetry, five novels, four collections of short stories, and a book of essays. He currently teaches at Boston University.

GEORGIA DOUGLAS JOHNSON (1880–1966) was born in Atlanta and attended Atlanta University. She went on to study music at the Oberlin Conservatory (Ohio) and the Cleveland College of Music. Her ambition was to be a composer, but to earn a living she taught high school in Alabama and Washington, D.C., and later worked for the federal government. She was prolific as a poet, fiction writer, playwright, songwriter, and journalist; in addition to writing a syndicated newspaper column from 1926 to 1932, she wrote twenty-eight plays, thirty-one short stories, and over two hundred poems. She was the most widely published of all the women poets of the Harlem Renaissance period. Beyond her importance as a writer, she played an influential role in Washington circles by providing a "salon" in her home as a meeting place for artists and writers.

HELENE JOHNSON (1906–1995) was born and raised in Boston. She attended Boston University and Columbia University. Her work began attracting attention when James Weldon Johnson and ROBERT FROST selected three of her poems for prizes in a 1926 competition. Although she was regarded in the early 1930s as one of the most gifted poets of the Harlem Renaissance, she had a limited poetic output: thirty-four poems in a range of forms and voices, published in small magazines. The last of her poems published during her lifetime was "Let Me Sing My Song," which appeared in *Challenge*, a journal founded by her cousin, the novelist Dorothy West, to revive the spirit of the Harlem Renaissance. She married in 1933 and from then on directed most of her energy and attention to motherhood and earning a living as a correspondent for *Consumer's Union*.

RICHARD JONES (b. 1953) was born in London, where his father was serving in the U.S. Air Force, and studied at the University of Virginia. Jones is the author of several books of poems, including *The Blessing: New and Selected Poems*, which received the Midland Authors Award for Poetry for 2000, and most recently, *The Correct Spelling & Exact Meaning* (2010). He has also produced a CD on the art of poetry, entitled *Body and Soul*. In addition, he has published two critical anthologies and edited the literary journal *Poetry East* since 1979. Jones taught at Piedmont College and the University of Virginia and presently is professor of English and director of the creative writing program at DePaul University in Chicago.

BEN JONSON (1572–1637) was born in London, the stepson of a bricklayer (his father died before he was born). He attended Westminster School and then joined the army. Jonson later worked as an actor and was the author of comedies such as *Everyman in His Humor* (in which Shakespeare acted the lead), *Volpone*, and *The Alchemist*. He wrote clear, elegant, "classical" poetry, contrasting with the intricate, subtle, "metaphysical" poetry of his contemporaries JOHN DONNE and GEORGE HERBERT. He was named poet laureate and was the idol of a generation of English writers, who dubbed themselves the Sons of Ben.

WEB: Further research this author with LitLinks at bedfordstmartins.com/rewritinglit.

A. VAN JORDAN (b. 1965) was born and raised in Akron, Ohio. He is a graduate of the M.F.A. Program for Writers at Warren Wilson College, where he taught in the undergraduate writing program and served as the 1999–2000 and 2000–2001 Joan Beebe Graduate Teaching Fellow. In 1995, he was awarded a D.C. Commission on the Arts and Humanities Literary Award. He was also a semifinalist for the 1999 "Discovery"/The Nation Award. He is the author of three collections of poetry, most recently *Quantum Lyrics: Poems* (2007). He teaches in the English department at the University of Michigan.

ALLISON JOSEPH (b. 1967) was born in London to Caribbean parents and grew up in Toronto and the Bronx. She earned her B.A. from Kenyon College and her M.F.A. from Indiana University. She is the author of five collections of poetry: *What Keeps Us Here* (winner of Ampersand Press's 1992 Women Poets Series Competition and the John C. Zacharis First Book Award), *Soul Train* (1997), *In Every Seam* (1997), *Imitation of Life* (2003), *Worldly Pleasures* (2004), *Voice* (2009), and *My Father's Kites* (2010). Her poems are often attuned to the experiences of women and minorities. She is editor of the *Crab Orchard Review* and holds the Judge Williams Holmes Cook Endowed Professorship and directs the M.F.A. program in creative writing at Southern Illinois University, Carbondale.

JAMES JOYCE (1882–1941) was born in Rathgar, a suburb of Dublin. His father, descended from an old, wealthy Cork family, drank his family into poverty. However, Joyce received an excellent classical education at a Jesuit school and University College, Dublin, where he studied modern languages and began writing. He became alienated from the Catholic religion and from Ireland, and in 1902 he left Dublin for Paris; he returned in 1903 to be with his mother, who was dying of cancer. From 1905 he lived on the Continent, in Trieste, Zurich, and from 1920 to 1939 as part of the vibrant colony of expatriate authors in Paris. Although he was not able to live in Ireland, all of his writings concern Ireland and his memories of it. His first book was a collection of poems, *Chamber Music*, published in 1907. His major collection of stories, *Dubliners*, appeared in 1914, followed in 1916 by the autobiographical novel that established his reputation as a major writer, *A Portrait of the Artist as a Young Man*. The novel regarded generally as his masterpiece, *Ulysses*, was published in 1922 in Paris. (*Ulysses* was not published in the United States until 1933 and not in England until 1937, because legal difficulties prohibited uncensored publication in those countries prior to that.) His final novel, *Finnegans Wake*, appeared in 1939. To escape the German occupation of France, he returned that year to Zurich, where he had lived while writing *Ulysses*, and died there slightly more than a year later.

WEB: Further research this author with LitLinks at bedfordstmartins.com/rewritinglit.

BEL KAUFMAN (b. 1911) was born in Berlin, Germany, and raised in Russia where she vividly remembers the Russian Revolution and its impact on her town, Odessa. She published her first poem as a child in the Odessa magazine *Little Bells*. She came to the United States when she was twelve. She received her B.A. from Hunter College and her M.A. from Columbia University. She taught in New York City high schools for over twenty years, where she gained the experience that informed her celebrated novel *Up the Down Staircase* (1965). It remained on the *New York Times* best-seller list for sixty-four weeks. She has taught and lectured at a number of colleges including The New School, Manhattan Community College, the University of Rochester, and the University of Florida. She describes herself as a teacher first, then a writer and has said that she would rather do anything but write. She is the granddaughter of famed Yiddish writer Sholem Aleichem and serves on the board of directors of the Sholem Aleichem Foundation and is honorary chair of the Yiddish Studies faculty at Columbia.

JOHN KEATS (1795–1821) was born in London. His father, a worker at a livery stable who married his employer's daughter and inherited the business, was killed by a fall from a horse when Keats was eight. When his mother died of tuberculosis six years later, Keats and his siblings were entrusted to the care of a guardian, a practical-minded man who took Keats out of school at fifteen and apprenticed him to a doctor. As soon as he qualified for medical practice in 1815, he abandoned medicine for poetry, which he had begun writing two years earlier. In 1818, the year he contracted tuberculosis, he also fell madly in love with a pretty, vivacious young woman named Fanny Brawne, whom he could not marry because of his poverty, illness, and devotion to poetry. In the midst of such stress and emotional turmoil, his masterpieces poured out between January and September 1819: the great odes, a number of sonnets, and several longer lyric poems. In February 1820, his health failed rapidly; he went to Italy in the autumn, in hopes that the warmer climate would improve his health, and died there on February 23, 1821. His poems are rich with sensuous, lyrical beauty and emotional resonance, reflecting his delight in life as well as his awareness of life's brevity and difficulty.

WEB: Further research this author with LitLinks at bedfordstmartins.com/rewritinglit.

JANE KENYON (1947–1995) was born in Ann Arbor, Michigan, and grew up in the Midwest. She earned her B.A. and M.A. from the University of Michigan. She was married to poet Donald Hall from 1972 until her death from leukemia in 1995. During her lifetime, she published four books of poetry—*From Room to Room* (1978), *The Boat of Quiet Hours* (1986), *Let Evening Come* (1990), and *Constance* (1993)—and a book of translation, *Twenty Poems of Anna Akhmatova* (1985). Two additional volumes were published after her death: *Otherwise: New and Selected Poems* (1996) and *A Hundred White Daffodils: Essays, Interviews, the Akhmatova Translations, Newspaper Columns, and One Poem* (1999). At the time of her death, she was New Hampshire's poet laureate.

WEB: Further research this author with LitLinks at bedfordstmartins.com/rewritinglit.

JAMAICA KINCAID (b. 1949) was born Elaine Potter Richardson in St. Johns, Antigua, the West Indies, and completed her British-style secondary education there. She lived with her stepfather, a carpenter, and her mother until 1965 when she was sent to Westchester, New York, to work as an au pair. After working for three years and taking night classes at a community college, she attended Franconia College in New Hampshire for a year. Because her family disapproved of her writing, she changed her name to Jamaica Kincaid when she began publishing stories in magazines. Her work drew the attention of William Shawn, editor of the *New Yorker*, who hired her as a staff writer in 1976. For the next nine years, she wrote columns for the "Talk of the Town" section. In 1978, she first published a story in the *New Yorker*; it later became part of her first book, a collection entitled *At the Bottom of the River* (1984), which won the Morton Dauwen Zabel Award of the American Academy and Institute of Arts and Letters.

She has also published five novels; a nonfiction book about Antigua, *A Small Place* (1988); and a memoir, *My Brother* (1997). She taught creative writing for many years at Bennington College and now is Josephine Olp Weeks Professor of Literature at Claremont McKenna College in Claremont, California.

WEB: Further research this author with LitLinks at bedfordstmartins.com/rewritinglit.

ETHERIDGE KNIGHT (1931–1991) was born in Corinth, Mississippi. He dropped out of school at age sixteen and served in the U.S. Army in Korea from 1947 to 1951, returning with a shrapnel wound that caused him to fall deeper into a drug addiction that had begun during his service. In 1960, he was arrested for robbery, convicted, and sentenced to eight years in an Indiana state prison. During this time, he began writing poetry. His first book, *Poems from Prison* (1968), was published one year before his release. The book was a success, and Knight joined other poets in what came to be called the Black Arts movement, the aesthetic and spiritual sister of the Black Power concept. He went on to write several more books of poetry and to receive many prestigious honors and awards. In 1990 he earned a B.A. in American poetry and criminal justice from Martin Center University in Indianapolis.

WEB: Further research this author with LitLinks at bedfordstmartins.com/rewritinglit.

RON KOERTGE (b. 1940) was born in Olney, Illinois. He earned his B.A. from the University of Illinois and his M.A. from the University of Arizona. He is author of many poetry collections including *Dairy Cows* (1982), *Life on the Edge of the Continent: Selected Poems* (1982), *Making Love to Roget's Wife* (1997), *Geography of the Forehead* (2002), and *Indigo* (2009). He is also a novelist, writing books for both adults and young adults, most of which have been chosen by the American Library Association as "Best Books" or "Best Books for Reluctant Readers." He was professor of English at Pasadena City College from 1965 to 2001 and also taught in the Vermont College M.F.A. Program in Writing for Children and Young Adults.

YUSEF KOMUNYAKAA (b. 1947) was born and grew up in Bogalusa, Louisiana. He earned degrees at the University of Colorado, Colorado State University, and the University of California, Irvine. His numerous books of poems include *Neon Vernacular: New and Selected Poems, 1977-1989* (1994), for which he received the Pulitzer Prize and the Kingsley Tufts Poetry Award, and *Thieves of Paradise* (1998), which was a finalist for the National Book Critics Circle Award. Other publications include *Blues Notes: Essays, Interviews & Commentaries* (2000), *The Jazz Poetry Anthology* (coedited with J. A. Sascha Feinstein, 1991), and *The Insomnia of Fire* by Nguyen Quang Thieu (co-translated with Martha Collins, 1995). He has taught at the University of New Orleans, Indiana University, and Princeton University, and currently is a professor in the Creative Writing Program at New York University.

WEB: Further research this author with LitLinks at bedfordstmartins.com/rewritinglit.

TED KOOSER (b. 1939) was born in Ames, Iowa. He received his B.A. from Iowa State University and his M.A. in English from the University of Nebraska–Lincoln. He is the author of twelve collections of poetry, including *Sure Signs* (1980), *One World at a Time* (1985), *Weather Central* (1994), *Winter Morning Walks: One Hundred Postcards to Jim Harrison* (2000, winner of the 2001 Nebraska Book Award for poetry), and *Delights & Shadows* (2004). His fiction and nonfiction books include *Local Wonders: Seasons in the Bohemian Alps* (2002, winner of the Nebraska Book Award for Nonfiction in 2003) and *Braided Creek: A Conversation in Poetry* (2003), written with fellow poet and longtime friend Jim Harrison. His honors include two NEA fellowships in poetry, a Pushcart Prize, the Stanley Kunitz Prize, and a merit award from the Nebraska Arts Council. He served as the United States Poet Laureate Consultant in Poetry to the Library of Congress from 2004-2006. He lives on acreage near the village of Garland, Nebraska, and is a visiting professor in the English department of the University of Nebraska–Lincoln.

MAXINE KUMIN (b. 1925) was born in Philadelphia and received her B.A. and M.A. at Radcliffe College. She has published many books of poetry, including *Up Country: Poems of New England* (1972), for which she received the Pulitzer Prize. Her most recent collection is *Where I Live: New and Selected Poems 1990-2010* (2010). She is also the author of a memoir, *Inside the Halo and Beyond: The Anatomy of a Recovery* (2000); five novels; a collection of short stories; more than twenty children's books; and four books of essays. She has taught at the University of Massachusetts, Columbia University, Brandeis University, and Princeton University and has served as Consultant in Poetry to the Library of Congress and as poet laureate of New Hampshire, where she lives.

WEB: Further research this author with LitLinks at bedfordstmartins.com/rewritinglit.

MARK LAMBECK is a director, producer, and sometime actor but primarily a playwright. His works have been produced throughout New York, New Jersey, and Connecticut. A member of Manhattan's Emerging Artists Theatre Company and the Stratford, Connecticut-based SquareWrights, his New York credits include productions at the Pulse Ensemble Theatre, the American Globe Theatre, Spotlight On Productions, and Genesis Rep, among others. He has directed with SquareWrights, the Oronoque Reader's Theatre, and the Greenwich House Theatre in New York City's Greenwich Village. In 1998 he launched the Temple Players in Stratford, to bring shows with "identifiable Jewish characters or themes" to Connecticut audiences.

LI-YOUNG LEE (b. 1957) was born in Jakarta, Indonesia, to Chinese parents. His father, who had been personal physician to Mao Tse-tung, relocated his family to Indonesia, where he helped found Gamaliel University. In 1959, the Lee family fled the country to escape anti-Chinese sentiment, and they settled in the United States in 1964. Lee studied at the University of Pittsburgh, the University of Arizona, and the Brockport campus of the State University of New York. He has taught at several universities, including Northwestern University and the University of Iowa. He is the author of four collections of poetry—*Rose* (1986), which won the Delmore

Schwartz Memorial Poetry Award; *The City in Which I Love You* (1991), which was the 1990 Lamont Poetry Selection; *Book of My Nights* (2001); and *Behind My Eyes* (2008)—and a memoir, *The Winged Seed: A Remembrance* (1995), which received an American Book Award from the Before Columbus Foundation. In his poems, one often senses a profound sense of exile, the influence of his father's presence, and a rich spiritual sensuousness.

WEB: Further research this author with LitLinks at bedfordstmartins.com/rewritinglit.

DENISE LEVERTOV (1923–1997) was born in Ilford, Essex. Her mother was Welsh and her father was a Russian Jew who became an Anglican priest. She was educated at home and claimed to have decided to become a writer at the age of five. Her first book, *The Double Image* (1946), brought her recognition as one of a group of poets dubbed the "New Romantics." Her poems often blend the sense of an objective observer with the sensibility of a spiritual searcher. She moved to the United States after marrying the American writer Mitchell Goodman. There she turned to free-verse poetry, and with her first American book, *Here and Now* (1956), she became an important voice in the American avant-garde. In the 1960s, she became involved in the movement protesting the Vietnam War. She went on to publish more than twenty collections of poetry, four books of prose, and three volumes of poetry in translation. From 1982 to 1993, she taught at Stanford University. She spent the last decade of her life in Seattle.

WEB: Further research this author with LitLinks at bedfordstmartins.com/rewritinglit.

PHILIP LEVINE (b. 1928) was born in Detroit and received his degrees from Wayne State University and the University of Iowa. He is the author of twenty books of poetry, including *The Simple Truth* (1994), which won the Pulitzer Prize. He has also published a collection of essays, *The Bread of Time: Toward an Autobiography* (1994), edited *The Essential Keats* (1987), and coedited and translated books of poetry by Spanish poet Gloria Fuertes and Mexican poet Jamie Sabines. He divides his time between Fresno, California, and New York City, where he taught at New York University.

LARRY LEVIS (1946–1996) grew up on a farm near Fresno, California. He earned a B.A. from Fresno State College (now California State University); an M.A. from Syracuse University; and a Ph.D. from the University of Iowa. He published six collections of poetry—several of them receiving major awards—and a collection of short fiction. He taught at the University of Missouri, the University of Utah, and Virginia Commonwealth University. Levis died of a heart attack at the age of forty-nine. PHILIP LEVINE wrote that he had years earlier recognized Levis as "the most gifted and determined young poet I have ever had the good fortune to have in one of my classes. . . . His early death is a staggering loss for our poetry, but what he left is a major achievement that will enrich our lives."

YIYUN LI (b. 1972) was born and grew up in Beijing. She came to the United States in 1996 to study medicine but gave it up after three years to become a writer. She has an M.F.A. from the University of Iowa Writers' Workshop and an M.F.A. in creative nonfiction from the University of Iowa. Her stories and essays have been published in *The New Yorker, Paris Review, Zoetrope: All-Story, Ploughshares, Gettysburg Review, Glimmer Train, Prospect,* and elsewhere. Her first book, *A Thousand Years of Good Prayers* (2006), won the Frank O'Connor International Short Story Award, the PEN/Hemingway Award, the California Book Award for first fiction, and the Guardian First Book Award. Since then she has published another collection of stories, *Gold Boy, Emerald Girl* (2010), and a novel, *The Vagrants* (2009), and was named a 2010 MacArthur fellow. She teaches at the University of California, Davis.

AUDRE LORDE (1934–1992) was born in New York City of West Indian parents. She grew up in Manhattan and attended Roman Catholic schools. While she was still in high school, her first poem appeared in *Seventeen* magazine. She earned her B.A. from Hunter College and her M.A. in library science from Columbia University. In 1968, she left her job as head librarian at the University of New York to become a lecturer and creative writer. She accepted a poet-in-residence position at Tougaloo College in Mississippi, where she discovered a love of teaching, published her first volume of poetry, *The First Cities* (1968), and met her long-term partner, Frances Clayton. Many other volumes of poetry followed, several of which won major awards. She also published four volumes of prose, among them *The Cancer Journals* (1980), which chronicled her struggles with cancer, and *A Burst of Light* (1988), which won a National Book Award. In the 1980s, Lorde and writer Barbara Smith founded Kitchen Table: Women of Color Press. She was also a founding member of Sisters in Support of Sisters in South Africa, an organization that worked to raise awareness about women under apartheid. She was the poet laureate of New York from 1991 to 1992.

WEB: Further research this author with LitLinks at bedfordstmartins.com/rewritinglit.

RICHARD LOVELACE (1618–1657) was born into a prominent family in Kent, England, and went to Oxford University, where his dashing appearance and wit made him a social and literary favorite. He fought in the English civil war on the Royalist side and was imprisoned and exiled. Later he fought in France against the Spanish and was again imprisoned on his return to England. After his release he spent ten years in poverty and isolation before his death. He was a leader of the "Cavalier poets," followers of King Charles I who were soldiers and courtiers but also wrote well-crafted, light-hearted lyric poetry. "To Lucasta, Going to the Wars" (p. 837) is an excellent example of the type.

WEB: Further research this author with LitLinks at bedfordstmartins.com/rewritinglit.

ROBERT LOWELL (1917–1978) was born in Boston into a prominent New England family. He attended Harvard University and then Kenyon College, where he studied under John Crowe Ransom. At Louisiana State University, he studied with Robert Penn Warren and Cleanth Brooks as well as Allen Tate. He was always politically active — a conscientious objector during World War II and a Vietnam protestor — and suffered from manic depression. Lowell's reputation was established early: His second book, *Lord Weary's Castle*, was awarded the Pulitzer Prize for Poetry in 1947. In the mid-1950s, he began to write more directly from personal experience and loosened his adherence to traditional meter and form. The result was a watershed collection of the "confessional" school, *Life Studies* (1959), which changed the landscape of modern poetry, much as T. S. ELIOT's *The Waste Land* had done three decades before. He died suddenly from a heart attack at age sixty.

WEB: Further research this author with LitLinks at bedfordstmartins.com/rewritinglit.

RICHARD MCGUIRE (b. 1957) was born in New Jersey and now lives in New York and Paris. He is a multitalented artist who has achieved success in a variety of forms. He shot to fame in the comic world with his groundbreaking graphic story "Here" (p. 223), which was originally published in *Raw* and republished in Ivan Brunetti's *An Anthology of Graphic Fiction, Cartoons and True Stories* (2006). But his work was already widely known and respected. He is a regular art contributor to *The New Yorker*, and his comics have appeared in the *New York Times*, *McSweeney's*, *Le Monde*, and *Libération*. He has designed and directed animated films and has designed toys and games, authored children's books, and created logos, posters, and artist's books. He is also the founder of and bass player for the punk-funk band Liquid Liquid.

HEATHER MCHUGH (b. 1948) was born to Canadian parents in San Diego and grew up in Virginia. She is a graduate of Radcliffe College and the University of Denver. McHugh has published numerous books of poetry, including *Upgraded to Serious* (2009) and *Hinge & Sign: Poems 1968–1993* (1994), which won both the *Boston Book Review*'s Bingham Poetry Prize and the Pollack-Harvard Review Prize, was a finalist for the National Book Award, and was named a "Notable Book of the Year" by the *New York Times Book Review*. She has also written a book of prose, *Broken English: Poetry and Partiality* (1993), and two books of translations. She was awarded a MacArthur Foundation grant in 2009. She teaches as a core faculty member in the M.F.A. Program for Writers at Warren Wilson College and as Milliman Writer-in-Residence at the University of Washington, Seattle.

WEB: Further research this author with LitLinks at bedfordstmartins.com/rewritinglit.

CLAUDE MCKAY (1890–1948), the son of poor farmworkers, was born in Sunny Ville, Jamaica. He was educated by his older brother, who possessed a library of English novels, poetry, and scientific texts. At age twenty, McKay published a book of verse in dialect called *Songs of Jamaica*, recording his impressions of black life in Jamaica. In 1912, he traveled to the United States to attend Tuskegee Institute. He soon left to study agriculture at Kansas State University. In 1914, he moved to Harlem and became an influential member of the Harlem Renaissance. After committing to communism and traveling to Moscow in 1922, he lived for some time in Europe and Morocco, writing fiction. McKay later repudiated communism, converted to Roman Catholicism, and returned to the United States. He published several books of poetry as well as an autobiography, *A Long Way from Home* (1937).

WEB: Further research this author with LitLinks at bedfordstmartins.com/rewritinglit.

EDUARDO MACHADO (b. 1953) was born in Havana, Cuba. He and his brother Jesus emigrated to the United States without their parents in 1961 as part of Operation Pedro Pan, which brought Cuban children to the United States in the early part of Fidel Castro's rule. They lived with relatives in Florida until their parents were able to emigrate and settle in California. Machado started acting professionally in California at seventeen and became a member of the Screen Actors Guild at twenty. He studied acting with David Alexander and began writing plays under the tutelage of María Irene Fornés in 1980. He moved to New York City in 1981. The author of many successful plays, he is regarded as one of the leading voices among contemporary Latino dramatic writers. He has taught playwriting at Columbia University, where he was the head of the graduate playwriting program, and now teaches at New York University, where he is head of playwriting.

CHRISTOPHER MARLOWE (1564–1593) was born in Canterbury, England, the same year as WILLIAM SHAKESPEARE. The son of a shoemaker, he needed the help of scholarships to attend King's School, Canterbury, and Corpus Christi College, Cambridge. He was involved in secret political missions for the government. He was one of the most brilliant writers of his generation, in narrative poetry, lyric poetry, and drama (his best-known play is *Doctor Faustus*). He died after being knifed in a bar fight, reportedly over his bill, at the age of twenty-nine. "The Passionate Shepherd to His Love" (p. 840) is among the most famous of Elizabethan poems.

WEB: Further research this author with LitLinks at bedfordstmartins.com/rewritinglit.

MÁRQUEZ, GABRIEL GARCÍA—See GARCÍA MÁRQUEZ, GABRIEL.

ANDREW MARVELL (1621–1678) was born in Hull, Yorkshire, and educated at Trinity College, Cambridge. After traveling in Europe, he worked as a tutor and in a government office (as assistant to JOHN MILTON) and later became a member of Parliament for Hull. Marvell was known in his lifetime as a writer of rough satires in verse and prose. His "serious" poetry, like "To His Coy Mistress" (p. 841), was not published until after his death. It is a famous exploration of the *carpe diem* theme (see the Glossary of Literary Terms, p. 1471).

WEB: Further research this author with LitLinks at bedfordstmartins.com/rewritinglit.

DAVID MEANS (b. 1961), a native of Michigan, now lives in Nyack, New York, and teaches at Vassar College. His first book of short stories, *A Quick Kiss of Redemption*, was published in 1991. His second, *Assorted Fire Events* (2000), won the Los Angeles Times Book Award and was a finalist for the National Book Critics Circle Award. His most recent book is *The Spot* (2010). His stories have appeared in the *New Yorker*, *Harper's*, *Esquire*, *The O. Henry Prize Stories*, *The Best American Short Stories*, and *The Best American Mystery Stories*.

JOHN MILTON (1608–1674), son of a well-off London businessman, was educated at St. Paul's School and at home with private tutors. After graduating with an M.A. from Christ's College, Cambridge, he spent the next six years reading at home. Milton had written verse since his university days, but he broke off to write prose tracts in favor of Oliver Cromwell, in whose government he later headed a department. The strain of long hours of reading and writing for the revolutionary cause aggravated a genetic weakness and resulted in his total blindness around 1651. He wrote his most famous works, *Paradise Lost* (1667), *Paradise Regained* (1671), and *Samson Agonistes* (1671), by dictating them to his daughter and other amanuenses.

WEB: Further research this author with LitLinks at bedfordstmartins.com/rewritinglit.

KATHERINE MIN (b. 1959) was born in Champaign-Urbana, Illinois, and grew up in Charlottesville, Virginia, and Clifton Park, New York. She graduated from Amherst College and the Columbia School of Journalism. Her short stories have appeared in numerous literary journals and anthologies. "Courting a Monk" (p. 247) won a Pushcart Prize in 1998. Her novel *Secondhand World* was selected one of the best books of 2006 by *School Library Journal*, one of the best debut novels of the year by the *Rocky Mountain News*, and was a winter guide pick on *MSNBC.com*. She lives in New Hampshire and teaches at Plymouth State University and in the Iowa Summer Writing Festival.

GARY MIRANDA (b. 1938) was born in Bremerton, Washington, and grew up in the Pacific Northwest. After spending six years in a Jesuit seminary, he went on to do graduate work at San Jose State College and the University of California, Irvine. He is the author of three collections of poetry, *Listeners at the Breathing Place* (1978), *Grace Period* (1983), and *Turning Sixty* (2001) and has published a translation of Rainer Maria Rilke's *Duino Elegies* (1981). He lives in Portland, Oregon.

MARIANNE MOORE (1887–1972) was born near St. Louis and grew up in Carlisle, Pennsylvania. After studying at Bryn Mawr College and Carlisle Commercial College, she taught at a government Indian school in Carlisle. She moved to Brooklyn, where she became an assistant at the New York Public Library. She loved baseball and spent a good deal of time watching her beloved Brooklyn Dodgers. She began to write imagist poetry and to contribute to the *Dial*, a prestigious literary magazine. She served as acting editor of the *Dial*

from 1925 to 1929 and later as editor for four years. Moore was widely recognized for her work, receiving among other honors the Bollingen Prize for Poetry, the National Book Award, and the Pulitzer Prize.

WEB: Further research this author with LitLinks at bedfordstmartins.com/rewritinglit.

PAT MORA (b. 1942) was born and grew up in El Paso, Texas. She is a descendant of four Mexican grandparents who came to Texas during the Mexican Revolution of 1910 and during the early twentieth century. She earned degrees at Texas Western College and the University of Texas, El Paso. She has published more than thirty volumes of poetry, nonfiction, and children's picture books and received many awards for her work, including the Kellogg National Leadership Fellowship, four Southwest Book Awards, and the Premio Aztlan Literature Award. She has been a distinguished visiting professor at the University of New Mexico, a museum director, and a consultant for U.S.–Mexico youth exchanges. She has spent much of her teaching time working with young writers. Now retired, but still teaching on her own, she lives in Santa Fe, New Mexico, and Cincinnati, Ohio.

TONI MORRISON (b. 1931) was born Chloe Anthony Wofford in Lorain, Ohio. She spent her childhood in the Midwest, reading widely in such classic authors as Leo Tolstoy, Feodor Dostoyevski, Gustave Flaubert, and Jane Austen on the one hand, and absorbing folktales and literary culture of the black community from her father on the other. She received her B.A. from Howard University (where she began using a shortened form of her middle name because "Chloe" was difficult for others to pronounce) and her M.A. from Cornell University. She taught at Texas Southern University and Howard University and then worked as an editor for Random House. In 1958, while teaching at Howard, she married Harold Morrison, a Jamaican architect, and she began writing fiction. Her first novel, *The Bluest Eye*, was published in 1970, followed by *Sula* in 1973. Her next novel, *Song of Solomon* (1977), brought her international recognition. It was the first novel by a black writer to be a main selection of the Book-of-the-Month Club since Richard Wright's *Native Son* in

1949. In 1984, she was appointed to an Albert Schweitzer chair at the University of New York at Albany. Her fifth novel, *Beloved* (1987), was awarded the 1987 Pulitzer Prize for Fiction. In 1987, Morrison was named the Robert F. Goheen Professor in the Council of Humanities at Princeton University, the first black woman writer to hold a named chair at an Ivy League university. Later novels are *Jazz* (1992), *Paradise* (1998), *Love* (2003), and *A Mercy* (2008). In 1993, she became the eighth woman and the first black woman to receive the Nobel Prize for Literature.

THYLIAS MOSS (b. 1954) was born in Cleveland. She attended Syracuse University and received her B.A. from Oberlin College and M.F.A. from the University of New Hampshire. She is the author of numerous books of poetry, most recently *Tokyo Butter* (2006); a memoir, *Tale of a Sky-Blue Dress* (1998); two children's books; and two plays, *Talking to Myself* (1984) and *The Dolls in the Basement* (1984). Among her awards are a Guggenheim Fellowship and a MacArthur Foundation Fellowship. She lives in Ann Arbor, where she is a professor of English at the University of Michigan.

WEB: Further research this author with LitLinks at bedfordstmartins.com/rewritinglit.

BHARATI MUKHERJEE (b. 1940) was born in Calcutta, India, into a wealthy traditional family. In 1947, her father was given a job in England and he brought his family to live in London until 1951, where Mukherjee perfected her English language skills. Her parents gave their children excellent educational opportunities, with Mukherjee earning a B.A. from the University of Calcutta and an M.A. from Baroda University. Having written stories since she was five, she knew she wanted to be a writer and entered the prestigious University of Iowa Writers' Workshop, intending to earn an M.F.A. and then return to India to marry a bridegroom of her father's choosing. However, while in Iowa City, she met a Canadian student from Harvard, Clark Blaise, and married him after a two-week courtship. After receiving her M.F.A., she went on to earn her Ph.D. in English and comparative literature from the University of Iowa in 1969. For ten difficult years, she and her husband lived in Canada where she experienced discrimination

and was treated as a member of a "visible minority." During that time she taught at McGill University and published her first two novels. In 1980, Mukherjee and her family moved to the United States, where she taught at a number of colleges and universities and published several more novels, two collections of stories, and two books with her husband about experiences in India. She is a professor of English at the University of California–Berkeley.

DAVID MURA (b. 1952), a third-generation Japanese American, was born in Great Lakes, Illinois, and graduated from Grinnell College in Iowa; he did graduate work at the University of Minnesota and Vermont College. Mura is a poet, creative nonfiction writer, critic, playwright, and performance artist. He is author of numerous books of poetry, including *After We Lost Our Way* (1989), which was selected as a National Poetry Series winner; two novels; and two memoirs: *Turning Japanese: Memoirs of a Sansei* (1991), which was a *New York Times* Notable Book of the Year; and *Where the Body Meets Memory: An Odyssey of Race, Sexuality & Identity* (1996).

WEB: Further research this author with LitLinks at bedfordstmartins.com/rewritinglit.

HARUKI MURAKAMI (b. 1949), one of the most popular and widely translated of all contemporary Japanese authors, is a novelist, short-story writer, essayist, and translator whose work combines postmodern techniques and fantasy with influences from American culture. He was born in Kyoto, but grew up in Ashiya, Hyogo, before moving to Tokyo in 1968 to study theater at Waseda University, graduating in 1975. From 1974 to 1981, Murakami and his wife managed a jazz club. He started to write in the 1970s and has published a dozen novels—most recently *1Q84* (2009)—in addition to many short stories. In 2006, Murakami became the sixth recipient of the Franz Kafka Prize from the Czech Republic for his 2002 novel *Umibe no Kafka* (*Kafka on the Shore*).

WEB: Further research this author with LitLinks at bedfordstmartins.com/rewritinglit.

MARILYN NELSON (b. 1946) was born in Cleveland, Ohio, and grew up on numerous military bases. Her father was a U.S. serviceman in the air force, one of the last Tuskegee Airmen, and her mother was a teacher. While still in elementary school, she started writing. She earned her B.A. from the University of California–Davis, her M.A. from the University of Pennsylvania, and her Ph.D. from the University of Minnesota. *The Homeplace* (1990), *The Fields of Praise: New and Selected Poems* (1997), and *Carver: A Life in Poems* (2001) were all finalists for the National Book Award. In addition to her many poetry collections for adults and children, she has translated from the Danish Halfdan Rasmussen's *Hundreds of Hens and Other Poems*. She is founder and director of Soul Mountain Retreat, a writer's colony that encourages and supports poets who belong to underrepresented racial or cultural groups. She is professor emerita of English at the University of Connecticut and was poet laureate of Connecticut from 2001 to 2006.

LORINE NIEDECKER (1903–1970) was born and died in Fort Atkinson, Wisconsin. She lived much of her life in a small cabin on Black Hawk Island on Lake Koshkonong. Though celebrated by many of the most acclaimed experimental/modernist/objectivist writers of the twentieth century, among them WILLIAM CARLOS WILLIAMS and Louis Zukofsky, she chose to remain isolated from the poetry world, living an all but reclusive life. Niedecker said that she spent her childhood outdoors and from that developed her keen eye and strong sense of place. In 1931, she discovered "objectivist" poetry, which called for sincerity and objectification, values that fit well with her own vision and influenced her poems from that time on. While living on Black Hawk Island, she worked in a local hospital cleaning the kitchen and scrubbing floors. Her books include *New Goose* (1946), *North Central* (1968), *My Life by Water* (published the year of her death), and *Blue Chicory* (published posthumously in 1976). Her selected poems, *The Granite Pail*, was not published until 1985.

DON NIGRO (b. 1949) was born in Malvern, Ohio. He received his B.A. in English from the Ohio State University and his M.F.A. in playwriting from the University of Iowa. He has written more than two hundred plays, twenty-eight of them produced off Broadway.

Two of them, *The Dark Sonnets of the Lady* (1992) and *Anima Mundi* (1994), were nominated for the National Repertory Theatre Foundation's National Play Award. The film *The Manor* (1999) was adapted from his play *Ravenscroft* (1991). His works have been performed throughout the United States and Canada as well as in London and Budapest. He has been the James Thurber Writer in Residence at Thurber House and has taught at several universities.

NAOMI SHIHAB NYE (b. 1952) was born in St. Louis of a Palestinian father and an American mother and grew up in both the United States and Jerusalem. She received her B.A. from Trinity University in San Antonio, Texas, where she still resides with her family. She is the author of many books of poems, most recently *You and Yours* (2005), which received the Isabella Gardner Poetry Award. She has also written short stories and books for children and has edited anthologies, several of which focus on the lives of children and represent work from around the world. She is a singer-songwriter and on several occasions has traveled to the Middle East and Asia for the U.S. Information Agency, promoting international goodwill through the arts. Nye's work often attests to a universal sense of exile, from place, home, love, and one's self, and the way the human spirit confronts it.

WEB: Further research this author with LitLinks at bedfordstmartins.com/rewritinglit.

JOYCE CAROL OATES (b. 1938) was born in Lockport, New York. She began storytelling in early childhood, composing picture stories even before she could write. Only after earning a B.A. from Syracuse University and an M.A. from the University of Wisconsin did she focus on writing as a career. Her first book was a collection of stories, *By the North Gate* (1963). Since then she has gone on to become one of the most versatile, prolific, and important American writers of her time, publishing more than a hundred books—novels, story collections, poetry, plays, children's books, and literary criticism. She has been nominated for the Nobel Prize for Literature three times. She is the Roger S. Berlind Distinguished Professor of Humanities at Princeton University.

WEB: Further research this author with LitLinks at bedfordstmartins.com/rewritinglit.

TIM O'BRIEN (b. 1946) was born in Austin, Minnesota, and grew up in Worthington, Minnesota. He attended Macalester College in Minneapolis and, on graduation, was drafted for military service in Vietnam. O'Brien served from 1969 to 1970 as an infantry foot soldier in the Americal division, which was involved in the My Lai massacre in 1968, an event that figures prominently in O'Brien's novel *In the Lake of the Woods* (1994). While in Vietnam he rose to the rank of sergeant and received the Purple Heart. After Vietnam he entered graduate school at Harvard University but left to become a newspaper reporter, a career he pursued until publication of his first book, *If I Die in a Combat Zone, Box Me Up and Ship Me Home* (1973). He has gone on to write several other novels, including *Going after Cacciato* (1978), which won the National Book Award. His collection of stories *The Things They Carried* (1990) was a finalist for the National Book Critics Circle Award and for the Pulitzer Prize and winner of the Heartland Award from the *Chicago Tribune* and of the French prize for the best foreign book of the year; it was chosen by the *New York Times Book Review* as one of the nine best books of the year in all categories. He lives in Texas and teaches alternate years in the creative writing program at Texas State University–San Marcos.

WEB: Further research this author with LitLinks at bedfordstmartins.com/rewritinglit.

FLANNERY O'CONNOR (1925–1964) was born in Savannah, Georgia. She earned her B.A. from Georgia State College for Women in Milledgeville, Georgia, and an M.F.A. from the University of Iowa Writers' Workshop. When she was twenty-five, she was found to have disseminated lupus, an incurable disease from which her father had died when she was thirteen. She returned to Milledgeville for treatments that slowed the progress of the disease. Living with her mother on the family dairy farm, she wrote in the mornings and rested, read, and carried on correspondence in the afternoons, and she traveled to give occasional lectures as health permitted. She wrote only two novels, *Wise Blood* (1952) and *The Violent Bear It Away* (1960); her literary output also includes two collections of stories, *A Good Man Is Hard to Find* (1955) and *Everything That Rises Must Converge* (1965); a collection of her lectures and essays, *Mystery and Manners* (published posthumously in 1969); and a volume of correspondence (published in 1979 as *The Habit of Being*). Despite her career being cut short, O'Connor is widely recognized as a major southern writer. Her short stories are generally considered to be her finest work; they are carefully crafted, often focusing on grotesque characters redeemed by grace, have a crisp humor, and reflect the influence of her Catholic faith. *Complete Stories*, a collection of the thirty-one stories she wrote, won the National Book Award for fiction in 1972.

WEB: Further research this author with LitLinks at bedfordstmartins.com/rewritinglit.

SHARON OLDS (b. 1942) was born in San Francisco and educated at Stanford and Columbia universities. She has written eleven books of poetry and received numerous important prizes and awards. Olds is known for writing intensely personal, emotional poetry that graphically depicts family life as well as global political events. "Sharon Olds is enormously self-aware," says critic David Leavitt. "Her poetry is remarkable for its candor, its eroticism, and its power to move." She lives in New York City and was New York State Poet from 1998 to 2000. She teaches in the graduate writing program at New York University.

MARY OLIVER (b. 1935) was born in Cleveland and educated at Ohio State University and Vassar College. She is the author of some twenty volumes of poetry, including *American Primitive* (1983), for which she won the Pulitzer Prize, and four books of prose. Her most recent book is *Swan: Poems and Prose Poems* (2010). She held the Catharine Osgood Foster Chair for Distinguished Teaching at Bennington College until 2001, and now lives in Provincetown, Massachusetts. Oliver is one of the most respected among poets concerned for the natural world.

WEB: Further research this author with LitLinks at bedfordstmartins.com/rewritinglit.

TILLIE OLSEN (1912?–2007) was born either near Mead, Nebraska, or in Omaha, Nebraska. Her parents were Jewish immigrants who fled from the Russian czarist repression after the revolution of 1905. In the 1920s, her father became a leader in the Nebraska Socialist Party. After the eleventh grade she had to leave school to help support her family during the Depression. She joined the Young Communist League and throughout her life was active politically, especially in causes rooted to her attachment to poor and oppressed workers. Early in 1932, she wrote four chapters of her first novel, *Yonnondio.* Part of one chapter was published as "The Iron Throat" in the *Partisan Review* in 1934 and was acclaimed critically. She wrote very little for the next two decades, during which she married, had a child, and had to care for the child alone, much as described in her story "I Stand Here Ironing" (p. 506). She then had three more children with Jack Olsen, a YCL comrade whom she moved in with in 1936 and married in 1944. When her youngest child entered school in 1953, she was able to take creative writing classes at San Francisco State College and Stanford University. "Tell Me a Riddle" won the O. Henry Award for Best Short Story of the Year (1961). It and three other stories were published in *Tell Me a Riddle* (1961), selected by *Time* magazine for its "best-ten-books" list in 1962. Olsen then went on to complete *Yonnondio* (1974) and a nonfiction work, *Silences* (1978). She played an important role in reclaiming the works of neglected women authors. Despite her limited literary output, she received wide recognition for the quality of her fiction and for the importance of her contributions to the feminist movement.

WEB: Further research this author with LitLinks at bedfordstmartins.com/rewritinglit.

MICHAEL OPPENHEIMER (b. 1943) was born in Berkeley, California, and grew up on a cattle ranch in Colorado. He earned his undergraduate degree at Antioch College and his master's degree at Lone Mountain College–University of San Francisco. In addition to writing fiction, Oppenheimer has worked as a reporter, teacher, and publisher. He currently lives in Bellingham, Washington.

SIMON J. ORTIZ (b. 1941) was born and raised in the Acoma Pueblo Community in Albuquerque. He received his early education from the Bureau of Indian Affairs school on the Acoma reservation, later attending the University of New Mexico and completing his M.F.A. at the University of Iowa, where he was a part of the International Writing Program. Unlike most Native American contemporary writers, Ortiz is a full-blooded Native American, and his first language is Keresan. By learning English, he found a way to communicate with those outside his immediate culture. His poetry explores the significance of individual origins and journeys, which he sees as forming a vital link in the continuity of life. His many writing accomplishments include poems, short stories, essays, and children's books. Ortiz has taught Native American literature and creative writing at San Diego State University, Navajo Community College, Marin College, the Institute for the Arts of the American Indian, the University of New Mexico, the University of Toronto, and most recently Arizona State University.

WEB: Further research this author with LitLinks at bedfordstmartins.com/rewritinglit.

WILFRED OWEN (1893–1918) was born in Oswestry, Shropshire, and went to school at Birkenhead Institute and Shrewsbury Technical School. He studied at London University but was forced to withdraw for financial reasons. After that he went to Dunsden, Oxfordshire, as a vicar's assistant. At Dunsden, Owen grew disaffected with the church and left to teach in France. He enlisted in 1915 and six months later was hospitalized in Edinburgh, where he met Siegfried Sassoon, whose war poems had just been published. Owen was sent back to the front and was killed one week before the armistice. He is the most widely recognized of the "war poets," a group of World War I writers who brought the realism of war into poetry.

WEB: Further research this author with LitLinks at bedfordstmartins.com/rewritinglit.

ZZ PACKER (b. 1973) was born in Chicago and grew up in Atlanta and Louisville. Her given name is *Zuwena*, Swahili for "good." After teachers kept mispronouncing her name, she began introducing herself as "ZZ" and, she says, "it just kind of stuck." She was nineteen when she published her first significant work in *Seventeen* magazine. She had planned to become an electrical engineer but decided to attend Yale University instead of Massachusetts Institute of Technology. She went on to earn an M.A. at Johns Hopkins and an M.F.A. from the University of Iowa Writers' Workshop. She was named a Stegner Fellow in Fiction at Stanford. Her first collection, *Drinking Coffee Elsewhere* (2004), was a finalist for the PEN/Faulkner Award. She has served on the creative writing faculty or served as writer-in-residence at California College of the Arts, Tulane University, San Jose State University, and Texas State University. In 2010 she was selected for the *New Yorker's* "20 under 40" fiction issue.

DOROTHY PARKER (1893–1967) was born in West End, New Jersey, and educated at a Catholic school. After the death of her mother, stepmother, and father, she moved to New York City and became a well-known short story writer, poet, and critic and an important figure in the New York literary scene. From 1917 to 1920 Parker worked for *Vanity Fair* and, with writers Robert Benchley and Robert Sherwood, she formed the nucleus of the Algonquin Round Table, an informal luncheon club held at New York City's Algonquin Hotel on Forty-Fourth Street where the most famous writers of the day gathered. Between the years 1927 and 1933 Parker wrote a highly popular column, "Constant Reader," for *The New Yorker*, and her work continued to appear in the magazine at irregular intervals until 1955. Her first collection of poems, *Enough Rope*, published in 1926, was a best seller and was followed by *Sunset Guns* (1928) and *Death and Taxes* (1931), which were collected in *Collected Poems: Not so Deep as a Well* (1936). During the 1920s Parker drank heavily and attempted suicide three times but maintained the high quality of her literary output. She spent the 1930s in Hollywood, working as a screenwriter. With Lillian Hellman and Dashiell Hammett, she helped found the Screen Writers' Guild. She was blacklisted during the McCarthy era but was never a member of the Communist Party.

SUZAN-LORI PARKS (b. 1964) was born in Fort Knox, Kentucky, and attended high school in West Germany and Maryland. She started writing plays at Mount Holyoke College, from which she graduated with a B.A. in English and German literature. Her numerous plays include *Imperceptible Mutabilities in the Third Kingdom* (1990 Obie Award for Best New American Play), *The Death of the Last Black Man in the Whole Entire World* (1990), *Venus* (1996 Obie Award), and *In the Blood* (2000 Pulitzer Prize finalist). She is the first African American woman to receive the Pulitzer Prize for Drama, for *Topdog/Underdog* (2002). She received a MacArthur Foundation Fellowship in 2001. In November 2002, she undertook the project of writing a short play each day for a year. *365 Plays/365 Days* was staged in nearly seven hundred theaters, in more than thirty cities across the United States in 2006–2007, one of the largest grassroots collaborations in theater history.

WEB: Further research this author with LitLinks at bedfordstmartins.com/rewritinglit.

LINDA PASTAN (b. 1932) was born in New York City, graduated from Radcliffe College, and earned an M.A. from Brandeis University. She has published many books of poetry—including *Traveling Light* (2011)—and received numerous awards for them, including a Dylan Thomas Award. Her deeply emotional poetry often has grief at its center. She is known for writing short poems that address family life, domesticity, motherhood, the female experience, aging, death, loss and the fear of loss, as well as the fragility of life and relationships. She served as Poet Laureate of Maryland from 1991 to 1994 and was a staff member at the Breadloaf Writers Conference for twenty years. She lives in Potomac, Maryland.

MARGE PIERCY (b. 1936) was born in working-class Detroit and studied at the University of Michigan and Northwestern University. She has published seventeen books of poetry, seventeen novels, a collection of essays on poetry, *Parti-Colored Blocks for a Quilt* (1982), and a memoir, *Sleeping with Cats* (2002). She has been deeply involved in many of the major progressive political battles of the past fifty years, including anti–Vietnam War activities, the women's movement, and most recently resistance to the war in Iraq.

WEB: Further research this author with LitLinks at bedfordstmartins.com/rewritinglit.

ROBERT PINSKY (b. 1940) was born in Long Branch, New Jersey. He is the author of many books of poetry, including *The Figured Wheel: New and Collected Poems 1966-1996* (1996), which won the 1997 Lenore Marshall Poetry Prize and was a Pulitzer Prize nominee. He has also published several books of criticism, two books of translation, a biography—*The Life of David* (2005)—several books on reading poetry, and a computerized novel, *Mindwheel* (1984). In 1999 he coedited with Maggie Dietz *Americans' Favorite Poems: The Favorite Poem Project Anthology*. He is currently poetry editor of the weekly Internet magazine *Slate* and teaches in the graduate writing program at Boston University. In 1997 he was named Poet Laureate Consultant in Poetry at the Library of Congress.

WEB: Further research this author with LitLinks at bedfordstmartins.com/rewritinglit.

SYLVIA PLATH (1932-1963) grew up in a middle-class family in Boston and showed early promise as a writer, having stories and poems published in magazines such as *Seventeen* while she was in high school. As a student at Smith College, she was selected for an internship at *Mademoiselle* magazine and spent a month working in New York in the summer of 1953. Upon her return home, she suffered a serious breakdown and attempted suicide, was institutionalized, and then returned to Smith College for her senior year in 1954. She received a Fulbright fellowship to study at Cambridge University in England, where she met poet Ted Hughes. They were married in 1956. They lived in the United States as well as England, and Plath studied under ROBERT LOWELL at Boston University. Her marriage to Hughes broke up in 1962, and from her letters and poems it appears that she was approaching another breakdown. On February 11, 1963, she committed suicide. Four books of poetry appeared during her lifetime, and her *Selected Poems* was published in 1985. The powerful, psychologi-

cally intense poetry for which she is best known (including "Daddy," p. 851) was written after 1960, influenced by the "confessional" style of Lowell.

WEB: Further research this author with LitLinks at bedfordstmartins.com/rewritinglit.

EDGAR ALLAN POE (1809-1849) was born in Boston. His parents were touring actors; both died before he was three years old, and he was taken into the home of John Allan, a prosperous merchant in Richmond, Virginia, and baptized Edgar Allan Poe. His childhood was uneventful, although he studied in England for five years (1815-1820). In 1826, he entered the University of Virginia but, because of gambling debts, stayed for only a year. He began to write and published a book of poems in 1827. He joined the army and gained an appointment to West Point but was dismissed after six months for disobedience of orders. He turned to fiction writing and journalism to support himself. He began publishing stories and was appointed editor of the *Southern Literary Messenger* in Richmond, but his job was terminated after two years because of his drinking. He achieved success as an artist and editor in New York City (1837), then in Philadelphia (1838-1844), and again in New York (1844-1849) but failed to satisfy his employers and to secure a livelihood, and thus lived in or close to poverty his entire adulthood. He is famous for his horror tales and is credited with inventing the detective story, as well as for writing poetry with a prominent use of rhythms, alliteration, and assonance that gives it a strongly musical quality.

WEB: Further research this author with LitLinks at bedfordstmartins.com/rewritinglit.

KATHERINE ANNE PORTER (1890-1980), a descendant of Daniel Boone, was born in Indian Creek, Texas. When she was two, her mother died; she was raised by her grandmother and attended convent schools. At sixteen, she ran away to get married, but left her husband a few years later to be an actress. She worked briefly as a reporter in Chicago and Denver. Between 1918 and 1921, she became involved in revolutionary politics and worked as a journalist and teacher in Mexico, the setting for several of her stories. She traveled in the late

1920s to Europe, settling in Paris during the early 1930s, and began publishing stories in magazines. Her first book, *Flowering Judas and Other Stories* (1930), won high praise. It was followed by *Noon Wine* (1937), *Pale Horse, Pale Rider: Three Short Novels* (1939), and numerous other books of essays, stories, and nonfiction. Her only novel, *Ship of Fools* (1962), on which she worked for twenty years, was published when she was seventy-two. Her *Collected Stories* (1965) won the Pulitzer Prize for Fiction and the National Book Award.

WEB: Further research this author with LitLinks at bedfordstmartins.com/rewritinglit.

EZRA POUND (1885–1972) was born in Idaho but grew up outside Philadelphia and began studying at the University of Pennsylvania at the age of sixteen. He was fired from a teaching job at Wabash College and left for Europe, where he lived for the next few decades in Venice and London. There, Pound founded several literary movements—including imagism and Vorticism—and began his major work, the *Cantos*. During World War II he did radio broadcasts from Italy in support of Mussolini, for which he was indicted for treason in the United States. Judged mentally unfit for trial, he remained in an asylum in Washington, D.C., until 1958, when the charges were dropped. Pound spent his last years in Italy.

A. K. RAMANUJAN (1929–1993) was an internationally renowned poet and scholar as well as a professor of linguistics, anthropology, the history of religions, folklore, and literary studies. He was one of India's most published authors with an international recognition for expertise as a writer and translator. He wrote in English and Kannada and translated works from Tamil and Kannada into English and from English into Kannada. At the time of his death, he was the William H. Colvin Professor in South Asian Languages and Civilizations at the University of Chicago.

MARCO RAMIREZ (b. 1983) is a native of Miami, Florida. He was only eighteen, a high school senior, when his one-act play *Domino* was performed at Miami's Coconut Grove Playhouse in 2001. He twice won the Heideman Award given by the Humana Festival for

New Plays at the Actors Theater of Louisville, once for *I Am Not Batman* (2007) and once for *3:59 A.M.* (2009). He is a graduate of the Juilliard School, where he studied under the instruction of playwrights Christopher Durang and Marsha Norman. He has had plays produced at the Kennedy Center, Julliard, the Arsht Center, Louisville's Humana Festival, and other venues.

DUDLEY RANDALL (1914–2002) was born in Washington, D.C., but lived most of his life in Detroit. His first published poem appeared in the *Detroit Free Press* when he was thirteen. He worked for Ford Motor Company and then for the U.S. Postal Service and served in the South Pacific during World War II. He graduated from Wayne State University in 1949 and then from the library school at the University of Michigan. In 1965, Randall established the Broadside Press, one of the most important publishers of modern black poetry. "Ballad of Birmingham" (p. 853), written in response to the 1963 bombing of a church in which four African American girls were killed, has been set to music and recorded. It became an "anthem" for many in the civil rights movement.

WEB: Further research this author with LitLinks at bedfordstmartins.com/rewritinglit.

HENRY REED (1914–1986) was born in Birmingham, Warwickshire, England, and was educated at the University of Birmingham, where his circle of friends included W. H. AUDEN and Louis MacNiece. His service in the British army during World War II provided the basis for his famous *Lessons of the War* (three related poems, of which "Naming of Parts" is the first). In addition to his one early volume of poetry, he is well known in Britain for his many radio plays; he also published translations and a book on the novel.

ADRIENNE RICH (b. 1929) was born in Baltimore, the elder daughter of a forceful Jewish intellectual who encouraged and critiqued her writing. While she was at Radcliffe College in 1951, W. H. AUDEN selected her book *A Change of World* for the Yale Younger Poets Award. She became involved in radical politics, especially in the opposition to the Vietnam War, and taught inner-city minority youth. In the 1970s,

Rich became a feminist, freeing herself from her old models and becoming an influential figure in contemporary American literature. She is the author of over twenty volumes of poetry, including *Diving into the Wreck* (1973), *Dark Fields of the Republic* (1995), and *The School among the Ruins: Poems 2000-2004* (2004), which won the Book Critics Circle Award, and several books of nonfiction prose. Her most recent books of poetry are *Tonight No Poetry Will Serve* (2011) and *Telephone Ringing in the Labyrinth* (2007). She edited Muriel Rukeyser's *Selected Poems* for the Library of America. *A Human Eye: Essays on Art in Society* appeared in 2009. She was awarded a MacArthur Foundation Fellowship in 1994 and in 1999 received the Lifetime Achievement Award from the Lannan Foundation. She was the 2006 recipient of the National Book Foundation's Medal for Distinguished Contribution to American Letters. She lives in California.

WEB: Further research this author with LitLinks at bedfordstmartins.com/rewritinglit.

JACK RIDL (b. 1944) was born and grew up in New Wilmington, Pennsylvania. His father was a basketball coach and his mother had family connections with circuses throughout the United States. He has said that he spent his life watching the big shows from behind the scenes. He has published five collections of poetry—*The Same Ghost* (1984), *Be tween* (1988), *Poems from* The Same Ghost *and* Be tween (1993), *Broken Symmetry* (2006), and *Losing Season* (2009)—and three chapbooks: *After School* (1988), *Against Elegies* (selected by BILLY COLLINS as winner of the Center for Book Arts 2001 Poetry Chapbook Competition), and *Outside the Center Ring* (2006). His poems have appeared in numerous anthologies and poetry journals. He taught at Hope College for thirty-four years before retiring in 2006; in 1996, he was named Michigan Professor of the Year by the Council for the Advancement and Support of Education.

ALBERTO RÍOS (b. 1952) was born to a Guatemalan father and an English mother in Nogales, Arizona, on the Mexican border. He earned a B.A. in English and one in psychology and an M.F.A. at the University of Arizona. In addition to ten books of poetry, he has published three collections of short stories, and a memoir, *Capirotada: A Nogales Memoir* (1999). His work often fuses realism, surrealism, and magical realism, as exemplified by "Nani" (p. 857). Since 1994, he has been Regents Professor of English at Arizona State University, where he has taught since 1982.

WEB: Further research this author with LitLinks at bedfordstmartins.com/rewritinglit.

EDWIN ARLINGTON ROBINSON (1869–1935) was born in Head Tide, Maine, and grew up in the equally provincial Maine town of Gardiner, the setting for much of his poetry. He was forced to leave Harvard University after two years because of his family's financial difficulties. He published his first two books of poetry in 1896 and 1897 ("Richard Cory" [p. 637] appeared in the latter). For the next quarter-century Robinson chose to live in poverty and write his poetry, supporting himself through temporary jobs and charity from friends. President Theodore Roosevelt, at the urging of his son Kermit, used his influence to get Robinson a sinecure in the New York Custom House in 1905, giving him time to write. He published numerous books of mediocre poetry in the next decade. The tide turned for him with *The Man against the Sky* (1916); the numerous volumes that followed received high praise and sold well. He was awarded three Pulitzer Prizes: for *Collected Poems* (1921), *The Man Who Died Twice* (1924), and *Tristram* (1927). Robinson was the first major American poet of the twentieth century, unique in that he devoted his life to poetry and willingly paid the price in poverty and obscurity.

LUIS J. RODRIGUEZ (b. 1954) was born in El Paso, Texas, but grew up in Watts and East Los Angeles, California. By eleven, he was already involved in gangs and by the time he was eighteen he had lost twenty-five friends to gang fights and killings. From this life came his best-selling memoir, *Always Running: La Vida Loca, Gang Days in L.A.* (1993), winner of the Carl Sandburg Award from the Friends of the Chicago Library Association. Rodriguez now lives in Chicago where he is also a journalist and critic, his work appearing in a wide variety of national magazines. He is regarded as one of the leading Chicano writers in the country, with fourteen published books in memoir, fiction, nonfiction, children's literature, and poetry. He is also known for helping start community organizations, like Chicago's Guild Complex, one of the largest literary arts organizations in the Midwest; Humboldt Park Teen Reach in Chicago; and Tia Chucha Press, one of this country's premier small presses. He is a founder of Youth Struggling for Survival, a Chicago-based nonprofit working with gang and non-gang youth. He works as a gang intervention specialist in Los Angeles, Chicago, and other cities as well as in Mexico and Central America.

THEODORE ROETHKE (1908–1963) was the son of a commercial greenhouse operator in Saginaw, Michigan. As a child, he spent much time in the greenhouse, and the impressions of nature he formed there later influenced the subjects and imagery of his verse. Roethke graduated from the University of Michigan and studied at Harvard University. Although he published only eight books of poetry, they were held in high regard by critics, some of whom considered him among the best poets of his generation. *The Waking* was awarded the Pulitzer Prize in 1954; *Words for the Wind* (1958) received the Bollingen Prize and the National Book Award. He taught at many colleges and universities and gained a reputation as an exceptional teacher of poetry writing, though his career was interrupted several times by serious mental breakdowns.

WEB: Further research this author with LitLinks at bedfordstmartins.com/rewritinglit.

WENDY ROSE (b. 1948) was born Bronwen Elizabeth Edwards in Oakland, California, of Hopi and Miwok ancestry. As a teenager, she dropped out of high school and became connected with the bohemian scene in San Francisco. Her experiences in the city and the struggle in finding her identity within her mixed lineage would be major influences on her poetry. Rose attended Costa College and the University of California–Berkeley, and completed a Ph.D. in anthropology. The author of a dozen volumes of poetry, she has taught American Indian studies at the University of California–Berkeley, and California State University–Fresno, as well as being coor-

dinator of American Indian studies at Fresno City College. Rose's poems often combine the world of the contemporary native culture with an elegiac voice, a quiet sense of reverence and loss.

MARY RUEFLE (b. 1952) was born near Pittsburgh but spent her early life moving around the United States and Europe as the daughter of a military officer. She graduated from Bennington College with a literature major. She has published ten books of poetry, including *Memling's Veil* (1982), *The Adamant* (1989, winner of the 1988 Iowa Poetry Prize), *A Little White Shadow* (2006), and *Selected Poems* (2010). She published her first collection of short stories, *The Most of It*, in 2008. Among awards she has received are a Guggenheim Fellowship, an American Academy of Arts and Letters Award in Literature, and a Whiting Foundation Writer's Award. She lives in Vermont, where she is a professor in the Vermont College M.F.A. program.

CARL SANDBURG (1878–1967) was born in Galesburg, Illinois, to Swedish inmigrant working-class parents. He left school after the eighth grade; he entered college later and did well as a writer, but did not take a degree. He traveled and worked at a variety of jobs, mostly in journalism, until he was able to support himself from his writing and lecturing (on Abraham Lincoln and Mary Todd Lincoln, as well as on poetry). He published more than fifty books, in many genres — poetry, fiction, prose, biography, children's stories, autobiography — and won two Pulitzer Prizes: in 1940 for the second volume of his Lincoln biography, *Abraham Lincoln: The War Years* (1939), and in 1951 for *The Complete Poems of Carl Sandburg* (1950). Sandburg gave American poetry a needed direction and intensity through his hard-hitting, energetic, often politicized verse, which was more notable for its content than for its craft.

MARJANE SATRAPI (b. 1969) was born in Rasht, Iran, and grew up in Tehran in a family that was involved with communist and socialist movements prior to the Iranian Revolution. She attended the Lycée Français and witnessed the growing suppression of civil liberties, the fall of the shah, the rise of the Khomeini regime, and the first years of the Iran-Iraq War. She was sent to Vienna when she was fourteen to escape the dictatorial government. Her career began when she met the French comics artist David B. (pen name of Pierre-François Beauchard). She has become known worldwide through her autobiographical graphic novels. She also is a writer and illustrator of children's books. The animated film adaptation of *Persepolis* was nominated for an Academy Award for Best Animated Feature. Satrapi lives in Paris.

CHERYL SAVAGEAU (b. 1950) was born in central Massachusetts and grew up in an island neighborhood on Lake Quinsigamond. She is of mixed French Canadian and Abenaki heritage. She graduated from Clark University in 1978, where she began writing "by accident": She signed up for a poetry class through Continuing Education to finish her degree, and it turned out to be a writing class. She is the author of three books of poetry, *Home Country* (1992), *Dirt Road Home* (1995), and *Mother/Land* (2006). Her children's book, *Muskrat Will Be Swimming*, was named a 1996 Notable Book for Children by the Smithsonian. She worked for several years as a poet and storyteller in the schools through the Massachusetts Artist in Residence program and was a member of Wordcraft Circle of Native Writers and Storytellers, working as a mentor to apprentice native writers. She also works as a textile artist: Her quilts have been exhibited at the University of New Hampshire in Durham. She now lives in New Hampshire.

WEB: Further research this author with LitLinks at bedfordstmartins.com/rewritinglit.

WILLIAM SHAKESPEARE (1564–1616) was born in Stratford-upon-Avon, England, where his father was a glovemaker and bailiff, and presumably went to grammar school there. He married Anne Hathaway in 1582, and sometime before 1592 he left for London to work as a playwright and an actor. Shakespeare joined the Lord Chamberlain's Men (later the King's Men), an acting company for which he wrote thirty-five plays, before retiring to Stratford around 1612. In addition to being a skillful dramatist, he was perhaps the finest lyric poet of his day, as exemplified by songs scattered through his plays, two early nondramatic poems (*Venus and Adonis* and *The Rape of Lucrece*), and the sonnet sequence expected of all noteworthy writers in the Elizabethan age. Shakespeare's sonnets were probably written in the 1590s, though not published until 1609.

WEB: Further research this author with LitLinks at bedfordstmartins.com/rewritinglit.

PERCY BYSSHE SHELLEY (1792–1822) was born into a wealthy aristocratic family in Sussex County, England. He was educated at Eton, then went on to Oxford University, but was expelled after six months for writing a defense of atheism, the first price he would pay for his nonconformity and radical (for his time) commitment to social justice. The following year he eloped with Harriet Westbrook, daughter of a tavern keeper, despite his belief that marriage was a tyrannical and degrading social institution (she was sixteen, he eighteen). He became a disciple of the radical social philosopher William Godwin, fell in love with Godwin's daughter, Mary Wollstonecraft Godwin (later the author of *Frankenstein*), and went to live with her in France. Two years later, after Harriet committed suicide, Shelley and Godwin married and moved to Italy, where they shifted about restlessly and Shelley was generally short on money and in poor health. Under such trying circumstances, he wrote his greatest works. He died at age thirty, when the boat he was in was overturned by a sudden storm.

WEB: Further research this author with LitLinks at bedfordstmartins.com/rewritinglit.

LESLIE MARMON SILKO (b. 1948) was born in Albuquerque of mixed Pueblo, Mexican, and white ancestry and grew up on the Laguna Pueblo Reservation in New Mexico. She earned her B.A. with honors from the University of New Mexico. In a long and productive writing career (she was already writing stories in elementary school), she has published poetry, novels, short stories, essays, letters, and film scripts. The best known of her works is her 1977 novel, *Ceremony*. She taught creative writing first at the University of New Mexico and later at the University of Arizona. She has been named a Living Cultural Treasure by the New Mexico Humanities Council and has received the Native Writers' Circle of the Americas Lifetime Achievement Award. She was awarded a MacArthur Foundation grant in 1981. Her work is a graphic telling of the life of native peoples, maintaining its rich spiritual heritage while exposing the terrible consequences of European domination.

WEB: Further research this author with LitLinks at bedfordstmartins.com/rewritinglit.

CHARLES SIMIC (b. 1938) was born in Belgrade, Yugoslavia. In 1953 he, his mother, and his brother joined his father in Chicago, where he lived until 1958. His first poems were published in 1959, when he was twenty-one. In 1961, he was drafted into the U.S. Army, and in 1966 he earned his B.A. from New York University. His first book of poems, *What the Grass Says*, was published in 1967. Since then, he has published more than sixty books of poetry, translations, and essays, including *The World Doesn't End: Prose Poems* (1990), for which he received the Pulitzer Prize for Poetry. Simic is a professor of English at the University of New Hampshire. In 2007, he was named Poet Laureate Consultant in Poetry to the Library of Congress.

WEB: Further research this author with LitLinks at bedfordstmartins.com/rewritinglit.

CATHY SONG (b. 1955) was born in Hawaii and lived in the small town of Wahiawa on Oahu. She left Hawaii for the East Coast, studying at Wellesley College and then at Boston University. Her first book, *Picture Bride*, was chosen by Richard Hugo for the Yale Series of Younger Poets in 1982. Since then she has published four other books of poetry, most recently *Cloud Moving Hands* (2007).

WEB: Further research this author with LitLinks at bedfordstmartins.com/rewritinglit.

SOPHOCLES (496?–406 B.C.E.), born the son of a wealthy merchant in Athens, enjoyed the advantages of the thriving Greek Empire. He studied all of the arts. By the age of sixteen, he was known for his beauty and grace and was chosen to lead a choir of boys at a celebration of the victory of Salamis. He served as a statesman, general, treasurer, and priest as

well as, with Aeschylus and Euripides, one of the three major authors of Greek tragedy. He was an accomplished actor and performed in many of his own plays. Fragments indicate that he wrote over 120 plays, of which only 7 are extant. His plays introduced several innovations to Greek theater, particularly adding a third actor, which allowed for more dialogue and greater complexity of action and reduced the role of the chorus. He also changed the form of drama. Aeschylus had used three tragedies to tell a single story; Sophocles made each play a complete and independent work, which required greater compression of action and resulted in greater dramatic intensity.

WEB: Further research this author with LitLinks at bedfordstmartins.com/rewritinglit.

GARY SOTO (b. 1952) grew up in Fresno, California. He earned his B.A. from California State University, Fresno, and his M.F.A. from the University of California, Irvine. At a young age, he worked in the fields of San Joaquin Valley. Much of his poetry comes out of and reflects his working background, that of migrant workers and tenant farmers in the fields of southern California, and provides glimpses into the lives of families in the barrio. Soto's language comes from earthy, gritty, raw everyday American speech. His first book, *The Elements of San Joaquin*, won the 1976 United States Award from the International Poetry Forum. He has published eleven collections of poetry, eight novels, four essay collections, and numerous young-adult and children's books and has edited four anthologies.

WEB: Further research this author with LitLinks at bedfordstmartins.com/rewritinglit.

EDMUND SPENSER (1552–1599), a contemporary of WILLIAM SHAKESPEARE, was the greatest English nondramatic poet of his time. Best known for his allegorical and national epic *The Faerie Queene*, Spenser wrote poems of a number of other types as well and was important as an innovator in metrics and forms (as in his development of the special form of sonnet and unique stanza form that bear his name—see the Glossary of Literary Terms, p. 1485). The sonnet included in this anthology, beginning "One day I wrote her name upon the strand" (p. 866), is number 75 in *Amoretti*, a sequence of sonnets about a courtship addressed to a woman named Elizabeth, probably Elizabeth Boyle, who became his second wife.

WEB: Further research this author with LitLinks at bedfordstmartins.com/rewritinglit.

ART SPIEGELMAN (b. 1948) was born in Stockholm, Sweden, to Polish-Jewish refugees. He immigrated with his parents to the United States in his early childhood and grew up in Rego Park in Queens, New York, and graduated from the High School of Art and Design in Manhattan. His parents wanted him to be a dentist. He attended what is now Binghamton University and, although he did not graduate, thirty years later they awarded him an honorary doctorate. He credits Harvey Kurtzman, the creator of *Mad Magazine*, as his inspiration for creating comics. In the 1960s and 1970s he was a major figure in the underground comics movement. He and his wife, Francoise Mouly, started the hugely influential magazine *Raw*, which first serialized *Maus*. *Maus* received unprecedented attention and critical acclaim including an exhibition of it at the Museum of Modern Art and a special Pulitzer Prize in 1992. In 2005, *Time* magazine named Spiegelman one of their "Top 100 Most Influential People." He is an advocate for comics and has taught courses on the history and aesthetics of comics at such schools as the University of California, Santa Cruz, and the School of Visual Arts in New York City. Together with his wife he has also published anthologies of comics for children, called *Little Lit*.

WILLIAM STAFFORD (1914–1995) was born in Hutchinson, Kansas, and studied at the University of Kansas and then at the University of Iowa Writers' Workshop. In between, he was a conscientious objector during World War II and worked in labor camps. In 1948, Stafford moved to Oregon, where he taught at Lewis and Clark College until he retired in 1980. His first major collection of poems, *Traveling through the Dark* (1962), was published when Stafford was forty-eight. It won the National Book Award in 1963. He went on to publish more than sixty-five volumes of poetry and prose and came to be known as a very influential teacher of poetry. From 1970 to 1971, he was Consultant in Poetry at the Library of Congress.

WEB: Further research this author with LitLinks at bedfordstmartins.com/rewritinglit.

JOHN STEINBECK (1902–1968) is one of the most widely read American novelists of the twentieth century. He was born in Salinas, California, and raised near Monterey in the fertile Salinas Valley, the setting of much of his fiction. He studied English literature at Stanford University off and on until 1925, when he decided to pursue his dream of being a writer. He supported himself by working at a variety of jobs, thus gaining insight into the problems faced by the working class. His first novel, *Cup of Gold* (1929), was unsuccessful, but he found his voice by writing about California and the struggles of rural workers during the Great Depression. Success arrived with *Tortilla Flat* (1935), *In Dubious Battle* (1936), *Of Mice and Men* (1937), and *The Long Valley* (1938), a collection of short stories including "The Chrysanthemums" (p. 320). His greatest work, *The Grapes of Wrath* (1939), won the Pulitzer Prize. He received the Nobel Prize for Literature in 1962.

WEB: Further research this author with LitLinks at bedfordstmartins.com/rewritinglit.

GERALD STERN (b. 1925) was born in Pittsburgh and studied at the University of Pittsburgh and Columbia University. Stern came late to poetry: he was forty-six when he published his first book. Since then he has published more than fifteen collections of poems, most recently *Save the Last Dance: Poems* (2008) and *Early Collected Poems, 1965-1992* (2010), and received many prestigious awards, including the 1998 National Book Award for Poetry for *This Time: New and Selected Poems*. Stern's work has often been compared to that of WALT WHITMAN and JOHN KEATS for its exploration of the self and the sometimes ecstatic exuberance of its verse. Stern taught at many universities, including Columbia University, New York University, Sarah Lawrence College, the University of Pittsburgh, and for many years the University of Iowa Writers' Workshop, until his retirement in 1995. He is currently serving as distinguished poet-in-residence at Drew

University's low-residency M.F.A. Program in Poetry.

WALLACE STEVENS (1879–1955) was born in Reading, Pennsylvania, and attended Harvard University for three years. He tried journalism and then attended New York University Law School, after which he worked as a legal consultant. He spent most of his life working as an executive for the Hartford Accident and Indemnity Company, spending his evenings writing some of the most imaginative and influential poetry of his time. Although now considered one of the major American poets of the twentieth century, he did not receive widespread recognition until the publication of his *Collected Poems* just a year before his death.

WEB: Further research this author with LitLinks at bedfordstmartins.com/rewritinglit.

MARK STRAND (b. 1934) was born on Prince Edward Island, Canada, and studied at Antioch College, Yale University, the University of Florence, and the University of Iowa. He is the author of numerous collections of poetry, including *Reasons for Moving* (1968), *The Story of Our Lives* (1973), *The Continuous Life* (1990), *Blizzard of One* (1998), which won the Pulitzer Prize for Poetry, *Man and Camel* (2006), and *New Selected Poems* (2007). He has also published several volumes of translation (of works by Rafael Alberti and Carlos Drummond de Andrade, among others), several monographs on contemporary artists, and many books for children. He received a MacArthur Foundation Fellowship in 1987, served as Poet Laureate Consultant in Poetry to the Library of Congress in 1990–1991, and is a former chancellor of the Academy of American Poets. He teaches literature and creative writing at Columbia University in New York.

KELLY STUART (b. 1961) is the author of several highly successful plays, among them *Demonology* (1996), *Mayhem* (2004), *The Life of Spiders* (2005), and *The Disappearing World* (2007). She received a Guthrie New Play grant and commission, which enabled her to spend extensive time in eastern Turkey to research and write *Shadow Language* (2007),

which deals with the Kurdish "problem," American idealism, and political asylum issues in the United States. She was the recipient of a Whiting Fellowship in 2000 (for *The Life of Spiders*) and a 2004 artists' fellowship from the New York Foundation of the Arts. Stuart currently lives in New York and teaches playwriting at Columbia University.

VIRGIL SUÁREZ (b. 1962) was born in Havana, Cuba. Eight years later he left with his parents for Spain, where they lived until they came to the United States in 1974. He received his B.A. from California State University, Long Beach, and his M.F.A. from Louisiana State University. He is the author of eight collections of poetry, five novels, a collection of short fiction, and a memoir titled *Spared Angola: Memories from a Cuban-American Childhood* (1997). He is editor or coeditor of several important anthologies, including *Iguana Dreams: New Latino Fiction* (1993), the first anthology of Cuban American writers, and *Paper Dance: 55 Latino Poets* (2000), a collection of contemporary Latino poetry. His work has been included in hundreds of magazines, journals, and anthologies. Presently he is a professor of creative writing at Florida State University.

WEB: Further research this author with LitLinks at bedfordstmartins.com/rewritinglit.

SEKOU SUNDIATA (1948–2007) was born and raised in Harlem. His work was deeply influenced by the music, poetry, and oral traditions of African American culture. A self-proclaimed radical in the 1970s, for the past several decades he used poetry to comment on the life and times of our culture. His work, which encompasses print, performance, music, and theater, received praise for its fusion of soul, jazz, and hip-hop grooves with political insight, humor, and rhythmic speech. He regularly recorded and performed on tour with artists such as Craig Harris and Vernon Reid.

WEB: Further research this author with LitLinks at bedfordstmartins.com/rewritinglit.

MAY SWENSON (1913–1989) was born in Logan, Utah, the eldest of ten children in a Mormon household where Swedish was spoken regularly and English was a second language. She graduated from Utah State University and worked as a reporter in Salt Lake City, then as an editor in New York City for the publisher New Directions. She published numerous volumes of poetry, three books of poetry for younger readers, a book of prose (*The Contemporary Poet as Artist and Critic*, 1964), and translations of contemporary Swedish poetry, including *Windows and Stones: Selected Poems of Tomas Tranströmer* (1972), which received a medal of excellence from the International Poetry Forum.

ARTHUR SZE (b. 1950) was born in New York City, a second-generation Chinese American. Educated at the University of California, Berkeley, he is the author of numerous collections of poetry, most recently *The Ginkgo Light* (2009), and a celebrated translator of Chinese poetry. He is professor emeritus at the Institute of American Indian Arts and has held residencies at Brown University, Bard College, and Naropa Institute. His work often assembles aspects of completely different cultures and has been described as lying within postmodern experimentation and Taoist contemplation. He is fascinated by the way disparate events happen simultaneously. His work has been translated into Dutch, Italian, Turkish, and Chinese. He is also the editor of *Chinese Writers on Writing* (2010).

MARY TALLMOUNTAIN (1918–1994) was born Mary Demonski in the interior of Alaska in Nilato. Her mother was a Koyukon-Athabaskan and her father a Scotch-Irish signal corpsman. Her mother died when she was six, and she was the first child from her village to be adopted by an Anglo-American couple. TallMountain's poetry was fully influenced by her spiritual connections to her birthplace, her family, and her native culture. She began every day by talking with her late grandmother, mother, and two aunts. She claimed both a Christian faith and "the ritual of the Indian. We have only one God—and we know that—but we follow two paths. Why not? Why not worship Him twice. Him or Her." The Mary TallMountain Circle in San Francisco produces and distributes her work and continues her support for Native American and Tenderloin writers.

AMY TAN (b. 1952) was born in Oakland, California. Her father had been educated as an engineer in Beijing; her mother left China in 1949, just before the Communist revolution. After her father's death, Tan and her mother lived in Switzerland, where Tan attended high school. She received her B.A. and M.A. in English and linguistics from San Jose State University, took a job as a language development consultant to the Alameda County Association for Retarded Citizens, and later directed a training project for developmentally disabled children. She became a highly successful freelance business writer specializing in corporate communications for such companies as AT&T, IBM, and Pacific Bell, but she found the work unsatisfying and began writing fiction. A visit to China with her mother in 1987, and meeting relatives there, gave her the realization, as she put it, that "I belonged to my family and my family belonged to China." Inspired by LOUISE ERDRICH's *Love Medicine* (1986), she began to write stories about her own minority culture. A literary agent read one of them and secured her an advance that allowed her to write full-time, resulting in her very successful first book, *The Joy Luck Club* (1989). She has gone on to write five more novels, two children's books, and a collection of essays, *The Opposite of Fate: A Book of Musings* (2003). She is also the lead singer for the Rock Bottom Remainders, a rock band made up of fellow writers who make select appearances at charities and benefits that support free-speech issues.

WEB: Further research this author with LitLinks at bedfordstmartins.com/rewritinglit.

ALFRED, LORD TENNYSON (1809–1892) was born in Somersby, Lincolnshire, and grew up there in the tense atmosphere of his unhappy father's rectory. He went to Trinity College, Cambridge, but was forced to leave because of family and financial problems, so he returned home to study and practice the craft of poetry. His early volumes, published in 1830 and 1832, received bad reviews, but his *In Memoriam* (1850), an elegy on his close friend Arthur Hallam, who died of a brain seizure, won acclaim. He was unquestionably the most popular poet of his time (the "poet of the people") and arguably the greatest of the Vic-

torian poets. He succeeded WILLIAM WORDS-
WORTH as poet laureate, a position he held
from 1850 until his death.

WEB: Further research this author with LitLinks
at bedfordstmartins.com/rewritinglit.

DYLAN THOMAS (1914–1953) was born in
Swansea, Wales, and after grammar school
became a journalist. He worked as a writer for
the rest of his life. His first book of poetry,
Eighteen Poems, appeared in 1934 and was followed by *Twenty-five Poems* (1936), *Deaths
and Entrances* (1946), and *Collected Poems*
(1952). His poems are often rich in textured
rhythms and images. He also wrote prose,
chiefly short stories collectively appearing as
Portrait of the Artist as a Young Dog (1940),
and a number of film scripts and radio plays.
His most famous work, *Under Milk Wood*,
written as a play for voices, was first performed in New York on May 14, 1953. Thomas's radio broadcasts and his lecture tours and
poetry readings in the United States brought
him fame and popularity. Alcoholism contributed to his early death in 1953.

WEB: Further research this author with LitLinks
at bedfordstmartins.com/rewritinglit.

JEAN TOOMER (1894–1967) was born in
Washington, D.C., of mixed French, Dutch,
Welsh, African American, German, Jewish,
and Indian blood. Although he passed for
white during certain periods of his life, he was
raised in a predominantly black community
and attended black high schools. He began
college at the University of Wisconsin but
transferred to the College of the City of New
York. He spent several years publishing poems
and stories in small magazines. In 1921, he
took a teaching job in Georgia and remained
there four months; the experience inspired
Cane (1923), a book of prose poetry describing the Georgian people and landscape that
became a central work of the Harlem Renaissance. He later experimented in communal
living and both studied and tried to promul-
gate the ideas of the Russian mystic George
Gurdjieff and later of Quakerism. From 1950
on, he published no literary works and began
withdrawing from public life.

WEB: Further research this author with LitLinks
at bedfordstmartins.com/rewritinglit.

NATASHA TRETHEWEY (b. 1966) was born in
Gulfport, Mississippi. She has degrees from
the University of Georgia, Hollins University,
and the University of Massachusetts. She has
won many awards for her poetry including the
inaugural Cave Canem Poetry Prize for her
first collection, *Domestic Work* (2000). Her
second collection, *Bellocq's Ophelia* (2002),
received the 2003 Mississippi Institute of Arts
and Letters Book Prize and was a finalist for
both the Academy of American Poets' James
Laughlin and Lenore Marshall prizes. In 2007
her collection *Native Guard* received the Pulitzer Prize. She has taught at Auburn University,
the University of North Carolina, and Duke
University. In 2009–2010 she was the James
Weldon Johnson Fellow in African American
Studies at Yale University's Beinecke Rare
Books and Manuscript Library. She presently
teaches at Emory University, as the Phillis
Wheatley Distinguished Chair in Poetry. Her
book of creative nonfiction, *Beyond Katrina:
A Meditation on the Mississippi Gulf*, was
published in 2010.

QUINCY TROUPE (b. 1943) was born in New
York City and grew up in St. Louis, Missouri.
He is the author of sixteen books, including
eight volumes of poetry, most recently *The Architecture of Language* (2006). He is recipient
of two American Book Awards, for his collection of poetry *Snake-Back Solos* (1980) and
his nonfiction book *Miles the Autobiography*
(1989). In 1991, he received the prestigious
Peabody Award for writing and coproducing
the seven-part Miles Davis Radio Project aired
on National Public Radio in 1990. *Trans-
circularities: New and Selected Poems* (2002)
received the Milt Kessler Award for 2003 and
was a finalist for the Paterson Poetry Prize.
Troupe has taught at the University of California, Los Angeles, Ohio University, the College of Staten Island (CUNY), Columbia
University (in the Graduate Writing Program), and the University of California, San
Diego. He is now professor emeritus of creative writing and American and Caribbean
literature at the University of California, San
Diego. He is the founding editorial director of
Code magazine and former artistic director of
"Arts on the Cutting Edge," a reading and
performance series at the Museum of Contemporary Art, San Diego. He was the first official poet laureate of the state of California,

appointed to the post in 2002 by Governor Gray Davis.

WEB: Further research this author with LitLinks at bedfordstmartins.com/rewritinglit.

JOHN UPDIKE (1932–2009) was born in Reading, Pennsylvania, but grew up in the small nearby city of Shillington. He earned his B.A. at Harvard University where he contributed to and later edited the *Harvard Lampoon*. He spent 1954–1955 at the Ruskin School of Drawing and Fine Arts in Oxford, England, then worked at *The New Yorker* until 1957 when he left to become a full-time writer. In 1959, he published his first book of stories, *The Same Door*, and his first novel, *The Poorhouse Fair*, and he moved from New York City to Massachusetts, where he lived most of the time until his death. A prolific writer, Updike published over sixty books — novels, collections of poems, short stories, essays, criticism, and a memoir. He received numerous awards, including the National Medal of Art and the National Medal for the Humanities. Two of his novels, *Rabbit Is Rich* (1981) and *Rabbit at Rest* (1990), won Pulitzer Prizes.

WEB: Further research this author with LitLinks at bedfordstmartins.com/rewritinglit.

HELENA MARÍA VIRAMONTES (b. 1954) was born and raised in East Los Angeles. She began writing poetry and fiction at Immaculate Heart College, from which she earned her B.A. in 1975 (one of five Chicanas in her class). In the next few years, several of her stories won prizes. She entered the M.F.A. program at the University of California, Irvine, in 1981, and completed her degree in 1994, after many years of successful writing. She has published two novels, most recently *Their Dogs Came with Them* (2007), and a collection of short stories. She is coeditor, with Maria Herrera-Sobek, of two anthologies, *Chicana Creativity and Criticism: Charting New Frontiers in American Literature* (1988) and *Chicana (W)rites: On Word and Film* (1995). Her stories are known for their vivid depictions of Chicano culture and especially of the struggles and sufferings of Chicana women. She is a professor of English at Cornell University.

WEB: Further research this author with LitLinks at bedfordstmartins.com/rewritinglit.

ALICE WALKER (b. 1944) was born in Eatonton, Georgia. Her parents were sharecropper farmers. When she was eight, she lost sight in one eye when one of her older brothers accidentally shot her with a BB gun. She was valedictorian of her high school class. Encouraged by her teachers and her mother to continue her education, she attended Spelman College in Atlanta, a school for black women, for two years, and graduated from Sarah Lawrence College. From the mid-1960s to the mid-1970s, she lived in Tougaloo, Mississippi. She was active in the civil rights movement of the 1960s and remains an involved activist today. Her first book was a collection of poetry, *Once* (1968). She is a prolific writer, having gone on to publish over thirty books of poetry, novels, short stories, and nonfiction. Her best-known novel, *The Color Purple* (1982), won the American Book Award and the Pulitzer Prize for Fiction and was made into a motion picture directed by Steven Spielberg.

WEB: Further research this author with LitLinks at bedfordstmartins.com/rewritinglit.

JAMES WELCH (1940–2003) was born in Browning, Montana. His father was a member of the Blackfoot tribe, his mother of the Gros Ventre tribe. He attended schools on the Blackfoot and Fort Belknap reservations and earned a degree from the University of Montana, where he studied under Richard Hugo. Welch published many books of poetry, fiction, and nonfiction. His hard, spare poems often evoke the bleakest side of contemporary Native American life. He received a Lifetime Achievement Award for Literature from the Native Writers' Circle in 1997.

WEB: Further research this author with LitLinks at bedfordstmartins.com/rewritinglit.

PATRICIA JABBEH WESLEY (b. 1955) was born in Monrovia, Liberia, and lived there until her father sent her and her siblings to the Tugbakeh Boarding Mission School in her father's hometown. She was teaching at the University of Liberia when civil war broke out in 1991. She immigrated with her family to the United States and received her Ph.D. in English and creative writing at Western Michigan University. Wesley is the author of four collections of poetry, *Before the Palm Could Bloom: Poems of Africa* (1998), *Becoming Ebony* (2003), *The River Is Rising* (2007), and *Where the Road Turns* (2010). Her poems also have appeared in many anthologies and literary journals. She is a faculty member at Pennsylvania State University, Altoona.

ROBERTA HILL WHITEMAN (b. 1947), a member of the Oneida tribe, grew up around Oneida and Green Bay, Wisconsin. She earned a B.A. from the University of Wisconsin and an M.F.A. from the University of Montana. Her poems have appeared in many magazines and anthologies. Her three collections of poetry—*Star Quilt* (1984), *Your Fierce Resistance* (1993), and *Philadelphia Flowers* (1996)—have been illustrated by her husband, Ernest Whiteman, an Arapaho artist.

WALT WHITMAN (1819–1892) was born in rural Long Island, the son of a farmer and carpenter. He attended grammar school in Brooklyn and took his first job as a printer's errand-boy for the *Long Island Patriot*. Attending the opera, dabbling in politics, participating in street life, and gaining experience as student, printer, reporter, writer, carpenter, farmer, seashore observer, and teacher provided the bedrock for his future poetic vision of an ideal society based on the realization of self. Although Whitman liked to portray himself as uncultured, he read widely in the King James Bible, SHAKESPEARE, Homer, Dante, Aeschylus, and SOPHOCLES. He worked for many years in the newspaper business and began writing poetry only in 1847. In 1855, at his own expense, Whitman published the first edition of *Leaves of Grass*, a thin volume of twelve long untitled poems. Written in a highly original and innovative free verse, influenced significantly by music and with a wide-ranging subject matter, the work seemed strange to most of the poet's contemporaries, but they did recognize its value: Ralph Waldo Emerson wrote to him, less than three weeks after Whitman sent him a copy, "I greet you at the beginning of a great career." He spent much of the remainder of his life revising and expanding this book. *Leaves of Grass* today is considered a masterpiece of world literature, marking the beginning of modern American

poetry, and Whitman is widely regarded as America's national poet.

WEB: Further research this author with LitLinks at bedfordstmartins.com/rewritinglit.

RICHARD WILBUR (b. 1921) was born in New York City and grew up in rural New Jersey. He attended Amherst College and began writing poetry during World War II, while fighting in Italy and France. Afterward, he studied at Harvard University and then taught there and at Wellesley College, Wesleyan University, and Smith College. He has published many books of poetry, including *Things of This World* (1956), for which he received the Pulitzer Prize for Poetry and the National Book Award, and *New and Collected Poems* (1988), which also won a Pulitzer Prize. He has always been respected as a master of formal constraints, comparing them to the genie in the bottle: The restraints stimulate the imagination to achieve results unlikely to be reached without them. He has also published numerous translations of French plays, two books for children, a collection of prose pieces, and editions of WILLIAM SHAKESPEARE and EDGAR ALLAN POE. In 1987, he was appointed Poet Laureate Consultant in Poetry at the Library of Congress. He now lives in Cummington, Massachusetts.

WEB: Further research this author with LitLinks at bedfordstmartins.com/rewritinglit.

NANCY WILLARD (b. 1936) was raised in Ann Arbor, Michigan, and educated at the University of Michigan and Stanford University. She has published twelve books of poetry, including *Water Walker* (1989), which was nominated for the National Book Critics Circle Award, and *Swimming Lessons: New and Selected Poems* (1996); two novels, *Things Invisible to See* (1984) and *Sister Water* (1993); and four books of stories and essays. She is the author of numerous children's books, including *A Visit to William Blake's Inn: Poems for Innocent and Experienced Travelers* (containing such delightfully titled poems as "The Wise Cow Enjoys a Cloud" and "The Marmalade Man Makes a Dance to Mend Us"), which was the first book of poetry to win the prestigious Newbery Medal. She lives in Poughkeepsie, New York, and teaches at Vassar College.

WEB: Further research this author with LitLinks at bedfordstmartins.com/rewritinglit.

TENNESSEE WILLIAMS (1911–1983) was born Thomas Lanier Williams in Columbus, Mississippi. He moved to New Orleans in 1939 to write for the WPA. It was there that he changed his name to the state in which his father was born. His father, a hard-drinking traveling salesman, favored Tennessee's younger brother. His mother was a borderline hysteric, and his sister was diagnosed as schizophrenic. It is thought that much of his work draws on his experiences with his family. He attended the University of Missouri and Washington University in St. Louis, then graduated from the University of Iowa. He later studied at the Dramatic Workshop of The New School. He said that theater was the only thing that saved his life. Two of his plays won the Pulitzer Prize for Drama: *A Streetcar Named Desire* in 1948 and *Cat on a Hot Tin Roof* in 1955. *The Glass Menagerie* won the New York Drama Critics Circle Award in 1945. In 1980 Williams received the Presidential Medal of Freedom.

WILLIAM CARLOS WILLIAMS (1883–1963) was born in Rutherford, New Jersey; his father was an English emigrant and his mother was of mixed Basque descent from Puerto Rico. He decided to be both a writer and a doctor while in high school in New York City. He graduated from the medical school at the University of Pennsylvania, where he was a friend of EZRA POUND and Hilda Doolittle. After an internship in New York, Williams practiced general medicine in Rutherford, writing poems between seeing patients. His first book of poems was published in 1909, and he subsequently published poems, novels, short stories, plays, criticism, and essays. Initially one of the principal poets of the imagist movement, Williams sought later to invent an entirely fresh—and distinctly American—poetic, whose subject matter was centered on the everyday circumstances of life and the lives of common people. Williams, like WALLACE STEVENS, became one of the major poets of the twentieth century and exerted great influence on poets of his own and later generations.

WEB: Further research this author with LitLinks at bedfordstmartins.com/rewritinglit.

AUGUST WILSON (1945–2005)—See page 959.

WILLIAM WORDSWORTH (1770–1850) was born and raised in the Lake District of England. Both of his parents died by the time he was thirteen. He studied at Cambridge University, toured Europe on foot, and lived in France for a year during the first part of the French Revolution. He returned to England, leaving behind a lover, Annette Vallon, and their daughter, Caroline, from whom he was soon cut off by war between England and France. He met SAMUEL TAYLOR COLERIDGE, and in 1798 they together published *Lyrical Ballads*, the first great work of the English Romantic movement. He changed poetry forever by his decision to use common language in his poetry instead of artificial poetic diction (see the Glossary of Literary Terms, p. 1481). In 1799, he and his sister Dorothy moved to Grasmere, in the Lake District, where he married Mary Hutchinson, a childhood friend. His greatest works were produced between 1797 and 1808. He continued to write for the next forty years but never regained the heights of his early verse. In 1843, he was named poet laureate, a position he held until his death in 1850.

WEB: Further research this author with LitLinks at bedfordstmartins.com/rewritinglit.

JAMES WRIGHT (1927–1980) grew up in Martin's Ferry, Ohio. He attended Kenyon College, where his study under John Crowe Ransom sent his early poetry in a formalist direction. After spending a year in Austria on a Fulbright fellowship, he returned to the United States and earned an M.A. and a Ph.D. at the University of Washington, studying under THEODORE ROETHKE and Stanley Kunitz. He went on to teach at the University of Minnesota, Macalester College, and Hunter College. His working-class background and the poverty that he saw during the Depression stirred a sympathy for the poor and "outsiders" of various sorts, which shaped the tone and content of his poetry. He published numerous books of poetry; his *Collected Poems* received the Pulitzer Prize for Poetry in 1972.

WEB: Further research this author with LitLinks at bedfordstmartins.com/rewritinglit.

JOHN YAU (b. 1950) was born in Lynn, Massachusetts, a year after his parents emigrated from China. He received a B.A. from Bard College and an M.F.A. from Brooklyn College, where he studied with John Ashbery. He has published over fifty books and pamphlets—among them artists' books, a great deal of art criticism, an anthology of fiction, and at least ten volumes of poetry, including *Corpse and Mirror* (1983), a National Poetry Series book selected by John Ashbery, and, most recently, *Paradiso Diaspora* (2006).

WEB: Further research this author with LitLinks at bedfordstmartins.com/rewritinglit.

WILLIAM BUTLER YEATS (1865–1939) was born in Sandymount, Dublin, to an Anglo-Irish family. On leaving high school in 1883, he decided to be an artist, like his father, and attended art school but soon gave it up to concentrate on poetry. His first poems were published in 1885 in the *Dublin University Review*. Religious by temperament but unable to accept orthodox Christianity, Yeats throughout his life explored esoteric philosophies in search of a tradition that would substitute for a lost religion. He became a member of the Theosophical Society and the Order of the Golden Dawn, two groups interested in Eastern occultism, and later developed a private system of symbols and mystical ideas. Through the influence of Lady Gregory, a writer and promoter of literature, he became interested in Irish nationalist art, helping to found the Irish National Theatre and the famous Abbey Theatre. He was actively involved in Irish politics, especially after the Easter Rising of 1916. He continued to write and to revise earlier poems, leaving behind, at his death, a body of verse that, in its variety and power, placed him among the greatest twentieth-century poets of the English language. He was awarded the Nobel Prize for Literature in 1923.

WEB: Further research this author with LitLinks at bedfordstmartins.com/rewritinglit.

AL YOUNG (b. 1939) was born in Ocean Springs, Mississippi, and lived for a decade in the South before moving to Detroit. He attended the University of Michigan and the University of California, Berkeley. He has been a professional guitarist and singer, a disk jockey, a medical photographer, and a warehouseman and has written eight books of poetry (most recently, *Something about the Blues: An Unlikely Collection of Poetry*, 2008), five novels, memoirs, essays, and film scripts. He has edited a number of books, including *Yardbird Lives!* (1978) and *African American Literature: A Brief Introduction and Anthology* (1995). He has taught literature and creative writing at numerous colleges and universities. In the 1970s and 1980s, Young cofounded the journals *Yardbird Reader* and *Quilt* with poet-novelist Ishmael Reed. From 2005 to 2007, he served as California Poet Laureate.

WEB: Further research this author with LitLinks at bedfordstmartins.com/rewritinglit.

RAY A. YOUNG BEAR (b. 1950) was born and grew up in the Mesquakie Tribal Settlement near Tama, Iowa. His poetry has been influenced by his maternal grandmother, Ada Kapayou Old Bear, and his wife, Stella L. Young Bear. He attended Pomona College in California as well as Grinnell College, the University of Iowa, Iowa State University, and Northern Iowa University. He has taught creative writing and Native American literature at the Institute of American Indian Art, Eastern Washington University, the University of Iowa, and Iowa State University. Young Bear and his wife cofounded the Woodland Song and Dance Troupe of Arts Midwest in 1983. Young Bear's group has performed traditional Mesquakie music in this country and the Netherlands. Author of four books of poetry, a collection of short stories, and a novel, he has contributed to contemporary Native American poetry and to the study of it for nearly three decades.

WEB: Further research this author with LitLinks at bedfordstmartins.com/rewritinglit.

PAUL ZIMMER (b. 1934) was born in Canton, Ohio, and educated at Kent State University. He is author of fifteen poetry collections, including *The Great Bird of Love*, which was selected for the National Poetry Series in 1998 and *Crossing to Sunlight Revisited: New and Selected Poems* (2007). His latest collection, *The Importance of Being Zimmer* (2010), brings together a selection from his more than 130 poems in the voice of the persona "Zimmer," a tragicomic everyman. He has also published several collections of personal essays. Zimmer directed the university presses at the University of Pittsburgh, the University of Georgia, and the University of Iowa, where he was responsible for the discovery and first publication of many of the finest contemporary poets.

Appendix on Scansion

This appendix returns to the use of meter in poetry, extending the discussion begun in Chapter 16. We say there that meter forms an important component of rhythm for poems using it, especially ones having a regular beat created by a repeating pattern of stressed and unstressed syllables. In Chapter 16, we indicate the beat in metrical lines by using capital letters for stressed syllables (i AM bic ME ter GOES like THIS) to show that you can hear meter by listening for the stressed (louder) syllables, those that get more emphasis than the unstressed syllables. That's the important thing for readers beginning to read poetry attentively: hearing a steady beat when it's present and being able to distinguish poetry that has such a beat from poetry that does not. As you read more poetry, however, you may want to deal with meter in a more sophisticated way. This appendix introduces the traditional system of scansion and shows how metrical analysis contributes to a fuller understanding and appreciation of a poem written in meter.

Here is a brief review of some basic concepts and terminology introduced in Chapter 16. Go back to pages 652–74 to review them if you need to.

FOOT A two- or three-syllable metrical unit made up (usually) of one stressed and one or two unstressed syllables. The most important metrical feet are these:

Iamb: unstressed, stressed: da DA (for example, "awake")

Trochee: stressed, unstressed: DA da ("wakeful")

Anapest: unstressed, unstressed, stressed: da da DA ("in a dream")

Dactyl: stressed, unstressed, unstressed: DA da da ("sleepily")

Spondee: stressed, stressed: DA DA ("dream house")

LINE LENGTH Line lengths are measured by the number of feet in the line and are labeled with names derived from Greek roots:

Trimeter: a line with three metrical feet

Tetrameter: a line with four metrical feet

Pentameter: a line with five metrical feet

Hexameter: a line with six metrical feet

These are the commonest line lengths; more rare are monometer (one foot) and heptameter (seven).

The meter in a poem is highlighted and clarified through a process called **scansion**. To scan a poem involves marking its stressed syllables — whether the stress is heavy or light — with an accent mark (´) and marking its unstressed syllables with a curved line (˘). You use a vertical line to indicate the way the lines divide up into feet. (You don't need to distinguish stronger from weaker stresses — only syllables that receive at least *some* stress from those that receive *none*.

Ĭám | bĭc mé | tĕr góes | lĭke thís.[1]

You then describe (or label) the type of foot used most often in the line and the line length — in this case, iambic tetrameter.

The ideal way to scan a poem is to listen for where you stress syllables. But read with a natural emphasis, not a singsong regularity. Where *you* stress syllables is important: Scansion is not a mechanical process; it involves your interpretation. Scansion reflects the way a poem actually is read and so will differ slightly from one reader to another. Practice hearing the stresses as a recurring background beat, somewhat like the bass guitar or drums. But do not emphasize the beat; instead, concentrate on the words as you feel the beat underneath them.

You can use logic to do a rough but generally adequate scansion. First, start with multisyllabic words, using a dictionary if necessary to put ´ on the accented syllables and ˘ on the unaccented ones. Then put stress marks on important shorter words (most nouns and verbs, for example). Rhyming syllables almost always are stressed. Helping words (such as *a, an, to*) are rarely stressed and can safely be given ˘ marks. Just examining a poem thoughtfully will show where at least three-fourths of the stressed or unstressed syllables fall. The remainder can be sounded or figured out: For example, in ˘ ˘ ? ˘ ˘, the ? will almost surely be stressed; five unstressed syllables in a row would be very unusual. After such an analysis, read the poem aloud to test how well the stress patterns you identified match what you hear.

To begin practicing scansion, read the following stanza, which describes the setting of the island of Shalott in the days of King Arthur.

---

[1]In dividing lines into feet, begin by looking for the way that yields the greatest number of identical groupings of twos or threes since most feet in a poem will be the same; then figure out the exceptions.

Notice that dividing lines into feet may involve breaking up words. Feet work primarily with syllables, not words. However, in a line like "Evening traffic homeward burns" (from Yvor Winters's "Before Disaster"), which could be scanned as either iambic or trochaic, trochaic seems preferable because it keeps the words together ("Évenĭng | tráffĭc | hómewărd | búrns" rather than "Evé | nĭng tráf | fĭc hóme | wărd búrns").

Alfred, Lord Tennyson   1809–1892

From The Lady of Shalott   [1832]

On either side the river lie
Long fields of barley and of rye,
That clothe the wold° and meet the sky;   *plain*
And through the field the road runs by
To many-tower'd Camelot;   5
And up and down the people go,
Gazing where the lilies blow
Round an island there below,
The island of Shalott.

Now read it again, the way we have scanned the lines:

Ŏn éi | thĕr síde | thĕ rí | vĕr líe
Lóng fíelds | ŏf bár | lĕy and² | ŏf rýe,
Thăt clóthe | thĕ wóld | ănd méet | thĕ ský;
Ănd thró' | thĕ fíeld | thĕ róad | rŭns bý
    Tŏ má | nŷ-tów | er'd Cá | mĕlŏt;   5
Ănd úp | ănd dówn | thĕ péo | plĕ gó,
Gáz | ĭng whére | thĕ líl | ĭes blów
Róund | ăn ís | lănd thére | bĕlów,
    Thĕ ís | lănd ŏf | Shălótt.

Notice how several metrical substitutions control emphasis and make the sound natural, not artificially "poetic." Lines 1, 3, 5, and 6 are in regular iambic feet and have the important role of establishing the prevailing "beat," but line 2 begins with a spondee ("Long fields"), and lines 7 and 8 lack the opening, unstressed syllable; unlike the opening six lines, they begin with a stressed syllable and have only seven syllables, instead of eight.

For practice, try scanning the following lines. Mark the stressed syllables with ´ and unstressed syllables with ˘, and use | to divide lines into feet. Try first to do it by hearing the beat; if that doesn't work, figure it out logically, following the steps we suggest above. To compare your result with the way we scanned it, see page 1431.

---

²A reversed accent [`] can be used for a very lightly stressed syllable, such as the slight stress a normally unstressed word (like *and*) receives when its position in a line calls for it.

Samuel Taylor Coleridge 1772–1834

Metrical Feet   [1806]
Lesson for a Boy

> Trochee trips from long to short.
> From long to long in solemn sort
> Slow Spondee stalks; strong foot! yet ill able
> Ever to come up with Dactyl trisyllable.
> Iambics march from short to long;—   5
> With a leap and a bound the swift Anapests throng.

To illustrate further, we will consider what scansion might add to our understanding, enjoyment, and appreciation of the following poem. Read it twice, once silently, once aloud, and listen for the beat.

Emily Dickinson 1830–1886

I like to see it lap the Miles   [c. 1862; 1891]

> I like to see it lap the Miles—
> And lick the Valleys up—
> And stop to feed itself at Tanks—
> And then—prodigious step
>
> Around a Pile of Mountains—   5
> And supercilious peer
> In Shanties—by the sides of Roads—
> And then a Quarry pare
>
> To fit its Ribs
> And crawl between   10
> Complaining all the while
> In horrid—hooting stanza—
> Then chase itself down Hill—
>
> And neigh like Boanerges[3]—
> Then—punctual as a Star   15
> Stop—docile and omnipotent
> At its own stable door—

---

[3]*Boanerges* ("sons of thunder") is the name Jesus gave to the brothers James and John, his disciples (see Mark 3:17).

This poem resembles a riddle—it forces the reader to supply the implied antecedent to the pronoun *it*. The answer would have been obvious to most readers in Emily Dickinson's day, and perhaps it was to you as you read it too; but cultural changes (especially the replacement of rail systems with freeways) make the riddle less obvious for many readers today. Because trains are not as much a part of our visual imagery as they were during the last century, we may be tempted to read "neigh" and "stable" as literal, rather than as parts of an extended implied metaphor. Scanning the poem can help us clarify why meter is an important aspect of this imaginative depiction of a train. Try scanning it yourself first and then compare your reading with ours.

The poem starts with a stanza of regular iambic feet, alternating lines of tetrameter and trimeter.

> Ĭ líke | tŏ sée | ĭt láp | thĕ Míles—
> Ănd líck | thĕ Vál | lĕys úp—
> Ănd stóp | tŏ feéd | ĭtsélf | ăt Tánks—

Not only is the meter regular, but the rhythm is steady as well; the short, simple words can be read at an even pace, with no internal punctuation interrupting or slowing them down; the dashes at the ends of lines 1 and 2 (Dickinson had her own, unusual ideas about punctuation) give just enough pause for a breath to keep the pace in the following line. Meter and rhythm together echo the repetitive, predictable, clickity-clack sound that train wheels make as they pass over the cracks between the rails.

In line 4 the meter remains regular—"Ănd thén— | prŏdí | giŏus stép"—but the rhythm slows down because the dash creates a pause and because the multisyllabic word "prodigious" takes longer to say than the short monosyllabic words "stop to feed." There is no punctuation at the end of stanzas 1 and 2; in fact, the entire poem is made up of one sentence. Some readers pause briefly at the end of a line even when there is no punctuation, and pause a bit longer at the end of a stanza that lacks end punctuation. That too slows the rhythm—just as, we find in the next line, the speed of the train decreases as it curls around mountains. (We may even sense the effect of having our eyes "step around" the end of the first stanza into the beginning of the second, in imitation of the train.)

Scansion can alert us to another way of slowing the rhythm, in line 5. The pattern established in the first stanza leads us to expect that first and third lines will have eight syllables, four iambic feet. When you read line 5, your ear should hear a difference, something unexpected. Here's an example of the tension between "expected" meter and "heard" meter. Scanning the line ("Ăroúnd | ă Píle | ŏf Moún | taĭns–") reveals that the difference is that it has only seven syllables and lacks the final stressed syllable the other lines have. We tend to linger a bit on the end of that line, slowing the rhythmic pace, partly because of the dash but partly out of respect for the syllable that our ear expects to hear.

The next three lines reestablish the expected pattern of iambic trimeter, tetrameter, trimeter, at a steady pace but slower than lines 1 to 3, slower largely because the combinations of sounds cannot be said rapidly: "Ănd sú | percíl | iŏus peér / Ĭn Shán | tiĕs—by | thĕ sídes | ŏf Róads—/ Ănd thĕn | ă Quár | rў paŕe."

Just as we become reaccustomed to the expected pattern, we are jolted out of it again. Stanza 3 has five lines instead of the usual four and it begins with two lines of only four syllables—two iambic feet—instead of the expected eight syllables, four feet:

Tŏ fít | ĭts Ríbs
Ănd cráwl | bĕtweén
Cŏmpláin | ĭng áll | thĕ whíle
Ĭn hór | rĭd–hoót | ĭng stán | ză—

Scanning the lines helps us notice that the unexpected line still fits the "pattern": Lines 9 and 10 are just an expected tetrameter line divided into two. With a playfulness typical of her, almost as a poetic joke, Dickinson has the stanza become visually narrower as the train peels along the edge of a quarry, fitting its metal "ribs" into the tight space. Line 9 is made tight by the sound of the "fit its" in the middle. As the train slows down for the narrow curves, the poem's rhythm does too, because of the pauses at the ends of the short lines 9 and 10, the long, slow *craaawwll* sound in the middle of line 10, and the length of words and the sound combinations of "Complaining" and "horrid—hooting."

The poem, like the train, hesitates at the end of line 12, which like line 5 lacks the final stressed syllable, then speeds up in regular meter as the train thunders downhill—

Thĕn cháse | ĭtsélf | dŏwn Híll—
Ănd neígh | lĭke Bó | anér | gĕs—

—only to pause sharply at the missing eighth syllable in line 14.

Scansion clarifies a final playful, but metrically effective, touch. After line 15 slows down, "Thĕn—púnc | tŭal aś | ă Stár," because of the spondee, the dash, and the extra syllable (though some readers may slur "púnc | tŭal" into two syllables and keep the meter regular), line 16 again does the unexpected. Thus far, most lines have begun with an unstressed syllable and an iambic foot, and our ears begin to expect that. This line jolts our ear, pulls us up short, by a metrical substitution—a spondee instead of an iamb: "Stóp—dóc | iĭe ănd | ŏmní | pŏtént / Ăt íts | ŏwn stá | blĕ doór." The substitution puts strong emphasis on "Stop," and that, together with the dash following it, interrupts the rhythm—stops us—as the train, now quiet though still powerful, stops at the end of its journey.

In this case it seems that Dickinson may have deliberately decided how meter would fit the shape and effects of the poem. However, poets who use meter do not always count syllables and decide consciously that it is time to make a substitution or to leave off a final stressed syllable. Their ears are attuned to meters, so they hear whether a line "sounds appropriate" or "right" or whether they need to make further changes. Looking back, they may be able to figure out (perhaps by scanning the line) what made it sound better, what made it "work." Scanning—and attention to meter generally—can be retrospective, part of the process of figuring out why what was done proved effective, or it can be part of the creative process.

Let's try this now on a more complex passage, a famous speech from Shakespeare's tragedy *Macbeth* (5.5.19–28). It occurs when Macbeth nears the end of his life. His evil deeds have been found out, his opponents are closing in on his castle, and he is told that his wife has just committed suicide. Full of grief and despair, Macbeth utters a bleak assessment of human existence. Read the passage and then scan it yourself before looking at the way we did it:

> Tomorrow, and tomorrow, and tomorrow
> Creeps in this petty pace from day to day
> To the last syllable of recorded time,
> And all our yesterdays have lighted fools
> The way to dusty death. Out, out, brief candle!   5
> Life's but a walking shadow, a poor player
> That struts and frets his hour upon the stage
> And then is heard no more. It is a tale
> Told by an idiot, full of sound and fury,
> Signifying nothing.   10

Here is the way we scan the lines, but it is important to realize that this is not *the one correct* way to scan it. Differences in pronunciation and interpretation can lead to entirely acceptable differences in scansion of a poem. (Acceptable differences do not include mispronunciations. You may need to look up pronunciations, as well as definitions, of unfamiliar words to be fair both to the sound and to the meaning of a poem.)

> Tŏmór|rŏw, ănd|tŏmór|rŏw, ănd|tŏmórrŏw
> Créeps ĭn| thĭs pét|tў páce| frŏm dáy| tŏ dáy
> Tŏ thĕ lást| sýllă| blĕ ŏf| récórd| ĕd tíme,
> Ănd áll| oŭr yés|tĕrdáys| hăve líght|ĕd fóols
> Thĕ wáy| tŏ dúst|ў déath.| Oút, oút,| bríef cán| dĭe!   5
> Life's bŭt| ă wálk| ĭng shád| ŏw, ă póor| pláyĕr
> Thăt strúts| ănd fréts| hĭs hóur| ŭpón| thĕ stáge
> Ănd thén| ĭs héard| nŏ móre.| Ĭt ĭs| ă tále
> Tóld bў ăn| ídĭŏt,| fúll ŏf| soúnd ănd| fúrў,
> Sígnĭ| fўĭng| nóthĭng.   10

The passage, like much of the poetry in Shakespeare's plays, is written in **blank verse** (unrhymed iambic pentameter). The first line is regular, except for the extra unstressed syllable on the final iamb. That syllable, together with the two caesuras and the time it takes to say each "tomorrow," lengthens the line and slows it down, so that rhythmically it creeps, the way Macbeth says life does. Stressing "and" twice adds to the sense of circularity and monotony Macbeth finds in life.

The second line begins with one of the most common metric substitutions, an initial trochee instead of an iamb, which puts extra emphasis on the key word "creeps." That the rest of the line is regular echoes the steady, plodding pace by which life proceeds, and it sets up the irregular, unexpected anapest and trochee of the first half of line 3 — to think of the very end, the final millisecond, of history ("recorded time") is jolting, and the meter jolts us as well. After two irregular lines the expected, regular iambics return for the rest of line 3, all of line 4, and half of line 5, again suiting the steady, plodding pace by which Macbeth says people follow one another through life toward death, the past like a lantern lighting the way as people foolishly imitate what those before them have done.

The rest of line 5 is irregular: two spondees and an extra unstressed syllable: "Out, out, | brief candle!" Although life may seem to plod, it is short; Macbeth expresses the wish that his would end. The double stresses of the spondees, emphasized by the caesuras that make one linger, give strength to the words "Out, out," and another spondee with an extra syllable and a definite end stop make us dwell on "brief candle!" The rhythm, which had been slow but steady, becomes broken and forceful here and in the following line. Line 6 also is irregular and unusual — a trochee, two iambs, an anapest, and a trochee. This is an unusual metrical combination, difficult to enunciate, just as its thought (that there is no reality, that life is empty and meaningless) is difficult for most people to accept. That slow, contorted line rhythmically leads into a line and a half that are metrically regular, reestablishing the expected meter. The mostly monosyllabic words, full of stops and fricatives, seem almost drumlike, booming their assertions about the brevity and unreality of people's stage-play lives: "That STRUTS and FRETS his HOUR upON the STAGE / And THEN is HEARD no MORE."

After the full-stop caesura, the iambs continue for two feet but the drum disappears with the lightly stressed "is." But these quieter, softer lines ("It is | a tale / Told by an | idiot, | full of | sound and | fury, / Signi | fying | nothing") are perhaps even more intense than those before them since they describe life as having no more shape and significance than the babblings of an insane person. The meter in lines 9 and 10 — two dactyls and six trochees — is madly unusual and amazingly effective. Emphasis on "tale | Told" is heightened by stressing both and linking them by alliteration. The two dactyls, "Told by an idiot," can only be read slowly, with difficulty, which places unmissable emphasis on "idiot." The dactyls and the six trochees following illustrate the anticlimactic potential of "falling meter," as with each foot we seem to sink lower than the one before.

The length of the ninth line, with its two extra syllables, makes an idiot's tale seem not only chaotic but also almost endless. The unifying sounds of the last six feet (alliteration linking "full" and "fury" and also "sound" and "signifying") makes them forceful; the rhythm, steady in line 9, becomes less steady in line 10 (the stress on "fy" is so light that one may hear "signifying") and almost fades away (to "nothing").

When you are watching *Macbeth*, you probably do not think about the fact that much of it is poetry and can be discussed for its figures, sounds, meter, and rhythm like the short poems we examine throughout this book. Even though you are not thinking about or realizing the presence of the poetry, however, it contributes in an important way to the intensity and emotional power of the play.

For additional practice, scan the following lines and label the prevailing metrical foot and line length without looking at page 1431 (cover it up).

> Woman much missed, how you call to me, call to me,
> Saying that now you are not as you were
> When you had changed from the one who was all to me,
> But as at first, when our day was fair.
>
> —Thomas Hardy

> That time of year thou mayst in me behold
> When yellow leaves, or none, or few, do hang
> Upon those boughs which shake against the cold,
> Bare ruined choirs, where late the sweet birds sang.
>
> —William Shakespeare

> "Good speed!" cried the watch, as the gate-bolts undrew;
> "Speed!" echoed the wall to us galloping through;
> Behind shut the postern, the lights sank to rest,
> And into the midnight we galloped abreast.
>
> —Robert Browning

> Piping down the valleys wild,
> Piping songs of pleasant glee,
> On a cloud I saw a child,
> And he laughing said to me:
>
> —William Blake

Now look at page 1431 and compare your results with ours.

Trochee | trips from | long to | short.   *trochaic tetrameter*

From long | to long | in sol | emn sort   *iambic tetrameter*

Slow Spon | dee stalks; | strong foot! |yet   *spondaic tetrameter plus*
    ill able   *two weak syllables*

Ever to | come up with | Dactyl tri | syllable.   *dactylic tetrameter*

Iam | bics march | from short | to long;—   *iambic tetrameter*

With a leap | and a bound | the swift An | *anapestic tetrameter*
apests throng.

   —Samuel Taylor Coleridge, "Metrical Feet"

Woman much | missed, how you | call to me, | call to me,

Saying that | now you are | not as you | were   *dactylic*

When you had | changed from the | one who was | all to me,   *tetrameter*

But as at | first, when our | day was | fair.

                   —Thomas Hardy

That time | of year | thou mayst | in me | behold

When yel | low leaves, | or none, | or few, | do hang   *iambic*

Upon | those boughs | which shake | against | the cold,   *pentameter*

Bare ru | ined choirs, | where late | the sweet | birds sang.

            —William Shakespeare

"Good speed!" | cried the watch, | as the gate | -bolts undrew;

"Speed!" ech | oed the wall | to us gal | loping through;   *anapestic*

Behind | shut the pos | tern, the lights | sank to rest,   *tetrameter*

And in | to the mid | night we gal | loped abreast.

                —Robert Browning

Piping | down the | valleys | wild,

Piping | songs of | pleasant | glee,   *trochaic*

On a | cloud I | saw a | child,   *tetrameter*

And he | laughing | said to | me:

       —William Blake

Appendix on
Reading Critical Essays

When you see a movie you really like, you may not only want to see it again but also to find out more about it—what other films an actor has appeared in (and perhaps some details about her or his life), some background on the director and information on the screenwriter, what changes were made from the work on which it was based (if adapted from another source), and what well-informed film critics said about it. As you look for information about these topics in newspapers, in magazines, or on the Internet, you are engaging in research. You can do the same for literary works. Even if you learn a lot about a work by reading it several times, reflecting on it and taking notes about it, listening to what is said about it in class, and discussing it with your classmates, for rich, complex works there is always more to learn, beyond the classroom.

THE ONGOING CONVERSATION   Learning more in this case can be interesting and even exciting as it brings you deeper into the great ongoing conversation about literature that we've referred to several times in this book. That conversation starts with people talking about works they like and sharing their enthusiasms, dislikes, and questions. It continues as they move that exchange to paper (or computer screens). It extends further through the efforts of literary scholars who publish their critical insights about a particular work or era or theme.

PARTICIPATING IN THAT CONVERSATION   Obviously, you can participate in early stages of that conversation. But it's important for you, as a student of literature, to enter the later stages as well by reading, reflecting on, and responding to the critical writings of literary scholars, thus incorporating them into your own literary experience. This appendix offers suggestions on how to read and assess critical essays about literary works, something that can be an important step toward an even more interesting and provocative involvement in the wider world of literary study.

WHAT ARE CRITICAL ESSAYS?

The word *critical* in its literary use (and in its use for the arts in general) does not mean "inclined to find fault or judge severely," as in "My uncle is such a critical person—always ripping somebody apart." Rather, it means exercising skillful and well-informed judgment as to the techniques, ideas, or merits in, for example, a work of literature or a play, a concert, a dance performance, or an art exhibit.

Literary critics are scholars who have learned a great deal about literature, usually through work toward academic degrees but sometimes through extensive reading on their own. When they prepare to write a critical essay on a work, they read the work many times; they read everything else the author has written; and they read critical essays and books written about the work and author by other critics. Through previous study they probably already have learned a good deal about the time and places in which the author lived, and about writers and works that influenced the author, but they may do additional study as preparation for a particular essay.

For us to read what such expert authorities write about a work can yield insights—which we otherwise might miss—and a fuller understanding of the work itself, its context, and how it came into being.

WHY READ CRITICAL ESSAYS?

Reading critical essays helps in a number of ways. However, you will find them most useful if you read them at the right point. We recommend strongly that you not begin reading critical essays about a story, poem, or play until you have read the work itself several times and formulated your own thoughts about it. If you start reading criticism before you know the text well and form your own ideas about it, the ideas in the essays may overwhelm your thoughts and lead you merely to accept or adapt what you read. With your own conclusions already in mind, you'll be better able to evaluate the criticism, to disagree with the critic as well as to agree, and to accept refinements of your own insights.

Once you know a work well and have begun shaping your ideas about it, there are five good reasons for reading critical studies of the work:

1. To see how your own ideas are like and unlike those of other readers
2. To have your attention drawn to parts or aspects of the work whose significance you haven't recognized and to begin to imagine new ways of reading a text—new interpretations of or perspectives on it

3. To learn where the literary conversation about an author or a work stands and what scholars regard as strengths and weaknesses in what other critics have written

4. To discover new ways of constructing a literary argument, refuting earlier positions, offering counterarguments, and using explanation, elaboration, and evidence effectively

5. To gain a better understanding of the background or culture or literary tradition of a work by reading the results of a scholar's primary research (since you don't have time to do research on everything yourself, you often learn through reading the results of other people's research)

Each of these reasons has a practical benefit when you are working on a paper. Reading critical essays can give you a more informed and balanced stance as you explore a work. You can be more confident about your ability to find support for a position you want to uphold, and for entering the ongoing discussion as you write your paper. If need be, you may be able to refine your tentative thesis into a more effective idea-based thesis by connecting it with points about which critics disagree or about which one modifies what another has said—the way Susan Farrell challenges prevailing views about "Everyday Use" in the sample essay later in this chapter.

ACTIVE READING: Critical Essays

In Chapters 2, 3, 9, 18, and 24, we describe a number of conventions you should follow in writing a literary paper—being sure that you state a thesis in the introduction, starting each paragraph with a topic sentence, and so on. There is a strategic reason for following those conventions: They enable your reader to grasp your paper easily and they establish confidence in you as a writer worth attending to. The importance of what we say in those chapters may become more evident as you read critical essays and find yourself using those conventions to trace the steps in the argument and to understand what is being said.

Here are some guidelines for reading critical essays. (For reading critical books, begin by looking at the table of contents, noticing the overall outline of the book, and reading the preface to find out the aims, approach, and outlook of the book; then apply the guidelines to each chapter.)

• *Pick out the thesis and identify the central idea the paper will explore.* The thesis is likely found near the end of the introductory paragraph or section.

Look also for references to previous studies and notice how the essay you are reading differs from or disagrees with them. Use such references to identify what is new about the central idea and about the essay.

- *Look for the topic sentence in each paragraph.* The first sentence usually states the central idea to be discussed in the paragraph. (The second sentence may do this instead if the first is mainly a transitional sentence.)

- *Watch for the way the ideas are advanced and supported.* Outline the steps in the argument (the thesis sentence and topic sentences may provide an outline). Consider the reasoning used in laying out ideas and connecting points to each other. Consider the nature and adequacy of the evidence provided in support of the reasoning.

- *Identify and take into account the theoretical approach being taken in the essay.* The appendix on theoretical approaches to literature (p. 1445) summarizes a number of ways scholars approach literature, such as doing literary analysis, literary interpretation, historical background research, or analysis from a Marxist, psychoanalytic, or feminist perspective. Knowing where a critical work is coming from—what its assumptions and intentions are—helps you to follow its arguments and to do justice to its ideas.

- *Look at the footnotes and/or Works Cited list to see if there are other studies you might want to read yourself.*

SAMPLE ESSAY

ENTRY POINTS   Try out those strategies in reading the following essay. If you did not read Alice Walker's story "Everyday Use" in Chapter 6 (p. 169) or if you do not remember it well, read it before going on to the essay. For the convenience of readers, we have changed the page numbers for quotations of "Everyday Use" originally given in the essay to the pages on which they are found in this book.

Notice as you read the essay that the first paragraph situates the study in the ongoing discussion of "Everyday Use." It sketches out the positions held by other critics, summarizing and quoting from a few representative analyses of the story and listing many other studies in a footnote. Then it states the thesis to be explored in this essay, one that clearly is argumentative because it asserts a position almost directly opposite to the one most critics hold. The rest of the essay elaborates on that argument and explains why the author adheres to it. As you read, it is important to differentiate between sentences that *advance* the argument and sentences that *support* and *illustrate* the argument. To make that easier, we have put the former in boldface and added some marginal notes.

Susan Farrell

Fight vs. Flight: A Re-evaluation of Dee in Alice Walker's "Everyday Use"   [1998]

Method: sum-
mary of views
held by other
critics.

Most readers of Alice Walker's short story "Everyday Use," published in her 1973 collection *In Love and Trouble*, agree that the point of the story is to show, as Nancy Tuten argues, a mother's "awakening to one daughter's superficiality and to the other's deepseated understanding of heritage" (125).[1] These readers praise the "simplicity" of Maggie and her mother, along with their allegiance to their specific family identity and folk heritage as well as their refusal to change at the whim of an outside world that doesn't really have much to do with them. Such a reading condemns the older, more worldly sister, Dee, as "shallow," "condescending," and "manipulative," as overly concerned with style, fashion, and aesthetics, and thus as lacking a "true" understanding of her heritage. **In this essay, conversely, I will argue that this popular view is far too simple a reading of the story. While Dee is certainly insensitive and selfish**

Thesis.

to a certain degree, she nevertheless offers a view of heritage and a strategy for contemporary African Americans to cope with an oppressive society that are, in some ways, more valid than those offered by Mama and Maggie.

Method: build-
ing on earlier
critics.

We must remember from the beginning that the story is told by Mama; the perceptions are filtered through her mind and her views of her two daughters are not to be accepted uncritically. Several readers have pointed out that Mama's view of Maggie is not quite accurate—that Maggie is not as passive or as "hangdog" as she appears.[2] **Might Mama's view of her older daughter, Dee, not be espe-**

Central idea for
Section I.

cially accurate as well? Dee obviously holds a central place in Mama's world. The story opens with the line: "I will wait for her in the yard that Maggie and I made so clean and wavy yesterday afternoon" (169). As Houston Baker and Charlotte Pierce-Baker point out, "The mood at the story's beginning is one of ritualistic waiting," of preparation "for the arrival of a goddess" (715). Thus, Dee seems to attain almost mythic stature in Mama's imagination as she and Maggie wait for the as-yet unnamed "her" to appear. Such an opening may lead readers to suspect that Mama has a rather troubled relationship with her older daughter. Dee inspires in Mama a type of awe and fear more suitable to the advent of a goddess than the love one might expect a mother to feel for a returning daughter.

Mama, in fact, **displaces what seem to be her own fears onto Maggie** when she speculates that Maggie will be cowed by Dee's arrival. Mama conjectures that

Maggie will be nervous until after her sister goes: she will stand hopelessly in corners, homely and ashamed of the burn scars down her arms and legs, eyeing her sister with a mixture of envy and awe. She thinks her sister has held life always in the palm of one hand, that "no" is a word the world never learned to say to her. (169)

But Mama here emphasizes the perceptual nature of this observation—she says that Maggie *thinks* these things, encouraging readers to wonder whether or not this first perception of Dee is true. We also find out in the next section, when Mama relates her Johnny Carson television fantasy, that she herself is the one who will be "nervous" until after Dee goes, that she is ashamed of her own appearance and very much seeks her daughter's approval. Mama confesses that, in "real life," she is "a large, big-boned woman with rough, man-working hands" (170). However, in her television fantasy, as Mama tells us,

Method: close reading of text.

Evidence: summary and quotation.

all this does not show. . . . I am the way my daughter would want me to be: a hundred pounds lighter, my skin like an uncooked barley pancake. My hair glistens in the hot bright lights. Johnny Carson has much to do to keep up with my quick and witty tongue. (170)

It is important to remember, though, that **this Johnny Carson daydream is Mama's fantasy of a mother-child reunion, *not* Dee's.** In fact, Mama even acknowledges that this particular scenario might not be to Dee's taste—she imagines Dee pinning an orchid on her even though Dee had previously told Mama she thinks orchids are "tacky flowers" (170). Thus, although Tuten equates Dee's values with those of "the white Johnny Carson society" (126), it seems to me that we have to question whether Mama's vision of her light-skinned, slender, witty self is actually Dee's wish or only Mama's perception of what she imagines Dee would like her to be.

Elsewhere, as well, we see that **Mama is often wrong about her expectations of Dee and her readings of Dee's emotions.** She writes that she "used to think" Dee hated Maggie as much as she hated the previous house that burned down (171). Mama implies, though, that she has since changed her mind about this. Further, as Mama and Maggie continue to wait for Dee's arrival, Mama "deliberately" turns her back on the house, expecting Dee to hate this house as much as Mama believes she hated the earlier one: "No doubt when Dee sees it she will want to tear it down" (171). When Dee does arrive, however, she has a camera with her and "never takes a shot without making sure the house is included" (172). Of course, most readers see this as evidence of Dee's fickle changing

Method: contrast with other critics.

with whatever fad happens to be current. Once it becomes fashionable to have rural, poverty-stricken roots, Dee wants a record of her own humble beginnings. This might very well be true. Yet **I would argue that we have only Mama's word for Dee's earlier haughtiness, and this could have been exaggerated,** much as Mama hints that her earlier suspicion of Dee's hatred for Maggie was inaccurate. The more subtle point here is that **Mama's expectations of Dee tell us more about Mama herself than they do about Dee.** Again, Mama seems to view Dee with a mixture of awe, envy, and fear. Although she resents Dee because she expects Dee will want "to tear the house down," Mama still takes her cue from her older daughter, herself turning her back on the house, perhaps in an effort to appease this daughter, who looms so large in Mama's imagination.

Central idea for Section II.

In contrast to her own fearfulness, **Mama, with grudging admiration, remembers Dee as a fearless girl.** While Mama imagines herself unable to look white people in the eye, talking to them only "with one foot raised in flight," Dee "would always look anyone in the eye. Hesitation was no part of her nature" (170). Mama remembers Dee as self-centered and demanding, yes, but she also remembers this daughter as **a determined fighter.** Dee is concerned with style, but she'll do whatever is necessary to improve her circumstances. For instance, when Dee wants a new dress, she

Method: accumulation of details.

"makes over" an old green suit someone had given her mother. Rather than passively accept her lot, as Mama seems trained to do, Dee "was determined to stare down any disaster in her efforts" (171). **Mama's fearful nature is also apparent in her reaction to knowledge.** Words for Mama are associated with "lies" and "other folks' habits" (171). She remembers feeling "trapped and ignorant" as Dee reads to her and Maggie "without pity" (171). This is partly because Mama never had an education herself. When her school was closed down in 1927, after she had completed only the second grade, Mama, like the other African Americans in her community, didn't fight: "colored asked fewer questions than they do now," she tells us (171). Again, Mama is trained in acquiescence while Dee refuses to meekly accept the status quo.

Method: contrast with other critics.

Most critics see Dee's education and her insistence on reading to Mama and Maggie as further evidence of her separation from and lack of understanding for her family identity and heritage. Tuten, for instance, argues that, in this story, "Walker stresses not only the importance of language but also the destructive effects of its misuse. . . . Rather than providing a medium for newfound awareness and for community, . . . verbal skill equips Dee to oppress and manipulate others and to isolate herself" (125). Similarly, Donna Winchell writes that "Dee tries to force on" Maggie and her mother "knowledge they probably do not need." She continues,

Mrs. Johnson can take an objective look at who and what she is and find not disillusionment but an easy satisfaction. Simple pleasures—a dip of snuff, a cooling breeze across a clean swept yard, church songs, the soothing movements of milk cows—are enough. (82)

But are these "simple pleasures" really enough for Mama in the story? When she imagines her future she seems vaguely unhappy and apprehensive about it: "[Maggie] will marry John Thomas (who has mossy teeth in an earnest face) and then I'll be free to sit here and I guess just sing church songs to myself. Although I never was a good singer. Never could carry a tune" (171). Not quite sure what she will do with herself when Maggie marries, Mama can only imagine herself alone, engaging in an activity which she feels she is not even very good at. Although she perhaps goes about it in the wrong way—Mama says that Dee "pressed us to her with the serious way she read," only to "shove us away at just the moment, like dimwits, we seemed about to understand" (171)—Dee at least tries to change what she foresees as Mama's fairly dismal future, a vision of her future Mama herself seems to reinforce rather than dispute. **Thus, I'd suggest the possibility that Dee's attempt to educate Mama and Maggie may be read much more positively than other critics have suggested.** Again, we must remember that Mama's perspective is the only one we see throughout the story. Told from Dee's point of view, we might expect a very different rendering of this incident. Rather than simply abandon her mother and sister in their ignorance and poverty, in their acquiescence to an oppressive system, Dee tries her best to extend her own education to them, which is surely not such a bad thing.

Method: showing other critics may be mistaken.

When Dee does finally arrive, **both Maggie and her mother react again with fear of the unknown, of something strange and different.** But as Dee approaches, Mama notices that the brightly colored African dress that Dee wears "throw[s] back the light of the sun" (172). Mama feels her "whole face warming from the heat waves it throws out" (172). She also admires the way that the "dress is loose and flows," and, despite her initial reaction, even decides that she likes it as Dee moves closer to her. In her admiration of the dress, **Mama illustrates Walker's point that everything new is not to be feared, that change can be positive, not only negative.** Maggie, however, remains fearful, even in the face of the friendliness of Dee's companion, who grins and greets Mrs. Johnson and Maggie warmly: "Asalamalakim, my mother and sister!" (172). When he tries to hug Maggie, though, she falls back against a chair and trembles. And later, when he tries to teach Maggie a new handshake, her hand remains limp and she quickly withdraws it from his.

Central idea for Section III.

Method: con- trast with other critics.

Shortly after this, Dee announces that she is no longer Dee but "Wangero Leewanika Kemanjo." She has newly adopted an African name since, as she explains: "I couldn't bear it any longer, being named after the people who oppress me" (172). Many readers point to Dee's proclamation of her new name as the turning point in the story, the point at which Dee pushes her mother too far. They point out that Dee is rejecting her family heritage and identity in this scene. **Yet it seems to me that Dee and Mama are *both* right here.** Mama's recounting of the family history of the name is surely ac- curate, but what the critics fail to point out is that Dee's assertion that the name comes from "the people who oppress" her is also ac- curate. While most readers see Mama and Maggie as having a "true" sense of heritage as opposed to Dee's false or shallow understanding of the past, both Mama and Dee are blind to particular aspects of heritage. Dee has much to learn about honoring her particular and individual family history, but Mama has much to learn about the history of African Americans in general, and about fighting oppres- sion. Although each is stubborn, both Dee and Mama do make a concession to the other here. Dee tells Mama that she needn't use the new name if she doesn't want to, while Mama shows her will- ingness to learn and to use the name.

Method: new way of reading the text.

Mama's secret admiration for Dee's fighting spirit leaks out again when she explicitly connects the "beef-cattle peoples down the road" to Dee and her boyfriend, "Hakim-a-barber." We see that the neighbors down the road, like Dee's boyfriend, are most likely black Muslims: they also say "Asalamalakim" when they meet, and Hakim explains that he accepts "some of their doctrines," although farming is not his style. Like Dee, these neighbors are also fighters. When "white folks" poison some of their cattle, they "stayed up all night with rifles in their hands" (173). Tellingly, Mama, who can't look white people in the eye and who never asked questions when her school closed down, is intrigued by this younger generation's refusal to acquiesce. She "walked a mile and a half" down the road "just to see the sight" of blacks armed for resistance (173). **Mixed with her resentment against her older daughter's worldliness and self- centered attitude, Mama also grudgingly respects and even envies the willingness to fight evinced both by Dee and the black Muslim neighbors.**

Maggie's forbearance in the story contrasts with Dee's boldness. When Dee haughtily insists that Maggie would ruin Grandma's quilts by using them every day, and that hanging the quilts would be the only way to preserve them, Maggie, "like somebody used to never winning anything, or having anything reserved for her," meekly re- plies: "She can have them, Mama, . . . I can 'member Grandma Dee without the quilts" (175). Mama, though, does not react so meekly. She sees Maggie standing with her scarred hands hidden in her skirt and says: "When I looked at her like that something hit me in the top of my head and ran down to the soles of my feet. Just like when I'm in church and the spirit of God touches me and I get happy and shout" (175). This powerful feeling causes Mama to do something she "never had done before": she "snatched the quilts out of Miss Wangero's hands and dumped them into Maggie's lap" (175). **Ironically, in acting against Dee's wishes here, Mama is truly behaving more like Dee, with her refusal to back down, her willingness to stand up for herself, than she is like the patient and long-suffering Maggie.** So perhaps, along with the younger, changing generation coming of age in the early 1970s that she is associated with, Dee, despite her outward obnoxiousness, has taught Mama something about fighting back. Or perhaps Dee has inherited more of her stubbornness and self-determination from her Mama than previously suspected. But, in any case, it seems too easy and neat a reading to simply praise Mama and Maggie for understanding their heritage while dismissing Dee as shallow and self-serving, when Mama's final courageous act ties her more closely to this older daughter than to the younger one she is trying to protect.

Walker raised similar problems concerning the willingness to fight for a cause versus the desire to remain passive in her novel _Meridian_, published in 1976, three years after _In Love and Trouble_. In this novel, Walker's main character, Meridian Hill, is at first passive and dreamy. She drifts into an early marriage and pregnancy, since these things seem to be expected of her, but she doesn't truly find direction in her life until she becomes involved with the early Civil Rights movement. As a movement worker, though, Meridian is tempted toward becoming a martyr for her cause. When asked if she would "kill for the revolution," Meridian remains unable to answer. Although readers see the complexities of Meridian's ambivalence here, other activists call her a coward and a masochist for her lack of commitment. In her forbearance and initial willingness to sacrifice her own needs if necessary, Meridian shares much in common with Maggie of "Everyday Use." Meridian's college roommate, Anne-Marion Coles, on the other hand, is similar to Dee. Aggressive and determined to change her life, Anne-Marion, unlike Meridian, easily asserts her willingness to kill if necessary. But, also like Dee in the way she treats Mama and Maggie, Anne-Marion is self-centered and at times unthinkingly cruel to the weaker, more fragile Meridian. While Meridian is certainly a more sympathetic character than Anne-Marion throughout the novel, just as Maggie and Mama are more appealing than Dee in many ways, by the end Walker shows us that Meridian has something to learn from Anne-Marion and her other militant colleagues in the movement....

Readers of these two works may at first be seduced into affirming the passive acquiescence of characters such as Mama, Maggie, and

Central idea for Section IV.

Method: parallel situation in another work by Walker.

Summary to bring out similarities between the two works.

Meridian because they are, in many ways, more palatable, more likeable, than such aggressive fighters as Dee and Anne-Marion. These determined, fierce women, however, have much to teach the more forbearing, self-sacrificing characters in both works. Yet, at the same time, we see that a spirit of rebellion, without a corresponding spirituality and respect for such traditional black institutions as the church or the folk arts of "Everyday Use," can be empty as well. Though defiant and aggressive, both Dee and Anne-Marion are selfish and capricious in their social activism. Finally, then, in "Everyday Use," **Walker shows that Mama's moment of triumph is achieved because she is able to attain a balance between the two types of her heritage represented by her very different daughters**—at the end Mama combines Maggie's respect for tradition with Dee's pride and refusal to back down, the combination Walker seems to feel is necessary if true social change is to come about.

Completion of thesis idea.

Notes

Informative endnotes.

1. See especially, along with Tuten's *Explicator* article, Houston Baker and Charlotte Pierce-Baker's "Patches: Quilts and Community in Alice Walker's 'Everyday Use,'" Margaret D. Bauer's "Alice Walker: Another Southern Writer Criticizing Codes Not Put to 'Everyday Use,'" and Donna Haisty Winchell's Twayne Series book on Alice Walker (80–84).

Note listing related critical studies.

2. Tuten, for instance, argues that the "action of the story . . . in no way supports Mama's reading of her younger daughter," that Maggie "conveys disgust with her sister rather than envy and awe" as Mama believes (127). Similarly, Baker and Pierce-Baker point out that, "in her epiphanic moment of recognition," Mama must perceive "the fire-scarred Maggie—the stay-at-home victim of southern scarifications—in a revised light," that she must reassess "what she wrongly interprets as Maggie's hang-dog resignation before Dee" (717).

Note providing further supporting evidence.

Works Cited

Baker, Houston, and Charlotte Pierce-Baker. "Patches: Quilts and Community in Alice Walker's 'Everyday Use.'" *The Southern Review* 21 (1985): 706–20. Print.

Bauer, Margaret D. "Alice Walker: Another Southern Writer Criticizing Codes Not Put to 'Everyday Use.'" *Studies in Short Fiction* 29 (1992): 143–51. Print.

Tuten, Nancy. "Alice Walker's 'Everyday Use.'" *The Explicator* 51.2 (Winter 1993): 125–28. Print.

Walker, Alice. "Everyday Use." *In Love and Trouble*. New York: Harcourt, 1973. 47–59. Rpt. in *Approaching Literature: Reading + Thinking + Writing*. Ed. Peter Schakel and Jack Ridl. 3rd ed. Boston: Bedford/St. Martin's, 2012. 169–75. Print.

——. *Meridian*. New York: Harcourt, 1976. Print.

Winchell, Donna Haisty. *Alice Walker*. New York: Twayne, 1992. Print.

OUTLINE   Most scholars, when they read such an essay, pick out the central idea in each paragraph and jot down an outline of the main steps in the argument. Here is an example of the sort of outline a reader might sketch out:

> Thesis: Dee offers a view of heritage and way of coping with society more valid than those of Mama and Maggie
> I.   Mama's view of Dee may not be reliable
>   A. She displaces her fears of Dee onto Maggie
>   B. The Johnny Carson daydream is Mama's fantasy, not Dee's
>   C. Mama is often wrong about Dee
> II.   Contrast between Dee's fearlessness and Mama's fearfulness
>   A. Dee as a determined fighter
>   B. Mama's fear of knowledge
>   C. Mama's fear of the future
> III.   Mama's attitude changes as she interacts with Dee
>   A. Mama seems more open to new things than Maggie
>   B. Both Mama and Dee need to gain a more adequate understanding of heritage
>   C. Mama admires Dee's fighting spirit
>   D. Mama behaves like Dee (not like Maggie) by fighting back against Dee's demands
> IV. The same pattern (passivity vs. fighting back) is evident in *Meridian*
> Restatement of thesis: Mama triumphs as she achieves a balance between the approaches and attitudes of Dee and Maggie.

Such an outline enables you to view the argument as a whole—what the individual points are and how they relate to each other. That's valuable in understanding the essay and in assessing the strength of what it says.

KINDS OF EVIDENCE   It's also important to notice the kinds of evidence an author uses to support her or his argument. In Farrell's essay, most of the evidence comes through close reading of the text, with supporting details and quotations from it. But the author also uses the authoritative opinions of other scholars in support of her own positions when she regards them as sound, and she argues against them when she believes their interpretations are not accurate or adequate. And the author uses as a further kind of supporting evidence a parallel situation in another work by Walker, the novel *Meridian*. (We include only the first paragraph of that section, to show how the author introduces the comparison, and omit the following three paragraphs because they discuss a work that is not included in this book and will be unfamiliar to many of you.)

REREADING: Critical Essays

An important step in reading critical essays is evaluation: After all, the essay is trying to persuade you, so it is crucial that you not simply accept automatically what has been written, that you have the skills necessary to decide how good the points and arguments in the essay are. Making that decision usually requires rereading all, or the key parts of, the essay. To evaluate the essay well, start by comparing the critic's ideas with your own. This is why it is important that you know the work itself well and that you formulate your own interpretation of it before reading any critical essay. Here are some suggestions for evaluating critical essays.

- *Compare the critic's interpretation with your own interpretation.* The first step in evaluation is to formulate your own judgment as clearly and substantially as you can. Then compare the critic's interpretations to your own—how convincing do they seem to you? Does the critic use the text accurately and fairly and draw sensible conclusions about details in it? Does the critic take everything into account or pass over details that don't support her or his conclusions? Do the steps in the critic's argument proceed logically, and is the case that is presented sound and convincing?

- *Compare what one critic says with what other critics say.* Perhaps comparison is the best method of evaluation. To assess fully what one critic says, read the interpretations of several or many other critics. By comparing what one says with what another says, you will begin to get a sense of what ideas need to be explored in a work, what sections or details need to be taken into consideration, what approaches prove to be most productive and illuminating. In some cases, you will find some critics agreeing with or replying to or refuting the interpretations of others (as you do in the sample essay above). What the critics say about each other will be very helpful in testing and shaping your own conclusions about a critical essay—though, of course, you will need to be evaluating the soundness of each as you make your comparisons.

Approaching
Critical Theory

This book is about approaching literature. It's valuable to realize that you always approach something from somewhere. We have tried to connect reading literature to your everyday life: You come to this course with prior interests and experiences, and the way you approach what you read, even your ability to relate to it at all, depends on where you're "coming from."

ALL READING IS THEORY BASED In addition to this personal way to approach a work, there is another sense of approaching literature from somewhere. All readers approach their reading from a critical or theoretical perspective, even though they may not be aware of it. There are many such perspectives—some practical, others more abstract and philosophical. This appendix, though it cannot cover all of them, does indicate the range of past and present approaches used by readers.

BENEFITS OF BEING AWARE OF THEORY Having an awareness of critical and theoretical perspectives helps as you read literary works themselves—helps you sharpen and refine your own approaches to reading, helps you become a more flexible reader, and helps you vary your approaches for different works and in different situations. And being familiar with critical theories is beneficial as you read scholarly books and essays about literature. As we said in "Appendix on Reading Critical Essays" (p. 1432), knowing where a critical work is coming from, what its assumptions and intentions are, can help in following its arguments and in understanding why two readers of the same text can arrive at quite different readings. (Note, however, that scholars usually do not limit themselves to only one approach; they often combine approaches, or elements from different approaches, to fit a particular work or problem.)

CHRONOLOGICAL APPROACH TO THEORY The following survey of approaches is arranged in roughly chronological order to provide a brief history of literary criticism and to indicate how some theories developed out of, or as a reaction to, other theories—though theories have often overlapped, or run simultaneously, with others.

BIOGRAPHICAL CRITICISM

BEGINNING WITH THE BEGINNINGS English literature didn't become a subject of academic study until the late 1800s. At that point the emphasis was on its beginnings, on the study of Old English and Middle English language and writings. The assumption was that students didn't need much help with literature from Shakespeare on: Those works were considered part of their reading for pleasure, not part of the academic curriculum.

FOCUSING ON AUTHORS By the 1930s, academic study of English literature had begun to include later authors, though still not contemporary literature, the attention focusing particularly on the historical backgrounds of works and on the lives of authors. Scholars used literary works as a source of information about authors (not always being careful to keep a first-person narrator or speaker separate from the author) and used details from an author's life to gain a better understanding of a work (not always being careful to remember that a writer can make things up).

INSIGHTS FROM BIOGRAPHY Biographical criticism today involves research into the details of an author's life to shed light on the author's works, an important and basic form of literary study. Publishers have recognized its value by publishing biographical encyclopedias for literary figures and by including biographical sketches of the authors in anthologies such as this textbook (see p. 1371). Knowledge about an author can enable us in many cases to notice details or ideas in a work we might otherwise miss.

DOING BIOGRAPHICAL CRITICISM Chapter 10 illustrates the kind of material a biographical approach draws upon. The chapter starts with a detailed biographical sketch of Sherman Alexie and includes excerpts from two interviews. These, combined with the personal essay by Alexie in Chapter 1, could form the groundwork for a paper on how Alexie's works relate to his life, though a thorough study would require additional reading and research. Likewise, the poems, personal writings, and interviews in Chapter 19 and the story "Nada" (p. 395) could be used toward a biographical study of Judith Ortiz Cofer. If you decide to attempt biographical criticism of Alexie, Ortiz Cofer, or another author, be sure it actually *is* criticism and not just a *report* on the author's life. The paper must involve analysis, and it must use biographical data to illuminate meaning and build its interpretations on what is in the text, not on extraneous material from outside the text.

HISTORICAL CRITICISM

FOCUSING ON CONTEXT   As biographical knowledge enhances your understanding of a work, so does awareness of the social, political, cultural, and intellectual context in which it was conceived and written. Literary historians research such backgrounds and bring what they find to bear on a work, explaining details used in the work and clarifying the meaning of the work as its original readers would have understood it. They research sources the author drew on and influences that shaped the form and content of the work. They connect the work to other works written at the time, to describe the literary environment that surrounds it, and compare it to works written earlier, to understand how it relates to the traditional handling of similar forms and ideas.

HEMINGWAY AND HISTORY   To see how historical criticism is used, look again at the discussion of "Hills Like White Elephants" in Chapter 7 (p. 201). There we describe the historical context and social milieu in which Hemingway wrote and in which the story was set. We show how awareness of events and attitudes of the time clarifies details in plot, characterization, and setting and proves helpful in understanding the story.

USING HISTORICAL APPROACHES   You can try using such an approach for a paper assignment, if you'd like—probably a research paper. Learning about history almost invariably involves doing research into the era you're interested in. As with biographical criticism, be sure what you write is actually criticism, not just a report on the time period. A historical study also must involve analysis and must use data to illuminate meaning and build its interpretations on what is in the text, not on extraneous material from outside the text.

PSYCHOLOGICAL CRITICISM

FOCUSING ON FREUD   Biographical criticism—or a good deal of it, at least—began to turn in a psychological direction during the 1940s and 1950s. This was a result of the growing interest in the parent of psychoanalysis, Sigmund Freud, who sought a scientific understanding of the mind and mental illness. His methods and conclusions were revolutionary and controversial and have been and continue to be both applied and challenged on many grounds. The field of psychoanalysis has now moved far beyond Freud — so far, in fact, that he is given slight attention in psychology courses today. However, his work had a great impact on twentieth-century literature and twentieth-century literary criticism.

THE CONSCIOUS AND THE UNCONSCIOUS A brief summary of Freud's thought is needed before we can consider its effect on literature. Crucial to its early phase is Freud's realization of a dynamic tension between the conscious and the unconscious in mental activity. This was a radical shift. Pre-Freudian belief held that one could *know* and *control* oneself. The idea that there are parts of the self knowable only through analysis is almost universally accepted now, but it was strikingly new when Freud advanced it. He described three areas of consciousness, each of which can contain causes for human behavior. First is the *conscious* level, the things we are aware of. Second is the *preconscious* level, feelings and sensations we are not presently aware of but that can be brought to the surface if we reflect on them. Third is the *unconscious* level, the realm of things we are not aware of, though they influence us greatly.

ID, EGO, SUPEREGO In his second phase, Freud replaced the conscious and unconscious with the very different and now familiar concepts of the id, ego, and superego. The *id*, a reservoir of biological impulses and drives, demands instant gratification of its needs and desires — for food, relieving ourselves, sexual gratification. But instant satisfaction is not always possible, and when satisfaction must be postponed, tensions build up that cause inner conflict. We are often unaware that such tensions and conflicts exert an influence on our lives and actions. The *ego* (rational, controlled, partially conscious) is concerned first with pleasure, through the elimination of inner tensions and conflicts, but also with self-preservation, which requires that urges and needs be dealt with in a practical, realistic way. The id, for example, tells us we need to eat, and the ego *wants* to concur, but the ego, balancing the id's desire with the restraint imposed by the *superego* (the rules and taboos internalized through parental and societal influences), tells us to wait until lunchtime.

OEDIPUS COMPLEX, ELECTRA COMPLEX In a third phase of his work, Freud focused on the development of the ego in children. Freud held that part of the normal emotional development of a child includes an unconscious wish to replace the parent of the child's sex in the affection of the parent of the opposite sex: A little boy wants to eliminate his father and marry his mother (Oedipus complex) and a little girl to eliminate her mother and marry her father (Electra complex). Although many aspects of his approach to the stages of early childhood development have been challenged or discredited, evidence of them is found in literary criticism, to clarify what lies behind a character's attitudes or actions, and in literary works, as authors influenced by Freudian theories apply them as they develop characters and plots.

REPRESSION   Another controversial Freudian theory important for literary study is that of *repression*. This theory holds that memories (that is, bundles of psychic energy) of situations with painful or threatening or guilt-laden associations are unconsciously pushed out of consciousness and sealed off so we will not have to deal with them consciously. When such matters are repressed, the pent-up energy has an effect on the personality—a repressed memory of childhood abuse, for example, may interfere with a person's adult relationships. It may take something of great force to break through the barrier, but only when it has been broken through is the person freed from the pain and its effects.

CHARACTER ANALYSIS   Psychological criticism is most commonly used to analyze characters in a work. The psychological critic attempts to clarify a character's actions, motivations, and attitudes by bringing modern psychoanalytical insights to bear on them. The critic does with characters what a psychoanalyst does with a patient: probes beneath the surface, exploring what unconscious conflicts and tensions, or repressed memories, may underlie the character's behavior.

YOUNG GOODMAN BROWN   This approach isn't profitable with every story, poem, or play: Some works don't give us enough in-depth information about its characters to undertake a psychological analysis. Such an analysis would be possible for the title character in "Young Goodman Brown" (p. 337). It's a fairly long story and we are told a good deal about Young Goodman Brown's background and behavior, enough to show in a convincing way that many of his actions and attitudes come not from his conscious thought but from unconscious and repressed guilt, fears, and conflicts.

PURSUING A PSYCHOLOGICAL APPROACH   That kind of analysis is what you will probably want to use if you decide to write a paper taking a psychological approach. Your approach does not need to be Freudian—other psychological theories also can be used to amplify literature. But to work responsibly, you will need to know a good deal about whichever one you use. If you haven't taken at least one psychology course, trying this approach might not be advisable.

MYTHOLOGICAL CRITICISM

FOCUSING ON MYTH   What Freud attempted for the individual consciousness, another group of theorists in the late 1940s began to do for cultures, or the human race as a whole. Theorists who came to be known as *mythological critics* (or *archetypal critics*) focused their attention on the myths that underlie many literary works. *Myth* here must be understood not in its popular sense of a "fictitious story, or unscientific account, theory, belief," but in its literary sense of an anonymous story arising from a culture's oral traditions that involves gods or heroic figures and explores matters beyond and above everyday life, concerning origins, endings, aspirations, purpose, and meaning. Myths often appear in the earliest and seemingly simplest stories told in a culture — folktales, fairy tales, or religious writings, for example.

THE ROLE OF ARCHETYPES   Myths usually build on literary **archetypes** — symbols, character types, and plot lines that have been used again and again in a culture until they come to carry a wide, nearly universal significance and thus move most readers at a very deep emotional level. Throughout the centuries, writer after writer has drawn on motifs such as the quest, the journey into experience, and the Cinderella pattern in developing the plot of a story. Such writers use a typical or recurring symbol, character type, or plot motif that, in the words of archetypal theorist Northrop Frye, "connects one poem with another and thereby helps to unify and integrate our literary experience."[1]

SEASONAL CYCLES   Among the most used and most important of such archetypal images are the seasonal cycle of spring, summer, autumn, and winter; the daily cycle of dawn, zenith, sunset, and night; and the life cycle of youth, adulthood, old age, and death. Throughout history, poets have seen analogies among these natural cycles. Each time we speak of the "sunset" and "golden" years of life in referring to old age or describe death as being "sleep," we are, consciously or unconsciously, invoking those archetypes.

THE MONOMYTH   Beyond the meaning of the individual cycles is the significance of the patterns as a whole. "In the solar cycle of the day," Frye explains, "the seasonal cycle of the year, and the organic cycle of human life, there is a single pattern of significance"; elsewhere he calls that pattern the "story of the loss and regaining of identity," which is "the framework of all literature," the single story or "monomyth" underlying it all.[2] Other

---

[1]*Anatomy of Criticism, Four Essays* (Princeton: Princeton UP, 1957), 99. Print.
[2]*Fables of Identity: Studies in Poetic Mythology* (New York: Harcourt, 1963), 15. Print; *The Educated Imagination* (Bloomington: Indiana UP, 1964), 55. Print.

theorists hold that the "single story" focuses on the earth mother[3] or on the hero.[4] All of the theories, however, share a belief in the close relationship between literature and life. "Putting works of literature in such a context gives them an immense reverberating dimension of significance..., in which every literary work catches the echoes of all other works of its type in literature, and so ripples out into the rest of literature and thence into life."[5]

For an example of an essay that uses a mythological approach, see Susan Koprince's "Baseball as History and Myth in August Wilson's *Fences*" (p. 1038), which explores baseball, together with its archetypal implications, as a metaphor for the American dream. Before trying this approach in a paper, you should review the sections on symbols in Chapter 7 (pp. 203–205) and perhaps do some additional reading on myths and archetypes. You could work with a story like Nathaniel Hawthorne's "Young Goodman Brown" (p. 337), a poem like William Shakespeare's "That time of year thou mayst in me behold" (p. 680) or A. E. Housman's "To an Athlete Dying Young" (p. 824), or a play like David Henry Hwang's *As the Crow Flies* (p. 1073), or look for a work in which the mythical and archetypal aspects are less obvious or more subtle.

NEW CRITICISM (FORMALISM)

FOCUSING ON THE TEXT   The literary approach most influential in the twentieth century, and still important today, is called New Criticism, or Formalism (from its concentration on the *formal* elements of a work). It originated in the 1930s and for over forty years it dominated the study of literature. New Criticism was in part a reaction against an approach that makes biography or history primary and treats the literary text as secondary, either regarding it merely as a source of information or as material to the interpretation of which biographical and historical knowledge provides all the clues we need. New Criticism insists on the primacy of the text, appreciated as worthwhile for its own sake, for its aesthetic beauty, for its way of considering and helping understand the human condition generally. New Criticism takes texts themselves very seriously, looks at them closely as self-contained works of art, and affirms that literature has its own epistemology, or theory of knowledge.

EXPLICATION AS METHOD   New Criticism borrowed from France a method of teaching literature called *explication de texte*. The word *explicate* comes from Latin roots meaning "to unfold, to give an account of" and

---

[3]Robert Graves, *The White Goddess: A Historical Grammar of Poetic Myth* (London: Faber, 1948). Print.

[4]Joseph Campbell, *The Hero with a Thousand Faces*, Bollingen Series XVII (Princeton: Princeton UP, 1949). Print.

[5]Frye, *Fables of Identity*, 37. Print.

means to explain in detail. A key method of New Criticism is to explain the interconnections and ambiguities (multiple meanings) within a work, or within an important passage from a work, through a detailed, close analysis of its language — the meanings, relationships, and complexities of its words, images, figures, and symbols. In all this, what the author *intended* to do is not relevant — what matters is what the work *actually* says and does. New Critics, therefore, read works repeatedly. The first reading is less important than the later ones because one does not yet know where the work is headed and cannot see how early parts tie in with things further along.

UNITY OF FORM AND MEANING   As one rereads, again and again, one begins to see connections and to grasp the way large and small features relate to each other. Central to New Criticism are unity and universality. In the words of Cleanth Brooks, one of the developers of the approach, "The primary concern of criticism is with the problem of unity — the kind of whole which the literary work forms or fails to form, and the relation of the various parts to each other in building up this whole."[6] The unity sought is unity of meaning; but meaning, for New Critics, cannot be separated from form. Thus, a New Critic focuses on the speaker (or persona), conflicts and tensions, the arrangement of parts and details, and the relationships between them. A New Critic pays particular attention to metaphors as ways of unifying dissimilar things and to irony and paradox as ways apparent contradictions can be resolved (and thus unified).

THEORY OF KNOWLEDGE   New Criticism tends to look especially for issues of significance to all people, in all times — issues of life and relationship, worth and purpose, love, aging, death, faith, and doubt. The foundation of New Critical theory is its claim that literature has its own kind of knowledge — experiential knowledge conveyed imaginatively — and that this knowledge is superior to the abstract, impersonal knowledge of science. An overreliance on scientific approaches, New Critics believe, has led to fragmentation and "dissociation" within society and even within individuals. In the face of such disintegration, New Criticism emphasizes wholeness and unity. Literature offers a hope of wholeness, of a "unified sensibility" combining intellect and feeling, of redemption from the disintegration — the division, specialization, and alienation — that science has sometimes inflicted on the modern world.

CRITICAL METHOD   Today New Criticism is viewed more as a critical method than as a way of knowing. Anyone who engages in detailed close reading of a text is a descendant of New Criticism, even if she or he doesn't look for universal meanings or think in terms of being a New

---

[6]"The Formalist Critics," *Kenyon Review* 13 (1951): 72. Print.

Critic. The method we have used in this book borrows from New Criticism in the way it teaches close attention to details in literary works, though we are more concerned with readers and the reading process than New Criticism itself is.

EXAMPLES IN THIS BOOK   Two of the student papers in this book offer good examples of New Critical readings. Sunkyo Hong's paper on "First Snow" (p. 714) is New Critical in the way it focuses on imagery, figures of speech, and rhetorical strategies to clarify how the poem enables the reader to imaginatively participate in the experience Mary Oliver is describing. And Julian Hinson's paper on *The New New* (p. 955) looks closely at the handling of language in a play about the use and misuse of words and the moral distortions language can cover up. If you want to try doing a paper with a New Critical approach, look at the Literary Analysis sections in the lists of writing prompts found in Chapters 5-10, 13-19, and 22-25 for suggestions of selections and topics you might use to explore them.

READER-RESPONSE CRITICISM

FOCUSING ON THE READER   Reader-response criticism (or reader-oriented criticism) contrasts sharply with New Criticism by focusing primarily on the reader instead of the text and on individual effect instead of universal meaning. The roots of reader-response criticism go back to the 1930s and were laid down as a reaction against historical and biographical approaches, which gave little consideration to the role of the reader. Louise Rosenblatt began developing a reader-response theory just about the time New Criticism was emerging. New Criticism caught on and became widely accepted, while for several decades Rosenblatt's work was mostly neglected. Interest in the reader reemerged in the 1960s as a reaction against New Criticism's text-centered neglect of the reader. Reader-response criticism has become increasingly popular and influential, especially as a classroom approach.

READING AS TRANSACTION   Reader-response criticism, as we say in Chapter 1, is based on the assumption that reading is a transaction between an author, a reader, and a text in a cultural context. Reader-response criticism studies the steps through which the reader, by interacting with a text, completes the work in her or his mind. It does not just *describe* the response a work elicits from a reader ("here's what the work makes me feel") but examines the *activity* involved in reading—*how* the work produces the effects and feelings it does as a reader interacts with it. Reader-response criticism focuses on the sequential apprehension of a work—on the experience of grasping each line or each paragraph without knowing what comes later and on the process of putting the pieces together. Rereading is just as important for reader-response criticism as for New Criticism, but unlike for New Criticism, the first reading is regarded as crucially significant.

READERS AND TEXTS Most reader-response theories have a more subjective view of a text than New Criticism does, thinking of a text as more like a musical score that is meant to be "performed," brought to life by a reader, than as a permanent artistic object. The degrees of subjectivity vary. Some versions see the reader's interaction with the text as controlled to some extent by formal structures included in the text. For these, the text is a stable and "objective" entity that sets limits on the reader. A work cannot mean just anything the reader says it does: The reader must pay close attention to the text to notice and follow the cues it supplies and must be able to provide evidence from within the text to support the way she or he interprets it.

INTERPRETIVE COMMUNITIES Other, more subjective reader-response approaches deemphasize the words on the page and place more emphasis on a text created in the reader's mind. This raises the question of whether there are any limits on the reader. Does a text then mean anything the reader says it does? Perhaps not. One way to consider that limits do exist, without giving up subjectivity of the text, is to recognize that reading occurs within "interpretive communities." In their broadest sense, interpretive communities are groups of readers who share a common situation, similar assumptions about how literary works are actualized, or an agreement about how literary conventions are used in approaching a text. The community provides a context within which individual experiencing of a work can be assessed. A class, for example, is an interpretive community. So are the readers of a professional journal and a group of scholars who specialize in a given area of literature.

COLLECTIVE JUDGMENTS The role of such a group is not to arrive at a single "best" reading or to judge which among several readings is the "right" one or is "better" than others. Rather, by its endorsements and discouragements, each interpretive community indicates which readings go too far for that community, which ones it regards as *unacceptable*. This too will vary. What is unacceptable to one group of readers may not be to another. It is the collective judgments of interpretive communities, in this view, not texts or readers, that create stability. Even within the same community readings will vary because texts are not objective and different readers enact them in individual ways. Constraints do exist: A text can "mean" many things, but not just anything. The constraints, however, are not *in* the text but grow out of the strategies, assumptions, and conventions of the community.

THE READER AND "RECITATIF" For an example of a paper specifically focused on a reader-response approach, see Kristina Martinez's student paper on "Recitatif" (p. 85). It looks closely at large-scale strategies in the work rather than at smaller details the way New Critical papers do. It focuses on discrepancies and ambiguities in the text and the way readers must sort out differences and attempt to figure out the way things really were. It brings up questions readers are forced to work through: "Which story is correct, Roberta's or Twyla's (or neither)? Are they remembering details about Maggie differently because one of them is the same race as Maggie and the other not? If so, which one is the same?" It points out how readers — like Twyla and Roberta in the story — may wrongly attempt to construct meaning out of their own contexts as a way to resolve the ambiguities, instead of acknowledging "that this story will not provide answers to their questions, and that acceptance of ambiguity itself answers the need to have answers." One can pay attention to readers and how readers process a work even without focusing specifically on a reader-response approach, and we think often one should. That has indeed been an emphasis throughout this book.

MARXIST CRITICISM

FOCUSING ON MARX'S IDEAS Although acceptance of Marxism has waned over the past few decades, Karl Marx's social and economic theories had a major impact across the world through much of the twentieth century. That was true for literature as well: While Marxist ideas influenced authors and literary critics from the 1920s on, they emerged more prominently in the 1960s. They remain an important strand in literary study, one with which students of literature should be conversant. A brief introduction to the basic tenets of Marx's thought is helpful in understanding the foundations of and procedures used in Marxist criticism.

CLASS CONFLICT Marx's main interest was in economic power and the ways in which it is disguised and manipulated. His analysis of society starts with the exploitation of workers by owners and capitalists, which creates class conflict between the bourgeoisie (the middle and upper classes — the owners and capitalists) and the proletariat (the workers, those who must sell their labor to the owners and capitalists). The subjugation of the workers, Marx held, is maintained by *ideology*, that is, the beliefs, values, and ways of thinking through which human beings perceive what they believe to be reality and carry out their roles in society. The ideology of an era (Marx called it the "superstructure") is determined by the contemporary socioeconomic system (the "base") and reflects the beliefs, values, and interests of the dominant class in it.

THE EFFECT OF IDEOLOGY   Ideology includes everything that shapes the individual's mental picture of life experience—not what life really is, but the way it is perceived. This ideology may seem to people at the time just the natural, inevitable way of seeing and explaining things. But Marxists claim that it seems that way only because ideology quietly, subtly works to legitimize and maintain the position, power, and economic interests of the ruling class and, for the working classes, to cover up the reality of their exploitation. Ideology helps preserve the status quo by making what is artificial and oppressive seem natural and inevitable. According to Marxists, such ideology must be exposed and overcome if people are to gain relief from their oppressors.

BRINGING IDEOLOGY INTO CONSCIOUSNESS   Early Marxist criticism concentrated on exposing the presence of bourgeois attitudes, values, and orientation in literary works. Later Marxist criticism became more sophisticated in analyzing the ideology underlying literature and societies: bringing out the beliefs, values, and ways of thinking through which people perceive what they believe to be reality and on which they carry out their roles in society. In the latter part of the twentieth century, Fredric Jameson used insights from psychoanalysis to reenergize Marxist criticism. The function of ideology, Jameson held, is to "repress" revolutionary ideas or tendencies, to push them into the "political unconscious."[7] As ideology works itself into a text, things must be omitted: "In order to say anything, there are other things *which must not be said*."[8] As a result, gaps and contradictions occur and generally go unnoticed. Like psychoanalysts, Marxist critics focus on the text's "unconscious," on what is unspoken and repressed, and bring it into "consciousness."

READING AGAINST THE GRAIN   To expose the ideology in literary works, the main approach of Marxist criticism is to read "against the grain." The metaphor comes from carpentry: It is easiest to plane a board by pushing "with the grain"; the plane moves easily, can glide over irregularities and inconsistencies in the wood, and produces smooth, pleasing results. Pushing "against the grain" is harder and usually causes rough edges. To apply the metaphor to reading, it is easiest and most natural to read a work "with the grain"—that is, to accept and follow the conventions and signals that correspond with the ideology behind it. Reading with the grain allows a reader to glide over problems and leads to smooth, reassuring results, compatible with what the dominant culture values and approves. It is harder to read "against the grain," to resist the conventions of the dominant culture's ideology, to challenge and question them instead of accepting

---

[7]*The Political Unconscious: Narrative as a Socially Symbolic Act* (Ithaca: Cornell UP, 1981). Print.
[8]Pierre Machery, qtd. in Raman Selden, *A Reader's Guide to Contemporary Literary Theory* (Lexington: UP of Kentucky, 1985), 41. Print.

and following them. The role of a Marxist approach to literature is to bring what is hidden into the open, to expose underlying ideology, and to make readers see its effect.

COMMITMENT TO THE CAUSE   Marxist criticism is committed criticism: It aims not only to illuminate readers but also to arouse them to involvement and action; it seeks to impact the lives and values of readers and effect changes in society. As with psychological criticism, you should not attempt writing a paper from a Marxist perspective unless you have read and understood a good deal from Marx's works and from works studying his positions. Attempting to do so without being well informed is likely to lead to superficial and even erroneous results. And it seems fair to point out that if you write a Marxist critique without sharing Marx's beliefs about class conflict and the need for rising up against the injustices of the capitalist system, though it might fulfill an academic assignment, your work will not be authentic Marxist criticism, which requires passionate commitment to a set of ideas designed to initiate significant societal change.

APPLYING THE APPROACH   The value of a Marxist approach can be illustrated by using it to consider "The Homes of England," a poem written around 1825 by Felicia Hemans (1793–1835) — and available online. The poem celebrates a variety of English homes, starting with the magnificent country houses of the rich: "The stately Homes of England, / How beautiful they stand! / Amidst their tall ancestral trees, / O'er all the pleasant land." Following stanzas go on to discuss "merry" and "blessed" homes in idyllic terms, moving down to "The Cottage Homes of England! / By thousands on her plains, / They are smiling o'er the silvery brooks / And round the hamlet fanes [churches]." A Marxist critic would expose the underlying ideology and point out what goes unsaid, and unseen, in the poem. Hemans, though not wealthy herself, saw her country through the lens of patriotic, upper-class landowners and capitalists. England was a land of "free, fair Homes" where all citizens lived with the "glad spirit" of children and loved their "country and its God."

But that is not how all of England was. It is how the upper classes perceived it. Hemans's setting is rural England; she makes no mention of the wretched homes in city slums where exploited factory workers and their families lived at the time. The lower classes are invisible to the upper classes, who profit from them but are oblivious to their lives and welfare. Rural areas had their poor as well, living not in romantic cottages but in huts and hovels. These homes, too, don't appear in the poem (the poem does refer to "hut and hall," but the very phrase seems to equate them, as equally pleasant, happy dwellings). A Marxist critic would bring out how acceptance of this ideology — this sense that all are free, happy, and content — is a way to keep the lower classes from realizing the inequity of their situation and from wanting to rebel against it.

FEMINIST CRITICISM AND
EXPANSION OF THE CANON

MALE DOMINANCE OF LITERARY STUDIES Prior to 1970, especially during the period in which New Criticism was in vogue, literary standards and agendas were dominated by white male academics. A large majority of college and university teachers and scholars were male; all of the founders of New Criticism were male; most of the writers studied and approved of by New Criticism were male. Cleanth Brooks and Robert Penn Warren's landmark New Critical textbook *Understanding Poetry* (1938) included poems by 89 men and 5 women (11 poems are anonymous). Of poems included, 220 were by men, 8 by women (one an example of a "bad" poem). In the original edition of a very influential formalist textbook on poetry, Laurence Perrine's *Sound and Sense* (1956), 107 male, but only 10 female, poets were represented (169 poems by men, 18 by women).

MALE ORIENTATION IN NEW CRITICISM The tendency of male critics to favor works by men was reinforced by the theoretical position of New Criticism. New Criticism looked in literature for universal themes — themes it assumed would apply equally to women and men of all classes, cultures, and times. The shapers of New Criticism, however, did not seem aware of the extent to which their own backgrounds and presuppositions — their ideologies — defined those "universal" issues: The issues were ones raised by well-educated, upper-class, conservative men. Just as their method of reading sought to unify and integrate aspects of literary works, so too the themes they found in the works involved social unity and integration. Issues of importance to marginal groups — women, people of color, lower classes — did not fit the mold and were overlooked (only one poem by an ethnic American author — Countee Cullen's "Incident" — appears in the original *Sound and Sense*; none is included in *Understanding Poetry*).

THE FEMINIST MOVEMENT Against this background arose a feminist protest movement, which initiated a radical rethinking of the canon. Pivotal in its development was Kate Millett's *Sexual Politics* (1970), which began to raise the consciousness of women to the fact that, generally speaking, all avenues of power in Western culture were under male control. That was true of the production and study of literature. White males set the criteria for what was good literature and decided whose books would be published and whose works would be anthologized. They, therefore, had the power to determine who would be read, who would receive attention, who would achieve fame.

BECOMING A RESISTING READER Feminist criticism reacted against this power initially by asking what happens to a work written by a male when it is read from a consciously feminine perspective instead of an assumed male perspective. The first act of a feminist reader, according to critic Judith Fetterley, is to become a "resisting reader" instead of an assenting reader[9] — that is, to question and challenge the assumptions of a work about roles, power, and values. A resisting reader exposes the masculine biases (the patriarchal ideology) in a work. This requires paying attention not only to what is said but also to what is not said. Even works in which no women are present may convey an attitude toward women: What does their absence say? How does the fact that no women are present shape and color the situation? Are there details that (perhaps unintentionally or unconsciously) demean women or treat subjects in a way that is potentially insulting to women?

ENLARGING THE CANON   From a reappraisal of works by men, feminist criticism moved on to the study of literature written by women — what Elaine Showalter has termed *gynocriticism*. This involves, on the one hand, the reexamination of women authors who have long been accepted in the canon, and on the other hand, even more significantly, the discovery or rediscovery of many neglected or forgotten women writers, past and present. The result has been to open up the literary canon to include works by women that earlier criticism had excluded.

INCLUDING THE "SOMETHING ELSE"   One criticism of early varieties of feminist criticism is that much of it treats *woman* as a universal category without recognizing differences among women — differences of race, economic and social class, and national origin — that contribute to their identity. Contemporary feminists such as Gayatri Spivak say that while all women are female, they are something else as well (such as working class or upper class, heterosexual or lesbian, African American or living in a postcolonial nation), and the "something else" is important to consider. Such an approach has led feminists to feel affinities with all those who are considered "the Other" or are marginalized on the basis of race, ethnicity, class, sexual orientation, or social background.

REACHING OUT TO OTHER MARGINALIZED GROUPS   Thus feminist critics took the lead in raising for ethnic minorities the same questions and concerns raised about women — particularly for African Americans at first, and then for Latinos, Native Americans, and other ethnic minorities: How are they treated in works by white authors? Are they stereotyped in insensitive and demeaning ways? Are there details that (perhaps unintentionally or unconsciously) demean minorities or treat subjects in a way that is potentially insulting to the minority group? Are ethnic characters rendered invisible? Are they not included at all? If so, what does their absence say? Ethnic critics began to point out the dearth of writers of color in anthologies and literature courses, to call attention to ethnic authors who had been

---

[9]*The Resisting Reader: A Feminist Approach to American Fiction* (Bloomington: Indiana UP, 1978). Print.

accepted in the canon or were on its fringes, and to discover or rediscover many neglected or forgotten writers of color, past and present. As the canon expanded to include woman writers, so it expanded to include ethnic authors. This textbook's table of contents is evidence of the result.

AN ORIENTATION, NOT A METHOD Feminist criticism, like Marxist criticism, does not focus on a *method* (the way New Criticism and reader-response criticism do). Instead, it is an orientation, a set of principles that can be fused with a variety of critical approaches. Thus there can be feminist-reader-response criticism, feminist-deconstructive criticism, and so on. Feminist criticism, in addition to indicating some things to *do* with a work of literature, points out issues to be aware of in a work. It is a committed criticism that aims to heighten awareness, to effect changes in attitudes and behavior, to correct injustices, and to improve society and individual situations. You can use a feminist approach yourself by experimenting with being a resisting reader, by being open to the writings and concerns of women authors, and by focusing papers and discussions on issues of the sort raised in this section.

FEMINISM IN "EVERYDAY USE" Susan Farrell's essay "Fight vs. Flight: A Re-evaluation of Dee in Alice Walker's 'Everyday Use'" (p. 1436) illustrates how awareness of theoretical approaches can help in understanding the premises on which a scholarly essay is based. Nowhere does the essay say that it is taking a feminist approach to the story, but that is its effect. The essay undertakes a reassessment of Dee, a character with modern feminist inclinations — she went to college to prepare herself for a career, she is fearless and a fighter, she stands up for herself and refuses to back down from what she believes in.

Most critics see the story as putting Dee down because she fails to recognize the difference between her own attitude toward her heritage (fashionable, though separate from her past experience) and that of her mother and sister, who continue to live in that heritage, with its values permeating their daily experiences. Farrell's essay, however, defends Dee, showing that she offers — through her feminist ways — a strategy for contemporary African Americans to cope with an oppressive society, a strategy, Farrell argues, that Dee's mother admires, envies, and eventually emulates.

GENDER STUDIES

FOCUSING ON SOCIALLY CONSTRUCTED DISTINCTIONS The protest movement that began as feminist criticism has moved on in large part to the more inclusive area of gender studies. Gender studies focus on the idea that gender is socially constructed on attitudes toward masculinity and femininity that are rooted in deeply but uncritically held beliefs of a society.

Most varieties of gender studies assume a difference between the terms *sex* and *gender*. *Sex* refers to the physical characteristics of women and men biologically; *gender* refers to traits designated as "feminine" and "masculine." One is born biologically female or male, but one *acquires* a "gender" (society's conceptions of "woman" and "man"). In Simone de Beauvoir's words, "One is not born a woman, one becomes one."[10]

BINARY OPPOSITIONS   Gender studies show that such distinctions in the West traditionally have been shaped through the use of binary oppositions:

masculine / feminine
father / mother
son / daughter
brother / sister
active / passive
reason / emotion
intelligent / sensitive

Through the centuries, the items on the left side of these pairings generally have been favored (or *privileged*) over those on the right side. Gender criticism exposes the pairings as false oppositions, contending that all these traits can be a part of one's identity.

ALL TYPES OF OPPRESSION   Gender criticism covers *all* "the critical ramifications of sexual oppression,"[11] including gay, lesbian, and queer studies. Just as early feminist critics brought attention to the way women traditionally have been forced to approach literature from a masculine perspective, so gay, lesbian, and queer studies have called attention to the way texts traditionally are read from a heterosexual viewpoint. Many readers assume that a relationship described in a work is heterosexual even when that is not indicated directly. It is not a valid assumption. Lesbian and gay critics have produced revisionist rereadings — often provocative and illuminating — of many texts that previously were read as straight.

DECONSTRUCTION

One of the best known contemporary literary theories, deconstruction, is also one of the most controversial and difficult. You may have heard of deconstruction, and maybe even used the verb *deconstruct* without realizing its use in literary studies.

---

[10]*The Second Sex* (1949), trans. H. M. Parshley (New York: Vintage, 1974), 301. Print.
[11]Jonathan Culler, *On Deconstruction: Theory and Criticism after Structuralism* (Ithaca: Cornell UP, 1982), 56. Print.

FOCUSING ON OPPOSITIONAL THINKING Deconstruction challenges the logical principles on which the thinking of the Western world since Socrates has been based. Fundamental to Western logic, for example, is the law of noncontradiction (that is, "A" is not the same as "not A") and the use of binary oppositions that have become deeply embedded in our thought: We try to understand things by considering them in pairs that differentiate them. Remember some of the binaries in the section on gender studies:

masculine / feminine

active / passive

reason / emotion

intelligent / sensitive

Here's another list similar to that one:

conscious / unconscious

being / nonbeing

reality / image

right / wrong

thing / sign

speech / writing

Western thinking, from the Greeks on, has privileged the left side of this list over the right side. Such privileging reflects the classical, or Hellenic (Greek), influence on Western philosophy, with its love of reason, logic, order, clarity, coherence, and unity. A key aspect of deconstruction is to challenge that impulse to divide and stratify. Things are not always separate and opposed. They can be different without being opposed; they can also be interdependent and interactive.

QUESTIONING PHILOSOPHICAL ASSUMPTIONS Deconstruction — like Marxist and feminist criticism — is not a critical *method* the way New Criticism is. Rather, it is a philosophical approach, a way of thinking, a critique of the assumptions that underlie such systems as New Criticism, which emphasize order, coherence, and unity. Deconstructionists posit that a text has no stable reference, and they therefore question assumptions about the ability of language to represent reality. Language is not fixed and limited: It always conveys meanings different from or beyond what we intend.

LOOKING FOR CRACKS Deconstruction focuses on gaps and ambiguities that expose a text's instability and indeterminacy, the "crack" in the seeming unity or coherence of its argument. "Meaning" is not present in the work but is filled in by the reader in the act of reading. According to deconstruction, meaning is totally contextual. A literary work does not *reflect* reality; rather, works *create* their own reality. One cannot go outside a text—to the author's intentions or to references to the outside world—to determine its signification. The text is "self-referential": Only as we look closely at a work and consider its full range of interplay and implication can its signification emerge.

CLOSE ANALYSIS OF LANGUAGE   A deconstructive reading, therefore, looks very closely at language, perhaps even more attentively than New Criticism does. It treats language "playfully," showing how the multiple meanings in words (the doubleness of language) contribute to the instability of texts. It picks out key binary oppositions, identifying which term in those oppositions is being privileged (given preference) and showing how such privileging imposes an interpretive template on the subject being examined. It watches for inconsistencies in the apparent unity and stability of a work, as exposed by gaps (comparing what is privileged and what is passed over, or "marginalized").

BINARY OPPOSITIONS IN "SONNY'S BLUES"   The values of a deconstructive reading can be illustrated through analyzing James Baldwin's "Sonny's Blues" (p. 362). The story is grounded in a binary opposition, between words and music. The narrator is strongly oriented toward words, while Sonny is oriented toward music. The story opens with the narrator reading about Sonny in a newspaper (that, ironically, is their only means of communication at that point). Also, the story shows the narrator reading, or attempting to read, not just words but people and situations.

VERBALIZING THE NONVERBAL   Keith E. Byerman has said of the narrator in "Sonny's Blues" that "the story, in part, is about his misreadings" or his "inability to read properly."[12] As Byerman explains, the narrator is constantly turning nonverbal experiences into words. For example, when the narrator listens in the nightclub, he declares that both the terribleness and triumph of music is that "it has no words." Yet, immediately afterward, he begins reading language into the music, describing it as a conversation: "The dry, low, black man *said* something awful on the drums, Creole *answered*, and the drums *talked back*. Then the horn insisted, sweet and high, slightly detached perhaps, and Creole listened, *commenting* now and then" (p. 385; italics added).

Byerman suggests that Baldwin uses the verbalizing of the nonverbal early in the story as a way to undercut the narrator and to show his need for deeper understanding. However, something more complex than that is

---

[12]"Words and Music: Narrative Ambiguity in 'Sonny's Blues,'" *Studies in Short Fiction* 19 (1982): 367. Print.

going on near the end. Byerman notes the lack of preparation for the narrator's sophisticated analysis of music in the final scene. The narrator throughout has expressed his antipathy to music and an inability to comprehend its appeal. Yet suddenly he expresses profound understanding of how music affects a listener. But Byerman does not deal fully with the contradictory nature of the narrator's sudden grasp of music, or with the "crack" this creates in the text.

DECONSTRUCTING THE STORY   A deconstructionist would recognize that what we are hearing, actually, is the author's voice breaking through the narrator's voice, conveying the meaning he finds in music. That, in turn, undermines the author's own undercutting of the narrator: The author himself cannot resist verbalizing the meaning of music. Or he cannot avoid it because the final section of the story rests on a binary opposition it attempts to deconstruct: Words and music are similar as well as different. Music, like objects and like words, must be "interpreted" — there is no escape from "reading." But the reading that music invites is open and indirect. Baldwin, however, gives a direct and closed reading in an attempt to convey openness and indirection. The story, thus, has a level of complexity, through its contradictions, which Byerman's New Critical reading does not pick up but which a deconstructive approach can bring out.

CULTURAL CRITICISM

FOCUSING ON CULTURES   From the 1980s on, much of literary study has been focused on culture, but not the promotion of "high culture" advocated by Matthew Arnold in the mid- to late 1800s. Cultural criticism explores the relationship between an author and her or his work and the cultural context in which they exist. An author, writing at a specific time in a specific place, inevitably is influenced by contemporary events and attitudes, whether she or he accepts and reflects prevailing attitudes or ignores, rejects, or challenges them.

CULTURAL INCLUSIVENESS   The work of anthropologists has changed the primary meaning of *culture* from a single, static, universal, elitist "high culture" to a set of dynamic, interactive, always-changing *cultures*. Contemporary cultural criticism (sometimes referred to as cultural studies) is inclusive ethnically, with a strong multicultural emphasis. It emphasizes that cultural achievements of worth are produced by people from a variety of social, economic, and ethnic backgrounds, past as well as present, and that criticism should enable us to appreciate this diversity of accomplishment. And it is inclusive regarding subject matter — it does not limit itself to the literature of "high culture" but also draws on popular culture as a valuable indicator of cultural values. It studies comic books as well as novels, hit movies as well as theater, MTV as well as public television, pop songs as well as jazz, graffiti as well as gallery art. The emphasis in cultural studies is on how people *relate to* all levels of art, rather than on their aesthetic standards and on getting them to recognize and work with "the best" literature, music, or art.

INFLUENCED AND INFLUENCING   Cultural criticism focuses on what a work conveys about social attitudes and social relations, focusing especially on the impact of such things as social background, sex, class, ethnicity, power, and privilege. Cultural critics concentrate on the way a work embodies a cultural context, how the events, ideas, or attitudes in a work were influenced by the economic conditions, political situation, or social conventions existing when it was written; but they also explore the way a work exists as *a part of* a culture and how it can influence, and perhaps change, the economic conditions, political situation, or social conventions of its time or later times.

INTERDISCIPLINARY   Thus the theory tends to work with interdisciplinary approaches. Cultural criticism often views works in relation to other works (literary works, especially ones outside the traditional canon, but also journals, memoirs, and diaries of ordinary people, church records, medical reports, architectural drawings, and so on); to social and economic conditions that affected them; to the way they were shaped by those who held power (including editors, publishers, and reviewers, for example); and to the way they reinforced conditions of power, intentionally or not.

For an example of a paper engaging in cultural criticism, see Harry J. Elam, Jr.'s "August Wilson" (p. 1034), which explores a variety of cultural influences on Wilson and discusses how his works have critiqued and influenced U.S. culture of the late twentieth and early twenty-first centuries.

NEW HISTORICISM

FOCUSING AGAIN ON HISTORY   An influential variety of cultural studies, New Historicism, grew out of a sense that New Criticism and deconstruction, through their neglect of the social and cultural milieu in which a work had been written, were leaving out something important and valuable. New Historicists would say that by focusing almost wholly on what occurs within a text, New Critics and deconstructionists cut themselves off from the ways historical context can clarify and illuminate a work. They lose referentiality. Despite many differences, the varieties of historicist critics have in common a belief in referentiality—that works of literature are influenced by, and influence, reality.

THE UNDERLYING THEORY New Historicism starts from a theory of history different from that which underlies "old historicism," with its emphasis on facts and events, its selective focus on the kinds of events that get recorded in official documents, and its explanations of causes and effects and of development toward an end. New Historicists assume that it is virtually impossible to reconstruct the past. We have only stories about the past, not objective facts and events existing independently; the stories are constructed by historians, reflecting the historians' assumptions and purposes and the choices they inevitably make about what to include, what to emphasize, what to omit. French philosophical historian Michel Foucault says that all historians are "situated." It is difficult for historians to recognize their own cultural practices and assumptions and even more difficult to get outside them and enter those of another age.

AN INTERDISCIPLINARY APPROACH The work of New Historicists is influenced by deconstruction and reader-response criticism, with their emphasis on subjectivity, and by cultural studies generally, with its attention to the myriad forces that shape events and motivations. New Historicists do not concentrate on economic and political forces or on the better-documented activities of the rich and famous, as the old historicism did. Like other types of cultural studies, New Historicism is open to other disciplines in its attempts to elucidate how art is shaped by, and shapes, social, historical, and economic conditions, and how art is affected by politics and has political effects itself.

NEW HISTORICISM AND "ODE ON A GRECIAN URN" Consider, for example, John Keats's 1819 poem "Ode on a Grecian Urn" (p. 829). The poem was a central text discussed in Cleanth Brooks's famous book of New Critical essays, *The Well Wrought Urn*.[13] In his close examination of the poem, Brooks suggests that it is proper for the personified urn to ignore names, dates, and special circumstances and to concentrate instead on universal truths. Brooks ignores historical context and influences as a whole; instead he takes a few details and orders them so that we better appreciate the beauty of the poem and its own impact as myth.

SITUATING THE POEM New Historicists, in contrast, would hold that it is important to situate the poem in its historical context and to ask, in this case, how economic and political conditions of early nineteenth-century England shaped Keats's image of ancient Greece. New Historicists tend to start their analysis by discussing a particular object or event and then proceed to connect that object or event to the poem so that readers come to see "the event as a social text and the literary text as a social event."[14]

---

[13]*The Well Wrought Urn: Studies in the Structure of Poetry* (New York: Reynal, 1947), ch. 8. Print.

[14]Brook Thomas, "The New Literary Historicism," *A Companion to American Thought*, ed. Richard Wightman Fox and James T. Kloppenberg (New York: Blackwell, 1995), 490. Print.

THE URN AND MUSEUMS   Brook Thomas, for example, asks where Keats would have seen such an urn. The answer—in a museum—leads into a discussion of the rise of art museums in eighteenth- and nineteenth-century Europe, as cultural artifacts from the past were placed in collections to be contemplated as art, isolated from their social setting. "In Keats's poem an urn that once had a practical social function now sparks aesthetic contemplation about the nature of truth, beauty, and the past." Thomas then says that reflecting on how the urn assumes a purely aesthetic function in a society that was becoming increasingly practical helps clarify "how our modern notion of art has been defined in response to the social order."[15]

SOCIAL IMPLICATIONS OF THE TEXT   To the New Historicist, even the urn's position in a museum raises political issues. The presence of a Grecian urn in an English museum can lead to reflections on the political implications of a cultural heritage. Englishmen in the nineteenth century, although they sympathized with the struggle for liberation in Greece, nevertheless took cultural treasures out of the country and put them on display in London. Thomas concludes that Keats's poem is "a social text, one that in telling us about the society that produced it also tells us about the society we inhabit today"[16] and should lead to reflection not just on present attitudes toward museums in the United States, but also on the implications of the way Keats's English poem has become a museum-type artifact in U.S. culture today.

POSTCOLONIAL CRITICISM

FOCUSING ON COLONIZATION   Postcolonial theory deals with cultural expression and behavior relating to the formerly or currently colonized parts of the world. Postcolonial criticism involves the analysis of literature by native writers who are living in colonized countries or who emigrated from such countries. We limit the discussion here to literature written in English in parts of the world that were colonized by Great Britain or the United States: primarily, then, Australia, New Zealand, and parts of the Caribbean, South America, Africa, and Asia. Postcolonial criticism focuses particularly on how colonized peoples attempt to assert their identity and to claim their heritage separate from, or other than, the colonizing culture. It also involves analysis of works written about colonized countries by writers from the colonizing countries, particularly as such writers misrepresent the cultures they describe, imposing on them their own cultural values and sense of cultural superiority.

---

[15]"The Historical Necessity for—and Difficulties with—New Historical Analysis in Introductory Literature Courses," *College English* 49 (1987): 518. Print.
[16]Ibid., 519. Print.

THE STRUGGLES OF COLONIZED PEOPLES Postcolonial criticism deals with all aspects of the struggle that occurs when one culture is subjugated by another, with what happens when one culture, because of the political power behind it, is able to dominate the other and to establish the impression of being superior to the other. It deals with the creation of Otherness, especially through the use of dialectical thinking to create pairs such as us/them, same/other, white/colored, rational/irrational, ordered/chaotic. Postcolonial criticism also addresses the way colonized peoples lose their past, are removed from history, and are forced to give up many of their cultural beliefs and practices. It confronts the way colonized peoples must forsake their language and cooperate with the conquerors if they want to get ahead economically. It reveals how the colonized peoples must cope with the memories and continuing legacy of being an occupied nation.

Glossary of Literary Terms

Abstract language Language that names general or intangible concepts, such as *love, truth,* and *beauty.* See also CONCRETE LANGUAGE.

Accent The emphasis, or stress, given a syllable in articulation. Metrical accent is the placement of stress as determined by the metrical and rhythmic pattern of a poetic line. See also STRESS.

Act One of the major divisions of a dramatic work. See also SCENE.

Alexandrine A poetic line with six iambic feet. Also called a *hexameter.*

Allegory A literary form or approach in which objects, persons, and actions make coherent sense on a literal level but also are equated in a sustained and obvious way with (usually) abstract meanings that lie outside the story. A classic example in prose is John Bunyan's *The Pilgrim's Progress;* in narrative poetry, Edmund Spenser's *The Faerie Queene;* in drama, the medieval English play *Everyman.* Nathaniel Hawthorne's "Young Goodman Brown" (p. 337) is a moral allegory, in which the names convey the abstract qualities developed in a second level of meaning beyond that of the literal events and characters in the story.

Alliteration The repetition of identical initial consonant sounds in the stressed syllables of words relatively near to each other. See also CONSONANCE.

Allusion Echoes or brief references to a literary or artistic work or a historical figure, event, or object, as, for example, the references to Lazarus and Hamlet in T. S. Eliot's "The Love Song of J. Alfred Prufrock" (see p. 796). It is usually a way of placing one's poem within, or alongside, a whole other context that is thus evoked in a very economical fashion.

Ambiguity (1) In expository prose, an undesirable doubtfulness or uncertainty of meaning or intention, resulting from imprecision in use of words or construction of sentences. (2) In poetry, the desirable condition of admitting more than one possible meaning, resulting from the capacity of language to function on levels other than the literal. Related terms sometimes employed are *ambivalence* and *polysemy.* See also PUN.

Anapest   A metrical foot consisting of three syllables, with two unaccented syllables followed by an accented one (*da da DA* — "in a dream"). In anapestic meter, anapests are the predominant foot in a line or poem.

Antagonist   The character who opposes the protagonist in a narrative or dramatic work. See also PROTAGONIST.

Antihero   A protagonist in a narrative or dramatic work who lacks the attributes of a traditional hero.

Antistrophe   (1) The second stanza in a three-stanza segment of a choral ode in Greek drama. It is preceded by (and identical in form to) the strophe, which is sung while the chorus moves from stage right to stage left. During the antistrophe, the chorus moves back to stage right before singing the epode. (2) The second stanza in a three-stanza segment of an ode (thus, stanzas two, five, eight, and so on). See also CHORUS; EPODE; ODE; STROPHE.

Antithesis   A figure of speech in which contrasting words, sentences, or ideas are expressed in balanced, parallel grammatical structures; for example, "She had some horses she loved. / She had some horses she hated" (Joy Harjo, "She Had Some Horses," p. 691).

Apostrophe   A figure of speech in which an absent person is addressed as though present or an abstract quality or a nonhuman entity is addressed. In the latter case, it is a particular type of PERSONIFICATION.

Approximate rhyme   See SLANT RHYME.

Archetype   An image, symbol, character type, or plot line that occurs frequently enough in literature, religion, myths, folktales, and fairy tales to be recognizable as an element of universal literary experience and thus to evoke a deep emotional response. See page 1450.

Aside   A convention in drama in which a character utters thoughts intended for the audience to hear that supposedly cannot be heard by the other characters onstage.

Assonance   The repetition of identical or similar vowel sounds in words relatively near to each other whose consonant sounds differ. See also SLANT RHYME.

Atmosphere   The feeling, or emotional aura, created in a reader or audience by a literary work, especially as such feeling is evoked by the setting or landscape.

Ballad   A poem that tells a story and is meant to be recited or sung; originally a folk art, transmitted orally from person to person and generation to generation. Many of the popular ballads were not written down and published until the eighteenth century, though their origins may have been centuries earlier. See "Sir Patrick Spens" (p. 763) for an example of a Scottish popular ballad.

Ballad stanza   A quatrain in iambic meter rhyming *abcb* with (usually) four feet in the first and third lines, three in the second and fourth.

Biographical criticism   See page 1446.

Blank verse   Lines of unrhymed iambic pentameter.

Cacophony   A harsh or unpleasant combination of sounds, as, for example, "But when loud surges lash the sounding shore, / The hoarse, rough verse should like the torrent roar" (Alexander Pope, "An Essay on Criticism," ll. 368–69). See also EUPHONY.

Caesura   A pause or break within a line of verse, usually signaled by a mark of punctuation.

Canon   In the Christian tradition, the books accepted by the church as divinely inspired and approved for inclusion in the Bible. In literary studies, it means (1) the list of works generally accepted as the authentic work of a particular author (e.g., the Shakespearean canon) or (2) literary works that are given special status by the literary establishment within a society as works most worthy of study and emulation.

Carpe diem   "Seize the day," a Latin phrase from an ode by Horace. It is the label for a theme common in literature, especially sixteenth- and seventeenth-century English love poetry, that life is short and fleeting and that therefore one must make the most of present pleasures. See, for example, Robert Herrick's "To the Virgins, to Make Much of Time" (p. 819) and Andrew Marvell's "To His Coy Mistress" (p. 841).

Catastrophe   The concluding section of a play, particularly of a tragedy, describing the fall or death of the protagonist that results from the climax. The term *dénouement* is more commonly used for comedy. See also DÉNOUEMENT.

Catharsis   Term used by Aristotle in the *Poetics* to describe the outcome of viewing a tragedy. The term has usually been translated as "purgation" or "purification," though what Aristotle meant by it is widely disputed. A tragedy, it seems to say, engenders pity and fear in its audience, then releases and quiets those emotions, a process that has a healthy effect, psychologically and physically: The audience goes away feeling not dejected but relieved.

Center of consciousness technique   A third-person limited point of view in which a narrator relates a story through what is thought, felt, seen, and experienced by one of the characters, showing only what that character is conscious of.

Character   (1) A figure, human or personified, in a literary work; characters may be animals or some other beings. (2) A literary genre that offers a brief sketch of a personality type or an example of a virtue or vice, such as a country bumpkin or a braggart soldier.

Characterization   The process or use of techniques by which an author describes and develops the characters in a literary work.

Chaucerian stanza   A seven-line iambic stanza rhyming *ababbcc,* sometimes having an alexandrine (hexameter) closing line. It was first used in English by Geoffrey Chaucer (c. 1343–1400) in *Troilus and Criseyde,* as well as in many of his later poems (thus the name *Chaucerian stanza*), and was widely used in English poetry of the fifteenth and sixteenth centuries. It is also referred to as RHYME ROYAL.

Chorus   In its literary sense, the group of performers in Greek theater whose dancing and singing provided exposition and comment on the action of a play. In later theater, a single character identified as "chorus" who has a function similar to that of the Greek chorus.

Climax   The moment of greatest tension or emotional intensity in a plot.

Closed form   A poetic organization that evinces any repetition of meter, rhyme, or stanza. See also OPEN FORM.

Closet drama   A play that is intended to be read rather than performed.

Colloquial language   The diction, syntax, and idioms characteristic of informal speech.

Comedy   In medieval times, a literary work that has a happy ending and is written in a style less exalted than that of tragedy (e.g., Dante's *Divine Comedy*). More broadly, a humorous and entertaining work, particularly such a work in drama. See also TRAGEDY.

Comic relief   A humorous scene, passage, or character in an otherwise serious play; sometimes described as providing an audience with a momentary relief from the emotional intensity of a tragedy but at the same time heightening the seriousness of the work.

Complication   One of the traditional elements of plot, describing the protagonist's entanglements resulting from plot conflicts.

Concrete language   Language that names material things. See also ABSTRACT LANGUAGE.

Concrete poem   A poem arranged in a shape suggestive of the poem's subject matter.

Conflict   A confrontation or struggle between opposing characters or forces in a literary work, which gives rise to and is a focal point for the action of the plot.

Connotation   The shared or communal range of associations and emotional implications a word may carry in addition to its dictionary definitions. See also DENOTATION.

Consonance   The repetition of consonant sounds in the same or nearby lines. See also SLANT RHYME.

Convention   A rule, method, practice, or characteristic established by usage; a customary feature.

Couplet   A unit consisting of two consecutive lines of poetry with the same end rhyme. See also HEROIC COUPLET.

Crisis   The turning point in a plot, the moment at which a situation changes decisively for better or for worse. See also CLIMAX.

Cultural criticism   See page 1464.

Dactyl   A metrical foot consisting of three syllables, an accented one followed by two unaccented ones (*DA da da*—"sleepily"). In dactylic meter, dactyls are the predominant foot of a line or poem.

Deconstruction   See page 1461.

Denotation   The basic meaning of a word; a word's dictionary definition. See also CONNOTATION.

Dénouement   From the French for "unknotting," the untangling of events at the end of a play that resolves the conflicts (or leaves them satisfyingly unresolved), clarifies what is needed for understanding the outcome, and ties up the loose ends. It can be used in tragedy, but is generally used in comedy. See also CATASTROPHE.

Deus ex machina From the Latin for "god out of the machine," refers to the mechanical device by which the actor playing a god was lowered to the stage in Greek drama to rescue characters from a seemingly impossible situation. It now denotes the use of any unexpected or artificial means to resolve an irresolvable conflict.

Dialect One of several varieties of a language, differing in vocabulary, grammar, and/or pronunciation, and identified with a certain region, community, or social, ethnic, or occupational group. Often one dialect comes to be considered the "standard."

Dialogue A conversation between two or more characters in a literary work.

Diction Choice of words; the kind of words, phrases, and figurative language that make up a work of literature. See also POETIC DICTION.

Dimeter A line of verse consisting of two metrical feet.

Double rhyme A rhyme in which the accented, rhyming syllable is followed by one or more identical, unstressed syllables: *thrilling* and *killing, marry* and *tarry.* An older label, *feminine rhyme,* is generally no longer used. See also SINGLE RHYME.

Downstage The part of the stage closest to the audience.

Drama (1) A literary composition that tells a story, usually involving human conflict, by means of dialogue and action rather than narration. (2) In modern and contemporary theater, any play that is not a comedy or a musical. (3) The dramas of a particular writer or culture, considered as a whole (e.g., Shakespearean drama, medieval drama). See also CLOSET DRAMA; PLAY.

Dramatic irony A situation in which a reader or audience knows more than the speakers or characters, either about future events or about the discrepancy between a meaning intended by a speaker or character and that recognized by a reader or an audience. See also IRONY; SITUATIONAL IRONY; VERBAL IRONY.

Dramatic monologue A poem consisting of speech by one speaker, overheard in a dramatic moment and usually addressing a character or characters who do not speak. The speaker's words reveal what is going on in the scene and expose significant depths of the speaker's temperament, attitudes, and values. See also SOLILOQUY.

Dramatis personae The characters in a play, or a list of such characters.

Dynamic character A character shown as changing and growing because of what happens to her or him. See also STATIC CHARACTER.

Elegy In Greek and Roman literature, a serious, meditative poem written in elegiac meter (alternating hexameter and pentameter lines); since the 1600s, a sustained and formal poem lamenting the death of a particular person, usually ending with a consolation, or setting forth meditations on death or another solemn theme. The adjective *elegiac* is also used to describe a general tone of sadness or a worldview that emphasizes suffering and loss. It is most often applied to Anglo-Saxon poems such as *Beowulf* or *The Seafarer* but also can be used for modern poems, as, for example, A. E. Housman's poems in *A Shropshire Lad.*

End rhyme   Rhyme at the ends of lines in a poem. See also INTERNAL RHYME.

End-stopped line   A line in which a grammatical pause (punctuation mark) and the completion of the meaning coincide at the end. See also RUN-ON LINE.

English sonnet   A sonnet consisting of three quatrains (four-line units, typically rhyming *abab cdcd efef*) and a couplet (two rhyming lines). Usually the subject is introduced in the first quatrain, expanded in the second, and expanded still further in the third; the couplet adds a logical, pithy conclusion or gives a surprising twist. Also called the *Shakespearean sonnet*. See also ITALIAN SONNET.

Enjambment   See RUN-ON LINE.

Epic   A long narrative poem that celebrates the achievements of great heroes and heroines, often determining the fate of a tribe or nation, in formal language and an elevated style. Examples include Homer's *Iliad* and *Odyssey*, Virgil's *Aeneid*, and John Milton's *Paradise Lost*.

Epic simile   An extended or elaborate simile in which the image used to describe the subject is developed in considerable detail.

Epigram   Originally, an inscription on a building, tomb, or gravestone; in modern usage, a short poem, usually polished and witty with a surprising twist at the end. (Its other dictionary definition, "any terse, witty, pointed statement," is a characteristic of some dramatic writing, for example, the comedies of Oscar Wilde.)

Epigraph   In literature, a quotation at the beginning of a poem, story, chapter, play, or book. See, for example, the epigraph from Dante at the beginning of T. S. Eliot's "The Love Song of J. Alfred Prufrock" (p. 796).

Epilogue   Final remarks by an actor after the main action of a play has ended, usually summing up or commenting on the play, or asking for critics and the audience to receive it favorably. In novels, an epilogue may be added to reveal what happens to the characters in future years, after the plot proper concludes.

Epiphany   An appearance or manifestation, especially of a divine being; in literature, since James Joyce adapted the term to secular use, a sudden sense of radiance and revelation one may feel while perceiving a commonplace object; a moment or event in which the essential nature of a person, a situation, or an object is suddenly perceived. The term is more common in the criticism of fiction, narrative poetry, and drama than in lyric poetry.

Epode   (1) The third stanza in a three-stanza segment of an ode in Greek drama, sung while the chorus is standing still. (2) The third stanza in a three-stanza segment of an ode. See also ANTISTROPHE; CHORUS; ODE; STROPHE.

Essay   A relatively brief discussion, usually in prose, of a limited, nonfictional topic or idea.

Euphony   Sounds that strike the ear as smooth, musical, and agreeable, as, for example, "Soft is the strain when Zephyr gently blows, / And the smooth stream in smoother numbers flows" (Alexander Pope, "An Essay on Criticism," ll. 366–67). See also CACOPHONY.

Exact rhyme   Rhyme in which the vowel sound and all sounds following it are the same: *spite* and *night* or *ache* and *fake*.

Exaggeration   See HYPERBOLE.

Explication   A method entailing close analysis of a text, opening it up line by line, clarifying how diction, images, figurative language, symbols, sounds, rhythm, form, and allusions contribute toward shaping the work's meaning and effect. See page 1451.

Exposition   A nondramatized explanation, often a speech by a character or the narrator, that describes things that occurred before the initial action of a narrative or drama, filling in background information the audience needs to make sense of the story.

Extended metaphor   A metaphoric comparison that is sustained and expanded over a number of lines.

Falling action   The action following the climax of a traditionally structured play as the tension lessens and the play moves toward the catastrophe or dénouement. See also RISING ACTION.

Falling meter   A foot (usually trochee or dactyl) in which the first syllable is stressed, followed by unstressed syllables that give a sense of stepping down. See also RISING METER.

Farce   A dramatic work intended to excite laughter that depends less on plot and character than on improbable situations, gross incongruities, coarse wit, and horseplay.

Feminine rhyme   See DOUBLE RHYME.

Feminist criticism   See page 1458.

Fiction   From the Latin verb "to make." (1) Narrated stories in prose — usually short stories, novellas, or novels — that are drawn from the imagination or are an imaginative reworking of actual experiences. Incidents and details in a work of fiction can originate in fact, history, or everyday life, but the characters and events as a whole are primarily invented, or altered, in the author's imagination. (2) The made-up situation underlying any literary work; the feigned or imagined situation underlying it. See also NOVEL; NOVELLA; SHORT STORY.

Figurative language   See FIGURE OF SPEECH.

Figure of speech   Use of language that departs from customary construction, order, or significance in order to achieve a special effect or meaning. It occurs in two forms: (1) trope (from a word for "turn"), or "figure of thought," in which a word or phrase is turned or twisted to make it mean something different from its usual significance; and (2) "rhetorical figure," which creates a surprising effect by using words in unexpected ways without altering what the words mean. See also METAPHOR; METONYMY; PERSONIFICATION; SIMILE; SYNECDOCHE.

First-person point of view   The *I* who tells a story from a first-person point of view, either as an outside observer or as someone directly or indirectly involved in the action of the story.

Fixed form   In poetry, definite, repeating patterns of line, rhyme scheme, or stanza.

Flashback   A literary device that interrupts a narrative to present earlier material, often something that occurred before the opening of the work, through a character's memories or dreams or through juxtaposition of earlier and later events.

Flat character   A character represented through only one or two main features or aspects that can often be summed up in a sentence or two. See also ROUND CHARACTER.

Foil   A character used as a contrast with another character, thus highlighting the latter's distinctive attributes or character traits.

Foot   The basic unit in metrical verse, comprised of (usually) one stressed and one or more unstressed syllables. See also ANAPEST; DACTYL; IAMB; SPONDEE; TROCHEE.

Foreshadowing   Words, gestures, or other actions that hint at future events or outcomes in a literary work.

Form   (1) Genre or literary type (e.g., the lyric form); (2) patterns of meter, lines, and rhymes (stanzaic form); or (3) the organization of the parts of a literary work in relation to its total effect (e.g., "The form [structure] of this poem is very effective"). See also STRUCTURE.

Formalist criticism   See page 1451.

Found poem   A passage from a nonpoetic source such as a newspaper, a magazine, an advertisement, a textbook, or elsewhere in everyday life that contains some element of poetry: meter (sometimes), effective rhythm, phrasings that can be divided into lines, imaginative uses of language and sound, and so on.

Fourth wall   The theatrical convention, dating from the nineteenth century and realistic drama, whereby an audience seems to be looking through an invisible fourth wall into the room of an actual house created by the other three walls of a box set.

Free verse   See OPEN FORM.

Gay and lesbian criticism   See page 1461.

Gender criticism   See page 1460.

Genre   A recurring type of literature; a literary form as defined by rules or conventions followed in it (e.g., tragedy, comedy, epic, lyric, pastoral, novel, short story, essay).

Gothic story   Fiction in which magic, mystery, and effects creating a sense of horror, or an atmosphere of brooding and unknown terror, play a major role.

Haiku   A lyric form, originating in Japan, of seventeen syllables in three lines, the first and third having five syllables and the second seven, presenting an image of a natural object or scene that expresses a distinct emotion or spiritual insight.

Hamartia   An error in judgment, a mistake, a frailty that, according to Aristotle's *Poetics*, results in a tragic hero's change in fortune from prosperity to adversity. *Hamartia* is sometimes mistakenly equated with tragic flaw. It does not, however, refer to a character flaw but rather to a central or defining aspect of the character. In reading plays critically, watching for an error or misstep (*hamartia*) is more advisable than looking for a defect in character (tragic flaw). See also TRAGIC FLAW.

Heptameter   A poetic line with seven metrical feet.

Hero, heroine   The protagonist, or central character, in a literary work.

Heroic couplet   Couplet in iambic pentameter with a full stop, usually, at the end. Also called *closed couplet*.

Hexameter   See ALEXANDRINE.

Historical criticism   See page 1447.

Hubris (hybris)   Greek for "insolence"; excessive pride that can lead to the downfall of the protagonist in a tragedy.

Hyperbole   Exaggeration; a figure of speech in which something is stated more strongly than is logically warranted. See also UNDERSTATEMENT.

Iamb   A metrical foot consisting of two syllables, an unaccented one followed by an accented one (*da DA* — "awake"). In iambic meter, iambs are the predominant foot in a line or poem.

Image   (1) A word or group of words that refers to a sensory experience or to an object that can be known by one or more of the senses. *Imagery* signifies all such language in a poem or other literary work collectively and can include any of the senses (visual imagery, auditory imagery, tactile imagery, kinetic imagery, imagery of smell or taste). (2) A metaphor or other comparison. *Imagery* in this sense refers to the characteristic that several images in a poem have in common, for example, the winter imagery in Judith Ortiz Cofer's "Cold as Heaven" (p. 646).

Imagery   See IMAGE.

Implied metaphor   Metaphor in which the *to be* verb is omitted and one aspect of the comparison is implied rather than stated directly, as, for example, "these dragonflies / filled with little men" in Julia Alvarez's "How I Learned to Sweep" (p. 647).

In medias res   Latin for "into the middle things"; used to describe the technique of starting a narrative at an engaging point well into the story and filling in the background events later as needed.

Interior monologue   The representation of unspoken mental activity — thoughts, impressions, and memories — as if directly overheard by the reader, without being selected and organized by a narrator, either in an associative, disjointed, nonlogical, nongrammatical way (stream of consciousness) or in a logical, grammatical flow of thoughts and memories moving through a person's mind, as if being spoken to an external listener. It is sometimes set off typographically, for example, by using italics rather than quotation marks.

Internal rhyme   Rhyme that occurs between words within a line, between words within lines near each other, or between a word within a line and one at the end of the same or a nearby line.

Irony   A feeling, tone, mood, or attitude arising from the awareness that what is (reality) is opposite from, and usually worse than, what seems (appearance). Irony is not the same as mere coincidence. Irony has different forms: What a person *says* may be ironic (see VERBAL IRONY); a discrepancy between what a character knows or means and what a reader or audience knows can be ironic (see DRAMATIC IRONY); a general situation can be ironic (see SITUATIONAL IRONY).

Italian sonnet   A sonnet composed of an octave (an eight-line unit), rhyming *abbaabba,* and a sestet (a six-line unit), often rhyming *cdecde* or *cdcdcd,* although variations are frequent. The octave usually develops an idea or a question or a problem; then the poem pauses, or "turns," and the sestet completes the idea, answers the question, or resolves the difficulty. Sometimes called a *Petrarchan sonnet.* See also ENGLISH SONNET.

Juxtaposition   Placement of things side by side or close together for comparison or contrast or to create something new from the union, without necessarily making them grammatically parallel.

Limited omniscient point of view   Use of a narrator who is omniscient in some areas or to some extent but is not completely all-knowing.

Line   A sequence of words printed as a separate entity on a page; the basic structural unit in poetry (except prose poems).

Literal   In accordance with the primary or strict meaning of a word or words; not figurative or metaphorical.

Litotes   See UNDERSTATEMENT.

Lyric   Originally, a poem sung to the accompaniment of a lyre; now a poem, usually short, expressing the personal emotion and ideas of a single speaker.

Marxist criticism   See page 1455.

Masculine rhyme   See SINGLE RHYME.

Melodrama   Originally, a drama with musical accompaniment that enhanced its emotional impact; it became in the nineteenth century a type of play relying on broadly drawn heroes and villains, suspenseful plots, improbable escapes, the triumph of good over evil, and an excessive appeal to the emotions of the audience.

Metaphor   A figure of speech in which two things usually thought to be dissimilar are treated as if they were alike and have characteristics in common, as, for example, "numbers were fractious beasts," in Anita Endrezze's "The Girl Who Loved the Sky" (p. 586). See also IMPLIED METAPHOR.

Metaphysical poetry   The work of a number of seventeenth-century English poets characterized by philosophical subtlety and intellectual rigor; subtle, often outrageous logic; imitation of actual speech, sometimes resulting in "rough" meter and style; and far-fetched analogies. Sometimes applied to modern verse sharing some of these characteristics.

Meter   A steady beat, or measured pulse, created by a repeating pattern of accents, syllables, or both.

Metonymy   A figure of speech in which the name of one thing is substituted for that of something closely associated with it, as in commonly used phrases such as "The *White House* announced today . . ." See also SYNECDOCHE.

Metrics   The study of the patterns of rhythm in poetry.

Monometer   A poetic line with one metrical foot.

Morality play   A form of drama that originated in the Middle Ages and presents a dramatized allegory in which abstractions (such as Mercy, Conscience, Perseverance, and Shame) are personified and engage in a struggle for a human soul.

Motif   A recurring element — image, idea, feature, action, or theme — that is elaborated or developed throughout a work.

Motivation   The combination of personality traits and circumstances that impel a character to act in a particular way.

Mystery play   A medieval play based on biblical history; a scriptural play.

Myth   Anonymous stories arising from a culture's oral traditions that involve gods or heroic figures, explore matters beyond everyday life, and concern origins, endings, aspirations, purpose, and meaning.

Mythological criticism   See page 1450.

Naive narrator   A narrator too young or too inexperienced to understand fully the implications of what she or he is talking about. See also NARRATOR; RELIABLE NARRATOR; UNRELIABLE NARRATOR.

Narrative   A narrated story, in prose or verse; an account of events involving characters and what they do and say, told by a storyteller (narrator).

Narrator   The storyteller through whom an author relates a narrative. See also FIRST-PERSON NARRATOR; NAIVE NARRATOR; POINT OF VIEW; RELIABLE NARRATOR; UNRELIABLE NARRATOR.

Naturalism   A literary movement of the late nineteenth and early twentieth centuries that applies the principles of scientific determinism to literature and views humans as animals in a natural world who respond to environmental forces — physical or socioeconomic — and internal stresses and drives, none of which they can control or understand.

Near rhyme   See SLANT RHYME.

New Comedy   Greek comedy of the fourth and third centuries B.C.E. that depicts the obstacles faced by young lovers and the unpredictable changes of fortune they encounter and pokes fun at the foibles and attitudes of the lovers as well as those around them.

New Criticism   See page 1451.

New Historicism   See page 1465.

Novel   Although the term can refer to any extended fictional narrative in prose, it is generally used for narratives that emphasize complexity of character and development of a unifying theme. See also FICTION; NOVELLA; SHORT STORY.

Novella   A fictional prose narrative longer than a short story but shorter than a novel; commonly fifty to one hundred pages in length. See also FICTION; NOVEL; SHORT STORY.

Objective point of view   A narrative approach in which a narrator describes events only from the outside, without looking into the mind of any of the characters or explaining why any of the characters do what they do.

Octameter   A poetic line with eight metrical feet.

Octave   The first, eight-line segment of an Italian sonnet.

Ode   (1) In Greek drama, a speech delivered by the chorus. (2) A long lyric poem, serious (often intellectual) in tone, elevated and dignified in style, dealing with a single theme. The ode is generally more complicated in form than other lyric poems. Some odes retain a formal division into strophe, antistrophe, and epode, which reflects the ode's origins in Greek drama. See also ANTISTROPHE; CHORUS; EPODE; STROPHE.

Off rhyme   See SLANT RHYME.

Old Comedy   Comedy, such as that of Aristophanes in the fifth century B.C.E., employing raucous (sometimes coarse) humor, elements of satire and farce, and often a critique of contemporary persons or political and social norms.

Omniscient point of view   The point of view in a work of fiction in which the narrator is capable of knowing everything about a story's events and characters, including their inner feelings.

One-act play   A short play that is complete in one act.

Onomatopoeia   The use of words whose sounds supposedly resemble the sounds they denote, such as *hiss* or *buzz,* or a group of words whose sounds help to convey what is being described.

Open form   A poetic form free of any predetermined metrical and stanzaic patterns. See also CLOSED FORM.

Orchestra   From the Greek word for "dance." In Greek theater, the area in front of the skene where the chorus performed its songs and dances. Later, a pit for musicians in front of the stage; still later, the group of musicians working there.

Ottava rima   An eight-line stanza in iambic pentameter rhyming *ababababcc.*

Overstatement   See HYPERBOLE.

Oxymoron   A figure of speech combining in one phrase (usually adjective-noun) two seemingly contradictory elements, such as "loving hate" or "feather of lead, bright smoke, cold fire, sick health" (Shakespeare, *Romeo and Juliet* 1.1.176–80). Oxymoron is a type of PARADOX.

Pantoum   A poem consisting of four-line stanzas rhyming *abab.* The second and fourth lines of one stanza serve as the first and third lines of the next stanza, and the first and third lines of the first stanza reappear as the fourth and second lines of the last stanza, so that the poem begins and ends with the same line.

Paradox   A figure of speech in which a statement initially seeming self-contradictory or absurd turns out, seen in another light, to make good sense. See also OXYMORON.

Parallelism   (1) A verbal arrangement in which elements of equal weight within phrases, sentences, or paragraphs are expressed in a similar grammatical order and structure. (2) A principle of poetic structure in which consecutive lines in open form are related by a line's repeating, expanding on, or contrasting with the idea of the line or lines before it, as in the biblical psalms or the poems of Walt Whitman (see p. 877).

Parody In modern usage, a humorous or satirical imitation of a serious piece of literature or writing. In the sixteenth and seventeenth centuries, poets such as George Herbert practiced "sacred parody" by adapting secular lyrics to devotional themes.

Partial rhyme See SLANT RHYME.

Pastoral (1) As an adjective, that which deals with a rural setting and affirms a rustic way of life. (2) As a noun, a literary type associated with shepherds and country living.

Pause See CAESURA.

Pentameter A poetic line with five metrical feet.

Persona Literally, the mask through which actors spoke in Greek plays. In some critical approaches of recent decades, the "character" projected by the author, the *I* of a narrative poem or novel, or the speaker whose voice is heard in a lyric poem. In this view, the poem is an artificial construct distanced from the poet's autobiographical self. See also VOICE.

Personification A figure of speech in which something nonhuman (an abstraction or a natural object) is treated as if it had human (not just living) characteristics or actions. See also APOSTROPHE.

Petrarchan sonnet See ITALIAN SONNET.

Play A drama intended for performance before a theatrical audience. See also CLOSET DRAMA.

Plot (1) The selection and arrangement of events in a narrative to present them most effectively to the reader and bring out their causal connections. (2) The action that takes place within a play, considered by Aristotle in the *Poetics* to be the most important of the six elements of drama. See also SUBPLOT.

Poem A term whose meaning exceeds all attempts at definition. Here is a slightly modified version of an attempt at definition by William Harmon and C. Hugh Holman in *A Handbook to Literature* (1996): A poem is a literary composition, written or oral, typically characterized by imagination, emotion, sense impressions, and concrete language that invites attention to its own physical features, such as sound or appearance on the page.

Poetic diction In general, a specialized language used in or considered appropriate to poetry. In the late seventeenth and the eighteenth centuries, a refined use of language that excluded "common" speech from poetry as indecorous and substituted elevated circumlocutions or archaic synonyms, or such forms as *ope* and *e'er*.

Point of view The vantage point from which an author presents a story, combining person (first, second, or third, named or anonymous) and perspective (objective, omniscient, limited). See also CENTER OF CONSCIOUSNESS TECHNIQUE; STREAM-OF-CONSCIOUSNESS TECHNIQUE.

Problem play A serious work that dramatizes a real-life, usually contemporary, social, political, or ethical problem. Although in a broad sense it covers all drama dealing with problems of human life, it is used more narrowly for the "drama of ideas" that emerged in the late nineteenth century in the work, for example, of Norwegian playwright Henrik Ibsen (see p. 1245).

Prologue   (1) The opening section of a Greek tragedy. (2) Words spoken before the beginning of a play, usually a monologue by one of the actors providing background information.

Property (prop)   A movable object used on stage, especially one handled by an actor while performing.

Proscenium   The part of the stage in a modern theater between the orchestra and the curtain. The proscenium arch is the arch over the front of the stage from which the curtain hangs and which separates the stage from the audience.

Prose poem   A poem printed as prose, with lines wrapping at the right margin rather than being divided through predetermined line breaks.

Prosody   The principles of versification, especially of meter, rhythm, rhyme, and stanza forms.

Protagonist   The most important or leading character in a literary work. See also ANTAGONIST.

Psychological criticism   See page 1447.

Pun   A "play on words" based on similarity in sound between two words having very different meanings, as when *fractious* in Anita Endrezze's line "numbers were fractious beasts" ("The Girl Who Loved the Sky," p. 586) suggests *fractions* in addition to its dictionary meanings of "unruly, readily angered, quarrelsome." Also called *paronomasia*. Often used to produce AMBIGUITY in sense 2.

Quatrain   A stanza of four lines or other four-line unit within a larger form, such as a sonnet.

Reader-response criticism   See page 1453.

Realism   (1) An approach to literature that attempts to depict accurately the everyday life of a time and place. (2) A literary movement that developed in the latter half of the nineteenth century characterized by an objective presentation of material and realistic depiction of setting, characters, and details.

Recognition   A significant realization or discovery by a character, usually the protagonist, that moves the plot forward by changing the circumstances of a play.

Refrain   One or more identical or deliberately similar lines repeated throughout a poem, sometimes with meaningful variation, such as the final line of a stanza or as a block of lines between stanzas or sections.

Reliable narrator   A narrator who tells her or his story accurately and honestly. See also NAIVE NARRATOR; NARRATOR; UNRELIABLE NARRATOR.

Resolution   The culmination of a fictional plot that resolves the conflicts or leaves them satisfyingly unresolved.

Rhyme   The repetition of the accented vowel sound of a word and all succeeding consonant sounds. See also EXACT RHYME; SLANT RHYME.

Rhyme royal   An alternative term for CHAUCERIAN STANZA because it was used by King James I of Scotland in his poem *The Kingis Quair* ("The King's Book"), written about 1424.

Rhyme scheme   The pattern of end rhymes in a poem or stanza; the recurring sequence is usually described by assigning a letter to each word sound, the same word sounds having the same letter (e.g., *abbaabba*).

Rhythm   The patterned "movement" of language created by the choice of words and their arrangement, usually described through such metaphors as fast or slow, smooth or halting, graceful or rough, deliberate or frenzied, syncopated or disjointed. Rhythm in poetry is affected, in addition to meter, by such factors as line length; line endings; pauses (or lack of them) within lines; spaces within, at the beginning or end of, or between lines; word choice; and combinations of sounds.

Rising action   The part of a plot leading up to the climax and marked by increasingly tense and complicated conflict. See also FALLING ACTION.

Rising meter   A foot (usually an iamb or an anapest) in which the final, stressed syllable is preceded by one or two unstressed syllables, thus giving a sense of stepping up. See also FALLING METER.

Romance   (1) In medieval narrative poetry or prose, a tale involving knights and kings, adventures, ladies in distress, courtly love, and chivalric ideals. (2) In modern fiction, a work characterized by remote and exotic settings, exciting and heroic action, passionate love, and mysterious or supernatural experiences. (3) In drama, a play neither wholly comic nor wholly tragic, often containing elements of the supernatural.

Round character   A complex, fully developed character either shown as changing and growing because of what happens to her or him or described in such rich detail that we have a clear sense of how she or he would, or will, change even though we don't see it happening. See also FLAT CHARACTER.

Run-on line   A line whose sense and grammatical structure continue to the next. The technique is called *enjambment*. See also END-STOPPED LINE.

Sarcasm   A harsh and cutting form of VERBAL IRONY, often involving apparent praise that is obviously not meant seriously.

Satire   A work, or manner within a work, that combines a critical attitude with humor and wit with the intent of improving human institutions or humanity.

Scansion   The division of metrical verse into feet in order to determine and label the meter of a poem. See also FOOT; METER; page 1422.

Scene   (1) A subdivision of an ACT in drama, or — in modern drama — a section of a play that is not divided into acts. (2) See SETTING. (3) A variant spelling of *skene*.

Script   The written text of a play, which includes the stage directions, dramatic monologues, and the dialogue between characters.

Sentimentality   A term used to describe a work seeking to elicit an emotional response in a reader or spectator that exceeds what the situation warrants.

Sestet   The last six lines of an ITALIAN SONNET.

Sestina   A lyric poem consisting of six six-line stanzas and a three-line concluding stanza (or "envoy"). The six end-words of the first stanza must be used as the end-words of the other five stanzas, in a specified pattern (the first line ends with the end-word from the last line of the previous stanza, the second line with that of the first line of the previous stanza, the third line with that of the previous fifth line, the fourth line with that of the previous second line, the fifth line with that of the previous fourth line, the sixth line with that of the previous third line). The three lines of the envoy must use the end-words of lines 5, 3, and 1 from the first stanza, in that order, and must include the other three end-words within the lines.

Set   The physical equipment of a stage, including backdrops, furniture, properties, and lighting.

Setting   The overall context—where, when, in what circumstances—in which the action in a fictional or dramatic work takes place.

Shakespearean sonnet   See ENGLISH SONNET.

Shaped poem   See CONCRETE POEM.

Short story   A brief prose work of narrative fiction characterized by a carefully crafted plot and style, complexity in characterization and point of view, and unity of effect. See also FICTION; NOVEL; NOVELLA.

Simile   Expression of a direct similarity, using such words as *like, as,* or *than,* between two things usually regarded as dissimilar (e.g., "His face was as white as a sheet."). It is important to distinguish *simile* from *comparison,* where the two things joined by *like* or *as* are not dissimilar.

Single rhyme   A rhyme in which the stressed, rhyming syllable is the final syllable in the rhyme: *west* and *stressed, away* and *today.* Formerly called *masculine rhyme.* See also DOUBLE RHYME.

Situational irony   A kind of irony in which a result turns out very different from, and usually more sinister than, what a character expected or hoped for. Unlike dramatic irony, in situational irony the reader does not necessarily know more than the characters and may be as surprised by what happens as the characters are. See also DRAMATIC IRONY; IRONY; VERBAL IRONY.

Slant rhyme   A form of rhyme in which words contain similar sounds but do not rhyme perfectly (usually involving assonance or—more frequently—consonance). See also ASSONANCE; CONSONANCE.

Soliloquy   A monologue delivered by a character in a play while alone on stage or otherwise out of hearing of the other characters, often revealing the character's inner thoughts or feelings. Sometimes applied to a poem imitating this feature. See also DRAMATIC MONOLOGUE.

Sonnet   A fourteen-line poem usually written in iambic pentameter. Originally lyrical love poems, sonnets came to be used also for meditations on religious themes, death, and nature and are now open to all subjects. Some sonnets have varied from the traditional form—using hexameter lines, fewer or more than fourteen lines, or an appended coda. Sometimes sonnets are grouped in a "sonnet sequence," with implied narrative progression in the situations imagined as underlying the successive utterances. See also ENGLISH SONNET; ITALIAN SONNET; SPENSERIAN SONNET.

Speaker   The imagined voice in a nonnarrative poem of someone uttering the words of the poem, either that of the poet quite directly or of a character expressing views or feelings the poet may or may not share.

Spenserian sonnet   A variation of the English sonnet that employs the structure of three quatrains plus a couplet, but joins the quatrains by linking rhymes: *abab bcbc cdcd ee.*

Spenserian stanza   A stanza of nine iambic lines, the first eight pentameter and the ninth hexameter, rhyming *ababbcbcc*. It was created by Edmund Spenser (1552– 1599) for his allegorical epic *The Faerie Queene* (1590, 1596) and was used frequently by English poets in the nineteenth century.

Spondee   A metrical foot made up of two stressed syllables (*DA DA* — "dream house"), with no unstressed syllables. Spondees cannot be the predominant foot in a poem; they are usually substituted for iambs or trochees as a way of increasing emphasis.

Stage directions   Written instructions in the script of a play, typically placed in parentheses and set in italics, telling actors how to move on the stage or how to deliver a particular word or speech.

Stage left, stage right   Areas of the stage seen from the point of view of an actor facing the audience. Stage left, therefore, is on the audience's right-hand side, and vice versa.

Stanza   A grouping of poetic lines into a section, either according to form — each section having the same number of lines and the same prosody — or according to thought, creating irregular units comparable to paragraphs in prose. Irregular stanzas are sometimes called STROPHES.

Static character   A character in a narrative or dramatic work who is not shown as changing. See also DYNAMIC CHARACTER.

Stichomythia   A form of repartee in dialogue originating in ancient Greek drama — brief, alternating lines that reply sharply to each other in wordings that echo and vary what the preceding character expressed.

Stock character   A traditional character defined by a single, stereotypical characteristic, such as an innocent young woman, a rakish young man, or a clever servant.

Story   Any account of a related series of events in sequential order, usually chronological order (the order in which they happened).

Stream-of-consciousness technique   An attempt to convey the unstructured, even at times chaotic, flow of random sense perceptions, mental pictures, memories, sounds, thoughts, and feelings — prerational mental activity, before the mind orders it into a coherent form or shape — through an associative rather than a logical style, usually without ordinary punctuation or complete sentences.

Stress   In metrics, the greater emphasis given to some words and syllables relative to that received by adjacent words and syllables. See also ACCENT.

Strophe   (1) The first part in a three-stanza segment of a choral ODE in Greek drama, sung while the chorus moves from stage right to stage left. (2) The first stanza in a three-stanza segment of an ode. (3) See STANZA. See also ANTISTROPHE; CHORUS; EPODE; ODE.

Structure   (1) The planned framework — the general plan or outline — of a literary work. (2) Narrower patterns within the overall framework. See also FORM.

Style   In writing, the distinctive, individual manner in which a writer uses words, constructs sentences, incorporates nonliteral expressions, and handles rhythm, timing, and tone; also, the manner characteristic of a group of writers (as in "period style").

Subplot   A subordinate or minor story in a dramatic or narrative work, often related thematically or structurally to the main plot. See also PLOT.

Substitution   The use of a different kind of foot in place of the one normally demanded by the predominant meter of a poem, as a way of calling attention to an idea, emphasizing the dominant foot by variation from it, speeding up or slowing down the pace, or signaling a switch in meaning.

Suspense   A sense of uncertainty and concern about how things in a literary work will turn out, when disaster will fall or rescue will occur, who did what, or what the effects on the characters or events will be.

Symbol   Something that represents both itself and something else. A literary symbol is a prominent or repeated image or action that is present in the poem, story, or play and is seen, touched, smelled, heard, tasted, or experienced imaginatively but also conveys a cluster of abstract meanings beyond itself.

Synecdoche   A special kind of METONYMY in which a part of a thing is substituted for the whole of which it is a part, as in the commonly used phrases "give me a hand," "lend me your ears," or "many mouths to feed."

Syntax   The arrangement of words in a sentence to show their relationship to one another.

Tercet   A stanza of three lines, each usually ending with the same rhyme. See also TERZA RIMA; TRIPLET.

Terza rima   A poetic form consisting of three-line stanzas (TERCETS) with inter-linked rhymes, *aba bcb cdc ded efe*, etc., made famous by Dante's use of it in *The Divine Comedy*.

Tetrameter   A poetic line with four metrical feet.

Text   Traditionally, a piece of writing. In recent READER-RESPONSE CRITICISM, *text* has come to mean the words with which the reader interacts; in this view, a literary work is not an object, not a shape on the page or a spoken performance, but what is completed in the reader's mind.

Theme   The central idea embodied or explored in a literary work, what it all adds up to; the general concept, explicit or implied, which the work incorporates and makes persuasive to the reader.

Thesis   A succinct statement of the central idea or proposition to be explored in an expository essay.

Third-person narrator   The type of narration with a storyteller who is not identified; uses the pronouns *he, she, it,* or *they* — but not *I* — in speaking of herself or himself; asserts no connection between the narrator and the characters in the story; and tells the story with some objectivity and distance.

Title   The name attached to a work of literature. Usually a title, when assigned by the author, is an integral part of a work and needs to be considered in interpreting it. In some cases, a title for a poem has been added as a means of identifying it and is not integral to its interpretation. Sometimes a poem is untitled and the first line is used as a convenient way of referring to the poem (e.g., in Emily Dickinson's poems), but it should not be thought of as a title and does not follow the capitalization rules for titles.

Tone   The attitude, or "stance," toward the subject and toward the reader or audience implied in a literary work; the "tone of voice" it seems to project.

Tragedy   A story recounting a causally related series of serious and important events that culminate in an unhappy ending for the protagonist. See also COMEDY.

Tragic flaw   The theory, attributed to Aristotle's *Poetics,* that the downfall of the hero in a tragedy is caused by a defect, or flaw, in her or his character. See also HAMARTIA and page 1102.

Tragicomedy   A play whose plot could be appropriate to tragedy until the final act, when it turns out unexpectedly to have the happy ending of a comedy. The tone and style of tragicomedy are serious and the outcome could well be disaster or death; but somehow the disaster is averted, and at the end order and harmony prevail. See also COMEDY; TRAGEDY.

Trimeter   A poetic line with three metrical feet.

Triplet   A group of three consecutive lines with the same rhyme, often used for variation in a long sequence of couplets. See also TERCET.

Trochee   A metrical foot consisting of two syllables, an accented one followed by an unaccented one (*DA da* — "wakeful"). In trochaic meter, trochees are the predominant foot in a line or poem.

Type   (1) See GENRE. (2) A character who represents a class or kind of person, either atypical and individualized, or stereotypical (see STOCK CHARACTER). (3) A variety of symbol, especially as used in religion for something that is to come, such as "a type of Christ."

Understatement   A figure of speech expressing something in an unexpectedly restrained way, which often has the effect of increasing rather than reducing emphasis. See also HYPERBOLE.

Unity   A sense of wholeness and cohesion in a literary work, as all of its parts work together according to some organizing principle to achieve common effect.

Unreliable narrator   A narrator who may be in error in her or his reporting or understanding of things, or who distorts things, deliberately or unintentionally. See also NAIVE NARRATOR; NARRATOR; RELIABLE NARRATOR.

Upstage   The part of the stage farthest from the audience.

Verbal irony   A figure of speech in which what is said is nearly the opposite of what is meant. See also DRAMATIC IRONY; IRONY; SARCASM; SITUATIONAL IRONY.

Verisimilitude   The semblance of truth; the use of abundant detail to create the appearance of reality in a literary work.

Verse (1) A unit of poetry, the same thing as a stanza or line. (2) A rhythmic composition, often in meter and rhyme, irrespective of merit (the term *poetry* is often reserved for verse of high merit).

Viewpoint See POINT OF VIEW.

Villanelle A nineteen-line lyric poem divided into five tercets and a final four-line stanza, rhyming *aba aba aba aba aba abaa*. Line 1 is repeated to form lines 6, 12, and 18; line 3 is repeated to form lines 9, 15, and 19. See, for example, John Yau's "Chinese Villanelle" (p. 701) and Dylan Thomas's "Do not go gentle into that good night" (p. 873).

Voice The supposed authorial presence in poems that do not obviously employ persona as a distancing device.

Acknowledgments (continued from p. iv)

Sherman Alexie, "Superman and Me" is reprinted by permission of Nancy Stauffer Associates. Copyright © 1998 by Sherman Alexie. All rights reserved. "This Is What It Means to Say Phoenix, Arizona" and "The Lone Ranger and Tonto Fistfight in Heaven" from *The Lone Ranger and Tonto Fistfight in Heaven*. Copyright © 1993 Sherman Alexie. Used by permission of Grove/Atlantic, Inc. "This Is What it Means to Say Phoenix, Arizona" and "The Lone Ranger and Tonto Fistfight in Heaven" from *The Lone Ranger and Tonto Fistfight in Heaven*. Copyright © 1993 and 2005 by Sherman Alexie. Used by permission of Grove/Atlantic, Inc.

Woody Allen, "Death Knocks," copyright © 1966, 1967, 1968, 1969, 1970, 1971 by Woody Allen, from *Getting Even* by Woody Allen. Used by permission of Random House, Inc.

Isabel Allende, "And of Clay Are We Created" reprinted with permission of Scribner, an imprint of Simon & Schuster Adult Publishing Group, from *The Stories of Eva Luna* by Isabel Allende, translated from the Spanish by Margaret Sayers Peden. Copyright © 1989 by Isabel Allende. English translation Copyright © 1991 by Macmillan Publishing Company. All rights reserved.

Julia Alvarez, "Daughter of Invention" from *How the Garcia Girls Lost Their Accents*. Copyright © 1991 by Julia Alvarez. Published by Plume, an imprint of The Penguin Group (USA) and originally in hardcover by Algonquin Books of Chapel Hill. Reprinted by permission of Susan Bergholz Literary Services, New York, NY and Lamy, NM. All rights reserved. "How I Learned to Sweep" from *Homecoming*. Copyright © 1984, 1996 by Julia Alvarez. Published by Plume, an imprint of The Penguin Group (USA) and originally published by Grove Press. Reprinted by permission of Susan Bergholz Literary Services, New York. All rights reserved.

Margaret Atwood, "you fit into me" from *Power Politics* by Margaret Atwood. Copyright © 1971, 1996 by Margaret Atwood. Reprinted by permission of House of Anansi Press, www.anansi.ca. "True Stories" from *Selected Poems II: Poems Selected and New 1976-1986* by Margaret Atwood. Copyright © 1987 by Margaret Atwood. Reprinted by permission of Houghton Mifflin Harcourt Publishing Company and Oxford University Press Canada. All rights reserved.

W. H. Auden, "Musée des Beaux Arts," copyright 1940 & renewed 1968 by W. H. Auden, from *Collected Poems* by W. H. Auden. Used by permission of Random House, Inc.

Jimmy Santiago Baca, "Family Ties" from *Black Mesa Poems*, copyright © 1989 by Jimmy Santiago Baca. Reprinted by permission of New Directions Publishing Corp.

James Baldwin, "Sonny's Blues" © 1957 by James Baldwin was originally published in *Partisan Review*. Copyright renewed. Collected in *Going to Meet the Man*, published by Vintage Books. Reprinted by arrangement with the James Baldwin Estate.

Toni Cade Bambara, "The Lesson," copyright © 1972 by Toni Cade Bambara, from *Gorilla, My Love* by Toni Cade Bambara. Used by permission of Random House, Inc.

Clive Barnes, "Fiery 'Fences': A Review" from the *New York Post*, March 27, 1989. Copyright © 1987 by Clive Barnes. Reprinted by permission.

Jim Barnes, "Return to La Plata, Missouri" from *American Book of the Dead: Poems*. Copyright © 1982 by Jim Barnes. Used with permission of the poet and the University of Illinois Press.

Lynda Barry, "Today's Demon: Magic" from *One Hundred Demons* by Lynda Barry. Copyright © 2002 by Lynda Barry. Reprinted courtesy of Darhansoff, Verrill, Feldman Literary Agents.

Anne Beattie, "Snow" is reprinted with the permission of Scribner, a Division of Simon & Schuster, Inc., from *Where You'll Find Me* by Ann Beattie. Copyright © 1986 by Irony and Pity, Inc. All rights reserved.

Wendell Berry, "The Peace of Wild Things" from *The Selected Poems of Wendell Berry*. Copyright © 1998 by Wendell Berry. Reprinted by permission of Counterpoint.

Elizabeth Bishop, "Sestina" and "In the Waiting Room" from *The Complete Poems 1927-1979* by Elizabeth Bishop. Copyright © 1979, 1983 by Alice Helen Methfessel. Reprinted by permission of Farrar, Straus and Giroux, LLC.

Peter Blue Cloud, "Crazy Horse Monument" from *Clans of Many Nations: Selected Poems 1969-1994*. Copyright © 1995 by Peter Blue Cloud/Aroniawenrate. Reprinted with the permission of White Pine Press, www.whitepine.org

Eavan Boland, "The Pomegranate," from *In a Time of Violence* by Eavan Boland. Copyright © 1994 by Eavan Boland. Used by permission of W. W. Norton & Company, Inc.

Anne Bradstreet, "To My Dear and Loving Husband" is reprinted by permission of the publisher from *The Works of Anne Bradstreet*, edited by Jeannine Hensley, Cambridge, Mass: Belknap Press of Harvard University Press, Copyright © 1967 by the President and Fellows of Harvard College.

Gwendolyn Brooks, "The Bean Eaters" and "We Real Cool" are reprinted by consent of Brooks Permissions.

Olga Broumas, "Cinderella" from *Beginning with O* by Olga Broumas is reprinted by permission of the publisher, Yale University Press. Copyright © 1977 by Olga Broumas.

Sterling Brown, "Riverbank Blues" from *The Collected Poems of Sterling A Brown*, edited by Michael S. Harper. Copyright © 1980 by Sterling A. Brown. Reprinted by permission of HarperCollins Publishers.

Dennis Brutus, "Nightsong: City" from *A Simple Lust: Selected Poems*. Copyright ©1973 by Dennis Brutus. Reprinted by permission of the author.

Charles Bukowski, "my old man" from *Love Is a Dog from Hell: Poems 1974-1977* by Charles Bukowski. Copyright © 1977 by Charles Bukowski. Reprinted by permission of HarperCollins Publishers.

Jo Carson, "I cannot remember all the times" from *Stories I Ain't Told Nobody Yet*. Copyright © 1989 by Jo Carson. Reprinted by permission of Orchard Books, an imprint of Scholastic Inc.

Raymond Carver, "What We Talk about When We Talk about Love," from *What We Talk about When We Talk about Love* by Raymond Carver, copyright © 1974, 1976, 1978, 1980, 1981 by Raymond Carver. Used by permission of Alfred A. Knopf, a division of Random House, Inc.

Lorna Dee Cervantes, "Freeway 280" in *Latin American Literary Review*, volume 5, issue # 10 Copyright © 1977. Reprinted by permission of Latin American Literary Review Press.

Tina Chang, "Naming the Light" from *Half-Lit Houses*. Copyright © 2004 by Tina Chang. Reprinted with the permission of Four Way Books, www.fourwaybooks.com

Marilyn Chin, "How I Got That Name" from *The Phoenix Gone, The Terrace Empty* (Minneapolis: Milkweed Editions). Copyright © 1994 by Marilyn Chin. Reprinted with permission from Milkweed Editions.

Sandra Cisneros, "The House on Mango Street" from *The House on Mango Street*. Copyright © 1984 by Sandra Cisneros. Published by Vintage Books, a division of Random House, Inc. and in hardcover by Alfred K. Knopf in 1994. Reprinted by permission of Susan Bergholz Literary Services, New York, NY and Lamy, NM. All rights reserved.

Lucille Clifton, "adam and eve" from *Good Woman: Poems and a Memoir 1969-1980*. Copyright © 1987 by Lucille Clifton. Reprinted with the permission of BOA Editions Ltd., www.boaeditions.org. "at the cemetery, walnut grove plantation, south carolina, 1989" from *Quilting: Poems 1987-1990*. Copyright © 1991 by Lucille Clifton. Reprinted with the permission of BOA Editions, www.boaeditions.org. "homage to my hips" from *Two-Headed Woman* (1980). Copyright © 1980 by Lucille Clifton. Reprinted by permission of Curtis Brown, Ltd.

Judith Ortiz Cofer, "And Are You a Latina Writer?" is reprinted with permission from the publishers of *Americas Review*, © 1980 Arte Público Press–University of Houston. "Silent Dancing" from *Silent Dancing: A Partial Remembrance of a Puerto Rican Childhood*, copyright © 1990 Arte Público Press–University of Houston. Reprinted by permission of the publisher. *The Latin Deli: Prose and Poetry* by Judith Ortiz Cofer is reprinted by permission of The University of Georgia Press. Copyright © 1993 by Judith Ortiz Cofer. "Cold as Heaven," "On the Island I Have Seen," and "The Birthplace" from *Reaching the Mainland and Selected New Poems*. Copyright © 1995 by Judith Ortiz Cofer. Reprinted by permission of Bilingual Press/Editorial Bilingüe. "The Changeling" first published in *Prairie Schooner*, volume 66, issue 3, Fall 1992, is reprinted by permission of the University of Nebraska Press. Copyright © 1992 by the University of Nebraska Press. "The Latin Deli: An Ars Poetica" is reprinted with permission from the publisher of *The Americas Review*. Copyright © 1992 Arte Público Press–University of Houston. "My Father in the Navy: A Childhood Memory" from *Triple Crown*. Copyright © 1987 by Judith Ortiz Cofer, Roberto Duran, and Gustavo Perez Firmat. Reprinted by permission of Bilingual Press/Editorial Bilingüe. "First Job: The Southern Sweets Sandwich Shop and Bakery" from *A Love Story Beginning in Spanish: Poems* by Judith Ortiz Cofer is reprinted by permission of The University of Georgia Press. Copyright © 2005 by Judith Ortiz Cofer.

Billy Collins, "I Chop Some Parsley While Listening to Art Blakey's Version of 'Three Blind Mice'" fom *Picnic, Lightning* by Billy Collins, copyright © 1998. Reprinted by permission of the University of Pittsburgh Press.

Joseph L. Coulombe, "The Approximate Size of His Favorite Humor: Sherman Alexie's Comic Connections and Disconnections in the 'The Lone Ranger and Tonto Fistfight in Heaven.'" Reprinted by permission of the author.

James Cox, "Muting White Noise: The Subversion of Popular Culture Narratives of Conquest in Sherman Alexie's Fiction," from *Studies in American Indian Literatures*, Series 2, Volume 9, Number 4 (Winter 1997): 52-70, Copyright © 1997. Reprinted by permission of the author.

Victor Hernandez Cruz, "Problems with Hurricanes" from *Maraca: New and Selected Poems, 1965-2000*. Copyright © 2001 by Victor Hernandez Cruz. Reprinted with the permission of Coffee House Press, www.coffeehousepress.org

Countee Cullen, "Incident" and "For a Lady I Know" from *Color* by Countee Cullen, copyright © 1925 by Harper & Brothers Copyright 1952 by Ida M. Cullen. Copyrights held by the Amistad Research Center, Tulane University. Administered by Thompson and Thompson, Brooklyn, NY.

E. E. Cummings, "next to of course god america i," copyright 1926, 1954, © 1991 by the Trustees for the E. E. Cummings Trust, copyright © 1985 by George James Firmage, from *Complete Poems: 1904-1962* by E. E. Cummings, edited by George J. Firmage. "Buffalo Bill 's" Copyright 1923, 1951, © 1991 by The Trustees for the E. E. Cummings Trust. Copyright © 1976 by George James Firmage from *Complete Poems: 1904-1962* by E. E. Cummings. Used by permission of Liveright Publishing Corporation.

Lydia Davis, "What She Knew" from *The Collected Stories of Lydia Davis* by Lydia Davis. Copyright © 2009 by Lydia Davis. Reprinted by permission of Farrar, Straus and Giroux, LLC.

Todd Davis, "Accident" from *The Least of These: Poems* by Todd Davis (2010). Reprinted with permission of Michigan State University Press.

Jerome DeNuccio, "Slow Dancing with Skeletons: Sherman Alexie's 'The Lone Ranger and Tonto Fistfight in Heaven,'" originally published in *Critique*, volume 44, issue #1 (Fall 2002): 86-96. Reprinted by permission of the author.

Toi Derricotte, "A Note on My Son's Face" from *Captivity* by Toi Derricotte, copyright © 1989. Reprinted by permission of the University of Pittsburgh Press.

Emily Dickinson, #311, #465, #712, #288, and #585 are reprinted by permission of the publishers and the Trustees of Amherst College from *The Poems of Emily Dickinson*, Thomas H. Johnson, ed., Cambridge, Mass.: The Belknap Press of Harvard University Press, Copyright © 1951, 1955, 1979, 1983 by the President and Fellows of Harvard College.

Chitra Banerjee Divakaruni, "Clothes" from *Arranged Marriage* by Chitra Divakaruni, copyright © 1995 by Chitra Divakaruni. Used by permission of Doubleday, a division of Random House, Inc. "Nargis' Toilette" from *Black Candle* by Chitra Banerjee Divakaruni (Calyx Books, 1991) is reprinted by permission of the publisher.

Mark Doty, "Tiara" from *Bethlehem in Broad Daylight* by Mark Doty. Reprinted by permission of David R. Godine, Publisher, Inc. Copyright © 1991 by Mark Doty.

Rita Dove, "Fifth Grade Autobiography" from *Grace Notes* by Rita Dove. Copyright © 1989 by Rita Dove. Used by permission of the author and W. W. Norton & Company, Inc.

Cornelius Eady, "My Mother, If She Had Won Free Dance Lessons" in *Victims of the Latest Dance Craze.* Copyright © 1985 by Cornelius Eady. Reprinted by permission of the author.

Dave Eggers, "Accident" by Dave Eggers was originally published in *The Guardian*, April 16, 2005. Reprinted by permission of the author.

Harry J. Elam Jr., From "August Wilson" from *Companion to 20th Century American Drama*, edited by David Krasner, is reprinted by permission of Harry J. Elam Jr.

T. S. Eliot, "The Love Song of J. Alfred Prufrock," from *Collected Poems 1909-1962.* Reprinted with the permission of Faber & Faber Ltd.

Ralph Ellison, "Battle Royal," copyright 1948 by Ralph Ellison, from *Invisible Man* by Ralph Ellison. Used by permission of Random House, Inc.

Gray Emerson, "The Indexer in Love" from *Time You Let Me In: 25 Poets under 25*, edited by Naomi Shihab Nye (Greenwillow Books, 2010) is reprinted by permission of the author.

Anita Endrezze, "The Girl Who Loved the Sky" in *At the Helm of Twilight* (Broken Moon Press). Copyright 1992. Reprinted by permission of the author.

Louise Erdrich, "The Red Convertible" from the book *Love Medicine, Newly Revised Edition* by Louise Erdrich. Copyright 1984, 1993 by Louise Erdrich. Reprinted by permission of Henry Holt and Company, LLC.

Martín Espada, "Latin Night at the Pawnshop," copyright © 1990 by Martín Espada, from *Alabanza* by Martín Espada. Used by permission of W. W. Norton & Company, Inc.

Susan Farrell, "Fight vs. Flight: A re-evaluation of Dee in Alice Walker's 'Everyday Use'" from *Studies in Short Fiction* 35:2 (Spring 1998): 179–186. Reprinted by permission of the author.

William Faulkner, "A Rose for Emily," copyright 1930 and renewed 1958 by William Faulkner, from *Collected Stories of William Faulkner* by William Faulkner. Used by permission of Random House, Inc.

Carolyn Forché, All lines from "The Colonel" from *The Country Between Us* by Carolyn Forché. Copyright © 1981 by Carolyn Forché. Originally appeared in *Women's International Resource Exchange.* Reprinted by permission of HarperCollins Publishers.

Vievee Francis, "1864, A Pocket Full of Rye" from *Blue-Tail Fly* by Vievee Francis. Copyright © 2006 Wayne State University Press, used with the permission of Wayne State University Press.

Robert Frost, "The Road Not Taken" and "Birches" from *The Poetry of Robert Frost* edited by Edward Connery Latham. Copyright 1916, 1969 by Henry Holt and Company. Copyright 1944 by Robert Frost. "After Apple Picking" and "Design" from *The Poetry of Robert Frost* edited by Edward Connery Latham. Copyright 1930, 1969 by Henry Holt and Company. Copyright 1936, 1958 by Robert Frost, copyright 1964, 1967 by Lesley Frost Ballantine. Reprinted by permission of Henry Holt and Company, LLC.

Tess Gallagher, "The Hug" from *Amplitude: New and Selected Poems.* Copyright © 1984 by Tess Gallagher. Reprinted with permission of Graywolf Press, Minneapolis, Minnesota, www.graywolfpress.org.

Richard Garcia, "Why I Left the Church" from *The Flying Garcias* by Richard Garcia, copyright © 1993. Reprinted by permission of the University of Pittsburgh Press.

Gabriel García Márquez, all pages from "A Very Old Man with Enormous Wings" from *Leaf Storms and Other Stories* by Gabriel García Márquez, translated by Gregory Rabassa. Copyright © 1971 by Gabriel García Márquez. Reprinted by permission of HarperCollins Publishers.

Dagoberto Gilb, "Love in L.A." from *Magic Blood* (1993) is reprinted by permission of the author.

Allen Ginsberg, All lines from "A Supermarket in California" from *Collected Poems 1947-1980* by Allen Ginsberg. Copyright © 1955 by Allen Ginsberg. Reprinted by permission of HarperCollins Publishers.

Nikki Giovanni, "Nikki Rosa" from *Black Feeling, Black Talk, Black Judgment* by Nikki Giovanni. Copyright © 1968, 1970 by Nikki Giovanni. Reprinted by permission of HarperCollins Publishers.

Aracelis Girmay, "Consider the Hands That Write This Letter" from *Teeth* (Curbstone Press, 2007) is reprinted by permission of the publisher Northwestern University Press.

Diane Glancy, "Emigrant" from *Iron Woman.* Copyright © 1990 by Diane Glancy. Reprinted with the permission of New Rivers Press, www.newriverspress.com.

Ray González, "The Jalapeño Contest" from *The Ghost of John Wayne and Other Stories* by Ray González. Copyright © 2001 Ray González. Reprinted by permission of the University of Arizona Press. "Praise the

Tortilla, Praise Menudo, Praise Chorizo" from *The Heat of Arrivals*. Copyright © 1996 by Ray González. Reprinted with the permission of BOA Editions, Ltd., www.boaeditions.org.

Angelina Weld Grimké, "A Winter Twilight" from the Angelina Weld Grimké papers. Reprinted by permission of the Moorland-Spingarn Research Center, Howard University.

Ha Jin, "Saboteur" from *The Bridegroom* by Ha Jin, copyright © 2000 by Ha Jin. Used by permission of Pantheon Books, a division of Random House, Inc.

Kimiko Hahn, "Mother's Mother" from *Volatile*. Copyright © 1999 by Kimiko Hahn. Reprinted by permission of Hanging Loose Press.

Lorraine Hansberry, *A Raisin in the Sun* by Lorraine Hansberry, copyright © 1958 by Robert Nemiroff, as an unpublished work. Copyright © 1959, 1966, 1984 by Robert Nemiroff. Copyright renewed 1986, 1987 by Robert Nemiroff. Used by permission of Random House, Inc.

Joy Harjo, "She Had Some Horses" from *She Had Some Horses*. Copyright © 2006. Reprinted by permission of the author.

Michael S. Harper, "Nightmare Begins Responsibility" from *Songlines in Michael Tree: New and Collected Poems*. Copyright © 2000 by Michael S. Harper. Used with permission of the poet and the University of Illinois Press.

Robert Hayden, "Those Winter Sundays," copyright © 1966 by Robert Hayden, from *Angle of Ascent: New and Selected Poems* by Robert Hayden. Used by permission of Liveright Publishing Corporation.

Terrance Hayes, "Talk" from *Wind in a Box* by Terrance Hayes, copyright © 2006 by Terrance Hayes. Used by permission of Penguin, a division of Penguin Group (USA), Inc.

Samuel Hazo, "For Fawzi in Jerusalem" in *Blood Rights*. Copyright © 1968. Reprinted by permission of the author.

Seamus Heaney, "Mid-Term Break" from *Opened Ground: Selected Poems 1966–1996* by Seamus Heaney. Copyright © 1998 by Seamus Heaney. Reprinted by permission of Farrar, Straus and Giroux, LLC and Faber & Faber Ltd.

Ernest Hemingway, "Hills Like White Elephants" reprinted with the permission of Scribner, an imprint of Simon & Schuster Adult Publishing Group, from *The Short Stories of Ernest Hemingway* by Ernest Hemingway. Copyright © 1927 by Charles Scribner's Sons. Copyright © renewed 1955 by Ernest Hemingway. All rights reserved.

Lance Henson, "vision song" from *another song for america* is reprinted by permission of the author.

David Hernandez, "The Butterfly Effect" in *A House Waiting for Music* by David Hernandez. Copyright © 2003. Reprinted by permission of Tupelo Press.

Bob Hicok, "In the loop" from *Words for Empty and Words for Full* by Bob Hicok, copyright © 2010. Reprinted by permission of the University of Pittsburgh Press.

Tomson Highway, "Interview with Sherman Alexie." Originally published in *Aboriginal Voices*, 4.1, Jan./Feb./March 1997. Reprinted by permission of Tomson Highway.

Jane Hirshfield, "To Drink" from *Of Gravity and Angels*, copyright © 1988 by Jane Hirshfield. Reprinted by permission of Wesleyan University Press.

Tony Hoagland, "History of Desire" from *Sweet Ruin*, copyright © 1993 by the Board of Regents of the University of Wisconsin System. Reprinted by permission of The University of Wisconsin Press.

Linda Hogan, "Crow Law" from *The Book of Medicines*. Copyright © 1993 by Linda Hogan. Reprinted with the permission of Coffee House Press, www.coffeehousepress.org.

Garrett Kaoru Hongo, "Yellow Light" by Garrett Kaoru Hongo from *Yellow Light*. Copyright © 1982 by Garrett Kaoru Hongo. Reprinted by permission of Wesleyan University Press.

Langston Hughes, "Harlem (2)" and "The Negro Speaks of Rivers" from *The Collected Poems of Langston Hughes* by Langston Hughes, edited by Arnold Rampersad with David Roessel, Associate Editor, copyright © 1994 by The Estate of Langston Hughes. Used by permission of Alfred Knopf, a division of Random House, Inc. "Thank You, M'am" from *Short Stories* by Langston Hughes. Copyright © 1996 by Ramona Bass and Arnold Rampersad. Reprinted by permission of Hill and Wang, a division of Farrar, Straus and Giroux, LLC.

David Henry Hwang, "As the Crow Flies" from *Between Worlds: Contemporary Asian-American Plays*, edited by Misha Berson, was originally produced by the Los Angeles Theatre Center in 1985 and directed by Reza Abdoh. Copyright © David Henry Hwang. Reprinted by permission of Paradigm Agency.

Henrik Ibsen, "A Doll House," from *The Complete Major Prose Plays of Henrik Ibsen* by Henrik Ibsen, translated by Rolf Fjelde, copyright © 1965, 1970, 1978 by Rolf Fjelde. Used by permission of Dutton Signet, a division of Penguin Group (USA), Inc.

David Ives, "Sure Thing" from *All The Timing: Fourteen Plays*. Copyright © 1989, 1990, 1992 by David Ives. Used by permission of Vintage Books, a division of Random House, Inc.

Randall Jarrell, "The Death of the Ball Turret Gunner" from *The Complete Poems* by Randall Jarrell. Copyright © 1969, renewed 1997 by Mary von S. Jarrell. Reprinted by permission of Farrar, Straus and Giroux, LLC.

Honorée Fanonne Jeffers, "Unidentified Female Student, Former Slave (Talladega College, circa 1885)" from *Outlandish Blues*, copyright © 2003 by Honorée Fanonne Jeffers. Reprinted by permission of Wesleyan University Press.

Georgia Douglas Johnson, "Wishes" from *Crisis* magazine, April 1927. Copyright 1927. Reprinted by permission of Crisis Publishing Co., Inc., We wish to thank the Crisis Publishing Co., Inc., the publisher of the magazine of the National Association for the Advancement of Colored People, for the use of this material.

Helene Johnson, "Sonnet to a Negro in Harlem" is reprinted from *This Waiting for Love*, edited by Verner D. Mitchell. Copyright © 2000 by Verner D. Mitchell and published by the University of Massachusetts Press.

Richard Jones, *"OED"* from *The Correct Spelling & Exact Meaning*. Copyright © 2010 by Richard Jones. Reprinted with the permission of Copper Canyon Press, www.coppercanyonpress.org.

A. Van Jordan, "From" from *M-A-C-N-O-L-I-A: Poems* by A. Van Jordan. Copyright © 2004 by A. Van Jordan. Used by permission of W. W. Norton & Company, Inc.

Allison Joseph, "On Being Told I Don't Speak Like a Black Person" from *Imitation of Life* by Allison Joseph. Copyright © 1999 by Allison Joseph. Reprinted by permission of Carnegie Mellon University Press.

Marilyn Kallet, from "The Art of Not Forgetting: An Interview with Judith Ortiz Cofer." Reprinted from *Prairie Schooner*, Volume 68, Issue #4 (Winter 1994) by permission of the University of Nebraska Press. Copyright © 1994 by the University of Nebraska Press.

Bel Kaufman, "Sunday in the Park" by Bel Kaufman from *PEN Short Story Collection* (Available Press, 1985) is reprinted by permission of the author.

Jane Kenyon, "A Boy Goes into the World "from *Collected Poems*. Copyright © 2005 by The Estate of Jane Kenyon. Reprinted with the permission of Graywolf Press, www.graywolfpress.org.

Bridget Kevane and Juanita Heredia, "The Poetic Truth: An Interview with Judith Ortiz Cofer" in *Latina Self Portraits* by Bridget Kevane and Juanita Heredia. Copyright © 2000 by the University of New Mexico Press.

Jamaica Kincaid, "Girl" from *At the Bottom of the River* by Jamaica Kincaid. Copyright © 1983 by Jamaica Kincaid. Reprinted by permission of Farrar, Straus and Giroux, LLC.

Etheridge Knight, "Hard Rock Returns to Prison from the Hospital for the Criminal Insane" from *The Essential Etheridge Knight* by Etheridge Knight, copyright © 1986. Used by permission of the University of Pittsburgh Press.

Ron Koertge, "Q and A" from *Geography of the Forehead*. Copyright © 2000 by Ron Koertge. Reprinted with the permission of the University of Arkansas Press, www.uapress.com.

Yusef Komunyakaa, "Facing It" by Yusef Komunyakaa from *Pleasure Dome: New and Collected Poems* (Wesleyan University Press, 2001). Copyright © 2001 by Yusef Komunyakaa and reprinted by permission of Wesleyan University Press.

Ted Kooser, "Student" from *Delights & Shadows*. Copyright © 2004 by Ted Kooser. Reprinted with the permission of Copper Canyon Press, www.coppercanyonpress.org.

Susan Koprince, "Baseball as History and Myth in August Wilson's *Fences*." Copyright © 2006 by Susan Koprince. Reprinted by permission of the author.

Missy Dehn Kubitschek, "August Wilson's Gender Lesson" from *May All Your Fences Have Gates: Essays on the Drama of August Wilson*, edited by Alan Nadel, pp. 183–199. Copyright © 1994 by Missy Dehn Kubitschek. Reprinted by permission of the author.

Maxine Kumin, "The Sound of Night" from *Halfway* by Maxine Kumin. Reprinted by permission of The Anderson Literary Agency, Inc.

Mark Lambeck, "Intervention" by Mark Lambeck is reprinted by permission of the author from *The Best 10-Minute Plays for 3 or More Actors*, edited by Lawrence Harbison (Smith & Kraus 2008).

Li-Young Lee, "Eating Alone" and "Visions and Interpretations" from *Rose*. Copyright © 1986 by Li-Young Lee. Reprinted with the permission of BOA Editions, Ltd., www.boaeditions.org.

Denise Levertov, "Leaving Forever" by Denise Levertov from *Poems 1960-1967*, copyright © 1964 by Denise Levertov. "Talking to Grief," from *Poems 1972-1982*, copyright © 1978 by Denise Levertov. Reprinted by permission of New Directions Publishing Corporation.

Philip Levine, "What Work Is" from *What Work Is* by Philip Levine, copyright © 1991 by Philip Levine. Used by permission of Alfred A. Knopf, a division of Random House, Inc.

Larry Levis, "The Poem You Asked For" from *Wrecking Crew* by Larry Levis, copyright © 1972. Reprinted by permission of the University of Pittsburgh Press.

Miles Marshall Lewis, "Talks with August Wilson" from *The Believer Book of Writers Talking to Writers*, edited by Vendela Vida. Copyright © 2005 by Vendela Vida. Reprinted by permission.

Yiyun Li, "The Princess of Nebraska" from *A Thousand Years of Good Prayers* by Yiyun Li, copyright © 2005 by Yiyun Li. Used by permission of Random House, Inc.

Lorraine M. Lopez, excerpts from "Possibilities for Salsa Music in the Mainstream: An Interview with Judith Ortiz Cofer" is reprinted from *Crab Orchard Review*, Fall 1999, with permission of the author.

Audre Lorde, "Hanging Fire" Copyright © 1978 by Audre Lorde, from *The Collected Poems of Audre Lorde* by Audre Lorde. Used by permission of W. W. Norton & Company.

Robert Lowell, "Skunk Hour" from *Collected Poems* by Robert Lowell. Copyright © 2003 by Harriet Lowell and Sheridan Lowell. Reprinted by permission of Farrar, Straus, and Giroux, LLC.

Bonnie Lyons, "An Interview with August Wilson," first published in *Contemporary Literature*, 40.1 (Spring 1999):1-21. Copyright © 1999 by Bonnie Lyons. Reprinted by permission.

Eduardo Machado, "Crossing the Border" from *The Best 10-Minute Plays for 2 or More Actors*, edited by Lawrence Harbison (Smith & Kraus, 2009) is reprinted by permission of Beacon Artists Agency.

Richard McGuire, "Here" by Richard McGuire from *An Anthology of Graphic Fiction, Cartoons & True Stories* (Yale 2006), edited by Ivan Brunetti, is reprinted by permission of the author. Copyright © 1989 by Richard McGuire.

Heather McHugh, "What He Thought" by Heather McHugh, from *Hinge and Sin: Poems 1968–1993*. Copyright © 1994 by Heather McHugh and reprinted by permission of Wesleyan University Press.

David Means, "The Secret Goldfish" from *The Secret Goldfish*. Copyright © 2004 by David Means. Reprinted by permission of HarperCollins Publishers, Ltd.

Katherine Min, "Courting a Monk" was first published in *Triquarterly Review*, 95, Winter 1995/1996, pp. 101–113. Copyright © 1995 by Katherine Min. Reprinted by permission of the author.

Gary Miranda, "Love Poem" from *Grace Period*. Copyright © 1983 Princeton University Press. Reprinted by permission of Princeton University Press.

Marianne Moore, "Poetry" (1967 version) and "Poetry" (original) reprinted with the permission of Scribner, a division of Simon & Schuster, Inc. from *The Collected Poems of Marianne Moore* by Marianne Moore. Copyright 1935 by Marianne Moore; renewed 1963, 1967 by Marianne Moore and T. S. Eliot. All rights reserved.

Pat Mora, "La Migra" from *Aqua Santa/Holy Water*, copyright © 1995 by Pat Mora. Reprinted by permission of Curtis Brown, Ltd.

Toni Morrison, "Recitatif," copyright © 1983 by Toni Morrison. Reprinted by permission of International Creative Management, Inc.

Thylias Moss, "Rush Hour" from *Small Congregations* (Ecco Press, 2003) is reprinted by permission of the author.

Bharati Mukherjee, "The Management of Grief" from *The Middleman and Other Stories*, copyright © 1988 by Bharati Mukherjee. Used by permission of Grove/Atlantic, Inc. and Penguin Group (Canada).

David Mura, "Grandfather-in-Law" from *After We Lost Our Way* by David Mura. Copyright © 1989 by David Mura. Reprinted by permission of the author.

Haruki Murakami, "Birthday Girl" translated by Jay Rubin, copyright © 2006 by Haruki Murakami, from *Blind Willow, Sleeping Woman: Twenty-Four Stories* by Haruki Murakami, translated by Philip Gabriel & Jay Rubin. Used by permission of Alfred A. Knopf, a division of Random House, Inc.

Marilyn Nelson, "Minor Miracle" from *The Fields of Praise* is reprinted by permission of Louisiana State University Press.

Lorine Niedecker, "My Life by Water" from *The Granite Pail*. Copyright © 1985 by Lorine Niedecker. Reprinted by permission of Bob Arnold, Literary Executor of The Estate of Lorine Niedecker.

Don Nigro, "Letters from Quebec to Providence in the Rain" from *The Best 10-Minute Plays for 2 or More Actors*, edited by Lawrence Harbison (2009). Professionals and amateurs are hereby warned that "Letters from Quebec to Providence in the Rain," being fully protected under the copyright laws of the United States of America, the British Commonwealth countries, including Canada, and the other countries of the Copyright Union, is subject to a royalty. All rights, including professional, amateur, motion picture, recitation, public reading, radio, television and cable broadcasting, and the rights of translation into foreign languages are strictly reserved. Any inquiry regarding the availability of performance rights, or the purchase of individual copies of the authorized acting edition must be directed to Samuel French, Inc., 45 West 25 Street, New York, NY 10010.

Naomi Shihab Nye, "The Small Vases from Hebron" from *Fuel*. Copyright © 1998 by Naomi Shihab Nye. Reprinted with permission of BOA Editions, Ltd., www.boaeditions.org.

Åse Nygren, "A World of Story-Smoke: A Conversation with Sherman Alexie" from *MELUS*, Volume 30, Number 4 (Winter 2005). Copyright © 2005 by MELUS. Reprinted by permission of MELUS: The Journal of the Society for the Study of Multi-Ethnic Literature of the United States.

Joyce Carol Oates, "Where Are You Going? Where Have You Been?" by Joyce Carol Oates, Copyright © 1970 Ontario Review, Inc. Reprinted by permission of John Hawkins & Associates, Inc. "When I Was a Little Girl and My Mother Didn't Want Me" by Joyce Carol Oates. Copyright © 1998 by Ontario Review, Inc. All rights reserved. Rights inquiries should be directed to Phyllis Wender, Gersh Agency, 41 Madison Ave., New York, NY 10010.

Tim O'Brien, "The Things They Carried" from *The Things They Carried* by Tim O'Brien, Copyright © 1990 by Tim O'Brien. Reprinted by permission of Houghton Mifflin Harcourt Publishing Company. All rights reserved.

Rafael Ocasio and Rita Ganey, "Speaking in Puerto Rican: An Interview with Judith Ortiz Cofer" by Rafael Ocasio and Rita Ganey from *Bilingual Review/Editorial Bilingüe*, May–Aug. 1992, 17, Issue # 2. Reprinted by permission of Bilingual Press/Editorial Bilingüe.

Flannery O'Connor, "A Good Man Is Hard to Find" from *A Good Man Is Hard to Find and Other Stories*, copyright 1953 by Flannery O'Connor and renewed 1981 by Regina O'Connor, reprinted by permission of Houghton Mifflin Harcourt Publishing Company.

Sharon Olds, "I Go Back to May 1937" from *The Gold Cell* by Sharon Olds, copyright © 1987 by Sharon Olds. Used by permission of Alfred A. Knopf, a division of Random House, Inc.

Tillie Olsen, "I Stand Here Ironing" from *Tell Me a Riddle*. Copyright © 1956, 1957, 1960, 1961 by Tillie Olsen. Reprinted by permission of the Elaine Markson Literary Agency, Inc.

Mary Oliver, "First Snow" from *American Primitive* by Mary Oliver, Copyright © 1983 by Mary Oliver. By permission of Little, Brown and Company.

Michael Oppenheimer, "The Paring Knife" by Michael Oppenheimer, first published in *Sundog*, Volume 4, Number 1 (1982) is reprinted by permission of the author.

Simon J. Ortiz, "Speaking" from *Woven Stone* by Simon J. Ortiz. Copyright © 1992 by Simon J. Ortiz. Reprinted by permission of the author.

ZZ Packer, "Brownies" from *Drinking Coffee Elsewhere* by ZZ Packer, copyright © 2003 by ZZ Packer. Used by permission of Riverhead Books, an imprint of Penguin Group (USA), Inc.

Dorothy Parker, "Resumé" copyright © 1926, 1928, renewed 1954 © 1956 by Dorothy Parker, from *The Portable Dorothy Parker*, edited by Marion Meade. Used by permission of Viking Penguin, a division of Penguin Group (USA), Inc.

Suzan-Lori Parks, From *365 Days/365 Plays*. Copyright © 2006 by Suzan-Lori Parks. Published by Theatre Communications Group. Used by permission of Theatre Communications Group.

Linda Pastan, "love poem" from *The Imperfect Paradise* by Linda Pastan. Copyright © 1988 by Linda Pastan. Used by permission of W. W. Norton & Company, Inc.

Marge Piercy, "Barbie Doll," from *Circles on the Water* by Marge Piercy, copyright © 1982 by Marge Piercy. Used by permission of Alfred A. Knopf, a division of Random House, Inc.

Robert Pinsky, "Shirt" from *The Want Bone* by Robert Pinsky. Copyright © 1990 by Robert Pinsky. Reprinted by permission of HarperCollins Publishers.

Sylvia Plath, All lines from "Metaphors" from *Crossing the Water* by Sylvia Plath. Copyright © 1960 by Ted Hughes. All lines from "Daddy" from *Ariel* by Sylvia Plath. Copyright © 1963 by Ted Hughes. Reprinted by permission of HarperCollins Publishers and Faber and Faber, Ltd.

Katherine Anne Porter, "The Jilting of Granny Weatherall" from *Flowering Judas and Other Stories*, copyright 1930 and renewed 1958 by Katherine Anne Porter. Used with the permission of Houghton Mifflin Harcourt Publishing Company.

Ezra Pound, "In a Station of the Metro" by Ezra Pound, from *Personae*, copyright © 1926 by Ezra Pound. Reprinted by permission of New Directions Publishing Corporation.

A. K. Ramanujan, "Self-Portrait" from *The Striders: Poems*. Copyright © 1966 by A. K. Ramnujan. Reprinted by permission of Oxford University Press.

Marco Ramirez, *I Am Not Batman*. Copyright © 2007 by Marco Ramirez. All rights reserved. Reprinted by permission of Playscripts, Inc. To purchase acting editions of this play, or to obtain stock and amateur performance rights, you must contact: Playscripts, Inc. Website: http://www.playscripts.com. e-mail: info@playscripts.com. Phone: 1-866-NEW-PLAY (639-7529).

Dudley Randall, "The Ballad of Birmingham" from *Roses and Revolutions: The Selected Writings of Dudley Randall*, edited by Melba Joyce Boyd (Wayne State University Press, 2009). Reprinted by permission of the Dudley Randall Literary Estate.

Henry Reed, "Naming of Parts" from *Collected Poems* of Henry Reed, edited by Jon Stallworthy (2007), is reprinted by permission of Carcanet Press Ltd.

Adrienne Rich, "Rape," copyright © 2002 by Adrienne Rich. Copyright © 1973 by W. W. Norton & Company, Inc. from *The Fact of a Doorframe: Selected Poems 1950-2001* by Adrienne Rich. Used by permission of the author and W. W. Norton & Company, Inc.

Frank Rich, "Family Ties in Wilson's *Fences*," from *The New York Times*, March 27, 1987. Copyright ©1987 by *The New York Times*. All rights reserved. Used by permission and protected by the Copyright Laws of the United States. The printing, copyright, redistribution, or retransmission of the material without express written permission is prohibited.

Lloyd Richards, "Introduction," from *Fences* by August Wilson, copyright © 1986 by Lloyd Richards, copyright © 1986 by August Wilson. Reprinted by permission of Dutton Signet, a division of Penguin Group (USA), Inc.

Jack Ridl, "First Cut" from *Losing Season* (CavanKerry Press Ltd., 2009) is reprinted by permission of the publisher.

Alberto Ríos, "Nani" from *Whispering to Fool the Wind*. Copyright © 1982 by Alberto Ríos. Reprinted by permission of the author.

Luis J. Rodriguez, "Running to America" from *Poems across the Pavement*. Copyright © 1998 by Luis J. Rodriguez. Published by Tia Chucha Press. By permission of Susan Bergholz Literary Services, New York, NY and Lamy, NM. All rights reserved.

Theodore Roethke, "My Papa's Waltz," copyright 1942 by Hearst Magazines, Inc., from *Collected Poems of Theodore Roethke* by Theordore Roethke. Used by permission of Doubleday, a division of Random House.

Wendy Rose, "Loo-Wit" from *The Halfbreed Chronicles*. Copyright © 1985 by Wendy Rose. Reprinted by permission of the author.

Mary Ruefle, "Barbarians" from *Life without Speaking* by Mary Ruefle (University of Alabama Press, 1987) is reprinted by permission of the author.

Carl Sandburg, "Fog" from *Chicago Poems* by Carl Sandburg, copyright © 1916 by Holt, Rinehart and Winston and renewed 1944 by Carl Sandburg, reprinted by permission of Houghton Mifflin Harcourt Publishing Company.

Marjane Satrapi, "The Cigarette" from *Persepolis: The Story of a Childhood* by Marjane Satrapi, translated by Mattias Ripa & Blake Ferris. Copyright © 2003 by L'Association, Paris, France. Used by permission of Pantheon Books, a division of Random House, Inc.

Cheryl Savageau, "Bones—A City Poem" from *Home Country* (Alice James Books, 1992) is reprinted by permission of the author.

William Shakespeare, Notes to "Othello, the Moor of Venice" from *The Complete Works of Shakespeare*, 3rd edition, by David Bevington. Copyright © 1980 by Scott, Foresman and Company. Reprinted by permission of Pearson Education, Inc.

Leslie Marmon Silko, "The Man to Send Rain Clouds," copyright © 1969 by Leslie Marmon Silko and "Prayer to the Pacific," copyright © 1981 by Leslie Marmon Silko. Used with permission of The Wylie Agency LLC.

Charles Simic, "Classic Ballroom Dances" from *Selected Poems: 1963–1983* (New York: George Braziller, Inc.). Copyright © 1983. Reprinted by permission of the publisher.

Cathy Song, "Heaven" from *Frameless Windows, Squares of Light: Poems* by Cathy Song. Copyright © 1988 by Cathy Song. Used by permission of W. W. Norton & Company, Inc.

Sophocles, "Antigone" from *Three Theban Plays* by Sophocles, copyright © 1982 by Robert Fagles. Used by permission of Viking Penguin, a division of Penguin Group (USA), Inc.

Gary Soto, "Moving Away" from *New and Selected Poems*, copyright © 1995 by Gary Soto. Used with permission of Chronicle Books LLC, San Francisco. Visit ChronicleBooks.com.

Art Spiegelman, from *Maus 1: A Survivor's Tale/My Father Bleeds History*, copyright © 1973, 1980, 1981, 1982, 1984, 1985, 1986 by Art Spiegelman. Used by permission of Pantheon Books, a division of Random House, Inc.

William Stafford, "Traveling through the Dark" from *The Way It Is: New and Selected Poems*. Copyright © 1962, 1980, 1998 by William Stafford and the Estate of William Stafford. Reprinted with the permission of Graywolf Press, Minneapolis, Minnesota, www.graywolfpress.org.

John Steinbeck, "The Chrysanthemums," copyright 1937, renewed © 1965 by John Steinbeck, from *The Long Valley* by John Steinbeck. Used by permission of Viking Penguin, a division of Penguin Group (USA), Inc.

Gerald Stern, "The Dog" from *Lovesick: Poems* by Gerald Stern. Copyright © 1987 by Gerald Stern. Reprinted by permission of HarperCollins Publishers.

Wallace Stevens, "Anecdote of the Jar" from *The Collected Poems of Wallace Stevens*, copyright 1954 by Wallace Stevens and renewed 1982 by Holly Stevens. Used by permission of Alfred A. Knopf, a division of Random House, Inc.

Mark Strand, "Eating Poetry" from *Selected Poems* by Mark Strand, copyright © 1979, 1980 by Mark Strand. Used by permission of Alfred A. Knopf, a division of Random House, Inc.

Kelly Stuart, "The New New" first published in *The Best 10-Minute Plays for Three or More Actors* (2004), editors Michael Bigelow and Liz Engelman is reprinted by permission of the author. Copyright © 2003 by Kelly Stuart.

Virgil Suárez, "Tea Leaves, *Caracoles*, Coffee Beans" from *90 Miles: Selected and New Poems* by Virgil Suárez, copyright © 2005. Reprinted by permission of the University of Pittsburgh Press.

Sekou Sundiata, "Blink Your Eyes" by Sekou Sundiata is reprinted by permission of the Estate of Robert Feaster.ar

May Swenson, "The Shape of Death" is reprinted with permission of the Literary Estate of May Swenson. All rights reserved.

Arthur Sze, "The Shapes of Leaves" from *The Redshifting Web: Poems 1970–1998* by Arthur Sze. Copyright © 1994 by Arthur Sze. Reprinted with the permission of Copper Canyon Press, www.coppercanyonpress.org.

Mary Tallmountain, "Matmiya" from *The Light on the Tent Wall: A Bridging* (1990): 84. Reprinted by permission of the American Indian Studies Center, UCLA. Copyright © 1990 Regents of the University of California.

Amy Tan, "Two Kinds" from *The Joy Luck Club* by Amy Tan, copyright © 1989 by Amy Tan. Used by permission of G. P. Putnam's Sons, a division of Penguin Group (USA), Inc.

Dylan Thomas, "Do not go gentle into that good night" by Dylan Thomas, from *The Poems of Dylan Thomas*, copyright © 1952 by Dylan Thomas. Reprinted by permission of New Directions Publishing Corporation.

Jean Toomer, "Face" from *Cane*, copyright © 1923 by Boni & Liveright, renewed 1951 by Jean Toomer. Used by permission of Liveright Publishing Corporation.

Natasha Trethewey, "History Lesson" from *Domestic Work*. Copyright © 2009 by Natasha Trethewey. Reprinted with the permission of Graywolf Press, www.graywolfpress.org.

Quincy Troupe, "A Poem for 'Magic'" from *Avalanche*. Copyright © 1996 by Quincy Troupe. Reprinted with the permission of Coffee House Press, www.coffeehousepress.com.

John Updike, "A & P" from *Pigeon Feathers and Other Stories* by John Updike, copyright © 1962 and renewed 1990 by John Updike. Used by permission of Alfred A. Knopf, a division of Random House, Inc.

Helena María Viramontes, "The Moths" is reprinted with permission from the publisher of *The Moths and Other Stories*. Copyright © 1995 Arte Público Press–University of Houston.

Alice Walker, "The Flowers" and "Everyday Use" from *In Love and Trouble: Stories of Black Women*, copyright © 1973 by Alice Walker, reprinted by permission of Houghton Mifflin Harcourt Publishing Company.

James Welch, "Christmas Comes to Moccasin Flat" from *Riding the Earthboy 40* Copyright © 1971 by James Welch. Reprinted by permission of the Elaine Markson Literary Agency, Inc.

Patricia Jabbeh Wesley, "There's Nothing You Can Do" from *Where the Road Turns*. Copyright © 2010 by Patricia Jabbeh Wesley. Reprinted with the permission of Autumn House Press, www.autumnhouse.org.

Roberta Hill Whiteman, "The White Land" from *Star Quilt*. Copyright © 1984 by Roberta Hill Whiteman. Reprinted with permission of Holy Cow! Press, www.holycowpress.org.

Richard Wilbur, "Love Calls Us to the Things of This World" from *Things of This World*, copyright © 1956 and renewed 1984 by Richard Wilbur, reprinted by permission of Houghton Mifflin Harcourt Publishing Company.

Nancy Willard, "Questions My Son Asked Me, Answers I Never Gave Him" from *Household Tales of Moon and Water*, copyright © 1978 by Nancy Willard, reprinted by permission of Houghton Mifflin Harcourt Publishing Company.

Tennessee Williams, "This Property Is Condemned" from *27 Wagons Full of Cotton*, copyright © 1945 by The University of the South. Reprinted by permission of New Directions Publishing Corporation.

William Carlos Williams, "The Red Wheelbarrow" and "Spring and All, Section 1" by William Carlos Williams, from *Collected Poems: 1909–1939, Volume I*, copyright © 1938 by New Directions Publishing Corporation. Reprinted by permission of New Directions Publishing Corporation.

August Wilson, "Fences" from *Fences* by August Wilson, copyright © 1986 by August Wilson. "Introduction" by Lloyd Richards, copyright © 1986 by Lloyd Richards. Used by permission of Dutton Signet, a division of Penguin Group (USA), Inc.

James Wright, "A Blessing" from *The Branch Will Not Break* by James Wright. Copyright © 1963 by James Wright. Reprinted by permission of Wesleyan University Press.

John Yau, "Chinese Villanelle" from *Radiant Silhouette: New and Selected Work 1974–1988*. Copyright © 1988 by John Yau. Reprinted by permission of the author.

Al Young, "A Dance for Ma Rainey," copyright © 1968, 1992, and 2007 by Al Young. Reprinted by permission of the author.

Ray A. Young Bear, "Green Threatening Clouds" from *The Invisible Musician*. Copyright © 1990 by Ray A. Young Bear. Reprinted with the permission of Holy Cow! Press, www.holycowpress.org.

Paul Zimmer, "Zimmer's Head Thudding against the Blackboard" is reprinted by permission of the author. Copyright by Paul Zimmer.

PHOTO AND ART CREDITS

Page 1: Photo of Julia Alvarez reprinted by permission of Cameron Davidson.
Pages 22, 31: Photo of Kortney DeVito courtesy of Kortney DeVito.
Page 28: Photo of Annie Otto courtesy of Annie Otto.
Page 32: Brainstorm clustering courtesy of Annie Otto.
Page 59: Photo of Kristina Martinez courtesy of Kristina Martinez.
Page 60: Screenshot reprinted by permission of Hope College Libraries.
Page 62: Screenshot reprinted by permission of the Modern Language Association.
Page 63: Screenshot reprinted courtesy of ITHAKA. ©2010 ITHAKA. All rights reserved.
Page 64: Image published with permission of ProQuest. Further reproduction is prohibited without permission.
Page 66: Screenshot reprinted by permission of Alan Liu, University of California, Santa Barbara.
Page 105: Photo of James Baldwin Copyright © Bettmann/Corbis.
Page 126: Photo of Louise Erdrich Copyright © Ulf Anderson/Getty Images.
Page 155: Photo of Lynda Barry Copyright © Guillaume Paumier/Wikimedia Commons, CC-by-sa
Page 160: Photo of Sandra Cisneros Copyright © Ulf Andersen/Getty Images.
Page 169: Photo of Alice Walker Copyright © Harcourt Brace/Getty Images.
Page 177: Photo of William Faulkner Copyright © Carl Mydans/Time Life Pictures/Getty.
Page 196: Photo of Ernest Hemingway Copyright © Bettmann/Corbis.
Page 247: Photo of Katherine Min by Julie Mento, courtesy of the New Hampshire State Council on the Arts.
Page 266: Photo of Alicia Abood courtesy of Alicia Abood.
Page 278: Photo of Sherman Alexie Copyright © Rob Casey.
Page 279: Photo from *Smoke Signals* Copyright © Miramax Films/Jill Sabella/Everett Collection. Reprinted by permission.
Page 280: Photo of Sherman Alexie Copyright © AP/Wide World Photos/Seth Wenig.
Page 563: Photo of Naomi Shihab Nye reprinted by permission of Ha Lam.
Page 574: Photo of Gwendolyn Brooks Copyright © Bettmann/Corbis.
Page 589: Photo of Cathy Song Copyright © John Eddy.
Page 596: Photo of Li-Young Lee Copyright © Paul Elledge Photography.

Page 607: Photo of Sekou Sundiata Copyright © Andrew Savulich/NY Daily News Archive via Getty Images.
Page 615: Photo of Jane Kenyon Copyright © Donald Hall.
Page 640: Photo of William Stafford courtesy of Kim Stafford.
Page 662: Photo of Lucille Clifton Copyright © AP/Wide World Photos.
Page 666: Photo of Robert Frost Copyright ©Lofman/Pix Inc./Time Life Pictures/Getty Images.
Page 691: Photo of Joy Harjo Copyright © Paul Abdoo/MPI/Getty Images.
Page 697: Photo of E. E. Cummings Copyright © The Granger Collection, New York.
Page 707: Photo of Sunkyo Hong courtesy of Sunkyo Hong.
Page 721: The book cover of "Silent Dancing" is reprinted with permission from the publisher of "Silent Dancing" by Judith Ortiz Cofer (© 1991 Arte Público Press–University of Houston).
Page 722: Portrait of Judith Ortiz Cofer Copyright © University of Georgia, Peter Frey.
Page 767: Painting "Landscape with the Fall of Icarus" by Pieter Brueghel the Elder reprinted by permission of Scala/Art Resource, NY.
Page 784: Photo of Billy Collins Copyright © Lynn Goldsmith/Corbis.
Page 795: Photo of Rita Dove Copyright © Christopher Felver/Corbis.
Page 865: Photo of Gary Soto used by permission of Gary Soto.
Page 873: Photo of Dylan Thomas Copyright © Rue des Archives/ The Granger Collection, New York.
Page 880: Photo of Nancy Willard Copyright © Eric Lindbloom.
Page 889: Photo of David Henry Hwang Copyright © Michael Romanos, www.MichaelRomanos.com.
Page 909: Photo of Eduardo Machado Copyright © Austin Irving.
Page 922: Photo of Susan Glaspell Copyright © The Granger Collection, New York.
Page 949: Photo of Julian Hinson courtesy of Julian Hinson.
Page 960: Photo of August Wilson performing Copyright © E. Pablo Kosmicki/AP/Wide World Photos. Photo of August Wilson in front of Ann's Restaurant in Boston Copyright © by Michael Romanos, www.MichaelRomanos.com.
Page 961: Photo of James Earl Jones Copyright © Photofest, Inc.
Page 962: Photo of Lynn Thigpen and James Earl Jones Copyright © Photofest, Inc.
Page 1091: Photo of Marco Ramirez Copyight © George Shiavone.
Page 1099: Classical Greek Theater drawing. (McGowan & Melnitz, The Living Stage: A History of the World Theater, illustration of a classical Greek theatre by Gerda Becker, p. 148, © 1982. Reproduced by permission of Pearson Education, Inc.).
Page 1145: A Conjectural Reconstruction of the Globe Theatre, 1599–1613. (Drawing by C. Walter Hodges from his Globe Restored, published by Oxford University Press © 1968 C. Walter Hodges. Reprinted with permission of Oxford University Press.)
Page 1149: Photo of William Shakespeare Copyright © Nathan Benn/Corbis.
Page 1300: Photo of Lorraine Hansberry Copyright © Bettmann/Corbis.

Index of Authors and Titles

A & P, 552
Accident (Davis), 315
Accident (Eggers), 787
adam and eve, 758
After Apple-Picking, 803
AI
  Why Can't I Leave You?, 761
ALEXIE, SHERMAN
  The Lone Ranger and Tonto Fistfight in
    Heaven, 291
  Superman and Me, 4
  This Is What It Means to Say Phoenix,
    Arizona, 282
ALI, AGHA SHAHID
  I Dream It Is Afternoon When I Return
    to Delhi, 762
ALLEN, WOODY
  Death Knocks, 1066
ALLENDE, ISABEL
  And of Clay Are We Created, 355
ALVAREZ, JULIA
  Daughter of Invention, 10
  How I Learned to Sweep, 647
And Are You a Latina Writer?, 738
And of Clay Are We Created, 355
Anecdote of the Jar, 866
ANONYMOUS
  Sir Patrick Spens, 763
  Western Wind, 758
Antigone, 1103
Approximate Size of His Favorite Humor,
    The: Sherman Alexie's Comic
    Connections and Disconnections in
    The Lone Ranger and Tonto Fistfight in
    Heaven, 300

Araby, 242
Art of Not Forgetting, The: An Interview with
    Judith Ortiz Cofer, 744
As the Crow Flies, 1073
at the cemetery, walnut grove plantation,
    south carolina, 1989, 662
ATWOOD, MARGARET
  True Stories, 764
  you fit into me, 758
AUDEN, W. H.
  Musée des Beaux Arts, 767
August Wilson, 1034
August Wilson's Gender Lesson, 1029

BACA, JIMMY SANTIAGO
  Family Ties, 768
BALDWIN, JAMES
  Sonny's Blues, 362
Ballad of Birmingham, 853
BAMBARA, TONI CADE
  The Lesson, 208
Barbarians, 760
Barbie Doll, 604
BARNES, CLIVE
  Fiery Fences: A Review, 1019
BARNES, JIM
  Return to La Plata, Missouri, 769
BARRY, LYNDA
  Today's Demon: Magic, 150
Baseball as History and Myth in August
    Wilson's Fences, 1038
Battle Royal, 402
Bean Eaters, The, 574
BEATTIE, ANN
  Snow, 314

Because I could not stop for Death, 790
BERRY, WENDELL
    The Peace of Wild Things, 588
Birches, 804
Birthday Girl, 471
Birthplace, The, 726
BISHOP, ELIZABETH
    In the Waiting Room, 770
    Sestina, 699
BLAKE, WILLIAM
    The Chimney Sweeper, 772
Blessing, A, 690
Blink Your Eyes, 607
BLUE CLOUD, PETER
    Crazy Horse Monument, 863
BOLAND, EAVAN
    The Pomegranate, 773
Bones — A City Poem, 883
Boy Goes into the World, A, 616
BRADSTREET, ANNE
    To My Dear and Loving Husband, 774
Break of Day, 793
BROOKS, GWENDOLYN
    The Bean Eaters, 574
    We Real Cool, 675
BROUMAS, OLGA
    Cinderella, 775
BROWN, STERLING A.
    Riverbank Blues, 776
Brownies, 512
BROWNING, ELIZABETH BARRETT
    How do I love thee? Let me count the
        ways, 777
BROWNING, ROBERT
    My Last Duchess, 622
BRUTUS, DENNIS
    Nightsong: City, 633
Buffalo Bill 's, 655
BUKOWSKI, CHARLES
    my old man, 598
Butterfly Effect, The, 806

CARSON, JO
    I Cannot Remember All the Times . . . ,
        777
CARVER, RAYMOND
    What We Talk about When We Talk
        about Love, 386
Cask of Amontillado, The, 528
CERVANTES, LORNA DEE
    Freeway 280, 663
CHANG, TINA
    Naming the Light, 779
Changeling, The, 725

Chimney Sweeper, The, 772
CHIN, MARILYN
    How I Got That Name, 780
Chinese Villanelle, 701
CHOPIN, KATE
    The Story of an Hour, 233
Christmas Comes to Moccasin Flat, 874
Chrysanthemums, The, 320
"Cigarette, The," from *Persepolis*, 185
Cinderella, 775
CISNEROS, SANDRA
    The House on Mango Street, 160
Classic Ballroom Dances, 864
CLIFTON, LUCILLE
    adam and eve, 758
    at the cemetery, walnut grove plantation,
        south carolina, 1989, 662
    homage to my hips, 782
Clothes, 328
COFER, JUDITH ORTIZ
    And Are You a Latina Writer?, 738
    The Birthplace, 726
    The Changeling, 725
    Cold as Heaven, 646
    First Job: The Southern Sweets Sandwich
        Shop and Bakery, 729
    The Latin Deli: An Ars Poetica, 727
    My Father in the Navy, 728
    Nada, 395
    On the Island I Have Seen, 726
    Silent Dancing, 731
Cold as Heaven, 646
COLERIDGE, SAMUEL TAYLOR
    Kubla Khan, 783
    Metrical Feet, 1425
COLLINS, BILLY
    I Chop Some Parsley While Listening to
        Art Blakey's Version of "Three Blind
        Mice," 785
Colonel, The, 801
Consider the Hands That Write This
    Letter, 810
COULOMBE, JOSEPH L.
    The Approximate Size of His Favorite
        Humor: Sherman Alexie's Comic
        Connections and Disconnections in
        *The Lone Ranger and Tonto Fistfight in
        Heaven*, 300
Courting a Monk, 247
COX, JAMES
    Muting White Noise: The Subversion of
        Popular Culture Narratives of
        Conquest in Sherman Alexie's
        Fiction, 305

Crazy Horse Monument, 863
Crossing the Border, 909
Crow Law, 822
CRUZ, VICTOR HERNÁNDEZ
    Problems with Hurricanes, 786
CULLEN, COUNTEE
    For a Lady I Know, 758
    Incident, 677
CUMMINGS, E. E.
    Buffalo Bill 's, 655
    "next to of course god america i, 697

Daddy, 851
Dance for Ma Rainey, A, 886
Daughter of Invention, 10
DAVIS, LYDIA
    What She Knew, 315
DAVIS, TODD
    Accident, 787
Death, be not proud, 793
Death Knocks, 1066
Death of the Ball Turret Gunner, The, 759
DENUCCIO, JEROME
    Slow Dancing with Skeletons: Sherman
        Alexie's *The Lone Ranger and Tonto
        Fistfight in Heaven*, 301
DERRICOTTE, TOI
    A Note on My Son's Face, 788
Design, 805
DICKINSON, EMILY
    Because I could not stop for Death,
        790
    I heard a Fly buzz, 790
    I like to see it lap the Miles, 1425
    I'm Nobody! Who are you?, 669
    It sifts from Leaden Sieves, 643
Director's Introduction, 1018
DIVAKARUNI, CHITRA BANERJEE
    Clothes, 328
    Nargis' Toilette, 791
Do not go gentle into that good night,
    873
Dog, The, 614
Doll House, A, 1245
DONNE, JOHN
    Break of Day, 793
    Death, be not proud, 793
DOTY, MARK
    Tiara, 794
DOVE, RITA
    Fifth Grade Autobiography, 795
Dulce et Decorum Est, 619
DUNBAR, PAUL LAURENCE
    We Wear the Mask, 659

EADY, CORNELIUS
    My Mother, If She Had Won Free Dance
        Lessons, 795
Eagle, The, 642
Eating Alone, 596
Eating Poetry, 867
EGGERS, DAVE
    Accident, 315
1864, A Pocket Full of Rye, 802
ELAM, HARRY J., JR.
    August Wilson, 1034
ELIOT, T. S.
    The Love Song of J. Alfred Prufrock, 797
ELLISON, RALPH
    Battle Royal, 402
EMERSON, GRAY
    The Indexer in Love, 800
Emigrant, 811
ENDREZZE, ANITA
    The Girl Who Loved the Sky, 586
ERDRICH, LOUISE
    The Red Convertible, 126
ESPADA, MARTÍN
    Latin Night at the Pawnshop, 628
Everyday Use, 169

Face, 874
Facing It, 620
Family Ties, 768
Family Ties in Wilson's *Fences*: A Review,
    1021
FARRELL, SUSAN
    Fight vs. Flight: A Re-evaluation of Dee
        in Alice Walker's "Everyday
        Use," 1436
Father Comes Home from the Wars (Part 1),
    1061
FAULKNER, WILLIAM
    A Rose for Emily, 176
Fences, 963
Fiery *Fences*: A Review, 1019
Fifth Grade Autobiography, 795
Fight vs. Flight: A Re-evaluation of Dee in
        Alice Walker's "Everyday Use," 1436
First Cut, 856
First Job: The Southern Sweets Sandwich
        Shop and Bakery, 729
First Snow, 644
Flowers, The, 20
Fog, 761
For a Lady I Know, 758
For Fawzi in Jerusalem, 817
FORCHÉ, CAROLYN
    The Colonel, 801

FRANCIS, VIEVEE
1864, A Pocket Full of Rye, 802
Freeway 280, 663
From, 828
FROST, ROBERT
After Apple-Picking, 803
Birches, 804
Design, 805
The Road Not Taken, 666

GALLAGHER, TESS
The Hug, 807
GARCIA, RICHARD
Why I Left the Church, 765
GARCÍA MÁRQUEZ, GABRIEL
A Very Old Man with Enormous Wings,
413
GILB, DAGOBERTO
Love in L.A., 113
GINSBERG, ALLEN
A Supermarket in California, 808
GIOVANNI, NIKKI
Nikki-Rosa, 809
Girl, 317
Girl Who Loved the Sky, The, 586
GIRMAY, ARACELIS
Consider the Hands That Write This
Letter, 810
GLANCY, DIANE
Emigrant, 811
GLASPELL, SUSAN
Trifles, 922
God's Grandeur, 682
GONZÁLEZ, RAY
The Jalapeño Contest, 316
Praise the Tortilla, Praise Menudo, Praise
Chorizo, 811
Good Man Is Hard to Find, A, 134
Grandfather-in-Law, 698
Green Threatening Clouds, 887
GRIMKÉ, ANGELINA WELD
A Winter Twilight, 635

HA JIN
Saboteur, 347
HAHN, KIMIKO
Mother's Mother, 812
Hanging Fire, 836
HANSBERRY, LORRAINE
A Raisin in the Sun, 1300
Hard Rock Returns to Prison from the
Hospital for the Criminal Insane,
831

HARDY, THOMAS
The Man He Killed, 814
HARJO, JOY
She Had Some Horses, 691
Harlem, 631
HARPER, MICHAEL S.
Nightmare Begins Responsibility,
815
HAWTHORNE, NATHANIEL
Young Goodman Brown, 337
HAYDEN, ROBERT
Those Winter Sundays, 572
HAYES, TERRANCE
Talk, 816
HAZO, SAMUEL
For Fawzi in Jerusalem, 817
HEANEY, SEAMUS
Mid-Term Break, 665
Heaven, 589
HEMINGWAY, ERNEST
Hills Like White Elephants, 196
HENSON, LANCE
song in january, 759
HERBERT, GEORGE
The Pulley, 818
Here, 223
HEREDIA, JUANITA
The Poetic Truth: An Interview with
Judith Ortiz Cofer, 751
HERNANDEZ, DAVID
The Butterfly Effect, 806
HERRICK, ROBERT
To the Virgins, to Make Much of Time,
819
HICOK, BOB
In the loop, 819
HIGHWAY, TOMSON
Interview with Sherman Alexie, 295
Hills Like White Elephants, 196
HIRSHFIELD, JANE
To Drink, 820
History Lesson, 585
History of Desire, 820
HOAGLAND, TONY
History of Desire, 820
HOGAN, LINDA
Crow Law, 822
homage to my hips, 782
HONGO, GARRETT KAORU
Yellow Light, 822
HOPKINS, GERARD MANLEY
God's Grandeur, 682
House on Mango Street, The, 160

HOUSMAN, A. E.
  To an Athlete Dying Young, 824
How do I love thee? Let me count the ways,
  777
How I Got That Name, 780
How I Learned to Sweep, 647
Hug, The, 807
HUGHES, LANGSTON
  Harlem, 631
  The Negro Speaks of Rivers, 826
  Thank You, M'am, 418
HURSTON, ZORA NEALE
  Sweat, 421
Hwang, David Henry
  As the Crow Flies, 1073

I Am Not Batman, 1090
I Cannot Remember All the Times . . . , 777
I Chop Some Parsley While Listening to Art
  Blakey's Version of "Three Blind
  Mice," 785
I Dream It Is Afternoon When I Return to
  Delhi, 762
I Go Back to May 1937, 848
I heard a Fly buzz, 790
I like to see it lap the Miles, 1425
I Stand Here Ironing, 506
IBSEN, HENRIK
  A Doll House, 1245
If we must die, 694
I'm Nobody! Who are you?, 669
In a Station of the Metro, 760
In the loop, 819
In the Waiting Room, 770
Incident, 677
Indexer in Love, The, 800
Intervention, 1054
Interview with August Wilson, An, 1023
Interview with Sherman Alexie, 295
It sifts from Leaden Sieves, 643
IVES, DAVID
  Sure Thing, 1046

Jalapeño Contest, The, 316
JARRELL, RANDALL
  The Death of the Ball Turret Gunner,
  759
JEFFERS, HONORÉE FANONNE
  Unidentified Female Student, Former
  Slave (Talladega College, circa 1885),
  827
Jilting of Granny Weatherall, The, 533
JIN, HA. See HA JIN

JOHNSON, GEORGIA DOUGLAS
  Wishes, 670
JOHNSON, HELENE
  Sonnet to a Negro in Harlem, 696
JONES, RICHARD
  OED, 580
JONSON, BEN
  On My First Son, 827
JORDAN, A. VAN
  From, 828
JOSEPH, ALLISON
  On Being Told I Don't Speak Like a Black
  Person, 582
JOYCE, JAMES
  Araby, 242

KALLET, MARILYN
  The Art of Not Forgetting: An Interview
  with Judith Ortiz Cofer, 744
KAUFMAN, BEL
  Sunday in the Park, 429
KEATS, JOHN
  Ode on a Grecian Urn, 829
KENYON, JANE
  A Boy Goes into the World, 616
KEVANE, BRIDGET
  The Poetic Truth: An Interview with
  Judith Ortiz Cofer, 751
KINCAID, JAMAICA
  Girl, 317
KNIGHT, ETHERIDGE
  Hard Rock Returns to Prison from the
  Hospital for the Criminal Insane, 831
KOERTGE, RON
  Q and A, 581
KOMUNYAKAA, YUSEF
  Facing It, 620
KOOSER, TED
  Student, 642
KOPRINCE, SUSAN
  Baseball as History and Myth in August
  Wilson's Fences, 1038
KUBITSCHEK, MISSY DEHN
  August Wilson's Gender Lesson, 1029
Kubla Khan, 783
KUMIN, MAXINE
  The Sound of Night, 576

La Migra, 617
Lady of Shalott, The, From, 1424
Lake Isle of Innisfree, The, 693
LAMBECK, MARK
  Intervention, 1054

Latin Deli, The: An Ars Poetica, 727
Latin Night at the Pawnshop, 628
Leaving Forever, 759
LEE, LI-YOUNG
    Eating Alone, 596
    Visions and Interpretations, 832
Lesson, The, 208
*Letters from Quebec to Providence in the
    Rain*, 938
LEVERTOV, DENISE
    Leaving Forever, 759
    Talking to Grief, 833
LEVINE, PHILIP
    What Work Is, 834
LEVIS, LARRY
    The Poem You Asked For, 835
LEWIS, MILES MARSHALL
    Miles Marshall Lewis Talks with August
        Wilson, 1027
LI, YIYUN
    The Princess of Nebraska, 432
Lone Ranger and Tonto Fistfight in Heaven,
    The, 291
Loo-Wit, 861
LÓPEZ, LORRAINE M.
    Possibilities for Salsa Music in the
        Mainstream: An Interview with Judith
        Ortiz Cofer, 747
LORDE, AUDRE
    Hanging Fire, 836
Love Calls Us to the Things of This
    World, 879
Love in L.A., 113
Love Poem (Miranda), 668
love poem (Pastan), 849
Love Song of J. Alfred Prufrock, The, 797
LOVELACE, RICHARD
    To Lucasta, Going to the Wars, 837
LOWELL, ROBERT
    Skunk Hour, 837
LYONS, BONNIE
    An Interview with August Wilson, 1023

McGUIRE, RICHARD
    Here, 223
McHUGH, HEATHER
    What He Thought, 839
McKAY, CLAUDE
    If we must die, 694
MACHADO, EDUARDO
    Crossing the Border, 909
Man He Killed, The, 814
Man to Send Rain Clouds, The, 540

Management of Grief, The, 459
MARLOWE, CHRISTOPHER
    The Passionate Shepherd to His Love, 840
MÁRQUEZ, GABRIEL GARCÍA. *See* GARCÍA
    MÁRQUEZ, GABRIEL
MARVELL, ANDREW
    To His Coy Mistress, 841
Matmiya, 870
Maus, *From*, 260
MEANS, DAVID
    The Secret Goldfish, 215
Metaphors, 670
Metrical Feet, 1425
Mid-Term Break, 665
Miles Marshall Lewis Talks with August
    Wilson, 1027
MILTON, JOHN
    When I consider how my light is spent,
        843
MIN, KATHERINE
    Courting a Monk, 247
Minor Miracle, 845
MIRANDA, GARY
    Love Poem, 668
MOORE, MARIANNE
    Poetry, 760, 843
MORA, PAT
    La Migra, 617
MORRISON, TONI
    Recitatif, 445
MOSS, THYLIAS
    Rush Hour, 844
Mother's Mother, 812
Moths, The, 557
Moving Away, 865
MUKHERJEE, BHARATI
    The Management of Grief, 459
MURA, DAVID
    Grandfather-in-Law, 698
MURAKAMI, HARUKI
    Birthday Girl, 471
Musée des Beaux Arts, 767
Muting White Noise: The Subversion of
    Popular Culture Narratives of
    Conquest in Sherman Alexie's
    Fiction, 305
My Father in the Navy, 728
My Last Duchess, 622
My Life by Water, 846
My Mother, If She Had Won Free Dance
    Lessons, 795
my old man, 598
My Papa's Waltz, 602

Nada, 395
Naming of Parts, 854
Naming the Light, 779
Nani, 857
Nargis' Toilette, 791
Negro Speaks of Rivers, The, 826
NELSON, MARILYN
    Minor Miracle, 845
New New, The, 899
"next to of course god america i, 697
NIEDECKER, LORINE
    My Life by Water, 846
Nightmare Begins Responsibility, 815
Nightsong: City, 633
NIGRO, DON
    Letters from Quebec to Providence in the
        Rain, 938
Nikki-Rosa, 809
Note on My Son's Face, A, 788
NYE, NAOMI SHIHAB
    The Small Vases from Hebron, 846
NYGREN, ÅSE
    A World of Story-Smoke: A Conversation
        with Sherman Alexie, 297

OATES, JOYCE CAROL
    When I Was a Little Girl and My Mother
        Didn't Want Me, 1062
    Where Are You Going, Where Have You
        Been?, 481
O'BRIEN, TIM
    The Things They Carried, 493
OCASIO, RAFAEL
    Speaking in Puerto Rican: An Interview
        with Judith Ortiz Cofer, 742
O'CONNOR, FLANNERY
    A Good Man Is Hard to Find, 134
Ode on a Grecian Urn, 829
OED, 580
OLDS, SHARON
    I Go Back to May 1937, 848
OLIVER, MARY
    First Snow, 644
OLSEN, TILLIE
    I Stand Here Ironing, 506
On Being Told I Don't Speak Like a Black
    Person, 582
On My First Son, 827
On the Island I Have Seen, 726
One day I wrote her name upon the
    strand, 866
OPPENHEIMER, MICHAEL
    The Paring Knife, 319

ORTIZ, SIMON J.
    Speaking, 848
Othello the Moor of Venice, 1149
OWEN, WILFRED
    Dulce et Decorum Est, 619
Ozymandias, 863

PACKER, ZZ
    Brownies, 512
Paring Knife, The, 319
PARKER, DOROTHY
    Résumé, 760
PARKS, SUZAN-LORI
    Father Comes Home from the Wars
        (Part 1), 1061
Passionate Shepherd to His Love, The,
    840
PASTAN, LINDA
    love poem, 849
Peace of Wild Things, The, 588
PIERCY, MARGE
    Barbie Doll, 604
PINSKY, ROBERT
    Shirt, 850
PLATH, SYLVIA
    Daddy, 851
    Metaphors, 670
POE, EDGAR ALLAN
    The Cask of Amontillado, 528
Poem for "Magic," A, 825
Poem You Asked For, The, 835
Poetic Truth, The: An Interview with Judith
    Ortiz Cofer, 751
Poetry, 760, 843
Pomegranate, The, 773
PORTER, KATHERINE ANNE
    The Jilting of Granny Weatherall,
        533
Possibilities for Salsa Music in the Mainstream:
    An Interview with Judith Ortiz Cofer,
    747
POUND, EZRA
    In a Station of the Metro, 760
Praise the Tortilla, Praise Menudo, Praise
    Chorizo, 811
Prayer to the Pacific, 685
Princess of Nebraska, The, 432
Problems with Hurricanes, 786
Pulley, The, 818

Q and A, 581
Questions My Son Asked Me, Answers I
    Never Gave Him, 881

Raisin in the Sun, A, 1300
RAMANUJAN, A. K.
    Self-Portrait, 669
RAMIREZ, MARCO
    I Am Not Batman, 1090
RANDALL, DUDLEY
    Ballad of Birmingham, 853
Rape, 855
Recitatif, 445
Red Convertible, The, 126
Red Wheelbarrow, The, 578
REED, HENRY
    Naming of Parts, 854
Résumé, 760
Return to La Plata, Missouri, 769
RICH, ADRIENNE
    Rape, 855
RICH, FRANK
    Family Ties in Wilson's *Fences:* A Review,
      1021
Richard Cory, 637
RICHARDS, LLOYD
    Director's Introduction, 1018
RIDL, JACK
    First Cut, 856
RÍOS, ALBERTO
    Nani, 857
Riverbank Blues, 776
Road Not Taken, The, 666
ROBINSON, EDWIN ARLINGTON
    Richard Cory, 637
RODRIGUEZ, LUIS J.
    Running to America, 858
ROETHKE, THEODORE
    My Papa's Waltz, 602
ROSE, WENDY
    Loo-Wit, 861
Rose for Emily, A, 176
RUEFLE, MARY
    Barbarians, 760
Running to America, 858
Rush Hour, 844

Saboteur, 347
SANDBURG, CARL
    Fog, 761
SATRAPI, MARJANE
    "The Cigarette" from *Persepolis,*
      185
SAVAGEAU, CHERYL
    Bones—A City Poem, 883
Second Coming, The, 885
Secret Goldfish, The, 215

Self-Portrait, 669
Sestina, 699
SHAKESPEARE, WILLIAM
    Othello the Moor of Venice, 1149
    Shall I compare thee to a summer's
      day?, 862
    That time of year thou mayst in me
      behold, 680
Shall I compare thee to a summer's
    day?, 862
Shape of Death, The, 868
Shapes of Leaves, The, 869
She Had Some Horses, 691
SHELLEY, PERCY BYSSHE
    Ozymandias, 863
Shirt, 850
Silent Dancing, 731
SILKO, LESLIE MARMON
    The Man to Send Rain Clouds, 540
    Prayer to the Pacific, 685
SIMIC, CHARLES
    Classic Ballroom Dances, 864
Sir Patrick Spens, 763
Skunk Hour, 837
Slow Dancing with Skeletons: Sherman
    Alexie's *The Lone Ranger and Tonto*
    Fistfight in Heaven, 301
Small Vases from Hebron, The, 846
Snow, 314
SONG, CATHY
    Heaven, 589
song in january, 759
Song of Myself, *From,* 877
Sonnet to a Negro in Harlem, 696
Sonny's Blues, 362
SOPHOCLES
    Antigone, 1103
SOTO, GARY
    Moving Away, 865
Sound of Night, The, 576
Speaking, 848
Speaking in Puerto Rican: An Interview with
    Judith Ortiz Cofer, 742
SPENSER, EDMUND
    One day I wrote her name upon the
      strand, 866
SPIEGELMAN, ART
    From Maus, 260
Spring and All, 882
STAFFORD, WILLIAM
    Traveling through the Dark, 639
STEINBECK, JOHN
    The Chrysanthemums, 320

STERN, GERALD
    The Dog, 614
STEVENS, WALLACE
    Anecdote of the Jar, 866
Story of an Hour, The, 233
STRAND, MARK
    Eating Poetry, 867
STUART, KELLY
    The New New, 899
Student, 642
SUÁREZ, VIRGIL
    Tea Leaves, Caracoles, Coffee Beans, 867
Sunday in the Park, 429
SUNDIATA, SEKOU
    Blink Your Eyes, 607
Superman and Me, 4
Supermarket in California, A, 808
Sure Thing, 1046
Sweat, 421
SWENSON, MAY
    The Shape of Death, 868
SZE, ARTHUR
    The Shapes of Leaves, 869

Talk, 816
Talking to Grief, 833
TallMOUNTAIN, MARY
    Matmiya, 870
TAN, AMY
    Two Kinds, 543
Tea Leaves, Caracoles, Coffee Beans, 867
TENNYSON, ALFRED, LORD
    The Eagle, 642
    From The Lady of Shalott, 1424
    Ulysses, 871
Thank You, M'am, 418
That time of year thou mayst in me behold,
    680
There's Nothing You Can Do, 875
Things They Carried, The, 493
This Is What It Means to Say Phoenix,
    Arizona, 282
This Property Is Condemned, 1083
THOMAS, DYLAN
    Do not go gentle into that good
        night, 873
Those Winter Sundays, 572
Tiara, 794
To an Athlete Dying Young, 824
To Drink, 820
To His Coy Mistress, 841
To Lucasta, Going to the Wars, 837
To My Dear and Loving Husband, 774

To the Virgins, to Make Much of Time, 819
Today's Demon: Magic, 150
TOOMER, JEAN
    Face, 874
Traveling through the Dark, 639
TRETHEWEY, NATASHA
    History Lesson, 585
Trifles, 922
TROUPE, QUINCY
    A Poem for "Magic," 825
True Stories, 764
Two Kinds, 543

Ulysses, 871
Unidentified Female Student, Former Slave
        (Talladega College, circa 1885), 827
UPDIKE, JOHN
    A & P, 552

Very Old Man with Enormous Wings, A,
    413
VIRAMONTES, HELENA MARÍA
    The Moths, 557
Visions and Interpretations, 832

WALKER, ALICE
    Everyday Use, 169
    The Flowers, 20
We Real Cool, 675
We Wear the Mask, 659
WELCH, JAMES
    Christmas Comes to Moccasin Flat,
        874
WESLEY, PATRICIA JABBEH
    There's Nothing You Can Do, 875
Western Wind, 758
What He Thought, 839
What She Knew, 315
What We Talk about When We Talk about
        Love, 386
What Work Is, 834
When I consider how my light is spent, 843
When I Was a Little Girl and My Mother
        Didn't Want Me, 1062
Where Are You Going, Where Have You
        Been?, 481
White Land, The, 876
WHITEMAN, ROBERTA HILL
    The White Land, 876
WHITMAN, WALT
    From Song of Myself, 877
Why Can't I Leave You?, 761
Why I Left the Church, 765

WILBUR, RICHARD
Love Calls Us to the Things of This
World, 879
WILLARD, NANCY
Questions My Son Asked Me, Answers I
Never Gave Him, 881
WILLIAMS, TENNESSEE
This Property Is Condemned, 1083
WILLIAMS, WILLIAM CARLOS
The Red Wheelbarrow, 578
Spring and All, 882
WILSON, AUGUST
Fences, 963
Winter Twilight, A, 635
Wishes, 670
WORDSWORTH, WILLIAM
The world is too much with us,
883
world is too much with us, The, 883
World of Story-Smoke, A: A Conversation
with Sherman Alexie, 297

WRIGHT, JAMES
A Blessing, 690

YAU, JOHN
Chinese Villanelle, 701
YEATS, WILLIAM BUTLER
The Lake Isle of Innisfree, 693
The Second Coming, 885
Yellow Light, 822
you fit into me, 758
YOUNG, AL
A Dance for Ma Rainey, 886
YOUNG BEAR, RAY A.
Green Threatening Clouds, 887
Young Goodman Brown, 337

ZIMMER, PAUL
Zimmer's Head Thudding against the
Blackboard, 888
Zimmer's Head Thudding against the
Blackboard, 888